CITIES IN
AMERICAN
POLITICAL HISTORY

Richardson Dilworth
editor

Andrew A. Beveridge
Matthew Crenson
Margaret Garb
Todd Gardner
David Goldfield
Mary Ryan
Associate Editors

Los Angeles | London | New Delhi
Singapore | Washington DC

Los Angeles | London | New Delhi
Singapore | Washington DC

For information:

CQ Press
An Imprint of SAGE Publications, Inc.
2455 Teller Road
Thousand Oaks, California 91320
E-mail: order@sagepub.com

SAGE Publications Ltd.
1 Oliver's Yard
55 City Road
London, EC1Y 1SP
United Kingdom

SAGE Publications India Pvt. Ltd.
B 1/I 1 Mohan Cooperative Industrial Area
Mathura Road, New Delhi 110 044
India

SAGE Publications Asia-Pacific Pte. Ltd.
33 Pekin Street #02-01
Far East Square
Singapore 048763

Development Editor: Andrew Boney
Production Editor: Mirna Araklian
Copy Editor: Sarah J. Duffy
Typesetter: C&M Digitals (P) Ltd.
Proofreader: Bonnie Moore
Indexer: Diggs Publication Services
Cover Designer: Myself Included Design
Marketing Manager: Ben Krasney

Printed in the United States of America

Dilworth, Richardson.

Cities in American political history / Richardson Dilworth.

p. cm.
Includes bibliographical references and index.

ISBN 978-0-87289-911-7 (cloth : alk. paper)

1. Cities and towns—United States—History.
2. United States—Politics and government. I. Title.

HT123.D53 2011

307.760973—dc23   2011032463

Library of Congress Cataloging-in-Publication Data

This book is printed on acid-free paper.

11 12 13 14 15 10 9 8 7 6 5 4 3 2 1

ABOUT THE EDITOR

RICHARDSON DILWORTH is associate professor of political science and director of the Center for Public Policy at Drexel University. He is the author of *The Urban Origins of Suburban Autonomy* and the editor of two books: *The City in American Political Development* and *Social Capital in the City: Community and Civic Life in Philadelphia*. He serves on the Philadelphia Historical Commission, where he is chair of the Historic Designation Committee.

ABOUT THE ASSOCIATE EDITORS

ANDREW A. BEVERIDGE is professor of Sociology at Queens College and the Graduate Center of The City University of New York. He is at work on several projects on long term urban change in the United States. He also is one of the developers of Social Explorer (www.social explorer.com), which allows the tracking of such change.

MATTHEW CRENSON is a native of Baltimore and professor emeritus of political science at The Johns Hopkins University, where he taught courses on urban politics. His is the author of seven books, including *Neighborhood Politics*, a study of Baltimore's residential communities.

MARGARET GARB is associate professor of history at Washington University in St. Louis, and the author of *City of American Dreams: A History of Home Ownership and Housing Reform in Chicago, 1871-1919*. She is currently working on a study of black politics in late nineteenth- and early twentieth-century Chicago.

TODD GARDNER is a survey statistician at the U.S. Census Bureau. He works in the Center for Economic Studies and oversees all of the demographic data available to researchers in the Census Bureau's national network of Research Data Centers. He received his Ph.D. in history from the University of Minnesota in 1998.

DAVID GOLDFIELD is the Robert Lee Bailey Professor of History at the University of North Carolina, Charlotte. He is the editor of the *Journal of Urban History* and the author of numerous books and articles on the urban South. He is a founder of the Museum of the New South in Charlotte and serves as a curatorial consultant to several urban history museums in the Southeast.

MARY RYAN is the John Martin Vincent Professor of American History at The Johns Hopkins University. Over the last four decades she has been mining two different veins of American History: women's history and the history of cities. Her most recent publications include *Mysteries of Sex: Tracing Women and Men through American History since 1500* and *Civic Wars: Democracy and Public Life in Nineteenth Century Cities*.

CONTRIBUTORS

JERRY ACKERMAN
Independent scholar

BRIAN ALNUTT
Northampton Area Community College

TRICIA BARBAGALLO
New York State Museum

JOHN BAUMAN
University of Southern Maine

BARBARA BERGLUND
University of South Florida

ALAN BLISS
University of Florida

JAMES CAMPBELL
University of Leicester

JAMES CONNOLLY
Ball State University

MATTHEW CRENSON
The Johns Hopkins University

NATHALIE DESSENS
Université de Toulouse–Le Mirail

RICHARDSON DILWORTH
Drexel University

ERICA ARMSTRONG DUNBAR
University of Delaware

IRIS ENGSTRAND
University of San Diego

KEONA K. ERVIN
Luther College

ROBERT B. FAIRBANKS
University of Texas at Arlington

KRISTEN FOSTER
Marquette University

CHARLES A. FRACCHIA
City College of San Francisco

MARGARET GARB
Washington University in St. Louis

MARK I. GELFAND
Boston College

LOUIS GERTEIS
University of Missouri, St. Louis

MICHAEL R. GLASS
University of Pittsburgh

JENNIFER L. GOLOBOY
Independent Scholar

C. MORGAN GREFE
Rhode Island Historical Society

ANDREW HEATH
The University of Sheffield

JOHN HEPP
Wilkes University

WILFRED HOLTON
Northeastern University

TOM HULME
University of Leicester

BRYAN JACK
Southern Illinois University, Edwardsville

FAYE JENSEN
South Carolina Historical Society

DENNIS KEATING
Cleveland State University

SCOTT KNOWLES
Drexel University

JOHN KRINSKY
The City College of New York

DAVID KRUGLER
University of Wisconsin–Platteville

GEORGE J. LANKEVICH
Bronx Community College

STEVEN LEITNER
Independent scholar

ALAN LESSOFF
Illinois State University

CHRISTOPHER P. MAGRA
University of Tennessee

KENNETH H. MARCUS
University of La Verne

JAMES MCWILLIAMS
Texas State University

EDWARD H. MILLER
Boston College

CHAR MILLER
Pomona College

DANE MORRISON
Salem State University

EDWARD MULLER
University of Pittsburgh

THOMAS K. OGORZALEK
Columbia University

DOMINIC PACYGA
Columbia College Chicago

MICHAEL PHILLIPS
Collin College

JOEL RAST
University of Wisconsin–Milwaukee

DE ANNA REESE
California State University, Fresno

ALEXANDER J. REICHL
Queens College, City University of New York

KEITH REVELL
Florida International University

RONALD J. SCHMIDT, JR.
University of Southern Maine

NANCY LUSIGNAN SCHULTZ
Salem State University

AMANDA SELIGMAN
University of Wisconsin–Milwaukee

ROGER D. SIMON
Lehigh University

TOM SITTON
Natural History Museum of Los Angeles County

LESTER K. SPENCE
The Johns Hopkins University

JUDITH SPRAUL-SCHMIDT
University of Cincinnati

DANA STEFANELLI
University of Virginia

HENRY LOUIS TAYLOR, JR.
University at Buffalo SUNY

PHILIP VANDERMEER
Arizona State University

DONNA PATRICIA WARD
University of North Carolina at Greensboro

AMY WIDESTROM
California State University, Long Beach

JAMES WOLFINGER
DePaul University

STEPHEN YODER
University of Maryland

ANDRE YOUNG
The Johns Hopkins University

JASON YOUNG
State University of New York (SUNY), Buffalo

CONTENTS

CONTENTS BY CITY

INTRODUCTION

This is a book about big American cities—more specifically, the ten largest cities in ten successive eras of United States history, stretching from the Revolution and Founding era (1776–1790), to the post–Cold War present (1989–2011). Each city in each chapter is discussed in a separate entry, resulting in a total of one hundred entries, covering twenty-nine separate cities that have at some point in U.S. history been among the ten biggest in terms of population size according to the U.S. Census.* At the time of the first census in 1790, the majority of those big cities were located in New England (Boston, Massachusetts; Salem, Massachusetts; Newport, Rhode Island; Providence, Rhode Island; Gloucester, Massachusetts; and Marblehead, Massachusetts). The largest of the cities, New York, had 33,131 residents, mostly living at the southern end of Manhattan Island. The smallest of the cities, Gloucester, had a population of 5,317. By the last census count in 2010, seven of the biggest cities in the United States were located in Texas, Arizona, and California. The largest city was still New York, with a population of approximately 8.2 million spread over 309 square miles. The smallest city was San Jose, California, with a population of nearly one million spread across approximately 170 square miles.

The trend evident in the nation's largest cities, of a steady southwesterly progression, is part of a larger story about the overall movement of the U.S. population westward, fueled first by the hunger for natural resources and cheap land and

---

*More specifically, the lists of largest cities used in this book come from the censuses of 1790 (chapter 1), 1820 (chapter 2), 1840 (chapter 3), 1870 (chapter 4), 1890 (chapter 5), 1920 (chapter 6), 1940 (chapter 7), 1950 (chapter 8), 1980 (chapter 9), and 2010 (chapter 10). While this book relies on only ten of the last twenty-three census counts of city population, it includes at least one entry on every city that has ever been counted by the census as being among the ten largest in the country, with the exception of Norfolk, Virginia (counted as the tenth largest city in 1800), and cities that were later annexed to other cities, such as Brooklyn, which is discussed as part of the entries on New York.

facilitated by an increasing network of canals and railroads. These new means of transportation in the nineteenth century facilitated western population growth into Ohio, Illinois, and Missouri, and cities in those states (namely Cincinnati, Chicago, and St. Louis, respectively) soon eclipsed in size and territory the New England towns and cities that had previously been among the largest in the country. Urban industrial growth in the Midwest proceeded into the twentieth century, as Cleveland, Ohio; Pittsburgh, Pennsylvania; and Detroit, Michigan, joined the ranks of the ten largest cities. Yet after World War II, companies were increasingly attracted to the southern and western states where, among other things, the relative lack of unions provided for cheaper labor costs, and the new Interstate Highway System decreased the advantages of traditional railroad hubs. Thus the postwar period, up to the present day, has witnessed a massive southern and western population shift, reflected in the rise of Los Angeles, San Diego, and San Jose in California; Houston, Dallas, and San Antonio in Texas; and Phoenix, Arizona—a constellation of cities that came to be known as the Sun Belt. By contrast, nearly every large city in the northeastern and midwestern United States—a constellation known as the Rust Belt—suffered a period of net population loss after World War II, even as the U.S. population overall was steadily increasing.

The rise of the Sun Belt and demise of the Rust Belt was not due to national population shifts alone, but also to the structures of the respective cities themselves. During the nineteenth century, Rust Belt cities routinely annexed outlying communities, thus expanding in terms of both territory and population size. By the twentieth century, these cities were increasingly surrounded by independent suburban municipalities whose residents and officials no longer wanted to be annexed to big cities, thus limiting the cities' potential for population growth. By contrast, the southwestern cities have been steadily annexing outlying land since World War II. They are thus larger in terms of territory and have more potential for population growth than the cities in the Rust Belt. In 1980, for instance, the census recorded the ten largest cities as being equally split between the Rust Belt (New York; Chicago; Philadelphia, Pennsylvania; Detroit; and Baltimore, Maryland) and the Sun Belt (Los Angeles, Houston, Dallas, San Diego, and Phoenix). Yet in that same year, the Sun Belt cities were on average more than twice the geographic size of the Rust Belt cities (400 versus 176 square miles).

Those Rust Belt cities that have managed to maintain their status as being among the largest in the nation (New York, Philadelphia, and Chicago) had more diversified economies, and were thus not as dependent on single industries that became increasingly globalized and moved beyond their original host cities, such as the automobile industry in Detroit and the steel industry in Pittsburgh. New York, Chicago, and Philadelphia have also all found economic niches in increasingly global industries, such as financial services and biomedical research.

Four cities that were at one point counted among the ten largest but later annexed to larger cities are not given their own entries in this book but are instead discussed in the entries for the cities to which they were annexed. Not including cities that were later annexed allowed for coverage of three additional cities that never quite made the "top ten," thus providing slightly broader coverage. The cities that were annexed, and thus which do not receive separate entries, were the Pennsylvania cities of Northern Liberties (counted as one of the ten largest cities from 1790 to 1840), Southwark (1790–1830), and Spring Garden (1850), all of which were absorbed into Philadelphia as part of a city-county consolidation in 1854, and Brooklyn, which was counted among the ten largest cities from 1840 to 1890 but was absorbed in the creation of the five-borough "Greater New York" in 1898. Foregoing entries on those cities that were later annexed allowed space for entries on Gloucester; Marblehead; and Richmond, Virginia, and for extra entries on Albany, New York; Buffalo, New York; Providence; and Washington, D.C.*

The choice to bundle cities that were annexed into the entries on the cities to which they were annexed is in part recognition that, even in the late eighteenth century, urban settlements spilled out beyond formal municipal boundaries. In the case of Philadelphia, residents and businesses concentrated in settlements along the Delaware River that spilled over into the neighboring districts of Northern Liberties and Southwark, contrary to William Penn's intention that the city extend in an orderly grid westward, away from the Delaware. And in his classic multivolume *History of the City of Brooklyn*, published by subscription between 1867 and 1870, Henry Stiles noted of his city's growth that "Candor certainly compels the acknowledgment that it was chiefly attributable to the overflowing prosperity and greatness of its giant neighbor, New York."

While this book thus acknowledges that urban areas extend beyond the formal boundaries of cities, the subject here is decidedly cities and not larger urban areas—or, as the census came to call them by 1910, "metropolitan districts," and later, "standard metropolitan statistical areas." Even in the entries on Philadelphia and New York where outlying areas are discussed, those outlying areas are included only because they would later be formally absorbed into their respective neighboring cities. Nor is this a book about "urban" issues—a term broad enough to encompass most aspects of modern life, and which after World War II became a synonym (one might even say a euphemism) for issues involving concentrated poverty, racial conflict and violence, blight, and crime. Many of the more notable events from that period that might be described as urban, such as the formation of the Black Panthers in Oakland, California, or the violence that confronted the nonviolent protest marchers in Birmingham, Alabama, in 1963 are not discussed herein because they did not occur in cities large enough to be included in this book. Readers will find a great deal of overlap between a general urban history and the histories of the cities covered in this book, but many urban events also occurred outside the boundaries of these cities.

There are several major themes in the history of American cities that in this book we have tried to capture under three headings in each entry: Government and Politics; Industry, Commerce, and Labor; and Race, Ethnicity, and Immigration. The first theme, government and politics, is central to the focus in this book on cities, which are formal institutions, endowed in almost every instance with charters that define the structures of their governments, the extent of their powers, and the specific territorial jurisdiction over which they exercise those powers.

---

*Foregoing separate entries on Northern Liberties, Southwark, Spring Garden, and Brooklyn allowed inclusion of additional entries in chapter 1 on Gloucester (twelfth largest city in 1790) and Marblehead (which, at 5,661 people, was tied with Southwark for being the tenth largest city in 1790); in chapter 2, Albany (eleventh largest in 1820) and Richmond (twelfth largest in 1820); in chapter 3, Washington, DC (thirteenth largest in 1840) and Providence (fourteenth largest in 1840); and, in chapters 4 and 5, Buffalo (eleventh largest in 1870 and 1890).

The history of American city government is marked by experimentation with new organizational forms and by a continuous struggle for authority with the states of which they are a part. As the entries in chapter 1 indicate, city government in the eighteenth century was a somewhat haphazard affair. In some cases, such as in Philadelphia; Baltimore; and Charleston, South Carolina, the city at some points had no government but was run as part of the state, and in other cases, a semi-official organization became the de facto government, as in the case of the Ancient and Honorable Mechanical Company of Baltimore or the Charles Town Board of Police.

After the Revolution, most big cities adopted charters that roughly mimicked the new national government, with a separate executive branch led by an elected mayor and a bicameral legislature consisting of an upper chamber of aldermen and a lower chamber most frequently called a common council. The reform period of the early twentieth century was marked by the introduction of new structures for city governance, namely the commission system (where the city was governed by a board of several commissioners, all elected at-large, sometimes with the commissioner who won the most votes designated the mayor) and the council-manager system (a quasi-parliamentary system with no independently elected executive but a "city manager" appointed by the elected council). The commission and council-manager systems were more readily adopted in smaller cities, with the result that most of the cities discussed in this book maintained the mayor-council structure, though with a unicameral council. However, the western cities in particular bear the marks of reform. San Jose, for instance, is governed under a council-manager system, though one that also incorporates a mayor.

The extent to which cities are actually governments exercising genuine sovereignty or merely administrative subunits of states has historically been a matter of contention. Two competing legal doctrines from the nineteenth century defined the conflict over the extent of city sovereignty: The "Cooley Doctrine" (named after Michigan Supreme Court judge Thomas Cooley) argued that local governments were constitutive elements of states, and states thus exercised only a limited authority over local government. "Dillon's Rule" (named after Iowa Supreme Court judge John Dillon, also later a federal circuit court judge) argued that states created local governments over which they thus exercised complete control. Dillon's Rule has largely prevailed over the Cooley Doctrine, yet cities also established some level of independence through "home rule" charters—state constitutional provisions that established some protections against legislative meddling in city affairs and which often resemble in their language the Tenth Amendment to the U.S. Constitution.

The second theme of the entries—industry, commerce, and labor—addresses the central role that big cities have played in the national and international economy. In the eighteenth and early nineteenth centuries, cities were centers of commerce, with life organized around bustling ports and city government functions centered around trade, such as regulating weights and measures, entry into vocations, and maintaining docks and central marketplaces. During the nineteenth century, and especially after the Civil War, cities blossomed into industrial manufacturing hubs, and as such they also provided fertile ground for the growing labor movement, starting with the Knights of Labor, which had its heyday in the 1880s but was quickly eclipsed by the American Federation of Labor. Of course, many of the biggest labor conflicts of the late nineteenth century occurred outside of big cities, such as the 1892 Homestead Strike, and many (especially those that involved railroads and their growing networks) were national in scope, such as the Great Railroad Strike of 1877, which began in West Virginia but spread to cities as far apart as Baltimore and San Francisco.

The previously noted population shift away from the Rust Belt and growth of the Sun Belt reflects as well a change in the labor movement. Though many Sun Belt cities have significant manufacturing sectors, their growth was premised more on high-tech and service industries, such as finance, insurance, and real estate, none of which require the same kind of labor force as did the traditional industrial manufacturing firms that were concentrated in the Rust Belt. These industries, however, have increasingly migrated overseas in search of lower labor costs. Corresponding with the shift away from manufacturing has been a decline in membership in the industrial unions, such as the United Auto Workers and the United Steel Workers of America, and a rise in unions more closely tied to service sectors, such as the American Federation of State, County, and Municipal Employees (AFSCME) and the Service Employees International Union (SEIU). Reflecting the changing nature of labor in the United States, the SEIU, in conjunction with six other more service-oriented unions, broke from the American Federation of Labor-Congress of Industrial Organizations in 2005 to form a new labor coalition, Change to Win.

The third theme—race, ethnicity, and immigration—focuses on cities' traditional roles as the points of destination for new arrivals to the United States who made cities ethnically and racially distinct from the rest of the country. The first Europeans who came over in notably large numbers were the Irish in the early nineteenth century, quickly followed by Germans. By the end of the nineteenth century, decreasing numbers of Irish and Germans were more than supplemented by swelling numbers from Italy, Austria-Hungary, and eastern Europe. The total number of new arrivals from abroad to the United States peaked at nearly nine million during the first decade of the twentieth century, after which the blockade of Europe during World War II, followed by more restrictive immigration laws, began to stem the tide. As new arrivals from abroad decreased, the number of African Americans migrating from rural areas in the South to northern and midwestern cities began to increase dramatically. In 1965 a new immigration law known as the Hart-Celler Act reduced the preferential treatment of Europeans seeking to immigrate to the United States which had the unintended effect of facilitating a massive increase in the number of immigrants coming from Asian and Latin American countries. Indeed, based on immigration trends since 1970, the census estimates that people of Hispanic origin will comprise nearly a quarter of the total U.S. population by 2050, which would be double their percentage of the population in 2000. And though people of Asian origin comprise a smaller proportion of the total U.S. population, they too are increasing in numbers far faster than the average—three times the rate of growth of the total U.S. population in the first decade of the twenty-first century. By contrast, the census estimates the African American population will remain relatively stable into the middle of the twenty-first century, at roughly 13 percent of the total U.S. population.

New arrivals to American cities, especially those belonging to an identifiable racial or ethnic group, have often faced hostility and violence, many times associated with fears that the new arrivals would threaten the economic positions of established residents. Thus the Irish confronted anti-Catholic violence, most notably in a series of riots in Philadelphia in 1844. As they moved in increasing numbers to cities in the early twentieth century, African Americans faced violence such as race riots in more than a dozen cities between 1917 and 1920. Similarly, the 1992 riot in Los Angeles was notable for the fact that Korean business owners were a target for violence. In part because of such hostility, including laws that prevented them from moving freely to different neighborhoods, but also no doubt from a desire to be among people with whom they shared a culture and language, immigrants often clustered in cities, creating "urban villages" and "ethnic enclaves." In some instances this provided them with greater political power as they then represented majorities in local electoral districts, but in other instances it made them easier to ignore, as was often the case with African American neighborhoods, especially after World War II.

Between the race riots of the earlier and latter parts of the twentieth century, the status of cities in the United States changed significantly. The increasing role of the federal government as a result of the Great Depression and World War II changed the relationship between cities and the nation, and cities became an active lobbying force through the U.S. Conference of Mayors, established in 1933, which was followed by the National League of Cities and other urban advocacy groups. The Lyndon Johnson administration was especially supportive of cities through its Model Cities Program and the establishment of the U.S. Department of Housing and Urban Development.

Other federally sponsored projects, including the Interstate Highway System and federally guaranteed home mortgages, also dramatically affected the fortunes of cities, mainly by spurring suburbanization. The effects are evident in the changing population distribution of the country. The U.S. Census today counts 366 metropolitan areas in the country, in which approximately 84 percent of the U.S. population lives. Yet an increasingly smaller proportion of the overall population lives in the ten largest cities. From a peak of 16 percent in 1930, the percent of the U.S. population living in the country's ten largest cities dropped to 8 percent by 2000.

In 1790 roughly 5 percent of the American population could be called "urban" in the sense that they lived in one of the twenty-four communities with populations over twenty-five hundred, the larger half of which are covered here in chapter 1, which included roughly 4 percent of the U.S. population. By contrast, we are today a decidedly urban nation, yet one in which the biggest cities are, just as they were in an earlier period of our history, demographically and economically distinct from the rest of the country, containing a greater degree of racial and ethnic diversity and a greater disparity in incomes. The continuity and change that marks the history of cities in the United States, and the variations between cities themselves, can be tracked in the entries in this book.

RICHARDSON DILWORTH

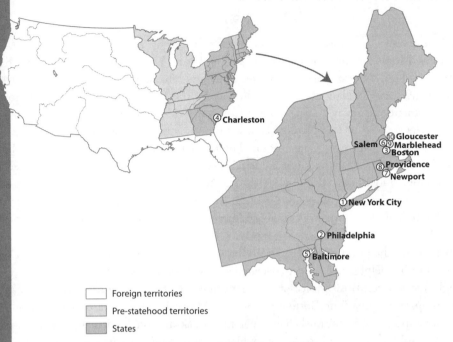

Includes states, territories, and population rankings as of 1790

CITIES IN THE
REVOLUTIONARY ERA,
1776–1790

After starting out as small villages in the seventeenth century, a few American cities had reached urban-scale populations by the latter half of the eighteenth century. By 1775 the population of Philadelphia, Pennsylvania, was approximately forty thousand—making it one of the largest in the whole British Empire. The population of New York City was twenty-five thousand, and that of Boston, Massachusetts, was sixteen thousand. City populations declined dramatically during the American Revolution, though afterwards cities once again became centers of growth. In 1790, in the first census authorized by the United States Congress, the ten largest cities in the country (all covered in this chapter) ranged in population from 33,131 (New York) to 5,317 (Gloucester, Massachusetts).[1] Collectively, they represented only 4 percent of the 3.9 million people then living in the United States.

---

1. Gloucester was actually counted as the twelfth largest city by the 1790 census, yet two larger cities, Northern Liberties and Southwark, were both later annexed to Philadelphia. For the purposes of this book, they are treated as part of Philadelphia and not provided with separate entries.

Of these cities, seven were located in states that had by 1790 at least formally abolished slavery or had passed gradual emancipation acts, and New York followed suit in 1799. By contrast, the two big southern cities, Baltimore, Maryland, and Charleston, South Carolina, both had increasing slave populations—indeed, throughout the 1770s and 1780s in Charleston there were approximately as many black slaves as there were white residents.

The years covered by this chapter begin with the Revolution and end during the first Congress under the United States Constitution. The Revolution has its origins in tensions between the colonies and the Crown over new imperial taxes and trade restrictions implemented in the 1760s, reaching a highpoint with the British Tea Act of 1773. The reaction on the part of colonial activists—stealing valuable quantities of tea from East India Company ships and dumping it into the harbors of New York, Philadelphia, Charleston, and, most famously, Boston—provoked the British government into a series of reprisals, known among the colonists as the Intolerable Acts, which had the effect of further increasing tensions. Thus the First Continental Congress convened in Philadelphia in 1774 and declared a boycott on British-produced goods.

Fighting between British forces and American colonists began in the spring of 1775 when British troops, marching from Boston to Concord, Massachusetts, to destroy a cache of American weapons and supplies, skirmished with colonists in Lexington, leaving eight Americans dead. The British soldiers retreated to Boston, which they occupied, though they were surrounded by American militia. In response, the Second Continental Congress convened in Philadelphia, declared the colonies in a state of defense, and appointed George Washington commander in chief of the Continental Army. That July Washington traveled to Massachusetts to join the militia in Cambridge, where they had retreated after the Battle of Bunker Hill. Nine months later, American forces captured Dorchester Heights, thus compelling the British to evacuate Boston.

By the summer of 1776, the British, having recognized that they were fighting a war and not merely quelling an insurrection, successfully invaded New York City, though their attempt to invade Charleston in that same month failed. In Philadelphia, a committee of the Continental Congress drafted the Declaration of Independence, copies of which were printed and sent to all thirteen states. By the end of the year, the U.S. Navy had suffered a severe defeat in the Battle of Valcour Bay; Washington and his troops had been defeated in the Battle of White Plains; the British had captured a naval base in Newport, Rhode Island; and the Continental Congress, fearing an invasion of Philadelphia, had left for Baltimore. 1776 ended on at least one positive note for the Americans, however: Washington's famous capture of Hessian troops in Trenton, New Jersey.

The Continental Congress returned to Philadelphia in March of 1777 only to leave for Lancaster, Pennsylvania, six months later. Philadelphia was occupied by the British in September, by which time the Continental Congress had relocated from Lancaster to the neighboring town of York, where they drafted and approved the Articles of Confederation. At nearly the same time, American troops won a major victory in the Battle of Saratoga, which helped Benjamin Franklin in the following year negotiate French allegiance and support for the United States. By the summer of 1778, British troops left Philadelphia to regroup in New York, the Continental Congress returned to Philadelphia, and French and American forces attempted a combined attack to recapture Newport from the British.

BY THE NUMBERS: **THE MOST POPULOUS CITIES IN 1790**							
	TOTAL POPULATION	NUMBER OF HEADS OF FAMILIES	WHITE POPULATION	"FREE COLORED" POPULATION	SLAVE POPULATION	% WHITE POPULATION	% "FREE COLORED" POPULATION	% SLAVE POPULATION
NEW YORK, NY	33,131	6,035	29,661	1,101	2,369	89.5	3.3	7.2
PHILADELPHIA, PA	28,522	4,312	26,892	1,420	210	94.3	5.0	0.7
BOSTON, MA	18,320	2,391	17,554	766	0	95.8	4.2	0.0
CHARLESTON, SC	16,359	1,933	8,089	586	7,684	49.4	3.6	47.0
BALTIMORE, MD	13,503	1,736	11,925	323	1,255	88.3	2.4	9.3
SALEM, MA	7,921	1,493	7,661	260	0	96.7	3.3	0.0
NEWPORT, RI	6,716	1,242	6,076	417	223	90.5	6.2	3.3
PROVIDENCE, RI	6,380	1,129	5,905	427	48	92.6	6.7	0.8
MARBLEHEAD, MA	5,661	1,104	5,574	87	0	98.5	1.5	0.0
GLOUCESTER, MA	5,317	1,006	5,276	41	0	99.2	0.8	0.0

Note: This list does not include Northern Liberties Township, PA, or Southwark, PA. See introduction for details.

Source: Heads of Families at the First Census of the United States in the Year 1790.

The attempt to recapture Newport failed, but the British left the city in 1779 as they gathered their forces for a major southern campaign that resulted in, among other things, the capture of Savannah, Georgia, at the end of 1778 and of Charleston in 1780. In general, however, the southern campaign went badly for the British, who surrendered at the Battle of Yorktown in October of 1781. Eight months earlier, the last of the new states, Maryland, had finally ratified the Articles of Confederation, which became the constitution of the emergent nation.

Despite the surrender at the Battle of Yorktown and the effective end of the war, small battles continued into 1782, and Charleston remained under British occupation until the end of that year. Britain and the United States did not declare an official end to the war until 1783, the last of the British troops did not leave New York until the end of that year, and the final peace treaty was signed in 1784.

The Articles of Confederation created a relatively weak national government, though it was one with significant war debts. By the summer of 1783, Congress was compelled to move from Philadelphia to Princeton, New Jersey, in order to avoid the disgruntled and increasingly threatening war veterans who had not been paid for their service. Two years later, the national capital moved to New York, where it stayed until 1790 when it moved back to Philadelphia while awaiting the construction of its permanent home along the Potomac. The new state governments were also heavily indebted, though they had a greater ability to levy taxes. Heavier taxes, combined with a postwar economic slump, led to public discontent, especially among poorer farmers and war veterans. The most notable discontent came from southwestern New England in the form of war veteran Daniel Shays and his followers. They engaged in armed protests against the Massachusetts court system and ultimately attempted to storm a federal arsenal in Springfield, though they were thwarted by state militia.

Shays's Rebellion highlighted the weakness of the national government and thus provided more support for a convention that had been planned for Philadelphia in the summer of 1787, the purpose of which was to discuss changes to the Articles of Confederation. The convention, which included fifty-five delegates representing every state but Rhode Island, met from May 25 to September 17, 1787, and overstepped its mandate by proposing a new constitution that included new restrictions on state power, a bicameral legislature with significantly more powers than the Confederation Congress, an independently elected president, and an independent national judiciary that would reign supreme over the state courts.

The proposed constitution was sent from Philadelphia to the states, with ratification contingent on the approval of at least nine of the thirteen legislatures. By the end of June 1788, eleven states had ratified the U.S. Constitution with the understanding that it would include a set of amendments—what would become the Bill of Rights—guaranteeing various additional rights to citizens and the states. It was only after the ratification of the Bill of Rights that North Carolina and Rhode Island finally agreed to join the Union, in 1789 and 1790, respectively.

The Confederation Congress adjourned in November of 1788, and the First Congress under the Constitution convened in March of 1789. The following month, George Washington was elected to serve as the first United States president and John Adams as the first vice president. A new government had been established.

NEW YORK, NY 1776–1790

FROM 1776 TO 1790 NEW YORK CITY first endured and then triumphed over enormous trauma, a process that secured its position as the nation's most pivotal municipality and one that anticipated its emergence as the American metropolis. City patriots had gleefully advanced the cause of independence for a decade before 1776, yet the great port on the Hudson River was easily conquered by Britain in the fall of that year. For seven years New York served as Britain's military headquarters, a garrison city under martial law that suffered privation and physical deterioration. After being liberated in 1783, it rapidly rebuilt its infrastructure, reunited its divided population, and served as capital of the United States for five years. Revived by 1790, it was poised to challenge Philadelphia, Pennsylvania, as the most populous American city.

GOVERNMENT AND POLITICS

On July 9, 1776, by order of General George Washington, the just-approved Declaration of Independence was read to cheering New York citizens and their defending soldiers. The ensuing celebrations, however, were held under an ominous cloud. Across the harbor on Staten Island, Lord William Howe was assembling the greatest military force that Great Britain would field before World War II. The first elements of Britain's invading army had arrived on June 29.

QUICK FACTS

NEW YORK, NY 1776–1790

MAYORS

David Matthews	(1776–1784)
James Duane	(1784–1789)
Richard Varick	(1789–1790)

MAJOR INDUSTRIES AND EMPLOYERS

Shipbuilding and related
   industries
Construction and carpentry
Prostitution
Textile factory of the
   Manufacturing Society
   (150 workers)
Lorillard Brothers Tobacconist

MAJOR NEWSPAPERS

*New York Gazette and the Weekly
   Mercury*
*New York Packet and the
   American Advertiser*
Royal Gazette
Royal American Gazette
New York Mercury
New-York Morning Post and Daily Advertiser
Independent Journal
New York Journal
Daily Advertiser
New-York Packet
New York Daily Gazette
Gazette of the United States

MAJOR EVENTS

August–November 1776: Lord William Howe inflicts great losses on American forces and secures control of Manhattan. The city remained the British military headquarters for the next seven years.

September 21–22, 1776: Fire destroys five hundred buildings and a third of city housing, a catastrophe George Washington attributes to "providence."

November 25, 1783: Evacuation Day marks America's re-occupation of New York, an event celebrated in Manhattan until World War I.

April 13–14, 1788: The "doctor's riot" leads to five deaths. Mobs fearful of grave robbery and autopsies of the dead attack Manhattan doctors and destroy their medical instruments.

March–April 1789: The federal government is organized in New York as Congress meets in Federal Hall. George Washington becomes president on April 30, but sixteen months later the capital leaves Manhattan forever.

"I thought all London was afloat" wrote one awed observer. Subsequent reinforcements increased England's expedition to five hundred ships, thirty-two thousand soldiers, and thirteen thousand sailors. Their target was New York, the city that John Adams called "a kind of key to the whole continent," and it was Washington's unenviable duty to defend the city with an untested army. A novice himself, Washington failed at the task.

A series of battles, beginning in Brooklyn on August 27 and culminating with the surrender of Fort Washington on November 16, confirmed Howe's possession of New York. Washington's major accomplishment was to preserve his army as a fighting force. Americans captured during

Lord William Howe's massive force captured New York City after a series of battles in the summer and fall of 1776. The British held the city for seven years. This print depicts the triumphant British forces marching in the city's streets.

Source: Library of Congress

that and later campaigns were incarcerated on ships in Wallabout Bay, Brooklyn; a memorial column honoring over 11,500 dead prisoners now stands in Fort Greene Park. Most importantly, after 1776 the "key" to North America was in British hands, and for seven years the metropolis was Britain's strongest bulwark. Manhattan's suffering was intensified by great fires in September 1776 and August 1778 that destroyed much housing. After the first of those catastrophes, Nathan Hale—often portrayed as a heroic patriot—was captured carrying diagrams of fortifications and incendiary matches. Hale was hanged by the British as a spy and suspected arsonist, and Washington's staff admitted the execution was "upon good grounds."

During the long British occupation, Loyalists from every colony flocked to the safety of the metropolis, as did escaped slaves drawn by British promises of freedom. Royalists proudly issued their Declaration of Dependency in November 1776, even as Manhattan patriots were forced to quarter British troops or live in a tented "Canvas-town." Alternately known as "Topsail Town," the area at the end of Broad Street gained a reputation as a place where prostitutes could be engaged, joining the "Holy Ground" behind St. Paul's Chapel as a place for illicit recreation. Military rule in Manhattan was harsh. Spies of both sides prowled the streets, and surrounding counties were areas of constant skirmishing; it is significant that fully a third of all Revolutionary battles were fought in New York State. Manhattan's civilian leaders were ineffective—Mayor David Matthews and Loyalist officials Joshua Loring and William Cunningham were overtly dishonest, and the city's wealth and its forests were ravaged to support the "Gibraltar of America."

New York endured as the Revolution was won elsewhere. After hostilities ended in 1781, it became the port from which thirty thousand Loyalists went into exile. The Treaty of Paris was formally signed on September 3, 1783, and on November 25 the last British contingents, resplendent in their red uniforms, left Manhattan and were replaced by Washington's "weather-beaten and forlorn" troops. Evacuation Day would be celebrated as a New York holiday for over a century, but the city faced many rebuilding challenges. Extending less than a mile north of the Battery, Manhattan's population of twelve thousand was only half its 1770 total, its nonmilitary docks were decrepit, its streets were filled with garbage, and Trinity Church, its most distinctive structure, was a burnt-out shell.

City revival began in December. General Washington bade farewell to his staff at Fraunces Tavern, the last British ships left the harbor, and elections were held for both the state legislature and a new city council. Patriots easily won both elections since only propertied males over twenty-one could vote and Tories were excluded. When the new assemblies convened in the ruined city in January 1784, Governor George Clinton appointed James Duane as New York's mayor. A prominent lawyer who had helped draft the national Articles of Confederation, Duane undertook the twin tasks of rebuilding and reconciliation. Over one thousand families needed relief, but in a city still one-quarter Tory, a greater issue was a vengeful spirit that demanded confiscation of Tory property. In the case of *Rutgers v. Waddington* (1784), newly minted lawyer Alexander Hamilton convinced the Mayor's Court that such action violated both the Articles of Confederation and the Treaty of Paris. Hamilton also was instrumental in founding the Bank of New York, which provided capital for reconstruction of docks and the business district. Ambitious city merchants resumed coastal commerce and instituted trade with China and the West Indies. Important social changes included the disestablishment of the Anglican Church, the opening of Manhattan's first Catholic church, and the transformation of King's College into Columbia College. The Confederation Congress added to New York's prestige by designating it the national capital in 1785. By the end of 1786, the population had doubled to twenty-four thousand and vibrancy had returned to the metropolis.

The national scene was less encouraging, however, as the deficiencies of the Articles of Confederation became apparent. The 1787 Constitutional Convention presented a new form of government to Americans: a federal republic supported by most city residents. Alexander Hamilton, John Jay, and James Madison explained the document in the *Publius* essays first published in the *Independent Journal* and then serialized in four city papers. Later compiled as *The Federalist*, their effort remains the best introduction to the American Constitution. Hamilton and Jay also played decisive roles in winning New York State's ratification of the Constitution, triumphing over a coalition led by Governor Clinton that sought to keep the weak confederation. Proving New York's centrality, the capital of the new government was located in Manhattan, and President-elect George Washington triumphantly returned to the city he had once lost and regained. He was inaugurated on April 30, 1789, and it was in New York that the first Congress met, the first Supreme Court convened, and the first Cabinet sessions were held. Distinguished New Yorkers such as Hamilton, Jay, and Duane were among the first federal appointees. Although Manhattan's tenure as national capital lasted only sixteen months, its emergence as the dominant American city was well advanced.

INDUSTRY, COMMERCE, AND LABOR

When peace returned to America in 1783, New York's entrepreneurial elite quickly restored vitality to their decimated city. Manhattan's forte had been, was, and remains making money. With the restrictions of wartime removed, its merchants, financiers, and investors resolutely turned to the restoration of commerce. The Paris peace treaty limited their access to the British Caribbean, but grain trade with other islands and stateside coastal shipping quickly resumed. Significant for future development was the first transshipment of Charleston cotton to Europe in 1785, a reorientation of natural trade routes quickly accepted by planters in Savannah, Georgia. In February 1784 the *Empress of China,* carrying furs and ginseng, sailed for Canton, China, and her return fifteen months later proved that American trade with Asia was both possible and profitable. By 1786 six more ships left New York for China and India. By 1790 Manhattan's revived merchant community dominated trade with the Caribbean and America's coasts; even more impressively, their prime European trading partner was Great Britain.

New city institutions were established to support the revival. Early in 1784 merchants meeting at the Tontine Coffee House suggested a bank, and Alexander Hamilton turned their hope into reality. By June the Bank of New York was in operation on Pearl Street, even as Hamilton won his justly famous court decision against the confiscation of Tory property. City credit availability increased as the rift between Loyalist and patriot merchants was healing. By 1787 all laws discriminating against Loyalists were abolished, and a leading Anglophile, William Johnson, assumed the presidency of Columbia College. Every entrepreneur hailed a revived chamber of commerce in 1784, the creation of Manhattan's first daily paper in 1785, the first city directory in 1786, and the founding of a fire insurance company in 1787. New docks and buildings increased citizens' enthusiasm, and land speculation, soon to become a city staple, began when the Sands brothers founded the "City of Olympia" across the East River.

Despite booming commercial activity, Manhattan's local economy was dominated by myriad small manufacturers whose business success lifted the postwar gloom. New York was still in a pre-industrial world, and artisan workshops existed in all areas of the city. In 1785 these artisans organized the General Society of Mechanics and Tradesmen to provide mutual assistance, educate apprentices, and guarantee standards. There was a near-medieval atmosphere in some Manhattan precincts, and not until January 1789 was the Society for the Encouragement of American Manufactures organized. Some tiny establishments would go on to greatness—Isaac Roosevelt supervised sugar refining operations, and the tobacconist Lorillard brothers initiated the nation's first advertising campaign in 1787 using an Indian logo and offering a money-back guarantee—but most remained resolutely master-apprentice operations.

Artisans and merchants shared common beliefs in property rights and security, and the ever-active Alexander Hamilton formed them into a single voting bloc favoring the proposed constitution. New York's Federal Procession of July 1788, organized to celebrate the ratification of the proposed constitution by other states and to demand approval of the new government by New York State's ratifying convention, featured ten marching divisions and over sixty trades and professions. The prosperous merchant elite came last in the marching order. Five thousand spectators cheered as a float of the "Great Ship Hamilton," constructed by Manhattan artisans, passed them by. Onlookers, artisans, and merchants remained loyal elements of the Federalist city coalition for years.

New York never overcame the poverty that afflicted a large proportion of its population, however. During the occupation British officers lived exceedingly comfortably; the ranks expropriated what they could, and thousands of Loyalists arrived to live in temporary exile and serve their king. Poverty increased for a general population that suffered price gouging, food shortages, and the coldest winter in city history in 1779–1780. Officials created a board of overseers to provide aid to the poor and raised £45,000 through taxes levied against the property of patriots. Nevertheless, thousands of Manhattan residents needed public assistance, and even after liberation, newspapers reported that one thousand families still had such a need. During the 1780s almshouse residency increased every winter and in poor sailing weather. New York's Humane Society was founded in 1787, but the persistence of poverty had the unfortunate effect of forcing some women into prostitution. Not surprisingly, New Yorkers in 1790 chose to emphasize public accomplishments such as the razing of Fort George, construction of Battery walking paths, and the consecration of a rebuilt Trinity Church when they discussed city growth.

RACE, ETHNICITY, AND IMMIGRATION

New York is the American city most noted for its diversity. As early as 1643 eighteen languages were spoken in the town; that multiplicity of accents still existed in 1770 when its population reached twenty-one thousand. Blacks constituted fully one-fifth of the population, a total exceeded in the colonies only by Charleston, South Carolina. Because so many frightened residents fled Manhattan during the Revolution, Lord Howe conquered a city whose population had fallen to five thousand, but the influx of Loyalists from every colony first restored, and then exceeded, its previous level (which fell again after British evacuation). Among the new arrivals were over four thousand blacks who agreed to fight for Great Britain in return for their freedom. Blacks were not treated equally and were forced to occupy separate barracks, yet they fought exceedingly well. Their military formations—the Ethiopian Regiment, the Black Pioneers, and particularly the Black Brigade—constantly engaged American units in contested areas outside the city. After Evacuation Day, Britain fulfilled its promise and transported black servicemen into exile from anchorages near Staten Island. A large majority of the refugees settled in Nova Scotia and established the Birchtown settlement.

New York retained a substantial black population, both slave and free, even after the British left, and during the 1780s that number grew. Trinity Church continued its practice of performing marriages for free blacks, but New York did not abolish slavery or ban slave ships from using its harbor. During the rebuilding years, blacks both slave and free labored in every brewery, ropeworks, shipyard, and construction crew in the city. Early in 1785 wealthy parishioners of Trinity Parish helped to found the New York Manumission Society, but many members of the new association themselves held slaves. Yet the New Yorkers most likely to own slaves and the most reluctant to free them were artisans—smaller shopkeepers who also opposed the creation of New York's African Free School in 1786. In 1787 black poet Jupiter Hammon issued a tract advising blacks to meekly obey their masters, and the state legislature enacted a slave code soon afterwards. By 1790, at the time of the first national census, New York's black population was recorded as 3,470, approximately one-third of who were freemen, and their percentage of the total population had fallen to 11 percent. Despite the implied promises of the Declaration of Independence, New York did not abolish slavery until 1827.

Peace and the end of the Revolution stimulated renewed European immigration to New York. In 1784 John Jacob Astor of Waldorf, Germany, arrived in the city and soon opened a musical instrument shop. He quickly discovered the fur business as a road to wealth and afterward speculated in city land, an endeavor that would make him the richest man in the nation. Catholic newcomers from Ireland included Dennis Lynch of Galway, a merchant who city legend credits with bringing in the greatest amount of hard cash. Catholics had been rare in Manhattan before 1776, but during the British occupation masses were performed by Reverend Ferdinand Steenmeyer. Increasing numbers of Catholic immigrants arrived after 1783, and their presence made construction of a church possible. In 1786 Lynch joined with Thomas Stoughton and Hector St. Jean Crevecoeur to build St. Peter's on Barclay Street, the first of many Catholic churches in Manhattan. By 1790 there were almost two thousand Irish in the city, a mere foretaste of future population shifts. Several other major city leaders of the 1780s were immigrants: financier William Duer came from the West Indies, merchant Archibald Gracie was a Scot, and Pierre L'Enfant, who remodeled city hall for the Federal Congress, was French. Moreover, the city population gained new vigor as dozens of Loyalists moved from other colonies, spurned British relocation offers, and chose to build new lives in Manhattan.

Despite the tumult of the revolutionary era and population churnings, New York in 1790 remained essentially a city ethnically dominated by its past. Most of Manhattan's elite leaders and its business leadership traced their roots to English and Dutch families present since the British conquest of 1664. The Revolution had empowered a younger generation of leaders, however, and in the 1780s the reality of opportunity had drawn upstate elites, immigrant entrepreneurs, and speculators to the city on the Hudson. The first national census in 1790 counted its population at 33,131, still perhaps trailing Philadelphia, yet a cohort already tested by adversity and sublimely confident of future greatness. An extraordinary period of New York City's growth was about to begin.

See also *New York, NY 1790–1828; New York, NY 1828–1854; New York, NY 1854–1877; New York, NY 1877–1896; New York, NY 1896–1929; New York, NY 1929–1941; New York, NY 1941–1952; New York, NY 1952–1989; New York, NY 1989–2011*

GEORGE LANKEVICH

BIBLIOGRAPHY

Burrows, Edwin, and Mike Wallace. *Gotham: A History of New York City to 1898*. New York, NY: Oxford University Press, 1999.

Cochran, Thomas C. *New York in the Confederation: An Economic Study*. Port Washington, NY: Kennikat Press, 1970.

Mohl, Raymond A. *Poverty in New York, 1783–1825*. New York, NY: Oxford University Press, 1971.

Pomerantz, Sidney. *New York: An American City, 1783–1793*. New York, NY: Columbia University Press, 1938.

Schecter, Barnet. *The Battle for New York: The City at the Heart of the American Revolution*. New York, NY: Walker & Co., 2002.

Stansell, Christine. *City of Women: Sex and Class in New York, 1789–1860*. New York, NY: Alfred A Knopf, 1986.

PHILADELPHIA, PA 1776–1790

PHILADELPHIA WAS THE EPICENTER of revolutionary activity in the mid-to-late eighteenth century. The city had matured over the course of the century from the plan for a "green country town" constructed by William Penn to a bustling, important trade center through the revolutionary era. Prior to 1750, Philadelphia was plagued with filth and disease and was lined by unpaved streets. However, the city's skyline began to change by midcentury as the Pennsylvania State House (Constitution Hall) was erected, streets were paved, and Philadelphia became a cultural and scientific center. Men such as James Logan worked to bring schools, libraries, and theatres to the growing city. Logan paved the way for men such as Benjamin Franklin and well-known botanist John Bartram to lead and further develop Philadelphia.

Franklin worked hard to protect the city and propel its growth by organizing Philadelphia's Union Fire Company. He also developed the first hospital for the American colonies, known as Pennsylvania Hospital, in 1751, and created the Academy and College of Philadelphia in 1749, which later became the University of Pennsylvania. By the era of the American Revolution, Philadelphia was a major city and an intellectual hotbed for activism and change.

GOVERNMENT AND POLITICS

Pennsylvania more generally was a complicated political landscape. By the late 1760s, the Provincial Assembly was viewed by a younger generation as overly conservative. During the early years of the 1770s, new faces and committees began to slowly take control of the commonwealth. In July of 1776 a state convention stripped control away from the "old government" and established the Pennsylvania Council of Safety to rule during the turbulent years of the American Revolution.

On September 28, 1776, the first state constitution of Pennsylvania was adopted. This document created an assembly that consisted of one house with a supreme executive council instead of a governor. Many men connected to the patriot cause were opposed to the new Pennsylvania constitution. Moderates led by John Dickinson, Robert Morris, and Benjamin Rush were willing to make accommodations for the British and worried about the impact that a war would have on the Pennsylvania economy. A more radical group known as the Constitutionalists included men such as William Findley, George Bryan, and Thomas Paine. These men were heavily involved in the governing of Pennsylvania throughout the revolutionary era, eventually removing more moderate voices from leadership positions.

While optimism and excitement grew following the famous meeting of the First Continental Congress and the issuance of the Declaration of Independence, the realities of war soon hit home in the nation's birthplace. On September 11, 1777, George Washington's Continental Army was badly beaten at Brandywine, and British troops moved to take the city of Philadelphia. Many residents fled to the countryside as three thousand British troops marched into the city. Fear and anxiety were palpable as smallpox devastated both British and patriot troops. Most

QUICK FACTS

PHILADELPHIA, PA 1776–1790

MAYORS

In 1776 the city government was abolished and city functions were controlled by the Provincial Assembly of Pennsylvania. The state government continued to run the city until a new charter for the city was granted in March of 1789. No change in the election of the mayor occurred from colonial practices

Samuel Powel   (1789–1790)
Samuel Miles   (1790–1791)

MAJOR INDUSTRIES AND EMPLOYERS

Maritime trade (sailmaking, porters, coopers, innkeepers)
Manufacturing textiles
Printing, publishing, and papermaking

MAJOR NEWSPAPERS

The Freeman's Journal
Gazette of the United States
The Pennsylvania Chronicle and Universal Advertiser
Pennsylvania Evening Herald, and the American Monitor
The Pennsylvania Evening Post
Pennsylvania Gazette and Weekly Advertiser
Pennsylvania Herald, and General Advertiser
The Pennsylvania Journal
Pennsylvania Ledger, or, The Philadelphia Market-day Advertiser
Pennsylvania Mercury and Universal Advertiser
Pennsylvania Packet, and Daily Advertiser

MAJOR EVENTS

July 1776: In a document written primarily by Thomas Jefferson, the Continental Congress adopts the Declaration of Independence. This document severs the ties between the thirteen colonies and the British Empire.

September 1776: Pennsylvania adopts its first state constitution.

1777: Philadelphia is invaded by British troops and endures a ten-month siege.

March 1780: Pennsylvania begins the process of dismantling slavery through the Gradual Abolition Act.

1783: The Pennsylvania Mutiny (also known as the Philadelphia Mutiny), an antigovernment protest issued by nearly four hundred men from the Continental Army, takes place. Congress eventually leaves the city of Philadelphia.

1787: The Constitutional Convention came together to address the problems of governing the United States of America. The result was the creation and adoption of the United States Constitution.

Philadelphians were unable to acquire common goods such as coffee, flour, and salt as they were either too expensive to purchase or impossible to find. British troops pulled out of the city some ten months later, but Philadelphians continued to live under difficult wartime conditions.

Philadelphia continued to play a major role in the shaping of politics during the early years of the Republic. Although the United States Congress left Philadelphia and moved to New York during the early 1780s, city and state politicians lobbied hard to have the permanent capital placed in Philadelphia. A permanent site along the Potomac River was chosen, however, though Philadelphia served as a temporary site for the United States capital beginning in 1790.

As citizens began to repair their city following the end of the Revolution, Philadelphia witnessed economic growth and expansion.

INDUSTRY, COMMERCE, AND LABOR

Throughout the latter decades of the eighteenth century, Philadelphia was perhaps the wealthiest American urban center. Although boom and bust years between 1776 and 1790 often created change and uncertainty, the city's economy was a fairly stable one with a clear dependence upon commerce. Most workers depended upon direct or indirect trade, not only among the states within the infant Republic, but also with a greater Atlantic world. Small apple farmers in rural Pennsylvania, city storekeepers, and larger manufacturers and merchants who shipped goods throughout the Caribbean and London were all involved in what became an expansive business of trade. Foreign ships found a natural home at the wharves of the nation's birthplace and were constantly releasing their cargo for distribution throughout the Delaware Valley. In return, these vessels were loaded with the grain and livestock products that were well known and sought after in the region.

Many Philadelphians engaged in work that was related to commerce, such as maritime trade. Twenty percent of the city's men were involved in maritime work, making them the largest occupational group in the city between 1756 and 1798. In addition to those who took to the open seas, merchants and clerk assistants accounted for nearly one-third of the free work force. Yet there was another large group of people dependent upon trade, including laborers, porters, coopers, shopkeepers, grocers, innkeepers, and sailmakers, all of whom made a living from the flourishing seaport. Carpenters and bricklayers who labored to build new homes in a rapidly growing city accounted for one-tenth of taxpayers, while nearly 20 percent of those who paid their taxes were involved in selling clothes, hats, and bread within the city and beyond. Others worked with leather and metal products, built ships, or were involved in municipal jobs such as constables, jail keepers, postal employees, and city governmental officials.

However, many of Philadelphia's laborers in the middle of the eighteenth century were classified as unfree and were bound by a system of indentured servitude or slavery. As European immigration into the city accelerated during the early colonial period, indentured servants became an integral part of the Philadelphia landscape. The majority of early colonial servants were English and skilled in a trade. In many instances indentured servitude became a vehicle by which family members and friends could be brought over to the colony and given an opportunity for success.

By the mid-eighteenth century, indentured servitude in Philadelphia changed along with the immigrating population. No longer were skilled English servants the majority of those who took on indenture contracts. Irish, German, and Scottish men and women quickly began to compose the majority of the servant population in the city. As Philadelphia became the commercial center of the Delaware River valley, servants became valuable commodities. Established English immigrants simply stopped offering their family members the favor of passage and indenture to Pennsylvania. The cost of labor continued to increase and the bonds of family and friendship failed to trump financial gain.

Following the Revolution, the British began to dismantle the servant trade in an attempt to fortify the labor pool at home in England. Fearing that the continuation of mass emigration to the United States would hurt the British labor force and leave parts of Ireland depopulated, the British passed two acts, in 1788 and 1803, severely limiting the number of indentured servants allowed to go from Britain to America. The emigration of the northern Irish was targeted in this movement, since they represented the largest block of indentured servants in the United States. The number of Irish indentured servants in Philadelphia was larger than the number of indentured servants from all other parts of Europe combined. Since Great Britain had served as Pennsylvania's primary source of servants, these acts brought about the end of white indentured servitude in the state.

The influx of Irish emigrants transformed labor scarcity into labor surplus and prompted Philadelphia servant holders to rethink the indenture system. As it became much more cost effective for masters to abandon the practice of supporting a servant and his or her family, wage labor became much more popular. Not only did masters prefer this transition, it also became much more difficult to find European men and women willing to become indentured servants. Free wage labor became the preferred labor system, but as indentured servants were displaced they were left vulnerable to a fluctuating labor market. As indentured servitude gave way, so did the institution of slavery.

RACE, ETHNICITY, AND IMMIGRATION

Although historians attribute abolition in Pennsylvania to the principles behind the American Revolution, it was not the primary reason for slavery's demise. Before the Revolution, slavery was being dismantled by both white Quakers and men and women of African descent in Philadelphia. The political ideology of the Revolution did provide a secular language to critique black slavery, but in itself it did not provide for immediate emancipation in Pennsylvania. Available cheap and abundant white labor following the war pushed city residents to abandon the expensive practice of slaveholding. Slaveholders in the countryside, some of whom had talked of abolishing slavery in the early eighteenth century, held on to the peculiar institution through the 1770s.

Philadelphians could purchase slaves at public auction throughout the 1770s. British ships captured by privateers were brought to the Philadelphia port to sell off their cargo. This was the case in 1779, when a ship loaded with coffee, molasses, sugar, and slaves found eager buyers. And although Quakers were freeing their slaves, non-Quakers continued to import black men and women. As the Society of Friends released their slaves in rural Pennsylvania, Anglicans, Episcopalians, and Presbyterians remained detached from abolitionist sentiment, especially if their trade was dependent on human labor.

Throughout the chaos of the Revolutionary War, artisans ended their relationship with the system of bound labor. Many artisans served in the militia, but their businesses were disrupted and teetered on the brink of bankruptcy. Upon their return from war, artisans were much more willing to hire labor, which was now a cheaper alternative. With a glut of white laborers, owners found ways to end their connections to slave labor without freeing their chattel: by death (either their own or the death of their slaves), by a slave's escape, or by selling their slaves to slave traders.

Slavery lived on for only another twenty-five years in Pennsylvania. (It lasted longer in the neighboring states of New Jersey and Delaware.) This was due to the Gradual Abolition Act of 1780. Two years earlier, in 1778, talk of a gradual abolition bill began to circulate in the city. George Bryan, a merchant and Irish immigrant to Philadelphia, prompted the assembly to establish a committee to draft a law by February 1779. In deference to the property rights of slaveholders, the original act did not call for the actual emancipation of slaves in Pennsylvania. Instead, the bill required the gradual emancipation of all slaves born on or after March 1, 1780. Children born of slaves would serve as indentured servants for a period of twenty-eight years. All slaveholders in the commonwealth were required to register their slaves with their county, and those slaves who remained unregistered were to gain freedom automatically. As for new residents, any slaveholder entering Pennsylvania with his or her slaves was required to release them within six months after their arrival, with congressmen and foreign ministers being the only exception to the rule.

The assembly passed the Gradual Abolition Act of Pennsylvania on March 1, 1780, yet slavery would not entirely end in Pennsylvania until 1847. Emancipation was a tricky business, and for slaveholders worried about financial loss, gradualism was the only remedy to their problems. Gradual emancipation allowed slave owners to exact as much free labor from their slaves as possible. Slaves would spend many of their early years—their most productive years— working for their masters, thereby reducing their masters' financial losses.

Many whites felt that blacks were simply unprepared for freedom and if left to their own devices would become indolent and lazy and bring crime and agitation to the city. By ensuring that blacks were owned, in one form or another, well into adulthood, gradual emancipation and lengthy indentures eased whites' distrust of black freedom.

In addition to the Gradual Emancipation Act, the revival of the Pennsylvania Abolition Society in 1784 created a hostile environment for slaveholders in Philadelphia. Founded earlier in the century, the revived society became a watchdog organization, ensuring that thousands of men and women of African descent were set free under the provisions of the new law.

Even prior to the end of slavery in the city, Philadelphia's free black community grew steadily and was significantly large for a northern city. The last decades of the eighteenth century witnessed a drastic reduction of the slave population within the city's limits. From 1763 to 1775 the slave population of Philadelphia reached its colonial peak at 1,481, and by 1770 there were between two hundred and three hundred free black men and women. In the five years before the war, the number of free blacks doubled, and by 1783 more than one thousand free black men and women called Philadelphia their home. Following the enactment of the Gradual Abolition Act, the slave population of Philadelphia began to diminish. By 1800 there were only fifty-five slaves in the city, and the total free black population was just over six thousand people.

As African Americans moved into the nineteenth century, they found themselves in a new system of bound labor: indentured servitude. Many slaveholders simply emancipated their slaves and quickly indentured them. Servitude elongated the transition from slavery to freedom. For African American women in particular, servitude was a difficult and lengthy experience. They used their extended period in bondage, however, as a time to gain skills, rudimentary education, and the means to improve the future conditions of their own freeborn children.

See also *Philadelphia, PA 1790–1828; Philadelphia, PA 1828–1854; Philadelphia, PA 1854–1877; Philadelphia, PA 1877–1896; Philadelphia, PA 1896–1929; Philadelphia, PA 1929–1941; Philadelphia, PA 1941–1952; Philadelphia, PA 1952–1989; Philadelphia, PA 1989–2011*

ERICA ARMSTRONG DUNBAR

BIBLIOGRAPHY

Dunbar, Erica Armstrong. *A Fragile Freedom: African American Women and Emancipation in the Antebellum City.* New Haven, CT: Yale University Press, 2008.

Nash, Gary B. *Forging Freedom: The Formation of Philadelphia's Black Community, 1720–1840.* Cambridge, MA: Harvard University Press, 1988.

Nash, Gary B., and Jean Soderlund. *Freedom by Degrees: Emancipation in Pennsylvania and Its Aftermath.* New York, NY: Oxford University Press, 1991.

Salinger, Sharon. *"To Serve Well and Faithfully:" Labor and Indentured Servants in Pennsylvania, 1682–1800.* New York, NY: Cambridge University Press, 1987.

Smith, Billy. *"The Lower Sort:" Philadelphia's Laboring People 1750–1880.* Ithaca, NY: Cornell University Press, 1994.

BOSTON, MA 1776–1790

BOSTON WAS FOUNDED IN 1630 BY PURITANS from the Massachusetts Bay colony and was established as the capital of the colony within two years, serving as the home of the colonial legislature, known as the General Court, and the colonial civil and criminal court, known as the Quarterly Courts. While religious issues were, unsurprisingly, paramount in the early decades of the city, over the course of the eighteenth century commerce and politics replaced religion as the primary interests and motivating factors of most Bostonians. Boston was a leader almost from its inception, establishing a free public school by 1635, poor relief and a private charitable aid society by 1657, and the first newspaper printed in the New World, the *Boston Newsletter*, in 1704. Boston was also at the forefront of the movement for independence, establishing and organizing committees of correspondence throughout the colonies and agitating for revolution. In 1775 British troops led by General Thomas Gage occupied the city and held it for over a year. By the time the British withdrew, the focus of the war had shifted to New York, and Massachusetts as a whole was spared further immediate conflict. While no further battles were fought in Massachusetts, the ongoing pressure to raise men, money, and supplies for American troops was a constant strain on the local economy. With the end of the war, Boston was able to rebuild. Privateering ships were sent in search of new international markets, and a new focus on manufacturing substantially changed the city's economy.

QUICK FACTS

BOSTON, MA 1776–1790

MAYORS

Boston had no mayors during this time period and was governed by town meetings.

MAJOR INDUSTRIES AND EMPLOYERS

Shipping
Textile manufacture
Ironworks
Fishing
Shipbuilding
Printing and bookselling

MAJOR NEWSPAPERS

The Boston Gazette
Massachusetts Spy
Independent Chronicle and the Universal Advertiser
Continental Journal and Weekly Advertiser
Independent Ledger and American Advertiser
The American Herald and the General Advertiser
Massachusetts Register and United States Calendar
The Massachusetts Centinel and the Republican Journal

MAJOR EVENTS

1775: Following the battles of Lexington and Concord, the Siege of Boston began on April 20. During the following winter, the British tore down over one hundred buildings for firewood.

1776: The British evacuate Boston on March 17, leaving the Boston harbor aboard 140 ships. On July 18 the Declaration of Independence is read at the Town House (today's Old State House) in Boston.

1778: The Massachusetts General Court passes the Test Act, which requires those suspected of continued loyalty to Britain to take an oath to support the revolutionary cause. This act is strengthened further in 1779 when the court passes the Banishment Act, confiscating the property of anyone who refused to take the loyalty oath and banishing them from the colony.

1779: Depreciation of the Continental currency and the high price of imported goods, as well as price gouging and speculating, leads the town meeting to set prices for food, textiles, leather goods, and labor.

1788: Three free black men are kidnapped from a ship in Boston Harbor and transported to Martinique to be sold as slaves. This act outrages much of Boston and prompts the General Court to finally address the issue of slavery. The resulting legislation declared the slave trade illegal and assessed real penalties on those found to be involved in it.

GOVERNMENT AND POLITICS

Boston was governed by the town meeting system that prevailed throughout most of the New England colonies. Eligible residents, men who held taxable property, would meet to elect town officers and to vote on issues that affected the town. Elections, which occurred yearly, included lesser offices like constable, justice of the peace, and fire wardens, as well as the more important offices of town clerk and selectmen. A moderator was elected at each meeting to oversee proceedings in the meeting itself. The moderator ruled on points of order and publicly announced voting results. The town clerk recorded minutes of town meetings and also served as recorder of deeds and vital statistics. The selectmen constituted the executive committee of the town meeting and were responsible for overseeing common land, summoning town meetings, announcing and overseeing state elections, and fulfilling any financial or legal duties required by the town.

In smaller communities, town meetings might be called as infrequently as once or twice a year. In Boston, town meetings were called almost monthly to vote on such issues as raising taxes, appointing schoolmasters, and deciding on poor relief and salaries for public officers. The selectmen of the city met even more regularly, and throughout the revolutionary period members of the local committee of correspondence would frequently attend their meetings and assist in planning to meet military quotas, appoint officers, and raise money for the financial inducement needed to recruit men as the war continued. As Boston continued to grow and expand this system of government became increasingly unwieldy and inefficient. The town meeting, however, was the only form of local government authorized under the 1780 state constitution and, despite repeated petitions for incorporation as a city—eleven between 1650 and 1822—Boston remained a town until 1822.

As a major port, Boston was acutely conscious of the growing presence of British troops and was among the first to be affected by the increasingly oppressive polices being imposed by Parliament. Early clashes with British troops, such as the Anti-Impressment Riots in 1747, the Boston Massacre in 1770, and the Boston Tea Party in 1773, demonstrated to the British the increasing hostility of Boston to the mother country. The British reacted in 1774 with the passage of the Intolerable Acts, which included the Boston Port Act that closed the port of Boston and put the overwhelming majority of Bostonians out of work. Boston, in particular, became a primary motivating factor in the nonimportation agreements passed by most of the colonies.

In May of 1774 General Gage moved a large contingent of British troops into Boston to seal the port and enforce the acts of Parliament. Many of Boston's wealthy elite joined the British, but the majority of the city's residents rallied around the leaders of the Boston Committee of Correspondence and Safety—Samuel Adams, John Adams, and John Hancock, most notably. Over the next year, Gage steadily expanded the troop presence in Boston and placed increasingly inflexible controls on the city. Boston's revolutionary leaders, called "the faction" by the British, maintained order in the city, intent on giving Gage no excuse to attack and on buying time to strengthen support for the revolutionary cause and to organize the colonial militias. Tensions continued to rise, culminating in the battles of Concord and Lexington in April of 1775. In the aftermath of the first battles of the Revolutionary War, British troops retreated to Boston and blocked the narrow land access to the city, beginning the Siege of Boston.

Over the next months life grew increasingly harsh under British martial law. In the early days of the siege, Gage struck an agreement with the selectmen, allowing residents to pass freely through the barricades so long as they did not carry arms with them. This was modified first to allow people to leave, but not to return. Then they were allowed to leave, but not to take any supplies with them. Eventually, residents were not permitted to leave the city at all. As Gage and his British troops established themselves in Boston, the city was surrounded by Continental

Boston's Faneuil Hall, built in 1742 and named for merchant Peter Faneuil, was used as a market and housed the city's town meetings. In 1805 the hall was greatly expanded in a design by celebrated architect Charles Bulfinch.   *Source: Library of Congress*

troops. With the Americans blocking overland supply routes, the British were forced to rely on their navy for supplies, though that was quickly complicated by the ever-growing numbers of American privateers who harassed the supply routes, capturing ships and blocking supplies. The situation in Boston quickly became untenable. Food shortages, extortionate prices for the few supplies that did make it into the city, and ongoing tensions between Boston's residents and the British troops and Loyalists made life increasingly difficult over the next year. In October, following the Battle of Bunker Hill, General Gage was recalled to England and replaced by General William Howe. Skirmishes and small pitched battles had given way to a stalemate, with both sides waiting for an opening. In March of 1776, the American troops, now under the command of George Washington, found such an opening with the arrival of sixty pieces of heavy artillery from Fort Ticonderoga in New York. Washington used the guns to convince Howe that his best option was retreat.

Within two weeks, the British troops, accompanied by the Loyalist population of the city, surrendered Boston. Before leaving, however, they collected all blankets and clothing and pillaged private homes, removing anything of value and breaking anything they could not carry. Oddly, they left the barracks and military battlements damaged but serviceable. They also left a number of heavy cannons and horses. Despite Howe's quick surrender, Washington was careful about which soldiers were allowed into the abandoned city to avoid the potential spread of smallpox. Statements issued by the town meeting report that Boston was not completely free of the disease until October of that year.

Boston had elected selectmen in March 1775 before the siege began. These men served as the town representatives and intermediaries throughout the occupation and were reelected in the first town meeting following the British withdrawal. The first order of business was to appoint committees to determine the extent of the damage to the city. There were larger, external issues to face as well. With the rejection of the royal charter as a governing document, the colony had no official government. In 1778 the General Court of Massachusetts sent a proposed state constitution to the towns for ratification. Boston's town meeting rejected it, as did the overwhelming majority of the towns, calling instead for a constitutional convention. The state constitution that finally passed in 1780 addressed most of the issues raised by the towns in 1778, mainly representation and the lack of a bill of rights. The first article of the constitution declared "all men are born free and equal" and opened the door for slaves to sue for freedom. Two cases, the Quock Walker case and the Mum Bett case, finally ended slavery in the state of Massachusetts when the Supreme Court of Massachusetts declared that the "free and equal" clause of the constitution negated slavery.

The next weighty political issue to come before the town council was the ratification of the federal constitution. The sharp division between merchants and farmers visible throughout the colonies was also clear in Massachusetts. Merchants were generally Federalists, favoring a stronger central government to provide better control of commerce and trade. Farmers were, for the most part, anti-Federalists, resenting any intrusion of the government into private affairs. Samuel Adams and John Hancock, leaders of the revolutionary movement and delegates to the state constitutional convention, were also delegates to the Massachusetts convention to consider ratification of the federal constitution. Both men were initially opposed to it, fearing that they would simply be substituting homegrown tyranny for British control, but they were swayed by a meeting of four hundred Boston tradesmen who supported it. Hancock suggested they ratify the document but include a list of amendments and recommendations they felt were necessary. The convention voted on February 6, 1788, ratifying the United States Constitution by a vote of 187 to 168. Three months later the Constitution was declared the official law of the country with the ratification of New Hampshire in June.

INDUSTRY, COMMERCE, AND LABOR

After the British withdrawal, the city also faced an uphill battle in reinvigorating the business sector. The closure of the port had put 90 percent of the population out of work. While the ships themselves employed a much smaller percentage of the population, the shipping and shipbuilding industries together were by far the largest employers in Boston. Martial law imposed by Gage had interrupted most of the rest of the city's industries, shuttering printing presses and schools and the majority of manufacturing and retail outlets. In addition, shipbuilding had shifted to smaller, less politically fraught ports years earlier. Trade with England and the English-controlled West Indies was no longer an option, and all available ships were needed for the fledgling Continental Navy. Local industry slowly began to fill the void, focusing on textile production, ironworks, paper manufacturing, and privateering. Privateering, especially, drove the economic future of the city. Throughout the war years, Massachusetts registered more than 365 privateers. Smaller ships patrolled the American coastline, interrupting British supply lines and running British blockades. Larger ships traveled to the West Indies and smuggled in forbidden goods. Still-larger ships sailed off the coast of England, Ireland, and Scotland, forcing the British to use military ships to escort merchant vessels. Building and fitting out privateers dominated the waterfront, and local manufacturers were kept busy supplying them. The shipbuilding industry employed or otherwise supported as many as thirty local industries. Textile workers produced canvas for sails. Ironworkers made anchors and brass cannons. Carpenters and rope manufacturers were central to maritime production. In addition, crews from the privateers filled the city's waterfront, requiring lodging, food, and entertainment. In 1779 Boston had twenty-one distilleries supplying rum for both local use and trading.

Two industries that came to dominate the manufacturing sector of the city were paper and textiles. The textile industry began in earnest with the nonimportation agreements. The colonists encouraged the local production of clothing and textiles to replace imported British goods. The fledgling industry produced linen, wool, canvas, and cordage, as well as employing a thriving side industry that made wool cards, which in turn employed wire cutters for the cards. The paper industry was healthy enough at this time that announcements were published in the local paper asking for donations of rags to be used in paper production. Printers, bookbinders, and booksellers were also part of a flourishing local industry, and wallpaper was big business in the city.

Despite their determined rebuilding, Bostonians faced considerable difficulties during this period. Demands for more men, money, and supplies for the military were a constant drain, and the town meeting members protested regularly that they had met their requirements and complained that other towns had not contributed their share. The steady depreciation of Continental currency was a significant problem, as was price gouging and speculating in commodities. In response, the Boston town meeting authorized the selectmen to set prices on goods ranging from salt and hay to rum and molasses. At the same time, they set wages for day laborers and criminalized not accepting Continental paper money. The paper money issue and the ensuing divide between rural and urban interests were the driving forces behind Shays's Rebellion in 1786. When smaller protest actions were largely ignored, Shays's ragtag group of farmers and militia veterans marched on Springfield, the home of the national armory. While they were easily put down, the popular support for Shays and the continuing furor over debt and currency were prime motivators to the Constitutional Convention.

The end of the war allowed privateers to return their focus to trade. As legitimate trade with England and the West Indies was unavailable, local merchants began looking for new markets. Boston ships reached Canton, China, and India in 1785 and Russia in 1787. They were the first American ships to reach the northwest coast in 1787. The China trade had enormous potential, but trading was difficult. China refused to accept American currency, and American traders had few goods of interest to the Chinese markets. With the opening of the northwest coast, Boston merchants were able to offer seal and otter skins in trade and became the first merchants to see steady profits from the China trade.

RACE, ETHNICITY, AND IMMIGRATION

Founded in 1630 by religious exiles from England, Massachusetts as a whole retained a remarkable homogeneity of population. By the eve of the Revolution, Boston was still overwhelmingly of English descent, though there were apparently substantial enough populations of Scots and Irish to support the founding of charitable aid societies, such as the Scots Charitable Society in 1657 and the Charitable Irish Society in 1737.

Slavery was introduced to Massachusetts as early as 1637, and despite early involvement in the slave trade, Boston was quickly overtaken by Salem, Massachusetts, and Newport, Rhode Island, as the northern centers of what was known as the "triangle trade." Molasses and sugar brought in from the West Indies was distilled locally into rum, which was then shipped to Africa and traded for slaves, who were taken to the West Indies and traded for gold to buy molasses. Boston played an integral role in this by supplying ships, rum, and insurance to merchants.

Boston began political action in favor of ending slavery as early as 1701, instructing the town's representatives to the General Court to push for a resolution encouraging the use of white indentured servants and an end to slavery. While the legislature did not act on that request, there were regular attempts to constrict and discourage slavery and the slave trade within Massachusetts over the coming decades.

Throughout the 1760s, slaves used the court system to sue for liberty and frequently won. By the 1770s public opinion had resulted in a steady decline in slave-holding. The Quaker Society of Friends barred members from owning slaves or being involved in the slave trade as early as 1758, and many found the Enlightenment rhetoric emphasizing the inherent rights and nobility of man to be at odds with the practice of owning slaves. Prompted by the British invitation to free blacks to join the British troops, Washington lifted a ban on blacks fighting with the Continental Army. The Continental Navy needed no such prompting. Short of men and supplies, they welcomed sailors, black or white, many of them from the Massachusetts coast. Privateers also welcomed black crewmen and generally paid better.

In 1780 the General Court passed the Declaration of Rights to the Constitution of the Commonwealth. While the declaration declared all men "born free and equal," it did not expressly refer to slavery. Beginning in 1781, a series of cases that would come to be known as the Quock Walker case challenged this declaration, resulting in Chief Justice William Cushing stating that "slavery is in my judgment as effectively abolished as it can be by the granting of rights and privileges wholly incompatible and repugnant to its existence" and instructing the jury in the case that slavery was unconstitutional in Massachusetts.

See also *Boston, MA 1790–1828; Boston, MA 1828–1854; Boston, MA 1854–1877; Boston, MA 1877–1896; Boston, MA 1896–1929; Boston, MA 1929–1941; Boston, MA 1941–1952*

JAMES MCWILLIAMS

BIBLIOGRAPHY

Adams, James Truslow. *New England in the Republic, 1776–1850*. Whitefish, MT: Kessinger Publishing, 2004.

Carr, Jacqueline Barbara. *After the Siege: A Social History of Boston 1775–1800*. Boston, MA: Northeastern University Press, 2005.

Frothingham, Richard. *History of the Siege of Boston and of the Battles of Lexington, Concord, and Bunker Hill*. Boston, MA: Little, Brown, and Company, 1903.

Hall, Van Beck. *Politics without Parties: Massachusetts, 1780–1791*. Pittsburgh, PA: University of Pittsburgh Press, 1972.

Nash, Gary B. *The Urban Crucible: The Northern Seaports and the Origins of the American Revolution*. Cambridge, MA: Harvard University Press, 1986.

Nelson, William. *Notes toward a History of the American Newspaper*. New York, NY: Charles F. Heartman, 1918.

Riess, Oscar. *Blacks in Colonial America*. Jefferson, NC: McFarland & Company, Inc., 2006.

Warden, G. B. "Town Meeting Politics in Colonial and Revolutionary Boston." In *Boston 1700–1980*, edited by Ronald P. Formisano and Constance K. Burns, 13–28. Westport, CT: Greenwood Press, 1984.

CHARLESTON, SC 1776–1790

THE YEARS BETWEEN 1776 AND 1790 were politically and economically turbulent in Charleston (originally named Charles Town)—an era of revolutionary battles, British occupation, and the fumbling start of the United States. During the British threat and its aftermath, the prewar planter and merchant elite that had dominated Charles Town and the rest of the colony was challenged by non-elites, the developing backcountry, and its own slaves. For a brief period, the egalitarian forces of the Revolution appeared to be making Charles Town a less aristocratic city.

GOVERNMENT AND POLITICS

In June 1776 the British attacked Charles Town, shelling an unfinished fort made of palmetto logs on Sullivan's Island. Bad sailing on the part of the British and the unexpected durability of the green palmetto logs against British cannon fire contributed to a decisive American victory. South Carolinians commemorated the event with a state flag showing an American palmetto dominating a British oak.

South Carolina was granted two years of peace until the British southern campaign began. On May 12, 1780, having stayed in the city until his troops had no chance for escape, General Benjamin Lincoln was forced to surrender on British terms. The patriot cause thus suffered one of its major defeats and the occupation of Charles Town began.

The British hoped that a well-governed Charles Town would serve as a beacon for Loyalists. In the summer of 1780, the British created a civilian board of police to serve alongside the military commandant in governing Charles Town. This board of police, composed of intendants headed by an intendant general, was supposed to be a temporary arrangement, soon to be replaced with a more traditional civilian government, but it continued to exist until the British began to evacuate.

MAYORS

Occupied Charles Town, intendant general of board of police:

James Simpson	(1780–1781)
William Bull	(1781–1782)

Charleston after 1783 incorporation:

Richard Hutson	(1783–1785)
Arnoldus Vanderhorst	(1785–1786)
John F. Grimké	(1786–1788)
Rawlins Lowndes	(1788–1789)
Thomas Jones	(1789–1790)

MAJOR INDUSTRIES AND EMPLOYERS

Agriculture

Exportation of rice, indigo, and naval stores

Importation of slaves and manufactured goods

MAJOR NEWSPAPERS

Charleston Evening Gazette
Charleston Morning Post and Daily Advertiser
Charlestown Gazette
The Columbian Herald, or, The Patriotic Courier of North-America
Gazette of the State of South-Carolina
Royal South-Carolina Gazette
South Carolina Gazette & General Advertiser
South Carolina Gazette & Public Advertiser

MAJOR EVENTS

1776: A failed British attack on Charleston gives the city a two-year hiatus from the war.
1780: In a massive setback for the American cause, the British successfully conquer and occupy Charleston.
1782: The British are forced to evacuate Charleston but bring thousands of slaves with them.
1785: As Charlestonians find themselves unable to pay for their postwar purchases, a disastrous economic downturn begins.
1790: The state capital moves to Columbia, signaling the end of low country control over state politics.

The intendants were career colonial officials, military personnel, and formerly exiled Loyalist Carolinians. Experienced but venal, they frequently wrote home to plead for higher salaries. One man complained that without the salary from a second office, he would have to "call in [his] own private monies for Subsistence." Many of them hoped to use their experience in Charles Town to trade up for more glamorous government jobs.

The board of police's original purpose was to provide a location to settle civil lawsuits that might arise, but as the war continued it began to address other issues such as fire prevention, regulation of the food markets, and sanitation. It also engrossed the responsibility for charity towards the poor (formerly organized by church parishes) and regulation of Charles Town's slave population. By 1782 the board had lost most of its momentum and its meetings occurred less regularly. Though increasingly ineffective, the board represented an important change from colonial precedent. Before the war, Charles Town had been governed by South Carolina's legislature, which met in Charles Town and was primarily focused on low country issues. The board of police represented its first city government.

During the British occupation, Charlestonians were under increasing pressure to swear loyalty oaths to the king and to obey these oaths. Despite this, the war was much more brutal in the backcountry than in the occupied city; the fact that it had already been conquered sheltered Charles Town from the destruction to the west.

By 1781 patriot military victories and the successful reconstitution of a patriot government signaled that the British were losing control of South Carolina. A series of battles in 1781 expelled the British from everywhere but Charles Town. A new patriot legislature was elected in November 1781, even though few Charlestonians were able to participate. This legislature, called the Jacksonborough Assembly for the location where it met, was most notable for passing confiscation and amercement acts punishing Loyalists by claiming all or a percentage of their estates. These names were not chosen fairly; some seem to have escaped punishment because they had friends serving in the assembly. However, these acts served one of their goals, which was to intimidate Loyalists living in Charles Town.

The British occupiers were forced to evacuate Charles Town in December of 1782. Over nine thousand people left, more than five thousand of who were African American. (In 1770 the population of the city as a whole had been about eleven hundred people, over half of whom were black.) Most evacuating Loyalists immigrated to Jamaica or East Florida, which were other British plantation colonies. They left behind a worn-out, impoverished city in a state that had seen too many farms and plantations destroyed and too many men lost.

In the economic, political, and demographic chaos of the postwar period, many Charlestonians questioned the wisdom of the planter-merchant elite that dominated political offices before the war and wished to hold onto its authority when the war was over. One particularly heated issue involved British merchants. In 1782 the state legislature allowed British merchants who had come to Charleston during the occupation to stay in town and sell their stock on hand for six months. These men were in much better shape economically than their American competitors, and their presence necessarily hurt patriot merchants.

Alarmed by disputes such as this, the legislature attempted to calm the situation by giving the city its own government in 1783. An intendant (mayor) and wardens were given broad power to act at "the appearance of tumult or riot." The legislature was especially concerned about controlling slaves, free blacks, and seamen. Charles Town was also officially renamed Charleston.

The opposition continued to rise, however. American merchant Alexander Gillon renamed a local club the Marine Anti-Britannic Society in late 1783 to encourage the development of South Carolina's maritime industry and to threaten mob action against British merchants, Tory sympathizers, and other symbols of British naval and commercial power. Enlisting the support of artisans, mechanics, and backcountry farmers, the society was an important sign of opposition to the planter-merchant elite as well as its more obvious targets.

An overenthusiastic contemporary observer explained that after 1784 "a violent opposition" in Charleston nearly "ruin[ed] the Aristocracy." The summer of 1784 witnessed "riots" on the streets of Charleston, none of which were actually very violent, though on July 8 intendant

Richard Hutson used what an uncomplimentary newspaper called "an envenomed band" of "American Tories [and] British Merchants" to break up a group parading with an American flag and search the houses of supposed rioters. Mostly Gillon's followers and the intendant's supporters conducted a paper war in the newspapers that flourished in postwar Charleston as they did throughout the country.

The mayoral contest in the summer of 1784 between Alexander Gillon and Richard Hutson exemplified a nationwide issue: the contest between old elites (Hutson) who presumed they would continue to rule after the Revolution, and self-made middling sorts (Gillon) who felt there should be a place for them in the new nation's government. Men of Gillon's type attacked the elites and defended the poor but seldom tried to bring the poor into political office, promising to be their faithful representatives instead. Despite Gillon's electoral defeat by Hutson, the Charleston opposition survived.

The planter-merchant elite also faced challenges on the state level. While Charleston would retain much of its power—local observers believed that the U.S. Constitution was approved in South Carolina because Charleston was able to outvote the underrepresented citizens to the west—backcountry Carolinians were increasingly influential, in part because of economic growth. As western South Carolinians discovered tobacco farming, they became a part of the plantation economy that had dominated the coast for nearly a century. A second reason was the changing demographics of the legislature. State constitutions in 1776, 1778, and 1790 gave the backcountry progressively more representation.

Backcountry legislators were quick to use their new power for their own benefit. In 1783 they first made an issue of the inequitable location of the state's capital in Charleston. Though the legislature agreed to move to Columbia in 1786, legislators dragged their feet. One man joked that the site should be called the "Town of Refuge" because it was so far from civilization that it would be the ideal haven for criminals. When the legislature actually moved to Columbia in January of 1790, it was a sign of the end of an era. No longer would Charleston and its planter-merchant elite dominate the state government, and in Charleston itself, the voices of nonelite whites increasingly demanded to be heard.

INDUSTRY, COMMERCE, AND LABOR

Colonial Charles Town's primary economic role was to ship rice and indigo from South Carolina's plantations back to the mother country and to import the goods South Carolina's planters needed. Charlestonians also imported enough slaves to make an island near their city what one historian called "the Ellis Island of black Americans." Though the city was wealthy, colonial Charles Town already showed signs of the backwardness in manufacturing relative to northern cities that plagued the antebellum south. After the Revolution, Charlestonians had to adapt to being outside Britain's mercantilistic embrace. The terrible inflation of the war years gave way to a brief postwar boom and profound bust that was just beginning to show signs of ending in 1790.

During the war, Charlestonians were faced with the effects of British invasion, the political disruption of trading patterns, and the problem of unpayable debts. Enormous inflation challenged Charleston's merchants and consumers. Revolutionary-era analysts found the paper currency to have devaluated by 8,000 percent by June of 1780. The scarcity of food and consumer goods after patriot successes in 1781 contributed to the inflationary trend. The occupying British authority combated inflation with regulation controlling the amount of paper currency that could be used to repay debts, as well as bans on exporting *specie* (gold and silver money) from the state. They also regulated the markets, attempting to prevent soldiers from buying all the produce from country farmers then selling it in the market at a higher rate.

After the war, South Carolinians were desperate to acquire the goods they had not been able to import during the war or that had been stolen or destroyed by the British Army. Though not as damaged as the backcountry, Charleston had suffered losses; one enterprising British soldier even took the bells from St. Michael's Church. Aided by the British merchants who had been allowed to remain in Charleston, imports boomed in the first two years after the war. More than £1 million worth of merchandise and slaves arrived in Charleston in 1784 and about £6,000 the following year. Enslaved people from Africa repopulated the low country plantations and the tobacco-growing backcountry. Nearly five thousand new slaves arrived in 1784.

By 1785 it was apparent to everyone that Americans might have been eager to buy from Charleston's importers, but they had no ability to pay their debts. In a world dominated by great powers such as Great Britain and France, a weak America had little ability to export its crops. No longer could South Carolinians sell rice to the Portuguese, and South Carolina's indigo crop lost its value when the British no longer subsidized it in order to compete with French colonial producers. Unexpected crop failures in rice and indigo also hindered planters' ability to pay for their purchases.

South Carolina's legislature acted to protect the debtors' interests. Following the war, several laws were passed delaying suits to recover debts. Two laws were especially notorious: the Pine Barren Act of 1785, which enabled planters to pay merchants in pine land, valued by biased appraisers at multiples of its real worth, and the Installment Act of 1787, which required that debts be paid back in installments. Debts contracted before January 1, 1787, were not due until March 1790.

Like much of the country, postwar Charleston appeared to be in serious decline. But a revival was on its way due to European wars that opened trading to the Americans, the post-Constitution development of financial institutions, and, most importantly, the rise of cotton.

RACE, ETHNICITY, AND IMMIGRATION

The relationship between white masters and black slaves was the largest racial issue before and after the Revolution. About half of Charles Town's population was African American, and most of them were slaves. In 1770, 5,833 slaves, twenty-four free blacks, and 5,030 whites lived in the city. In 1790, 7,684 slaves, 586 free blacks, and 8,089 whites lived there. According to a sample drawn from 1730 to 1799, most enslaved men practiced a trade, including some very skilled ones such as goldsmithing. A large number of enslaved men were also watermen who transported goods on small boats. More enslaved women than men worked as household slaves; some also worked as washerwomen or cooks. Charleston was unusual among American cities in that most of its artisans were enslaved.

TO BE SOLD, on board the Ship *Bance-Island*, on tuesday the 6th of *May* next, at *Ashley-Ferry*; a choice cargo of about 250 fine healthy NEGROES, just arrived from the Windward & Rice Coast. —The utmost care has already been taken, and shall be continued, to keep them free from the least danger of being infected with the SMALL-POX, no boat having been on board, and all other communication with people from *Charles-Town* prevented.

Austin, Laurens, & Appleby.

N. B. Full one Half of the above Negroes have had the SMALL-POX in their own Country.

Thousands of enslaved Africans entered through Charleston in the late eighteenth century. Working on low country indigo and rice plantations, in tobacco fields further inland, and in a number of urban jobs, slaves constituted a significant portion of the region's population. The announcement above for a Charleston-area sale highlights previous exposure to smallpox as a selling point to buyers.   *Source: Library of Congress*

Enslaved South Carolinians endured considerable wartime turmoil. Both Whigs and Tories in the state agreed that the system of slavery must not be ended by the war, because the state would prove valueless to its possessor without its plantations. However, both sides also sought to use slaves to promote their cause, which sometimes gave unprecedented opportunity to the slaves. Though the system of slavery was more entrenched and more widely spread throughout the state after the war, slaves never forgot the freedom that the Revolutionary War provided.

Perhaps the greatest effect that the Revolution had on slaves in South Carolina was the way it promoted slave mobility as runaways or captives. The British acted first to loosen restraints on slaves. The 1779 Philipsburg Proclamation allowed rebel slaves, if they could escape, to stay unmolested behind British lines. In practice, many Loyalist-owned slaves escaped as well, and the British often found it too much trouble to return them. For the British, slaves were useful laborers, and their loyalty could be purchased with the promise that they would be free at the end of the war if they worked diligently. Runaway slaves served the army in construction projects, in the army hospitals, and as spies.

Determined not to challenge the system of slavery, both Whigs and Tories resisted the idea of slave combatants. John Laurens promoted this measure in the patriot legislature with no favorable response. The British did create a few African American battalions at the end of the war, the success of which may have encouraged similar efforts in the Caribbean.

As the center of British occupation, Charles Town absorbed a flood of runaways. Escaping to Charles Town offered many slaves unprecedented freedoms, not the least of which was the freedom of leisure for people who were accustomed to arduous agricultural labor, such as working in South Carolina's malarial rice swamps. Other runaway slaves discovered the pleasures of visiting public houses. The quieter enjoyments of urban life—such as the ability to choose one's companions and to practice one's chosen trade—are less likely to appear in the records, but one can speculate that runaway slaves discovered them as well.

Running away to Charleston was not necessarily a safe choice. The British took little interest in protecting the African American men and women who labored for them. A smallpox epidemic ripped through Charleston in 1779 and 1780, hitting the unvaccinated runaways particularly hard, and death rates seem to have been much higher among black than white members of the British Army.

Some slaves had little say about where the war took them. Both the British and American forces were eager to use slaves as a reward for white combatants. The British believed that the spoils of war were a natural benefit of military service; the Americans wished to induce men to join the army and lacked the money to pay them. Slaves were captured and taken away from their homes by both sides, and many seem to have been illicitly shipped out of the state through Charleston.

The British evacuation was a milestone in slave immigration. In 1782 Lieutenant General Alexander Leslie agreed to leave Charleston with only the slaves who were promised freedom or feared for their lives. Since this depended on slave testimony, many had the opportunity to leave with the British. At least five thousand of the approximately nine thousand people who evacuated the city were slaves. All in all, between 1775 and 1782, more than a quarter of the slaves in the low country left the region—either as captives or runaways—or died.

After the war, planters were eager to rebuild their workforce. Between 1783 and 1787, over ten thousand slaves were imported into South Carolina from Africa, mostly through the port of Charleston. Importation levels seem to have been especially high in 1784 and 1785. In 1787 both the international and domestic slave trades were closed in South Carolina. Possibly due to protests from the backcountry, the domestic slave trade was revived the following year, but the international slave trade was banned in South Carolina until 1803. By the end of this mass migration, the plantation system had spread far into the backcountry, entrenching the system of slavery across the state. The period after the Revolution saw the growth and spread of slavery in South Carolina.

Ironically, the revolutionary-era promulgation of egalitarian ideals began to erode the legitimacy of slavery. At the Constitutional debates, South Carolina's delegates looked increasingly peculiar in demanding a continued international slave trade and a fugitive slave law. Back in Charleston in 1791, three free black artisans wrote a petition to the legislature that turned the Constitution's three-fifths clause on its head. Since they were counted as citizens under the three-fifths clause, they queried, didn't they deserve all the rights of citizens? Though their petition was denied, it serves as a reminder that many of Charleston's African Americans never forgot the freedoms the war promised.

See also *Charleston, SC 1790–1828; Charleston, SC 1828–1854*

JENNIFER L. GOLOBOY

BIBILIOGRAPHY

Coclanis, Peter A. *The Shadow of a Dream: Economic Life and Death in the South Carolina Low Country, 1670–1920*. New York, NY: Oxford University Press, 1989.

Fraser, Walter J. *Charleston! Charleston!: The History of a Southern City*. Columbia: University of South Carolina Press, 1989.

Frey, Sylvia R. *Water from the Rock: Black Resistance in a Revolutionary Age*. Princeton, NJ: Princeton University Press, 1991.

Klein, Rachel N. *Unification of a Slave State: The Rise of the Planter Class in the South Carolina Backcountry.* Chapel Hill: University of North Carolina Press, 1990.

McCowen, George Smith, Jr. *The British Occupation of Charleston, 1780–1782.* Tricentennial Studies, no. 5. Columbia: University of South Carolina Press, 1972.

McMillan, James A. *The Final Victims: Foreign Slave Trade to North America, 1783–1810.* Columbia: University of South Carolina Press, 2004.

Morgan, Philip D. "Black Life in Eighteenth-Century Charleston." *Perspectives in American History* 1 (1984): 187–232.

———. "Black Society in the Lowcountry, 1760–1810." In *Slavery and Freedom in the Age of the American Revolution,* edited by Ira Berlin and Ronald Hoffman, 89. Urbana: University of Illinois Press, 1986.

Nadelhaft, Jerome J. *The Disorders of War: The Revolution in South Carolina.* Orono: University of Maine at Orono Press, 1981.

Nash, R. C. "Urbanization in the Colonial South: Charleston, South Carolina as a Case Study." *Journal of Urban History* 19 (1992): 3–29.

Olwell, Robert. *Masters, Slaves, and Subjects: The Culture of Power in the South Carolina Low Country, 1740–1790.* Ithaca, NY: Cornell University Press, 1998.

BALTIMORE, MD 1776–1790

COLONIAL MARYLAND HAD LITTLE USE FOR CITIES. The Chesapeake Bay and its many navigable tributaries provided easy access to shipping channels, and some plantations had their own dock facilities where British merchant ships tied up to exchange manufactured goods for tobacco, the colony's principal crop. Across the ocean in London, tobacco merchants provided credit and banking services for the planters of the Chesapeake. As long as the settlers were concentrated in tidewater Maryland, they did not need a city to store and ship their crops, to supply them with manufactured clothing and farm implements, or as a place to bank and borrow.

Baltimore was a late bloomer. Its population only stood at forty-three when it received its town charter in 1729—almost a hundred years after the colony's founding. The town's commissioners were appointed, not elected. They were authorized to purchase sixty acres on the Patapsco River, divide it into one-acre lots, and sell them to prospective townsmen. It was decades before they were empowered to legislate or impose taxes. Early public works such as a public wharf and a "market house" were financed by lotteries or voluntary subscription, not taxes.

Meanwhile, two other settlements, Jonestown and Fell's Point, emerged nearby as potential rivals. But Baltimore, in spite of its slow growth, outpaced its competitors. In 1745 it absorbed Jonestown and in 1773 its boundaries were extended to include Fell's Point.

Since the provincial assembly granted such limited powers to the town's official government, residents improvised an unofficial government to provide public services. The Ancient and Honorable Mechanical Company of Baltimore discharged nearly all of the duties needed for the government of the town. The company was responsible for policing and magisterial functions and also acted as firemen. Two years after its founding in 1763, the company provided the membership base for Baltimore's Sons of Liberty, one of the colony's fiercest protest organizations formed in response to the Stamp Act.

Public meetings also operated as unofficial governing bodies. As they lacked legitimate authority, they sometimes resorted to mob violence to enforce their decisions. In 1774 such a meeting became one of the first political assemblies in the colonies to call for the creation of a continental congress. Another gathering later in the same year elected representatives to a provincial convention in Annapolis, Maryland, that had all but displaced the institutions of British government. The convention's most significant act was to order the formation of a state militia. Baltimore was the first jurisdiction in Maryland to organize a militia company.

GOVERNMENT AND POLITICS

Baltimore's merchants and mechanics moved more rapidly toward revolution than most other Marylanders. Samuel Purviance, chair of the Baltimore Committee of Observation, hatched an unsuccessful plot to kidnap the colonial governor, but the Maryland Convention was not ready to strike so directly at British authority, and it formally censured Purviance. Purviance's committee had been elected by the Baltimore Association of the Freemen of Maryland. Signing on as an "associator" signified one's willingness to stand in defense of American liberty, but the "nonassociators" who refused to sign were a particular concern of Purviance's committee.

The committee tacitly supported a new organization—the Whig Club—that informally policed people of questionable loyalties. One of the club's more prominent targets was Baltimore county sheriff Robert Christie, who had refused to read the Declaration of Independence aloud from the steps of the courthouse. Christie fled after receiving a letter signed "Legion"—the Whig Club's code name—warning him that he would be killed if he did not leave the colony within six days.

The Whigs did not stop at threats. They engaged in running gun battles with Loyalists through the streets of Baltimore. Complaints against the club mounted, and the Maryland Assembly passed a resolution condemning the group. The violence soon subsided, possibly because many of the militiamen in the club were called to active service beyond Baltimore.

Militia membership seemed to trigger political activism among laborers and tradesmen once too obscure to claim political standing. Maryland's revolutionary-era constitution was one of the least revolutionary in the new United States, however. About half of the state's free white males still stood outside the electorate.

For Baltimore, the most significant by-product of Maryland's state-building was representation of two seats in the lower house of the state legislature, but even these were given grudgingly. The legislature kept Baltimore firmly in check. Instead of expanding the powers of the town commissioners to meet the needs of a growing community, the assembly created special commissioners to perform limited functions with designated resources. Special commissioners for street paving were appointed in 1782 and were empowered to grade and pave streets and to collect a variety of fees and taxes. The revenue covered not only street paving, but the hiring of street cleaners, constables to collect fines and assessments, and a treasurer to handle the money. The proliferation of special commissions may have stimulated proposals

QUICK FACTS

BALTIMORE, MD 1776–1790

MAYORS

Baltimore was governed by commission during this period. No mayors were elected until Baltimore received its city charter in 1797.

MAJOR INDUSTRIES AND EMPLOYERS

Shipping and trade
Flour milling
Shipbuilding
Iron forging
Textiles

MAJOR NEWSPAPERS

Maryland Journal and Baltimore Advertiser (weekly)
Baltimore had no daily newspaper until 1794.

MAJOR EVENTS

1729: Baltimore Town is chartered with a population of forty-three.
1776: The Continental Congress moves to Baltimore when Philadelphia, Pennsylvania, is threatened by British troops.
1777: The Whig Club is formed.
1782: A special commission is appointed to pave the streets.
1784: The town is authorized to build three public markets.

to convert Baltimore into a municipal corporation with expanded powers of self-government. Two such proposals were defeated, one in 1782 and one in 1784, allegedly by the town's "laboring classes," who worried that municipal government might raise their taxes higher without proportionate benefits.

After the Revolution, Baltimore's manufacturers failed twice in their effort to get the state assembly to enact a tariff on imported goods to protect them from the postwar resurgence of trade in British manufactures. By 1787 they had become ardent advocates of a federal constitution, hoping that a national congress might give more sympathetic treatment to the interests of urban manufacturers than did the landed gentry who dominated the state's legislature. It was a view that they shared with the town's established mercantile elite, who supported the proposed constitution because they expected it to bring uniform tariffs and improve American credit abroad.

Statewide turnout to elect delegates to the Maryland ratifying convention was less than 25 percent, but in Baltimore it was well over 100 percent—an early portent of electoral frauds to follow. Property and residency requirements for voters were routinely ignored. Federalist mobs took possession of polling places until driven off by anti-Federalist mobs. The mobs were led by prominent citizens, occasionally the candidates themselves. The election repeated a pattern of political action that had emerged at the time of the Stamp Act crisis and the founding of the Ancient and Honorable Mechanical Company of Baltimore, which continued to operate as an unauthorized institution of government.

INDUSTRY, COMMERCE, AND LABOR

Baltimore's commerce improved as prices for Maryland tobacco fell, and settlers moved west toward the Alleghenies, taking with them the investment capital of the colony's leading families. Western land was not suitable for growing tobacco, but it was good for grain. The first Baltimorean to grasp the commercial possibilities in the grain trade was town physician Dr. John Stevenson. He contracted with nearby farmers to purchase their wheat crops, and then he negotiated with ship owners to carry the cargoes to his original homeland of Ireland, where the grain was consigned to one of his old acquaintances for sale. According to a customs official of the province, Stevenson's profits were so impressive that "persons of a commercial and enterprising spirit emigrated from all quarters to this new and promising scene of industry." Pennsylvania farmers from the Susquehanna Valley found Baltimore a more accessible destination for their crops than Philadelphia. By about 1745, a road connected Baltimore and the Monocacy Valley, near Frederick, extending the territory from which grain flowed into town.

Growth was not immediate. A sketch of Baltimore drawn by a local resident in 1752 shows only twenty-five houses, one church, two taverns, and a pair of small sailing ships in the harbor. The town's population at the time was about two hundred. The market for Baltimore's wheat and corn soon expanded to the Mediterranean, however, especially when European grain harvests failed, and the Caribbean, where sugar had become so profitable that planters found it disadvantageous to divert land to the production of food for their slaves. Commercial contacts with the West Indies and Latin America added sugar, coffee, and guano to the commodities traded by the town's merchants.

The grain trade stimulated other local businesses. Baltimore's location on the fall line made it an ideal location for water-powered flour mills. It was more efficient to ship grain as flour or as baked bread than as raw wheat. The biscuit and bread business added jobs and profits to the town's economy. Ship and wagon builders produced the vehicles that carried wheat to Baltimore and from Baltimore to foreign markets. As the town's hinterland expanded, many farmers and drovers were unable to complete the round trip from farm to town in one day. Local taverns provided overnight accommodations. Farmers could not haul their crops all the way to Baltimore on the chance that a ship would be waiting to load it. They depended on merchants to buy their crops, store them in warehouses, and sell them manufactured goods in exchange. Cargoes of raw sugar picked up in the Caribbean were refined in Baltimore. Local iron ore deposits fed forges in and around Baltimore. The homes, inns, mills, workshops, foundries, refineries, and warehouses needed to house all these activities provided work for the construction trades.

The Revolution proved a powerful stimulus of Baltimore's commerce. By war's end, the permanent residents numbered about nine thousand. Baltimore was the only major port in the United States not to suffer disruption by battle or occupation. The concentration of merchants made it possible to manage the uncertainties of wartime trade by dividing the risk of any particular venture among a large number of investors. Privateering became a growth industry as the town's merchants combined commerce with legally authorized piracy. Over two hundred privateers were commissioned in Baltimore during the Revolution. And Baltimore's flour trade, the old standby of local commerce, benefited when the British crippled the town's competitors with their destruction of Norfolk, Virginia, and their success in closing trade on the Delaware River.

The war freed Baltimore from British restrictions on trade and manufacturing. Foreign merchants and consuls converged on the town to facilitate the conduct of commerce. For the first time, Baltimore ships began to trade with China. In 1784 the town created three public markets, one for each of the three former villages that had come together to form Baltimore.

Craftsmen, manufacturers, entrepreneurs, and apprentices also poured into Baltimore during the war. The population of Fell's Point alone doubled between 1771 and 1783, and the town's slave population quadrupled, a reflection of the shipbuilding industry's dependence on slave labor. Smaller enterprises grew through diversification. A saddler branched out into making chairs and chaises; a printer went into bookbinding; a goldsmith hired a few clockmakers. Manufacturing in general expanded to occupy the void that was left when British goods disappeared from American ports and to meet the needs of the Continental Army and Navy. In 1785 the members of the fledgling industrial sector organized the Association of Tradesmen and Manufacturers of Baltimore.

RACE, ETHNICITY, AND IMMIGRATION

Direct migration from England, Scotland, Ireland, and Germany accounted for some of the early growth of Baltimore, but for many more new arrivals, the town was a second or third landing place in the New World. In 1756, for example, nine hundred French-speaking Acadians expelled from Nova Scotia produced a sudden jump in local population. They formed the nucleus for Baltimore's first Roman Catholic Church congregation. Scots and Scotch-Irish merchants arrived in Baltimore by way of Pennsylvania, bringing capital to invest in slaves, ships, waterfront real estate, and flour milling. German settlers moved from York and Lancaster counties in Pennsylvania to Frederick County, Maryland, and began to reach Baltimore around 1748. Their numbers grew rapidly during the 1760s, and by the 1780s they were sufficiently numerous to divide into distinct church congregations—one Calvinist and one not. English and Irish millers came from Pennsylvania, Delaware, and Maryland's Cecil County. Many of the town's more prosperous citizens brought slaves with them to Baltimore or purchased them after they arrived. By 1790 about twelve hundred African American slaves worked in Baltimore, many of them in crafts like brickmaking, ship caulking, and iron forging. Some of these were hired out by their owners and others were allowed to hire themselves out, a practice that opened a pathway to emancipation. Another opportunity came with the introduction of "term slavery," which promised slaves freedom after a fixed term of servitude.

See also *Baltimore, MD 1790–1828; Baltimore, MD 1828–1854; Baltimore, MD 1854–1877; Baltimore, MD 1877–1896; Baltimore, MD 1896–1929; Baltimore, MD 1929–1941; Baltimore, MD 1941–1952; Baltimore, MD 1952–1989*

MATTHEW CRENSON

BIBLIOGRAPHY

Barker, Charles A. *The Background of the Revolution in Maryland*. New Haven, CT: Yale University Press, 1940.

Brugger, Robert J. *Maryland, a Middle Temperament, 1634–1980*. Baltimore, MD: Johns Hopkins University Press, 1988.

Crowl, Philip A. *Maryland During and After the Revolution: A Political and Economic Study*. Baltimore, MD: Johns Hopkins University Press, 1943.

Clarence, P. Gould. "The Economic Causes of the Rise of Baltimore." In *Essays in Colonial History Presented to Charles McLean Andrews by His Students*, 225–251. New Haven, CT: Yale University Press, 1931.

Hoffman, Ronald. *A Spirit of Dissension: Economics, Politics, and the Revolution in Maryland*. Baltimore, MD: Johns Hopkins University Press, 1973.

Klingelhofer, Herbert E. "The Cautious Revolution: Maryland and the Movement toward Independence." *Maryland Historical Magazine* 60 (September 1965): 268–269.

Land, Aubrey C. *Colonial Maryland: A History*. Millwood, NY: KTO Press, 1981.

Nash, Gary B. *The Urban Crucible: The Northern Seaports and the Origins of the American Revolution*. Cambridge, MA: Harvard University Press, 1986.

Olson, Sherry. *Baltimore: The Building of an American City*. 2d ed. Baltimore, MD: Johns Hopkins University Press, 1997.

Scharf, J. Thomas. *Chronicles of Baltimore, Being a Complete History of "Baltimore Town" and Baltimore City from the Earliest Period to the Present Time*. Baltimore, MD: Turnbull Brothers, 1874.

Steffen, Charles G. *The Mechanics of Baltimore: Workers and Politics in the Age of Revolution, 1763–1812*. Urbana: University of Illinois Press, 1984.

SALEM, MA 1776–1790

SALEM, MASSACHUSETTS, WAS FOUNDED BY PURITANS in 1626 at the mouth of the Naumkeag River on the Atlantic coast of what would become the Massachusetts Colony. Salem's location on a deep, protected harbor made the city a natural site for fishing, trading, overseas commerce, and shipbuilding. Until the establishment of Boston, Salem was the largest, most prosperous city in the region. The latter half of the seventeenth century was difficult for Salem due to continuing conflict with Native Americans and, later, the notorious Salem witchcraft trials. By the dawn of the eighteenth century, Salem had largely overcome these obstacles and was growing in population and prosperity. Over the next decades Salem was repeatedly forced to reinvent itself in the face of new challenges.

GOVERNMENT AND POLITICS

While the entire period was rife with political tension, Salem saw little intracommunity conflict during the Revolutionary War and immediately after. The town was governed through the traditional town meeting structure that had been in place since 1637. The freemen of the community

QUICK FACTS

SALEM, MA 1776–1790

MAYORS

Under Salem's town meeting system, there was no executive. Instead the selectmen served as an executive committee, but their power was limited. Most major decisions had to be made by a vote of the freeholders.

MAJOR INDUSTRIES AND EMPLOYERS

Privateering
Overseas trade
Shipbuilding

NEWSPAPERS

The Salem Gazette and Newbury
   & Marblehead Advertiser
The American Gazette or
   Constitutional Journal
The Salem Gazette & General
   Advertiser
The Salem Gazette
The Salem Chronicle & Essex Advertiser
The Salem Mercury

MAJOR EVENTS

1776: On June 12 Salem's town meeting passes a resolution calling for independence from Great Britain and pledging support for the American cause.

Fort Lee on Salem Neck is reinforced with stone gun walls and shoulder-high earthworks and garrisoned with one hundred artillery men.

1777: Food shortages lead to riots in Salem and across Massachusetts. In response, the legislature bans distilleries from processing grain that might be used as food. As problems worsen and shortages drive up prices—tea reaches $7 a pound in Salem at one point—the legislature votes to give town governments the right to set prices on staple items.

Growing hostility between farmers and merchants over the use of paper money explodes as a Salem merchant is beaten for refusing to accept paper money and local farmers threaten to starve the town by refusing to sell their products for paper money.

1782: Salem's town meeting votes to instruct its representatives to emphasize the importance of securing the coastline and fishing rights to those negotiating the peace treaty.

1785: Elias Hasket Derby's ship *Grand Turk* sets sail from Salem for Canton, China. She returns nineteen months later, in June 1787, with established trade routes to China and a cargo of tea and silk.

met at least once a year to elect officers. Elections included lesser offices like constable, fence viewer, and justice of the peace, as well as the more important offices of moderator, town clerk, and selectmen. The moderator oversaw proceedings in the meeting itself, ruling on points of order and publicly announcing voting results. The town clerk recorded minutes of town meetings and also served as recorder of deeds and vital statistics. The selectmen constituted the executive committee of the town meeting and were responsible for overseeing common land, summoning town meetings, announcing and overseeing state elections, and fulfilling any financial or legal duties required by the town. This structure remained in place with very little alteration until well into the nineteenth century.

The strongest political shake-up came with the beginning of the Revolution. The majority of the established commercial and social elite remained loyal to the Crown, even as the majority of the population was turning against it. This elite segment of Salem's community had been remarkably stable prior to this, with birth or marriage into a wealthy, powerful family very nearly the only way to gain status. Due to the Revolution, however, many of the families that made up that class lost their wealth and power and survived only by relocating to England. This widening divide between the common people and the elite that generally made up the elected officials is clear as early as 1767, when Salem's representative to the Massachusetts legislature William Browne voted to rescind a resolution protesting the Townshend Act and was subsequently asked to resign his position. Most of the leading men of Salem fled to England but still faced increasingly severe consequences for their political beliefs back home. The Banishment Act of 1778 called for their arrest and imprisonment should they return to Massachusetts, and the Conspiracy Act of 1779 confiscated any property held by Loyalists.

With the closure of Boston's port in 1774, shipbuilders, merchants, printers, and other related laborers shifted their bases of operations to Salem, newly named the capital of Massachusetts. This sudden shift in population combined with the growing power vacuum to create a new elite class, defined by revolutionary politics and business success rather than established family authority. The resulting community was strongly supportive of the American cause. As tensions mounted, committees of correspondence were formed across the state to maintain contact throughout the region, and committees of inspection were organized to enforce compliance with anti-British policies. Those found to be working against American interests faced harsh penalties. The Sons of Liberty, who worked with local committees of safety, ransacked homes, forcibly evicted people from towns, and, in the case of one British informer discovered in Salem, tarred and feathered people and deposited them on ships bound for England. Throughout the war, Salem regularly recruited men for the American Army, often voting to pay them a salary out of town funds.

INDUSTRY, COMMERCE, AND LABOR

The period from 1774 to 1790 contained a series of sharp reversals and recoveries for Salem. During the mid-1770s, Salem was growing and profitable. The town's economy had always been focused on the sea, but this period also saw the establishment of twelve coopers, sixteen cigar makers, six cigar and tobacco shops, three distilleries, several tanneries, and even a chocolatier. Salem was sufficiently literate at this time to support a number of libraries and booksellers, as well as local printers that produced books, almanacs, political pamphlets, religious tracts, and philosophical essays. One popular book of the period was *The Revolution in America* by Abbé Reynal, published in 1781. Salem also had two public schools, the Latin, or grammar, school begun in 1642, and the English school founded in 1712. Both schools were supported by the town government and by taxes levied on parents, though both accepted children of poor families for no charge.

Salem thrived as a major maritime shipping center in the late eighteenth century, with ships sailing as far as Canton in the late 1780s and returning with cargoes of silk and tea.

Source: Library of Congress

Maritime occupations thrived through international trade that supplied fish, lumber, and livestock to the British West Indies and coastal trade among the colonies that traded locally produced goods. Shipbuilders had steady employment producing trading ships for colonial interests and masts, spars, and other goods for the British Navy. Salem, along with other small sheltered ports, profited significantly as the growing political tensions drove industrial clients and maritime traders out of Boston and down the coast in search of reduced political strain and royal scrutiny. With the closure of Boston's port in 1774, shipbuilders, merchants, and traders moved down the coast, boosting Salem's merchant community and commercial activity.

With the outbreak of war, Salem's fortunes changed dramatically. Salem's fishing vessels were needed to fight the British Navy. The British West Indies were no longer available as a market for the fishing industry, and British blockades and warships decimated both international and coastal trade. The shipbuilding industry suffered a similar fate with the sudden removal of the British Navy as a corporate client. By 1776 Salem's economic situation was so dire that the town was granted a tax abeyance, with the General Court (the legislature of the Commonwealth of Massachusetts) noting that "in whole or part, [most] rely on commerce, fishery and the various handicrafts; that many have houses for shelter, and nothing more; that there are but few incomes of the ablest, which will support their families" (Felt, p. 387).

With the advent of the Revolutionary War, Salem turned from a fishing and trading community to a center of privateering. This "legalized piracy" served the dual purpose of bringing in needed supplies and damaging the British war effort by crippling their maritime trade, forcing them to divert ships from the conflict to escort trading vessels, and preventing supplies from reaching their troops. Salem's privateering fleet would eventually number well over 150 ships, but it began with refitted fishing vessels. Merchants refitted their own ships as fighting ships, recouping the expense through the profits from captured ships and cargo. Refitted fishing vessels could not compete for long against the British Navy, however. Recognizing this disadvantage, Salem shipbuilders, led by merchant Elias Hasket Derby, introduced innovations in ship design that allowed the new vessels to travel farther faster while carrying more cargo. While these engineering advances gave America an advantage against the British fleet, allowing Salem's privateers to capture as many as 445 ships, their real benefits would not become obvious until after the war.

The last years of the war saw an ever-tightening blockade around Salem's port, sharply reducing the inflow of both profit from captured ships' cargo and necessities such as food and clothing. After the cessation of hostilities, Salem suffered further, for while peace brought an end to the constant need to raise money and men for military efforts, it also ended the need for a privateering fleet. Moreover, the West Indies were no longer available as a market, and most of the slower fishing vessels used by privateers had either been captured or dry-docked. Without a fleet of fishing vessels or a market to sell to, Salem was in dire straits, forced to rely on what coastal trade could be accomplished with smaller boats and through barter with neighboring communities. Privateering vessels, freed from the demands of war, led Salem's economic revival. Engineered to be lighter, faster, and more agile, these ships had significant advantages in long voyages, and Salem's fortunes began to recover as a new breed of merchants gambled on opening new trading routes. That gamble paid off in 1787 with the opening of the China trade when Elias Hasket Derby's ship *Grand Turk* returned from a seventeen-month voyage to Canton. Derby's ships were also the first American ships to reach the Cape of Good Hope in Africa in 1781, Russia in 1784, and India in 1787. Other Salem merchants, such as Jonathan Peele, Benjamin Pickman, and Nathaniel Rogers, opened trade routes into Madagascar, Indonesia, and the Philippines, firmly establishing Salem as a center of international trade.

Six shipbuilders were among the original settlers in Salem, and they established an industry that continued to grow. By 1677 Salem was noted as one of the main centers of shipbuilding in the colony. During the war, shipbuilders were kept busy working with merchants, first to refit fishing vessels as fighting ships, and later to produce new ships with engineering advances that made them faster, more agile, and capable of carrying far more cargo. With the end of the war, shipbuilding again became a major industry in Salem. Salem's shipbuilding industry was a diverse community, encompassing both long-established companies like Beckett's Beach, a family business that built ships in the same shipyard from 1655 to 1800, and newcomers like Enos Briggs, who built the *Grand Turk* for Elias Haskett Derby. Briggs also later built the *Essex*, the largest vessel and only warship ever produced in Salem.

RACE, ETHNICITY, AND IMMIGRATION

Salem was founded by English Puritans in 1628, and in 1776 its population remained overwhelmingly homogeneous. While indentured servitude and a growing urban economy brought in Scots, Irish, German, French, and Dutch immigrants, the population remained largely British.

While slavery had been introduced to Massachusetts as early as 1637, the following decades would see a contest between support and opposition of the practice. Despite strong involvement in the slave trade by merchants, Salem began political action in favor of ending slavery as early as 1755, authorizing a church deacon to petition the General Court to ban the importation of slaves. Throughout the 1760s slaves used the court system to sue for liberty and frequently won. By the 1770s public opinion had resulted in a steady decline in slaveholding. The Quaker Society of Friends, which had a strong presence in Salem, abolished slavery in 1770, and many others found the Enlightenment rhetoric emphasizing the inherent rights and nobility of man to be at odds with the practice of owning slaves. This period saw the growth of a free black community within Salem, as more and more residents freed their slaves, often offering bonds on their behalf. Free blacks were primarily employed in the fishing and shipbuilding industries, though their opportunities expanded with the advent of war. Prompted by the British invitation to free blacks to join the British troops, Washington lifted a ban on blacks fighting with the Continental Army. The Continental Navy needed no such prompting. Short of men and supplies, they welcomed sailors, black or white, many of them from the Massachusetts coast. Privateers also welcomed black crewmen and generally paid better. In Salem a slave named Titus operated a business recruiting free blacks to serve with privateers.

Salem's role became more central to the issue of slavery in Massachusetts in 1776 when a privateer brought in a prize ship carrying two slaves to be offered for sale. In response the General Court passed a resolution banning the sale and ordering the men to be treated as any other prisoners of war. Shortly thereafter the issue was taken up by the Continental Congress, which appointed a committee to consider the fate of blacks captured by American ships.

In 1780 the General Court passed the Declaration of Rights to the Constitution of the Commonwealth. While the declaration declared all men "born free and equal," it did not expressly refer to slavery. Beginning in 1781, a series of cases that would come to be known as the Quock Walker case challenged this declaration, resulting in Chief Justice William Cushing stating that "slavery is in my judgment as effectively abolished as it can be by the granting of rights and privileges wholly incompatible and repugnant to its existence" and instructing the jury in the case that slavery was unconstitutional in Massachusetts.

See also *Salem, MA 1790–1828*

JAMES McWILLIAMS

BIBLIOGRAPHY

Cushing, John D. "The Cushing Court and the Abolition of Slavery in Massachusetts: More Notes on the 'Quock Walker Case.'" *American Journal of Legal History* 5, no. 2 (April 1961): 118–144.

Fairlie, John A. *Local Government in Counties, Towns and Villages.* New York, NY: The Century Company, 1906.

Felt, Joseph B. *Annals of Salem.* Salem, MA: W. & S.B. Ives, 1849.

Hurd, D. Hamilton. *History of Essex County, Massachusetts, with Biographical Sketches of Many of Its Pioneers and Prominent Men.* Philadelphia, PA: J. W. Lewis & Co, 1888.

Morison, Samuel Eliot. *The Maritime History of Massachusetts, 1783–1860.* Boston, MA: Houghton Mifflin Company, 1921.

Morris, Richard J. "Redefining the Economic Elite in Salem, Massachusetts, 1759–1799: A Tale of Evolution, Not Revolution." *The New England Quarterly* 73, no. 4 (December 2000): 603–624.

Osgood, Charles S., and H. M. Batchelder. *Historical Sketch of Salem 1626–1879.* Salem, MA: Essex Institute, 1879.

Powell, Lyman P., ed. *Historic Towns of New England.* London: G. P. Putnam's Sons, 1898.

Stark, James Henry. *The Loyalists of Massachusetts: The Other Side of the American Revolution.* Boston, MA: J. H. Stark, 1910.

Weedon, William. *Economic and Social History of New England, 1620–1789.* New York, NY: Hillary House Publishers, 1963.

NEWPORT, RI 1776–1790

NEWPORT WAS FOUNDED IN 1639 BY RELIGIOUS exiles from Massachusetts. Roger Williams, the founder of Rhode Island, established the colony on the basis of freedom of conscience. The wide-ranging and pluralistic society that grew in Newport was emblematic of that goal, with Anglican, Congregationalist, Baptist, Quaker, Moravian, and Jewish populations living side-by-side. This pluralistic attitude fostered cooperation and led Newport to nearly unrivaled commercial success in the decades leading up to the Revolutionary War. While Newport was among the first to espouse the cause of independence, the city would ultimately have no real role in the revolution itself, as it was occupied by British troops for much of the war. Following the withdrawal of British troops, Newport was devastated physically and commercially and left with only a fraction of its former population.

GOVERNMENT AND POLITICS

Newport was governed through the traditional town meeting structure until 1784 when it was incorporated as a city. Under town meeting governance, the freemen of the community met at least once a year to elect officers. Elections included lesser offices like constable, fence viewer, and justice of the peace, as well as the more important offices of moderator, town clerk, and selectmen. The moderator oversaw proceedings in the meeting itself, ruling on points of order and publicly announcing voting results. The town clerk recorded minutes of town meetings and also served as recorder of deeds and vital statistics. The selectmen constituted the executive committee of the town meeting and were responsible for overseeing common land, summoning town

QUICK FACTS

NEWPORT, RI 1776–1790

MAYORS

During most of this period Newport operated under the town meeting system, in which there was no executive. Instead the selectmen served as an executive committee, but their power was limited. Newport was incorporated briefly in 1784, but the city charter was repealed by the state legislature in 1787 as part of a political dispute and the town went back to the town meeting.

MAJOR INDUSTRIES AND EMPLOYERS

Shipping
Slave trade
Distilleries
Privateering
Whale oil

MAJOR NEWSPAPERS

The Rhode Island Gazette
Newport Mercury
The Newport Gazette
Gazette Française
Newport Herald

MAJOR EVENTS

1776: On May 4 the Rhode Island General Assembly votes to formally renounce allegiance to Great Britain. In the same session the assembly passes the Test Act requiring all freemen to take an oath of loyalty to the American cause.

A company of ten thousand British troops marches into Newport and occupies it without firing a shot. With the British fleet stationed in Narragansett Bay and British troops quartering in the city, Newport is effectively shut off from the rest of the colonies.

1778: In their first joint military effort, France and the colonies attempt to retake Newport and force the British out. The effort fails due to miscommunication and a lack of coordination.

1779: British troops abandon Newport in October to concentrate their efforts on the conflicts in the southern colonies.

1780: Continued attacks on Narragansett Bay and Newport Harbor emphasize the need for increased security. The French fleet arrives to help clear the harbor and protect the coastline.

1784: Newport's citizens vote to abandon the town meeting form of government and incorporate as a city. The new arrangement lasts only three years, and the state legislature repeals the city charter in 1787 in a dispute over property rights between the city and an influential Newport politician.

meetings, announcing and overseeing state elections, and fulfilling any financial or legal duties required by the town. In 1784 the town voted to incorporate under a city charter, and in June of that year voters elected a mayor, George Hazard, along with four aldermen, six councilmen, and a city clerk. Three years later, a controversy over control of a beach between the owner, Nicholas Easton, and the city council resulted in a petition to the state legislature to repeal the city's charter. Despite being signed by only a minority of residents the petition passed, largely due to Easton's political influence, and Newport returned to the traditional town meeting structure which remained in place until 1853.

Newport was especially affected by political factionalism early in the Revolution. Newport's prosperity and its position as a major shipping center made many of the leading merchants of the city extremely wary of upsetting the status quo. The divide between Loyalists and growing revolutionary sentiments was apparent as early as 1764, when a group of Loyalists that came to be known as the "Newport Junta" petitioned the king to revoke Rhode Island's charter. Growing distrust led to the Test of Loyalty Act, passed by the Rhode Island General Assembly in 1776, which allowed anyone to be denounced as a Loyalist by a member of the assembly and brought before a summary court. Anyone refusing to take the prescribed oath in support of American independence was subject to search, arrest, banishment, and seizure of property. The act was strengthened in 1780, resulting in thirty-seven men being banished from Rhode Island, all but five of who were from Newport. Despite the Loyalist stance of some members of the elite, public support was firmly with the American cause, as was made glaringly obvious with the deposition of Loyalist governor Joseph Wanton.

Rhode Island's actions against Loyalists and its patriots' increasingly sharp rhetoric concerning independence led to devastation for Newport. British customs officials, convinced Rhode Island was a haven for smugglers, had long directed their ships to pay special attention to maritime traffic in and out of Newport. The conspicuous presence of British customs ships and their harassment of trading vessels sparked ever-growing hostilities between Great Britain and Newport. Simmering tensions erupted into actual conflict in 1769 when Newport residents attacked the British customs ship *Liberty*. Three years later, in 1772, the Gaspée Affair, in which the British customs ship the *Gaspée* was driven out of Newport Harbor and subsequently run aground and burned in Narragansett Bay, placed Newport in particular, and Rhode Island in general, at the center of British opposition. Tensions continued to escalate, finally reaching their zenith in the summer of 1775 when Captain James Wallace of the British Navy stationed his fleet, led by the *HMS Rose,* in Narragansett Bay and demanded Newport provision his ships, threatening to fire on the town if they refused.

Over the next few months, Wallace continued to demand supplies, often simply sending men to take what was not surrendered. In September, anticipating fresh depredations from the British fleet, three hundred members of the local militia moved in and drove off the remaining livestock to prevent Wallace from stealing them. Wallace again threatened to destroy the city if his demands were not met. Newport, with the agreement of both the Rhode Island legislature and the Continental Congress, signed a treaty agreeing to keep Wallace's fleet provisioned with meat and beer. By November the number of British ships had reached twelve and had successfully destroyed all merchant activity into or out of the port, forcing the majority of the Newport merchants to abandon the city to save their businesses. This caused concern among the more radical elements in Providence, such as the Sons of Liberty, that the lack of patriots in Newport could allow Tories loyal to the British to gain control of the city. These fears turned out to be justified when ten thousand British troops marched into Newport and occupied the town without firing a shot in December 1776.

Newport remained in British hands for the next three years. No serious action was taken to free the city until 1778 and the Battle of Rhode Island. The battle was the first proposed joint venture between French and American forces, and its overall failure was due to miscommunication and a lack of coordination. While American troops did manage to gain some ground and force the British troops to the outskirts of town, they were ultimately compelled to retreat, leaving Newport still under British control. The city did not factor heavily into subsequent events of the Revolutionary War. In 1779 the British abandoned the already devastated city to concentrate their efforts on the growing conflicts in the southern colonies, and the city they left behind was very different from the one they had entered. The barracks the troops had occupied at Fort Adams were burned, as were all the wharves and docks on the harbor. Wells had been filled in, and virtually all of the trees and surrounding forests had been cut down for either firewood or for defense purposes. As many as nine hundred private homes had been burned and more than half the population had fled, including almost the entire commercial segment. Further complicating the rebuilding process, the British also took with them all the town records, including the Registry of Deeds and all court and town meeting records. Shortly after the British withdrawal, the Rhode Island General Assembly voted $500 to the town of Newport and granted them a tax abeyance. Other colonies also came to Newport's aid, with Connecticut raising $4,300 in relief funds and both Connecticut and New York lifting their grain embargoes to allow shipments of grain to Rhode Island.

With the end of the Revolutionary War, the colonies faced the task of creating their own government. State politics in Rhode Island during this period was dominated by warring factions of farmers and merchants. The economic destruction of Newport had driven most of the wealthy merchants to other cities and few returned after the war. Newport's lack of commercial power resulted in a lack of political power, leaving it at the mercy of outside forces. In 1786 the so-called Country Party, dominated by agricultural and farming interests, won in statewide elections and overturned the balance of power in the legislature. The issue of paper money would take center stage at this point, with farmers and planters supporting the new currency and the remaining merchants opposing it.

One of the first acts of the new government was to issue $100,000 in new bills and encourage farmers to mortgage land for the new currency, thus allowing them to profit on otherwise unprofitable land. The new money lost value almost as soon as it was printed, however, and Newport merchants refused to accept it at face value. The Country Party, heavily invested in the success of the new system, passed a "forcing act" imposing a $100 fine on anyone who refused to accept payment in paper bills. A standoff between farmers holding paper currency and merchants who refused to accept it developed across the region, with merchants closing up shop rather than accepting the devalued currency and farmers attempting to starve them out by refusing to bring goods to market. In Newport the standoff devolved into riots in the street, with people attacking farmers to force them to sell their grain. With the already fragile economy stagnating further and the state poised on the edge of violence, the legislature acted again, authorizing anyone whose paper money was not accepted to bring a case before a court of summary judgment. The issue was eventually decided by the case of *Trevett v. Weedon*. Newport resident John Trevett brought suit against a butcher, John Weedon, for refusing to accept paper currency. The court found that the legislation requiring merchants accept paper currency was unconstitutional and held that no one could be forced to accept the devalued money.

The new power faction in Rhode Island also proved to be exceptionally wary of Federalists and their desire for a strong central government, refusing to even send delegates to the Federal

Convention in Philadelphia in 1787. When the U.S. Constitution was sent to the states for ratification, Rhode Island put it before the local town meetings for a vote, which almost guaranteed defeat. The U.S. Senate eventually proposed taxing all trade from Rhode Island as goods from a foreign port and passed a bill barring all trade with Rhode Island. In 1790 the Rhode Island legislature finally relented, voting to ratify the Constitution by a vote of 34–32 despite overwhelming public sentiment against ratification.

INDUSTRY, COMMERCE, AND LABOR

A 1774 census estimated the population of Newport at over nine thousand, with a thriving economy based on both trade and production. The census of 1782, following British occupation and war, showed a very different city. The population had fallen to less than six thousand, and the economic and physical destruction was nearly total.

During Newport's "golden age" in the decades directly preceding the Revolution, its merchant fleet consisted of two hundred ships involved in international trade and as many as three or four hundred ships engaged in coastal trade. The slave trade was highly lucrative, with nearly two-thirds of the ships sailing out of Newport dedicated to what was known as the "triangle trade." Molasses brought in from the West Indies was distilled locally into rum, which was then shipped to Africa and traded for slaves, who were taken to the West Indies and traded for gold to buy molasses. Due to the enormous profits being generated, the majority of the population was employed in some way by the merchants. The ships themselves employed more than two thousand seamen, and dockworkers, shipbuilders, and sales agents were all directly employed by merchants. Even those who worked at a remove from the shipyards were ultimately dependent on the merchants and traders for their livelihood. Newport was home to thirty distilleries and three sugar refineries that supplied the triangle trade, as well as a robust whaling industry that produced everything from lamp oil to candles to soap for sale in Great Britain. In addition, Newport had a small but highly regarded community of artisans. Silversmiths such as Samuel Vernon and Jonathan Otis and furniture makers such as John Goddard and the Townsend family led a community of artisans whose distinctive work was still sought after in the twenty-first century.

The diversity that characterized Newport's population was especially obvious in the commercial sector. In 1658 a small group of Sephardic Jews from Barbados was granted permission to settle in Newport. By the mid-seventeenth century, the Jewish community in the city consisted of as many as sixty families and had established the Touro Synagogue, the second oldest synagogue in the colonies. It also included some the most well-regarded and prosperous merchants in town. Aaron Lopez arrived in Newport from Portugal in 1752 and became a valued member of the merchant community. He owned as many as thirty ships engaged in foreign trade. Even more important to the commercial success of Newport was Rodriguez Rivera, who is credited with founding the spermaceti industry. The industry came to support seventeen firms manufacturing whale oil and candles.

British occupation destroyed Newport, not just by decimating its maritime trade and driving off the majority of the merchant community, but also by forcing the city to keep the British ships provisioned and by razing many of the buildings and trees in the town and destroying the surrounding docks. A 1782 assessment of the damage caused by the British estimated the damage to private property at £125,000. Following the war, few of the merchants who had fled returned. The prospect of rebuilding the docks, the city, and the merchant fleet, as well as clearing the harbor, was daunting. Those merchants that did attempt to revive Newport's Caribbean trade were stymied by the British closing of the West Indies. Some tried to break into the now largely illegal slave trade or the nascent trade in China, but competition from more established and prosperous cities such as New York; Boston, Massachusetts; and Salem, Massachusetts, prevented any substantial economic development.

RACE, ETHNICITY, AND IMMIGRATION

The Newport community was primarily of English origin, but it did include a small number of Irish, Scots, and Germans. Real diversity in Newport was religious, with large contingents of Congregationalists, Quakers, Anglicans, and, later, Baptists. A small but prosperous community of Spanish and Portuguese Jews also contributed to the diversity of the population and to Newport's commercial success.

Newport's commercial success was built largely on the slave trade. Rhode Island was the center of the slave trade in the northern colonies, and Newport was the center of the Rhode Island slave trade. While most of the slaves were sold in the West Indies for molasses to be distilled into rum, enough were brought into Newport to give it the largest slave population in the state. A 1774 census noted that out of 3,668 slaves in Rhode Island, 1,246 were in Newport. The next-largest slave population, in South Kingstown, totaled only 440. Most of Newport's wealthier families had anywhere from five to forty slaves, with the bulk of the slave population employed in manufacturing and distilleries. While there was a small community of free blacks, efforts within Newport to end slavery or interfere with the slave trade were actively discouraged. Individuals who wanted to free their slaves found the process difficult and expensive, as slave owners were required to post a fairly significant bond against any crimes the slave might commit or charity the town might be required to pay. In addition, the rules regulating the behavior of former slaves were detailed and intrusive, and any failure to comply with them nullified the manumission.

During the late 1750s and throughout the 1760s, Newport's political machine succeeded in passing a number of laws protecting slavery and supporting slave owners' rights. Newport's waning political influence from the early 1770s onward allowed the growing abolition movement to take hold and begin to affect reform. The strongest force behind the abolition movement was the Quakers, who barred members from owning slaves or having involvement in the slave trade as early as 1758. Movement within the Newport town meeting on the issue was slow, as the vast majority of the population was employed, directly or indirectly, by the slave trade. Stephen Hawkins, a prominent Quaker politician, was evicted from the meeting for his refusal to free his slaves, while another man, Moses Brown, freed his slaves prior to being admitted to the meeting. Despite the overwhelming presence of the slave trade in southern

Rhode Island, by 1782 no Quakers at the yearly New England meeting owned or were involved in the sale of slaves.

The clash between abolitionists and powerful shipping interests over slavery was long and hard fought. Numerous pamphlets from around the region found their way to Newport and the *Newport Mercury* published a number of articles and editorials between 1768 and 1775 condemning slavery.

In 1774, recognizing the disconnect between fighting for personal freedom on the one hand and owning slaves on the other, the colonial legislature, led by Governor Joseph Wanton, passed legislation barring the slave trade. The measure was largely symbolic and had little effect on Newport merchants. The bulk of slaves carried on Newport ships were sold in the West Indies. Following the 1774 legislation, slavers merely disposed of cargo brought into the colonies in southern ports where the slave market was stronger and continued home with the profits. Over the next decade, northern abolition interests maintained a firm hold on the state legislature and used it to continue to act against slavery. In 1779 an act was passed barring an owner from selling a slave out of state against his will. While of much narrower focus than the 1774 bill addressing the slave trade, the 1779 bill did have a much more tangible effect. Slaves to be sold out of state had to appear before a panel of judges, alone, and state their agreement with being sold and with the destination. In 1784 the legislature reached a compromise of "gradual emancipation." Children of slaves born after March 1 were to be considered "apprentices" who would age out of slavery, the girls at eighteen, the boys at twenty-one. Written and passed primarily by northern interests and actively fought by Newport commercial interests, the bill also outlawed the selling or importing of slaves, though it imposed no penalties on those who failed to comply. In 1787 the legislature attempted to add teeth to the regulations by assessing considerable fines on merchants and ships found to be involved with the importation or sale of slaves. While the slave trade was injured through these actions, it was by no means destroyed and continued well into the nineteenth century.

JAMES McWILLIAMS

BIBLIOGRAPHY

Adams, James Truslow. *New England in the Republic, 1776–1850.* Gloucester, MA: Peter Smith, 1960.

Bicknell, Thomas Williams. *The History of the State of Rhode Island and Providence Plantations.* Vol. 2. New York, NY: The American Historical Society, Inc., 1920.

Birmingham, Stephen. *The Grandees: America's Sephardic Elite.* New York, NY: Dell, 1972.

Carp, Benjamin L. *Rebels Rising: Cities and the American Revolution.* New York, NY: Oxford University Press, 2007.

Federal Writers' Project of the Works Progress Administration for the State of Rhode Island. *Rhode Island: A Guide to the Smallest State.* American Guide Series. St. Clair Shores, MI: Somerset Publishers, 1973.

Johnston, William Dawson. *Slavery in Rhode Island, 1755–1776.* Providence: Rhode Island Historical Society, 1894.

Peterson, Edward. *History of Rhode Island and Newport.* New York, NY: J. S. Taylor, 1853.

PROVIDENCE, RI 1776–1790

FOUNDED IN 1636 BY ROGER WILLIAMS, Providence is situated at the north end of Narragansett Bay at the junction of the Providence and Seekonk Rivers. Settled primarily by religious dissenters and based on freedom of conscience, Rhode Island was largely snubbed by most of the surrounding colonies. Poor soil, distance from the ocean, and political turmoil all combined to slow Providence's development into a political or economic power. Though its commercial interests began to grow in the eighteenth century, Providence remained in a distant second place to Newport until the Revolutionary War. Newport's occupation by the British and its resulting physical and economic destruction allowed Providence to develop politically, demographically, and economically.

GOVERNMENT AND POLITICS

After fleeing the strict dogma of Massachusetts Bay, Roger Williams was determined to craft a different type of settlement. His only firm political belief was that of the separation of church and state; Williams felt the church should be completely free of secular matters. Without religious authority to strengthen and define civil government, the political system of Providence developed haphazardly. Quarrels over suffrage and apportionment of land characterized the early development of the city, as the original settlers sought to maintain political control in the growing community. Town government eventually settled into a more-or-less traditional town meeting structure with freemen, defined as freeholders of land, qualifying for participation in town government. The freemen would meet at least once a year to elect officers. Elections included lesser offices like constable, fence viewer, and justice of the peace, as well as the more important offices of moderator, town clerk, treasurer, and deputies. The moderator oversaw proceedings in the meeting itself, ruling on points of order and publicly announcing voting results. The town clerk recorded minutes of town meetings and also served as recorder of deeds and vital statistics. The treasurer collected local taxes and fines and oversaw town funds and expenditures. The town deputies constituted the executive committee of the town meeting and were responsible for overseeing common land, summoning town meetings, announcing and overseeing state elections, and fulfilling any legal duties required by the town. Deputies also served as judges in the local criminal court and arbitrators of civil disputes. This structure remained in place with little alteration until well into the nineteenth century.

The individualistic nature of Rhode Island settlers in general led to early and vehement support of colonial rights. Whereas Newport saw a number of its leading men denounced as Loyalists, little if any sympathy for the British cause existed in Providence. Public support across Rhode Island was firmly with the American cause, as was made glaringly obvious with the deposition of Loyalist governor Joseph Wanton.

Providence was placed at the center of the growing conflict with the destruction of the British customs ship the *Gaspée* in 1772. The *Gaspée* was run aground in Narragansett Bay and

QUICK FACTS

PROVIDENCE, RI 1776–1790

MAYORS

During this period Providence operated under a town meeting style of government. Under the town meeting system, there was no executive. Instead the selectmen served as an executive committee, but their power was limited. Most major decisions had to be made by a vote of the freeholders.

MAJOR EMPLOYERS AND INDUSTRIES

Agriculture (primarily farming and horse breeding)
Shipping (international and domestic trading and the slave trade)
Distilleries
Ironworks
Shipbuilding
Privateering

MAJOR NEWSPAPERS

The Providence Gazette & Country Journal

The American Journal and General Advertiser
The United States Chronicle: Political, Commercial, Historical

MAJOR EVENTS

1776: On May 4 the Rhode Island General Assembly votes to formally renounce allegiance to Great Britain. In the same session the assembly passes the Test Act requiring all freemen to take an oath of loyalty to the American cause.

The British occupation of Newport, Rhode Island, and the blockade of Narragansett Bay have serious consequences for Providence. Providence officials and residents fortify their harbor, take in refugees from Newport, and become the center of financial and naval operations for Rhode Island.

1788: The conflict between Federalists supporting ratification of the Constitution and anti-Federalists opposing it is brought into sharp focus when city leaders in Providence host a public feast celebrating New Hampshire's ratification of the Constitution and anti-Federalists from the surrounding countryside attempt to stop the celebration with armed force.

1790: The conflict over ratification continues as the Rhode Island General Assembly steadfastly refuses to call a convention to vote on the Constitution. Providence threatens to secede from Rhode Island and join the Union alone if a convention is not called.

Moses Brown, a leading merchant of Providence, invests in Samuel Slater, who builds the first water-powered textile mill in the United States at Pawtucket and establishes the cotton manufacturing industry in Rhode Island.

---

destroyed by men from Providence led by John Brown, one of the leading merchants of the city, and Abraham Whipple, who would become a naval hero during the Revolution. Providence continued to be at the forefront of the resistance to British rule, instructing its delegates to the Rhode Island General Assembly to move for the colonies to come together to resist the British. This made the Providence town meeting the first formal body in the colonies to call for a continental congress. Continued support for resistance came in March 1775 when the residents of Providence gathered at Market Square and burned three hundred pounds of tea in support of the nonimportation agreements passed by the colonies. As tensions continued to rise and the British first blockaded Newport Harbor, then occupied the city itself, Providence grew increasingly concerned that Newport was meant to serve simply as a staging area to allow the British to move on to the rest of Narragansett Bay and New England. In response, Providence strengthened its defenses by installing barricades to block entry into its harbor and stationing an armed fleet equipped with fire ships at the northern end of Narragansett Bay. These defenses were tested in 1775 when British ships attempted to move north from Newport and were forced to withdraw.

During the Revolution, Providence served as a temporary home to American troops en route to various campaigns and as a more permanent home to a contingent of nearly one thousand who remained as a protective force. Providence also provided a home to the fledgling Continental Navy, proposed by Rhode Island delegates and led by Providence native Esek Hopkins. Providence contributed men, money, and arms to the war effort, but its most important contributions came at sea through the navy and through privateering. This "legalized piracy" served the dual purpose of bringing in needed supplies and damaging the British war effort by crippling their maritime trade, forcing them to divert ships from the conflict to escort trading vessels and preventing supplies from reaching their troops. Providence's merchants refitted their own trading ships as fighting ships, recouping the expense through the profits from captured ships and cargo. These ships ran the British blockade of Narragansett Bay, bringing in needed supplies and allowing the merchants to continue doing business.

With the end of the Revolutionary War, the colonies faced the task of creating their own government. Rhode Island chose to continue operating under its original charter rather than creating a new state constitution. While this decision was popular with the existing power structure as it permitted considerable self-governance at the local level, problems quickly became obvious. The charter, written for a much smaller population, fixed the numbers of representatives each town sent to the state legislature, allowing no means to address demographic shifts. Newport, the commercial and political center prior to the Revolution, sent six delegates, while smaller towns were allotted four. Despite the growing political and commercial importance of Providence and its growing population, there was no mechanism in the existing charter to address such changes. The inherent problems in this system were exemplified by the growing struggles between commercial and agricultural interests over the paper money issue and ratification of the Constitution. In 1786 the so-called Country Party, dominated by agricultural and farming interests, won in statewide elections and overturned the balance of power in the legislature. The issue of paper money took center stage at this point, with farmers and planters supporting the new currency and merchants opposing it. Providence, as a commercial center, joined Newport's merchants at the forefront of the opposition to paper money, preferring hard currency of gold or silver. One of the first acts of the new government was to issue $100,000 in new bills and encourage farmers to mortgage land for the new currency, thus allowing farmers to profit on otherwise unprofitable land. The new money lost value almost as soon as it was printed, however, and merchants refused to accept it at face value. A standoff between farmers holding paper currency and merchants who refused to accept it developed across the region, with merchants closing up shop rather than accept the devalued currency and farmers attempting to starve them out by refusing to bring goods to market. The Country Party, heavily invested in the success of the new system, passed a "forcing act" imposing a $100 fine on anyone who refused to accept payment in paper bills, later strengthening the act to bar anyone refusing to accept paper currency from voting or holding political office at the state or local level. The issue was eventually decided by the case of *Trevett v. Weedon,* in which the court found that legislation requiring merchants to accept paper currency was unconstitutional and held that no one could be forced to accept the devalued paper money.

The new power faction in Rhode Island also proved to be exceptionally wary of Federalists and their desire for a strong central government, refusing to even send delegates to the Federal Convention in Philadelphia in 1787. The town-versus-country divide was again the primary distinction between those who advocated ratification and joining the United States and those who opposed it. Commercial areas like Providence were the center of efforts to push for ratification, most publicly through the press. When the Constitution was sent to the states for ratification, Rhode Island's legislature refused to call for a convention to vote on it, choosing instead to put it before the local town meetings for a vote, which almost guaranteed defeat.

Despite celebrations in Providence for ratification in other states, the Rhode Island General Assembly held firm. When the United States Senate finally proposed taxing all trade from Rhode Island as goods from a foreign port and eventually passed a bill barring all trade with the state, Providence threatened to secede from Rhode Island and join the Union as an independent state if the assembly continued to defer the vote. In 1790 the legislature finally relented, calling a convention to meet in Newport to vote on the Constitution. The convention met in May of that year, voting to ratify the U.S. Constitution with a vote of 34–32 despite overwhelming public sentiment against ratification.

INDUSTRY, COMMERCE, AND LABOR

Commerce in Providence began slowly. Though the area was settled in 1636, it struggled economically until the beginning of the eighteenth century. Poor soil and the lack of an ocean harbor, as well as the political chaos that defined Providence's early decades, prevented most commercial development. Farming was the dominant occupation throughout the colonial period. The surrounding countryside was dominated by plantation agriculture, which used black and American Indian slaves to grow apples, corn, and hay, as well as raise horses and sheep. As commerce began to overtake agriculture in importance early in the eighteenth century, the town of Providence formally separated from Providence Plantations, which remained dominated by agricultural interests.

Despite a slow start, Providence showed a steady growth in commercial enterprises from the early eighteenth century forward, with tradesmen and artisans representing more than thirty-five different services and skills. While trading and shipping were the most important industries during this period, local manufacturing interests included six distilleries, two spermaceti candle works, two tanneries supplying shoemakers and glove makers, a slaughterhouse, two sugar refineries, iron ore mines and forges, an anchorsmith, a potash works, a chocolatier, a snuff mill, and two paper mills. Many local merchants traded out of Providence but built production facilities in nearby Pawtucket to take advantage of the easily accessible water power of Pawtucket Falls.

Providence's trading fleet included as many as five hundred ships prior to the Revolutionary War. Domestic shipping interests included coastal trade and whaling, as well as packet ships that traveled between Providence, Boston, and New York carrying goods, mail, and cargo. Shippers also developed an extensive land-based transportation system that mostly followed established Indian trails. These trails had been widened to accommodate carts and stagecoaches by the middle of the eighteenth century and kept Rhode Island connected to the rest of the colonies during the war. Following the war, Providence served as the main transfer point for overland goods between Boston and New York, which encouraged the development of travelers' inns and common rooms.

Prior to the war, Providence's overseas trade included nearly two hundred ships, mostly employed in the slave trade. In a system known as the "triangle trade," trading ships brought in sugar or molasses from the West Indies to be refined into rum, which was then taken to Africa and traded for slaves. The slaves were then sold in the West Indies for sugar or molasses that was taken to Rhode Island, completing the triangle. After the war, as tightening legislation steadily criminalized the slave trade, most merchants turned to the newly opened East India trade or to manufacturing. One of the few Providence merchants to reenter the slave trade, John Brown, would be the first man prosecuted under the United States antislavery importation laws in 1796.

The Brown family had been a central part of the commercial life of Providence for five generations. The earliest shipyard in Providence was begun in 1646 by Nicholas Brown. During the post-Revolution period, the four Brown brothers—Nicholas, John, Moses, and Joseph—dominated both shipping and manufacturing interests. International trade during this period focused on new shipping routes opened by Newport merchants. Ships left Providence carrying exports of horses, sheep, dried fish, and lumber for Canton, Calcutta, Indonesia, and the Philippines and returned with cargoes of spices and pepper, porcelain and china, silk, tea, and coffee that brought stunning profits. The mercantile trade firm Brown & Ives (founded by Nicholas Brown's son and a former clerk named Thomas Poynton Ives) further expanded business by having fleets of smaller vessels based in central foreign ports that were responsible for assembling goods from smaller ports to be loaded and shipped on larger vessels of the firm.

The biggest turning point for commercial interests in Providence came in 1790. The textile industry in Great Britain had exploded with the invention of water-powered mills. Anxious to gain a foothold in this new industry, desperate American manufacturers were offering cash incentives to anyone with knowledge of the British textile industry. Moses Brown had been experimenting with secondhand versions of British textile equipment unsuccessfully when he began corresponding with a young man named Samuel Slater. Slater had been an apprentice at a cotton mill in England and brought that knowledge with him to the United States. The two men went into partnership, building a cotton mill in Pawtucket that is credited with sparking the Industrial Revolution in America. Within twenty years, the overwhelming majority of commercial interests in Providence and the surrounding area would be focused on textile manufacturing.

RACE, ETHNICITY, AND IMMIGRATION

The Providence community was primarily of English origin, but did include a small number of Irish, Scots, French Huguenots, and Germans. Real diversity in Providence could be found in its religious congregations, with large contingents of Unitarians, Sabbatarians, Congregationalists, Quakers, Anglicans, and Baptists represented.

Rhode Island's commercial success was built largely on the slave trade, and while Newport was its uncontested center, Providence did take part. Of the 184 ships from Providence involved in overseas trade, fewer than sixty seem to have been employed in the triangle trade. While most of the slaves were sold in the West Indies for molasses to be distilled into rum, enough were brought into Rhode Island to give it the largest slave population in New England. A 1774 census noted that out of 3,668 slaves in Rhode Island, 1,246 were in Newport. Providence, in contrast, had only 303. During the late 1750s and through the 1760s, Newport's political machine succeeded in passing a number of laws protecting slavery and supporting slave owners' rights. Newport's waning political influence from the early 1770s onward allowed the growing abolition movement to take hold and begin to affect reform. The strongest force behind the abolition movement was the Quakers, who barred members from owning slaves or being involved in the slave trade as early as 1758. Providence merchant Moses Brown freed his slaves prior to being admitted to the local meeting, despite his family's continued involvement in the slave trade. After joining the Quakers, Brown founded the Providence Abolition Society and became a leader in the growing antislavery movement.

In 1774, recognizing the disconnect between fighting for personal freedom on the one hand and owning slaves on the other, the colonial legislature, led by Governor Joseph Wanton, passed legislation barring the slave trade. The measure was largely symbolic and had little effect on merchants. The bulk of slaves carried on trading ships were sold in the West Indies. Following the 1774 legislation, slavers merely disposed of cargo brought into the colonies in southern ports where the slave market was stronger and then continued home with the profits. Over the next decade, northern abolition interests maintained a firm hold on the state legislature and used it to continue to act against slavery. In 1779 an act was passed barring an owner from selling a slave out of state against his will. While of much narrower focus than the 1774 bill addressing the slave trade, the 1779 bill did have a much more tangible effect. Slaves to be sold out of state had to appear before a panel of judges, alone, and state their agreement with being sold and with the destination. In 1784 the legislature reached a compromise of "gradual emancipation." Children of slaves born after March 1 were to be considered "apprentices" who would age out of slavery, the girls at eighteen, the boys at twenty-one. Written and passed primarily by northern antislavery activists and actively fought by commercial interests, the bill also outlawed the selling or importing of slaves, though it imposed no penalties on those who failed to comply. In 1787 the legislature attempted to add teeth to the regulations by assessing considerable fines on merchants and ships found to be involved with the importation or sale of slaves. While the slave trade was injured through these actions, it was by no means destroyed and continued well into the nineteenth century.

See also *Providence, RI 1828–1854*

JAMES McWILLIAMS

BIBLIOGRAPHY

Arnold, Samuel Greene. *History of the State of Rhode Island and Providence Plantations: 1701–1790.* Vol. 2. New York, NY: D. Appleton & Co., 1874.

Field, Edward. *State of Rhode Island and Providence Plantations at the End of the Century.* Boston, MA: The Mason Publishing Company, 1902.

Rappleye, Charles. *Sons of Providence: The Brown Brothers, the Slave Trade, and the American Revolution.* New York, NY: Simon & Schuster, 2006.

Staples, William R. *Annals of the Town of Providence from its First Settlement to the Organization of the City Government in 1832.* Providence, RI: Knowles and Vose, 1843.

Withey, Lynn. *Urban Growth in Colonial Rhode Island: Newport and Providence in the Eighteenth Century.* Albany: State University of New York Press, 1984.

MARBLEHEAD, MA 1776–1790

MARBLEHEAD HAS A RICH MARITIME HISTORY. It is a coastal community located northeast of Boston, Massachusetts. Unlike nearby Pilgrim and Puritan settlements, Marblehead was founded so that merchants in England could have a permanent base of operations near Atlantic waters teeming with fish. English fishermen first settled Marblehead around 1630, and the port was officially incorporated as a town in Massachusetts in 1649. Its rocky beaches and proximity to fertile fishing waters in the Atlantic Ocean made Marblehead an ideal location for catching and drying fish. Dried, salted cod was a particularly valuable early modern commodity. It was an inexpensive source of protein that could remain on consumers' shelves for years in an age without refrigeration. As a result, this cod became the most valuable export in all of New England. By the American Revolution, "saltfish," as it was known, was the fourth most valuable trade good that the British produced in the Western Hemisphere, behind sugar, tobacco, and grain.

The fishing industry lured laborers and merchants. By 1765 Marblehead boasted a population of five thousand. The only place larger in Massachusetts was Boston. Moreover, at this time Marblehead ranked first among fishing towns in British North America in terms of the number of fishermen and fishing vessels.

There were dramatic changes in Marblehead between 1776 and 1790. Commercial fishing communities sacrificed much to break away from the British Empire. Conflict with one of the strongest naval powers in the world severely disrupted the American fisheries. Economic hard times did not stall the port's steady population growth, however. More and more people kept

QUICK FACTS

MARBLEHEAD, MA 1776–1790

MAYORS

Marblehead had town meetings run by selectmen

MAJOR INDUSTRIES AND EMPLOYERS

Cod fisheries
Whale fisheries
Merchant marine
Taverns
Shipbuilding

MAJOR NEWSPAPERS

Essex Gazette
Salem Gazette and Newbury and Marblehead Advertiser

MAJOR EVENTS

1776: Elbridge Gerry, a Marblehead fish merchant, signs the Declaration of Independence.

1780: Voters in Marblehead ratify a new state constitution, which is the oldest state constitution still in use, and they vote to elect John Hancock the first governor of Massachusetts.

1787: A Marblehead town meeting resolves to support the Massachusetts government in its suppression of Shays's Rebellion.

1787: Marblehead elects Elbridge Gerry as one of four Massachusetts delegates to attend the Constitutional Convention in Philadelphia. This convention brings together representatives from the states.

1788: Elbridge Gerry is one of sixteen delegates at the Constitutional Convention in Philadelphia to refuse to ratify the new U.S. Constitution, chiefly due to its lack of a bill of rights.

1788: Marblehead delegates to the Massachusetts convention unanimously vote to ratify the new Constitution. Gerry is not among the delegates who attend this state convention.

coming to Marblehead. The Revolutionary War also gave rise to the United States of America and a newer, more democratic federal political system, which paved the way for townspeople to gain access to new elected offices.

GOVERNMENT AND POLITICS

Prior to the American Revolution, Marbleheaders had limited access to political power. Wealthy, educated, property-owning fish merchant families such as the Gerrys, Glovers, Hoopers, and Lees held local elected offices such as selectmen, surveyors, and justices of the peace. As selectmen, they administered local town meetings that met on a regular basis. They could also win election to the colony's bicameral legislature. However, this elected body could only propose new laws. Massachusetts was a royal colony with a Crown-appointed governor. Royal governors and Parliament maintained oversight powers that enabled them to veto bills that local elites proposed. Those without real estate, such as the many fishermen that worked for the wealthy merchant families, could only access political power by attending and voting at the town meetings.

The Revolution altered political institutions in America and expanded access to political power. Revolutionary activities brought martial law, General Thomas Gage, and the British

Army to Massachusetts in 1774. Gage dissolved the famous New England town meetings. As a result, committees of safety consisting of prominent town members ideologically committed to defending American rights essentially ran local affairs in Marblehead during the Revolution. Patriots such as the Glovers, Gerrys, and Lees purged local Tories such as the Hoopers from the committee. The Hoopers had maintained strong commercial ties to England while the other families had not. The purge made room for new local elites to fill the power vacuum.

Revolution brought institutional changes at the colony-state level, as well. The royal governor of Massachusetts, Thomas Hutchinson, went to England with his family for safety. The British government, acting through Gage, disbanded the Massachusetts legislature. The duly elected members of this legislature continued to meet illegally as the Massachusetts Provincial Congress, however. These elected officials essentially coordinated military resistance to the British in Boston at the very start of conflict. In 1780 this congress drafted a constitution for a new state government that was then distributed to towns for ratification. Marblehead's political elite voted immediately in favor of creating a new state government, and they voted for John Hancock as the first democratically elected governor of the state of Massachusetts. While the same men served in the Massachusetts Provincial Congress that had served in the legislature, the Revolution vested town members in places such as Marblehead with heretofore unknown political powers.

The war also resulted in new, more centralized national political institutions in America. The Continental Congress that met in Philadelphia from 1774 to 1781 organized and financed the American war effort at a national level, and it provided political and diplomatic leadership as well. Marblehead voters elected local fish merchant and Harvard graduate Elbridge Gerry to represent Massachusetts at the Continental Congress. There, Gerry signed the Declaration of Independence in 1776, which officially converted colonial resistance into a rebellion aimed at separation from the British Empire.

Elbridge Gerry went on to play a prominent role in the ratification of the U.S. Constitution after the Revolution. During the ratification process in the years 1787–1789, Gerry was one of the most outspoken anti-Federalists. This pushed Marblehead's favorite son into national prominence. He opposed the Federalists' plan for a strong, centralized national government because of his classical republican fear of tyranny. Despite Gerry's recalcitrance, Marblehead delegates to the Massachusetts ratification convention unanimously resolved to ratify the Federalists' plan at the beginning of 1788. By the middle of this year, enough states voted to accept the Constitution of the United States of America that it legally replaced the Articles of Confederation as the bedrock of the new nation's democracy. Town members then voted for the president and vice president in the nation's first presidential election.

The new federal system fundamentally expanded political horizons at the local level. From Gerry's activities in the Continental Congress to Marbleheaders' participation in Massachusetts' ratification convention to the first presidential election in United States history, Marblehead town members' political ambitions and political powers changed dramatically as a direct result of the American Revolution. Indeed, Elbridge Gerry eventually became vice president under James Madison. Such national leadership, and the prestige and power that went along with it, were unavailable to colonists in the British Empire.

Not everyone shared in this efflorescence of civic power, however. Certain groups were politically marginalized in America during the early years of the Republic. Women were not given the right to vote or hold office in Marblehead, in Massachusetts, or anywhere in the United States. Moreover, Federalists promoted the ideal of republican motherhood, in which a woman's civic duty was to stay at home and raise children to be law-abiding citizens. This classical republican political ideal worked in tandem with preexisting restrictive gender norms to further solidify a cult of domesticity in which women were excluded from the public sphere, including politics.

Nonproperty holders, which included many poorer workers, were also denied access to political power at the local, state, and national levels. Those without property could not vote or hold elected office in Marblehead throughout the colonial era, and this tradition was maintained and fiercely defended during the early years of the Republic. Selectmen, the political leaders in Marblehead, continued to be men who owned real estate. Land ownership and political power remained conjoined twins following the birth of the United States of America.

At the same time, racial norms and restrictive voter laws prevented African Americans and Native Americans from fully realizing the political mandate set forth in the Declaration of Independence that all men are created equal. Although both groups lived and worked in Marblehead, members of neither could vote. Nor could members of either group hold elected office. Much had changed in terms of the political climate in Marblehead, and, indeed, in America, but much remained the same.

INDUSTRY, COMMERCE, AND LABOR

Marblehead was a commercial port that maintained the typical maritime enterprises found in coastal communities around the Atlantic. It had a commercial fishing industry that launched watery expeditions for cod and whales. There were shipbuilders in Marblehead that maintained yards for constructing and repairing vessels of sundry sizes and sorts. Sailmakers labored in sail lofts crafting the enormous gossamer wings that enabled wooden vessels to fly across the ocean. A ropemaking industry in Marblehead manufactured the sinews that linked these wings and vessels together. Local ship riggers ensured that these sinews were properly placed. Taverns abounded in the seaport, as they did in most coastal communities. In all these ways, Marblehead looked and felt like any other commercial port of its size.

Marblehead was atypical, however, in the fact that it was the premiere commercial fishing port in North America on the eve of the American Revolution. This seaport maintained more fishing vessels and fishermen than any other colonial community directly involved with the Atlantic fisheries in the Western Hemisphere.

The export of dried, salted cod was the principal commercial enterprise in town. The cod fisheries connected Marblehead to overseas markets in the Iberian Peninsula and the Caribbean. Catholics in Spain and Portugal paid New World gold and silver for the best grades of saltfish, which they consumed during Lent and other meatless holy days of obligation. Sugar plantation owners in the Caribbean purchased the lowest grades of saltfish to feed black African slave laborers. In this manner, the Atlantic cod trade tied Protestant free laborers in North America to Catholics and slaves.

Commercial cod fishing had a widespread reputation for being among the most trying and dangerous forms of employment. In colonial British North America, fishermen tended to be young men between the ages of twelve and thirty. Skippers recruited crews from local labor pools for vessel-owning fish merchants. Experienced workers, or "sharesmen," earned shares of the profits from the sale of catches to the fish merchants. Younger lads, known as "cuttails" for the fact that they marked the tails of the fish they caught, earned a set amount for each fish hauled in from the ocean. Crews of seven men worked offshore waters stretching northeast from Cape Cod, Massachusetts, to Newfoundland in Canada between spring and fall months. Once skippers determined the most promising fishing waters through past experience and communications with fellow fishermen, anchors were thrown overboard of schooners. Schooners were two-masted vessels that could carry between twenty and one hundred tons. These hardy vessels had revolutionized the industry around the turn of the eighteenth century by allowing larger crews to work waters further from shore for extended periods of time. With the schooner secured on the Atlantic Ocean, crews stood hanging over the sides of schooners with handlines hauling in fish for eighteen-to-twenty-hour shifts in all sorts of weather. Strong gale force winds were common on the Atlantic. Even moored wooden sailing vessels could rock violently on the ocean, and it was not unusual for the sudden pitch of a deck to shatter a man's leg bone or to throw an exhausted worker overboard. Fishermen doggedly pursued their craft until they filled holds with salted filets, however. They then returned to port to dry the filets in the sun on wooden platforms called fish flakes. Once the catch had been cured through this combination of salting and drying, fish merchants employed their vessels, both schooners and larger craft, and their fishermen, along with professional, full-time sailors, on trade voyages to overseas markets.

The Revolution spoiled the lucrative fishing industry in Marblehead. Colonists' demands for liberty brought the wrath of the British government down on their heads. In 1775 Parliament made it illegal for colonists to fish anywhere in the Atlantic Ocean until they agreed to behave as obedient subjects.

Instead of acquiescing, there is strong evidence that businessmen and workers in Marblehead chose to fight for independence. Fish merchant ledgers, which recorded wages paid and the cost of equipment and provisions fishermen used on fishing expeditions, are blank for the war years. Fishing vessels were converted to privateers and warships for the pursuit of the American war effort. Overseas business contacts and trade routes were converted to military suppliers and supply lines. Fishermen became fighting men and participated in every single one of the American armed forces, both on land and at sea. As a result of Parliament's closure of the colonial fisheries and the military mobilization of the fishing industry, which led to workers' deaths and the wreck and capture of fishing vessels, American fishing communities suffered in the postwar years. According to historians Richard Wilkie and Jack Tager, at the start of the Revolution in Marblehead and nearby Gloucester alone there were fishing vessels displacing 7,500 and 5,530 tons of water, respectively. In 1790 there remained fishing vessels in all of Massachusetts that displaced only ten thousand tons.

The newly established United States government began to improve the situation for American fishing communities in 1790. As Secretary of State, Thomas Jefferson issued a series of bounties aimed at subsidizing commercial fishing. These bounties stimulated economic expansion in American ports such as Marblehead. Wilkie and Tager note that the tonnage of fishing vessels increased more than sixfold in Massachusetts as a result, rising from ten thousand in 1790 to sixty-two thousand in 1807. With the federal government's aid, then, commerce eventually returned to Marblehead.

RACE, ETHNICITY, AND IMMIGRATION

Marblehead's Atlantic commerce brought people as well as goods into town. The port was a thriving center of commercial fishing prior to the Revolution, and fishermen from Ireland, England, Scotland, France, and Spain uprooted their families and settled in the area. Fish merchants trading with Caribbean plantations purchased black African slaves and brought them home to Marblehead primarily for ostentatious attempts to gain prestige and status. British surnames dominate pre-Revolution tax lists, to be sure, but one can find slaves and surnames belonging to non-British peoples in this source as well.

Prior to the Revolution, attitudes toward race almost certainly hardened in Marblehead. A pejorative social construction of blackness probably prevailed in the port. The commercial cod fishing industry, the economic engine in Marblehead, was almost exclusively white at this time. Slaves were allowed to perform menial tasks hauling dried, salted filets around town. On exceptionally rare occasions they were allowed to sail on fishing expeditions. Native Americans and black Africans were also integrated into the town's whaling industry, which paid less and entailed longer durations at sea. However, the norm in Marblehead was that the cuttails and sharesmen who worked in the community's most important industry, the cod fisheries, were white.

Revolutionary ideals associated with liberty and freedom certainly impacted attitudes towards race in Marblehead. Town members did manumit their black African slaves during the Revolution out of a heightened social awareness of the benefits accruing to society from a free citizenry. Marblehead's regiment, which became amalgamated into the Continental Army after George Washington became commander in chief, also had a reputation for being exceptionally well integrated in terms of race during the war. Employment in the commercial cod fisheries remained the exclusive province of whites, however, even during the postwar economic doldrums.

The white, primarily English, Irish, and Scottish population continued to expand in Marblehead over the course of the late eighteenth century. Between 1765 and 1810, Massachusetts' population grew by 92 percent, adding over 226,000 souls to the region. At the end of this period, according to Wilkie and Tager, one in fifteen Americans lived in Massachusetts. Many new immigrants flocked to Marblehead to reap the benefits of the government's fishing subsidies. This coastal community has always existed in symbiosis with the sea.

CHRISTOPHER P. MAGRA

BIBLIOGRAPHY

Billias, George Athan. *Elbridge Gerry: Founding Father and Republican Statesman*. New York, NY: McGraw Hill Book Co., 1976.

———. *General John Glover and His Marblehead Mariners*. New York, NY: Henry Holt and Co., 1960.

Magra, Christopher P. *The Fisherman's Cause: Atlantic Commerce and Maritime Dimensions of the American Revolution*. New York, NY: Cambridge University Press, 2009.

Roads, Samuel, Jr. *The History and Traditions of Marblehead*. 3d ed. Marblehead, MA: N. Allen Lindsay & Co., 1897.

Tagney, Ronald N. *The World Turned Upside Down: Essex County during America's Turbulent Years, 1763–1790*. West Newbury, MA: Essex County History, 1989.

Vickers, Daniel. *Farmers and Fisherman: Two Centuries of Work in Essex County, Massachusetts, 1630–1830*. Chapel Hill: The University of North Carolina Press, 1994.

Wilkie, Richard W., and Jack Tager. *Historical Atlas of Massachusetts*. Amherst: University of Massachusetts Press, 1991.

GLOUCESTER, MA 1776–1790

GLOUCESTER IS LOCATED ON CAPE ANN, a broad, rocky promontory jutting into the Atlantic Ocean located approximately twenty-four miles northeast of Boston, Massachusetts. The land consists of granite outcroppings and thin soils poorly suited for farming and often strewn with glacial erratics. Gloucester's natural jewel is its wide, sheltered harbor that faces southward into Massachusetts Bay, earning Cape Ann the name "le Beau Port" from French explorer Samuel de Champlain after his visit in 1606. A second major water feature is the Annisquam River, a broad tidal inlet that opens onto Ipswich Bay on the north and transects Cape Ann across almost its entire six-mile width. The headwaters of the Annisquam stop short of reaching the harbor by just a few hundred feet, leaving only a narrow neck of land connecting the mainland and the "island" where most of Gloucester's eighteenth-century population lived. It was almost inevitable that the town should boast an insular outlook in which outside government was often ignored and sometimes defied.

Thus set apart from the rest of Massachusetts, Gloucester avoided the outright conflicts of the Revolutionary War. Only one open skirmish was fought in the town, in 1775, when residents fended off an assault by the British sloop of war the *Falcon*. Geographic isolation along with economic reliance on fishing and merchant shipping, however, made Gloucester exceptionally vulnerable to the blockade imposed by the British at the war's outbreak. Vessels carrying needed provisions were often seized by the British and their cargoes confiscated. A handful of privateers—vessels fitted out to conduct what was in effect legalized piracy—did venture out, seizing more than two dozen British merchant ships over the course of the war, but many of the privateers ultimately were captured, and hundreds of Gloucester mariners were lost at sea or captured. While a few merchants and seafarers reaped financial gains, much of the remaining population was hungry and destitute. At one low point during the war, nearly one-fifth of all Gloucester families were receiving charitable aid, and during the bitter winter of 1776–1777, John Murray, a local preacher who knew General George Washington, trekked to the Continental Army camp at Cambridge to solicit funds. Washington himself is said to have given £10.

QUICK FACTS

GLOUCESTER, MA 1776–1790

MAYORS

During this time the city was overseen by selectmen who were elected at town meetings to serve for one-year terms

MAJOR INDUSTRIES AND EMPLOYERS

Merchant shipping
Fishing

MAJOR NEWSPAPERS

None published in Gloucester
Salem Gazette
Salem Mercury

MAJOR EVENTS

1777: The town meeting orders John Murray, leader of the breakaway Independent Christian Society (Universalists), to depart the town. Murray ignores the order.

1778: Privateering reaches its zenith with as many as eighteen vessels active; the privateer *Gloucester* is lost at sea with sixty men.

1777–1779: Smallpox epidemics sweep Gloucester in three waves, each more severe than before. The town at first rejects inoculation, then in 1778 reverses its position and encourages it.

1782: Town assessors seize and sell at auction goods belonging to three leading members of John Murray's Universalist Church after they refuse to pay taxes to support the First Parish. Four years later, the state's highest court rules that compulsory support of the "established church" violates the principles of religious freedom set forth in the 1780 state constitution.

1783: Peace is celebrated; Gloucester vessels sail to the Grand Banks, where the Treaty of Paris has guaranteed fishing rights to Americans. Overseas trade also builds, reaching a high point in 1790 when trade begins between Gloucester and Suriname.

Battle losses also occurred. Beginning with the 1775 Battle of Bunker Hill, nearly sixteen hundred Gloucester men took up arms or went to sea over the course of the war. More than 375 Gloucester men died as soldiers, at sea, or in prisons. Meanwhile, smallpox swept through the town for three consecutive years, from 1777 through 1779. Records are incomplete but at least one hundred people died of the disease. A growing city before the war, Gloucester saw its population fall from 4,945 in 1775 to 3,893 in 1782, a loss of more than 20 percent. The first federal census, in 1790, found the populace had rebounded to 5,317. Significantly, however, one-sixth of the 983 households counted that year were headed by females, suggesting that Gloucester was home to as many as one thousand widows and orphans.

GOVERNMENT AND POLITICS

As in other Massachusetts towns, Gloucester was governed by town meetings. Freeholders, almost entirely adult male property owners, each had one vote. Votes were tallied by voters walking from one side of the meeting room (the First Parish Church Meeting House) to another.

Records indicate that attendance was sparse and meetings were dominated by leading citizens. An annual meeting in March set the stage for governing the town for the ensuing year, including election of the seven-member Gloucester Board of Selectmen and representatives to the General Court (the Massachusetts legislature). Selectmen oversaw routine affairs through the year or, if faced with larger issues, referred them to reconvened or special town meeting sessions for resolution.

Names associated with leading landowners and merchant families dominated the elected leadership. These included the Coffin, Foster, Ellery, Low, Pearce, and Rogers families. John Low held office as a selectman for twelve of the fifteen years between 1760 and 1776 and was also sent eight times to the General Court. Peter Coffin, descendant of a prominent early Massachusetts Bay Colony settler, was elected selectman nineteen times between 1753 and 1776, and, between 1774 and 1792, represented Gloucester in the General Court for nine one-year terms. Town and church governance were thickly intertwined and church elders played leading roles. The First Parish, the most populous of the town's five parishes, headed by formidable pastor Eli Forbes, carried the most weight.

The town meeting was responsible for raising taxes to support town needs such as road upkeep and charitable support, as well as for raising money to pay a tax to the provincial government or, after 1780, the newborn Commonwealth of Massachusetts. Town meetings also had to respond to wartime demands from the General Court to recruit more soldiers or raise additional funds. As fighting wore on, the town meeting often appropriated bounties to recruit soldiers or to pay for replacement soldiers. As economic circumstances grew dire, the town meeting also often petitioned the General Court for charitable help and relief from provincial taxes, usually with little success.

Wartime vigilance also produced another level of political governance: the committee for safety, appointed by the selectmen to keep watch on strangers and hunt for British sympathizers. Gloucester's disdain for the Crown predated hostilities and was heightened by colonial authorities' efforts to tame rampant smuggling that had grown to make up a significant part of the merchant marine economy. These ill feelings had led to violence in 1770 when, less than three weeks after the Boston Massacre, a band of men disguised as Indians and blacks descended in the night on Jesse Saville, a resident and sometime customs officer whose Tory allegiance was no secret. Pulling Saville from his bed, they dragged him by his heels for four miles through snow and mud then placed him in a cart stripped nearly naked and for four hours wheeled him through the streets. They then tarred him and beat him again. Only one person, a slave owned by the town's physician, ultimately was prosecuted.

Politically, Gloucesterites tended to support the Federalists as the new nation took shape. On such major issues as a constitution for Massachusetts and, later, one for the new republic, voters usually left final decisions to the cadre of establishment leaders that represented the town's moneyed merchant class and men tightly tied to the established church, which held strong sway over local behavior. Nevertheless there was social ferment afoot. In 1773 a few dissident members of the established First Parish Church began to break away and recruited John Murray as their leader. His views rejected the dominant Calvinist doctrine of hellfire and eternal damnation, promised universal salvation, and presented God as all-loving. Successive

First Parish pastors branded such Universalist preachings as "dangerous errors," and in 1777 the committee on safety and later the town meeting (pushed by First Parish elders) ordered Murray to leave town. Murray defied the directive and, with his supporters, endured continuing harassment and censure. His following grew, and in 1779 some sixty Gloucesterites organized the Free and Independent Church of Christ, later known as the Independent Christian Society. This was the first American church of the Universalist denomination (now part of the Unitarian Universalist Association).

The struggle did not end there. In 1782 several Universalists refused to continue paying taxes to support the "established church." Gloucester's assessors responded by seizing silver plates and personal goods from three of the most prominent Universalist members and selling the items at auction. Murray and the breakaway church members sued for damages and in 1786 won a significant court ruling that declared all citizens were entitled to freedom of belief under the 1780 Massachusetts Constitution—a principle that later was incorporated into the First Amendment to the United States Constitution.

INDUSTRY, COMMERCE, AND LABOR

Settled in 1623 as a fishing outpost, Gloucester was largely a sustenance agrarian community until around 1700, when local mariners began shipping dried saltfish for sale to the southern colonies and the West Indies, mostly as food for slaves. Fishing as a commercial enterprise grew after the introduction of a new vessel design, the schooner, by Gloucester mariner Andrew Robinson. Schooners were larger and faster and capable of longer voyages, able to sail up to three months to destinations such as the rich Grand Banks fishing grounds off Newfoundland, Canada, and to make cargo trips to more distant ports. By the outbreak of the war, more than a dozen Gloucester merchant families that owned ships employed captains and crews who sailed to the southern colonies, the Caribbean, Europe, and sometimes Africa. After carrying saltfish south, the ships typically returned with corn, wheat flour, and hogs for local sale, or, from the West Indies, molasses, sugar, and rum. Trade also was sometimes triangular, with ships turning toward Europe with cargoes taken on in the south or the Caribbean, then returning to North America with salt needed by the fishing, wine, and finished goods industries. Anecdotes suggest some slave trade was likely, although there is no documentation of this.

Gloucester's ocean trade never approached that of Salem, Boston, or Marblehead, but it was undisputedly the town's economic life force until interrupted by hostilities and the British blockade. Gloucester, dependent as it was on shipping, was devastated by the blockade. Most mariners did not dare leave port. For a few, privateering was an opportunity. The Sargents, the Pearces, the Rogerses, and others, individually and in partnerships, fitted out at least eighteen privateers that hunted offshore for British ships loaded with goods or arms. The hope was to take these ships hostage and profit from sale of their cargoes or the vessels themselves. Several prizes were captured, but just as often the privateers themselves were seized by the enemy and their crews taken prisoner. Many seafarers, possibly hundreds, were lost at sea; in 1777 David Pearce's privateer *Gloucester* went to sea with a crew of sixty but, after capturing and sending back two prizes, was never seen again.

Despite the activity of the privateers, the bulk of Gloucester's population—the shipwrights, riggers, sailmakers, carpenters, blacksmiths, chandlers, and others who kept the fleet afloat, as well as the men and women who caught, dried, salted, and packed fish for export—had little work or income during the blockade. Worse, food was scarce. Gloucester was unable to feed itself without imports. By one estimate the town's annual harvest was only enough to supply the population for two months, and grist mills were in disrepair. As the war wore on, the town fathers in January 1780 counted 291 widowed women and 437 fatherless children as qualifying for charity and noted another 305 families in need. Four months later, in May, twenty desperate Gloucester women marched on Colonel Joseph Foster's warehouse demanding groceries. Under duress, Foster complied and emptied his stores. With no other help in sight, the town beseeched the Massachusetts General Court for aid. Despite a delegation's report of "half starved miserable women and naked children," the best that body could offer was a temporary reduction in taxes.

The end of the war with the Treaty of Paris in 1783 was justly celebrated in Gloucester. Among other provisions, the treaty guaranteed Americans fishing rights on the Grand Banks. Within months vessels from Gloucester were again sailing to the Banks to fill their holds with cod and haddock. Over the next decade the Gloucester offshore fishing fleet grew to more than 150 boats. Shipping, too, began to return, and by 1790 thirty-six Gloucester vessels were counted in ocean trade—four ships, nine brigs, and twenty-three schooners. After reconnecting with the West Indies, Gloucester mariners also somehow cornered trade between Massachusetts and Suriname on South America's northern coast. Inspired by this commercial coup, a syndicate of Gloucester merchants set their sights on the East India trade alongside the more prosperous Salem fleet, but they met with limited success. Nevertheless, as Samuel Eliot Morison concluded in his 1980 *Maritime History of Massachusetts*, "Gloucester [at the end of the decade] was a thriving and prosperous town . . . boasting a bank with a vault carved out of solid rock, a schoolhouse with cupola, and a two-story 'artillery house' or armory, with four field pieces and a bell procured from Denmark."

RACE, ETHNICITY, AND IMMIGRATION

The vast majority of Gloucester's people were of English ancestry, probably mostly from the west of England. A smaller number emigrated from coastal locations around the North Atlantic rim, including Scots and Irish coming by way of Canada's Maritimes and men who arrived as fishermen from a wide mixture of ports, including Portugal and the Azores.

Relatively few residents were not Caucasian. Until the new state constitution ended the practice in 1780, slave ownership was common among wealthier Massachusetts landowners and merchants, and Gloucester was no exception. The exact number and even the race of individuals who were owned by others in Gloucester are uncertain. Writing in the 1890s, Gloucester historian James R. Pringle estimated there were once as many as three hundred slaves in the town. "Some of the attics of the large houses were fitted up with slave pens for the accommodation of the blacks," he wrote. "The negroes, as was characteristic of their race, were very convivial and once each year were granted a holiday when they held a merry carnival at the Pine Tree Tavern."

Researchers at the Cape Ann Museum in Gloucester, however, dispute the notion of attic pens and place the maximum number of men and women in slavery at about forty, citing the 1790 census that listed forty-one African Americans. Nor is it clear how slaves got to Gloucester. Pringle speculated most came from Virginia, where local vessels traded. More recently, historian Joseph E. Garland has said some likely came from Charleston, South Carolina, also a port of call for Gloucester mariners and a major slave trade center.

Peter Coffin, the aristocrat who held more than five hundred acres in west Gloucester, is known to have owned at least six slaves. Dr. Samuel Plummer, the town's physician between 1748 and 1778, had at least two, one of whom, known as George and identified as a "molatto man-slave," was the lone person prosecuted for the tarring of Jesse Saville. Though he pleaded innocent, George nevertheless was sentenced to be whipped, imprisoned for two years, and fined £100.

After the slaves were freed, their population diminished; by 1890 there were only two African American families in Gloucester.

Native Americans, long driven back by the advancing American frontier, remained regular summertime visitors to Gloucester into the nineteenth century. Champlain had reported finding about two hundred natives when he visited in the summer of 1606. Records after that are limited but seldom mention natives and never hint at conflict. The natives who visited in the early 1800s were from the Pennacook tribe in New Hampshire and came by water to fish. At some point a number of natives made claims for reparations from European settlers in Gloucester, but how many, and for how much, is not recorded. The last such mention in town records was in 1700 when a settlement for an unstated amount was paid to Samuel English, described only as "an Indian."

JERRY ACKERMAN

BIBLIOGRAPHY

Babson, John J. *History of the Town of Gloucester, Cape Ann, Including the Town of Rockport.* Gloucester, MA: Peter Smith Publisher, Inc., 1972.

Brooks, Alfred Mansfield. *Gloucester Recollected: A Familiar History.* Gloucester, MA: Peter Smith Publisher, Inc., and the Cape Ann Historical Association, 1974.

Copeland, Melvin T., and Elliott C. Rogers. *The Saga of Cape Ann.* Freeport, ME: The Bond Wheelwright Co., 1960.

Eddy, Richard. *Universalism in Gloucester, Mass.: An Historical Discourse on the One Hundredth Anniversary of the First Sermon of Rev. John Murray in that Town, Delivered in the Independent Christian Church, November 3, 1874.* Gloucester, MA: Proctor Brothers, 1892.

Garland, Joseph E. *The Fish and the Falcon: Gloucester's Resolute Role in America's Fight for Freedom.* Charleston, SC: The History Press, 2006.

Hart, Albert Bushnell, ed. *Commonwealth History of Massachusetts.* Vol. 3. New York, NY: The States History Company, 1929.

Heyrman, Christine Leigh. *Commerce and Culture: The Maritime Communities of Colonial Massachusetts.* New York, NY: W. W. Norton & Company, 1984.

Morison, Samuel Eliot. *The Maritime History of Massachusetts.* Boston, MA: Northeastern University Press, 1980.

Pringle, James R. *History of the Town and City of Gloucester, Cape Ann, Massachusetts.* Gloucester, MA: City of Gloucester Archives Committee and Ten Pound Island Book Co., 1997.

Ray, Mary, and Sarah V. Dunlap. *Gloucester, Massachusetts, Historical Time-Line 1000–1999.* Gloucester, MA: The Gloucester Archives Committee, 2002.

Tagney, Ronald N. "Fought for Their Faith; How Universalism Was Planted On Cape Ann." *New York Times,* Aug. 22, 1892. Available online at http://query.nytimes.com/mem/archive-free/pdf?res=9401 E2D71331E033A25751C2A96E9C94639ED7CF (accessed May 18, 2011).

———. *The World Turned Upside Down: Essex County during America's Turbulent Years, 1863–1790.* West Newbury, MA: Essex County History, 1989.

Foreign territories

Pre-statehood territories

States

Includes states, territories, and population rankings as of 1820

CHAPTER 2

CITIES IN THE EARLY REPUBLIC, 1790–1828

The period from 1790 to 1828 was marked by the establishment of new government institutions such as a national bank, massive western expansion in terms of both population growth and the acquisition of new territory, the introduction into the Union of eight new states, the abolition of slavery in all of the northern states and the end of the importation of slaves from abroad, and the emergence of at least the outlines of the two-party system. In 1790 the population of the United States was approximately four million, with only some two hundred thousand people living in the twenty-four communities with populations over twenty-five hundred. Of the biggest cities in the country, the majority were located in New England. By the 1830 census, the population of the United States was almost thirteen million, with nearly 9 percent of those people living in the ninety communities with populations greater than twenty-five hundred. By this time the only city in New England to rank among the ten largest in the country was Boston,

Massachusetts. However, New England was still heavily urban and industrial, and it became the center of the textile industry. This industry grew in part from increased cotton production in the South.

By 1790 the first Congress under the United States Constitution was actively legislating in what was at that point the country's second largest city, Philadelphia, Pennsylvania. During its term (from March 1789 to March 1791) it authorized a national census, settled on the permanent location of the national capital as a stretch along the Potomac River, and established the First Bank of the United States.

Alexander Hamilton and Thomas Jefferson quickly came to represent two opposing political philosophies. Hamilton's Federalists favored a stronger national government and envisioned the United States as a commercial republic. Jefferson's Republicans favored stronger state governments and visualized an agrarian republic. The Federalists were more "urban" in the sense that much of their support came from the bigger cities and also because they were stronger supporters of industrial development. Jefferson, by contrast, was notoriously anti-urban, as reflected in one oft-cited letter he wrote to Benjamin Rush in 1800, in which he declared that cities were "pestilential to the morals, the health and the liberties of man."

In the first Congress, the Federalist vision prevailed. The national government assumed the debts of the states and established the First Bank. It also authorized taxes on imports and domestically produced "luxuries," most notably whiskey. Furthering the vision of a commercial republic in the private sphere, the first toll road in the United States was completed in 1794—the turnpike that connected the Pennsylvanian cities of Philadelphia and Lancaster—and hundreds more were built in the following decades.

George Washington, who had the support of both Federalists and Republicans, refused to run for a third term as president, and 1796 thus marked the nation's first competitive presidential election, with John Adams as the Federalist candidate and Jefferson as the Republican. Adams was elected the second president of the United States, and the Federalists maintained majority control over Congress. Yet the Federalists in Congress overstepped themselves by passing the notorious Alien and Sedition Acts, which were used to convict several Republican newspaper editors.

In the 1800 presidential election, in which Adams and Jefferson once again ran against each other, the Republicans secured some big-city support by allying with New York City's Aaron Burr and the political organization he controlled, the Society of Saint Tammany (later known as Tammany Hall). The Republicans carried the vote in New York, which swung the national election, though the final choice of president ultimately came down to a vote in the House of Representatives between Jefferson and Burr, with Jefferson emerging as the winner.

Jefferson and the congressional Republicans eliminated taxes on domestically produced goods, decreased government spending and the national debt, and reduced the size of the army and navy. Yet Jefferson also vastly expanded the size of the United States in 1803 through the Louisiana Purchase, in part a defensive move to protect the port of New Orleans and to prevent a potential French empire on the continent. The Louisiana Territory covered land that would later become part of fourteen states, but more importantly for this book, it also included New Orleans, Louisiana; St. Louis, Missouri; Detroit, Michigan; and Fort Dearborn, Illinois, the future site of Chicago.

BY THE NUMBERS: **THE MOST POPULOUS CITIES IN 1820**

	TOTAL POPULATION	WHITE POPULATION	FREE "COLORED" POPULATION	SLAVE POPULATION	% FREE POPULATION
NEW YORK, NY	123,706	112,820	10,368	518	99.6
PHILADELPHIA, PA	63,802	54,917*	8,782*	3	100.0
BALTIMORE, MD	62,738	48,055	10,326	4,357	93.1
BOSTON, MA	43,298	41,558	1,690	0	99.9
NEW ORLEANS, LA	27,176	13,584	6,237	7,355	72.9
CHARLESTON, SC	24,780	10,653	1,475	12,652	48.9
WASHINGTON, DC	13,247	9,606	1,696	1,945	85.3
SALEM, MA	12,731	12,437	294	0	100.0
ALBANY, NY	12,630	11,876	645	109	99.1
RICHMOND, VA	12,067	6,445	1,235	4,387	63.6

	% SLAVE POPULATION	PERSONS ENGAGED IN MANUFACTURES	% ENGAGED IN MANUFACTURES	FOREIGNERS NOT NATURALIZED	% FOREIGNERS NOT NATURALIZED
NEW YORK, NY	0.4	9,523	7.7	5,390	4.4
PHILADELPHIA, PA	0.0	6,100	9.6	777	1.2
BALTIMORE, MD	6.9	4,601	7.3	1,359	2.2
BOSTON, MA	0.0	2,891	6.7	1,836	4.2
NEW ORLEANS, LA	27.1	2,704	9.9	1,500	5.5
CHARLESTON, SC	51.1	887	3.6	425	1.7
WASHINGTON, DC	14.7	865	6.5	293	2.2
SALEM, MA	0.0	887	7.0	134	1.1
ALBANY, NY	0.9	909	7.2	237	1.9
RICHMOND, VA	36.4	1,305	10.8	324	2.7

*Due to an error in the census volume, these figures do not add up to the total population given for the city as a whole.

Note: This list does not include Northern Liberties Township, PA, or Southwark, PA. See introduction for details.

Source: Census for 1820. Published by authority of an act of Congress, under the direction of the secretary of State.

At the end of his presidency, in 1807, Jefferson and Congress instituted an embargo restricting American ships from traveling to foreign ports. This resulted in an economic depression that hit the urbanized, mercantile areas of the Northeast especially hard. The embargo was in reaction to aggressive action by the British Navy, which was itself a reflection of a deteriorating relationship between the United States and Britain, especially with regard to British support of Indian tribes along the western frontier. The midterm elections in 1810 (after James Madison's election as president in 1808) brought new members of Congress—Henry Clay and John Calhoun among them—eager for a military solution. Thus, Madison signed the bill sent to him from Congress in 1812 that declared war with Britain.

The War of 1812 was for the most part a failure for the United States. It had even worse consequences for the Indian tribes, who lost much of their ability to thwart the western advance of white Americans. One notable American military success was the Battle of New Orleans, which was possibly most significant not for thwarting advancing British troops, but for making the major general in charge, Andrew Jackson, a war hero. The battle, however, actually occurred in 1814 after Britain and the United States had agreed on a peace treaty.

Madison was reelected president in 1812, and his secretary of State, James Monroe, was elected president in 1816, by which time the Federalist Party had all but disappeared. The Republicans had, at any rate, incorporated many Federalist policies as their own. In 1816 Congress enacted new protective tariffs and chartered the Second Bank of the United States, the original bank's charter having not been renewed in 1811. The president after Monroe, John Quincy Adams (elected in 1824), had been a Federalist, and Speaker of the House Henry Clay was pursuing the "American System"—a notably Hamiltonian program of domestic improvements financed through protective tariffs—and support for a strong role for the national bank.

By 1824 the party system had largely fallen apart, and the presidential election that year was marked by a fractured factionalism, with four candidates running: John Quincy Adams, Henry Clay, William Crawford, and Andrew Jackson. Though Jackson won the most popular and electoral votes, the election was decided by the House of Representatives, which chose Adams. In response, Jackson's supporters ramped up their support of states' rights and popular democracy. Therefore, the new Democratic Party became in many respects the heir to the Jeffersonian legacy. When Jackson succeeded in being elected as the first Democratic president in 1828, it marked the emergence of a second party system and a new era in American history.

NEW YORK, NY 1790–1828

FROM 1790 TO 1828, NEW YORK CITY WAS THE DRIVING ENGINE of the United States economy and one of the fastest-growing cities in the world. During the 1790s, even though New York ceased to serve as national (1790) and state (1797) capital, its population soared by 80 percent and then rose another 60 percent from 1800 to 1810. Despite the traumas of war and depression, Manhattan was home to two hundred thousand people by 1828. Led by its innovative and aggressive merchant elite, the city achieved domination of the import and export trade of the nation even before 1800, and its position became unassailable once the Erie Canal opened in 1825. During this period New York was the largest and richest American city and the most important metropolis in the Western Hemisphere.

GOVERNMENT AND POLITICS

On June 20, 1790, Secretary of the Treasury Alexander Hamilton and House leader James Madison met for dinner at Thomas Jefferson's leased home on Maiden Lane. The three negotiated an arrangement that provided crucial southern votes to enact Hamilton's program whereby the new federal government would assume the debts of the state governments. In return, Hamilton agreed that the national capital would be temporarily transferred to Philadelphia and ultimately located in a yet-to-be constructed Washington, D.C. Hamilton, the intellectual leader of the

QUICK FACTS

NEW YORK, NY 1790–1828

MAYORS

Richard Varick	(1790–1801)
Edward Livingston	(1801–1803)
De Witt Clinton	(1803–1807)
Marinus Willett	(1807–1808)
De Witt Clinton	(1808–1810)
Jacob Radcliff	(1810–1811)
De Witt Clinton	(1811–1815)
John Ferguson	(1815)
Jacob Radcliff	(1815–1818)
Cadwaller D. Colden	(1818–1821)
Stephen Allen	(1821–1824)
William Paulding	(1825–1826)
Philip Hone	(1826–1827)
William Paulding	(1827–1828)

New York Gazette and General Advertiser
Time Piece
Commercial Advertiser
Tablet and Weekly Advertiser
Spectator
The Shamrock
Truth Teller
New York Mercantile Advertiser
Porcupine's Gazette
New York Columbian
New York Evening Post
Freedom's Journal
National Advocate
New York American
New York Enquirer

MAJOR INDUSTRIES AND EMPLOYERS

New York Customs House
Shipbuilding
Shoemaking
Tanning
Sugar refining

MAJOR NEWSPAPERS

New York Daily Advertiser
New York Morning Post
New York Weekly Museum
Gazette of the United States
New York Journal and Patriotic Register
Loudon's Register
Columbian Gazette
American Minerva
American Citizen
Greenleaf's New York Journal
New York Commercial

MAJOR EVENTS

June 20, 1790: After dinner at Thomas Jefferson's, Alexander Hamilton and James Madison agree on a "deal" that transfers the national capital to Philadelphia, Pennsylvania, and ultimately to Washington, DC, in return for approval of Hamilton's financial plan.

May 17, 1792: The *New York Evening Post*, founded by Alexander Hamilton, begins publication with William Coleman as editor. Later edited by William Cullen Bryant, it still publishes as New York City's oldest newspaper.

August 17, 1807: Robert Fulton's *North River Steamboat* (*The Clermont*), a "sawmill on a raft spitting fire," travels north to Albany, New York. Regular passenger service to the capital begins in September and initiates a transportation revolution.

August 10, 1811: New York's city hall, designed by John McComb and Joseph Mangin, opens and the council meets there the next day. It remains one of the finest municipal structures in the United States.

November 4, 1825: The *Seneca Chief* arrives in Manhattan after completing the first trip though the Erie Canal from Buffalo, New York. Governor De Witt Clinton presides over the "wedding of the waters" as Lake Erie is joined to the Atlantic Ocean.

George Washington administration, thereby furthered his goal of creating a strong national government at the expense of his home city. However, operating as the leader of Manhattan's Federalists, he simultaneously built a municipal coalition of artisan and merchant voters that secured his party's control of New York City for a decade. Although the federal government vacated New York, Federalists controlled the city during the crucial first years of the American experiment.

Federalist mayor Richard Varick, like his predecessor James Duane an appointee of Governor George Clinton, continued to repair the ravages of British occupation during the Revolution. A bit of a snob and a bully—he once ordered a ferryman whipped for "insolence"—Varick used his office to consolidate the merchant-artisan alliance. Varick coordinated city responses against outbreaks of yellow fever (1791, 1795, 1796), cholera (1798), and a "bawdy house" riot (1793). He also accelerated Manhattan's development. New arrivals in the city averaged three thousand annually during the 1790s, and the mayor implemented a house numbering system. Mayors of New York did not receive a salary until 1813, but Varick gained a substantial income from his licensing authority (every businessman from butcher to barman had to apply to City Hall for a license). Federalist investors controlled the two city banks that provided funds for port improvements, the demolition of old Fort George, and the opening of new streets. Statistics revealed that Manhattan surpassed Philadelphia to lead American import and export trade by 1797, and Congress approved construction of a naval yard along the East River in 1801 to take advantage of city expertise in shipbuilding.

Not until 1799, when the administration of John Adams splintered into factions, was there an effective challenge to Federalist control. Democratic leader Aaron Burr obtained a state charter for the Manhattan Company, ostensibly a water supply utility, but in fact an institution that he quickly converted into a Jeffersonian bank. Burr also transformed the benevolent and patriotic Society of St. Tammany into a political force active in local elections. New York had barely four thousand voters, since only property-owning males could vote, but financial aid from Tammany gradually created additional Democratic voters. In 1800 Burr and the Democrats sponsored a municipal ticket that delivered New York's electoral vote to Thomas Jefferson. When the ever-ambitious Burr subsequently attempted to deprive Jefferson of the presidency in 1801, he was thwarted by Alexander Hamilton, who considered it a "religious duty" to oppose such a scoundrel. The political rivalry between the two culminated in the most famous duel in American history and Hamilton's death in 1804.

Manhattan's extraordinary growth continued in the new century under Democratic leadership. Mayor Edward Livingstone openly appealed for the support of labor, but Federalists defeated his proposed jobs program. After Livingstone resigned his post in 1803, De Witt Clinton left the U.S. Senate to succeed him. Clinton served ten terms as mayor and was a dominant figure in city history. He helped found the New York Historical Society in 1804 and the Free School Society in 1805, and he established the first health department in 1805. City population continued its amazing growth, with seven hundred new homes built in 1803 alone. As Manhattan replaced Philadelphia as the nation's biggest city, the mayor ordered that the Collect Pond, a source of drinking water in Dutch days but now polluted by industrial waste, be filled. Unfortunately, tenements constructed there would become part of the notorious Five Points slum. City growth was so rapid that a three-man commission was named to plan its northward extension; the grid pattern they mandated in 1811—north-ward avenues crossed by numbered streets—determined the future construction of two thousand city blocks.

Washington Irving's *Salmagundi Essays* (1807) first referred to New York as "Gotham," and many residents adopted his nickname for their busy city. New York already ranked as America's "queen of commerce" when Robert Fulton's *Clermont* pioneered steam travel on the Hudson in 1807. Rising tensions between London and Washington over the imperial impressment of American seamen temporarily dashed entrepreneurial hopes, however. New York's port was sorely impacted by Jefferson's Embargo Act of 1807, a national program denounced by local merchants as "O Grab Me." As fears of war escalated, "fortification fever" swept the city, and Mayor Clinton supervised construction of a series of forts to protect against assault from the sea. The Southwest Battery that was built then is now known as Castle Clinton and is a national monument. Another survivor of that exciting era is New York's city hall, which opened for business in 1811. Expectations of future growth placed the building far uptown, and the council refused to place marble on its northern façade as they believed no one would ever see it.

America's second war with Great Britain began in 1812, and the economy of Manhattan

In response to rapid growth, New York's City Council received state approval to begin devising a comprehensive City Plan. The result was the Comissioner's Plan of 1811, seen above, which created the grid system on which Manhattan was developed.

Source: Granger Collection

declined precipitously and poverty came to its streets. By the time the Treaty of Ghent restored the *status quo ante,* one of every seven city residents was receiving welfare aid administered by the Humane Society. Yet when Great Britain attempted to undermine infant American industries by "dumping" goods on New York's reopened piers, city merchants brilliantly responded with an auction market that distributed goods nationally. Philip Hone made a fortune that allowed him to retire, become mayor in 1826, and write his two-million-word *Diary* that chronicled city life. Not all city residents prospered, however, and the severe economic collapse caused by the panic of 1819 put seventeen hundred unemployed into the poor house. Full prosperity for workers did not return until the opening of the Erie Canal in 1825. By 1828 political reform had broadened the electorate, workingmen's parties had been formed, and the city supported Andrew Jackson's election by more than six thousand votes.

INDUSTRY, COMMERCE, AND LABOR

In 1790 Manhattan's local economy was dominated by artisan manufacturing. Craftsmen within this community were conservative and voted as part of Hamilton's Federalist coalition. Their work patterns followed almost medieval norms of development. Labor was performed in small shops and men progressed from helper to journeyman; some attained master status and owned their own shops. As New York grew in wealth and population, this system of manufacturing endured and remained largely in place by 1828. Although rivers surrounded Manhattan, the island lacked sufficient water power to achieve the industrialized factory life that transformed New England and parts of the Hudson Valley early in the nineteenth century. It is significant that from 1790 to 1819 the legislature issued a mere dozen grants of incorporation to city firms, and only one of these lasted into the 1820s. Historian Carl Kaestle found 52 percent of all city workers in 1796 were artisans and that apprenticeship remained vital to manufacturing into the 1820s. The career of Duncan Phyfe, master of the Regency Style of cabinetmaking, epitomizes the system. He opened his business in 1792, owned three shops by 1815, and became famous and wealthy enough to speculate in land, yet he never employed more than one hundred journeymen. New York had vast manufacturing capabilities but they remained small scale—the value of its products came from the ancient expertise and the sheer number of tanners, shoemakers, tailors, brewers, cabinetmakers, and dozens of other tradesmen who peopled the city.

Although industrialization may have lagged, the city led all rivals in finance, banking, real estate, and insurance. A brief monetary panic early in 1792, caused by speculation in federal bonds offered at auction, convinced city brokers who regularly met in coffee houses that regulation of financial transactions was necessary. That May twenty-four brokers drew up rules for a securities market, and their Buttonwood Agreement eventually became the New York Stock Exchange in 1817. Manhattan's five banks of 1815 were soon joined by the Emigrant Savings Bank in 1819 and the Chemical Bank in 1824. Not to be outdone, merchants such as Archibald Gracie and Nicolas Low organized marine insurance companies to mitigate the dangers of seaborne commerce. Even more vital was Manhattan's introduction of scheduled transatlantic packet service by the Black Ball (1818) and Red Star (1821) lines. City merchants expanded their position as transshippers of southern cotton and their ships dominated the sea lanes, while banks and insurance companies financed new enterprise. Despite the national panic of 1819, New York continued to outpace all economic competition. Former mayor De Witt Clinton served four terms as governor, during which he drove the 363-mile Erie Canal to completion. The "governor's gully" gave Manhattan access to the produce of the American Midwest and guaranteed greater future prosperity. By 1828 the city handled almost one-third of America's exports and received two-thirds of its imports, ratios it maintained for a century. Most of the revenue collected by the federal government was generated on the docks of New York.

Large returns, ample credit, and a more secure market drew ambitious men, including many New Englanders, to the growing city. Manhattan's merchant class quadrupled by 1830, yet this intense commercial activity occurred in a congested city that extended barely two miles from the harbor. John Jacob Astor was at first a fur merchant, but he foresaw the future growth of the metropolis and began to speculate in uptown Manhattan real estate. His insight was quickly matched by representatives of the Dodge, Goelet, Lorillard, Rhinelander, Ruggles, and Schermerhorn families. Fortunes in Manhattan could be made (or lost) in a myriad of commercial endeavors but land values always rose.

Labor's role in the New York economy was less dynamic. Before 1788 there were no more than three attempts at withholding labor from Manhattan employers. Only in 1794 did journeyman printers form the Franklin Typographical Society—the first attempt to create a union that might strike for better conditions. The model was slowly adapted by other crafts, but worker unity was difficult to attain when most journeymen were normally unemployed up to half a year. When the embargo impacted commerce, workers depended on municipal soup kitchens or their personal relationship with their master rather than unions. One historian counted only twenty-five strikes from 1795 to 1825. Stoppages by carpenters in 1810, cordwainers in 1811, construction workers in 1816, printers in 1817, and masons in 1819 made minor gains. By 1825, however, dockworkers achieved the ability to virtually shut down the port. In 1828, even as stevedores and ship riggers again crippled waterfront commerce, striking weavers destroyed looms to back their wage demands.

During the first decades of the Republic, Manhattan's dominant commercial class created vast personal wealth, freely performed public service, and cared for the less fortunate members of society through a myriad of public institutions. Yet by the 1820s their firm control of political life had ended. From 1821 to 1824, Stephen Allen, a rich businessman who won office by saying he was a simple maker of sails, served as mayor. He faced an electorate that had quadrupled in size since 1800 because property requirements for voting had ended for most males. New York's social structure was in constant flux as seven thousand newcomers arrived annually, and its traditional journeyman system of manufacturing could no longer meet consumer demands. Wealth in America's metropolis was unevenly distributed—the top 4 percent of the population held half the wealth—and poverty was increasing.

RACE, ETHNICITY, AND IMMIGRATION

During America's colonial period, one-fifth of New York's population was black, a percentage exceeded only by that of Charleston, South Carolina. Yet the national census revealed that

Manhattan's percentage of blacks, both slave and free, fell to 10 percent by 1800. Although many New York merchants remained active in the lucrative slave trade, a Manumission Society formed in 1785 and led by John Jay and Alexander Hamilton strongly advocated the abolition of slavery. Because the state enacted a gradual emancipation law in February 1799, 84 percent of all New York blacks were free by 1810. Most blacks belonged to the laboring class, but many began their own businesses, and a black neighborhood formed east of city hall. The Manumission Society organized a free school for blacks in the 1790s, and the community organized its first African Methodist Episcopal Zion congregation in 1797. The Abyssinian Baptist Church was formed in 1808, and in 1809 St. Philip's Episcopal Church was founded by secessionists from Trinity. By 1820 only 518 New York blacks remained in slavery, and after July 4, 1827, all were freed. *Freedom's Journal* began publication that year, speaking for almost fourteen thousand blacks who comprised only 7 percent of New York's population.

In his New Year's address of 1790, President Washington had predicted that the "highly favored situation of New York will . . . attract numerous emigrants, who will gradually change its ancient customs." His insight was proven correct during the 1790s as the city received influxes of refugees from Haiti, Ireland, and Germany. Most Haitians were slaveholders who shortly left the city, but Pierre Toussaint stayed to become Manhattan's leading hairdresser and stylist. The Irish who came were largely northern Protestants fleeing the failed United Irishmen's uprising of 1798, while the Germans were largely artisans. Subsequent decades would see different motives for emigration, but the flow of people towards "the grand emporium of the Western World" faltered only during the War of 1812. In the 1820s the number of immigrants reached an average of seven thousand annually. Despite all these immigrants, the city in 1825 remained English-dominated and 80 percent native-born.

Irish immigrants had already made substantial contributions to the fabric of New York. The Tammany Society that William Mooney created in 1786 as a benevolent organization for Revolutionary War veterans had become a political element within the Jacksonian coalition. Thomas Emmet, who left Ireland after being jailed for his part in the rebellion of 1798, became a leading Manhattan lawyer and the first president of the Irish Immigrant Society in 1817. Another Ulsterman, Alexander Stewart, arrived with bundles of lace and began a successful business career; he created New York's first department store. The bulk of early Irish immigrants were Protestant (Scotch-Irish), but poorer Irish Catholics began emigrating after 1800. These newcomers organized a second Catholic parish; "old" St. Patrick's Cathedral was dedicated in May 1815, and New York's first Catholic bishop, John DuBois, is buried beneath its doorstep. As Catholics increased in number, old religious hostilities surfaced, and in 1824 there was a riot when Orangemen marched through Catholic areas of Greenwich Village. Emmet's defense of imprisoned Catholics made him a hero to almost all Irishmen, and his death in 1827 was marked by a half-day's business closure.

Undeniably the immigrants of the 1820s were poorer and less skilled than their predecessors. Irishmen found employment as dockworkers or laborers on the Erie Canal, and Germans often worked in breweries or sugar refineries near the East River. Both groups were unwelcome in the fashionable wards of lower Manhattan, so many found lodging in the Five

Points, which became a slum even before 1830. Yet blacks, Irish, Germans, and others lived there in peace and with a sense of optimism about the future. Few even aspired to dine at the Delmonico brothers' restaurant that was established in 1827. It catered to the wealthy elite, but most could agree with the judgment of civic leader John Pintard: "This city is the wonder of every stranger."

See also *New York, NY 1776–1790; New York, NY 1828–1854; New York, NY 1854–1877; New York, NY 1877–1896; New York, NY 1896–1929; New York, NY 1929–1941; New York, NY 1941–1952; New York, NY 1952–1989; New York, NY 1989–2011*

GEORGE LANKEVICH

BIBLIOGRAPHY

Albion Robert G., and Jennie Barnes Pope. *The Rise of New York Port, 1815–1860.* New York, NY: Scribner's, 1939.

Dolan, Jay. *The Immigrant Church: New York's Irish and German Catholics, 1815–1865.* Baltimore, MD: The Johns Hopkins University Press, 1975.

Gellman, David. *Emancipating New York: the Politics of Slavery and Freedom, 1777–1827.* Baton Rouge: Louisiana State University Press, 2006.

Wilentz, Sean. *Chants Democratic: New York City and the Rise of the American Working Class, 1788–1850.* New York, NY: Oxford University Press, 1984.

Young, Alfred. *The Democratic Republicans of New York: The Origins, 1763–1797.* Chapel Hill: University of North Carolina Press, 1967.

PHILADELPHIA, PA 1790–1828

ON APRIL 17, 1790, A MAN AS DIVERSE AND ADAPTABLE AS THE CITY HE CALLED HOME died at the age of eighty-four. Benjamin Franklin, in many ways the quintessential American, was gone. A somber group of interdenominational clergy led his funeral cortege four days later. The estimated twenty thousand mourners in attendance (nearly half the city) gathered to watch the procession, which included printers and their apprentices, members of the American Philosophical Society, and members of the College of Physicians of Philadelphia, all honoring the man's contributions to the city and the country. He was laid to rest next to his wife, Deborah, in the Christ Church burial ground on Second Street above Market. The death of Benjamin Franklin, a man who embodied the energy and spirit of Philadelphia and of eighteenth-century America, marked the end of an era. By the start of the War of 1812, both the national and state capitals would leave America's premier eighteenth-century city, and Philadelphia would be left to adapt to New York's ascendance as the young Republic's largest city. Despite its lost title, Philadelphia continued to set both industrial and cultural standards in the early nineteenth century.

QUICK FACTS

PHILADELPHIA, PA **1790–1828**

MAYORS

Samuel Powel	(1789–1790)
Samuel Miles	(1790–1791)
John Barclay	(1791–1792)
Matthew Clarkson	(1792–1796)
Hilary Baker	(1796–1798)
Robert Wharton	(1798–1800)
John Inskeep	(1800–1801)
Matthew Lawler	(1801–1805)
John Inskeep	(1805–1806)
Robert Wharton	(1806–1807)
John Barker	(1807–1810)
Robert Wharton	(1810–1811)
Michael Keppele	(1811–1812)
John Barker	(1812–1813)
John Geyer	(1813–1814)
Robert Wharton	(1814–1819)
James Nelson Barker	(1819–1820)
Robert Wharton	(1820–1824)
Joseph Watson	(1824–1828)

MAJOR INDUSTRIES AND EMPLOYERS

Seth Craige's cotton mill
Oliver Evans' flour mill
Mars Iron Works
Gilpin Paper Mill
Binny and Richardson's foundry
Lehigh Coal and Navigation Company

MAJOR NEWSPAPERS

The Federal Gazette and Philadelphia Daily Advertiser
Gemeinnützige Philadelphische Correspondenz
The General Advertiser and Political, Commercial, Agricultural and
 Literary Journal
Independent Gazetteer or the Chronicle of Freedom
National Gazette
Philadelphia Minerva
Pennsylvania Packet and Daily Advertiser
Universal Asylum and Columbian Magazine

MAJOR EVENTS

1793: A yellow fever epidemic rages in the late summer and early fall, at which point nearly half the city flees.
1795: The Philadelphia and Lancaster Turnpike opens as the first such road in the United States.
1799: Work begins on the Schuylkill Water Works to bring water to the city.
1800: The nation's capital moves from Philadelphia to the District of Columbia.
1817: Richard Allen's Mother Bethel Church becomes the first African Methodist Episcopal church in the United States.
1826: Philadelphia's council wins the right to elect any Philadelphia citizen—not just a member of the council—to serve as mayor.

GOVERNMENT AND POLITICS

Philadelphia's city government was a mixture of elected offices, appointed positions, and voluntary organizations. City government included a mayor elected for a one-year term. The mayor served as a kind of chief of police, dealing with riots and other disturbances himself. The legislative power of the city was vested in the select and common councils, both of which became elected bodies in 1789. The select council had the responsibility of electing the mayor until 1839 and also appointed city officers until 1885. Both councils represented ward-based constituencies; the select council consisted of one member from each ward, and the common council had one member for every two thousand taxable residents in each ward. By 1796 the two councils had a collective membership of thirty-two men. The city government also included a board of city commissioners, which appointed tax collectors and assessors, furnished lists of voters to election officers, and helped the sheriff select jurors (based on taxpayer lists). In the early nineteenth century, the city commissioners also leased polling places and provided ballot boxes. The city registrar kept the city's official records. Constables and watchmen reinforced around-the-clock order on the streets. Volunteer fire companies protected the city, but only in 1811 did the city councils appropriate $1,000 to help support these companies. A council of twelve "viewers" planned new streets, and a separate group determined the cost of these municipal improvements. The city also had the Watering Committee to oversee Philadelphia's water needs. Poor relief was left to municipal benevolent groups like the Guardians of the Poor. The state's responsibility for the administration of the bustling port of Philadelphia fell largely to city inhabitants. In 1803 Pennsylvania reorganized the administrative duties to include a master warden and six (later twelve) assistants, and Philadelphians filled a majority of these positions.

Perhaps one of Philadelphia's greatest civic achievements between 1790 and 1828 was the completion of the nation's first municipal waterworks. Previously, city inhabitants had gotten their water from wells and cisterns that were easily contaminated, and two deadly yellow fever epidemics had broken out in the 1790s. This, along with arguments that the growing city needed more water to fight fires, prompted Philadelphians to petition the two city councils for a new water source. Engineer and architect Benjamin Henry Latrobe proposed a plan to build a basin on the Schuylkill River above Chestnut Street. The water from the basin was lifted and forced by steam pumps to a canal and tunnel between Chestnut Street and a pump house in Centre Square. Another steam pump in Centre Square lifted the water to a sixteen-thousand-gallon reservoir from which wooden pipes delivered the water throughout the city. The operation began with some success in 1801, and in 1805 Frederick Graff took charge of improvements, such as installing iron pipes instead of wooden ones. He soon found his plan for the waterworks at Fairmount followed by nearly thirty-five other cities.

In the 1790s, the city's political life was overshadowed by the workings of a national government that had just returned to Philadelphia after Senator Robert Morris, Representative Thomas FitzSimons, and Tench Coxe worked their political magic to wrest it away from New York City. The presidencies of George Washington and John Adams supported the development of a pro-English Federalist party that included the city's former army officers, militiamen from the city's elite voluntary company known as MacPherson's Blues. This company had formed in 1794 to help Washington quell the Whiskey Rebellion in western Pennsylvania. Those who supported France even after the beginning of the bloody Reign of Terror in 1793 included national notables like Thomas Jefferson, Benjamin Rush, David Rittenhouse, Thomas McKean, and Thomas Mifflin. As ordinary Americans voiced their own opinions about the French Revolution, the Democratic-Republican Party developed. This party included Irish immigrants such as Mathew Carey and William Duane, the city's free black population, and a majority of French immigrants. Party politics had come to Philadelphia.

In response to major disease
outbreaks in the 1790s
and other city needs, a
major municipal project
was undertaken to bring
clean drinking water to the
residents of Philadelphia.
A system of steam pumps
and canals was designed
by architect Henry Latrobe
to raise water from the
Schuylkill River, store it,
and deliver it to residents
of the city. Pictured above
is Latrobe's Centre Square
waterworks building, which
began operation in 1801.

Source: Library of Congress

By 1800, when the nation's capital moved to the District of Columbia, the Federalist dominance of Philadelphia had ended. Governor Thomas McKean had helped the Democratic-Republicans secure control of Pennsylvania, not to mention the United States presidency, by late 1800. Dr. Michael Leib, arguably Philadelphia's first political boss, organized a coalition of Jeffersonians, vociferously anti-English (and thus anti-Federalist) Irish immigrants, and all those Philadelphia voters who feared the recent rise of what appeared to be an aristocracy of wealth and privilege into a working opposition party. To aid this process, Jeffersonian William Duane used his bitterly partisan newspaper, the *Aurora*, to voice a rising democratic spirit. A revolt of small farmers, free blacks, and the city's working poor in general, guided by middling liberals against a ruling elite, brought the Revolution of 1800 to Philadelphia. The city's Federalists found that their best chance for election came when the Democratic-Republicans fought among themselves. In 1808 Federalists noticeably demonstrated against the embargo of 1807, but by the end of the War of 1812, the party had disappeared as a viable opposition. In 1828 the city supported the ascendancy of Andrew Jackson's Democratic Party, which sealed the power shift.

INDUSTRY, COMMERCE, AND LABOR

In 1789 Philadelphia adopted a municipal coat of arms that sported a plow with sheaves of wheat atop a ship under full sail. Not knowing the future, of course, the city fathers could not have known how quickly these iconic choices would suggest more of the city's past than its future. Between 1789 and 1828, Philadelphia would shift its economic emphasis from agriculture and shipping to manufacturing and begin its ascent to the notable distinction of America's first major industrial city.

A healthy relationship between Philadelphia's hinterland farmers and its maritime commerce had powered the city's eighteenth-century economy. As the city ushered in a new century, merchants enjoyed trade both within and beyond the British Empire. Their ships brought goods from Holland, Germany, and Russia, and eventually Philadelphian Robert Morris even opened up the China trade. The first threat to Philadelphia's economic preeminence came from Baltimore, Maryland, which, between 1798 and 1800, boasted more exports than Philadelphia. Philadelphia responded by building a turnpike west to Lancaster, Pennsylvania, so the hinterland could be more readily included in commercial growth. Economic competition with both Baltimore and New York, in fact, fueled growth and led to the state's transportation revolution, which included the construction of turnpikes, canals, and eventually railroads that better connected Philadelphia's port to the hinterland. Oliver Evans built the first completely automated flour mill in the city in 1784, and by 1805 flour production dominated the city's economy, with four hundred thousand barrels exported during that year alone.

In the meantime, the Napoleonic Wars took so much of Europe's shipping power away from trade that the United States became the world's primary neutral carrier. Philadelphia's primary market had been the Caribbean sugar islands, but with English and French abuses to the country's neutral shipping rights, this trade became problematic at best. Earlier, in 1784, Robert Morris paired with New Yorker Daniel Parker to send the first American ship, the *Empress of China*, to Canton in China. That year, the *United States* sailed from Philadelphia into India and opened trade there as well. West Indian trade soon became less important as merchants like Tench Coxe, Mordecai Lewis, and Robert Morris looked to Asia, Europe, and even South America for other opportunities. Silk, tea, and porcelain from China all came to Philadelphia and opened the eyes of the city's residents to new worlds and new cultural possibilities. These cargoes were first sold in the auction style of the eighteenth century, but as a market revolution rumbled through the Republic, warehouses and retail shops multiplied in the city. While the China trade reached new heights by 1805, the 1807 embargo quickly brought it to a halt. In 1808 angry seamen marched to city hall to ask Mayor John Barker for help. When he could offer little respite, many left the city. Just four years later, the War of 1812, which featured a British blockade that bottled up Philadelphia shipping, ushered in the country's first experiments in domestic manufactures and spurred Philadelphians to build manufactories.

Philadelphia had always prided itself on its artisan production. Prior to the War of 1812, citizens produced floor cloth, carpets, cotton, linen wool, calico cloth, soap, earthenware goods, window glass, and a number of other items. In 1792 the very same Oliver Evans who changed flour milling in the state established Mars Iron Works, the first significant foundry and ironworks in the United States, which by 1801 was building steam engines for commercial sale. Thanks to the Gilpin Paper Mill on the Brandywine River, Philadelphia was also home to papermaking, which, along with Binny and Ronaldson's type foundry, helped the city become the country's printing center before the War of 1812.

While these manufacturing changes promised economic growth, they also dislocated artisans and changed the face of labor relations. The move to manufactories led to the de-skilling and displacement of trained craftsmen. The artisan shop with its communal commitments soon became a thing of the past. In 1805 journeymen cordwainers went on strike for higher wages. They were found guilty and convicted of a conspiracy to combine, or strike. The first round of the struggle to industrialize Philadelphia thus went to the shop owners, encouraging the shift from craft to factory production.

After the War of 1812, waterpower and canal fever revolutionized Philadelphia. In 1818 the Lehigh Coal and Navigation Company formed to speed the city's shift from turnpikes and horse-powered railroads to water-powered transportation. In 1809 Josiah White and Erskine Hazard built a rolling mill and wire factory at the falls of the Schuylkill River. They first used bituminous coal from Virginia to fuel their furnaces, but by 1815 they had discovered that the abundant anthracite coal found in their own state could be used in its place. Philadelphia had three canal projects—two to get anthracite coal from the beds north of the city to Philadelphia and a third that reached westward to the Susquehanna River—by which coal started to come into the city in 1820, and in 1827 the Lehigh Coal and Navigation Company's canal project began. The industrial revolution was underway, and the city eagerly, though sometimes uncomfortably, embraced the changes.

RACE, ETHNICITY, AND IMMIGRATION

Philadelphians lived in a walking city between 1790 and 1828, and so they tended to live within easy distance of their livelihoods, making class and ethnic segregation difficult. Yet class, race, and ethnicity all helped define the city's living arrangements. One could hear many different languages and accents on the streets. Germans were visible enough to warrant bilingual signposts in the late eighteenth century. Wealthier Philadelphians tended to live on the main thoroughfares, and the laboring or "lower" sort (including immigrant German and Irish and native-born free black men and women) lived behind them on narrow streets and alleyways. Because of their proximity to one another, Philadelphians interacted regularly with other classes, races, faiths, and ethnicities. When they celebrated public holidays such as the Fourth of July, they might come together, but for more personal socializing, Philadelphians tended toward more comfortable, ethnically defined gatherings.

In the summer of 1793, when ships arrived in the city's wharves they brought more than coffee and French refugees from Saint-Domingue. Yellow fever came to Philadelphia in August, and the crisis magnified the city's social tensions. News of the fever, diagnosed by doctors Benjamin Rush, Hugh Hodge, and John Foulke, soon created a panic. From late August to mid-September, about six hundred people died, and by the end of September, half the city had fled, business had come to a halt, and the government had evacuated. While wealthy, white, native-born inhabitants left the city promptly, Philadelphia's poorest remained, as did its free black population and a scattering of community-minded notables that included Mayor Mathew Clarkson and Dr. Rush.

The tension between the city's growing free black population and its white native-born and immigrant inhabitants was exacerbated by the epidemic. Led by Absalom Jones and Richard Allen, Philadelphia's free black community heroically tended to the sick and dying throughout the crisis. While successful printer Mathew Carey, an Irish immigrant, accused these men of taking advantage of the dying, Jones and Allen later printed a persuasive pamphlet in their defense. Just as the yellow fever began its rampage, Jones and Allen celebrated the beginning of work on the city's first black church, St. Thomas's African Church of Philadelphia. Between 1794 and 1796, Allen split from this church and formed his own

Mother Bethel Church, which in 1817 became the independent African Methodist Episcopal Church.

Between 1820 and 1830, Philadelphia boasted the largest, most economically successful, and most dynamic free black community in the United States. Slavery had all but disappeared between 1790 (three hundred slaves noted in the census) and 1820 (three slaves noted), and the city's free black population grew from ten thousand to fifteen thousand from 1820 to 1830. With this growth, however, came an increase in racial tension. While the 1790 state constitution had recognized the right of free black men to vote, by 1838 that right was gone. So slim was the promise of American life for Philadelphia blacks that in 1824 Richard Allen's son left with other emigrants to try their luck in the new Haitian republic.

Federal Philadelphia lost its primacy to New York City by the census of 1810, but it managed to retain its charm as it moved towards industrial growth. While the city remained a predominantly Anglo-American city, Philadelphia had been the favorite port of non-English immigrants in the eighteenth century because so many German and Scotch-Irish were attracted to the agriculturally rich hinterland. After 1825, however, when New York completed the Erie Canal and connected the seaboard to the interior more cheaply, Philadelphia lost its primary immigrant pull. In the 1820s the city took in roughly 12 percent of new immigrants to the United States, but those who came through Philadelphia suggested a kind of chain migration from Ireland in particular. Word of mouth and the McCorkell and Company shipping line from Londonderry, Ireland, brought a regular stream of Irish immigrants to Philadelphia well into the nineteenth century. While the economy of the walking city did not facilitate hardened racial and ethnic segregation, ethnic enclaves grew in the first decades of the nineteenth century: Germans and German Americans congregated in the northwest section of the city, while free blacks tended to the southeast where Mother Bethel grew. Between 1790 and 1828, Philadelphia remained a primarily Anglo-American city, but its struggles with ethnic and racial diversity foreshadowed the problems of nineteenth-century America.

See also *Philadelphia, PA 1776–1790; Philadelphia, PA 1828–1854; Philadelphia, PA 1854–1877; Philadelphia, PA 1877–1896; Philadelphia, PA 1896–1929; Philadelphia, PA 1929–1941; Philadelphia, PA 1941–1952; Philadelphia, PA 1952–1989; Philadelphia, PA 1989–2011*

A. KRISTEN FOSTER

BIBLIOGRAPHY

David, Allen F., and Mark H. Haller, eds. *The Peoples of Philadelphia: A History of Ethnic Groups and Lower-Class Life, 1790–1940.* Philadelphia: University of Pennsylvania Press, 1998.

Nash, Gary. *Forging Freedom: The Formation of Philadelphia's Black Community, 1720–1840.* Cambridge, MA: Harvard University Press, 1991.

Scharf, J. Thomas, and Thompson Westcott. *History of Philadelphia, 1609–1884.* Philadelphia, PA: L. H. Everts Co., 1884.

Schultz, Ronald. *The Republic of Labor: Philadelphia Artisans and the Politics of Class, 1720–1830.* New York: Oxford University Press, 1993.

Weigley, Russell F., ed. *Philadelphia: A Three Hundred Year History.* New York, NY: Norton, 1982.

Wolf, Edwin. *Philadelphia: Portrait of an American City.* Philadelphia, PA: Camino Books, 1990.

BALTIMORE, MD 1790–1828

IN 1790 BALTIMORE'S POPULATION OF 13,500 MADE IT THE FOURTH LARGEST CITY in the United States. Under Maryland law, however, it was still just a town, not an incorporated, self-governing municipality, but a dependency of the state legislature, which spent much of its time managing Baltimore's affairs. The town's legislative representatives exercised little influence in these deliberations; they were only two voices among more than sixty in the state's House of Delegates. The last years of the eighteenth century were marked by intense struggles over the political status of Baltimore Town, and the first quarter of the nineteenth century was a period of turbulent economic growth and recession.

GOVERNMENT AND POLITICS

Baltimoreans had high hopes for their town to become the capital of the United States under the newly ratified Constitution. The city's geographic location at mid-Republic seemed a decisive asset, but the honor went instead to a notional city on the Potomac—worse yet, a city that might compete with Baltimore for western trade. Baltimoreans blamed their state's congressional delegation for insufficient exertions on their behalf. Maryland had six congressional districts. Representatives had to reside in their districts, but Marylanders voted for all six in a statewide, at-large election. In 1790 angry Baltimoreans drew up their own slate of "Chesapeake" candidates in opposition to the "Potomac" ticket selected at a convention of county delegates. Baltimore's large population and suspicious 99 percent turnout, together with votes from nearby counties, sent all six of its candidates to Congress. The legislature convened at the end of the year and voted to substitute district balloting for the statewide election of congressmen. Baltimore City and Baltimore County would have only one congressional representative, and thus became once again a dependency of the tidewater tobacco aristocracy.

Baltimore began to turn Jeffersonian and Republican in the mid-1790s, while the state government remained Federalist until 1801. Unlike their counterparts in other cities, Baltimore's merchant elite did not succumb to Federalism's aristocratic appeals. Baltimore had merchants, but no merchant aristocracy. The town's Jeffersonian unity was conditional, however, and Baltimore Republicans turned against one another over the issue of municipal incorporation. The more substantial citizens—mostly merchants and professionals—sought to consolidate their control of the town. In 1793 they renewed an earlier drive for municipal home rule and won legislative approval, but the vote had to be confirmed at the following session of the assembly. The residents of Fell's Point rose in vigorous opposition, fearing that a strong city government would tax them to dredge old Baltimore Town's basin, negating the navigational advantages of moorings at the point where the water was twice as deep. The mechanics' and carpenters' societies sided with Fell's Point, and the artisans and shopkeepers of the Republican Society split with their merchant leaders and joined the opposition. The bill failed. The fight was not simply about social class—it was a battle of neighborhoods. The homes of the merchant elite were arrayed on the slopes just north of the basin. Most of their opponents lived in Fell's Point and the town's

QUICK FACTS

BALTIMORE, MD **1790–1828**

MAYORS

James Calhoun	(1797–1804)
Thorowgood Smith	(1804–1808)
Edward Johnson	(1808–1816)
George Stiles	(1816–1819)
Edward Johnson	(1819–1820)
John Montgomery	(1820–1822)
Edward Johnson	(1822–1824)
John Montgomery	(1824–1826)
Jacob Small	(1826–1831)

MAJOR INDUSTRIES AND EMPLOYERS

Shipping
Shipbuilding
Iron and copper smelting
Flour milling
Cotton textiles and sail cloth

MAJOR NEWSPAPERS

Maryland Journal and Baltimore Universal Daily Advertiser
Baltimore American and Daily Advertiser
The Baltimore Daily Repository
Federal Intelligencer and Baltimore Daily Gazette
The Telegraph and Daily Advertiser
Federal Republican and Commercial Advertiser
Baltimore Whig

MAJOR EVENTS

1797: Baltimore receives a municipal charter that makes the city a self-governing polity.
1802: The first independent black congregation, the Sharp Street Methodist Church, is founded.
1812: The *Federal Republican* riot gives Baltimore a national reputation for mob violence.
1814: Defense against the British troops at Fort McHenry and the Battle of North Point turn back the British invasion.
1827: The Baltimore and Ohio Railroad is chartered as the first railroad in the United States.

outlying districts, where residents worried that they might get the short end of city services, but not city taxes.

The mercantile elite made another, more devious attempt in 1795. A town meeting at the exchange, where merchants and traders congregated, produced a draft city charter. However, the version that later surfaced in Annapolis differed sharply from the one presented to the public in Baltimore. The Annapolis version specified high property qualifications for officeholders and made the mayor and the upper house of the city council indirectly elected. The stealth charter produced an immediate uproar in Baltimore, but the state assembly adopted it in 1796, perhaps precisely because it promised conservative government immune to radical tendencies among the town's lower orders. Two serious fires, a yellow fever epidemic, and a major flood also created support for an internal power necessary to preserve order, health, and safety.

Apprehensions about elitist government proved justified, at least at first. Merchants and men of property made up nine-tenths of the first, bicameral city council, and the first mayor,

James Calhoun, was one of the leading lights of the mercantile elite and a member of the Ancient and Honorable Mechanical Company. Calhoun's five successors, like him, would all be members of the private association that had served as Baltimore Town's informal government since 1763.

In spite of the potential for political tension between the city's elitist government and its less prominent inhabitants, Baltimore did not divide along class lines. The maintenance of cross-class political alliances was partly the work of Baltimore's congressman, wealthy merchant, and Revolutionary notable General Samuel Smith. Smith had fallen out with Federalists, who had threatened to unseat him in the congressional election of 1796. Although he did not abandon his rich friends, he reached out for support to the Baltimore Republican Society, the Carpenters' Society, and the Society of French Patriots. He also used his military background to create a base of support among Baltimore's militia companies.

In 1798 Smith fought the most difficult political campaign of his long career. The Federalists began their attack months before the election, raising one charge after another designed to portray Smith as unpatriotic, pro-French, and perhaps even Jacobin. The contest drew to a close, in the Baltimore manner, with mob violence. When a Federalist and a Republican parade crossed paths, Smith's supporters charged the Federalists and drove them from the streets. Some of his partisans broke into a private home to disrupt a Federalist meeting and beat up its participants. Smith himself led a mob attack on a Federalist rally—not the first time the congressman had been associated with violence. More than twenty years earlier he had been identified as the leader of a mob attack on the office of an unpopular editor. The *Federal Gazette* brushed off the violence: "Unfortunately, heated as the minds of the people were at the election, and as they ever will be in large cities where votes are taken *viva voce* and at but one poll, we can for the honor of Baltimore say but one house was assaulted, and that the contest terminated more peaceably than could reasonably have been expected." The next year the state legislature mandated the creation of eight polling places in Baltimore, one in each ward, and in 1801 voice voting was abandoned for paper ballots.

Smith won reelection in 1798, though not by an overwhelming margin. He took 59 percent of the vote in the city and 56 percent in the remainder of Baltimore County. In 1800 Baltimore went for Jefferson by more than 75 percent. The city's population had more than doubled since 1790 and now exceeded thirty thousand, and the state itself increased its representation in the U.S. House of Representatives from six to nine seats. The city of Baltimore and its county got two of these seats. Both went to Republicans, and the Republican capture of the House of Delegates in the legislature elevated Samuel Smith to the U.S. Senate. The House also abolished all property qualifications for voters in state and local elections and won the assent of the state senate's Federalist majority by threatening to call a constitutional convention to consider the direct popular election of the senators, who as it stood were chosen indirectly by electors. Four years later, in 1805, Baltimore's two representatives in the House of Delegates proposed that the city be granted an additional delegate in view of its large population. Every legislator except for the two Baltimoreans voted in the negative. The Republican affinities of the body's majority could not overcome the state's aversion toward its biggest city.

In 1807 the merchants of Baltimore presented the U.S. Navy with two sloops of war. One, the *Chesapeake,* on its maiden voyage and even before its guns were mounted, was attacked by a much larger British warship. The city's merchants called a town meeting, the resolutions of which informed President Thomas Jefferson that Baltimoreans would support whatever actions he decided to take in response to the outrage. Mercantile support for Jefferson's embargo of 1807 came at a time when it would add little to the burdens borne by commerce. French privateers and British warships were already devastating the city's merchant fleet. Senator Smith's own firm suffered serious losses. He argued that total cessation of American commerce would starve French and British Caribbean colonies and force both nations to treat American shipping more respectfully.

As the city's economy declined, support for the embargo faded, but animosity toward the British thrived. At the end of 1808, an English journeyman shoemaker expressed views partial to his homeland. A mob that included many of his fellow journeymen tarred and feathered him and carried him in a cart from the center of the city to the tip of Fell's Point and back again. Several members of the mob were apprehended and sentenced to fines and imprisonment. All were pardoned. In 1812, one month before Congress declared war on Britain, exasperated Baltimoreans were ready to fight and not especially particular about whom the adversary might be. Delegates elected in a town meeting sent a resolution to President James Madison urging that the country go to war with Britain or France or both, with a slight preference for Britain. As soon as war was declared, local merchants lined up for the letters of marque that would authorize them to arm their ships and operate as privateers. Within six months, forty-two privateers had sailed from Baltimore. Eventually, about one-fifth of the city's population had investments or livelihoods in legal piracy.

Baltimore's most immediate act of war, however, was yet another riot—the most deadly in the city's history and a shocking abandonment of traditional restraints on mob behavior. The spark was an editorial attack on President Madison and the American declaration of war against Britain published by Alexander C. Hanson, editor of the Baltimore *Federal Republican*. Hanson fled after a crowd attacked his office, but he continued to publish his paper from Georgetown, stoking the fury of the mob, which reassembled almost every night for more than a month to attack targets that sparked its members' racial, class, ethnic, and religious animosities. The mob actions prompted protest meetings far from Baltimore, and in the state elections three months later, reaction to the riot helped the Federalists to take a majority of the House of Delegates, the governorship, and one seat in the U.S. Senate. Alexander Hanson himself was elected to the House of Representatives. The riot, wrote J. Thomas Scharf in his 1874 *Chronicles of Baltimore*, "left a stigma on the city, which bore for a long time the name of 'mobtown.'"

Baltimore may have reduced the stain left by the riot with its performance in resisting a British invasion two years later. The English troops arrived fresh from their rout of the American militia at Bladensburg, Maryland, and their unopposed entry into Washington, D.C., where they burned the Capitol, the White House, and a number of public buildings. Baltimore, with its warehouses and merchant ships, represented an even richer prize, and in addition the city's privateers had captured or sunk about five hundred British ships since the war's start. Waiting for the British in Baltimore was the commander of more than sixteen thousand sailors, marines, militiamen, and regulars, Senator and Major General Samuel Smith. The city's resistance against land assaults and bombarding warships provided Francis Scott Key with the occasion to write the lyrics for the song that would become the national anthem.

Baltimore had incurred heavy costs in preparing its defenses for the British attack and petitioned the state assembly to cover the expense. The legislature refused, but the city eventually recovered its expenditures from the federal government. In 1816 the legislature compelled the city to absorb outlying districts—the "precincts"—with a population of more than sixteen thousand. Neither the residents of the city nor the population to be annexed desired the consolidation, and though Baltimore's population increased substantially as a result of the action, it continued to send only two representatives to the House of Delegates. The city held about one-fifth of the state's population, but only one-fortieth of the seats in the lower house. As compensation, perhaps, the Federalist legislature enlarged Baltimore's municipal authority in 1818 to remove restrictions on the city's taxation powers, to increase its debt limit, and to grant it the power of eminent domain for public improvements. This enhancement of the city's political status was followed by the panic of 1819, which was a severe setback for Baltimore's economy.

Samuel Smith came close to financial ruin as a result of the 1819 panic, but he retained his political status. The Federalist-turned-Republican emerged as a key leader of the Jacksonian faction in Baltimore politics. The panic was a political setback for Smith and his merchant allies. A rival faction led by former congressman and Maryland attorney general John Montgomery mobilized Irish Catholic and ethnic German voters who propelled him into the mayor's office in 1820. For six years, Montgomery and Smith's man, Edward Johnson, took turns serving as mayor. In 1826 housing contractor Jacob Small challenged Smith's leadership by mobilizing middle-class property owners. He also drew Irish and German voters away from Montgomery and successfully turned them against Smith's Quaker, Presbyterian, and Scotch-Irish supporters. Smith fought his way back by recasting his coalition as the political champion of Baltimore's "workingmen" and by linking issues of local politics to the Jacksonian creed that was unfolding in national politics. Smith, according to Gary Browne in his 1980 *Baltimore in the Nation, 1789–1861*, introduced "the Jacksonian-party machine into local elections." His control of federal patronage provided it with essential political resources. As a latecomer to the Jacksonian fold, Smith may not have seemed politically deserving, but as chair of the Senate Finance Committee, he was a valuable ally for an administration concerned about the tariff and the fate of the Second Bank of the United States. As merchant, congressman, senator, and rioter, Smith had been the embodiment of his city. His last public office was a fitting culmination of his Baltimore-based career. He became mayor in 1835 at the age of eighty-three.

INDUSTRY, COMMERCE, AND LABOR

The Jeffersonian embargo contributed to a new enthusiasm for manufacturing in Baltimore as a means of compensating for the decline of commerce. Enthusiasm, however, was not actuality. While a few factories appeared in and around Baltimore, the embargo stimulated only early steps toward an industrial future. Instead, it may have stimulated the spirit of invention, as Baltimore moved to the cutting edge of early nineteenth-century technology. In 1813 the first steam-powered flour mill was built at the end of a wharf where it could receive raw wheat and transfer ground flour to the hold of a ship. In the same year Baltimore launched its first steamboat service between the city and Philadelphia, Pennsylvania. The first steam-powered textile mill opened in 1814, and in 1817 the city became the first to light its streets and houses with gas.

The burst of innovation coincided with a decline of the local economy. With the close of the Napoleonic Wars, Britain and France reimposed mercantilist restrictions on trade with their colonies in the Western Hemisphere. Manufactured goods from England and Germany flooded the city, driving down prices for locally manufactured products. Trade in western agricultural produce suffered from falling prices and the devaluation of currency by western banks. Baltimore plunged into the panic of 1819.

The panic was nationwide, but the shady practices of Baltimore merchants added a local component to the distress. Some of the city's traders, for example, had invested illegally in privateers supposedly sponsored by Latin American revolutionaries. In fact, the ships sailed from Baltimore. Congress cracked down on the maritime desperadoes in 1817, and civil suits filed by Spanish and Portuguese ship owners stripped Baltimore investors of the gains they had won as financiers of piracy. The collapse of their enterprises fed the larger panic.

Bank shenanigans added to Baltimore's troubles. Several mercantile firms took effective control of the local branch of the Bank of the United States and used its assets to finance their speculative ventures. Congressional investigations and the dismissal of the president of the Bank of the United States helped to bring the Baltimore irregularities to light. The new president of the bank insisted that the Baltimore branch settle up its accounts in *specie*, forcing the bank to call in its loans to other banks. One after another, they collapsed, and the Baltimore branch itself went down in May 1819. In June the national panic arrived and merged with its local counterpart.

A new era of prosperity began for Baltimore with the 1827 chartering of the Baltimore and Ohio Railroad, which was jointly financed by private investors and city government. It made the city the starting point on the nation's rail network. The railroad also made the city a center for the distribution and consumption of coal and the manufacture of steam locomotives and steel rails.

RACE, ETHNICITY, AND IMMIGRATION

By 1828 Baltimore's population was nearing one hundred thousand. Foreign immigration was limited. In 1815 editor Hezekiah Niles reported that eight hundred immigrants were settling in Baltimore each month. Many of these came from other parts of the United States or the Western Hemisphere. Though predominantly from Britain, they were not English, but mostly Irish, Scots, and Scotch-Irish. They were also not English Anglicans, but dissenting Methodists, Presbyterians, Quakers, and Roman Catholics. About fifteen hundred refugees produced by the revolution in Haiti augmented the city's existing Francophone population, the Acadians who had stopped at Baltimore instead of proceeding to Louisiana. Small numbers of Germans, who would eventually become the city's largest ethnic group, also arrived during the first quarter of the nineteenth century. The town's ethnic composition may help to account for its endemic Anglophobia. Pro-French sentiment ran so strong in the town that one of the local militia companies called itself the Baltimore Sans Culottes.

Newcomers were seldom slaveholders. Perhaps for that reason, the number of slaves decreased by about 20 percent during the decade of the 1820s. The number of free blacks, however, increased sharply. In 1790 they accounted for only 1.3 percent of all households in Baltimore, but by 1830 they amounted to more than 15 percent. Free blacks achieved a critical mass in Baltimore so early that they began to create their own independent community with its own institutions long before African American populations elsewhere were able to do so. The first all-black congregation formed in 1802 with the founding of the Sharp Street Methodist Church.

In that same year, the church took over a private school founded by Quakers for the education of African Americans. In 1815 a portion of the Sharp Street congregation seceded to form Bethel Methodist Church, which was completely independent of any white denomination. Its pastor, Daniel Coker, was one of the founders of the African Methodist Episcopal denomination.

See also *Baltimore, MD 1776–1790; Baltimore, MD 1828–1854; Baltimore, MD 1854–1877; Baltimore, MD 1877–1896; Baltimore, MD 1896–1929; Baltimore, MD 1929–1941; Baltimore, MD 1941–1952; Baltimore, MD 1952–1989*

MATTHEW CRENSON

BIBLIOGRAPHY

Browne, Gary Lawrence. *Baltimore in the Nation, 1789–1861.* Chapel Hill: University of North Carolina Press, 1980.

Cassell, Frank A. *Merchant Congressman in the Young Republic: Samuel Smith of Maryland, 1752–1839.* Madison: University of Wisconsin Press, 1971.

Clark, Dennis Rankin. "Baltimore 1729–1829: The Genesis of a Community." PhD diss., The Catholic University of America, 1974.

Renzulli, L. Marx. *Maryland, the Federalist Years.* Rutherford, NJ: Fairleigh Dickinson University Press, 1972.

Scharf, J. Thomas. *Chronicles of Baltimore; Being a Complete History of 'Baltimore Town' and Baltimore City from the Earliest Period to the Present Time.* Baltimore, MD: Turnbull Brothers, 1874.

Steffen, Charles G. *The Mechanics of Baltimore: Workers and Politics in an Age of Revolution, 1763–1812.* Urbana: University of Illinois Press, 1984.

BOSTON, MA 1790–1828

BY 1828 BOSTON WAS NO LONGER THE RELATIVELY TYPICAL PROVINCIAL eighteenth-century maritime town it had been, but it was not yet the bustling cosmopolitan nineteenth-century city that it would become. Three major transformations—one each in the area of politics, industry, and demography—occurred within this time period to alter the distribution of political power along Boston's traditional class lines and diversify its economy. These changes proved crucial in Boston's ability to successfully integrate the large-scale population growth of the mid-nineteenth century. No event was more indicative of Boston's transition than the jettisoning of its traditional town meeting political structure in favor of a city charter.

GOVERNMENT AND POLITICS

Boston's town meeting governance structure administered the town from its Puritan founding in 1630 until 1822. Town meetings were informal events where all male church members of a certain age took part in governing the settlement's affairs. Officials were elected annually to municipal boards that regulated certain economic and public health needs, generally serving on

BOSTON, MA **1790–1828**

MAYORS

Boston had no mayors from 1790–1822 and was governed by town meetings

John Phillips   (1822–1823)
Josiah Quincy   (1823–1828)

MAJOR INDUSTRIES AND EMPLOYERS

Maritime-related trade
Clothing manufacturing
Book printing
Suspender and neck sock
  manufacturing
Marble, stone, and granite
  manufacturing

MAJOR NEWSPAPERS

Daily Advertiser
Independent Chronicle
Columbian Centinel
New-England Palladium
New-England Galaxy
Boston Patriot
Boston Gazette
Boston Commercial Gazette
*Bostonian and Mechanics
  Journal*
American Apollo
Argus
Constitutional Telegraph
Boston Courier
Repertory
Boston Recorder
Boston Spectator
Castigator
Weekly Messenger
Boston Weekly Report
Yankee

MAJOR EVENTS

1776–1810: Boston's population swells from six thousand to well over thirty thousand.

1800: Thomas Jefferson's election marks the decline of Federalist Boston's influence in national politics. With the exception of John Quincy Adams, not one Massachusetts resident would have a significant influence in national politics until the ascendancy of Daniel Webster.

1807–1815: Jefferson's 1807 embargo and the War of 1812 profoundly cripple both Boston and the state's eastern maritime-based economy. As a direct result of the British barricade, Francis Cabot Lowell and a handful of investors known as the "Boston Associates" open a cotton textile mill in Waltham in 1813 that serves as the model for future New England industrialization.

1822: Boston abandons its town charter and is incorporated into a city—Massachusetts' first. John Phillips becomes Boston's first mayor.

1823–1828: Boston's "Great Mayor," Josiah Quincy, is consecutively elected for six terms, during which he builds Quincy Market, professionalizes the fire and police departments, erects the House of Industry to house displaced debtors, and reforms the sanitation department.

a volunteer basis. Community affairs were decided by a voice vote of all freemen. The electorate was expanded over the years when the church membership requirement was replaced by one dictated by property, but little else about the town meeting structure had changed through Independence.

Aristocratic dominance of the town meeting began in 1720 when the Caucus, a semisecret group of young merchants and doctors, gained election through canvassing and the spoils system. The Caucus oftentimes supported the public will, particularly when serving as a foil for the royal government, but it also acted to prevent any change in the town meeting system—such as election of officials by ward—that might challenge its hold on power.

The politics of the Federalist period presented little change in the class of men who held power. Well-heeled patriots from adjacent Essex County, located about thirty miles to the north of Boston, had rushed to fill the power vacuum left with the forced departure of the British military and its Loyalists in 1776. Revolution to these aristocrats—the "Boston Brahmins," those wealthy families whose lineage stretched to the initial Puritan landing—meant the driving out of the British; they were content with the existing hierarchy of wealth and class and with their position atop it. They easily transferred their wealth and social class into political power at the local, state, and federal levels. Neither class nor personal enrichment was the driving force for Brahmin control of government; rather, they touted their civic mindedness, born of Puritan morality, in governing for the benefit of the lesser classes.

These aristocrats' great success in seizing and retaining political power under the auspices of the Federalist Party made Boston a one-party town. The public's relation to these power elites was one of deference marked by little political participation. In 1822 Boston's seven thousand vote-eligible citizens participated at rates as high as 70 percent for some highly contested national elections, but as few as one hundred citizens might vote on town matters, and those who did vote were not assured a voice as vote outcomes were often ignored by the ruling elite.

The aristocracy ruled Boston with the cooperation of the lesser merchants and the consent of the middle class. This changed in 1822 when an interparty, populist-backed revolt by upper-class, but not aristocratic, Federalists splintered this compact and ended Boston's one-party rule. The initial uprising centered on the matter of incorporating the Town of Boston as a city, a move that the Federalist oligarchy supported but, in rare setbacks, they had been unable to prevail over popular will in referenda in 1784, 1792, 1804, and 1815. In 1822, however, the evidence was increasingly clear that the town's growth could no longer be properly administered by volunteers. Boston had grown beyond its small community origins, as was evident in citizens' unwillingness to organize into bucket brigades to put out fires or to aid peace officers in making arrests.

The motion to incorporate Boston saw extensive debate in a fully packed Faneuil Hall. After three days, the charter making Boston the first community incorporated as a city in Massachusetts passed, as did seemingly lesser amendments to repeal a height restriction on wooden buildings and to elect state legislators by ward. The Federalist leadership was opposed to these latter measures and dismissed them. This deafness to the public's appeals came amidst a profound economic depression whose brunt was borne unequally by the middle and lower classes, and it ignited a revolt. A group of middle- and upper-class Federalists who supported both dismissed measures splintered off to create the Middling Interest, a political party that, according to its slogan, stood for the common good against the interest of "any one man, family, or class of men." An opposing faction had confronted Boston's aristocratic hegemony.

The new party set its sights on Boston's inaugural contest for mayor. The Federalists chose aristocrat and perennial Federalist candidate Harrison Gray Otis. The Middling Interest countered by selecting Josiah Quincy, an upper-class, but not aristocratic, Federalist and an expert on the city's social problems. The election returns were split amidst high turnout, with Boston's heretofore moribund second party, the Republicans, splitting their small vote share, which resulted in neither candidate winning a majority. The parties came to an agreement on John Phillips, a popular nonpartisan. The next year, with Phillips refusing to run for reelection, the Federalists picked Quincy as their candidate, a sign that the elites realized that middle-class popular opinion now factored in city politics.

This class revolt destroyed Boston's Federalist Party, politically awakened its middle class, and created a power vacuum into which Quincy quickly stepped. Quincy's later renown as Boston's "Great Mayor" was well-earned and founded upon two main feats that would later prove essential for Boston's growth into a modern city. First, Quincy consolidated power in his office over six consecutive one-year terms by either abolishing outright or by placing himself at the head of the old municipal boards that had retained power after the city's chartering. This centralization of power was accompanied by a thorough modernization and professionalization of the city's municipal services that had far-reaching effects on Boston's political culture, changing it from one

Josiah Quincy (1772–1864), a Federalist, served as Boston's mayor for six terms in the 1820s. During his tenure as the "Great Mayor," Quincy consolidated power in the mayoral office and modernized the city's municipal services.   *Source: Library of Congress*

dependent upon unaccountable civic voluntarism (such as bucket brigades) to one based upon expertise (professional firefighters) responsible to the mayoralty. This shift moved Boston from a system of direct democracy to one of representative governance wherein the city's officials were accountable to the people.

Second, whereas in the past private capital would take on the initiative—and the profits—of public works projects, Quincy's backing of several massive infrastructure projects, most ambitious of which was the addition of a new building to Faneuil Hall Market (later renamed Quincy Market), seized for municipal government the commission of municipal investment. Quincy's projection of the value of the expansion forward through increased tax revenue created the precursor for the tax-increment financing mechanism still in use by municipalities today.

The lower and middle classes that had risen up to defeat the aristocratic Federalists in 1822 formed Quincy's electoral base, and he worked hard to expand it. His reduction of the minimum election qualifications from those males who owned property to those who had paid any sort of city tax enlarged the electorate from seven thousand at the beginning of his first term to twelve thousand by 1827, but it was these new voters who were responsible for replacing him in the

1828 election with Otis, a figure much more malleable to public will. These tumultuous seven years proved the downfall of one-party rule in Boston and the ascension of a degree of popular participation in the city's democracy.

Boston entered the years 1790–1828 firmly in the grasp of a one-party, aristocratic rule whose power was wielded, ironically, through a system of direct democracy. The political system that emerged granted Boston's ordinary citizens a greater degree of choice in their leadership, while providing the administrative structure necessary to provide municipal services for a flourishing urban center. The tremendous upheaval in Boston's political strata, underwent from 1790 to 1828, set the stage for increased populist activism and participation in the upcoming decades, but these changes should not be overstated. In reality, the revolt garnered from the upper class only nominal acknowledgement that they could not fully disregard the opinions of the middle and lower classes. This lesson learned, Boston's Brahmins would remain in power for the next three decades.

INDUSTRY, COMMERCE, AND LABOR

Boston's industry in 1790 reflected the town's isolated riparian geography and existed wholly to meet local needs. By 1829 Boston had become a domestic commercial power by creating America's first great industry, textile manufacturing. Even as the factories moved outside the city to take advantage of the country's vast hydropower resources, money continued to flow into Boston, transforming its streets, buildings, and culture and providing the tax dollars needed for the expansion of municipal government that would later provide services and jobs for the large influx of Irish immigrants at midcentury.

Until the late eighteenth century, Boston's population grew slowly. Trade with Europe, and particularly with Great Britain, provided manufactured goods in exchange for raw materials. Boston's role in this transatlantic trade was as shipbuilder and port, maritime trades passed down from generation to generation that created little demand for additional labor. As a result, Boston's hierarchical class structure was, in contrast to the usual pyramid, diamond shaped: the largest group was the merchant middle class, flanked by smaller numbers of aristocrats above and the lower class below.

The merchant and aristocratic classes were fully invested in the transatlantic trade, and the Federalist Party nationally and locally focused on repairing ties with Great Britain following Independence. They succeeded, and transatlantic trade once again flourished, but this was soon undone by increased bellicosity with England at the national level. Great Britain's restrictions on trade with France, support of Native Americans in the Pacific Northwest, and drafting of U.S. citizens into the Royal Navy led Democratic president James Madison to convince Congress to declare war in 1812. This move proved disastrous to the nation's and Boston's maritime industry. Boston's port was barricaded by the British Navy, and the city lost its only viable industry. Americans, cut off from needed manufactured goods, became desperate for finished items at any price.

Here the aristocratic class split along generational lines, with older patriarchs sticking true to, and often failing alongside, maritime industry, while their scions diversified their holdings into manufacturing to provide America with much-needed commodities. Seen as a temporary wartime measure at the time, ramshackle cotton textile factories backed by Boston financing sprung up around New England. Introduction of European industrial methods, particularly the power loom by Francis Cabot Lowell in 1810, produced greater efficiency in production and, subsequently, more profit. By the 1820s, the great factories had moved outside of Boston to take advantage of the abundant hydropower necessary for further gains in efficiency, but the Boston textile magnates of this period, the "Boston Associates," controlled America's first great multi-million dollar industry. In the 1830s and 1840s, they gained control of New England's railroads as a means to deliver finished textiles throughout the region and to Boston's port. This great wealth was funneled into improving Boston and its arts and culture, as well as into domination of state and local politics.

The rise of textile manufacturing did not signal the death knell of shipping; rather, shipping greatly complemented Boston's new industry by creating an avenue by which finished products could travel to markets. Further, diversification of assets into both sectors helped to stabilize the city economy. Boston entered this period a small maritime town fully dependent upon trade and seafaring industries, but it entered the 1830s as the home of the nation's first great industry.

RACE, ETHNICITY, AND IMMIGRATION

The homogeneity of its industry in 1790 was largely mirrored in, and partly responsible for, Boston's racial and ethnic homogeneity. Boston in 1790 was almost wholly white and middle class, a mix of Nordic and English Puritan nicknamed "Yankee." By 1830 predominantly Irish immigration had positioned the lower class to numerically overtake the middle class.

Considering the enormous role that the Irish have played in the history of Boston, it may come as a surprise that until 1815 Boston had few Irish residents. Those who came before this time arrived in the early to mid-eighteenth century and were predominantly Protestants from Northern Ireland whose support of the Revolution gained them recognition as loyal patriots. This immigration stream petered out in the early nineteenth century as the immigrants themselves started to obtain political power and economic influence in Massachusetts, most notably with the election of James Sullivan as governor in 1807. Around this time the Protestants were joined by a second but distinct Irish immigrant stream, Catholics from southern Ireland. This new wave, a result of England's onerous agricultural policies, was poorer than the first, and more numerous. Boston had a population of forty-four thousand by 1822, some two thousand of whom were poor Irish Catholics. That latter number grew to over five thousand by 1825 and comprised eight thousand of sixty-one thousand Bostonians by 1830.

The large influx of poor Catholic immigrants taxed city social services and created tensions with the Protestant majority. The mid-to-late 1820s saw a rise of violence toward Irish property and persons, culminating in almost nightly riots that shook Irish neighborhoods in the summer of 1825. This early anti-Catholic sentiment was a harbinger of things to come, blossoming into large-scale violence in the 1830s and the full-on political movement of the Know-Nothing Party following the resulting explosion in Irish immigration wrought by the Great Potato Famine of 1847.

Boston's black population also saw great growth during this period, virtually doubling in number, but this increase was largely missed amid the city's rapid growth. Though many of Boston's seafaring merchants made their fortunes in the eighteenth- and nineteenth-century slave trade, few Bostonians held slaves. A census taken in 1776 found that about thirteen hundred of the two thousand or so slaves in Massachusetts were held in Boston and its environs. Enumerations of the full black population of Boston at this time are little more than rough estimates, as blacks were not counted as persons until Massachusetts abolished slavery in 1783, partially in response to the offer of freedom to slaves who fought for the state militia in the Revolution. A 1784 census lists 4,377 blacks in Massachusetts, about 2 percent of the commonwealth's population, but numeric estimates of blacks in Boston at this time are absent.

Black Bostonians had few prospects for economic success following emancipation. Blacks found themselves competing with lower-class whites for jobs, and doing so without formal education, training, or monetary funds. They also had to face rampant discrimination. Many became vagabonds, resulting in a 1788 state law requiring all blacks who were not citizens of any state to leave Massachusetts. Those who stayed formed organizations aimed at improving their status. The African Society, formed in 1796 as a closed organization existing for the mutual benefit and charity of its members, listed forty-two members by 1809. In 1798 black Bostonians established the first school for black children; this segregation, which lasted until 1855, was institutionalized in 1812 when the city gained control of the school and gave $200 annually for its operation. Boston's first black church, the African Baptist Church, started holding services within the African Meeting House in 1806. Black social life of this period revolved around these institutions, but their economic lives focused on just one industry: textiles. Facing increasing competition from low-skilled Irish immigrants in the 1820s, black Bostonians moved their community away from its traditional center in the North End and closer to available low-skilled textile jobs in the West End.

Boston would later become the center of the abolitionist movement, but not until 1831, when newspaper publisher William Lloyd Garrison's *The Liberator* exchanged the placid, gentile tone that had previously marked discussion of abolition for rhetoric that was more brazenly accusatory. The movement did begin to attract a trickle of free blacks to Boston, but the greater heterogeneity of industry and importance as stops on the Underground Railroad of Philadelphia, Pennsylvania, and New York City caused those cities to draw far larger shares. The black population in Boston had only grown from about one thousand in 1755 to 1,833 in the mid-1830s.

Boston saw three major transformations from 1790 to 1828, all of which prepared it for the massive onslaught of Irish immigration at midcentury that would forever change the nature of the city. Modernization of city government enabled efficient provision of municipal services at grander scales and created a space for middle- and lower-class involvement in the city's governance; diversification of the city's industry into textile production provided both the wealth needed to transform the city and employment for the city's expanding lower class; and immigration-driven population growth created a deep workforce for the city's construction and municipal employment, trades for which the Irish would later become renowned.

See also *Boston, MA 1776–1790; Boston, MA 1828–1854; Boston, MA 1854–1877; Boston, MA 1877–1896; Boston, MA 1896–1929; Boston, MA 1929–1941; Boston, MA 1941–1952*

STEPHEN YODER

BIBLIOGRAPHY

Crocker, Matthew H. *The Magic of the Many: Josiah Quincy and the Rise of Mass Politics in Boston, 1800–1830.* Amherst: University of Massachusetts Press, 1999.

Cromwell, Adelaide M. *The Other Brahmins: Boston's Black Upper Class, 1750–1950.* Fayetteville: University of Arkansas Press, 1994.

Formisano, Ronald P. "From Deferential-Participant to Party Politics, 1800–1840." In *Boston, 1700–1980: The Evolution of Urban Politics,* edited by Ronald P. Formisano and Constance K. Burns, 34–35. Westport, CT: Greenwood Press, 1984.

Holli, Melvin G. *The American Mayor: The Best & the Worst Big-City Leaders.* University Park: Pennsylvania State University Press, 1999.

Jaher, Frederic Cople. "The Politics of Boston's Brahmins: 1800–1860." In *Boston, 1700–1980: The Evolution of Urban Politics,* edited by Ronald P. Formisano and Constance K. Burns. Westport, CT: Greenwood Press, 1984.

Kirker, Harold, and James Kirker. *Bulfinch's Boston, 1787–1817.* New York, NY: Oxford University Press, 1964.

Lane, Roger. *Policing the City: Boston, 1822–1885.* New York, NY: Atheneum, 1977.

O'Connor, Thomas H. *The Athens of America: Boston, 1825–1845.* Amherst: University of Massachusetts Press, 2006.

Warden, G. B. "Town Meeting Politics in Colonial and Revolutionary Boston." In *Boston, 1700–1980: The Evolution of Urban Politics,* edited by Ronald P. Formisano and Constance K. Burns. Westport, CT: Greenwood Press, 1984.

Whitehall, Walter Muir, and Lawrence W. Kennedy. *Boston: A Topographical History.* 3d ed. Cambridge, MA: Belknap Press, 2000.

NEW ORLEANS, LA 1790–1828

THE YEARS 1790–1828 WERE AMONG THE MOST EVENTFUL IN NEW ORLEANS'S HISTORY, in part because the city was under the control of three nations in these four decades. Named after Philippe, Duc d'Orléans, the regent of France, la Nouvelle-Orléans became the capital of the French colony of la Louisiane from its founding by Jean Baptiste Le Moyne de Bienville in 1718. When, at the end of the Seven Years' War in 1762, la Louisiane became Luisiana through its cession to Spain by the 1762 Treaty of Paris, la Nouvelle-Orléans became Nueva Orleans. Nonetheless, the city remained dominated by the Gallic population throughout its almost forty years of Spanish rule. Louisiana was secretly retroceded to France in 1800 through the Treaty of San Ildefonso before being sold by Napoleon to the United States in 1803. The city then became New Orleans after only twenty-one days of official French rule.

During the first three decades of the nineteenth century, Americans who were migrating in great numbers to the city and attempting to Americanize it were met with staunch resistance by the Creole population, assisted by the massive influx of the Saint-Domingue refugees fleeing the

MAYORS

New Orleans had no mayors during 1790–1803 until the Louisiana Purchase was made.

Etienne de Boré	(1803)
James Pitot	(1804)
John Watkins	(1805–1807)
James Mather	(1807–1812)
Charles Trudeau	(acting mayor; 1812)
Le Breton Dorgenois	(acting mayor; 1812)
Nicholas Girod	(1812–1815)
Augustin de MacCarty	(1815–1820)
Louis Philippe Joseph de Rouffignac	(1820–1828)

MAJOR INDUSTRIES AND EMPLOYERS

Trade in agricultural products (cotton, tobacco, sugar)
Sugar refining
Rum distilling
Rope and brick manufacturing

MAJOR NEWSPAPERS

L'Abeille
L'Ami des Lois (name slightly changed in 1815, 1819, and 1822)
L'Argus (from 1827 known as The Argus)
Le Courrier de la Louisiane
The Louisiana Advertiser
The Louisiana Gazette
Le Moniteur de la Louisiane
The Orleans Gazette and Commercial Advertiser

MAJOR EVENTS

1800: The secret retrocession of Louisiana by Spain to France through the Treaty of San Ildefonso occurs. The Cabildo, the Spanish unit of municipal organization, remains the main municipal government until the fall of 1803.

1803: The United States purchases the territory from France. New Orleans becomes a city of the young American Republic.

1805: The act incorporating the City of New Orleans is passed by the territorial government of Louisiana.

1812: Louisiana is admitted as a state by an act of Congress to take effect on April 30. New Orleans becomes the first capital of the new state, a position it still occupied in 1828, although attempts were already in progress to get the capital transferred to Baton Rouge.

1815: The Battle of New Orleans occurs in Chalmette in January and is marked by a dazzling victory against the English. Word of the signing of the Treaty of Ghent, which ended the War of 1812 on December 24, 1814, had not yet reached New Orleans.

revolution in Haiti. These were also decades of extraordinary development for the city, which grew from a population of eight thousand inhabitants in 1803 to one of 17,242 in 1810, a number that ranked it seventh in size among American cities. In 1820 and 1830, it was the fifth largest American city, with a population of 27,176 (+57.6 percent) and 46,082 (+69.6 percent), respectively. By 1810 New Orleans was already by far the largest city south of Baltimore, Maryland. By 1820—despite the epidemic of yellow fever that reportedly took the lives of approximately six thousand people in 1817–1818—the population had more than doubled.

GOVERNMENT AND POLITICS

Between 1790 and 1828, Louisiana changed hands twice, which had important repercussions on the city's administration and political life. The Spanish mode of government had been a mixture of centralized power and self-government. According to a system of administration implemented from the Middle Ages and codified through the 1680 Recopilación de Las Leyes de las Indias, Louisiana was administered by the viceroy of New Spain. It was one of the eight captaincies-general of the Spanish Americas. The captain-general was assisted by a privy council called the Audiencia and, after 1782, by an intendant. Colonial authorities were directly responsible to the Crown through the Superior Court of the Indies at Sevilla. The colony also had military or civil governors, six of them for the post–1790 colonial period.

New Orleans was administered by a municipal council based on the Roman system, the Cabildo, which held all the city's administration agencies. It managed public welfare; had police and taxation powers; and dealt with public works, building regulations, land distribution, price and market regulation, and everything pertaining to health and justice (civil and criminal). There was no equivalent to a mayor, although every year the council elected two *alcaldes ordinaries* to lead the debates, as well as an equivalent to an attorney general (*sindico procurador general*) and a city treasurer (*mayordomo de propios*).

When the French regained possession of Louisiana, and thus of New Orleans, they did so secretly. The Cabildo thus pursued its maintenance of municipal affairs until 1803. France did not send Pierre Clément de Laussat as colonial prefect until March 1803, and the latter did not reclaim possession of Louisiana until the fall, when news of the purchase was already reaching New Orleans and provoking turmoil in the city. The retrocession ceremony took place in New Orleans on November 30 and inaugurated the shortest colonial period in the history of New Orleans. On the same day, Etienne de Boré was appointed the first mayor of New Orleans. During the twenty-one days of French rule that followed, the French authorities abolished the Cabildo and instituted a municipality according to the French republican model.

On December 20, 1803, the formal transfer of Louisiana to the United States took place in New Orleans. After a brief territorial period, Louisiana gained statehood in 1812. New Orleans uninterruptedly remained the seat of the state government, which was patterned after other state governments in the country, at least until the late 1820s. A council ruled the city under the supervision of a mayor. In 1805 the city was incorporated and divided into seven wards, to which a new ward was added in 1812, the year of statehood when the ward boundaries were redefined. The city divided into three municipalities, each subdivided into wards. City council members were elected by ward.

The next two decades were marked by a constant struggle for power between the old French-speaking Creole population—assisted by the refugees of Saint-Domingue and immigrants from France—and the new American leaders, as attested by the succession of Gallic and Anglo names in the list of mayors. It was the only city in the South, or even in the United States, where political life was marked by a linguistic and cultural divide. Tensions increased under the term of Governor Villeré (1816–1820), especially since a de facto residential segregation embittered relationships between Creoles, who were mainly living in the Old Quarter, and Anglo-Americans, who lived mainly to its west, when the distribution of public funding for urban improvement was concerned.

New Orleans functioned under a unique legal and judicial system—partly originating in its colonial past—that distinguished it from other cities. Spanish laws concerning slavery, for instance, were maintained after the failed attempt by the French to reinstate the *Code noir* during the brief 1803 French rule. Some persisted even after the issuing of the new legal codes of 1806 and 1808. Louisiana was also the only state to be governed by a civil law code inspired by the Roman-based Napoleonic Code (1808), while the rest of the country was committed to English common law. The 1825 penal code of Louisiana was also influenced by colonial traditions and laws—such as the inheritance laws giving stronger economic power to women—and remained unaffected by the transition from colonial to American rule. Some institutions, however, were altered by the end of colonial rule. To give a single instance, the American institution of the separation between church and state made marriage a civil contract, which legalized divorce.

The first twenty-five years of American rule were also a period of intense modernization of the city and development of new services. It was the early period of urban expansion out of the Vieux Carré, or Old Quarter, mostly through the impulse of the Saint-Domingue refugees who settled in the east (Faubourg Marigny) and of the American migrants in the west (Faubourg Sainte-Marie). As soon as New Orleans became a municipality under United States rule, the municipal services developed at a very rapid pace, confirming government (state and city) as the main employer in the city. The New Orleans city police force and New Orleans fire department were created in 1806 and 1807, respectively. City markets were built; the meat market, for instance, was erected in 1813. In 1825 the Internal Improvement Board was founded to oversee construction of roads, bridges, levees, and canals. The streets were paved, *banquettes* (New Orleans's very distinctive sidewalks) were built, and a water pumping system was installed by Benjamin Latrobe in 1819. A sanitation reform program was also implemented during this time. New Orleans also had an organized militia, inherited from the colonial period and including troops of free people of color, which insured the safety of the city in times of peace and war. This militia played an important part in the Battle of New Orleans in January 1815.

INDUSTRY, COMMERCE, AND LABOR

New Orleans was essentially a slave society based on plantation agriculture. Although it had remained relatively undeveloped during French rule, due to a chronic shortage of manpower that the French had not attempted to solve, Louisiana became a far more successful plantation economy under Spanish rule. The late eighteenth century was marked by a period of renewed importation of enslaved manpower, which provoked a substantial development of the agricultural yield, indigo and tobacco first, then cotton and sugar from the late Spanish period onward.

Like other cities that relied heavily on slave labor, New Orleans's economy was dependent upon the plantation region around it rather than an industrialized urban center, although, by the end of the Spanish period, it counted several sawmills, cotton mills, sugar refineries, distilleries, and even a cordage factory and a small rice mill. These light industries developed during the early

American rule and, by the late 1820s, modern techniques were already reaching New Orleans, as exemplified by the building of the first steam-powered cotton mill in 1828.

New Orleans, however, remained essentially a port town whose main activity revolved around commerce and exchanges. The largest port in the American South by far, its growth was due to several factors. First, it was favored by its location at the mouth of the Mississippi River, which was then the main outlet of what was at that time the northwestern United States. New Orleans was the gateway to the Caribbean, Latin America, and even Europe for produce from the American Northwest. The second factor was geopolitical. Due to Louisiana's poor integration in the Spanish colonial system, the authorities legally sanctioned the development of commerce with the other nations. In 1795, for instance, through the Treaty of San Lorenzo, the Spanish government allowed the United States to use neutral foreign ships to trade in New Orleans and authorized navigation of the Mississippi River by both nations. Although this treaty was revoked in 1799—to the utter dismay of the Cabildo and governor who asked the intendant to ignore the law—New Orleans thus became the main outlet of western North American production and a pivot in the Atlantic trade. The third factor was purely economic, since the principle of a staple-crop-based economy did not favor economic diversification and thus tended to mainly develop exchanges.

Once New Orleans had become a city of the young Republic, the growth of the harbor activity went unchecked, making it the second most important port in the country by 1820. The vitality of the port was also enhanced by the development of steam transportation on the Mississippi River and its tributaries. The first steamboat, symbolically named the *New Orleans*, reached the city in 1812, inaugurating a new era. Not surprisingly then, after the government the second main employer of the city was the port, with all its infrastructures and services (stevedores, dockworkers, customs authorities, carters, and others). The shipping power of New Orleans was, by the late 1820s, largely equivalent to that of New York City or Philadelphia, Pennsylvania.

The early American period was also marked by the coming of financial services to the city. A banking system was rapidly organized. The Bank of Louisiana was chartered in 1804 and, shortly thereafter, the New Orleans branch of the First Bank of the United States was created, as well as the Bank of Orleans and the Louisiana Planters' Bank. In 1824 the Louisiana State Bank was founded. Many new forms of capitalistic enterprise also came to the city early after the U.S. purchase. In 1805, for instance, the New Orleans Insurance Company was founded, followed by the New Orleans Fire Assurance Company and the New Orleans Navigation Company.

RACE, ETHNICITY, AND IMMIGRATION

The racial and ethnic composition of New Orleans at the turn of the nineteenth century was a complex web of sometimes antagonistic relationships. While the Anglo-Saxon United States had developed a vision of relationships largely based on a biracial order, despite a certain degree of racial mixing New Orleans was a three-tiered society. The majority of the city's population was white. It had a solid, although relatively small, slave population. It also had a socially and economically powerful free black population, which occupied a middle ground between the whites and the enslaved. Free blacks owned property—even property in slaves—and very often possessed a formal education and held certain legal rights and privileges (although not the right to hold public office or to vote).

Because of its active maritime activities, New Orleans was also the main southern port of entry for new immigrants and the only southern city in the period to attract large influxes of foreign-born populations. Beginning with 5,056 in 1785, the city's number of inhabitants slowly rose to 8,056 in 1799 and reached 46,082 in 1830, according to the U.S. Census. The French-speaking population still prevailed in Louisiana in the 1790s; the Spanish colonial period had only slightly altered its composition. The immigration of a few hundred migrants from the Spanish city of Málaga and some one thousand Canary Islanders in the years 1779–1783 merely added to the cosmopolitan character of the city without bringing much change to its cultural fabric. Spurred by the promulgation of Governor Miró's 1786 land grant policy, however, a large influx of Anglo-Americans started altering the composition of the New Orleans population.

After the Louisiana Purchase, there was a continuous influx of new immigrants from the United States. At the turn of the nineteenth century, the main demographic factor was thus the Americanization of both white and slave populations. The first decade of the nineteenth century, however, brought to New Orleans a new French-speaking population—Saint-Domingue refugees fleeing the revolution and proclamation of the Haitian republic in January 1804. The flow of refugees started slowly with the slave rebellion in the early 1790s, speeded up in the early 1800s (with a new wave of arrivals from Saint-Domingue in 1803 and one from Jamaica in 1803–1804), and climaxed with the deportation from Cuba of about ten thousand former inhabitants of Saint-Domingue who had found temporary refuge there. Altogether, more than fifteen thousand French speakers came to Louisiana—90 percent of them to New Orleans. This reinforced the Gallic population and New Orleans's three-tiered order, the refugee flux being composed of an almost equally distributed population of slaves, free people of color, and whites. Immigrants also arrived from France and other European countries. Contingents of German migrants came on cotton ships trading between New Orleans and Bremen. Greeks, Italians, and Irish also came to New Orleans, many of whom had been recruited for the building of canals and other public works.

Although extremely varied populations arrived in New Orleans between 1790 and 1828, none were as significant as the ones from the United States and from Saint-Domingue. Both significantly influenced racial and ethnic relationships in the city. Two conflicts marked the period. The first one was obviously ethnic, or more specifically linguistic and cultural, and pitted the new Anglo-American masters of Louisiana against the Gallic population. It was a struggle for economic, political, and cultural domination over the city, with the French-speaking population struggling to maintain its cultural domination and managing to do so until the 1830s.

The first three decades of American rule in New Orleans were marked by the attempt of the new American authorities to impose their biracial order on New Orleans's society. Due to the arrival of the free refugees of color from Saint-Domingue (whose last wave, in 1809–1810, increased the free population of color by 143 percent), the group managed to resist those attempts and to make the three-tiered order remain a feature of the city of New Orleans throughout the antebellum period.

During this period American authorities also attempted to diminish the power of the free population of color and to limit their rights and prerogatives. The free blacks resisted these attempts and continued to thrive, thanks to the addition of the last wave of free refugees from Saint-Domingue and those from the prior, though numerically less important, waves. Experienced in the exercise of a certain degree of political activism and intent on preserving their special status, free blacks made their mark on the New Orleans fabric.

See also *New Orleans, LA 1828–1854; New Orleans, LA 1854–1877*

NATHALIE DESSENS

BIBLIOGRAPHY

Clark, John G. *New Orleans, 1718–1812: An Economic History.* Baton Rouge: Louisiana State University Press, 1970.

Dessens, Nathalie. *From Saint-Domingue to New Orleans: Migration and Influences.* Gainesville: University Press of Florida, 2007.

Din, Gilbert C., and John E. Harkins. *The New Orleans Cabildo: Colonial Louisiana's First City Government, 1769–1803.* Baton Rouge: Louisiana State University Press, 1996.

Fossier, Albert E. *The New Orleans Glamour Period 1800–1840. A History of the Conflicts of Nationalities, Languages, Religion, Morals, Culture, Laws, Politics and Economics during the Formative Period of New Orleans.* New Orleans, LA: Pelican Publishing Company, 1957.

Hanger, Kimberly. *Bounded Lives, Bounded Places: Free Black Society in Colonial New Orleans, 1769–1803.* Durham, NC: Duke University Press, 1997.

Hirsh, Arnold R., and Joseph Logsdon. *Creole New Orleans: Race and Americanization.* Baton Rouge: Louisiana State University Press, 1992.

Pitot, James. *Observations on the Colony of Louisiana from 1796 to 1802.* Translated by Henry C. Pitot. Baton Rouge: Louisiana State University Press, 1979.

Rowland, Dunbar. *The Official Letter Books of W. C. C. Claiborne 1801–1816.* 4 vols. Jackson, MS: Printed for the State Department of Archives and History, 1917.

CHARLESTON, SC 1790–1828

PERCHED ON THE EASTERN SEABOARD WITH A HARBOR SERVED BY TWO RIVERS, Charleston served as the economic and cultural center of South Carolina's plantation society. The period from 1790 to 1828 has been called the "golden age of Charleston." The city was a major port for agricultural goods and enjoyed a reputation for its affluent and refined population. Noting the important role that local aristocrats, such as the Pinckneys and Rutledges, played in the new nation, at least one historian has commented that Charleston was at the peak of its importance in these three decades. After the post-Revolution economic recession, Charleston experienced substantial prosperity in the early 1790s. The city council built an orphan house and the College of Charleston opened its doors. A second wave of French immigrants arrived, increasing the town's population and adding to its cultural diversity. After the invention of the cotton gin in 1793, cotton production exploded throughout the southern United States. As a major export center for both rice and cotton, Charleston also benefited from

QUICK FACTS

CHARLESTON, SC 1790–1828

INTENDANTS (MAYORS)

Arnoldus Vanderhorst	(1790–1792)
John Huger	(1792–1794)
John Bee Holmes	(1794–1795)
John Edwards	(1795–1797)
Henry William DeSaussure	(1797–1799)
Thomas Roper	(1799–1801)
John Ward	(1801–1802)
David Deas	(1802–1803)
John Drayton	(1803–1804)
Thomas Winstanley	(1804–1805)
Charles Cochran	(1805–1806)
John Dawson Jr.	(1806–1808)
Benjamin Boyd	(1808–1809)
William Rouse	(1809 –1810)
Thomas H. McCall	(1810–1812)
Thomas Bennett Jr.	(1812–1813)
Thomas Rhett Smith	(1813–1815)
Elias Horry	(1815–1817)
John Geddes	(1817–1818)
Daniel Stevens	(1819–1820)
Elias Horry	(1820–1821)
James Hamilton Jr.	(1821–1822)
John Geddes	(1823–1824)
Samuel Prioleau	(1824–1825)
Joseph Johnson	(1825–1827)
John Gadsden	(1827–1829)

MAJOR INDUSTRIES AND EMPLOYERS

City Market
Holbeck's brickyard
Chisholm's mill
Shipping (indigo, rice, cotton, and naval stores)

MAJOR NEWSPAPERS

Charleston Courier
Charleston Mercury
City Gazette
South Carolina State Gazette
South Carolina Weekly Gazette

MAJOR EVENTS

1790: The College of Charleston opens.
1799: The Charleston Water Works is established as the city's first public utility.
1808: The U.S. Congress passes an act which closes the foreign slave trade, adversely affecting the economy of Charleston.
1822: Denmark Vesey, a free black man, is convicted of plotting a slave insurrection and is hanged in Charleston.
1824: The Medical College of South Carolina is founded in Charleston—the first medical school in the southern United States.

the reopening of the foreign slave trade in 1803. The state prohibited the importation of slaves in 1787, but the demand for cotton created a need for field hands in the piedmont. Cotton farmers appealed to the state legislature and the international slave trade was reopened. In the five years between 1803 and 1808, nearly forty thousand African slaves arrived in the city.

During the War of 1812, Charleston was home to a number of privateers. Two local forts were garrisoned and a new line of fortifications was constructed across the neck of the peninsula, along what became Line Street. After the war, the European demand for cotton increased, and the value of Charleston's exports was second only to that of New York City. Planters enjoyed their prosperity and built large "single houses" with wide piazzas to capture the sea breezes.

Organized by the South Carolina Jockey Club, race week was the highlight of the town's social season. Each October planters and merchants crowded the city for races, balls, and theatre. The season lasted until April and also attracted portrait painters, dressmakers, and entertainers to the area. As early as 1790, Charleston boasted a symphony, a chorus, and at least two theatre companies. The coastal city was known to many as the cultural center of the South. However, the plantation system did not support large urban development, and Charleston's growth was slower than other major cities during this period. The only southern city that experienced large-scale urban expansion was New Orleans, Louisiana, which had a more diverse economic base than Charleston.

The city's boom times ended in the spring of 1819. Overproduction of cotton led to a collapse of prices and Charleston's economy suffered. Planters' sons headed to more fertile soil in the Southwest, and more cotton was shipped from New Orleans and Mobile, Alabama, than from Charleston. With the rise of steamboats, farmers shipped their goods to other towns. Local merchants and skilled laborers suffered from a lack of business. With an economy that relied heavily on the export of cotton, Charleston lacked the economic diversity that could help it weather financial hardship. As the white population left to find employment and fertile soil, homes stood empty. The panic of 1819, emigration, and a fear of slave insurrections took their toll on the local economy. By 1828 land values had decreased by 50 percent and a number of local businesses had closed or moved from the area.

GOVERNMENT AND POLITICS

In the 1790s the City of Charleston was divided into thirteen wards. City wardens were elected by free, white, male citizens who were able to pay three shillings a year in taxes. The voters also elected the city's chief executive, called the intendant, from among the wardens. Together the wardens formed the city council, which had authority to regulate the harbor, buildings, roads, markets, and workhouses. In addition, the council could discipline any and all disorderly persons. In October the council elected constables for each ward. Originally, two were elected for each ward, but in 1810 the number was expanded based on population. Constables made up the voluntary police force and were fined if they refused to serve. In 1809 Charleston's thirteen wards were consolidated into four larger ones in an effort to make them easier to administer.

Landowners and merchants dominated the city government in the late eighteenth and early nineteenth centuries. Many of the local elite were Federalists, such as John Rutledge and Charles Cotesworth Pinckney. In 1786 South Carolina relocated its capital from Charleston to Columbia. Political leaders in Charleston continued to resent that move well into the nineteenth century. When the state drafted a new constitution in 1790, the town's elite fought for preferential representation for the coastal area. There were few who spoke out in opposition to the city's leaders. However, during the 1790s, several tradesmen organized the Republican Society of Charleston that sympathized with Citizen Genet and the French Revolutionaries. This placed them at odds with large landholders who favored order and tradition.

CLASS No. 1.

Comprises those prisoners who were found guilty and executed.

Prisoners Names.	Owners' Names.	Time of Commit.	How Disposed of.
Peter	James Poyas	June 18	
Ned	Gov. T. Bennett,	do.	Hanged on Tuesday
Rolla	do.	do	the 2d July, 1822,
Batteau	do.	do.	on Blake's lands,
Denmark Vesey	A free black man	22	near Charleston.
Jessy	Thos. Blackwood	23	
John	Elias Horry	July 5	Do. on the Lines near
Gullah Jack	Paul Pritchard	do.	Ch.; Friday July 12.
Mingo	Wm. Harth	June 21	
Lot	Forrester	27	
Joe	P. L. Jore	July 6	
Julius	Thos. Forrest	8	
Tom	Mrs. Russell	10	
Smart	Robt. Anderson	do.	
John	John Robertson	11	
Robert	do.	do.	
Adam	do.	do.	
Polydore	Mrs. Faber	do.	Hanged on the Lines
Bacchus	Benj. Hammet	do.	near Charleston,
Dick	Wm. Sims	13	on Friday, 26th
Pharaoh	— Thompson	do.	July.
Jemmy	Mrs. Clement	18	
Mauidore	Mordecai Cohen	19	
Dean	— Mitchell	do.	
Jack	Mrs. Purcell	12	
Bellisle	Est. of Jos. Yates	18	
Naphur	do.	do.	
Adam	do.	do.	
Jacob	John S. Glen	16	
Charles	John Billings	18	
Jack	N. McNeill	22	
Cæsar	Miss Smith	do.	
Jacob Stagg	Jacob Lankester	23	Do. Tues. July 30.
Tom	Wm. M. Scott	24	
William	Mrs. Garner	Aug. 2	Do. Friday, Aug. 9.

Denmark Vesey, a free black living in Charleston, was found guilty of organizing a slave rebellion in the city in 1822 and executed along with thirty-five others. The list above includes all those found guilty, their date of execution, and, for those enslaved, their owners.

Source: The Granger Collection

In 1790 the city council built the Charleston Orphan House to support and educate poor orphans. The city's first board of health was organized in 1796 and acted as an advisory board to city leaders. Most of its members were from the Medical Society and all were selected by the city council. In December of 1799 the town's first public utility, the Charleston Water Company, was chartered. Like other towns of the time, Charleston was faced with frequent outbreaks of cholera, yellow fever, malaria, and dysentery. The board of health convinced the council to prohibit goats and pigs inside city limits and demanded that low areas be drained or filled. Laws were passed that prohibited dumping trash in the streets. The city marshal and commissioners of streets enforced these regulations. Thirteen commissioners of streets were appointed by the city council and served without pay for a year. Funds were appropriated to pave and widen the streets and to wash down the wharves and market. In September of 1804 a hurricane caused massive flooding on the peninsula that was followed by an outbreak of disease.

When the slave trade reopened in 1803, the influx of more enslaved Africans into the city concerned the local government, which responded with stricter regulations in an effort to maintain control. In 1806 the city council passed a slave code that limited assembly, required a license for business, and prohibited a number of activities such as smoking, dancing in the street, or walking with a cane or club. The penalties for such actions were whippings and fines. That same year the council supplemented its constables with a paid city guard. The guard numbered seventy men who drilled daily and carried muskets and bayonets. In 1818 the council passed an ordinance requiring all owners to register slaves that were hired in the city, and those slaves were required to carry a pass that indicated their occupation. In 1822 Denmark Vesey, a free black man, was accused of organizing a slave rebellion. Vesey and thirty-four others were hanged and the council demolished the church he attended. They also organized an additional force of 150 men to protect public property and safety and petitioned the state legislature for an arsenal.

A large fire destroyed much of the city in 1812. The council considered several measures to curtail fires, but their efforts were interrupted by the war with the British. The effort resumed after a rash of fires in early 1826. At that time, the city council added six horses to the city guard and offered a reward for the capture of arsonists. Fires continued to plague Charleston and were followed by mobs that threatened to hunt down and lynch suspected arsonists.

INDUSTRY, COMMERCE, AND LABOR

Charleston epitomized a market center of the plantation system. South Carolina's staple crops were grown on large plantations that depended on the manual labor of African slaves. Planters emulated British gentry and built manor houses surrounded by gardens and acres of planting fields. They dominated the cultural and political life in South Carolina, and many had homes in town for business and social reasons. Although they sometimes looked down upon men of business, planters depended on merchants to move their products. By 1760 a number of wealthy and influential merchants infiltrated Charleston's elite society. Lawyers, bankers, shipbuilders, and mechanics assisted the planters and merchants in the harbor town.

In the early 1790s, Charleston was the fourth largest port in America in terms of value and the largest one south of Philadelphia, Pennsylvania. Its major exports were indigo, rice, cotton, and naval stores (tar, pitch, and turpentine). When France and England went to war in 1793, Charleston benefited from an increase in trade with both countries, as well as with the French West Indies. In the late 1790s, the indigo trade diminished as British India produced a superior product. However, South Carolina's production of cotton soared, and by 1800 Charleston exported twenty million pounds of cotton. That same year the Santee Canal opened, providing another transportation link from the agricultural hinterland to the port of Charleston. Many local planters supported the reopening of the slave trade, which was approved by the state legislature in 1803. Obviously, Charleston's shipping companies and merchants benefited.

A branch of the First Bank of the United States opened in Charleston in 1792. The First Bank of South Carolina was established in 1798. The First Bank of the United States building was converted to city hall around 1818. However, a branch of the Second Bank of the United States, the charter for which was written by John C. Calhoun, opened in Charleston in 1817. South Carolina's largest planters deposited their funds in this bank, which handled international transactions that were critical to the area's trade. The state's first two incorporated insurance companies, the Mutual Insurance Company and the Charleston Insurance Company, were established in Charleston in 1797.

The town's prosperity attracted businessmen and mechanics. Coopers, carpenters, bricklayers, silversmiths, and cabinetmakers established themselves as skilled laborers and frequently became entrepreneurs with their own apprentices and slaves. As the homes of merchants and planters grew more ostentatious, many of Charleston's craftsmen became known for their skill and talent. Slaves made up the majority of laborers, working as artisans, domestics, and market workers.

After Congress closed the slave trade in 1808, Jefferson's embargo on trade with France and England dealt the port city another blow. While other harbor towns turned to industry,

Charleston continued to rely on cotton exports. Some merchants and planters realized the importance of rice and lumber, but the majority were totally dependent on cotton. When cotton prices began to fall in 1819, the city faced economic distress. The panic of 1819, the Missouri Compromise of 1820, and the Denmark Vesey episode of 1822 changed Charleston's attitude and future. Production of cotton in South Carolina was superseded by that of the rich fields of Alabama and Mississippi, and shipments left from New Orleans, not Charleston.

RACE, ETHNICITY, AND IMMIGRATION

The 1790 Charleston census reported 8,089 white persons, 7,684 slaves, and 586 free blacks. Charleston's first European settlers were British, but French Huguenots, Scottish, Irish, and Germans migrated to the city as well. Ethnic societies, including the St. Andrews and Hibernian societies, were formed by successful individuals who wanted to aid immigrants from their native countries. By the eighteenth century, the town was home to the largest and wealthiest Jewish community in North America. In 1824 members of Kahal Kadosh Beth Elohim formed the Reform Society of Israelites, making Charleston the birthplace of Reform Judaism in the United States.

African slaves and free blacks made up a large contingent of the population. Ships carrying West African slaves arrived in Charleston regularly and provided a handsome profit for investors. Most Africans were sold as field hands and house servants, but a few were purchased for work in town. Slaves endeavored to preserve their heritage through songs, stories, rituals, and foods. In an effort to be understood by both English- and French-speaking residents, Africans developed their own Creole dialect known as Gullah. Because it is a spoken, and not written, language, the arrangement of words and cadence are important aspects of Gullah. Linguistic studies have found that many Gullah vowels are similar to those spoken in Nigeria.

By 1720 there were two blacks for every white in South Carolina. In 1696 South Carolina adopted the Barbadian slave code that was originated to control the black majority in that colony. The code designated slaves as property and permitted masters to discipline them in any way they deemed appropriate. The slave code was tightened in 1740 with a number of laws that prohibited slaves from selling certain items in the market, wearing decorative clothing, or carrying weapons. Charleston was also home to a small but active free black community that dated from the 1690s. Many of these individuals were carpenters, brick masons, painters, butchers, coopers, tailors, barbers, shoemakers, and blacksmiths. German and Irish workers competed with blacks for skilled and semiskilled labor.

The debate over Missouri's admission to the Union caused a great deal of anxiety among Charleston's white population. Rumors of slave insurrections circulated throughout the South, and the state passed a new patrol law in 1820. Then, on May 30, 1822, a slave reported to his master that he had been asked to join an uprising spearheaded by a free black man, Denmark Vesey. Vesey was born a slave but was allowed to hire himself out as a laborer. In 1800 he won a lottery ticket and purchased his freedom. He was a carpenter and taught Sunday school at the African Methodist Episcopal Church in Charleston. It was believed that Vesey's plot involved hundreds of blacks in the Charleston area. Three days before the planned rebellion, the plot was revealed, and the city's intendant, James Hamilton Jr., notified the governor. They decided to call out the militia. In the midst of growing hysteria, seventy-nine blacks were tried. Thirty-five of those tried were sentenced to death, and thirty-seven were sold out of state. Vesey was hanged on July 2. Some white Charleston residents questioned the lack of evidence in the trial, but most supported harsh and immediate action. The African Methodist Episcopal Church was closed and the building demolished, and free black sailors were jailed while their ships were in port. Emphasizing a need for "public order," the city built an armory in 1825 that would later house the Citadel Military College.

See also *Charleston, SC 1776–1790; Charleston, SC 1828–1854*

FAYE L. JENSEN

BIBLIOGRAPHY

Bellows, Barbara L. *Benevolence among Slaveholders: Assisting the Poor in Charleston, 1670–1860.* Baton Rouge: Louisiana State University Press, 1993.

Coker, P. C., III. *Charleston's Maritime Heritage, 1670–1865: An Illustrated History.* Charleston, SC: Coker-Craft, 1987.

Edgar, Walter B. *South Carolina: A History.* Columbia: University of South Carolina Press, 1998.

Egerton, Douglas R. *He Shall Go Out Free: The Lives of Denmark Vesey.* Madison, WI: Madison House Publishers, 1999.

Fraser, Walter J., Jr. *Charleston! Charleston! The History of a Southern City.* Columbia: University of South Carolina Press, 1990.

Hagy, James William. *This Happy Land: The Jews of Colonial and Antebellum Charleston.* Tuscaloosa: University of Alabama Press, 1993.

Powers, Bernard E., Jr. *Black Charlestonians: A Social History, 1822–1885.* Fayetteville: University of Arkansas Press, 1994.

Rosen, Robert. *A Short History of Charleston.* Columbia: University of South Carolina Press, 1997.

WASHINGTON, DC 1790–1828

UNCERTAINTY CHARACTERIZED THE EARLY YEARS of Washington, D.C., history. During the 1780s, lawmakers and community leaders throughout the United States competed to bring the federal seat of government to their locales, expecting that considerable political influence and economic strength would accrue to the host city. For Washington, this competition to secure the federal seat meant little aid from Congress for city construction and many attempts to move the government to another location.

George Washington, James Madison, and other Potomac boosters believed the capital could overcome these challenges if it became a commercial center capable of financing its own development. Washington, D.C., lost the contest for mercantile primacy, but during the first forty years of its history the city became a vital part of the Potomac regional economy. The government's presence combined with private investment to create a community with the physical and financial infrastructure necessary to resist efforts to remove the federal seat of government. Congress's

QUICK FACTS

WASHINGTON, DC **1790–1828**

MAYORS

Robert Brent	(1802–1812)
Daniel Rapine	(1812–1813)
James Blake	(1813–1817)
Benjamin Orr	(1817–1819)
Samuel Smallwood	(1819–1822)
Thomas Carbery	(1822–1824)
Samuel Smallwood	(1824)
Roger Weightman	(1824–1827)
Joseph Gales Jr.	(1827–1830)

MAJOR INDUSTRIES AND EMPLOYERS

United States government
United States Navy Yard
Indian Queen Hotel
Printing trade
Banking and finance

MAJOR NEWSPAPERS

Alexandria Daily Advertiser
   (later the *Alexandria Gazette*)
Alexandria Expositor
Alexandria Times
Columbian Chronicle
National Intelligencer
Washington Federalist
Washington Gazette

MAJOR EVENTS

1790: Congress passes the Residence Act mandating the removal of the federal government from Philadelphia, Pennsylvania, to a permanent seat on the banks of the Potomac River.

1791: The federal district on the Potomac is demarcated to include Georgetown, Maryland, and Alexandria, Virginia; Washington City, future seat of the federal government, is founded between Rock Creek and the eastern branch of the Potomac (the Anacostia River).

1800: The federal government moves from Philadelphia to Washington City.

1814: Washington, DC, is occupied by the British during the War of 1812. Government buildings are burned.

1828: Construction begins in Georgetown on the Chesapeake and Ohio Canal, which, when completed, stretches west to Cumberland, Maryland.

decision after the War of 1812 to stay in Washington City put to rest concerns the government might move elsewhere and spurred an economic boom that helped make the city more politically and commercially relevant than ever before.

GOVERNMENT AND POLITICS

In the Compromise of 1790, James Madison agreed to support Alexander Hamilton's plan for federal government assumption of state debts in exchange for Hamilton's support for a permanent seat of government on the Potomac. The resulting Residence Act of 1790 required the government stay in Philadelphia for ten years prior to settling on the banks of the Potomac, a move other cities' leaders were confident would be preventable.

In 1791, in accordance with the provisions of the Residence Act, President George Washington delineated the boundaries of the federal district. Georgetown, Maryland, and Alexandria, Virginia, were included within the district but remained separate municipalities. Soon after demarcating the federal district, the president appointed a three-member board of commissioners to administer the federal city. He also asked Peter Charles L'Enfant to explore the hilly and thinly populated forest, farm, and pastureland between Rock Creek and the Potomac's eastern branch (now the Anacostia River) to determine the best location for the government buildings.

L'Enfant's survey inspired his plan of the city. Designed to boost land values in the area, it enticed local landowners into a property-sharing agreement with the federal government. Sales of land appropriated by the public were expected to fund construction of government buildings, eliminating dependence on congressional financial support. Officials hoped the proprietors would use proceeds from sales of their retained land to develop the city. The board of commissioners was charged with overseeing civil affairs, finance, and the construction of federal buildings until the arrival of Congress. Vacancies on the board were filled by presidential appointment. Most of the commissioners' time was spent fundraising and managing disputes between construction workers, managers, city residents, and proprietors. In September 1791 they officially named the seat of government the City of Washington.

L'Enfant was dismissed from the building project in 1792, and proceeds from land sales proved an inadequate source of funding. L'Enfant's plan, however, had an enduring influence over city development. Construction of the government buildings moved forward with financing through loans and donations from Maryland and Virginia and a loan from the federal treasury. A public contest inviting submissions for plans for the President's House and the Capitol began in 1792. James Hoban's plan for the executive mansion was selected in July 1792, and a modified version of William Thornton's Capitol design was selected in 1793.

When the federal government moved from Philadelphia to Washington City in 1800, the President's House was not quite finished and the Capitol was far from complete, but an office had been constructed for the executive departments. In 1803 Congress made its first direct appropriation to fund Capitol construction. In 1807 the south wing of the Capitol was completed, but no action was taken to erect the center section of the building.

The dominance at the federal level of Jefferson's Republicans directly influenced politics in Washington City. In 1802 the commissioners were replaced by a mayor appointed by the president and an elected twelve-member bicameral city council. In 1804 the council expanded to eighteen members and then to twenty in 1812 when it was empowered to select the mayor. After 1820 city residents directly elected the mayor, a system which lasted until 1871. Each of the federal district's separate jurisdictions was governed under the laws of its state of origin, but after 1800 only Congress could amend these statutes. This arrangement created distinct judicial systems north and south of the Potomac. This changed in 1847 when Alexandria City and County (now Arlington County) retroceded to Virginia. Georgetown and Washington City combined in 1871.

Social life was muted in the largely rural capital during its early years, reflecting President Thomas Jefferson's desire to avoid events which bestowed an air of grandiosity upon the federal government. Federal officials and foreign envoys left town when Congress was not in session.

In August 1814 British forces occupied Washington, burning government buildings including the capitol, seen above after the siege, and the White House.

Source: Library of Congress

Enforcing public order was a minor concern, and half of the city's revenues were devoted to poor relief. Maintenance on streets and other public improvements claimed the remainder of funds. A public school opened in 1806 that the city soon discovered it could not afford. The school continued with private funding in a modified form, and in 1807 a privately funded school was founded to educate black children.

In 1808 Congress rejected a provision removing the seat of government from Washington City, and in 1809 it repealed the Embargo Act that had depressed the district's economy. These actions, combined with the election of James Madison to the presidency, boosted the city's prospects and invigorated Washington society. Madison's inauguration featured some of the first balls held in the city, and the president's wife, Dolley, quickly became the city's arbiter of social graces. The Madisons held weekly receptions in a newly renovated President's House, which locals started calling "the white house."

Few thought the federal district would tempt an invading army, but the War of 1812 proved otherwise. Paradoxically, the British Army's capture of Washington and the incineration of the government buildings in August 1814 had a long-term positive effect on the city. Rebuilding became a point of pride for both Washingtonians and federal lawmakers, and considering that the Capitol was unfinished before the fire, rebuilding offered a real opportunity to produce a city grander than before. Some congressmen again tried and failed to move the seat of government from the district. For the first time, it was clear that the federal government was in Washington to stay.

INDUSTRY, COMMERCE, AND LABOR

Washington's founders expected that the proprietors of land would play an active role in the city's physical and financial development, and some proprietors did invest in the federal city in its early days. Uriah Forrest offered to partner with the city to finance construction of commercial wharves, and, in order to build houses, Samuel Davidson started a brickmaking enterprise. Many of these first proprietors were discouraged from further involvement by the city's slow progress and differences with the commissioners, especially after L'Enfant's dismissal. In later years, city growth revived urban development by original proprietors like William Prout and proprietary heirs like John Van Ness.

Despite the city's sporadic expansion, public and private building projects were ongoing during the first four decades of the city's history, and many laborers worked in construction trades. Skilled labor was difficult to find at prices the city budget could accommodate, and the commissioners had mixed success attracting the necessary stonecutters, masons, and carpenters. In order to meet labor needs, they hired slaves from the region's plantations. Over the course of the 1790s, slave laborers became the core of the city's workforce.

Private improvement efforts were sometimes more successful than public works. In 1793 the commissioners, short of money, seized on an opportunity presented by speculators James Greenleaf, Robert Morris, and John Nicholson to sell a large quantity of lots at a bargain price on the condition that the investors develop every third lot. Morris, Greenleaf, and Nicholson did not fulfill the terms of their agreement with the commissioners, but their construction crews built many of the city's first permanent private buildings.

Entrepreneurial individuals ran lotteries and formed companies to finance improvements like bridges, streets, hotels, and the city canal. The Long Bridge over the Potomac was completed in 1809 without federal assistance. In 1813 work started again on the city canal after twenty years of inaction. In 1815 Potomac steamboat service began between Aquia Creek in Virginia and the district's three municipalities.

Confirmation in 1815 that the federal government would stay in the district produced a postwar boom in the city. A strike briefly delayed Capitol rebuilding, but soon construction started on both old and new federal buildings. Newfound congressional interest in military defense spurred expansion of facilities at the Navy Yard, which in 1819 launched the *Columbus*, a seventy-four-gun ship. Real estate prices in some parts of the city climbed 500 percent. Banking flourished in the district when the Treasury Department began using local banks for deposits after the First Bank of the United States closed its doors in 1811. Local businessmen were disappointed when the Second Bank of the United States was chartered in Philadelphia in 1816, but concerns were ameliorated somewhat when a branch of the Bank of the United States opened in the district. Georgetown Seminary began granting academic degrees in 1815. Columbian College, now George Washington University, was chartered in 1821.

Printing evolved into one of the city's major businesses in the 1820s as the size of official Washington expanded. The Columbia Typographical Union soon became one of the city's most influential organizations. The beginnings of a significant federal government patronage system emerged during this period. Newspaper circulation increased and government contracts served as a major source of income for area printers. The Indian Queen Hotel and Washington Hotel flourished, as did smaller lodgings like the Woodward and Myer's City taverns and boarding houses that had long been a mainstay of visitor housing.

By 1820 it was clear that the Potomac River by itself could not be the major commercial corridor envisioned by the founders of Washington City. The Potomac Company built locks around Great and Little Falls and had worked since 1784 with mixed success to keep the river channel open. The company ceased operations, and in 1824 its stockholders took shares in the newly established Chesapeake and Ohio Canal Company. President John Quincy Adams presided over Chesapeake and Ohio's groundbreaking, which was held in Georgetown on July 4, 1828. On the same day in Baltimore, Maryland, the inaugural ceremony was held for the Baltimore and Ohio Railroad. By the time the completed Chesapeake and Ohio Canal opened in 1851, Washington's quest to become the primary east-west commercial entrepôt had been eclipsed by more quickly developed and effective transportation systems in cities to the north.

RACE, ETHNICITY, AND IMMIGRATION

A significant number of immigrants from outside North America came to Washington in its early years when skilled and unskilled workers from abroad were hired to construct the public buildings, but it was the city's large African American population that made it racially diverse. Most whites in the district were Protestants, although St. Patrick's Catholic Church, established west of Capitol Hill in 1794, was one of the city's first congregations. The city commissioners sought out English, French, Scottish, Irish, German, and Italian laborers with mixed success. Recruitment was difficult as the commissioners could promise few rewards. In the early nineteenth century, Washington's relatively small commercial and manufacturing sectors did not attract large numbers of foreign workers seeking economic opportunity.

Slaves were present in the district from the time it was carved out of Maryland and Virginia. During the early years of the city's history, the number of free black residents was small relative to the size of the slave population. In 1800 over two thousand slaves lived in the area, comprising nearly one-fourth of the district's population, while free blacks accounted for just one-twentieth of inhabitants. During the first decade of the nineteenth century, both the slave and free black populations began a period of steady growth, but the number of free blacks increased more rapidly. By 1830 equal numbers of slave and free African Americans lived in the district, comprising close to one-third of its thirty thousand inhabitants. After 1830 the slave population began falling, but the number of free blacks continued to increase.

Nonresident slaves proved a highly visible presence since slave trading near the Washington City and Alexandria waterfronts became one of the district's most profitable enterprises. Concerns about the city's ability to control the expanding black population led to passage in 1808 of the first of the city's black codes. The measure set a 10:00 p.m. curfew, levied fines on free black violators, and prescribed whippings for transgressions by slaves. In 1812, with the country at war, authorities thought it prudent to stiffen penalties for blacks violating the law, to add rules regulating the assembly of black residents, and to require that free blacks carry documentation of their status. Despite these restrictions, Washington law continued to permit slave education and manumission and to allow freed slaves to stay in the district, provisions which helped explain the constant increase in the free black population.

General manumission was suggested by some leaders early in the nineteenth century but not seriously considered. The American Colonization Society, which advocated slave emancipation followed by expatriation to Africa, was established in Washington in 1816. Few of the city's blacks were interested in the society's agenda. African Americans started their own community organizations, such as the Resolute Beneficial Society that paid medical and burial fees for the poor and helped educate black children. Several African American churches were founded after 1814. In 1820 a new ordinance passed requiring that free black male residents obtain a $20 bond that was forfeited if they or their families engaged in begging, disorderly conduct, or criminal activity. Mulatto bank messenger William Costin challenged the bond measure in court, but a modified version of the law remained in place.

African Americans in the district labored in a variety of occupations. Many were employed in the city's modest manufacturing enterprises or at the Navy Yard. Some worked in trades such as bricklaying, carpentry, fishing, and blacksmithing. Others worked in service occupations as hairdressers, tailors, cooks, and waiters. Black women worked predominantly as domestic servants. The few black bank messengers represented the pinnacle of black social achievement in Washington.

In 1827 restrictions on the movement of African Americans in the city became more severe. This may have occurred in response to increasingly strident abolitionist condemnation of slavery in the capital, which became harder to ignore as the printing industry flourished. The peace bond was increased to $500 and the curfew was more strictly enforced, but the number of free blacks sold into slavery to pay forfeited bonds did not seem to increase.

The district's white population had diversified somewhat by the end of the 1820s. Irish immigrants were employed to dig the Washington City Canal in 1814–1815, and many more were employed as digging began for the Chesapeake and Ohio Canal. The Irish presence in Georgetown would prove a source of social tension in the district for years to come.

See also *Washington, DC 1828–1854; Washington, DC 1941–1952*

Dana John Stefanelli

BIBLIOGRAPHY

Arnebeck, Bob. *Through a Fiery Trial: Building Washington, 1790–1800.* Lanham, MD: Madison Books, 1991.

Bowling, Kenneth R. *The Creation of Washington, DC: The Idea and Location of the American Capital.* Fairfax, VA: George Mason University Press, 1991.

Bryan, Wilhelmus Bogart. *A History of the National Capital from Its Foundation through the Period of the Adoption of the Organic Act, 1790–1814.* Vol. 1. New York, NY: MacMillan Company, 1914.

———. *A History of the National Capital from Its Foundation through the Period of the Adoption of the Organic Act, 1815–1878.* Vol. 2. New York, NY: MacMillan Company, 1916.

Green, Constance McLaughlin. *The Secret City: A History of Race Relations in the Nation's Capital.* Princeton, NJ: Princeton University Press, 1967.

————. *Washington: Village and Capital, 1800–1878.* Princeton, NJ: Princeton University Press, 1962.

Young, James Sterling. *The Washington Community, 1800–1828.* New York, NY: Columbia University Press, 1966.

SALEM, MA 1790–1828

A CURIOUS BLEND OF GENUINE ACHIEVEMENT, ROMANCE, AND MYTH, Salem often has been called one of America's truly remarkable cities. Infamous for the witch trials of 1692–1693, Salem reached its economic and, some say, cultural prime during the years 1791–1807, when its seafaring merchants contributed 5 percent of the revenue of the United States government. The years 1790 to 1828 were perhaps the brightest in Salem's nearly four-hundred-year history. Responding to the country's wrenching economic depression after it achieved independence, Salem's merchants and mariners charted innovative courses to markets that had previously been closed to Americans, including India, Sumatra, Mauritius, and Ceylon. Opening these markets infused the national treasury with desperately needed revenues. The town celebrated its achievements in a cultural florescence marked by the founding of the East India Marine Society and the Salem Athenaeum.

By 1828, however, Salem was entering a period of transition, if not decline. Jefferson's 1807 Embargo Act, the silting up of the harbor, and industrialization channeled Salem's wealth to new markets and its most entrepreneurial citizens to other cities where fresh opportunities awaited. This generation turned its talent to politics, education, and the enjoyment—rather than creation—of wealth. Decaying wharves and Nathaniel Hawthorne's sour portrayal in the opening pages of *The Scarlet Letter* were the most discernable symbols of antebellum Salem.

GOVERNMENT AND POLITICS

Salem continued to be governed by town meetings throughout the period, becoming a city only in 1836, after its maritime prominence had passed. Town officials (selectmen), state and county officials (judges, sheriffs), and national officials (customs officers) carried out most administrative functions. They were complemented by an array of voluntary associations such as fire companies, militia, and marine societies. One such organization was the Salem Marine Society, formed in 1766 to aid the indigent and their families. Many public projects were financed through subscriptions both public and private. The Salem Marine Society raised funds to erect a series of buoys around the harbor in the 1790s, and a public subscription raised funds to drain the town commons in 1801.

Prosperity did not insulate the town from the political and economic growing pains of a new nation or the maelstrom of international conflict. The town divided itself between established Federalist families—led by the Derbys, Grays, and Pickmans—that increasingly congregated in the town's West End and the up-and-coming Jeffersonian Republican households of the East End led by the German Crowninshield family. Through the War of 1812 and the secessionist Hartford Convention of 1814, pro-British Federalist households sported white

QUICK FACTS

SALEM, MA 1790–1828

MAYORS

None during this period; Salem was governed through a town form of government, with selectmen and occasional town meetings making the major decisions

MAJOR INDUSTRIES AND EMPLOYERS

Maritime commerce (fishing, shipbuilding and repair, sailmaking, ropeworks, blockmaking, and pumpmaking)

MAJOR NEWSPAPERS

Salem Gazette
Salem Mercury
Salem Register
Impartial Register

MAJOR EVENTS

1787: The first Salem vessel, the *Grand Turk*, returns from China.
1793: Captain Jonathan Carnes of Salem discovers pepper on the island of Sumatra.
1799: The Salem East India Marine Society is established. It is the forerunner of today's celebrated Peabody Essex Museum.
1807: Thomas Jefferson signs the Embargo Act, idling New England shipping.
1810: The Salem Athenaeum, the town's premier private library, is established.

cockades that signaled their opposition to the extremes of the French Revolution. Republican families favored "Jacobin" red, white, and blue ribbons to display their alignment with Jefferson's pro-French policies. When the nation's political alignments shifted in the Era of Good Feelings that followed, Salem split between Whigs and Jacksonians.

Salem's political concerns were informed primarily by its commercial and maritime position, and its representatives pressed the new national government to provide for the protection of commerce and fishing and for provisions for coastal improvements such as lighthouses and buoys. At a time when duties brought in over 90 percent of federal revenues, Federalists in Salem lobbied for a larger navy to protect shipping from North African pirates and European privateers, while Republicans advocated for lower taxes and smaller government. The town was more of a mirror of the nation's political trajectory than one might expect of a New England seaport. As early as 1796, Dr. William Bentley was reporting the emergence of a Jeffersonian opposition party. This was followed in 1800 by the founding of a Republican newspaper, the *Impartial Register*. The town grew divided by parochial squabbles and party friction rather than class or policy.

As early as 1790, the wars of the French Revolution had begun to hamper American commerce, and the federal government responded with an evolving menu of neutrality, nonintercourse, and eventually war, albeit an undeclared one. Impressment and confiscation affected Salem's mariners and crippled the country's efforts at neutrality. Hundreds of Salem vessels were confiscated by warships and privateers of the warring parties and their allies from the Caribbean to the Indian Ocean. During the 1790s, American vessels were subject to search and seizure in the Caribbean, and Salem enthusiastically supported the quasiwar against France after 1797. After Congress authorized the construction of three frigates, Salem residents filled a subscription of $74,700 to support the building of the *Essex*, which launched in September 1799. The Crowninshield family offered two of their own vessels to the cause, but Navy Secretary Solomon Stoddard demurred; the family's turn toward republicanism may be traced to Stoddard's refusal.

Congress's passage of a partial nonintercourse act in April 1806, banning trade with Europe's warring parties, created anxiety throughout the maritime community. At the end of December 1807, word reached Salem that Jefferson's policy prevented any vessel from leaving an American port for any foreign port. This was followed by more restrictive acts to plug loopholes, and excessive bonds were eventually required for the coastal trade. The policy immediately affected the overseas trade and idled some 185 vessels and two thousand mariners, decimating both the coastwise trade and fishing fleet. Salem's three shipyards were silenced; no ships were launched the next year and only a couple in 1809. This crippled attendant industries such as sailmaking, ropeworking, blockmaking, and pumpmaking. By spring, farmers who depended on commerce to move their goods to lucrative overseas and coastal markets felt the pinch.

Surprisingly, however, Salem's merchants were not universally opposed to Jefferson's Embargo Act of 1807, which precluded all American overseas commerce. Prominent pro-Jefferson figures such as the Crowninshield family, William Gray, and Joseph White vocally supported it. The federal government's selective permission to sail to other ports further divided the town, as Federalists complained that those who supported the embargo benefited most from the loopholes in it. With the replacement of the embargo in March 1809 with less restrictive regulations, the town's merchants again sent their ships out to Sumatra, China, the Caribbean, and South Africa.

Salem's ruling citizens were involved in commerce, with families such as the Derbys, Crowninshields, and Forresters helping to develop innovative strategies for a national economic recovery. In this way, Salemites stepped onto the political stage of the new nation. Timothy Pickering moved to Philadelphia, Pennsylvania, during this period, serving as George Washington's secretary of State and attorney general. Others filled the void in local politics. Jacob Crowninshield served in the Massachusetts legislature and in the U.S. House of Representatives from 1803 to 1808, chairing the U.S. House Committee on Commerce and Manufactures. His brother Benjamin Williams Crowninshield, who also served in the state legislature intermittently and was elected to four terms in Congress from 1823 to 1831, became secretary of the U.S. Navy in January 1815. Nathaniel Silsbee served in the Massachusetts legislature and U.S. House of Representatives from 1817 to 1821 and the Senate from 1826 to 1835.

INDUSTRY, COMMERCE, AND LABOR

Salem's rise to prominence from a modest diversified seaport of fishing, shipbuilding, and Atlantic commerce to a major contributor to the antebellum economy was the result of its expansion into the East Indies and Baltic trades. This was not an even ascent, however. By 1790 foreign wars and piracy, punctuated by the French Revolution and defensive actions against North African pirates, triggered episodes of economic volatility.

The period began amidst signs of gradual recovery. As in other New England ports, the fisheries and commerce had struggled throughout the economic depression of the 1780s. The fishing fleet had dropped to one-third of its prewar levels and only numbered 160 men by 1790. However, the pioneering efforts of Derby and others in opening eastern and Baltic markets helped build the wealth of Salem's merchants. Selling off their wartime privateers—large, swift, heavily manned ships ill-fitted for trade—they pulled the town out of the wrenching economic depression of the previous decade.

Salem was not the first American seaport to send a vessel to the East. By the 1786–1787 trading season, however, the *Grand Turk* of Salem was one of five American ships reported at Canton, China. From this start, its vessels sailed the globe in search of goods to bring home, and this period saw the first Salem visits to Sumatra, Burma, Arabia, Indochina, Japan, and the Philippines, and the first American vessels were reported at Calcutta and Bombay, Batavia, Mocha, and St. Helena. For a brief period, Jonathan Lambert of Salem took possession of Tristan da Cunha in the South Atlantic and created a trading post for passing vessels. Salem opened the sandalwood trade with Fiji and the pepper trade with Sumatra. In fact, by the early 1800s, Salem vessels so dominated the Sumatran pepper trade that for generations the South Pacific was known as the Salem East Indies.

After 1790 shipbuilding prospered as men such as Ebenezer Mann, Retire Becket, and Enos Briggs launched ships of over one hundred tons that were known as Indiamen. Lucrative commerce with the East also supported a local economy that revived ropeworks and sail lofts and once again employed blacksmiths, blockmakers, pumpmakers, small boat builders, wood carvers, and instrument makers. An iron foundry established in 1795 made anchors. By 1828 Salem boasted fifty wharves.

In the early days of the Republic, Salem's brand of entrepreneurship was a mix of continuation and innovation. The Custom House continued to be run, as it had been during and following the Revolution, by Major Joseph Hiller until Jefferson installed a Republican in 1802. Many of the families who had been financially successful before the Revolution became even wealthier after the war. In 1792 a group of merchants established the Essex Bank, formally consolidating an earlier ad hoc arrangement. Similarly, seven years later, merchants formalized their previous insurance practices, and in 1800 they founded the Salem Marine Insurance Company, capitalized at $400,000, and in 1803 the Essex Fire and Marine Insurance Company, capitalized at $300,000. These were enormous sums at the time, representing about $6–7 million each in modern-day currency.

For a brief period, Salem exerted a remarkable influence on American life. The port introduced exotics such as the elephant and giraffe to Americans and filled Yankee pantries with pepper, tea, and porcelain. The city's exploits shaped national character and did so at a critical moment. Nowhere else, outside of the largest cities, did one encounter the richness of Salem's commercial and cultural resources: banks, publishers, insurance companies, charitable organizations, libraries, bookstores, a municipal water system, a museum of Orientalia and natural history, concert halls and assembly rooms, marine societies, free schools, private schools for adults and children, and choral and instrumental groups.

Two institutions in particular illustrate Salem's cultural tone and commitment to civic culture. The Salem Athenaeum traces its origins back to the port's Social Library, established in 1760, and the Philosophical Library, organized in 1781 after the privateer *Pilgrim* captured a British merchantman carrying 116 volumes of scientific literature to Royal Society member Richard Kirwan. In 1810 the two merged to form the private library with a limited membership of one hundred patrons. Other libraries, including the Library of Arts and Sciences and the Fourth Social Library, were also established in Salem, along with the Essex Institute.

The Marine Society at Salem had already been founded in 1766 to provide assistance for the families of men lost at sea, but in 1799 a unique institution came together. The Salem East India Marine Society, open only to captains who had sailed beyond the Atlantic, reflected the ideals of the early Republic and the experience of encounters with the East. In addition to the conventional social functions, its members promoted "one great object of their institution, which was the acquiring of nautical knowledge" and required its mariners to maintain journals "to be returned at the end of his voyage, with a regular diary of the winds, weather, and remarkable occurrences, during his voyage." Eventually, members were also asked to donate souvenirs collected in their travels to "form a museum of natural and artificial curiosities, particularly such as are to be found beyond the Cape of Good Hope and Cape Horn." In 1825 the society dedicated an impressive museum to house its collections. This later became the site of the renowned Peabody Essex Museum.

RACE, ETHNICITY, AND IMMIGRATION

Like other early American seaports, Salem drew hundreds of transients each year, primarily from the ranks of merchant seamen and fishermen. Consequently, its visitors were a largely dispersed and mobile people who resided along the peripheries of the town center while waiting for the next voyage. Salem was not so much a magnet for immigrants as it was a stopover for diverse crews from European ports. A notable exception was the enclave of Franco-American households that specialized in the maritime trades and congregated along the town's eastside waterfront. Drawn principally from the Isle of Jersey in the English Channel, many of these families had been in Salem since the 1660s.

Also of importance was an active enclave of African Americans whose homes abutted the shipyards of so-called Knockers' Hole. This population largely constituted the 260 "nonwhite" residents (about 3 percent) of the 1790 census. While Salem's white population grew steadily, if modestly, however, the number of its African Americans fluctuated in relation to economic conditions, falling to 202 in 1800 and to 167 in 1810 before rising to above 200 again by the end of the period. Less able to participate in Salem society than the families from Jersey, they formed an African Society in 1805. Although the town's schools had been integrated through the 1790s, in 1807 a period of segregation began and continued until 1844. In that year Salem became the first Massachusetts municipality to permanently integrate its schools.

Salem's economic prosperity and cultural prominence in this period grew out of its capacity to send its citizens abroad to establish communities of expatriate traders and missionaries, creating, in effect, an extended city. One could find Salem men and women in the most far-flung regions, freighting a bit of Salem life on virtually every sea and in every port, from Canton to Calcutta and from Macao to Mauritius. As a consequence of this, Salem was not only a place transformed by contact with the East, but also a place transferred.

The practical effects of the Enlightenment, guilt about the witch trials, and the influence of material prosperity and consumerism led to increasing toleration and expanding religious diversity. In the late eighteenth and early nineteenth centuries, liberals such as Unitarian cleric and public figure William Bentley pointed to the witch trials as an example of what happened when supernaturalism and irrationality spun out of control. Bentley arrived in Salem from Boston, Massachusetts, in 1783 and served as minister of the Second Congregational (East) Church until his death in 1819. A progressive thinker, he lobbied for the Freedom of Religion Act of 1811 and was a vocal proponent of public schooling for all, including Salem's African American children.

As Bentley moved his Congregationalist flock toward Unitarianism, the First and North Churches followed, reflecting the town's growing acceptance of expansive views. Others, particularly the Episcopalians at St. Peter's Church, remained staunchly conservative. These developments emerged not without the tensions that foreshadowed the religious turmoil of antebellum America, and even the open-minded Bentley found limits to ecumenism. He staunchly opposed revivalists and revivals and condemned "the stupid ass at the Tabernacle"—Joshua Spaulding, minister of the Tabernacle Church—for embroiling local churches in controversy and schism and for bringing other illiterate and ill-informed preachers to town. When a Baptist congregation was assembled in Salem in 1805, Bentley called it "a dark day." Salem's sense of religious exceptionalism also found its way into overseas missions, and when Adoniram Judson and Samuel Newell sailed to Calcutta with their families on February 26, 1812, the city's Tabernacle Church became one of the earliest American denominations to send missionaries to the East.

By 1828 Salem was established as one of America's remarkable sites, a global city that had charted an innovative course out of economic depression and enriched both the national treasury and national culture. A generation later, in 1850, Salem's son Nathaniel Hawthorne, in his introduction to *The Scarlet Letter*, bemoaned the decaying warehouses and dilapidated wharves that were then mere shadowy reminders of the city's bustling trade with China, in the days when the world was Salem's market.

See also *Salem, MA 1776–1790*

DANE MORRISON AND NANCY SCHULTZ

BIBLIOGRAPHY

Adams, Gretchen A. *The Specter of Salem: Remembering the Witch Trials in Nineteenth-Century America.* Chicago, IL: University of Chicago Press, 2009.

Flibbert, Joseph, K. David Goss, Jim McAllister, Bryant F. Tolles, and Richard B. Trask. *Salem: Cornerstones of a Historic City.* Beverly, MA: Commonwealth Editions, 1999.

Morrison, Dane A., and Nancy L. Schultz, eds. *Salem: Place, Myth, and Memory.* Hanover, NH: Northeastern University Press, 2004.

Phillips, James Duncan. *Salem and the Indies: The Story of the Great Commercial Era of the City.* Boston, MA: Houghton Mifflin, 1947.

ALBANY, NY 1790–1828

ALBANY GAINED NEW DISTINCTION IN THE 1790s when it became the seat of state government and after the completion of an extensive harbor along the Hudson River. Many manufactories, mills, and a lumber district redefined the economy and made Albany a haven for laborers. New England migrants flocked to the city and brought innovative skills and vision, which changed the once-Dutch port town into a diverse cultural community and a commercial capital. Albany residents lived crowded among forty blocks that surrounded the Dutch Reformed Church at the city's core—an important edifice that symbolized the city's history and cultural traditions. What gave Albany notoriety was the state-funded Erie Canal, which opened there in 1825. The canal increased settlement, diversified the economy, and was a key resource for merchants in Canada, New Jersey, New England, and Pennsylvania. By 1830 Dutch identity had declined and there was a migration to the countryside. Because it was the seat of state government and boasted progressive industry and shipping interests, Albany became known as a center for politics and modernity and was considered a pioneer of innovations in industry and commerce.

GOVERNMENT AND POLITICS

Albany's political history was distinct because the community was settled by the Dutch and not by the British like most other colonies. What shaped the government the most was that Albany was the largest northern inland settlement and the closest community to the frontier. After the New Netherland Dutch established a fort in 1624, Fort Orange (Albany) became a center for trade and political action. Buying and selling, land negotiations, and Indian relations defined politics and led to the development of the municipal political structure. In 1790 Albany was a key location for the transfer of natural resources from the West, a commercial hub for merchants and craftsmen, and a center for Native American affairs. In 1664 Dutch provincial leaders surrendered the colony to Great Britain. The Dutch maintained influence, but their authority weakened after 1674 when Britain established the English legal and government system and a court of sessions at Albany. Albany magistrates abided by English policies, but even in 1790 they remained driven to maintain community autonomy and—most importantly—their political traditions and commercial interests.

In 1686 New York's provincial governor, Thomas Dongan, granted Albany a charter that declared it an independent city and allowed for corporate privileges and the formation of a municipal government. This charter established the offices of a mayor, appointed by the governor to oversee operations; a recorder (deputy mayor); a clerk; and a treasurer. After the 1777 state constitution passed, the mayor was chosen by the state's council of appointment. In 1790 three common councilmen or alderman, one for each city ward, wrote local ordinances and decided on civic issues. Eligible freemen elected aldermen and assistant aldermen, which made government participatory and diverse. The mayor and aldermen held a Mayor's Court, and a sheriff and constables assisted with legal matters.

QUICK FACTS

ALBANY, NY 1790–1828

MAYORS

John Lansing Jr.	(1786–1790)
Abraham Yates Jr.	(1790–1796)
Abraham Ten Broeck	(1796–1799)
Philip S. Van Rensselaer	(1799–1816)
Elisha Jenkins	(1816–1819)
Philip S. Van Rensselaer	(1819–1821)
Charles E. Dudley	(1821–1824)
Ambrose Spencer	(1824–1826)
James Stevenson	(1826–1828)
Charles E. Dudley	(1828–1829)

MAJOR INDUSTRIES AND EMPLOYERS

New York State government
Lumber district
Iron production
Silk production
Copper production
James Caldwell's mill complex
Stevenson, Douw, and Ten Eyck Nail Factory
John Wendell's hat factory
Albany Chair Factory

MAJOR NEWSPAPERS

Albany Gazette
Albany Chronicle
Albany Centinel
Albany Register
Albany Journal
Republican Crisis
Guardian
Albany Argus
Albany Advertiser
Plough Boy
Microscope

MAJOR EVENTS

November 17, 1793: Slaves Bet, Dean, and Pomp set fire to a stable. The fire spreads and damages two city blocks. The slaves confess that they were lured to set the fire by whites and are publicly hanged.

1797: The state legislature convenes permanently at Albany.

April 21, 1807: Politicians cane and punch each other on State Street. A riot ensues, and one hundred onlookers watch three Republicans attack Federalist Solomon Van Rensselaer. Five politicians sue each other for assault and battery.

September 5, 1807: The North River steamboat *Clermont* docks at Albany after its first successful run. Residents celebrate this first steam-powered vessel, which was designed by Robert Fulton.

March 31, 1817: The Gradual Emancipation Law of 1817 is enacted and grants freedom to all slaves after July 4, 1827.

October 26, 1825: The "wedding of the waters" ceremony is held to celebrate the completion and opening of the Erie Canal. The canal extends 363 miles from Albany to Buffalo, New York.

Officials met in the common council room in the Stadt Huys, or city hall. The Mayor's Court was held there, and the basement served as the jail and housed the jailer and his family. City officers annually appointed public servants such as watchmen, firemasters, and poormasters, as well as a chimney sweep, bullkeeper, ferrymaster, and a town crier. State political ideology influenced city politics and ultimately controlled regional politics. Between 1786 and 1828, the city was a center for anti-Federalism and democratic republicanism. The leaders of this movement were Abraham Yates and John Lansing. Most eligible voters were Clintonians, called Democratic-Republicans. These voters supported Governor George Clinton—a man who objected to any aristocratic control of government or class favoritism. Clinton was against policies that Federalists endorsed, as his party felt such endorsements represented sympathy to British strategy. Philip Schuyler, Alexander Hamilton, and members of the Van Rensselaer and Ten Broeck families led the Federalist faction in Albany. Mayor Abraham Yates and his council primarily focused on an economic strategy to overcome the postwar debt. By 1794 they had improved over two miles of docks and established numerous stagecoach lines and a post office. The wharf made Albany more competitive with New York City; Boston, Massachusetts; and Philadelphia, Pennsylvania. Yates and the council also expanded government and added salaried positions for street cleaners and lamplighters. City leaders contended with urban problems, mostly a population boom, which resulted in the development of nine city blocks. Albany suffered two fires (1793 and 1797) and a yellow fever scare (1792), and smallpox was endemic. These problems increased unemployment, poverty, and homelessness—more urban issues that were new to Albany. Nearby towns of Watervliet, Colonie, Guilderland, and Bethlehem had been incorporated and separated from the city, which relieved many political burdens. Albany continued to be the prime locale to resolve Indian affairs. Between 1788 and 1828, the leaders of the Oneida, Onondaga, and Cayuga nations frequented Albany to argue terms to cede land to the state.

Albany's mayor was appointed, making the position influential and a key to maintaining power in partisan politics. In 1799 Federalist John Jay was elected New York's governor, and his council appointed Philip Van Rensselaer mayor. Although the common council remained Democratic, its members initially trusted Van Rensselaer because they respected his ideas and social position. He focused on public improvements and the economy and can be credited with transforming Albany into a modern urban center. Improvements were made to increase commerce and to accommodate state leaders. In 1797 these leaders declared Albany the permanent location for state government. With this designation, city officials aimed to make Albany more orderly and contemporary, and they facilitated plans for modern amenities that would help transform it from a town to a city. They retained engineers to build a water system using the latest technology. Water was piped in through specially treated, hollowed-out logs from five miles away. Dirt roads were paved with stone, sidewalks were overlaid with brick, and gutter systems were installed. Tax revenue was used to complete projects, which made Albany an expensive place to live. Ordinances were passed to control roaming pigs and to regulate taverns and liquor production and the recreational activities of slaves. Albany was compelled to turn away strangers to control poverty and to license criers (vendors)—marginal people who sold baked goods and produce from street carts. By 1803 a state capitol was built, which was also used as the quarters for city government until 1831. A state bank was also constructed, and in 1806 Albany's first poorhouse was completed.

Albany became a hotbed of political conflict after Mayor Van Rensselaer was ousted by Republican governor Daniel Tompkins. In 1816 Tompkins influenced the appointment of Elisha Jenkins as the first mayor who was not a native of Albany. When De Witt Clinton became governor, Van Rensselaer was re-appointed mayor, but city aldermen tried to remove him from office twice, citing "disagreeable" political issues. Political factions developed over the mayoral issue and the construction of the Erie Canal. Democratic factionalism influenced the establishment of the Albany Regency, one of the first political machines in the United States, which was led by Martin Van Buren. The Regency was formed as Dutch aristocrats passed away and a younger generation of Irish and English began taking office. It controlled local and state politics until 1838. Van Rensselaer was finally ousted in 1821, and the Albany Regency influenced the aldermen at their first mayoral election to select English-born Charles E. Dudley. In 1820 ten elected common council members served five city wards and were assisted by twenty-five city officers. These officers worked in eighteen city departments and included two police justices, two city physicians, and three captains of the city watch.

INDUSTRY, COMMERCE, AND LABOR

Private enterprise continued to be the basis of the Albany economy. The Erie Canal and Albany's close proximity to waterways and turnpikes made the transportation of goods more widespread and expedient. Merchants improved their wealth by selling imports and by exporting produce and natural resources, most of which was bound for Europe (grain and timber) or the lower Hudson River valley. Goods from Canada, New England, and New York were transported to Albany, making waggoneers, boatmen, and dockworkers a major part of the labor system and central to a successful economy. Albany was home to large mercantile firms, "copartnerships," which were owned by multiple merchants such as the Bleeckers, Ten Broecks, and James Caldwell and William James. Merchants gained prominence by owning docks in Albany and New York City; having suppliers in England, the West Indies, or Canada; and owning stores in Vermont, Montreal, or western communities. They built storehouses on the waterfront, owned boats and farms, and supplied local and regional taverns and inns as far west as Niagara Falls. Smaller firms were family-owned specialty stores that sold only foods or liquor or local goods produced by city bakers, butchers, and distillers. Thomas Shipboy, John Robison, and Henry and Robert McClallen were major retailers. Hundreds of craftsmen sold goods from their homes or shops, while others provided services in the trades or did repairs. There were over thirty-eight inns or boarding houses by 1813, fourteen of which were owned by women. Women sold homespun goods, clothes, and linens from their homes and two operated millinery shops in 1803. Most women served as day laborers and were hired to care for the infirm or to nurse infants, but some earned money doing laundry, housecleaning, and cooking for wealthier families. In 1813 two women ran a leather-dressing business. Many freed women ran private businesses. One example of this was Volkie Speck, a gardener and poultry dealer who sold geese and chickens.

North Albany was an industrial district and earned national recognition in 1790 for industry. The designation was attained because of immigrants like James Caldwell, who hailed from Ireland and profited as a merchant during the American Revolution. He built mills that were described as "the most extensive factory in the nation." Caldwell's Mills opened in March 1790 and processed 150,000 barrels of tobacco annually. He produced snuff, cigars, mustard, and chocolate, which he labeled with his name. The mills were a technological sensation and many marveled at the engineering. Multiple conduits provided

The advent of the steam-powered ship by Robert Fulton in the first decade of the nineteenth century, coupled with the completion of the Erie Canal in 1825, revolutionized the movement of people and goods in the Northeast and greatly facilitated Albany's growth. Fulton's *Clermont*, seen above, first docked at Albany in 1807.

Source: Library of Congress

separate power sources and allowed milling to continue in one area while it was halted in another. In 1793 Caldwell and his engineer, Christopher Batterman, received a United States patent for tobacco production.

Oil mills and gristmills were also built in northern Albany. During the War of 1812, the first federal arsenal was established at Watervliet for the production of ordnance and military accouterments. Five smaller manufactories were established, which created a sense of modernism in the city and enticed job seekers and entrepreneurs. Factories included the Stevenson, Douw, and Ten Eyck Nail Factory; Thomas Barry's Tobacco Factory; and iron and copper factories. Owners employed newcomers and boys between the ages of nine and fifteen. No industry surpassed the lumber district, which was established near the Erie Canal basin.

In addition to having the most factories, Albany also had more slaves, lawyers, and physicians than any community in the region. In 1827 seventy-seven lawyers were in practice and served both locals and the government, and many traveled to Albany to seek their services. People also traveled to the city to receive medical treatment from a number of surgeons, dentists, apothecaries, and cancer doctors. Slaves worked as domestics, practiced trades, or were laborers in stores or on the waterfront. Freed blacks established their own businesses, including Ned Davis, a house painter, and Samuel Schuyler, a famed and wealthy skipper.

RACE, ETHNICITY, AND IMMIGRATION

The 1790 census enumerated 3,498 people in Albany, but the city could not be considered as culturally diverse as larger cities. The population increased each decade by at least 30 percent, and in 1820 the population reached 12,541. Dutch, English, and African Americans were the dominant ethnic groups, and slaves and freed blacks constituted one-third of the city's population. The Dutch were known to be large slaveholders, and Albany's slave population peaked at 572 in 1790. The largest ethnic section in Albany was a free black neighborhood at Bassett Street and South Pearl Street. The area was home of the Jackson, Thompson, and Lattimore families, who intermarried and did business together. Black neighborhoods also existed in north Albany where the Davis and Speck families established businesses. By 1827, when all slaves were manumitted, more blacks settled in the south end neighborhood. More than fifty black households existed in Albany in 1825, and many blacks lived in multifamily dwellings near the northern Arbor Hill section. Most blacks joined the Episcopal or African churches but celebrated Pentecost at the Pinkster celebration, an outdoor festival that included music, dancing, food, and vendors. The celebration was banned in 1811 because white and black attendees were said to be drunk and boisterous. Black children attended either the New York African Free School or a school for "colored" children.

The Dutch as an ethnic group remained strong in 1790, but they were being overshadowed in both population and wealth by New Englanders. Albany was known for its "fine Dutch girls," who favored marrying newcomer English, Irish, and Scots, effectively breeding the "Dutch" out of Albany but leaving many of its traditions. Many Dutch left Albany to farm in the countryside because the urban core became too commercial and crowded for family life. The Dutch who remained in the city held on to cultural traditions but were mainly wealthy merchants or state or city politicians. Many converted family homes into businesses, lived in west Albany, and only came to the city to work. The city appeared Dutch because the architecture remained intact, and the Dutch Church was popular and remained a significant cultural practice.

New Englanders and migrants from nearby states settled in Albany, as did a few European immigrants. One such European family was the James family of Ireland, who became well known in commerce and American literature. Newcomers settled in the south section on the former city pasture, which was developed for housing. Most newcomer males enlisted in the militia and served in the War of 1812. In 1815 the city annexed forty-seven blocks in the north that became a center for the working-class Irish. German, Scots, and Scotch-Irish also congregated in many sections of Albany but formed no distinct neighborhood. All groups created an identity for themselves by establishing institutions such as societies, schools, and churches, and by 1825 this eclipsed any Dutch aristocracy or culture. The Irish established St. Mary's in 1797—Albany's first Catholic church—and a relief society called St. Patrick's. The Scots who settled west of the city core founded First Presbyterian Church and the St. Andrew's Society, to aid the impoverished. German Lutherans built a new church and settled in the northwest section. Many newcomers opened import stores and sold goods from their homeland, giving the city a culturally diverse appeal by 1825. The English built a new edifice for the Episcopal St. Peter's Church, and many reformed Dutch joined the parish. English citizens sponsored the establishment of schools such as the Albany Academy, the Female Academy, the African Free School, and the Lancaster School. They also were involved in the Mechanics Society, and many Scots and Irish joined the Masonic Temple.

In a move of particular note, Albany's first significant Jewish population established the Beth El Society in 1822. Jews ran stores in Albany's south end and lived near free blacks. Shakers founded the city's first Friends of the Shakers meetinghouse. Newcomer English, Irish, and Jews made Albany distinct because they ushered in a new economy that featured specialized crafts and services. Many benefited from custom-ordered coaches, saddles, wigs, watches, furniture, and stoves. Albany earned new recognition as a center for exclusive services and goods. By 1828, due to progress in industry and transportation, there was opportunity for economic improvement, so the city experienced a population boom and became a place known for diversity and opportunity.

See also *Albany, NY 1828–1854*

TRICIA BARBAGALLO

BIBLIOGRAPHY

Barbagallo, Tricia, Cynthia Sauer, and John Warren. *A Historical Orientation to Albany, New York: Historic Crossroads, State Capital, and City of Neighborhoods*. Albany, NY: National Council on Public History, 1997.

Bielinksi, Stefan. *Government by the People: The Story of the Dongan Charter and the Birth of Participatory Democracy in the City of Albany*. Albany, NY: Albany Tricentennial Commission, 1986.

———. "A Middling Sort: Artisans and Tradesmen in Colonial Albany." *New York History* 73, no. 3 (July 1992) 261–290.

Howell, George R., and Jonathan Tenney, eds. *Bicentennial History of the County of Albany, N.Y. from 1609 to 1886*. Albany, NY: W. W. Munsell, 1886.

Munsell, Joel. *Annals of Albany*. 10 vols. Albany, NY: Munsell and Rowland, 1850–1871.

———. *Collections on the History of Albany*. 4 vols. Albany, NY: J. Munsell, 1876.

RICHMOND, VA 1790–1828

BETWEEN 1790 AND 1828, RICHMOND, VIRGINIA, EXPERIENCED SUBSTANTIAL EXPANSION of its population, geographical boundaries, and economy as it developed into a prominent commercial and political center. The capital of Virginia since 1780, Richmond's population stood at little more than one thousand people when it was incorporated in 1782, but within a decade around thirty-seven hundred people lived in the city. Forty years later, this figure had more than quadrupled to sixteen thousand, and the Richmond landscape had expanded to cover more than 2.4 square miles and evolved to reflect the city's growing political and economic status. The neoclassical state capitol, designed by Thomas Jefferson, was completed in 1798. An imposing state penitentiary, built in the west of the city, admitted its first prisoners in 1800. A striking city hall was constructed in 1816, and a new city jail followed within a decade. The city's first stage coach lines were founded in 1813, and steamboat services were inaugurated two years later, connecting Richmond to Manchester across the

QUICK FACTS

RICHMOND, VA **1790–1828**

MAYORS

Alexander Robert	(1789–1790)
Robert Boyd	(1790)
Robert Mitchell	(1790–1791)
John Barrett	(1791–1792)
Robert Mitchell	(1792–1793)
John Barrett	(1793–1794)
Robert Mitchell	(1794–1795)
Andrew Dunscomb	(1795–1796)
Robert Mitchell	(1796–1797)
James McClurg	(1797–1798)
John Barrett	(1798–1799)
George Nicholson	(1799–1800)
James McClurg	(1800–1801)
William Richardson	(1801–1802)
John Foster	(1802–1803)
James McClurg	(1803–1804)
Robert Mitchell	(1804–1805)
William DuVal	(1805–1806)
Edward Carrington	(1806–1810)
David Bullock	(1810–1811)
Benjamin Tate	(1811–1812)
Thomas Wilson	(1812–1813)
John Greenhow	(1813–1814)
Thomas Wilson	(1814–1815)
Robert Gamble	(1815–1816)
Thomas Wilson	(1816–1817)
William H. Fitzwhylson	(1817–1818)
Thomas Wilson	(1818)
Francis Wicker	(1818–1819)
John Adams	(1819–1826)
Joseph Tate	(1826–1839)

MAJOR INDUSTRIES AND EMPLOYERS

Flour milling
Iron manufacturing
Slave trading
Tobacco processing

MAJOR NEWSPAPERS

Richmond Commercial Compiler
Richmond Enquirer
Virginia Argus
Virginia Gazette and General Advertiser

MAJOR EVENTS

1800: A planned rebellion involving as many as one thousand slaves, led by the slave Gabriel, is uncovered and crushed by city and state authorities.

1802: The public guard is established to protect state buildings and aid in slave control.

1807: Aaron Burr, former vice president of the United States, stands trial in a federal court in Richmond and is charged with treason.

1811: A fire at the Richmond Theatre kills seventy-two people, including Virginia governor George W. Smith. Enslaved blacksmith Gilbert Hunt rescues a dozen people from the blaze.

1824: Revolutionary War hero General Lafayette visits Richmond and is feted throughout a week of celebrations.

James River. Lining the city's streets were banks, law firms, slave auction houses, and grog shops that were interspersed among residential properties. The city also boasted theatres, churches, a synagogue, and a museum. The riverfront was lined with flour mills, tobacco factories, and iron foundries.

At the heart of Richmond life was slavery. The city was not only a place where slaves lived and worked, it was a place that was shaped in its politics, economics, and social order by the significance of slavery as an institution throughout the state of Virginia. In this respect, Richmond was an unusual and almost unique urban location, for it was one of the few cities in the nation where slavery and manufacturing developed in a relationship of mutual dependence. Indeed, by 1828 Richmond stood on the brink of further expansion that would see it emerge as the sixth largest manufacturing center in the nation before the Civil War.

GOVERNMENT AND POLITICS

The Democratic-Republican Party of Jefferson, James Madison, and James Monroe controlled Virginia politics at the state level in the early national period, reflecting the regional power of the slaveholding planter class. Richmond, however, was a Federalist stronghold. Although many of the city's growing white artisanal class held Republican sympathies, the city government, which comprised a popularly elected common council of twelve men from whose number was chosen the city mayor, was mostly controlled by lawyers, merchants, and speculators who supported core elements of the Federalist platform. These elements included protective tariffs and government-sponsored internal improvements to protect and develop the nascent American economy. Even after the Federalists ceased to be a viable national party after the War of 1812, the Richmond electorate continued to buck the trend of Virginia state politics, and under the second party system the city routinely elected Whig candidates to local office even though Democrats controlled the state government.

As the Federalist capital of a state dominated by Democratic-Republicans, Richmond was a site of intense political conflict in the early national period. Partisan sentiment in and around the city was especially acute during the tumultuous election year of 1800. John Adams, a Federalist, was in the White House, and for two years his administration had pursued controversial policies that stopped just short of war with France and included on the domestic front the hugely unpopular Alien and Sedition Acts. Republicans perceived that the national government was overreaching its authority and threatening state liberties for partisan ends. Richmond became a focal point for their outrage when James Thomson Callender, a journalist, stood trial in the city in June 1800. Callender was charged with sedition for publishing anti-Federalist writings. Fears of Federalist domination were further fuelled by the stationing of a federal force of four hundred men close to Richmond, a move that Virginia governor James Monroe interpreted as evidence that the government planned to commandeer the city's federal armory. Republicans, however, were not unprepared for such an eventuality. In 1799 the Republican-controlled Virginia state government was accused by pro-Federalist newspapers in Richmond of preparing for an armed uprising when it imported large numbers of guns from Europe.

In any event, it was not partisan violence but the specter of slave rebellion that posed the most serious threat to Richmond's political establishment at the turn of the nineteenth century. In August 1800, the city's white society was shaken by news of an armed uprising organized by Gabriel, an enslaved African American blacksmith. Inspired by religious faith, the revolutionary rhetoric of the age, the ongoing slave rebellion in Saint-Domingue, and the party political divisions within the urban white community, Gabriel recruited hundreds of slaves to his cause and drew up a plan to plunder the state armory, seize control of Richmond, and capture white hostages whose lives he intended to trade for the freedom of himself and his followers. Gabriel's ambitious designs never came to fruition. Bad weather caused the attack to be postponed, and when one of the enslaved conspirators subsequently revealed the plot to a local white man, Governor Monroe initiated a brutal crackdown that resulted in the execution of Gabriel and twenty-six other rebel slaves.

State and municipal authorities responded to Gabriel's uprising by providing increased police protection for Richmond. A public guard of around one hundred men, armed with muskets and stationed permanently in the city, was established by Governor James Monroe in 1802 to patrol the state capitol, penitentiary, and armory and to supplement slave control in times of rebellion. The guardsmen also contributed to more routine policing of the urban slave population, a task for which Richmond's small night watch was ill equipped. Accusations of negligence and corruption plagued the night watch, and there were repeated calls to increase the number of watchmen. However, as with other aspects of city government, these were usually trumped by concerns about cost, and during the 1820s municipal spending on policing fell.

Law enforcement was a major function of the city council. The mayor, city recorder, and aldermen held a Hustings Court (the equivalent of a county court for towns and cities in Virginia) to try misdemeanor cases in the city, and in 1825 the mayor also took control of the night watch. Substantial police reforms, including the establishment of a day police force, did not occur until the 1830s, however. The council's record in other public services was mixed; few roads were paved and gas street lighting was not introduced until the 1850s, but early in the nineteenth century Richmond established one of the South's first poorhouses, mainly for poor whites, which also served as a public hospital and later encompassed a public burial ground. By the early 1820s, the city government additionally funded outdoor relief for more than two hundred residents, though it struggled to finance this expense. Other services were primarily provided by private or benevolent institutions, such as the Mutual Assurance Society against Fire in Buildings, founded in 1794, and the Lancastrian School.

INDUSTRY, COMMERCE, AND LABOR

A felicitous location at the falls line of the James River facilitated both commercial and, later, industrial economic growth in Richmond. The city was originally established as a trading post in the 1640s, and mercantile activities remained an integral part of the Richmond economy into the nineteenth century. During this period the city provided facilities for the storage and sale of goods produced on tidewater plantations and across the Virginia interior. At the same time, the waterpower generated by the James River rapids, combined with the easy access that Richmond enjoyed to the eastern Virginia coal deposits, helped provide for the development of milling and manufacturing enterprises in the city.

In the early national era, Richmond's economy developed in accordance with the changing demands and interests of rural Virginia, as well as in response to and in conjunction with national and transatlantic markets. When the U.S. economy flourished, Richmond invariably prospered, yet it was equally susceptible to the frequent periods of economic instability that plagued the United States in the early decades after the Revolutionary War. The 1810s, and more specifically the years immediately after the War of 1812, were a prosperous time in the city. In the wake of heavy investment from speculators, the value of city lots and buildings soared, as did the price of tobacco. Richmond's prosperity was short lived, however, and with the nationwide panic of 1819 the city entered a period of depression that saw property values halve, and from which recovery had scarcely begun by the end of the 1820s.

At the state level, as Virginia farms and plantations that traditionally had been used to grow tobacco were increasingly turned over to the cultivation of wheat and grain in the late eighteenth century, Richmond's merchant class and investors responded accordingly. In the 1790s major flour mills were established, including the Haxall Mills and the Gallego Mills that within decades would be among the largest in the world. In turn, demand from the mills and surrounding plantation regions, and later from ironworks and other factories, encouraged the growth of subsidiary industries such as transportation and the supply and repair of machinery. European immigrants were among the founders of some of Richmond's earliest and most important manufacturing enterprises, and French, German, Irish, and Scottish settlers also contributed to the growth of a substantial class of white workers and artisans in the city in the early nineteenth century. This development, however, was tempered and complicated by the reliance of many Richmond businesses on the labor of African American slaves. By the 1830s, tobacco factories and flour mills employed hundreds of slaves, and thousands more toiled in stores and dockyards or on ships and building sites. Many others served as cooks and house servants.

While Richmond's economic success was closely tied to the demands of Virginia agriculture and the availability of slave labor, the strength of rural slaveholding interests in state politics also compromised urban growth, notably by hindering internal improvements and restricting the availability of credit. The first bank was chartered in the city in 1804, and by 1828 Richmond was home to the headquarters of both the Bank of Virginia and the Farmer's Bank, as well as an office of the Second Bank of the United States. Nonetheless, a majority of white Virginians concurred with the Jeffersonian view that the banking system was unconstitutional, immoral, and a source of corruption in American life, and overall credit supplies remained limited. Most Virginians were similarly antagonistic toward manufacturing, and the state failed to support internal improvements that might have enabled Richmond to keep pace with the many towns and cities across the northern states that far outstripped it in terms of economic development. George Washington had recognized the importance that transportation links to the West would play in Richmond's economic future as early as the 1780s, and in 1784 the James River Navigation Company had been chartered with the aim of constructing a canal to connect Richmond to the Ohio River. The first sections of the canal were built in the 1790s, but by 1820 little progress had been made and the company was bought out by the state government. Over the next fifteen years, Virginia invested more than $1 million in the canal, but as late as the Civil War it remained incomplete. While larger cities to the north, such as New York City and Philadelphia and Pittsburgh in Pennsylvania, benefited from extensive state-sponsored internal improvements, Richmond's national economic standing plummeted, stymied by the political power of Virginia's agrarian interests.

RACE, ETHNICITY, AND IMMIGRATION

African Americans comprised approximately 50 percent of Richmond's population in the early national era. Most black men and women in Richmond were slaves, but approximately one in five was free, and the anonymity of the urban environment and the demands for a flexible and mobile labor force in the city were such that many were able to forge a significant degree of independence in their working and personal lives. Owners routinely required their slaves to move about the city to run errands, buy and sell goods, collect and deliver merchandise, or simply to travel from their living quarters to the factories, stores, and dockyards where so many worked. By 1830 hundreds of slaves in the city were hired out to persons besides their owners, sometimes on one-year contracts, but often under more sporadic and short-term arrangements. This enabled slaveholders to maximize the returns from their investments in human property, and it provided a means for city merchants and manufacturers to meet what were often changeable and short-term labor needs without engaging in the high-cost commitment of slave ownership. Yet the hiring of slaves also had unsettling implications for white Virginians. Although self-hire was prohibited by law in the early 1800s, many slaves in Richmond were permitted to negotiate terms of hire that, in the most advantageous of cases, could include the payment of wages and even the right to live independently.

Slaves, free African Americans, and poor whites formed an interracial subculture in Richmond that could be violent and racist. However, it was also based on a degree of friendship and even intimacy that developed in the workplaces and grog shops and on the streets and entered into the private sphere of the home and the bedroom. African Americans were subject to strict controls in the city. Hundreds were arrested each year and sentenced by the mayor to be whipped for offenses including drunkenness, keeping a disorderly house, illegal assembly, and even suspicious conduct. Furthermore, African Americans who were freed from slavery after the passage of new legislation in 1806 could be arrested and re-enslaved if they remained in Virginia more than twelve months after obtaining their liberty. By the mid-1820s, this was also the fate proscribed for free African Americans convicted of noncapital felonies. For both enslaved and free African Americans, therefore, Richmond was a city where black autonomy was always temporary, fragile, and subject to brutal repression.

The complexities and vulnerability of black life in Richmond were encapsulated in African Americans' experiences of religion and the church. By 1824 the First Baptist Church had a majority black membership among its eight-hundred-strong congregation, as well as black deacons and preachers. The church served as an important meeting place for African Americans, a source of black community leadership, and the basis for black-controlled institutions such as the African Burial Ground Society and the African Missionary Society, both founded in 1815. Even so, for many black Richmond residents the church spurred flight from the city rather than progress within it. In the 1820s about one hundred free blacks, representing some of the city's best-educated and most-skilled black families, left Richmond for Liberia. One of the migrants was Lott Cary, a Richmond slave who converted to Christianity and became a member of the First Baptist Church before buying his own freedom and assuming a leading role in the founding of the city's African Missionary Society. Cary sailed for Liberia in 1821 and remained a leading advocate of colonization until his death seven years later.

The exodus of free African Americans from Richmond in the 1820s was more than just a response to the conditions of black life in the city, but it was nonetheless a reflection of the oppression, violence, and instability that characterized the black experience even in a place that simultaneously offered opportunities and freedoms that were unknown to African Americans throughout most of the South. Over the following decade, the situation would deteriorate further as new laws to restrict the rights of all African Americans were introduced in the wake of Nat Turner's slave rebellion in Southampton County, Virginia, in 1831. Yet, at the same time, the reality of race relations on the street of Richmond grew ever more complex as industrial expansion exacerbated class and ethnic divisions among the city's whites in ways that challenged the primacy of race to the social order.

JAMES CAMPBELL

BIBLIOGRAPHY

Dabney, Virginius. *Richmond: The Story of a City*. New York, NY: Doubleday, 1976.

Green, Elna C. *The Business of Relief: Confronting Poverty in a Southern City, 1740–1940*. Athens: University of Georgia Press, 2003.

Kimball, Gregg D. *American City, Southern Place: A Cultural History of Antebellum Richmond*. Athens: University of Georgia Press, 2000.

Mordecai, Samuel. *Richmond in By-Gone Days*. Richmond, VA: George M. West, 1856.

Rothman, Joshua. *Notorious in the Neighborhood: Sex and Families across the Color Line in Virginia, 1787–1861*. Chapel Hill: University of North Carolina Press, 2003.

Sheldon, Marianne B. "Black-White Relations in Richmond, Virginia, 1782–1820." *Journal of Southern History* 45 (1979): 27–44.

Sidury, James. *Ploughshares into Swords: Race, Rebellion, and Identity in Gabriel's Virginia, 1730–1810*. New York, NY: Cambridge University Press, 1997.

Takagi, Midori. *"Rearing Wolves to Our Own Destruction": Slavery in Richmond, Virginia, 1782–1865*. Charlottesville: University Press of Virginia, 2002.

Whitman, T. Stephen. *Challenging Slavery in the Chesapeake: Black and White Resistance to Human Bondage, 1775–1865*. Baltimore: Maryland Historical Society, 2007.

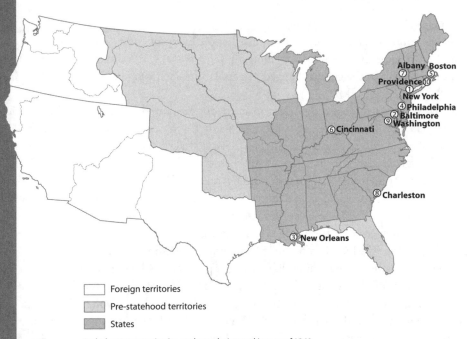

Albany Boston
⑦ ⑤
Providence⑩
① New York
④ Philadelphia
② Baltimore
⑨ Washington
⑥ Cincinnati

⑧ Charleston

③ New Orleans

☐ Foreign territories
▨ Pre-statehood territories
▨ States

Includes states, territories, and population rankings as of 1840

CHAPTER 3

CITIES IN THE AGE OF JACKSON, 1828–1854

In the quarter century covered in this chapter, the United States expanded across the continent through four major land acquisitions, and six additional states were admitted into the Union. The Erie Canal was completed in 1825, and, largely as a result, the 1830 census marked the first time that a northwestern city, Cincinnati, Ohio, was counted among the country's ten largest cities. The 1830s also saw the introduction of some of the first railroads, and, by the 1850s, the telegraph was poised to revolutionize long-distance communication. The period was also one of rapid industrialization fueled by a growing population, the increased use of coal as a power source, the development of interchangeable parts in manufacturing machinery, and new inventions such as the sewing machine.

In 1830, of the approximately 12.9 million people living in the United States, nearly 9 percent lived in communities with populations greater than twenty-five hundred. By 1854 the country's population had roughly doubled to approximately twenty-seven million, and the percent of those people living in communities with over twenty-five hundred persons had increased to more than 15 percent. According to the 1850 census, the ten largest cities in the country ranged in population size from 515,547 (New York City) to 50,763 (Albany, New York).

Nearly six hundred thousand immigrants came to the United States in the 1830s, which was more than had arrived in any previous decade. Nearly three times as many arrived in the 1840s, and the numbers increased dramatically in the 1850s as well. A hostile response to the new immigrants took organizational form in the Native American Association—the Know-Nothings—founded in 1837 and organized formally into the American Party for the 1854 midterm elections. In these elections the party had significant victories in the northeastern states and briefly became a major party in the U.S. House of Representatives.

The electoral success of the Know-Nothings was part of a revolution in popular democracy, the beginning of which is often dated to Andrew Jackson's election as president in 1828. The newer states entering the Union disavowed property and poll tax requirements for suffrage, and the older states followed suit. With the expansion of suffrage came the increased power of political parties, as those organizations could organize the new mass of voters. The parties themselves were democratized through the establishment of the presidential nominating convention, first used by the Democrats in 1832. The Whig Party, established in reaction to the Jacksonian democracy and led by Henry Clay, John Calhoun, and Daniel Webster, generally supported commercial and industrial development and a stronger federal government. The Democrats, by contrast, supported greater western expansion and states' rights.

Despite Democrats' generally stronger support for states' rights, Jackson defended federal supremacy against the position, argued most effectively by Calhoun, that states had the right to nullify federal laws they deemed unconstitutional. Calhoun argued for nullification specifically with regard to the national tariff that he believed harmful to his beloved home state, South Carolina (though he was known to dislike Charleston). A second major issue during Jackson's first term in office was the role of the Second Bank of the United States, headquartered in Philadelphia, Pennsylvania, and led by stalwart Philadelphia aristocrat Nicholas Biddle. The bank's charter was up for renewal in 1836, and Jackson, as a states' rights advocate, was inclined to let its charter lapse. Henry Clay ran for president against Jackson in 1832 on the platform that he would save the bank. Jackson was reelected, however, and he withdrew all federal deposits from the bank and declined to renew its charter.

Jackson's opponents blamed his decision regarding the bank for being at least partly responsible for the financial panic of 1837 and the ensuing depression that largely defined the presidency of Jackson's chosen successor, Martin Van Buren. Van Buren did little to mitigate the depression, and he thus lost the 1840 election to Whig candidate William Harrison. Harrison died after his first month in office and was succeeded by vice president John Tyler, a former Democrat. Repudiated by the Whigs after he vetoed internal improvement bills, Tyler ran for president as a third-party candidate in 1844 but ultimately withdrew in support of Democratic candidate James Polk. Polk supported western expansion, particularly the annexation of Texas. However, it was Tyler who accomplished the annexation of Texas in his last year in office, while Polk negotiated with Britain for the Oregon territory and entered into a war

BY THE NUMBERS: **THE MOST POPULOUS CITIES IN 1840**							
	TOTAL POPULATION	WHITE POPULATION	FREE "COLORED" POPULATION	SLAVE POPULATION	% FREE POPULATION	% SLAVE POPULATION	NUMBER EMPLOYED IN MANUFAC- TURES AND TRADES	% OF THE WHITE POPULATION LITERATE
NEW YORK, NY	312,710	296,352	16,358	0	100.0	0.0	43,390	95.3
BALTIMORE, MD	102,313	81,147	17,967	3,199	96.9	3.1	8,847	97.2
NEW ORLEANS, LA	102,193	59,519	19,226	23,448	77.1	22.9	4,593	99.5
PHILADELPHIA, PA	93,665	83,158	10,507	0	100.0	0.0	8,917	97.7
BOSTON, MA	93,383	90,956	2,427	0	100.0	0.0	5,333	97.7
CINCINNATI, OH	46,338	44,098	2,240	0	100.0	0.0	10,287	98.8
ALBANY, NY	33,721	32,835	886	0	100.0	0.0	1,621	97.3
CHARLESTON, SC	29,261	13,030	1,558	14,673	49.9	50.1	1,025	99.9
WASHINGTON, DC	23,364	16,843	4,808	1,713	92.7	7.3	886	95.7
PROVIDENCE, RI	23,171	21,869	1,301	1	100.0	0.0	3,948	93.7

Note: This list does not include Brooklyn City, NY; Northern Liberties, PA; Spring Garden, PA; or Southwark, PA. See introduction for details.

Source: Census for 1840. Enumeration of the Inhabitants and Statistics of the United States, as Obtained at the Department of State, from the Returns of the Sixth Census.

with Mexico. The war resulted in a treaty in which Mexico ceded much of its territory to the United States in 1848.

With westward expansion came the entry of new states into the Union, and each one threatened to disrupt the balance of power in the Senate between the free and slave states. Members of Congress from the free states proposed that slavery be prohibited in any states formed from the land acquired from Mexico, while those from slave states contended that slave owners should have the right to move with their property wherever they pleased. As both presidential candidates in 1848 (Zachary Taylor for the Whigs and Lewis Cass for the Democrats) avoided the issue during their campaigns, antislavery interests formed the Free-Soil Party and chose Martin Van Buren as their candidate.

Taylor won the 1848 election, and by the time of his inauguration, the population of California had swelled as a result of the gold rush, ultimately turning what had been a small town founded by Spanish soldiers and priests in 1776 into the city of San Francisco (covered in chapters 4 and 5 of this book). Taylor requested Congress admit California as a free state in 1849. As members of Congress negotiated a deal to allow this by providing concessions to the slave states such as a stronger fugitive slave law, Taylor died and Millard Fillmore became president.

The Whig Party was increasingly divided over the issue of slavery, and many of its former members defected to the Free-Soil Party, especially in New York and Ohio. Thus, though he likely would have lost regardless, the presence of a Free-Soil candidate (John Hale) in the 1852 presidential election hurt the Whigs, whose candidate, Winfield Scott, lost to Franklin Pierce. Pierce was inaugurated as president of a country increasingly divided over the issue of slavery, especially after Stephen Douglas, a U.S. senator representing Illinois, in an effort to facilitate a northern route for the transcontinental railroad, pressed to introduce Nebraska as a new state into the Union. As Nebraska was north of the line dividing free and slave territory that was agreed upon in the 1820 Missouri Compromise, Douglas negotiated that the compromise line would be repealed, that the Nebraska territory would be divided into two states (Kansas and Nebraska), and that the residents of both prospective states would decide in elections whether or not the states would be free or slave. The Kansas-Nebraska Act, as it came to be known, was deeply unpopular in the North, and it split the Whig Party apart. In 1854 both former Whigs and Democrats who were antislavery formed the Republican Party, which in that same year won enough seats in the House of Representatives that it allied with the American Party to form a majority in that chamber. This ushered in a new party era and set the stage for the Civil War.

NEW YORK, NY 1828–1854

AMERICAN HISTORIANS OFTEN ASSERT THAT THE ERA OF THE COMMON MAN began in 1828 with the election of Andrew Jackson. The victory of Old Hickory, however, was no harbinger of political peace. Jackson was not a uniter; he hated abolitionists, banks, Indians, and opposition and happily wielded executive authority. Despite the many New York supporters of Jackson's policies, the newly formed Whig Party closely contested all Manhattan elections for the next generation. The city suffered from the long economic depression that began in 1837, yet it grew increasingly dominant as industrial production replaced its artisan economy. Waves of new immigrants flooded the city, and the government's role expanded to improve urban services, prevent ethnic violence, and provide jobs. Tammany Hall allied itself with the newcomers and emerged as the prime political organization in America's metropolis. Its wealth and population made New York the logical choice to host the first world's fair held in the United States (1853–1854). Over one million people came to marvel at America's mechanical genius and the city that best embodied its ambitions.

GOVERNMENT AND POLITICS

New York politics had been dominated by business and social elites for two centuries before the "common man" rose to power in 1828. Although remnants of elite authority remained influential for decades, the tone of city politics changed in the 1830s as workingmen's parties agitated for greater democracy and economic justice. Gradually, popular demands were incorporated into city law as imprisonment for debt and mechanic lien laws were abolished in 1831 and 1832, respectively; payment for members of the city council and single member districts was established; the use of prison labor ended; and tax levies increased for schools. The General Trades Union was formed in 1833 and, though it failed to immediately achieve a ten-hour workday or the right to unionize, it did succeed in pressuring the government for reform. In 1834 Manhattan voters elected their mayor for the first time, sending Democrat Cornelius Van Wyck Lawrence to city hall. In a foretaste of future competitions, however, voters selected a Whig city council.

QUICK FACTS

NEW YORK, NY 1828–1854

MAYORS

William Paulding	(1827–1829)
Walter Browne	(1829–1833)
Gideon Lee	(1833–1834)
Cornelius Lawrence	(1834–1837)
Aaron Clark	(1837–1839)
Isaac Varian	(1839–1841)
Robert Morris	(1841–1844)
James Harper	(1844–1845)
William Havemeyer	(1845–1846)
Andrew Mickle	(1846–1847)
William Brady	(1847–1848)
William Havemeyer	(1848–1849)
Caleb Woodhull	(1849–1851; first two-year mayor under 1849 charter reform)
Ambrose Kingsland	(1851–1853)
Jacob Westervelt	(1853–1855)

MAJOR INDUSTRIES AND EMPLOYERS

Shipbuilding (one thousand workers employed in twenty yards)

U.S. Customs House (750 government employees)

Harper Brothers (350 printing employees, 250 salesmen)

Devlin and Company (350 clothing employees)

Shoemaking

MAJOR NEWSPAPERS

New York Evening Post
New York Morning Post
New-York American, for the Country
New York Journal of Commerce
New York Daily Whig
New York Evening Express
New York Gazette and General Advertiser
Daily News
Freedom's Journal
Working Man's Advocate
Free Enquirer
Penny Press
Transcript and Wasp
True National Democrat and Morning Star
True Sun
Truth
New York Arena
New Yorker Staats-Zeitung
New York Transcript
Washingtonian Daily News
Weekly Advocate
New York Sun
New York Morning Herald
New York Herald
Courier and Enquirer
New York Herald
New York Standard
New York Statesman
New York Times

MAJOR EVENTS

1834: Jacksonian Democrat Cornelius Van Wyck Lawrence defeats Gulian Verplanck by 174 votes in New York's first direct mayoral election.

December 16–17, 1835: A great fire devastates the East Side of Manhattan, destroying a quarter of the business district (seven hundred buildings) and incinerating the last remnants of Dutch New Amsterdam.

October 14, 1842: The Croton System begins operation. Designed by Charles King, it provides the city with clean drinking water, makes indoor plumbing possible, and eliminates most epidemic threats.

May 10, 1849: In Astor Place, a riot spurred by the rival appearances of competing Shakespearean actors, one British and one American, results in twenty-two deaths.

July 14, 1853: America's first world's fair begins as the Crystal Palace, topped by a dome 123 feet high, opens at Fortieth Street and Sixth Avenue.

Popular voting inaugurated a generation of chaotic city elections. After a brief period of independent existence, labor parties were undermined by economic decline that began in 1836 and lasted for a decade. During this time the supporters of the labor parties were incorporated into the major parties. Democrats emerged as the major city party, but their unity was fragile and shattered by successive factional disputes between Locofocos, Spartans, Tammany Hall, Barnburners, Hunkers, and Mozart Hall. Whigs, who organized originally to oppose the "dictatorship" of Jackson, proved almost equally self-destructive. Over the next twenty years, Democrats won twelve of eighteen mayoral races, the Whigs five, and the American Republicans (the nativist party) one. In retrospect, the most important development of these years was the gradual emergence of Tammany Hall as the primary Democratic force in Manhattan. Tammany built its political clubhouse on Nassau Street in 1812, and its leaders learned to accommodate voter concerns. The hall overcame its initial disdain for immigrants and built alliances with Irish ward leaders such as Constantine Donaho and Felix O'Neil. It also empowered labor advocates such as Mike Walsh. Despite some setbacks for good government—the Democratic council that served from 1851–1853 was known as the "Forty Thieves"—Tammany learned how to govern a city that was nearing 750,000 in population. After a reform movement led by Peter Cooper expelled the "Forty Thieves," Democrats elected Fernando Wood as mayor in November 1854. Wood was a rich rogue who bonded with Manhattan's Irish and German voters and became their "model mayor."

Democracy meant that voter concerns in America's metropolis were heeded by politicians. After the fire of December 1835 swept through Manhattan, reconstruction was funded almost immediately. Yellow fever and cholera plagues had long ravaged the city, the latter having killed four thousand New Yorkers in 1832, and quarantine and health codes were expanded. When the Croton Water System opened on October 14, 1842, Manhattan residents enjoyed the finest drinking water in the nation. The sewer system begun in 1849 materially improved public health by getting hogs off the streets. Manhattan's appalling death rate fell from one in twenty-seven (1840) to one in forty (1855). Mayor James Harper authorized the formation of a municipal police force in 1845, and his successor, William Havemeyer, made the department work. Havemeyer also instituted garbage collection.

Harper's civil servant list numbered 3,691 persons, from one mayor to ninety lamplighters to 976 watchmen, but Manhattan's expanding services demanded an ever greater bureaucracy. New York's amended city charter of 1849 created ten city departments and increased patronage jobs. Every politician advocated major improvement, one example of which was the Harlem High Bridge that completed the Croton System in 1849. Mayor Ambrose Kingsland, who tolerated the depredations of the "Forty Thieves," committed Manhattan to the construction of Central Park, the greatest public art project of the century. Even potential voters were worthy of consideration; in 1855 Castle Clinton, which had served the city as a fort and a theatrical venue, was transformed into an immigrant reception center.

Economic decline and the growing number of immigrants in the city complicated administrative problems. Hunger accompanied the serious depression that began in 1837 and caused the "flour riot." Newcomers turned Five Points into a gang-ridden slum, and Charles Dickens recorded his distasteful visit there in *American Notes*. Competing factions used gangs to control

A great fire in December 1835 swept across Manhattan's East Side, burning hundreds of buildings and erasing architectural remnants of colonial Dutch architecture.   *Source: Library of Congress*

voting, and each city election carried the possibility of violence. It was ethnic tension, not theater criticism, which led to bloodshed at Astor Place in May 1849. From 1845 to 1855, Manhattan doubled in population, with half its residents now foreign-born. Most Americans and even many New Yorkers considered such a huge, diffuse city to be ungovernable. It was Tammany that mastered the art of mobilizing ethnic voters and providing them with a stake in the city. The hall turned politics into a profession and provided the leaders, from Havemeyer to Wood to "Boss" Tweed, who confirmed Manhattan's standing as America's only world metropolis.

During this period New York's growing neighbor, Brooklyn, ranked among the most populous cities in the country. Brooklyn developed separately but in tandem with New York City, and both had roots in colonial New Amsterdam. In 1834 Brooklyn's city charter was granted, and the installation of gas (1848) and horse railroad (1854) systems soon followed. By 1855 the adjoining towns of Williamsburg and Bushwick were annexed, and Brooklyn, with a population of 205,000, became the third largest city in the United States. Among its greatest attractions were Greenwood Cemetery, where prominent Manhattanites were buried; its elegant city hall, designed by carpenter Gamaliel King; the nation's most famous preacher (Henry Ward Beecher of Plymouth Church); and the vast Havemeyer sugar factory along the East River.

INDUSTRY, COMMERCE, AND LABOR

New York's preeminent position in domestic and international trade and commerce continued to grow from 1828 to 1854. Statistics show the city handled 58 percent of American imports in the 1830s, 60 percent in the 1840s, and 65 percent in the 1850s. Equally impressive, the city's share of exports rose from 26 percent to 33 percent. In 1830 it had more ships at sea than the rest of the nation combined and built the greatest amount of tonnage at its fourteen shipyards. One thousand ships from 150 ports approached Manhattan through the Narrows in 1835. Building America's finest vessels was a New York specialty; its shipwrights built the yacht *America* and the clipper ships (*Rainbow*, *Sea Witch*, *Flying Cloud*) that were the fastest boats in the world from 1840 until the Civil War.

In 1838 the city established steamship routes to British, French, and German cities and soon offered service to Cuba and Panama. Cunard Lines found it expedient to relocate its offices to Manhattan in 1839 because New York had seized yet another portion of world trade. Andrew Jackson's destruction of the Second Bank of the United States allowed city bankers to supplant Philadelphia as the money center of the nation by 1840. Business loans made by Manhattan's 152 banks in 1846 fueled entrepreneurial initiatives from international trade to retail stores to manufacturing. In 1852, 80 percent of United States federal revenue was collected on city docks.

The adaptability of city businessmen also raised Manhattan to manufacturing primacy. Its republican craft system of production had brought prosperity before the Erie Canal opened, yet after 1825 the city developed what historian Sean Wilentz has described as a "bastard artisan" system. Manhattan entrepreneurs never built huge factories but cut manufacturing costs by subdividing work, contracting out stages of production, and exploiting labor. Great fortunes were made in specific industries (Peter Cooper in glue and metals, James Allaire in ship engines, William Colgate in soap, William Havemeyer in sugar refining), but in 1854 the bulk of city hiring was still done by small proprietors. Fully one-third of these enterprises were German owned and a fifth were Irish, and they produced clothing, shoes, furniture, pianos, jewelry, tools, musical instruments, artificial flowers, and other goods for the nation. Fine craft work was never eliminated from Manhattan, it was simply relegated to secondary status as four thousand workplaces produced an immense diversity of products for world and domestic consumption. The most productive part of the city was still the downtown Second Ward, which employed 15 percent of city laborers, but every ward in the expanding city contained scores of workshops that employed twenty to thirty persons who coordinated webs of outworkers. Although no more than 3.7 percent of Manhattan workers were ever employed in "heavy" industry, the city produced 8 percent of all American manufactures by 1855.

Mastery of the oceans and the creation of a new manufacturing paradigm joined with New York's access to the agricultural wealth of the United States to solidify its economic supremacy. Manhattan's docks were the fulcrum of the "cotton triangle" and the Erie Canal brought Midwestern produce to the city. The agricultural revolution of the 1830s, fostered by the development of Cyrus McCormick's reaper in 1831 and John Deere's steel plow in 1837, increased grain production immensely, but canal flow towards Manhattan was halted in winter. When the Erie

Railroad completed tracks to Buffalo, New York, in 1851, however, even this seasonal decline was erased.

Every American innovation seemed to enhance Manhattan's domination. In New York the "penny press" was created with the publication of Benjamin Day's *New York Sun* in 1833. Its appearance was quickly followed by the *Transcript* in 1834 and the *Herald* in 1835. Led by publishers such as Harper Brothers, the city replaced Boston, Massachusetts, as the leader of the American printing industry. The appearance of the *New York Tribune* in 1841 and the *New York Times* in 1851 provided Manhattan with two of the world's great newspapers. The creation of Elias Howe's sewing machine in 1846 facilitated the outsourcing of piecework and produced both the sweatshop and garment industries. Migration to the city provided the cheap labor force that mass-manufacturing techniques needed. Horace Greeley, editor of the *Tribune*, declared in 1845 that two-thirds of New Yorkers lived on $1 a week—a conclusion published even before a new influx of impoverished immigrants entered the city. The harsh fact was that the panic of 1837 and the depression that followed destroyed New York's labor movement. A series of strikes in 1850–1851 signaled a brief revival, but the return of hard times in 1854 kept labor subservient. By 1850 the poet Nathaniel Willis could write that an "Upper 10,000" controlled the destiny of the city.

After 1800 the farms and businesses of Brooklyn provided provisions, workers, and manufacturing sites for a growing Manhattan. Ferry service had always connected the two shores, but Robert Fulton's steam ferry, built in 1814, provided such transportation reliability that it spurred an exodus of rich New Yorkers to land free of city clamor. Brooklyn Heights became America's first suburb, a development featuring fabulous vistas of Manhattan. After the Erie Canal opened in 1825, ropeworks, slaughterhouses, breweries, and docks quickly dotted the shoreline of the Village of Brooklyn and increased its prosperity.

RACE, ETHNICITY, AND IMMIGRATION

The abolition of slavery in 1827 legitimized a black community that had been essential to Manhattan life for two centuries. Although their numbers continued to decline, blacks initiated the springtime celebration of Pinkster in the 1830s, and during its revelry a black "king" presided over a carnival that featured African music. Blacks and Irish comprised the lowest tier of Manhattan's working class but lived together peacefully in the Five Points during this period; they even merged their traditional rhythms to create tap dancing. A prominent community leader of the time was the Reverend Peter Williams of St. Philips Episcopal, but an anti-abolitionist mob destroyed his church in 1834. Blacks continued to decline in absolute and proportionate numbers, and job tensions with new immigrants increased their isolation. Many moved to the northern reaches of Manhattan to escape contact with whites.

The greatest ethnic change in Manhattan during this period was the emergence of Irish Catholics as a major city force. During the 1830s over two hundred thousand Irish arrived in the United States through New York's port, and many of them stayed to change city politics. Before this influx, Protestant leaders had dominated the Irish community. The newcomers were Catholic, poorer, and less educated. New York counted ninety thousand Irish Catholics by 1845, and to serve their needs the Ancient Order of Hibernians (1836), the Irish Emigrant Society (1841), and a dozen more parish churches were organized. Transfiguration Parish was established in 1836 in the Five Points, and Manhattan's "Bloody Ould Sixth" ward ranked as the largest Irish community in America.

Bishop John Hughes ministered to this growing flock and attempted to combat the tide of prejudice they encountered. As early as 1834 "American" mobs fought the Five Points Irish in Election Day battles, and in 1840 Samuel F. B. Morse ran for mayor on a nativist platform. Morse lost, but "No Irish Need Apply" signs became common in Manhattan as newcomers sought to enter its crowded job market. Hughes believed that the arriving Irish needed education, but the Public School Society was dominated by Protestant clerics who were not above proselytizing. From 1839 to 1842, Hughes demanded but failed to obtain state funding for Catholic schools. In response the inventive bishop founded two colleges and initiated a parochial school system. When city voters elected James Harper on a nativist platform in 1844, Hughes almost despaired; he informed officials that if mobs attacked any of his churches New York would become "another Moscow." Although Harper's prejudiced views made him mayor, his political ineptness limited him to one term. He created a police department that was corrupt and whose members refused to wear uniforms, and he alienated voters by attempting to limit liquor sales on Independence Day. The election in 1845 of a Democratic mayor dependent on Irish votes signaled a permanent change in politics; in a very short time Irish cops patrolled Manhattan streets.

In 1845 the first waves of Irish fleeing the famine in their country began to arrive on New York's wharves. The flood became so great that it almost overwhelmed Hughes, who in 1849 opened St. Vincent's Hospital to treat the poor. By 1855, 85 percent of New York laborers and 75 percent of its domestic servants were Irish, as were most of the felons and prostitutes in the city. Aided by Tammany Hall, many became naturalized citizens, and in 1854 Fernando Wood became mayor of an electorate that was only half native-born. Irishmen comprised fully one-fourth of the total city population. They included an elite class led by retailers like A. T. Stewart and Daniel Devlin, a middle class, and those dwelling in the slums of the Five Points.

The Irish dominated the central wards of Manhattan, but eastward towards the river German immigrants built *Kleindeutschland*. Newcomers from Prussia to Bavaria clustered in a neighborhood that later would be known as the Lower East Side. Catholics, Lutherans, and Jews lived there in harmony and were aided by the Leiderkrantz Society, founded in 1847; German newspapers such as the *Staats-Zeitung*; and the German Society, found jobs for them from Manhattan to the Midwest. German artisans dominated the cabinetmaking and upholstery sectors of the city economy. They also built beer gardens that served happy customers along the East River. Moreover, German farmers developed a local industry in northern Manhattan and Brooklyn that supplied city tables for half a century. Germans comprised the third largest immigrant population in the city in 1854, trailing only the English and the Irish, and they often seemed the most content.

Immigration fundamentally altered New York from 1828 to 1854 and made it a diverse metropolis. Compassionate concern for less-fortunate citizens had always characterized New York, and an 1853 city directory listed twenty-two asylums, eight hospitals, seven medical dispensaries, ninety benevolent societies, and seventy-five benefit societies that continued the tradition.

The city was the richest in the nation, yet it had the largest number of poor people. It was a conglomerate of different groups who somehow managed to live together. In 1856 *Harper's Monthly Magazine* celebrated its uniqueness: New York is "notoriously the largest and least loved" city for "it is never the same city for a dozen years together." The modern image of Manhattan was clearly established during these decades.

See also *New York, NY 1776–1790; New York, NY 1790–1828; New York, NY 1854–1877; New York, NY 1877–1896; New York, NY 1896–1929; New York, NY 1929–1941; New York, NY 1941–1952; New York, NY 1952–1989; New York, NY 1989–2011*

GEORGE LANKEVICH

BIBLIOGRAPHY

Anbinder, Tyler. *Five Points: The Nineteenth-Century Neighborhood that Invented Tap Dance, Stole Elections and became the World's Most Notorious Slum*. New York, NY: Penguin Putnam, 2002.

Bridges, Amy. *A City in the Republic: Antebellum New York and the Origins of Machine Politics*. New York, NY: Cambridge University Press, 1987.

Ernst, Robert. *Immigrant Life in New York City, 1825–1863*. New York, NY: the King's Crown Press, 1949.

Nevins, Allan, ed. *The Diary of Philip Hone, 1828–1851*. New York, NY: Dodd Mead, 1936.

Pessen, Edward. *Riches, Class and Power before the Civil War*. Lexington, MA: Heath, 1973.

Spann, Edward K. *The New Metropolis: New York, 1840–1857*. New York, NY: Columbia University Press, 1981.

Wilentz, Sean. *Chants Democratic: New York City and the Rise of the American Working Class, 1788–1850*. New York, NY: Oxford University Press, 1984.

BALTIMORE, MD 1828–1854

ANTEBELLUM BALTIMORE WAS A SEMIPROFESSIONAL CITY. It had a police force that worked during the day, and after dark the night watch took over. In 1834 the city created the Baltimore United Fire Department, but it was only a conglomeration of volunteer fire companies that continued to engage one another in gang violence. The city's water was supplied by a private company whose service extended only to those neighborhoods that yielded a profit until the city finally purchased it in 1854. Baltimoreans were moving gradually toward a sense of their collective identity as an urban public with a full-time government.

GOVERNMENT AND POLITICS

Internal improvements became a preoccupation in Baltimore during the 1820s. The country's population was moving west beyond the reach of saltwater shipping. In the competition for

QUICK FACTS

BALTIMORE, MD **1828–1854**

MAYORS

Jacob Small	(1826–1831)
William Steuart	(1831–1832)
Jesse Hunt	(1832–1835)
Samuel Smith	(1835–1838)
Sheppard C. Leakin	(1838–1840)
Samuel Brady	(1840–1842)
James O. Law	(1843–1844)
Jacob G. Davies	(1844–1848)
Elijah Stansbury Jr.	(1848–1850)
John Hanson Thomas Jerome	(1850–1852)
John Smith Hollins	(1852–1854)

MAJOR INDUSTRIES AND EMPLOYERS

Cotton textiles
Ironworks and copper refining
Railroad locomotives, cars, rail, and hardware
Brickmaking
Chemicals (alum, chrome, copper sulfate)

MAJOR NEWSPAPERS

The Baltimore Sun
The American
Baltimore Clipper (later *The American Republican*)
Niles' Register
Baltimore Patriot and Evening Advertiser
Daily Evening Gazette

MAJOR EVENTS

1828: Construction begins on the Baltimore and Ohio Railroad.

1835: A bank riot targets directors and officers of a bankrupt savings institution.

1844: Samuel F. B. Morse sends the first telegraph message from Baltimore.

1851: Baltimore City becomes independent of Baltimore County.

1853: The Baltimore and Ohio Railroad reaches the Ohio River.

western markets, cities invested heavily in roads and canals to carry goods overland between the interior and eastern ports. Baltimore's search for a connection with the Ohio River intensified after New York's completion of the Erie Canal in 1825, a development that practically negated Baltimore's locational advantage as the westernmost of the port cities. In addition, Philadelphia, Pennsylvania, was simultaneously engaged in projects designed to capture more trade in the Susquehanna Valley—an area in which Baltimore had long enjoyed an advantage.

In an effort to lift itself out of the prolonged economic slump that followed the War of 1812, Baltimoreans conceived two canal projects. A distinct political faction lined up behind each of the imagined waterways. Former mayor Edward Johnson, backed by Senator Samuel Smith, led the supporters of a canal that would run from Baltimore to the Susquehanna River, entering the city from the east. John Montgomery, also a former mayor, led another faction whose members favored a canal from Baltimore to the new Chesapeake and Ohio Canal along the Potomac River. A third faction formed behind Mayor Jacob Small, who would eventually win over Samuel Smith. Its membership included property-owning tradesmen worried about the taxes needed to finance expensive canal projects.

Engineering surveys demonstrated that both canal projects were financially impractical. Some merchants abandoned the city for New York and the advantages of the Erie Canal. Those who remained eventually succeeded in building a modest Susquehanna canal that paralleled the lower course of the river, where swift currents and navigational obstacles prevented shipping from moving upstream. Work started on the Susquehanna Tidewater Canal in 1835, and it was completed in 1840. The canal company was insolvent by 1842.

Although they proved ultimately fruitless, canal politics helped to transform Baltimore. In the city's era of mercantile prosperity, Baltimoreans had mostly engaged in trade singly or in small partnerships, though larger groups of investors had sometimes collaborated in risky ventures like privateering. However, the internal improvements needed to maintain the city's position in relation to its competitors were large-scale, collective enterprises, as much political as economic. When Baltimore's business class seized on the railroad system as an alternative to canals, they sought government support as an essential component in the new effort. In 1832 the president of the Baltimore and Ohio Railroad presented an engineering survey for the proposed line between Baltimore and Washington, D.C., to the state legislature. The assembly authorized Baltimore City to purchase up to five thousand shares in the company but deferred any state investment until 1833. The city used property tax revenues to finance the railroad and depended on it to enhance both property values and its revenues. The traditional distinction between public and private enterprise evaporated. All this, according to Baltimore historian Gary Browne in his 1980 book *Baltimore in the Nation, 1789–1860*, was part of a "larger transition away from the private and individual basis of the old order toward the public and group basis of the new one." The culmination of the new order came in 1851 when a state constitutional convention reluctantly made Baltimore City independent of Baltimore County and increased its representation in the Maryland General Assembly.

The new order included new political party organizations. In the era of the Jeffersonians and Federalists, loosely integrated parties had been led by self-nominated notables who gathered support through nonparty organizations such as the militia. Parties of the Jacksonian period developed organizational structures of their own and sponsored a variety of activities—nominating conventions, for example—through which new men could rise to leadership positions. In effect, the party became an alternative status system that enabled men from nonprominent families and of middling wealth to acquire political influence. The old oligarchs were not rejected, however. Many simply grew old and retired or died. Others such as Senator Smith and Congressman Isaac McKim defined their leadership in national terms and left local affairs to men who had earned local prominence.

In the city council, votes on local issues generally reflected ward interests rather than party politics. The parties—especially the Jacksonians—took their bearings from national, not local, concerns, but the two kinds of issues were not completely distinct. National conflicts had local repercussions that strained party loyalties. President Jackson's opposition to the federal financing of internal improvements lost him some support in Baltimore and threw the burden of financing railroads and canals almost completely on private investors and state and local governments. The national administration's refusal to support the renewal of the charter of the Second Bank of the United States had even more significant implications for the city.

The expected demise of the Second Bank of the United States and the redistribution of federal deposits encouraged the founding of several local banks in Baltimore. One of them, the Bank of Maryland, adopted the then-novel practice of paying interest on savings accounts. This inducement drew deposits from thousands of tradesmen and workingmen who could not afford to buy securities or invest in trading ventures. The failure of the bank in the recession of 1834 injured not just a handful of wealthy stockholders, but a large portion of the city's working- and middle-class households. These depositors did not react immediately, but frustrations grew as they waited more than a year for the settlement of the bank's affairs, at which point they would find out how much remained of the money they had entrusted to the institution. One of the bank directors had claimed in a pamphlet that the depositors could get most of their money back, but courts had impounded the bank's books while they worked their way through the lawsuits, some of which were filed by the bank's other directors.

One of these privileged litigants, Reverdy Johnson, owned a conspicuous mansion near the city center on Monument Square. In the summer of 1835, the square outside his house became the nightly gathering place for a mob of Baltimoreans. Some of these residents were bank depositors, but many others were boys, young men, or various other curious spectators. A full-blown riot finally erupted in August 1835. Jacksonian mayor Jesse Hunt recruited a force of civilian guards to resist the mob, but their wooden clubs were no match for the bombardment of bricks and paving stones they met. With the assent of a local judge, the guards resorted to firearms and fired a single volley into the crowd. It killed five people, including at least one who was trying to calm the mob. Mayor Hunt disavowed all responsibility for the shooting, thus seeming to repudiate the same volunteer peacekeepers that he had mobilized. Many of the guards, fearing mob retaliation, left town with what belongings they could carry. Hunt called out the militia, but only a handful responded. The mob continued rioting unopposed.

Baltimore's bank riot was one of many civil disturbances to erupt in American cities during 1834 and 1835. These outbursts have been attributed in part to the polarizing attacks by Jacksonians on the stockjobbers, speculators, and aristocrats—those people who supposedly exploited or demeaned the solid Americans who worked with their hands. The mobs may also have been a symptom of frictions attendant on urbanization, such as the compression of potentially hostile groups in dense settlements. In one respect, however, the Baltimore riot was distinctive. Instead of attacking blacks, abolitionists, Mormons, or Catholics, Baltimore's mob went after some of their city's wealthiest and most distinguished citizens. As Seth Rockman points out in his 2003 article for *Common-Place*, "unlike the other urban centers of the new nation (Boston, Philadelphia, New York, and Charleston), Baltimore had no meaningful colonial past to shape its institutions or people." The city's relative youth had given it little time to establish an aristocracy that commanded the deference of the ordinary citizens who composed its mobs.

INDUSTRY, COMMERCE, AND LABOR

The working-class riot undermined working-class organization. In 1833, just two years before the bank riot, thirty journeymen's associations had been formed and had threatened or carried out eleven strikes to protest wage cuts. Seventeen trades had joined in an interracial movement to demand a ten-hour workday. A citywide labor organization, the Union Trade Society, brought together workingmen from a variety of crafts. And, when the Jacksonians failed to nominate legislative candidates satisfactory to the party's labor wing, the Workingmen's Party briefly formed to nominate candidates of its own on the so-called mechanical ticket. Both of these candidates were elected. Many of the workers' job actions also enjoyed widespread public support. However, the bank riot was a setback for unionism as it caused a public backlash against crowd actions. Due to this inconsistency of public support, Baltimore's union movement lost its momentum and collapsed during the panic of 1837.

Labor activism was a response to the early stages of industrialization. Beginning in the 1820s, Baltimore's master craftsmen had begun to recast themselves as manufacturers and reduce their journeymen and apprentices to the status of wage laborers. By the 1830s journeymen tobacconists complained that local cigar manufacturers were employing young boys and blacks who had not served a regular apprenticeship. Steam-powered textile factories appeared at about the same time, some of which employed hundreds of workers, but the industry did not prosper until the 1840s, after the recovery from the panic of 1837. Steam power also drove a sugar refinery, a flour mill, two planing and grooving mills, a glass cutting operation, a plaster mill, and a mill for grinding chocolate, ginger, mustard, and castor oil beans. Chemical plants found customers in the local metals industry, which achieved success earlier than textiles, largely because of its role as a supplier of the materials needed to construct internal improvements, especially railroads. One Baltimore coach manufacturer had already converted to the production of passenger cars.

The Baltimore and Ohio Railroad reached Harper's Ferry by 1834 but lacked the capital to push further west. Once again, it turned to the state for financing. The legislature authorized Baltimore to invest another $3 million in the railroad, in addition to the $2 million it had already provided. The Baltimore and Susquehanna Railroad would eventually connect the city with Harrisburg, Pennsylvania, but it ran out of money well short of its objective until the city supplied $600,000, then $150,000 more, then a promise of another $100,000. Meanwhile, the Philadelphia, Wilmington, and Baltimore Railroad and the Baltimore and Washington lines had been completed in 1838, apparently without municipal subsidies.

Between 1830 and 1844, the city's debt increased from $500,000 to more than $5 million, and from 1835 to the end of the antebellum period, interest charges accounted for one-third to one-half of the municipal budget. At first the state tried to curb the city's financial growth. In 1831, in response to a petition submitted by Baltimore's eighty-five largest property owners, the legislature limited the city's tax revenues to $220,000 a year and restricted its total borrowing authority. In 1832 the Maryland General Assembly reversed course and removed all limits on the city's taxing powers. In 1834, however, the assembly once again imposed a limit, but only on Baltimore's general property tax revenues, and, for the first time in thirty years, it allowed Baltimore to reassess property. The tenfold increase in assessments permitted the city to lower its tax rate while generating sufficient revenue to finance its growing debt, although it had to neglect other municipal needs such as water supply. In 1839 and 1853, the city was again able to persuade the assembly to raise the limits on property tax revenues.

More money was needed to finance the Baltimore and Ohio Railroad's final push to the Ohio River at Wheeling, Virginia. The railroad reached Cumberland, Maryland, and the surrounding coal-mining region in 1842. Baltimore provided a loan guarantee of $5 million to pay for the line to Wheeling, as well as branch lines that would draw trade from the regions flanking the railroad's route. Later the guarantee would become a direct loan, but the Baltimore and Ohio would not reach the Ohio River until 1853. In the short run, the investment paid off for Baltimore. The railroad had 190 locomotives, thirteen hundred railroad cars, steel bridge components, rails, wheels, and axles built in the city. Perhaps the most conspicuous by-product of the city's railroad economy was Canton, a twenty-five-hundred-acre development just outside Baltimore's eastern limits. It was the first planned industrial park in the United States—a railroad hub with warehouses, copper smelters, iron foundries, coal and lumber yards, and access to the waterfront. Inland contained blocks of two-story row homes for workers.

Antebellum Baltimore was becoming not only an industrial powerhouse but one of the leading developers of the era's high technology. It had pioneered the use of gas lighting. Its application of steam power extended from factories to railroads to shipping. Maryland's first experiments with steamboats occurred in 1798, and the first steamer was built in Baltimore in 1813. Ten steamship companies formed in the city between 1831 and 1843. And, on a single day in 1844, Samuel F. B. Morse sent the first telegraph message from Baltimore to Washington and a local dentist offered the first public exhibition of the use of laughing gas as a means of painless tooth extraction.

RACE, ETHNICITY, AND IMMIGRATION

In 1830, with a population of over eighty thousand, Baltimore was the second largest city in the United States. In 1850 it was still in second place, but its population had more than doubled to almost 170,000. Much of this increase was the result of immigration. During the 1820s, only about 10,500 foreigners landed in Baltimore, but in the next decade the figure rose nearly 425 percent to 55,000. Germans were the most numerous; by 1839 they accounted for about 20 percent of the city's residents. Next in size was the Irish population.

Irish and German newcomers competed with one another for jobs on the railway gangs that fanned out from the city, and they engaged in fierce competition for unskilled jobs on the waterfront. Black employment suffered most from immigrant pressure, which was exerted through mob action in addition to labor market competition. Black brickyard workers in Canton and Federal Hill were driven off by white gangs. Mobs made repeated attacks on black caulkers in the shipyards and eventually drove them out of a trade in which they had enjoyed a near-monopoly. One of these black caulkers was Frederick Douglass, who had been badly beaten by white coworkers during his apprenticeship because they did not want to labor alongside African Americans.

By 1830 Baltimore's black population was diminishing as a proportion of the total, but its slave population had been shrinking even more rapidly. Four-fifths of the African Americans living in Baltimore were free. The city held the largest concentration of free black people in the United States, a distinction that it retained until emancipation. Notwithstanding the racial antagonism and violence perpetrated by white immigrants, Baltimore's dominant mood concerning race and slavery was one of profound ambivalence. When wealthy British social reformer

James Silk Buckingham visited Baltimore in 1840, he found that Baltimoreans did not defend slavery, as residents of New York and other cities had. In fact, they tolerated a variety of opinions on matters of race, but their overriding inclination was to avoid the subject.

Maryland's seventeenth-century Act of Toleration had brought many Quakers to the colony, and by mid-nineteenth century some of their abolitionist descendants were numbered among the most successful businessmen of Baltimore. These abolitionists lived, socialized, and did business with other prominent citizens who either owned slaves or took slavery for granted. When avoiding the issue was impossible, Baltimoreans tried to straddle it. At the time of Buckingham's visit, for example, the city was a center of the African colonization movement. Its adherents proposed to moderate America's divisions over race by sending the slavery issue back to Africa.

See also *Baltimore, MD 1776–1790; Baltimore, MD 1790–1828; Baltimore, MD 1854–1877; Baltimore, MD 1877–1896; Baltimore, MD 1896–1929; Baltimore, MD 1929–1941; Baltimore, MD 1941–1952; Baltimore, MD 1952–1989*

MATTHEW CRENSON

BIBLIOGRAPHY

Browne, Gary Lawson. *Baltimore in the Nation, 1789–1860.* Chapel Hill: University of North Carolina Press, 1980.

Olson, Sherry H. *Baltimore: The Building of an American City.* 2d ed. Baltimore, MD: Johns Hopkins University Press, 1997.

Ridgway, Whitman H. *Community Leadership in Maryland, 1790–1840: A Comparative Analysis of Power in Society.* Chapel Hill: University of North Carolina Press, 1979.

Rockman, Seth. "Mobtown U.S.A.: Baltimore." *Common-Place* 3, no. 4 (July 2003). Available online at www.common-place.org/vol-03/no-04/baltimore/ (accessed May 22, 2011).

Sutton, William R. *Journeymen for Jesus: Evangelical Artisans Confront Capitalism in Jacksonian Baltimore.* University Park: Pennsylvania State University Press, 1998.

NEW ORLEANS, LA 1828–1854

FROM 1828 TO 1854, NEW ORLEANS GREW FROM A RELATIVELY SMALL CITY to an urban center with a population and shipping interests that rivaled northeastern and southern cities such as Philadelphia, Pennsylvania, and Baltimore, Maryland. The growth of commerce was due to the city's importance as a connecting point for trade from the Ohio and Mississippi River valleys, and as the nation expanded to the south and west, people were drawn to New Orleans to seek opportunities more present in the growing city than in more rural areas.

New Orleans's growth was characterized by growing strife between the city's French and Spanish Creole inhabitants and the influx of new American settlers, struggles with disease

QUICK FACTS

NEW ORLEANS, LA 1828–1854

MAYORS

Denis Prieur	(1828–1838)
Paul Bertus	(1838)
Charles Genois	(1838–1840)
William Freret	(1840–1842)
Denis Prieur	(1842–1843)
Paul Bertus	(1843)
William Freret	(1843–1844)
Joseph E. Montégut	(1844–1846)
Abdiel D. Crossman	(1846–1854)

MAJOR INDUSTRIES AND EMPLOYERS

Freret Brothers Cotton Mill

Cooperage

Boot and shoemakers

Wholesale grocers and importers

Steamboat workers and cotton
   screwmen

MAJOR NEWSPAPERS

Courieur de la Louisiane

The Daily Picayune

The Louisiana American

The Native American

The New Orleans Bee

MAJOR EVENTS

1832: Andrew Jackson visits the city to celebrate the Battle of New Orleans, and a statue is dedicated to him.

1832: A cholera epidemic kills approximately five thousand people out of the city's forty thousand total residents.

1836: The city is divided into three municipalities, separating the Creoles, Americans, and free people of color or immigrants.

1852: Three municipalities are consolidated into one city, and the city of Lafayette is annexed.

1852: Work begins on the New Orleans, Opelousas and Great Western Railroad and the New Orleans, Jackson and Great Northern Railroad.

outbreaks such as cholera and yellow fever, floods that threatened to engulf the city, economic depression following the panic of 1837, and difficulties containing urban disorder.

GOVERNMENT AND POLITICS

Following the United States' purchase of Louisiana, the territory was administered by territorial governors dispatched from the nation's capital. These representatives, of whom William C. C. Claiborne (served 1804–1822) was the most important, faced the challenge of converting a French-derived civil code of government to a more republican and American form. Until an influx of American settlers arrived around 1820, the governors managed these tensions by honoring the principles of the former civil code. By 1830 the burgeoning population necessitated the division of new municipalities, or wards, and settlement patterns became differentiated such that Creoles inhabited the original square of what is now the French Quarter, while Americans settled above and west of this region. Free people of color and a smattering of immigrants settled in the region east of the Creole center of population.

In 1832 the Louisiana state legislature invested New Orleans with extensive powers, including the rights to lay out streets, improve public places, and develop the suburbs, but little growth occurred. The wharves in front of the French Quarter attracted most of the shipping from Mexico and other foreign ports, and the accretion of sediment blocking access to wharfage in the American sector of the city aroused tensions over economic competition and access to trade. By 1836 these tensions led to the division of the city into three distinct municipalities, or wards, that functioned as separate corporations answerable to the city's general council, which consisted of two representatives from each municipality, and to the authority of the mayor. This organization endured until 1852. The general council had few powers, but the representatives were able to levy taxes for the whole city. However, they had almost no power to enforce payment of these taxes. During this period the French Quarter became the city's First Municipality, boasting a primarily Creole population; the Faubourg Sainte Mary, or Second Municipality, west of the French Quarter, became a stronghold of the growing American population; and the region east of the French Quarter, the Faubourg Marigny, became known as the "Immigrant Sector" and contained free people of color and Irish and German immigrants.

This period of three municipalities, which has been dubbed a curious experiment in city government, had the roots of its demise in the diminishment and divisions of power it created and in debts caused by the expense of running, in effect, three separate cities. City services such as sanitation, road building, and wharf repair withered during this period because of financial difficulties. The municipalities were governed by a recorder and a council elected by the wards. Recorders had to be at least thirty years of age, have a family, and own a minimum of $3,000 worth of property. The members of the separate municipal councils had to be twenty-one years of age or older and own property valued at no less than $1,000. In this way, participation in municipal government was reduced to a fraction of the city's male population. The general council only had the power to make decisions that interested all of the three municipalities, and it had no financial power. The mayor had to balance the concerns of all the municipalities and had limited ability to effect change without the cooperation of a sector's particular council.

By the mid 1840s, the problem of debt for the three municipalities had begun to achieve the proportions that would lead to the city's consolidation in 1852. The First Municipality had acquired a debt of $400,000 in judgments against it, one of which sprang from that sector's attempt to block the American (or Second Municipality) sector's access to wharfage rights. Other debts for the First Municipality, including unpaid interest on loans and unpaid taxes, amounted to approximately $900,000. After the consolidation of the separate municipalities, the city's debt amounted to $7.7 million. The consolidation rendered all parts of New Orleans on the left bank of the Mississippi River a single corporation that was divided into nine wards. The emerging legislative branch of the new city government included a board of eleven aldermen and a twenty-four-member board of assistant aldermen who held office for two years and were elected from three districts divided into three wards each. The mayor's financial and other powers, which had been severely restricted under the former city organization, were strengthened.

The Creole elite that dominated municipal politics displayed Whiggish tendencies and eschewed the inclusion of national concerns in local elections. This elite showed its strong loyalty to its roots and its sensitivity to insult when Joseph Montégut defeated his American rival, Paul Bertus, for the office of mayor after local newspapers attributed a slanderous remark about the ignorance of the city's Creoles to Bertus. Bitter disagreements erupted throughout the period when efforts were made to restrict the franchise to only American-born eligible males, a prospect that angered naturalized inhabitants and recently arrived Creoles.

Before the establishment of free public schools in 1841, the Capuchin monks and Ursuline nuns educated wealthy white boys and girls, respectively. After 1841 each municipality had its own school board and executive officer. The boards consisted of one representative from each ward and worked with the city's general council and each sector's common council. By 1848, though total school appropriation reached $105,000, schools were unevenly distributed. Few schools existed in the Third Municipality, a mixture of public and private schools were present in the Second Municipality, and the largest amount, including a high school, was found in the American sector. Despite this, the education system garnered compliments from professional national critics.

INDUSTRY, COMMERCE, AND LABOR

By 1828 New Orleans was a small city whose wealth came primarily from the profits of agricultural production outside of the city limits in either Louisiana's southern coastal parishes or those near the border of Mississippi where cotton was cultivated. This commerce began to prosper between the 1830s and 1840s, but experienced a significant increase after means were devised to navigate the Mississippi River due to the advent of steam power and the increased use of steamboats. Before this innovation, produce from the outlying parishes was shipped down the Mississippi River on barques or flatboats to New Orleans. The flatboats, after delivering their cargo, were destroyed and the timber used to construct homes and other structures. Some ships were returned to the outlying parishes through a complicated process in which shipmen would pull the flatboat against the current by means of a rope.

Despite the panic of 1837, which caused a run on *specie* and a depression as severe in New Orleans as anywhere else, the city by 1840 had developed a robust trade. Most of the trade occurred with Mexico and was conducted through foreign merchants. Goods made in Europe and destined for Mexico came through New Orleans where they were forwarded to Tampico, Metamoros, and Veracruz. In return for these exports, the city received gold, silver, precious woods, hides, and tropical fruit. Wholesale and retail trade also flourished with merchants in Arkansas, Mississippi, Alabama, and Tennessee. These merchants received long-term credits payable at the harvest. Former mayor William Freret's cotton mill, located at St. Charles Avenue and Poydras, was one of the largest and most profitable in the city.

With so much importance attached to waterborne trade, disputes about access to wharfage and water rights plagued the different sectors of the city, especially during the period of three municipalities from 1836 to 1852. In 1840 a dispute arose between the (Creole) First Municipality and the (American) Second Municipality. The dispute arose when sediment from the Mississippi River blocked the Second Municipality's access to waterborne commerce, making the landing of trading vessels in that area virtually impossible. The First Municipality, to exacerbate matters, argued for their right to build wharves into the river along Canal Street, instead of parallel with it, as was usual. Such construction would further limit the Second Municipality's access to waterborne commerce. When the Second Municipality's petition requesting that the wharves be extended was rejected, a chain of events began that included the Second Municipality's filing of a lawsuit that it won, garnering it a fee of $10,000 from the First Municipality. The destruction of the wharves came toward the time of the consolidation of the municipalities.

New Orleans began to recognize the importance of city improvements in the 1830s and instituted several over the next decade. Numerous plans were undertaken to enhance access to the city and to construct public and other buildings that would distinguish the urban landscape. Under Mayor Abdiel Crossman, initiatives began to build more railroads out of the city. These included plans for the construction of the New Orleans, Opelousas and Great Western Railroad and the New Orleans, Jackson and Great Northern Railroad. These lines would connect the city to commerce from the west and the north, respectively. Construction of both began in 1852.

Banks, improvement companies, public buildings, and hotels were also involved in efforts to attract commerce and to make New Orleans a city that would rival Philadelphia, Baltimore, and New York, all of which it competed with for trade and prominence. Banks and improvement companies, often working interchangeably, provided much of the capital necessary for city improvements. In 1831 the New Orleans Improvement and Banking Company was chartered to build the St. Louis Hotel in what became the First Municipality. The initial capital raised exceeded $500,000 for the project. The company received a charter in 1832 to build the St. Charles Hotel in the Second Municipality with starting capital of $1 million. Both the St. Charles and St. Louis Hotels were luxury establishments, and their architecture, barrooms, and exchanges prompted comparisons to hotels in other American or foreign cities. The hotels functioned as sites for social and business interactions. They catered to the French and English communities and helped establish two competing commercial centers in the city. In the exchanges, merchants contracted business while slaves were sold beneath the buildings' rotundas. After the construction of these structures, the streets adjacent to them became concentrated locations where slave traders had their pens or offices. While both hotel companies had banking privileges, they never used them.

In addition to wealth garnered by the transshipment of goods from foreign ports to Mexico and small cities to the west, a good deal of the city's prosperity arose from trading slaves. After the close of the Atlantic slave trade, the commerce in slaves for the South shifted from Charleston, South Carolina, to New Orleans. Slaves were brought over land or by ship to New Orleans and then sold to the sugar or cotton parishes outside of the city or to southwestern cities such as Pensacola, Florida; Galveston, Texas; and Biloxi, Mississippi. Despite sporadic attempts to regulate the movements of slaves, a substantial amount of them worked in the city and rented rooms where they lived without their masters. Male slaves were river pilots, cotton screwmen, deckhands, and ship caulkers, while female slaves worked in domestic or market jobs. The influx of Irish immigration spurred competition for these jobs and almost completely displaced female slaves from domestic work.

RACE, ETHNICITY, AND IMMIGRATION

New Orleans's origins as both a French (1718–1762) and Spanish (1763–1800) territory led to attitudes toward race and ethnicity that varied considerably from those at work in the rest of the nation. The influence of both of these European regimes, combined with aspects of Catholicism and particular racial codes, created a city in which complete spatial or social segregation of whites and blacks did not exist. Though many consider the city primarily French in style, it was during the Spanish regime that most innovations in architecture occurred. This was also when the largest portion of enslaved blacks earned their freedom through self-purchase. The Spanish regime kept in place most civil codes and laws instituted by the French, and the main concession made by Spanish authorities was the publication of city ordinances in both French and Spanish.

Two cultural aspects that prevented a strict separation of the races came from godparentship, a custom important to the Catholic Church, and plaçage, a system of concubinage between free women of color and white males. The system of godparentship allowed people to expand their social connections—often across races, ethnicities, and nationalities—through the formal recognition of a type of fictive kinship. Godparents were responsible for the religious upbringing of their godchildren, and these arrangements were often made public at christenings and preserved in documents. In many cases, free people of color had white godparents, a connection that had its benefits. In St. Louis Cathedral, free people of color were allowed to worship alongside whites. During the 1840s the Irish so strongly objected to this practice that they had St. Patrick's Cathedral erected so they could worship without African Americans.

The system of plaçage began at masquerade balls held in hotels and dancehalls throughout the city. The women at these balls were primarily free women of color, often of such light pigmentation that custom was the only system that established their identities as other than white. At these balls white men, married and unmarried, had the opportunity to make connections with these women. Legend asserts that the women's mothers arranged unions between them and interested suitors so that the women received shelter, the means to support themselves, and sometimes guarantees of financial support for their children. This system, combined with Spanish self-purchase of slaves, led to a growth in the population of free people of color. Free people of color often performed artisan work. While they lived dispersed throughout the city, a concentration of them existed in the Third (or Immigrant) Municipality.

The influx of Irish immigrants in the 1840s complicated the makeup of the city. New Irish immigrants were considered relatively uncouth by the Irish population that had long been a part of New Orleans's composition. The older Irish population disliked the new immigrants because they were poor—a factor that led to the new arrivals competing with free people of color and slaves for work related to the waterfront industries and domestic services. Although much emphasis is placed on the French and Spanish origins of the city, even before 1828 the city contained significant populations of Jews, Germans, and settlers from the northeastern United States.

Tensions between Americans and Creoles escalated through the 1830s and contributed to the division of the city into three separate municipalities. By the consolidation of the city in 1852, the American population had grown to overpower most other groups in New Orleans.

From 1828 to 1854, political contests grew particularly volatile, particularly in the 1840s when attempts were made to restrict the voting population to only males who had been born in the United States. This did not occur due to the size and importance of foreign immigrants in New Orleans.

See also *New Orleans, LA 1790–1828; New Orleans, LA 1854–1877*

ANDRÉ F. YOUNG

BIBLIOGRAPHY

Hirsch, Arnold, and Joseph Logsdon. *Creole New Orleans: Race and Americanization.* Baton Rouge: Louisiana State University Press, 1992.

Johnson, Walter. *Soul by Soul: Life inside the Antebellum Slave Market.* Cambridge, MA: Harvard University Press, 1999.

Kellman, Ari. *A River and Its City: The Making of Landscape in New Orleans.* Berkeley: University of California Press, 2003.

Kendall, John. *The History of New Orleans.* Chicago, IL: The Lewis Publishing Group, 1922.

Lewis, Peirce. *New Orleans, the Making of an Urban Landscape.* Charlottesville: The University of Virginia Press, 2003.

PHILADELPHIA, PA 1828–1854

THE YEARS 1828 TO 1854 WERE AMONG THE MOST TUMULTUOUS in Philadelphia's three-hundred-year history. After Andrew Jackson's election as president in 1828, the city's hopes of reclaiming commercial and financial primacy from New York City withered, in part due to Jackson's refusal to renew the charter of the Philadelphia-based Second Bank of the United States. Jackson's assault on the bank, however, was far from the only problem Philadephians faced. The local economy struggled to recover from the depression that followed the panic of 1837, and a fragmented system of municipal government fought to deal with the challenges posed by riot and disorder.

Discernible amidst the turbulence, however, were the roots of the modern industrial metropolis. Before and after the depression, the city's manufacturing sector grew dramatically. Ward politicians laid the foundations for the emergence of machine politics and political reforms, culminating in the city-county consolidation of 1854 that strengthened the power and reach of the municipal government.

GOVERNMENT AND POLITICS

Philadelphia in 1828 was not one city but a cluster of separate municipalities. The original settlement founded by William Penn extended approximately two square miles between the Delaware and Schuylkill Rivers, but beyond its boundaries the city councils had no authority. By the 1830

QUICK FACTS

PHILADELPHIA, PA **1828–1854**

MAYORS

George Mifflin Dallas	(1828–1829)
Benjamin Wood Richards	(1829)
William Milnor	(1829–1830)
Benjamin Wood Richards	(1830–1832)
John Swift	(1832–1838)
Isaac Roach	(1838–1839)
John Swift	(1839–1841)
John Morin Scott	(1841–1844)
Peter McCall	(1844–1845)
John Swift	(1845–1849)
Joel Jones	(1849–1850)
Charles Gilpin	(1850–1854)

MAJOR INDUSTRIES AND EMPLOYERS

Cornelius and Baker (chandeliers and lamps)
Isaac Norris and Company
Matthias Baldwin and Company
   (locomotives)
Alfred Jenks and Company (machinery)
Wm. Sellers and Company (machinery)

MAJOR NEWSPAPERS

Item
Mechanics' Free Press
North American
Pennsylvanian
Public Ledger
Spirit of the Times
Sun
Sunday Dispatch
United States Gazette

MAJOR EVENTS

1834: Mayor John Swift leads anti-abolitionist protestors in dumping abolitionist literature in the Delaware River.
1839: The first direct election for mayor is held. John Swift wins a plurality of votes, but a lack of majority sends the election to the city councils—the system by which mayors had previously been chosen. Swift emerges victorious.
1845: Philadelphian radical George Lippard publishes *The Quaker City, or the Monks of Monk Hall*. The work, a thinly veiled attack on the city's upper class, is the greatest-selling American novel until the appearance of *Uncle Tom's Cabin* seven years later.
1846: Vice President George Mifflin Dallas, a former mayor of Philadelphia, is burned in effigy in the city for casting the deciding vote in the Senate to lower tariff duties. Manufacturers and mechanics believed these duties were crucial to the prosperity of local industry.
1849: A cholera epidemic claims 386 lives.

census, the population of these outlying districts, boroughs, and townships already outnumbered that of the city proper by 108,335 to 80,462. The lack of a united response to epidemics and riots impeded effective municipal administration throughout the era, leading to calls for the annexation of the contiguous suburbs after 1844.

The city proper was governed by a mayor (elected directly from 1839) and a bicameral system of councils. The lower branch, the common council, had twenty members around midcentury, while the upper branch, the select council, had a dozen. In contrast, most of the outlying districts were run by unicameral boards of commissioners that chose a president from among their number. Despite their different structures, the municipal authorities in the city and districts had similar responsibilities. The bulk of their work was taken up with the regulation of wharves and markets, the lighting and cleaning of the streets, and maintaining order through the night watches and police forces. Other functions, including relief for the poor, establishing quarantines during epidemics, and, after 1834, public schooling, fell under the auspices of countywide bodies. The boundaries between legislative and executive authority in the city proper were blurry, and joint subcommittees of councils increasingly took responsibility for the water supply, highways, street cleaning, city property, and the administration of the gas works, thus relegating the mayor to a peripheral role in government. The expenses incurred were met through a mixture of real estate taxes and bonds—popular investments for the city's elite—with other improvements, including the opening, grading, and paving of streets, funded through special levies on the property holders benefiting from the work being undertaken.

In 1828 a gentlemanly elite, accustomed to public service as a civic duty, still dominated local politics. As late as the 1840s, merchant prince Thomas Pym Cope and the son of celebrated attorney Horace Binney sat on the municipal councils. Stephen Girard, one of America's wealthiest citizens, even trusted the city enough to leave most of his estate to the corporation for the establishment of a school for orphans and the improvement of a major thoroughfare along the Delaware River.

By the 1830s, however, new men challenged the authority of the gentlemen politicians. Figures such as Joel Bartholomew Sutherland of Southwark cultivated alliances among the journeymen and laborers of the city and districts. Taking advantage of the egalitarian ethos of the Jacksonian era; the opening of offices like mayor, alderman, and judge to election; and heightened partisan competition, these men began to specialize in politics as a vocation. Whether the old elite were pushed out or gave way willingly to the new order is still a matter for debate, but by 1854 men with the social standing of a Cope or Binney were unlikely to run for the city councils. Only prestigious offices like the mayoralty continued to attract them.

The rise of the ward politician was entwined with the emergence of the second party system in Philadelphia. A number of factors made the city proper a bastion of the new Whig Party that coalesced to oppose the presidency of Democrat Andrew Jackson after 1834. Jackson's hostility to the Second Bank of the United States—an institution located on Chestnut Street—worried many Philadelphians. Local manufacturers supported the tariffs and internal improvements that lay at the heart of the Whigs' economic program, and the party's cultural conservatism chimed with the outlook of a predominantly Protestant city. In outlying suburbs like Northern Liberties and Moyamensing, however, the white egalitarianism of the Democrats found a receptive audience. By midcentury it was commonplace to refer to the city as a "Whig Gibraltar" surrounded by Democratic suburbs.

Philadelphia's two-party system was on its last legs by 1853. The emergence of a strong nativist movement in response to Irish immigration in the 1840s drew votes away from both the Democrats and the Whigs. After riots in 1844, the anti-Catholic American Republican party won office in a number of suburban districts, and in 1849 an unlikely coalition of Democrat and nativist reformers even managed to wrest the mayoralty from the Whigs. In 1853 a number of independent candidates, including locomotive builder Matthias Baldwin and real estate attorney Eli Kirk Price, won election to the state legislature to push for consolidation with the help of nativist votes. Few realized at the time that this marked the beginning of the end for the second party system in the city.

The reform Baldwin and Price were sent to enact had its roots in the 1840s. In the aftermath of the 1844 Bible riots—pitting nativist Protestants against Catholic Irish immigrants—Philadelphians from across the city and suburbs demanded improvements to a system of policing that left little room for coordination between the divided jurisdictions. Opposition to the amalgamation of the Whig city with the Democratic suburbs led to a series of compromises. A law was passed in 1845 in the capital of Harrisburg mandating each municipality retain one policeman for every 250 taxable residents, and a metropolitan-wide police force under an elected marshal was created in 1850. Neither measure appeased reformers, however, who concluded by 1853 that a countywide consolidation of the city and districts was imperative. Early the following year, the governor signed into law a measure that united the twenty-nine townships, boroughs, and districts of the county with the city.

INDUSTRY, COMMERCE, AND LABOR

By 1828 New York had already superseded Philadelphia as the commercial center of the Republic, and the fortunes of the city's mercantile and financial sectors did not improve markedly over the ensuing decades. Philadelphians looked instead to cement their advantages as a manufacturing center, and by midcentury it had become clear this was where the city's future lay.

Hopes of reclaiming commercial primacy from New York City nevertheless lingered through the era. Envisaging a rival to the Erie Canal, Philadelphia's merchants persuaded state legislators to fund a series of canals and railroads, which were mostly constructed in the 1830s, to the Ohio River valley at Pittsburgh. Hampered by the state's mountainous interior and the need to appease remote rural districts with unprofitable branch lines, however, the Main Line of Public Works proved an expensive failure. And while the port of Philadelphia continued to grow, New York and Baltimore, Maryland, drew more of the lucrative foreign trade.

Philadelphia's status as a financial center seemed to offer a better route for challenging New York's ascent. The city was home to a number of major banks and insurance companies. However, President Jackson's refusal to renew the federal charter of Nicholas Biddle's Second Bank of the United States hurt the sector. Then, in the aftermath of the panic of 1837, a number of the city's financial institutions suspended *specie* payments (the redemption of paper money or bank notes in metal coin). In the rocky years that followed, seven institutions, including the Second Bank (rechartered as a state institution), failed.

The relative decline of Philadelphia as a commercial and banking center was offset to an extent by the expansion of the city's manufactures. Rich reserves of anthracite coal and iron to the north, coupled with ample building land in the suburbs, gave entrepreneurs the power and space to expand. In contrast to the factory towns of New England, the city boasted a diverse manufacturing base by the 1830s, with particular strengths in textiles, iron, and the building of locomotives. Joseph Harrison's commission to build steam engines for Russia in the 1830s proved an especial point of pride for city boosters and indicated the international renown of Philadelphia's engineers. Most of the expansion in manufacturing capacity, however, rested on trade with a prosperous hinterland rather than lucrative contracts from further afield.

Philadelphia's manufacturing establishments were characterized more by the diversity of their wares than their scale. Thousands of workshops employed no more than a dozen hands, and even in the larger factories workforces exceeding five hundred were rare. Women often found industrial work, especially in the textile mills of Manayunk and Kensington, though skilled jobs remained largely the preserve of Protestant white journeymen. Rather than seeking incorporation, most of the city's enterprises were run as family firms or partnerships. Only a handful of manufacturers were welcomed into the social circles of wealthy merchants and lawyers, and cultural divisions between the predominantly Episcopalian upper class and upstart Presbyterian mechanics persisted through the era.

From the workshops and neighborhoods of manufacturing Philadelphia came a series of challenges to the new industrial order. In 1828, following the formation of the Mechanic's Union of Trade Associations the previous year, the Workingmen's Party formed in the city and demanded free public education and restrictions on working hours. Unions throughout the era were usually limited to skilled workers and organized along craft lines, but in 1835 the newly formed General Trades' Union managed briefly to overcome these divisions. A series of successful strikes culminated a year later with unskilled laborers joining a citywide walkout. Mayor John Swift's attempt to prosecute the leaders of the stoppage failed, but the mass unemployment that followed the panic of 1837 succeeded where the city authorities had failed and fractured the union.

The years that followed the panic were marked more by ethnocultural conflict than labor struggles, as an influx of Irish Catholic immigrants polarized working-class Philadelphians. Even in these lean years, however, major strikes among the predominantly Irish weavers of Kensington and coal heavers along the Schuylkill wharves troubled employers. By 1850, with the economy once more on the upswing, another wave of organizing saw the brief reemergence of a Workingmen's Party, though the strikes of the early 1850s lacked the broad participation of the struggles of 1836–1837.

The economic recovery coincided with the chartering of the Pennsylvania Railroad in 1846. Intended to supplant the Main Line of Public Works with a direct rail link to Pittsburgh, the line was funded largely by local investors. The city government became the largest single shareholder, but only after a bitter municipal election that October that split the major parties over the wisdom of purchasing stock. Both merchants and manufacturers saw the venture as Philadelphia's best hope of reclaiming metropolitan primacy from New York, and, with the line just two months from completion at the end of 1853, the urban economy seemed poised for years of expansion.

RACE, ETHNICITY, AND IMMIGRATION

Although Philadelphia remained a predominantly Protestant city between 1828 and 1854, migration from within the United States and abroad altered its ethnic complexion and spurred a dramatic period of demographic growth. Between 1830 and 1850, the population of the city and the outlying districts more than doubled from 188,797 to 408,762. The religious and racial hostilities exacerbated by this expansion boiled over in a series of riots.

Philadelphia's population in 1828 was principally white, Protestant, and descended from British stock. Alongside the white majority, African Americans—with slavery all but extinct in the state—created a small but resilient free black community. Migrants over the ensuing decades continued to come from these sources, although disfranchisement in the state constitution of 1837, job discrimination, and persistent violence contributed to a decline in the black population between 1840 and 1850.

Along with British immigrants, Americans from rural Pennsylvania and New Jersey, and transient journeymen and laborers, more newcomers arrived from other countries. Philadelphia's German population increased markedly in the era. In even greater numbers came Irish Catholics, especially during the potato famine of the 1840s. By 1850 more than one in four of the county's residents had been born outside the United States, and 72,312—or 18 percent of the county's population—hailed from Ireland.

These immigrants were not distributed evenly into the city's economy. New arrivals from England and Germany were often able to use their Old World training to find skilled work in the workshops of the manufacturing suburbs. In contrast, Irish and African Americans, often sharing a common rural background, tended to be absorbed into the ranks of unskilled labor and domestic service.

Philadelphia's neighborhoods lacked the ethnic segmentation of the city's workplaces. While parts of the metropolis, such as the southern suburbs of Moyamensing and Southwark, boasted a larger-than-average Irish community, homogeneous neighborhoods were not the norm. Even those suburbs also housed significant populations of blacks and white Protestants, and other districts were similarly diverse. Although wealthier residents tended to cluster in the city proper, segregation by class was rare. Instead of harboring distinct ethnic and social enclaves, the city at midcentury was marked more by distinctions between wealthier residents, who occupied the row houses fronting onto the main streets of the rectangular grid, and the poor, who were relegated to the warren of courts and alleys behind the impressive facades. Epidemics, including the cholera outbreaks that struck the city in 1832 and 1849, were more likely to claim lives in these insalubrious backstreets.

Heterogeneous residential patterns did not prevent the formation of robust ethnic communities. African Americans had organized their own network of churches, benevolent associations, and schools long before 1828, and in the 1830s and 1840s, black abolitionists and temperance campaigners defied white hostility by parading through the streets. In communities containing Protestants, Irish Catholics, and Germans, volunteer fire companies, street gangs, taverns, churches, fraternal lodges, and mutual aid organizations bound residents together and often provided an institutional springboard for political participation.

Such communities did not always coexist peacefully. The sense of territoriality that institutions like fire companies cultivated fused with religious and racial prejudices to create a combustible environment. Between 1828 and 1849 a series of major riots pitted whites against African Americans and Protestants against Irish Catholics. In May and July of 1844, two disturbances in the suburbs of Kensington and Southwark—instigated by Protestants angry at Catholic demands for the removal of their Bible from the public schools—led to twenty deaths and the first calls for a consolidation of the city and its districts. In 1849 another riot, this one targeting a mulatto owner of a Moyamensing tavern who was married to a white woman, spurred renewed calls for municipal reform.

Partisan politics proved one way to channel this riotous spirit, although with Election Day riots commonplace, political enthusiasm hardly guaranteed social peace. Ward bosses like Moyamensing fireman William McMullen helped deliver ethnic votes to their favored candidates and provided a muscular presence at the polls. Broadly speaking, Protestants tended to favor the cultural conservatism of the city's Whig Party, and Catholics preferred the white egalitarianism of the Democrats, but there were many exceptions to the rule. The Bible riots of 1844, moreover, drew native-born supporters away from both parties. By 1853 cultural issues such as temperance, which Irish critics saw as a way to attack their taverns, had become topics for major political debate.

The demand for temperance, the abolition of the turbulent volunteer fire companies, and stronger policing helped proponents of consolidation win the 1853 election. The reform they pushed through made Philadelphia the largest city in territorial terms in the world. Ethnic and social divisions, however, proved far harder to override than the boundaries of the old district system.

See also *Philadelphia, PA 1776–1790; Philadelphia, PA 1790–1828; Philadelphia, PA 1854–1877; Philadelphia, PA 1877–1896; Philadelphia, PA 1896–1929; Philadelphia, PA 1929–1941; Philadelphia, PA 1941–1952; Philadelphia, PA 1952–1989; Philadelphia, PA 1989–2011*

ANDREW HEATH

BIBLIOGRAPHY

Clark, Dennis. *The Irish in Philadelphia: Ten Generations of Urban Experience.* Philadelphia, PA: Temple University Press, 1973.

Dawson, Andrew. *Lives of the Philadelphia Engineers: Capital, Class, and Revolution, 1830–1890.* Burlington, VT: Ashgate, 2004.

Feldberg, Michael. *The Philadelphia Riots of 1844: A Study of Ethnic Conflict.* Westport, CT: Greenwood Press, 1975.

Laurie, Bruce. *Working People of Philadelphia, 1800–1850.* Philadelphia, PA: Temple University Press, 1980.

Warner, Sam Bass, Jr. *The Private City: Philadelphia in Three Periods of Its Growth.* Philadelphia: University of Pennsylvania Press, 1987.

Weigley, Russell F., ed. *Philadelphia: A 300-Year History.* New York, NY: Norton, 1982.

Wright, Robert E. *The First Wall Street: Chestnut Street, Philadelphia, and the Birth of American Finance.* Chicago, IL: University of Chicago Press, 2005.

BOSTON, MA 1828–1854

BOSTON UNDERWENT AN EXTREME TRANSFORMATION on several fronts between 1828 and 1854, as its population more than tripled and the English Protestant city became half foreign-born. The influx of immigrants was met by prejudice and violence. The city's economy had been built on maritime trade from its beginnings, and by the 1840s, trade had declined and the city was the financial center for the burgeoning manufacturing industries in New England. The tiny peninsula upon which the city was built was expanded physically by landfill to create new land for commerce and housing. Boston became the American equivalent of Athens, Greece, during this period: a center for literature, culture, and social reform movements. By 1854 the city was a successful metropolis with growing suburbs.

GOVERNMENT AND POLITICS

In 1828 Boston had only been an incorporated city for six years, and Federalist mayor Josiah Quincy was in his last one-year term in office. Quincy had completed ambitious development projects and had become known as a reformer in public safety, public health, social welfare, and the prison system. In 1828 Quincy withdrew from the race for reelection when he failed to win on the first two ballots because no candidate had a majority; some blamed his loss on his haughty republican manners and the labor-class vote. Quincy went on to become the fifteenth president of Harvard College and the author of several books. At this time, Boston's city government structure comprised the mayor; an eight-member board of aldermen, elected at large; and forty-eight members of the common council, four elected from each of twelve wards.

Harrison Gray Otis, another Federalist and member of a prominent Boston family, followed Quincy as mayor. Throughout most of this period, Boston's mayors were of English Protestant descent. These wealthy men mostly represented business interests but also sought to meet the social needs of the poor and working people who voted for them. These reform efforts were designed to make Boston a model modern city.

Two mayors in the 1830s were faced with violence in the city. Mayor Theodore Lyman, a graduate of Harvard and an old-style Federalist, organized a meeting in 1834 at which he was joined by former mayors Quincy and Otis to denounce the burning of an Ursuline convent and school in nearby Charlestown. A year later, Lyman intervened to rescue abolitionist leader William Lloyd Garrison when he was grabbed at an event of the Boston Female Anti-Slavery Society by a mob of business leaders. In 1837 Mayor Samuel Eliot handled the Broad Street riot that began with a clash between a Catholic funeral procession and a Protestant fire company returning from a fire; after an estimated fifteen thousand rioters joined the fray, the mayor personally led the militia to subdue them.

The only exception to the rule of Old Yankee mayors before 1855 was Martin Brimmer, a German American merchant and the fourth Whig mayor of Boston. Whigs held that office for eighteen years during this time period. As anti-immigration sentiment rose due to the massive

QUICK FACTS

BOSTON, MA **1828–1854**

MAYORS

Josiah Quincy	(1823–1828)
Harrison Gray Otis	(1828–1831)
Charles Nells	(1831–1834)
Theodore Lyman	(1834–1836)
Samuel Armstrong	(1836–1837)
Samuel Eliot	(1837–1840)
Jonathan Chapman	(1840–1843)
Martin Brimmer	(1843–1845)
Thomas Davis	(1845)
Josiah Quincy Jr.	(1845–1849)
John Bigelow	(1849–1852)
Benjamin Seaver	(1852–1854)
Jerome Van Crowninshield Smith	(1854-1856)

MAJOR INDUSTRIES AND EMPLOYERS

Shipbuilding and nautical supplies
Banking and insurance
Ironworks and metalworking
Piano manufacturing
Publishing and printing

MAJOR NEWSPAPERS

Boston Bee
Boston Courier
Boston Daily Advertiser
Boston Daily Atlas
Daily Chronicle
Daily Chronotype
Daily Mail
Boston Daily Times
Boston Herald
Boston Journal
Boston Post
Boston Recorder
Boston Transcript
Boston Traveler

MAJOR EVENTS

1832: The New England Anti-Slavery Society and the Boston Female Anti-Slavery Society are founded.

1835: Railroads open to Providence, Rhode Island, and Worcester, Massachusetts, and soon to the north and northwest. This greatly improves transportation since previously Boston was only served by one short canal.

1848: Water is brought to Boston from Lake Cochituate near Framingham, Massachusetts, about twenty miles to the west, replacing the inadequate supply from Jamaica Pond in nearby Roxbury, Massachusetts.

1850: A special census report sponsored by the city of Boston reveals that 47 percent of the population consists of foreign-born people and their children.

1852: The Commonwealth (State) of Massachusetts appoints a three-man commission to make plans to fill the Back Bay former tidal marsh.

influx of new immigrants, one mayor was elected from the Native American or Know-Nothing Party, Dr. Jerome Van Crowninshield Smith. Smith did not institute anti-immigrant measures like those passed at the state level in Massachusetts, however. Instead he reduced taxes and passed laws that targeted deceptive market sales and eliminated tolls on bridges.

In 1854 voters approved changes in the city government. The mayor was given limited veto powers but was removed from meetings of the board of aldermen that convened to approve appointments and initiatives. Additionally, the board was increased from eight to twelve members, still elected at large.

Public education for boys began in 1635 when the Boston Latin School was established, and after 1789 Boston provided elementary education for girls six months per year. Boys attended school all year. Boston established the nation's first public high school for girls in 1826. It served thirty-five students, but Mayor Quincy closed it in 1828 on the grounds that no city could stand the expense. In 1835 white merchant Abiel Smith donated a building for a public elementary school for African Americans; the Smith School operated for twenty years until state law prohibited school segregation by race.

After Mayor Quincy's public construction projects in the 1820s led to the completion of Quincy Market, a large workhouse, and other institutions, Boston was well positioned to meet its economic and social needs. Quincy Market handled the city's wholesale food demands into the twentieth century. As the population grew, more social service facilities, such as orphanages and residences for the elderly poor, were built by philanthropic organizations to serve specific needy populations.

Following completion of the city's Quincy Market project, which filled the former Town Cove, Boston encouraged the filling of more coves and marshlands by private ventures in the 1830s and 1840s. In 1837 the city established the Boston Public Garden by granting a petition to Horace Gray and others to create a botanical garden on twenty-four acres of marsh. Over a ten-year period, Mill Cove was filled between modern-day Haymarket Square and Causeway Street for business purposes, and the Church Street District (now Bay Village) was filled by property owners along the shore of the Back Bay. In the 1840s the South Cove was filled for commercial uses and new railroad stations.

In about 1850 the city began a large development in the new South End by laying out streets on the desolate Boston Neck to connect the city to Roxbury and filling in around the shore. Boasting several elegant park streets, the new neighborhood attracted many wealthy Protestant families. As the Back Bay former tidal marsh became severely polluted, the city of Boston wanted to fill it and develop the new land for housing. The project to fill in the Back Bay was taken over by the state legislature, which appointed a three-man commission in 1852 for that purpose. The city objected at several points, but the Commonwealth of Massachusetts prevailed. Boston benefited in the long run by having over five hundred acres of valuable taxable land added to its territory.

INDUSTRY, COMMERCE, AND LABOR

By 1828 Boston's economy had been based on maritime trade for nearly two hundred years. Local merchants sent ships to ports all over the world. Boston, as a trading town, supported businesses for investments in shipping, supplying ships for voyages, insuring ships and cargoes, and wholesaling goods brought in by ship. The large granite and brick wharf buildings along Atlantic Avenue and Commercial Street today are reminders of Boston's strong position in maritime trade until about 1850. Families such as the Cabots, Lowells, and Appletons made their first fortunes as merchants. Banks and insurance companies thrived on mercantile wealth and contributed to Boston's economic success.

The building of sailing ships came to Boston quite late when Donald McKay established a shipyard in eastern Boston. He launched his first large ship in 1845 and soon was building clipper ships for the China trade and sailing to California during the gold rush. His fastest ship, the *Flying Cloud* of 1851, once sailed around the tip of South America to San Francisco, California, in the record time of eighty-nine days and twenty-one hours. But as shipping was leaving Boston, McKay's clipper ships would mostly sail from New York City. Boston had lost much of its advantage in maritime trade by the 1840s because New York and other ports farther south had better access to inland resources and markets. The hills and mountains west of Boston prevented the construction of canals and early railroads far inland from the city, while New York's Erie Canal and railroads reached the Great Lakes and opened up lucrative markets. The use of the Middlesex Canal to Lowell, Massachusetts, on the Merrimack River dropped off in the 1830s when a railroad was completed.

As Boston's dominance in maritime trade began to slip, the Industrial Revolution reached New England. Although Boston did not have a fast-flowing river to generate waterpower for factories, families and banks holding wealth from the trade era were eager to invest in the new industries. Textile mills in other New England cities were the key to making Boston a successful machine metropolis. The new town of Lowell had several large cotton mills by 1828 when the Lowell and Appleton companies were established. Boston provided investments for the factories, handled the shipping of cotton from the South, insured the facilities and products, and housed the wholesaling functions for the profitable new industry. Factories all over New England increased the profits of Bostonians and their businesses.

Boston itself grew to be an industrial center of a different kind. By the mid-1800s, it was noted for its garment, leather goods, and machinery industries. The estimated or actual value of Boston's annual industrial products grew from $25 million in 1830 to $58 million in 1855. Organs and pianos were produced in Boston in large numbers, and the Chickering Piano Company factory in the South End became the second largest building in the country in 1853.

Boston banks thrived due to shipping and industry until 1837, at which point there were thirty-four banks with capital totaling $21,350,000. Then a banking crisis and depression hit, which caused thirteen Boston banks to fail.

In 1834 four thousand artisans in sixteen crafts formed a citywide union of trades and issued a declaration of rights claiming that workmen had the right to associate together. However, the prevailing legal view in Massachusetts was that unions were conspiracies that threatened society. A lawsuit against the Boston Society of Journeymen Bootmakers in 1840 was decided against the union and appealed based on the judge's instructions to the jury. The eminent chief justice of the State Supreme Judicial Court, Lemuel Shaw, heard the appeal. Shaw ruled in favor of the bootmakers and upheld the workers' right to organize and strike as long as they did so peacefully and without violating contracts.

Massachusetts took the lead in the movement for the ten-hour workday in the 1830s. As the market for textiles suffered from heavy competition, machines were sped up and workers handled more machines, making thirteen- and fourteen-hour workdays even more onerous. The movement for a shorter workday included efforts to improve conditions for children as young as eight or nine who worked the same long hours in the mills. Boston journeymen, demanding rights and better treatment for workers, wrote the *Ten Hour Circular* of 1835. The depression of 1837 temporarily suppressed unions, but a region-wide 1844 convention in Boston on the ten-hour day resulted in the establishment of the New England Workingmen's Association (NEWA). Middle-class reformers participated in the NEWA and privileges were extended to women's labor groups.

RACE, ETHNICITY, AND IMMIGRATION

In the late 1820s, most residents of the small city of Boston had English roots. Although this situation underwent drastic change by 1854, Boston's cultural and educational life continued to be dominated by the more affluent Protestant families. By the beginning of this period, Mayor Josiah Quincy's new public buildings and architect Charles Bulfinch's elegant designs had transformed Boston into a much more impressive city. The two decades starting in about 1825 saw Boston come to be called the Athens of America. Writers and philosophers, including Ralph Waldo Emerson, Nathaniel Hawthorne, Henry Wadsworth Longfellow, Henry David Thoreau, and John Greenleaf Whittier, brought the city cultural fame. The Protestant leadership elite took responsibility for improving the community and sponsoring the arts. Statesmen, artists, physicians, lawyers, ministers, teachers, and leaders from all walks of life also joined the effort toward a better Boston.

Social and humanitarian reforms were also part of this effort to make Boston a model for America and the world. Male and female writers and philosophers who valued human integrity and nature founded the Transcendentalist Movement in 1836. Elizabeth Peabody and Margaret Fuller, among others, developed women's-rights values that led to the first Women's Rights Convention in Boston in 1854. A growing prohibition movement led to a state law banning alcohol sales in 1852, but it proved difficult to enforce and was repealed about fifteen years later. In 1843 Dorothea Dix's report on horrendous conditions in the state's insane asylums led to better care for the mentally ill.

Boston's African American community had its roots in the 1650s and was centered on the north slope of Beacon Hill in the early-to-mid-nineteenth century. This community opposed slavery in the South—a sentiment shared by liberal whites in Boston. In 1829 William Lloyd Garrison, a local white abolitionist leader, gave his first antislavery speech in the Park Street Church. In that same year, Boston African American businessman David Walker published *An Appeal to the Colored Citizens of the United States*, in which he urged slaves to fight for their freedom. Governors in the South demanded Walker's arrest, and he was found dead on the street a year later. In 1831 Garrison launched *The Liberator* newspaper to promote the abolition of slavery.

Organized abolitionist activity in the country began in January 1832 when white and African American Bostonians founded the New England Anti-Slavery Society at the African Meeting House on Beacon Hill. In October of the same year, the Boston Female Anti-Slavery Society was established. The antislavery movement met with a cold reception and opposition, however. Much of the support for the South came from the textile industry's reliance on cheap cotton produced with slave labor. Acceptance of abolitionist views increased gradually.

In 1842 the Underground Railroad was created by Boston African Americans to help fugitive slaves escape to freedom in Canada. When runaway slave George Latimer was arrested in Boston in 1842, sixty thousand signatures were secured on a petition to free him, and that freedom was purchased for $400. In the next year a state law made it illegal to arrest or hold fugitive slaves. In 1850 conflict between abolitionists and adherents of slavery erupted over the Fugitive Slave Act supported by Massachusetts Senator Daniel Webster. Also in 1850 the Boston Vigilance Committee was formed, which was chaired by Unitarian minister Theodore Parker. The committee raised money to aid more than one hundred runaway slaves. A meeting in Faneuil Hall to voice opposition for the Fugitive Slave Act and Daniel Webster was broken up by anti-abolitionists. Boston native Harriet Beecher Stowe's *Uncle Tom's Cabin*, published in 1852, fueled abolitionist sentiments throughout the northern states when it became the most popular book in United States history. When runaway slave Anthony Burns was captured in Boston and ordered returned to the South in 1854, fifty thousand demonstrators lined the streets as two thousand armed militia members, police, and soldiers escorted him to a ship. The passage of the Kansas-Nebraska Act that year turned most Bostonians into abolitionists.

Incidents of violence against Catholic Irish American immigrants occurred as their numbers began to increase in the 1830s. The most rapid influx of Irish came during the potato famine in the 1840s. Contrasting reactions occurred in Boston. In 1847 prominent Protestant and Catholic Bostonians established the Irish Famine Relief Committee, which sent four shiploads of food and other supplies to Ireland. On the other hand, many Protestants held deep prejudices against Irish Catholics that originated in England. In the popular press and cartoons, both the Irish and African Americans were portrayed as stupid, dirty, and even subhuman. Economic discrimination against Irish Americans was symbolized by the phrase "no Irish need apply" that appeared on job notices. By 1854 about half of Boston's population consisted of foreign-born citizens and their children, and an estimated 80 percent of them were of Irish origin. Only 1.9 percent of Boston's population in 1850 consisted of German-born immigrants and their children. In 1854 the virulently anti-immigrant American (Know-Nothing) Party held nearly every elected office in Boston and Massachusetts. In spite of the anti-Irish sentiment, the large and growing Irish American population was laying the groundwork for the political dominance of Irish Catholics in Boston by early in the twentieth century.

See also *Boston, MA 1776–1790; Boston, MA 1790–1828; Boston, MA 1854–1877; Boston, MA 1877–1896; Boston, MA 1896–1929; Boston, MA 1929–1941; Boston, MA 1941–1952*

WILFRED E. HOLTON

BIBLIOGRAPHY

Adams, Russell B. *The Boston Money Tree*. New York, NY: Thomas Y. Crowell Company, 1957.

Green, James R., and Hugh Carter Donahue. *Boston's Workers: A Brief History*. Boston, MA: National Endowment for the Humanities Learning Library Program, Boston Public Library Program, Publication Number 8, 1979.

Juravich, Tom, William Hartford, and James R. Green. *Commonwealth of Toil: Chapters in the History of Massachusetts Workers and Their Unions*. Amherst: University of Massachusetts Press, 1966.

O'Connor, Thomas H. *The Athens of America: Boston 1825–1845.* Amherst: University of Massachusetts Press, 2001.

———. *Bibles, Brahmins, and Bosses: A Short History of Boston.* 3rd ed. rev. Boston, MA: Trustees of the Public Library and the City of Boston, 1991.

———. *Eminent Bostonians.* Cambridge, MA: Harvard University Press, 2002.

———. *The Hub: Boston Past and Present.* Boston, MA: Northeastern University Press, 2001.

Vrabel, Jim. *When in Boston: A Time Line & Almanac.* Boston, MA: Northeastern University Press, 2004.

CINCINNATI, OH 1828–1854

BY 1828, THE FORTIETH ANNIVERSARY OF THE CITY'S 1788 FOUNDING on the shores of the Ohio River, Cincinnati justly claimed the title "Queen City of the West." One of the nation's fastest-growing urban centers, it became a major destination for immigrants, particularly from Ireland and the German states. The thirteenth largest American city in 1820, Cincinnati ranked seventh in population by 1830 and was the sixth largest city by 1840. By this time it was also the third largest manufacturing center.

After the opening of the Miami and Erie Canal in the 1820s, the city's trade routes were dramatically expanded. As an educational, printing, and fine arts center, Cincinnati was the focus of cultural and intellectual activity in the interior West. Located due north of the slave state of Kentucky, but with its most vital trading done with New Orleans, Cincinnatians straddled both sides of the growing debate over slavery. However, the city restricted the lives of its African American residents by law and practice.

GOVERNMENT AND POLITICS

Cincinnati was first chartered as a town in 1802 and then in 1819 as a city with a mayor-council form of government. The primary responsibility of this early city government was maintaining order to facilitate commerce and trade. City elections tended to focus on local issues, yielding temporary groupings like the Coffee House Party, unless there were also national elections being held at the same time. Over the next decades, Democrats maintained a more consistent structure, though the Whig Party, which was anti-Andrew Jackson and pro-Bank of the United States, found strong support. The practice in Cincinnati of avoiding the slavery question to maintain trade with the South largely ended in 1854 with the Kansas-Nebraska Act's provision to allow slavery in land north of the 1820 line. (This line dividing slave and free states was created as part of the Missouri Compromise.) Many Cincinnatians, including Salmon P. Chase and Free-Soiler, city solicitor, and future president Rutherford B. Hayes, participated in the formation of the Republican Party.

In 1850 Cincinnati began to annex adjoining developed land and continued to do so until about 1920. In many cases, residents of the communities annexed were eager to obtain the city services that were becoming common, such as police and fire fighting forces.

QUICK FACTS

CINCINNATI, OH 1828–1854

MAYORS

Isaac G. Burnet	(1819–1831)
Elisha Hotchkiss	(1831–1833)
Samuel W. Davies	(1833–1843)
Henry Evans Spencer	(1843–1851)
Mark P. Taylor	(1851–1853)
David T. Snelbaker	(1853–1855)

MAJOR INDUSTRIES AND EMPLOYERS

Clothing manufacturing (including outworkers and seamstresses)
Iron foundries and works
Furniture
Pork processing, packing, and shipping
Printing and publishing

MAJOR NEWSPAPERS

Cincinnati Daily Commercial
Cincinnati Daily Enquirer
Cincinnati Daily Gazette
Cincinnati Daily Times
Daily Cincinnati Chronicle
Liberty Hall
Volksblatt
Volksfreund

MAJOR EVENTS

1825–1845: Construction of the Miami and Erie Canal and the Whitewater Canal connects Cincinnati's water routes through the Ohio River to the Great Lakes and to fertile Indiana, vastly expanding the city's hinterland and fostering agricultural development.

1829: Race riots and the enforcement of strict black codes drive nearly half of Cincinnati's black population to leave the city.

1834: Debates on the slavery question and colonization take place at the Lane Seminary, headed by Lyman Beecher, and a number of faculty and students leave Cincinnati for Oberlin College, where both African American and women students are soon admitted.

1830s–1840s: Cincinnati becomes known as the nation's "Porkopolis"—the largest center of pork processing and distribution in the country. The use of pork by-products, particularly lard, to produce candles and soap, leads to the development of major producers, most notably Procter and Gamble.

1840s–1850s: Cincinnati grows to be the third largest manufacturing city in the United States and the third largest city in population. It becomes a major destination for immigrants, particularly a diverse group of peoples from the German states and from Ireland.

Throughout the 1830s, Cincinnati expanded parts of its infrastructure and began to issue bonds. The city also purchased railroad and canal stock. One of the most expensive city enterprises undertaken during this era was the purchase of an ineffective waterworks, payments for which were charged to the user as "water rent." This was consistent with the practice of charging property owners who wanted their streets paved for the expense incurred. In making the water available to potential purchasers, the city government protected the public interest of the municipality by providing protection from the threats of fire and epidemic disease. By 1847 the city expanded its waterworks and thus its responsibility for providing regular ongoing residential services and fire protection and protecting commerce. It had also begun collecting water rents twice yearly through a water commission.

Another expensive project the city undertook during this period was the creation of common schools. Cincinnati asked the Ohio legislature for authority to create these schools only when it could not convince the legislature to do so statewide. The 1829 amendment to the city charter allowed Cincinnati to create common schools and collect taxes for their support. The schools served the public interest of the commercial city by educating all white children. It would be another twenty years before common schooling for African American children would be addressed.

INDUSTRY, COMMERCE, AND LABOR

After 1828 Cincinnati's commercial and industrial sectors advanced dramatically. The 1830s and 1840s saw new mechanization, including the assembly-line processing of meat, particularly beef and pork. Indeed, Cincinnati became the nation's largest meat packing and shipping center and acquired the nickname "Porkopolis." Pigs arrived from the vast hinterland—particularly Ohio and Indiana—by foot, canal, or railroad. The increasing number of plants making glue, chemicals, leather, brushes, and lard oil from pork by-products raised the value of hogs sold in Cincinnati. Entrepreneurs William Procter and James Gamble built their soap and candle business by using pork by-products.

Commerce increased rapidly, most notably due to steamboat travel on the Ohio and Mississippi Rivers to New Orleans. Trade was also facilitated with northern areas through a series of canals, roads, and, ultimately, railroads. European travelers to the United States, including Alexis de Tocqueville and Charles Dickens, visited Cincinnati and reported on its progress. Michel Chevalier called it "the capital, or great interior mart of the West," noting its vast agricultural hinterland. The industries that employed the most workers included meatpacking and processing; iron foundries; furniture and other wood products; the printing of books and other publications; the making of soap and lard; the production of whiskey and beer; jobs relating to the steamboat trade; and the manufacturing of boots, shoes, textiles, and clothing. These latter businesses employed a workforce of approximately 20 percent women who worked as seamstresses or did piecework.

Local business leaders founded the Cincinnati Chamber of Commerce in 1830, then expanded it significantly following the financial panic of 1837. They also created the Cincinnati Merchants' Exchange, hired a paid clerk, and created and regulated standards with regards to weights and measures, quality of goods, and prices. The exchange also offered banking and bonding services. By 1850 the exchange functioned as the center of Cincinnati's local economic activity, publishing weekly information on the market and pricing. It facilitated and secured transactions and produced an annual report that listed transactions on the docks. It also assessed the state of the market as manufacturing expanded in the 1840s.

As manufacturing expanded and began the shift from small establishments to factories employing hundreds of workers, artisans expressed concerns about their place in the changing commercial landscape. Tailors, cabinet makers, printers, and building carpenters led Cincinnati workers in forming trade unions beginning in the mid-1820s. They demanded fair wages and

Situated on the Ohio River, Cincinnati became a major commercial center in the early nineteenth century. Steamships quickened the movement of Cincinnati's goods, most notably the pork products that gave the city its nickname of "Porkopolis."   *Source: Library of Congress*

the recognition of their rights as citizens of the Republic. By the mid-1830s, they had joined together to form a General Trades Union and launched a general strike in 1836. The panic that began the next year thwarted their efforts and union organizing in general. In 1841 a Working Men's Association emerged that supported the creation of trade unions to advocate for the artisan against the violations of his rights by larger businesses and their investors. The association also published a newspaper.

Little successful organizing occurred until 1850, when a group of printers began to publish a new daily newspaper called the *Nonpareil.* They advocated for the formation of trade unions and the rights of laborers in America and spoke against capitalists and aggressive city-building activity that would further compromise the standing of workers. By 1853–1854, a rise in prices prompted strike activity for the first time in nearly two decades. As they had earlier, union members challenged what they saw as threats to their rights to equal opportunity in the changing Republic. The large number of recent immigrants from the German states and Ireland were well represented among Cincinnati's laborers. A significant number of Germans succeeded economically in the city. By the 1850s Cincinnati was home to 3,382 factories, employing some thirty-three thousand people. A large proportion of Cincinnati residents maintained their optimism about the city's potential for further growth and hoped it would in turn provide them with individual opportunity.

RACE, ETHNICITY, AND IMMIGRATION

The dramatically growing city of Cincinnati attracted a large number of immigrants. They came from western farms and eastern cities. Some were free African Americans or fugitive slaves from Kentucky and Virginia. Others were immigrants from Europe, particularly from the 1830s onward. The 1850 census reported that immigrants from the German states accounted for 28 percent of the city's population and immigrants from Ireland 12 percent. Immigrants from these two groups, combined with English, Scottish, and other settlers, composed more than half the city's population. African American migration north to Cincinnati soared, especially after 1826. That population then decreased from 2,258 in 1829 to 1,090 in 1830, following a focused race-based attack—a three-day riot—in 1829. The African American population rose back to the pre-riot level after 1840 and then to 3,237 in 1850.

Slavery was never legal in Cincinnati, yet with the practice already in place across the river in Kentucky, race was always an issue in the city. In 1804 the year-old state of Ohio prepared to limit citizenship by race and discourage African Americans from settling within its borders by passing the first of its "black laws." The Act to Regulate Black and Mulatto Persons required those persons to register with the county, pay a $12 fee, and hold a Certificate of Freedom from their county of residence. It also made it illegal for anyone to hire a person of color who did not have a freedom certificate and provided fines for violations.

Though Cincinnati's African American population grew little before 1826, an influx of arrivals in the next three years raised the number from approximately 700 to 2,258 by 1829. Constrained by legal, economic, and personal restrictions, African Americans in Cincinnati began to build communities of their own. They found themselves largely relegated to the least-desirable residential locations, which included an area on the edge of town to the southwest that came to be called "Bucktown" and one to the east known as "Little Africa." In this densely packed walking city, however, these areas were never completely segregated from white city residents. African Americans also faced discrimination in white churches, and by the 1820s they had established an African Methodist Episcopal Church where they could worship without being demeaned. They also used the church to create a vehicle for public statements opposing racist practices as violations of their rights as Americans. Cincinnati established a series of common schools at the end of the decade but barred African Americans from attending them.

1829 marked an organized attack on African American residential enclaves after local whites called for the enforcement of the black laws. In response, more than a thousand African Americans elected to participate in the formation of a new colony in Canada, named for Anglican antislavery activist William Wilberforce, or to leave Cincinnati for other places in Ohio. Riots occurred again in 1836, with an attack on the printing press of abolitionist publisher James G. Birney, and again in 1841. African Americans refused to tolerate these attacks and began working with political leaders to settle the issues. The rest of the decade saw relative peace, and in 1848 Ohio loosened its black law requirements.

While many African Americans found work in unskilled jobs, including work on steamboats, a smaller component worked as skilled or semiskilled artisans or entrepreneurs. Others were clergymen, schoolteachers, or physicians. Several built widely respected careers, including photographer J. P. Ball, maker of beds Henry Boyd, hairdresser to the city's elite women Eliza Potter, and artist Robert Duncanson. Duncanson painted murals in the home of the city's richest man and philanthropist, Nicholas Longworth. At the African American-owned Dumas Hotel, freemen rented rooms, but so did the enslaved personal servants of southern visitors who were in Cincinnati for entertainment or business. This situation provided opportunities for exchanging information on freedom and slavery.

Throughout this period, Cincinnati leaders avoided antagonizing their commercial partners in the South even as the city became a major locus of Underground Railroad activity. In 1836 debates on the slavery question and colonization that were held on the campus of Lane Seminary became so controversial that a number of theology students, led by Theodore Weld, left Lane and moved to Oberlin College. The president of Lane Seminary at the time was Lyman Beecher, whose daughter Harriet married seminary professor Calvin E. Stowe. Harriet lived in Cincinnati for several more years, observing the return of fugitive slaves to their masters, and incorporated those observations into her famous book *Uncle Tom's Cabin*.

Immigrants, whose opportunities were less limited than those of African Americans, arrived in large numbers beginning in the 1820s and comprised more than half of the city's population by midcentury. Irish immigrants, who made up some 12 percent of the city's population by 1850, were largely refugees from the 1840s potato famine. They were poor, Catholic, and from rural backgrounds, lacking the skills necessary for urban work. Immigrants came from England, Scotland, and other countries as well, although in smaller numbers. The most important immigrant group, however, was the Germans, who constituted some 29 percent of Cincinnati's population by the 1850s. The first large group of Germans arrived in the 1830s. Many of them were political liberals from the German states, and their numbers included curriers, hatters, tanners, and shoemakers, as well as unskilled laborers. Immigration accelerated in the 1840s and brought a heavier concentration of skilled artisans, including furniture makers, masons, and brewers, as well as political radicals from the revolutions of 1848. By 1850 more than half of the German population had settled in the area north of the central city, above the Miami Canal, in a neighborhood that thus became known as "Over-the-Rhine." Like other Americans, when they achieved economic success, most German families opted to move out to the developing suburbs.

While Cincinnatians participated in the Know-Nothing Party nativism of the 1850s, large numbers of German residents rose to prominence, including furniture manufacturers Mitchell and Rammelsberg, whose innovative six-floor mechanized factory set a new standard for production. Germans in the city held places in all socioeconomic ranks, and, unlike their African American counterparts, they were accepted as Americans when they prospered. The first German daily newspaper, the *Volksblatt*, served the interests of the more liberal arrivals of the 1830s. In the 1850s conservative Catholics started the *Volksfreund* in opposition to the *Volksblatt*. Though some two-thirds of the city's Germans were Catholic, members of several Protestant sects and German Jews joined their ranks. Dr. Isaac M. Wise played a pivotal role in the development of Reformed Judaism in America and laid the foundations for the first Reform rabbinical center, Hebrew Union College in suburban Cincinnati. German civic leaders from these diverse branches joined the Democratic and Whig Parties, and many played prominent roles in politics. Some even joined the Know-Nothing Party briefly in the 1850s. Like other Cincinnatians, most tried to remain publicly neutral on the issue of slavery to avoid disturbing trade with the South, but a significant number joined the new Republican Party as well.

See also *Cincinnati, OH 1854–1877; Cincinnati, OH 1877–1896*

JUDITH SPRAUL-SCHMIDT

BIBLIOGRAPHY

Aaron, Daniel. *Cincinnati, Queen City of the West: 1819–1838.* Columbus: Ohio State University Press, 1992.

Abbott, Carl. *Boosters and Businessmen: Popular Economic Thought and Urban Growth in the Antebellum Middle West.* Westport, CT: Greenwood Press, 1981.

Marcus, Alan I. *Plague of Strangers: Social Groups and the Origins of City Services in Cincinnati.* Columbus: Ohio State University Press, 1991.

Ross, Steven J. *Workers on the Edge: Work, Leisure, and Politics in Industrializing Cincinnati, 1788–1890.* New York, NY: Columbia University Press, 1985.

Shapiro, Henry D., and Jonathon D. Sarna, eds. *Ethnic Diversity and Civic Identity: Patterns of Conflict and Cohesion in Cincinnati since 1820.* Urbana: University of Illinois Press, 1992.

Stradling, David. *Cincinnati: From River City to Highway Metropolis.* Charleston, SC: Arcadia Publishing, 2003.

Taylor, Henry Louis, ed. *Race and the City: Work, Community, and Protest in Cincinnati, 1820–1970.* Urbana: University of Illinois Press, 1993.

Taylor, Nikki M. *Frontiers of Freedom: Cincinnati's Black Community, 1802–1868.* Athens, OH: Ohio University Press, 2005.

Wade, Richard C. *The Urban Frontier: The Rise of Western Cities, 1790–1830.* Columbus: Ohio State University Press, 1996.

ALBANY, NY 1828–1854

IN 1828 ALBANY WAS MOST REMARKABLE for its commercialism and government structures, and the city was also noteworthy because it retained a unique position as the head of sloop navigation in the region. Immigrants considered Albany ideal because it was not congested like larger cities and because of job opportunities and its "salubrious air." The first decades of the nineteenth century could be characterized as a period of substantial wealth, prosperity, and social diversity. Of great note was the completion of the Erie Canal in 1825. It was a time when the city earned respectable status as a center for the advancement of natural and biological sciences and as a hub for public and private industry. Banking, insurance, and education became principal enterprises, and, because Albany was a major commercial port, it developed as a regional center for railroads and shipping. What was important during these decades was that there was an accord among businesses. Companies worked together to accommodate political and commercial needs, and many firms became so

QUICK FACTS

ALBANY, NY **1828–1854**

MAYORS:

James Stevenson	(1826–1828)
Charles E. Dudley	(1828–1829)
John Townsend	(1829–1831)
Francis Bloodgood	(1831–1832)
John Townsend	(1832)
Francis Bloodgood	(1833)
Erastus Corning	(1834–1837)
Teunis VanVechten	(1837–1839)
Jared Rathbone	(1839–1841)
Teunis VanVechten	(1841–1842)
Barent Staats	(1842–1843)
Friend Humphrey	(1843–1845)
John Keyes Paige	(1845–1846)
William Parmelee	(1846–1848)
John Taylor	(1848–1849)
Friend Humphrey	(1849–1850)
Franklin Townsend	(1850–1851)
Eli Perry	(1851–1854)
William Parmelee	(1854–1856)

MAJOR INDUSTRIES AND EMPLOYERS

Lumber
Brewing
New York State government
Cattle

MAJOR NEWSPAPERS

Albany Gazette
Albany Argus
The Guardian
American Masonic Record and Albany Literary Journal
Albany Evening Journal
Farmers, Mechanics, and Workingmen's Advocate
Daily Patriot
Albany Atlas
Daily Knickerbocker
Albany Morning Express
Albany Daily Messenger
Albany Evening Atlas
Albany Daily Times
Temperance Recorder

MAJOR EVENTS

1831: The Hudson and Mohawk Railroad launches the *DeWitt Clinton*, the first passenger rail train engine in New York.

1832: A cholera epidemic infects about 766 people and kills over 320. Barrels of tar are burned in the streets to contain the disease, and stores, schools, and the waterfront are closed.

1832: A riot occurs at Lodge Street, led by "indignant citizens" upset over a "disreputable house" of blacks and whites displaying raunchy behavior who disturb the peace. The mayor and constables are unable to contain the crowd, and they tear down the house.

1839: The "anti-rent wars" commence when tenant farmers organize to riot against Albany's Van Rensselaer heirs, who tried to collect payments on overdue leaseholds. The county sheriff and the militia fail to quell the protests. The conflict continues periodically until 1845 when a state law dissolves all manor rights.

1840: The drawbridge at State Street falls into the Hudson River injuring many; twenty people drown.

1844: The Albany State Normal School is established to educate teachers. It is the founding institution of the State University of New York system.

successful they incorporated and formed conglomerates. This changed the political, physical, and social dynamics of Albany. Abundant commercial capital fueled the formation of a significant wealthy class. Albany looked regal, but, as in other cities, officials contended with immigration, disaster, and disease, which caused hardship and presented political challenges. Big business and state, county, and local governments expanded, and with that expansion came the development of the hospitality industry. New public policies were passed to accommodate local economic endeavors, but Albany was seen as a link to the West, so the state supported improvements to benefit all citizens of the state.

GOVERNMENT AND POLITICS

Publicly elected members of the city's common council and the president of the council ran the government in Albany, in accordance with the 1686 charter. The council elected a mayor, but partisan politics caused conflicts between the mayor and common council, and the council president held more power than the mayor. Thirteen different mayors held office within a sixteen-year period. As immigration and business flourished, public improvements became a major priority, but politicians could not always come to terms over which improvements best suited the city. However, this turmoil seemed balanced after 1840 when the public, instead of the common council, began to elect mayors.

The city was a Democratic (Jacksonian) stronghold from 1828 until the early 1850s. The most influential politicians were wealthy businessmen and lawyers, such as Erastus Corning, William Parmelee, and Franklin Townsend. A few Dutchmen still were active in government, inlcuding Barent Staats and Teunis VanVechten. Developing the Hudson River was the most significant political and commercial priority for the city, and it was necessary to accommodate increasing demands as western New York was settled. The city and state funded the construction of the Albany Basin, which consisted of four docks that extended into the river and were connected to a wharf. The change was necessary so larger steam vessels could dock at the wharf in deeper water, while small ships could dock at the shore or along the four docks. Storehouses were built in the middle of the Hudson on a wharf, and the city charged shippers dock and storage fees. Most importantly, parts of the river were dredged to prevent freezing and flooding, but a freshet continued to inundate the city each spring. Improvements encouraged the designation of Albany as an official U.S. port of entry in 1833, and William Seymour served as customs officer. The city funded the development of Steamboat Square to accommodate nine steamboat companies. These improvements were partially in response to New York's first railroad, the Mohawk and Hudson, which launched it first locomotive, *The DeWitt Clinton*, from Albany in 1831.

By the late 1820s, the county government of Albany had formed and held more authority in legal and social matters than the city government. The county oversaw road construction, transportation, land issues, and taxing issues. Facilitated by state law, the county built and operated key institutions the city once solely controlled, such as the Albany County Penitentiary (built in 1846) and the County Alms House, which by the 1830s the county and city both managed. A new city hall was completed in 1833, and by 1835 it housed the common council, which was comprised of ten aldermen and ten assistants; the mayor; recorder; and treasurer. Municipal government then reorganized into branches that included superintendents, committeemen, and commissioners. There were nineteen committees and an attorney and a watch staff of about forty men. The most active committees included the buildings committee, the accounting committee, and the schools committee.

Albany's health commission expanded during cholera epidemics in 1832 (about seven hundred cases and 320 deaths) and 1849 (twenty-two deaths). The commission ordered the usual precautions: the halting of shipping, the closing of offices and stores, the provision of vaccinations, and the burning of tar in the streets to contain the disease. Cholera caused a mass exodus and an economic slump, and Albany was referred to as the "city of the dead." Health officers believed the disease originated in a public school, but they also focused on "Shanty Town," a neighborhood near the Beaverkill Creek where Irish immigrants congregated in shacks. The epidemic prompted the incorporation in 1833 of the Albany Orphan Asylum, St. Vincent's Female Orphan Asylum, St. John's for male orphans, and the Home for the Friendless. Controlling cholera forced political action to remove some pastoral features. Creeks were filled, wells eliminated, and animals (mostly pigs and goats) were killed. Laws were also passed disallowing people to keep pigs, chickens, or goats in the city center.

By 1840 Albany had numerous government and commercial structures in the city core. The city passed legislation in 1841 that ordered the demolition of all Dutch-style and pre-1800 structures on prime streets, which many felt was necessary to make room for commercial space and create a downtown business district. It was a move to make Albany more modern and commercially efficient.

Although it was becoming more urban and commercial, Albany still contended with flooding and too many hogs. City officials passed ordinances to control swine. Records show that constables and watchmen captured four thousand hogs in 1849 and ten thousand in 1854. By 1854 a sewer system was built with underground gutters, and streets were paved with stone. Spring floods continued to bury at least two blocks every year and slowed river and rail traffic. By 1850 water supply had become a priority, and the city established a municipal waterworks, which supplied ten wards and had two reservoirs on the outskirts of the city.

Albany had only private schools until a state mandate in 1851 established free schools. The city taxed residents to build the new schools ($5,000 in 1852), of which there were thirteen by 1853, including the Wilberforce School for black children. A city school board formed in 1853 to manage programs and operations. In addition to the local schools, in 1844 the Normal School was established in the city to better educate and professionalize teachers. It was the founding institution for the State University of New York's college and university system.

The Albany Gas Light Company, which was reorganized by 1825 with municipal support, installed lines for streetlights and household use. The company built a gasworks near Charles and Grand Streets, making that neighborhood more industrial. Due to the use of natural gas and the development of more neighborhoods, the city built firehouses. By 1845 eleven engine companies and two hook and ladder companies had formed. Companies were called to the South End in 1848 when over six hundred homes covering thirty-seven acres burned in the city's largest fire. Citizens complained that disagreements among firefighters intensified the damage, and that year the first fire chief was appointed. He was paid $700 annually to oversee all engine companies.

After the fire, the city mandated that only brick structures could be built downtown. By 1854 a police department formed, and the police chief oversaw four districts, each of which had two captains, a doorman, and an average of ten policemen.

INDUSTRY, COMMERCE, AND LABOR

Because of the Albany Basin, the Erie Canal, and steamboat and railroad companies, Albany evolved as the largest center in the region for exchanging, producing, and transporting commodities. The largest new businesses were in manufacturing, railroads, hospitality, education, and science. In 1830 private industry remained a chief force in the economy. Business became diverse as a rush of immigrants brought ingenuity and capital and also provided a labor force and specialty skills that made the city a commercial haven. Crafts and trades dominated the economic and labor systems until 1845 and typically included the production and repair of shoes, clothes, hardware, and furniture that supplied the local market. Farmers from surrounding counties sold produce, grains, and meat at the public market and to dealers. Steam-powered vessels kept goods moving and shipping lucrative, which led to more merchants, laborers, and seamen settling in the city.

As commerce increased, the city center, located east of Eagle Street and surrounding State and Court Streets (Broadway), became a commercial district. Most small shops and stores were established in homes dating from the colonial period and positioned on main thoroughfares. Larger mercantile firms had storehouses and supplied produce, fruit, flour, and grains to western New York. Industry defined the city, and the period before 1850 could be described as an era of custom-made merchandise. Specialty craftsmen sold furs, cutlery, confections, silk suits, infant clothing, and jewelry—new businesses that reflected increasing consumerism, wealth, expert trades, and labor. Lawyers and physicians were the largest professional occupations, but the incorporation of banks and private schools increased vocations.

Albany's position as the largest inland port and its access to New York's thirty-two canals and railroads promoted the success of business and characterized the labor system. Albany was known for commerce, but by 1840, due to the establishment of eight banks, four insurance and railroad companies, and eight steamboat companies, the city was also identified with industry. As businesses became more centered on banking and insurance, native-born youths sought desk jobs, while immigrants took on manual labor posts. There were gas and wood stove dealers in the city's North End who in 1850 sold seventy-five thousand stoves annually at a return of $1 million. Coach and sleigh firms were founded, the most notable of which was John Kingsbury's, which patented a coach spring. German and Irish immigrants operated most of the specialty shops. There were many stonecutters and marble dealers, but Albany was known for plaster, piano, and stove manufacturers, all of which drove up the lumber industry, the production of natural resources, and factory and trade labor.

State government as a source of labor expanded in the late 1840s, as new state departments were created. State office buildings included the Department of Agriculture, the Department of Weights and Measures, the office of the attorney general, and the Banking Department. Each office had enough assistants and support staff to make the government the largest employer next to lumber and breweries. Major brewers included the Dobler Brewing Company and the Hinkle

Brewing Company. Albany exported over 30,000 gallons of beer annually in 1830 and a reported 162,000 gallons by 1850.

Women worked in food service, widows ran boarding houses, and Sylvia Zebra was the city's fortune teller for decades. More than ten women in 1842 set up inns before marriage. They competed with larger hotels, such as Delavan House, Stanwix Hall, and Knickerbacker Hall. Adam Blake, an African American, operated one of Albany's most exclusive establishments, Congress Hall, which catered to politicians.

The biggest industry outside the city core was the New York Central Railroad, which was founded by Erastus Corning. By 1854 the railroad acquired 350 acres of land for an engine house and repair and production shops, which provided labor to immigrants, trained machinists, car operators, and brakemen. At Exchange Street, Albany looked like the West, because more than thirteen hundred cattle roamed the railroad cattle yard. It was reported that sixty-nine cattle cars left Albany daily. By 1850 eighty thousand tons of merchandise were exchanged in Albany, mostly grain, lumber, sleighs, stoves, and glass.

Albany was renowned for advances in medicine and science, which created new institutions and jobs in education, research, and nursing. The most well-known scientific advancement was in 1829 when Albany native Joseph Henry used the intensity magnet to transmit an electrical current for one mile. Physicians flocked to Albany to learn anatomy and surgery. By 1845 fifty-seven doctors settled in the city. Most of them were traditionalists who had trained at universities, and they competed with the city's homeopaths and botanical physicians. Traditionalists founded Albany Medical College in 1839 and Albany Hospital in 1849, both of which were noted for training students in nursing and surgery. The Dudley Observatory was founded in 1854 and was noted for its research in astronomy.

RACE, ETHNICITY, AND IMMIGRATION

In 1828 the Dutch remained a prominent ethnic group in Albany. In 1830 the city's population reached 24,238, of which African Americans constituted one-third. By 1840, at which time the population reached 33,721, the Dutch had been eclipsed by large numbers of Irish and German immigrants and New Englanders. The presence of the foreign immigrants led to the formation of ethnic neighborhoods, and it also led many Albany natives to move out of the downtown area. Many immigrants lived in multiple-family dwellings. Some found job opportunities in factories, but most worked in trades and for the railroads. The Irish and English took city posts in the fire and police departments by 1855. The Irish settled mostly in the northwest quarter along Clinton Avenue near Sacred Heart Church. Another group settled south of Madison Avenue and north of Pearl Street. The Irish established Catholic churches and schools and attended the Cathedral of the Immaculate Conception (1852) and Holy Cross, which was the center of the neighborhood and enticed immigrants to settle the area. By 1850 Albany was known as "McAlbany" due to its large Irish Catholic population.

Germans and Jews were the second largest group of immigrants and established three ethnic neighborhoods. Jews settled east of South Pearl Street around Franklin Street and established three synagogues and several businesses. These businesses included tailor shops, specialty food and cigar stores, and furniture and upholstery stores. Many were involved in banking and law and in the newspaper business. Temple Beth El Jacob (1841) and Anshe Emeth (1850) incorporated and offered Hebrew lessons. The Jews lived near German immigrants in the South End and established an Evangelical Lutheran church. After the 1848 fire, many families moved west. A German neighborhood formed north of Central Avenue and featured import stores, specialty meat shops, and two Lutheran churches.

Albany also had a sizable population of African American residents, all of whom were emancipated in 1827. Most were New Englanders and former Albany-born slaves who were middle class. Black neighborhoods existed in the South End near Bassett and South Pearl Streets and in two areas in Arbor Hill. Most blacks worked as laborers or on the waterfront, and many worked in the service industries as cooks and waiters. Others operated lucrative businesses as barbers, tailors, fruit dealers, and hairdressers. In 1842 there were eighty-five black families in Albany. By 1850 the city's most famous African Americans were abolitionist Stephen Myers and wealthy skipper Captain Samuel Schuyler. The black population increased naturally, but mostly because blacks migrated from New York City and the Hudson Valley. There were two black schools and Baptist and Methodist black churches in the city by 1840.

By 1850 there were 50,700 people living in Albany, and the majority of them were immigrants. In 1854 an average of thirty-four immigrant trains passed through Albany daily headed to western New York. Many people, however, changed their destination plans and settled in Albany. They found it ideal for family life because it was not as crowded as larger cities and because the professional and unskilled labor opportunities in breweries, factories, and foundries and in public service were optimal.

See also *Albany, NY 1790–1828*

TRICIA BARBAGALLO

BIBLIOGRAPHY

Barbagallo, Tricia, Cynthia Sauer, and John Warren *A Historical Orientation to Albany, New York: Historic Crossroads, State Capital, and City of Neighborhoods.* Albany, NY: National Council on Public History, 1997.

Bowers, Virginia. *The Texture of a Neighborhood: Albany's South End, 1880–1940.* Albany, NY: South End Historical Society, 1991.

Howell, George R., and Jonathan Tenney, eds. *Bicentennial History of the County of Albany, N.Y. from 1609 to 1886.* Albany, NY: W. W. Munsell, 1886.

Kennedy, William. *O Albany!: Improbable City of Political Wizards, Fearless Ethnics, Spectacular Aristocrats, Splendid Nobodies, and Underrated Scoundrels.* New York, NY: Viking Press, 1983.

Munsell, Joel. *Annals of Albany.* 10 vols. Albany, NY: Munsell and Rowland, 1850–1871.

———. *Collections on the History of Albany.* 4 vols. Albany, NY: J. Munsell, 1876.

Reynolds, Cuyler. *Albany Chronicles: A History of the City Arranged Chronologically, From the Earliest Settlement to the Present Time.* Albany, NY: J. B. Lyon, 1906.

Rowley, William E. "Albany: A Tale of Two Cities, 1820–1860". PhD diss., University of Southern California, 1973.

Weise, Arthur. *History of the City of Albany.* Albany, NY: E. H. Bender, 1884.

Worth, Gorham. *Random Recollections of Albany from 1800 to 1808.* Albany, NY: J. Munsell, 1866.

CHARLESTON, SC 1828–1854

BETWEEN 1828 AND 1854, CHARLESTON UNDERWENT MOMENTOUS CHANGES. Although it was once a critical theater during the Revolutionary War and an important port city for the emerging nation, many of Charleston's leaders turned increasingly to local and regional concerns in the antebellum period. Epidemic disease, economic stagnation, and the constant fear of slave rebellions threatened the city. As the Civil War approached, the Charleston elite secured its place atop a teetering social system marked by intense political, economic, and racial inequality.

By the mid-eighteenth century, a mere 3 percent of the free heads of household controlled nearly half of Charleston's wealth. Most free citizens owned neither land nor slaves, and, although they were shut out of the halls of governance and privilege, many poorer whites found common cause with the city's elite as both maintained a strict adherence to white supremacy and the plantation system. When war came, threatening an end to that way of life, Charlestonians both rich and poor answered the call with their own declaration of independence, which they defended with their lives. Meanwhile, Charleston's blacks, both slave and free, saw the impending conflict as the much-awaited day of Jubilee and expressed their disdain for slavery when they responded—sometimes in arms, oftentimes with their feet—to the institution's final death knell.

GOVERNMENT AND POLITICS

In the immediate aftermath of the Revolutionary War, Charleston officials set about the task of reorganizing the local government. The chief executive officer of the city, known as the intendant, presided over a representative council comprised of Charleston's thirteen legislative districts. In 1836 the title of intendant was dropped when Robert Y. Hayne became the first chief executive officer of the city to be called mayor. Property restrictions limited the eligible electorate to white males who paid at least 3 shillings per year in taxes. By the antebellum period, the tax requirements for voters had been eliminated, although property restrictions on officeholders remained until after the Civil War. In effect, local politics was controlled by an oligarchy of wealthy, influential men drawn principally from the planter class. In its goal to protect the interests of the planters, the city council proved quite successful in keeping at bay a rising class of merchants and industrialists. At the same time, the council devoted itself to the social control of blacks, both slave and free, and of the city's poor whites, including a wave of new immigrants who entered the city during the 1830s and 1840s.

As memories of the Revolutionary War receded in the minds of many Americans, an important sector of the Charlestonian elite began to shift its loyalties away from the national unity so often lauded during the Revolution toward a new emphasis on regional unity. Perhaps nothing exemplifies this shift better than southern reaction to the Tariff of 1828, which raised fees on a range of manufactured goods. Fearful that the tariff would make international consumers less likely to buy southern cotton, many planters cried foul, dubbing the unpopular tax the "Tariff of Abominations." In 1827 Robert J. Turnbull, a wealthy Charlestonian lawyer, charged that the

QUICK FACTS

CHARLESTON, SC 1828–1854

MAYORS

Mayors in Charleston were
called "intendants" until 1836

John Gadsden	(1827–1829)
Henry Laurens Pinckney	(1829–1830)
James Pringle	(1830–1831)
Henry Laurens Pinckney	(1831–1833)
Edward North	(1833–1836)
Robert Young Hayne	(1836–1837)
Henry Laurens Pinckney	(1837–1840)
Jacob Mintzing	(1840–1842)
John Schnierle	(1842–1846)
Thomas Leger Hutchinson	(1846–1850)
John Schnierle	(1850–1852)
Thomas Leger Hutchinson	(1852–1855)

MAJOR INDUSTRIES AND EMPLOYERS

Cotton and rice exporting
Milling (West Point Mill and Charleston
   Cotton Manufacturing Company)

MAJOR NEWSPAPERS

Carolina Weekly Messenger

Charleston Courier
Charleston Daily Republican
*Charleston Evening Post and Commercial and Political
   Gazette*
Charleston Mercury
Charleston News and Courier
Charleston City Gazette
Charleston Observer
South Carolina and American General Gazette
South Carolina Gazette and General Advertiser
South Carolina Gazette
South Carolina Weekly Gazette
State Gazette of South Carolina

MAJOR EVENTS

1824: The Medical College of South Carolina opens.

1828: John C. Calhoun anonymously publishes the *South Carolina Exposition and Protest.*

1830: The first passenger steam locomotive in America, the *Best Friend*, begins regular service between Charleston and Hamburg, South Carolina.

1832: An epidemic of cholera is brought to Charleston, carried on the *Amelia* from New York City.

1838: A yellow fever epidemic devastates Charleston.

---

protective tariff was little more than "a scheme for rendering the South tributary to the North." Rather than submit to the measure, Turnbull and others argued for the right of states to nullify any federal law deemed contrary to the better interests of the state.

In April 1830, while celebrating the birthday of the late president Thomas Jefferson, Andrew Jackson raised his glass for a toast: "Our Federal Union—It must be Preserved." His vice president, John C. Calhoun of South Carolina, retorted with "The Union—next to our liberties most dear." Earlier in that same year, Daniel Webster of Illinois confronted Robert Y. Hayne in an epic debate on the floor of the Senate concerning states' rights. Hayne, a well-known lawyer, senator, and mayor from Charleston, defended the "Carolina doctrine" of nullification and secession, while Webster ardently championed the primacy of the Union. Over the course of eight days, the two men engaged in what would become one of the best-known debates in American history. From his perch as president of the Senate, John C. Calhoun presided over the debate with a marked neutrality, though behind the scenes he coached Hayne, who served, at least in some measure, as the mouthpiece for Calhoun's developing theories of nullification and secession. Indeed, Calhoun often found himself at odds with President Jackson. As early as 1828, Calhoun publicly defended nullification in the anonymously written *South Carolina Exposition and Protest*. In the end, his ideological differences with the president could not be reconciled, and he resigned his post as vice president, later mounting a successful senatorial campaign.

As talk of nullification reached a fever pitch throughout the South, Charleston's elite quickly found itself divided. A significant portion of the city's leaders counseled moderation and maintained a staunch adherence to the Union. Nullifiers expressed their opposition, not only to federal tax policies as represented by the Tariff of 1828, but also to the very idea of federal authority over the individual states. In the legislative elections of 1832, the nullifiers won the day and, convening at Columbia, rejected both the Tariff of 1828 and the more moderate Tariff of 1832. Tensions continued to rise as President Jackson moved troops to federal forts in South Carolina to intimidate the nullifiers. In addition, he engineered the passage of the Force Bill, which authorized the president to call up troops in the enforcement of federal laws. Jackson articulated his opposition to the very idea of secession as he implored South Carolinians to rally "under the banners of the union whose obligations you in common with all your countrymen have . . . and which must be indissoluble as long as we are capable of enjoying freedom." Eventually, a compromise was reached in the form of the Tariff of 1833, which further reduced the duty imposed on imported items. In response, the South Carolina legislature repealed its nullification of the tariff but nullified the Force Bill.

In the end, both sides proclaimed victory. For his part, Jackson reasserted federal power in all regions and rejected both nullification and secession as the product of "ambitious, deluded, and designing men." In South Carolina, the crisis resulted in the fullest articulation of the logic and right of nullification and secession. Indeed, Charleston provided many of the principle theorists for southern independence. This is certainly true of well-known men like John C. Calhoun and Robert Hayne, but is equally true of lesser-known Charlestonians like James Hamilton Jr., who coined the term "nullification" and predicted the eventual dissolution of the Union. Many institutions that proved critical in the lead-up to war were also located in Charleston. *The Charleston Mercury* newspaper, for example, served as the mouthpiece of the southern cause throughout the region.

INDUSTRY, COMMERCE, AND LABOR

Visitors to antebellum Charleston often commented on the breathtaking beauty of the city. Francis Asbury, a well-known Methodist minister, traveled through the region at the turn of the nineteenth century and noted the "beautiful deep sands, live oaks, lofty pines, palmetto swamps, with intermingled gums and cypresses, variegated by evergreens of bay and laurel, and twining jessamine flinging its odours far and wide around." Indeed, many regarded the city as a paragon of the plantation South, idyllic in its natural beauty and presumed social order. If Charleston fed planters' fantasies of a romantic South, however, it also dashed those same dreams. Throughout the 1830s and 1840s, the city experienced a series of debilitating disasters that killed hundreds of Charleston's residents, while nearly crippling the local economy. Throughout the 1830s and 1840s, several outbreaks of epidemic disease, including yellow fever and cholera, riddled the city and had a horrendous effect on trade. Fearful that the city was unhealthy, investors shied away from Charleston and opted to take their capital investments elsewhere. Significant economic stagnation resulted. Due to this, in 1828, despite the fact that Charleston shipped its greatest crop of rice and its second largest crop of cotton up to that time, the Charleston Chamber of Commerce lamented the future prospects of a city that had earlier been an economic juggernaut.

Adding to the city's economic problem was the reluctance of Charleston's elite to industrialize. Despite its fortuitous location, Charleston did not have railroads to connect the city's port with the emerging markets in the West. Moreover, the Charleston elite restricted the construction of all mills to the periphery of the city. Perhaps too-closely wedded to the idea of Charleston as a pastoral paradise, some planters rejected suggestions to industrialize the city, fearing that the natural beauty of the place might be lost under the weight of technological progress. At least one observer noted wryly that the delicate Charleston elite looked askance at industrialization "lest the smoke of an engine should disturb the delicate nerves of an agriculturalist; or the noise of the mechanic's hammer should break in upon the slumber of a real estate holder . . . while he is indulging in fanciful dreams of building on paper, the *Queen City of the South*."

From the planters' point of view, the lack of industrial development in the city had the added benefit of providing an important means of social control. Nearly 60 percent of Charleston's workforce was comprised of slaves. By limiting industry to the outskirts of the city, many planters and merchants hoped to reduce the number of blacks on Charleston's streets, thereby reducing the risk of slave uprisings in the city. And the Charleston elite had reason enough to fear. Throughout the antebellum period, arsonists, comprised mainly of rebellious poor whites and blacks, both slave and free, wreaked havoc in the city. Between 1825 and 1858, more than two hundred fires were reported in Charleston; nearly half of these were reported as arson by local authorities. And so, beneath the assurances of social order that many planters presumed were characteristic of southern slave society, a seething underclass of slaves, free blacks, and poor whites resisted the dominance of the planter elite.

All told, Charleston's leaders faced many obstacles as they attempted to industrialize and modernize the city. As a result, Charleston's economy proceeded in fits and starts throughout the antebellum period. Not until the 1850s did a small group of young businessmen emerge to tackle some of the city's toughest economic difficulties. Largely unaffiliated with the plantocracy of the city, these young entrepreneurs underwrote railroad production, the development of a merchant marine, and the deepening of the Charleston harbor. In addition, local businessmen organized the South Carolina Institute for the Promotion of Art, Mechanical Ingenuity, and Industry. Speaking before an annual conference of the institute in 1851, William Gregg implored his fellow Southerners not to "stand in the same relation to the Northern States and the balance of the manufacturing world, that Ireland . . . does to England—hewers of wood and drawers of water." Indeed, Gregg argued, the establishment of industry in the South would benefit that class of poor whites who "are wholly neglected, and are suffered to while away an existence but one step in advance of the Indian in the forest."

Eventually, the city's elite came to view southern modernization as a way to mobilize poor whites who might otherwise find common cause with slaves and free blacks, and in the end, the program of southern industrialization was a success in Charleston. By 1850 the city reigned as the industrial center of South Carolina, boasting as it did a vast array of mills, foundries, and distilleries. The success of this industrialization was due in large part to a rising cadre of entrepreneurs, businessmen, and investors who saw in Charleston development opportunities for real economic gain. In particular, these investors were successful in expanding rail development and modernizing the shipping industry in the city. These developments not only enriched members of the merchant class, they also enabled planters to ship cotton more effectively to the West by rail and across the Atlantic.

RACE, ETHNICITY, AND IMMIGRATION

At the heart of virtually all of the political and economic debates riddling the city during the antebellum era was the constant and persistent conflict over slavery. The principal example of this conflict is the 1822 slave conspiracy in which bondmen, under the leadership of former slave Denmark Vesey, planned a massive slave uprising. When the elaborate scheme came to the attention of Charleston planters, a ferocious response lay in wait for the would-be rebels. In the end, thirty-five blacks were hanged, including Vesey. Recent scholarship has questioned the extent, and even the reality, of the Vesey conspiracy. Some historians suggest that the entire event constituted little more than angry talk among a small group of blacks. Nevertheless, the swift and violent response of local authorities reflects clearly the constant fear and trepidation under which many Charleston residents lived.

In many ways, the Vesey conspiracy galvanized the city council. For years after the rebellion was quelled, the council persistently sought to curtail the movement and freedoms of the city's population of blacks and poor whites. The first steps in this process were several repressive measures. City officials made it unlawful for blacks to congregate in large numbers. Further, the council mandated that all free blacks be attached to a white steward, lest they be subject to enslavement. In addition, the council established a municipal guard of 150 men that would eventually develop into the city's police force and successfully petitioned the legislature to construct an arsenal, or "citadel," to protect and preserve the city's safety. Construction of a permanent arsenal began in 1825, and in 1842 the state legislature officially chartered the South Carolina Military Academy, more commonly known as the Citadel. At least one Charleston resident justified the city's mounting militarism by observing "the nature of our institutions of domestic slavery and its exposure of us to hostile machinations . . . render it doubly incumbent on us to cherish a military spirit and to diffuse military science among our people." These local measures mirrored the state's attempt to limit black mobility. In December 1822 the legislature passed the Negro Seaman Act that required all black sailors who entered Charleston's port to be officially detained until their vessels left the city. Black sailors found on shore could be summarily sold into slavery.

Notably, the extension of social control applied not only to blacks but to poor whites as well. Recent immigrants, along with poor whites and criminals, increasingly found themselves bound in the city's prison house, which stood adjacent to the workhouse for blacks. While city officials deemed it suitable to place poor whites in close proximity with blacks, however, they still deemed it important to draw sharp distinctions between the two oppressed groups. For example, the city council rejected a request to have a treadmill installed in the local poorhouse on grounds that the device was a punishment deemed suitable for slaves, and the council was "unwilling to break down any of the distinctions between that class of persons and the white population by subjecting them to a common mode of punishment." Despite its increasingly repressive measures, Charleston boasted a fairly diverse ethnic and religious landscape. The city had long been a haven of religious toleration for all Protestants, and it became a key site for the emergence of modern Reform Judaism with the establishment of the Reformed Society of Israelites in the city in 1824.

As the antebellum period continued and the contest against abolitionists reached a fever pitch, many Charlestonians adopted even harder lines on the question of slavery. While many city residents had formerly supported the American Colonization Society in its effort to transport free blacks out of the South and into Africa, they now looked at the same idea as an abolitionist scheme. When, in 1835, Charleston planters learned that some antislavery tracts were in the federal post office, bound for distribution throughout the South, they formed a mob, stormed the post office, and burned the papers and pamphlets. The city council posted a $1,000 reward for the arrest and conviction of anyone who possessed or distributed antislavery materials. Also in 1835, the state legislature passed a law making it illegal for slaves to learn to read or write. This last measure is particularly significant because it coincided with the efforts of missionaries, principally Baptists and Methodists, to proselytize slaves. Without easy access to literacy and education, slaves were almost wholly reliant on white preachers to receive the Gospel. The result was a skewed theology that emphasized submission, duty, and obedience. For their part, slaves emphasized a god of deliverance and identified with the children of Israel who were led out of Pharaoh's house of bondage.

Despite all of these efforts, the force of antislavery literature was still felt throughout the South. In 1829 David Walker, a free black man living in Boston, published his *Appeal to the Colored Citizens of the World*, in which he called on slaves to rise up in arms against their masters. Though his work was outlawed in the slave South, smuggled copies appeared frequently, especially in port cities where black sailors took advantage of their mobility to spread the word. In 1852 Harriet Beecher Stowe's classic *Uncle Tom's Cabin* was published to the ire of many of southerners who continued to defend the institution of slavery.

Despite the growing success of the city's industrial base and the rising international pressure to end slavery, most of Charleston's whites held doggedly to their deep commitment to a society based on human bondage. Indeed, in 1853 Charleston officials briefly considered measures that would have reopened the transatlantic slave trade. That talk was hushed, however, by planters who saw a potential loss in value for the slaves they already owned. Charleston's leaders focused ever more on social control, and in the decade leading up to the Civil War, the city's police force ballooned, the poorhouse exceeded capacity, and public whippings and hangings proceeded apace.

See also *Charleston, SC 1776–1790; Charleston, SC 1790–1828*

JASON YOUNG

BIBLIOGRAPHY

Egerton, Douglas R. *He Shall Go Out Free: The Lives of Denmark Vesey.* Madison, WI: Madison House, 1999.

Fraser, Walter, Jr. *Charleston! Charleston!: The History of a Southern City.* Columbia: University of South Carolina Press, 1989.

Meffert, John, and Sherman E. Pyatt. *Charleston, South Carolina.* Charleston, SC: Arcadia Publishing Co., 2000.

Molloy, Robert. *Charleston: A Gracious Heritage.* New York, NY: D. Appleton-Century Co., 1947.

Rosen, Robert. *A Short History of Charleston.* Columbia: University of South Carolina Press, 1997.

Smythe, Augustine. *The Carolina Low-Country.* New York, NY: The MacMillian Co., 1931.

Steele, John Carson Hay. *Charleston: Then and Now.* Orangeburg, SC: Sandlapper Publishing Co., 1996.

WASHINGTON, DC 1828–1854

OF THE MAJOR AMERICAN CITIES, ONLY WASHINGTON IS DEVOTED TO GOVERNMENT, rather than commerce, industry, or finance. In 1828, in an attempt to broaden the local economy, the three towns then comprising the District of Columbia—Washington City and Georgetown on the Maryland side of the Potomac River and Alexandria on the Virginia side—pledged $1.5 million for the construction of the Chesapeake and Ohio Canal. President John Quincy Adams broke ground on July 4, 1828, the same day that rival Baltimore, Maryland, commenced work on the Baltimore and Ohio Railroad. The canal proved a financial disaster for the capital city, which in 1836 required one of its periodic federal bailouts to avoid defaulting on canal bonds.

Despairing it would never thrive under federal control, Alexandria successfully petitioned to rejoin Virginia in 1846. The remaining sixty-nine square miles of the original one-hundred-square-mile federal district did grow into a consequential city, with the District of Columbia's population leaping from under forty thousand in 1830 to nearly fifty-two thousand in 1850, despite the Virginia retrocession. Major federal projects—the new treasury and patent buildings, begun in the 1830s; the Smithsonian Institution building, commenced in 1849; and the Washington Aqueduct, started in 1853—portended the city's emergence as an attractive, thriving national capital in the late 1800s. Prior to these advancements, however, the inability to finance the completion of the Washington Monument—abandoned half-finished in its scaffolding in 1854—fed the sense that antebellum Washington was a disappointment. Far from the majestic

QUICK FACTS

WASHINGTON, DC **1828–1854**

MAYORS

Joseph Gales Jr.	(1827–1830)
John P. Van Ness	(1830–1834)
William A. Bradley	(1834–1836)
Peter Force	(1836–1840)
William W. Seaton	(1840–1850)
Walter Lenox	(1850–1852)
John W. Maury	(1852–1854)
John Thomas Towers	(1854–1856)

MAJOR INDUSTRIES AND EMPLOYERS

Federal agencies (notably the Treasury Department, post office, and patent office)

Washington Navy Yard

Printers and publishers (notably John C. Rives and Ritchie and Company)

Hotels and boarding houses

Chesapeake and Ohio Canal trade in coal and agricultural products

MAJOR NEWSPAPERS

Congressional Globe
National Era
National Intelligencer
National Journal
Madisonian
Washington Union
Whig Standard

MAJOR EVENTS

1828: On July 4 President John Q. Adams breaks ground for the Chesapeake and Ohio Canal. In 1836, a looming default on municipal canal bonds prompts a federal bailout that dramatizes the chronic fiscal weakness of the Washington City government.

1846: Congress passes an act founding the Smithsonian Institution, based on a bequest by wealthy British inventor James Smithson. Architect James Renwick's Norman Revival Smithsonian Castle is constructed between 1849 and 1855.

1846: Alexandria successfully petitions for retrocession to Virginia of portions of the District of Columbia south of the Potomac, leaving only sixty-nine of the one hundred square miles authorized in the Constitution for the federal district.

1848: After the thwarting of a mass escape by seventy-six local slaves aboard the schooner *Pearl*, proslavery mobs along Pennsylvania Avenue threaten to lynch the crew and then attack the offices of the *National Era*, a weekly abolitionist newspaper.

1851: A Christmas Eve fire burns two-thirds of the Library of Congress. This leads, in part, to the Army Corps of Engineers beginning construction in 1853 of the innovative Washington Aqueduct.

embodiment of American republicanism envisioned in the 1790s by engineer Pierre Charles L'Enfant and his patron, George Washington, the capital had become a focal point for conflicts of region and principle that threatened to tear the country apart.

GOVERNMENT AND POLITICS

The Constitution reserves to Congress "exclusive legislation in all cases whatsoever" in the federal district—jurisdiction at least as broad as that which state governments exercise over their cities. Indeed, in the 1870s the federal government began governing Washington directly through an appointed commission. In the antebellum period, however, certain officials, led by the House and Senate committees on the District of Columbia, exercised authority in a piecemeal fashion. These officials included the architects of the Capitol and the treasury building, the commissioner of public buildings, and members of various congressional committees. In 1802 Congress incorporated the new municipality of Washington City. The federal capital as platted by L'Enfant was an area bounded by the Potomac and Anacostia Rivers and the modern-day Florida Avenue, then known as Boundary Street. Georgetown and Alexandria retained colonial-era municipal governments. Outlying, unincorporated areas of the federal district fell under the jurisdiction of appointed boards for Alexandria (now Arlington) County on the Virginia side and Washington County on the Maryland side.

Though only a portion of the entire District of Columbia, Washington City encompassed an enormous area, especially given the dense patterns of work and life in early nineteenth-century walking cities. Until the Civil War, visitors and residents routinely described the place as "straggling" or, in the derisive words of British author Charles Dickens, as a "city of magnificent intentions." Due to their limited commerce and resources, Washingtonians could not hope to maintain the L'Enfant plan, with its radiating, 160-foot-wide avenues and its majestic parks and squares. The plan set aside over half the capital city for streets, public spaces, and public buildings on the assumption that the nation would underwrite construction, which it did sporadically before the Civil War.

In Washington's early years, Congress tinkered frequently with municipal structure. The original city charter of 1802 provided for a mayor appointed by the president and a twelve-member council elected by white property holders. The council divided itself into a five-member upper house and a seven-member lower house. The charter was amended in 1804 to establish a directly elected bicameral council—each house having nine members—and then was amended again in 1812 to provide for an eight-member board of aldermen and a twelve-member common council, both elected by wards. The city council in turn elected the mayor. In 1820 a new charter provided no regular federal support, but it did for the first time authorize popular election of the mayor and also expanded city powers over public health, sanitation, street improvements, and oversight of the poor. Property restrictions on white male voting remained in place until an 1848 charter revision that enfranchised all white men who paid a school tax of $1 per year.

Municipal politics reflected tension between a local elite with cultural roots in Virginia and Maryland and newcomers with a national orientation. Of the seven mayors between 1828 and 1854, three were born in Virginia or the district, two came from the North, and one came from England (with one undetermined). Joseph Gales Jr., the son of a Sheffield printer and mayor from 1827 to 1830, published the *National Intelligencer*, the local voice of the Whigs. Gales's copublisher, Virginia native William W. Seaton, dominated city politics as mayor from 1840 to 1850. Other local politicians had backgrounds in national politics and publishing, including John Peter Van Ness, mayor from 1830 to 1834, a banker and former New York congressman, and New Jersey-born Peter Force, mayor from 1836 to 1840 and editor of the Whig *National Journal*. The first Washington-born mayor, Walter Lenox, who served from 1850 to 1852, was the first truly local figure in decades and the last of Washington's miniature Whig dynasty. His successors were a Democrat and a Know-Nothing.

Whig partisanship complicated dealings with Democrats in Congress and the executive branch. Certainly the anticentrist Jacksonian Democrats had little sympathy with President Adams's vision of Washington as a Paris-style metropolis of science and learning. Still, architect Robert Mills's treasury, patent office, and post office buildings all won authorization during the presidencies of Andrew Jackson and Martin Van Buren, and the Smithsonian was established during James Polk's administration. The Whig administration of Millard Fillmore sponsored landscape architect Andrew Jackson Downing's 1851 plan to improve the neglected Mall. Jefferson Davis himself, secretary of war under Democrat Franklin Pierce, oversaw the start of the Washington Aqueduct, which was designed and supervised by army engineer Montgomery Meigs. Meigs and Davis would later become nemeses after Meigs became Union quartermaster general.

INDUSTRY, COMMERCE, AND LABOR

Washington hinged on the federal government, which was a remarkably small set of institutions until the Civil War. National totals for civilian employees of the United States rose from 11,491 in 1831 to 26,274 in 1851 to 36,672 in 1861. There was one federal employee for every 1,120 Americans in 1831 and one for every 857 Americans in 1861. The post office—the primary way that antebellum Americans encountered their government—accounted for over three-fourths of federal employees, totaling 76 percent in 1831 and rising to 83 percent in 1861. The limited size and scope of federal activity explains the small federal workforce in Washington: 666 people in 1831; 1,014 in 1841; 1,533 in 1851; and 2,199 in 1861. To illustrate the Civil War's centrality in American governmental history and in Washington's development, between 1861 and 1881 total federal employment leapt 2.7 times, reaching 100,020 in 1881, and federal employment in Washington increased around six times, reaching 13,124 in 1881. From 1831 to 1861, an average of 5.7 percent of all federal employees worked in Washington. By 1871 this figure doubled to around 12 percent, where it stayed with minor fluctuations through the 1990s.

In the antebellum period, the treasury, patent office, and post office became substantial bureaucracies, but most federal agencies had rudimentary staffs. Washington's research and educational establishment was still embryonic. Physicist Joseph Henry, the Smithsonian's first secretary, supervised a pair of laboratories and a small exhibit hall when the institution's building opened in 1855. The Library of Congress contained fifty-five thousand volumes in a cramped room in the Capitol, two-thirds of which burned in a Christmas Eve fire in 1851. Among the destroyed were two-thirds of the 6,487 volumes acquired from Thomas Jefferson after the British burned the Capitol in 1815. Higher education amounted to Georgetown College, a small Catholic school founded in 1789, and Columbian College, a Baptist school opened in 1821 that also offered medical and legal training. Columbian later grew into George Washington University.

While still fairly small during the antebellum period, the number of federal employees in the nation's capital grew from 666 people in 1831 to 1,533 in 1851. Despite these relatively low numbers, symbolic structures were constructed during this time to house the bureaucracy. The United States Patent Office, pictured above, was designed by Robert Mills in the Greek Revival style with the first wing constructed between 1836 and 1842.

Source: Library of Congress

The only significant federal industry in the antebellum capital was the Washington Navy Yard, situated along the Anacostia River. In preceding years the yard had become a center for the research and manufacture of naval equipment and ordnance. By the late 1800s, the federal government would oversee immense printing and publishing operations, but the Bureau of Printing and Engraving and the Government Printing Office both trace their origins to the Civil War. Public printing on contract had become a major enterprise, and the firms of John Rives (which printed the *Congressional Globe*) and Ritchie and Company were among the few well-capitalized businesses in the city. Employing around eighty employees, the Ritchie firm was huge by local standards—most private employers engaged fewer than fifteen people.

Antebellum Washington did develop the foundations for its distinctive economy, which were rooted in activities derived from or serving the federal government. These activities and services included real estate development, hotels and boarding houses, retail and wholesale trade, law, claims agencies, and lobbying. Founded in 1840, the firm of Georgetown natives William W. Corcoran and George W. Riggs formed the nucleus of Washington banking after earning a rumored $1 million by arranging financing for the Mexican War. Underwriting a variety of philanthropic and cultural ventures, these two bankers helped give Washington's pre-Civil War elite its southern tone. Northern entrepreneurs also filtered into the city, including brothers Henry and Edwin Willard, who in 1850 bought what became the famous Willard Hotel on Pennsylvania Avenue.

Business and civic leaders hoped that the Chesapeake and Ohio Canal would help in the realization of the L'Enfant plan's vision of Washington as a metropolis for trade as well as government. The Baltimore and Ohio Railroad, however, diverted commerce to Baltimore, whose regional dominance was dramatized by the fact that Washington's only rail connection to the North was a branch of the Baltimore and Ohio, opened in 1835. By the 1830s the so-called Washington Canal—planned by L'Enfant along the north side of the Mall to bring Potomac commerce into the city's heart—had degraded into a squalid open sewer. Apart from lumber and coal yards and the Center Market on the site of the present-day National Archives, little trade ever ventured beyond the riverfront docks. Federal assumption in 1836 of Washington's debts for the faltering Chesapeake and Ohio Canal partially shielded the city during the panic of 1837, and federal payrolls and expenditures and the intertwining of the city's banks with government finance seemed to limit the ensuing depression.

The river ports of Georgetown and Alexandria, meanwhile, struggled against competition from the railroads. Between 1833 and 1843, Alexandria constructed an extension of the Chesapeake and Ohio Canal that included the unusual Aqueduct Bridge, which enabled barges to cross the Potomac uninterrupted. The hope that Virginia would relieve its debts and help revive the town prompted Alexandria's petition for retrocession in 1846. Observers speculated that an unarticulated motive on Virginia's part was protection of Alexandria's slave markets, which channeled slaves from the Chesapeake toward the cotton-producing South.

RACE, ETHNICITY, AND IMMIGRATION

Nineteenth-century Washington stood out for its high percentage of black residents and small proportion of immigrants. Until the Civil War, around 30 percent of the District of Columbia's population was black. In Baltimore—another border city with a historically large African American presence—free and enslaved blacks together accounted for between 15 and 20 percent of the population. In 1850 only around 9.5 percent of Washingtonians had been born overseas. Washington's relative paucity of immigrants reflected its distinctive economy, which did not supply the laboring, artisan, and small-business opportunities available elsewhere. The 2,373 Irish-born residents of the federal district in 1850 worked mainly in construction, with the remainder scattered in crafts and small businesses such as groceries and taverns. Occupation patterns among the 1,415 German-born residents—3 percent of the population in 1850—also reflected Washington's special economy. At a time when technical training in the United States was rudimentary, federal agencies such as the Coast Survey, the U.S. Patent Office, and the Washington Navy Yard all had contingents of German specialists. Yet most Washington Germans worked in crafts and small business, as they did elsewhere in the United States.

When Washington became the capital in 1800, slaves outnumbered free blacks by around 4 to 1. Free blacks outnumbered slaves by 1830, and by 1850 around three-fourths of black Washingtonians were free. The approximately ten thousand free blacks in the federal district at midcentury totaled nearly 20 percent of the population. The ratio of free blacks to slaves increased partly through sales of slaves to the Southern states. Alexandria was the main slave-trading center, but slave-trading firms and auctions were spread throughout the capital, including ones near both Lafayette Square and Center Market. Of greater statistical significance were the fairly liberal manumission laws and practices that spread across the Chesapeake region during the Revolutionary Era. Despite black codes, curfews, and other restrictions and humiliations, freed slaves from the Chesapeake found Washington an attractive place to migrate. The more oppressive atmosphere and tighter restrictions that faced free blacks in Virginia and Maryland after the 1830s increased Washington's relative appeal.

Washington slave owners employed or hired out slaves for typical urban slave occupations: service in households, restaurants, and hotels, as well as work in artisan shops, small businesses, docks, and construction. Construction gangs for the Capitol and other federal buildings included slaves. As in other slaveholding cities, the daily lives of slaves in Washington afforded a measure of autonomy and mobility, with slaves carving out their own space in backyard houses provided by employers or in scattered, quasi-legal shanty settlements.

The abundance of inexpensive free labor accelerated the turn from slavery in services, construction, and dockwork. Free black entrepreneurs overcame discriminatory licensing practices to start small businesses, especially restaurants, groceries, barbershops, shoemaking shops, hack stands, and vending stalls, all of which were typical business opportunities available to urban African Americans in the mid-1800s. The White House and other federal buildings had free blacks on their domestic staffs, and blacks held messenger positions and other assorted federal jobs. At midcentury, women outnumbered men among the district's free blacks, 4,760 to 3,398. Free black women most often labored as domestic servants, laundresses, and seamstresses, which again were typical occupations of urban black women in the mid-1800s.

Despite the constraints they faced, free black residents acquired property and established neighborhoods throughout the city, especially in southeast Washington. Washington's best-known antebellum black activist came from the network of the city's black churches. An exslave, shoemaker, and federal messenger, John F. Cook served as the city's first ordained black Presbyterian minister and headmaster of the Columbia Institute, which offered free education to African American children. Despite municipal refusal to fund black education, Washington's African Americans ran dozens of schools.

Understandably, given the city's location and distinctive status, the struggle over slavery moved regularly from the Capitol into the community. Antislavery activists targeted Washington's slave trade, leading to its abolition in the Compromise of 1850. Despite the risks, black Washingtonians organized against slavery and cooperated with white sympathizers to help escaped slaves travel northward. Such efforts sparked antebellum Washington's most notorious racial clash. In April 1848, near the mouth of the Potomac River, a posse from a pursuing steamship boarded the schooner *Pearl*, which carried seventy-six slaves who had escaped from Washington and the surrounding environs. After threatening to lynch the crew as they were taken to jail along Pennsylvania Avenue, proslavery rioters attacked the offices of an abolitionist weekly newspaper, the *National Era*, and tried to force the editor, Gamaliel Bailey, to leave town. The paper survived to publish the serialized version of Harriet Beecher Stowe's *Uncle Tom's Cabin* in 1851 and 1852. The 1848 *Pearl* rioters largely left local blacks alone, in contrast to the "Snow riot" of 1835, when an attempted murder by a slave sparked attacks on black houses, institutions, and businesses, including a restaurant owned by Beverly Snow, who allegedly made insulting remarks about whites.

Not all of Washington's mob violence stemmed from race. In 1854 Know-Nothings attacked the unfinished Washington Monument, seizing marble donated by the pope and throwing it into the Potomac. In 1857 seven people died when marines fired into a crowd during a Know-Nothing-related election riot. By midcentury, however, unfinished, disappointing, conflict-ridden Washington embodied the country's accelerating and paralyzing clash of race and region.

See also *Washington, DC 1790–1828; Washington, DC 1941–1952*

ALAN LESSOFF

BIBLIOGRAPHY

Bryan, Wilhelmus Bogart. *A History of the National Capital: Volume 2: 1815–1878*. New York, NY: Macmillan, 1916.

Cary, Francine Curro, ed. *Urban Odyssey: A Multicultural History of Washington, D.C.* Washington, DC: Smithsonian Institution Press, 1996.

Diner, Steven J. *Democracy, Federalism, and the Governance of the Nation's Capital, 1790–1974.* Washington, DC: Center for Applied Research and Urban Policy, University of the District of Columbia, 1987.

Gillette, Howard, Jr. *Between Beauty and Justice: Race, Planning, and the Failure of Urban Policy in Washington, D.C.* Baltimore, MD: Johns Hopkins University Press, 1995.

Green, Constance McLaughlin. *Washington: Village and Capital, 1800–1878*. Princeton, NJ: Princeton University Press, 1962.

Gutheim, Frederick, and Antoinette J. Lee. *Worthy of the Nation: Washington, DC, from L'Enfant to the National Capital Planning Commission*. 2nd ed. Baltimore, MD: Johns Hopkins University Press, 2006.

Harrold, Stanley. *Subversives: Antislavery Community in Washington, D.C., 1828–1865*. Baton Rouge: Louisiana State University Press, 2003.

Pacheco, Josephine F. *The Pearl: A Failed Slave Escape on the Potomac.* Chapel Hill: University of North Carolina Press, 2005.

PROVIDENCE, RI 1828–1854

IN 1828 PROVIDENCE WAS THE LARGEST TOWN IN THE STATE OF RHODE ISLAND, and within four years it became the state's first incorporated city. It served as one of two seats of the Rhode Island legislature, or the Rhode Island General Assembly, the other being Newport. These were not easy years for Providence and Rhode Island. As in other urban centers throughout the expanding nation, the population in Providence grew and became increasingly heterogeneous in the years from 1828 to 1854. A sizable and influential African American community constituted a progressively smaller proportion of the city population in the face of mass immigration from Ireland, Catholicism was well on its way to becoming the predominant religion of this formerly Baptist stronghold, and industry replaced maritime trade as the leading economic force in the city.

The tensions that existed between people of various races, ethnicities, and religions informed the political events that culminated in the 1842 Dorr Rebellion. A movement begun in the 1820s for free suffrage and reapportionment in the general assembly turned into a near-war that would involve a United States president and Tammany Hall. For a brief time in 1842, Rhode Island was in open rebellion; it was a state with two constitutions and two popularly elected governors. Providence was the political locus of this divide. This was a fight that would set a precedent in the U.S. Supreme Court and inform the arguments surrounding states' and individuals' rights in the decades to come.

GOVERNMENT AND POLITICS

By 1828 Providence had the largest population of any town in Rhode Island, and it was growing rapidly as mills and factories took hold of the town and state economy. Just after the American Revolution, there were 4,312 individuals living in Providence; by 1830 the number had quadrupled to 16,836. Race riots in the 1820s and early 1830s brought the shortcomings of the town meeting system of government to light for the general assembly, the state's main body of governance as detailed in the charter of 1663. For safety, Providence had night watchmen to patrol the streets after sundown—the same form of protection that had been in place since the Revolution. Fire control was still reliant upon volunteers and had not advanced far past the bucket system that had been used in the colonial period. By 1830 the town meeting style of government was not sufficient for this growing, heterogeneous population.

In January 1830 the legislature granted Providence a city charter, but it was unsuccessful in garnering the three-fifths vote from the legislature necessary to ratify its passage. A deadly four-day race riot broke out in the Olney's Lane section of Providence on September 21, 1831, which helped to convince the public and the general assembly that the town council and a night patrol were no longer sufficient to keep the peace. In 1831 the charter went to the general assembly again. This time it passed, making Providence the first city in Rhode Island and confirming Samuel Bridgham as its first mayor. The charter created a city council system for Providence that

QUICK FACTS

PROVIDENCE, RI **1828–1854**

MAYORS

Providence had no mayors until its incorporation as a city in 1832

Samuel W. Bridgham	(1832–1840)
Thomas M. Burgess	(1841–1852)
Amos C. Barstow	(1852–1853)
Walter R. Danforth	(1853–1854)
Edward P. Knowles	(1854–1855)

MAJOR INDUSTRIES AND EMPLOYERS

Base metal industry (Corliss Steam Engine Co., Providence Iron Co., American Screw Co.)

Precious metal industry (Gorham Silver)

Woolen textiles (two mills)

Maritime industry

MAJOR NEWSPAPERS

Daily Advertiser (later the *Daily Advertiser and American*)

Independent Inquirer and Rhode Island Journal

Manufactures' and Framers' Journal (Providence and Pawtucket Advertiser)

Morning Courier and General Advertiser

Providence Daily Journal

Providence Daily Journal and General Advertiser

Providence Daily Post

Providence Patriot and Columbian Phenix

Republican Herald (two independent papers)

Rhode Island Country Journal and Independent Inquirer

MAJOR EVENTS

1828: Construction of the Arcade commences between Westminster and Weybosset Streets in Providence. This Greek Revival structure was the first indoor shopping mall in Rhode Island. It was built by Cyrus Butler, who hired architect Russell Warren to design the Weybosset Street façade and James C. Bucklin to design the Westminster edifice. It marks the expansion of the city's commercial district and the growth of its economic base.

1828: The *Lady Carrington* is the first boat to travel from Providence to Worcester, Massachusetts, via the Blackstone Canal. This canal was first proposed by prominent Providence businessman John Brown in 1796, but it took until the nineteenth century to gain funding and broad support.

1832: The Rhode Island General Assembly grants Providence city status, thus making it the first city in Rhode Island.

1835: The first railroad serving Rhode Island reaches Providence from Boston, Massachusetts. This helps to solidify the role of Providence as a hub of transportation in southern New England.

1842: The Dorr Rebellion reaches its zenith with the election of a second governor for the state of Rhode Island and places the state in open rebellion—making Rhode Island the only state to have two popularly elected governors at one time.

included a board of alderman and a common council. A thirty-three member school committee was formed and with the city council, governed the public schools. The charter also called for the creation of a much-needed police force. In its first full year of operation, 1833, it cost $43,205 to run the city.

The state's general assembly, at the behest of education activist and historian John Howland, passed the School Act of 1828. Providence was already offering public primary and writing schools, but this act gave state money to cities and towns, allowing Providence to expand its already significant educational system. Although it was a revolutionary bill, it made segregated education the law in the state. In spite of this, education flourished in the 1830s and 1840s with the aid of men such as Mayor Bridgham, Nathan Bishop, and Thomas Wilson Dorr. By 1832, when Providence was incorporated as a city, it housed twelve schools to educate twelve hundred students, including girls and boys of all races. The city's education system was seen by surrounding towns as something to emulate, and in 1845 the state hired Henry Barnard as the first state commissioner of education. He stayed until 1849, later becoming the first United States commissioner of education.

Like other cities of this time, the population of Providence was embroiled in aggressive political debate over the fairly apportioned representation of individuals and regions in state and city politics. In 1818 Rhode Island became the last state to be governed by its original charter. In the seventeenth century, this document had created a more democratic colony than any other, but by the nineteenth century many residents believed the charter to be woefully archaic. As dictated by the antiquated document, most of the state's representatives came from Newport, a town still rebuilding from the Revolution. Many Rhode Islanders held that a new constitution was needed to better represent the geographic and demographic realities of their state in the nineteenth century. That would mean giving increased representation to northern Rhode Island sites such as Providence. The 1663 charter did not contain a procedure for amendment, so any changes would have to come from the general assembly. Asking those in power to voluntarily abdicate that authority was a struggle. Throughout the 1820s, constituencies from each side fought vociferously to either maintain or broaden the power base.

By 1828, under the leadership of Seth Luther, a carpenter and head of the Rhode Island Workingmen's Party, the debate widened to encompass not only reapportionment, but also suffrage. In 1798 the legislature reaffirmed a freehold requirement for voting and set $134 worth of real estate as the threshold. At the state level, prior to the Revolution, 75 percent of white male residents in the state were qualified to vote. By the 1830s, less than half owned adequate property to vote, and that number was tumbling. This fight, however, was not one for franchising African American males, who had been disfranchised in 1822, or women. Its focus was to broaden the vote for adult, white males.

Beginning in 1834, Thomas Wilson Dorr, a young Providence lawyer from a prominent family, led the Rhode Island Constitutional Party, a short-lived combination of middle-class reformers and working-class men. Little was accomplished at a constitutional convention and the party folded, yet Dorr gained notoriety and lit a fire under those who wanted change.

The panic of 1837 fueled the discontent many Rhode Islanders felt as banks suspended lending and businesses closed. New England's recession, however, was less severe than those of other regions. Providence and other New England cities fared better than those to the south. Scholars argue that private lenders, such as the Suffolk Bank in Massachusetts, aided this by clearing notes for other banks and acting as a "lender of last resort." Thus, even though Providence's economy was heavily dependent on cotton, it was able to rebound well. Banks were opening by 1838, and, while textile production growth slowed, it did not stop. Despite

Providence's relative success during this period, political and economic tensions remained high as the city recovered. Members of the working class, also gaining inspiration from the 1840 presidential campaign, were increasingly aware of their precarious financial and political position in the city and state.

In 1840 the American public elected William Henry Harrison president, but in Rhode Island all political attention was turned inward as debates raged over the creation of a state constitution and expanding voting rights. Suffragists wanted to take action, and, not trusting the legislature to do any better than they had in 1824 and 1834, called the People's Convention. Here the 58 percent of white men who were currently disfranchised had a voice, and some hoped African American men would find the same. In October 1841 elected delegates drafted what they called the People's Constitution. This document mandated a more balanced political system, but it retained some property qualifications for the franchise for both native-born and naturalized Rhode Islanders, and it denied the vote to all African Americans. A popular vote to ratify the constitution was held over three consecutive days in December. It was ratified by a vote of 13,944 to 52.

Although reformers contended that the public wished to have this new constitution replace the old charter, the state, or, as they were known, "charter," legislature did not agree. The Law and Order Party formed in 1842 and set itself apart from both the legislature and the Dorrites. Party members proposed their own replacement for the charter, which they called the Freeman's Constitution, and which gave African American men the right to vote. The Freeman's Constitution was ratified and put into effect, yet the supporters of the People's Constitution still believed their document had the true backing of the people of Rhode Island. Law and Order Party member Samuel Ward King was elected governor in April of 1842 and took up where the former charter government had left off.

In an unprecedented move, the People's Party held an election and chose Thomas Wilson Dorr to be the governor. Therefore, in April 1842, Rhode Island became the first, and only, state to have two popularly elected governors. It was a state in open rebellion against itself, and in early May of 1842 the fallout led both Governor King and Governor Dorr to seek the help of President John Tyler. Tyler demurred, holding that this was a state issue and that the National Guard would not get involved. Dorr also appealed to New York's Tammany Hall, which promised that its men would come to the Dorrites' aid.

On May 18, 1842, Dorr led his men to an armed confrontation at the Cranston Street Armory in Providence, but when a cannon misfired, the men dispersed in confusion and fear. After a series of missteps and interceptions, a planned military conflict with the state militia in the summer of 1842 was canceled by Dorr. The "Dorr War," as it was called, never amounted to a physical confrontation. What it did yield, however, was the state's first constitution in 1842, a series of riots, a jailed pseudogovernor in Dorr (later posthumously recognized by the state as a true governor), and a franchised African American male population. And, through the U.S. Supreme Court case of *Luther v. Borden* (1849), the conflict set precedent regarding illegal search and seizure rights and affirmed that the guarantee of a republican form of government is a political question to be resolved by the president and the Congress, not the courts.

INDUSTRY, COMMERCE, AND LABOR

In the first quarter of the nineteenth century, Rhode Island, and Providence County in particular, became the seat of textile production in the United States. Begun in Rhode Island in 1793 at Slater's Mill on the Blackstone River, the cotton textile industry flourished as entrepreneurs shifted their focus from shipping to manufacturing. This was also the end of Providence's previously lucrative role as a leading port in the China trade. Although water was still used to power the textile industries, Samuel Slater introduced steam power to the industry in 1827. The city housed four cotton textile mills in 1832 that employed more than 350 employees.

To better compete with the ports in Massachusetts, industrialists in Providence backed the development of the Blackstone Canal, which opened in 1828. The first boat to traverse the canal, the *Lady Carrington*, made its way from Providence to Worcester, Massachusetts, that year and ushered in a brief canal career for the new city. The cotton industry boomed, and by 1840 there were thirty mills with over two thousand employees. The city's woolen industry grew as well, albeit more slowly.

While the textile industries were growing and maritime trades were waning, base metal, machinery, jewelry, and silverware production were gaining prominence. Providence's George Corliss improved upon the reciprocating engine developed by Oliver Evans in Philadelphia. The Corliss Steam Engine Company became one of the largest firms in the city and was joined by the American Screw Company, Providence Iron Company, and Providence Machine Company. Just prior to the Civil War, the city had twenty-five active machine and base metal shops. The precious metal industries were also growing rapidly in this period, with John Gorham's company becoming the most nationally and internationally renowned. Metal industries, in fact, far surpassed the textile industries in terms of capitalization by 1850.

Many of the labor issues of this period led directly to the Dorr Rebellion. Those that did not were typical of national trends in labor, and the advanced industrialization of this region meant that labor unions formed early and strikes were common. Much of the labor activity was actually taking place to the north and west of the city in Providence County, where factory towns were becoming the norm. The village of Pawtucket, then part of the town of North Providence, saw some of the nation's earliest strikes. Seth Luther's Workingmen's Association formed with the help of local barber William Tillinghast, but its focus was suffrage and reapportionment—the demands of the future Dorr Rebellion—more so than day-to-day struggles in the workplace.

Providence grew during this period not only because of the increasing prevalence of factories, but because it was a center of finance, banking, and transportation. It was, indeed, a transportation hub of southern New England. Many industrialists held that the Blackstone Canal would shape the future of industry in the state, but it was late on the scene in 1828. Just seven years later, the first railroad of many would reach Providence, headed south from Boston. The 1840s became a heyday for rail building in Rhode Island. In 1847 the Providence-Worcester Line opened, spelling the end for the canal, and the next year the city began to fill in the tidal estuary known as the Cove and on it built the impressive Union Passenger Depot designed by Thomas Tefft. Water traffic, however, was not passé. In 1853 the U.S. Army Corps of Engineers surveyed the Providence River and began a dredging project to make it navigable for larger vessels needed for modern coastal trade. This allowed Providence's disparate products to be shipped to foreign and domestic markets.

After 1855 Providence lost its status as one of the largest cities in America, but this was not because of the attenuation of its economy. Despite a brief downturn before the Civil War, Providence's prominence as an industrial powerhouse was growing. By 1900 it was one of the wealthiest cities in the nation, but it was small in size. This adherence to the self-determination of towns and avoidance of annexation kept Providence from increasing its landmass. It was not until the 1920s, when a majority of textile mills in the United States relocated to the American South, that deindustrialization began to chip away at the industrial and economic strength of this city.

RACE, ETHNICITY, AND IMMIGRATION

In 1828 there were still black slaves in the city of Providence. The Gradual Emancipation Act of 1784 only applied to those individuals born after March 1, 1784, and then it put these boys and girls into a state of servitude that lasted until the ages of twenty-one and eighteen, respectively. Thus, by 1828 the mixture of free, permanently enslaved, and temporarily enslaved people of African descent comprised 7.2 percent of the city's population. Within this group there was also a mixture of Native American peoples who had been intermarrying with the black community since slaves had first been brought to the colony. The long history of African peoples in Providence did not mean that it was an easy or comfortable situation as the diminution of slavery gave way to industrialization, aggravating class issues and straining the demand for jobs, housing, and other resources.

Over several decades, African American communities developed in a handful of areas in Providence. Hard Scrabble, Olney's Lane, and Snowtown were three neighborhoods with high concentrations of people of African descent. Because of their long presence in the town, African Americans had created strong neighborhoods with their own social, religious, and educational organizations. Many people within these communities were employed and owned property. Homeowner Elleanor Eldridge, however, became a *cause célèbre*. She was a successful African American woman whose home was unjustly taken from her after rumors of her death and the subsequent illness of a family member, which required her presence out of state. She brought a suit against the man who held her loan and sold her property, but the court costs and funds needed to buy back her property forced her into poverty. Eldridge's story ignited reformist fires throughout the city and state, and her highly successful memoir helped to fund her fight and buy back her home.

Other whites, however, were angered by African Americans' presence. On September 21, 1831, a group of white sailors entered the Olney's Lane neighborhood. They instigated a confrontation and residents fought back. A bloody riot ensued that lasted for four days, and troops were sent in by the state. Five people died and countless were injured. The general assembly responded by passing the Providence city charter. The new city, the legislators argued, needed a true police force to manage its increasingly large and diverse population.

Industrialization was about to change the demographic landscape of Providence. In the third decade of the nineteenth century, the Irish population of Rhode Island was so small that only one priest resided in the entire state, making his parish in Newport in 1828. The number of Irish swelled at an unprecedented rate over the next three decades due to a surplus of jobs in Rhode Island and the devastating potato famine in Ireland. By 1855 the population of Providence was 47,785, 30 percent of which were people of Irish descent. These recent arrivals were relegated to unskilled labor in manufacturing, often performing the most dangerous jobs. The dominant religion of the Irish immigrants was Roman Catholicism, which also put them at odds with the Protestant majority.

Providence was expanding and began to build housing on formerly agricultural land. Wealthier community members, predominantly those of Anglo descent, moved to larger homes farther away from the first settlement of Providence on the river. Mimicking this move to more salubrious surroundings, in 1847 the new Swan Point Cemetery was constructed on the Seekonk River on what had been Moses Brown's farm. This beautifully located and landscaped cemetery became the most desired final address for Providence residents.

This increasingly urban and industrial community needed social institutions to fill in where previous networks no longer provided enough support for whites or people of color. The Children's Friend Society was formed in 1835 to help orphaned youth. The Association for the Benefit of Colored Children began in 1848, and the Roman Catholic Sisters of Mercy opened the St. Aloysius Home just five years later. The Providence Reform School, located in the impressive Tockwotton House, took in its first child in 1850. In this same period, in 1847, the first hospital for the mentally ill in Providence, Butler Hospital, saw its initial patient. It was a new and institutional era.

See also *Providence, RI 1776–1790*

C. MORGAN GREFE

BIBLIOGRAPHY

Botelho, Joyce. *Right and Might: The Dorr Rebellion and the Struggle for Equal Rights.* Providence: Rhode Island Historical Society, 1992.

Brown, William J. *The Life of William Brown of Providence, R.I.: With Personal Recollections of Incidents in Rhode Island.* Durham: University of New Hampshire Press, 2006.

Coleman, Peter. *The Transformation of RI, 1790–1860.* Providence, RI: Brown University, 1963.

Conley, Patrick T. *An Album of Rhode Island History, 1636–1986.* Virginia Beach, VA: The Donning Company Publishers, 1992.

Conley, Patrick T., and Paul R. Campbell. *Providence: A Pictorial History.* Norfolk, VA: The Donning Company/Publisher, 1982.

Gilkeson, John S., Jr. *Middle-Class Providence, 1820–1940.* Princeton, NJ: Princeton University Press, 1986.

Kirk, William. *A Modern City: Providence, RI and its Architecture.* Chicago, IL: University of Chicago Press, 1909.

McLoughlin, William G. *Rhode Island: A History.* New York, NY: W. W. Norton & Co., 1986.

Pre-statehood territories

States

Includes states, territories, and population rankings as of 1870

CITIES IN THE CIVIL WAR AND RECONSTRUCTION, 1854–1877

The period covered in this chapter begins with the dissolution of the Whig Party and the rise of the Republicans, a financial crisis, and the Civil War, followed by the abolition of slavery, the assassination of Abraham Lincoln, another financial crisis (the worst to date), the end of Reconstruction, and the first nationwide strike.

Between 1854 and 1877, the population of the United States approximately doubled, from roughly twenty-seven to fifty million people, in large part due to the ever-increasing number of immigrants arriving. Most of these immigrants came from England, Ireland, and elsewhere in Europe. Of the hundreds of officially "urban places" (defined by the census as anywhere with over twenty-five hundred people and accounting for approximately a quarter of the U.S. population by 1877), the ten cities covered in this chapter (including Brooklyn, which was a separate city, though included here in the discussion of New York) represented more than one-third of the country's total urban population. New York City's population surpassed one million people during the 1870s. San Francisco, California, was the smallest of the ten cities in the 1850s, with a population of less than forty thousand, yet by the late 1870s its population had exploded to more than two hundred thousand.

The rapid growth of San Francisco, and of all western cities, was made possible in part by the expansion of railroads. Tens of thousands of new rail lines were laid during the 1850s, 1860s, and 1870s, including the transcontinental railroad, which was completed in 1869 by two federally chartered railroad companies. The railroads were increasingly organized into large, consolidated corporations, as were other industries closely related to railroad expansion, such as steel and oil.

The 1850s were marked by the sectional crisis that became the Civil War. The violence and widespread fraud that accompanied the vote in Kansas in 1855 as to whether the territory would enter the Union as a free or slave state, which resulted in the establishment of two separate and hostile provisional governments, one proslavery and one antislavery, indicated the intractability of the conflict. President Franklin Pierce supported Kansas's proslavery government. In part for this taking of sides in the divisive battle, Democrats passed over Pierce in 1856 and nominated James Buchanan as their presidential candidate. Republicans nominated their first-ever presidential candidate, John Fremont, and what was left of the Whigs and the Know-Nothings joined together to nominate Millard Fillmore. Buchanan won by a slim margin, and as president he was quickly confronted with the financial crisis of 1857 and the Supreme Court's divisive 1857 *Dred Scott* decision that denied citizenship to black people and the ability of northern states to ban slavery within their borders.

Deep divisions on the topic of slavery among Democrats were evident in their 1860 presidential nominating convention in Charleston, South Carolina. Southern delegates walked out, reconvened in Richmond, Virginia, and nominated John C. Breckinridge. The other delegates reconvened in Baltimore, Maryland, and nominated Stephen Douglas. The Republicans nominated Lincoln, who had made a name for himself nationally by running for the Senate against Douglas in 1858.

Lincoln lost his senatorial bid, but, with the Democrats divided, he won the presidency with a plurality. Before his inauguration, South Carolina declared itself an independent state and was quickly joined by Mississippi, Florida, Alabama, Georgia, Louisiana, and Texas, all of which formed the Confederate States of America. When Confederate troops seized Fort Sumter, a federal military installation in Charleston's harbor, they did so as a declaration of war. Rapidly thereafter, Virginia, Arkansas, Tennessee, and North Carolina joined the Confederacy. Lincoln instituted a naval blockade of the South and began recruiting troops, at first through voluntary enlistment, but by 1863 by conscription—a decision that led to riots in several cities, including Boston, Massachusetts; Detroit, Michigan; and, most famously, New York.

Union forces made little progress in attempting to capture the Confederate capital of Richmond, though they captured New Orleans, Louisiana, in 1862 and western Virginia, which was admitted into the Union as West Virginia, in 1863. In the same year, under the direction of Robert E. Lee, Confederate troops marched into Pennsylvania and met Union troops in

BY THE NUMBERS: **THE MOST POPULOUS CITIES IN 1870**

	TOTAL POPULATION[1]	WHITE POPULATION[1]	"COLORED" POPULATION[1]	OTHER POPULATION[1]	% WHITE POPULATION[1]
NEW YORK, NY	942,292	929,199	13,072	21	98.6
PHILADELPHIA, PA	674,022	651,854	22,147	21	96.7
ST. LOUIS, MO	310,864	288,737	22,088	39	92.9
CHICAGO, IL	298,977	295,281	3,691	5	98.8
BALTIMORE, MD	267,354	227,794	39,558	2	85.2
BOSTON, MA	250,526	247,013	3,496	17	98.6
CINCINNATI, OH	216,239	210,335	5,900	4	97.3
NEW ORLEANS, LA	191,418	140,923	50,456	39	73.6
SAN FRANCISCO, CA	149,473	136,059	1,330	12,084	91.0
BUFFALO, NY	117,714	117,018	696	0	99.4

	% "COLORED" POPULATION[1]	% OTHER POPULATION[1]	% OF THE POPULATION FOREIGN-BORN[1]	% OF THE LABOR FORCE EMPLOYED IN MANUFACTURING[2]	% OF THE POPULATION 10+ LITERATE[2]
NEW YORK, NY	1.4	0.0	44.5	22.2	90.2
PHILADELPHIA, PA	3.3	0.0	27.2	30.4	90.7
ST. LOUIS, MO	7.1	0.0	36.1	21.2	90.9
CHICAGO, IL	1.2	0.0	48.4	15.9	95.4
BALTIMORE, MD	14.8	0.0	21.1	22.8	87.3
BOSTON, MA	1.4	0.0	35.1	19.6	87.0
CINCINNATI, OH	2.7	0.0	36.8	24.3	93.1
NEW ORLEANS, LA	26.4	0.0	25.3	10.3	79.3
SAN FRANCISCO, CA	0.9	8.1	49.3	16.5	92.3
BUFFALO, NY	0.6	0.0	39.3	22.1	94.7

Note: This list does not include Brooklyn, NY. See introduction for details.

[1]*Source:* The Statistics of the Population of the United States: Ninth Census - Volume I. Table III - Population of Civil Divisions Less Than Counties

[2]*Source:* Steven Ruggles, J. Trent Alexander, Katie Genadek, Ronald Goeken, Matthew B. Schroeder, and Matthew Sobek. Integrated Public Use Microdata Series: Version 5.0 (Machine-readable database). Minneapolis: University of Minnesota, 2010. (1850 sample)

Gettysburg in what became a devastatingly bloody defeat for the Confederacy. Union forces then captured Atlanta, Georgia, in 1864, burned the city to the ground, and marched toward Savannah, Georgia, destroying most things in their path. General Ulysses S. Grant's troops captured an important railroad line that cut off supplies to Richmond. The Confederate government fled the capital, burning the city down as they left. In April of 1865, Confederate generals Lee and Sherman surrendered.

With the end of the Civil War came the end of slavery. Lincoln had issued his Emancipation Proclamation in 1863, declaring all slaves in Confederate territory free. Slavery itself was officially outlawed by the Thirteenth Amendment to the Constitution, which was adopted in 1865. The Fourteenth Amendment, adopted in 1868, was designed to protect the rights of newly emancipated slaves by expressly forbidding states to deny their citizens rights and "equal protection" without "due process of law." The Fifteenth Amendment, adopted in 1870, forbid suffrage restrictions on the basis of "race, color, or previous condition of servitude."

While industry in the North had been bolstered by government spending during the war, the South had been devastated. More than a quarter of a million Confederate troops had died (the war was made more deadly through technological innovations in weaponry, including Winchester's repeating rifle), cities and plantations had been burned, plantation owners had lost their investments in slaves, and emancipated slaves had no evident prospects. Congress provided only modest support such as food and new schools through the Freedmen's Bureau.

In the same month as Lee and Sherman surrendered, Lincoln was assassinated, thus making Vice President Andrew Johnson president. With Congress on summer recess, Johnson established rules for the reentry of Southern states to the Union, including abolishing slavery and ratifying the Thirteenth Amendment. When Congress reconvened, its Republican-majority members discarded Johnson's plan, established stronger military control over the Southern states, and set new reentry requirements. All adult black men and all white men who had not been involved in the war effort were eligible to vote for delegates to state constitutional conventions, and the constitutions drafted therein had to be approved by Congress. The governments elected under those constitutions had to ratify the Fourteenth Amendment. By 1870 all of the Southern states had complied with Congress's rules for reentry, and the Union had been restored.

As an unelected president who had only weak ties to both major parties and a hostile relationship to Congress (he was impeached by the House and only avoided conviction in the Senate by one vote), Johnson was politically weak. Both major parties passed him over for the presidential nomination in 1868, the Democrats choosing Horatio Seymour and the Republicans Ulysses Grant. Grant won, and as president presided over the beginning of the Gilded Age, a term coined by Mark Twain to refer to the extreme wealth and corruption that came with industrialization after the Civil War. The age was defined by such events as the Tweed Ring (discussed in the entry on New York), frequent corruption scandals in the Grant administration (despite which Grant was reelected by a wide margin in 1872), and the economic collapse of 1873, which was brought about in large part by overspeculation in railroads.

As the depression following 1873 turned public attention to the economy, support for Reconstruction waned. In 1874 Democrats captured majority control of the House of Representatives, and in 1876 a Democratic candidate won the popular vote for president—though not the presidency. Republicans passed on nominating Grant for a third term and nominated Rutherford Hayes, while the Democrats nominated former New York governor (and active participant in exposing the Tweed Ring) Samuel Tilden. Tilden won the popular vote by a slim margin, yet the results in four states were challenged. The election was turned over to a special commission, which, voting along straight party lines, awarded the election to Hayes. Soon after assuming office, Hayes withdrew the remaining federal troops from the Southern states.

The 1876 presidential election was followed by the largest strike in the history of the United States. By the 1870s, railroads were the country's largest industrial employer, and when many of them announced a wage reduction of 10 percent in 1877, the effects were widespread. Disgruntled workers in West Virginia and Maryland refused to move freight, and officials in those states called in state militia and the National Guard. The conflict escalated to violence in Baltimore and spread first to the Pennsylvania cities of Pittsburgh, Philadelphia, and Reading, where more workers joined the struggle. The strike eventually reached as far west as Illinois and Missouri, with especially large demonstrations occurring in Chicago. President Hayes sent federal troops across the country to quell the conflicts, and the strike eventually lost momentum after more than a month.

NEW YORK, NY 1854–1877

BY 1880 NEW YORK CITY'S POPULATION WAS 1.2 MILLION—approximately double what it had been in the period from the 1850s to the 1870s. It had annexed three towns in Westchester County and bolstered its position as the country's center for trade, finance, and manufacturing. Yet the rate of growth in New York was slight compared to that of Brooklyn, whose population more than quintupled to more than five hundred thousand (in part because it annexed the neighboring towns of Williamsburg and Bushwick in 1855), making it the third-largest city in the United States. Reflecting its new prominence, Brooklyn's water system, which rivaled New York's eminent Croton system, commenced operation in 1858.

Explosive growth was a profoundly destabilizing process, and New York in the mid-nineteenth century was marked by violence, corruption, political factionalism, class conflict, and economic crises. The Civil War was especially contentious in the city, which was intimately linked financially to the Southern states. The National Conscription Act led to a devastating riot in the city in 1863. By the late 1870s, as the federal government was ending its military occupation of the Southern states, Tammany Hall, chastened by the fall of the Tweed Ring, had become a more disciplined organization under the direction of John Kelly; class divisions had grown and hardened; and the nation was still in the grips of a recession that had originated with a financial panic in New York City.

GOVERNMENT AND POLITICS

New York City politics in the 1850s was characterized by factionalism. The city government was decentralized, which provided various opportunities for entrepreneurial politicians to create independent organizations. The organization to beat was Tammany Hall, named after the meeting place of the fraternal society that also served as the main headquarters for the city's Democrats. In 1853 the state legislature passed a new charter for New York City, which, among other things, consolidated the bicameral city council into a single chamber, provided stronger veto powers for the mayor, and required that city police wear uniforms. The charter also authorized the city's use of eminent domain to create a 778-acre park between Fifth and

QUICK FACTS

NEW YORK, NY **1854–1877**

MAYORS

Jacob A. Westervelt   (1853–1855)
Fernando Wood   (1855-1858)
Daniel F. Tiemann   (1858–1860)
Fernando Wood   (1860–1862)
George Opdyke   (1862–1864)
Charles G. Gunther   (1864–1866)
John T. Hoffman   (1866–1868)
Thomas Coman   (1868)
A. Oakey Hall   (1869–1872)
William Havemeyer   (1873–1874)
Samuel B. H. Vance   (1874)
William H. Wickham   (1875–1876)
Smith Ely Jr.   (1877–1878)

MAJOR INDUSTRIES AND EMPLOYERS

Apparel manufacturing
Banking and finance
Ironworks
Piano manufacturing (Steinway and Sons)
Shipping

MAJOR NEWSPAPERS

New-York Commercial Advertiser
New York Sun
New York Herald
New York Times
New York Daily News
New York World
Daily Commercial Bulletin and Auction Record
Evening Telegram
New York Daily Register
City Record
Hotel Reporter

MAJOR EVENTS

1857: The New York State legislature passes a new charter for New York City that transfers significant powers, including control over the port, public works, and the police, to state-appointed commissions.

1857: The New York branch of the Ohio Life Insurance and Trust Company fails on account of bad investments and outright theft by management, leading to a larger financial panic and an ensuing depression that spreads as far as London and Paris.

1857: Final authorization is granted for the establishment and construction of Central Park. The state legislature had originally authorized the use of eminent domain to create the park in 1853. The common council voted to cut the size of the proposed park in half in 1855.

1863: In response to the implementation of a national conscription law in the city, residents break out in a massive riot that lasts for three days, leading to more than $1 million in damages and more than one hundred deaths.

1871: An exposé in the *New York Times* reports massive financial improprieties on behalf of city officials William Tweed, A. Oakey Hall, Peter Sweeny, and Richard Connolly, who become known as the "Tweed Ring." Connolly and Sweeny fled the country, Hall survived four trials, and Tweed went to jail, where he died in 1878.

1873: Overspeculation in railroads on behalf of New York banks contributes to a widespread financial panic, resulting in the worst depression in United States history to that date, which lasts through most of the decade.

Eighth Avenues and Fifty-Eighth and 116th Streets. In 1854 Fernando Wood, a successful businessman, former member of Congress, and Tammany Democrat, was elected mayor, and the following year a small group of elite New Yorkers formed a chapter of the Republican Party.

Mayor Wood announced an aggressive reform agenda, including the establishment and construction of Central Park, the design for which was awarded to Calvert Vaux and Frederick Law Olmsted. This pair also went on to design Brooklyn's Prospect Park after the Civil War. Yet the Republican legislature in 1857 passed a new city charter that took patronage resources away from Democrats by placing the city's port, the construction of Central Park, most public works, and the police under the authority of state-appointed, nonelective commissions. The legislature passed a similarly disempowering charter for Brooklyn in the same year, removing the police, Prospect Park, and public works from city control. Under Mayor Martin Kalbfleisch, Brooklyn gradually began to regain some formal authority over public works starting in 1869.

New York's new charter forced Wood to stand for election early, in 1857. He lost, probably as a result of both the financial crisis of that year and the fact that he had been expelled from Tammany Hall by Democrats who were concerned about his increasing power. Yet Wood established his own Democratic organization, Mozart Hall, and was reelected in 1859, beating Tammany candidate (and former mayor) William Havemeyer and Republican George Opdyke.

Mozart Hall temporarily eclipsed Tammany as the regular Democratic Party organization in the city. It became a bastion for "Peace Democrats" who wanted to reconcile with the Confederate states. Indeed, Wood famously made the public suggestion in 1861 that New York become a "free city," independent of New York State and the Union, so that it could continue to trade with the South. Tammany became the base for "War Democrats" who supported the Union cause even as they opposed Republicans. With the Democrats divided, Republican Opdyke was elected mayor in 1861. It was during Opdyke's mayoralty, in 1863, that the highly unpopular National Conscription Act, a new draft initiated to build up declining troop levels, was instituted in New York. Passage of the act was met with mass protests that turned violent and resulted in three days of rioting and more than one hundred casualties.

Meanwhile, the state-appointed Central Park Commission had been gradually increasing its authority to resemble a metropolitan planning agency. From 1859 to 1870, the legislature extended the authority of the commission to cover the planning and construction of all streets north of 155th Street, north of 110th Street to St. Nicholas Avenue, west of Eighth Avenue and north of Fifty-Ninth Street, and in lower Westchester County in what would later become the Bronx.

The Central Park Commission's authority over streets beyond the confines of Manhattan Island foreshadowed New York City's annexation of lower Westchester County in 1874. Prior to this, the city had had jurisdiction only in Manhattan, having been granted authority over the entire island by a colonial governor in 1665. By the time of the 1874 annexation, however, the commission was no longer an independent entity. The legislature passed a new city charter in 1870 under which the functions of the Central Park Commission and the Croton

Aqueduct Department were absorbed into the new departments of Public Parks and Public Works, respectively.

The new commissioner of the Department of Public Works, through which some of the most lucrative city contracts were issued, was William Tweed, who was also simultaneously serving as a state senator. Tweed had previously served as a city alderman, U.S. House representative, member of the New York County Board of Supervisors, and a deputy street commissioner. In at least the latter two positions, Tweed began to build up what would come to be known as his "ring"—the extensive system of kickbacks on city contracts orchestrated by Tweed, Mayor A. Oakey Hall, City Chamberlain Peter Sweeny, and City Controller Richard Connolly, starting approximately in 1866. The largest source of kickbacks, according to later reports, was the construction of a new courthouse, for which the city was vastly overcharged by contractors. The contractors then passed much of the surplus along to the Tweed Ring and its associates.

A campaign against Tweed and his associates led by the *New York Times*, which

Perhaps the most famous of New York City's 19th-century political figures was William "Boss" Tweed, here caricatured by cartoonist Thomas Nast. The cartoon illustrates Tweed's widespread far-reaching power with a caption that reads, "'No prison is big enough to hold the Boss.' In on one side, and out at the other." Tweed used his positions in city government to reap significant financial kickbacks that landed him in jail twice in the 1870s.   *Library of Congress*

revealed the shockingly broad scope of malfeasance, marked the beginnings of a reform movement that led to the temporary electoral defeat of Tammany Hall in the early 1870s and the indictment of the members of the Tweed Ring and their associates. In response, Sweeny and Connolly both fled the country. Connolly's replacement as comptroller, chosen by reformers, was Andrew Green, formerly the leading member of the Central Park Commission during its expansionary period. Hall survived unscathed through four trials. Tweed was brought to trial twice in 1873, sentenced to a jail term of twelve years, and released in 1875. He was immediately re-arrested on civil charges and sent back to jail, after which he escaped for a year, was captured, and died in jail in 1878.

The necessity of restoring the city's credit and meeting bond payments and payroll with a treasury depleted from five years of graft, combined with the financial panic of 1873 and the ensuing economic depression, demanded severe government retrenchment. A new city charter in 1873 created the Board of Estimate and Apportionment (composed of the mayor, comptroller, head of the Department of Taxes and Assessment, and the president of the board of aldermen) that controlled the city budget. Mayor Havemeyer and Green joined to ruthlessly cut the city budget, which, ironically, led to the ultimate electoral defeat of reformers to candidates aligned with a more centralized Tammany Hall, led by the respectable John Kelly. Only a few years after the fall of the Tweed Ring, Tammany Democrat William Wickham was back in the mayor's office. (Havemeyer had died in office and been replaced briefly by the president of the board of aldermen, Samuel Vance.) Tammany officials promised a new round of public works in order to create jobs, yet Green, with the backing of Governor Samuel Tilden, remained as comptroller and vigorously contained city spending. At the end of Green's term, in 1876, Kelly himself became comptroller, yet even he was forced to cut the budget.

The instability engendered by the depression of the 1870s bolstered class divisions, which, combined with the rise of machine politics and increasingly strident labor demands, moved many of the city's elite to reconsider the benefits of universal white male suffrage. Thus, when Governor Tilden established a state commission to propose municipal government reforms, the elites on the commission recommended that cities in New York State be governed primarily by appointed commissions, that they only be allowed to take on debt in exceptional circumstances, and that most of their governing power should be vested in local boards of finance, the members of which would be elected only by city residents who paid at least $500 annually in property taxes. The proposed amendments to the state constitution were passed by the legislature in 1877, but a new legislature, elected in November of that year with the support of a coalition of working-class interests in New York City and upstate farmers, soundly voted them down in 1878.

INDUSTRY, COMMERCE, AND LABOR

By 1860 approximately two-thirds of all goods imported into the country, and one-third of the goods leaving the country for export, went through New York's port. At the center of this mercantile activity was cotton, though as farm production increased in the West, railroads stretched further into the continent, and Southern farm production decreased during the Civil War, as increasing number of merchants turned to wheat and corn.

Merchants often had to extend credit in order to facilitate trade, making them de facto bankers, and it is thus not surprising that the mercantile center of the country also became the largest center for banking and finance. By 1858 approximately one-fifth of all capital controlled by American banks was held by the fifty-four banks in New York City.

Just as with trade and finance, New York was, by the 1850s, the center of manufacturing in the United States. By 1860 there were more than four thousand factories of various sorts in the city, most relatively small, but employing collectively more than ninety thousand workers. The largest industry was men's clothing, which employed over twenty thousand workers in slightly more than three hundred shops. The largest private employers were ironworks, several of which employed more than one thousand workers apiece. Steinway and Sons, which sold its first piano in 1853, also rapidly became one of the city's largest employers.

As components of the economic center of the country, New York City institutions also shared a disproportionate responsibility for financial crises and the ensuing depressions, such as in the summer of 1857 when the New York branch of the Ohio Life Insurance and Trust

Company failed on account of bad investments and outright theft on the part of its manager. Realizing that they would not be recovering the millions of dollars they had loaned to Ohio Life and that other money they loaned may have also been invested just as badly, banks called in their outstanding loans. This led to a financial panic that spread as far as London and Paris. By the end of the summer, the number of unemployed in both New York and Brooklyn was estimated at one hundred thousand. By the end of the year, crowds of several thousand people marched on Wall Street to demand loans to businesses in order to increase employment, and on city hall to demand public relief programs.

The crisis of 1857 decimated the relatively small labor movement in the city, though unions returned to the city during the Civil War and increased more than tenfold in number to total roughly 160 by the end of the war. Indeed, it was in 1864 in New York City that a young Samuel Gompers joined his first union, the Cigar Makers' National Union Local 15. During the 1860s and 1870s, hundreds of strikes were held by workers in various trades throughout the city. Two of the largest of these were the 1869 bricklayers' strike and, in 1872, the largest strike to date, which involved roughly one hundred thousand workers, mostly from manufacturing establishments. At Steinway and Sons, workers went on strike five times between 1863 and 1869.

Unionization depended on a resurgent economy. Between 1860 and 1870, the number of workers in New York's factories increased from 39,373 to 129,577, thus creating far more fertile ground for labor organizing. Manufacturers after the war often acceded to workers' demands, and radical Republicans in the legislature were able to pass an eight-hour workday law (albeit one with weak enforcement power) in 1867.

Industrial growth in Manhattan was actually somewhat slower than that occurring nationally. The number of factories in Manhattan had only increased by approximately 75 percent during the 1860s, reaching 7,624 in number by 1870, while nationally the number of factories approximately doubled. Heavy industries such as ironworks were moving to more affordable locations outside the city. The city increasingly became a place for the manufacture of lighter items, such as clothing, cutlery, and sewing machines, and of carriages and printing presses, while it also secured its position as the financial center of the country.

Indeed, it was immediately after the war that the New York Stock Exchange moved into its new headquarters near Broad and Wall Streets. The majority of companies traded on the exchange after the war were railroads. By 1870 bankers had become the wealthiest New Yorkers, and it was in New York financial institutions that the financial panic of 1873 began (in part from overspeculation in railroads), inaugurating the worst depression in American history to that date. Approximately one-fourth of all New York City workers had lost their jobs by 1874. The unemployed held mass demonstrations in 1873 and 1874 to demand public relief, but to little avail as the city was busy cutting its own budget in the wake of the Tweed Ring.

During the depression of the 1870s, class tensions were exacerbated, employers became less amenable to labor demands, and the city's union rolls declined sharply. City officials were especially wary of the possibility of a violent riot when labor organizers planned a meeting in Tompkins Square Park in 1877 in support of the nationwide railroad strike, yet the only significant violence occurred when police, apparently unprovoked, began clubbing some of the twenty thousand attendees.

RACE, ETHNICITY, AND IMMIGRATION

New York by the 1850s was the largest point of entry in the United States for immigrants, who started to arrive in truly massive waves in the 1840s. Particularly large groups came from Ireland and Germany as millions fled those countries on account of disastrous potato crops and repressive governments. Of the more than four million immigrants that arrived in the United States in the twenty years after 1840, approximately 75 percent arrived in New York. Both the Irish and German waves of immigration reached high points during the 1850s, though Germans came over in even greater numbers after the 1870s. Immediately after the Civil War, and before the depression of the 1870s, more than two hundred thousand immigrants arrived in New York City every year. The vast majority moved further inland toward the frontier, but the shear mass of new arrivals swelled the population of the city.

Many German immigrants resumed the trades they had practiced in Europe and worked as bakers, butchers, brewers, and makers of pianos (such as the Steinways). Additionally, although the profession was dominated by the native-born, there were a significant number of German physicians in the city. By the 1850s, the city's garment industry was almost entirely run by immigrants, the majority of which were German, but many Irish worked in these jobs as well. The Irish were more likely than the Germans to work as unskilled laborers (through which many came to own construction companies), teamsters, hostlers, and dockworkers. The rise of John Kelly to the leadership of Tammany Hall was also indicative of the increasing presence of the Irish in city politics. Indeed, immigrants were a real political force in New York in the 1850s, as they accounted for almost half of the city's legal voters. And though the majority of the new arrivals were poor or working class, nearly half of the members of the city's upper class (depending on how they were measured) were also foreign-born, a statistic which remained relatively stable into the late nineteenth century and provided a cosmopolitan feel to the city.

Largely at the behest of organized German and Irish groups, the state legislature in 1847 created the Board of Commissioners of Emigration, which established the Emigrant Refuge and Hospital on Ward's Island. This hospital was the largest medical complex in the world in the 1850s. In 1855 the commission established the first-ever immigrant reception center, Castle Garden, which was replaced by Ellis Island in 1892.

Many Germans lived in a concentrated area known as *Kleindeutschland* in what is today the Lower East Side, or they moved to the more northern settlement of Yorkville. Irish immigrants were more widely dispersed throughout the city, though they were especially numerous in the lower portions of Manhattan, such as the Five Points, where they increasingly pushed out the city's relatively small African American population (approximately 12,500 in 1860). However, small enclaves of blacks existed in Greenwich Village, the northern reaches of the city past Twenty-Third Street, and in Crow Hill and Fort Greene in Brooklyn.

New York had a long history of anti-abolitionist riots, such as the sacking of Lewis Tappan's house in 1834. The 1863 draft riots were to some extent a continuation of that tradition, as rioters beat and lynched African Americans and destroyed any identifiable Republican institutions. Most evidence suggests that the rioters were predominantly Irish, despite the fact that Irish had also been some of the most enthusiastic to first volunteer for war, joining New York's Irish 69th Regiment. On account of the war and the hostility they faced, the African American population was still very small after the war, representing only a bit more than 1 percent of the overall city population. Their numbers began to expand significantly after the war, however, in part because the migration of freedmen north. The largest concentration of black New Yorkers became that in the northwestern neighborhood of Hell's Kitchen.

Among the German immigrants there was a small but significant Jewish population, whose members established their own institutions, including synagogues. The Irish who arrived were largely Catholic, though enough of them were Protestant to warrant celebration of the 1690 Battle of the Boyne, in which Protestant forces defeated Catholics. Their loss of this battle resulted in restricted rights for the Catholics. The celebration, generally held on July 12 and known as the Orange Parade, was taken, and was often meant, as an offense to Irish Catholics. Thus, as "Orangemen" marched through New York in 1870, singing songs meant to provoke Irish Catholics, the Catholics attacked, resulting in eight deaths. The following year, the Orangeman once again marched. They had at first been denied permission by the city, but that decision was reversed. The parade, which marched with the protection of five thousand troops, was met with a barrage of stones and other projectiles and some sniper fire. The troops returned fire, which resulted in sixty-three people being killed and more than a hundred injured.

See also *New York, NY 1776–1790; New York, NY 1790–1828; New York, NY 1828–1854; New York, NY 1877–1896; New York, NY 1896–1929; New York, NY 1929–1941; New York, NY 1941–1952; New York, NY 1952–1989; New York, NY 1989–2011*

RICHARDSON DILWORTH

BIBLIOGRAPHY

Beckert, Sven. *The Monied Metropolis: New York City and the Consolidation of the American Bourgeoisie.* New York, NY: Cambridge University Press, 2001.

Bersntein, Iver. *The New York City Draft Riots: Their Significance for American Society and Politics in the Age of the Civil War.* New York, NY: Oxford University Press, 1990.

Burrows, Edwin G., and Mike Wallace. *Gotham: A History of New York City to 1898.* New York, NY: Oxford University Press, 2000.

Callow, Alexander B., Jr. *The Tweed Ring.* New York, NY: Oxford University Press, 1966.

Foord, John. *The Life and Public Services of Andrew Haswell Green.* New York, NY: Doubleday, Page, and Company, 1913.

Hershkowitz, Leo. *Tweed's New York: Another Look.* Garden City, NY: Anchor Press, 1977.

Mushkat, Jerome. *Fernando Wood: A Political Biography.* Kent, OH: The Kent State University Press, 1990.

Rosenzweig, Roy, and Elizabeth Blackmar. *The Park and the People: A History of Central Park.* Ithaca, NY: Cornell University Press, 1992.

PHILADELPHIA, PA 1854–1877

PHILADELPHIA'S CONSOLIDATION IN 1854 TRANSFORMED THE CITY from a cluster of divided districts, boroughs, and townships into what was in territorial terms the largest municipality in the nation. In the years that followed, industrial development gathered pace. Factories and working-class row homes expanded onto the land annexed by the 1854 reform, and by the 1870s Philadelphia boasted the most diverse manufacturing base in the nation.

The city weathered the war years relatively well. No civil disorders on the scale of the riots of the 1830s and 1840s disturbed the peace, and the local economy benefited from the local and national ascendancy of the new Republican Party. Yet beneath the surface problems persisted. Though fighting between nativists and Irish immigrants abated, many whites resisted the postwar extension of civil rights to African Americans. Meanwhile, manufacturing workers revived the labor movement after 1865, which shifted the site of social tension from ethnically diverse neighborhoods to the city's factories.

GOVERNMENT AND POLITICS

The consolidation of 1854 overrode the old municipal boundaries and extended the city limits to the county line. The act enlarged more than the territorial reach of the local state, however. The new charter strengthened the powers of the mayor, increased the city's tax base, and gave city council members new responsibilities, including the provision of parks and open spaces. Philadelphia's consolidation, according to both contemporary reformers and recent historians, modernized the city's municipal government.

By merging the Whig stronghold of the old city proper with the predominantly Democratic suburbs, consolidation left open the question of who would win control of the new metropolis. Supporters of the reform, led by real estate attorney Eli Kirk Price, had only won the crucial election on an independent ticket the previous October due to the support of nativist voters disillusioned with the major parties. In the first mayoral election of the new city in May 1854, the Whigs reluctantly backed the anti-immigrant Know-Nothing poet and playwright Robert T. Conrad. The same year long-serving Whig congressman Joel B. Chandler—a convert to Catholicism—failed to secure his party's nomination, which went instead to a candidate more attuned to nativist sensibilities. The Whig Party, having ruled the city proper for much of the preceding two decades, had all but disappeared by 1856.

Philadelphia's Democratic Party proved more durable. In 1856 Democrat Richard Vaux defeated Conrad in the race for city hall. Vaux, a wealthy attorney from a Quaker family, used the promise of patronage to cultivate alliances with local bosses like the Fourth Ward's William McMullen, who in turn helped deliver Irish and working-class voters.

National politics helped the Democrats after Vaux's election. In the summer of 1856, the Republican Party held its first presidential nominating convention in Philadelphia. Many former Whigs, however, including the president of the Philadelphia Board of Trade, Frederick Fraley,

QUICK FACTS

PHILADELPHIA, PA 1854–1877

MAYORS

Robert Thomas Conrad	(1854–1856)
Richard Vaux	(1856–1858)
Alexander Henry	(1858–1866)
Morton McMichael	(1866–1869)
Daniel Fox	(1869–1872)
William S. Stokley	(1872–1881)

MAJOR INDUSTRIES AND EMPLOYERS

Textiles
Iron and steel
Boots and shoes
Machine and locomotive building
Carpentry and building

MAJOR NEWSPAPERS

Age
Daily News
Evening Bulletin
Philadelphia Inquirer
North American and United States Gazette
Pennsylvanian
Philadelphia Press
Public Ledger

MAJOR EVENTS

1857: Unemployed residents gather in Independence Square to demand employment on public works projects. This was the largest public meeting ever held in the city up to that point.

1860: The first-ever Japanese mission to the West sees dignitaries visit the Federal Mint in the city.

1864: The Great Sanitary Fair is put together by wealthy Philadelphians to raise money for aspects of the war effort. The fair inspired organizers of the Centennial Exhibition twelve years later.

1867: The state legislature gives the Fairmount Park Commission responsibility for the city's extensive park land and open spaces.

1871: Octavius Catto, a prominent African American activist, is shot through the heart on Election Day in October. The Democrat accused of his murder was finally brought to trial in 1877 but was acquitted by an all-white jury.

found a new home in the Democratic Party, as they were unwilling to back the radical antislavery platform of the Republican candidate John C. Fremont.

Democratic ascendancy did not last long. Two years later, merchant Alexander Henry won the mayoralty on a Republican ticket. He did so in part by downplaying the antislavery message. The ticket even eschewed the name Republican in favor of "People's Party" to distance itself from abolitionists in a city notoriously hostile to its disfranchised black minority. An economic crisis in 1857—which many Philadelphians blamed on the low protective tariffs favored by Democrats—together with the Republicans' ability to draw nativist support proved crucial to the party's victory.

Sectional conflict may not have helped the Republicans rise to power in Philadelphia, but it certainly helped the party maintain it. Upper-class Democrats, many of whom had strong business and family ties to the South, were often highly sympathetic to the cause of the rebel states.

Wealthy Republicans, allied with a few loyal Democrats, formed the Union League in 1862 to isolate Confederate sympathizers. Northern victories disgraced the pro-Southern "copperhead" faction, whose advocacy on behalf of the Confederacy allowed local Republicans to brand the Democrats with the stigma of treason.

The vast resources of the consolidated city also proved vital to cementing Republican rule. William McManes's Gas Trust and Mayor William Stokley's Public Buildings Commission both served as huge patronage machines that dispensed financial rewards in exchange for support. The powers vested in the mayor to hire and fire policemen offered another route to reward loyal backers. And infrastructure improvements undertaken in the burgeoning suburbs won votes for the party on the metropolitan periphery. Democrat Daniel Fox's election in 1868 proved the only interruption to Republican hegemony.

Fox's police force tried to stop a group that would become a bulwark of the Republican coalition—African Americans—from casting their ballots for the first time after passage of the Fifteenth Amendment in 1870. African American men had demanded the vote as far back as January 1867, when black veterans from across the nation gathered in the city to push for enfranchisement, but it took the presence of federal troops on polling day to safeguard nonwhite voters from violent Democrats. Despite their participation in wartime voluntary movements like the Sanitary Commission, however, women proved less successful in securing political rights. Philadelphia abolitionist Lucretia Mott was among the founders of the American Equal Rights Association in 1864 that called for women's suffrage, and feminists did try to cast ballots in Reconstruction elections in the city, but their efforts proved unsuccessful.

These debates over citizenship took place against the backdrop of growing middle-class opposition to active government in Philadelphia. Successive city administrations faced criticism from property owners who feared the huge increase in city debt over the Civil War years—a result of expensive civic improvements on either side of the conflict and the cost of recruitment bounties and defending the city during the sectional struggle—would lead to higher taxes. Many also complained that the new city charter of 1854 was not functioning as its framers had intended. Despite consolidators' attempts to strengthen the position of the mayor, the bicameral municipal councils found ways to usurp executive powers for themselves. State legislators, moreover, often overrode the stated wishes of the city. After 1856 Harrisburg politicians granted a number of street railway companies the rights to lay tracks down the city streets despite the opposition of councilmen. Then, in the postbellum era, state legislators created commissions empowered to erect a new city hall and establish a system of parks with little or no oversight from the city councils.

By the early 1870s, many Philadelphians had joined the call for cheap, efficient government, and between 1871 and 1872, taxpayers organized the Citizens Municipal Reform Association (CMRA) and Reform League to challenge Republican rule. Some of the reformers' suggestions, such as restrictions on municipal debt, were incorporated into a new state constitution in 1873. Politicians, however, found ways to circumvent such measures, and support for the reform cause remained largely limited to the city's wealthier residents. Thus Republican hegemony endured, and by 1877 the position of the party in the city appeared unassailable.

INDUSTRY, COMMERCE, AND LABOR

Philadelphia's consolidation took place at the moment the economic boom of the late 1840s was coming to an end. Citizens nonetheless had good reason to be optimistic in 1854. In February the Pennsylvania Railroad, chartered in 1846, finally completed its direct link to the Ohio Valley at Pittsburgh. And the real estate market, aided by annexation, continued to offer rich rewards for investors.

The years after 1854 nevertheless saw the local economy slow down, and in the fall of 1857, a financial panic that began in New York brought down the Bank of Pennsylvania. Within a few weeks, hundreds of factories shut their doors, placing thousands of operatives out of work. The panic destroyed many of the labor unions that had organized in the 1850s, but the common experience of hardship drew the unemployed together across ethnic and trade divisions in a series of huge meetings to demand employment on local improvements.

Philadelphia's economy recovered relatively quickly from the panic. By 1860 industry and commerce in the city were on the rise again, but the secession crisis and outbreak of war led to a mini-recession. Over the following years, however, the conflict benefited many of the city's factory owners. Republican control of the national government finally won locomotive builders and iron interests the protective tariff they had long demanded. Government contracts helped industries like textiles expand. Although manufacturing output increased 70 percent between 1860 and 1870, much of the growth took place after 1866. Philadelphians nevertheless played a vital role in the war effort. Thomas Scott, a postbellum president of the Pennsylvania Railroad, used his expertise to coordinate the transportation of troops and supplies, while financier Jay Cooke pioneered the selling of government bonds to thousands of middle- and working-class Americans. The precise impact of the conflict on the city's industry remains a matter for debate; it is clear, however, the local economy emerged from the storm in better health than many of its rivals.

The experience of war rarely led to consolidation in the manufacturing sector. Throughout the era, though, the corporate form of organization remained rare. Even larger enterprises, such as locomotive builders Matthias Baldwin and Company, were run as partnerships or family firms. Far more common were small factories that employed no more than a few dozen employees and produced goods as diverse as stoves, hats, and furniture. These were the enterprises that flourished in the suburbs annexed by the Act of Consolidation, and their expansion into rural villages like Germantown drew the city outwards. The frequent claim of boosters across the era that Philadelphia was the leading manufacturing center of the continent rested on the small scale and diversity of its industry, not the large-scale concentration commonly associated with the Gilded Age.

The Pennsylvania Railroad, which at the outset of the Civil War was the nation's largest corporation, proved an exception to this rule. By the 1870s, after a wave of corporate consolidations, the line had outposts in Chicago, Illinois; St. Louis, Missouri; and New York City, and for a time its postwar president Thomas Scott headed the Union Pacific, the nation's first transcontinental railroad. In 1876 the Pennsylvania Railroad ferried in many of the ten million visitors to Philadelphia who attended the Centennial Exhibition world's fair in Fairmount Park. The fair provided an opportunity for the city to display its manufacturing strength.

The exhibition's festivities took place against a backdrop of economic turmoil, however. In 1873 the failure of Jay Cooke's bank triggered a nationwide recession, and the long depression that followed drew converts to working-class radicalism. But the revival of Philadelphia's labor movement predated the 1870s. During the Civil War, *Finchers' Trades' Review*, published in the city by a mechanic at the Baldwin Works, had become one of the nation's leading labor journals. Then, in 1866, iron molder William Sylvis helped to organize the progressive National Labor Union (NLU). Although reformist rather than militant—Sylvis preferred cooperation to strikes—the organization was the first nationwide labor federation. The NLU disbanded in 1872, but another movement that first took root in Philadelphia, the Knights of Labor, endured rather longer. Founded by tailors Uriah Stevens and James Wright in 1869, it quickly spread to the rest of the country and arguably became the most important labor organization in the United States prior to the American Federation of Labor.

Philadelphia, however, did not witness the violent clashes between labor and capital that were evident elsewhere in America during the Gilded Age. Even when the nationwide railroad strike of 1877 spread to the city, most workers stayed at home. Despite the relative calm, however, the strike profoundly troubled the civic elite, many of whom feared socialism had finally arrived as a force to be reckoned with in America.

Such fears were probably exaggerated. Working-class Philadelphians after the Civil War were more likely to join a building society in order to secure a home rather than join a labor union. The member-run building societies loaned money on mortgage to their members, who then used it to secure property. Pioneered in Britain, they first appeared in Philadelphia in 1849 and by 1877 had expended an estimated $50 million in turning the metropolis into a "city of homes." In 1877 Mayor Stokley and the press appealed to members of the associations to stand firm as property holders on the side of order. The houses the societies' capital was used to construct helped the city's manufacturing economy expand into new space on the metropolitan frontier.

RACE, ETHNICITY, AND IMMIGRATION

The relative calm of the Civil War years suggested the city authorities had found a way to contain the endemic violence of the preceding decades. Certainly battles between Irish Catholic immigrants and Protestants were more likely to be fought at the ballot box than in the street after midcentury, and the channeling of ethnocultural hostility into political conflict may help account for the decline in rioting. Nonetheless, the strength of the nativist Know-Nothing Party in the mid-1850s and the importance of its voters to the Republican majority that emerged after 1858 suggest cultural tensions persisted despite a marked drop in immigration from Ireland over the course of the decade. Nor did the rise of the antislavery Republican Party necessarily suggest white citizens were warming to the presence of the city's black population.

The Civil War slowed immigration to the city further and left a significant mark on ethnic and race relations. Irishmen such as Democratic Party ward boss William McMullen demonstrated their loyalty to the Union by enlisting, winning plaudits from the city's elite.

Unlike New York, no antidraft riots broke out in the city—a testimony both to the strength of Philadelphia's consolidated police and the readiness of the municipality and wealthy citizens to offer hefty bounties that allowed the city to fill its quota of troops without conscription. Black military service, meanwhile, challenged longstanding racial hostilities. With the help of the Union League, African American regiments recruited among the free black population. Camp William Penn, established on the northern edge of the city, trained black troops. In the aftermath of the conflict, Sylvis tried to draw African American workers into the National Labor Union.

However, hostility to blacks persisted in a metropolis Frederick Douglass called the most racist in America. Until a change in state law in 1867, African Americans were barred from the passenger railways that had crisscrossed the city since 1856. Republican mayors Alexander Henry and Morton McMichael both refused to condemn the discrimination. And the coming of black suffrage in the late 1860s heightened racial antagonisms, especially among Democrats who feared black voters would help the Republican cause. In 1871 a turbulent election day concluded with the murder of African American activist and Union veteran Octavius Catto, allegedly at the hands of one of McMullen's political allies.

The city Catto fought to integrate was becoming more segregated, though never to anything like the degree familiar to historians of the mid-twentieth-century metropolis. African Americans remained concentrated in the city proper and inner suburbs, while suburban expansion paved the way for some whites to move outwards. Many upper-middle-class Philadelphians left the central wards for leafy enclaves like West Philadelphia. For the working class, meanwhile, in an era where most still walked to work, outmigration to manufacturing suburbs was sometimes a necessity, though many white laborers moved into central areas vacated by wealthy residents. Clerks and white-collar workers who moved out commuted into the center along the street railway lines. Distinctive ethnic neighborhoods were yet to emerge, but some patterning was evident. McMullen's crowded Fourth Ward, in the 1830s and 1840s the scene of fighting between blacks and Irish Catholics, continued to serve as an immigrant entrepôt, though after the Civil War newcomers often arrived from southern and eastern Europe. Italian migration in particular took off in the 1870s, though Philadelphia's foreign-born population remained a far smaller proportion of the city's residents than in New York and Chicago.

While boosters frequently proclaimed Philadelphia a "city of homes," inequality in the provision of housing persisted. Although Philadelphia averaged half the number of residents per dwelling in 1870 than New York, within the city the family homes built on the urban periphery contrasted strongly to the rickety tenements in the overcrowded courts and alleys of the inner suburbs and Delaware waterfront. Cholera hit the city hard in 1866, and such outbreaks helped spur reformers to buy houses in the Fourth Ward's notorious Alaska District and rebuild them as more salubrious dwellings. Concerns over public health were also used to justify the expansion of Fairmount Park in 1867, which gave Philadelphia the largest public park in America. The park stretched along the Schuylkill River, northwest of the downtown area. Proponents of Fairmount's extension envisaged the park eventually becoming the center of a vast city built around the row home and factory. However, the problems of the 1870s—poor government, economic turbulence, and labor strife—combined to threaten that vision.

See also *Philadelphia, PA 1776–1790; Philadelphia, PA 1790–1828; Philadelphia, PA 1828–1854; Philadelphia, PA 1877–1896; Philadelphia, PA 1896–1929; Philadelphia, PA 1929–1941; Philadelphia, PA 1941–1952; Philadelphia, PA 1952–1989; Philadelphia, PA 1989–2011*

ANDREW HEATH

BIBLIOGRAPHY

Dawson, Andrew. *Lives of the Philadelphia Engineers: Capital, Class, and Revolution, 1830–1890.* Burlington, VT: Ashgate, 2004.

Diemer, Andrew. "Reconstructing Philadelphia: African Americans and Politics in the Post-Civil War North." *Pennsylvania Magazine of History & Biography* 133, no. 1 (2009): 29–58.

Dunbar, Eric Armstrong. *A Fragile Freedom: African-American Women and Emancipation in the Antebellum City.* New Haven, CT: Yale University Press, 2008.

Gallman, J. Matthew. *Mastering Wartime: A Social History of Philadelphia during the Civil War.* New York, NY: Cambridge University Press, 1990.

Hershberg, Theodore, ed. *Philadelphia: Work, Space, Family, and Group Experience in the 19th Century.* New York, NY: Oxford University Press, 1981.

Jones, Martha S. *All Bound up Together: The Woman Question in African-American Public Culture, 1830-1900.* Chapel Hill: University of North Carolina Press, 2007.

Lane, Roger. *Roots of Violence in Black Philadelphia, 1860–1900.* Cambridge, MA: Harvard University Press, 1986.

McCaffery, Peter. *When Bosses Ruled Philadelphia: The Emergence of the Republican Machine, 1867–1933.* State College: Pennsylvania State University Press, 1993.

Warner, Sam Bass, Jr. *The Private City: Philadelphia in Three Periods of Its Growth.* Philadelphia: University of Pennsylvania Press, 1987.

ST. LOUIS, MO 1854–1877

BY 1854 ST. LOUIS HAD BECOME A NORTHEASTERN-ORIENTED CITY IN A SLAVE STATE. The city's older French Creole elite retained its wealth (including property in slaves) and social prominence, but newly arrived merchants and manufacturers from the Northeast dominated public life. Substantial amounts of German immigrants strengthened the city's antislavery perspective and provided the electoral base for the emerging Republican Party.

GOVERNMENT AND POLITICS

In the late 1840s and early 1850s, Francis P. (Frank) Blair Jr. and his cousin Benjamin Gratz Brown transformed the Jacksonian *St. Louis Democrat* into the city's prominent Free-Soil, and

QUICK FACTS

ST. LOUIS, MO 1854–1877

MAYORS

John How	(1853–1855)
Washington King	(1855–1856)
John How	(1856–1857)
John Wimer	(1857–1858)
Oliver Dwight Filley	(1858–1861)
Daniel G. Taylor	(1861–1863)
Chauncy I. Filley	(1863–1864)
John S. Thomas	(1864–1869)
Nathan Cole	(1869–1871)
Joseph Brown	(1871–1875)
Arthur B. Barret	(1875)
James H. Britton	(1875–1876)
Henry Overstolz	(1876–1881)

MAJOR INDUSTRIES AND EMPLOYERS

Empire Stove Works
Excelsior Stove Works
Fulton Iron Works
St. Louis Compress Company (cotton)
Valle Rolling Mills

MAJOR NEWSPAPERS

Anzeiger des Westens
Globe-Democrat
Missouri Democrat
Missouri Republican
Post-Dispatch
Westliche Post

MAJOR EVENTS

May 10, 1861: The capture of Camp Jackson by federal forces commanded by Nathaniel Lyon ends the pro-Southern state militia muster in St. Louis and marks the assertion of federal control in the city.

1864: Frustrated by what they view as the degradation of their trades, workingmen in St. Louis launch widespread strikes in the spring of 1864. On April 29, 1864, General William Rosecrans places the workingmen of St. Louis under martial law and forces an end to the strikes.

1868: James B. Eads completes plans for a steel and iron carriage and railway bridge across the Mississippi River. The bridge opened in 1874 and provided St. Louis with its first rail link across the river.

October 1875: Missouri voters ratify a new state constitution that grants St. Louis a good deal of home rule but divorces the city from St. Louis County and prohibits future expansion of the city.

1876: Federal investigators uncover the "Whiskey Ring" fraud that diverted millions of dollars of federal tax revenues, initially to support St. Louis's leading Republican newspaper, but later to profit the ring's leaders.

later Republican, newspaper. The two leading German language dailies, the *Anzeiger des Westens* and the *Westliche Post*, promoted the Republican perspective in the German community. A distinctive feature of the city, the creation of southern St. Louis as a working-class neighborhood in the 1850s, took shape as a public committee sold off common lands, originally plotted out by the Spanish and French, and created new subdivisions south of the city center.

In the presidential election of 1856, St. Louis's most prominent political leader, former Democratic senator Thomas Hart Benton, supported Democratic candidate James Buchanan over his son-in-law, Republican nominee John C. Fremont. As a result, Fremont failed to carry St. Louis and the state. However, following Benton's death in 1858, antislavery Democrats quickly coalesced with antislavery Whigs. In 1858 St. Louis voters elected a Republican mayor: Connecticut-born manufacturer Oliver Dwight Filley. In the presidential election of 1860, Abraham Lincoln won a plurality of the city's vote. Only five hundred voters cast ballots for the Southern Rights Party candidate John Breckinridge, compared with ninety-five hundred votes for Lincoln. Unionist Democrat Stephen A. Douglas won eighty-five hundred votes, and conditional unionist John Bell won forty-five hundred votes. The conservative Unionist majority briefly broke with the Republicans in April 1861 and elected as mayor a self-proclaimed "Union Anti-Black Republican" candidate. Republicans regained control of the mayor's office in 1863, however, and remained in power until 1871.

A key figure in the unfolding secession crisis in St. Louis was the pro-secessionist governor of Missouri, Claiborne Jackson. Jackson hoped to control St. Louis and the federal arsenal located in the city. To that end, he secured the passage of state legislation creating the police board to control the St. Louis police. The city had long been governed by an elected mayor and a board of aldermen. The new Missouri law (which remains in place to this day) denied the mayor direct control over the police force. The law made the mayor a member of the police board but empowered the governor to appoint the other four members. Jackson also called out the state militia shortly after he rejected Lincoln's call for troops following the fall of Fort Sumter. Under the circumstances, most of the men who joined the St. Louis militia muster—commanded by Daniel Frost at Camp Jackson on the western edge of St. Louis—supported the Southern cause.

Frank Blair led the opposition to Jackson and Frost. Blair worked closely with Nathaniel Lyon, who commanded a detachment of regular U.S. troops charged with protecting federal property in St. Louis. With support from Lincoln's administration, Blair and Lyon raised several regiments of Home Guard, composed largely of recent German immigrants. The senior U.S. military commander in St. Louis, General William S. Harney, opposed the arming of the Home Guard and lobbied against it. In early May 1861, when Harney went to Washington, DC, to argue his case, Blair and Lyon took decisive action. Lyon led a force of nearly ten thousand men to surround and force the surrender of less than one thousand militiamen at Camp Jackson.

Harney, on his return to St. Louis, continued his policy of conciliation. To avoid conflicts between federal forces in St. Louis and the militia elsewhere in the state, Harney entered into an agreement with Missouri's militia commander, Sterling Price. Price proposed to maintain order in the state, and Harney agreed not to move federal forces out of St. Louis. It quickly became evident to Blair and Lyon that the Price-Harney agreement worked to the benefit of Governor Jackson, who maneuvered to align Missouri with the Confederacy. Acting on Blair's advice, Lincoln replaced Harney with Lyon. Lyon then drove Price and Jackson from the state capital. Under federal military protection, unionists controlled the state government for the duration of the war.

Until the fall of Vicksburg, Mississippi, in July 1863, St. Louis was the anchor for federal military operations west of the Mississippi River and south into the Tennessee and lower Mississippi River valleys. It was a measure of the importance Lincoln attached to St. Louis that he appointed John C. Fremont to be the first commander of the newly created military Department of the West. Fremont had close political and personal ties to the powerful Blair family, and Lincoln had already placed a great deal of reliance on Frank Blair in St. Louis. With the appointment of Fremont the president clearly hoped to strengthen the hand of Blair and his unionist allies.

Fremont quickly proved to be inadequate to the task. The commander alienated Frank Blair in St. Louis, and Fremont's wife, Jessie, traveled to Washington, DC, to defend her husband and angered both Francis P. Blair Sr. and President Lincoln. Fremont's command lasted just one hundred days from his arrival in St. Louis in July 1861 until his removal in October. Federal losses at the Battle of Wilson's Creek in August 1861 (where Lyon died) and the Battle of Lexington in September took place under Fremont's command, although they were largely beyond his control. Fremont did, however, effectively reinforce Ulysses S. Grant at Cairo, Illinois, and slowly reasserted federal control in western Missouri. Most famously, Fremont issued an emancipation proclamation and declared martial law in August. Lincoln rescinded the emancipation edict but allowed martial law to stand. Civil courts remained open in St. Louis throughout the Civil War, but martial law trumped civil law from August 1861 until General John Pope rescinded it in March 1865.

Insulated by martial law and buoyed by a strict loyalty oath that limited suffrage, Republican rule became hegemonic and corrupt. Liberal Republicans in St. Louis led the call for reform and reshaped the political landscape across the state. For Frank Blair and Gratz Brown, the Liberal Republican movement restored a degree of personal and political harmony. Early in the war the two men had parted company as Brown embraced emancipation and Blair, although a Union field commander eager to defeat the Confederacy, became a bitter opponent of racial equality. Their paths began to converge after the war as both men opposed the loyalty oath and the corruption that prevailed among Grant stalwarts. The Whiskey Ring scandal, exposed during Grant's second administration, vindicated the reformers and hastened the end of Reconstruction.

James O. Broadhead became a central figure in uncovering the Whiskey Ring in St. Louis. Broadhead had worked closely with Frank Blair during the secession crisis and, like Blair, he had returned to the Democratic Party after the war. In 1876 Broadhead became a special U.S. counsel in the prosecution of the Whiskey Ring cases. His investigation focused on St. Louis internal revenue inspector John McDonald. Closely allied with McDonald was William McKee, the editor and principal owner of the pro-Grant *Missouri Democrat*. Broadhead soon discovered that McDonald and McKee had collaborated with President Grant's personal secretary to control federal patronage in St. Louis, and that they manipulated the federal whiskey tax to help fund their fight against the Liberal Republicans. In 1872 McKee diverted this tax money to launch the St. Louis *Globe* as a rival to the increasingly reform-minded *Democrat*. In 1875, again with whiskey tax revenue, McKee bought out the rival *Democrat* and began publishing the pro-Grant *St. Louis Globe-Democrat*. The diversion of whiskey tax revenue for political purposes led McDonald, McKee, and others to pocket funds for personal gain. Broadhead's investigations resulted in more than two hundred indictments and over one hundred convictions, including those of McDonald and McKee.

Liberal Republicans also led the successful effort to eliminate the test oath and restore suffrage to former rebels. In October 1875 Missouri voters formally adopted a new constitution, marking the end of the Reconstruction era. The new constitution permitted the city to separate from St. Louis County—a move of great importance to the future of St. Louis. This provision offered the home rule that the city had long sought, but it also defined a western boundary for St. Louis that limited the city's future expansion.

INDUSTRY, COMMERCE, AND LABOR

The census of 1850 revealed that St. Louis, with a population of over one hundred thousand, had emerged as one of the ten largest cities in the country. The censuses of 1860 and 1870 showed the city continuing to grow in absolute and relative terms. St. Louis's geographical advantages were particularly evident in the 1850s and 1860s, when river commerce knit together developing economic regions in the West. Located at the confluence of the Missouri, Mississippi, and Illinois Rivers, St. Louis became the center of trade and manufacturing for much of the area drained by these rivers and their tributaries. Although St. Louis's ties to Memphis, Tennessee; New Orleans, Louisiana; and Mobile, Alabama remained healthy, by 1850 the city's economic links to the Northeast (particularly to Philadelphia, Pennsylvania, and New York City) had become stronger than its ties to the South. One of the city's wealthiest citizens, fur-trader-turned-merchant and real estate investor Robert Campbell, illustrated this affinity with the Northeast. He built a new home on the city's first private street (Lucas Place) in the early 1850s and decorated it with furniture, carpets, mirrors, and drapes purchased in Philadelphia.

The Mississippi River served St. Louis as a corridor of commerce, but it also became increasingly a barrier as railroads supplanted riverboats in the transportation of commodities across the interior of the country. The vested interests of steamboat and ferryboat companies discouraged the construction of a railroad bridge in St. Louis, and the scouring currents of the river and the frequency of floods also posed daunting challenges. Eventually, James B. Eads succeeded in utilizing caissons to construct massive stone piers on bedrock hundreds of feet beneath the river and its silt. An experienced river man, Eads had constructed ironclad gunboats in St. Louis during the Civil War. By 1868 he completed his engineering plans for the bridge that would bear his name, and he joined in the celebration of its opening in 1874. By that time, however, numerous rail bridges had been constructed across the relatively shallow and slow Mississippi River above the falls at Keokuk, Iowa. These rail lines all led to Chicago, Illinois, which, by the 1880s, quickly replaced St. Louis as the great emporium of the West.

Designed by James B. Eads and completed in 1874, the St. Louis bridge was a marvel of steel construction that permitted train travel across the Mississippi River. In spite of this effort to generate local commerce, St. Louis would fall far short of Chicago which quickly became the Midwest's commercial hub in the late 19th century.

Source: Library of Congress

St. Louis's Northern-oriented merchants and manufacturers became the leaders of the Republican Party and of the Union war effort. The war disrupted commerce with Memphis, Vicksburg, and New Orleans, but the demands of the Union Army increased business for whole-sale grocers such as Carlos Greeley, a native of New Hampshire, and the Connecticut-born iron manufacturers Giles and Oliver Filley. The Filley brothers were also at the forefront of the struggle between capital and labor. They established the Excelsior Stove Works in St. Louis in 1849 and incorporated the Excelsior Manufacturing Company in 1865. In the spring of 1864, workers in a wide array of trades protested against wartime inflation. Indexed to 1860, prices rose 56 percent by 1864. Wages rose only 30 percent in the same period. Workers also protested against what they viewed to be the degradation of their trades. At a mass meeting of workingmen in the rotunda of the court house in April, machine molders, brass finishers, and other tradesmen protested that there were too many "boys" in their workshops. The strike against the Filley brothers' Excelsior Stove Works became particularly bitter. Strikers complained that the Filleys hired apprentices at low wages with no intention that they should learn the trade. The secretary of the National Union of Machinists and Blacksmiths visited St. Louis and urged his members to strike to keep their trade "perfect."

As strikes spread in St. Louis, General William Rosecrans, commander of the Department of the Missouri, issued General Orders No. 65 on April 29, 1864. Because the strikes interrupted the production of articles "required for use in the navigation of the Western waters, and in the military, naval and transport service of the United States," all persons seeking employment were to be provided with military protection against harassment or intimidation by union men. Moreover, Rosecrans directed that all employers in the city provide him with lists of the names and addresses of strikers and "all who have taken an active part in any combination." The military order stunned the workingmen. Timidly and unsuccessfully, they petitioned Rosecrans asking that his order include a requirement that employers hire no more than five apprentices for each journeyman. For Carl Bernays, editor of the *Anzeiger des Westens*, the military order contradicted his belief that the Union war effort widened the sphere of freedom in America. The editor sent a copy of the order to Lincoln with a lengthy letter of protest. Bernays accepted the need for martial law and supported the suspension of the writ of *habeas corpus* as part of the "paramount right of the President to take extraordinary measures to put down this rebellion." However, he claimed Rosecrans's order threatened to change "the entire character of industrial life in the American nation." In Bernays's view, "slave and free labor have created all the capital." He believed the destruction of slavery should be a boon to free labor. Instead, martial law threatened to destroy free labor "in order to maintain capital alone."

Tensions between labor and capital continued to grow as the Civil War came to an end, and St. Louis, like many communities across the country, experienced a general strike in 1877. After several days of work disruptions, mass rallies at the city's central market, and boisterous marches by workingmen, leading merchants and manufacturers formed a militia, captured the strike leaders, and restored order and control.

RACE, ETHNICITY, AND IMMIGRATION

Coinciding with the rise of a new class of merchants and manufacturers in the 1840s and 1850s was a large influx of German and Irish immigrants who transformed the ethnic composition of St. Louis. The 1850 census showed that slightly more than half of the city's 105,000 residents were born outside of the United States. The total foreign-born population rose to 96,000 in 1860 and reached 124,000 in 1870. As a percentage of the total population, the foreign population remained at about 50 percent in 1860 but dropped to 35 percent in 1870. In 1870 the German-born population stood at 65,936, or nearly 19 percent of the city's population. The Irish-born community numbered 34,803, or slightly less than 1 percent of the city's population. However, in St. Louis as in other industrial cities, nearly 72 percent of the population reported that one or both parents were foreign-born.

The African American population of St. Louis also changed dramatically over the years. In 1850 the nearly six thousand slaves living in the city comprised about 7 percent of the state's slave population. By contrast, 56 percent (1,470) of the state's free black population lived in St. Louis. In 1850 the total black population of St. Louis (7,437) comprised 7 percent of the city's total population. By 1860 the total black population in the city had dropped to 6,211, or about 3 percent. By 1870, however, the black population stood at 26,387, or 7.5 percent of the city's population. Undoubtedly, many of the city's new black residents had settled in St. Louis as a result of wartime migration out of the lower Mississippi Valley, but many others probably came from rural Missouri. Between 1860 and 1870, the state's black population dropped by several hundred; in the same period, St. Louis's black population grew by more than twenty thousand. The declining importance of slavery in antebellum St. Louis, together with the strength of the city's free black population, combined to sustain a strong African American community after emancipation. The St. Louis black community enjoyed sufficient political and institutional strength to maintain equity in public education and to resist the legal segregation that took hold in the rest of the state.

See also *St. Louis, MO 1877–1896; St. Louis, MO 1896–1929; St. Louis, MO 1929–1941; St. Louis, MO 1941–1952*

LOUIS S. GERTEIS

BIBLIOGRAPHY

Adler, Jeffery S. *Yankee Merchants and the Making of the Urban West: The Rise and Fall of Antebellum St. Louis.* New York, NY: Cambridge University Press, 1991.

Cain, Marvin R. *Lincoln's Attorney General: Edward Bates of Missouri.* Columbia: University of Missouri Press, 1965.

Chambers, William Nisbet. *Old Bullion Benton, Senator from the New West: Thomas Hart Benton, 1782–1858.* Boston, MA: Little, Brown, 1956.

Gerteis, Louis S. *Civil War St. Louis.* Lawrence: University Press of Kansas, 2001.

Kremer, Gary R. *James Milton Turner and the Promise of America: The Public Life of a Post-Civil War Black Leader.* Columbia: University of Missouri Press, 1991.

Peterson, Norma Lois. *Freedom and Franchise: The Political Career of B. Gratz Brown.* Columbia: University of Missouri Press, 1965.

Primm, James Neal. *Lion of the Valley: St. Louis, Missouri.* Boulder, CO: Pruett Publishing Company, 1990.

Sandweiss, Eric. *St. Louis: The Evolution of the American Urban Landscape.* Philadelphia, PA: Temple University Press, 2001.

Smith, William E. *The Francis Preston Blair Family in Politics.* New York, NY: The Macmillan Company, 1933.

Spencer, Thomas M. *The St. Louis Veiled Prophet Celebration: Power on Parade, 1877–1995.* Columbia: University of Missouri Press, 2000.

CHICAGO, IL 1854–1877

DURING THE DECADES SURROUNDING THE CIVIL WAR, Chicago grew from a thriving trading center for the West into a rapidly industrializing city. Even in the 1850s, Chicago was widely seen as a "frontier town" where a hardworking young man could make his fortune. Just two decades earlier, the Illinois Potawatomi, after nearly fifteen years of war and a handful of treaty payments, had been pushed to lands further west, and the French fur-trading families who had built the swampy village's first tavern and hotel had moved on. In the years before the Civil War, the city was a jumble of houses, shops, and warehouses stretching just four miles along the lakefront and west across the Chicago River to Western Avenue. The streets were dirt, "often seas of mud or beds of thick dust, sometimes leading into a deep, impeding slough," and littered with animal carcasses and broken wagons. "Sidewalks were merely more mud," remembered one early resident. "Even women wore boots."

By 1870 Chicago's population had grown to nearly three hundred thousand, and it was the nation's fifth-largest city—just twelve thousand residents behind rival St. Louis, Missouri. A decade later, the city's population hit more than five hundred thousand. Demand from Union forces during the Civil War had fueled industrialization. Immigrants from Europe and African American refugees from slavery and the war-torn South sped population growth and provided the labor for the city's expanding industries. The 1848 construction of a shipping canal that provided a continuous water route between Chicago and the Mississippi River had expanded Chicago trade into western prairies. In the following decades, the networks of rail lines linking the city to both the agricultural West and eastern port cities made Chicago the nation's primary market for corn, wheat, and lumber and a major producer of farm implements, bricks, fire-proof safes, ready-made clothing, boots, and barrels.

GOVERNMENT AND POLITICS

Chicago politics in the mid-nineteenth century was governed by a few white men, largely of New England birth, who made fortunes in Illinois real estate and local commerce. They were self-made men with interlocking business interests and, eventually, family ties. City government in the nineteenth century remained fairly small. Most authority rested with city council members who pursued the interests of their wards. Democrats, Whigs, and Republicans competed for political office, but until the Civil War, party differences were unimportant in local politics as civic boosters agreed on the goal of attracting outside investors to speed economic growth.

The city's charter, approved by the state legislature on March 4, 1837, established a common council composed of a mayor and aldermen and divided the city into wards from which the aldermen were elected. In 1837 the city was divided into six wards; a decade later, that number increased to nine with two aldermen to represent each ward, their terms extended from one to two years. A new city charter in 1875 lengthened the mayor's term from one to two years. Cook County was organized January 15, 1831, with Chicago as its county seat. Most of the

MAYORS

Isaac Lawrence Milliken	(1854–1855)
Levi D. Boone	(1855–1856)
Thomas Dyer	(1856–1857)
John Wentworth	(1857–1858)
John C. Haines	(1858–1860)
John Wentworth	(1860–1861)
Julian S. Rumsey	(1861–1862)
Francis Cornwall Sherman	(1862–1865)
John B. Rice	(1865–1869)
Roswell B. Mason	(1869–1871)
Joseph E. Medill	(1871–1873)
Lester Legrant Bond (acting mayor following Modill's resignation)	(1873)
Harvey Doolitte Colvin	(1873–1876)
Monroe Heath	(1876–1879)

MAJOR INDUSTRIES AND EMPLOYERS

Chicago Rolling Mills Company
Union Car and Bridge Works
Pullman Palace Car Company
McCormick Harvesting Machine
   Company
Chicago Packing and Provision
   Company
The United States Clock and Brass
   Company

MAJOR NEWSPAPERS

Chicago Daily Tribune
Chicago Daily News
Chicago Daily Times (consolidated with
   the *Herald* in 1860)
Chicago Times and Herald (later the
   Daily Chicago Times)
Daily Chicago Times
Chicago Post
Chicago Evening Mail (later became *Post & Mail*)
Chicago Evening Post (later became *Post & Mail*)
Chicago Post & Mail
Illinois Staats-Zeitung
National Demokrat
Irish Republic
Workingman's Advocate
Chicago Evening Journal
Chicago Daily Journal
Chicago Inter-Ocean
Chicago Democrat

MAJOR EVENTS

December 1869: The Union Stock Yards open. The yards were first proposed in 1864 after Chicago's nine largest railroads and members of the Chicago Pork Packers Association formed a corporation called the Union Stock and Packers Association.

1865: Responding to a campaign led by Chicago entrepreneur John Jones, the state legislature repeals the series of laws barring black people in Illinois from owning property, serving on juries, testifying against whites, or serving in the state militia.

October 1871: The Great Chicago Fire starts on the city's West Side, jumping the south branch of the Chicago River and racing through the city's business district before leaping the river again to destroy many of the homes in the North Division. The fire destroyed 17,420 buildings, left nearly one hundred thousand Chicagoans homeless, killed at least three hundred, and caused financial losses of nearly $200 million.

July 1877: On July 22 and 23, Chicago workers, responding to the first nationwide strike, walk off the job. The strike had started on the East Coast when the Baltimore and Ohio Railroad announced a wage cut of 10 percent, and within days rail service across the nation was halted. In Chicago, street battles between police and strikers lasted several days until federal troops and two regiments of the state militia joined local officers to use force to end the strike. By July 28, an estimated fifty civilians had been killed and many others injured, and the military was escorting trains leaving the rail yards.

governing elite were successful businessmen with investments in real estate, railroads, breweries, and banking. Only two of the city's nineteen mayors before the Civil War—a bartender and a blacksmith—were of the laboring classes.

The outbreak of the Civil War sparked overwhelming support for the Union cause. Democrats and Republicans united in a Union Party, electing John Wentworth mayor as a "fusion" Republican candidate. A series of vitriolic editorials in the Confederate-sympathizing *Chicago Times* helped the Democrats to reorganize.

State law aimed to bar black men from politics. Illinois's black codes forbid black men from serving on juries, testifying against white men, serving in the state militia, and voting. The law required free African American men and women entering Illinois to carry their freedom papers or to post a $1,000 bond. A campaign against the black codes was led by John Jones, a tailor who made a fortune in real estate. In 1871 he was the first black man elected to political office when he became a member of the Cook County Board. The war and emancipation sped efforts to abolish the black codes, and the legislature revoked the law in 1865. Black men, however, did not get the vote until the addition of the Fifteenth Amendment to the U.S. Constitution in 1870.

The Great Fire of 1871 laid waste to much of the city; the burnt district covered more than three-and-a-half square miles, more than one-third of the city's population was left homeless, and at least three hundred people were killed by the flames. Mayor Roswell Mason turned to the Chicago Relief and Aid Society, a private organization founded in 1857 and run by Chicago's business leaders and most affluent professionals, to oversee the relief effort. A ladies' auxiliary, the Ladies' Relief and Aid Society, formed just after the fire, but its members became frustrated with oversight from the men's group. This caused several prominent women to establish their own relief efforts, which became some of the earliest of the city's philanthropic and political organizations led by women.

Debates over reconstruction prompted the organization of another fusion ticket, the Fireproof-Reform Party led by Joseph Medill, the Republican editor of the *Chicago Daily Tribune*. Medill and his supporters largely blamed the fire's devastation on the wood-frame houses that had made homeownership affordable for working-class immigrants. The Fireproof Party sought eastern capital for reconstruction and demanded the passage of a fire limits ordinance to ban wood construction in the city. A limited version of the ordinance was passed but hardly enforced. The debate furthered growing tensions between laboring immigrants and the city's booster elite.

City government expanded after the conflagration. Legislation passed in the wake of the fire gave city officials the authority to regulate building materials and review construction plans. In the late 1870s, Mayor Monroe Heath established the city's first permanent Department of Health, which was charged with protecting the city's growing populace from contagious diseases through the inspection of housing and workshops.

Decentralized governance, coupled with the growing power of real estate interests, led to unequal distribution of the municipal government's primary responsibility: urban infrastructure. Services like street paving and garbage removal were allocated through tax assessments of "interested" property owners. Most streets were paved only after a group of property owners petitioned the council, agreed to an assessment of their property, and then paid the assessment to cover the cost of paving the street. Construction of sidewalks followed a similar pattern, which was typical of antebellum cities.

In the mid-1850s, in response to an 1854 cholera epidemic, the common council established the Board of Sewage Commissioners and the Board of Water Commissioners, later combined into the Board of Public Works. Over the following decades, the council floated bonds and levied water taxes and hook-up fees to finance the construction of sewer and water lines and pumping stations. By the late 1870s, Chicago had one of the most advanced drainage, sewage, and water systems in the nation, yet the assessment system persisted through the nineteenth century. That, along with fees for hooking up sewage lines and for water usage, meant that wealthier neighborhoods acquired sidewalks, paved streets, and indoor plumbing while poorer blocks often lacked those basic amenities.

The most divisive political issue of the era was temperance, which typically pitted the city's Yankee elite against the immigrant working classes. The "lager beer riot" erupted in 1855 when anti-immigrant Know-Nothings won control of the common council and mayor's office, hiked the liquor license fee from $50 to $300, and arrested tavern owners under an old but rarely enforced Sunday closing law. North Side Germans led the opposition, which viewed the temperance campaigns as an attack on their immigrant cultures and the earning power of local brewers and saloonkeepers. The issue flared again in the early 1870s when reformers attempted to close taverns on Sundays. An anti-temperance People's Party, led by German Republican Anton Hesing, editor of the *Illinois Staats-Zeitung*, won control of the common council and the mayor's office in 1873. In the following years, Democrats and Republicans, vying for support from Catholic immigrant voters, tended to overlook violations of the Sunday closing laws and avoided temperance crusades.

INDUSTRY, COMMERCE, AND LABOR

Chicago in the mid-nineteenth century grew to become a leading industrial producer, a center of labor strife, and the transportation hub for much of the nation's commerce. New technologies for production and transportation of goods helped drive this transformation. More important, however were the ambitions, energy, and political skills of the men and women who settled in Chicago. It took the combined efforts of William Ogden and a group of young entrepreneurs to persuade eastern capitalists to invest in rail lines into the city. In the 1850s, Stephen Douglas, the Democratic senator from Illinois aptly known as the "Little Giant" and an early investor in Chicago real estate, adeptly maneuvered the U.S. Congress to set aside western lands for rail lines to Chicago. His work effectively secured Chicago's preeminence among the western cities vying for commercial growth.

The railroad transformed the city and the countryside. In the city, silos were built along the lakefront to hold the thousands of bushels of wheat and corn shipped by rail cars each year. Cyrus Hall McCormick's mechanical reaper came to represent the link between hinterland

and urban economy and the dramatic growth in manufacturing fostered by the railroad. The young inventor, who was born in Virginia, opened his first reaper works in Chicago in 1848. By 1860 McCormick's plant was producing over four thousand reapers a year. To sell the new machines, he sent salesmen to farming towns across the Midwest, each traveling by rail with a "sample" machine. McCormick was among the first nineteenth-century entrepreneurs to use a deferred payment system: with just $30 dollars down, farmers could pay the balance in six months with only 6 percent interest on the $120 price. As reapers and other farm machinery, such as John Deere's steel plow, sped the cultivation and harvesting of grains, young men and women whose labor was no longer needed on the farm headed to Chicago, often by rail, in search of work.

The Civil War triggered the rapid industrialization of the late nineteenth century. Ready-made clothing firms, for example, were established during the war to manufacture uniforms for Union soldiers and sailors and were producing $12 million in goods annually by 1863. But it was the opening of the Union Stock Yards on Christmas Day 1865 that signaled, in many ways, the emergence of the industrial city. The stock yards, which were built in the town of Lake just south of the city (later annexed to Chicago), introduced the mass-production techniques that would be widely used in the following years, though the slaughtering and meatpacking plants used a "disassembly" line to transform livestock into packages of beef and pork. Chicago did not become a center for slaughtering and packing until refrigerated rail cars were introduced in the 1880s. However, by 1875 the Union Stock Yards contained twenty-three hundred pens on one hundred acres that were capable of handling twenty-one thousand head of cattle, seventy-five thousand hogs, twenty-two thousand sheep, and two hundred horses, all at the same time. The packing plants, like the reaper factory, planing mills, brass and iron foundries, breweries, and workshops making such items as wagons, gloves, pumps, and saddles, employed the growing numbers of skilled and unskilled laborers arriving in the city.

By 1880 Chicago had the largest industrial workforce—seventy-five thousand people—west of the Appalachians. Manufacturing and mechanical industries employed more than any other sector of the city's economy, and immigrants made up 64 percent of the total workforce. The wholesale and retail trade made up the second-largest sector. More than half of those engaged in trade were native-born white Americans. Germans were the largest group of skilled workers, while 54 percent of Irish immigrants worked in unskilled positions.

Wages for unskilled men often were not enough to sustain a household, spurring women and children to enter the labor force. Significant numbers of immigrant women worked for wages, most as domestic servants or seamstresses, though many left waged work when they got married. The 1870 census found 3,763 women working in manufacturing and typically earning lower wages than men. That number increased in the following decade. Children ages ten to fifteen made up less than 3 percent of wage earners in the city—a percentage lower than the national average.

Labor organizing came early to Chicago. Printers organized one of the city's first labor organizations in the early 1850s. By 1860 the union had eighty-four members—more than one-third of all printers in Cook County. By the end of the Civil War, Chicago laborers had created nineteen new unions, including ones for sailors, carpenters, painters, cigar makers, musicians, sewing women, harness makers, iron puddlers, and boot and shoemakers. Along with higher wages, most of these unions demanded closed shops and sometimes the establishment of apprenticeship systems. Membership included Irish, German, and Scandinavian immigrants and native-born white men. African Americans, with few exceptions, were barred from labor organizations. Most unions excluded women, except in the garment trades. Many Chicago laborers would in the 1870s join the Knights of Labor.

The eight-hour workday was the central issue for Chicago workers. Agitation began in the mid-1860s. In March 1867, after a long lobbying effort by labor leaders, Republicans who controlled both the city and state governments pushed through eight-hour workday laws. While workers celebrated, their employers simply shifted from paying by the day to paying by the hour and refused to pay ten hours' wages for eight hours of work.

The nationwide economic depression of the 1870s put new pressure on Chicago workers and generated new strife between labor and industrial employers. Reconstruction after the fire had employed thousands of laborers in the building trades, but by the winter of 1873, a series of bank failures, and falling land values left many small businesses bankrupt and land speculators holding worthless property. By 1876 Chicago newspapers were reporting that even skilled laborers were willing to work for board alone in order to eat. Workers responded with strikes and mass demonstrations. The most violent was the 1877 railroad strike, which began on the East Coast and hit Chicago on July 23, prompting massive street protests and leading to the deaths of at least thirteen people and scores of injuries. The 1877 strike marked the height of the decade's labor violence and signaled the rise of the "labor question" as a powerful and divisive issue in urban politics for the coming decades.

RACE, ETHNICITY, AND IMMIGRATION

Chicago's population expanded rapidly in the years between 1854 and 1877, fed largely by immigrants from northern and western Europe, along with a steady flow of Yankee strivers and a small but growing number of African American refugees from the slave South. In 1860 foreign-born residents made up 50 percent of Chicago's population; ten years later the foreign-born totaled slightly less than half of the population. However, the foreign-born and their American-born children would make up close to 80 percent of Chicago's population from the 1870s through World War I. The 1850 census found just 323 people of African descent in Chicago; that number would jump to nearly six thousand in 1880, but it was still less than 2 percent of the city's total population.

African Americans in this period consisted of a tiny group of successful businessmen and professionals and many more skilled and unskilled workers. Until 1865, black Chicagoans were barred under state law from owning property, but several purchased houses and started businesses. If they were not property owners or tradesmen, black men typically held low-skill, low-wage jobs, working as waiters or stevedores for the ships docking at the pier jutting into Lake Michigan. African American women, who were even fewer in number, often worked as servants in white homes or as laundresses and seamstresses for white clientele.

The outbreak of the Civil War sparked new tensions between black and white workers and between immigrants and the native-born. *Chicago Times* editor Wilbur F. Storey published a series of vicious attacks on black Chicagoans and on President Lincoln. In 1864 the Republican *Tribune*, describing a violent assault by Irish laborers on black men working on the lumber docks, warned against "mobocrats."

The Catholic Irish experienced hostility from the city's Protestant Germans and Yankees. The *Tribune* editorial called the Irish the "most illogical people on the face of the earth." Irish immigrants expressed their grievances on Election Day, making the Democratic Party their primary weapon.

African Americans supported the Republicans, though by the 1870s many were angered that Republicans nationally had turned away from the promises of Reconstruction. In Chicago, despite an ordinance banning racial discrimination in education, the public schools remained segregated and all of the city's teachers were white.

By 1877 the city's labor force was increasingly segmented by race and nationality, and, as the city emerged into the industrial era, ethnic and racial rivalries continued to confound labor organizers and divide urban politics.

See also *Chicago, IL 1877–1896; Chicago, IL 1896–1929; Chicago, IL 1929–1941; Chicago, IL 1941–1952; Chicago, IL 1952–1989; Chicago, IL 1989–2011*

MARGARET GARB

BIBLIOGRAPHY

Cronon, William. *Nature's Metropolis: Chicago and the Great West.* New York, NY: W. W. Norton & Co., 1991.

Einhorn, Robin. *Property Rules: Political Economy in Chicago, 1833–1872.* Chicago, IL: University of Chicago Press, 1991.

Miller, Donald L. *City of the Century: The Epic of Chicago and the Making of America.* New York, NY: Simon & Schuster, 1996.

Pacyga, Dominic A. *Chicago: A Biography.* Chicago, IL: University of Chicago Press, 2009.

Pierce, Bessie Louise. *A History of Chicago: From Town to City, 1848–1871.* Vol. 2. New York, NY: Knopf, 1940.

Sawislak, Karen. *Smoldering City: Chicagoans and the Great Fire, 1871–1874.* Chicago, IL: University of Chicago Press, 1995.

Schneirov, Richard. *Labor and Urban Politics: Class Conflict and the Origins of Modern Liberalism in Chicago, 1864–97.* Urbana: University of Illinois Press, 1998.

Smith, Carl S. *Urban Disorder and the Shape of Belief: The Great Chicago Fire, The Haymarket Bomb, and the Model Town of Pullman.* Chicago, IL: University of Chicago Press, 1995.

Wade, Louise Carroll. *Chicago's Pride: The Stockyards, Packingtown, and Environs in the Nineteenth Century.* Urbana: University of Illinois Press, 1987.

BALTIMORE, MD 1854–1877

TRAUMATIC AS IT WAS FOR THE REST OF THE COUNTRY, the Civil War may have been a more dramatic turning point for Baltimore than for other cities. Much of the war was fought on its doorstep. Before the war, it had been the nation's fastest-growing city; afterwards, it struggled and slowed. The city's politics went from violent to venal, and it ceased to be a major destination for European immigrants. Black migrants from other parts of Maryland and points south accounted for most of its population growth.

GOVERNMENT AND POLITICS

In 1854 Baltimoreans broke out of the national two-party system to elect a Know-Nothing city government. Mayor Samuel Hinks and a majority of the Baltimore City Council belonged to secret, nativist, anti-Catholic lodges of the American Party. Hinks won even though he had never held public office, announced his candidacy only two weeks before the election, and did almost no public campaigning. Like his party, his election was an underground affair. Hinks was reelected in 1855 with an even larger majority in the council, and the Know-Nothings swept the state elections. In 1856 Maryland became the only state in the Union to give its electoral votes to Know-Nothing presidential candidate Millard Fillmore. Baltimore gave him a bigger percentage of its vote than any of the counties. By 1858 the city was "a political barony controlled by the Know-Nothings."

The sudden eruption of the new party was most obviously a reaction to foreign immigration. By 1860 one in four of the city's 212,000 residents had been born in Europe. Throughout the 1840s, most of the foreigners arriving in Baltimore had been German, but at the end of the decade Irish immigration rose abruptly. Most came from rural Ireland and lacked the literacy and skills to be suited to an urban, industrial economy. To native-born Protestants, the supposed obedience of the Irish to the Roman pope made them a threat to the autonomy and democracy of the United States.

In addition to the virulent nativism that energized them, the Know-Nothings also benefited from Baltimoreans' growing estrangement from the old parties. The town's aristocratic, literary politician John Pendleton Kennedy longed for the deference and civility of political life in a younger, smaller Baltimore, and he resented the party organizations formed in the 1830s that had mobilized "the profoundly ignorant, the vicious and dissolute, the frequenters of tippling houses, the idle, the unthrifty, the fraudulent debtors, the decayed and brokendown workmen, the outlawed and cast off members of society under bar for incorrigible faults."

Kennedy shared the nativist sensibilities that animated many Know-Nothings, though only a few of them were politically disaffected aristocrats. However, politically disaffected aristocrats with nativist sympathies—such as Kennedy—supplied the new party with the measure of political legitimacy needed to stand up against older parties. An inciting spark for mobilization was a piece of legislation introduced in the state's general assembly in 1852 by Baltimore Democratic delegate Timothy Kerney that would have authorized the payment of public funds to church

QUICK FACTS

BALTIMORE, MD **1854–1877**

MAYORS

Samuel Hinks	(1854–1856)
Thomas Swann	(1856–1860)
George William Brown	(1860–1861)
John C. Blackburn	(1861–1862)
John Lee Chapman	(1862–1867)
Robert T. Banks	(1867–1871)
Joshua Vansant	(1871–1875)
Ferdinand C. Latrobe	(1875–1877)

MAJOR NEWSPAPERS

Baltimore Sun
Baltimore Argus
Baltimore Daily Republican
Daily Exchange
Baltimore American
Evening Transcript
Evening Bulletin
Baltimore Patriot

MAJOR INDUSTRIES AND EMPLOYERS

Apparel manufacturing
Brick manufacturing
Canning (oysters, fish, fruits, and
    vegetables)
Iron (forged and rolled)

MAJOR EVENTS

1854: Baltimore elects a Know-Nothing (American Party) government.
1858: The state of Maryland takes control of the city's police force.
1861: Mob attack on Union troops passing through Baltimore marks the first bloodshed of the Civil War.
1871: Boss Isaac Freeman Rasin consolidates control over the Democratic machine and the city.
1877: A violent railroad strike paralyzes the Baltimore and Ohio Railroad. Federal forces intervene.

schools. The fiery debate that ensued spread to the Baltimore City Council when the local archbishop petitioned to grant a portion of the school budget to parochial schools.

Similar controversies inflamed nativist sentiments elsewhere in America, but Baltimore and Maryland were different. In most states, the party collapsed when the slavery issue trumped the immigration issue, but in Maryland the Know-Nothings soldiered on. Their cause, however, evolved. The vehement anti-Catholicism of the party steadily subsided. It had always been a bit awkward; Maryland's founders and first families had been Catholic. Now Protestant nativism was replaced by a fervent devotion to the preservation of the Union. For Baltimoreans, at least, Know-Nothingism was the solvent of sectionalism, a party ready "to stand by the Union as it is and the Constitution as it is." Like many residents of their border state, Baltimoreans desperately wanted to avoid the looming choices between North and South, slavery and abolition. Baltimore congressman and premier Know-Nothing orator Henry Winter Davis embodied his city's ambivalence. Though he owned slaves, his misgivings about that peculiar institution moved him to offer his slaves their freedom—but only if they would emigrate to Liberia. Davis shared Baltimoreans' longstanding preference for saying as little as possible about slavery, at least in public.

Though Davis's Know-Nothing party was new, it carried on the Baltimore custom of political violence, but with much more intensity. By using their allied gangs and volunteer fire companies, Know-Nothings and Democrats turned Baltimore elections into pitched battles. The political contests of 1856, for example, produced twenty-eight fatalities and hundreds of injuries. The Know-Nothings generally got the best of the fighting. The objective was to control the city's twenty polling places, with violence when necessary. The Know-Nothings' characteristic weapon, the shoemaker's awl, became a party symbol in Baltimore. Occasionally conflicts to control the polls expanded into quasi-military engagements involving organized volleys of gunfire and even small artillery pieces.

Baltimore's gangs—the Plug Uglies, Rip Raps, Rough Skins, Tigers, Black Snakes, and Blood Tubs—became famous. Know-Nothing mayor Thomas Swann attempted to restore the city's reputation and safety by replacing its night watch and twenty daytime police officers with a force of 397 armed and uniformed officers, but the fix was a failure. Many of the police officers appointed by the mayor were members of his own party; some were the very thugs who fought over polling places. They did little to diminish Election-Day violence and intimidation, though fatalities fell because Democrats were afraid to go to the polls. The police did nothing to stop the stuffing of ballot boxes.

The City Reform Association sent bills to the general assembly that would place the police force under the control of a state-appointed metropolitan police board, place election judges under police control, and assure that juries could not be rigged to acquit Know-Nothing thugs. The bills passed, and a purge of Baltimore's police eliminated most Know-Nothing officers. In 1859 the City Reform Association fielded candidates to challenge the nativist politicians of Baltimore and won six of the thirty seats in the two chambers of the city council. In 1860 the Democrats obligingly stood aside in all but one ward to allow the City Reform Association to confront the Know-Nothings. Reformer George William Brown won the mayor's office by a margin of more than two votes to one. The Know-Nothings were finished.

The reformers were not simply Democrats in disguise, but they tilted heavily toward the party, and John Brown's raid on Harper's Ferry had solidified their strength in Baltimore. They were in charge of the town in April 1861 when the first Union troops passed through Baltimore on their way to defend Washington against Confederate attack. The mob that met the soldiers killed four members of the Massachusetts Sixth Regiment and suffered twelve deaths themselves. The city government, determined to prevent any more Union troops from passing through the city, dispatched the Maryland Guard, a militia force of doubtful loyalty to the Union, to burn railroad bridges north and east of Baltimore. President Lincoln wanted to avoid provoking Baltimoreans, according to his aide John Hay, because "if quiet was kept in Baltimore a little longer, Maryland might be considered the first of the redeemed" for the Union. With the outbreak of war, some of the city's most dangerous Confederate sympathizers left Baltimore as young men of military age went south to join the Confederate Army.

Unionist sentiment rebounded in the city, even though (or perhaps because) federal authorities arrested and imprisoned Mayor Brown, the marshal of police, and all four members of the police board. The remnants of the Know-Nothing Party allied themselves with the local branch of the Constitutional Unionists. The new Union Party held itself apart from the small contingent of local Republicans because they regarded Republican Free-Soilers with as much distaste as secessionist fire-eaters. Their object was to sidestep the issues that would divide the city and turn the state into a battleground. The party recruited some leaders without clear partisan attachments. Baltimorean Augustus Bradford had been clerk of the city's circuit court, but he retired from politics during the 1850s and was fortunately free of any record on the nasty divisions of that decade. He was elected governor overwhelmingly at the end of 1861, succeeding the last Know-Nothing governor of Maryland, who went on to become a Union Party U.S. senator. The Union Party (including many former Know-Nothings) also swept the state legislature and judicial elections. There was little evidence that the result reflected military interference. Even sympathizers of states' rights described the election as "quiet" and "free from molestation."

Former Know-Nothing champion Henry Winter Davis did not fare so well as his fellow unionist partisans. In mid-1861, President Lincoln had called for a special meeting of Congress to consider the challenge to the Union. All of Maryland's unionist candidates won the ensuing special election, except Davis in Baltimore, who lost to Henry May, a former Democrat who advocated conciliation with the Confederates. Davis had incurred local enmity in the previous session of Congress for having supported a Northerner for speaker of the House. Federal military authorities arrested Henry May in September, and an unsuccessful effort was made to expel him from the House. Davis had his seat back by 1863, but he faced another rival in Montgomery Blair, Lincoln's postmaster general and a leader in state politics. Davis headed the Unconditional Unionists; Blair, the Conservative Unionists. Both leaders supported emancipation but disagreed on how to achieve it and what should follow. Blair wanted slave owners compensated for their slaves, opposed the recruitment of black soldiers for the Union Army, and recommended that free blacks be required to emigrate to Africa. Davis and the "Unconditionals" disagreed with Blair on all three issues and advocated racial equality. The division was so intractable that two unionist candidates ran against one another in Baltimore's 1864 mayoral election. As postmaster general, however, Blair controlled five hundred patronage jobs in Maryland, and Davis's political career ended with his death in 1865. Blair became principal leader of the Unionists and continued his effort to strengthen the new political organization by appealing to Democrats and former Democrats who could not abide Republicans.

By the war's end Blair's leverage with the Democrats had evaporated. A state constitutional convention had approved emancipation without compensation in 1864, and the Fourteenth Amendment pushed the Democrats even further away from Blair and his party. Moreover, Maryland Democrats could now win elections on their own, as they did in 1866 when they carried Baltimore and sixty of the eighty seats in the House of Delegates. Baltimore unionists put up a fight. However, Thomas Swann, formerly the city's Know-Nothing mayor and now the state's ostensibly unionist governor, recognized that his party was sinking and denounced the Unconditional Unionists and began redirecting state patronage to Democrats. He fired the unionist police commissioners in Baltimore that were responsible for appointing election judges and replaced them with Democrats. A unionist judge, Hugh Bond, then had the Democrats arrested. Swann, fearing a return to the violent electoral practices of the 1850s, asked President Johnson for federal troops. Ulysses S. Grant dispatched a regiment to the city, where the polls remained quiet and

Democrats triumphed. The unionists abandoned their political quest and their name in 1867 and began to call themselves Republicans. Swann became a Democrat.

Baltimore's diminished Republican forces sealed their doom by making war with one another. Holders of federal patronage jobs under the Johnson administration turned against their party's own gubernatorial candidate, former Unconditional Unionist judge Hugh Bond. After more than a decade in the wilderness, Baltimore's Democrats were back in firm control of the city, and they were employing some new organizational tools. They were building a machine. Its principal architect was Isaac Rasin, son of a prominent Eastern Shore family. Rasin had moved to Baltimore, gotten elected from the Seventh Ward to the city's Democratic Executive Committee, and became clerk of the Court of Common Pleas in 1867. He built his organization by recruiting neighborhood leaders and brawlers such as John J. "Sonny" Mahon of the tough Ninth Ward on Baltimore's waterfront. The price of Mahon's loyalty was a $2-a-day job in a state tobacco warehouse. Rasin consolidated his control over the city in 1871 when his candidate for mayor, local hatmaker Joshua Vansant, swept into office. Ferdinand C. Latrobe, Rasin's next mayor, held office for twenty years. The new boss also had assets outside the city. In 1870 he had met Howard County's Arthur Pue Gorman in a back room of city hall and later helped him to become speaker of the House of Delegates. He was also close to William Pinkney Whyte, an antebellum congressman from Baltimore who became governor in 1871. They helped Rasin to compensate politically for the city's gross underrepresentation in the state legislature. Although Baltimore contained half the state's population, it held less than 20 percent of the seats in the House of Delegates and 12 percent of the Maryland State Senate.

Muscle still mattered in Baltimore politics. Gang leaders like Sonny Mahon were vital members of the Democratic coalition. But money and jobs assumed a more prominent role in city politics, and ethnicity remained a factor. Immigrants were not sufficiently numerous in Baltimore to carry elections, but in combination with the city's "Southron"-slanted Democrats, they could master the municipality. They were told that the nation's treatment of the South during Reconstruction was no different from England's occupation of Ireland.

INDUSTRY, COMMERCE, AND LABOR

Baltimore's economy had been powered for twenty years or more by the project of building the Baltimore and Ohio Railroad from the Patapsco River to the Ohio River. When the work was completed in 1853, the industrial core of the railroad economy collapsed as the demand for rails, locomotives, and cars abruptly declined. Even much of the repair and replacement work left Baltimore when the railroad established shops in the West Virginia towns of Martinsburg and Wheeling. The city was still growing, but not as fast as other cities, and its economic climate dimmed. Conditions got abruptly worse at the beginning of the Civil War when Baltimore was isolated from its Southern markets, but the local recession eased in 1862 when government war contracts began to revive Baltimore businesses. The city's status as a transportation hub for the Union Army increased the revenues of local railroads and steamboat companies. Manufacturers of men's clothing, the largest employers in town, began to turn out military uniforms, and local

Against a recession and two pay cuts, employees of the B&O Railroad led a massive strike in 1877 snarling traffic throughout the state. Over 2,000 federal troops were called in to break up the strike. Confrontations left 9 dead and the strike eventually collapsed yielding no gains from management.

Source: Library of Congress

boot and shoemakers equipped federal soldiers for long marches. Shipbuilders helped to outfit the U.S. Navy.

Railroads and shipping soon spawned other industries. Rail connections with the new Pennsylvania oil fields carried crude oil to new petroleum refineries in Baltimore. The city's traditional trade connections with the Caribbean and Latin America brought in the raw material for several local sugar refineries and coffee roasters. Guano mined on islands off the coast of Peru came to Baltimore for processing in new fertilizer plants. The canning of oysters had been an obvious outgrowth of Chesapeake's bounty, and as farmers on the eastern and western shores switched from tobacco to vegetables and fruits, canning became one of the city's leading industries.

The recession of 1877 ignited some of the fiercest labor conflicts in almost forty years. Employers tried to stay afloat by cutting workers' wages, and the workers responded by going on strike. Box and can makers—essential suppliers to the city's canneries—walked out. Even before the recession, Baltimore and Ohio Railroad wages had been substantially lower than those employed by other railroads. The workers' dissatisfactions erupted into rage in mid-1877, when Baltimore and Ohio president John Work Garrett increased his stockholders' dividends by 10 percent while cutting his workers' wages by the same amount—the second such reduction in eight months. On the line west of Baltimore, striking workers blocked trains, and three hundred federal troops arrived at Martinsburg to put down what the secretary of war called an "insurrection." Baltimore's trainmen stopped all freight moving in Maryland. President Garrett met with Maryland's governor to discuss sending two Baltimore volunteer regiments to open the line as far as Cumberland. In East Baltimore, a crowd supporting the strikers blocked one regiment just outside its armory. In the ensuing melee, some of the troops fired on the crowd, killing nine. The other regiment reached the rail depot only to discover that a crowd had forced the engineer and fireman to abandon the locomotive and then tore up track to prevent the train from moving. Two thousand federal troops and five hundred marines were called in to reinforce the local regiments, and a federal revenue cutter patrolled the warehouses along the waterfront. The strike collapsed. Management made no concessions.

RACE, ETHNICITY, AND IMMIGRATION

The heavy foreign immigration of the 1850s increased the city's alien population by almost 50 percent; by 1860 Baltimore held 68 percent of Maryland's foreign-born population. The African American population scarcely increased at all, however, and the absolute number of slaves actually declined. Before Lincoln emancipated a single slave, 92 percent of the city's black population was already free.

The Civil War abruptly reversed these patterns. Foreign immigration virtually ceased during the war, and immigrants from abroad played only a secondary role in the postwar development of Baltimore's industrial workforce. Most of the new workers were migrants from agricultural areas of Maryland and the Middle Atlantic. Foreigners continued to land at the Baltimore and Ohio Railroad's immigrant dock on Locust Point, but most boarded the trains for destinations further west. From 1870 to the end of the century, foreigners accounted for only 5 percent of the city's population growth. During the same period, African Americans accounted for almost 90 percent of Baltimore's growth.

Freedom did not bring Baltimore's African Americans equality of citizenship. They could not serve on juries in Maryland, were not allowed to testify in cases involving whites, and did not have the right to practice law in Maryland courts. A new state constitution in 1867 removed the disqualification for black witnesses, and the U.S. Supreme Court eventually declared that restricting the practice of law to whites was a violation of the Fourteenth Amendment. Maryland followed many states further south in its imposition of Jim Crow restrictions on its black residents, but there were omissions. The terror, mob violence, and lynchings that whites visited on blacks in the Deep South were rare in Maryland, and almost absent in Baltimore. In 1867 the city created a free public school system for black children. It was segregated and not as well financed as the white system, but expenditures for black schools were far more generous than in towns further south. The city departed from the regime of Jim Crow in one other respect. After the ratification of the Fifteenth Amendment, it never deprived its black citizens of the right to vote, though the state made several attempts to do so. The city not only accommodated its black electorate, it permitted an elaborate procession of its newly enfranchised citizens to march through the streets in celebration of the ratification of the Fifteenth Amendment. A local printer issued a colored lithograph to commemorate the occasion.

The city's support was less than adequate for the thousands of ex-slaves and black soldiers who arrived in Baltimore after the end of the war. By 1866 the city's trustees of the poor conceded that they were unable to care for "all worthy persons without regard to nation or color," and the federal Freedmen's Bureau provided no relief to black Baltimoreans. The local Quakers did what they could, but the Friends' Association for the Aid of Freemen was able to find employment for only a few hundred migrants out of the thousands who poured into the city and provide clothing for about one thousand more. The principal burden of caring for the newly freed blacks was taken up by the well-established free black community of Baltimore. Black orphan asylums, a home for aged women, several black churches, and the Lincoln Zouaves all raised money for the ex-slaves. Frederick Douglass returned to town after a quarter century as a runaway to deliver a lecture sponsored by the Colored State Fair Association; the proceeds went to sick and wounded black veterans. Baltimore's well-developed black civic community took care of its own.

See also *Baltimore, MD 1776–1790; Baltimore, MD 1790–1828; Baltimore, MD 1828 –1854; Baltimore, MD 1877–1896; Baltimore, MD 1896–1929; Baltimore, MD 1929–1941; Baltimore, MD 1941–1952; Baltimore, MD 1952–1989*

MATTHEW CRENSON

BIBLIOGRAPHY

Baker, Jean H. *The Politics of Continuity: Maryland Political Parties from 1858 to 1870.* Baltimore, MD: Johns Hopkins University Press, 1973.

Bruchey, Eleanor. "The Industrialization of Maryland, 1860–1914." In *Maryland: A History, 1632–1974,* edited by Richard Walsh and William Lloyd Fox, 396–498. Baltimore: Maryland Historical Society, 1974.

Brugger, Robert J. *Maryland: A Middle Temperament, 1634–1980.* Baltimore, MD: Johns Hopkins University Press, 1988.

Evitts, William J. *A Matter of Allegiances: Maryland from 1850 to 1861.* Baltimore, MD: Johns Hopkins University Press, 1973.

Towers, Frank. *The Urban South and the Coming of the Civil War.* Charlottesville: University of Virginia Press, 2004.

BOSTON, MA 1854–1877

IN SEVERAL WAYS THE YEARS BETWEEN 1854 AND 1877 FORETOLD THE EMERGENCE OF MODERN BOSTON. Territorially, the size and shape of the city in the twentieth century was cemented with the annexation of Roxbury in 1867; Dorchester in 1869; and Brighton, Charlestown, and West Roxbury in 1873; with the only further acquisition being Hyde Park in 1911. The population consequently rose from 177,840 in 1860 to 362,839 in 1880, with half the increase coming from these communities. Many new immigrants, who made up the rest of the increase, found employment in the burgeoning industries of the city, as Boston confirmed its role as a regional center of manufacturing and finance. Perhaps most important, the last years of the period saw the increasing promise of a peaceful Irish ascendancy, after two decades wracked by tensions emanating from immigration, abolition, and prohibition. In both social mobility and politics, the Irish made increasing inroads, as the seeds of an Irish and Yankee Democrat alliance were sown. From 1854 to 1877, therefore, a realignment of both party politics and civic control, affected as much by national events like the Civil War as by demographic change, was beginning to change the face of politics in Boston.

QUICK FACTS

BOSTON, MA **1854–1877**

MAYORS

Jerome V. C. Smith	(1854–1856)
Alexander H. Rice	(1856–1858)
Frederic W. Lincoln Jr.	(1858–1861)
Joseph Wightman	(1861–1863)
Frederic W. Lincoln Jr.	(1863–1867)
Otis Norcross	(1867–1868)
Nathaniel B. Shurtleff	(1868–1871)
William Gaston	(1871–1873)
Henry L. Pierce	(1873)
Leonard R. Cutter	(1873–1874)
Samuel C. Cobb	(1874–1877)
Frederick O. Prince	(1877–1878)

MAJOR INDUSTRIES AND EMPLOYERS

Ready-made clothing

Boots and shoes

Sugar refining

Machinery

Shipbuilding

Construction

MAJOR NEWSPAPERS

Boston Daily Advertiser

Boston Evening Transcript

Boston Globe

Boston Herald

Boston Journal

Boston Post

MAJOR EVENTS

1854: Richmond slave Anthony Burns is captured in Boston, fueling antislavery sentiment locally and across the North. A U.S. Marshall also loses his life as outraged abolitionists storm the courthouse to free Burns.

1863: A crowd of angry women in the North End attack provost marshals serving official papers, leading to the Boston Draft Riot. The riot only dissipates after the growing mob is confronted by the mayor and the militia.

1869: The first Irish alderman, Christopher Connor, is elected from South Boston.

1872: The Great Boston Fire kills at least twenty people, destroys 776 buildings, including most of the financial district, and results in $73.5 million of damage.

1876: New Mayor Frederick O. Prince selects Irishman Thomas Gargan for the Board of Police, the highest office yet to be held by an Irish Catholic.

GOVERNMENT AND POLITICS

That the Irish were to develop as the controlling political force in Boston was not apparent in the 1850s. After the total dissolution of the Whigs both nationally and locally over the issue of slavery, beginning with the Conscience Whig Revolt in 1848 and climaxing with a terminal split regarding the Kansas-Nebraska Act in 1854, a new era in politics began. First was the the rapid rise of the virulently anti-Irish Know-Nothing American Party in 1854. Sweeping to power overnight in Massachusetts—capturing the governorship, mayoralty in Boston, every congressional seat, the entire state senate, and 376 out of 379 seats in the lower state house—their success displayed the level of mistrust toward Irish Catholics nationally and in immigrant centers like

Boston. Their power was to be extremely short-lived, however. The Irish were not yet important enough politically to be a consistent target, the Know-Nothing administration made several public blunders, and in 1855 the party split over its inability to reconcile northern and southern attitudes regarding slavery. With the formation of the Republican Party in 1854, a more organized, united, and consistently electable party entered into nationwide and Boston politics, essentially replacing the Know-Nothings.

Yet Boston was never fully "Republicanized." A degree of nonpartisanship had been part of the mayoralty before 1854 and continued to be so during this period. Alexander Hamilton Rice (1856–1858), Frederick Walker Lincoln (1858–1861), Henry Lillie Pierce (1873), and Samuel Crocker Cobb (1874–1877) were all elected as nonpartisan mayors. Representatives of different parties would form a convention, such as at Fanueil Hall in 1857, and nominate a candidate on a "Citizens" ticket. Even those elected on a party ticket usually stressed their nonpartisanship in politics, with those who did show a strong allegiance being criticized by the local press. Boston government was a three-tiered system of the mayoralty, aldermen, and a common council. In contrast to the mayoralty, there was a strong partisan current in the common council throughout the period. This democratically elected body of seventy-two men was much more predisposed to declaring its partisan allegiances, and its members were elected on a straight party ticket. Republicans, being more evenly spread out over the city, dominated the council for most of the period.

Following the Civil War especially, though electing five mayors in Boston, the Democrats were political underdogs in Massachusetts. With the election of Republican Abraham Lincoln to the presidency in 1860 and 1864, and the end of the war in favor of the Union, the Republicans assured their dominance. In contrast, the Democrats were criticized for their previous sympathy toward slaveowners and secession as well as their opposition to the Lincoln government, and were consequently viewed with mistrust by northern voters. The best chance for the Democratic Party in Boston clearly lay in the incorporation of the growing Irish vote. For some time already the Irish in Boston had been invariably Democratic, seeing the party as an ally against the moralism of middle-class Yankee Protestants, particularly of the Republican Party, who crusaded against the urban saloon and slavery. With obvious links to the saloon as a meeting place and respite from industrial toil, and fears of competition from African Americans should slavery be repealed, the Irish had little in common with the Republicans and their supporters. Consolidating this support after the Civil War was key for the Democrats.

With the formation in 1868 of the Young Man's Democratic Club by two Irishmen, Patrick Collins and Thomas Gargan, enthusiasm began to grow. Spurred on by the weekly meetings held to plan campaign strategy, there was a revival in local party culture. Through his chairmanship of the Democratic City Committee, Collins then set about reorganizing the city's local machinery by creating an elected central committee. In 1876 the Irish in Boston showed their party loyalty by voting for a straight Democratic ticket, even though they disagreed with the choice for governor, Charles Francis Adams. Though this was another unsuccessful year in the state and national elections for the Democrats, the success that local Irish leadership had in securing loyalty and getting voters to the ballot box showed how important they were to the Democratic Party. In the December election of 1876, Frederick Octavius Prince (1877–1878) won the mayoralty in

Boston with an unprecedented twenty-six thousand votes, with nine out of twelve Democratic aldermen also elected. With this victory and the promise of an increasingly organized local party machine, the future for both the Irish and Democrats in the city was much more encouraging in 1877 than either group could have possibly imagined in 1861.

Outside of politics, municipal government increasingly professionalized during this period, as the apparatus of the city responded to modern industrial conditions. In an 1854 revision to the city charter, the board of aldermen was enlarged from eight to twelve members, and the executive powers of Boston government transferred to this board from the former combination of the common council, the mayor, and the aldermen. While the mayor retained his right to appoint police officers, he now had to gain the official approval of the aldermen, who also had control of the fire department, the health department, the markets, the streets, and the granting of licenses.

By the 1870s, however, it was seen as unattractive to unpaid councilmen and aldermen to maintain such an arduous day-to-day responsibility. Another amendment to the charter in 1870 therefore transferred the powers of the aldermen in deciding the laying out, altering, and discontinuing of streets to a board of elected street commissioners. In 1872 the creation of a three-man health commission took the supervision of the health department away from the aldermen, and following the disastrous Great Fire in 1873, another three-man commission took charge of the fire department. In 1875 two final significant changes were made. First, a park commission was given the power to take lands and form rules for the recreational areas of the city. Second, the Boston Water Board took control of the city's water supply. Municipal expenditures had already been increasing before these changes. After almost doubling between 1860 and 1865, it then more than doubled between 1865 and 1869, reaching $13 million, as municipal government in its modern form began to emerge.

INDUSTRY, COMMERCE, AND LABOR

In terms of manufacturing, commerce, and output, Boston and its hinterland grew impressively during the period, with only two significant blips affecting the city. First, a financial panic in 1857, due to a declining international economy and overexpansion of the domestic economy, was felt particularly keenly in the railroad industry. Second, an international depression in 1873 was set in motion by a series of financial collapses in Europe due to a diminishing demand for silver; this was more serious, lasting until 1878–1879, with widespread business failures and unemployment across the country. In general, though, the overall picture of the period was one of industrialization, growth, and commercial health. Taking the total value of products from Suffolk County, which Boston dominated, the state census of industries in 1855 gave a figure of $58 million. By 1875 this had more than doubled to nearly $141 million. It was further estimated that manufactures dependent on Boston capital totaled $300 million by the beginning of the 1880s—more than double the production of the city itself. If, by the end of the period, it was struggling to directly compete with the emerging giants of industry in cities such as Chicago, or the financial hub of New York, Boston was certainly still an important city, being fifth in terms of manufacturing in 1880, down just slightly from fourth a decade or so earlier.

Many industries rose rapidly, as the surplus of cheap labor provided by high rates of immigration in the 1840s combined with developments in machinery, technique, and industrial organization to create productive and economically efficient factories, most of which were on the east and south sides of the city. With the application of new sewing machines in the 1850s, and the concentration of labor into factories, boot and shoe production grew rapidly. By 1880 over one-half of the boots and shoes made in the United States came from Massachusetts, with Boston being the center of production and sale. By 1875, fifteen thousand people were involved in manufacturing ready-made clothing, the leading employer in the city. Technological developments and a demand for quickly and ready-made uniforms during the Civil War stimulated the industry especially. In sugar refinery before 1845, there had been only one hundred persons employed. With the introduction of new plants and bigger refineries, however, the industry proliferated on a large scale in Boston, with the number of employees—most of whom were Irish—tripling within ten years. After 1858 the industry increased further with the building of the Adams Sugar Refinery, the second largest in the United States. Across the country, smaller refineries closed as they could not compete with what was increasingly termed the Boston System, defined as the replacement of technically skilled craftsmanship with mechanization and mass cheap labor.

Boston also developed in functional complexity, continuing and expanding its role as a center of finance, commerce, and markets. Following the growth of canals and railroads in the 1830s and 1840s, New England became easily accessible to the city, and the city to New England. Increasingly, there were more factories located outside the city than within. The downtown district of the city consequently evolved from an area dominated by commercial wharves, public buildings, and expensive houses into a classic central business district complete with financial, retail, wholesale, and governmental areas. Brokers and merchants imported raw materials—Boston still being the second-largest port in the country—and distributed them to factories in the city or hinterland. The city also provided the arena for sale of manufactured goods, with contemporary descriptions boasting that Boston controlled the largest wool market in the country, as well as being the home of the headquarters of the fish business.

While showing constant improvement throughout the period, Boston's commercial functions were starting to be eclipsed by the continuing monumental growth of New York. The exchanges of the Boston Clearing House in 1856, made up originally of thirty-two banks, totaled just over $1 billion. While impressive, this was only one-seventh of the total cleared in New York. By 1880 the amount had increased to more than $3 billion, yet Boston's clearings were now only one-twelfth of New York's. After the depression of 1873–1878 lifted, however, Boston contemporaries still had much to be pleased with and reason to believe that the city would continue to maintain its role as a source of both capital and production.

RACE, ETHNICITY, AND IMMIGRATION

By 1855 there were fifty thousand Irish in Boston, a fifteen-thousand-person climb from 1850 alone. Demographically, Boston had been transformed from a bastion of those who could trace their lineage to England to a dichotomous and emotionally segregated city, with other nationalities making up only a small proportion of the city. Though after 1854 the amount of Irish immigration remained fairly low, apart from some temporary rises in the 1860s with new landlord troubles and reappearance of the potato blight, the period of 1854–1877 was when the problems of such a mass transference of people and culture became wholly apparent.

Discrimination was both common and overt with, for example, job advertisements frequently stating "No Irish Need Apply" or educators undermining the Roman Catholic faith in schools. Due to this prejudice, and a lack of training and skills, Irish workers were limited to a narrower range of occupations than their native counterparts, with unskilled labor being the most common. With low earnings, little or no job security, and a high demand for housing, living conditions were particularly dire. Old warehouses and mansions near the industrial heart of the city were quickly converted into spaces that packed in as many human bodies as possible, with unscrupulous landlords showing more concern for profit than welfare. Formerly mixed-class nativist neighborhoods, particularly those close to the emerging industries, became Irish ghettoes as the previous inhabitants took flight to the West End and beyond, facilitated by improved transport services. Disease was endemic, with the cholera epidemic of 1849 affecting the Irish community to a remarkable degree. In the middle of the century, 60 percent of Irish children did not live past their sixth birthday. Frequent Irish intoxication (regardless of the prohibition law passed in 1855) and a high representation among crime statistics (most likely a natural response to the uncontrollable economic conditions, exploitation, and the general desperation of the situation) further damaged relations between the old and new elements of Boston.

Yet in time, and especially following the Civil War, the Irish community came of age, growing to become a more accepted part of Boston society. Nativist concerns that the Irish were disloyal were much less tenable when faced with widespread tales of Irish courage on the battlefield. Combined with the almost complete disappearance of the Know-Nothings in the 1850s, and the settling of the slavery issue, there were fewer points of contention between traditional Yankees and Irish newcomers. Gradually, an independent associational culture, including clubs, churches, schools, and newspapers, provided both a sense of identity and permanence in the city and a safety net against discrimination. The position of the Irish in economic hierarchies improved also, as occupations that were previously shut off began to open up, and an Irish middle class began to materialize. The acceptability of Irish employment in the police is one way of measuring this improvement; before the Civil War there was only one Irishman on the force, despite the community having made up a significant part of the city for more than three decades. By the end of the 1870s, however, there were 100—though still an unrepresentative amount considering that the force consisted of 715 police. Irish representation on the city common council also grew; by 1870 there were eleven Irish members out of a council of seventy-two.

If the position of the Irish improved in the decades after the Civil War, it was not as simple for African Americans in the city, a group that rose from 2,261 in 1860 to 3,496 in 1870. Following the abolition of slavery and the cessation of the war, black citizens had reason to be hopeful in Boston. Two African Americans were elected to the state House of Representatives in 1866, and until the end of the nineteenth century at least one African American was elected to serve in the state legislature each year. Yet African Americans remained segregated, both physically and socioeconomically. Remaining firmly in the same district as they had been for over a hundred years, dubbed "Nigger Hill," and struggling to move up the economic ladder, the situation for African Americans remained frustrating. That before the Civil War these two groups had occupied much a similar rung on the social ladder shows how far the Irish had come. Yet their ascendancy was not an uncontested and foregone conclusion by 1877. In the following decades, as the Irish made increasing social and political gains, an undercurrent of nativist and Republican fears, and ethnocultural conflict, was still never far from the surface.

See also *Boston, MA 1776–1790; Boston, MA 1790–1828; Boston, MA 1828–1854; Boston, MA 1877–1896; Boston, MA 1896–1929; Boston, MA 1929–1941; Boston, MA 1941–1952*

TOM HULME

BIBLIOGRAPHY

Blodgett, Geoffrey T. "Yankee Leadership in a Divided City: Boston, 1860–1910." In *Boston, 1700–1980: The Evolution of Urban Politics*, edited by Ronald P. Formisano and Constance K Burns. Westport, CT: Greenwood Press, 1984.

Bugbee, James M. "Boston Under the Mayors, 1822–1880." In *The Memorial History of Boston, Including Suffolk County, Massachusetts, 1630–1880*, Vol. III, edited by Justin Winsor. Boston, MA: James R. Osgood, 1881.

Conzen, Michael P., and George K. Lewis. *Boston: A Geographical Portrait*. Cambridge, MA: Ballinger, 1976.

Formisano, Ronald P. "Conclusion." In *Boston, 1700–1980: The Evolution of Urban Politics*, edited by Ronald P. Formisano and Constance K. Burns. Westport, CT: Greenwood Press, 1984.

Handlin, Oscar. *Boston's Immigrants, 1790–1880: A Study in Acculturation*. Cambridge, MA: Belknap Press of Harvard University Press, 1991.

Hill, Hamilton A. "The Trade, Commerce, and Navigation of Boston, 1780–1880." In *The Memorial History of Boston, Including Suffolk County, Massachusetts, 1630–1880*, Vol. III, edited by Justin Winsor. Boston: James R. Osgood, 1881.

Jaher, Frederic Cople. "The Politics of Boston's Brahmins: 1800–1860." In *Boston, 1700–1980: The Evolution of Urban Politics*, edited by Ronald P. Formisano and Constance K. Burns. Westport, CT: Greenwood Press, 1984.

Kleppner, Paul. "From Party to Factions: The Dissolution of Boston's Majority Party, 1876–1908." In *Boston, 1700–1980: The Evolution of Urban Politics*, edited by Ronald P. Formisano and Constance K. Burns. Westport, CT: Greenwood Press, 1984.

Lane, Roger. *Policing the City: Boston, 1822–1885*. New York: Atheneum, 1977.

O'Connor, Thomas H. *The Boston Irish: A Political History*. Boston: Northeastern University Press, 1995.

———. *Civil War Boston: Home Front and Battlefield*. Ann Arbor, MI: Edwards Brothers, 1997.

Wright, Carroll D., and Horace G. Wadlin. "The Industries of the Last Hundred Years." *The Memorial History of Boston, Including Suffolk County, Massachusetts, 1630–1880*, Vol. III, edited by Justin Winsor. Boston: James R. Osgood, 1881.

CINCINNATI, OH 1854–1877

BETWEEN 1854 AND 1877, CINCINNATI CONTINUED TO GROW in population and to expand both its railroad connections and its manufacturing. However, it grew at a rate slower than many of its midcontinent urban rivals, most prominently Chicago and St. Louis. While its population more than doubled from 115,435 in 1850 to 255,139 in 1880, Cincinnati, the sixth-largest city in the nation from 1830 to 1850, saw its rank decline to the seventh-largest city in the 1860 census, and to the eighth largest in 1870 and 1880. At the same time, Cincinnati grew to be the third-largest American manufacturing city in 1860, behind only New York City and Philadelphia, Pennsylvania. With Cincinnati's commerce tied prominently with the South via the Ohio River, residents faced the slavery politics of the 1850s with real trepidation. Throughout the Civil War, most Cincinnatians supported the Union, and military contracts bolstered the local economy. Population growth to the west and the importance of east-west road and railway connections were already signaling the rising importance of Chicago as the major center of commerce in the Midwest.

Conscious of their city's relative decline, especially compared to what Mayor Johnston referred to in 1869 as "our rival cities, St. Louis and Chicago," Cincinnatians launched a series of attempts to shore up its position. They created a municipal railway and a series of arts-related institutions and organizations. The latter included the construction of a grand music hall, which also served as a convention center; a symphony orchestra; a music college; an arts school; a university; an art museum; and an early zoological garden. Cincinnatians also constructed a series of parks and, through 1888, held annual industrial expositions that addressed a midcontinent market. All of these endeavors boosted the profile of the city, yet none were capable of restoring Cincinnati to its former position as "Queen City of the West."

GOVERNMENT AND POLITICS

As in other mid-nineteenth-century American cities, municipal services began to grow in Cincinnati in the 1850s, expanding from the encouragement and regulation of commerce to the promotion of the welfare of urban society through the provision of regular services. Like other cities, Cincinnati became an explicitly public, governmental body, providing a series of regular ongoing services to a diverse city population on a daily basis. These services were largely supported by taxation and bond issues and were administered by a salaried bureaucracy. Over the 1860s and 1870s, Cincinnati expanded its waterworks, redesigned and expanded its police force, instituted a paid fire department, installed gas street lights, and expanded streets. It also built its first city sewers, formed a permanent health department, took responsibility for a free public library, participated in planning for a municipal university, and created a park commission. Concurrently, Cincinnati also launched a period of land annexations that expanded the city limits from some seven to twenty-five square miles.

While Cincinnatians had obtained their earliest city charter in 1819 by special act of the Ohio legislature and appealed directly to the legislature for subsequent charter amendments and

QUICK FACTS

CINCINNATI, OH 1854–1877

MAYORS

David T. Snelbaker	(1853–1855)
James J. Faran	(1855–1857)
Nicholas W. Thomas	(1857–1859)
Richard M. Bishop	(1859–1861)
George Hatch	(1861–1863)
(Col.) Leonard A. Harris	(1863–1866)
Charles F. Wilstach	(1866–1869)
John F. Torrence	(1869–1871)
S. S. (Simon) Davis	(1871–1873)
George W. C. Johnston	(1873–1877)
Robert M. Moore	(1877–1879)

MAJOR INDUSTRIES AND EMPLOYERS

Clothing manufacturing

Iron foundries and metalworks (Eagle Iron Works)

Furniture (Mitchell and Rammelsberg Furniture Company)

Shoes and boots

Printing and publishing

MAJOR NEWSPAPERS

Cincinnati Chronicle

Cincinnati Commercial

Cincinnati Enquirer

Cincinnati Gazette

Cincinnati Star

Cincinnati Times

Tägliches Cincinnati Volksblatt

Cincinnati Volksfreund

MAJOR EVENTS

1855: Three days of rioting follow the Know-Nothing attacks on immigrants—including liberal Protestant Germans who had supported the Know-Nothings in previous elections. This ends the party's ascendancy in the city.

1867: The Roebling suspension bridge is completed, connecting Cincinnati to its southern hinterland through neighboring Covington. The plans for the bridge had been held until after the resolution of the Civil War to avoid providing easy access to the city to Confederate troops.

1869–1873: The city of Cincinnati, after receiving authority from the Ohio legislature, launches a municipal railroad, the Cincinnati Southern Railway, to Chattanooga, Tennessee. The railroad is an effort to shore up the city's economic decline relative to faster-growing cities such as St. Louis, Missouri, and Chicago, Illinois.

1869–1873: The Cincinnati "Bible wars" resolve the conflict raised by the Catholic Archdiocese over the use of the King James Bible in public schools by ending Bible reading, though not prayer and religious singing, in the schools.

1871: The 43-foot-high fountain called the "Genius of Waters" on Fifth Street in the center of the city is dedicated. The fountain, which was donated to the people of Cincinnati as an iconic symbol of the new city, yields the creation of a signature public space: Fountain Square.

replacements, Ohio's new constitution of 1851 changed that system to deny special legislation for municipal corporations and promote general acts instead. In 1852 Ohio adopted an extensive law classifying municipal corporations and granting them the authority to impose taxes and issue bonds to pay for services. Basing this system on city population, Ohio designated specific powers and responsibilities for cities of the first class (twenty thousand residents), second class (five hundred to twenty thousand), and villages (five hundred). Cincinnati was the only "city of the first class" for nearly a decade. In 1869 the Ohio legislature revised the provisions of the 1852 law into the nation's first formal municipal code, the provisions of which recognized the expansion of city activities.

The politics of city governance remained volatile between 1854 and 1877, with single-term mayors dominating. The rotation of mayors between Whigs, Democrats, Republicans, and Citizen's Party candidates reflected the turmoil of the 1850s and the issues of slavery and secession in this border city. It was not slavery (prohibited in Cincinnati from its founding in the Northwest Territory), nor racism (the subject of earlier rioting in the city), but immigration issues that set off the greatest political violence of the 1850s. As one of the nation's fastest-growing cities, the center of trade west of the Appalachian Mountains, and a large manufacturing hub of the mid-nineteenth century, Cincinnati drew a large immigrant population. The census of 1860 reported 46 percent of city residents as foreign-born. This number was dominated by Germans (30 percent), and Irish (12 percent). Though liberal German Protestant immigrants had earlier joined them in politics, crowds of Know-Nothings launched an attack in 1855 on the area of densest German settlement. The violent conflict lasted for three days and led to the demise of the Know-Nothing Party in Cincinnati. Between the end of the Civil War and 1873, a series of Republicans held the mayor's office during a period of reorganization of city services through a series of boards.

Two important structural changes, one legislative and one administrative, occurred in the 1870s under the provisions of the 1869 municipal code. The 1869 code mandated in cities of the first class the election of a mayor, solicitor, treasurer, street commissioner, police judge, prosecuting attorney, clerk of the police court, and a city council consisting of two members from each of twenty-five wards. State legislation in 1870 created a new board of alderman, which served as the upper chamber of the city council and was comprised of five representatives for each of five districts created from the twenty-five wards. In 1876 the elected Board of Public Works took control of the boards or commissions of the waterworks, city improvements, sewers, platting, and parks. This board was reconfigured and realigned in the decades after 1879. While charges of machine politics and grafting persisted throughout the era, the city provided services and granted franchises to establish its first regularly scheduled streetcars in the 1850s. In the 1870s five separate inclined planes were created to take passengers to the hilltop suburbs above the city center to Mt. Auburn, Price Hill, Clifton, Mt. Adams, and Fairview.

INDUSTRY, COMMERCE, AND LABOR

Though commerce remained essential to this western entrepôt, manufacturing gained ascendancy by the 1850s. More manufacturing every year was occurring in larger factories, and by 1850 one-third of Cincinnati's industrial workers were employed in factories with more than fifty workers. By 1870 that percentage shifted to nearly half. However, the stunning growth of Chicago as the commercial center of a new West, tied as it was to vast agricultural lands and a series of smaller cities and bolstered by aggressive railroad connections expanded further during the Civil War, soon allowed it to supplant Cincinnati not only as the nation's meat-packing capital, but also as the western center of commerce and industry. The borders of the new Great Lakes industrial corridor stopped north of Cincinnati, which continued to grow, but at a significantly lower rate.

By the 1870s, as space within the city was sorted out for particular uses—residential, commercial, industrial—larger factories tended to be constructed on the edges of town or near the riverfront where large lots were cheaper. The largest of these, including Mitchell and Rammelsberger Furniture Company, built separate retail buildings in the center of town on Fourth and Fifth Streets, near the new Fountain Square. The square was built around the donated Tyler Davidson Fountain, and together they formed a civic space and icon that identified Cincinnati as a forward-reaching city. Mitchell and Rammelsberger were joined by other businesses, as well as the new department stores, including the large and dramatic Shillito Department Store that John Shillito built in the late 1870s.

In the 1850s, a large percentage of stores and factories remained relatively small and were owned by individuals or small groups of partners. Many produced artisanal products. By the 1870s, these businesses were generally replaced, or at least superseded, by large operations funded and controlled by corporations or investors. Their workforces included large numbers of women both in the factories and the retail stores.

Throughout the 1850s Cincinnatians dreaded secession and civil war for commercial as well as political reasons. City officials, residents, and business owners feared the potential destruction of their Southern-oriented Ohio River trade. The city's production of pork, machinery, steamboats, furniture, clothing, soap, candles, whiskey, ales, and printed materials had raised it to the rank of America's third-largest manufacturing city by 1860. Once the war began, local manufacturers and merchants obtained significant contracts for military supplies, and boots, clothing, pork, and bacon found ready markets. The thirty-year-old steamboat works on the Ohio River built war vessels, refitted passenger boats for military supply and transfer, and clad ships with iron. Eagle Iron Works manufactured cannons and gun carriages and also retrofitted muskets into rifles—a dozen years before the establishment of the important milling machine companies of the 1880s. The Union Army made use of a series of camps as military training grounds; most notable was Camp Dennison on the northeast side of town. Cincinnati leaders also used their years of experience holding Ohio Mechanics Institute annual exhibitions to host the Great Western Sanitary Fair in 1863.

The Ohio Mechanics Institute fairs and exhibitions held between 1838 and 1860 and the expositions the institute cosponsored between 1870 and 1888 with the chamber of commerce and the newly organized Board of Trade were designed specifically to advance industry and illustrate changing industrial practices and perceptions. The early fairs solicited the admission of goods typically made in city stores, including machinery, books, stationery, chairs, upholstery, and other goods. By the tenth exhibition, in 1850, the organizing committee had begun to differentiate between categories of items and to rank them in a hierarchical order. It recommended that only submissions from the highest ranked "classes" be eligible for gold medals and created new gold medals for inventions relating to land or sea steam engines.

Subsequent expositions continued to reflect the ascendancy of industry and the hardening of social class lines. The panic of 1873 tested the economy of a defensive Cincinnati, and industrial laborers were hit hardest. By 1877 workers in increasingly consolidated industries went on strike, though with no resultant increase in their wages. From that point on, factory workers proved more likely to join unions, but they also faced more bureaucratic, entrenched management forces. Tellingly, at this same time the sorting of neighborhoods into concentric circles (with the housing closest to the center inhabited by the poorest residents, including African Americans, and the strivers in the zone beyond them) left lower-paid workers with far fewer residential choices at the same time that their owners and investors were moving their homes further away in increasing numbers.

RACE, ETHNICITY, AND IMMIGRATION

In the two decades after 1854, immigrants from the German states continued to dominate Cincinnati's foreign-born population. The next-largest immigrant group was the Irish Catholics. German immigrants in Cincinnati never formed a monolithic or homogenous community; they were diverse in politics, religion, economic background, skills, and practices. By 1850, 40 percent of Cincinnatians were first- or second-generation Germans. They included large numbers of Catholics—as many as two-thirds of them—but also counted members of Protestant congregations, Conservative and Reform Jews, and some nonbelievers (*Freeimanner*, or "freethinkers"). Many became successful economically and politically, establishing businesses or finding employment in companies or the expanding city government. They lived throughout the growing city and even persuaded the public schools to include German-language instruction, which lasted until the beginning of World War I. Even before 1854, the area of town just north of the central business district and the Miami and Erie Canal had been labeled "Over the Rhine" by Cincinnatians who noted its heavy concentration of Germans. In fact, many arrivals from the German states first settled in that neighborhood, though nearly one-third of them present in the 1850 census do not appear in 1860, as by then they had moved within or beyond Cincinnati. Many who moved within the city left their churches and joined institutions in their new neighborhoods, but others returned for decades to their original places of worship for religious services. Of note were the freethinkers who became Know-Nothing Party members, then fell under nativist attack in the deadly three-day riot of 1854.

Although Cincinnati already housed a conservative synagogue, arriving Drs. Isaac M. Wise and Max Lilienthal played pivotal roles in the development of Reformed Judaism in America. In the 1860s the leaders asked their congregations to build an impressive new temple in a prominent position on Ninth Street near the Catholic cathedral and city hall. By the 1870s, the foundations had been laid for the first Reform rabbinical center, Hebrew Union College, in suburban Clifton. They worked closely on civic activities with Christian Cincinnatians.

Irish arrivals advanced in smaller numbers, but many of them also made their way in politics and business, and they too demonstrated some religious diversity. In 1837 Methodist James Gamble from Ireland and his brother-in-law William Procter from England created a soap and candle business that grew rapidly through the war years, filling military contracts for its products.

The issue of religion in public life emerged in 1869 when a disagreement arose over the exclusive use of the King James Bible in the Cincinnati public schools, which many saw as a denial of the rights of Catholic, Jewish, and some Protestant families. At issue also were requests from the archbishop for public funding for Catholic parochial schools. School board members addressed the heated conflicts with two separate plans: consolidating parochial schools with the public schools and eliminating the use of the Bible in the public schools. Noting the significant differences between the Roman Catholic and the King James Bibles, including several books that appear in only one of them, the school board agreed that required use of the latter in the schools could violate First Amendment rights. The board's solution was to abandon the compulsory reading of the Bible in the schools, but not "sacred song" or "Christian literature." After several years of litigation, known nationally as the Cincinnati Bible Wars, in 1872 the Ohio Supreme Court ratified this compromise decision and determined that the board had acted within its authority.

African Americans continued to face more difficulty in assimilating into civic society than either immigrant or religious groups. Throughout the 1850s, Cincinnatians continued to allow visitors from slave states to bring their "servants" with them to the city. Due to its position as the most important western city on the border between free and slave states, Cincinnati became a major center for escaping slaves fleeing alone or with the help of others via the Underground Railroad. Most dramatically, when Margaret Garner and her family were thwarted in their attempt to escape slavery by crossing the frozen Ohio River to Cincinnati in 1856, she killed her own child rather than have her returned to slavery. The case drew national attention, divided citizens on both sides of the river, and left most Cincinnatians opposed to the institution of slavery. However, even in the late 1850s many local white antislavery advocates still looked to colonization in Africa or some other place outside the United States as a reasonable alternative for the freeperson.

Accordingly, Cincinnatians of color continued to wage their own campaign for their rights. Peter Clark, a leader in education, fought to obtain a black public school, the promise of which was inherent in the legislation creating tax-supported common schools in Cincinnati in 1829. By 1849 Clark began to see results, and by 1859 the city had opened a public school that was supported by the taxes paid by its African American citizens and under the direction of an elected, segregated, black school board. Clark continued to serve an important public role as professional teacher and advocate for African Americans in Cincinnati. Women played prominent activist roles as well; the Anti-Slavery Sewing Society made clothing for fugitive slaves and made a statement with their name.

African American men attempted to serve in the military before President Lincoln's preliminary Emancipation Proclamation began to open that door, but they were denied. When Cincinnati feared a Confederate attack in 1862 and called for a Home Guard, African American volunteers were denied participation and rounded up under a police directive to build defensive fortifications in northern Kentucky along the expected route. In response, the commander of the Department of Ohio sent Major General Lewis Wallace to command the forces, and he released the African Americans. This led to the formation of the one-thousand-member Black Brigade. The attack did not take place and the troops were disbanded, but many of the Black Brigade members later served in Ohio regiments. Others left for Massachusetts as soon as the

54th Regiment formed. Racism persisted after the war's end, but African Americans continued to organize to assert their rights.

See also *Cincinnati, OH 1828–1854; Cincinnati, OH 1877–1896*

JUDITH SPRAUL-SCHMIDT

BIBLIOGRAPHY

Abbott, Carl. *Boosters and Businessmen: Popular Economic Thought and Urban Growth in the Antebellum Middle West.* Westport, CT: Greenwood, 1981.

Ford, Henry A., and Kate B. Ford. *History of Cincinnati, Ohio.* Cleveland, OH: L. A. Williams & Co., 1881.

Hurley, Daniel. *Cincinnati: The Queen City.* Cincinnati, OH: the Cincinnati Historical Society, 1982.

Kenny, D. J. *Illustrated Cincinnati: a Pictorial Hand-Book of the Queen City.* Cincinnati, OH: Robert Clarke & Co., 1875 and 1879.

Miller, Zane L. *Boss Cox's Cincinnati: Urban Politics in the Progressive Era.* New York, NY: Oxford University Press, 1968.

———. *Visions of Place: The City, Neighborhoods, Suburbs, and Cincinnati's Clifton, 1850–2000.* Columbus: The Ohio State University Press, 2001.

Ross, Steven J. *Workers on the Edge: Work, Leisure, and Politics in Industrializing Cincinnati, 1788–1890.* New York, NY: Columbia University Press, 1985.

Shapiro, Henry D., and Jonathon D. Sarna, eds. *Ethnic Diversity and Civic Identity: Patterns of Conflict and Cohesion in Cincinnati since 1820.* Urbana: University of Illinois Press, 1992.

Stradling, David. *Cincinnati: From River City to Highway Metropolis.* Charleston, SC: Arcadia Publishing, 2003.

Taylor, Henry Louis, ed. *Race and the City: Work, Community, and Protest in Cincinnati, 1820–1970.* Urbana: University of Illinois Press, 1993.

Taylor, Nikki M. *Frontiers of Freedom: Cincinnati's Black Community, 1802–1868.* Athens, OH: Ohio University Press, 2005.

NEW ORLEANS, LA 1854–1877

THE YEARS 1854 TO 1877 BROUGHT TO NEW ORLEANS A PERIOD OF TURMOIL AND A DECREASE IN SHIPPING as a result of the Civil War that would destroy the city's attempts to compete for prominence with cities such as New York, Philadelphia, and Baltimore. The period began with a devastating yellow fever epidemic, in the summer of 1853, that killed more than eleven thousand people. The city then cast its lot with the Confederacy following a period of instability that culminated in the Know-Nothing riot of 1858. Owing to excessive confidence in the city's natural protection from Union invasion due to the difficulty of navigating the Mississippi River and the piecemeal garrisons at Forts Jackson and Phillip, New Orleans fell easily in 1862 to the Union Army's ships that successfully evaded the protection of the forts.

QUICK FACTS

NEW ORLEANS, LA 1854–1877

MAYORS

Charles M. Waterman	(1856–1858)
Gerard Stith	(1858–1860)
John T. Monroe	(1860–1862)
George F. Shepley	(1862)*
Godfrey Weitzel	(1862)*
Jonas H. French	(1862)*
Henry C. Deming	(1862–1863)*
James F. Miller	(1863)*
Edmund H. Durell	(1863)*
James F. Miller	(1864)*
Stephen Hoyt	(1864–1865)*
Hugh Kennedy	(1865)*
Samuel Miller Quincy	(1865)*
Glendy Burke	(1865)*
Hugh Kennedy	(1865–1866)*
Joseph Rozier	(1866)*
George Clark	(1866)*
John T. Monroe	(1866–1867)
Edward Heath	(1867–1868)
John R. Conway	(1868–1870)
Benjamin Franklin Flanders	(1870–1872)
Louis A. Wiltz	(1872–1874)
Charles J. Leeds	(1874–1876)
Edward Pilsbury	(1876–1878)

*Appointed military mayors

MAJOR INDUSTRIES AND EMPLOYERS

Dockwork and shipping
Cotton processing
Municipal government
Domestic work

MAJOR NEWSPAPERS

L'Union
New Orleans Bee
New Orleans Crescent
New Orleans Delta
New Orleans Louisianian
New Orleans Times
New Orleans Tribune
Republican

MAJOR EVENTS

1858: The Know-Nothing riot occurs, during which time a Committee of Vigilance temporarily gains control of the city.

1861: Louisiana secedes from the Union.

1862: New Orleans is captured by the Union Army.

1866: Republican efforts to convene a constitutional convention erupt in the Riot of 1866, killing more than nine hundred people.

1877: The White League bands with former Confederates to stage a coup taking over the city, only to be put down by the Louisiana militia.

With financial hardships resulting from the devaluation of Confederate currency, conflicts over the enfranchisement of former slaves, and difficulties relating to the reestablishment of a state constitution, New Orleans descended into civil disorder following the Civil War and into the end of Reconstruction in 1877. Rather than being excluded from the franchise and participation in municipal government, many former Confederates became involved in local politics, setting the stage for the exploitation of the freedmen and stifling attempts to institute government reform.

GOVERNMENT AND POLITICS

The 1858 Know-Nothing riot and the city's capture by Union forces were indicative of the social and governmental instability that defined New Orleans during this period. Even after the Civil War, the city endured several riots, most notably in 1866 and 1874. The 1858 riot arose from disputes over the election that year in which Gerard Stith, who had the support of the Know-Nothings, was elected mayor in a race against P. T. Beauregard. Prior to the election, a "crowd of rowdies" (as John Kendall described them in his *History of New Orleans*) took over the Registrar of Voters office in order to alter the registration rolls. In response, a Vigilance Committee—organized along the same lines as a similar committee formed in San Francisco in 1851 and revived in 1856, in response to rampant civil disorder and crime—effectively took control, by force, of a majority of the City of New Orleans.

The Vigilance Committee, which may have had primarily nativist sympathies, refused to disband, ostensibly to maintain order during the election, though the city's official police force was also trying to do the same thing. Mayor Waterman, still in office and apparently fearful for his safety, effectively abandoned his post and was impeached by the city council. Eventually, with the help of the state militia, the Vigilance Committee was defeated and disbanded, thereby returning control of the city to the police force and supporting the installment of Mayor Stith.

During the war, and after the seizure of New Orleans by Union forces, the city was governed under martial law by Major General Benjamin Butler, who established order and maintained a fairly remarkable level of cleanliness in the city. Butler also antagonized city residents with harsh laws—including a notorious general order that any local woman who insulted or showed offense to Union troops would be "treated as a woman of the town plying her avocation"—that undoubtedly created even greater sympathy for the Confederate cause. Butler was later replaced by Major General Nathaniel Banks. Federal troops remained in the city until the end of Reconstruction in 1877.

After the Civil War, the paramilitary activities of former confederate soldiers thwarted attempts to hold a state constitutional convention in New Orleans, through which Louisiana could accept the federal government's terms for reentry into the Union. This violence erupted into what is known as the Riot of 1866. Union veterans, prominent free blacks, and freedmen gathered at the Mechanics Institute in 1866 in an attempt to draft a new state constitution that would grant blacks the franchise and to allow them relatively equal participation in state and municipal government. Angered by the Confederate defeat, Union occupation, and possible enfranchisement of blacks, a large segment of the population disagreed with the terms of reinstatement of Louisiana into the Union. In an attempt to preserve order during the protests of the constitutional convention, the mayor authorized the deputization of ordinary citizens. This action backfired when members of the deputized force opened fire on demonstrators outside the Mechanics Institute on July 30. The deputized force then tried to storm the hall inside which convention members had barricaded themselves. Attempting to negotiate a surrender of the conventioneers, the mayor promised them safe passage, only to witness the police force storm the building and slaughter those inside. These events received national and international attention from the journalistic efforts of Jean-Charles Houzeau, editor of the *New Orleans Tribune*, and helped the Republicans nationally, as the riots turned public opinion in their favor and got more of them elected to Congress.

As with other Southern cities, many former Confederates who had been involved in government before the Civil War returned to prominence and elected office in New Orleans after the end of Reconstruction in 1877. These circumstances ensured that African American politicians such as Pinckney B. S. Pinchback and others would see themselves stripped of the right to participate as state and city representatives. Disputes over the conditions under which Louisiana would rejoin the Union continued to erupt in riots through the 1860s and 1870s.

The growth of the White League—a paramilitary organization opposed to the rights of the freedmen and Louisiana's concessions during Reconstruction—would cause riots in 1874 and 1875, and culminate in the Street Battle of 1877. The riot of 1874 arose when White League members attempted to arm themselves against the state militia and then overthrow William Kellogg, Louisiana's governor and a Republican who hailed from the North. A search for arms found that the White League had amassed a respectable arsenal. In the riot of 1875, another White League insurgency was suppressed by the Union Army, and order was restored to the city in the wake of mayoral and gubernatorial elections. Yet in 1877 the White League rallied more successfully in the absence of federal military intervention so that the offices of mayor and governor were filled by either former Confederates or enemies of black enfranchisement.

INDUSTRY, COMMERCE, AND LABOR

By 1854, thanks to the successful use of steamboats to navigate the Mississippi River and steam power to facilitate the shipment of goods upstream, New Orleans was enjoying a strong wave of prosperity that held despite the economic downturns of the 1840s. In addition to the booming commerce in sugar that was often shipped from the outlying parishes of Louisiana to New Orleans for redistribution and sale in other cities, the production of cotton increased to rival the sale and cultivation of sugar. The largest cotton mill, owned by the Freret brothers, one of whom served as mayor of the city in 1840, processed a majority of the crops that arrived in the city. Although the city began to produce its own manufactured wares, the volume of this commerce never rivaled the importation and redistribution of manufactured goods from Mexico and Europe. With the focus of agricultural production on sugar or cotton, few plantations cultivated foodstuffs, which the city was forced to import in significant quantities. Consequently, some of the most numerous professions included grocers, wholesalers, and commission agents who engineered the redistribution of goods. This commerce shaped the growth of the port so that warehouses, cotton factories, and storage facilities crowded the wharves; shops where imported goods were sold lined Canal Street because of its access to river traffic.

The city's shipping interests and waterborne commerce suffered severely following Louisiana's secession from the Union, federal blockages, and the curtailment of shipping from Europe and Mexico. In addition, the instability of confederate currency undermined a good deal of the prosperity and wealth that had accumulated in New Orleans. During the Union occupation,

Major General Butler's quarantine of all ships thwarted what trade continued from parts of Mexico and Europe. The Union occupation plunged the city into debt and financial disorder from which it would scarcely recover, even into the 1870s.

With the capture of the city by the Union army, jobs such as river pilot, cotton screwman, and longshoreman severely decreased or disappeared entirely until the port was once again open to trade around 1864. The Union occupation brought not only federal troops, but also a sizable influx of slave refugees. This influx, combined with the slowing of waterborne commerce and a population of recently arrived Irish immigrants created conditions of severe competition for jobs or unemployment. Yet one advantage of the closed port was a decrease in yellow fever. It was only after Reconstruction, in 1878, that New Orleans once again had a major outbreak.

Agricultural production slowed to almost a standstill in Louisiana during the Civil War as slaves fled plantations for New Orleans, where they were designated as contraband by Major General Butler. Initially the slaves were placed in what was effectively a refugee camp, uptown near what is now Audubon Park, where they performed manual labor and assisted Union troops. So many were destitute that the federal troops found themselves supplying rations to approximately ten thousand African Americans by 1862. As the fugitive slave population increased beyond the capacity of the camp, the slaves were sent back to plantations, where they were made to work to cultivate sugar cane and cotton. This forced labor boosted agricultural production in the state, and consequently the wealth of New Orleans, during Union occupation.

Despite the financial setbacks of the Civil War, the port became one of the largest and most vital employment sectors in New Orleans. The city's dockworkers displayed an unusual ability to organize in pursuit of higher wages and improved working conditions as well as the tendency to form successful and enduring coalitions and systems of cooperation that crossed racial lines. In more than one instance, black and white dockworkers successfully struck to gain higher wages and resisted the temptation to riot caused by attempts on the part of the port to employ scabs. Even though port activities represented important sectors of commerce, the city's trade in sugar and cotton did not recover from the prominence and volume it had had before the Civil War. Instead, competitors such as Cuba displaced Louisiana as one of the biggest producers of sugar, especially when protective tariffs no longer stabilized the price of sugar produced in the United States. Similarly, following the Civil War a bumper crop of cotton produced in Europe flooded the market and prevented Louisiana producers from again garnering the prices they had formerly commanded before the war.

RACE, ETHNICITY, AND IMMIGRATION

By 1854 the ethnic and racial composition of New Orleans consisted of a mosaic of different populations, including French and Spanish Creoles; descendants of refugees from Germany, Ireland, and Haiti; and a mixture of free people of color, urban slaves, and newly arrived Americans. During the early 1860s, when the city was under military control, roughly 40 percent of New Orleans's residents were German and Irish immigrants, whose sympathies tended to lie with the Union. These different groups tended to live in separate areas of the city, with the Creoles in the French Quarter, Americans in what is now the lower Garden District, and immigrants and free people of color in the Faubourg Marigny, east of the French Quarter. Despite this spatial segregation, however, institutions such as godparentship—a type of fictive kinship among Catholics—united different peoples so that none of these communities were separate and unrelated to one another. In addition to godparentship, restrictions established in the 1850s that required a white person to vouch for the integrity and character of emancipated slaves created bonds of interdependence and obligation between freed people and whites.

As a result of sectional tensions regarding the continuation of slavery and the approach of the Civil War, the 1850s witnessed severe restrictions on the ability of slaves to gain emancipation through self-purchase or by the grace of their masters. In addition to requiring each slave in pursuit of emancipation to have a white person to vouch for his integrity, a $1,000 bond, paid by the white person or the slave, was also required. In the 1860s the government of Louisiana went so far as to specify that slaves emancipated in Louisiana were required to leave the state. Despite the apparent strictness of this requirement, it was subject to lax enforcement, and many slaves emancipated during the period were allowed to remain in Louisiana.

In 1860 the number of free blacks in Orleans parish was 10,939, and the slave population amounted to 14,484, while whites in that same year numbered 149,063. The approach of the Union army in the 1860s and the capture of the city brought an influx of runaway slaves to New Orleans that would add to the already significant black population. In 1870 the "colored" population in the city was 50,456, or 26 percent of the total population, while whites numbered 140,923. The influx of slaves and the change in status and prominence for free people of color following the Emancipation Proclamation and the end of the Civil War exacerbated strained race relations and led to tensions that would erupt in riots, the first of which occurred in 1866 over the issues of enfranchising former slaves and the terms of a new state constitution required to reinstate Louisiana into the Union.

Despite strong opposition to bolstering the rights and liberties afforded to former slaves, people of color in New Orleans experienced advantages and opportunities that were different from those in other parts of the country. The political career of Pinckney B. S. Pinchback provides valuable information about the experiences and advantages of people of color in New Orleans during the Civil War and Reconstruction. After working as a deckhand on steamboats from 1854 to 1861, Pinchback enlisted in the Union Army and served as captain of Company A, Second Louisiana Native Guard. Pinchback then recruited and organized the Corps d'Afrique of black volunteers. His military experience and organizational skills helped launch him into a career in politics. He formed the Fourth Ward Republican Club in 1867 and was elected as a delegate to the national Republican convention the following year. From 1868 to 1871 Pinchback served as a member of the Louisiana Senate; the following year he was president pro tem of the state senate and lieutenant governor. From 1872 to 1873 he was governor of the state, but his election to the U.S. Congress in 1872 was contested and thwarted by increased resistance to the participation of blacks in national government and the deterioration of radical Reconstruction.

See also *New Orleans, LA 1790–1828; New Orleans, LA 1828–1854*

ANDRÉ F. YOUNG

BIBLIOGRAPHY

Bell, Caryn Cossé. *Revolution, Romanticism, and the Afro-Creole Protest Tradition in Louisiana, 1718–1868.* Baton Rouge: Louisiana State University Press, 1997.

Blassingame, John. *Black New Orleans, 1860–1880.* Chicago, IL: University of Chicago Press, 1973.

Caper, Gerald. Occupied City: *New Orleans Under the Federals, 1862–1865.* Lexington: University of Kentucky Press, 1965.

Hogue, James. *Uncivil War: Five New Orleans Street Battles and the Rise and Fall of Radical Reconstruction.* Baton Rouge: Louisiana State University Press, 2006.

Hollandsworth, James. *An Absolute Massacre: The New Orleans Race Riot of July 30, 1866.* Baton Rouge: Louisiana State University Press, 2001.

Kelman, Ari. *A River and Its City: The Nature of Landscape in New Orleans.* Berkeley: University of California Press, 2006.

Kendall, John S. *History of New Orleans.* New York, NY: Lewis, 1922.

Lewis, Peirce. *New Orleans: The Making of an Urban Landscape.* Charlottesville: University of Virginia Press, 2003.

Towers, Frank. *The Urban South and the Coming of the Civil War.* Charlottesville: University of Virginia Press, 2004.

Vandal, Gilles. *The New Orleans Riot of 1866: Anatomy of a Tragedy.* Lafayette: Center for Louisiana Studies, 1983.

SAN FRANCISCO, CA 1854–1877

FOUNDED IN 1776 AS A SPANISH GARRISON AND MISSION, San Francisco became part of the Republic of Mexico in 1822. By mid-1846 the settlement on the cove had about two hundred inhabitants. On July 9 of that year, what is today San Francisco was seized by U.S. naval forces during the Mexican-American War. The fate of the small settlement was forever changed in January 1848 when the foreman of a group constructing a sawmill on the south fork of the American River, about 150 miles away, discovered gold. The ensuing gold rush attracted some 350,000 to 500,000 individuals (the vast majority of which were men) from around the world to California, and many of them traveled through San Francisco. Very quickly, San Francisco became the financial, merchandising, and manufacturing center of the West, changing from a trading village of several hundred inhabitants into an instantaneous, heterogeneous city—a city with one of the busiest ports in the United States.

Although supplies of easily extractable gold had greatly diminished by 1854, the period 1854–1877 saw San Francisco develop into a major commercial center and destination for immigrants. The period was also a volatile one for San Francisco both politically and economically as the city's population surged from nearly 35,000 residents in 1852 to over 149,000 in 1870. The Civil War, the completion of the transcontinental railroad, and metal speculation all contributed to a wave of booms and busts during this period, and the political scene saw little party loyalty or stability and was affected by the lasting influence of the Second Committee of Vigilance.

QUICK FACTS

SAN FRANCISCO, CA **1854–1877**

MAYORS

Cornelius K. Garrison	(1853–1854)
Stephen P. Webb	(1854–1855)
James Van Ness	(1855–1856)
George J. Whelan	(1856)
Ephraim W. Burr	(1856–1859)
Henry F. Teschemacher	(1859–1863)
Henry P. Coon	(1863–1867)
Frank McCoppin	(1867–1869)
Thomas H. Selby	(1869–1871)
William Alvord	(1871–1873)
James Otis	(1873–1875)
George Hewston	(1875)
Andrew J. Bryant	(1875–1879)

MAJOR INDUSTRIES AND EMPLOYERS

Shipping
General manufacturing (mining goods, food processing, apparel)

MAJOR NEWSPAPERS

Alta California
San Francisco Bulletin
San Francisco Chronicle
San Francisco Examiner
Golden Era
San Francisco Herald
Overland Monthly
Pacific Appeal
Picayune

MAJOR EVENTS

1854: Due to the difficulty and expense of transferring gold to eastern mints for creating coins, the U.S. government opens the San Francisco mint.

1854–1855: San Francisco endures a significant economic depression caused in part by the growing scarcity of easily mined gold.

1856: The Second Committee of Vigilance seizes power in San Francisco, tries suspects in extrajudicial trials, and hangs four people.

1856: The California state legislature passes the Consolidation Act, which creates a new county and provides San Francisco with a coterminous city and county government.

October 21, 1868: A major earthquake strikes the Bay Area, causing significant damage in San Francisco.

1875: The market in mining stocks collapses. The Bank of California, the premier bank in the West, closes its doors for two months following a run on the institution.

GOVERNMENT AND POLITICS

The instability engendered by the nearly instantaneous growth of San Francisco from a small trading village into a large city and busy port after the discovery of gold resulted in a generally corrupt city government that ruled until 1856. This government followed the process that had begun immediately after the seizure of California by the United States during the Mexican-American War in 1846. Members of the city council had long used their political power to enrich themselves and their friends at the expense of the community as a whole. Such corruption was made possible by the transience of a city population largely attracted by the chance to get rich quick.

Some of the principal forms of municipal corruption involved land grants and construction of the city's infrastructure. As early as 1847, the military governor of California auctioned land in San Francisco based on the city survey by Jasper O'Farrell. Those who bought the lots had to fulfill certain obligations to obtain title. Lists of the land sales showed extensive purchases by San Francisco's politicians, who then abolished the restrictions and conditions for title—a form of "land-grabbing" that lasted well into the 1850s. In terms of infrastructure, contracts for street grading on the city's myriad hills, the planking of the streets, the building of the wharves that extended from the Yerba Buena Cove into the bay, and the filling in of the cove between 1849 and 1855 were awarded to politically connected contractors that charged outrageous prices for their work and who then kicked back some of their profits to their political patrons. The municipal bonds issued to pay for these inflated contracts put the city government into massive debt.

The California state legislature chartered San Francisco as a municipal corporation in April 1850 and issued new charters subsequently in attempts to aid the city to control its municipal expenditures and out-of-control debt. Until a reform movement obtained control of the city in 1856, however, these city charters were ineffective at curtailing corruption.

The party divisions during most of the 1850s were between Democrats (divided into two factions), Whigs, and Know-Nothings. With the demise of the Whigs and the Know-Nothings by the end of the decade (their constituencies merging into the newly formed Republican Party) and the collapse of the "chivalric" wing (the Southern faction) of the Democratic Party at the beginning of the Civil War, two parties—the reconstituted Democrats and the Republicans—competed for municipal governmental power. From the 1850s to the 1880s, national parties struggled to stay in power for more than a couple of years, which resulted in high party turnover in the city's government.

The year 1856 witnessed two major changes in San Francisco's political landscape. The first was the passage in the state legislature of the Consolidation Act. This legislation sought to diminish the political corruption and high expenditures of a city and a county of San Francisco. The city's boundaries were expanded to its present dimensions, and it was created coterminously a city and a county. A new county—San Mateo—was created out of the old County of San Francisco.

The second major change was a seminal event in San Francisco's political development: the founding of the Second Committee of Vigilance on May 15, 1856. The first vigilance committee was founded in 1851 to fight perceived election fraud and political corruption. This original group, numbering some seven hundred people, had an official headquarters and, although their ambition was not a usurpation of government power, their extrajudicial "trials" stripped suspects of their constitutional rights and resulted in several hangings. The group disbanded in 1853. The second committee was something of a continuation of the earlier one and included some of the same leaders. In contrast to its predecessor, the second committee attracted thousands of members. The organization's aim was to fight perceived corruption in the government, and it attracted the allegiance of city militias. Its leadership consisted primarily of merchants, although committee membership included a diverse group of skilled and unskilled workers. The group held show trials, including the trial of California's chief justice, cast aside constitutional protections, and hanged those they found guilty. A large parade marked the committee's disbanding several months later on August 18, 1865, but its lasting legacy was the creation of the People's Party. This party swept the municipal elections and effectively and economically governed San Francisco until the mid-1870s.

INDUSTRY, COMMERCE, AND LABOR

The discovery of gold in 1848, and of silver in the Comstock Lode eleven years later, transformed the small trading village of San Francisco into a large metropolis with one of the busiest ports in the world. By 1852 San Francisco was second only to New York City in terms of tonnage entering its port. The city served as a critical entry point for moving goods into the interior of California.

Almost immediately after the discovery of gold, ships coming from New England and the Mid-Atlantic states arrived in San Francisco, pouring into the city significant quantities of manufactured goods, agricultural products, and commodities for the burgeoning city and for the market towns and mining camps of California. Such imported goods were supplemented by local manufacturing companies (such as the Union Iron Works, founded in 1849) and met the needs of the instant city and its hinterland.

However, unlike New York City; Chicago, Illinois; Philadelphia, Pennsylvania; Boston, Massachusetts; and its surrounding area, San Francisco never became a large manufacturing center. The shortage of labor in the city after the discovery of gold (which caused wages to be much higher than in other parts of the country), a lack of coal and iron resources necessary for manufacturing, and a comparative lack of a highly dense population all combined to make San Francisco dependent on East Coast manufactured items.

The Civil War years brought commercial opportunity to the city as turmoil in the eastern United States made shipping goods risky for foreign buyers. San Francisco merchants benefited as European markets increasingly looked to California goods, particularly agricultural products, as a safer alternative.

The completion of the transcontinental railroad in 1869 had a mixed effect on the economy of the city. While the railroad did facilitate movement of goods from California inland and also from the United States to Asian markets through San Francisco, it had the net effect of loosening the city's stranglehold over western commerce. The railroad also further reduced San Francisco's status as a manufacturing center due to a significant lowering of transportation costs. Additionally, the railroad brought an influx of Chinese rail workers into the city's labor market, bolstering competition for jobs.

San Francisco relied on a substantial, mostly water-based, transportation system to deliver goods to Washington, Oregon, southern California, and the towns and mining camps of northern California. Stagecoach lines and wagon trains completed this distribution system. With the development of an extensive railroad system in the 1870s, under the aegis of the San Francisco–based Southern Pacific Railroad Company, the earlier patterns of the distribution of goods began to change.

San Francisco's development as the financial center of the West began immediately after the discovery of gold. The earliest banks appeared in 1849, and throughout the 1850s both locally owned banks and insurance companies were founded. Savings banks came into existence in the mid-1850s. The federal government opened a mint in San Francisco in 1854 to process gold into coinage and to alleviate currency shortages. Prior to this, transactions were paid for by a combination of gold dust, foreign and domestic coins, and the coins minted by several local assay firms.

The boom created by the Comstock discovery—a boom that lasted throughout the 1860s and most of the 1870s—further increased the number of financial institutions in San Francisco, one of which was William Ralston's Bank of California, one of the premier banks in the country. The boom also increased the city's importance as a financial center. In the 1860s and 1870s, for example, individuals and businesses in Southern California sought loans from San Francisco banks. However, along with the booms that gold and silver brought to the economy of San Francisco, speculation in metals also brought devastating busts in the 1850s and 1870s.

San Francisco's reputation as a "union town" began in the early days of the gold rush. As early as 1849, San Francisco carpenters had organized and sought a wage increase. When denied, they went on strike. Soon thereafter, printers, teamsters, sailors, and musicians also initiated strikes. Similar to patterns seen in the East, unions appeared, fell apart, and reappeared in a different form sometime later. The scarcity of labor, however, almost always kept the city's labor market at a high level of wages; the abundance of cheap labor upon which the great manufacturing centers of the rest of the country depended was never really present in San Francisco.

A significant exception to this general rule was San Francisco's sizable Chinese labor force. In the 1860s, for example, Charles Crocker, one of the owners of the Southern Pacific Railroad and the head of its construction, fired all the Caucasian workers building the railroad and hired Chinese laborers at much lower wages. Manufacturers in industries such as cigarmaking and textiles did likewise.

As a counterpoint to the rising union movement in the United States and Europe during the second half of the nineteenth century, the Chinese, who had had no experience in organizing for better working conditions and higher wages, happily took the jobs of striking Caucasian workers or were hired initially because they were willing to work for less than Caucasians.

This situation led to great antagonism between the Chinese and Caucasians, which was manifested in attempts to boycott companies that employed Chinese workers and popular agitation against the Chinese in the depression years of the late 1870s. It also led Congress to pass the Page Act in 1875 (restricting certain forms of Asian immigration) and the Chinese Exclusion Act in 1882.

RACE, ETHNICITY, AND IMMIGRATION

Even while under Mexican rule, the tiny town of Yerba Buena (renamed San Francisco in 1847) had a polyglot population, a tradition that continued after the discovery of gold. San Francisco's population was derived by simultaneous immigration from every part of the United States and from almost every corner of the world. The majority of midcentury settlers were male, creating a marked gender imbalance in the city. According to the 1852 state census, only 15 percent of the city's population was female, although this number rose to 39 percent by 1860. Immigrants seeking economic opportunity and aided by advances in transportation came by the tens of thousands, primarily from the northeast United States, Europe, China, and Central and South America. The foreign-born population of the city was significant and represented a formidable bloc of eligible voters during this period. By 1870, foreign-born persons represented nearly 50 percent of the city's population.

California entered the Union as a free state in 1850. However, African Americans could neither vote nor testify against whites in court. African Americans in San Francisco started their own newspapers, including the *Mirror of the Times,* the *Pacific Appeal*, and the *Elevator*, and petitioned for the right to testify against whites. In 1863 the state of California passed legislation giving them that right.

San Francisco served as a major port of entry for Chinese immigrants during the gold rush and throughout the period. In 1860 some three thousand Chinese residents lived in San Francisco, and by the 1870s some 25 percent of California's Chinese population lived in the city. It was primarily after the Civil War that the board of supervisors began to take discriminatory legislative action against the Chinese residents of the city. An 1870 "Cubic Air" law, for example, regulated the amount of open space necessary in a dwelling, largely directed at Chinese tenements. In 1873 the city passed a zoning ordinance banning laundries from certain areas of the city, which represented another attempt to limit the settlement of Chinese residents. One regulation even prohibited city residents from walking with poles on sidewalks, something commonly associated with Chinese residents transporting goods around the city.

San Francisco in the 1850s saw some aspects of the nativism that gripped the United States during that decade, albeit in a much milder form. There was some hostility towards foreign-born residents, towards Roman Catholics, and certainly towards Native Americans, Hispanics, and Chinese, but such bigotry never reached the pitch that it had in other cities, where harm to persons and property was an occasional occurrence.

Not surprisingly, San Francisco's various ethnic groupings lived in distinctive neighborhoods and often were drawn to certain occupations. The Chinese lived close to the city's downtown area, along Grant Avenue from California to Broadway. Across Broadway were Latinos and the fledgling Italian community. The patrician Anglo-Saxons, along with a handful of successful Irish businessmen, inhabited Rincon Hill briefly and then, in the 1870s, Nob Hill. The rapidly growing Irish population lived in the area south of Market Street and also in the Mission district, where they were joined by smaller numbers of Germans and Scandinavians.

This heterogeneous population produced a colorful mosaic in San Francisco due to its celebration of various festivals, its entertainments, the frequent use of various languages, and the numerous organizations, both business and philanthropic, that grew from the needs and desires of the various ethnic groups.

See also *San Francisco, CA 1877–1896*

Charles A. Fracchia

BIBLIOGRAPHY

The Builders of a Great City: San Francisco's Representative Men, the City, Its History and Commerce. San Francisco, CA: The Journal, 1891.

Camp, William Martin. *San Francisco: Port of Gold*. Garden City, NY: Doubleday, 1947.

Decker, Peter R. *Fortunes and Failures: White-Collar Mobility in Nineteenth Century San Francisco*. Cambridge, MA: Harvard University Press, 1978.

Ettington, Philip J. *The Public City: The Political Construction of Urban Life in San Francisco, 1850–1900*. New York, NY: Cambridge University Press, 1994.

Fracchia, Charles A. *Fire and Gold: The San Francisco Story*. Encinitas, CA: Heritage Publishing Co., 1994.

Hittell, John S. *A History of the City of San Francisco*. San Francisco, CA: A. L. Bancroft & Co., 1878.

Issel, William, and Robert Cherny. *San Francisco, 1865–1932: Politics, Power, and Urban Development*. Berkeley: University of California Press, 1986.

Kinnaird, Lawrence. *History of the Greater San Francisco Bay Region*. 3 vols. New York, NY: Lewis Historical Pub. Co., c. 1966.

Lockwood, Charles. *Suddenly San Francisco: The Early Years of an Instant City*. San Francisco, CA: Examiner Special Projects, 1978.

Lotchin, Roger W. *San Francisco, 1846–1856: From Hamlet to City*. New York, NY: Oxford University Press, 1974.

McDonald, Terrence J. *The Parameters of Urban Fiscal Policy: Socio-Economic Change, Political Culture, and Fiscal Policy in San Francisco, 1860–1906*. Berkeley: University of California Press, 1986.

Mullin, Kevin J. *Let Justice Be Done: Crime and Politics in Early San Francisco*. Reno: University of Nevada Press, 1989.

Young, John P. *San Francisco: A History of the Pacific Coast Metropolis*. Chicago, IL: S. J. Clark, 1912.

BUFFALO, NY 1854–1877

BECAUSE OF ITS LOCATION ON THE ERIE CANAL, Buffalo, New York, seemed poised to become a hub of transportation and commerce in the mid-nineteenth century. Despite a devastating cholera outbreak in 1854 and the nationwide economic slowdown of 1857, Buffalo's population grew, and the canal attracted workers and entrepreneurs throughout the 1850s, 1860s, and 1870s. The Civil War provided an economic boost, and industrialization hastened in the postwar decades.

GOVERNMENT AND POLITICS

A rapidly increasing population strained Buffalo's early city charters. The initial charter, passed in 1832, provided for a popularly elected common council but not for an elected mayor. Laws passed in 1840 established an elected executive, and the revised charter of 1853 codified a popularly elected mayor in the city charter. However, the charter limited mayoral power by declaring that the mayor could not succeed himself, and establishing a president of the common council. The council had formerly been presided over by the mayor. The new charter also extended the city boundaries to incorporate the nearby town of Black Rock, which expanded the city to forty

QUICK FACTS

BUFFALO, NY 1854–1877

MAYORS

Eli Cook	(1853–1855)
Frederick Stevens	(1856–1857)
Timothy T. Lockwood	(1858–1859)
Franklin A. Alberger	(1860–1861)
William G. Fargo	(1862–1865)
Chandler J. Wells	(1866–1867)
William F. Rogers	(1868–1869)
Alexander Brush	(1870–1873)
Lewis P. Dayton	(1874–1875)
Philip Becker	(1876–1877)

MAJOR INDUSTRIES AND EMPLOYERS

Shipping
Grain/milling industry
Tanning industry
Iron industry
Shipbuilding

MAJOR NEWSPAPERS

Buffalo Commercial Advertiser
Buffalo Daily Courier
Buffalo Morning Express
Buffalo Evening Post

MAJOR EVENTS

1853: Charter revision establishes an elected mayor and a president of the common council and expands the size of the city to forty square miles.

1854: The most devastating cholera epidemic in Buffalo to date hits. It results in the acquisition of the Buffalo Water Works by the city in 1868, which allowed the city to provide safe drinking water and proper sewage disposal to prevent future epidemics.

1860s and 1870s: Buffalo's shipping and iron industries experience an economic boom as a result of the Civil War, giving citizens hope that Buffalo will become a major urban center in America in subsequent decades.

1862 and 1863: Draft, labor, and race riots reveal sharp racial and ethnic tension in Buffalo, despite a very small African American population. The tension is due primarily to frustration over strike-breaking policies of the major shipping and grain interests and the Civil War among immigrant communities in the city.

1866: To combat concerns over local corruption, control of the police department is transferred to the governor, who establishes the Frontier Police Department. Control was reinstated at the local level in 1871 because local issues and concerns were not being properly addressed.

square miles and thirteen wards. Citizens elected two aldermen from each ward to serve on the common council.

Democrat Eli Cook was the first mayor elected under the new charter. Cook, along with his successors, had to cope with a rapidly expanding population and a growing commercial sector. The annexation of Black Rock brought thirty thousand new residents to Buffalo, and the Erie Canal spurred population growth by drawing native- and foreign-born laborers and entrepreneurs to the city. The canal also expanded commerce and industry in Buffalo by increasing the flow of goods and raw materials through the city. This growth and expansion made quality-of-life and economic issues central to governance in Buffalo.

To accommodate this growth, mayors had to find a balance between funding municipal improvements and services while keeping taxes low. A primary issue in the city was education. In 1839 Buffalo became the first city in the state of New York to offer free public education to every school-aged white child. (The city did not establish the first public school for African American students until 1848.) This mandate, coupled with the growing number of school-aged children, put schools at the top of the mayoral list of priorities. Schools had to be built and maintained to keep pace with the growing population. As the school system grew, its administration became independent from city hall. The superintendent became an elected position after passage of the laws of 1840, which were codified in the 1853 city charter, and the common council lost control of the school board in the revised charter of 1870.

Other issues facing elected officials were the safety and health of the citizens of Buffalo. Prior to the 1853 charter, police duties were carried out by justices of the peace, a position that became popularly elected with the laws of 1840. These men were in charge of watch houses throughout the city. More systematic policing became necessary as the population grew, and a chief of police position was introduced in the charter of 1853.

Public health was also a major concern for elected officials and citizens. Buffalo experienced severe cholera outbreaks in 1832 and 1849. In response to the 1832 outbreak, the Buffalo Board of Health was established. The worst cholera epidemic was in 1854 and primarily affected the Irish community in the southeastern First Ward. Cholera and typhoid fever presented the greatest public health challenge to the city, and the provision of potable water and a safe sewer system were part of every mayor's agenda, beginning with the administration of Democrat Frederick Stevens in 1856. This effort culminated with the city purchasing the Buffalo Water Works in 1868, thus ensuring the provision of safe water.

Despite a commitment to address these issues, concerns among citizens over corruption and patronage in city hall grew throughout the 1850s, 1860s, and 1870s. Indeed, the public's commitment to school funding began to wane in the 1870s when school-building and maintenance began to be seen as an outlet for corruption. The police force was also identified as an agency with rampant patronage and corruption. Due to this, during the late 1850s, the position of chief of police vacillated between being elected and appointed. Yet corruption concerns persisted, and in 1866 control of the police force was transferred to the governor. This new Frontier Police Force lasted for only five years, and in 1871 control over the police department was transferred back to the city.

The Civil War also greatly affected Buffalo's development. More than two dozen regiments were drawn from Buffalo and Erie County, contributing a total of 15,249 men to the Union Army during the Civil War. The majority of the men were volunteers, though the draft was required on two occasions. Although Buffalo was largely a Democratic stronghold, President-elect Lincoln was well received when he passed through Buffalo on his way to Washington, D.C., in 1861. In fact, Buffalonians initially supported the war effort because of strong antislavery sentiments in the city. However, the toll of the war on families and labor unrest in the city quickly soured residents on the war. As a result, power in city hall switched between Democrats and Republicans between 1865 and 1877, largely reflecting concerns about corruption and uncertainty over which party would best address local concerns.

INDUSTRY, COMMERCE, AND LABOR

Prior to the mid-1850s, commerce in Buffalo was largely dependent on the Erie Canal. The majority of work along the canal was loading, unloading, and processing corn and wheat being transported from the East to points in the West. Shipping in and out of Buffalo brought grains to the city, and the corn and wheat mills established in the city employed mill hands to process the grains. In the 1820s and 1830s, stevedores could move about two thousand bushels of grain a day. In 1842 Joseph Dart built the nation's first grain elevator, which could unload one thousand bushels an hour. This invention attracted domestic- and foreign-born white and African American laborers to work as stevedores and mill hands during the shipping boom of the 1850s.

The economic success of shipping and grain interests along the waterfront in Buffalo was good for business owners, but often difficult for workers, especially foreign-born Irish and African Americans. In the 1850s, the Irish engaged in frequent work stoppages or strikes to demand better wages and working conditions. Black laborers were brought in to break these strikes, which caused frequent riots and fights between the Irish and black workers. The Civil War complicated matters further. Many of Buffalo's immigrants, and the Irish and Polish Catholics in particular, fought in the Civil War for a cause (the abolition of slavery) they felt was given too much attention by abolitionists and Protestants, and they resented the fact they were fighting for a black population who took their jobs during strikes. In 1863 the tension was so high that the Sixty-Fifth and Seventy-Fourth militia regiments were activated in Buffalo, along with local police, to quell the violent riots and return order to the waterfront.

In the early 1850s the Erie Canal brought to Buffalo the first shipment of raw materials necessary to produce iron. Sherman S. Jewett and F. H. Root established the Jewett and Root Stove Factory. They then partnered with O. Follett to open the Eagle Iron Company, which made elevators and general machinery. Other major ironworks manufactured cast-iron furnaces, steam engines, and bank vaults. In the 1850s iron manufacturers employed sixteen hundred workers and were the largest industrial employer in the city during this time. This industry experienced a boom during the Civil War, and continued to expand in the late 1870s and 1880s.

Buffalo's commercial and manufacturing base was also complemented by smaller industries. The tanning industry was a major employer in Buffalo. Leatherworking businesses, such as Forbush and Brown's Shoe and Boot Manufactory, dotted the waterfront along with small shipbuilding and agricultural machinery factories. Together, various small manufacturers employed approximately five hundred people in the city. Buffalo's geographic location—centrally located in a barley-growing region—supplied brewers with the natural ingredients for making beer. There were at least thirty-seven breweries in Buffalo during the 1850s and 1860s, and they produced approximately 109,000 barrels of beer a year. Clothing manufacturing began in Buffalo in 1854 and became a small but strong component of the city's business sector. Furniture-making began in the 1820s and remained an important part of Buffalo's commercial life in the mid-nineteenth century.

In the decades following the Civil War, citizens hoped that Buffalo would become a major industrial center in the United States. Transportation of goods was easy, labor was plentiful, and a relatively small but vibrant manufacturing and industrial base was in place. The only piece missing was capital investment. In 1860 John Bell founded the Association for the Encouragement of Manufactures (AEM), and the Civil War did spur production and some investment, but Buffalo was not catapulted onto the national scene. In 1869 the AEM hosted the first annual Industrial Exposition. Organizers of the event thought it necessary to shift the focus of the economy from canal-driven commerce to industries that took advantage of Buffalo's proximity to the coal, iron ore, and timber regions of Pennsylvania. This economic reorientation was necessary because railroads had been challenging the Erie Canal as the main source of goods transport since the mid-1850s.

RACE, ETHNICITY, AND IMMIGRATION

In 1855 the population of Buffalo was 74,214—up 75 percent from 42,261 in 1850. The rapid population growth was due in large part to the rising immigrant population, primarily Irish and German, who came to Buffalo for work. Indeed, 60 percent of the residents in Buffalo were foreign-born by 1855. Half of those were German (approximately twenty-two thousand), and one-fifth were Irish (approximately nine thousand). The vast majority of the remaining 40 percent were native-born white Protestants, with African Americans making up less than .01 percent of the population during this era. Despite the rapid increase of the foreign-born population in Buffalo, native-born Protestants dominated the economic life of the city, as well as its medical, legal, and political professions.

Irish and German immigrants settled into Buffalo in different ways; they lived in different neighborhoods, worked different jobs, and participated at different levels in Buffalo's civil society. Irish immigrants lived primarily in the First Ward in the southeast, which bordered the Erie Canal and the harbor, as well as in the Second and Third Wards to the north. This clustered the Irish very near to the industrial center of the city and away from other immigrant populations and native-born Americans. These Irish neighborhoods were densely populated mostly by uneducated and unskilled workers who worked on the waterfront and in factories. Unlike other parts of Buffalo, which were primarily residential, these neighborhoods were both residential and commercial—houses and schools were located among taverns, grain elevators, railroad tracks, and breweries. Indeed, the overcrowded and industrial nature of these neighborhoods combined with the low-lying and waterside location to create prime environments for the spread of cholera. Thus, in addition to being among the poorest in Buffalo, the Irish community was the hardest hit in the cholera epidemic of 1854.

The Irish community was strongly Catholic, and the church provided a site for growing Irish nationalism during the mid-nineteenth century. Prior to 1848 the German Catholics and the Irish Catholics had limited contact with each other. German Catholics had their own priests and churches in the Fifth, Sixth, and Seventh Wards, while the majority of church services in the Irish neighborhoods were conducted by priests in the homes of Irish families. In 1848 John Timon, an Irish Catholic, was appointed the first bishop of Buffalo. He attempted to unite the city's Catholic community, but he quickly found that tensions between the Germans and Irish were too strong to overcome. Timon turned his focus to improving the lives of the Irish in Buffalo by developing parochial schools, advocating for poor relief and jobs for the Irish who were most affected by the depression in the late 1850s, and building St. Joseph's Cathedral.

One reason for the rift between the Irish and Germans in Buffalo was that most of the Germans were better educated and better skilled at trades like tailoring, shoemaking, and black-smithing. Moreover, German neighborhoods were physically isolated from the Irish community, as well as from the native-born population in Buffalo. Their neighborhoods were quiet, residential, burgeoning middle-class communities located in the Fifth, Sixth, and Seventh Wards.

By the mid-1850s, the German community of Buffalo had several German-language news-papers and churches and had established numerous cultural and social organizations. Members of the German community were also actively engaged in local politics, with the first German common council member elected in 1838 and the first German citywide officeholder elected in 1854 to the office of comptroller. German civic engagement in the 1850s increased due to an influx of Germans fleeing the failed European revolutions of 1848. These new immigrants were nicknamed "the '48ers" and were more politicized. They spurred community engagement in the growing union movement: the German-American Workingman's Union was formed in 1849 and the German Workingman's Sick Benefit Society in 1850. This shift from social and cultural activities to political and civic activity is evidence that by the mid-1850s the German community had become more engaged in Buffalo civil society and local politics. Thus, during the mid-nineteenth century, the Irish became more isolated and nationalistic, while the Germans became more integrated into Buffalo society.

The African American population in Buffalo was relatively small during this time. In 1850 there were roughly three hundred black residents in the city; this number grew to approximately seven hundred in the decades following the Civil War. The African American community in Buffalo was largely comprised of free blacks—those who had come to Buffalo through Canada or who were born free and came to Buffalo to find work on the Erie Canal. The black community, along with the Irish and the Germans, lived on the east side of town, mostly in enclaves within the German-dominated Fifth, Sixth, and Seventh Wards. Blacks maintained a small but vibrant community with two churches and one school, and during the Civil War free blacks and sympa-thetic whites maintained stops on the Underground Railroad.

Though the abolitionist movement was strong in Buffalo, racism still existed in the city. Tensions were particularly high between the black community and the Irish community, and many native whites also held low opinions of African Americans. This was due in part to the labor politics of Buffalo, as well as the fact that the native-born population blamed the increas-ing crime, poverty, and lax morals in the city on the black and immigrant communities alike. The native-born population also believed pseudoscientific ideas that white people were innately superior to African Americans. Thus, during the mid-nineteenth century, Buffalo was highly segregated along racial and economic lines and rife with racial and class tension.

Despite these tensions, however, by 1877 Buffalo was poised to become a great industrial city. It had the Erie Canal and railroads, a large labor force, and a burgeoning industrial base. In the mid-1870s, Buffalo resident Frank H. Goodyear began opening vast tracts of timber, coal, and iron ore in Pennsylvania that would spur major industrialization in Buffalo. As a result,

Buffalo in the last quarter of the nineteenth century experienced tremendous growth, positioning it to emerge as a prominent urban center in twentieth-century America.

See also *Buffalo, NY 1877–1896*

AMY WIDESTROM

BIBLIOGRAPHY

Cotter, John V., and Larry L. Patrick. "Disease and Ethnicity in an Urban Environment." *Annals of the Association of American Geographers* 71, no. 1 (March 1981): 40–49.

Goldman, Mark. *High Hopes: The Rise and Decline of Buffalo, New York.* Albany: State University of New York Press, 1983.

Gredel, Stephen. "People of Our City and County." In *Adventures in Western New York.* Vol. 13. Buffalo, NY: Buffalo and Erie County Historical Society, 1971. Available online at http://bechsed.nylearns. org/pdf/low/People%20of%20our%20City%20and%20County.pdf.

Hill, Henry Wayland. *Municipality of Buffalo, New York: A History 1720–1923.* Vol. 1. New York, NY: Lewis Historical Publishing Company, Inc., 1923.

Merrill, Horace Samuel. *Bourbon Leader: Grover Cleveland and the Democratic Party.* Boston, MA: Little, Brown Co., 1957.

Nevins, Allan. *Grover Cleveland: a Study in Courage.* New York, NY: Dodd, Mead & Co., 1934.

Rizzo, Michael, comp. "Through the Mayors' Eyes: the Only Complete History of the Mayors of Buffalo, New York." *The Buffalonian.* Available online at www.buffalonian.com/history/industry/mayors/ index.html (accessed June 16, 2011).

Smith, H. Perry. *History of the City of Buffalo and Erie County.* Vol. 2. Syracuse, NY: D. Mason & Co. Publishers, 1884.

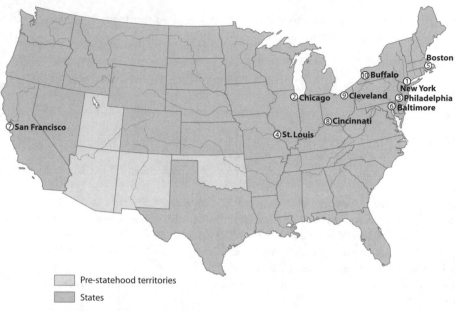

Pre-statehood territories

States

Includes states, territories, and population rankings as of 1890

CITIES IN THE GILDED AGE, 1877–1896

The year 1877 is known to historians as one of the most violent in American history. It marked the formal end of Reconstruction, providing white Southerners a new freedom to intimidate blacks; the acme of the depression of the 1870s; and the first nationwide strike, in which several cities became battlegrounds between workers and the National Guard. And while the economy recovered in the 1880s, by the end of the period, in 1896, the country was once again in the grips of a depression more severe than that of the 1870s. The era was marked as well by the publication of Englishman James Bryce's influential treatise *American Commonwealth* (1888), in which he announced that "There is no denying that the government of cities is the one conspicuous failure of the United States."

Every decade of the late nineteenth century saw an increasing rate of population growth nationally and an increasing proportion of the population living in urban places. The cities covered in this chapter (including Brooklyn, counted here as part of New York, though it was still an independent city) included within their borders nearly 10 percent of the total U.S. population in 1880 and nearly 11 percent in 1890. By 1896 approximately 38 percent of the seventy million people in

CHAPTER 5

282

the country lived in urban places. "Urban places" are defined by the census as anywhere with a population over twenty-five hundred; the smallest city covered in this chapter, Buffalo, had a population of 255,664 in 1890. By 1896 Chicago, Illinois; Philadelphia, Pennsylvania; and New York City, all had populations in excess of one million people.

The westward growth of the country was reflected in the rising populations of San Francisco, California, and Chicago and highlighted by the choice of Chicago to host the 1893 world's fair, which celebrated the four-hundredth anniversary of Christopher Columbus's arrival in America. The Columbian Exposition drew record-breaking crowds and was notable, among other reasons, for the extensive use of a new technology, electric lighting, and for historian Frederick Jackson Turner's lecture, in which he announced the closing of the western frontier and a new stage in American development.

The unsettled West had always offered freedom from wage labor, and its disappearance thus represented a new age of proletarianization and class conflict. In the late 1870s, the Knights of Labor (K of L) was the largest workers' organization, yet it was rapidly eclipsed by the American Federation of Labor (AFL), founded in 1881. The K of L began as a clandestine organization in 1869, went public in the 1870s, and expanded rapidly in the 1880s. While the K of L welcomed all workers and espoused a socialist philosophy, the AFL was a confederation of trade unions with the practical mission of gaining its members better wages and working conditions.

Labor-related clashes at Haymarket Square in Chicago in 1886, in Homestead (a borough close to Pittsburgh) in 1892, and in Pullman (a town near Chicago) in 1894 illustrate the nature of class conflict in the late nineteenth century. The Haymarket case involved a demonstration in conjunction with the AFL's call for a nationwide strike for an eight-hour workday. A bomb was thrown at police attempting to forcibly disperse the crowd, killing seven officers and injuring scores more. The police opened fire, killing four demonstrators. Eight anarchists were tried for the bombing in a notoriously unfair trial, seven of whom received death sentences.

The image of anarchist bombers burdened labor organizers, hurting especially the K of L. For that and other reasons, the organization had all but disappeared by the time of the Homestead strike, which involved workers at a steel mill owned by Andrew Carnegie. The workers struck over wage reductions, and Carnegie hired the notoriously brutal Pinkerton Detective Agency to protect the workers hired in place of those striking. After a deadly battle with the striking workers that involved guns and dynamite, the Pinkertons retreated in defeat. Yet the workers' victory was short-lived, as the governor of Pennsylvania brought in the National Guard to protect the replacement workers.

Pullman was both a company that manufactured railroad cars and a town owned almost entirely by the company. As the economy sank in 1893, the company cut wages, but it did not cut the rents it charged workers in the town. The workers responded by striking and allied themselves with the American Railway Union (ARU), whose members refused to work on trains with Pullman cars, thus halting a large portion of the nation's rail traffic. When the governor of Illinois refused to send in state militia to resolve the conflict, President Grover Cleveland sent in federal troops to protect nonunionized replacement workers, and the ARU leadership was arrested and jailed for defying a court order to end the strike, which collapsed as a result.

BY THE NUMBERS: THE MOST POPULOUS CITIES IN 1890

	TOTAL POPULATION	WHITE POPULATION	"COLORED" POPULATION	OTHER POPULATION	% WHITE POPULATION	% "COLORED" POPULATION	% OTHER POPULATION	PERCENT OF THE POPULATION 10+ EMPLOYED IN MANUFACTURING	VALUE OF MANUFACTURED PRODUCTS	% OF THE POPULATION FOREIGN-BORN
NEW YORK, NY	1,515,301	1,489,627	23,601	2,073	98.3	1.6	0.1	29.3	$ 777,222,721	42.2
CHICAGO, IL	1,099,850	1,084,998	14,271	581	98.6	1.3	0.1	25.0	$ 664,587,923	41.0
PHILADELPHIA, PA	1,046,964	1,006,590	39,371	1,003	96.1	3.8	0.1	30.7	$ 577,234,446	25.7
ST. LOUIS, MO	451,770	424,704	26,865	201	94.0	5.9	0.0	26.6	$ 229,157,343	25.4
BOSTON, MA	448,477	439,887	8,125	465	98.1	1.8	0.1	24.4	$ 210,936,616	35.3
BALTIMORE, MD	434,439	367,143	67,104	192	84.5	15.4	0.0	24.4	$ 141,723,599	15.9
SAN FRANCISCO, CA	298,997	270,696	1,847	26,454	90.5	0.6	8.8	19.2	$ 135,625,754	42.4
CINCINNATI, OH	296,908	285,224	11,655	29	96.1	3.9	0.0	41.1	$ 196,063,983	24.1
CLEVELAND, OH	261,353	258,318	2,989	46	98.8	1.1	0.0	25.2	$ 113,240,115	37.2
BUFFALO, NY	255,664	254,495	1,118	51	99.5	0.4	0.0	26.5	$ 100,052,208	35.0

	% OF THE POPULATION LITERATE	LAND AREA (SQ. MI.)	POPULATION DENSITY (PER SQ. MI.)	PARKS AS A % OF AREA	SEWER (MILES)	SALOONS	SALOONS PER 1,000 PEOPLE	TRAINS TO AND FROM THE CITY DAILY	STREET RAILWAY (LENGTH OF ALL TRACKS IN MILES)	AVG. NUMBER OF RIDES PER INHABITANT
NEW YORK, NY	92.3	40.2	37,675.0	19.8	464	7,579	5.0	1135	377.4	297
CHICAGO, IL	95.4	160.6	6,849.6	0.9	525	5,200	4.7	448	390.3	164
PHILADELPHIA, PA	95.0	129.4	8,091.8	3.7	370	1,203	1.1	636	351.1	158
ST. LOUIS, MO	94.1	61.4	7,361.6	5.4	328	1,600	3.5	179	192.5	150
BOSTON, MA	94.3	37.9	11,845.4	4.7	291	595	1.3	854	305.8	225
BALTIMORE, MD	90.2	29.5	14,736.9	4.6	(x)	1,900	4.4	159	156.6	94
SAN FRANCISCO, CA	94.7	42.2	7,087.3	5.1	193	2,900	9.7	369	156.2	270
CINCINNATI, OH	95.7	23.2	12,809.8	3.6	98	2,090	7.0	162	122.2	128
CLEVELAND, OH	93.5	24.9	10,504.7	0.6	146	1,300	5.0	38	158.9	150
BUFFALO, NY	94.6	39.0	6,549.7	2.6	219	1,997	7.8	126	66.3	65

Note: (x) indicates that no data was available.

Note: This list does not include Brooklyn, NY. See introduction for details.

Source: Report on Vital and Social Statistics in the United States at the Eleventh Census: 1890. Part II - Vital Statistics. Cities of 100,000 Population and Upward.

Grover Cleveland was the first Democrat to serve as president after the Civil War and the last to serve before the Democrats moved in a populist direction, as evidenced by the nomination of William Jennings Bryan in 1896. This nomination had the overall effect of diminishing, and shifting westward, the party's electoral support. After the end of Reconstruction, the two major parties were practically indistinguishable on policy grounds, though they divided the country roughly equally. Democratic support was strongest in the South and among the working class and immigrants in big cities in the North, and Republican support was strongest among middle-class Protestants in the North.

Presidents during the nineteenth century were relatively powerless in relation to Congress, though they did have an immense patronage responsibility, with authority over nearly one hundred thousand federal appointments. To ease the patronage burden, Rutherford Hayes attempted to establish a federal civil service, replacing some of the presidential appointments with a competitive examination system, but he failed to get Congress interested in the initiative. When the next president, James Garfield, was shot and killed by a mentally unstable man who had been denied a federal position, Congress finally saw fit to establish a civil service in 1883.

In 1884 Cleveland, a former New York governor with reform instincts, was elected president. He pushed for a lower tariff, and, in response, the Republican presidential candidate in 1888, Benjamin Harrison, campaigned on the basis of establishing a higher tariff in order to protect domestic industries against imports. Harrison won the majority of electoral votes and thus became president, although Cleveland won the popular vote. Congressional Republicans followed through on the higher tariff, with disastrous electoral results. In 1890 the Republicans lost their majorities in both the House and Senate, and in 1892 the presidency went once again to Cleveland.

Democratic electoral success was short-lived, however. As his second administration commenced, Cleveland confronted a stock market collapse in 1893, followed by the closure of thousands of businesses and mass unemployment. With their electoral prospects thus looking dim for the 1896 election, Democrats from states in the South and West were eager to absorb much of the platform of the People's Party, known as the populists, an alliance formed from farmer organizations in the West and South. The People's Party supported greater regulation of railroads, an inflationary monetary policy, and other measures designed to help agricultural regions. The populists ran a candidate for president in 1892 and succeeded in electing their members to the House, Senate, three governorships, and many state legislative seats, yet their party platform put it at odds with industrial and business interests in the North. This made the choice of a presidential nominee in 1896 a divisive one for Democrats. The populists prevailed with the nomination of William Jennings Bryan, though they were badly defeated in the general election. Republicans won every state in the highly populated (and vote-rich) northeastern states, and no Democrat won the presidency again until Woodrow Wilson's election in 1912.

NEW YORK, NY 1877–1896

THE FINAL DECADES OF THE NINETEENTH CENTURY IN NEW YORK were defined by Democratic control (though with factional feuding), a resurgent economy after the 1870s that was once again brought down by a panic and depression in the 1890s, and typically explosive population growth that was fueled in large part by immigration. New York was the first American city to reach a population of more than one million by the late 1870s, and it had a population of approximately 1.5 million by 1890, the number of residents having increased by more than 50 percent in twenty years. In Brooklyn the population had more than doubled, totaling 806,343 in 1890. Two of the most significant events for the city in the 1890s were the financial collapse of 1893 and the referendum in 1894, in which voters in New York City and surrounding municipalities voted on whether they would like to be included in a "Greater New York." The voters approved the measure in 1894, the legislature finalized a consolidation plan in 1896, and Greater New York came into being in 1898.

MAYORS

Smith Ely Jr.	(1877–1878)
Edward Cooper	(1879–1880)
William Russell Grace	(1881–1882)
Franklin Edson	(1883–1884)
William Russell Grace	(1885–1886)
Abram S. Hewitt	(1887–1888)
Hugh L. Grant	(1889–1892)
Thomas F. Gilroy	(1893–1894)
William L. Strong	(1895–1897)

MAJOR INDUSTRIES AND EMPLOYERS

Banking and finance
Manufacturing (garments, sugar
   refining, pianos, cigars)
Publishing and advertising
Shipping and trade
Legal firms

MAJOR NEWSPAPERS

City Record
Evening Telegram
Evening World (later the *New York
   World-Telegram*)
Hotel Reporter
L'Eco d'Italia
Las Novedades
Le Courrier des Etats-Unis
New York Daily News
New York Herald
New York Times
New Yorker Staats-Zeitung (later the
   *New Yorker Staats-Zeitung und
   Herold*)
New Yorker Volkszeitung (later the *Neue Volks-Zeitung*)
Wall Street Journal
World
Yiddisches Tageblatt (later *Der Morgen Zhurnal and Yidishes
   Tageblat*)
Yudishe Gazeten

MAJOR EVENTS

1885: Construction of the New Croton Aqueduct begins in 1885, and it is in service by 1890, tripling the amount of water piped into New York.

1892: The federal government establishes a new immigration processing station on Ellis Island in New York Harbor, thus replacing the New York State immigration depot in Manhattan. Ellis Island becomes the busiest immigration center in the country.

1893: Declines in domestic prices for farm goods, in railroad expansion, and in other forms of construction combine with a financial crisis in England to lead to a financial "panic" in the United States. This panic leads to massive business closures and sustained unemployment. As New York City is a leading financial and manufacturing center, its residents and businesses are hit particularly hard by the recession.

1894: Following the advice of the state Consolidation Inquiry Commission, residents in New York City and the surrounding communities vote on whether they would like to be included in a "Greater New York." The measure is approved by a majority of approximately 55 percent. The legislature thus drafted a consolidation bill in 1896 that authorized nine commissioners, appointed by Governor Levi P. Morton, to draft a charter for the new city. The resultant charter, approved by the legislature in 1897, created the five-borough system that is still in place today.

1894: The New York State senate establishes a committee to investigate corruption in the New York City Police Department. The Lexow Committee, as it came to be known, reveals widespread corruption and leads to a new wave of reform, including the election of William Strong as mayor.

GOVERNMENT AND POLITICS

After the fall of the Tweed Ring in the early 1870s, John Kelly became the acknowledged "boss" of the preeminent Democratic organization in the city, Tammany Hall. Under Kelly's control, Tammany became a more disciplined outfit, though it by no means held a political monopoly. Kelly also served as city controller from 1876 to 1880, in which role he is generally credited with creating sound fiscal policy and reducing the city's debt. Under his direction, Tammany delegates broke with upstate Democrats by withdrawing their support for Governor Lucius Robinson's renomination in 1879, opting instead to nominate Kelly to run for governor. The purpose of this was to split the Democratic vote in the general election so that Robinson, with whom Kelly was feuding, would lose. The plan was successful, and Republican Alonzo Cornell was elected governor. Under Cornell, New York cast its electoral votes for Republican James Garfield in the presidential election of 1880—an outcome for which Kelly was blamed. Indeed, angered by Kelly's maneuvering at the state level, Mayor Edward Cooper refused to reappoint him controller.

By 1880 there were two main Democratic rivals to Tammany Hall in New York: Irving Hall and the New York County Democracy, otherwise known as the Swallowtails. Irving Hall had been formed by John Morrissey, who had been expelled from Tammany in 1875 for a lack of discipline. Morrissey, however, went on to beat a Tammany candidate for a state legislative seat in the same year. Morrissey died in 1878, but Irving Hall remained a headquarters for powerful Democrats estranged from Tammany, including Samuel Tilden. The New York County Democracy was organized in 1880 by industrialist Abram Hewitt and others, in large part in reaction to Kelly's role in the election of President Garfield in 1880. The three organizations united in 1882 to nominate, and successfully elect, merchant Franklin Edson as mayor.

Kelly suffered a nervous breakdown in 1884 and died in 1886, and his close associate Richard Croker quickly established himself as Tammany's new boss. In 1886 Henry George, author of the popular classic *Progress and Poverty* (1879), joined forces with the city's labor movement and ran for mayor on the United Labor Party ticket. Tammany allegedly tried to buy George off with a nomination to another office, and, when that failed, joined with the New York County Democracy to nominate the highly respected Hewitt to run for mayor. The Republicans nominated a young Theodore Roosevelt, who came in third place behind George and Hewitt. Hewitt won the election, though George supporters claimed that their candidate would have won in the absence of widespread electoral fraud.

With the economic slump of the 1870s finally over, Mayor Hewitt announced in 1888 an ambitious plan for a coordinated system of public works and improvements, including a proposal to create a publicly owned underground passenger rail system. Hewitt, whose nativism angered many of the Democrats' ethnic supporters, failed to get reelected in 1888. He lost to Tammany candidate Hugh Grant, who became the city's first Catholic mayor. Yet Hewitt's call for a coordinated system of public works was in part responsible for passage of the 1891 Rapid Transit Act, generally credited as the legal basis upon which the city's modern subway system was constructed, and for a new push toward the consolidation of New York with surrounding municipalities into a single city.

The idea for a consolidated city was pursued most vigorously by Andrew Haswell Green, former city controller and Central Park commissioner. Largely due to Green's efforts, the state legislature created the Consolidation Inquiry Commission in 1890, which proposed that Greater New York include the Town of Westchester and portions of the Towns of Eastchester and Pelham in Westchester County; the Towns of Flushing, Jamaica, Jamaica Bay, Newtown, part of the Town of Hempstead and Long Island City in Queens County; the Towns of Flatbush, Flatlands, Gravesend, New Utrecht and Jamaica Bay and the City of Brooklyn in Kings County; and the Towns of Castleton, Middletown, Northfield, Southfield and Westfield on Staten Island. The legislature approved a referendum on consolidation in 1894 in all the areas proposed for inclusion in Greater New York. In total, approximately 55 percent voted in favor of consolidation. Staten Island showed the greatest support, with 79 percent voting in the positive. In Queens County, 62 percent of the total vote was in favor of consolidation, although the Town of Flushing voted by 55 percent against the measure. In New York City, the vote was 58 percent in favor of consolidation. In Kings County, consolidation won with only a 277-vote lead, or less than 1 percent of the total vote, with most of the opposition coming from the City of Brooklyn. In Westchester County, the Town of Westchester registered a majority of one vote against consolidation, while the Towns of Pelham and Eastchester voted in favor of consolidation by 62 and 59 percent, respectively.

The referendum itself was vaguely worded, so the meaning of the majority vote is unclear, though there were pretty obvious reasons in some places why residents would want to be part of a larger city. In Long Island City, for instance, the municipal government was so notoriously corrupt that residents were clearly looking for an alternative. By the time of the referendum vote, which Long Island City residents overwhelmingly approved, the city had a massive debt and a correspondingly high tax rate.

In Brooklyn, the only reason that a slim majority of voters approved of the referendum was because three outlying towns that had been annexed to the city earlier in 1894—Flatbush, Gravesend, and New Utrecht—provided large majorities for consolidation. Still, the city had its problems—namely a high tax rate—that many residents obviously hoped would be alleviated by joining Greater New York. Advocates for Greater New York argued that consolidation would equalize taxes between New York and Brooklyn, lowering Brooklyn's tax rate in the process.

In New York itself, by the time of the referendum vote, Irving Hall and the New York County Democracy had dwindled away, as had the United Labor Party, which succumbed to internal feuding. Increasing charges of fraud and corruption in the city, combined with the strength of a Republican reform coalition after 1893, provided the state legislature with the political power to form an investigative committee in 1894, known generally by the name of its chair, Clarence Lexow. The Lexow Committee spent almost a full year collecting testimony from hundreds of witnesses and exposed widespread electoral fraud, police abuse, and kickbacks for every kind of government transaction, including bribes for operating gambling houses and brothels, obtaining government employment, and awarding franchises and contracts.

The Lexow hearings provided the impetus for the formation of a new elite reform organization, the Committee of Seventy, which ran wealthy banker and stalwart Republican William Strong for mayor in 1894—the same year that the consolidation referendum was also on the ballot. Tammany ran Hugh Grant for mayor again, and he was beaten soundly by Strong. As mayor, one of Strong's most successful moves was to appoint well-known sanitation engineer and Civil War veteran George Waring as head of the Department of Street Cleaning. Waring implemented a strict code of conduct and ruthless oversight to the city's street cleaners, with the result that city streets became dramatically cleaner. Waring even instituted a mandatory household recycling program in 1896.

Though select areas had voted by majorities against the measure in 1894, the entire area originally proposed as Greater New York was included in the final consolidation bill that passed the legislature and was signed by Governor Levi P. Morton in May of 1896. The state Republican boss, Thomas C. Platt, conceived that the creation of Greater New York under Republican auspices would enhance the power and prestige of his party and himself and possibly create a Republican-majority city. Platt's opposition came from Mayor Strong of New York and Mayor Wurster of Brooklyn, as well as organized groups from the Towns of Flushing, Jamaica, and Hempstead in Queens. The state constitution granted the mayors of New York and Brooklyn veto powers over bills affecting their cities, which they used against the 1896 consolidation bill. However, Platt was able to get enough votes in the legislature to override the mayoral vetoes. The 1896 consolidation bill authorized nine commissioners, appointed by Governor Morton, to draft a charter for the new city. The charter passed the 1897 legislature, once again over the veto of New York's Mayor Strong, and Greater New York came into existence in 1898.

INDUSTRY, COMMERCE, AND LABOR

By 1879 the depression was over and a new wave of railroad speculation had begun, leading ultimately to another series of bank collapses and a panic in 1884, though one that was not followed by a deep recession. After the panic of 1884, John Pierpont Morgan emerged as New York's (and the country's) preeminent banker. In the 1880s and 1890s, as New York further cemented its role as the banking center of the country, corporate headquarters, especially those of the railroads and the new industrial holding companies, began to move to New York in increasing numbers in order to have better access to capital. Along with corporations and banks, New York also became a center for the legal profession, especially, and not surprisingly, corporate law. Responding to an increasingly national press, the number of advertising agencies increased dramatically as well, from some forty firms in the 1870s to more than four hundred during the 1890s.

The increase in economic fortunes also revived the city's labor movement. The largest union during this period became the formerly clandestine Knights of Labor, which reached its highest membership ever in 1886 and was a major force behind the mayoral campaign of Henry George. The Knights of Labor was an ideologically socialist organization that included both skilled and unskilled workers and was a mix of Protestants, Catholics, both genders, and all racial groups. The influential cigar makers' union, on the other hand, led by Samuel Gompers, was designed as a business, collecting dues in order to deliver specific benefits to its members such as higher wages and shorter hours. It dispensed with any pretense of an ideology, and, as its name suggests, was strictly a craft union.

Many of the unions in the Knights of Labor also affiliated themselves with an umbrella organization, the Central Labor Union (CLU), which was organized in 1882 and by 1886 had more than two hundred member organizations. In 1886 the CLU was able to orchestrate a citywide transit strike involving tens of thousands of workers. The biggest strike of that year, however, was on May 1, when some forty-five thousand workers walked off their jobs as part of a nationwide general strike in support of an eight-hour workday. It was in 1886 as well that the Knights of Labor attempted to intervene in the midst of a cigar makers' strike, offering the cigar manufacturers a lower-wage agreement if the manufacturers recognized a competitor cigar makers' union. In response, a national convention of craft unions, held in Columbus, Ohio, organized into the American Federation of Labor (AFL). Samuel Gompers was elected president, a position he held for twenty years. As the AFL increased in size, it eclipsed the rapidly declining Knights of Labor.

Unionization suffered a severe blow with the economic crash of 1893 and the ensuing recession that defined the rest of the 1890s. The recession had its origins in London, though it was certainly helped by overspeculation fueled by New York's bankers, combined as well with declining prices for farm goods and declines in domestic manufacturing levels. In both New York and Brooklyn, tens of thousands were left unemployed as thousands of companies and hundreds of banks collapsed and went out of business.

RACE, ETHNICITY, AND IMMIGRATION

During the 1880s, the number of immigrants arriving in the United States nearly doubled from the previous decade, and their main point of arrival was New York City. Some of the newer immigrant groups, such as Italians, Eastern European Jews, and Chinese, were the subjects of journalist Jacob Riis's famous account of tenement life in *How the Other Half Lives* (1890). Riis's descriptions were hardly generous, as evidenced in his claim that "With all his conspicuous faults, the swarthy Italian immigrant has his redeeming traits . . . . The Italian is gay, lighthearted and, if his fur is not stroked the wrong way, inoffensive as a child."

The federal government took over the job of processing immigrants in New York, establishing a center for the Bureau of Immigration on Ellis Island in 1892. In its first year of operation, the center processed almost half a million new arrivals. The greatest numbers of immigrants in the 1880s were from Germany, where farmers, farm workers, and artisans were being pushed out by industrialization and agricultural commercialization. By 1890 the German-born population in New York City totaled 210,723 and was concentrated in the *Kleindeutschland* neighborhood on the south side of Manhattan, below Fourteenth Street. Brooklyn also had a large German population, concentrated most notably in Williamsburg.

Another notable wave of immigrants to New York consisted of East European Jews, many of whom were forcibly pushed out of their homelands. These arrivals were not particularly large in number nationally, but a disproportionate amount arrived and stayed in the city. By the early 1890s, there were more than 170,000 Eastern European Jews in New York, causing some consternation among the city's established, more upper-class and culturally distinct German Jewish population. However, since German Jews had to a great extent taken over the city's large garment industry, they found the newer Eastern European arrivals a good source of cheap labor.

Despite the fact that German immigration was nationally nearly twice the level of Irish immigration during the 1880s, the Irish were the largest group of foreign-born residents in New York, representing approximately 12 percent of the city's total population. There were significant concentrations of Irish in the Hell's Kitchen neighborhood, which was located on the western side of New York proper, and also in the Navy Yard and Red Hook neighborhoods of Brooklyn. The city's black population continued to slowly expand as well, though not so much that they ever increased their overall percentage of total city population. By 1900 black residents of both Brooklyn and New York represented only 2 percent of the total populations of both cities combined.

Italians, especially from southern Italy, started to arrive in substantial numbers in the 1880s and 1890s and became a significant presence in many sectors of the unskilled labor force—taking the place of the Irish. Italians were recruited to work on the docks by bosses during strikes by the predominantly Irish longshoremen. Lastly, though they were relatively small in numbers, Chinese immigrants were a visible and distinct presence in the city. Indeed, it was during the 1880s that a distinct Chinatown came into existence in lower Manhattan, centered on Mott Street. While the city's Chinese population was still small (though official counts are likely inaccurate), it dominated the laundry industry after taking it over from Irish women who had been demanding higher wages. One of the most socially isolated communities that suffered both official and unofficial discrimination, the Chinese community organized its own quasi-local government, an organization incorporated in 1890 as the Chinese Consolidated Benevolent Association.

See also *New York, NY 1776–1790; New York, NY 1790–1828; New York, NY 1828–1854; New York, NY 1854–1877; New York, NY 1896–1929; New York, NY 1929–1941; New York, NY 1941–1952; New York, NY 1952–1989; New York, NY 1989–2011*

RICHARDSON DILWORTH

BIBLIOGRAPHY

Beckert, Sven. *The Monied Metropolis: New York City and the Consolidation of the American Bourgeosie, 1850–1896*. New York, NY: Cambridge University Press, 1993.

Burrows, Edwin G., and Mike Wallace. *Gotham: A History of New York City to 1898*. New York, NY: Oxford University Press, 1999.

Hammack, David C. *Power and Society: Greater New York at the Turn of the Century*. New York, NY: Russell Sage Foundation, 1982.

Henschel, Albert E. *Municipal Consolidation: Historical Sketch of the Greater New York*. New York, NY: Press of Stettiner, Labert and Co., 1895.

Homberger, Eric. *Mrs. Astor's New York: Money and Social Power in a Gilded Age*. New Haven, CT: Yale University Press, 2002.

Riis, Jacob A. *How the Other Half Lives: Studies Among the Tenements of New York*. New York, NY: Charles Scribner's Sons, 1890.

Syrett, Harold Coffin. *The City of Brooklyn, 1865–1898: A Political History*. New York, NY: AMS Press, 1968.

CHICAGO, IL 1877–1896

CHICAGO EMERGED FROM THE CIVIL WAR AND THE GREAT FIRE OF 1871 and undertook its greatest period of expansion—capitalizing on its geographical location as a midway point between the finance capital of the East and the supply of raw materials in the nation's Midwest and West. In these years the city saw a population explosion, fueled by the arrival of hundreds of thousands of immigrant laborers who took up jobs in the industrializing economy. While poverty and labor unrest plagued the era, the World's Columbian Exposition of 1893 demonstrated the aspirations of what had become (behind New York) the nation's "second city."

GOVERNMENT AND POLITICS

Due to the explosion of its population from three hundred thousand in 1870 to 1.7 million in 1900, Chicago's government and politics in this period were defined by the rapidly expanding demands placed on city services such as the provision of clean water, sewerage, fire and police protection, as well as the struggle to assimilate immigrants and the demands of organized labor into the political culture.

The Great Chicago Fire of 1871, though it claimed three hundred lives and horrified the nation, did not slow the city's economic growth. The fire did clear the downtown of many wooden and masonry structures. With rising property values in a concentrated downtown commercial district (know as the "Loop"), architects and developers began looking for ways to do more with less land. The result was the first modern skyline in the world, as Chicago hosted the rise of the skyscraper in these years. Sharp political debates in the years after the 1871 fire left a legacy of concern over how to control the built environment of the city. While advocates of brick over wooden construction won rhetorical battles with regards to safety, they lost the war as the city continued to see wooden-frame construction and a lack of zoning whereby industrial, residential, and commercial districts rose in close proximity. Construction was good business and therefore good politics in Chicago in the late 1800s.

Despite the continued use of wood in building construction, William Le Baron Jenney's Home Insurance Building, erected in 1885, led the way in demonstrating the use of structural iron and steel rather than wood or masonry. The "Chicago School" of architecture evolved around the works of Louis Sullivan and Dankmar Adler, with the Auditorium Building, constructed in 1889, recognized as a masterpiece of the period. John Wellborn Root and Daniel H. Burnham became famous for their high-rise buildings, especially the Montauk Block in 1880 and the Rookery in 1886.

Neither Republicans nor Democrats managed to create a durable political machine in these years, in large part because of the power of the aldermen who comprised the city council and the corresponding weakness of the mayor's office. Another factor was the shifting power bases in a city undergoing such rapid expansion. Democratic mayor Carter Harrison Sr. held on to power longer than any other mayor in the era. Harrison eagerly courted the immigrant vote, campaigning in

QUICK FACTS

CHICAGO, IL **1877–1896**

MAYORS

Monroe Heath	(1876–1879)
Carter Harrison Sr.	(1879–1887)
John A. Roche	(1887–1889)
DeWitt Clinton Creiger	(1889–1891)
Hempstead Washburne	(1891–1893)
Carter Harrison Sr.	(1893)
(assassinated in office)	
George Bell Swift	(1893)
(mayor pro tempore)	
John Patrick Hopkins	(1893–1895)
George Bell Swift	(1895–1897)

MAJOR INDUSTRIES AND EMPLOYERS

Agricultural implements
Textiles
Construction
Electrical machinery
Meatpacking
Printing and publishing
Railroad and streetcar manufacturing and
  repair
Iron and steel manufacturing

MAJOR NEWSPAPERS

Chicago Daily News
Chicago Herald
Chicago Inter-Ocean
Chicago Journal
Chicago Republican
Chicago Times
Chicago Tribune

MAJOR EVENTS

1877: A major railroad strike, the first major national labor action, affects numerous cities, including Chicago.

1886: A bomb is thrown in Haymarket Square during a protest march. The incident was blamed on political anarchists who were convicted in a show trial. Several years later the surviving accused were pardoned.

1893: Chicago hosts the World's Columbian Exposition, the greatest world's fair of the era, which served as a showcase for Chicago's meteoric rise.

October 28, 1893: Popular mayor Carter Harrison Sr. is assassinated by Patrick Eugene Prendergast, a disgruntled job seeker.

1894: Labor unrest hits the "model" planned industrial community of Pullman, built by the railroad car manufacturer south of Chicago.

immigrant neighborhoods and speaking the languages of his supporters. He took a lax attitude towards alcohol sales in the city and encouraged saloons and brothels to operate in the South Side "Levee" vice district. Harrison also supported organized labor and showed reluctance towards the use of police power in breaking strikes. Reelected in time for the 1893 World's Columbian Exposition, an event he promoted with great enthusiasm as a showcase for the city and an economic growth generator, Harrison was assassinated in his home in 1893 by a man seeking a city job. Half a million people lined the streets during Harrison's funeral procession.

Republicans were generally divided between staunch reformers who wanted to crack down on drinking in the city and were critical of immigrant ethnic culture and more "pragmatic," tolerant Republicans. Chicago Republicans built a power base around Cook County congressman William Lorimer, who actively sought immigrant Catholic support.

Corruption in the city council was widespread in this era and centered on the lucrative awarding of public contracts to private real estate developers and construction firms organized by the so-called Gray Wolves, in particular First Ward alderman "Bathhouse" John Coughlin. The prerogatives of the city council over construction and the use of patronage in filling city positions made Chicago notorious in these years for lax and unreliable building code and fire code inspections.

The population growth of the city was matched by growth in land area as well. A citywide election in 1889 authorized the annexation of Hyde Park, Jefferson, Lake, and Lake View townships, adding 125 square miles to the city along with 225,000 new citizens. This expansion moved Chicago into first place among cities by geographic area and second in population, ahead of Philadelphia, Pennsylvania.

INDUSTRY, COMMERCE, AND LABOR

This period was undoubtedly the greatest era of innovation and industrialization in Chicago's history. Major manufacturing companies opened in the city, serving as magnets for immigrant workers from Europe and the American South. Innovations in science and technology emerged in transportation, manufacturing methods, materials, and retailing.

The role of Chicago as a national hub for transshipment was cemented in these years, as the transcontinental railroad network expanded. With raw materials flowing in from the farms and forests of the Midwest, Chicago was also growing into a dynamic manufacturing hub. One major industry of the period was meatpacking, with the Armour and Swift companies being the largest. This industry utilized continuous process manufacturing—featuring a moving assembly line—a method that would be replicated by the auto industry in the twentieth century.

The manufacturing of farm implements was also a major industry, epitomized by the McCormick Harvesting Machine Company and its network of sales and service distributors throughout the Midwest. The electrical industry emerged in these years, marked by the creation of an electric grid and electric street traction. Major entrepreneurs in this industry were Samuel Insull and Charles Tyson Yerkes. Electrification brought light to the city and made possible a tremendous wave of consumer product innovation, including Edison phonographs, Westinghouse lamps, Bell telephones, and electric irons. Railroad car manufacturing grew enormously; just south of the city George Pullman established a "model town" around his Pullman Palace Car Company. The town housed his four thousand workers in 1880.

In the realm of retailing, Chicago witnessed a revolution in catalog ordering houses, led by Montgomery Ward and Sears Roebuck. With their catalogs going out to farm households across the country, these companies built systems to fill and deliver orders thousands of miles away from Chicago—a consumer revolution for customers who wanted the goods of the city but could not afford the trip.

In the city, shopping became centralized in department stores, with Marshall Field's leading the way. This "palace of consumption" featured childcare and entertainment and carefully cultivated upper-class trappings for middle- and working-class shoppers who saw a trip to the department store as recreation. Legions of young women—working as secretaries in the offices of the Loop and clerks in the burgeoning retail trade—shopped and ate lunch in the new commercial core of the city.

Labor union organization proceeded rapidly, especially in the railroad industry. The national railroad strike of 1877 hit Chicago in late July of that year, with railroad workers walking off the job. They were also joined by workers in other industries. At least eighteen people died in clashes between strikers and police. With the founding of the Knights of Labor, Chicago workers of all genders and skill levels organized in great numbers. The movement spawned newspapers, cooperative associations, and a political party, the United Labor Party.

In 1886 eighty-eight thousand laborers staged over three hundred strikes for an eight-hour workday. Following rallies held on May 1, the general strike resulted in violence at the McCormick plant, with police firing at strikers and killing two. On May 4 at the West Randolph Street Haymarket, anarchists assembled a protest meeting. A bomb was thrown at police, killing one, and the police returned fire into the crowd. When the Haymarket riot was over, eight policemen were dead and sixty were injured. An indeterminate number of protesters were also dead or injured. Mayor Carter Harrison—who had shown support for laborers in his political tenure—cracked down immediately on union protests and assemblies, and a sensational trial followed, with eight anarchists convicted and seven sentenced to death. Four of these were executed before Governor John Peter Altgeld pardoned the rest, citing a complete miscarriage of justice in the trial. The Haymarket episode demonstrated both the radical potential of labor as an organizing political and economic force in the city and the anger and fear directed against this new urban industrial class by owners and managers, the police, and traditional elites. The friction was exacerbated further when employees of the Pullman Company went on strike in 1894. A sympathetic boycott by the American Railway Union slowed rail traffic nationwide and led to a federal injunction and the jailing of union leader Eugene Debs. Pullman's attempts at creating a well-planned and harmonious factory town were destroyed, again demonstrating the conflicts inherent in the rapid industrialization and immigration that were shaping modern Chicago.

The greatest showcase for the city's remarkable economic growth was the World's Columbian Exposition—a display of a "White City" that hosted twenty-seven million visitors in 1893–1894 and was designed and managed by Daniel H. Burnham. So many speeches were delivered and so much ink spilled by Chicago's boosters that New York Sun writer Charles Henry Dana coined it the "windy city." The city's wealthy elites, such as Cyrus McCormick, Charles Yerkes, and Philip Armour, made the fair their cause, subscribing to millions of dollars worth of stock in the enterprise. Such support was necessary as the original budget of $5 million dollars was continually raised, topping out at a final cost of $28 million. This was the renewal of Chicago's image as a commercial and industrial dynamo—the rise of the Phoenix foretold after the great fire and now demonstrated on a stage that attracted a world of visitors.

The nation's foremost architects and builders were brought in for the exposition, among them Frederick Law Olmsted to design the grounds; Dankmar Adler and Louis Sullivan to construct the Transportation Building; William Le Baron Jenney to build the Horticulture Building; and McKim, Mead, and White to construct the Agriculture Building. The structures were

The World's Columbian Exposition, held in Chicago in 1893–1894, attracted millions of visitors who marveled at Daniel Burnham's "White City." Local business elites supported the fair as a way of showcasing the city's might after its miraculous recovery from the devastating fire of 1871.   *Source: Library of Congress*

executed on an enormous scale and built on an extremely tight schedule in order to complete Burnham's grand vision. A workforce of approximately thirteen thousand workmen labored in the spring of 1893 to bring the White City to completion. The only way to complete the buildings on time was to make them impermanent, and this is exactly what Burnham intended to do. Though the exposition was dedicated in front of 125,000 people in October 1892, the grand opening had to wait until May 1, 1893.

The main buildings in the exposition's Court of Honor were situated around the Grand Basin, from which rose the Statue of the Republic, a gilded figure standing one hundred feet high. Behind this was the Peristyle, a group of forty-eight columns representing the states and the territories. Burnham wanted to present a unity in the architecture, which he achieved by setting height limits for the main buildings and utilizing a neoclassical Beaux-Arts motif. Numerous "theme" buildings and attractions intended to take the visitor on a tour of the world were also constructed. Another major attraction was the Ferris wheel, which featured a circumference of 825 feet and lifted fairgoers 250 feet in the air.

The White City vision—like Chicago itself—focused on technology presented on a grand scale. The Manufactures and Liberal Arts Building showcased the use of structural steel in a building that covered forty-four acres. Spectators also saw machinery from around the world and for nearly every conceivable purpose, from textile manufacture to printing to metal working and even firefighting. The technological heart of the White City, however, was most enamored with a force that was rapidly transforming American life in 1893: electricity. The Machinery Building contained the Westinghouse central plant, rumbling with the work of sixteen generators, supplying far more power than was used in the entire Chicago central business district or any other city in the world at the time. General Electric supplied the light for the entire building, more than any visitor had ever seen up to that time.

At night, the spectacle of electricity took center stage. From the earliest planning meetings in 1891, Frederick Law Olmsted had intended to outline the main buildings around the Grand Basin with incandescent lights at night. The plan was elaborated upon, to the point at which the exposition was as much an attraction at nighttime, if not more so, than it was during the day. The American public was still largely unaccustomed to electric light at night, especially such a planned electrical spectacle. The Ferris wheel was also illuminated and searchlights lit up the sky.

The World's Columbian Exposition was the most consequential cultural, architectural, and technological event in the United States in its day, and it served as a utopian foil to the realities of struggle and strife in the real industrializing Chicago that hosted the fair. The money and the innovations that fueled the city also fueled the exposition, but whether or not the real city could rise to Burnham's vision remained an open question in the late nineteenth century.

RACE, ETHNICITY, AND IMMIGRATION

With industrialization at a peak, Chicago saw waves and waves of arriving immigrants enter the city. In fact, it is fair to say that industrializing Chicago was, almost entirely, a city of newcomers. The city's population from its founding in 1837 into the early 1870s was dominated by migrants from New England, the Northeast, Britain, Germany, Ireland, and Scandinavia. The next wave saw Czechs, Italians, Lithuanians, Poles, Serbs, Croats, Greeks, and Chinese arriving in large numbers. Among these immigrants, Judaism, Catholicism, and Eastern Orthodox religions were practiced—religions that were (except for the Irish Catholics) new to the city. By 1890 the population stood at 1.1 million, a remarkable 118 percent leap from 1880, with roughly 40 percent of residents foreign-born. Within a decade the great majority of the city's residents were either foreign-born or the children of immigrants. The African American population remained comparatively small until the "Great Migration" of the 1910s.

Assimilation presented a contentious issue in a city where ethnic identity provided immigrants with networks for religious and social life, as well as work and political representation. White Protestant Chicagoans of northern European heritage expressed mistrust and fear of immigrants who brought folkways that were foreign. Repression of political radicalism and labor organization are evidence of this concern.

The so-called Settlement House Movement emerged as a way to provide humane assistance to immigrants, while at the same time funneling them into channels of assimilation that were designed to promote traditional middle-class and elite values. Hull House, founded by social reformer Jane Addams, provides a clear example of the settlement house phenomenon. In its work to assist immigrants, Hull House advocated for issues that would become core to the new progressive mindset and which were broadly shared by reformers in other cities. Child labor, safe living and working conditions, sanitation, political corruption and reform, judicial reform, libraries, and education were all areas of concern to Addams and her team of women working at Hull House.

See also *Chicago, IL 1854–1877; Chicago, IL 1896–1929; Chicago, IL 1929–1941; Chicago, IL 1941–1952; Chicago, IL 1952–1989; Chicago, IL 1989–2011*

SCOTT GABRIEL KNOWLES

BIBLIOGRAPHY

Cronon, William. *Nature's Metropolis: Chicago and the Great West*. New York, NY: W. W. Norton, 1992.
Grossman, James, Ann Durkin Keating, and Janice L. Reiff, eds. *The Encyclopedia of Chicago*. Chicago, IL: University of Chicago Press, 2005.
Knowles, Scott Gabriel. *Experts in Disaster: A History of Risk and Authority in the Modern United States*. Philadelphia: University of Pennsylvania Press, 2011.
Rosen, Christine Meisner. *The Limits of Power: Great Fires and the Process of City Growth in America*. New York, NY: Cambridge University Press, 1986.
Smith, Carl. *Urban Disorder and the Shape of Belief: The Great Chicago Fire, the Haymarket Bomb, and the Model Town of Pullman*. Chicago, IL: University of Chicago Press, 1996.

PHILADELPHIA, PA 1877–1896

AFTER THE CROWDS LEFT THE CENTENNIAL EXHIBITION IN 1876, Philadelphians returned to the patterns of life they had established earlier in the century. Despite the social and economic upheavals of the Gilded Age, the city continued to produce an extraordinarily diverse array of manufactured goods, maintained its reputation as a Republican stronghold, and housed its burgeoning population by building outwards rather than upwards. By the start of the Gilded Age, the centering of the nation's financial markets on Wall Street had all but ended boosters' hopes of reclaiming metropolitan status from New York, but they could still boast that their city was the "workshop of the world."

GOVERNMENT AND POLITICS

In the last three decades of the nineteenth century, the local ascendancy of the Republican Party persisted in Philadelphia. The period witnessed the maturation of machine politics, as the ward bosses who had dominated city politics in the antebellum era gave way to centralized metropolitan and state organizations. Although a few of the old upper-class families and portions of the

QUICK FACTS

PHILADELPHIA, PA 1877–1896

MAYORS

William S. Stokley	(1872–1881)
Samuel George King	(1881–1884)
William Burns Smith	(1884–1887)
Edwin H. Fitler	(1887–1891)
Edwin Sydney Stuart	(1891–1895)
Charles Franklin Warwick	(1895–1899)

MAJOR INDUSTRIES AND EMPLOYERS

Textiles

Iron, steel, and machine/locomotive building

Construction

Printing

Brickmaking

MAJOR NEWSPAPERS

Evening Bulletin

Evening Telegraph

Philadelphia Inquirer

North American and United States Gazette

Philadelphia Press

Public Ledger

Philadelphia Times

Philadelphia Tribune

MAJOR EVENTS

1879: At least sixty thousand citizens welcome ex-president Ulysses S. Grant to Philadelphia in a parade through the city. The parade takes six hours to pass any given point along the route.

1883: The *Philadelphia Tribune*, the first lasting African American newspaper in the city, is founded by Christopher Perry.

1891: Anthony J. Drexel founds the Drexel Institute of Art, Science and Industry, which later becomes Drexel University.

1893: The terminus of the Pennsylvania Railroad, originally built in 1881, is extended under the direction of the architect Frank Furness. His Gothic Broad Street Station was one of the largest stations in the world.

1896: The $30-million merger of the People's Traction Company and the Electric Traction Company and Peter A. B. Widener's Philadelphia Traction Company forms the Union Traction Company, which enjoys a virtual monopoly on the city's public transport.

Irish American community clung to the Democrats, Philadelphia was effectively a one-party city. Republicans maintained power by liberally dispensing patronage in exchange for financial and electoral support. The new city hall at the intersection of Broad and Market Streets—the largest and most expensive municipal building in the nation—was an emblem of the machine, and the commission empowered to raise the money to build it provided a springboard for the ascent of William Stokley, who was mayor for much of the 1870s. Stokley was closely allied for much of the period with James McManes, whose control of the city's gas works allowed him to build a vast patronage network. Peter A. B. Widener, a city treasurer and one of the nation's richest men, illustrated the close connection between business and politics. After profiting from a contract to supply the Union Army with meat during the Civil War, he began to invest in suburban real estate and street railways, eventually consolidating the entire network into the Philadelphia Traction Company.

Reformers troubled by the spendthrift practices of the city fathers pushed the cause of retrenchment and reform throughout the period, but even their most notable success—the new city charter (also known as the Bullitt Bill)—has been seen as a victory for machine politicians. Figures like medieval historian and publisher Henry Charles Lea, who had been active in the Citizens Municipal Reform Association of the early 1870s, continued to challenge Republican rule. Such men, who generally hailed from the upper echelons of Philadelphia society, lacked popular appeal. Most of their victories therefore depended on improbable alliances, and they were willing to court African American voters and Democrats to unseat Republican regulars. In 1881, for example, reformers and Democrats defeated Stokley and over the following decade helped elect two more reform mayors, the "two Edwins," Fitler and Stuart. The Bullitt Bill, passed in 1885 after years of agitation from the wealthy members of the Committee of One Hundred—a group of wealthy reformers who came together in 1880 in opposition to McManes and the Republican bosses—supposedly marked the high point of their efforts. Designed to strengthen the hand of the mayor by giving him the right to appoint the heads of a streamlined set of city departments, the measure found an unlikely champion in Matthew Quay, head of the state Republican Party. Quay had been at war with local bosses for many years, and he saw the bill as an opportunity to reduce the influence of his enemies and tighten the state party's grip on city politics. Rather than eradicating boss rule, then, the charter strengthened the hand of Harrisburg Republicans at the expense of their local counterparts.

In focusing on the machinations of bosses and reformers, it is too easy to forget what city government actually did. Schooling remained one of its principal functions, yet even this was touched by the workings of the Republican Party. In keeping with the centralization of the political machine, the boards of education, hitherto organized by district, were consolidated into one body in the 1880s. Consolidation may have delivered greater efficiencies, but the quality of teaching remained low. Teachers, like policemen, were political appointments and often had to pay a portion of their meager salaries to the party in exchange for their position. Meanwhile, a deteriorating water supply polluted by the mines and industries that dotted the Schuylkill basin concerned advocates of public health. Reformers could point to ample evidence that boss rule was failing to deal with the challenges rapid urban growth presented, but their prescription of economy and efficiency hardly promised to modernize the city's increasingly antiquated infrastructure. As the period drew to a close, attempts to improve the water supply continued to founder in councils.

INDUSTRY, COMMERCE, AND LABOR

Philadelphia in the late nineteenth century was an industrial city that, despite its large working-class population, avoided the most painful labor conflicts of the era. Large factories coexisted alongside small workshops, and heavy industry stood side by side with specialist production. As in the preceding decades, perhaps the most striking feature of the city's manufacturing output was its diversity. From steam engines to cigars and from hats to carpets, Philadelphia led the way.

The Pennsylvania Railroad stood out as the biggest corporation in the city. Under the aggressive leadership of Thomas A. Scott and George B. Roberts, the railroad increased its traffic to

"AMERICA'S GRANDEST RAILWAY TERMINAL"
— PENNSYLVANIA RAILROAD —
NEW PASSENGER STATION. BROAD STREET. PHILADELPHIA. U.S.A.

Frank Furness's Broad Street Station served as a grand portal for the Pennsylvania Railroad. His expansive Gothic-style addition opened in 1893.   *Source: Library of Congress*

New York City; Washington, D.C., and Chicago, Illinois, while developing real estate along its main line into suburban retreats for the city's wealthy citizens. Its potentially ruinous competition with William Vanderbilt's New York Central compelled banker J. P. Morgan (a protégé of the Philadelphia financier Anthony J. Drexel) to bring the presidents of the railroads together in the 1885 to force a rapprochement. The city's other main railroad, the Reading, fared less well in the era, suffering one of its many bankruptcies in 1880, but it did carry along its tracks the anthracite coal that, along with iron, lay at the foundation of the city's prosperity.

This mineral wealth fuelled some of Philadelphia's most important industries. Along the Delaware River at Philadelphia's port—known to contemporaries as the American Clyde and the nation's second busiest in this period—vast shipbuilding enterprises like William Cramp and Sons, most of which converted from wood to iron in the Civil War era, built up America's navy and merchant marine. A little to the northwest of the new city hall, the Baldwin Locomotive Works and William Sellers and Company turned out the engines and machines that powered the economy of the Gilded Age. By 1880 well over ten thousand employees labored in the city's iron and steelworks, foundries, and machine shops.

These industries benefited heavily from government assistance. For much of the period, only American-built ships were allowed to ply the coastwise trade, and in the last two decades of the nineteenth century, naval contracts provided an important source of income for the shipyards. Philadelphia's long-serving congressman, William D. Kelley, proved one of the most steadfast advocates of protective tariffs in Washington. The city's large-scale manufacturing interests therefore continued to benefit from the national ascendancy of the Republican Party.

As during much of the century, however, large enterprises whose fortunes were tied to the production of iron and coal may have impressed visitors, but they did not represent the typical Philadelphia manufactory. The sheer diversity of the scale and output of local industry makes generalizations about the local economy in the period fraught with difficulty. Cramp and Sons, with twenty-three hundred employees in 1880, was more of an outlier than the norm. Textiles remained the largest sector, but workshops rarely employed more than a couple of dozen hands. The 473 cigar makers recorded in the 1880 census operated on an even smaller scale, with just a little over two thousand employees citywide working in the trade. Sugar, books, hats, and carpets were just a handful of the dozens of products Philadelphia was renowned for in a period in which it had good reason to claim the mantle of America's preeminent manufacturing city. However, firms in these industries did have something in common with the likes of the Baldwin Locomotive Works insofar as the vast majority rejected incorporation. With the notable exception of the railroads, Philadelphia's businessmen tended to prefer partnerships or family firms to the corporate form of organization gaining ground elsewhere in the nation.

Labor relations in these workplaces were not characterized by the violence common elsewhere in America during the Gilded Age. In part perhaps due to the efficient response of the municipal authorities, Philadelphia had largely avoided pitched battles between strikers and police in the Great Railroad Strike of 1877. Although first the Knights of Labor and later the American Federation of Labor established a significant presence in many of the city's trades, violent conflict between workers and employers was generally avoided. One notable exception, a stoppage in 1895 on the part of the Amalgamated Association of Street Railway Employees, involved minor rioting and led to some improvements in pay and working conditions. Historians have often pointed to the high level of homeownership among the working class to account for the relative peace in Philadelphia during a turbulent era nationwide.

Employers nevertheless pushed their workforces hard. In the 1890s Frederick Winslow Taylor, a mechanical engineer from the suburb of Germantown, established a practice in Philadelphia. Taylor's time and motion studies of the work process, which he pioneered as an employee of Midvale Steel in the northwestern part of the city, put him at the forefront of the efficiency movement of the Progressive era and made him one of the founders of management consultancy. In an economy still characterized by small workshops and face-to-face contact between employers and employees, Taylor's scientific management must have seemed more of a curiosity than a harbinger of the future. In many ways, indeed, the city's economy in the late nineteenth century was more a continuation of earlier patterns than a new departure.

RACE, ETHNICITY, AND IMMIGRATION

Philadelphia's demographic growth continued between 1876 and 1896 as the city doubled in size. New residents continued to arrive from northern and western Europe, with the industrial suburb of Kensington providing a home to thousands of British weavers. Migrants came in greater numbers from the surrounding countryside. The most noticeable change in the city's demography was an influx of newcomers from southern and eastern Europe, however.

The arrival of Italians that had begun in the early 1870s continued, with over six thousand in the city by 1890 and about eighteen thousand a decade later, but mass migration did not take off until the early twentieth century. Polish Catholics came to Philadelphia in the era too, but forced to compete with Irish and blacks in a swollen market for unskilled labor, most quickly moved on. Jews from Eastern Europe, fleeing the pogroms of the 1880s, stayed in greater numbers. In 1882 alone two thousand arrived, and more than forty thousand came between 1880 and 1890.

Although the percentage of foreign-born residents in the city was the lowest among major metropolitan centers in the North and Midwest and actually declined from its peak of around 27 percent in 1870 to 23 percent at the turn of the century, the "New Immigration" shaped the city's residential geography and social structure. Italians settled in South Philadelphia; Jews in the southern wards or the northeast. These groups quickly established community institutions. By 1895, for example, the area south of Spruce Street boasted forty-five synagogues. Ethnic enclaves were not an entirely new phenomenon in the city—in the Civil War era, Irish and German immigrants had tended to cluster around South Street and Girard Avenue, respectively—but the late-nineteenth-century arrivals created neighborhoods that still endure to the present day.

Many of the newcomers were thrown into the casual labor market, but immigrants managed to establish ethnic niches in some occupations. Irish Americans had already won a foothold in the building trades, while Italians moved from railroad building (the Pennsylvania had recruited migrants) into construction; many worked, for example, on the new city hall. Some found work through the *padrone* system, in which a contractor, often with ties to the Republican machine, hired out teams of workers. Jews, who were often already accustomed to the rhythms of the urban economy, were more likely to enter the handicrafts. Although ethnocultural solidarities helped migrants adjust to Philadelphia, recent studies have emphasized community divisions as well. American Jews raised in the Reform tradition were not necessarily natural allies of the Orthodox arrivals from Eastern Europe, and among Germans class cleavages sometimes weakened ethnic consciousness.

The city's black population, augmented by migrants from the post-Reconstruction South, grew threefold between 1870 and 1900 and remained the largest African American population of any northern city through this period. Blacks found homes across the metropolis, following the white middle class in search of service work, but they continued to cluster around Lombard Street in the Seventh Ward, a few blocks south of Center City. Here they were close to both the mansions of fashionable Rittenhouse Square and to the docks, where they found work as help and longshoremen. Such unskilled and low-paid positions were typical, since African Americans were largely excluded from industrial pursuits and organized labor. Frederick W. Taylor's willingness to hire blacks at Midvale Steel in the 1890s was unusual, for most of the larger employers like Baldwin and Cramp kept the shop floor a white man's domain. When the Hod Carriers Union organized black and white workers in the 1880s, it marked a rare moment of interracial cooperation.

Republican ascendance did offer some political benefits to African Americans, who made up roughly 10 percent of the party's vote in the era. Community leaders were able to use the split between reformers and party regulars in the 1880s to trade their influence for patronage, which resulted in the appointment of the first black policemen, and by 1884 there were thirty-five in a force of about fourteen hundred. In the same decade, voters sent an African American to council in the Seventh Ward. A handful of other blacks won office on Republican tickets in the ensuing years, but, once the reform agitation subsided, party loyalty offered diminishing returns. The black community was perhaps more important for the African American population than the white-dominated machine. Along with the churches, which were dominated by the African Methodist Episcopals and the Baptists, there were three hundred black-owned businesses at the end of the era; a newspaper for black readers, the *Philadelphia Tribune*, founded in 1883; and a growing network of black professionals.

Housing the residents of the growing city proved challenging, but Philadelphia still coped better than many cities in the period. Newcomers and African Americans were often consigned to renting in overcrowded and disease-ridden neighborhoods. Fears of another cholera epidemic in 1892 and other public health scares led to calls for a better water supply and slum clearance. Despite these anxieties, the metropolis lacked the tenement houses of New York, and home-ownership, abetted by the hundreds of building societies that sprung up in the period, was more commonplace among the better-off industrial workers and clerks than in cities of comparable size. By 1895 there were over two hundred thousand dwellings in the metropolis. Nevertheless, if civic boosters liked to imply the city was uniformly middle class, growing social segregation suggested otherwise, as wealthy Philadelphians decamped to West Philadelphia and the prosperous suburbs of the Main Line that lay beyond the city's western border. Suburban outmigration on the part of less-wealthy, nonmanual workers also helped lead to a decline in population in the historic center. The geography of the twentieth-century metropolitan area was taking shape.

See also *Philadelphia, PA 1776–1790; Philadelphia, PA 1790–1828; Philadelphia, PA 1828–1854; Philadelphia, PA 1854–1877; Philadelphia, PA 1896–1929; Philadelphia, PA 1929–1941; Philadelphia, PA 1941–1952; Philadelphia, PA 1952–1989; Philadelphia, PA 1989–2011*

ANDREW HEATH

BIBLIOGRAPHY

Bjelopera, Jerome P. *City of Clerks: Office and Sales Workers in Philadelphia*. Urbana: University of Illinois Press, 2005.

Burt, Nathaniel, and Wallace E. Davies. "The Iron Age." In *Philadelphia: A 300 Year History*, edited by Russell Weigley, 471–523. New York, NY: W. W. Norton, 1982.

Heinrich, Thomas R. *Ships for the Seven Seas: Philadelphia Shipbuilding in the Age of Industrial Capitalism*. Baltimore, MD: Johns Hopkins University Press, 1997.

Hepp, John Henry. *The Middle Class City: Transforming Space and Time in Philadelphia, 1876–1926*. Philadelphia: University of Pennsylvania Press, 2003.

Juliani, Richard N. *Building Little Italy: Philadelphia's Italians before Mass Migration.* University Park: Pennsylvania State University Press, 1998.

Kazal, Russell A. *Becoming Old Stock: The Paradox of German-American Identity.* Princeton, NJ: Princeton University Press, 2004.

Lane, Roger. *Roots of Violence in Black Philadelphia, 1860–1900.* Cambridge, MA: Harvard University Press, 1986.

ST. LOUIS, MO 1877–1896

THE YEARS 1877–1896 WERE AMONG THE MOST IMPORTANT IN ST. LOUIS'S LONG HISTORY, as the city attempted to move beyond the Civil War years and claim its place as a leading American city. New technology, architecture, and businesses brought energy to St. Louis and created its appearance as a modern city. It was a time of great optimism for the city, as St. Louis leaders and boosters worked to position it as the center of trade and commerce for the growing, industrializing United States. However, it was also an era of worry and insecurity, as St. Louis tried to keep pace with its fast-growing rival, Chicago, Illinois, which was quickly becoming the most important city in the Midwest. There was also internal turmoil as immigration, political infighting, class conflict, racial strife, and labor upheaval contributed to St. Louis's growing pains. Additionally, a devastating tornado in 1896 damaged as many as eight thousand homes, affecting an area from fashionable Lafayette Square to the slums along the river and causing an estimated $10 million in damage. Despite the difficulties, the city rebuilt the affected areas and continued to grow.

During the second half of the nineteenth century, St. Louis achieved its status as America's fourth largest city, and many of its most powerful companies (Anheuser-Busch, Ralston Purina, Burroughs Corporation) either were founded or grew rapidly during these years. However, it was also during this time period that the seeds of St. Louis's eventual decline were sown as the city separated from St. Louis County and the tax base that the county would eventually provide.

GOVERNMENT AND POLITICS

In 1875 St. Louis adopted the first home-rule city charter in the United States. The Missouri Constitution of 1875 allowed city home rule, which meant that large cities, if they chose, could eliminate oversight from the counties in which they were located. Essentially, the concept allowed for cities to formally secede from their counties. For years, there had been conflict between the city and county of St. Louis over issues of taxation, land use, and city representation on county boards. After the passage of home rule, the city officially separated from St. Louis County in 1876. The city charter created a total area of the city of 61.37 square miles, including nineteen miles fronting the Mississippi River. This new boundary more than tripled the existing city area; included now were the recently completed city parks, as well as abundant farmland. Many county residents were upset at the generous boundaries for the city,

QUICK FACTS

ST. LOUIS, MO 1877–1896

MAYORS:

Henry Overstolz	(1876–1881)
William L. Ewing	(1881–1885)
David R. Francis	(1885–1889)
Edward A. Noonan	(1889–1893)
Cyrus P. Walbridge	(1893–1897)

St. Louis Times
Evening Chronicle
Tribune
The Missouri Immigrant
Anzeiger Des Westens
The Amerika
The Westliche Post

MAJOR INDUSTRIES AND EMPLOYERS

Brewing
Tobacco processing
Boot and shoe manufacturing
Furniture manufacturing
Dress manufacturing

MAJOR NEWSPAPERS

Globe-Democrat
Missouri Republican
Post-Dispatch
St. Louis Republican

MAJOR EVENTS

1877: A railroad workers' strike becomes a general strike in St. Louis. Strikers shut down the city for nearly a week before they are arrested by police and community leaders.

1879: Thousands of former slaves land in St. Louis during the Exodus of 1879 as they flee the post–Reconstruction South for homes in Kansas.

1880: The first electric lights are installed in St. Louis.

1894: Union Station opens. At the time, it was the largest railroad station in the United States.

1896: The Republican National Convention is held in St. Louis; William McKinley wins the presidential nomination.

1896: A tornado devastates much of the city, killing at least 140 people and injuring over one thousand.

and some city residents complained that the city was including too much empty space that had little tax value. At the time, it was assumed that the boundary included enough physical space to accommodate the city indefinitely. However, what it meant was that the city was essentially hemmed in on three sides by St. Louis County and on the fourth side by Illinois, bounded by the Mississippi River. As development occurred, St. Louis was precluded from physically growing its boundaries, and eventually the population of surrounding St. Louis County dwarfed the population of the city proper. So, politically, the time period after the charter was one of optimism and a sense of freedom for the city, but most importantly it was also a time of modernization.

Henry Overstolz was the first St. Louis mayor elected to a four-year term under the new charter. Overstolz, who had been declared the winner of a closely contested election to a two-year term in the 1875 election, received the nomination of both the Democrats and the Republicans when he ran for reelection in 1877. A German immigrant who had become a successful businessman, Overstolz represented both the large immigrant community in St. Louis and the business establishment. As the first mayor under the new charter, he sought to establish working relationships with both the state of Missouri and St. Louis County and strived to organize the new government under the charter's terms. Overstolz was criticized by some for not responding more forcefully to the general strike of 1877, and Republican William Ewing defeated Overstolz when he ran for a third term.

In 1888 David Francis, the Democratic mayor who defeated Ewing's reelection bid, became the only St. Louis mayor to be elected Missouri governor. During his time as mayor, Francis initiated many public works projects to improve the city's streets and water system. These improvements were continued by Francis's successor, Democrat Edward Noonan. During Noonan's tenure, the city underwent many environmental changes. Perhaps most importantly, the city passed its first smoke ordinance, which sought to eliminate the heavy concentration of manufacturing smoke that continually clouded the city and made breathing difficult. Additionally, Noonan began a program to better purify the city's drinking water, which had long had a reputation for being filled with river sediment.

Republican Cyrus Walbridge continued the environmental changes that Francis and Noonan had begun by enforcing garbage collection in the city and creating underground wires for telephones and telegraphs in the downtown area. But Walbridge's changes moved beyond the physical environment as he also became the first St. Louis mayor to appoint women to government office. He appointed women to the boards of the public library, the charity commissioners, and the House of Refuge. Walbridge was like the other St. Louis mayors during the Gilded Age; he believed that St. Louis was a city of limitless potential, and he worked to try to create an environment conducive to the city's growth.

INDUSTRY, COMMERCE, AND LABOR

The general strike of 1877 was a defining moment in St. Louis labor history and set the stage for labor relations in the city for the rest of the century. Brought on by wage cuts and unsafe working conditions, the strike was part of a larger railroad strike that took place in Pittsburgh, Pennsylvania; Baltimore, Maryland; and other cities. On July 23, 1877, the strike moved to St. Louis and quickly expanded from a railroad strike to a general strike carried out by workers in such diverse jobs as river boatmen, gas workers, factory workers, and coopers. For nearly a week, the strikers controlled much of the city, shutting down most industries.

Although the strike remained rather nonviolent and there was little property damage or injuries, the sight of the workers marching through the streets panicked the local leaders. The United States Army was put on alert in barracks outside of the city, and a citizens' militia led by two former generals was raised and began drilling in anticipation of a retaking of the streets. Eventually, as the strike began to lose momentum, the citizens' militia, led by the police cavalry and Mayor Overstolz, marched on the strikers' headquarters and effectively ended it. Very little tangible gain had been achieved by the strike, but it was, however, a wake-up call to St. Louis business leaders, who had, for a short time, lost control of the city. In the years after the strike, the St. Louis business elite would develop the "Veiled Prophet" parade, which was

The year after a significant labor strike in 1877, a group of St. Louis businessmen formed the Veiled Prophet organization for professional development, to encourage agricultural commerce in the city, and to reestablish dominance after the strikes. The focal point was an annual parade that continues to this day.

Source: Library of Congress

designed to instruct the city's workers in their rights and responsibilities and also served as a show of force, demonstrating who controlled the city's streets.

St. Louis industry changed significantly during the late 1880s and early 1890s, paradoxically widening the scope of its influence while also losing ground to competing cities. Before the Civil War, the St. Louis economy was tied closely to the South, especially in the shipping and wholesaling of cotton. However, the blockade of the southern portion of the Mississippi River during the war halted the trade and hurt St. Louis's economy. At the same time, Chicago was growing quickly as the key shipping point for the booming farm economy of the upper Midwest. After the war, St. Louis worked to regain its lost status by rebuilding its connections with the cotton economy in the South. By 1880 St. Louis was the third largest cotton market in the nation behind New Orleans, Louisiana, and Savannah, Georgia. Its receipts, which had ballooned to 496,750 bales a year, made it the largest interior cotton market in the world.

Connections to the Southwest, in addition to the South, also boosted St. Louis's economy in the second half of the nineteenth century. St. Louis became a major shipping and processing point for raw materials moving east and for finished products moving west. During the Gilded Age, St. Louis ranked among the largest cities producing a range of different products. It became the leader in production of lead paint pigments, plug chewing tobacco, and flour milling. It was also the largest producer west of the Mississippi River in industries such as coffee distribution and had substantial operations in groceries, lumber, and meat processing. By 1890 St. Louis was among the country's most important cities from an economic perspective. It was ranked fourth in the gross value of its manufactured products and fifth in the amount of capital invested in manufacturing. Industrial establishments grew rapidly during the 1880s, increasing in number from 2,984 to 6,148. The number of employees in manufacturing grew from 41,825 to 82,911. As another indicator, manufacturing capital rose from $50.8 million to $141 million during the decade and industrial production from $114.3 million to $229.1 million. However, although St. Louis was growing economically, it was also losing ground to some of its rivals. For example, it was surpassed by Minneapolis, Minnesota, in flour milling in 1890, and dropped from fifth to sixth place in meatpacking in the next decade.

St. Louis's German heritage meant that there was a strong beer-brewing tradition in the city, and it became famous worldwide for its breweries. In the middle of the nineteenth century, beer gardens became popular in St. Louis, and there were forty breweries in operation in the city. Although the number of breweries declined in the second half of the century, production increased, and by 1900 there were still nineteen breweries in operation. Anheuser-Busch was the largest, producing nearly one million barrels a year, and the Lemp Company produced nearly five hundred thousand. Within a decade of becoming president of his wife's family's company, Adolphus Busch pioneered the use of refrigerated railroad cars and pasteurized bottled beer to increase Anheuser-Busch's sales. In 1876 he introduced Budweiser, which became the most popular beer in the world and cemented St. Louis's place as a brewing center.

RACE, ETHNICITY, AND IMMIGRATION

St. Louis underwent dramatic changes in terms of race and ethnicity between 1877 and 1896. The African American population of the city increased rapidly, and St. Louis had one of the largest percentages of foreign-born residents of any city in the United States. In 1860 the African American population of St. Louis stood at 3,297 people, or 2 percent of the total population. By 1880 that number had increased to 22,256, or 6 percent of the population, making St. Louis the city with the third largest urban African American population in the country, behind Baltimore and Philadelphia.

Despite the strictures of the developing Jim Crow segregation system, the African American population of St. Louis was able to exert influence both politically and socially in the city. An example of this occurred in the general strike of 1877. Although African American workers had been barred from the labor unions that organized the strike, they joined in the strike and played a very prominent role. Some strike opponents blamed the strike leaders for allowing African Americans to participate, arguing that the strike allowed black workers to challenge the racial hierarchy of the city in addition to workers challenging the economic status quo.

African Americans also exerted their influence politically and socially. Politically, since white voters were relatively balanced between the Republicans and Democrats, blacks were able to use their political leverage, most often supporting Republican candidates. Although St. Louis had been a slave city in a slave state, before emancipation there had been an active free black community that built social networks and social power. African Americans founded churches, owned businesses, and became educated in various ways despite the limitations of the slave society. During the second half of the nineteenth century, these social networks were useful as the

African American community organized to combat segregation in the public school system, in housing, and in public transportation. For example, in 1877 the St. Louis school board refused to hire African American teachers for black schools, so black parents staged a boycott of the schools. When the school board insisted that there were no qualified African American teachers, the black community recruited some from outside St. Louis. St. Louis still developed Jim Crow laws, but its African American community was able to retain a level of influence not seen in cities further south.

St. Louis was, in many ways, a city of immigrants, and in the Gilded Age it was one of the most multicultural cities in the United States. The 1880 census showed that of its 350,518 residents, 54,901 were born in Germany, 28,566 in Ireland, and 8,762 in Great Britain. Additionally, a total of six thousand residents came from France, Sweden, and Bohemia. A full 28 percent of the children in public schools had been born outside of the United States. There were German language newspapers and German social clubs, and the German influence on St. Louis could best be seen in the over forty breweries that were in business in the 1880s. German influence was so great that there were some discussions that German should be the language of instruction in some of the city's schools.

In the early 1880s, only one-fifth of St. Louis residents owned their own homes. The rest lived in boarding houses, rented houses, and tenements that were notorious for their unsanitary, crowded conditions. Many Irish lived in one- and two-room shacks in the poor squatters' neighborhood of "Kerry Patch." Although most of the residents of the tenements and neighborhoods like Kerry Patch were employed, the low wages of their jobs and the transient nature of their housing kept them on the fringes of St. Louis society.

See also *St. Louis, MO 1854–1877; St. Louis, MO 1896–1929; St. Louis, MO 1929–1941; St. Louis, MO 1941–1952*

BRYAN JACK

BIBLIOGRAPHY

Belcher, Wyatt Winton. *The Economic Rivalry between St. Louis and Chicago, 1850–1880*. New York, NY: AMS Press, 1968.

Corbett, Katherine, and Howard S. Miller. *Saint Louis in the Gilded Age*. St. Louis: Missouri Historical Society Press, 1993.

Hurley, Andrew, ed. *Common Fields: An Environmental History of St. Louis*. St. Louis: Missouri Historical Society Press, 1997.

Jack, Bryan M. *The Saint Louis African American Community and the Exodusters*. Columbia: The University of Missouri Press, 2007.

Primm, James Neal. *The Lion of the Valley: St. Louis, Missouri, 1764–1980*. 3d ed. St. Louis: Missouri Historical Society Press, 1998.

Sandweiss, Eric, ed. *St. Louis in the Century of Henry Shaw: A View beyond the Garden Wall*. Columbia: The University of Missouri Press, 2003.

Spencer, Thomas. *The St. Louis Veiled Prophet Celebration: Power on Parade 1877–1995*. Columbia: The University of Missouri Press, 2000.

BOSTON, MA 1877–1896

DURING THE LAST THREE DECADES OF THE NINETEENTH CENTURY, Boston experienced interconnected commercial, social, and political changes. A high birthrate, a city-wide annexation program, the continued influx of "old" immigrants from western and northern Europe (especially Ireland), and the arrival of "new" immigrants from southern and eastern Europe combined to more than double Boston's population. Between 1870 and 1900, Boston's number of residents grew from 250,526 to 560,892. While the city's status as a banking and financial epicenter diminished, its industries remained sound, despite two depressions. The new public utility companies, which provided essential services for Boston's annexed neighborhoods, created new opportunities for labor. In politics, Boston was a Democratic island in a Republican sea. While Massachusetts regularly returned Republican delegations to Congress, Democrats controlled the Boston mayoralty for all but six years between 1877 and 1896. Relying on Irish American voters who had been loyal to the Democratic Party since the tenure of Andrew Jackson, a precarious and incongruous alliance of Irish Democrats and Yankee Democrats shared power. While Yankee and Irish Democrats found common ground, deep ethnocultural conflict between them remained an undercurrent, flaring up in politics and beyond the ballot box.

GOVERNMENT AND POLITICS

The Irish became an even more powerful political cohort in Boston between 1877 and 1896. The ability of Irish leaders to mobilize Irish laborers with the promise of work for votes accounted in part for the era's extraordinarily high level of voter turnout, which averaged 75 percent for all mayoral elections between 1876 and 1885. The mayoralty in Boston during the Gilded Age was largely ceremonial; it was the bicameral city council that ran the city. The council consisted of a twelve-member board of aldermen and a seventy-two-member common council. The Irish constituted 42 percent of the city's population in 1885 and a majority by 1900, and it was largely due to their strong numbers that their presence in the city council grew. Only eleven men of Irish descent served on the council in 1870, but by 1883 that number had increased to twenty-five. The Irish simultaneously assumed other powerful positions in the Democratic Party. In 1882 Democrat Patrick Collins became the first Boston Irishman elected to Congress. Patrick Maguire, a newspaper and real estate man, was a Hibernian rainmaker who wielded his power behind the scenes in Boston's dark and smoky saloons. Though he faced competition from a rising group of younger ward bosses, such as Martin Lomasney, John F. Fitzgerald, and Patrick J. Kennedy—all of whom were talented managers of political organizations in their own right—Maguire controlled the Democratic City Committee from 1876 to 1896. He was, according to historian John Galvin in his 1982 book *Patrick J. Maguire: Boston's Last Democratic Boss*, the "only city-wide boss Boston ever had." Galvin concluded that for twenty years, "party decisions were made in the back room of Maguire's real estate office."

QUICK FACTS

BOSTON, MA 1877–1896

MAYORS

Frederick Prince	(1877–1878)
Henry Pierce	(1878–1879)
Frederick Prince	(1879–1882)
Samuel Green	(1882–1883)
Albert Palmer	(1883–1884)
Augustus Martin	(1884–1885)
Hugh O'Brien	(1885–1889)
Thomas Hart	(1889–1890)
Nathan Matthews	(1891–1894)
Edwin Curtis	(1895)
Josiah Quincy	(1896–1899)

MAJOR INDUSTRIES AND EMPLOYERS

Men's clothing

Sugar

Meat

Printing and publishing

Malt liquors

MAJOR NEWSPAPERS

Boston Advertiser

Boston Globe

Boston Herald

Boston Transcript

The Pilot

The Republic

MAJOR EVENTS

1882: Patrick Collins becomes the first Boston Irishman elected to Congress.

1884: The state legislature passes a civil service reform law to increase efficiency and restrict the spoils system.

1884: Hugh O'Brien is elected as the first Irish-born mayor of Boston.

1885: Underscoring the ethnocultural conflict of the period, the Republican state legislature transfers control of Boston's heavily Irish police force to the state.

1895: The American Protective Association campaigns against Catholic candidates for political office.

In the late 1870s and early 1880s, Maguire and other Irish political leaders supported Yankee Democrats for mayor. In 1876 Maguire and the Democratic City Committee nominated Frederick Prince, who defeated his Republican opponent and ascended to the mayoralty. Mayor Prince understood that a politician's electoral survival rested on how well he could deliver the patronage. He lavished his supporters with patronage plums and substantially increased the number of Irish policemen in the city. During the mayoral race of 1877, in which Republican Henry Pierce ran against Prince, the Republican *Herald* assailed the mayor's generous distribution of patronage. Prince and his cronies, the *Herald* asserted, were "a ring." The Democratic *Pilot* disagreed, condemning the efforts of "Republican editors" to defeat Prince. Although Pierce won in 1877, Prince reclaimed city hall in 1878 with the backing of Maguire's machine and was reelected in 1879 and 1880. Maguire and the committee tapped another Yankee Democrat, Albert Palmer, for the mayoral nomination in 1881. Samuel Green, a physician, was his Republican opposition. "The Republican Party is sick," *The Boston Globe* quipped, "and a physician has been called in to prescribe for it." Although a temperance advocate in a "wet" city, Green had a record of treating the Irish with benevolence and attracted some Irish support, defeating Palmer. In 1882, however, with Maguire's new weekly, *The Republic*, attacking Green as "thoroughly incompetent," Palmer vanquished the incumbent mayor.

The most significant political event in Boston during the Gilded Age was the election of the first Irish-born mayor. Hugh O'Brien, who had served ably as alderman chair, was the Democratic nominee in 1883. After being narrowly defeated in 1883 by Republican Augustus Martin, O'Brien became mayor of Boston in 1885 and was reelected three times. While Yankee Republican newspapers such as the *Boston Transcript* initially fretted that O'Brien would set back "the cause of good government," he proved a talented and conscientious administrator, receiving in the process the respect and votes of many Yankee Republicans. In 1885 one Republican newspaper even praised his "honest and economical administration." But ethnocultural animosities still persisted beneath the surface. O'Brien faced an unfriendly Republican state legislature, which transferred control of Boston's heavily Irish

Hugh O'Brien, a Democrat, served as Boston's first Irish-American mayor for four terms between 1885 and 1888. Anti-Irish sentiment in the city contributed to his loss when he sought reelection for a fifth term.

Source: Library of Congress

police force to the state. Just prior to O'Brien's election, the legislature regulated city hiring with a civil service reform law, thus limiting the Irish patronage appointments. Ethnocultural conflict erupted during O'Brien's bid for a fifth term in 1888. The "Committee of One Hundred," established in the summer of 1888 to counter the growing influence of the Irish, campaigned against O'Brien and other Catholic candidates. Eliza Trask Hill, a member of the Women's Christian Temperance Union, helped register twenty thousand Protestant women for the fall elections. Many of the new female voters, who since 1879 could vote for the school committee, encouraged their husbands to oppose Catholic candidates. The rise in turnout accounted in part for O'Brien's defeat.

In the face of anti-Irish sentiment, Irish Democrats in the 1890s turned back to supporting Yankee Democratic mayoral candidates. In 1890 thirty-seven-year-old Yankee Democrat Nathan Matthews beat Republican Moody Merrill and became the city's youngest mayor since 1840. Reelected in 1891, 1892, and 1893, Matthews completed Boston's first park plan and laid the groundwork for the nation's first subway. His hands-off philosophy and fondness for balanced budgets, however, made him reluctant to use the full powers of the mayoralty to battle the depression of 1893, the century's most devastating downturn, which lasted until 1897. The depression itself caused a political power shift from Maguire's city committee to the ward bosses. During hard times when employment opportunities were scarce, a ward boss's control of a growing share of the patronage plums augmented his clout.

Ethnocultural conflict again took center stage in the 1895 mayoral race. The American Protective Association (APA), which attracted many British Americans, assailed both the "old" and "new" immigrants and campaigned against Catholic candidates. In East Boston, following a Fourth of July parade in 1895, one Catholic was killed when APA members confronted a crowd of spectators. Another event during that year's mayoral campaign stoked memories of 1884, when, during the presidential contest, an imprudent clergyman called the Democrats the party of "Rum, Romanism, and Rebellion," thus helping to swing the Irish vote and the presidency to Grover Cleveland. On the Sunday prior to voting, APA acolyte Reverend James Boyd Brady announced to his congregation that a vote for Yankee Josiah Quincy, the Democratic candidate, was a vote for "the rum-sellers." Democratic newspapers published the remarks, and in Boston's heaviest turnout to date, Quincy was elected to Boston's first two-year term. Unlike Matthews, Quincy rejected the belief that expanding the powers of government would destroy the virtue of self-reliance. Quincy combated the 1893 depression with a strong dose of municipal socialism, expanding patronage in public works, building new playgrounds, and establishing public bath facilities.

INDUSTRY, COMMERCE, AND LABOR

While America's railroads and factories reaped record-breaking profits and increased production in the 1870s and 1880s, Boston was not keeping pace with the nation's leading industrial metropolises, like New York City and Chicago, Illinois. One of the nation's epicenters for banking and investment in industry during the antebellum era, Boston provided the capital that underwrote the textile mills and shipyards of America, but never itself became a significant center for manufacturing, industry, or railroading. In the 1870s and 1880s, the new titans of big business who built empires of steel and oil collected the bulk of their treasures from locales other than Boston, thus eclipsing the wealth of the city's antebellum Brahmin businessmen.

To be sure, Boston was not relegated to relic status by the new urban giants. Although the city's great fire of 1872 decimated the business district and the economic downturns of 1873 and 1893 reduced the earnings of entrepreneurs and slowed the Boston economy, as a whole industries in the Hub remained healthy. With clothing, sugar, candy, iron, and printing sustaining its economy, Boston still ranked among the country's top five manufacturing cities in 1880, though it slipped a notch into sixth place by 1890. Nearby textile communities also bolstered Boston's economy. The factories of Lowell and Lawrence required cotton and leather to produce clothes and shoes. Boston businessmen successfully sold the manufactured wares and imported the cotton and leather. Boston also benefited from trade with Cuba and Puerto Rico, which provided Boston's refineries and candy companies with the sugar that satisfied America's sweet tooth.

Boston's success in navigating the shoals of two economic downturns in the last decades of the century did little to brighten the forecasts of many Boston Brahmins now shorn of their economic primacy. The remarkable changes in population and commerce were bewildering for the Yankee Brahmins. Born into prominent New England families, Brahmins viewed themselves as the "best men." By 1870 many of these distinguished Bostonians were living in the Back Bay, the premiere enclave for the city's affluent elite. Fiercely proud of the city their ancestors had helped build, many Brahmins yearned for an earlier Boston and had trouble relinquishing an ideal that no longer corresponded with reality. Social critic Charles Eliot Norton remarked in 1897 that "New England during the first thirty years of the century, before . . . the invasion of the Irish" was the ideal era. While some Brahmins raised their standards and expectations of the Irish, who had served loyally in the Civil War, others remained suspicious, scorning them as loafers prone to fighting and malingerers too fond of the bottle. Many Brahmins denounced universal suffrage. Contemporary historian Francis Parkman called it a "questionable blessing." Some questioned the wisdom of leaving the "gates unguarded" for immigrants. Many Brahmins regarded their own prospects as inauspicious. "We are vanishing into provincial obscurity," one Boston Brahmin cursed in the 1890s. "America has swept from our grasp. The future is beyond us."

If many Brahmins looked ahead with dread, greater employment opportunities in the last decades of the century gave other Boston citizens, especially the Irish, reason for optimism. To be sure, many still dug ditches, mixed cement, and worked as domestics. And workers always had to contend with the possibility of unemployment, which peaked at 15 percent—forty thousand Bostonians—during the downturn of 1893–1897. During the 1870s, 1880s, and 1890s, however, more ethnic Bostonians were finding work as merchants, saloonkeepers, and construction managers, thus raising their daily wages; fleeing from the downtown's dilapidated waterfront sections of Fort Hill, the North End, and the West End; and settling in the more affluent environs of Charleston, East Boston, and South Boston. The horse-drawn streetcar accelerated the city's expansion in the 1860s and 1870s, and new suburban communities were established, such as Dorchester, Jamaica Plain, Roxbury, West Roxbury, and Brighton. Boston's new neighborhoods required schools, hospitals, roads, and police and fire departments, as well as electricity. The new municipal service jobs provided steady work for thousands of Bostonians. In the 1880s, the incorporation of new public utilities, such as the Boston Consolidated Gas Company, the New England Telephone and Telegraph Company, Edison Electric Illuminating Company, and the Massachusetts Electric Company, provided thousands of higher paying and more secure work opportunities.

RACE, ETHNICITY, AND IMMIGRATION

Between 1865 and 1875, Boston's population nearly doubled, climbing from 192,318 to 341,919, primarily due to annexation. For the remainder of the nineteenth century, the city's population continued to surge with the arrival of thousands of new immigrants in the Hub. While they were the most numerous, the Irish were only one community in a diverse assortment of immigrant groups. The 1880s marked the beginning of a significant change in the character of immigration. The "new immigrants" arriving in the 1880s and 1890s included Italians, Poles, Jews, and two hundred Chinese Americans. These immigrants were more likely to hail from southern and eastern Europe and to speak in tongues other than English.

Italians began moving into the North End in the 1870s, numbering one thousand in 1880 and seven thousand in 1895, and then they moved into East Boston. "Little Italy" in the North End soon included Italian social clubs, which held annual festivals to honor their own patron saints. While Irish initially predominated in the North End, by 1895 Italians outnumbered their Hibernian neighbors by one thousand. Mostly illiterate, the early Italians made a precarious living, working on construction crews and as longshoremen before rising to claim work as cobblers, barbers, and craftsmen. They relied significantly on the labor boss, the *padrone*, whose facility with both English and Italian provided labor opportunities for his Italian brothers. For many Italians and Irish living in Boston at the end of the nineteenth century, the Catholic Church was a unifying force. St. Leonard's was built in the North End in 1873, and Sacred Heart Church was constructed in 1888.

If Catholicism gave immigrant communities a distinctive flavor and unique quality of life, the Jewish faith offered an equally powerful bond for Polish and Russian immigrants. German Jews had begun coming to Boston in the 1850s; many of them became middle-class shopkeepers and merchants and lived in the South End. Jews from Poland and Russia began arriving in the 1880s when minority populations in the Old World became increasingly susceptible to persecution by high-handed regimes. Four thousand Jews lived in Boston by 1890, many of whom had fled cruel repressors and brutal pogroms that took their loved ones as well as their homes. Substantial numbers of these Jewish immigrants settled alongside Irish and Italian neighbors in the North End before moving to East Boston, the South End, and Roxbury. Unlike the other "new immigrant" groups, however, many Jews had already gained invaluable work experience in European cities and carried these skills with them to Boston, where they found employment as tailors, shopkeepers, and peddlers. Divisions remained, however, between German Jews and non-German Jews. German Jews, who sought the social acceptance and respect of the Brahmins, feared that the Polish and Russian Jews would hamper their prospects and sometimes treated their fellow worshippers with suspicion.

If Russian and Polish Jews sometimes received a cold reception from German Jews, blacks migrating from the South were even less welcome in Boston. While only representing 2 percent of the city's population at the turn of the century, Boston's black population had grown from 3,496 in 1870 to 11,591 in 1900. Boston blacks, many of whom had migrated from the American South, were relegated to the poor west side of Beacon Hill, where they remained until 1895. Although at least one African American represented the West End on the common council for every year between 1876 and 1895, this political achievement belied the harsh reality of being black in Boston. Due to severe segregation policies, one-third of Boston's black children attended two elementary schools in the West End. Black adults, denied adequate educational and occupational training, worked the most menial jobs as longshoremen, laborers, waiters, and shoe shiners. Because of their meager remuneration, blacks were more likely than other Bostonians to take in boarders, and married black women were six times more likely to work than married white women. Blacks, who received lower wages than any of the immigrant groups and consistently were denied opportunities for upward mobility, lost what limited political influence they enjoyed when the legislature redistricted the West End in 1895.

Blacks, immigrants both "old" and "new," and the native-born residents of Boston constituted a motley array of different accents, cultures, and values. Boston was growing more diverse and cosmopolitan with each new immigrant arrival. Stubborn provincial predilections and ethnocultural antipathies were being challenged. As Boston entered a new century, it remained an open question whether its citizens would embrace or abandon the old divisions of the Hub's past.

See also *Boston, MA 1776–1790; Boston, MA 1790–1828; Boston, MA 1828–1854; Boston, MA 1854–1877; Boston, MA 1896–1929; Boston, MA 1929–1941; Boston, MA 1941–1952*

EDWARD H. MILLER

BIBLIOGRAPHY

Blodgett, Geoffrey T. "Josiah Quincy, Brahmin Democrat." *The New England Quarterly* 38 (December 1965): 435–453.

———. "Yankee Leadership in a Divided City: Boston, 1860-1910." In *Boston, 1700–1980: The Evolution of Urban Politics*, edited by Ronald Formisano and Constance Burns, 87–110. Westport, CT: Greenwood Press, 1984.

Galvin, John T. "The Dark Ages in Boston City Politics." In *Proceedings of the Massachusetts Historical Society, Volume LXXXIX, 1977*, edited by Robert Joseph Taylor, 88–111. Portland, ME: The Anthoensen Press, 1978.

———. "Patrick J. Maguire: Boston's Last Democratic Boss." *The New England Quarterly* 55 (September 1982): 392–415.

Green, James R., and Hugh Carter Donahue. *Boston's Workers: A Labor History*. Boston, MA: Boston Public Library, 1979.

Handlin, Oscar. *Boston's Immigrants, 1790–1880: A Study in Acculturation*. Cambridge, MA: Belknap Press of Harvard University Press, 1991.

Kleppner, Paul. "From Party to Factions: The Dissolution of Boston's Majority Party, 1876–1908." In *Boston, 1700–1980: The Evolution of Urban Politics*, edited by Ronald Formisano and Constance Burns, 111–132. Westport, CT: Greenwood Press, 1984.

O'Connor, Thomas H. *Bibles, Brahmins, and Bosses: A Short History of Boston*. Boston, MA: Trustees of the Public Library of the City of Boston, 1984.

———. *The Boston Irish: A Political History*. Boston, MA: Northeastern University Press, 1995.

———. *The Hub: Boston Past and Present*. Boston, MA: Northeastern University Press, 2001.

Silverman, Robert A. "Nathan Matthews: Politics of Reform in Boston, 1890-1910." *The New England Quarterly* 50 (December 1977): 626–643.

Warner, Sam B. *Streetcar Suburbs: The Process of Growth in Boston 1870–1900*. New York, NY: Atheneum, 1974.

BALTIMORE, MD 1877–1896

THE POLITICAL VIOLENCE THAT SCARRED ANTEBELLUM BALTIMORE subsided as the city settled down to the predictable regularities of machine politics after the Civil War. The war had also helped to energize Baltimore's sluggish manufacturing sector—but not for long. The city's industries fared poorly in the era of great corporate "trusts."

GOVERNMENT AND POLITICS

The alliance between Isaac Freeman Rasin and Arthur Pue Gorman—known to their opponents as the Gorman-Rasin Ring—was a formidable presence in Baltimore throughout this era and breached the boundary between city and state politics. Their regime took hold in the gubernatorial election of 1871, when the two bosses engineered the victory of William Pinkney Whyte.

Rasin managed to run Baltimore while remaining almost invisible. He reached the pinnacle of his career in electoral politics as clerk of the Court of Common Pleas. He held the job for eighteen years, then got a customhouse appointment during the first Grover Cleveland administration and later served as state insurance commissioner. He made his career in politics largely by advancing the careers of others. Rasin's support helped to lift Howard County's Arthur Pue Gorman from a seat in the House of Delegates to House majority leader, then Democratic boss of Maryland, and finally to the U.S. Senate.

Railroad politics figured prominently in Whyte's election and in the formation of the Gorman-Rasin Ring. The incumbent governor and Whyte's rival for the nomination was Odin Bowie. Bowie had earlier secured a charter for a railroad that would break the Baltimore and Ohio (B&O) Railroad's monopoly on rail traffic between Baltimore and Washington, D.C. The Pennsylvania Railroad backed Bowie's election as a way of assuring state approval for the new line and provided a $400,000 loan to help with its construction. The B&O wanted Bowie out of the governor's mansion before the line could be built. William Pinkney Whyte was a good friend of B&O president John Work Garrett, and the railroad put its considerable resources behind Whyte's campaign to win the governorship from Bowie.

According to Frank Kent, the *Baltimore Sun*'s foremost commentator on state and local politics, the election of 1871 marked a seismic shift in the character of Baltimore politics. It was the first, he claims, in which vote-buying played a significant role. The practice coincided with the implementation of the Fifteenth Amendment, which made African American men members of the local electorate. The city's Democratic organization countered black voters' affinity for the party of Abraham Lincoln by paying them to stay away from the polls. Isaac Rasin routinized the arrangement. Thomas A. Smith, his chief operative in Baltimore's black community, would appear at Rasin's office after an election to count up the registered black voters who had cast their votes. Smith would be paid according to the number of black voters who failed to show up at the polls. The buying of white votes was not far behind. Vote-buying was corrupt, but it was a far

QUICK FACTS

BALTIMORE, MD 1877–1896

MAYORS

George P. Kane	(1877–1878)
Ferdinand C. Latrobe	(1878–1881)
William P. Whyte	(1881–1883)
Ferdinand C. Latrobe	(1883–1885)
James Hodges	(1885–1887)
Ferdinand C. Latrobe	(1887–1889)
Robert C. Davidson	(1889–1891)
Ferdinand C. Latrobe	(1891–1895)
Alcaeus Hooper	(1895–1897)

MAJOR INDUSTRIES AND EMPLOYERS

Men's clothing
Canning
Brickmaking
Cotton goods
Foundry and machine shop products
Tin, sheet iron, and coppersmithing

MAJOR NEWSPAPERS

Baltimore Sun
Baltimore News
Star
Baltimore American
Baltimore Herald
World
Der Deutsche Correspondent

MAJOR EVENTS

1878: Rasin machine stalwart Ferdinand C. Latrobe is elected to his second of five terms as mayor.
1882: Isaac Rasin's organization loses the "new judges" campaign.
1888: The Maryland legislature approves new election law applying only to Baltimore.
1895: The Gorman-Rasin Ring suffers defeat.
1896: The Baltimore and Ohio Railroad goes into receivership.

more civilized way of managing the electorate than the homicidal violence that had terrorized voters before Rasin imposed his businesslike regime.

Arthur Gorman profited far more handsomely from the election of Governor Whyte than did black nonvoters. Whyte fired the incumbent president of the Chesapeake and Ohio (C&O) Canal and appointed Gorman in his place. Gorman gained a substantial salary and control of the numerous jobs connected with the canal's maintenance and management. The appointment had a peculiar effect on Gorman's (and Rasin's) corporate affiliations. The C&O operated in competition with the B&O. Although it had just helped to elect a friend of the B&O as governor, the Gorman-Rasin organization now leaned toward the Pennsylvania Railroad and away from the B&O.

Republicans, by themselves, posed no threat to the Gorman-Rasin Ring. They were so weak, according to political historian Frank Kent in his 1911 book *The Story of Maryland Politics*, that "they would fuse with most any disgruntled element of the Democrats that chose to put up a set of candidates." And there were always disgruntled Democrats. In 1875 the first coalition of Republicans and "Independent" Democrats challenged the Gorman-Rasin ticket from governor down to city council. One of their most distinguished leaders and orators was Severn Teackle Wallis, a Baltimore attorney and literary figure whose Confederate sympathies had earned him fourteen months' imprisonment during the Civil War—and the admiration of the city's numerous ex-Confederates who leaned toward the Independents. John K. Cowen provided more than oratory skills. He was the chief counsel (and later president) of the B&O. His corporate interests set him at odds with the Gorman-Rasin organization, which fed on the resources of the C&O. A state tax on Cowen's railroad's income, enacted in 1872, probably intensified his enmity toward the Gorman-Rasin Ring.

The Gorman-Rasin Ring swept both the state and municipal elections in 1875, but the victors had been chastened by the battle. Isaac Rasin adopted the practice of nominating reformers for visible municipal offices in order, he said, to "perfume" the ticket. In 1877 he named George P. Kane, a friend of the Independents, as candidate for mayor and "perfumery" for the Democratic slate.

George Kane died after a year in office, and Ferdinand Latrobe, the Rasin organization's "default" mayor, easily won a special election and became mayor once again. Latrobe obligingly stood aside from the mayoral contest in 1881 so that William Pinkney Whyte could take his place. Arthur Gorman had incurred Whyte's enmity by taking his seat in the Senate. According to Frank Kent, Gorman believed that making Whyte mayor "would be the most effective way of permanently sidetracking him as a political factor and preventing him from coming again to the front as a State leader."

Whyte, however, still exercised influence in some quarters. Several of the city's trial judges—known collectively as the Supreme Bench—stood ready to do the bidding of the mayor and the Rasin organization that stood behind him. One of the judges was Whyte's brother. In 1882 the terms of four judges expired. Leading attorneys among the Independent Democrats and their Republican allies launched a "new judges" campaign to place the court beyond the "polluting touch of politics," as one of them put it, by defeating three of the judges most clearly identified with Whyte and Rasin. Although the Rasin organization united with Whyte in defense of the old judges, Gorman remained inactive and remote, and he was rumored to be backing the reformers in secret. In a campaign illuminated by the pyrotechnic oratory of the city's best attorneys, the reformers handed Isaac Rasin his first political defeat, while serving Gorman's purposes by destroying what was left of Mayor Whyte's influence.

The "new judges" victory raised hope among the Independent Democrats that they might be able to win a controlling share in local government. A showdown came in 1885. "By long odds," wrote Frank Kent, "it was the fiercest municipal election ever fought in Baltimore." The Independents, who had been steadily narrowing the victory margins of the Gorman-Rasin Ring's candidates, seemed to be closing in on electoral triumph. The most distinguished political orators in the city spoke on their behalf, and they were backed by John K. Cowen—no mean orator himself—and his B&O Railroad. But the Independents came up short once again. Their defeat was due in part to the meticulous management of John J. "Sonny" Mahon, leader of the Ninth Ward, who negotiated patronage deals with Republicans assuring that many of them would "lie down" on Election Day.

The Independents and their Republican allies charged that the organization had fabricated its triumph through electoral fraud. Fraud became the leading issue in Baltimore's elections. By 1888 the pressure for electoral reform was so powerful that the Maryland General Assembly, prodded by the city's Independent Democrats, enacted new electoral safeguards applying only to Baltimore. The legislation required precinct-level voter registration every two years. The minority party was guaranteed a spot among the three election judges in each precinct, and minority representation was also mandated for the citywide Board of Election Supervisors that selected the judges. Each supervisor was to have a veto over proposed appointments. A final touch was the requirement that all of Baltimore's ballot boxes be made of clear glass.

The reformers were encouraged, but not satisfied, and immediately began campaigning for the secret ballot. But the battle for and against reform was condensed and personalized in the white-hot animosity between Arthur Gorman and John Cowen. In the 1889 campaign Gorman ignored all of his reform opponents except Cowen. In a vigorous stump speech, he accused Cowen of using the reform movement as a vehicle to advance the corporate interests of the B&O. Cowen responded with a four-column letter in the *Baltimore Sun,* and the exchange of charges and insults continued until Election Day.

Rasin's candidates carried the city as usual, but the struggle against the machine continued, and the fight over electoral reform became even more entwined with the interpersonal battle between Gorman and Cowen. In 1892 Gorman's second term in the U.S. Senate was set to end, and he wanted to be elected to a third. His ongoing feud with John Cowen cast a shadow over his prospects. Through an intermediary, he offered Cowen a truce. Cowen agreed to end his attacks on Gorman so long as the Democratic legislators in Annapolis looked kindly on the interests of his railroad.

Isaac Rasin was not covered by the treaty between Gorman and Cowen. He achieved a similar peace, however, by surrendering much of the Baltimore City Democratic ticket to the Independents. His strategy virtually silenced charges of manipulation in the city elections of 1893.

The peace was brief, and although many pressures contributed to the political eruption of 1895, Arthur Gorman's conduct in the U.S. Senate led most clearly to the downfall of the Gorman-Rasin Ring. In 1894 Gorman used his position as chair of the Democratic caucus to block legislation favorable to the B&O. Cowen regarded Gorman's act as a violation of their truce and, with renewed bitterness, prepared for an all-out showdown with the Gorman-Rasin Ring during the elections of 1895.

Gorman undermined his support among regular Democrats in Maryland by breaking with President Cleveland on the issues of silver coinage and the tariff. Cleveland pointedly demonstrated his alienation from Gorman by pressuring Isaac Rasin to arrange the election of John K. Cowen to the House of Representatives.

Maryland's Democrats were solid Cleveland supporters. So was Isaac Rasin, but he now bore the burden of his long partnership with Arthur Gorman. Gorman would not face reelection to the Senate until 1897, but Rasin had to endure a municipal election in 1895, and many Baltimoreans regarded the defeat of the Rasin organization as the first step toward unseating Gorman. On the defensive, the Rasin organization reverted to election-day violence not seen since the era of the Know-Nothings. Frank Kent declared it the "last disorderly election" in the city.

In a departure from the usual practice of quietly inducing African Americans to stay away from the polls, the Democrats made strident, racist appeals to the city's white majority. Republicans took control of both city and state governments, however, and they only grew stronger after the election of William McKinley in 1896, at which point they gained the federal patronage that the Democrats lost.

INDUSTRY, COMMERCE, AND LABOR

In 1877 the Baltimore City Council appointed a commission to consider how to encourage the growth of local manufacturing. After a lengthy inquiry, the commission recommended that all machinery, tools, and "implements of manufacture" be exempted from municipal taxation. In 1881 the council transformed the recommendation into law.

Baltimore industry seemed to need encouragement. The city's principal business was shipping things, not making them. After its disruption during the Civil War, Baltimore's trade resumed its rapid expansion. Between 1870 and 1900, the value of the city's foreign trade grew enough to lift Baltimore from fifth to third place among American cities. In its seaborne trade with domestic ports, the city was outranked only by New York.

The same railroads and steamship lines that carried goods in and out of Baltimore could just as easily be carrying goods *made* in Baltimore, enabling the city to add the profits of manufacture to those of transport. To Ferdinand C. Latrobe, the city's perennial postbellum mayor, the opportunities seemed obvious. By 1887 he felt that his fellow citizens had come to share his view. According to Latrobe, "it seems at last to be generally conceded that the future wealth and prosperity of the city is dependent on manufacturing industries."

In many cases, manufacturing was an outgrowth of the city's commerce. When Baltimore ships unloaded their cargoes of flour in the Caribbean, there was little to refill their holds save the sugar cane that provided the raw material for Baltimore's sugar refineries. Baltimore ships sailed past guano-encrusted islands in the Caribbean and off the west coast of Latin America. Gangs of black laborers from Baltimore were sent to these desolate places where, under hot sun and white overseers, they mined guano for shipment to the city's fertilizer plants, where the bird manure was processed and shipped out to enrich soil depleted by cotton and tobacco crops. The business eventually expanded from natural to chemical fertilizers. Just outside the city limits in Canton, smelters refined Cuban copper ore. By the close of the nineteenth century, Cuban iron ore and Pennsylvania coal converged in a massive mill in Sparrows Point to be used in the production of steel. The Chesapeake Bay itself provided the raw material for industrial enterprise. Baltimore canneries processed the bay's oysters so that they could be consumed far from salt water, and the canning business later extended to local vegetables and fruits.

The Civil War, while disrupting commerce, had fostered manufacturing. Government contracts enabled immigrant tailors from central and eastern Europe to convert their shops into factories for producing military uniforms. This required the tailors to abandon made-to-order production for standardized sizing, and, after the war, the manufacture of ready-to-wear men's and boy's clothing became Baltimore's biggest industry. The war also boosted shipbuilding and the production of sheet iron. A foundry in Canton produced the armor plating for the *U.S.S.*

Monitor and other Union ironclads. Textile plants just outside the city limits increased their output of sail cloth. By the 1880s Baltimore and its environs accounted for about 80 percent of all the sail cloth produced in the United States.

Growth prospects for the sail cloth industry, of course, were not promising. In fact, most of Baltimore's industries—even the most expansive—lagged behind competitors in other cities. Some historians argue that the Civil War had traumatized the city's business community and sapped the vitality of its residents. Baltimore had been the financial capital of the South, and the destruction of the Confederacy made local bankers and investors more conservative and less willing to take chances. There were also more tangible signs of the city's economic conservatism. In Baltimore, for example, manufacturing firms were less likely to incorporate and issue stock than in other East Coast cities. Baltimore businesses tended to be privately held and family owned. Although the city's industrial output was growing, it was not growing as rapidly as in other cities. After 1880, in fact, its rank as a manufacturing center began to decline. Perhaps most tellingly, Baltimore factories invested less money in machinery than factories elsewhere. This shortfall suggests not just technological backwardness but an impaired capacity to compete. Machinery usually meant lower prices.

Baltimore paid for its backwardness. Its manufacturing sector grew sluggishly, in relative terms, at a time when monopolistic trusts were gobbling up their weaker competitors. John D. Rockefeller was the first to strike the city's industrial base. He bought or drove out of business all of the independently owned oil refineries in Baltimore and later absorbed the survivors into Standard Oil. Rockefeller and Jay Gould joined forces to purchase the B&O Railroad's telegraph company and added it to Western Union. The two largest manufacturers of cigarettes and cigars were taken over by the American Tobacco Company. The capital stock of the Baltimore Sugar Refining Company was acquired by the American Sugar Refining Company. The largest cracker factory south of New York was bought out by the company that later became Nabisco. Eight local fertilizer factories were taken over by the American Agricultural Chemical Company. Perhaps the most jarring shock to Baltimore's economy was the failure of the Baltimore and Ohio Railroad, the city's signature enterprise. The company could not cover the bonds that it had issued to cover its construction costs. It stopped paying dividends from 1888 to 1890 and went into receivership in 1896. The railroad emerged from bankruptcy in 1899, but by then its owners were the New York and Chicago investors who had been the railroad's creditors.

Baltimore became a branch office town. The city's workers suffered a parallel loss of status. Industrial consolidation and mechanization undermined their bargaining power. Industrial machinery often made it possible for factories to reduce their labor costs by replacing skilled men with unskilled women and children. In 1880, for example, Baltimore's canneries introduced a machine that could substitute one man and one boy for five skilled makers of cans.

Trade unions multiplied along with the factories. In 1886 alone Baltimore workers formed sixteen new unions, and the Maryland Bureau of Industrial Statistics and Information counted a total of ninety-six unions in the city that had a combined membership of about twenty-five thousand. On May Day 1886, eleven thousand union members marched through Baltimore demanding an eight-hour workday. Less than a week after the parade, however, came the Haymarket riot in Chicago. Like the Baltimore bank riot fifty years earlier, the Haymarket affair diminished public support for labor activism in Baltimore and seemed to legitimize employers' resistance to the "radical" demands of organized labor. Only ten of the unions formed in the 1880s survived into the 1890s. A brief resurgence in the labor movement during 1892 was cut short by the panic of 1893, which thinned the ranks of almost all Baltimore unions, some of which simply disappeared.

RACE, ETHNICITY, AND IMMIGRATION

Between 1870 and 1900, more than six hundred thousand foreign immigrants landed in Baltimore, but the vast majority of them remained only briefly in the city before moving to destinations further west, where urban economies were growing more rapidly than Baltimore's. After 1870, in fact, the proportion of foreign-born residents in Baltimore's population actually declined. The in-migrants who accounted for most of Baltimore's population growth in the late nineteenth century came not from abroad, but from rural communities in the United States. Most came from Maryland itself. About a third of the American-born in-migrants were black. After 1880 Baltimore's African American population equaled or exceeded that of its foreign-born residents.

In the labor market, however, African Americans and foreign immigrants were not equal. Oyster shucking, for example, had traditionally been a job for black men, but immigrant women took over that niche in the local economy during the late 1870s, and by the 1880s, they were being hired as domestic servants. In the city's shipyards, racial conflict had erupted a generation before the Civil War, especially in ship caulking, where African Americans had gained a foothold. After emancipation, the position of the black caulkers became more precarious. In order to protect their jobs, African American workers raised $40,000 in capital to finance their own shipyard, which employed as many as three hundred caulkers. But neither they nor the white caulkers who ousted them could secure their jobs when wooden hulls were replaced by steel. The black-owned shipyard went out of business in 1883.

The white immigrants themselves were far from unified. From 1870 through 1890, Germans accounted for about 60 percent of Baltimore's foreign-born population. They outnumbered Irish-born residents by more than two to one, but the German population was internally divided. German Protestants generally voted for Republicans, while German Catholics joined the Irish in backing Democrats. Aside from voting, however, neither Catholic nor Protestant Germans became fully engaged in local politics. They founded their own churches, schools, choral groups, shooting clubs, fraternal organizations, and newspapers. Baltimore accommodated their separateness. In 1868 the Maryland General Assembly required that all public laws and ordinances be published in at least two Baltimore newspapers, one of which had to be in German. The practice continued until World War II. In the 1870s, the Board of School Commissioners opened an experimental school that offered instruction in both English and German. By 1897 there were seven German American public schools enrolling almost seven thousand pupils.

Baltimore's African American children had no public schools at all until 1867, and for many years thereafter the city spent far less on the education of black children than on the education of its white children. The city also discriminated against adult blacks. The city's hotels and schools were rigidly segregated. Public transportation was supposed to follow the same practice, but white riders were not sufficiently patient to wait for white horse cars—or sufficiently averse to traveling with African Americans. In addition, Baltimore's black community was largely spared the terror, mob violence, and lynchings that whites in the Deep South visited on African Americans, and black Baltimoreans were permitted to vote after the ratification of the Fifteenth Amendment even though the Maryland General Assembly had refused to ratify it.

See also *Baltimore, MD 1776–1790; Baltimore, MD 1790–1828; Baltimore, MD 1828–1854; Baltimore, MD 1854–1877; Baltimore, MD 1896–1929; Baltimore, MD 1929–1941; Baltimore, MD 1941–1952; Baltimore, MD 1952–1989*

MATTHEW CRENSON

BIBLIOGRAPHY

Bruchey, Eleanor. "The Industrialization of Baltimore, 1860–1914." In *Maryland: A History, 1632–1974*, edited by Richard Walsh and William Lloyd Fox. Baltimore: Maryland Historical Society, 1974.

Crooks, James. "The Baltimore Fire and Baltimore Reform." *Maryland Historical Magazine* 65 (1970): 1–17.

Hirschfeld, Charles. *Baltimore, 1870–1900: Studies in Social History*. Baltimore, MD: Johns Hopkins University Press, 1941.

Kent, Frank R. *The Story of Maryland Politics*. Baltimore, MD: Thomas and Evans, 1911.

Lambert, John R. *Arthur Pue Gorman*. Baton Rouge: Louisiana State University Press, 1953.

SAN FRANCISCO, CA 1877–1896

THE ALMOST TWENTY YEARS BETWEEN 1877 AND 1896 WERE A PERIOD OF INDUSTRIAL DEVELOPMENT marked by dramatic ebbs and flows of the business cycle, elite consolidation, urban expansion, population growth, and intense class and racial conflict. By 1880 San Francisco had climbed to hold the rank of the ninth most populous city, one of the most industrially productive cities in the nation, and the largest city on the West Coast. During this decade the city responded to its increasing growth by doubling its inhabited area. By 1890 its diverse population stood at three hundred thousand. During these years, San Franciscans witnessed the rise and fall of the Workingmen's Party of California, the heyday of the machine-style political organization led by Christopher Augustine Buckley, and the ascendancy of a new breed of businessmen reformers, symbolized by James Phelan's mayoral victory in 1896.

GOVERNMENT AND POLITICS

From 1877 to 1896, San Franciscans, like other Americans, conducted politics in three primary arenas: on the local city scene, on the state and national stage, and through less-formal vehicles such as parades, petitions, riots, uprisings, reform efforts, and fraternal and benevolent associations that frequently gave a political voice to the socially marginalized or disenfranchised.

QUICK FACTS

SAN FRANCISCO, CA 1877–1896

MAYORS

Andrew Jackson Bryant	(1875–1879)
Isaac Smith Kalloch	(1879–1881)
Maurice Carey Blake	(1881–1883)
Washington Bartlett	(1883–1887)
Edward B. Pond	(1887–1891)
George Henry Sanderson	(1891–1893)
Levi Richard Ellert	(1893–1895)
Adolph Sutro	(1895–1897)
James Phelan	(1897–1902)

MAJOR INDUSTRIES AND EMPLOYERS

Central-Southern Pacific Railroad

Union Iron Works

Pacific Rolling Mills

California Sugar Refinery (one of three firms controlling the nation's sugar business in the 1890s)

The Palace Hotel

MAJOR NEWSPAPERS

San Francisco Morning Call

San Francisco Evening Bulletin

San Francisco Chronicle

San Francisco Examiner

MAJOR EVENTS

1877: The Workingmen's Party of California, an explicitly anti-Chinese political party, emerges and dominates city politics for four years.

1882: Congress passes the Chinese Exclusion Act, the first law to label a specific group of people as undesirable for immigration to the United States.

1889: The majority of black workers at the Palace Hotel are fired due to accusations of theft and replaced by white workers. This was more than likely the result of pressure from the Cooks' and Waiters' Protective and Benevolent Union, formerly the Cooks' and Waiters' Anti-Coolie Association.

1894: The California Midwinter International Exposition is held in Golden Gate Park—the first ever held west of Chicago.

1896: Banker James Phelan's election as mayor marks the rise of businessmen reformers on the city's political scene.

1877 was both a year of departure from local political norms and a watershed year that signaled how solidly intertwined San Francisco's economic and political conditions were with those of the nation. The country hurtled headlong into a massive economic depression coupled with mounting class conflict that had begun with the panic of 1873. In San Francisco the economic crisis was exacerbated by declining yields from the silver mines of the Comstock, a drought that caused the grain harvest to fail, and the completion of the transcontinental railroad in 1869, which opened new opportunities for expanded commerce and economic growth but left the workforce that constructed it without gainful employment. By sloughing large numbers of unemployed workers into an already stressed economy, all of these factors—the results of the combined effects of industrial capitalism and nature—fueled longstanding fears among many white workers of unfair labor competition from Chinese immigrants. The year 1877 marked a point of intensification in the long history of cross-class anti-Chinese racism in San Francisco. In the context of heightened economic tensions in the city, this intensification pushed local politics in a new direction, and a political party with an explicitly anti-Chinese platform, the Workingmen's Party of California (WPC), emerged on the scene and came to dominate city politics for nearly four years.

The WPC's leader, Denis Kearney, rose to prominence espousing a message that combined familiar anti-Chinese political rhetoric with a new anticapitalist twist. It could be boiled down to the following key points: The rich used the Chinese to drive down wages, workers suffered due to both millionaires atop Nob Hill and their minions in Chinatown, monopolies must be destroyed, and, always his closing remark, "the Chinese Must Go."

By early 1878 the WPC had become a major political force both in San Francisco and elsewhere in the state. It reached the height of its state power in mid-1878 and remained a potent force in city affairs through the end of 1879. I. S. Kalloch, a prominent Baptist minister, was elected mayor of San Francisco in 1879 on the WPC ticket. The Democratic Party virtually disappeared as the WPC seized the support of normally Democratic voters and commanded the loyalty of half the voters in the city. Moreover, support for the WPC divided more starkly across class lines than it had for the Democratic Party. In working-class neighborhoods, the WPC had consistently stronger voter support than the Democrats; in middle-class and upper-class areas, the WPC did worse. Yet by 1881 the party was defunct, and its loyalists were absorbed back into the political order. The WPC ultimately did not provide realistic solutions to the complex problems it critiqued, and better economic times made its critiques seem less necessary.

Despite its brief existence, the WPC had done something extraordinary. It had piqued the interest of national politicians who picked up the anti-Chinese issue and began manipulating it in order to garner greater electoral support among working-class voters and to deflect attention from genuine national problems such as economic depression, mass poverty, and growing unemployment. Politicians across the country started denouncing the Chinese with a kind of antipathy once only heard among westerners. The result was the Chinese Exclusion Act of 1882, which set a significant legal precedent in that it was the first law to label a specific group of people as undesirable for immigration to the United States. In doing this, it departed from the traditional American policy of unrestricted immigration.

Throughout the last quarter of the nineteenth century, the Democratic Party was the leading electoral force in San Francisco politics. Beginning with victories in 1875 and again in 1877, in which the party won all city offices and most legislative seats, for the next twenty-five years Democrats usually won the mayoralty and majorities on the San Francisco Board of Supervisors. Sometimes these were narrow victories, and three times Democrats were defeated by strong third-party or independent candidates.

San Francisco's business elite tended to steer clear of local city politics, which they generally left to men of the working and middle classes, and which they viewed as profoundly limited in its powers due to the effects of the Consolidation Act of 1856. Instead, for the most part, San Francisco's railroad, banking, and mining tycoons turned their attention to the national government in Washington and the state government in Sacramento, which they saw as having the power to aid their business interests. As a result, in the 1880s, San Francisco had the unique distinction of having three sitting U.S. Senators—John F. Miller (1881–1886), Leland Stanford (1885–1893), and George Hearst (1886–1891)—among its residents.

From 1882 to 1891, a machine-style party organization dominated city government and concentrated power in the hands of Christopher Augustine Buckley, the undisputed boss of San Francisco's Democratic Party. The foot soldiers of Buckley's organization came from the working classes south of Market where firehouses, militia companies, saloons, and fraternal associations served as important sites of operation, but slates of candidates came from the middle-class business community and had enough respectability and ethnic cosmopolitanism (with identifiable Irish, German, French, Jewish, and Italian surnames) to give them citywide appeal.

The 1890s, however, gave rise to the emergence of a new kind of political culture that initially coexisted with, but was ultimately a reaction against, Buckley's political machine. Within the Democratic Party, these years reflected both a climate of increasing class tensions and a new style of politics organized along the lines of business, science, and professional expertise that sought to bring together upwardly mobile working-class voters and younger voters from the city's commercial upper class. This stood in stark contrast to the practices of Buckley and his associates and predecessors, who had emphasized personal relationships rather than specialized training. In 1894 fifty members of the city's business elite launched the nonpartisan Merchant's Association, dedicated to applying business principles to city government. Soon this organization was a major player in a campaign for a revised city charter that would not only release city government from the limitations of the 1856 Consolidation Act, but also further the Merchant Association's own agenda. The charter that emerged advocated a strengthened, more centralized city government and an enhanced civil service. It was undergirded by corporate principles and possessed a suspicious attitude toward working-class civic participation. San Franciscans voted it down in 1896, but they elected James Phelan to the office of mayor. Phelan had not only supported the charter but had campaigned on a platform that advocated intertwining the principles of corporate management with those of municipal administration. Phelan typified the new businessman reformer—a sharp contrast to the city's longstanding culture of personal politics and decade of boss Buckley—and his election established a political culture grounded in coalition-building and a corporate style that endured well into the twentieth century.

INDUSTRY, COMMERCE, AND LABOR

By the early 1870s, San Francisco had emerged as an industrial city as well as a commercial and financial center. During the 1860s, as manufacturing output's value quadrupled, capital investments in industry saw a tenfold increase, and the growing number of people employed in industrial jobs expanded to eighteen times greater than what it had been at the beginning of the decade. Indeed, nearly half of the city's workforce labored in industrial jobs. The capital necessary for the expansion of manufacturing originated principally within San Francisco. Some funding came from local industrialists, but the bulk of requisite investment came from profits from speculation—primarily in mining and especially the silver boom of the Comstock Lode. Prior to the 1860s, shortages of labor and raw materials, limited demand, and transportation hurdles had hampered speculation in manufacturing enterprises in the city. By the 1870s, the end of the Civil War, the transcontinental railroad, growing local markets, and increasing flows of labor and raw materials combined to make San Francisco more attractive as a site of industrial speculation and contributed to the city's industrial development. These economic and demographic trends continued into the 1880s as San Francisco advanced to rank ninth among the nation's cities in both population and industrial output.

From January 27 to July 4, 1894, San Francisco business elites produced an extravaganza that displayed the city's technological achievements and heralded a vision of social order associated with the level of industrial progress the city had recently attained: the California Midwinter International Exposition, also known as the Midwinter Fair. It was the first American international exposition ever held west of Chicago. The fair was designed, in part, to boost the image, morale, and finances of the city in trying times, as the ravages of the panic of 1893 brought skyrocketing levels of economic ruin and unemployment to the local economy. While the Midwinter Fair itself was deemed a success, the depression's effects played out next door to its grounds in Golden Gate Park in a huge citywide work-relief project, and the thousands of unemployed men who gathered on a daily basis could not help but present an ironic, mocking contrast to the exposition's overall celebration of capitalist progress.

Throughout the nineteenth century, the fate of San Francisco's workers was tied to the ups and downs of the business cycle. The city's increasing industrial production, for example, did not bode well for labor since the same conditions that favored labor—primarily labor scarcity which kept wages high and made workers reluctant to accept industrial employment—actually hindered the development of manufactures. Up until the 1870s, although labor unions remained unstable, frequently forming, dissolving, changing, and reappearing, labor had enjoyed a comparatively favorable position in the city and developed a reputation for both radicalism and an explicitly political orientation. Late in the 1860s, labor scarcity decreased as the city's population grew. These new residents—many of whom were foreign-born—had fewer choices about the kinds of work they could do and, as a result, effectively increased the labor pool for large manufacturing enterprises.

During the stronger economy of the 1880s, however, the number of unions not only grew but organizations also began to more successfully weather depressions, lost strikes, and employer opposition, in part due to increasing levels of national affiliation. It was during this period that the anti-Chinese agitation that had emerged as a force in city politics was explicitly transferred to labor groups. Founded in the late 1870s, the Cooks' and Waiters' Anti-Coolie Association, which became the Cooks' and Waiters' Protective and Benevolent Union in the early 1880s, had considerable success in using boycotts and threats of walkouts to convince restaurant owners to employ only white help. In all likelihood, it was also behind the firing of the majority of the black workers at the Palace Hotel under the cover of accusations of theft in 1889. That year, white workers rapidly replaced the black workforce. Service jobs at the Palace, the city's finest hotel, had represented well-paying, respectable work among the city's black community, which had staffed the hotel without incident since its opening in 1875.

However, by the early 1890s, many of the advances made by unions in the 1880s were stymied by the combination of an employer-led, citywide open-shop drive and a national economic depression. As a result, by the mid-1890s, labor organization in San Francisco was at its lowest point in fifteen years. With renewed prosperity in the late 1890s, however, the city witnessed an unprecedented renaissance of union activity.

San Franciscans responded to the increase in the density of settlement that followed population growth by doubling the city's inhabited area in the 1880s. During the 1870s, the city had begun its transformation from a traditional nineteenth-century walking city into an industrial metropolis—the opposite of a walking city in terms of its size, complexity, and spatial and social geographies. As the metropolis replaced the walking city, social segregation and spatial separation became increasingly prevalent forms of urban organization and had far-reaching implications for the way residents used and conceptualized public space. Residential, commercial, and entertainment districts became distinct parts of town. The boundaries of affluent suburbs, middle-class neighborhoods, and crowded working-class districts became more clearly defined and, even with advances in transportation, encounters among their residents diminished.

RACE, ETHNICITY, AND IMMIGRATION

According to the censuses of 1870, 1880, and 1890, San Francisco had a higher percentage of foreign-born residents than any other major American city—including New York City; Boston, Massachusetts; Chicago, Illinois; Milwaukee, Wisconsin; Detroit, Michigan; and Cleveland, Ohio. The Massachusetts mill towns of Fall River, Lowell, and Lawrence were the only places nationally with proportionally more foreign-born residents. By 1870 Chinese immigrants made up 8 percent of San Francisco's inhabitants. By 1900, reflecting both increased Japanese immigration after 1890 and the out-migration and decreased immigration of Chinese as a result of the Chinese Exclusion Act, Chinese and Japanese San Franciscans made up 4.6 percent of the population. In 1870, 41.5 percent of the white population was foreign-born, but that percentage had dropped to 30.4 by 1900. Most of these people had immigrated from Ireland, Germany, England, Scotland, Wales, Scandinavia, or Italy. Latinos, primarily Californios, Mexicans, Chileans, and Peruvians, were also a significant presence throughout this period. African Americans, most from New England and the Mid-Atlantic states like their Euro-American counterparts, represented a relatively small portion of the population, comprising .9 percent in 1870 and .5 percent in 1890. In terms of the balance between men and women, the sex ratio of seven men for every five women in the 1880s and 1890s—which meant women comprised about 45 percent of the population—was much closer to national norms than was the three-to-two ratio that prevailed in the 1860s or the nearly eleven-to-one ratio at the height of the gold rush.

While in many ways the broad patterns of San Francisco's racial order in the late nineteenth century followed national norms of white supremacy, the city also possessed unique local inflections. San Francisco's inclusive circle of whiteness drew Irish, Italian, and Jewish immigrants more quickly into ethnic white identities than in other cities like Boston or New York. This was in part because in San Francisco ethnic whites united against the Chinese across lines that often otherwise divided them. Although in many other American cities African Americans were often the group that bore the full brunt of white antipathy during this period, in San Francisco, the Chinese occupied this place in the racial hierarchy.

See also *San Francisco, CA 1854–1877*

BARBARA BERGLUND

BIBLIOGRAPHY

Berglund, Barbara. *Making San Francisco American: Cultural Frontiers in the Urban West, 1846–1906.* Lawrence: University Press of Kansas, 2007.

Bullough, William A. *The Blind Boss and His City: Christopher Augustine Buckley & Nineteenth-Century San Francisco.* Berkeley: University of California Press, 1979.

Daniels, Henry Douglas. *Pioneer Urbanites: A Social and Cultural History of Black San Francisco.* Philadelphia, PA: Temple University Press, 1980.

Gyory, Andrew. *Closing the Gate: Race, Politics, and the Chinese Exclusion Act.* Chapel Hill: University of North Carolina Press, 1998.

Issel, William, and Cherny, Robert W. *San Francisco, 1865–1932: Politics, Power, and Urban Development.* Berkeley: University of California Press, 1986.

Ryan, Mary P. *Civic Wars: Democracy and Public Life in the American City during the Nineteenth Century.* Berkeley: University of California Press, 1997.

CINCINNATI, OH 1877–1896

SITUATED ON THE BANKS OF THE OHIO RIVER at the borderline separating the North from the South, Cincinnati underwent dramatic changes in the late nineteenth century. Driven by economic transformation and population growth, this remarkable change process produced a "new city," characterized by technological innovation, crisis and disorder, and chaotic and unplanned patterns of growth and development. For example, the population leapt by 68.1 percent between 1870 and 1900 as the city grew from 216,239 to 363,591 residents and expanded its boundaries from six square miles in 1850 to 35.27 square miles by 1900. Even so, Cincinnati still lost ground in the urban rivalry, as it dropped from the sixth largest city in 1850 to the tenth largest in 1900. After 1900 it was never again listed in the top ten largest American cities.

The city's volatile change process was characterized by the emergence of a modern manufacturing system and intense battles between workers and employers as they fought over declining work conditions and contending visions of the "new city" and the role of the workers in it. As the business elites and workers collided, two additional subplots painted the evolving urban landscape with even more texture and color. First, the city's changing socioeconomic structure caused blacks to lose ground. The abolishment of the colored school system in 1887 symbolized the growing marginalization of African Americans in the new urban environment and also demonstrated the inability of these schools to stop or even slow the downward trajectory of black life in the city. Between 1870 and 1900, for example, the proportion of blacks in low-paying, semiskilled, and unskilled jobs grew dramatically.

Second, the influx of thousands of newcomers combined with the building of large factories triggered the unplanned and chaotic growth of the city. This development, coupled with the growing inability of the municipal institutions to grapple successfully with the problems of water, sewage, transportation, schooling, housing, and police and fire protection, produced an

QUICK FACTS

CINCINNATI, OH 1877–1896

MAYORS

Robert M. Moore	(1877–1879)
Charles Jacobs Jr.	(1879–1881)
William F. Means	(1881–1883)
Thomas J. Stephens	(1883–1885)
Amor Smith Jr.	(1885–1889)
John B. Mosby	(1889–1894)
John A. Caldwell	(1894–1897)

MAJOR INDUSTRIES AND EMPLOYERS

Apparel

Leather goods

Carriages, furniture, and wood products

Food products (e.g., pork)

Alcohol and tobacco

Glycerin

Printed materials

MAJOR NEWSPAPERS

Commercial Gazette

Cincinnati Enquirer

Cincinnati Times-Star

Weekly Cincinnati Times

Volksblatt

Volksfreund

Der Sonntagmorgen

MAJOR EVENTS

1884: The burning of the county jail and county court house and the subsequent riots, which last for three nights, reflect the growing tension between business elites and the working class, as well as the elites' ongoing effort to co-opt the working-class movement.

1870–1888: Sponsored by the Ohio Mechanics Institute and Cincinnati's Chamber of Commerce and Board of Trade, the Cincinnati Industrial Expositions are held to promote arts and manufactures, as well as the economic development of the city.

1878–1884: In this six-year period, Cincinnati workers organize one hundred new unions and membership increases from one thousand to twelve thousand.

1886: Republican governor Joseph B. Foraker selects George Cox to serve as his chief advisor on patronage and political affairs in Hamilton County. Cox used this position to build a political machine that dominated Cincinnati politics until 1911.

1887: Ohio law abolishes segregated schools, thereby closing Cincinnati's renowned colored schools.

---

unprecedented set of urban problems. These issues demonstrated the need for redefining the urban problem and for city planning and land-use regulation, while simultaneously highlighting the inefficiency of government. These pressures wrought by industrialization and population growth played out on all fronts—government and politics; industry, commerce and labor; and race, ethnicity, and immigration.

GOVERNMENT AND POLITICS

In the late nineteenth century, city governance emerged as a critical issue. Cincinnati was confronting unprecedented levels of crime, prostitution, labor turmoil, political corruption, and governmental inefficiency. Increasing industrialization combined with continued foreign and domestic migration produced a new type of city. As Cincinnati's population grew and the city became physically enlarged, the population became increasingly segregated along class and racial lines, and political and social problems took on a spatial dimension. Municipal institutions and agencies established to deal with the walking city became overburdened, outmoded, and dilapidated. Concurrently, the splitting of the city into distinct residential districts that reflected its varied class, ethnic, and racial make-up complicated the quest of business and professional elites to gain control over the political system. So, throughout much of the late nineteenth century, factionalism dominated Cincinnati politics. This fragmentation could only be overcome by the triumph of a social group with the unity and power to create an alliance based on neighborhood leaders that were willing to unite regardless of party affiliation. Three forces emerged during this period to usher in new political leadership that gained control over the city's political apparatus near the century's end.

The transformation of the business and professional elites into a conscious group played the critical role in shaping politics and government in the late nineteenth century. Throughout the period, the elites built cultural institutions, commercial clubs, and good government associations, which brought them together regardless of where they lived or the economic sector in which they worked. Through their interactions, the elites diluted their rivalries, and by collectively grappling with issues such as smoke abatement, street cleaning, and civil service reform, they begin to understand how their mutual interests were a foundation for unity. Prominent attorney Julius Dexter epitomized the business and professional elites of this era. He supported cultural institutions and charities and was prominent in political reform movements. Dexter was involved in many organizations and associations: he was secretary of the Committee of One Hundred, a founding shareholder of the city's art museum and music hall association, treasurer of the exclusive Queen City Club, and active in the Commercial Club of Cincinnati.

Participation in these institutions, organizations, and associations gave business and civic elites like Dexter a generalized identity and consciousness of themselves as a group, and this "consciousness" morphed into the ideal of "business citizenship" and a business-based notion of the "public good." These ideals made it possible for the elites to function as a team on common issues, in spite of the differences that separated them. Moreover, through a process of cultural transposition, the business elites were able to imbue the working class with these ideals as well. Anchoring these ideals were two interactive values: nonpartisanship, which meant the placement of the public good over individual and business interests, and a disdain for favoritism and political corruption. Within this context, government was viewed as a neutral arbitrator of justice that stood above the partisan fray, and only a nonpartisan approach could end corruption and guarantee a just city.

The working class, on the other hand, despite their radicalism and flirtation with socialist ideas, never developed class consciousness, and they never turned the unrest, numerous protests, and organizing activity into a sustainable political movement. One reason is the workers were divided along the lines of national origin, race, and ethnicity, as well as by the occupational categories to which they belonged. For example, about 57 percent of the workforce in 1870 and

38 percent in 1880 was foreign-born, and the entire working class was segmented into skilled, semiskilled, and unskilled cohorts. Therefore, culture, life in different neighborhoods, and varied work experiences created divisions within the working class that were difficult to overcome. At the same time, by embracing the conceptual frameworks of the business and professional classes, the working class negated their own political agenda by viewing the world through the same set of lenses as the elites.

The United Labor Party represented an effort of workers to translate their concerns into political power, but in Cincinnati and elsewhere this effort could not be sustained. The party and the politicization of workers failed because they were co-opted. The most intense years of working-class radicalism took place between 1886 and 1889. This coincided with the rise of George B. Cox as the driving force behind politics in Cincinnati.

In 1886 Republican governor Joseph B. Foraker appointed Cox as his chief advisor on patronage and political affairs in Hamilton County. Cox developed a powerful ward-based political machine and then forged an alliance with the business and professional elites to ensure the sustainability of this machine. To cement the alliance, Cox agreed to the political reforms advocated by the elites. He promoted a series of reforms, including the secret ballot, voter registration, and a series of state laws that, though retaining the mayor-council form of government with ward representation, were designed to give the city a stable and more centralized government. He also endorsed the building of a professional police force, the expansion and equipping of the fire department, and other initiatives designed to make Cincinnati a stable, orderly, and well-run city. In exchange, the elites helped Cox build and sustain his political machine, which remained in power until the second decade of the twentieth century.

INDUSTRY, COMMERCE, AND LABOR

Manufacturing and the machine drove Cincinnati's development in the late nineteenth century and spawned significant changes in the city's life and culture. New forms of production and the growing mechanization of industry altered the realities of factory workers and owners alike. To survive and remain competitive, business owners in all economic sectors had to develop new labor processes and introduce managerial innovations that decreased costs and increased their control over the inner workings of the factory. As production became increasingly routinized and dependent on the machine, the importance and status of skilled workers declined and unskilled laborers, including women and children, came to dominate factory work.

Concurrently, the vast amount of capital required to start or expand a factory caused owners to abandon their financially limited family firms or small partnerships in favor of organizing highly capitalized corporations. This led to the emergence of a new industrial elite and a separation between the ownership and the management of factories. The reason is that most factory owners had limited or no experience in plant operations, so they hired managers to run the factories for them. Thus, as the late nineteenth century progressed, industrial production grew more efficient and more impersonal. These changes notwithstanding, Cincinnati still fell from third in manufacturing to seventh in overall production in 1880. However, unlike smaller, one-industry towns like Lynn, Massachusetts, Cincinnati was a multi-industrial city. So, even though it fell in overall production after 1860, the city was either still the first or among the top five national producers of carriages, furniture, glycerin, coffins, plug tobacco, whisky, safes, clothing, boots and shoes, beer, printed materials, pork and pork by-products, sawed lumber, harnesses, and various leather goods.

These economic changes had a differential impact on the working class, with both gender and racial implications. The growing mechanization of industry led to the growth of unskilled labor and a dramatic increase in female and child labor. By 1890 women constituted more than half the laborers in the city's clothing, fur, textile, regalia and society banner, box, bag, and canned food establishments. Because women and children workers were unskilled, they were also cheap labor. Manufacturers typically paid women and children one-quarter to one-half the wages of a man. Consequently, their widespread use in factory work depressed the wages of all industrial workers.

The continued proletarianization and degradation of workers produced ongoing confrontations between labor and capital. The growing unrest among Cincinnati workers was part of a broad national trend, with Queen City workers participating in the national struggles locally. Workers in big and small factories organized and joined in battles to improve their plight. Initially, their efforts focused on economic issues, but during the 1880s these struggles took on an increasingly political tone. For example, in 1877 Cincinnati workers joined the Great Railroad Strike, which spawned an epoch of intense worker rebellion in the city. Between 1878 and 1884, workers formed over one hundred unions as the number of trade unionists leapt from one thousand to twelve thousand men and women.

The 1884 courthouse riot represented the first step toward the development of working-class consciousness in Cincinnati. Frustrated by a decade of economic injustice, the misuses of state power, and political and judicial corruption, the workers marched upon and set fire to the county jail and the courthouse—both popular symbols of injustice. The triggering event was the murder trial of Joseph Palmer, a mulatto, and William Berner, a German immigrant, accused of beating their employer to death in the act of stealing $285. To workers, the conviction of the men for manslaughter instead of murder was symptomatic of the injustice and political corruptions characteristic of the period. They took action by burning down the courthouse and jail. The ensuing three-day uprising left thirty-five dead and two hundred wounded.

This battle was followed by the participation of Cincinnati workers in an 1866 May Day general strike for an eight-hour workday, followed by the establishment of a local chapter of the United Labor Party in February 1887. Under the party's banner, Cincinnati workers waged a political crusade for worker control of the city government. Ironically, in terms of their years of economic and political struggles, Cincinnati workers never viewed their radicalism as a battle between capital and labor; rather, they viewed these fights as battles between the law-abiding class and the law-breaking class. In this sense, the workers placed their struggle in a cultural war rather than a labor-versus-capital framework. Given the resources and cultural institutions controlled by the elites, workers had no chance of winning a cultural war, void of rhetoric that clearly outlined the distinctions between capital and labor. Hence, the cultural war was a fight the workers were doomed to lose from the start. This is why the business and professional elites were able to develop class consciousness and the working class was not.

RACE, ETHNICITY, AND IMMIGRATION

Race was also a defining feature of the nineteenth-century world of work. During this period, although many white workers experienced job dislocation and a number of white-owned business establishments disappeared, there were still many whites that took advantage of the new opportunities created by industrialization. Equally important, while declining wages pushed many white workers to the economic edge, the employment of large numbers of white women and children kept them from falling off.

Black workers, however, experienced a different reality. All black workers occupied a deteriorating position in the labor force. From 1870 to 1890, the more prestigious black occupations, such as barber and teacher, declined as laborer and domestic servant came to dominate the black job ladder. In Cincinnati in 1890 there were virtually no blacks—male or female—working as painters, carpenters, boot and shoemakers, iron- and steelworkers, or cabinetmakers. Few were employed in clerical or sales positions as well. Instead, black men worked as laborers or servants, while black women worked mostly as servants and laundresses.

Occupationally, blacks and the Irish dominated common labor and personal and domestic service. Germans and southern and eastern Europeans obtained white-collar jobs and gravitated to the small business and professional fields. The exclusion of blacks from the growing number of white-collar jobs in the clerical and sales area was particularly damaging, since these jobs generally offered upward mobility in the nineteenth century. These jobs required literate workers, and although thousands of black children attended the public schools from the 1850s on, there were only fifty-eight black bookkeepers and clerks, seven black sales workers, and three black stenographers in Cincinnati in 1890—altogether, a mere 1 percent of the black labor force.

Blacks and European immigrants formed a significant proportion of the population during the era when Cincinnati transitioned from a commercial to industrial city. Yet, between 1870 and 1900, while the proportion of blacks in the population increased, the proportion of immigrants in the city declined in relative and absolute terms. In this time span, the number of blacks increased from 5,904 to 14,498, or by 146 percent. Concurrently, the number of immigrants in the city fell from 79,612 to 57,961—a decrease of 27 percent. In 1900 blacks and immigrants comprised about 22 percent of the city's total population.

Blacks and immigrants, for the most part, shared residential space in the Basin, an area situated along the city's waterfront. Some low-income, native-born whites lived here as well. Within this shared space, blacks built their institutions and lived in residential clusters, which were scattered throughout a setting dominated by native-born and foreign-born whites. Even though blacks shared space with immigrant and native-born whites, their location at the bottom of the economic ladder placed them at a greater disadvantage than other groups in the quest for good housing and neighborhood conditions.

In the Basin, blacks lived in the most undesirable sections of the community and were disproportionately represented in the worst housing units. Irregular and low incomes made life difficult for all workers trapped in the Basin, but racism and economics combined to worsen the situation for blacks and to make them the last group to leave this congested and declining residential area. These were transitional years for African Americans. The old institutional structure anchored by the colored schools and churches was giving way, and blacks would have to construct a new institutional framework to guide them in the coming century.

See also *Cincinnati, OH 1828–1854; Cincinnati, OH 1854–1877*

HENRY LOUIS TAYLOR JR.

BIBLIOGRAPHY

Bertaux, Nancy. "Structural Economic Change and Occupational Decline among Black Workers in Nineteenth-Century Cincinnati." In *Race and the City: Work, Community, and Protest in Cincinnati, 1820–1970*, edited by Henry Louis Taylor Jr., 126–155. Urbana: University of Illinois Press.

Bertaux, Nancy, and Michael Washington. "The 'Colored Schools' of Cincinnati and African American Community in Nineteenth-Century Cincinnati, 1849–1890." *Journal of Negro Education* 74, no. 1 (Winter 2005): 43–52.

Duggan, E. P. "Markets and Labor: The Carriage and Wagon Industry in Late-Nineteenth-Century Cincinnati." *The Business History Review* 51, no. 3 (1977): 308–325.

Haydu, Jeffrey. "Business Citizenship at Work: Cultural Transposition and Class Formation in Cincinnati, 1870–1910." *The American Journal of Sociology* 107, no. 6 (2002): 1424–1467.

Haydu, Jeffrey, and Caroline Lee. "Model Employers and Good Government in the Late 19th and Late 20th Centuries." *Sociological Forum* 19, no. 2 (2004): 177–202.

Miller, Zane L. *Boss Cox's Cincinnati*. New York, NY: Oxford University Press, 1968.

Peirce, Donald C. "Mitchell and Rammelsberg: Cincinnati Furniture Manufacturers 1847–1881." *Winterthur Portfolio* 13 (1979): 209–229.

Ross, Steven J. *Workers on the Edge: Work, Leisure, and Politics in Industrializing Cincinnati, 1788–1890*. New York, NY: Columbia University Press, 1985.

Taylor, Henry Louis, Jr. "Creating the Metropolis in Black and White: Black Suburbanization and the Planning Movement in Cincinnati, 1900–1950." In *Historical Roots of the Urban Crisis: African Americans in the Industrial City, 1900–1950*, edited by Henry Louis Taylor Jr. and Walter Hill, 51–71. New York and London: Garland Publishing, Inc., 2000.

———. "The Use of Maps in the Study of the Black Ghetto-Formation Process: Cincinnati, 1802–1910." *Historical Methods* 17, no. 1 (1984): 44–58.

Taylor, Henry Louis, Jr., and Vicky Dula. "The Black Residential Experience and Community Formation in Antebellum Cincinnati." In *Race and the City: Work, Community, and Protest in Cincinnati, 1820–1970*, edited by Henry Louis Taylor Jr., 96–125. Urbana: University of Illinois Press, 1993.

CLEVELAND, OH 1877–1896

POST–CIVIL WAR CLEVELAND, LOCATED AT THE JUNCTURE OF LAKE ERIE AND THE CUYAHOGA RIVER, almost tripled in population from 1870 to 1890, with its number of residents increasing from 93,000 to 261,000. The heavy manufacturing nature of the city's booming economy attracted waves of immigrants from Europe. Economic growth was led by entrepreneurs and inventors. John D. Rockefeller's Standard Oil Trust, which controlled oil refining, was the most notable example of monopolistic

QUICK FACTS

CLEVELAND, OH **1877–1896**

MAYORS

William G. Rose	(1877–1878)
Rensselaer R. Herrick	(1879–1882)
John H. Farley	(1883–1884)
George W. Gardner	(1885–1886)
Brenton D. Babcock	(1887–1888)
George W. Gardner	(1889–1890)
William G. Rose	(1891–1892)
Robert Blee	(1893–1894)
Robert E. McKisson	(1895–1898)

MAJOR INDUSTRIES AND EMPLOYERS

Iron ore and steel
Meatpacking
Petroleum
Machinery
Clothing
Paint

MAJOR NEWSPAPERS

The Plain Dealer
Cleveland Press
Cleveland Leader
Cleveland News
Cleveland Herald

MAJOR EVENTS

1877: A national railroad strike paralyzes the country until the federal government intervenes, although Cleveland avoids any violent incidents.

1882 and 1885: Cleveland Rolling Mill strikes characterize the struggle of the emerging labor movement to improve working conditions.

1882: John D. Rockefeller forms the Standard Oil Trust—the most powerful monopoly in the country. It is headquartered for several years in Cleveland.

1891: The Hungarian-language newspaper with the largest circulation in the United States, *Szabadsag* (*Liberty*), is founded in Cleveland. This reflects the growing Hungarian immigrant population.

1892: Cleveland adopts the "strong mayor" form of government.

business practices. Amidst such prosperity, however, immigrants were mostly poor and struggled to survive in ethnic enclaves in their new home. Periodic economic depressions, such as those in 1877 and 1893, led to strikes and social unrest. Major strikes occurred in Cleveland in 1877, 1882, 1885, and 1889, as the labor movement fought for a shorter workday, better wages and working conditions, and the recognition of unions. In 1892 Cleveland adopted a "strong mayor" system of government. In 1881 assassinated president James Garfield was buried in Lake View Cemetery and a monument was dedicated to him there in 1890. In 1894 the Civil War Soldiers and Sailors Monument was dedicated in Public Square. In 1895 the Cleveland Orchestra was formed.

GOVERNMENT AND POLITICS

Prior to 1892, Cleveland was governed by a "weak mayor" system, a city council, and numerous boards. With the rapid growth of the city, this system became increasingly inefficient and was unable to cope with the increased population and demands for infrastructure improvements and services. The city was also plagued by corruption, particularly in the police and fire departments.

After lobbying the state legislature for several years, in 1892 civic leaders finally won reform through a new city charter that changed the growing city's government according to the "federal plan," which reflected the federal governmental structure. It unified administrative authority under a strong mayor. The mayor had a cabinet of six department directors. To address prior corruption in the police and fire departments, a civil service system was adopted. The judicial system was separated from the executive and legislative branches.

The assumption that the federal plan would lead to better government was challenged with the election of Republican Robert McKisson in 1895. McKisson used his authority to build a patronage-based political machine. He attempted to wrest control of the Republican Party from Mark Hanna and only narrowly lost his bid against Hanna for a U.S. Senate seat in 1897. McKisson was defeated for reelection in 1899.

INDUSTRY, COMMERCE, AND LABOR

Cleveland's economy depended largely on iron and steel manufacturing, with shipping and railroads providing the key transportation hubs. With the rapid growth in the use of petroleum, John D. Rockefeller consolidated his control over oil refining, which was centered in Cleveland. In 1882 he and his partners formed the Standard Oil Trust. In 1884 Cleveland had eighty-six oil refineries. However, Standard Oil soon decentralized its operations, and in 1885 Rockefeller moved his company's headquarters to New York City.

Cleveland's chemical industry, which was dominated by the Grasselli Chemical Company (taken over by DuPont in 1929), also rose in importance during this period. In 1894 Herbert Dow founded Dow Chemical, for which he had laid the groundwork in the 1880s at the Case Institute of Technology.

Cleveland was home to numerous inventors. Among them was Charles Brush, whose mechanical generator of electricity (the dynamo) was patented in 1877. He then went on to arc lighting and batteries. Brush's company was eventually merged with the General Electric Corporation. Mergers leading to the emergence of large firms and so-called trusts characterized many of Cleveland's industries. For example, in 1893 the Cleveland Iron Company merged with the Iron Cliffs Company to form a single company. Cleveland was also the home of some of the early pioneers of the automobile industry. Walter Baker and Elmer Sperry developed electric cars. Alexander Winton, a bicycle manufacturer, developed a car powered by a gasoline engine, which he unveiled in 1896 and first sold in 1898. In 1884 the world's first electric streetcar appeared in Cleveland.

Cleveland's growth in manufacturing attracted many immigrants, mostly from Europe, seeking freedom and jobs. These immigrants poured into the city, attracted by the availability of employment in these burgeoning industries. Poor working conditions and low pay led to labor strife. In 1877 railroad workers in Cleveland joined the nation's first general strike. Although the strikers protested peacefully, the mayor called up militia to maintain order with a preemptive show of force. Elsewhere in the United States, violence led to the use of federal troops to confront strikers. There were also failed strikes that year in Cleveland at Standard Oil and the Cleveland Rolling Mill. In 1882 the mill witnessed another strike by workers demanding unionization. In response, the owner imported Polish and Czech strikebreakers. Ironically, these same workers then joined a strike in 1885 to protest wage cuts. Locked-out strikers eventually prevailed on the wage issue but failed to gain union recognition.

In 1882 workers organized the Federation of Organized Trades and Labor Unions in Cleveland. This gave birth to what would become the American Federation of Labor (AFL). That year steelworkers struck for the first time. The next major management-labor confrontation during this period in Cleveland came in 1889 when the streetcar workers went on strike. When the companies imported strikebreakers, violence ensued and lasted over several days. Despite a passenger boycott, this strike failed. Workers were hit hard by the panic of 1893. The lack of relief for the unemployed and destitute led to rioting on May Day in 1894. This type of economic hardship contributed to the founding by philanthropists and reformers of several settlement houses to assist poor immigrants in the 1890s.

In contrast to the poverty and economic hardship among immigrants and the working-class population, Cleveland also became home to great wealth. Industrialists like John D. Rockefeller built mansion homes along Euclid Avenue in downtown Cleveland. By the end of the century, Euclid Avenue became known as "Millionaires Row" and "The Showplace of America."

RACE, ETHNICITY, AND IMMIGRATION

In 1870, 42 percent of the city's population of ninety-three thousand was foreign-born. By 1890 the number of foreign-born residents (ninety-seven thousand) would more than equal the city's 1870 total population. In 1890 three-fourths of the city's population was either foreign-born or the children of foreign-born parents. The largest immigrant groups in 1870 remained the German and the Irish. However, in this and following decades, most of the European immigrants began to come from southern and eastern Europe. They populated the many ethnic neighborhoods that sprang up around industrial areas. Cleveland was then a walking city, with workers living close to the factories where most were employed. An example was Warszawa, later known as Slavic Village, which was heavily populated by Polish immigrants. These immigrants worked primarily as laborers in the nearby factories.

Although most immigrants were forced to take low-paying jobs as unskilled day laborers, some did achieve success in their new country. One example of this was Hungarian Theodor Kundtz, who prospered as a manufacturer of cabinets. Kundtz supplied the White Sewing Machine Company and eventually employed more than two thousand of his fellow countrymen as craftsmen. The center of the immigrant Hungarian community was located in the Buckeye neighborhood on the city's east side. In 1891 the Hungarian-language newspaper with the largest circulation in the United States was founded in Cleveland.

During this period many of the city's Jewish synagogues and ethnic churches representing various Christian religions were built by their largely immigrant congregations. For example, in 1892 the first Hungarian Catholic priest arrived and supervised the building of St. Elizabeth's Church in the Buckeye neighborhood.

The 1890s saw the opening of several neighborhood settlement houses modeled on Jane Addams' Hull House in Chicago. One such organization was Hiram House, which was opened by George Bellamy in 1896. Settlement houses provided social services, recreational activities, and education to many of the immigrants, including classes in English for those still speaking in their native tongues.

From 1870 through 1890, Cleveland's black population was tiny—totaling only about 1 percent. It increased from thirteen hundred in 1870 to about three thousand in 1890. This period preceded the era of the great migration from the South. Compared to many other cities in the North, Cleveland offered better employment and educational opportunities to blacks. In 1881 Republican lawyer John Green became the first African American elected to the Ohio legislature, and in 1891 he became the first and only black politician from the North elected to a state senate in the nineteenth century.

See also *Cleveland, OH 1896–1929; Cleveland, OH 1929–1941; Cleveland, OH 1941–1952*

DENNIS KEATING

BIBLIOGRAPHY

Campbell, Thomas F., and Edward M. Miggins. *The Birth of Modern Cleveland, 1865–1930*. London and Toronto: Associated University Presses, 1988.

Kusmer, Kenneth L. *A Ghetto Takes Shape: Black Cleveland, 1870–1930*. Urbana: University of Illinois Press, 1978.

Miller, Carol Poh, and Robert Wheeler. *Cleveland: A Concise History, 1796–1990*. Bloomington and Indianapolis: Indiana University Press, 1990.

Rose, William Ganson. *Cleveland: The Making of a City*. Cleveland and New York: World Publishing, 1950.

Van Tassel, David D., and John J. Grabowski, eds. *The Encyclopedia of Cleveland History*. Bloomington: Indiana University Press, 1987.

BUFFALO, NY 1877–1896

WHILE OTHER CITIES HAD DEVELOPED VIBRANT MANUFACTURING SECTORS before and during the Civil War, in 1865 only 5 percent of Buffalo's economy was based on manufacturing. Elected officials, industrial leaders, and citizens, however, believed that Buffalo's large labor force and its location on the Erie Canal—a water route that connected the Atlantic Ocean to the Great Lakes and made the city a key player in the transportation of raw materials and goods—rendered it a perfect location for major manufacturing. Thus, they launched a public relations campaign to promote Buffalo as an ideal place to do business. To do this, and to address the needs of a growing city, elected officials focused their efforts on eradicating corruption and patronage in local government and establishing practices of good governance. By the end of the century, despite the economic downturn of the mid-1890s, Buffalo had become a major commercial and manufacturing center in the United States. In recognition of the city's economic growth and development, Buffalo was selected as the site of the 1901 Pan-American Exposition, a world's fair aimed at showcasing current technological discoveries and advancements, such as innovations in transportation, machinery, and electricity.

QUICK FACTS

BUFFALO, NY 1877–1896

MAYORS

Solomon Scheu	(1878–1879)
Alexander Brush	(1880–1881)
Grover Cleveland	(1882)
(resigned in Nov.)	
Marcus M. Drake	(1882)
(resigned December 22)	
Harmon S. Cutting	(1882)
(appointed to succeed	
Drake until special election	
held January 9, 1983)	
John B. Manning	(1883)
Jonathan Scoville	(1884–1885)
Philip Becker	(1886–1889)
Charles F. Bishop	(1890–1894)
Edgar B. Jewett	(1895–1897)

MAJOR INDUSTRIES AND EMPLOYERS

Iron and steel manufacturing
Railroad companies
Brewing industry
Milling/grain industry
Furniture-making industry

MAJOR NEWSPAPERS

Buffalo Commercial Advertiser
Buffalo Daily Courier
Buffalo Times
Buffalo Morning Express
Buffalo Evening Post
Buffalo (Evening) News

MAJOR EVENTS

1883 and 1884: Statewide civil service reform creates the New York State Civil Service Commission, which allows Buffalo mayor Jonathan Scoville to create rules governing competitive and noncompetitive examinations for candidates running for some elected offices in the city. This creates a merit-based system for filling public offices in Buffalo.

1891: The charter revision of 1891 creates a three-year term for the mayor and a bicameral city legislature comprised of a board of alderman and a board of councilman. It also divides the city into twenty-five districts, each represented by one alderman, and establishes at-large elections for council members.

August 15, 1896: The first electric current is sent from Niagara Falls to Buffalo, attracting both national attention and industry. Many companies build new facilities or relocate to Buffalo to be near cheap and unlimited electrical power.

Mid-1890s: Despite a nationwide economic depression, the declining importance of the Erie Canal, and the rising importance of the railroad in Buffalo make the city the second largest railroad terminus in the United States. It also allows Buffalo's economy to diversify and expand so rapidly that in 1901 the city hosts the Pan-American Exposition, which serves to highlight Buffalo as an exemplary industrialized U.S. city.

GOVERNMENT AND POLITICS

The politics of mid-nineteenth-century Buffalo were dominated by concerns of corruption and inefficient government. In response, elected officials and candidates running for office in the late nineteenth century made good governance central to their campaigns, as well as a top priority while in office. Local and state politicians aimed to replace the corrupt politics that had dominated local governance for decades with a style of governance that promoted nonpartisan and business-like efficiency and responsiveness to local needs.

One way leaders in the city of Buffalo attempted to address corruption, as well as promote public safety, was to reform the police department. In 1866 widespread corruption led to the removal of police oversight from city officials and its placement in the hands of a state-level commission appointed by the governor. While control of the police department transitioned back to local authorities in 1871, concern over proper policing remained, and the mayor and two appointed commissioners were granted police oversight. This commission proved unsatisfactory, however, and soon after the creation of the Municipal Court in 1880 another act created a new commission to oversee the police department. This new commission was comprised of the mayor, a commissioner appointed by the mayor, and a superintendent of police appointed by the mayor and the commissioner. This arrangement was also insufficient to stem perceived corruption and lasted only three years, at which time a board was created that was comprised of three commissioners. While viewed as an improvement, this commission was quickly changed by an act signed in 1884 by the governor. It then consisted of three commissioners appointed by the city's comptroller.

In 1882 Grover Cleveland was elected mayor by a majority of voters—57 percent—and was charged with leading the fight against corruption and implementing a nonpartisan and business-like form of government in Buffalo. Though he only served as mayor for a short time, leaving in November of 1882 after being elected governor of New York State, he was able to usher in an era of good governance during his tenure. When the act of 1880 failed to produce any real improvement in the Buffalo police department, it was Cleveland who advocated a bipartisan police commission to oversee its operations. Additionally, he signed a civil service act into law and oversaw the 1883 creation of the New York State Civil Service Commission, which led to broad civil service reform in Buffalo. Following Cleveland's example, Mayor Jonathan Scoville, who served the first full term following Cleveland's abbreviated term, immediately established rules for competitive and noncompetitive examinations when filling some municipal offices.

Elected leaders and citizens worked to establish good government practices even while the city was growing. To accommodate this growth, the city charter was revised in 1891 to divide the city into twenty-five wards. Under the new charter, residents in each ward elected one alderman, and residents of the entire city elected nine councilmen. This new arrangement created a bicameral legislature in Buffalo and empowered the board of aldermen to originate, and the city council to amend, legislation. The new charter also revised the length of terms for elected officials: aldermen were to be elected for a term of two years, while councilmen and the mayor were to be elected for terms of three years, though this quickly changed and in 1895 these terms were extended to four years. These measures were aimed at removing corruption from politics; alternate elections for officials prevented overt collusion on the campaign trail among those running for alderman and councilman, and longer terms in office allowed elected representatives to focus on citywide concerns rather than electoral goals.

Active civic life in Buffalo existed beyond municipal and electoral politics as well, and many of the efforts in this arena were led by women. In 1867 Mrs. John C. Lord helped the founder of the Society for the Prevention of Cruelty to Animals (SPCA), Henry Bergh, secure passage of legislation to formally establish the SPCA, and she served as president of the Buffalo SPCA chapter, the second chapter in the state. Additionally, in the late 1860s, a group of philanthropic Christian women formed the Union Missionary Sunday School Aid Society to help clothe, feed, house, and educate children living in some of the poorest neighborhoods of Buffalo. In 1870 the society reformed to become the eleventh Women's Christian Association in the United States (now called the Young Women's Christian Association), with Emma Haines serving as its president.

Taken together, government, politics, and civil society in Buffalo during the decades following the Civil War were dominated by a concern for fair and efficient governance, as well as a commitment to the humane treatment of residents and animals living in Buffalo. This led to the reform of the police department, municipal hiring practices, and the city charter, as well as the establishment of prominent civic organizations. Elected officials and citizens believed that a compassionate, good-governance approach to local issues would ensure the best and most efficient response to demands on city resources that were growing as a result of an expanding manufacturing base and an increasing population.

INDUSTRY, COMMERCE, AND LABOR

Industry and commerce in Buffalo had long been dominated by the Erie Canal, the completion of which in 1825 opened a water route for trade and commerce from the Atlantic Ocean to the Great Lakes, and raw material and goods moving on the canal had become the basis of various industries in Buffalo. Yet the dominance of the Erie Canal as the primary mode of goods delivery and transportation was challenged by railroads as early as the 1850s, when railways opened shipping lines from Buffalo to Chicago and into the South and West. Though Buffalo was still dependent on lake commerce in the last half of the nineteenth century, the importance of railways had increased, not just because of their greater flexibility in transportation, but also because of the jobs they provided. By 1900 the canal was largely obsolete, and Buffalo had become the second largest railway terminus in the United States, behind Chicago.

To the residents of Buffalo, the city's location, transportation, and labor force seemed ideal for creating a booming industrial sector in the city. These components were not enough to spur economic growth, however. The city also needed to attract entrepreneurs and funding to capitalize on these resources. To do this, city boosters launched a campaign to create an image of the city as an ideal place to do business. This campaign began with the First Annual Industrial Exposition in 1869, which was sponsored by the Association for the Encouragement of Manufactures, and it culminated in the Pan-American Exposition of 1901. There was also a communitywide effort to attract industry: aldermen repeatedly dredged the canal to help industries bring in their raw materials and ship their goods, newspapers helped spread the idea that the city was a good place to do business and raise a family, and citizens were encouraged to always speak positively of their town. Their efforts paid off in the short term.

The increasing number of rail lines that connected Buffalo to other parts of the United States, coupled with its geographic location, did attract many entrepreneurs. Buffalo's location caught the attention of Frank H. Goodyear, who moved to the city in 1872. Throughout the

1870s, Goodyear slowly acquired several large timber tracts and lumber mills in western Pennsylvania. Lumber had the possibility to be a lucrative business, but transporting it was difficult, as no good way had been developed to move heavy logs from the timber tracts to the waterways where the timber could then float downstream to sawmills. To address the first problem, Goodyear developed a loader that could mechanically load and unload large logs onto flat cars. To address the second problem, he built a railroad that connected western Pennsylvania to Buffalo. The Sinnemahoning Valley Railroad was completed in the mid-1880s. It not only provided a way for Goodyear to move timber, it also made accessible huge tracts of coal fields and iron ore that Goodyear had also bought in Pennsylvania.

This development single-handedly positioned Buffalo to become a major producer of iron and steel in the coming decades. In 1880 Buffalo ranked eleventh in the United States for number of manufacturing establishments, but by the end of the decade it challenged Pittsburgh, Pennsylvania, as the iron and steel capital of the United States. Between 1890 and 1905, 412 new factories were established in Buffalo, most of which were iron and steel factories.

In addition to attracting businessmen, Buffalo's industrial boom attracted workers. In the 1870s and 1880s, a new wave of eastern European immigrants moved into Buffalo seeking employment. Importantly, one of the selling points for businessmen to set up shop in Buffalo was the fact that a strong unionization movement had not taken root in the city. Indeed, this is one of the main reasons that the Lackawanna Iron and Steel Company announced in 1899 that it was relocating from Scranton, Pennsylvania, to an area just outside of Buffalo's city boundaries.

Despite the depression of the mid-1890s, Buffalo became a major industrial center in the United States in the waning decades of the century because of the influx of capital, the developments in transportation, the innovations in energy provision using Niagara Falls, and its rapidly expanding and relatively compliant labor force. The Pan-American Exposition of 1901 was supposed to showcase these attributes of Buffalo. Unfortunately, the millions expected to attend the exposition never materialized. The tragedy of President William McKinley's assassination while attending the exposition overshadowed the event, and ultimately the development and economic growth that characterized Buffalo in the late nineteenth century proved unsustainable in the long run.

RACE, ETHNICITY, AND IMMIGRATION

What is most remarkable about Buffalo between the years of 1877 and 1896 is how similar it was to other U.S. cities. During this time the city was rapidly industrializing, as were other cities throughout the country. Politically the city was caught up in the good-governance movement that was sweeping other major cities. The population of Buffalo was also changing in ways that mirrored broader trends in the United States; it was growing rapidly, and new waves of immigration were creating an increasingly diverse populace. As railroads replaced the Erie Canal and the granaries and mills supplied by the canal were replaced by iron and steel factories, these new factories needed more workers. The population of Buffalo increased to 182,511 residents by 1882 and to 255,664 by 1890.

Part of this population growth was an expansion of Buffalo's traditional ethnic enclaves. By 1877 Irish and German immigrants had been living in Buffalo for at least a generation, and their numbers continued to increase during the last quarter of the nineteenth century. Indeed, in an 1880 survey of the parents of pupils in Buffalo's public schools, 9,088 were German, 2,834 were Irish, and 2,072 were listed as "other." Only 4,612 parents were listed as native-born Americans. This suggests that, at least among the students of the public school system, there were three times as many children of immigrant parents as there were children of native-born parents. Raw census data also supports this picture of demographic change in Buffalo: in 1892 there were 10,000 Irish-born city residents, up from 6,307 in 1850, and between the 1890s and 1910, the German-born population reached 40,000, up from 6,800 in 1850.

New immigrant groups were also arriving and settling in the city, hoping for work. One of the largest of these groups to settle in Buffalo during this time period was from Poland. There had been a small number of Polish immigrants in Buffalo prior to the Civil War, and Catholic immigrants from Poland moved through Buffalo following the war to settle in cities further west. In the early 1870s, however, Polish families began to settle in Buffalo. They built churches and schools and started a Polish-language newspaper in 1885. By the 1890s, thirteen thousand Polish-born residents lived in the city. One attraction for immigrants from eastern Europe was the readily available work in iron and steel factories, with the railroad companies, and in construction. These were primarily unskilled labor positions, and, as such, the Irish and the Polish often found themselves living in neighborhoods near one another, competing for the same jobs and working in the same factories. In fact, the largest Polish enclave in Buffalo was located just north of the First Ward, the largest Irish enclave in the city.

Italian immigrants also began moving into Buffalo in large numbers during this period. A small number of Italians lived in the city during the mid-nineteenth century, but in the 1890s a large wave of immigration brought twenty-five hundred Italians to Buffalo. Initially, these immigrants moved into traditionally Irish neighborhoods, sparking conflict between the Irish and the Italians. However, the Italians, much like the Germans, quickly assimilated into Buffalo society, thanks to their rapidly increasing numbers and quick language adaptation. Over time, the Italians displaced the Irish in some parts of town, creating their own Italian enclaves by the turn of the century.

Finally, Buffalo continued to have a small but significant black population. While there were only a little more than three hundred African Americans in the city in 1850, there were one thousand in 1892. Many of the black residents of Buffalo—like the Irish and Polish—found work in the factories of heavy industry or with the railroad. Although African Americans comprised the largest minority group in Buffalo by the early twenty-first century, this was not the case at the end of the nineteenth century, and, despite the labor and racial unrest of the mid-nineteenth century, race relations in Buffalo were fairly calm as the century came to a close.

Thus, the end of the nineteenth century found Buffalo poised to become a major industrial and commercial center in the United States. Elected officials worked to attract businesses and entrepreneurs while cleaning up corruption and patronage in city governance; heavy industry had finally come to Buffalo, with iron and steel dominating the commercial sector; and the city's population was rapidly growing, in part because more diverse groups of immigrants were coming to Buffalo to find work in its expanding industrial base. Together, citizens and elected leaders looked toward the twentieth century with optimism and hope for the success of their city.

See also *Buffalo, NY 1854–1877*

AMY WIDESTROM

BIBLIOGRAPHY

Goldman, Mark. *High Hopes: The Rise and Decline of Buffalo, New York*. Albany: State University of New York Press, 1983.

Gredel, Stephen. *People of Our City and County*. Buffalo, NY: Buffalo and Erie County Historical Society, 1971.

Hill, Henry Wayland. *Municipality of Buffalo, New York: A History 1720–1923*. Vol. 1. New York, NY: Lewis Historical Publishing Company, Inc., 1923.

Merrill, Horace Samuel. *Bourbon Leader: Grover Cleveland and the Democratic Party*. Boston, MA: Little, Brown Company, 1957.

Nevins, Allan. *Grover Cleveland: A Study in Courage*. New York, NY: Dodd, Mead & Company, 1934.

Rizzo, Michael, comp. "Through the Mayors' Eyes: the Only Complete History of the Mayors of Buffalo, New York." *The Buffalonian*. Available online at www.buffalonian.com/history/industry/mayors/index.html (accessed June 16, 2011).

Smith, H. Perry. *History of the City of Buffalo and Erie County*. Vol. 2. Syracuse, NY: D. Mason & Co. Publishers, 1884.

CHAPTER 6

Population rankings based on the 1920 census

CITIES IN THE PROGRESSIVE ERA, 1896–1929

In 1896 the United States was emerging out of a major economic depression, and 1929 marks the beginning of the Great Depression. The period between these two depressions saw the invention and mass production of the automobile and the radio; the election of two progressive reform presidents; U.S. intervention in World War I; the ratification in 1913 of both the Sixteenth Amendment, empowering Congress to levy an income tax, and the Seventeenth Amendment, providing for the direct election of U.S. senators; and in 1920 the ratification of both the Eighteenth Amendment, prohibiting the manufacture and sale of alcohol, and the Nineteenth Amendment, providing women the right to vote in national elections.

In addition, the 1920 census recorded for the first time that a majority, 51.2 percent, of the U.S. population lived in urban places, defined as those with populations over twenty-five hundred. The 15,355,250 people who in 1920 lived in the ten largest cities represented 14 percent of the total U.S. population, and 28 percent of the total U.S. urban population. By 1910 the census also recognized that urban places were no longer confined to single cities, and it thus invented the "metropolitan district," defined as central cities with populations over two hundred thousand (of which there were then twenty-eight) and neighboring "minor civil divisions." The census broadened this definition in each subsequent decade, with the result that it counted twenty-nine districts in 1920 and ninety-six in 1930.

The majority of people who lived in big American cities in the 1890s were foreign-born, mostly from Ireland, England, and Germany. Hundreds of thousands of new immigrants also came from Austria-Hungary, Italy, Sweden, and Russia, and they soon made up the majority of new arrivals, as the number of immigrants swelled from fewer than 4 million during the 1890s, to nearly 9 million in the 1900s. This population then declined in the 1910s (5.7 million) and 1920s (4.1 million), in part because of new federal laws, passed in 1921 and 1924, that limited the number of immigrants coming from any country to a small percentage of their total population already in the United States, and also because of the blockade of Europe during World War I.

Increasingly restrictive immigration laws indicated a public backlash against newcomers. The Ku Klux Klan experienced a rebirth in the 1910s. The organization reached a peak membership of roughly four million in 1924—focusing its energies more on Catholics than on African Americans—with a membership that spanned the country, in both rural and urban areas.

Despite the conservative sentiments reflected in Prohibition and the Klan, the period from 1896 to 1929 was also notably progressive, as reflected in the Nineteenth Amendment and progressive political and social reform, including the settlement movement (exemplified by Jane Addams's Hull House in Chicago, founded in 1889); workplace safety rules (in New York a result of the 1911 Triangle Shirtwaist Company fire that killed 146 workers); and political reforms such as nonpartisan elections, personal voter registration, primary elections, the official ballot, the commission system of city government (first adopted in Galveston, Texas, in 1901), and the council-manager system (first adopted in small cities in the South and later by Dayton, Ohio, in 1913).

At the national level, the Progressive movement is most closely associated with the presidencies of Theodore Roosevelt and Woodrow Wilson. Roosevelt, a hero of the Spanish-American War and governor of New York, was selected as the Republican vice presidential candidate on the William McKinley ticket in 1900. As he had done in 1896, McKinley defeated Democratic candidate William Jennings Bryan, though he was assassinated shortly thereafter, and Roosevelt, at age forty-one, became president.

In his first term, Roosevelt broke apart a railroad monopoly organized by J. P. Morgan, among others, and he intervened in a large coal miners' strike, getting the miners a wage increase and a shorter workday. He soundly defeated Democratic candidate Alton Parker in 1904, in an election that was significant for being the first time that labor leader Eugene Debs ran, on the Socialist ticket, garnering 3 percent of the popular vote. In his second term, Roosevelt focused on "trust-busting" (especially with regard to railroads), food and drug safety, and environmental conservation, adding extensive tracts of public lands to the national forest system.

	TOTAL POPULATION[1]	WHITE POPULATION[1]	BLACK POPULATION[1]	OTHER POPULATION[1]	% WHITE POPULATION[1]	% BLACK POPULATION[1]	% OTHER POPULATION[1]
NEW YORK, NY	5,620,048	5,459,463	152,467	8,118	97.1	2.7	0.1
CHICAGO, IL	2,701,705	2,589,169	109,458	3,078	95.8	4.1	0.1
PHILADELPHIA, PA	1,823,779	1,688,180	134,229	1,370	92.6	7.4	0.1
DETROIT, MI	993,078	952,065	40,838	775	95.8	4.1	0.1
CLEVELAND, OH	796,841	762,026	34,451	364	95.6	4.3	0.0
ST. LOUIS, MO	772,897	702,615	69,854	428	90.9	9.0	0.1
BOSTON, MA	748,060	730,485	16,350	1,225	97.7	2.2	0.2
BALTIMORE, MD	733,826	625,130	108,322	374	85.2	14.8	0.1
PITTSBURGH, PA	588,343	550,261	37,725	357	93.5	6.4	0.1
LOS ANGELES, CA	576,673	546,864	15,579	14,230	94.8	2.7	2.5

	FOREIGN-BORN WHITE POPULATION[1]	% WHITE POPULATION FOREIGN-BORN[1]	AVG. NUMBER EMPLOYED IN MANUFACTURING[2]	VALUE OF MANUFACTURED PRODUCTS[2]	% POPULATION 7–13 YEARS OLD ATTENDING SCHOOL[3]	LAND AREA (SQ. MI.)[4]	POPULATION DENSITY (PER SQ. MI.)[4]
NEW YORK, NY	1,991,547	36.5	638,775	$ 5,260,707,577	93.7	299.0	18,796.1
CHICAGO, IL	805,482	31.1	403,942	$ 3,657,424,471	93.9	192.8	14,013.0
PHILADELPHIA, PA	397,927	23.6	281,105	$ 1,996,481,074	94.0	128.0	14,248.3
DETROIT, MI	42,827	4.5	167,016	$ 1,234,519,842	94.7	77.9	12,755.8
CLEVELAND, OH	239,538	31.4	157,730	$ 1,091,577,490	96.2	56.4	14,128.4
ST. LOUIS, MO	103,239	14.7	107,919	$ 871,700,438	94.8	61.0	12,670.4
BOSTON, MA	238,919	32.7	88,759	$ 618,921,962	94.7	43.5	17,196.8
BALTIMORE, MD	83,911	13.4	97,814	$ 677,878,492	96.1	79.0	9,288.9
PITTSBURGH, PA	140,200	25.5	83,296	$ 614,726,978	94.5	39.9	14,745.4
LOS ANGELES, CA	121,530	22.2	47,118	$ 278,184,143	95.0	365.7	1,576.9

[1] Source: Fourteenth Census of the United States Taken in the Year 1920, Volume II: Population 1920. Table 16.
[2] Source: Fourteenth Census of the United States Taken in the Year 1920, Volume IX: Manufactures 1919. Table 6.
[3] Source: School Attendance in 1920 (Census Monograph V). Table 8.
[4] Source: Campbell Gibson, *Population of the 100 Largest Cities and Other Urban Places in the United States: 1790 to 1990.* (1998) Table 15.

Following tradition, Roosevelt declined to run for a third term in 1908. His handpicked successor, William Howard Taft, handily beat William Jennings Bryan, who ran again, and for the last time, as the Democratic nominee (Debs also ran, once again getting 3 percent of the vote). The Taft administration was a disappointment to progressives, including Roosevelt, who decided to run for president again, in 1912. Failing to win the Republican nomination (which went to Taft), he ran on the Progressive ticket, thus dividing the Republican vote, allowing the progressive Democratic candidate, Woodrow Wilson, to win with a plurality (Debs, running for the final time, captured 6 percent of the vote).

Wilson initiated sweeping reforms, including a lowering of the protective tariff (thus using foreign competition to weaken the power of corporate trusts), a progressive income tax, the establishment of the Federal Reserve banking system and the Federal Trade Commission, and new punitive taxes on goods produced with child labor (later declared unconstitutional by the Supreme Court). Running for reelection in 1916, Wilson campaigned on having kept the United States out of the war that was engulfing much of Europe. Yet German aggression prompted Wilson to commit the United States to World War I in 1917. Congress established a new draft, through which almost three million men were enlisted in the army. U.S. involvement in the war was brief, as Germany surrendered in 1918, though long enough to take the lives of approximately one hundred twelve thousand American troops (and nine million others).

The U.S. government actively suppressed dissent against its war effort. Congress passed the Espionage Act (1917) and the Sedition Act (1918), both of which were used to prosecute antiwar activists, including Eugene Debs, who was imprisoned in 1919, though his sentence was commuted in 1921 by President Warren Harding.

By the end of his presidency, Wilson had suffered a stroke and had become an invalid, Congress refused to join the new League of Nations, and the country was lurching painfully from a wartime to peacetime economy. Employers rescinded wartime worker benefits, wages were hurt by rampant inflation, and labor disputes became increasingly violent. A steel strike in 1919 involving hundreds of thousands of workers in several cities resulted in a riot in Gary, Indiana, and eighteen steelworkers killed; and a general strike in Seattle effectively shut the city down for nearly a week. The years from 1917 to 1921 were also characterized by race riots in several cities, in part a result of increasing black migration northward. The most violent, in Chicago in 1919, resulted in thirty-eight deaths, and dozens more fatalities occurred in other cities.

Despite the turbulence and upheaval, the country by the 1920s entered a period of remarkable prosperity, characterized by technological development, including the invention of the radio in 1923, the spread of the telephone (invented in 1890), and, most notably, the mass production of the automobile (the Ford Motor Company produced more than fifteen million Model Ts between 1908 and 1927), and the accompanying explosive growth of Detroit, which surged from ninth to fourth largest city in the country between 1910 and 1930.

The 1920s were also in many respects remarkably conservative years. Labor union membership declined from approximately five to three million between 1920 and 1929. Conservative Republicans were consistently elected president. Warren Harding's administration was marked mostly by scandal. Calvin Coolidge, Harding's vice president, assumed the presidency upon Harding's death in 1924, was elected in the same year, but declined to run again. Herbert Hoover, elected in 1928 in a race against the first-ever Irish Catholic major party candidate (New York governor Alfred Smith) was possibly the most qualified president elected in the 1920s, yet his administration would be overshadowed by the dramatic decline in stock prices that began in 1929, inaugurating the Great Depression and the end of the Roaring Twenties.

NEW YORK, NY 1896–1929

IN THE THREE DECADES BEFORE THE GREAT DEPRESSION, New York continued its transformation from dense mercantile city to sprawling corporate metropolis, maintaining its dominance in both manufacturing and finance. New waves of immigration and industrial decentralization transformed the city's social geography as the population grew from 3.4 million to nearly 7 million residents. The upward and outward growth of the city prompted the creation of new policies and institutions as public officials and interest groups wrestled with the political and physical implications of the creation of Greater New York in 1898, which created a centralized municipal government with representation of the five boroughs (Manhattan, Brooklyn, Richmond, Queens, and the Bronx) in the city's legislative and administrative bodies.

GOVERNMENT AND POLITICS

As home to the nation's most notorious political machine and intellectual center of Progressive-era reform, New York City witnessed a lively battle among political groups for the favor of an increasingly diverse and mobile electorate. After trading victories with Tammany Hall between 1894 and 1909, the "Fusion" coalition (composed of reform Democrats, Republicans, and Independents) led local government for eight crucial years before Tammany Democrats, partially refashioned as the progenitors of modern urban liberalism, reestablished citywide control until the landslide victory of Republican mayor Fiorello La Guardia in 1933.

A struggle within Tammany Hall—between its traditional pursuit of spoils and a growing interest in the nascent welfare state—was propelled by its inconsistent electoral performance. Boss Richard Croker's blatant sponsorship of police corruption was exposed by the 1894 Lexow investigation, ushering in Republican Mayor William Strong, but a four-way race among opposition candidates assured the election of Tammany stalwart Robert Van Wyck as the first mayor of the Greater City in 1897. An investigation into corruption that was headed by state senator Ferdinand Mazet, the findings from which were published in 1900, again exposed Tammany excesses, leading to the election of reformer Seth Low as mayor in 1902 and Croker's resignation as boss. Low alienated immigrant voters with enforcement of blue laws and peddler licensing, and a chastened Tammany Hall, under the leadership of "Silent Charlie" Murphy, took advantage of Low's errors by shifting toward "honest graft" and granting more district positions to new ethnic groups. Murphy also chose "respectable" candidates George B. McClellan and William J. Gaynor for mayor in 1903 and 1909, even though both operated with little regard for Murphy's wishes. After newspaper mogul William Randolph Hearst's Municipal Ownership League won borough president seats in Brooklyn and Queens in 1905, losing the mayoralty by fewer than thirty-five hundred votes, Murphy allowed younger Tammany operatives to champion the progressive causes that increasingly appealed to voters. But Murphy overreached by engineering the impeachment of Democratic Governor William Sulzer, a raw display of machine power that inspired the Fusion victory of John Purroy Mitchel as mayor in 1913. After running one of the

QUICK FACTS

NEW YORK, NY 1896–1929

MAYORS

William L. Strong	(1895–1897)
Robert Van Wyck	(1898–1901)
Seth Low	(1902–1903)
George B. McClellan	(1904–1909)
William J. Gaynor	(1910–1913)
Ardolph L. Kline	(1913)
John Purroy Mitchel	(1914–1917)
John F. Hylan	(1918–1925)
James J. Walker	(1926–1932)

MAJOR INDUSTRIES AND EMPLOYERS

Women's clothing
Printing and publishing
Men's clothing
Bakery products
Foundry and machine-shop products

MAJOR NEWSPAPERS

Irish World
Jewish Daily Forward
New York American
New York Evening Journal
New York Herald
New York Sun
New York Times
New York World
Progresso Italo-Americano
Staats-Zeitung

MAJOR EVENTS

1898: Greater New York City is established by act of the state legislature, bringing the five boroughs together with a central city government.

1904: The first leg of the subway opens, and in subsequent years the system grows dramatically.

1911: A fire at the Triangle Shirtwaist Factory kills 146 garment workers. Consequently, comprehensive industrial and labor regulations are established.

1914: The start of World War I propels the city into an acute financial crisis, yet allows New York to move ahead of London in managing several key components of international trade.

1927: The Holland Tunnel opens; it is the first underwater vehicle tunnel to connect both sides of the Hudson.

most enlightened administrations in the city's history, Mitchel then repelled the multiethnic electorate in his disastrous 1917 reelection bid by emphasizing loyalty and Americanism as the country entered World War I.

Tammany's tenuous victory in 1917 (with Brooklyn Judge John F. Hylan winning with fewer than half the votes) initiated sixteen years of Democratic rule, but the party's influence was circumscribed by the fickle electorate. A growing Socialist movement elected Meyer London to Congress in 1914 and gave Morris Hillquit almost as many votes as Mayor Mitchel in 1917. New Yorkers punished Democratic presidential candidates for Woodrow Wilson's peace by voting for Republicans Harding and Coolidge, even as they polled 11 percent for Socialist Eugene Debs in 1920 and 18 percent for Progressive Robert LaFollette in 1924. Although Governor Al Smith (aided by collaborators such as Robert Moses and Belle Moskowitz) became the new face of the Democrats in the 1920s, Tammany corruption resurfaced under boss George Olvany (who succeeded Murphy in 1924), and the subsequent Seabury investigations led to the resignation of Tammany Mayor Jimmy Walker in 1932, even though voters had given the affable Walker a plurality of half a million votes over La Guardia in 1929.

During these tumultuous years, city government expanded into many areas, thanks in part to the extensive network of social scientists and reformers that made New York City a national center of study and experimentation, including settlement house activists Florence Kelley and Lillian Wald, civil rights leader W. E. B. Du Bois, and Edward Devine, who helped establish the first school of social work under the auspices of the Charity Organization Society. Although New York was in the forefront of social welfare provision, prior to the 1930s the city's most impressive and lasting achievements occurred in building regulation and public works. The landmark Tenement Law of 1901 made it illegal to construct "dumbbell" tenements and established a new city agency to enforce extensive new design requirements. After the heartbreaking Triangle Shirtwaist fire in 1911 killed 146 garment workers, the New York State Factory Investigating Commission headed by up-and-coming Tammany leaders Robert F. Wagner and Al Smith produced the nation's most advanced industrial and labor regulations. And in 1916, the city adopted the country's first comprehensive zoning ordinance, which shaped the distinctive "setback" skyscrapers of midtown Manhattan while fostering the growth of single-family homes in the outer boroughs.

To accommodate population growth, unite the five boroughs, and link the city to the region, the city invested lavishly in the world's most elaborate urban infrastructure: borrowing over a billion dollars for public works between 1898 and 1914 before the fiscal crisis of that year temporarily halted government spending. In 1917, the city celebrated the completion of a massive new water system (begun in 1905) reaching 160 miles into the Catskill Mountains. The Interborough Rapid Transit Company opened the first leg of the city's publicly funded, privately operated subway in 1904; with the addition of the Brooklyn Rapid Transit Company lines after 1913, and the publicly operated Independent Subway after 1917, the system grew to over six hundred miles by the early 1930s. The consolidated city added three bridges over the East River—Williamsburg (1903), Queensboro (1909), and Manhattan (1909)—and began work on the Triborough Bridge complex in 1929. The Holland Tunnel (the first vehicular tunnel under the Hudson River) was completed in 1927 by a joint state commission. And the Port of New York Authority, a bi-state commission established in 1921, built three bridges connecting Staten Island and New Jersey— Goethals Bridge (1928), Outerbridge Crossing (1928), and Bayonne Bridge (1930)—and initiated construction on the monumental George Washington Bridge (completed 1931) between Fort Lee, New Jersey, and Washington Heights, in northern Manhattan.

INDUSTRY, COMMERCE, AND LABOR

This public infrastructure, when combined with privately constructed rail terminals, facilitated both the specialization of economic activity in lower Manhattan and the decentralization of industry throughout the city and region. Penn Station at 31st Street (1910), Grand Central Station at 42nd Street (1913), and the Hudson and Manhattan Railroad tunnels between New

Jersey and lower Manhattan (1908) eased commuting to midtown and accelerated the northward movement of factories and offices. One-third of the city's labor force was still employed in manufacturing in 1930, down from a peak of 40 percent in 1910, with 27 percent involved in transportation and trade, while clerical and professional workers increased from 17 to 25 percent. New York thus remained a manufacturing and commercial center even as it expanded its role as corporate headquarters and financial capital.

A remarkably diverse array of industries prospered below 59th Street, where they employed over four hundred thousand workers in 1922. Those requiring face-to-face contact among buyers, suppliers, and subcontractors, and those making unstandardized products or responding to unpredictable trends in fashion, filled loft buildings and speculative skyscrapers downtown, while less time-sensitive industries, those requiring more space or producing standardized goods, fled Manhattan in search of lower rents, resulting in a selective dispersal of industrial activities outward from the city center. Food processing (of chocolate, tea, sugar, and coffee) shifted to the Brooklyn waterfront, but meat slaughtering remained in Manhattan to serve the kosher trade. Three-quarters of machinery was produced in Brooklyn and Queens by the 1920s, but nearly twelve thousand workers made technical instruments south of Central Park. The New York region led the nation in chemical production, with the world's largest petroleum refining center in New Jersey, pharmaceutical producers in Brooklyn, and soap and perfume manufacturers in Manhattan. Newspapers were printed in midtown for rush-hour customers, but bookbinding moved increasingly to the outer boroughs. Three-quarters of garment workers were employed below Central Park, with over fifty thousand making women's dresses alone in 1922, even though production of menswear had begun to relocate to larger plants outside Manhattan.

With about one in every four workers in the New York region employed in garment-making in 1912, the needle trades became an area of intense union activity. New York had a long history of conservative craft unionism dominated by Irish and German men. Between 1909 and 1914, however, the United Hebrew Trades (1888), the Women's Trade Union League (led by the fiery Rose Schneiderman), and the International Ladies Garment Workers Union (1900) were energized by wildcat strikes, with over three hundred thousand garment workers (many of them young women) on the picket lines in 1913. This burst of activism culminated in the short-lived but influential Protocols of Peace, which improved hours, wages, and working conditions with a new labor management accord, but internal ideological conflicts sapped labor's strength during the 1920s.

By 1930, New York was also home to over five hundred thousand clerical workers and a quarter million professional service workers, many of whom labored in the skyscrapers that made the city's skyline unique in the world. A prewar building boom produced landmarks like the Woolworth Building (1913), while the prosperous 1920s saw the construction of modernist gems such as the Barclay-Vesey Building (1926). Gotham boasted nearly twenty-five hundred buildings over ten stories by 1929.

The city's commercial banks continued to provide specie, notes, and credit to all parts of the country, serving as intermediary between American industry and European investment capital. The creation of the Federal Reserve in 1913 and the financial crisis of World War I allowed New York to assume a larger role in international trade, previously managed through London. The key actors in the financial sector clustered in their historic neighborhood between the Battery and Fulton Street, where the closely packed skyscrapers of the financial district facilitated the exchange of information. In 1926, forty of the ninety-five main offices of the commercial banks engaged in national and international transactions were still below Fulton Street, as were the Clearing House, Federal Reserve Bank, Sub-Treasury, Custom House, and all seven formally organized exchanges. All but 5 of the 970 members of the New York Stock Exchange were located in the same area, along with 60 percent of the city's lawyers and the offices of 70 percent of the country's largest corporations (with assets over $100 million).

The financial sector had developed in lower Manhattan largely because of the port, which allowed the city to maintain its position as a commodity processing and distribution center. Although New York's share of the nation's foreign commerce had declined from its post–Civil War zenith, two-thirds of imports arrived there at the time of consolidation, and half the value of foreign trade (and about a fifth of the tonnage) still passed through the harbor in the early 1930s.

RACE, ETHNICITY, AND IMMIGRATION

In the mid-1890s, New York still resembled what it had been for much of the nineteenth century, a German/Irish city with a majority of its population in Manhattan. Three decades later, it had become an Italian/Jewish city with a majority of its population in Brooklyn and the Bronx. Thanks to consolidation, by 1930 over 5 million people lived outside Manhattan but still within the city limits. With just over 1.8 million residents, Manhattan was almost exactly as populous in 1930 as in 1900, while Queens and the Bronx experienced more than sixfold increases in population, and by 1925 Brooklyn, with 2.5 million residents, had became the city's most populous borough. Although restrictive immigration laws reduced the percentage of foreign-born residents from 41 in 1910 to 34 by 1930, there were still almost 2.4 million non-natives in Gotham. The religious composition of the city swung from predominantly Protestant (47 percent) and Catholic (35 percent) in 1900 to mainly Catholic (49 percent) and Jewish (31 percent) by 1935.

By 1910 the city's large German population had long since abandoned *Kleindeutschland* on the Lower East Side for new enclaves like Yorkville. Although 60 percent remained in Manhattan in 1900, a decade later the figure had declined to 42 percent as Germans dispersed to Brooklyn and Queens. This familiar combination of outward and upward mobility included a shift of most Germans into skilled labor or middle-class occupations by 1920. And while the German language daily *Staats-Zeitung* had a circulation of ninety-five thousand in 1919, many German institutions had changed their names due to ethnic hostility during World War I.

The Irish achieved less upward mobility than the Germans, resulting in an even more stratified population. A "lace curtain" class of doctors and other professionals had emerged by World War I, though most Irish were still found among the working class, where they dominated many craft unions in addition to holding about a third of all public-sector jobs and a majority of leadership positions in the Democratic Party. Irish success in politics was not confined to Tammany Hall: the leading Fusion candidates in 1913 were all Irish. Irish women, though highly represented among domestic laborers, moved into new fields, such as nursing. And while 60 percent of the city's Irish residents remained in Manhattan in 1910, new enclaves developed in the Bronx, Brooklyn, and Queens.

Russia, Austria-Hungary, and Romania were the main sources of Jewish immigration to New York City, swelling the population from five hundred thousand in 1900 to nearly two million by 1930. After 1900, over half of Jewish immigrants came from urban areas where many worked in skilled trades, especially garment making. With high rates of literacy and naturalization, Jews wielded increasing power in both Democratic and Fusion coalitions. Yiddish served as a unifying language and facilitated the growth of an extensive network of voluntary institutions. With its dense collection of Yiddish-language theaters and publishers, the Lower East Side, where half a million Jews lived in 1910, remained a cultural center for decades in spite of the rapid pace of outward migration. By 1925 Manhattan was home to fewer than 30 percent of Jews, whose burgeoning skilled and professional classes moved

The federally operated immigration facility on Ellis Island opened in 1892. The facility grew over the years to handle the influx of immigrants through its doors. In 1907, some 1.25 million immigrants were processed at the facility.

Source: Library of Congress

to Harlem, Brownsville, Washington Heights, and Williamsburg, making Brooklyn the most populous Jewish borough by the 1920s.

Initial waves of Sicilian and southern Italian peasants, many of them young male sojourners, gave way to families from different parts of Italy after 1900. More than half a million Italians lived in the city by 1910, about 60 percent in Manhattan and often in regional clusters. Drawn by employment opportunities, Italians scattered to more than two dozen districts throughout the city, and by 1930 half the Italian population resided in Brooklyn. About 50 percent of Italians worked in low-skill occupations in 1916, falling to about 30 percent by 1930, thanks to the growth of a middle class of bankers, shopkeepers, and newspaper publishers. Italian women dominated the needle trades by the 1920s. Geographical dispersion, lower rates of naturalization, and reduced participation in associational activities diluted Italian political strength during this period. Although initially suspicious of the Irish-dominated Catholic Church, by 1911 the Italian community counted some fifty churches and dozens of local *festa* celebrating particular saints.

African Americans experienced considerably less of the geographic and economic mobility that New York City offered other newcomers. Blacks numbered only 60,666 in 1900 but swelled to 327,706 in 1930 (4.7 percent of the city's total population). While other ethnic groups dispersed from gateway neighborhoods like the Lower East Side, assaults by white populations and police on black enclaves in Manhattan between 1900 and 1905 pushed the population into Harlem. By 1930 two-thirds of African Americans lived there, with another large community in Bedford-Stuyvesant (Brooklyn). Racism confined many black women to domestic work and black men to manual labor, although a small class of lawyers, teachers, and shop owners grew along with ghetto populations. The leading figures of the Harlem Renaissance, including philosopher Alain Locke, writers Langston Hughes and Zora Neale Hurston, sculptor Meta Vaux Warrick Fuller, and photographer James Van Der Zee, helped make New York City the national center of African American culture. This profusion of cultural achievement took place against a backdrop of extreme poverty and discrimination, highlighting the paradox of the African American experience in New York City.

See also *New York, NY 1776–1790; New York, NY 1790–1828; New York, NY 1828–1854; New York, NY 1854–1877; New York, NY 1877–1896; New York, NY 1929–1941; New York, NY 1941–1952; New York, NY 1952–1989; New York, NY 1989–2011*

KEITH D. REVELL

BIBLIOGRAPHY

Binder, Frederick W., and David M. Reimers. *All the Nations Under Heaven: An Ethnic and Racial History of New York City.* New York, NY: Columbia University Press, 1995.

Doig, Jameson W. *Empire on the Hudson: Entrepreneurial Vision and Political Power at the Port of New York Authority.* New York, NY: Columbia University Press, 2001.

Greenwald, Richard A. *The Triangle Fire, the Protocols of Peace, and Industrial Democracy in Progressive Era New York.* Philadelphia, PA: Temple University Press, 2005.

Hood, Clifton. *722 Miles: The Building of the Subways and How They Transformed New York.* Centennial Edition. Baltimore, MD: Johns Hopkins University Press, 2004.

Revell, Keith D. *Building Gotham: Civic Culture and Public Policy in New York City, 1898–1938.* Baltimore, MD: Johns Hopkins University Press, 2003.

Sacks, Marcy S. *Before Harlem: The Black Experience in New York City before World War I.* Philadelphia: University of Pennsylvania Press, 2006.

CHICAGO, IL 1896–1929

CHICAGO FROM 1896 TO 1929 CONTINUED ITS REMARKABLE GROWTH, with population standing at 1.1 million in 1890 and expanding to 3.3 million by 1930. The rapid expansion of the city's infrastructure and population opened the way to political corruption, a subject with which the city became synonymous, while at the same time Chicago emerged as a national epicenter of the Progressive movement, with a focus on reforming government and providing relief and opportunity to the working poor, largely immigrant population of the city. On the eve of the Great Depression, Chicago's role as the great industrial metropolis of the American West was secure.

MAYORS

George Bell Swift	(1895–1897)
Carter Henry Harrison II	(1897–1905)
Edward Fitzsimmons Dunne	(1905–1907)
Fred A. Busse	(1907–1911)
Carter Henry Harrison II	(1911–1915)
William Hale Thompson	(1915–1923)
William Emmett Dever	(1923–1927)
William Hale Thompson	(1927–1931)

MAJOR INDUSTRIES AND EMPLOYERS

Agricultural implements
Electrical industry
Meatpacking
Railroad and streetcar manufacturing/
   repair
Iron and steel manufacturing

MAJOR NEWSPAPERS

Chicago Defender
Chicago Daily News
Chicago Herald
Chicago Inter-Ocean
Chicago Journal
Chicago Republican
Chicago Times
Chicago Tribune

MAJOR EVENTS

December 30, 1903: The fire at the Iroquois Theatre causes the largest loss of life in any fire in a building in the twentieth century, killing 602 people and bolstering Progressive-era reform efforts in the built environment.

1915: The *S.S. Eastland*, a passenger ship, rolls over in the Chicago River while loading for a vacation cruise, killing 844 people.

1916–1920s: Chicago is a major destination city of the Great Migration, a major influx of African American migrants from the American South.

1919: The worst race riot in Illinois history points to strife resulting from segregation and rapid demographic change in the city.

1929: The St. Valentine's Day Massacre, a grisly Prohibition-era mob murder, comes to symbolize the violence of the 1920s in "gangland" Chicago.

GOVERNMENT AND POLITICS

Continuing the trends of previous years, the "Grey Wolves" of the city council—"Bathhouse" John Coughlin and Michael "Hinky Dink" Kenna—were famous for the lengths to which their corrupt practices ("boodling," as it was called) proliferated in turn-of-the-century Chicago. This was facilitated through aldermanic privilege and the sale of valuable utility franchises throughout the city. At the same time, perhaps unsurprisingly, the urban political reform movement was sweeping through Chicago. Corruption in the city became the stuff of legend when it was taken up in Lincoln Steffens's 1904 book *The Shame of the Cities*. The City Club of Chicago was founded in 1903 and epitomized the city's Progressive tradition. The City Club held weekly meetings and created committees to report on local government. After the Iroquois Theatre fire (1903), City Club member and millionaire Charles Crane helped sponsor a thorough investigation of the fire that turned up staggering corruption in the building inspection process of the city. Other members included settlement house founder Jane Addams, architect Louis Sullivan, and philosopher George Herbert Mead. While urban bosses and power brokers proved relatively immune to the reform spirit, tangible results of Progressive-era reforms in the city included construction of parks and playgrounds as well as enhancements to trash collection, water quality, and sanitation.

Chicago's intellectual elites proved nationally influential in these years. The University of Chicago was founded in 1892 by John D. Rockefeller, and William Rainey Harper served as its first president. John Dewey served on the faculty of the university from 1894 to 1905, thus making it a center of the "pragmatist" philosophical movement—a school that ranged across theories on politics and education, and included George Herbert Mead. Dewey's approach to education drew wide acclaim, focused on his innovative approaches to education, including a model kindergarten he established. Sociology was also a major new field of study developed at the University of Chicago, with much of the early work in the "Chicago School" focused on urban life, immigration, ethnicity, and community/identity formation studies.

The Progressive movement's precepts of meaningful representative government, limits on the power of money in politics, and the assimilation of immigrants into the American mainstream percolated through Chicago's universities, unions, immigrant neighborhoods, and elite clubs in these years, resulting in a strong base for the founding of the Progressive Party. The Progressive Party held its convention in Chicago in 1912 and nominated former Republican Theodore Roosevelt. In Illinois—with Chicago as the population center, housing 75 percent of the state's residents—Roosevelt pulled 33.7 percent of the popular vote to Woodrow Wilson's 35.3 percent, with Socialist Eugene Debs taking 7.1 percent. As these numbers indicate, at the high point of American reformist politics, Chicago was at the vanguard of the movement. Considering the rapid population growth, chronic struggles over the role of immigrants, and the intellectual ferment of the Progressives, it is fitting that Chicago set the trend for the nation in rethinking the possibilities and the perils to industrial democracy in these years.

Carter Henry Harrison II was one of the dominant political figures of the era, serving four terms as mayor. Harrison, son of the popular mayor Carter Harrison who was assassinated in 1893, pushed a progressive agenda in his time in office. This was most famously exemplified by an attempt by street traction magnate Charles Tyson Yerkes to use political contacts to expand his franchise in the city. Harrison blocked Yerkes in his effort. Like his father, Harrison was friendly to labor and immigrant coalitions.

William Hale Thompson was another popular mayor in these years. A Republican, Thompson was also a progressive and a supporter of women's suffrage. The women's suffrage movement had been very active in Chicago, and a new state law in 1913 gave women the right to vote in local elections. In 1914 more than one hundred fifty thousand women registered to vote in Chicago. Thompson also was widely thought to be tolerant of organized crime during the 1920s Prohibition "gangster era." With Prohibition underway, the city faced a new type of corruption, this time with powerful gang leaders—running illegal smuggling and saloon operations—finding their way into influence throughout the city. The gangs were often led by charismatic figures like Al Capone and Bugs Moran. On Valentine's Day, 1929, seven gang members were gunned down in an event that became a sensationalized symbol of the sometimes lawless and corrupt Second City.

INDUSTRY, COMMERCE, AND LABOR

Continuing in the pattern established after the Civil War, Chicago continued to build itself into one of the major industrial centers in the world. Meatpacking, steel manufacturing, traction, and electrical products were all major employers. Meatpacking provides a good microcosm of the industrial character of the city's workforce, made up as it was by a cross-section of European immigrants, with ethnicities of long standing in the city such as Germans often in foremen roles, and more recent immigrants such as Poles and Lithuanians starting in the least desirable posts. The Amalgamated Meat Cutters Union was organized by the American Federation of Labor in 1897, and at the time of a major strike over wages in 1904 the union boasted eighteen thousand members. The strike culminated in a riot, when a mob of union members surrounded strikebreakers, and eventual defeat for the union's demands—not an uncommon chain of events in labor activity of the period.

The physical location of the city proved more and more strategic as infrastructures like the transcontinental rail network and a canal system linking the city to the Mississippi River opened markets east and west, north and south. Industrial education flourished in Chicago, symbolized by the founding of the Armour Institute of Technology. Originally founded by Philip Armour in 1893, the institute grew rapidly after the turn of the century, providing a mixture of laboratory courses and more practical engineering courses. Majors included mechanical and electrical engineering as well as fire protection engineering. The institute was located in south Chicago and was aimed in its early years at educating working-class students, especially through its innovative extension and evening classes. The institute evolved rapidly, however, into an engineering college that catered primarily to young men going into the electrical and mechanical industries of the city.

Chicago continued to play host to innovations in high-rise construction in these years. However, the city was best known for a building tragedy—a fire in the Iroquois Theatre that claimed 602 lives. The Iroquois was advertised as absolutely fireproof, but was in fact a fire trap, with poorly marked exits, narrow landings, doors that opened inward, insufficient fire escapes, and no fire sprinkler as mandated by city fire code. A traveling Christmastime play—*Mr. Blue Beard*—was on at the Iroquois when a fire started on stage. Unable to escape in time, many of the dead were burned or asphyxiated in their seats, while others were trampled trying to escape. It was yet another tragedy in a line of Chicago fire tragedies stretching back to the Great Fire of 1871. The tragedy at the Iroquois gave rise to a thorough examination of all theaters in Chicago, an examination that revealed none to be up to code. Several lengthy trials found the theater owner and manager blameless, and no damages were paid to victims' families, except years later in a settlement by the Fuller Construction Company. The fire was a landmark in the area of fire safety, and it was in Chicago that the first major electrical and fire safety testing laboratory—Underwriters Laboratories—was founded in the late 1890s.

The City Beautiful Movement took shape in Chicago in these years with the publication of architect/planner Daniel H. Burnham's 1909 Plan of Chicago. This plan was a complete reimagining of the city's waterfront, transportation, and park systems. Burnham had opened the way for his plan with the stunning success of the 1893 World's Columbian Exposition. Returning to many of the same ideas, Burnham's plan was widely hailed—though the only portion of it completed was the Chicago waterfront. Architectural innovation likewise continued to be a major feature of Chicago life, exemplified by the works of Frank Lloyd Wright, such as the Robie House (1909), Wrigley Field (1914) and Soldier Field (1925) were completed, as was the Tribune Tower (1925). An elevated train system, begun in the nineteenth century, had encircled the downtown "loop" of the city by the 1910s, and an integrated subway system was underway by 1913.

RACE, ETHNICITY, AND IMMIGRATION

Chicago literature in these years was strongly influenced by the major themes of urban life—immigration and industrial labor. Upton Sinclair's 1906 novel *The Jungle* remains the most influential book from Chicago in these years. *The Jungle* chronicles the ups and downs of Jurgis, Ona, and their Lithuanian family as they arrive in the South Side of Chicago and take up meatpacking labor. Ultimately their family is destroyed, and Jurgis takes up socialist politics. Aside from its political ambitions—the book was more successful in provoking revulsion against poor sanitation in meatpacking than in the labor movement—*The Jungle* beautifully documents conditions in the immigrant ethnic culture of industrial Chicago and remains a paragon of the "muckraking" style. The most tangible impact of the book, other than fame for Sinclair, was that it in part inspired the federal government to pass the Meat Inspection Act.

Working-class politics aside, the narrative of the immigrant, either from abroad or merely from a smaller town or the countryside, became a dominant literary genre of the era. *Sister Carrie*, for example, was written by Theodore Dreiser in 1900 and follows the story of Caroline Meeber as she leaves the countryside and enters the rough-and-tumble life of the modern big city. Chicago nurtured the careers of writers like Dreiser and also Sherwood Anderson, Carl Sandburg, and Edgar Lee Masters. Many of these writers themselves were newcomers to the city, most notably perhaps Milwaukeean Carl Sandburg, who in his descriptions of the city—rendered in a free-verse, unadorned style—brought a social realism to bear that imagined its character as an amalgamation of its polyglot and multitalented immigrant workforce.

A look at the city's demographics in 1910 reveals a tapestry of ethnicities, with almost half of the residents being foreign-born. Germans led the way, with Europeans in general making up the great majority, but there was also a large Canadian population. The rapid influx of immigrants into the city that had begun in the 1860s had led to fierce competition for work, especially in unskilled industries. Beginning in the 1910s, as a result of Jim Crow–era violence and discrimination in the American South, a "great migration" of African Americans began, and Chicago was one of the primary destinations for these migrants. They soon found that they faced not only the perils of being migrants, but also the same color line that ruled the South.

Competition for housing and work at the end of World War I brought into relief racial tension already present in the city for over a generation, and a major race riot rocked the city in the summer of 1919. After an incident at a segregated beach in which an African American teenager was struck by a rock and died, fighting and eventually the full-scale riot erupted. In the incident thirty-five people were killed, including fifteen whites, and five hundred people were injured. The South Side of the city was especially impacted. Seventeen African Americans and no whites were ultimately indicted for rioting.

Despite this episode, African Americans found institutions, churches, and newspapers like the *Chicago Defender* as welcoming and assimilating agents on their behalf. The African American cultural ferment of Chicago in the 1920s produced or added to some of the nation's most important works of literature, such as Richard Wright's novel *Native Son*. The explosion of jazz and blues music in the city was led by artists like Blind Lemon Jefferson, Tampa Red, and Big Bill Broonzy, all influential bluesmen whose work would influence American music for generations to come. In the pressure cooker of the American industrial metropolis of the west, a new America was being forged. Diverse, profitable (for some), and magnetic, Chicago defined America in these years.

Perhaps the most influential meeting ground of Progressive-era reform traditions in Chicago in these years was the Hull House settlement, founded by Jane Addams. Strongly informed by Toynbee Hall in London, Hull House was established as a sort of refuge for immigrant working-class men, women, and especially children in the city. At Hull House, Addams and her staff provided services ranging from legal aid and health care to translation services and kindergarten instruction. In this setting, one could see the coming together of the major trends in Chicago: immigration, industrialization, intense urbanization, and reform. At the same time, Hull House was a meeting ground for feminists, educational reformers like John Dewey, and sociologists who were eager to understand the immigrant communities who were so rapidly remaking the city. Hull House spawned imitators across the country, and Addams won a Nobel Peace Prize in 1931.

See also *Chicago, IL 1854–1877; Chicago, IL 1877–1896; Chicago, IL 1929–1941; Chicago, IL 1941–1952; Chicago, IL 1952–1989; Chicago, IL 1989–2011*

Scott Gabriel Knowles

BIBLIOGRAPHY

Adler, Jeffrey S. *First in Violence, Deepest in Dirt: Homicide in Chicago, 1875–1920*. Cambridge, MA: Harvard University Press, 2006.

Bulmer, Martin. *The Chicago School of Sociology: Institutionalization, Diversity, and the Rise of Sociological Research*. Chicago, IL: University of Chicago Press, 1984.

Cronon, William. *Nature's Metropolis: Chicago and the Great West*. New York, NY: W. W. Norton, 1991.

Crunden, Robert. *Ministers of Reform: The Progressives' Achievement in American Civilization, 1889–1920*. Urbana: University of Illinois Press, 1985.

Garb, Margaret. *City of American Dreams: A History of Home Ownership and Housing Reform in Chicago, 1871–1919*. Chicago, IL: University of Chicago Press, 2005.

Grossman, James R., Ann Durkin Keating, and Janice L. Reiff, eds. *The Encyclopedia of Chicago*. Chicago, IL: University of Chicago Press, 2004.

Sandburg, Carl. *Chicago Poems*. New York, NY: H. Holt and Company, 1916.

Simpson, Dick. *Rogues, Rebels, and Rubber Stamps: The Politics of the Chicago City Council from 1863 to the Present*. Boulder, CO: Westview Press, 2001.

PHILADELPHIA, PA 1896–1929

THE TRENDS THAT BEGAN IN PHILADELPHIA AT THE MIDDLE OF THE NINETEENTH CENTURY reached their full articulation between 1896 and 1929. The combination of William Penn's grid-pattern streets and small brick row houses covered more of the region, and Philadelphia remained the "City of Homes." With greater transit options coupled with low fares and rising working-class income, economic and ethnic segregation became more common in housing. As an already diverse manufacturing base expanded, Philadelphia justifiably claimed it was the "Workshop of the World." The municipal government continued its expansion and its shift toward a strong-mayor model. The Republican machine remained in power, and Philadelphia earned its infamous distinction of being "corrupt and contented." The population became more diverse, but discrimination remained an unsolved problem. Although Center City Philadelphia's offices and stores rose in both size and prominence, the consolidation of New York City in 1898 ended Philadelphia's long attempt to overtake its nearby rival.

Philadelphia would remain the third largest city in the United States (after New York and Chicago) from 1890 to 1950. Although the second largest city on the Atlantic coast, Philadelphia would always be in the shadow of its larger northern neighbor. The city's long period of growth effectively ended in 1930 with a population of just under two million. In addition to continuity, there was also change. In the early twentieth century the city undertook projects that represented dramatic breaks with the past, from the Benjamin Franklin Parkway that cut a diagonal swath across Center City's grid to the towering Delaware River Bridge that tied Philadelphia to the New Jersey hinterland and was the longest suspension bridge in the world when it opened. In the opinion of many, the last remnants of William Penn's old Quaker City would disappear under the booming industrial metropolis.

GOVERNMENT AND POLITICS

Formally, the early twentieth century was a period of an evolving city government under almost exclusively Republican control trying to cope with the demands of a larger and more diverse population. The 1854 consolidation of the city with the county had created a complex government structure with a weak mayor and a relatively strong—yet unpaid and large—bicameral city council. Although the movement to a strong-mayor system began with the City Charter of 1887, that reform also increased the membership of the two chambers of city council to 146. It was not

QUICK FACTS

PHILADELPHIA, PA **1896–1929**

MAYORS

Charles Franklin Warwick	(1895–1899)
Samuel Howell Ashbridge	(1899–1903)
John Weaver	(1903–1907)
John E. Reyburn	(1907–1911)
Rudolph Blankenburg	(1911–1916)
Thomas B. Smith	(1916–1920)
J. Hampton Moore	(1920–1924)
W. Freeland Kendrick	(1924–1928)
Harry Arista Mackey	(1928–1931)

MAJOR INDUSTRIES AND EMPLOYERS

Department stores

Knit goods

Electrical machinery

Printing and publishing, newspaper and
  magazine

Foundry and machine shop products

MAJOR NEWSPAPERS

Evening Bulletin

North American

Philadelphia Inquirer

Public Ledger

Record

MAJOR EVENTS

1904: Muckraker Lincoln Steffens concludes that Philadelphia is "the most corrupt and contented" city in the United States in *The Shame of the Cities*.

1907: The Market Street subway-elevated opens as the city's first rapid transit line.

1911: President William Howard Taft dedicates the new John Wanamaker department store, which was then the largest department store in the world.

1918: The global influenza pandemic ravages Philadelphia in the fall and kills over twelve thousand people.

1926: Ten million people attend the Sesquicentennial international exposition running from May to November, but it is a financial failure.

---

until the 1919 Charter that the city council was reduced to one chamber with a more reasonable twenty-one members and became a paid body.

As with many other cities during the late nineteenth and early twentieth centuries, Philadelphia saw a rise in governmental functions as it took on new responsibilities. The Market Street Subway was a public-private partnership, with the city providing much of the capital financing and the private Philadelphia Rapid Transit operating the trains, it served as a model for all future rapid transit projects in Philadelphia. The city's most significant example of the City Beautiful movement was the Benjamin Franklin Parkway, which linked the Art Museum in Fairmount Park with City Hall via a diagonal boulevard that cut across the city's traditional grid. After a decade of discussion, the project was begun in 1907 and completed in 1926. By 1929 a zoning commission was appointed to create Philadelphia's first comprehensive zoning plan, which came into effect in 1933.

As with other major cities, what truly ran Philadelphia during this period was a corrupt political machine. In Philadelphia's case it was a Republican machine. Political corruption was in fact rife throughout Pennsylvania, and perhaps the worst excess in the city—the thirty-year-long

Designed by John McArthur Jr., and completed in 1901, Philadelphia's City Hall was an architectural marvel that took some three decades to complete. The statue of William Penn atop the building is over 30 feet tall.

Source: Library of Congress

construction of Philadelphia's City Hall from 1871 to 1901 at the cost of $24 million—was orchestrated by a corrupt state government commission. The construction of City Hall took so long that it was retrofitted for elevators and electric lights while being built. Of the nine men who served as mayor from 1896 to 1929, only one, Rudolph Blankenburg, who served from 1911 to 1916, was not part of the political machine. Perhaps the figure from this period that best represents the Republican machine was Boies Penrose, who became a powerful U.S. senator.

After Mayor Blankenburg, the best-known reformer was Smedley Butler, an outspoken, decorated Marine officer who became Philadelphia's Director of Public Safety in 1924. He was appointed by Mayor W. Freeland Kendrick to battle corruption in the police department. An already corrupt police department had become even less scrupulous since the enactment of Prohibition. Many bars had reopened as restaurants and freely served alcohol as long as payments were made to the police. Butler fired openly corrupt police officers and began a series of well-publicized raids that targeted not only working-class saloons but upper-class locations like the Union League (a Republican businessman's club) and the Ritz-Carlton Hotel. Butler was forced out of his job at the end of 1925 when he openly criticized the mayor.

Although Lincoln Steffens's claim that Philadelphia was "the most corrupt and contented" city in the United States was likely accurate, the city government dealt with a broad range of problems in a municipality that nearly doubled in population between 1890 and 1930. The city government became more centralized and hired more professionals to deal with issues like planning, zoning, law enforcement, and public health.

INDUSTRY, COMMERCE, AND LABOR

Philadelphia's economy did not change dramatically between 1896 and 1929. It remained a complex and diverse global industrial center and a regional financial and commercial center. Philadelphia justifiably promoted itself as "the Workshop of the World" based on its broad range of manufacturers and the sheer volume of goods it produced. Unlike the ties between steel and Pittsburgh or automobiles and Detroit, Philadelphia had no single dominant industry during this period. Most of Philadelphia's businesses were small to medium in size. Only a handful were large, such as the Baldwin Locomotive Works, Cramp Shipbuilding, Disston Saw, Midvale Steel, and Stetson Hat. In Philadelphia new industries, such as electronics, were added to the nineteenth-century mix of textiles, apparel, printing, publishing, and foundry and machines.

One trend in manufacturing that began in the 1920s was the movement of companies from smaller sites in the old industrial core around Center City to larger structures in outlying sections of the city and its suburbs. The best-known example is the movement of the Baldwin Locomotive Works from its longtime home in lower North Philadelphia to Eddystone in nearby Delaware County, Pennsylvania, in 1928.

Philadelphia was also one of the traditional centers of American shipbuilding, and this continued through this period. In the nineteenth century, the Delaware River became known as "America's Clyde," a reference to the dominance of Glasgow and its hinterland in British marine engineering. During World War I, Philadelphia shipyards set records for the size of their physical plant and the volume of their production. American International Shipbuilding at Hog Island was the largest shipyard in the world at that time, completing some 122 military vessels for the war effort. The city had two other giant shipyards: William Cramp & Sons in Kensington and the U.S. Navy Yard on League Island. Cramp, once America's largest shipbuilder, closed in 1927.

Although Philadelphia was often known as a retail center during this period because of the size of its main department stores, it also served as a wholesale center not just for the region but also in competition with New York City and Chicago for national markets. Philadelphia's department stores, led by John Wanamaker, Gimbel Brothers, and Strawbridge & Clothier, were dominant institutions from the 1890s through the 1920s. Each one would construct a building that would make it the "largest in the city" and often—albeit briefly—the largest department store in the world.

One reason for Philadelphia's industrial and commercial strength was its excellent port (usually the second busiest on the Atlantic coast after New York) and its well-developed rail freight facilities. Two major railroads, the Pennsylvania (the wealthiest and most powerful railroad in the country) and the Reading (a strong regional carrier affiliated with the New York Central and the Baltimore & Ohio), were headquartered in the city, and both developed complex systems that served the port, the city, and its hinterland.

Another factor often overlooked in Philadelphia's commercial success was the establishment of nonprofit institutions focused on supporting trade and industry in the city. The Franklin Institute continued to encourage scientific debate and practical engineering, as it had throughout the nineteenth century. The Commercial Museum was a unique institution that helped businesses study world trade. The University of Pennsylvania's Wharton School of Business would take over this function as higher education replaced museums as centers of learning in America.

A final factor in Philadelphia's manufacturing success was its anti-union policies that tended to suppress wages. Although this period was known for a number of important and large strikes, in general the smaller manufacturers of Philadelphia resisted unionization during this period reasonably effectively. In 1903 a textile workers strike against six hundred firms in the region involved approximately one hundred thousand workers. As part of the action, Mother Jones led a contingent of child laborers on a march from Philadelphia to President Theodore Roosevelt's home on Long Island. In 1910 a strike against the universally disliked Philadelphia Rapid Transit (the operator of the subway and almost all of the city's trolleys) escalated to a brief general strike in the city. Overall, however, most Philadelphia businesses remained nonunion during this period.

RACE, ETHNICITY, AND IMMIGRATION

Although immigration has played an important role in its growth and development, Philadelphia during this period had less foreign immigration than any other major city. The number of foreign-born reached its (rather low) peak in the 1870 census at a mere 27 percent (compared to 45 percent in New York City). Philadelphia's foreign-born population ranged from a low of 19 percent in 1930 to a high of 25 percent in 1910. The ethnic composition of Philadelphia's foreign-born changed dramatically between 1900 and 1930. In 1900 the five largest nationalities were Irish (95,080), German (71,399), English (40,691), Russian (28,339), and Italian (24,111). By 1930, Russian was the largest nationality (82,820), followed by Italian (67,367), Irish (49,187), German (34,239), and Polish (31,411).

A variety of reasons may have restricted greater settlement by immigrants in Philadelphia than in other major cities. The small and often specialized manufacturers tended to require skilled rather than unskilled labor. Only Midvale Steel, Disston Saw Works, and the leather industry had any significant demand for unskilled labor. Another factor was Philadelphia's growing African American population that, due to discrimination, competed for many of the same entry-level positions as immigrants. Certain skilled workers, such as textile workers from Scotland and Ireland and apparel workers from central Europe, found low-paying employment in traditional industries. The last wave of unrestricted immigration before 1924 would shape Philadelphia's ethnic landscape for decades. The Irish remained, and the Italians and Eastern European Jews became visible and dominant ethnic groups in the region.

Throughout the nineteenth century, Philadelphia had a relatively large African American population for a northern city. In 1900, there were 62,613 blacks in the city, slightly more than New York City (which was over twice as large) and double that of Chicago (which had a total population approximately 25 percent greater than Philadelphia's). The lure of jobs and the hope for better treatment spurred the Great Migration, and by 1920 the African American population had increased threefold to 191,222 (a little over 10 percent of the total population of the city), reaching 299,898 in 1930 (15 percent, and only slightly less than the total foreign-born population at 19 percent).

Philadelphia, and Pennsylvania as a whole, had retreated from their more progressive positions on race that had characterized both city and state in the decade after the Civil War. Although both Philadelphia and Pennsylvania had laws that restricted racial discrimination, a combination of nonenforcement and a tendency to ignore private contracts and actions limited the opportunities for African Americans during this period. Because of the Republican Party's desire to court black voters, the local, state, and federal governments tended to provide some opportunities for educated African Americans. Private employers tended to restrict black employment to service positions like waiters, porters, and elevator operators. Some employers, like John Wanamaker, shifted from a progressive position on race relations in the 1870s and 1880s to a more restrictive one in the 1920s. While some labor unions championed the rights of all workers, others struck to keep employers from hiring African American workers.

See also *Philadelphia, PA 1776–1790; Philadelphia, PA 1790–1828; Philadelphia, PA 1828–1854; Philadelphia, PA 1854–1877; Philadelphia, PA 1877–1896; Philadelphia, PA 1929–1941; Philadelphia, PA 1941–1952; Philadelphia, PA 1952–1989; Philadelphia, PA 1989–2011*

JOHN H. HEPP IV

BIBLIOGRAPHY

Cutler, William W., III, and Howard Gillette Jr., eds. *The Divided Metropolis: Social and Spatial Dimensions of Philadelphia, 1800–1975.* Westport, CT: Greenwood Press, 1980.

Davis, Allen F., and Mark H. Haller, eds. *The Peoples of Philadelphia: A History of Ethnic Groups and Lower-Class Life, 1790–1940.* Philadelphia: University of Pennsylvania Press, 1998.

Hepp, John H., IV. *The Middle-Class City: Transforming Space and Time in Philadelphia, 1876–1926.* Philadelphia: University of Pennsylvania Press, 2003.

McCaffery, Peter. *When Bosses Ruled Philadelphia: The Emergence of the Republican Machine, 1867–1933.* University Park: Pennsylvania State University Press, 1993.

Miller, Fredric M., Morris J. Vogel, and Allen F. Davis. *Still Philadelphia: A Photographic History, 1890–1940.* Philadelphia, PA: Temple University Press, 1983.

Warner, Sam Bass, Jr. *The Private City: Philadelphia in Three Periods of Its Growth.* Philadelphia: University of Pennsylvania Press, 1987.

Weigley, Russell F., ed. *Philadelphia: A 300-Year History.* New York, NY: W. W. Norton, 1982.

DETROIT, MI 1896–1929

FOUNDED AS A FRENCH FUR-TRADING OUTPOST by Antoine de la Mothe Cadillac in 1701, captured by the British in 1760, and later transferred to the United States in 1796, Detroit became an industrial powerhouse between 1896 and 1929. Augustus Woodward, directed by President Thomas Jefferson to organize Michigan as a territory, arrived in Detroit shortly after a fire destroyed much of the town in 1805. Woodward laid out the city in a pattern of large boulevards radiating out from a circular center, influenced by L'Enfant's plan of Washington, D.C. The geographic location across the Detroit River from Canada made the rebuilt city a natural international port and a destination for invention and innovation.

QUICK FACTS

DETROIT, MI 1896–1929

MAYORS

Hazen S. Pingree	(1890–1897)
William Rickert	(1897)
William C. Maybury	(1897–1904)
George P. Codd	(1905–1906)
William Barlum Thompson	(1907–1908)
Philip Breitmeyer	(1909–1910)
William Barlum Thompson	(1911–1912)
Oscar Marx	(1913–1918)
James J. Couzens	(1919–1922)
John C. Lodge	(1922–1923)
Frank Ellsworth Doremus	(1923–1924)
Joseph Martin	(1924)
John C. Lodge	(1924)
John Smith	(1924–1928)
John C. Lodge	(1928–1929)

MAJOR INDUSTRIES AND EMPLOYERS

Pharmaceutical manufacturing
Cigar and chewing tobacco
Iron, brass, and copper production
Heating and cooking stoves
Automobile, bus, and truck
   manufacturing

MAJOR NEWSPAPERS

Detroit Free Press
*Detroit News**
Detroit Times
*Detroit Tribune**
Evening News
* Merged in 1915

MAJOR EVENTS

1896: Illustrating the movement into the automotive age, the last horse-drawn streetcar shutters operation on November 9.

1907, 1908, 1909: Baseball's Detroit Tigers lose the World Series three years in a row, twice to the Chicago Cubs and once to the Pittsburgh Pirates.

1919: Accommodating the increased population of African Americans, the first all-black hospital opens in Detroit.

May 21, 1927: Detroit-born Charles Lindbergh becomes the first person to fly solo, nonstop in a single-engine plane from Long Island's Roosevelt Field to Paris's Le Bourget Air Field. The feat ushers in the age of air transportation, and by October 24 air service begins between Detroit and Cleveland and Detroit and Chicago.

1928: The Ambassador Bridge, connecting Detroit and Canada, opens as the longest suspension bridge in the world. The new Fox Theater, Detroit's most lavish, opens as the largest and most opulent of the theater chains, with a seating capacity of five thousand.

Located in Wayne County, Detroit experienced tremendous population growth between 1896 and 1929. The 1900 U.S. Census listed the total population of Detroit at 285,704. By 1920 the population had grown to 993,678, and by 1930 the population had reached 1,568,662. As industry and production expanded, immigrants and migrants supplied the demand for labor, carving out ethnic neighborhoods during a time of economic prosperity, prohibition, and progressivism. On the eve of the Great Depression, Detroit had established itself as a city of industry and growth. The 1920s witnessed the construction of ornate high-rise office buildings, entertainment facilities, and modest bungalow homes to meet the demand of an increasing population.

GOVERNMENT AND POLITICS

Chartered by the state of Michigan in 1857, Detroit had a unicameral, single legislative chamber, a common council elected by wards. In 1889 the common council consisted of thirty-two council members, holding office for two-year terms, representing sixteen wards. Candidates ran without party affiliations, with half of the ward elections held during even-numbered years and the mayoral and remaining ward elections held during odd-numbered years. The mayor appointed board commissioners for numerous departments, such as welfare, parks, and health, that required approval of the ward-elected city council members. The mayor also held the power of a veto, which took a two-thirds majority vote by the city council to override.

Hazen Pingree, mayor from 1890 to 1897, began the process of strengthening the power of city government. Elected as both mayor of Detroit and governor of Michigan, Pingree resigned his post as mayor in 1897 when the Michigan supreme court ruled he could not hold both offices. As governor, Pingree continued instituting changes through the state legislature to make city governments stronger. In 1908 the Michigan state legislature approved a change to the way that cities could organize their governments. No longer chartered by statewide offices, the Home Rule Act allowed cities to create a commission to frame a new city charter, with voters declaring their approval in a citywide election.

In 1918 Detroit voters approved a new city charter that organized their city government as a mayor–council system. The new elected city officials now controlled the day-to-day governance of Detroit, and through this new powerful mayoral office passed a city ordinance outlawing the production or sale of alcohol. Concerned with the increased population of non-Anglo-Saxons and combined with the nativism movement affecting the entire country, which associated Eastern European immigrants and southern migrants, both black and white, with immorality, the wealthy elite petitioned for a prohibition ordinance. Led by Henry Ford and other wealthy whites, the ordinance represented the attempts at control over the lower socioeconomic population by instilling perceived notions of morality. The citywide ordinance, passed two years before the National Prohibition Act, prohibited the production and sale of all alcoholic items as well as shut down the working-class and ethnic saloons where, after long days of monotonous work, members of the same ethnic strata gathered to exchange news from home, speak their native tongue, and talk politics.

The failed attempts of Detroit's new immigrants and migrants to furnish a powerful political candidate eliminated challenges to the Anglo-Saxon-controlled city government. As the prohibition ordinance forced saloons and bootlegging underground, the city's government was unable to enforce the control of the outlawed vice. Working-class white police officers, less than a generation removed from immigrant status, often ignored the smuggling of liquor from Canada and the distribution of bathtub gin.

INDUSTRY, COMMERCE, AND LABOR

Almost from its founding, Detroit had been a "break and bulk" city. Raw materials entered the city, and they left as manufactured products in the form of wearable furs, stoves, horse carriages,

Existing infrastructure for the manufacturing of carriages in Detroit facilitated the transition to producing automobiles around the turn of the 20th century. Innovators such as Henry Ford established factories and implemented new assembly line techniques to increase productivity. Due to high demand the industry soon began to migrate its factories to the suburbs.

Source: Library of Congress

cigars, and chewing tobacco. The geographic location of Detroit provided easy access to international waterways that were the bloodline of early settlement. With the arrival of the railroad in the mid-nineteenth century, Detroit became a destination settlement for people seeking employment, manufacturers, inventors, and bankers.

With Detroit a key manufacturer of horse-drawn carriages, the foundation for the automobile industry was already in place. In 1896 the first automobile appeared on the city's streets, and soon several innovative carriage makers began constructing automobiles on the carriage body foundation. Early manufacturing of open-air cars contributed to the already diverse manufacturing landscape of Detroit. Iron stoves, furniture building, pharmaceuticals, chemical production, paint, beer, steel mills, salt mines, and later typewriter and adding machine manufacturing made Detroit a labor destination for thousands of European immigrants fleeing turmoil in the early part of the twentieth century as well as for southern blacks.

As the demand for automobiles increased, innovative men such as Henry Ford, John and Horace Dodge, Walter O. Briggs, and Walter Chrysler constructed factories that increased efficiency by instituting the assembly line. Influenced by his 1893 tour of Chicago's Union Stockyards and the efficient manner of disassembling livestock, Henry Ford applied the same technique, only in reverse, in the automobile plant he opened in Detroit. The success of the Model-T, however, demanded a larger factory to increase production. In 1914 Ford opened his factory complex in Highland Park, a northern suburb of Detroit, thus beginning the move of factories into the undeveloped suburban landscape, where housing and peripheral industry would follow.

With the mundane, unskilled monotony of assembly line work compounded with low pay, high labor turnover plagued the automobile industry. In an attempt to thwart turnover and unionization, Ford offered workers in his assembly plants $5 per day, almost twice the going rate. While the raise in pay accomplished Ford's goals, it also acted as a beacon to immigrants and migrants searching for better economic opportunities. As such, thousands of immigrants flooded into Detroit to escape increasing turmoil in Europe. With the onset of World War I, European immigration ceased. To fill the labor needs of the automobile factories, company managers solicited southern blacks to travel north. Once the United States entered the war in 1917, automobile plants began producing equipment for the war effort, which made their owners very wealthy from government contracts.

Immigrants and southern migrants found employment as laborers in the automobile, iron, and steel factories and in the building trades. Hired into semiskilled and unskilled positions, both blacks and whites found benefits in the wartime economy. White women broke into the industrial trades in smaller manufacturing companies and as secretaries and clerks for large companies. Black females, however, remained employed primarily in domestic roles as cooks, servants, laundresses, and housekeepers, with much smaller numbers finding employment in factories.

After the Great War, demand for automobiles, trucks, and buses increased, requiring a larger workforce to supply the demand. In the years between the end of World War I and the 1924 Immigration Act, the European immigration numbers did not increase to the level before the war. The ethnic white labor force consisted of Poles, Hungarians, Germans, Irish, Italians, and Russians, but their fellow countrymen did not enlarge Detroit's labor force. To fill the labor shortage, once again African Americans traveled from the rural South to Detroit to work in hazardous and physically demanding jobs. Even after those who had traveled north notified family and friends remaining in the South of the working conditions and low wages, the negative reports did not deter hundreds of thousands of southern rural blacks from migrating northward.

By 1920 the automobile industry was the largest employer in Detroit, yet light manufacturing and assembling remained constant. These smaller manufacturing plants tended to remain within the city limits at a time when the automakers moved to larger factory complexes in the suburbs. Oil refining, garment manufacturing, chemical production, stove making, and adding machine and typewriter production continued, while new manufacturing came online to supply the automobile factories with equipment and parts for cars. Initially implementing de facto segregation, automobile companies had hired only a few African Americans. However, with the increased demand in cars, buses, and trucks, blacks filled the growing demand for labor. By 1921 the Ford Motor Company had become the largest employer of black workers.

At the onset of the twentieth century, Detroit remained the main producer of cooking and heating stoves, with the Detroit Stove Company, Peninsula Stove Company, and Michigan Stove Company as large employers. Manufactured tobacco became a large industry, and Detroit became the largest producer of chewing tobacco in the United States. Parke-Davis and Company produced pharmaceuticals requiring a more skilled labor force in Detroit. While the older avenues of manufacturing remained in the chemical, pharmaceutical, and stove-making industries, the automobile industry grew, thereby siphoning workers from other industrial sectors. Not only did new workers gravitate to the city, but long-time residents saw the new industry as an opportunity to make higher wages. They left their old production jobs for the new assembly line work of the automobile industry, and new workers entering the city filled the vacant spots of the old production jobs.

Many of the assembly line jobs in the automotive industry remained primarily for men. Women worked in light industry, as domestics, and conducted business from home as seamstresses or laundresses while caring for their children. For rural southern black women seeking domestic work, the Detroit Urban League provided year-long training programs to instruct on the use of gas and electric household appliances as well as provide guidance in appropriate behavior for working in the homes of Detroit's middle-class and elite whites.

RACE, ETHNICITY, AND IMMIGRATION

At the turn of the twentieth century, Detroit had become a powerhouse of industrial employment opportunities. The demand for semiskilled and unskilled labor established Detroit as a port-of-entry for European immigrants prior to World War I. By 1930 the city had become the fourth most important destination for southern African American migration, behind New York, Chicago, and Philadelphia. As native Detroit residents and Anglo-Saxons continued to adjust to the large influx of immigrants from Russia, Hungary, Italy, Finland, Bohemia, Poland, and even Germany and Ireland, African Americans from the rural South began trickling into the city to fill the demand for labor.

Immigration between 1896 and 1929 consisted of two ethnic waves, the first being European and the second being American southern. European immigration existed in Detroit from the early days of settlement, but the numbers remained stagnant and consisted primarily of German and Irish laborers. As these "old" ethnic groups assimilated and moved into the bungalow belts of Detroit, "new" white ethnic immigrants, from Poland, Hungary, and Russia, filled the older housing of early working-class neighborhoods, primarily single-family homes situated on small city lots with yards large enough to plant a small garden. These new residents often let out rooms in their homes to ensure that they met their monthly financial obligations. The boarders usually shared the same ethnic background with their landlords and maintained the same ethnic identity of the neighborhood. Within these ethnic enclaves, shop owners catered to the specific demands of the new white ethnic groups by offering foods from their native countries, and neighborhood saloons acted as gathering places for recent immigrant families to speak their native tongue and listen to news of their homeland. When the city council and mayor instituted prohibition, they forced the closure of the ethnic saloons, eliminating legal social gathering places for the new European immigrants. Forced to find alternative entertainments, these white ethnic groups established speakeasies in basements and storerooms of grocery stores and pharmacies while serving bathtub gin, homebrewed beer, and smuggled liquor from Canada.

Filling in the boarding houses and apartments of the Black Bottom neighborhood, rural southern African Americans, lured by the prospect of industrial jobs, laid the foundation of a black ghetto with businesses, professionals, churches, and social service agencies catering to the mostly migrant population. In 1900 Detroit's black population numbered 4,100, and by 1910 it had increased to 5,740, whereas the total population of Detroit increased from 285,704 to 465,766 in the same time period. During the first fifteen years of the twentieth century, the black population was a minor contribution to the overall Detroit population. However, by 1914 blacks began arriving in larger numbers, and by 1920 the black population increased to 41,000, drastically overcrowding the Black Bottom section of Detroit.

As with the European immigrants before them, rural southern African Americans viewed Detroit as the Promised Land containing numerous employment opportunities in the growing industrial sector of unskilled labor. With the onset of World War I, European immigration came to a virtual standstill, leaving factory owners and managers with an enormous labor shortage at a time when production increased as the United States crept closer to war. Witnessing lynchings and suffering from the whims of white creditors, rural African Americans defiantly protested the Jim Crow South and moved north. Labor agents traveled to the South to recruit workers and occasionally paid the expensive train fare on Jim Crow cars. Slowly at first, rural blacks began working for lower wages in jobs usually reserved for ethnic whites. The Detroit Urban League worked with Detroit's industrial complex, placing rural blacks in urban factory jobs and assisting with assimilation to urban life by holding instructional classes in preparing home meals using gas stoves, modern appliances, and sewing classes. As with the new European ethnic groups, Detroit's prohibition forced black residents to establish underground entertainments, some called "blind pigs," in back rooms of businesses where jazz music, illegal booze, and vice flowed freely.

The juxtaposition of immigrant whites attempting to Americanize and obtain citizenship rights, African Americans, and Anglo-Saxons sparked xenophobic battles in residential neighborhoods and in factories. Detroit's immigrant working-class whites, as in many other industrial cities, lived on meager wages from mundane assembly line jobs, and black workers earned even less while working in more hazardous jobs. These working-class residents of first- and second-generation immigrants were the backbone of the economic successes of factory owners yet received none of the credit. Homes became sanctuaries and a means of escaping the overcrowded, industrial conditions of Detroit. In the early 1920s, white homeowners and tenants fiercely fought for control of their neighborhoods by organizing homeowners and neighborhood improvement associations and placing racially restrictive deeds on property to prevent the sudden ethnic change of their enclaves. Coupled with the increased African American population and the Immigration Act of 1924, working-class whites strongly, and sometimes violently, attempted to hold on to the ethnic hegemony of their neighborhoods.

Since the 1863 Draft Riots, racial violence had been relatively minor, until 1925 when Ossian Sweet, a black doctor, purchased a home for his wife and young daughter in a traditionally white working-class neighborhood. The Sweets moved in on the first day of school. Concerned about what might happen, Dr. Sweet contacted the Detroit Police Department requesting some type of protection from his new neighbors. On the second night, hundreds of whites gathered outside the Sweet home and began throwing rocks. The police stood guard, keeping the white mob in the street away from the home. Someone from the street shattered the upstairs windows, and shortly afterward machine gun fire came from the home, wounding one and killing another in the all-white mob. The police arrested the Sweets and their friends and charged them with murder. Hired by the National Association for the Advancement of Colored People and a few weeks removed from his victory at the Scopes Monkey Trial, Clarence Darrow argued the innocence of the accused, and the trial resulted in a hung jury. Eventually acquitted, the Sweets never returned as a family to the bungalow home they had purchased. Racial tensions that led to the mob mentality outside the Sweet home in 1925 resembled the scenes of southern lynch mobs that occurred with more frequency as blacks laid legal claim to the city.

See also *Detroit, MI 1929–1941; Detroit, MI 1941–1952; Detroit, MI 1952–1989*

DONNA PATRICIA WARD

BIBLIOGRAPHY

Boyle, Kevin. *Arc of Justice*. New York, NY: Henry Holt and Co., 2004.

Farley, Reynolds, Sheldon Danziger, and Harry J. Holzer. *Detroit Divided*. New York, NY: Russell Sage Foundation, 2000.

Holli, Melvin G. *Reform in Detroit*. New York, NY: Oxford University Press, 1969.

Poremba, David Lee, ed. *Detroit in Its World Setting*. Detroit, MI: Wayne State University Press, 2001.

Sugrue, Thomas J. *The Origins of the Urban Crisis*. Princeton, NJ: Princeton University Press, 2005.

Thomas, Richard W. *Life for Us Is What We Make It*. Bloomington: Indiana University Press, 1992.

Zunz, Olivier. *The Changing Face of Inequality*. Chicago, IL: University of Chicago Press, 1982.

CLEVELAND, OH 1896–1929

CLEVELAND BECAME THE SIXTH LARGEST CITY in the United States by 1910. Immigrants, not only Europeans but also blacks from the American South, swelled the population in search of jobs and a better life. The city's economy was led by industrialists, who congregated on Euclid Avenue or "Millionaire's Row." They would later endow such cultural institutions as the Cleveland Museum of Art and the Cleveland Orchestra and create the charitable Cleveland Foundation and United Way. Many of the city's residents lived in poverty, however.

Under Progressive mayor Tom L. Johnson, Cleveland gained a national reputation for municipal reforms, including the creation of a downtown civic center proposed by famed Chicago architect Daniel Burnham. Political turmoil, however, led to opposition to reform and a return to patronage politics, which in turn led to a short-lived experiment with the city manager form of government. The Socialist and Labor movements became prominent for a while during World War I. In 1924 the Republican national convention was held in Cleveland. In the postwar period Cleveland prospered and continued to grow as an industrial city until the economic crash of 1929. However, its spatial growth by annexation ended as several adjoining suburbs voted to remain independent communities. A highlight was the Indians baseball team's victory in the 1920 World Series after its shortstop was tragically killed on the field during the season.

GOVERNMENT AND POLITICS

In 1896 Cleveland's politics were dominated by Republicans. That year Cleveland businessman Mark Hanna engineered the election of William McKinley as president of the United States. In 1895 Robert E. McKisson, aged thirty-two, was elected mayor (and was known popularly as the "Boy Mayor"). He organized his own political machine and challenged Hanna for the Republican Party leadership and a U.S. Senate seat but was unsuccessful. Meanwhile, in 1896

QUICK FACTS

CLEVELAND, OH **1896–1929**

MAYORS

Robert E. McKisson	(1895–1898)
John H. Farley	(1899–1900)
Tom L. Johnson	(1901–1909)
Herman C. Baehr	(1910–1911)
Newton D. Baker	(1912–1915)
Harry L. Davis	(1916–1919)
William S. Fitzgerald	(1920–1921)
Frederick Kohler	(1922–1923)

CITY MANAGER

William R. Hopkins (1924–1929)

MAJOR INDUSTRIES AND EMPLOYERS

Iron and steel
Machinery
Clothing
Meatpacking
Electrics
Automobiles
Chemicals/oil refining
Shipbuilding

MAJOR NEWSPAPERS

The Plain Dealer
Cleveland Press
Cleveland Leader and News

MAJOR EVENTS

1896: Cleveland celebrates its centennial.

1901: Progressive reformer Tom L. Johnson is elected and gains national acclaim for his ideas and reforms.

1903: A committee led by the City Beautiful architect Daniel Burnham recommends the Group Plan for construction of public buildings around a new downtown mall.

1911: The U.S. Supreme Court orders the breakup of John D. Rockefeller's Standard Oil Trust.

1921: By charter amendment, Cleveland adopts the city manager form of government.

reform-minded citizens formed the Municipal Association and chose Harry Garfield, son of the assassinated president, as its head. In 1899, along with disgruntled Republicans and Democrats, this association helped to defeat McKisson.

1901 saw the election of Tom L. Johnson, later called by muckraker Lincoln Steffens "the best Mayor of the best-governed city in the United States." His was a rags-to-riches story, becoming a wealthy businessman through his invention and patent of the streetcar fare box. He then competed against Mark Hanna for streetcar railway franchises in Cleveland. In 1890 Johnson was elected as a Democratic congressman representing a Cleveland district. He was converted to the ideas of economist and political reformer Henry George, advocate of the single tax. In 1901 Johnson campaigned on a reform platform, holding tent meetings to argue for home rule, a three-cent fare on the streetcars, and just taxation. He was reelected for three more terms.

As mayor, Johnson instituted reforms in the police department and the criminal justice system. He expanded the city's parks and recreation centers, opening them to the city's poorest residents. He supported the 1903 plan for the grouping of public buildings around a grand downtown mall proposed by a committee led by architect Daniel Burnham, famous for his planning efforts in Chicago, Washington, D.C., and elsewhere.

With a group of dedicated reformers in his administration, Johnson fought to lower streetcar fares against the opposition of private owners, including Mark Hanna. Frustrated, Johnson finally advocated municipal ownership of the streetcars. Likewise, challenging the privately owned electric company monopoly, Johnson advocated municipal ownership to reduce rates in order to make them more affordable to the city's poorer residents. However, Johnson's ideas were hampered by the Republican-controlled state legislature's restrictions on the city's powers. In 1909 Johnson was defeated by populist German American Republican Herman C. Baehr, whose campaign manager, Maurice Maschke, became the Republican party boss for the next two decades.

However, Baehr served only one term, defeated by Johnson protégé and former city law director Newton D. Baker. In his two terms, Baker achieved reforms long advocated by Johnson, who had died in 1911. In 1912 the Ohio Constitution was amended to authorize home rule. Cleveland adopted a new charter in 1913, which meant that it was no longer subject to the power of the state legislature. In 1914 Baker opened a voter-approved power plant that finally realized Johnson's dream. Cleveland's Municipal Light would act as a yardstick to measure the rates charged by the dominant private utility, the Cleveland Electric Illuminating Company. Baker retired in 1916 to found a prominent law firm and served as President Woodrow Wilson's Secretary of War as the United States entered World War I.

Johnson-era reformer and pacifist Peter Witt failed to carry on the Progressive tradition. He was defeated in the 1916 mayoral election by Republican Harry L. Davis, who reinstituted spoils-style politics. His administration was criticized by the Civic League (the renamed Municipal Association) and led to calls for the city manager system of municipal government. Also during this time, female activists devoted their efforts to women's suffrage.

With the entry of the United States into World War I, local politics became internationalized. There was a strong Socialist movement in Cleveland, led by Charles E. Ruthenberg. Patriotic organizations formed to oppose what they considered radical politics, particularly socialists and those involved in the labor movement, and foreign-born immigrants. These organizations included the Americanization Board to promote citizenship for aliens and a branch of the American Protective League, which informed on "un-American" activities to the U.S. Justice Department during the war. A postwar May Day (May 1, 1919) parade of Socialists and sympathizers with the new Bolshevik Communist regime in Russia sparked rioting in downtown Cleveland, resulting in two deaths and hundreds of arrests. Ruthenberg, who had become head of the Communist Party of America, was jailed and the city banned displays of red flags. The bombing of Mayor Davis's home that spring heightened anti-foreigner and anti-Socialist feelings.

This political climate contributed to a reaction against what was considered corrupt, ward-based government supported by immigrants. In 1921 the city's charter was amended by the voters to institute the city manager form of government. In 1913 Dayton, Ohio, had become the first major city to adopt this reform. The campaign for this reform was led by the Civic League, reformers dedicated to good government. The last mayor elected before this change took place was Frederick Kohler. Kohler had been Progressive Mayor Tom Johnson's police chief but was ousted in 1913. Ironically, he was known for his anti–political patronage policies. After much political jockeying, in 1924 William R. Hopkins was selected as Cleveland's first city manager with the support of both major political parties. A lawyer and businessman, he was a former Republican city councilman. Hopkins went on to dominate local government, with the city council playing only a secondary role. As elsewhere, the intended result was the transfer of power to a professional bureaucrat and a reduction of the role of city council members, especially those representing immigrant constituents, seen as too often engaged in petty parochial issues and prone to corrupt practices. Hopkins promoted development, including parks, public buildings to complete the Group Plan, an airport, and the construction of the Terminal Tower on Public Square by the Van Sweringen brothers (the developers of the planned suburb of Shaker Heights) and the Cleveland Stadium on the lakefront. His most vocal critic on the city council was Peter Witt. Hopkins was ousted by his city council opponents in January 1930.

Cleveland's spatial expansion ended in the 1920s. Growing suburbs such as Cleveland Heights, East Cleveland, and Lakewood that bordered the city rejected annexation. In 1917 the Cleveland Metroparks ringing the city were created. This was the brainchild of William Stinchomb, who served as the park district's director from 1921 until 1957.

INDUSTRY, COMMERCE, AND LABOR

The period of the late nineteenth and early twentieth centuries marked Cleveland's emergence as a premier industrial city. Following the Civil War, Cleveland grew rapidly on the basis of heavy industries. For a time, with its prime location on Lake Erie and the Cuyahoga River for transportation and raw materials, it became a center of the fledgling oil-refining industry under the direction of Standard Oil's John D. Rockefeller. Standard Oil's monopolistic success, however, led to its breakup by court decree in 1911 by the U.S. Department of Justice. This followed exposés by the muckraking journalist Ida Tarbell.

Cleveland had a flourishing central business district emanating from Public Square as well as a busy port. Railroads carried much of the raw products and manufactured goods in and out of the city. In 1900 about 30 percent of businesses in Cleveland were manufacturers, and a quarter of the labor force worked in manufacturing. These businesses were located not only in the Industrial Valley along the Cuyahoga River but also in other areas of the sprawling city, its spatial expansion fueled by the streetcar. This sector included leaders in the metal industries, electrical products, the garment industry, meatpacking, and the paint and varnish industry. In 1909 Cleveland held an Industrial Exposition heralding the output of more than two thousand manufacturers employing over one hundred thousand workers.

Leading entrepreneurs contributed to Cleveland's industrial prosperity. Charles Brush achieved success with arc lamps and batteries, and his company eventually merged with the

General Electric Corporation. Thomas White created a sewing machine company, and a son would later become a leader in the production of first cars and then trucks. Ambrose Swasey and Worcester Warner had won world recognition for their machine tools when they won the contract for the telescope in the Lick Observatory in California in the 1880s.

As occurred in the Civil War, the First World War contributed to Cleveland's industrial growth. The city was also home to some of the early pioneers of the auto industry and was second only to Detroit for a while in the production of automobiles. The industrial and commercial boom continued in the 1920s, with commercial and residential construction reflecting the city's growth in population from seven hundred ninety-seven thousand in 1920 to nine hundred thousand by 1930, not to mention the growth of adjacent suburbs.

With the rise of industry, Cleveland also became a center of the labor movement, with one hundred fifty unions mostly affiliated with the American Federation of Labor. Among the more prominent unions were several representing railroad workers.

In the downtown, many new office buildings arose. Over the course of almost three decades, many of the civic buildings envisioned by Burnham were constructed around the mall he had proposed. These included city hall, the city library, and the headquarters of the public school district. With the creation of the Federal Reserve banking system, Cleveland became the site of one of its regional banks, located across from the library. In 1912 a new west-side public market building was dedicated in Ohio City.

Accumulated wealth led to the creation of such cultural institutions as the Cleveland Music School Settlement (1912), the Playhouse Settlement (Karamu House; 1915), the Cleveland Art Museum and the Cleveland Playhouse (1916), the Cleveland Orchestra (1918), and the Cleveland Institute of Music and the Cleveland Museum of Natural History (1920). In addition, several vaudeville theaters opened downtown in an area later known as Playhouse Square.

RACE, ETHNICITY, AND IMMIGRATION

Cleveland's phenomenal growth, in one century, from a small village to the fifth largest city in the United States included hundreds of thousands of emigrants from Europe, followed by the great migration north by African Americans from the post–Civil War South. The first two major groups before the Civil War had been Germans and Irish. Following the Civil War, a succession of ethnic groups followed: Italians, Poles, Hungarians, Czechs (Bohemians), Jews, and other primarily eastern European nationalities. In particular, Cleveland became a center for Hungarian and Slovenian immigrants in the United States.

In 1910 one-third of the city's five hundred sixty-one thousand residents were foreign-born. These groups settled in urban villages, usually speaking their native tongue, and numerous native-language newspapers were published in Cleveland. Despite their poverty, these residents built churches and synagogues in their ethnic enclaves. The waves of immigration, and the resulting diversity of languages and cultures, led to Cleveland being called "Baghdad on the Cuyahoga." These immigrants provided the labor to fuel the factories that symbolized Cleveland's growth.

World War I and the postwar nativist reaction that led to nationality quotas for immigrants cut off this European mass migration to American cities like Cleveland. As previously recounted, the war also led to nationalistic efforts at Americanizing aliens and alarm at the radical politics of those immigrants sympathetic to the Socialist and Communist movements. The settlement house movement funded by philanthropists served some of the needs of poor immigrants.

In addition to European groups, Cleveland also saw a rise in its African American population. Before and during the Civil War, Cleveland was pro-Abolition and a stop on the Underground Railroad for fugitive slaves. However, its African American population was small (only one thousand three hundred by 1870). In the late 1890s, the city saw this population grow rapidly as blacks fled the segregated South, coming mostly from the rural areas of this region. Cleveland's black population almost tripled (from three thousand to eight thousand seven hundred) from 1890 to 1910. These new migrants clustered in the Central neighborhood (previously occupied largely by Italians) as the black population began to meet discrimination in employment, housing, and even public accommodations and schools that resembled what they had previously encountered in the South. In general, blacks could only find menial labor jobs rather than better-paying jobs in the manufacturing and commercial sectors. By 1920 the black population had tripled again to more than thirty-four thousand. The poet Langston Hughes recounted the discrimination and terrible slum housing conditions experienced by blacks living in the now visible black ghetto. Like their European counterparts, they founded churches (from seventeen in 1915 to one hundred fifty by 1930), mostly Baptist. Jane Edna Harris Hunter founded the Phyllis Wheatley Association to house and assist unmarried African American women and girls migrating from the South. Her boarding house was the alternative to the racially segregated YWCA.

Cleveland's growing black community was split between gradualists who followed the self-help ideas of Booker T. Washington and those who in the 1920s became more militant in their opposition to racial discrimination, such as the NAACP. Among the former was the first African American elected to the Cleveland City Council—Republican Thomas Fleming, a barber elected in 1909. He was reelected in 1915 and served until 1929. He would not be joined there by other African Americans until two were elected in 1927.

See also *Cleveland, OH 1877–1896; Cleveland, OH 1929–1941; Cleveland, OH 1941–1952*

DENNIS KEATING

BIBLIOGRAPHY

Campbell, Thomas F., and Edward M. Miggins. *The Birth of Modern Cleveland, 1865–1930*. London and Toronto: Associated University Presses, 1988.

Kusmer, Kenneth L. *A Ghetto Takes Shape: Black Cleveland, 1870–1930*. Urbana: University of Illinois Press, 1978.

Miller, Carol Poh. *Cleveland Metroparks, Past and Present*. Cleveland, OH: Cleveland Metroparks, 1992.

Miller, Carol Poh, and Robert Wheeler. *Cleveland: A Concise History, 1796–1990*. Bloomington: Indiana University Press, 1990.

Morton, Marian J. *Women in Cleveland: An Illustrated History*. Bloomington: Indiana University Press, 1995.

Phillips, Kimberley L. *Alabama North: African-American Migrants, Community, and Working-Class Activism in Cleveland, 1915–45*. Urbana: University of Illinois Press, 1999.

Rose, William Ganson. *Cleveland: The Making of a City*. Cleveland, OH and New York, NY: World Publishing, 1950.

Van Tassel, David D., and John J. Grabowski, eds. *The Encyclopedia of Cleveland History*. Bloomington: Indiana University Press, 1996.

ST. LOUIS, MO 1896–1929

FRONTIER CITY AND "GATEWAY TO THE WEST," St. Louis witnessed vigorous industrial growth in the decades after the Civil War. Manufacturing clothes, shoes, groceries, and beer, the city gained a reputation as an important center of trade and commerce. Its political climate dominated by machine politicians, St. Louis created immense wealth for a select few who wielded control over the city's government and economic institutions. Embarrassed by this activity, local elites developed a campaign to revitalize the city's appearance and initiated a bid for an international World's Fair. Among the most notable events of its history, St. Louis hosted the Louisiana Purchase Exposition (World's Fair) in the spring of 1904. That same year, it became the first American city to host the Games of the III Olympiad. The World's Fair attracted millions, especially immigrants whose increased visibility underscored growing class and ethnic divisions between old immigrants and new. In 1927 St. Louis received worldwide recognition for its support of aviator Charles Lindbergh, who flew the "Spirit of St. Louis" on the first nonstop solo flight from New York to Paris.

GOVERNMENT AND POLITICS

A city dominated by machine politics, St. Louis's political culture developed in relation to its geography, party politics, and immigration patterns. In the summer of 1896, the city was chosen to host the Republican National Convention, where party members gathered to discuss the gold standard and protective tariffs, as well as confirm the nomination of Ohio congressman and governor William McKinley in the auditorium of Washington Square Park, near City Hall. St. Louis was also the meeting place for the Populists, who supported a fusion ticket with Democratic presidential nominee William Jennings Bryan and Populist candidate Tom Watson. While the Populist Party's hopes for national power were dashed with the loss of the presidential election, its members found the Gateway City an ideal location to broaden their political platform.

With a fragmented and factional government, St. Louis operated under the concept of "home rule" in which the city's voters were responsible for choosing constables, judges, and administrative officials to perform county functions such as treasurer and sheriff. This structure was adopted in 1876 when the City of St. Louis separated from the county. After the split, city elections became increasingly partisan and machine politicians exerted new control. However,

QUICK FACTS

ST. LOUIS, MO 1896–1929

MAYORS

Cyrus Walbridge	(1893–1897)
Henry Ziegenhein	(1897–1901)
Rolla Wells	(1901–1909)
Frederick Kreismann	(1909–1913)
Henry Kiel	(1913–1925)
Victor Miller	(1925–1933)

MAJOR INDUSTRIES AND EMPLOYERS

Anheuser-Busch
Norvell Shapleigh Hardware Company
Famous-Barr Company
Stix, Baer and Fuller
C. F. Blanke Tea and Coffee Company

MAJOR NEWSPAPERS

Post-Dispatch
Globe Democrat
St. Louis Republic
Missouri Democrat

MAJOR EVENTS

1896: The Republican National Convention and People's Party Convention are held in St. Louis.
1904: The third modern Olympic Games are held in St. Louis during the Louisiana Purchase Exposition (World's Fair), attracting millions of visitors.
1915: St. Louis adopts a residential segregation ordinance.
1926: Charles Lindbergh, with funding from St. Louis businessmen, flies the first transatlantic flight from New York to Paris.
1927: A powerful tornado hits St. Louis, causing significant damage.

St. Louis's political machine was rarely controlled by one boss; power was found in the wards, where committee men called the shots. These men selected patronage employees for city and county offices and aligned themselves with other officials to form factions that competed for power. Even as Progressives attempted to make government and political parties more efficient and less corrupt, St. Louis remained committed to this political system.

The spoils system of machine politics also offered prestige and power to municipal leaders who advanced the idea of "boodle" to new levels. A term given to the practice of bribing city officials or legislators to win utility franchises, licenses, contracts, and other special privileges, boodle defined the relationship between politicians, bankers, investors, and financial institutions, especially banks, real estate companies, and utility firms. Among the power brokers of such deals were businessmen Charles Huttig, Adolphus Busch, David R. Francis, and Julius Walsh, also known as the "Big Cinch," who dominated the city's economic and political landscape. While there was no formal coordination of their activities, they played a key role in nominating Mayor Rolla Wells in 1901. Yet the business community's well-known graft and corruption did not escape the watchful eye of muckraking journalists in magazines like the *Iconoclast* and the *Globe Democrat* newspaper. Amid a public campaign to expose the problems of corporate power, local elites offered their support to finance the most notable event of its history, the Louisiana Purchase Exposition, or World's Fair, in 1904.

From the end of Reconstruction in 1877 until the entry of America into the First World War, Americans attended world's fairs. Intended to stimulate economic development in the host cities and provide manufacturers an opportunity to showcase their products, the World's Fair in St. Louis was the largest of its kind. With more than nineteen million visitors and over seventy thousand exhibits, the fair was held in celebration of the centennial of the 1804 Louisiana Purchase. The city enhanced its chances for hosting the fair when it raised ten million dollars in private subscription before a matching five million dollars was appropriated by Congress. United under a spirit of Progressive reform initiated by Mayor Rolla Wells, St. Louis found the fair to be of great benefit, boosting its reputation beyond a city of ward bosses to one known for orderly, responsible government and a clean, friendly environment.

While the city worked to improve its image in the years prior to the First World War, its reactionary racial policies limited its potential as a progressive city. With an African American population of around 6 percent, St. Louis was grudgingly tolerant and less hostile toward its black residents than other border state cities. Nonetheless, segregation remained an ever present and inconsistent part of the social landscape. Schools were segregated, libraries were not. Excluded from white hotels, restaurants, and barber shops, African Americans could ride department store elevators and sit where they pleased on streetcars, though most whites preferred to stand rather than sit next to them. Following its southern neighbors, St. Louis adopted a residential segregation ordinance in 1915. Opposed by the majority of the city's aldermen, the mayor, and major newspapers, St. Louis residents voted overwhelmingly in favor of its passing. Under the law, no person of any race could move to a block where 75 percent of the residents were of another race. Although the 1917 *Buchanan v. Warley* decision put an end to residential segregation by law, racial segregation continued through private practice and discriminatory provisions in rental services, terms, and conditions.

In the 1920s St. Louis enjoyed the conveniences of a modern industrial city. Changes to the city's transit system began with increased use of private automobiles and bus lines that gradually replaced trolley cars. The redevelopment and restoration of Forest Park after the World's Fair also brought additional attractions, including a zoo, an art museum, and the Jefferson Memorial building, which was partially constructed with World's Fair funds in remembrance of the Louisiana Purchase. It was also during this period that residents passed the largest bond issue adopted by an American city. The 1923 bond funded twenty proposals, all of which were designed to improve the civic life of the community.

As part of the Progressive effort to make St. Louis more attractive, women reformers had a tremendous impact on the city. At the end of the nineteenth century, many began to identify the city's most visible problems, including pollution, sanitation, and the safety of consumer goods. Like in other urban areas, St. Louis club women were among the earliest and most effective supporters of the City Beautiful campaign. The campaign encouraged the overall aesthetic improvement of the city, including the planting of trees, trash pick-up, the removal of unsightly billboards, and an appreciation for public art and architecture.

Often white, and middle and upper class, these women had the time and material resources to form social groups for both individual and community improvement. Integrating traditional female roles with that of public service, St. Louis reformers represented a new generation of educated professionals. Nonetheless, their record of improving race relations in the city was no better than other white residents. In their push for civic reform and later women's suffrage, many chose to exclusively ally themselves with white middle-class men rather than working-class or African American women. Such choices severely limited the degree of civic cooperation and Progressive idealism that defined their original goals. By the end of the decade, many projects remained incomplete as the city braced itself for the slowdown of industry and the social distress that accompanied the Great Depression.

INDUSTRY, COMMERCE, AND LABOR

A leading industrial center and commercial hub, St. Louis witnessed major changes to its industrial growth by the end of the nineteenth century. No longer forwarding raw materials and shifting the manufacture of goods to smaller cities within its trade territory, the city lost business in the meatpacking industry with the introduction of refrigerated railroad cars that replaced the long-distance shipping of livestock. The city was home to thriving wheat and cotton farms, so the economic depression of the 1890s had a dramatic effect on farmers who, after years of overproduction, witnessed sharp declines in the price of grain and increasing competition in the international market.

St. Louis was also the starting point for one of the nation's leading city planners, Harland Bartholomew. Arriving in St. Louis in 1915, Bartholomew's vision and organization of the city was later used to develop the methodology and professional practices that came to define the profession. An author and instructor, Bartholomew assembled plans for hundreds of cities across the world based on the St. Louis model.

The Progressive years also witnessed change in the city's largest industry, beer brewing. The introduction of pasteurized bottled beer and national advertising by its largest manufacturer, Anheuser-Busch, created a national market and a drastic reduction of local breweries across the city. Fewer competitors meant enhanced success of the Anheuser-Busch company in St. Louis, which began in 1876 with the making of Budweiser, a bottled beer named after a German town in the homeland of creator Adolphus Busch. Among the era's most ingenious entrepreneurs, Busch found his partnership with father-in-law Eberhard Anheuser a success both personally and professionally. Married for more than fifty years to Anheuser's daughter Lilly, Busch served as president of the Anheuser-Busch Brewing Association for more than thirty years, having earned a reputation as one of the city's most extravagant and wealthiest leaders.

Upon U.S. entry into World War I, the brewing industry in St. Louis experienced intense scrutiny and mistrust. As questions loomed about the loyalty and patriotism of brewery owners, many of German descent, attempts were made to dispel such rumors with the purchase of newspaper ads, liberty bonds, and donations to the American Red Cross to gain public favor. Brewery owners even offered aid to the U.S. government. Anheuser-Busch turned its highly profitable engine plant over to the government for the construction of submarine engines. Despite this support, anti-German sentiment remained constant, with attacks by prohibitionists who damaged beer sales and reputations. With the passage of the Eighteenth Amendment, smaller beer companies were forced to dramatically reduce their manufacture of stills while competing with bootleg distributors whose operations in cellars and garages cut into profits. Among the city's "moonshine kings" were Italians in the Hill section of the city, who brought to America not only their family distilling secrets, but a heritage of craftsmanship that aided their production of undercover stills.

The fourth largest city behind New York, Chicago, and Philadelphia by 1900, St. Louis developed the largest railway network outside Chicago. The first railroad line west of the Mississippi River, the Pacific Railroad was chartered by city leaders to extend the city's boundaries to the western end of the state. With subsidiary lines later constructed, trains under the Missouri Pacific Railway Company pushed volumes of goods across the plains to small towns and retailers who relied on St. Louis wholesalers for their supplies. Grocery distribution was the largest of this trade, with multimillion-dollar sales in staples such as sugar, coffee, rice, flour, soap, tobacco, spices, and other household items. With its river connections to staple-producing areas across the Midwest and New Orleans, St. Louis gained a competitive advantage in the wholesale market. Second only to the grocery trade was the dry goods market, in which Hargadine and McKittrick, Ely and Walker, and Rice-Stix were well known. Modern technology also brought male and female laborers to St. Louis to operate the era's newest gadgets, including the telegraph, typewriters, and telephones.

In 1900 Hargadine and McKittrick bought the William Barr Company, St. Louis's first and largest department store. Department stores not only encouraged women to be more active consumers, they also created new female workplaces. By 1930 downtown stores in St. Louis had created thousands of jobs for female salesclerks, waitresses, elevator operators, clerical workers, and seamstresses. Although women had worked behind the counters of neighborhood stores, selling had been primarily a male occupation until department stores revolutionized urban retailing. Like other department stores, Barr designed its store specifically for the female shopper. Customers received personal attention from "sales ladies" hired to greet middle-class women in separate merchandising departments. Store seamstresses customized ready-to-wear clothing, and female customers met friends and relatives for lunch in store tearooms.

The depression also hit St. Louis harder than other cities. With over a billion dollars in products by 1929, the St. Louis industrial district ranked seventh in manufacturing, just ahead of Cleveland and Los Angeles. Discrimination, Prohibition, and the relocation of key industries were among the factors that threatened the economic survival of residents. The local unemployment rate soared above the national average, and black unemployment nearly doubled that of white unemployment. The exclusion of black workers from craft unions and few opportunities in construction left many black youth without the skills needed to move elsewhere. For white workers, Prohibition all but shut down the brewing industry and its suppliers. A major city industry, the shoe trade moved its plants to small towns outside Missouri where people needed work, did not believe in unions, and rarely welcomed non-white workers. Though shoe company officers remained in the city, where they continued to make profits for stockholders, business declined throughout the 1930s.

RACE, ETHNICITY, AND IMMIGRATION

Slave or free, African Americans had a profound impact on the city of St. Louis. The slave of William Clark, Ben York proved an invaluable resource to both Clark and Meriwether Lewis on their exploration of the territories that were part of the Louisiana Purchase. Close to a half century later, Dred Scott began the battle to obtain his freedom at the Old Courthouse at Fourth and Market Streets, a case that would later become one of the most important in American legal history. After the Civil War, St. Louis was a destination city for thousands of African Americans, or "Exodusters," who left the South in search of greater freedom and opportunity out West. Yet the reality of life in urban areas fell short of expectations.

A city more segregated by custom than by law, St. Louis upheld the discriminatory practices of its southern neighbors through real estate covenants, realtor practices, and government policy. After moving into downtown flats that second- and third-generation Germans and Irish left behind, African Americans moved to Elleardsville, or "the Ville," and to the Mill Creek Valley. A small town later known as the center of the black community, the Ville was named for horticulturalist Charles Elleard and stretched from Goode to Newstead and from Old St. Charles Rock Road (later Dr. Martin Luther King Drive) to Cote Brilliante. Among its most prominent institutions were Sumner High School, which relocated to the Ville in 1910, and Poro College. The founder of Poro products, Annie Turnbo Malone established Poro College, a beauty school and manufacturing plant in 1918. The building occupied an entire city block and included an auditorium, cafeteria, dining room, guest rooms, dormitory, and rooftop garden. It was later used as the principal emergency relief unit for the American Red Cross after the 1927 tornado, the city's worst natural disaster since 1896.

A racially mixed neighborhood near Union Station, Mill Creek Valley was also home to African American residents. With an abundance of low-income housing, Mill Creek and Chestnut Valley were part of a thriving music district where Scott Joplin and other musicians played ragtime and jazz at Thomas Turpin's Rosebud Café. The home of civil rights leader Roy Wilkins and acclaimed dancer and expatriate Josephine Baker, Mill Creek Valley and the riverfront inspired other artists to reflect on the city's roots. W. C. Handy recalled the sounds of the levee in his world famous song "St. Louis Blues," and poet and essayist Langston Hughes drew upon the city's history in his poem "The Negro Speaks of Rivers."

During the last decades of the nineteenth century, St. Louis became a city of rich ethnic diversity. With a smaller immigrant population than other major cities, St. Louis was nevertheless greatly influenced by the culture and politics of immigrants. Immigrants from other continents comprised about one-third of the city's population. Most of these ethnic communities were located in the north and south sections of town by the river, surrounding the city's business district.

During the early twentieth century, "new" immigrants came to St. Louis seeking employment opportunities in downtown shoe factories, garment shops, and fruit and vegetable markets. For Italians the Hill, in the Cheltenham district of southwest St. Louis, provided a stable community for residents who continued to settle in such ethnic neighborhoods for generations to come. The targets of economic exploitation and nativism by American-born workers frustrated by economic depression and the growing presence of immigrants in southern Illinois, Italians came to St. Louis, where many found jobs in the city's clay mines, brickyards, and shoe factories. Having formed cohesive communal networks through their political, religious, and recreational organizations, Italians, like other new immigrants, found ways to adapt and resist America's new urban culture.

Like the Italians, the Chinese were among many new arrivals at this time seeking opportunities after their circumstances worsened elsewhere in the country. Having long established Chinatowns in the nation's largest cities, some Chinese came to St. Louis from coastal areas, while others came directly from China. Without clearly defined physical boundaries, Hop Alley sprang up during Reconstruction in the southern section of the business district and until the mid-1960s served as the Chinese community's primary commercial, residential, and recreational center. With a steady population of only several hundred by the early twentieth century, the first Chinese in St. Louis worked in laundries, groceries, tea shops, and restaurants. While their businesses served a diverse clientele, many found their economic contributions to the city did little to allay the fears of native-born residents who, after the passage of the Chinese Exclusion Act in 1882, were less tolerant of interracial unions.

Irish immigrants also found the Gateway City an appropriate location to call home. Having arrived in St. Louis during the mid-nineteenth century, the Irish formed ethnic enclaves along the northwest edge of downtown. Predominantly Catholic and among the city's poorest and unskilled laborers, residents gathered in Kerry Patch, a neighborhood named after the county in western Ireland where many had fled famine and rural poverty. Having labored under poor conditions in the garment industry, Irish women were among the city's most celebrated union leaders, particularly Hannah Hennessey, organizer of the St. Louis chapter of the Women's Trade Union League, and Fannie Mooney Sellins, a dressmaker who succeeded her as president. Transforming the local struggle for garment workers into a national campaign, both raised money for the relief of striking workers and promoted a national boycott.

Known for its steamboats, railroads, and factories, St. Louis also attracted large numbers of German immigrants, many of whom lived in the Soulard district close to the breweries. Like in other Midwestern cities, language bonded the German community together, and for years St. Louis had a program of German instruction in public elementary schools in addition to the publication of several German newspapers. Evangelical, Lutheran, and Catholic churches were also bastions of the German language until the early twentieth century, when many began to limit the number of services due to increased anti-German sentiment during the First World War. Nonetheless, Germans preserved their heritage through a variety of associations, or *vereine*, which upheld cultural traditions and maintained a variety of social services. Among them were benevolent associations that paid benefits for illness and death, craft unions, and the *turnverein*, which emphasized physical fitness, fellowship, and occasional political activity.

See also *St. Louis, MO 1854–1877; St. Louis, MO 1877–1896; St. Louis, MO 1929–1941; St. Louis, MO 1941–1952*

De Anna J. Reese

BIBLIOGRAPHY

Corbett, Katherine T. *In Her Place: A Guide to St. Louis Women's History*. St. Louis, MO: Historical Society Press, 1999.

Davis, Ronald L. F., and Harry D. Holmes. "Insurgency and Municipal Reform in St. Louis, 1893–1904." *The Midwest Review* I (1979): 1–18.

Faherty, William B., S. J. "The St. Louis Irish: An Unmatched Celtic Community." *Gateway Heritage* 21, no. 3 (2000/2001): 16–21.

Faherty, William B., S. J., and NiNi Harris. *St. Louis: A Concise History*. St. Louis, MO: Print/Graphics, 2004.

Heathcott, Joseph. " 'The Whole City Is Our Laboratory': Harland Bartholomew and the Production of Urban Knowledge." *Journal of Planning History* 4 (2005): 322–355.

Ling, Huping. *Chinese St. Louis: From Enclave to Cultural Community*. Philadelphia, PA: Temple University Press, 2004.

Miller, Eoghan P. "St Louis German Brewing Industry: Its Rise and Fall." MA thesis, University of Missouri-Columbia, 2008.

Mormino, Gary Ross. *Immigrants on the Hill: Italian Americans in St. Louis, 1882–1982*. Urbana: University of Illinois Press, 1986.

Primm, James Neal. *Lion of the Valley: St. Louis, Missouri*. Boulder, CO: Pruett, 1981.

Stein, Lara. "Home Rule for St. Louis." *Gateway Heritage* 22, no. 2 (2001): 74–77.

BOSTON, MA 1896–1929

BOSTON UNDERWENT DECISIVE CHANGES Between the end of the nineteenth century and the onset of the Great Depression. The city substantially restructured and centralized its government. The Democratic Party, led by the Irish, emerged as the dominant political institution in the city, a position it would maintain into the twenty-first century. Boston's status as a port city declined and manufacturing growth slowed considerably as well, particularly during the 1920s, trends that set the stage for a stagnant local economy that would endure until the late twentieth century. These changes took place against a backdrop of cultural conflict generated by the ascendance of the city's Irish Catholic majority, a shift evident not only in local politics but in the city's cultural life.

GOVERNMENT AND POLITICS

Two things defined Boston's public life between 1896 and 1929: Yankee-Irish conflict and the effort to reform and modernize local government and politics. The two were interconnected, as most reform efforts reflected at least in part an attempt to unseat Irish Democratic bosses from positions of authority. While the Irish dominated politics in lower- and middle-class sections of the city during the late nineteenth century, only one of their ranks had served as mayor before the election of Patrick Collins in 1901. From that point until 1993 only three of the fifteen men elected mayor were not Irish (and only two were Republican). Alarm over this shift in power

QUICK FACTS

BOSTON, MA **1896–1929**

MAYORS

Josiah Quincy	(1896–1899)
Thomas N. Hart	(1900–1902)
Patrick Collins	(1902–1905)
Daniel Whelton	(1905–1906)
John F. Fitzgerald	(1906–1908)
George A. Hibbard	(1908–1910)
John F. Fitzgerald	(1910–1914)
James M. Curley	(1914–1918)
Andrew J. Peters	(1918–1922)
James M. Curley	(1922–1926)
Malcolm Nichols	(1926–1930)

MAJOR INDUSTRIES AND EMPLOYERS

Wholesale trade
Transportation
Textiles
Boots and shoes
Domestic service

MAJOR NEWSPAPERS

Boston Daily Advertiser
Boston Daily Globe
Boston Daily Journal
Boston Evening American
Boston Evening Globe
Boston Evening Transcript
Boston Herald
Boston Post
Boston Traveler

MAJOR EVENTS

1903: Businessmen form the Good Government Association to pursue the restructuring of city government.
1907: William O'Connell, a proponent of a more assertive Catholicism, becomes Archbishop of Boston.
1909: Voters approve a new City Charter that centralizes city government.
1914: The colorful, provocative Irish Democrat James Michael Curley is elected mayor.
1919: The Boston Police Strike fails, dealing a blow to labor power locally and nationally.

helped spur campaigns for municipal reform designed to limit working-class Irish power and restore authority to the native-born elite. These efforts first developed during the 1890s but accelerated considerably with the formation of the Good Government Association (GGA), a body consisting of representatives from seven commercial and professional associations, in 1903. The GGA, a tightly knit, highly centralized organization run by prominent business and professional men, remained active into the 1930s. It was a major presence in local politics throughout this period, striving continually to limit the power of party machines, particularly the Irish-dominated Democrats. The conflict between vocal businessmen-reformers and party bosses—which frequently, though not always, fell along ethnic fault lines—had an impact on nearly every major issue debated in the city during these years.

People of Irish descent constituted the largest ethnic group in Boston at the beginning of the twentieth century, assuring that the Democratic Party would dominate local elections. Their numerical supremacy, geographic spread, and overwhelming loyalty to the Democrats meant that few Republicans had a chance to serve in city offices. Newer Jewish and Italian immigrants provided some voting support for Republicans, but the low participation rates among these groups, along with the growing power and appeal of Democrats, meant they had limited effect. Only in the upper-crust Back Bay and Beacon Hill districts did Republicans remain a majority through the first decades of the twentieth century, and only when Democrats quarreled among themselves did Republicans have any chance to capture the mayor's office.

The greater challenge to Irish Democratic dominance came from reformers seeking to restructure city government and undercut the power of Irish ward bosses. They succeeded in this effort in 1909 when the state legislature imposed some changes to the city charter and city voters approved others. The new governmental structure resulted from a proposal by the Boston Finance Commission, a municipal body formed in 1907 to investigate local expenditures and taxation. Its investigations found considerable corruption and inefficiency in city government, and it offered a series of proposals to remedy the problems. These included an increase in state control of municipal finances, civil services rules applied to city employment, expert-run administrative departments, a stronger mayor (with sole power to initiate expenditures) and a weaker city council, the substitution of a petition process in place of party nominations for municipal office, and a shift from a bicameral, district-based city council with eighty-seven members to a unicameral council with just nine members, all elected on an at-large basis. The state legislature imposed the administrative changes but permitted a referendum on the alterations to the electoral process and the strengthening of the mayor's office. That plan passed in 1909, transforming the city's political and governmental structure.

Local government also began to take greater responsibility for addressing social problems during the early twentieth century, a shift spurred by agitation among middle-class women. Working through organizations such as the Women's Municipal League, the Women's Educational and Industrial Union, and several settlement houses, they demanded a range of social reforms. They helped unskilled workers organize, established employment bureaus for those seeking work, and pushed for housing and sanitary regulations. Activist women often persuaded the city and state government to take on new responsibilities in these areas. The growing presence of women in public life also fueled demands for women's suffrage, spurring some, though by no means all, politicians to endorse female voting rights. But when granted nationally in 1920, voting rights for women did not induce further expansion of the local welfare state, partly because women divided their political loyalties along the same lines as men.

Neither suffrage nor other reforms altered the social and cultural conflicts that drove Boston's public life. If anything, the new electoral system, which placed a premium on mass mobilization, intensified ethnic conflict. Irish politicians such as John F. Fitzgerald (1906–1908, 1910–1914) and James Michael Curley (1914–1918, 1922–1926, 1930–1934, 1946–1950), both of whom would serve as mayor, proved adept at crafting media appeals and playing on ethnic identity in a manner that won them ethnic and working-class support and stoked group conflict. Fitzgerald captured the mayor's office in 1906 and again in 1910, when the first election under the new charter took place—a result that confounded reformers. Curley, whose antics and evident corruption provoked outrage from most native-born Protestants, or Yankees, and even some Irish, became a fixture in local politics, succeeding Fitzgerald as mayor and serving four terms between

1914 and 1950. Their success undercut the appeal of the GGA and, ultimately, the at-large city council elections. Responding to complaints from working-class ethnic sections of the city that at-large elections too often left them unrepresented at city hall, the state legislature authorized a new referendum that, if successful, would restore ward-based voting. Boston voters approved that measure in 1924.

Along with municipal reform, several other issues predominated in Boston's public life between 1896 and 1929. Perhaps the most persistent was the expansion of mass transit. Controversies over the laying of tracks, the influence of streetcar companies, strikes, and fare increases bubbled up regularly during this period. Intense debates about social welfare policies, education, and city planning also arose at various times as well. In most cases, these disputes intersected with the ethnic and class conflicts that defined so much of the city's public life. Streetcar service to poorer ethnic districts, demand for social assistance to the poor, the curriculum and character of public schools, the question of regulating parochial schools, and Curley's emphasis on developing ethnic neighborhoods at the expense of downtown all became elements of the larger drama about which group dominated the city and would shape its public policies.

INDUSTRY, COMMERCE, AND LABOR

Boston was first and foremost a port city at the end of the nineteenth century, though its economy also included a wide range of smaller manufacturing operations. Industrialization had developed in New England earlier than in any other region of the United States, and the region benefitted from early and efficient rail connections running westward, developments that placed Boston in the first rank of American ports. At the end of the nineteenth century, it remained the second largest foreign trade port in the United States, trailing only New York City. Textiles and shoes were among the largest local industries, and the city was home to several important trading houses and publishing firms.

Broad shifts in the American economy undermined Boston's economic position during the opening decades of the twentieth century. Industrialization accelerated in other regions, the nation's rail network had expanded so that cities such as Philadelphia and Baltimore had equal access to the West, and the nation's output shifted from agricultural to industrial goods, developments that lessened Boston's role in international commerce. Wool and leather exports remained strong, but Boston's share of trade in other sectors declined steadily. Civic leaders were well aware of the decline and worked to improve the city's harbor facilities, but the broader trends that undercut Boston's competitive position proved too great to overcome with enhanced infrastructure. By 1920 Boston was only the sixth largest port in the country, and it would continue to lose ground throughout the ensuing decade.

Other sectors of the economy were also too small to offset the city's loss of trade. Manufacturing during the late 1920s tended to be small and diverse, in contrast to cities such as Pittsburgh, Detroit, and Cleveland, where a particular industry dominated during this era, and even in comparison to commercial cities such as Chicago and Baltimore, where a handful of industries constituted the bulk of local production. Clothing, textiles, shoe production, and food processing were the largest Boston industries, but in 1929 none accounted for more than 4 percent of the city's total labor force of three hundred fifty-five thousand. The city remained an important center for retail, education, publishing, and medicine, which gave the city a substantial number of professional, salaried, and clerical workers. But these sectors of Boston's economy were not large enough to counter the city's economic stagnation, a fact of local economic life that would persist into the late twentieth century.

Boston's labor movement reflected the city's economic diversity. At the close of the nineteenth century, the city featured small but vocal groups of Socialists and a larger contingent of more conservative trade unionists with connections to the American Federation of Labor (AFL). Under the umbrella of the Boston Central Labor Union (BCLU), the trade unionists exercised a fair amount of clout, forcing the city to adopt an eight-hour day for municipal workers in 1899 and supporting some political reform efforts. But the BCLU's emphasis on craft unionism, a category that did not encompass most of the city's unskilled wage earners, and its expulsion of Socialists meant that it represented only a fraction of the city's workers. Other organizations, most notably the Women's Trade Union League, the United Hebrew Trades, and the Italian Laborers Union, formed to represent those left out. Those groups eventually persuaded the BCLU and the AFL to accept some unskilled workers. By 1913 BCLU affiliates represented over ninety-six thousand workers—a considerable number, though still not a majority of the city's wage earners.

As was the case in the nation as a whole, labor conflict slowed working-class organization in Boston after World War I. Perhaps because of its diverse economy and its relative lack of industry, Boston did not experience as many strikes or as much labor violence as did other cities before the war. Streetcar workers walked out in 1912 to gain recognition for their newly formed union, an event that sparked some violence when the Boston Elevated Company brought in scabs. The same workers struck again in 1919, as did the city's telephone operators and, most famously, its police. The Boston Police Strike proved a key event in the Red Scare that swept the country. The city's police struck in September, when the police commissioner, an appointee of ambitious Massachusetts Governor Calvin Coolidge, suspended nineteen union activists. Initially backed but then abandoned by the AFL and BCLU, the striking police failed to win concessions and the city ultimately hired an entirely new police force. Early in the strike, a few sections of the city experienced violence and looting, and one clash resulted in three deaths and eight injuries, events that undercut the public sympathy the walkout had generated. Their defeat reinforced anti-labor sentiment throughout the country and made union organizing more difficult. Labor's momentum slowed in Boston as elsewhere, further hurt by the furor surrounding the trial and execution of Italian anarchists Nicola Sacco and Bartolomeo Vanzetti, who had links to Boston labor radicals. The BCLU continued to represent skilled workers, but efforts to organize unskilled workers diminished.

RACE, ETHNICITY, AND IMMIGRATION

Ethnic and racial diversity increased in Boston between 1896 and 1929, and the Irish became the dominant group. At the end of the nineteenth century, Boston was a city comprised chiefly of Irish Catholics, British Americans (Protestant immigrants from the British Isles who had arrived in significant numbers after the Civil War), and native-born Yankees. In 1895 first- and second-generation Irish constituted more than 40 percent of the city's population, and any count that included third- and fourth-generation Irish would show a majority for the group. Irish hegemony in Boston took shape during the early twentieth century, although an influx of eastern and southern Europeans complicated that process After 1880 and especially after 1900, Jewish, Italian, Lithuanian, and other immigrant groups began arriving in the city at a steady clip, a flow that continued until the outbreak of World War I. It resumed after the war until Congress passed new immigration laws in 1924 that brought it to a close. The city's African American population also increased, although Boston was never as popular a destination for black migrants as were other northern cities.

The city's social geography was in flux as well. Irish Catholics predominated in the central city—the North, South, and West Ends—through the 1890s, though they would give way to Jewish and Italian newcomers during the early twentieth century. Supplanted Irish moved outward in growing numbers, with working- and lower-middle-class members of the group heading to nearby neighborhoods such as Charlestown, East Boston, and South Boston. By the 1910s the more upwardly mobile Irish began to take up residence in more distant middle-class suburban districts (though still within city limits) such as West Roxbury and Brighton, as well as in residential communities beyond Boston. Jews began to move from the West End after 1910 to Dorchester and other suburban locales. The well-heeled Back Bay and Beacon Hill remained enclaves of the Brahmin elite, but Yankee Protestants otherwise retreated to suburban locales. African Americans congregated in the West and South Ends before 1900 but began moving in substantial numbers to portions of Roxbury during the early twentieth century.

This ethnic and racial churning generated considerable tension before the Great Depression, but it did not produce much violence. Anti-Catholic nativism remained intense at the end of the nineteenth century. An 1895 clash between members of the nativist American Protective Association and Irish residents of East Boson reflected the cultural antagonisms at work in the city. The arrival of large numbers of Russian and Polish Jews, as well as many Italians, set the stage for political and social conflicts between newcomers and the dominant Irish. But aside from the occasional gang fight or political fisticuffs, the only significant outbreaks of ethnic violence before World War I involved Jewish housewives, who twice—in 1902 and 1912—rioted over price increases for kosher meat. The heightened nativism and antiradicalism surrounding the war sparked a fierce attack on Socialists parading against U.S. involvement in 1917, and a brief clash between police and labor radicals in 1919. Though ideological in nature, these clashes had ethnic dimensions as well. In each instance, local nativists blamed immigrants for importing dangerous ideas that threatened American institutions. Many observers also blamed the police strike and the violence associated with it on the machinations of dishonorable and radical Irish officers, an interpretation given added weight when the Boston Police Commissioners replaced the strikers with an overwhelmingly Yankee force.

Although immigrants were the scapegoats in these controversies, they were also triumphant in the larger battle to define Boston during the early twentieth century. The Irish in particular emerged from the period as the dominant cultural force in the community. Their ascendance was evident not only in municipal politics but in the emergence of a more militant Catholic Church.

With the appointment of William O'Connell as archbishop of Boston (he became a cardinal in 1911), the Church took increasingly aggressive action, expanding the number of parochial schools and taking conservative stances on issues such as child labor. O'Connell's 1909 declaration that "the Puritan has passed, the Catholic remains" signaled this new militancy, and Irish Catholic attitudes increasingly set the tone for Boston's cultural and political life. By the end of the 1920s, other ethnic and racial groups had expanded their influence as well. Both Jews and Italians had established a substantial network of ethnic institutions, and considerable numbers of the second generation had reached the middle class. By the time the Great Depression arrived, Boston was no longer a Yankee city.

See also *Boston, MA 1776–1790; Boston, MA 1790–1828; Boston, MA 1828–1854; Boston, MA 1854–1877; Boston, MA 1877–1896; Boston, MA 1929–1941; Boston, MA 1941–1952*

JAMES J. CONNOLLY

BIBLIOGRAPHY

Connolly, James J. *The Triumph of Ethnic Progressivism: Urban Political Culture in Boston, 1900–1925*. Cambridge, MA: Harvard University Press, 1998.

Deutsch, Sarah. *Women and the City: Gender, Space, and Power in Boston, 1870–1940*. New York, NY: Oxford, 2000.

Green, James R. and Hugh Carter Donahue. *Boston's Workers: A Labor History*. Boston, MA: Trustees of the Public Library of the City of Boston, 1979.

Kane, Paula M. *Separatism and Subculture: Boston Catholicism, 1900–1920*. Chapel Hill: University of North Carolina Press, 1994.

Kennedy, Lawrence W. *Planning the City Upon a Hill: Boston since 1630*. Amherst: University of Massachusetts Press, 1992.

O'Connor, Thomas. *The Boston Irish: A Political History*. Boston, MA: Northeastern University Press, 1995.

Russell, Francis. *A City in Terror: Calvin Coolidge and the 1919 Boston Police Strike*. Boston, MA: Beacon Press, 2005.

Tager, Jack. *Boston Riots: Three Centuries of Social Violence*. Boston, MA: Northeastern University Press, 2001.

Traverso, Susan. *Welfare Politics in Boston: 1910–1940*. Amherst: University of Massachusetts Press, 2003.

BALTIMORE, MD 1896–1929

IN THE EARLY TWENTIETH CENTURY, BALTIMORE CONFIRMED ITS STATUS AS A CITY OF SMALL-TIME OPERATORS. The Democratic machine fragmented into "machinelets" commanded by "bosslets" at the ward and neighborhood level whose abrupt realignments undermined stable leadership. In business, Baltimore could boast few captains of industry. Even its largest firms were owned by outsiders. The city could not break out of its role as a branch-office town.

QUICK FACTS

BALTIMORE, MD 1896–1929

MAYORS

Alcaeus Hooper	(1895–1897)
William T. Malster	(1897–1899)
Thomas G. Hayes	(1899–1903)
Robert M. McLane	(1903–1904)
E. Clay Timanus	(1904–1907)
J. Barry Mahool	(1907–1911)
James H. Preston	(1911–1919)
William F. Broening	(1919–1923)
Howard W. Jackson	(1923–1927)
William F. Broening	(1927–1931)

MAJOR INDUSTRIES AND EMPLOYERS

Clothing
Copper, tin, and sheet iron
Cars
Canned fruits and vegetables
Foundry and machine shops

MAJOR NEWSPAPERS

Baltimore Afro-American
Baltimore American
Deutsche Correspondent
Baltimore Herald
Baltimore News
Baltimore Sun

MAJOR EVENTS

1898: The legislature approves a new city charter for Baltimore enhancing the powers of the mayor.
1904: Fire destroys most of Baltimore's commercial district.
1907: Isaac Freeman Rasin dies, and John "Sonny" Mahon succeeds him as leader of the city's Democratic organization.
1910: The city council approves an ordinance mandating the racial segregation of residential areas.
1912: The Baltimore branch of the NAACP is founded.

POLITICS AND GOVERNMENT

The electoral uprising against the Gorman-Rasin Ring in 1895 gave Republicans control of both state and city governments. In Baltimore the putative Republican boss was William F. Stone, chair of the city's Republican committee. Until the downfall of the Democrats, Stone and his Republican colleagues had relied almost exclusively on federal patronage. Their party, though an underdog at the local level, generally dominated presidential politics during the Gilded Age. The Baltimore party's internal factions were organized around federal patronage. "Post Office" Republicans squared off against "Customhouse" Republicans.

Stone stood with the Post Office crowd, and when Republican McKinley succeeded Democrat Cleveland in 1897, Stone gathered endorsements to support his own appointment as the city's postmaster. The incumbent, however, was an Independent Democrat who had campaigned vigorously for McKinley, and the president was persuaded to reappoint him. Stone would be named Baltimore's customs collector, positioned to unite the party's two tribes.

Instead, the Republicans, unaccustomed to access to city and state jobs, multiplied their quarrels about patronage. Mayor Alcaeus Hooper, a promoter of municipal efficiency, was soon at loggerheads with his fellow Republicans on the city council over city jobs. The council wanted paying jobs for the Republican loyalists who had been steadfast party workers during the barren years of Democratic hegemony. The mayor wanted competence. In 1896 the council passed an ordinance, over the mayor's veto, depriving the mayor of his appointive power. The council appointed a slate of department heads. Hooper refused to administer the oaths of office. The dispute migrated to the courts, where the mayor prevailed. It was an empty victory, however. He still had to get council approval for his appointments.

Baltimore's Reform League fought for a more substantial triumph in the state legislature: a civil service law limited to Baltimore that would embody Mayor Hooper's commitments to expertise and nonpartisanship. A statewide referendum on the merit system lost decisively, especially in Baltimore, and its rejection may have emboldened the Post Office and Customhouse Republicans, now united behind William Stone, to deny Mayor Hooper renomination in 1897. The Republican organization turned instead to millionaire businessman Theodore Marburg. Stone's candidate, however, was shouldered aside by William T. Malster, a local shipbuilder and the aggressive leader of a relatively new Republican organization: the Columbian Club. The Reform League, though uncertain of Malster's progressive credentials, preferred him to the candidate of the Gorman-Rasin Ring, whose inclinations were well known.

Malster won and promptly confirmed the reformers' worst suspicions. A legion of Republican office-seekers marched behind him into City Hall. Local reformers, usually advocates of municipal improvements, were leery of Malster's proposals for public works. They suspected that the projects were simply pretexts for patronage. But they welcomed Malster's appointment of a bipartisan commission to draft a new city charter that would overcome the administrative disjointedness of ward-based government. The committee's draft, approved by the General Assembly in 1898, was a significant step toward the centralization of Baltimore's government. It extended the mayor's term in office from two to four years and increased his control of budgets, contracts, and appointments. By redrawing the boundaries of the city's wards, the charter disrupted the neighborhood power bases of the ward bosses, another step toward political centralization.

By the time Baltimore got its new charter, Arthur Pue Gorman had lost his Senate seat to a Republican. The "Ring" seemed fully vanquished. "By the time it was all over," one ward boss recalled, "you couldn't find a Democratic officeholder with a fine-tooth comb." Baltimore's Democratic organization had begun to unravel. Isaac Rasin's chief lieutenant, John "Sonny" Mahon, had drifted away from the boss to become a boss in his own right, and Arthur Gorman seemed ready to part company with Rasin, too.

But the Republicans had problems of their own. Mayor Malster's eleven stalwarts in the General Assembly session of 1898 refused to enter the Republican caucus, thus preventing the Republican majority from electing a speaker. The Malster Republicans combined with the Democratic minority to place a Malster man in the leadership position. (The new speaker was later convicted as a jewel thief.) Malster himself was alleged to have frustrated his party's attempt at legislative leadership with his unannounced ambitions for a seat in the U.S. Senate.

By the municipal election in 1899, Baltimore's voters were fed up with Malster. Freeman Rasin was shrewd enough to realize that his open sponsorship of a Democratic mayoral aspirant might decisively handicap the candidate. He made a great show of indifference concerning the contest, and deferred to a new Democratic Association of Baltimore City, headed by a popular ex-governor, which would select a candidate and orchestrate a "people's campaign." In fact, Rasin stayed in close but quiet touch with the group's leader. But his power had clearly diminished. From this time forward, he would support Democratic mayoral candidates designated by the Independent Democrats, and he would settle for just a portion of city patronage.

The Democratic Association's mayoral candidate was Thomas G. Hayes, a former U.S. attorney for Maryland and one-time Democratic candidate for governor. Gorman and Rasin privately gave their assent. Hayes's past denunciations of Arthur Gorman gave him credibility as a reform candidate. In the ensuing election, the Democrats won not only the mayor's office, but also the comptroller's, every seat in the upper chamber of the city council, and all but six of the twenty-four seats in the lower chamber. Racial animosity played a visible role in the Democratic comeback. Malster's Republican administration, wrote Frank Kent, "with its political pirates and negro office-holders, had pretty well disgusted the public."

To his regret, Freeman Rasin discovered that Hayes was not only a progressive reformer but a potential rival as the city's Democratic boss. He gave municipal offices to reformers and respected professionals and used them to win over some lesser Democratic bosses, like Sonny Mahon, in an effort to build his own machine for the next mayoral election. But Hayes was no good at preserving alliances. A young City Hall reporter for the *Baltimore Herald*, H. L. Mencken, later described him as "an extremely eccentric and rambunctious fellow, so full of surprises that he had already acquired the nickname of Thomas the Sudden. . . . There never lived on this earth a more quarrelsome man."

In the city council primaries of 1901, Rasin Democrats challenged Hayes Democrats, and in the general election Democrats of the two factions turned on one another, enabling the Republicans to win control of the city council once again.

The Republican resurgence in Baltimore resulted not just from Democratic disarray, but also from a new election law enacted earlier in 1901 by a special session of the General Assembly. Arthur Gorman, plotting his return to the U.S. Senate, sought to shrink the Republican electoral base by disenfranchising some of the state's fifty-three thousand African American voters, most of whom turned out reliably for the party of Lincoln. The new election law was ostensibly aimed at illiterate voters, who were disproportionately black. It eliminated all party emblems from the ballot and grouped candidates by the offices that they sought. Illiterate voters were barred from receiving any assistance at the polls. But in Baltimore, at least, the ploy backfired. Republicans held coaching sessions for illiterate black voters so that they could recognize the names of Republican candidates for the council. The Democrats offered similar classes for whites, but Democratic illiterates were apparently less willing to accept instruction than black Republicans. However, Democrats won sufficient support outside of Baltimore to send Gorman back to the Senate.

The Democratic determination to reduce the Republican party's African American electoral base continued nevertheless. The most ambitious Democratic effort was the "Poe Amendment" drafted by John Prentiss Poe, dean of the University of Maryland Law School, under the general direction of Senator Gorman. His constitutional amendment would have granted unconditional voting rights to men who had been qualified to vote before the Fifteenth Amendment extended the franchise to blacks, or who were lineal descendants of such voters. All others would have to demonstrate that they could explain a portion of the state constitution to the satisfaction of the election judges.

In 1905 Maryland voters defeated the Poe Amendment by slightly less than thirty-five thousand votes out of one hundred four thousand cast. Almost two-thirds of the margin of defeat had been rolled up in Baltimore, where the measure was rejected by almost two to one and lost in twenty-three of the city's twenty-four wards. States farther south had successfully used the "grandfather clause" to disenfranchise African Americans, but Baltimore's electorate included a sizable number of foreign-born whites and voters with foreign-born fathers. The grandfather clause would threaten their voting rights along with those of their black fellow citizens. Most of the immigrant voters were Democrats, and an array of white ethnic organizations joined forces with the black Maryland Suffrage League to oppose the Poe Amendment. Freeman Rasin quietly shifted the weight of his organization against the measure. Four ward bosses openly disowned the Poe Amendment. Rasin advised the city's Democratic candidates not to take positions on it. The Gorman-Rasin alliance was finished. An embittered Arthur Gorman died a year after the defeat of his amendment, for which he blamed Rasin.

The Rasin machine's noncooperation with the movement for black disenfranchisement may have reflected the fact that not all of Baltimore's African American voters were Republicans. The first of several black Democratic clubs in Baltimore had formed as early as the 1870s. Democratic candidates routinely won between 30 and 40 percent of the city's African American votes, and seven-time mayor and old-guard Democrat Ferdinand Latrobe was one of the few Democratic politicians who openly campaigned for the black vote. Backing the grandfather clause would alienate not only the city's white immigrants, but a sizable number of African Americans who were Democratic voters.

The same special session of the General Assembly that attempted to disenfranchise illiterate black voters in 1901 had also approved a request from Baltimore to issue $10 million in municipal bonds for the construction of a sanitary sewer in the city. Almost every big city in the world already had such a system, but Baltimore continued to rely on below-ground cesspools and a fragmented collection of half a dozen neighborhood sewers. Baltimore also had the highest typhoid rate of any major American city. Repeated proposals had been advanced for the construction of a sanitary sewer, but the city council had rejected every one.

One major beneficiary of the council's stubborn resistance to sewers was the Odorless Excavating Apparatus Company, a firm that had patented a system for pumping the waste from septic tanks so that it could be carted away to the edge of the city. The company employed hundreds of workers.

The construction of an adequate sanitary sewer was a top priority for Baltimore's next mayor, Robert M. McLane, one of the Democratic patricians that Rasin had adopted to "perfume" his ticket at the request of his party's reform wing. But Rasin, after his unhappy experience with Mayor Hayes, insisted that the remaining positions on the Democratic ticket be assigned to loyal organization men. The reformers agreed. Rasin chose two relatively obscure adherents as candidates for the presidency of the upper chamber of the city council and for city comptroller.

Robert McLane won his election by a narrow margin. William Stone's Republican candidates for comptroller and president of the council defeated McLane's Democratic running mates who were fatally tainted by their association with Freeman Rasin.

McLane took office, therefore, with two city officials of the opposition party and a Republican opponent who challenged his victory margin of five hundred twenty votes as a product of electoral fraud. Things soon got even worse. On February 7, 1904, a fire broke out in a dry goods store on the western side of Baltimore's business district. When the fire finally burned its way to the Jones Falls and the harbor more than a day later, one hundred forty acres of the city lay in ruins—virtually the entire commercial district.

Mayor McLane, at the recommendation of prominent local businessmen, appointed a sixty-three-member Citizen's Emergency Committee to devise a rebuilding program for the "Burnt District" and later got authorization from the General Assembly to appoint a bipartisan five-member Burnt District Commission, on which he would serve, to carry out the reconstruction plans of the Emergency Committee.

Plans for municipal improvement, like the proposed sewer system, were set aside so that the city could concentrate on repairing the fire's destruction. Simply finding property lines and street levels beneath the rubble kept city surveyors busy for months. The task of removing the debris occupied ten thousand workers. The Burnt District Commission was empowered to take property by eminent domain or private purchase, but the exercise of these and other powers was complicated by the mayor's need to win the approval of the Republican majority in the upper chamber of the city council. At the end of May, Mayor McLane took his own life.

Under the city charter, the Democratic mayor was succeeded by the president of the upper chamber of the city council, Republican E. Clay Timanus, who was a loyal lieutenant of party boss Stone. The city charter prevented them from replacing McLane's Democratic department heads.

After some dithering, Freeman Rasin approached former governor Frank Brown about the Democratic candidate for mayor. Rasin pledged his organization's support to any candidate that Brown chose. After extensive discussions with the members of Baltimore's political class, Brown settled on J. Barry Mahool, a city council member who had aspired only to become president of the council's upper chamber. Rasin agreed to the selection. Shortly after discussing his choice with the *Sun*'s Frank Kent, Rasin collapsed, and a few days later he was dead.

Rasin and Sonny Mahon had reconciled after the election of Robert McLane. It was Mahon who now succeeded to the leadership of Baltimore's Democratic organization and stage-managed Mahool's defeat of Mayor Timanus.

In 1908 Mahool and Mahon both supported the campaign of the Baltimore-based Equal Suffrage League to grant women the right to vote in Maryland's municipal elections. Though the measure enjoyed strong support in the city, the bill never got to the floor of the legislature. In the same session of the General Assembly, the Democratic majority renewed its campaign to disenfranchise illiterate black voters. This time the amendment was drafted to exempt foreign-born citizens. Though the new version stirred less controversy than its 1905 predecessor, the outcome was similar. The proposal was rejected by the state's voters, and Baltimoreans accounted for almost three-fourths of the margin of defeat. The next racial controversy faced by the Mahool administration erupted within the city itself.

In 1910 a Yale-educated African American attorney, George W. F. McMechen, moved into one of the city's fashionable neighborhoods. The reaction of Baltimore's white residents was so threatening that the police posted a round-the-clock guard to protect McMechen's house from ruffians. A mass meeting demanded that city officials do something to protect white neighborhoods from black "incursions." Mahool and the city council responded with an ordinance that prohibited African Americans from moving to blocks where a majority of the residents were white, and vice versa. The law, the first of its kind in the United States, reflected the political elite's attempt to eliminate some of the flashpoints that ignited the race issue in local politics. Baltimore was a border town, where white racial attitudes were hardly monolithic. Race issues generated contention among whites while unifying African Americans. Additional complications arose in the state courts, which threw out two successive versions of the ordinance as unconstitutional until the city finally produced a legally acceptable version in 1913, only to be ruled unconstitutional by the U.S. Supreme Court in a case from Louisville in 1917. In the meantime, the city's black leaders established a local branch of the National Association for the Advancement of Colored People in 1912.

While city officials drafted and redrafted the segregation ordinance, Sonny Mahon was organizing a major political offensive. During his estrangement from Rasin, Mahon had frequently cooperated with the progressives in his party, and his alliances with them continued for the duration of Mahool's term, in part because Mahon personally supported some progressive causes, such as women's suffrage and city planning. Therefore, the reformers mistrusted him less than they did Freeman Rasin. Ever since the Democratic catastrophe of 1895, the organization had deferred to the party's reform wing in the selection of mayoral candidates and settled for a modest share of city patronage. Mahon overrode the apprehensions of his lieutenants to promote the candidacy of James H. Preston, a respectable businessman and organization loyalist. He had served two terms in the House of Delegates and was briefly its speaker.

Mahon's backing of Preston galvanized his followers. They knew that defeat meant complete exclusion from City Hall and its emoluments. Turnout in the Democratic primary reached a record high of 80 percent. Preston defeated Mayor Mahool by nine thousand votes and vanquished Republican Mayor Timanus in the general election, by only six hundred thirty votes. Mahon placed one of his lieutenants, Danny Loden, in charge of City Hall patronage, and Mahon himself received some of it as a bonding agent for city contractors. His business expanded as the Preston administration carried out a long-delayed program of public improvements, much talked about during the terms of progressive mayors, but actually carried out under Mahon's machine.

The Preston administration won over some of the city's leading progressive Democrats, who supported the machine candidates in the state legislative election of 1913. All twenty-eight of the organization's General Assembly candidates were successful. In 1915 Mayor Preston was unopposed in the Democratic primary and carried eighteen of the city's twenty-four wards in the general election. During his second term, in 1918 Preston presided over Baltimore's last annexation of suburban territory. It added sixty-five thousand residents to the city's population. The mayor also demonstrated that his vision rose above street paving and sewers. The Baltimore City Symphony Orchestra was organized with his aid and municipal support.

But the impression of political consensus was misleading. Discord was growing within the Democratic machine itself. One of the organization's lesser bosses, Frank Kelly, chafed under the alliance between Preston and Mahon. Lacking his own mayoral ally, Kelly stood in Mahon's shadow but overcame this disadvantage by attaching himself to a gubernatorial patron. In 1915 Mahon and Preston had supported the nomination of gubernatorial candidate Blair Lee, Maryland's first popularly elected U.S. senator. The state's senior senator and former governor, John Walter Smith, backed state comptroller Emerson Harrington. Frank Kelly kept his own counsel until the last moment, when he instructed his ward leaders to turn out the voters for Harrington, who won the nomination decisively, and then the governorship. Kelly's access to state patronage permitted him to challenge Preston in the mayoral primary of 1919, when Kelly's candidate defeated Preston in the primary, but then lost to the Republican, William F. Broening, in the general election.

Kelly and Mahon had not spoken in four years. The gubernatorial campaign of Democrat Albert Ritchie in 1919 provided the occasion for a fragile, expedient truce to assure the party's control of state patronage. By 1920 Mahon and Kelly were sparring again, competing for seats on the Democratic State Central Committee. By an evenhanded treatment of the two bosses and division of state patronage, Governor Ritchie attempted to mend their differences. In 1923 Ritchie brought the bosses together in support of mayoral candidate Howard W. Jackson, one of Mahon's adherents, who was successful in his bid for mayor.

Mayor Jackson's leadership may have been impaired by the restlessness and ambition of the Kelly and Mahon loyalists. The two leaders were aging, and their lieutenants were jockeying in preparation for politics without the bosses. Jackson tried to create his own base, but was criticized for his drinking and absenteeism, and for awarding about a third of the city's fire insurance coverage to his own firm. Governor Ritchie and John Kelly denied him renomination in 1927 and chose instead one of Kelly's more promising adherents, William Curran, a successful attorney and former state senator and city council representative. Curran faced no opposition in the primary, but lost the general election to the resurrected Republican William F. Broening. Democratic ward and district leaders saw Curran's elevation as a threat to their own ambitions for organizational leadership when the current leaders were gone. That time came a year later, when both Kelly and Mahon died and Baltimore entered a new era of political factionalism.

INDUSTRY, COMMERCE, AND LABOR

A 1914 industrial survey of Baltimore concluded the city's industrial growth had been less than it should have been, especially considering the general state of the country and other similar cities. The city's "industrial retardation," the report explained, was a lingering effect of the economic disruption of the Civil War, which had abruptly ended the city's steady growth. Fifty years after the war, Baltimore was still struggling to make the transition from trade to manufacturing. Though some local industries were expanding, the city had lost ground in construction, sugar refining, pig iron, pottery, boots and shoes, wallpaper, and soap. On one measure—value added by manufacturing—Baltimore had ranked eighth among American cities in 1880, but the city stood at eleventh in 1914 when the survey was conducted. Baltimore was, however, the nation's leading producer of rye whiskey and straw hats.

The industrial mainstays of the city's economy were copper smelting, clothing, canning, and steel. The Baltimore Copper Smelting and Rolling Company ran the world's largest copper refinery on the waterfront in Canton, but in 1907 it was bought by the American Smelting and Refining Company. The massive steel mill southeast of the city at Sparrows Point employed thousands of Baltimoreans, but in 1916 the mill was taken over by Charles Schwab's Bethlehem Steel Company, which sought to exploit the locational advantages of the mill in reducing shipping costs.

One major industry—clothing—was still locally owned, and by any measure it was Baltimore's largest. But clothing production was rather fragmented. The industry consisted of "inside shops" and "contract shops." The inside shops occupied large lofts in West Baltimore where every process from cutting to finishing took place inside the building. The largest of the lofts was a ten-story structure opened by Henry Sonneborn in 1905—the world's biggest building for the manufacture of clothing. The owners of the West Baltimore lofts were primarily German Jews who had been Americans since birth.

The contract shops in East Baltimore usually occupied single rooms, often the same rooms where families lived. The contractors picked up bundles of cut cloth from the lofts and took them to their rooms, where their employees or family members did the sewing needed to produce a completed piece of clothing. According to a state survey conducted in 1900, Baltimore had about four hundred contract shops, and they produced about half of the clothing manufactured in the city. The annual reports of the Maryland Bureau of Industrial Statistics detailed the squalor and overcrowding in these contract shops, where the bosses and workers were disproportionately recent arrivals from Russia, Poland, Lithuania, Bohemia, and Italy. Contract shops were also more likely to employ women than the inside shops, and women were practically excluded from jobs requiring the highest-level skills.

The cutters and trimmers, almost all of whom worked in the inside shops, were the aristocrats of the clothing trades, and virtually all of them were men. If they went on strike, there would be no work for the less highly skilled employees who sewed and finished garments. The cutters became the vanguard of the United Garment Workers (UGW), an American Federation of Labor craft union that challenged both the industry and the Knights of Labor for the right to represent the garment workers in collective bargaining during the early 1890s. The Knights were already on the decline, but both the contract and inside shops stood fast against the UGW.

The Knights soon disappeared, and the UGW withdrew to its core constituency among the cutters and trimmers, but in 1914 the Amalgamated Clothing Workers (ACW), an industrial rather than craft union, arrived in Baltimore to contest the UGW's representation of the garment workers. The ACW's first test came with a walkout by more than three thousand workers at the Sonneborn factory to protest a new system of "scientific management" that would cost some of them their jobs. The strike brought ACW president Sidney Hillman to town, along with organizers who spoke the native languages of immigrant workers. A number of women also emerged as strike leaders. The UGW sought to undercut the upstart union by making a separate agreement with Sonneborn under which the cutters would return to work with a small wage increase. Instead, fifteen hundred of the remaining strikers surrounded Sonneborn's loft and refused to let the cutters leave. Only police escorts finally convinced them to come out. Sonneborn made a settlement with the ACW that guaranteed the jobs previously slated for elimination and gave workers representation on committees that would review changes in the production process. During the following two years, the ACW targeted other clothing manufacturers, and by 1916 it could claim about 75 percent of Baltimore's garment workers as members, including a contingent of cutters who had previously been the mainstay of the UGW.

ACW workers were soon sewing thousands of overcoats for the Doughboys in France. World War I generated orders for Baltimore industry even before the country became a combatant. The Bethlehem Steel plant at Sparrows Point embarked on its largest expansion ever, adding a second shipyard to its facilities and building two steamships for the British and fifty freighters for the U.S. Navy. Other companies manufactured munitions.

Baltimore came out of the Great War riding a wave of economic and territorial expansion. The city attracted 103 new plants during the 1920s. It became a center for the new aircraft industry, and it recovered some of the ground that it had lost to other industrial centers before the war. Bethlehem Steel's Charles Schwab declared that there "is no place in the United States so susceptible for successful industrial development." Still, the city of trade and commerce never disappeared beneath the city of industry. Baltimore's ranking in export-import trade rose along with its status as an industrial powerhouse. And the transport of coal was essential to the city's industrial prosperity.

RACE, ETHNICITY, AND IMMIGRATION

In 1900, foreign-born residents accounted for only 13.5 percent of Baltimore's population, much less than in Boston, New York, Philadelphia, Chicago, or Cleveland. Germans accounted for the largest group of immigrants, followed by Russians, Irish, and English. By 1930, only 9.4 percent had been born abroad, and Russia produced more in-migrants than Germany, which was followed closely by Poland and Italy. The proportion of the city's residents who were African American scarcely changed during the first third of the twentieth century, though it was smaller than it had been in 1880. Even so, African Americans outnumbered foreign-born Baltimoreans. The city had a larger black population than any other city in the North.

Before 1890 Baltimore had no distinctly African American neighborhoods. Many of the city's black and white residents lived in close proximity to one another. Blacks often occupied "alley houses," while the homes of whites fronted on the street. Crowding and poor sanitation in the alley houses of South Baltimore prompted a gradual movement of African Americans to the northwest part of the city beginning in the mid-1880s. By 1904 about half of the black residents lived in the emerging ghetto of West Baltimore. White immigrants lived in their own ghettoes on the other side of town. Once concentrated, the black population of West Baltimore created or attracted black institutions—churches, an entertainment district, black-owned businesses, and social organizations. The new racial geography also facilitated the segregation of schools. By 1907, in response to demands from Baltimore's African Americans, all black children were instructed by black teachers. The residential segregation ordinances of 1910–1913 had simply codified a developing status quo.

As segregation consolidated Baltimore's black population, immigration divided its Jews. The flight of Russian and Eastern European Jews from pogroms beginning in the 1880s brought a wave of new arrivals to Baltimore and other American cities. During the 1890s an average of two thousand Jewish immigrants arrived in Baltimore each year. From 1900 to 1905, the figure rose to five thousand. In a town where the entire Jewish population had been only ten thousand as recently as 1880, the flow of immigration seemed a tidal wave. Many of the German Jews already established in Baltimore were deeply apprehensive about the newcomers. Just below the surface was a fear that the immigrants would trigger an anti-Semitic reaction that would make no distinctions between the impoverished in-migrants and the established and "respectable" German Jews. But the philanthropy of German Jewish millionaires, employment opportunities in the garment industry, and upward mobility of the Yiddish speakers eventually combined to blur, if not eliminate, the divisions within Baltimore's Jewish community.

Though the number of new German immigrants declined at the end of the nineteenth century, the German community, numbering about eighty thousand in 1900, was the largest of Baltimore's white ethnic groups, and though many were second- and third-generation Americans, they maintained a distinct cultural identity. German social organizations, choral groups, gymnastic societies, and shooting clubs knit them together and separated them from the rest of Baltimore's population. The rest of the population not only accepted this separateness, but accommodated it. America's entry into World War I would change all of that. Between 1914 and 1917, the local German press had energetically backed the Central Powers and predicted their victory. But a week after America's declaration of war, the German-language *Baltimore Correspondent* published a statement in English above its masthead affirming its status as an American newspaper. Its subsequent turn toward patriotic Americanism failed to save it. After seventy-seven years of publication, the paper went out of business in 1918. Clubs, churches, and other German organizations also dissolved.

See also *Baltimore, MD 1776–1790; Baltimore, MD 1790–1828; Baltimore, MD 1828–1854; Baltimore, MD 1854–1877; Baltimore, MD 1877–1896; Baltimore, MD 1929–1941; Baltimore, MD 1941–1952; Baltimore, MD 1952–1989*

MATTHEW CRENSON

BIBLIOGRAPHY

Argersinger, Jo Ann E. *Making the Amalgamated: Gender, Ethnicity, and Class in the Baltimore Clothing Industry, 1899–1939.* Baltimore, MD: Johns Hopkins University Press, 1999.

Calcott, Mary Law. *The Negro in Maryland Politics, 1870–1912.* Baltimore, MD: Johns Hopkins University Press, 1969.

Crooks, James B. *Politics and Progress: The Rise of Urban Progressivism in Baltimore, 1895–1911.* Baton Rouge, MD: Louisiana State University Press, 1968.

Euchner, Charles C. "The Politics of Urban Expansion: Baltimore and the Sewerage Question, 1859-1905." *Maryland Historical Magazine* 86 (Fall 1991): 270–291.

Kent, Frank Richardson. *The Story of Maryland Politics.* Baltimore, MD: Thomas and Evans, 1911.

Olson, Sherry H. *Baltimore: The Building of an American City.* 2d ed. Baltimore, MD: Johns Hopkins University Press, 1997.

Rosen, Christine M. *The Limits of Power: Great Fires and the Process of City Growth in America.* New York, NY: Oxford University Press, 1986.

PITTSBURGH, PA 1896–1929

IN THE INITIAL THREE DECADES OF THE TWENTIETH CENTURY, Pittsburgh expanded industrial production and increased its population by two hundred twenty thousand. African American migrants from the South as well as eastern and southern European immigrants swelled the workforce and established vibrant communities. Public officials modernized the city's infrastructure, improving sanitary conditions, accommodating the automobile, and providing recreational space. Nonetheless, civic leaders worried about the city's future during the 1920s. The economy grew more slowly as the period of dramatic industrial expansion seemed to have passed. The dominant Republican Party staggered under rampant factionalism and corruption. Smoke-laden skies caused health problems and cost businesses money, but initial smoke-control regulation was ineffective. Social problems of poverty, poor health, and inadequate housing abounded. All told, Pittsburgh entered the Great Depression years with many issues yet to be successfully addressed.

GOVERNMENT AND POLITICS

The Republican Party dominated politics in Pittsburgh and Pennsylvania from the Civil War to the Roosevelt transformation in 1932. A Republican political machine controlled city government until it encountered internal dissension and the wrath of reformers in the late 1890s. Christopher Lyman Magee, a street railway magnate, and contractor William Flynn lorded over the tightly run organization. Through traditional machine practices of patronage and favors, they obtained the loyalty of lower-income, often ethnic populations and the complicity of businessmen. The city opened and paved new streets, extended water lines, built sewers, erected street lighting, and initiated a park system. At the same time, Magee and Flynn benefited handsomely from the manipulation of public funds, public works contracts, and distribution of franchises.

Middle- and upper-class Protestant reformers grew tired of rising taxes, bloated budgets, egregious graft, and unbridled vice. They created organizations such as the Civic Club of Allegheny County and the Citizens Municipal League, through which they expressed moral condemnation, demanded expertise in city government, and aimed to regain political power. To successfully address social, environmental, and political problems, they believed it necessary to challenge the machine at the polls, nearly winning the mayoral election of 1896. While reform gained momentum, dissension within the machine, Magee's death, and perennial battles with the state Republican Party resulted in the 1901 "Ripper Bill" enabling the governor to abolish

QUICK FACTS

PITTSBURGH, PA 1896–1929

MAYORS

Henry P. Ford	(1896–1899)
William J. Diehl	(1899–1901)
Adam M. Brown	(1901–1901)
Joseph Owen Brown	(1901–1903)
William B. Hays	(1903–1906)
George Guthrie	(1906–1909)
William A. McGee	(1909–1914)
Joseph G. Armstrong	(1914–1918)
Edward Babcock	(1918–1922)
William A. Magee	(1922–1926)
Charles H. Kline	(1926–1933)

MAJOR INDUSTRIES AND EMPLOYERS

Carnegie Steel Company
Jones & Laughlin Steel Company
National Tube Company
Pittsburgh Coal Company
Westinghouse Electric & Manufacturing
    Company

MAJOR NEWSPAPERS

Pittsburgh Chronicle-Telegraph
Pittsburgh Courier
Pittsburgh Dispatch
Pittsburgh Gazette-Times
Pittsburgh Post
Pittsburgh Press
Pittsburgh Post-Gazette (1927)
Pittsburgh Sun-Telegraph (1927)

MAJOR EVENTS

1901: The United States Steel Corporation is formed under the financial auspices of J. P. Morgan and includes the purchase of Carnegie Steel and several other smaller plants in the Pittsburgh area. U.S. Steel is the largest corporation in the nation.

1907: The Pennsylvania state legislature approves the annexation of Allegheny City by Pittsburgh, despite the fact that the residents of Allegheny City voted overwhelmingly against the annexation. In *Hunter v. Pittsburgh,* the U.S. Supreme Court upholds the act of the Pennsylvania legislature.

1911: The Pennsylvania legislature passes a bill that reduces the two city councils to one much smaller nine-member council, with all members elected from the city at large, and a bill that creates a city planning commission and a municipal art commission.

1919: A national steel strike is met in Pittsburgh by the steel companies with brutal, repressive tactics that defeat the workers and return the industry to the harsh working conditions that existed before World War I.

1929: Voters in Pittsburgh and Allegheny County narrowly defeat a new charter that would have maintained a federated structure of municipalities while consolidating many functions into a metropolitan government.

the mayoral office and appoint a recorder with full executive authority. The machine's disarray allowed the reformers to win council seats in 1902 and finally elect George Guthrie to a three-year term as mayor in 1906.

During the first decade of the twentieth century, the reformers and other progressive civic leaders scored several achievements. They followed earlier social initiatives such as the establishment of settlement and public bath houses with regulatory housing ordinances and the creation of playgrounds. With typhoid fever and other water-related diseases running rampant, the city opened a state-of-the-art water treatment plant in 1907. The Civic Club railed against unsightly billboards and urged the large-scale planting of trees on barren hillsides and in neighborhoods. Amid this wave of civic progress, reformers supported an unprecedented, multiyear social survey that exposed harsh working conditions for men and women, abhorrent social ills, pervasive corruption, and fragmented governance. The Pittsburgh Survey advocated through exhibits, published articles, and book-length studies typical progressive solutions of greater efficiency, centralization, and expertise.

With the exposure of city council scandals and high-profile convictions, calls for governmental reform finally yielded fruit. Legislation in 1911 scrapped the bloated, ward-based two councils for a single, salaried nine-member council elected at large. The Republican political machine adapted successfully to these changes, however, and remained in power. Concomitant reformist legislation also created a unified school district, a planning commission, and a municipal art commission to advise on the aesthetic quality of public works.

Local governance in the Pittsburgh metropolitan area was fragmented among the city and dozens of outlying municipalities. The suburbanization of industry began in the 1870s, so industrial towns lined the region's three rivers and smaller stream valleys. Residential suburbs close to the city spread out along railroad and streetcar lines. The Chamber of Commerce initiated a Greater Pittsburgh campaign in the mid-1890s designed to rationalize local governance, enhance business growth, and convey nationally the "true" size of the city. The Pittsburgh Survey and city planning advocates also argued for consolidation of coterminous communities. The city steadily annexed adjacent communities into the 1920s, but the real prize was the 1907 annexation of Allegheny City, the large sibling city across the Allegheny River. With Allegheny City's transition to Pittsburgh's North Side, many suburban communities banded together to fight absorption. Many civic leaders kept alive the dream of merging Pittsburgh with Allegheny County until a referendum on a federated governmental structure narrowly failed in 1929.

Although a coalition of church groups doggedly pursued social and labor reforms well into the 1920s, the burst of reform accomplishments wound down with the resurgence of the Republican machine after 1910 and the demands of World War I. The city's economic structure, imbalanced labor relations, and one-party governance remained intact as the post–World War I era unfolded. The public's embrace of the automobile challenged planners and public works officials to retrofit the city's infrastructure with new bridges, tunnels, and boulevards, and plans to construct a subway never got off the shelf. Slowing economic growth worried civic leaders.

Prohibition had little impact on the consumption of alcohol, but it extended opportunities for corruption among ward politicians and the police. Internecine battles among state Republican powers further embroiled Pittsburgh politics. One such imbroglio led to Charles H. Kline's (1926–1933) mayoral victory in 1925 over William A. Magee (1909–1914, 1922–1926), who had lost the support of the Mellons. But Kline soon built his own organization, further dividing the party, and oversaw the expansion of Prohibition-fueled corruption. Meanwhile, a drift away from the Republicans was apparent in the presidential races of 1924 and 1928. In the presidential election of 1924, ethnic voters in the city displayed surprising support for Progressive Party candidate Robert LaFollette, who vigorously attacked the U.S. secretary of the treasury, Pittsburgh's own Andrew W. Mellon, and in the presidential election of 1928, Democrat Alfred Smith garnered 48 percent of the vote. Despite the weak presence of the local Democratic Party, Pittsburghers were increasingly dissatisfied with the aging, rotting Republican machine when the stock market crashed in 1929.

INDUSTRY, COMMERCE, AND LABOR

Pittsburgh came out of the depression of the mid-1890s determined to resume the tremendous industrial growth of the previous twenty years. The city and its metropolitan area dominated the nation's iron and steel industry. In 1904 the region produced more than a quarter of U.S. pig iron output and three-eighths of all steel ingots. Andrew Carnegie had assembled an imposing complex of mills by the late 1880s, and with the appointment of Henry C. Frick to the helm in 1889, Carnegie Steel grew even more impressively. It produced 29 percent of the nation's ingots in its final year before being sold in 1901 to J. P. Morgan's newly created United States Steel Corporation. After the sale of his company, Carnegie focused on philanthropy, while Frick moved to New York, where he dabbled in several business projects and intensified his art collecting. These two entrepreneurs, who had been instrumental in Pittsburgh's dramatic rise as an industrial power, no longer towered over the local scene.

Despite the imposing presence of U.S. Steel, Pittsburgh's economy comprised many iron and steel firms, metalworking businesses, and nationally important companies in other industries. Numerous specialty steel firms complemented several large integrated operations such as Jones & Laughlin Steel Company. Besides the region's many coal mines and coke works, prominent industries included glass (American Window Glass), railroad equipment (Westinghouse Air Brake), heavy machinery (Mesta Machine), aluminum (Aluminum Company of America), electrical equipment (Westinghouse Electric & Manufacturing), and food processing (H. J. Heinz). Pittsburgh was a center of banking and venture capital, notably the financial empire of brothers Andrew W. and Richard Beatty Mellon. As the core of the nation's fifth largest metropolitan area, Pittsburgh also contained a diverse complex of business and professional services.

With the resumption of vigorous economic activity at the beginning of the new century, few civic leaders would have predicted that their city's era of rapid growth was almost over. Trouble began with the devastating flood of March 1907, which inundated downtown and many manufacturing facilities located along the riverbanks. No sooner had business begun to recover than the panic of October 1907 swept through the nation's financial system. The city's stock exchange closed, some banks and investment houses experienced financial embarrassment, and several manufacturing firms went bankrupt. The disruptions were felt for several years, and eventual economic recovery failed to reignite earlier growth rates. Changing national economic conditions began to undermine Pittsburgh's position. Markets for steel continued to move westward, attracting new plants with it, especially to Chicago. The demand for the city's steel products such as railroad rails and cars slowed, and the adoption of new coke-making technologies diminished

At the turn of the 20th century, Pittsburgh was a major industrial center producing a significant portion of America's iron and steel. The incredible wealth generated by these industries was offset by the detrimental environmental impact that they had on the city and its inhabitants.

Source: Library of Congress

the advantage of nearby Connellsville coke. Increased mechanization and a switch to natural gas led glass firms to leave the city for sites throughout the region and beyond.

In the years after the 1907 crises, Pittsburgh continued to grow, but its status relative to other cities slipped. The city's population rose to six hundred seventy thousand in 1930, while the metropolitan region's population nearly doubled since 1900 to two million. Although World War I stimulated industrial production, the 1920s resulted in uneven economic performance. Civic leaders expressed concern about the future. Continued specialization in iron and steel, coal, and glass rendered the region vulnerable to the nation's economic vicissitudes. Electrical equipment and aluminum buffered the diminishing rate of growth, but not enough to halt a relative decline. By 1930 the region's proportion of national output had fallen in iron and steel, glass, and coal. The city lost manufacturing as companies decentralized to suburban sites. Its proportion of manufacturing in the region declined from 55 percent in 1899 to 27 percent in 1929. Reflecting the slower growth of the 1920s, most of this change occurred before World War I.

Labor unrest accompanied Pittsburgh's rapid industrialization. The transition to large corporations and mass production from small partnerships and craft-based shop floors diminished the roles of skilled workers in the manufacturing process. Craft unions fought to preserve the wages and rights of their highly skilled members, but by the mid-1890s the large companies had gained the upper hand. The failure of the violent Homestead Strike of 1892 at Carnegie's Homestead Works left the Amalgamated Association of Iron and Steel Workers severely weakened.

The companies hired droves of unskilled immigrant laborers. In the mines, mills, and factories these workers toiled long hours at backbreaking jobs under unhealthy and dangerous conditions for low wages. Cyclical downturns, injury or death, and the capriciousness of bosses caused employment insecurity. Employers exercised unfettered control over the workplace, firing workers for union activity or minor transgressions. Workers and their families lived near their places of employment in overcrowded housing, where unsanitary conditions complicated life.

In the face of these harsh circumstances, workers developed a sense of pride and mutualism, which they manifested in resistance to the work regime. The United Mine Workers, the Amalgamated, and a number of other unions, including radical ones like the Industrial Workers of the World, organized strikes against the most intransigent employers. With police forces and local authorities on their side, companies ruthlessly put down strikes. The three-month 1919 Steel Strike was notoriously violent in the region's mill towns. Smearing the strike as a foreign radical conspiracy won over public support and divided American and British-born skilled workers from unskilled immigrant laborers. The companies resisted union organizing, instituted some paternalistic benefits, and sponsored company-based workers councils. In the wake of the failed 1916 Westinghouse Electric and 1919 Steel

Strikes, these tactics, along with unsettled economic conditions, left labor relatively impotent during the 1920s.

RACE, ETHNICITY, AND IMMIGRATION

Pittsburgh was a city of migrants. White and black native-born citizens along with European immigrants flocked to the Steel City's burgeoning employment opportunities. While British, Irish, and German immigrants dominated the European migration before 1900, southern and eastern Europeans prevailed after that date. By 1910 immigrants and those American-born of foreign parents comprised more than 60 percent of the city's population. World War I and congressionally imposed restrictions in the early 1920s nearly shut off the flow of immigrants. Consequently, the immigrant proportion of the city's population declined from 30 percent in 1900 to 16 percent in 1930. However, growth in the number of children and adults of foreign parentage kept the foreign stock population above 50 percent.

As immigration declined, the migration of African Americans increased. Pittsburgh had a sizable black community of more than twenty thousand in 1900. With the war's disruption of immigration and American workers joining the armed services, many employers recruited southern black men to fill labor shortages. When the war ended, many blacks lost their positions to returning veterans. Others who had been hired as replacement workers during strikes not only were fired when labor issues were resolved, but also encountered the enmity of white workers who viewed them as "scabs." Despite the postwar deterioration of economic conditions and the relatively flat growth of the city's number of industrial workers during the 1920s, the spike in black migration continued. The black community grew to fifty-five thousand by 1930, almost doubling from 4.5 percent of the city's population at the turn of the century.

These southern migrants, often impoverished and illiterate, encountered not only racial discrimination but also the disdain of the established black community. Although relatively few members of this older community had worked in the city's mills and most found employment in unskilled and personal service jobs, some had carved out occupational niches as barbers, caterers, or hack drivers, while others were successful entrepreneurs. They had also established a rich variety of cultural organizations. In contrast, the newcomers did not fare well in the wobbly economy of the 1920s. Hostile employers and unions deterred blacks from developing a solid foundation in the major industries. Those who worked in the mines and mills toiled at dirty, burdensome, and dangerous jobs such as helpers in blast furnace departments. Further, several traditional black businesses lost their white clientele, eroding older occupational niches. Growth of the community, unstable economic foundations, and high turnover engendered low homeownership rates as well as overcrowded and dilapidated housing. While the lower Hill district adjacent to downtown grew as the primary black community, the city's rugged topography and the need for pedestrian access to jobs dispersed blacks into four other areas. The Hill had long displayed residential mixing among immigrants and blacks, but by 1930 it is estimated that nearly three-quarters of blacks in Pittsburgh would have to have moved to achieve desegregation.

Despite the deprivation, the Hill district was a vibrant community. Entertainers playing venues between New Orleans and New York passed through Pittsburgh and interacted with local talent in the numerous clubs. A number of nationally renowned jazz musicians emerged from this creative mixture. The famous Pittsburgh Crawfords professional black baseball team and the nearby Homestead Grays grew out of a vigorous sandlot sporting life. Just as these ballplayers and musicians spread the renown of Pittsburgh's black community, Robert L. Vann's newspaper, the *Pittsburgh Courier*, became a staple in many black communities around the nation.

Pittsburgh's new immigrants experienced some of the same difficulties that black migrants did, but they made deeper inroads into the major industries, which provided a more stable foundation for their communities. While immigrants of northwest European ancestry dominated skilled industrial positions and several governmental occupations, Poles, Croatians, Slovaks, Serbians, Hungarians, Italians, and other national groups labored in the mills and mines, rising over the years to semiskilled and operative positions. At the price of deteriorating health, they often had the satisfaction of procuring employment in the mills for their grown children. Along with the income from daughters who worked until marriage in routine jobs at companies such as Heinz and Westinghouse Electric and wives who also contributed from piecework or taking in boarders, this modest employment stability supported increasing rates of home ownership, neighborhood businesses and services, and vital community institutions. Ethnic churches ministered to the spiritual needs of their congregations; fraternal organizations provided social outlets and financial services such as insurance and mortgages.

The city's topographical complexity, with industries and adjacent neighborhoods confined to river floodplains and narrow stream valleys, fragmented immigrant groups and sometimes led to surprisingly heterogeneous residential areas. Some groups predominated in a few neighborhoods, such as Poles in Lawrenceville or Italians in Larimer, but fragments of most ethnic groups were found in many sections of the city. The diversity of churches on the South Side, for example, reflected the residential mixing where religious institutions and fraternal organizations, not proximity, provided an ethnic community's cohesion. In addition to the growing black population, the lower Hill district housed Italians, Eastern European Jews, people from Syria and what is now Lebanon, and pockets of other immigrants, some of whom worked in garment shops, small cigar factories, and bakeries. The improving economic foundations, rising home ownership rates, growth of second-generation members, and community businesses and institutions all undergirded more stable and politically active ethnic communities before the Great Depression.

See also *Pittsburgh, PA 1929–1941*

EDWARD K. MULLER

BIBLIOGRAPHY

Bauman, John F. and Edward K. Muller. *Before Renaissance: Planning in Pittsburgh, 1889–1943.* Pittsburgh, PA: University of Pittsburgh Press, 2006.

Bodnar, John, Roger Simon, and Michael P. Weber. *Lives of Their Own: Black, Italians, and Poles in Pittsburgh, 1900–1960.* Urbana: University of Illinois Press, 1982.

Cannadine, David. *Mellon: An American Life*. New York, NY: Alfred A. Knopf, 2006.

Gottlieb, Peter. *Making Their Own Way: Southern Blacks' Migration to Pittsburgh, 1916–1930*. Urbana: University of Illinois Press, 1987.

Greenwald, Maurine W., and Margo Anderson, eds. *Pittsburgh Surveyed: Social Science and Social Reform in the Early Twentieth Century*. Pittsburgh, PA: University of Pittsburgh Press, 1996.

Lubove, Roy. *Twentieth-Century Pittsburgh: Government, Business, and Environmental Change*. New York, NY: John Wiley & Sons, 1969.

Tarr, Joel, ed. *Devastation and Renewal: An Environmental History of Pittsburgh and Its Region*. Pittsburgh, PA: University of Pittsburgh Press, 2003.

LOS ANGELES, CA 1896–1929

BETWEEN 1896 AND 1929, LOS ANGELES DEVELOPED INTO A DIFFERENT SORT OF AMERICAN METROPOLITAN CENTER. Political and business elites employed boosterism and national advertising to sell Southern California real estate, broken down into towns that were subdivided and sold before they were built. *Los Angeles Times* publisher Harrison Gray Otis, railway magnate Henry Huntington, and Moses Sherman made fortunes by selling the land and the urban infrastructure of newly imagined towns like Glendale and Sherman Oaks. The city politics of Los Angeles thus extended miles beyond the actual city, and even county, limits.

GOVERNMENT AND POLITICS

Four-time mayor Meredith "Pinkie" Snyder developed a popular type of political leadership for Los Angeles. Although he was a fixture of Angeleno civic life between the mid-1890s and the aftermath of World War I, Snyder characterized himself as a political reformer, the sort of energetic and unconventional figure well suited to a new city on the make. His reputation grew throughout the state, and at one point he considered a run for the governor's chair. More characteristic of turn-of-the-century Los Angeles elites, however, was Mayor Fred Eaton. Eaton played a part in the creation of the Los Angeles Aqueduct, growing the city and making his fortune through political misdirection.

In 1875 Eaton became superintendent of the Los Angeles City Water Company, a private concern. In 1903, under Mayor Snyder, Los Angeles purchased the company, thereby securing municipal possession of the city's water supply. At the same time, the city procured the services of the company's leading engineer, William Mulholland. Mulholland had secured his reputation by repairing the slipshod water system that had been installed while the company was under private ownership, and then set to work trying to find additional water supplies for a city that was quickly expanding, in a sprawling fashion, throughout Southern California. To that end, the engineer joined forces with his former boss—and soon to be mayor—Fred Eaton, and Joseph Lippincott, an engineer for the Federal Reclamation Service. Lippincott had been

QUICK FACTS

LOS ANGELES, CA 1896–1929

MAYORS

Frank Rader	(1894–1896)
Meredith P. Snyder	(1896–1898)
Fred Eaton	(1898–1900)
Meredith P. Snyder	(1900–1904)
Owen McAleer	(1904–1906)
Arthur C. Harper	(1906–1909)
William D. Stephens	(partial term 1909)
George Alexander	(1909–1913)
Henry Rose	(1913–1915)
Charles E. Sebastian	(1915–1916)
Frederick T. Woodman	(1916–1919)
Meredith P. Snyder	(1919–1921)
George E. Cryer	(1921–1929)

MAJOR INDUSTRIES AND EMPLOYERS

Southern Pacific Railroad
Sampson Tire Company
Ford Motor Company
Oil industry
Film industry

NEWSPAPERS

Los Angeles Times
Los Angeles Examiner
The Breeze
The Van Nuys Call
La Opinión
Pasadena Star News
Long Beach Press-Telegram

MAJOR EVENTS

1905: A bond is passed for the creation of a Los Angeles Aqueduct after the *Los Angeles Times* warns of an impending drought.

1910: The *Los Angeles Times'* building is partially destroyed by a bomb. The event, and the subsequent trial, served as the climax of *Times* publisher Harrison Gray Otis's anti-union campaign.

1910: The Los Angeles Harbor at San Pedro and Wilmington is completed.

1911: Job Harriman, a viable Socialist candidate for mayor, is defeated in the anti-labor backlash following the trial of the *Times* bomber.

1924: Voters approve the Major Traffic Street Plan, which would modernize the city's infrastructure.

assigned to report on the irrigation potential of the Owens Valley, in south-central California. He lobbied against the use of the valley for the federal government, while secretly serving as a go-between for the Los Angeles Department of Water and Power and the Owens Valley community; meanwhile Mulholland began providing Los Angeles media with dire—and fictional—predictions of drought in the city. Frightened voters supported several bonds for the creation of an aqueduct that would draw Owens River waters to Los Angeles and the unincorporated San Fernando Valley. Eaton, Otis, and a small circle of others invested in real estate throughout the valley and made millions when the land was required for the aqueduct and the San Fernando Valley was assimilated into metropolitan Los Angeles.

The aqueduct was not uncontroversial, however. Indeed, it was the central issue in what almost became a successful run for mayor by Job Harriman, a Socialist attorney. Harriman ran against the city's tiny political elite and its support of the aqueduct. Otis had employed a booster and advertising organization, the Merchants and Manufacturers' Association (known as the M&M), to transform Los Angeles into an "open-shop" city, thereby undercutting San Francisco's natural advantages as a West Coast business hub. Eighty percent of the city's major firms had joined the M&M to fund civic festivals and advertising campaigns; Otis used the subscription list and treasury to hire strikebreakers and scab labor and to punish any companies in the city that were willing to negotiate with unions. With the cooperation of a wide swath of the Angeleno business community, the M&M could withhold bank loans and supplies, delay payments, cancel newspaper advertisements, and boycott employers that didn't cooperate. The police facilitated M&M campaigns, and in July 1910 the city council, under M&M direction, unanimously passed a ban on all picketing and "certain" public meetings. There was also support in Los Angeles for unions, however; mass parades accompanied the opening of the State Labor Convention in 1910, and Harriman's candidacy for mayor the following year was assisted by Otis's high-handed methods, the ruthlessness of M&M strikebreakers, and the revelation (in the *Los Angeles Herald-Tribune*) that Otis, Eaton, and others stood to profit from taxpayer investments in the aqueduct.

INDUSTRY, COMMERCE, AND LABOR

Los Angeles at the turn of the twentieth century was known as "Otistown"; it was a central battleground in a national war over the representation of labor. By 1929 the physical mapping of the city into suburbanized enclaves had been completed; Otis's son-in-law, Harry Chandler, had assumed control over his small circle of economic and political elites; and the city's national profile was increasingly crafted in the incorporated town of Hollywood.

The victorious conclusion of Otis's open-shop campaign was secured, ironically, during Job Harriman's run for mayor and via a violent attack on the *Times* itself. On the night of October 1, 1910, the *Los Angeles Times'* building was destroyed in a fiery explosion. John J. McNamara, president of the International Association of Bridge and Structural Iron Workers' Union, and his brother James B. McNamara, were arrested and charged with the crime; Clarence Darrow and Harriman defended them. The latter's attack on the aqueduct and his role defending the McNamaras increased his popularity. The case against the brothers was suspicious, and hundreds of sympathetic workers in the city wore "McNamaras Innocent! Vote for Harriman!" buttons, while contributions to the McNamara Defense Fund poured in from all over the nation. But Darrow was increasingly convinced that his clients were guilty, and on December 1, 1911, just four days before the mayoral election, he convinced the brothers to accept a plea agreement and changed their pleas to "guilty." Republican incumbent Mayor George Alexander was reelected, and organized labor in Los Angeles lost credibility. The M&M pushed its advantage; labor did not return to the fight with the same degree of enthusiasm until the Great Depression.

Water and real estate marked the first major intersection between politics and economics in Los Angeles during this period; oil and celluloid marked the next two. Edward Doheny sank the first successful Los Angeles oil well in 1892. In 1896 the city was experiencing an oil boom; derricks in downtown were, in the words of one local native, "as thick as holes in a pepperbox." By the early 1900s, Doheny and his partner, Charles Canfield, successfully lobbied the

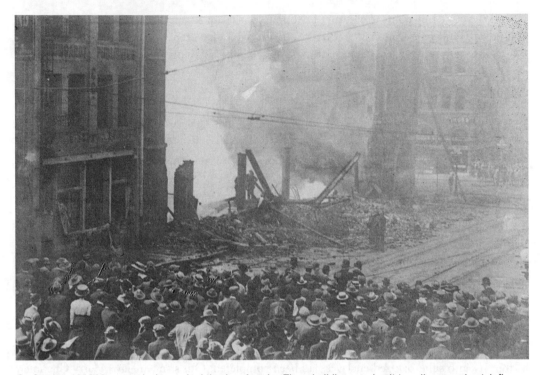

On October 1, 1910, an explosion rocked the *Los Angeles Times* building causing it to collapse and catch fire. The dynamite attack targeted the anti-union newspaper during a strike of metal workers that had been ongoing for several months.

Source: Library of Congress

Southern Pacific Railroad to switch to petroleum fuel from coal, a switch that made the two men extremely wealthy. By 1923 the Los Angeles metropolitan area was producing one quarter of the world's total supply; in local politics, the power of the oil lobby fueled the growth of Southern California urban sprawl, as petroleum-powered trolley lines and automobiles facilitated greater suburban development. In 1924, Los Angeles voters approved the Major Traffic Street Plan, which widened the city's streets, implemented modern traffic enforcement, and crafted a countywide highway system, thereby creating the necessary infrastructure for a petroleum-based, private automobile transit system. The Teapot Dome Scandal briefly tarnished Doheny's reputation in 1924, when he was accused of offering a $100,000 bribe to Secretary of the Interior Albert Fall to secure additional drilling rights. The influence of the oil industry in Southern California continued to spread throughout the 1920s nonetheless.

The movie industry settled in Southern California originally in 1914, when Cecil B. DeMille directed *The Squaw Man*. Filmmakers first moved into the Los Angeles area to avoid Pinkerton detectives hired by Thomas Alva Edison, who had the monopoly on the technology for film production in the United States. Once Edison's patent was successfully challenged in the courts, producers like Adolph Zukor (founder of Paramount Pictures), remained in Hollywood for its cheap real estate and frequent good weather (which facilitated year-round filming). By 1925 MGM's Irving Thalberg had perfected the "studio system" of film production. Each studio built extensive sound stages: fancy "old European" sets at Paramount and MGM, Transylvanian villages at Universal, East Coast urban sets at Warner Brothers, and so on. Having such extensive sets in place made it cost-effective for the studios to specialize in particular genres. The same steps were taken with the "talent"—actors, directors, and screenwriters signed multiyear contracts at particular studios and specialized in particular storylines and characters—and with the technical crew of carpenters, grips, set and production designers, and others.

By 1929 American film had become a highly profitable industry, and American audiences associated film with the Hollywood studios. Labor struggles began by the late 1920s. In 1927 the Academy of Motion Picture Arts and Sciences was founded (by MGM's Louis B. Mayer, among others) as a way to offer a "company union" alternative to the independent Screenwriters Guild and Screen Actors Guild. The struggle over film profits and labor representation would only increase as the nation entered the Great Depression in October 1929.

RACE, ETHNICITY, AND IMMIGRATION

As the Los Angeles Aqueduct was under construction, work crew foremen assured Angeleno voters that the work force would be "100 percent American," by which they meant that no Latino, Asian, or African American workers would be involved in the transportation of the city's drinking water. At the city's eighteenth century founding, the population was very ethnically diverse, but the new homeowners drawn to the Southland by the burgeoning real estate market were overwhelmingly midwestern, white, and Protestant. This process was already underway in the 1890s; by 1926 Los Angeles was more than 90 percent white; the total population of 1.3 million included only forty-five thousand Latinos and thirty-three thousand African Americans. Despite that fact, racial diversification was again on the rise.

African Americans accounted for less than 3 percent of the population of Los Angeles by 1929, but their numbers had doubled in the 1920s as a result of migration from the South. Segregationist real estate covenants and restrictive trust deed clauses kept black Angelenos limited to particular neighborhoods, but homeownership was on the rise in those areas, a result of the suburban spread of the city and the economic opportunities during a boom time for oil and land prices. African Americans were legally allowed to matriculate at the University of California's Los Angeles campus, which added to the growing black middle class. Black homeownership and voting registration rates rose so quickly in the town of Watts that, in 1926, white citizens voted to be annexed by Los Angeles in the hopes of foiling black political power. Segregationist policies directed at the black community would worsen after World War II; by 1950 the 1920s would be remembered with nostalgia by older African Americans.

The Latino population of Los Angeles tripled during the 1920s; Los Angeles County had a Mexican American population of one hundred sixty-seven thousand by 1929, a larger Latino presence than anywhere else in the United States. Most of the population growth in this community had come from the rising Mexican American birthrate rather than immigration, which meant that the increasing population would lead to a direct rise in the Latino electorate. Latinos were the object of the same policies of segregation that confronted African Americans, however. Mexican Americans bought homes at a relatively high rate, but were forced to do so within particular neighborhoods by discriminatory lending and purchase policies. The number of *barrios* increased, however; despite the Major Traffic Street Plan, Los Angeles still had an extensive network of metropolitan rail and streetcars, and Mexican Americans moved along their routes, buying suburban homes while working on farms out in the San Fernando Valley or at manufacturing and domestic jobs in the city center. Many Latinos worked in meatpacking plants, and increasing numbers were hired by the growing automobile industry, either in steel and auto assembly plants or for the Sampson Tire Company. Mexican Americans had a peculiar position in the public imagination of white Los Angeles. The old Mission Era provided the material for Protestant tourist faux-history, and Mexican American laborers were increasingly important to the Southern California economy, but public policy and political narrative rendered Latino Angelenos as perennial outsiders.

Only the Asian American population in Los Angeles declined by the end of the 1920s. The city had a thriving Chinatown into the 1890s, with Chinese-language newspapers, telephone exchanges, businesses, and theater, but immigration bans and police harassment shrank the city's Asian population to just two thousand by 1924. National immigration bans targeted specifically at Japan limited the numbers of new Japanese immigrants to California, and increasingly restrictive real estate covenants were employed to restrict business and homeownership for Nisei (second-generation) and Sansei (third-generation) Japanese Americans.

Jewish migration to Los Angeles was primarily upwardly mobile and working class, and it quickly centered in the garment trade and the film industry. In the words of historian Kevin Starr, "whatever strength the labor movement possessed after 1910 in the open-shop city belonged to Jewish-dominated unions such as the International Ladies' Garment Workers Union (ILGWU) and the Amalgamated Clothing Workers." In 1929 Congregation B'Nai B'rith moved from Downtown to the Wilshire Boulevard Temple. Rabbi Edgar Magnin led the congregation from 1915 until his death in 1984 and helped establish it as the wealthiest, and one of the most influential, in the United States. But despite the increased wealth and influence in the early twentieth century, Los Angeles's Jewish community would be locked out of the WASP political elite for another fifty years.

In addition to the *Times* publicity machine, Los Angeles owed its stream of tourism to the mythmaking of Helen Hunt Jackson, whose 1884 novel *Ramona* created a mythic landscape of gentle Catholic friars and hardworking Indians. Local towns held Ramona festivals; tourists came from around the country to participate and, more frequently, to stay. Though there were successful women boosters, however, women were denied positions of power in the downtown establishment. The International Ladies' Garment Workers Union (ILGWU) was almost alone in beginning to create the institutional support for cross-racial and cross-gender political organization in 1920s Los Angeles. ILGWU Local 52 achieved a membership of fifteen thousand by the time it was chartered, which elicited a visit from union Vice President Mollie Friedman in 1926. The ILGWU was primarily controlled by male (ethnically Jewish and Irish) leaders, but it was increasingly becoming a potential source of political agency for women, and Friedman upbraided the local leadership for largely ignoring the growing population of Latina dressmakers in the Southland. These early faltering steps toward political organization by the outcasts of the Otistown circle laid foundations for the coalitions of modern Los Angeles.

See also *Los Angeles, CA 1929–1941; Los Angeles, CA 1941–1952; Los Angeles, CA 1952–1989; Los Angeles, CA 1989–2011*

RONALD J. SCHMIDT JR.

BIBLIOGRAPHY

Brownlow, Kevin. *The Parade's Gone By*. New York: Ballantine Books, 1968.

Davis, Mike. *City of Quartz*. New York, NY: Vintage, 1991

Escobar, Edward. *Race, Police, and the Making of a Political Identity*. Berkeley: University of California Press, 1999.

Laslett, John, and Mary Tyler. *The ILGWU in Los Angeles 1907–1988*. Inglewood, CA: Ten Star Press, 1989.

Sanchez, George. *Becoming Mexican American*. New York, NY: Oxford University Press, 1995.

Schmidt, Ronald J., Jr. *This Is the City: Making Model Citizens in Los Angeles*. Minneapolis: University of Minnesota Press, 2005.

Starr, Kevin. *Material Dreams: Southern California Through the 1920s*. New York, NY: Oxford University Press, 1990.

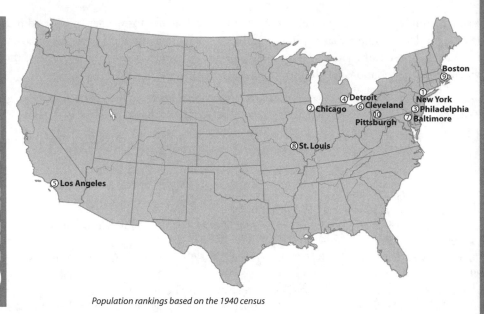

CHAPTER 7

Population rankings based on the 1940 census

CITIES IN THE GREAT DEPRESSION, 1929–1941

The period covered in this chapter starts with the onset of the Great Depression—the culmination of an economy increasingly concentrated in a few industries, weak consumer demand combined with high debt, and bankrupt European nations defaulting on debts, punctuated by a dramatic decline in stock market prices in October 1929—and it ends with the Japanese bombing of Pearl Harbor in December 1941. Between 1929 and 1941, the role of the federal government was radically transformed as it attempted to resuscitate a moribund economy and alleviate the suffering of millions of Americans who were unemployed, underemployed, or destitute.

For large American cities, a decade of economic stagnation (combined with stricter immigration laws) was accompanied by historically low population growth or, in some instances, net population loss. Between 1930 and 1940, the total population of the ten cities covered in this chapter increased by approximately 5 percent, from 19,042,823 to 19,906,825, which was slightly lower than the national growth rate during the 1930s of roughly 7 percent, from 123 million to 132 million people. As a result, the proportion of the total U.S. population living in the country's ten largest cities declined during the decade by roughly half a percent, to 15 percent, by 1940.

By contrast, however, the Census counted 56.5 percent of the country's population as living in "urban" places (those with populations greater than two thousand five hundred) in 1940, which was an increase of approximately half a percent from 1930. Thus urban population growth during the 1930s was greater in smaller cities, most notably those in the emergent Sunbelt. For instance, five of the ten largest cities in the country (Philadelphia, Cleveland, St. Louis, Boston, and Pittsburgh) either declined in population or stayed basically the same size during the 1930s. Of the remaining five that grew in size, only Los Angeles increased by more than 10 percent. Indeed, during the 1930s Los Angeles increased its population by nearly one-quarter, and smaller southwestern cities followed a similar trajectory. Houston, for instance, expanded in population by more than 30 percent, and San Diego by more than 35 percent, during the 1930s.

The population growth of southwestern cities during the 1930s was fueled in part by the migration of a destitute farm population as a result of the devastating drought and heat wave that transformed the region from Texas to the Dakotas into, as it came to be known, the Dust Bowl. Refugees of the Dust Bowl flooded into California, Southern California in particular, overwhelming local relief agencies and leading them to call on the federal government for assistance.

The Hoover administration sought to reverse the economic tide by negotiating with business and labor, increasing federal public works expenditures, increasing aid to farmers, and providing loans to businesses through a new federal agency, the Reconstruction Finance Corporation. Yet it was all too little to reverse both the economic collapse and the collapse of national Republican dominance. In 1930 Democrats won a majority in the U.S. House of Representatives, and in 1932 (by which time unemployment had settled at more than 20 percent nationally, with many more underemployed, thousands of banks bankrupt or voluntarily closed, and industrial output cut to half of what it had been in the 1920s), Democrats won majorities in the House and Senate, and the Democratic nominee for president, Franklin D. Roosevelt, won the presidency with nearly 60 percent of the popular vote. Between Roosevelt's election and inauguration, thousands more banks closed, and on the morning of his inauguration, the New York Stock Exchange announced that it would not be opening, thus signaling the near total collapse of the nation's financial system. The new president declared a national bank holiday.

Under Roosevelt and his New Deal programs, the national government took on previously unimaginable responsibilities. In 1933 alone, Congress passed, and the president signed, the National Industrial Recovery Act (NIRA), allowing businesses to set industry-wide agreements under government supervision regarding pricing and production, establishing collective bargaining rights for workers, and creating a program for public works through the Public Works Administration (PWA); the Agricultural Adjustment Act (AAA), taxing the processors of farm goods in order to pay subsidies to farmers who agreed to government production controls; the Glass-Steagall Act, separating commercial from investment banking and creating the Federal Deposit Insurance Company (FDIC); and the Securities Act, providing for federal regulation of interstate sales of securities. To top it all off, the Twenty-First Amendment was ratified that

BY THE NUMBERS: THE MOST POPULOUS CITIES IN 1940

	TOTAL POPULATION[1]	WHITE POPULATION[1]	BLACK POPULATION[1]	OTHER POPULATION[1]	% WHITE POPULATION[1]	% BLACK POPULATION[1]	% OTHER POPULATION[1]	FOREIGN-BORN POPULATION[1]
NEW YORK, NY	7,454,995	6,977,501	458,444	19,050	93.6	6.1	0.3	2,138,657
CHICAGO, IL	3,396,808	3,114,564	277,731	4,513	91.7	8.2	0.1	675,147
PHILADELPHIA, PA	1,931,334	1,678,577	250,880	1,877	86.9	13.0	0.1	292,546
DETROIT, MI	1,623,452	1,472,662	149,119	1,671	90.7	9.2	0.1	322,688
LOS ANGELES, CA	1,504,277	1,406,430	63,774	34,073	93.5	4.2	2.3	227,037
CLEVELAND, OH	878,336	793,417	84,504	415	90.3	9.6	0.0	179,784
BALTIMORE, MD	859,100	692,705	165,843	552	80.6	19.3	0.1	61,698
ST. LOUIS, MO	816,048	706,794	108,765	489	86.6	13.3	0.1	59,647
BOSTON, MA	770,816	745,466	23,679	1,671	96.7	3.1	0.2	184,080
PITTSBURGH, PA	671,659	609,235	62,216	207	90.7	9.3	0.0	84,903

	% POPULATION FOREIGN-BORN[1]	% LABOR FORCE UNEMPLOYED[2]	% LABOR FORCE ON PUBLIC EMERGENCY WORK[2]	% EMPLOYED POPULATION IN MANUFACTURING[3]	% POPULATION 7–13 YEARS OLD ATTENDING SCHOOL[4]	LAND AREA (SQ. MI.)[5]	POPULATION DENSITY (PER SQ. MI.)[5]
NEW YORK, NY	28.7	15.3	3.0	26.3	96.9	299.0	24,933.1
CHICAGO, IL	19.9	11.3	3.9	33.3	97.7	206.7	16,433.5
PHILADELPHIA, PA	15.1	17.0	2.7	35.3	97.0	127.2	15,183.4
DETROIT, MI	19.9	10.7	4.0	47.2	97.8	137.9	11,772.7
LOS ANGELES, CA	15.1	11.8	2.7	18.2	97.8	448.3	3,355.5
CLEVELAND, OH	20.5	12.7	7.5	40.5	97.8	73.1	12,015.5
BALTIMORE, MD	7.2	8.4	1.9	31.6	97.1	78.7	10,916.1
ST. LOUIS, MO	7.3	11.4	3.8	33.0	97.4	61.0	13,377.8
BOSTON, MA	23.9	13.3	6.6	22.0	98.2	46.1	16,720.5
PITTSBURGH, PA	12.6	17.6	4.6	26.9	94.5	52.1	12,891.7

[1] *Source:* Sixteenth Census of the United States: 1940, Population, Volume II, Characteristics of the Population. Table 36.
[2] *Source:* Sixteenth Census of the United States: 1940, Population, Volume II, Characteristics of the Population. Table 41.
[3] *Source:* Sixteenth Census of the United States: 1940, Population, Volume II, Characteristics of the Population. Tables 41 & 42.
[4] *Source:* Sixteenth Census of the United States: 1940, Population, Volume II, Characteristics of the Population. Table 38.
[5] *Source:* Campbell Gibson, *Population of the 100 Largest Cities and Other Urban Places in the United States: 1790 to 1990.* (1998) Table 17.

same year, making the distribution and sale of alcohol once again legal. Two years later, Congress and the Roosevelt administration established the National Labor Relations Act (protecting the rights of workers to organize into unions for the purpose of collective bargaining) and the Social Security Act (establishing, among other things, federal relief and insurance programs for the poor, unemployed, disabled, and elderly).

The scope of the New Deal is evident in the sheer number of new agencies that were created during the first Roosevelt administration, which, besides those already listed, included the Federal Emergency Relief Administration, the Rural Electrification Administration, the

Civilian Conservation Corps, the National Labor Relations Board, the Securities and Exchange Commission, the massive Works Progress Administration, and the Home Owners Loan Corporation. This last agency, which was replaced by the Federal Housing Administration in 1936, was responsible for refinancing over one million mortgages at risk of default. In the process it established the thirty-year mortgage as the standard home loan and helped to institute new lending standards among banks—appraisal criteria that tended to downgrade homes in the central city (especially those in diverse or non-white neighborhoods) and look more favorably on newer construction in the suburbs that often lay outside the official borders of the city.

Roosevelt was elected again in 1936, beating republican candidate Alf Landon in a landslide and bringing a larger Democratic majority into both the House and Senate. Yet despite massive majorities, Roosevelt faced resistance, especially as the economy once again slipped into recession. In 1937 he proposed to Congress his famous court-packing plan that would have allowed him to appoint additional justices to the Supreme Court. This was in part an obvious retaliation against the Court's rulings in 1935 and 1936 that large portions of the New Deal, including the AAA and NIRA, were unconstitutional. Congress rejected Roosevelt's plan, yet the Supreme Court also switched in favor of the New Deal, ruling, for instance, that the Social Security and National Labor Relations Acts were constitutional.

Roosevelt would go on to be reelected president twice more after 1936, but after 1938 the New Deal had effectively ended and the focus of the government shifted to the crisis in Europe. In 1939 Germany invaded Poland, and France and Britain declared war on Germany. In 1940 Italy and Germany invaded and captured France. After his reelection in 1940, Roosevelt ended American neutrality, began providing both Britain and the Soviet Union with arms and other supplies, and directed American ships to patrol Atlantic trade routes. The government also cut off supplies to Japan (an ally of Germany and Italy) by freezing Japanese assets in the United States. Japan retaliated in 1941 by bombing the naval base at Pearl Harbor, killing more than two thousand four hundred troops. The United States declared war against Japan, Germany and Italy declared war against the United States, and the country was thus fully embroiled in World War II.

NEW YORK, NY 1929–1941

NEW YORK CITY'S INFRASTRUCTURE, POLITICS, AND BASES OF SOCIAL AND POLITICAL POWER underwent momentous changes in the twelve years between the Wall Street crash on October 29, 1929, and the United States' entry into World War II. And yet New York remained a city of stark contrasts. The 1930s saw the development of major landmarks, including the Empire State and Chrysler Buildings and Rockefeller Center, as well as the nation's first public housing projects. It saw the development of major bridges between New York and New Jersey, and between Manhattan, the Bronx, and Queens, and the consolidation of the city's subway system under public auspices.

Fiorello La Guardia won the mayoral election of 1933 on a Fusion line, joining Republicans with reform Democrats. A fierce supporter of the New Deal, La Guardia circumvented the

QUICK FACTS

NEW YORK, NY **1929–1941**

MAYORS

James J. Walker	(1926–1932)
Joseph V. McKee	(1932)
John P. O'Brien	(1933)
Fiorello H. La Guardia	(1934–1945)

MAJOR INDUSTRIES AND EMPLOYERS

City of New York

Federal government

Garment manufacture

Longshoring and transportation

Printing and publishing

Food and beverage service and
  manufacture

Wholesale and retail trade

Finance and insurance

MAJOR NEWSPAPERS

Daily News

New York Post

New York Times

Herald Tribune

Journal American (merged 1936 from the
  American and *Evening Journal*)

Daily Mirror

World Telegram (beginning 1931)

New York Evening Graphic (until 1932)

PM (beginning 1940)

MAJOR EVENTS

1929: Wall Street crashes on "Black Tuesday," ushering in the Great Depression, stopping the supply of credit, and leading to bank collapses in New York and nationally over the next several years.

1930 and 1931: Chrysler and Empire State Buildings opened, respectively, altering the skyline of New York City and becoming permanent icons.

1932: Mayor Jimmy Walker resigns in a corruption scandal, and business-led reformers found the Citizens' Budget Commission, which remains a respected and influential good government watchdog organization.

1933: Fiorello La Guardia is elected mayor on a fusion ticket, leading to strong cooperation with Washington on the New Deal and dealing a strong blow to Tammany Hall, Democratic clubhouse politics.

1934: First Houses (nation's first public housing project) opens, leading the way to the national public housing program sponsored by New York Senator Robert F. Wagner in 1937: Transport Workers Union is founded, giving a strong, militant voice to workers spanning public and private employment.

1936: The Triborough Bridge opens, joining Manhattan, the Bronx, and Queens, facilitating interborough travel and access to the suburbs while also consolidating the power and reputation of the Triborough Bridge and Tunnel Authority's chairman, Robert Moses.

power of Tammany Hall (as the machine-wing of the Democratic Party was known) by drawing in federal resources and diminishing the influence of patronage. Concurrently, the city's parks commissioner—who also held two state jobs—was the powerful Robert Moses, who planned and built hundreds of playgrounds, thousands of units of housing, and hundreds of miles of highways with federal money. In so doing, Moses also established urban-suburban links and internal urban spatial patterns that entrenched patterns of segregation, and an expert-driven style of governance and accompanying institutions that were increasingly removed from democratic accountability.

GOVERNMENT AND POLITICS

The Great Depression weakened Tammany Hall. The city's budget suffered declining tax revenues, making the Tammany-controlled mayor and Board of Estimate (one of the legislative bodies at the time) unable to sustain its patronage. The fiscal crisis that ensued from the pressures of declining revenues and increasing demands for unemployment relief strengthened a longstanding business-led reform coalition. One of the coalition's organs was the Citizens' Budget Commission, a budget-watchdog group that retains a good deal of power even into the twenty-first century. Moreover, President Franklin D. Roosevelt's New Deal programs provided an alternative to locally generated patronage jobs, expanding and changing the nature of municipal government employment and the stakes of local politics along with it.

As the depression began, Mayor Jimmy Walker and the Tammany-dominated Board of Estimate sought to mitigate its effects on the city's budget by converting short-term bonds into long-term bonds. While banks allowed the city to roll over some debt, the budgets in the first two years of the decade relied on unrealistic real estate tax projections and even increased public spending, including a million-dollar allocation for unemployment relief. In 1932 Mayor Walker resigned in a corruption scandal and fled to Mexico. Joseph McKee, the president of the Board of Aldermen, filled in for a few months until a special election. John O'Brien, Tammany's candidate, won the special election and filled out Walker's term. The city's powerful banking community was able to force O'Brien to pare the city's workforce and, with it, many of the patronage jobs that had fuelled Tammany's power.

Tammany's split over O'Brien's inability or unwillingness to defy the bankers' demands enabled Fiorello La Guardia—half-Italian, half-Jewish, and a beloved congressman from East Harlem—to win the 1933 mayoral election with only 40 percent of the vote. When La Guardia came into office the city averaged more than one hundred fifty thousand evictions a year for the previous several years; nearly 40 percent of African Americans in Harlem were unemployed; more than one-third of the city's manufacturing firms had closed since 1930, or would close in the next two years; and 60 percent of public clinic visits were related to malnutrition. So-called Hoovervilles sprang up around the city, housing mainly single men—often men who left their families, no longer able to provide support.

La Guardia's alliance with President Roosevelt (who had been the governor of New York State before taking office as president in 1933) was instrumental in drawing millions of dollars in federal relief funds to the city. Beyond being the largest recipient of federal aid, New York City was a crucial site for the development of the policies that defined the New Deal. Even before New York's Senator Robert F. Wagner Sr. introduced the National Labor Relations Act in 1935 and the National Housing Act of 1937, and before the passage of the 1935 Social Security Act, New Yorkers had pioneered many of the programs that would be embodied in Roosevelt's legacy. Al Smith, governor of New York before Roosevelt, developed state-level unemployment insurance and workers' compensation insurance. Roosevelt continued in this vein, forming the Temporary Emergency Relief Administration (TERA) in 1931. TERA provided work-relief to the unemployed and, with a $25 million allocation, became a model for the Federal Emergency Relief Administration, a key element of the early New Deal. Tenement-house reformers prevailed on the city government under La Guardia to develop public housing for the working class. Using donated land and federal work-relief labor, the New York City Housing Authority opened the 122 units in First Houses in 1934 and expanded to nearly 2,000 units in several developments even before the first federal housing funds were applied three years later. By 1941 the New York Public Housing Authority had developed almost 13,000 units of housing and contributed almost a quarter of all the housing that had been developed for New York City's growing population between 1934 and the American entry into World War II.

During the depression, the development of New York's infrastructure owed at least as much to Robert Moses as it did to La Guardia or Roosevelt. More than just the city parks commissioner, Moses held the parallel post for the state government and three additional posts in the city. A tireless government reformer and administrator, he had begun to expand his power in the 1920s under Governor Smith. Though most frequently tied to the reform Republicans, Moses became close to the popular Tammany-supported Smith. By the mid-1920s Smith sought to increase the state support given to working-class and poor people and knew that the state's business had to be rationalized to make this fiscally possible. He turned to Moses, who developed an intricate knowledge of state administrative law in the process of rewriting it. As Parks Commissioner under La Guardia, Moses wrote legislation consolidating the five boroughs' parks departments into a single one (which he headed) and legislation allowing some city employees to work in state posts simultaneously. Over the course of the years 1934–1941, as Parks Commissioner— and as head of both the Triborough Bridge Authority and the State Parks Commission—Moses oversaw most of the city's projects in housing, transportation, and parks, and he transformed the city's economy and its residents' daily lives.

Moses's redevelopment activities entailed several ironies. First, they secured ongoing public support for the New Deal, which he regarded as socialistic and anathema. Second, his success rubbed off on his boss, whom he disliked; La Guardia benefited politically from Moses's bridge, park, and housing construction, and Moses's popularity accrued, as well, to the mayor's supporters, including the American Labor Party, a left-wing third party active in New York City politics during the mid-1930s. Third, while Moses connected the city to its region, his manner of doing so—with highways—fed the automobile-dependent suburbanization of the region. While New Yorkers hailed him for his accomplishments in the city, Moses was simultaneously laying the groundwork for larger demographic shifts that would ultimately harm the city's economic health and political clout.

INDUSTRY, COMMERCE, AND LABOR

The influx of federal funding largely resolved the city's fiscal crisis and put thousands of New Yorkers back to work. Nevertheless, New York City's dominant small-scale industrial sector did not recover until World War II. Its real estate industry also slumped, having been caught in a speculative hysteria at the end of the 1920s that led to a race among millionaires to raise the world's tallest building. The spires of the Chrysler and the Empire State Buildings were built, while other contenders for that title were shortened or left unbuilt, their investors chastened by the Empire State Building's high vacancy rate and dependence on public agencies' tenancies.

Rockefeller Center, a complex of office buildings on the west side of Manhattan's midtown, also depended on government tenants.

Residential real estate suffered as mass unemployment made it difficult for people to meet rents and mortgages. With almost one million people unemployed in New York State in 1931, court-ordered evictions more than tripled between 1930 and 1932, when they averaged thirty-seven thousand per month. New York City renters were likely to face multiple eviction proceedings over the course of the period between 1929 and 1941.

In spite of the real estate market, the banking industry began to stabilize as the federal government regulated it and founded several risk-spreading bodies. In 1933 Roosevelt took the United States off the gold standard, which allowed the Federal Reserve to loosen the money supply. Further, the Glass-Steagall Act of 1933 separated commercial banks from investment banks and thus limited the risks that the former could take with their depositors' money. From 1933 to 1938, several measures passed to ease the credit crisis that had precipitated the depression: Bank deposits were guaranteed by the Federal Deposit Insurance Corporation, and the development of secondary markets in mortgage debt helped to pool risk and provide mortgage guarantees. The depression, therefore, resulted in a shake-out of New York's banking industry. Though a New York City bank was among the first large bank failures in 1930, and several other banks subsequently failed in the city, others either formed or thrived during the Roosevelt era, due at least in part to its stabilization policies.

Most New Yorkers did not feel the benefits of this stabilization. And they did not take the circumstances of their privation sitting down. New York City was a center of left-wing politics, where the Socialist and Communist Parties were often rivals—and sometime collaborators—in organizing among the poor and unemployed. A rally of the unemployed, called by Communists in March 1930 in Union Square, drew thirty-five thousand people before being attacked by police. In October of the same year, another large rally convinced the city's Board of Estimate to allocate a million dollars toward unemployment relief, even in the midst of the fiscal crisis. Similarly, in 1931 and 1932 Communists organized bands of people in neighborhoods to resist evictions, keeping U.S. Marshals at bay or moving tenants back in when the law had departed. Such tactics often drew large crowds.

Public-sector labor unions formed that decades later would reshape the power base of New York City politics. Communists played an important role in their development. The city's buses and subways, schools, and relief bureaus were areas in which Communist and Communist-affiliated organizing were strong. The Transport Workers Union, for example, was led by Michael Quill, a flamboyant Fenian, sometime Communist, and key activist in the American Labor Party. Similarly, Communists helped to organize what would be the largest public employee union in the city until the 1950s, the State, County, and Municipal Workers of America. Though they were relatively few in number, Communist Party members were energetic organizers. Anti-Communist and conservative state officials attacked public unionism, and Communist involvement bolstered the conviction even among friends of labor such as La Guardia and Roosevelt that the public sector should not be unionized. Communists fared less well in New York City's major private industries. Socialist leaders of the garment workers had purged Communists from their ranks in the 1920s, and they failed to gain a strong foothold on the docks, which were controlled

The Great Depression had a devastating effect on New York City. With eviction rates skyrocketing, manufacturing firms shuttering, and crippling unemployment, many had to seek public assistance, like these people standing in a bread line beside the approach to the Brooklyn Bridge.

Source: Library of Congress

by anti-Communist Irish Catholics and the Mafia. An effort to fight mob rule on the docks, supported by Vito Marcantonio, the charismatic American Labor Party congressman from La Guardia's old East Harlem district, ran aground when its leader, Pete Panto, was murdered. Mob control of the docks persisted and deepened, and New York was free of the radicalism that characterized longshoring on the West Coast.

RACE, ETHNICITY, AND IMMIGRATION

Racial and ethnic segregation magnified New Yorkers' privation in the depression. Though at the beginning of the period African American New Yorkers composed less than 10 percent of the city's population, much of Manhattan's Central Harlem had already become identified with its large African American majority. Though Harlem taken as a whole—the area above Manhattan's 96th Street—remained ethnically diverse in the 1930s, it was largely because of the presence of overlapping but more concentrated ethnic niche neighborhoods of African Americans in Central and West Harlem, along with Finns, Puerto Ricans, Italians, and Jews in East Harlem. All were poor and working-class neighborhoods, but Central Harlem was hardest hit by unemployment because of what sociologist Roger Waldinger calls the "ethnic division of labor." African Americans were concentrated in domestic service and manual labor; 60 percent of employed black women were in the former field in 1940, ten years after the onset of the depression. Citywide, black unemployment was double that of whites, reaching 40 percent in 1934.

African Americans were not alone in hardship. Italians, who were concentrated in lower-skilled, blue-collar jobs, also fared poorly, and 20 percent were on relief during the depression.

Jews were better educated as a whole and present throughout the professions and as proprietors. But as the 1930s began, as many as 20 percent were blue-collar workers, especially concentrated in the garment trades. Second-generation Jews were widely employed as teachers. The Irish were also highly present in the blue-collar trades, but also in small businesses and, especially, in government jobs, where Tammany was a crucial supplier of ethnic niche employment. In all jobs gender segregation and niche markets also structured access. Historian Cheryl Lynn Goldberg reports that white men experienced longer spells of unemployment in part because they made themselves less available for manual labor. White women began to compete with black men for some of their service-sector jobs and, as the depression wore on, also began to compete even for the low-paid domestic work dominated by African American women. Even though domestic work was less devastated than were male-dominated industries like construction, wages fell as the supply of labor grew.

African Americans' increasing segregation in a ghetto characterized by poor and deteriorating housing and their large-scale exclusion from many areas of employment were among the causes attributed by sociologist E. Franklin Frazier to a night-long riot in Harlem in 1935. The riot, which some historians use to date the end of the Harlem Renaissance, was sparked by unfounded rumors of a police shooting of a teenager. Unlike so-called race riots in many other cities during the depression, however, New York's did not spread or last, in part because of the character of the political response. Mayor La Guardia appealed for calm, did not blame either Harlem residents or the police, and announced that he would appoint a commission, headed by Frazier, an African American, to study its causes.

Further, after the riot the newly created New York City Housing Authority accelerated plans for a housing project in Harlem. Having conducted an international architectural design competition for a planned whites-only project in Williamsburg, Brooklyn, it hired the first black graduate of the Columbia University School of Architecture to design the Harlem River Houses in 1937, which became, with Williamsburg Houses, the first federally funded public housing in the country, a distinction in spite of the projects' segregation.

La Guardia's policies, while helping to contain unrest in Harlem and give African Americans an increasing stake in politics (reflected in a near-doubling of voter registration numbers during the Depression), also scaled back Tammany's power. By converting many appointed city jobs to competitive civil service jobs, La Guardia helped to usher many Jews into relatively stable civil service employment and to deprive Tammany of its main source of patronage. While Jews had previously been present in large numbers as teachers in the public schools, they now entered all areas of government employment and became a secure constituency advocating for the expansion of regulation and social services. Together with a politicized black community—which would grow significantly in the postwar decades—Jews formed the core of a liberal alliance that would define New York City's particular brand of racially inclusive, liberal politics until the late 1960s.

See also *New York, NY 1776–1790; New York, NY 1790–1828; New York, NY 1828–1854; New York, NY 1854–1877; New York, NY 1877–1896; New York, NY 1896–1929; New York, NY 1941–1952; New York, NY 1952–1989; New York, NY 1989–2011*

JOHN KRINSKY

BIBLIOGRAPHY

Abu-Lughod, Janet L. *New York, Chicago, Los Angeles: America's Global Cities.* Minneapolis: University of Minnesota Press, 1999.

———. *Race, Space and Riots in Chicago, New York, and Los Angeles.* New York, NY: Oxford University Press, 2007.

Caro, Robert. *The Power Broker: Robert Moses and the Fall of New York.* New York, NY: Vintage Books, 1975.

Crouse, Joan M. *The Homeless Transient in the Great Depression: New York State, 1929–1941.* Albany: The State University of New York Press, 1986.

Edsforth, Ronald. *The New Deal: America's Response to the Great Depression.* Maldon, MA: Blackwell, 2000.

Freeman, Joshua B. *In Transit: The Transport Workers' Union in New York City, 1933–1966.* New York, NY: Oxford University Press, 1992.

Fuchs, Ester R. *Mayors and Money: Fiscal Policy in New York and Chicago.* Chicago, IL: University of Chicago Press, 1992.

Greenberg, Cheryl Lynn. *"Or Does It Explode?" Black Harlem in the Great Depression.* New York, NY: Oxford University Press, 1997.

Kimeldorf, Howard. *Reds or Rackets: The Making of Radical and Conservative Unions on the Waterfront.* Berkeley: University of California Press, 1992.

Maier, Mark. *City Unions: Managing Discontent in New York City.* New Brunswick, NJ: Rutgers University Press, 1987.

Naison, Mark. *Communists in Harlem During the Depression.* Urbana: University of Illinois Press, 2004.

Nelson, Bruce. *Divided We Stand: American Workers and the Struggle for Black Equality.* Princeton, NJ: Princeton University Press, 2001.

Piven, Frances Fox, and Richard A. Cloward. *Poor People's Movements: Why They Succeed, How They Fail.* New York, NY: Vintage Books, 1979.

Waldinger, Roger. *Still the Promised City? African-Americans and New Immigrants in Post-Industrial New York.* Cambridge, MA: Harvard University Press, 1999.

Wenger, Beth S. *New York Jews in the Great Depression.* New Haven, CT: Yale University Press, 1996.

CHICAGO, IL 1929–1941

AT THE BEGINNING OF THE 1930s, CHICAGO WAS IN MANY WAYS APPROACHING ITS PEAK: it was the fourth largest city in the world and the manufacturing engine and industrial transportation hub of the nation, linking the resources of the American heartland to the world. In raw numbers, the city itself had been growing in leaps and bounds for decades, welcoming a diverse group of immigrants from all regions of Europe as well as from the American South and annexing surrounding lands to grow in territory as well. As a marker of this seemingly boundless growth, the city planned the 1933 Century of Progress Exposition to mark its centennial. In the same year, the city's municipal airport at Midway Field opened, and the first traffic cruised down Lakeshore Drive not long after.

QUICK FACTS

CHICAGO, IL **1929–1941**

MAYORS

William Thompson   (1927–1931)
Anton Cermak   (1931–1933)
Frank Corr   (1933)
Edward Kelly   (1933–1947)

MAJOR INDUSTRIES AND EMPLOYERS

Steel
Meatpacking
Garment manufacture
Other manufacturing
Printing and publishing

MAJOR NEWSPAPERS

Chicago Tribune
Chicago Defender
Chicago Daily News
Daily Times
Chicago Sun
Daily Southtown

MAJOR EVENTS

1929: The St. Valentine's Day Massacre, one of the most famous murders by Chicago's infamous organized crime syndicates, leaves seven men dead. Within two years, Al Capone—who was responsible for the crime—is imprisoned for tax evasion.

1931: Chicago's most famous Progressive reformer, Jane Addams, wins the Nobel Peace Prize.

1933–1934: The Century of Progress Exposition is held downtown in Grant Park. Many of the landmark buildings in Grant Park (Adler Planetarium, Shedd Aquarium, and Soldier Field) are constructed for this event. Other major city landmarks, including the Museum of Science and Industry, Lakeshore Drive, and the Brookfield Zoo, are constructed by mid-decade.

1933: Mayor Anton Cermak, who mobilized and unified diverse European ethnic voters throughout Chicago to found the city's Democratic machine, is shot and killed in Miami in an attempted assassination of President Franklin Roosevelt.

1937: The Memorial Day Massacre at Republic Steel kills ten and wounds dozens as striking workers clash with police in the city's most violent labor unrest since the turn of the century.

By the time the Century of Progress Exposition opened in 1933, however, it had become clear that Chicago's growth would not in fact continue unabated forever. The depression hit the manufacturing heart of the city hard, as national demand for consumer and industrial goods plummeted. In a sense, Chicago had reached its plateau—its geographic extent and population have remained relatively stable since the 1920s (the city has actually shrunk a bit since midcentury, though the metropolitan area has continued to grow steadily)—but the 1930s marked a moment of political and social discontinuity as well; the decade saw both the culmination of a long process of industrialization and population growth, and a shift in trajectory.

Politics in the Second City, which had gained national notoriety for the close collaboration between city hall and organized crime during Prohibition, became known in later decades for a softer form of political corruption, that of the urban machine. The Democratic political machine forged a monopoly of local political control that would endure for decades and set up the institutional patterns of political exchange in "the city that works." At the same time, the cross-ethnic alliance that fueled this machine worked its way toward a panethnic white identity through selective cultural assimilation, political and economic incorporation through the machine and labor unions, and shared Catholic religious identity. Chicago shifted from a multicultural society organized around ethnicity and nativity to a much more polarized one whose central cleavage was race.

GOVERNMENT AND POLITICS

The decade of the "long 1930s," from 1929 to 1941, marked a sharp, durable shift in Chicago's local politics. The previous era had generally been characterized by frequent partisan rotation in office and battles between "good government" progressive reformers and deeply corrupt "boodlers," who had close ties to both organized crime and legitimate business. By the onset of World War II, however, the Democratic machine, with its ethnic white base in outlying wards of the city and patronage politics, had become the only game in town. The Democratic organization dominated local politics and maintained a tight grip on city hall without interruption for over forty years.

William "Big Bill" Thompson began his second tenure in office in 1927 and served until 1931. During his first term in office, from 1915 to 1923, he campaigned as a pro-consumer reformer; in 1927 he positioned himself as a friend of Chicago's diverse European ethnic groups, taking symbolic stands on international issues important to these immigrant communities and making appeals to newly arrived African Americans on the South Side as well. A brash and charismatic personality, he was the last Chicago mayor to rely on personal connection with voters for electoral success—as opposed to the strong organizational base of the machine. He was also the last Republican to lead the city.

In 1931 Anton Cermak, a Czech (Bohemian) immigrant who had worked his way up to become chair of the Cook County Democratic Party (CCDP), defeated Thompson in an election in which the city's first- and second-generation immigrants, largely from central, southern, and eastern Europe (though also Irish) took center stage in the local Democratic Party in an alignment that has never weakened. The electoral centrality of these groups was a two-way process: the passing of time and tighter national immigration policies saw the first generation of immigrants give way to the second (the proportion of Chicagoans born abroad diminished from about a quarter to about a sixth during the 1930s) and made a greater share of these "white ethnic" groups eligible voters, and increasing mobilization efforts by the Democratic organization made them less alienated from the political process. Cermak's political genius was organizational, rather than charismatic. He united several local factions into a coherent party, dispensing material and symbolic goods in order to court groups and solidify alliances.

Cermak's tenure at the head of the machine, however, was short-lived, as he was fatally wounded in Miami while accompanying the newly elected President Franklin Roosevelt in early 1933 (the original target of the assassination is most widely believed to have been Roosevelt, rather than Cermak, though this is a subject of recurring controversy). In the wake of

Cermak's death, the era of Irish American machine leadership began, starting with Ed Kelly as mayor and Patrick Nash as CCDP leader. Kelly served as mayor from 1933 to 1947, navigating the city and the party through the tough times of the depression and the relative boom of the later period.

Over the course of the 1930s, Democratic dominance in local and national elections helped to forge an enduring, mutually beneficial bond between local and national party organizations. Presidential and mayoral elections in the 1920s were relatively competitive in Chicago: in 1928 only 49 percent of Chicago votes were cast for presidential candidate Al Smith, and Thompson had been elected mayor the year before. By 1936 Franklin Roosevelt won 65 percent of Chicagoans' votes—an impressive total, but one that actually trailed the 82 percent won by Kelly the year before. Illinois would be closely contested in the Electoral College for decades, but typically wound up in the New Deal Democrats' column on the strength of Chicago's machine-mobilized votes. In return for this electoral support, Roosevelt channeled the national resources of the Public Works Administration (PWA) and Works Progress Administration (WPA) through Kelly and Nash's organization, bypassing the typical administrative procedures of the relief programs. Fueling a local machine with largely federal resources (Cermak and Kelly both faced a tax revolt and chronic shortages to pay civil servants) was an innovative adjustment to modern conditions by the Chicago machine.

In creating and solidifying a Democratic machine politics based on a cross-ethnic working-class alliance, Chicago in the 1930s was simultaneously typical and distinctive. The partisan shift toward the Democrats at this moment was hardly unique, as the ethnic white working class shifted in huge numbers to the Democratic Party of Al Smith and Franklin Roosevelt in many cities across America from 1928 to 1936. This demographic group, which overlapped substantially with organized labor, was the electoral backbone of the New Deal alliance for a generation. African Americans in Chicago and elsewhere also became Democratic stalwarts locally and nationally at this time, and that relationship has proved even more enduring despite being fraught with tension and doing little to remedy the material deprivation of most African Americans' lives. On the other hand, most big-city machines were fading away at this time in the face of continued efforts at reform and the continued growth of the national government. In Chicago, however, this was the moment in which the machine was established, and it would prove to be resilient over decades.

INDUSTRY, COMMERCE, AND LABOR

Chicago's local economy, closely tied to its role as a national industrial and transportation hub, followed, and magnified, trends in the national economy as a whole, declining swiftly during the onset of the Great Depression and remaining weak until the boom of the war years, when it rebounded particularly well. As industrial production declined, layoffs left Chicago particularly hard hit during the early years of the depression; from 1929 to 1933 home foreclosures in the city increased fivefold, and many city parks were transformed into Hooverville camps, which were frequent sites of conflict between police and the homeless. By 1932 unemployment in the city had reached 40 percent, outpacing the national average of about 25 percent, with rates even higher among African Americans and other marginalized groups. Between 1934 and 1937, approximately one million Cook County residents received government relief.

The end of prosperity also meant an end to the housing boom of the 1920s. While Chicago's population increased dramatically over the course of the 1920s, with tens of thousands of new home starts a year, the 1930s saw a drastic reduction in residential expansion. In that decade, fewer than two thousand new homes were built each year, and overall population growth stagnated, though the city would reach its maximum population after World War II.

To some extent, hardship was eased by public works spending. The early 1930s saw the construction of many of the city's downtown landmark buildings—the Shedd Aquarium, Adler Planetarium, and Soldier Field—in preparation for the Century of Progress Exhibition in 1933, as well as the Merchandise Mart, then the world's largest building. Many of the city's parks were also built or refurbished through the PWA and WPA. Federal funding flowed into the Democratic machine's coffers, serving the dual function of relief for workers and patronage for the party.

The depression hit the city's business elite quite hard, most of whom did not recover until war mobilization spurred national and global demand for the heavy manufactured goods and food products that were the city's lifeblood. While manufacturing was the engine of Chicago's development, its role as a national center of financial services underpinning the nation's vast agricultural production was also weakened during this period with the passage of the Agricultural Marketing Act of 1929, which brought the federal government into commodities markets as a major buyer, pushing the Chicago markets (such as the Chicago Board of Trade and the Chicago Mercantile Exchange) out of the central role in agricultural commerce they had occupied for decades.

While the Kelly administration sought to navigate the depression with strategic use of federal largesse, the labor and industrial climate in Chicago was generally one of confrontation. With the passage of the National Labor Relations Act in 1935 (the "Wagner Act") and its later being upheld by the Supreme Court, unionization rates skyrocketed across the country, and Chicago was a notable hotbed of union organizing activity. The Congress of Industrial Organizations made huge membership gains, particularly among the large steel and meatpacking industries of the South Side, though the vast majority of union labor was still affiliated with the American Federation of Labor.

In 1937 violent conflict erupted between police and striking workers at Republic Steel on the city's southeast side. In what became known as the Memorial Day Massacre, ten steelworkers were killed, and thirty wounded, by police. In the aftermath of the strike, a federal investigation found that the blame for the violence fell with the police. The Kelly administration reversed its typically pro-management position and began to allow strikes in the city. In the ensuing decades, the city administration was typically sympathetic to labor, its main electoral base.

In a concurrent and related development, Saul Alinsky and his allies began the Back of the Yards Neighborhood Council in 1939, which became the prototypical community organization, joining with radical labor and Roman Catholic leaders to address community needs. These two developments—community organizing and growing labor power—would shape the patterns of conflict and conflict resolution in the city and nation for decades to come.

RACE, ETHNICITY, AND IMMIGRATION

Chicago in the 1930s was marked by the acceleration of two parallel but seemingly paradoxical sociological phenomena: (1) the construction of a common racial identity between mostly Catholic white ethnic immigrant groups, and (2) a deepening racial divide between white and black Chicagoans, whose spatial separation remained stark. Over the course of the 1930s, these developments were in a holding pattern, as economic stagnation and barriers to immigration slowed the influx of all groups, including immigrants and African Americans, that had led to Chicago's rapid growth in the preceding decades. Disinvestment in the city's poorer neighborhoods over the course of the decade and gains made by the predominantly white working class, who benefitted most from New Deal social policies and the material benefits of the local machine, also set the stage for the increasingly divergent outcomes among racial groups in the postwar era.

Chicago's polyglot community of European "second-wave" immigrants came of political and civic age in the 1920s and 1930s. Socially, members of these groups sought to both "Americanize"—effectively transforming themselves from members of the Polish, Italian, or Lithuanian "races"—and adopt the newer, more expansive "white" racial identity. At the same time, these first- and second-generation Americans also sought to preserve their cultural identities, often supported by ethnically based Catholic parishes. These same Catholic institutions that sought to preserve distinctive European identities, however, also served as bridges between these groups and as integrative institutions in the city, linking their parishioners to both the growing labor movement and local politics.

The incorporation of these immigrant groups into the American white racial category was spurred by the labor unions' efforts to organize along class lines, a process that grew by leaps and bounds in the late 1930s. These cross-ethnic alliances further eroded the notion of distinctive and antagonistic European identities that had been highly conflictual just a decade before, and they strengthened race-based working-class solidarity.

Politically, ethnic whites were the electoral backbone of the consolidated Democratic machine built by Czech-born Anton Cermak and maintained by his Irish American successors—wresting control of city politics from the "old-stock" northern Europeans. While the machine did maintain racial and ethnic hierarchies in city politics and the distribution of material goods, it also served as an integrative institution, providing benefits for some and opportunities for advancement for others, and resolved for decades some questions of governance in a modern multicultural city.

Between 1910 and 1930, the growing African American populations of most northern cities had become increasingly isolated. Chicago's pattern of development was an extreme example of this phenomenon: by 1930 Chicago was the most racially segregated city in America, and this segregation deepened throughout the decade. Though the famous Chicago School of sociology identified "ethnic enclaves" of many varieties around the city, white ethnic groups were in fact far less residentially separated from each other than racial groups were, and the dominant racial divide was between white and black. There was (and still is) a small Chinatown just west of the Loop, and small *colonias* of Mexicans developed in industrial neighborhoods on the South and West Sides—though Mexicans were generally far more integrated into white neighborhoods than were African Americans. As the city's African American population grew, however, it also became a political force that downtown elites could not afford to ignore. While at first the black electorate supported Republicans such as Bill Thompson, Chicago's African American community realigned with the Democratic Party of Roosevelt over the course of the 1930s. By the end of this decade, the black South Side had been effectively incorporated into the machine as a submachine headed by then-alderman William Dawson, before he took his seat in the U.S. House of Representatives.

While African American Chicagoans gained and held descriptive representation within the machine and in Congress early on, they were effectively subordinated junior partners within the institution. As local politics shifted to a monopoly on power by the Democrats, black leaders opted to remain within the machine in this subordinate role rather than make stronger demands for substantive goods. In doing so, they effectively maintained their own personal positions and brought home meager benefits for their constituents, but this arrangement also served to exacerbate the differences in socioeconomic outcomes among racial groups.

See also *Chicago, IL 1854–1877; Chicago, IL 1877–1896; Chicago, IL 1896–1929; Chicago, IL 1941–1952; Chicago, IL 1952–1989; Chicago, IL 1989–2011*

THOMAS OGORZALEK

BIBLIOGRAPHY

Cohen, Lizabeth. *Making a New Deal: Industrial Workers in Chicago, 1919–1939*. New York, NY: Cambridge University Press, 1990.

Gosnell, Harold. *Machine Politics: Chicago Model*. Chicago, IL: University of Chicago Press, 1937.

———. *Negro Politicians: The Rise of Negro Politics in Chicago*. Chicago, IL: University of Chicago Press, 1935.

Newell, Barbara. *Chicago and the Labor Movement: Metropolitan Unionism in the 1930s*. Urbana: University of Illinois Press, 1961.

Pinderhughes, Dianne. *Race and Ethnicity in Chicago Politics*. Urbana: University of Illinois Press, 1987.

PHILADELPHIA, PA 1929–1941

FOR MOST PHILADELPHIANS, THE GREAT DEPRESSION WAS A SHATTERING EXPERIENCE that called into question the basic structures of society. Unemployment surged to 40 percent or higher, ruining people's finances, causing them to lose their homes, and undermining their family stability. Unlike Detroit and Pittsburgh, which depended heavily on a single industry, Philadelphia's diverse manufacturing base initially lessened the depression's blow. But hard times could not be kept at bay, and the depression led Philadelphians to challenge the Republican Party that had dominated their city's politics for generations. In the process, they built a shaky but substantial Democratic coalition that existed largely to support Franklin D. Roosevelt. Immigration to the city slowed to a trickle with the

PHILADELPHIA, PA **1929–1941**

MAYORS

Harry Mackey	(1928–1932)
Joseph Hampton Moore	(1932–1936)
Samuel Davis Wilson	(1936–1939)
George Connell	(1939)
Robert Lamberton	(1940–1941)
Bernard Samuel	(1941–1952)

MAJOR INDUSTRIES AND EMPLOYERS

Nondurable goods manufacturing
(textiles, apparel, food)

Durable goods manufacturing (metals,
furniture, machinery)

Clerical/secretarial work

Paper and publishing

Sales (wholesale and retail)

MAJOR NEWSPAPERS

Philadelphia Evening Bulletin

Philadelphia Inquirer

Philadelphia Public Ledger

Philadelphia Record

Philadelphia Tribune

MAJOR EVENTS

1930: Bankers Trust Company fails, bringing the Great Depression home to thousands of Philadelphians.

1932: Democratic coalition begins to coalesce under the leadership of John B. (Jack) Kelly, Albert Greenfield, and J. David Stern.

1933: Unemployment reaches its height at 40 percent or higher in many communities.

1936: President Franklin Roosevelt, at the height of his popularity, carries Philadelphia with some 62 percent of the vote.

1940: Federal defense spending leads to Philadelphia firms receiving approximately $1 billion in contracts, which finally ameliorates unemployment and pulls the city out of the Great Depression.

economic downturn, and housing as well as jobs emerged as critical issues for the city's racial and ethnic minorities.

GOVERNMENT AND POLITICS

Philadelphia was known as a politically conservative city in the late nineteenth and early twentieth centuries. Its mayors, J. Hampton Moore in particular, generally believed in a laissez-faire approach that limited government's role to setting the rules and getting out of the way so business could make money and lead society. Such views matched well the tenor of the 1920s, but the onset and deepening of the Great Depression led many Philadelphians to find that approach woefully inadequate. In the stony soil of the depression, the Democrats began to grow a coalition that finally took power two decades later.

When the depression first began in 1929, the city had limited official reaction to the want of its citizens. Philadelphia had stopped providing public outdoor relief in 1879, and there was little will to begin any programs. Instead, Mayor Harry Mackey appointed the banker H. Gates

Lloyd to head a relief committee in 1930 that identified the "worthy poor" and provided them with shelter, hot breakfasts, and vouchers for food and fuel. The Lloyd committee and its successor, the Bureau of Unemployment Relief, ultimately disbursed $14 million raised from private donations and, later, contributions from the city of Philadelphia and the state of Pennsylvania, but the money ran out in June 1932. Subsequent mass marches on City Hall, protests by unions as well as the Communist Party, and public testimony that Philadelphians were scavenging for food on the docks and some were starving led the state to provide more assistance.

As the city's economic problems worsened, J. Hampton Moore, who embodied the laissez-faire political worldview, won the mayoral race in 1931. At a time when reform candidates were capturing other cities, Moore received 92 percent of the vote. This was due in part to his politics and in part to the fact that the Republican Party dominated Philadelphia, as it was run relatively efficiently by the political machine built up by the Vare brothers (most notably William Vare), the construction contractors and politicians from South Philadelphia. Once in office, Moore announced that there was no depression in the city and that people inhabiting dilapidated houses were "merely living within their means." Over his four years in office, the city refused to contribute to relief for the unemployed and in fact fired three thousand five hundred city workers to save $12 million in salaries. Moore and other conservative political leaders so despised the New Deal that they at first refused to participate in any of its programs, and the city always contributed as little as it could to federal projects.

Such intransigence opened space for the moribund local Democratic Party to rebuild itself. While Moore won the 1931 mayoral race by an overwhelming margin, Franklin D. Roosevelt captured a remarkable 45 percent of the city's vote a year later, although he lost the state of Pennsylvania. His promise of a New Deal appealed to thousands of Philadelphians who needed government assistance. And with the contractor John B. "Jack" Kelly, businessman Albert Green-field, and newspaper publisher J. David Stern leading the way, the local Democrats finally made themselves viable and even helped elect George H. Earle III as governor in 1935. He was the first Democrat to hold that position in forty years.

Federal programs greatly boosted the Democrats' appeal. The Works Progress Administration (WPA) and Civilian Conservation Corps employed tens of thousands of people to build the city's airport and refurbish its schools, the National Youth Administration provided health screenings for children, and the Home Owners' Loan Corporation (HOLC) helped thousands of Philadelphians keep their homes. Working-class people flocked to the Democratic Party, more than tripling its registration numbers to a total of 364,259 (only 86,000 behind the Republicans). Philadelphia's largest racial and ethnic groups—Jews, African Americans, Italians, and Irish—increasingly shifted their allegiance to the Democrats in the 1930s, and Roosevelt carried the city and by extension the state in 1936, 1940, and 1944.

Although Roosevelt did well in the city, other Democratic candidates could not yet break through in the 1930s. Jack Kelly ran a close race but lost by thirty thousand votes to the Democrat-turned-Republican S. Davis Wilson in 1935, and Robert White lost to Robert Lamberton by a similar amount four years later. Still, the strength of the New Deal meant that in the mid-1930s Wilson did accept WPA money and even helped bring the Democratic National Convention to Philadelphia in 1936. But at the end of the decade, Lamberton turned away federal funds and the Republicans, aided by internal divisions in the Democratic Party, resolidified their hold on city politics. Democrats did not reclaim the mayor's office until Joseph Clark became mayor in 1952.

INDUSTRY, COMMERCE, AND LABOR

Philadelphia in the late 1920s still enjoyed a strong economy, although even without the Great Depression, clouds lurked on the horizon. In 1927 the city ranked third in the United States in both wealth and the value of products produced. The textile industry was the city's largest, employing some ninety thousand people, but Philadelphia also played a large role in the production of apparel, metals, chemicals, railroad cars, and electronic equipment. It was the second largest sugar refiner in the world and a national leader in printing and publishing. The Delaware River offered the largest freshwater port on the Atlantic, and a well-developed rail network facilitated the distribution of goods. Rather than being dominated by a single industry, the city had a diverse economic base that cushioned many residents from the worst of the depression in its first few years. Yet business leaders worried that the city's industries had peaked. The proportion of the population working in manufacturing had dropped from about half in 1890 to under a third by 1930. Some of these workers found clerical positions in the city's burgeoning service economy, but in Kensington, South Philadelphia, and other dense working-class communities, unemployment periodically reached 30 percent before the depression even began.

When the full weight of the depression hit Philadelphia in the early 1930s, it devastated the manufacturing and financial sectors of the city's economy. Between 1929 and 1933 business activity fell by a third and manufacturing output by half. Major employers such as Cramp's Shipyard, Baldwin Locomotive, Brill, Budd, Disston, and Philco either closed their doors or laid off thousands. Smaller concerns, especially in textiles and garments, had an even more difficult time. Some fifty banks, including Albert Greenfield's Bankers Trust Company with one hundred thousand depositors and $35 million in deposits, and nearly two thousand savings and loan societies collapsed. Philadelphians, many of whom had lost their jobs, found their life savings swept away.

Unemployment presented the greatest problem to most Philadelphians. A survey before the stock market crashed in October 1929 found that 10 percent of the city's workers were unemployed, with the problem concentrated in industrial areas. That number grew to 15 percent in 1930 and hit its peak when 40 percent were unemployed and another 20 percent were underemployed in 1932–1933. Per capita income fell to half what it had been before the depression began. Black Philadelphians were hit hardest, with some communities experiencing 50 percent unemployment. Women tended to have an easier time than men in finding employment, chiefly because they often worked in service jobs or the low-paying garment industry. Overall, unemployment was a persistent problem for a decade: as late as 1940, despite federal programs, 20 percent of Philadelphians were looking for work. Across the city, people grew accustomed to soup kitchen lines and shantytowns, known as Hoovervilles, springing up on vacant land.

Hard times led to a surge in working-class activism. Marches on City Hall, some led by the Communist Party, roiled the city, especially after Mayor Moore used the police to violently repress them. Other workers sought to organize unions—no mean feat in a city known as "the graveyard of unionism"—in response to the dire economic circumstances that saw even those with jobs have to work longer hours for lower pay. Strikes became common at employers such as Aberle Hosiery Mill and Exide. And while Philadelphia witnessed less violence than other large cities like Chicago and Detroit, the use of sit-down strikes (where workers took over the plant and refused to leave) made many middle-class observers fear anarchy's approach. In the past, Philadelphia employers had crushed unionism with the police, hired thugs, and legal injunctions, but the 1930s offered a different context. Workers knew that the National Labor Relations Act of 1935 and Pennsylvania's subsequent "Little New Deal" protected their rights to organize. Moreover, the new Congress of Industrial Organizations (CIO) pushed a militant industrial unionism that brought tens of thousands of Philadelphia's workers into the fold in 1936 and 1937. By 1939 the CIO had one hundred thousand members in the metropolitan area, and unions overall counted some two hundred fifty thousand people.

While unions helped some people, it took World War II contracts to pull Philadelphia out of the economic doldrums. With war looming in Europe and the Pacific, the federal government placed some $1 billion in war contracts in Philadelphia in 1940. Production in the city's factories shot up by 33 percent as Baldwin Locomotive began building light tanks, Brill produced gun carriages, Bendix made airplane instruments, and the textile and apparel industries turned out blankets, uniforms, and many other goods. Employment climbed quickly, finally ending a decade of joblessness. In fact, by late 1940 business writers, noting rising industrial production and the enlistment of tens of thousands of men in the armed forces, worried that Philadelphia would soon have a shortage of workers. Within a few years women and African Americans, who usually had to take the lowest-paying jobs, happily filled the void. World War II revitalized the city's economy, but it was unclear to most Philadelphians whether the good times would continue once the conflict ended.

RACE, ETHNICITY, AND IMMIGRATION

Philadelphia never experienced the levels of immigration that shaped New York City and Chicago. Still, in 1930 nearly one in five Philadelphians was foreign-born and one in three had at least one foreign-born parent. The largest of these groups (combining immigrants and first-generation Americans) were Russian (one hundred ninety-one thousand, generally Eastern European Jews), Irish (one hundred eighty-five thousand), Italian (one hundred eighty-one thousand), Polish (one hundred forty-four thousand), and German (one hundred thirty-one thousand). African Americans represented the other large population, accounting for approximately two hundred twenty thousand residents. The bad economy of the 1930s, along with changes in federal immigration law, meant that Philadelphia attracted few new residents over the decade. In fact, the city lost some twenty thousand people, although the black population climbed to two hundred fifty thousand. That meant that in 1940 Philadelphia's foreign-born population fell to 15 percent while its African American population climbed from 11.3 to 13 percent.

Although the built-up area of Philadelphia had expanded to the west and north, most immigrants and their families lived in the old city between the Delaware and Schuylkill Rivers and south of Allegheny Avenue. The Irish and Germans tended to be spread out across the city, while Italians were more concentrated in South Philadelphia, Jews in North and West Philadelphia, and Poles in industrial areas such as Port Richmond and Manayunk. The city's major African American community began in South Philadelphia not far from Center City, but by the 1930s had branched out to lower North Philadelphia and northern West Philadelphia. Segregation shaped the experience of African Americans' more than that of any other group, and they routinely had to take older, rundown properties as better-off Philadelphians of European ancestry moved into newer homes.

Along with jobs, housing was one of the most vital issues for racial and ethnic minorities in the 1930s. Studies showed that some eighty thousand houses, mostly on the edge of Center City and occupied by African Americans and recent immigrants, were substandard, and some even lacked running water. A horrific tenement collapse in December 1936 that killed six black Philadelphians highlighted the problems facing the city and led to a push for federal money for public housing. That money helped build a few projects such as the Hill Creek, James Weldon Johnson, Tasker, and Richard Allen Homes that added 2,859 new dwellings to the city's housing stock. But two problems plagued public housing from the start. The first was the issue of race, namely that white communities fought any housing projects that promised to desegregate their neighborhoods. The second was the anti–New Deal local Republican Party that tried to make any public housing cheaply and turned down funds when politically possible. In 1940 city leaders rejected $19 million in federal aid for housing, making Philadelphia the only city to say no to Washington. A program that could have helped Philadelphia's racial and ethnic minorities never gained much traction.

Despite the problems in housing and pervasive unemployment, the Great Depression and New Deal did energize the politics of Philadelphia's minorities. The city's largest minority populations—African Americans, Jews, Italians, and Irish—had voted strongly Republican for decades. But Al Smith's run for president in 1928 laid the groundwork for an electoral shift that made Roosevelt viable in the city in 1932 and then helped him win in the next three races. FDR's personal popularity certainly helped, but voters more frequently pointed to government programs such as the WPA and the HOLC that provided them with jobs and helped save their homes as the reason for their Democratic votes. Such Democratic support generally ran shallow, however, rarely extending beyond the presidential election. Moreover, the Democratic coalition had deep racial tensions over jobs and housing from the start, which persistently threatened to pull the new tenuous multiethnic alliance apart.

See also *Philadelphia, PA 1776–1790; Philadelphia, PA 1790–1828; Philadelphia, PA 1828–1854; Philadelphia, PA 1854–1877; Philadelphia, PA 1877–1896; Philadelphia, PA 1896–1929; Philadelphia, PA 1941–1952; Philadelphia, PA 1952–1989; Philadelphia, PA 1989–2011*

JAMES WOLFINGER

BIBLIOGRAPHY

Bauman, John. *Public Housing, Race, and Renewal: Urban Planning in Philadelphia, 1920–1974.* Philadelphia, PA: Temple University Press, 1987.

Licht, Walter. *Getting Work: Philadelphia, 1840–1950*. Cambridge, MA: Harvard University Press, 1992.

Miller, Fredric, Morris Vogel, and Allen Davis. *Philadelphia Stories: A Photographic History, 1920–1960*. Philadelphia, PA: Temple University Press, 1988.

———. *Still Philadelphia: A Photographic History, 1890–1940*. Philadelphia, PA: Temple University Press, 1983.

Ryan, Francis. *AFSCME's Philadelphia Story: Municipal Workers and Urban Power in the Twentieth Century*. Philadelphia, PA: Temple University Press, 2010.

Scranton, Philip, and Walter Licht. *Work Sights: Industrial Philadelphia, 1890–1950*. Philadelphia, PA: Temple University Press, 1986.

Simon, Roger. *Philadelphia: A Brief History*. University Park: Pennsylvania Historical Association, 2003.

Weigley, Russell, ed. *Philadelphia: A 300-Year History*. New York, NY: W.W. Norton & Company, 1982.

Wolfinger, James. *Philadelphia Divided: Race and Politics in the City of Brotherly Love*. Chapel Hill: University of North Carolina Press, 2007.

DETROIT, MI 1929–1941

THE YEARS FROM 1929 TO 1941 SAW DETROIT BECOME ONE OF THE MOST IMPORTANT CITIES in America, and the world, as it became the country's manufacturing hub. In 1929 almost half of the nation's automotive workers lived in Detroit, at that time the fourth largest city in the country. During this decade, labor and race were the most important political and economic issues that the city and its leaders faced, in part because the Great Depression devastated Detroit's finances as well as the quality of life of its citizens. Detroit become ground zero in the labor movement, and the creation of the United Auto Workers (UAW) eventually gave workers an opportunity to negotiate with management for increased salary, better working conditions, and increased benefits.

GOVERNMENT AND POLITICS

Between 1920 and 1940 Detroit's population grew 63 percent, and this growth came with significant political challenges. The city struggled under the weight of corruption and the growing demands of its citizenry.

In 1918, to make city government more accountable and less corrupt, Detroit citizens approved a new city charter that mandated nonpartisan elections, a "strong" mayor able to appoint commission members, and a significantly smaller city council (from forty-two members elected in districts to nine elected at-large). Corruption in the city was rife, particularly before the reform. After the reform, gangs continued to be a significant problem as many were often either in league with, or in many cases *were,* police officers. Approximately 33 percent of the police academy class of 1926 either had been dismissed or were forced to resign by 1932.

QUICK FACTS

DETROIT, MI **1929–1941**

MAYORS

John C. Lodge	(1927–1929)
Charles Bowles	(1930)
Frank C. Murphy	(1930–1933)
Frank Couzens	(1933–1938)
Richard Reading	(1938–1940)
Edward Jeffries	(1940–1948)

MAJOR INDUSTRIES AND EMPLOYERS

Automotive industry

MAJOR NEWSPAPERS

Detroit News
Detroit Free Press
Detroit Times

MAJOR EVENTS

1929: The Great Depression profoundly shapes Detroit's political and economic context; over 50 percent of the city's population is placed on public relief rolls by the mid-1930s.

1930: The Communist Party organizes a protest against unemployment that draws fifty thousand people downtown.

1935: United Auto Workers (UAW) is founded, increasing the wages and quality of life for tens of thousands of Detroit automotive workers.

1937: Members of Ford Motor Company's internal security department attack UAW organizers pushing for better wages and shorter hours in The Battle of the Overpass. The clash makes headlines around the world, generating support for the union.

1941: Ford recognizes the UAW.

In 1927 the Good Citizens League (formed in 1912 with the express purpose of ending corruption) ran John C. Lodge for mayor. Lodge, whose knowledge of the city was formidable given his previous experience on the common council, won. By 1930 citizens felt that the reforms enacted in 1918 had not worked, blaming the Good Citizens League among others. Lodge was a victim of anti-League sentiment and lost in 1930 to Charles Bowles. Yet the election of Bowles did nothing to reduce the tide of violence. Indeed, some felt that he was part of the problem and attempted to recall him. The League led this effort, and its support caused auto magnate Henry Ford to come to Bowles's support, unsuccessfully. Judge Frank C. Murphy replaced Bowles in the succeeding election.

Murphy's mayoral reign was marked by attempts to modernize Detroit's law enforcement efforts and wrestle with the poverty and misery caused by the Great Depression by shifting millions of city dollars to poverty relief. Under Murphy's reign and the leadership of police commissioner James Watkins, the police force shrank in size but became much more efficient and law-abiding. The economy was another issue.

By 1931 almost 33 percent of the city's population had neither income nor any means of visible support. The effect this had on city coffers was catastrophic. By the time Murphy entered office, the city's debt had increased to $255 million. Furthermore, because the budget itself was fixed, the proportion devoted to debt service grew from 21.6 percent in 1930 to 42.5 percent in

1933. Finally, a combination of shoddy budgetary procedures—the result of city officials being in the habit of short-term borrowing and lax tax collection—significantly exacerbated Detroit's fiscal crisis.

In this political and economic context, the Common Council and the mayor clashed. Mayor Murphy urged a combination of efforts to force poor Detroit residents to leave the city and to provide assistance for Detroiters who decided (or had no choice other than) to stay. The mayor went so far as to suggest that residents plant gardens in their backyards in order to deal with the diminished food supply. Simultaneously, he pursued radical means to reduce Detroit's debt burden. He took the unprecedented step of getting city department heads to agree without amendments to an austere spending plan for fiscal year 1931 that slashed the city's operating budget. To give some sense of how deep the cuts were, the total expenditures of the Department of Public Works saw its operating budget drop from $25.5 million to $4.9 million. In 1932 the Department of Health eliminated dental and medical services for school-aged Detroit children. At the same time, Murphy stressed that welfare relief continue, a propitious decision given the fact that Detroit's welfare rolls were the highest they had ever been in the city's history.

Murphy recognized that the problems his city faced were not solely Detroit problems. Inasmuch as the Ford Motor Company formerly employed many of the Detroiters that were now on the welfare rolls, it was complicit. Furthermore, because many of the automotive plants were located in the county, but outside the city, Murphy argued that the problem of unemployment was a metropolitan, rather than a city, one. However, neither the county nor the state was willing to contribute the resources required to help Detroit deal with the economic crisis, in part because of structural hurdles (the county required a two-thirds majority to centralize relief efforts) and in part because politicians outside of the city believed that Detroit's central problem was actually inefficient government. Murphy's pleas to private foundations fell on similarly deaf ears.

Murphy was forced to go to Washington, arguing that it was the federal government's responsibility to assist cities. Convening the first-ever national conference of mayors for this purpose (itself an outgrowth of a statewide conference of mayors Murphy chaired in May 1932), he sought to invoke a tide of public opinion to support what would in effect be the first attempt to create a direct relationship between the federal government and cities. A year later the conference became a permanent organization, and Murphy was named its first president.

The election of Franklin Delano Roosevelt changed the political context of Detroit in two important ways. First, Roosevelt was more amenable to directly disbursing aid to cities than Herbert Hoover had been. Although while mayor, Murphy was not able to get Roosevelt to deal with Detroit's issues directly, in 1934 the president oversaw the passage of the Municipal Debt Readjustment Act, which provided some relief to hard-hit cities. The second political change that came as a result of Roosevelt's election was the election of Detroit's youngest mayor, Frank Couzens, formerly president of the common council. In April 1933, President Roosevelt appointed Detroit Mayor Frank Murphy governor-general of the Philippines, causing Couzens to become mayor.

As mayor, Couzens had to contend with the growing divide between wealthy and poor Detroit citizens. But by the time he was elected in 1933, he was overtaken by national events, and although some credit him for putting Detroit back on its feet financially and politically, in the major books written about early-twentieth-century Detroit, he appears as less than a footnote. Indeed, Father Coughlin—a lightning rod of a Catholic preacher with his own local radio station that reached ten million listeners a week—was far more influential nationally and locally, preaching anti-Communist rhetoric at the same time as he blasted Wall Street bankers for causing the depression. Couzens was perhaps best known for helping to oversee the plan that Murphy created to deal with Detroit debt, a plan that called for a moratorium on debt payments.

Couzens' successor, Richard Reading, was a very different mayor than either Couzens or Murphy. Whereas both Couzens (particularly as president of the common council) and Murphy had expressed strong support for the premise that the good of Detroit citizens should come before other interests, Reading acted almost purely out of self-interest. Previously the city clerk, Reading argued that his salary did not befit his responsibilities as mayor. Naming his son executive secretary, Reading earned the nickname "Double Dip" Dick because he supplemented his income by taking a cut of various city deals (both legal and illegal). Reading almost singlehandedly reversed the gains Murphy had made in law enforcement, opening top jobs in the police department to open bidding. Running the numbers racket from his office, a former Reading girlfriend who committed suicide revealed his activities in her suicide note, indicting him and several others (135 all told, including 80 police officers). Although he wasn't sentenced—police incompetence led to his acquittal—he was voted out of office in 1940 and replaced by Edward Jeffries.

INDUSTRY, COMMERCE, AND LABOR

By 1929 Detroit was defined by the automotive industry. Ford and General Motors (GM) were the two largest employers. But as noted above, when the country was hit by the Great Depression, the automotive industry suffered significantly. The automobile was the lynchpin of American industry—it was responsible for one out of every six or seven jobs nationwide. And when the economy crashed, the automobile industry and Detroit were affected disproportionately. By November 1929 over two hundred thousand people in Michigan were out of work, and between 1929 and 1930 the automotive industry alone lost more than one hundred twenty thousand jobs. By January 1931 one out of every three families in Detroit—some one hundred twenty-five thousand residents—had no visible means of support. Further, because individuals were out of work they saved the little money they had. Their rational decision to save rather than spend money had even more harmful effects on the economy as this behavior was reproduced up the income scale.

Two phenomena increased as a result of the jump in unemployment. The first was bootlegging. In the absence of gainful employment, a number of Detroiters—particularly from white ethnic groups—looked to bootlegging to replace and in some cases supplement gainful income. Almost 1.2 million gallons of liquor made its way to Detroit by way of Windsor, Ontario. But bootlegging was accompanied by high levels of inter-gang violence. Indeed, the crime and gang warfare (especially that connected with the Purple Gang) associated with bootlegging was so vicious that it was one of the primary reasons Frank Murphy was elected mayor.

The second was growing union support. Before the stock market crash of 1929, industrial productivity was at its highest point. And although unions had begun to organize, government at all levels sided with management. Police officers and corporate gangs routinely broke strikes. Workers were forced to sign "yellow dog" contracts that specified that they could be fired if they attempted to join a union. After the crash, however, the federal government strengthened the rights of labor to organize. The passage of the Norris-LaGuardia Act in 1932 made it illegal to force workers to sign "yellow dog" contracts. The passage of the National Industrial Recovery Act in 1933 established a forty-hour work week along with a minimum wage and made employer harassment of unions illegal. The passage of the National Labor Relations Act two years later granted workers the right to collective bargaining. But these rights did not trickle down to Detroit workers immediately. As late as 1936, a year after a young Walter Reuther returned to Detroit from a sojourn in Russia, auto workers had enough organizing power that almost thirty thousand GM workers were on strike, but not enough for Detroit auto workers to start their own union—over 90 percent of Detroit Ford workers in 1935 voted against the establishment of a union. Union victories over Chrysler and GM meant that two of what came to be known as the Big Three were now union companies. But Ford did not relent, causing skirmishes between union supporters and Ford strikebreakers, with the most infamous of these being the 1937 Battle of the Overpass. Only in 1941, after more than fifty thousand auto workers walked out of the River Rouge Plant (after all of the company's legal and nonlegal attempts to prevent unionization), were workers finally able to organize at Ford.

RACE, ETHNICITY, AND IMMIGRATION

As Detroit became a hub for industrial labor, it also became a central hub for immigration. Irish, Italian, Polish, and German immigrants (among others) swiftly found homes in the city. It was often the members of these ethnic groups who formed the various bootlegging gangs that sprang up in response to Prohibition and the Great Depression—the Purple Gang, for example, was Jewish. But when the United States instituted strict immigration quotas as a result of World War I, foreign immigration declined.

In 1910 there were fewer than six thousand black men and women in Detroit. But African Americans began to arrive in Detroit in large numbers, and just ten years later there were twenty times as many, with black men and women attracted to the North by the promise of increased economic opportunity and freedom. In 1930, 39 percent of black males in Detroit worked in the automotive industry, compared to 9 percent of American-born whites and 17 percent of foreign-born whites. Ford in particular employed a significant number of black workers. In part this was because Ford had a sophisticated program designed to employ both whites and African Americans, using ministers to screen potential job candidates. But it was also due to the work of the Detroit Urban League and other black professional organizations. However, while the treatment blacks received in Detroit was much better than that which they had received in the South, they were rarely hired to perform the same jobs as their white counterparts. Furthermore, they lived in substandard housing (particularly on Detroit's East Side), a dynamic compounded by government policy that purposely devalued black residential areas. And as the number of black residents increased, the number of threats they faced from the general population increased as well. Although Ford employed black as well as white ethnic Detroit residents as strikebreakers, the River Rouge strike that finally broke Ford's anti-union stance was only possible because white union leaders were able to successfully change the attitudes of white workers (who, against UAW regulations, discriminated against black workers) as black civil rights leaders saw the benefit of union membership.

See also *Detroit, MI 1896–1929; Detroit, MI 1941–1952; Detroit, MI 1952–1989*

LESTER SPENCE

BIBLIOGRAPHY

Conot, Robert E. *American Odyssey*. New York, NY: Morrow, 1974.
Fine, Sidney. *Frank Murphy*. Ann Arbor: University of Michigan Press, 1975.
Thomas, Richard Walter. *Life for Us Is What We Make It: Building Black Community in Detroit, 1915–1945*. Bloomington: Indiana University Press, 1992.

LOS ANGELES, CA 1929–1941

DURING THE GREAT DEPRESSION LOS ANGELES BEGAN ITS TRANSITION from a Far West regional center to the modern urban and economic powerhouse it would become by mid century. Spurred by federal New Deal spending, the city witnessed notable economic growth during trying times and the increasing power of organized labor. At the same time municipal reformers eliminated corruption in city government while civil rights advocates fought less successfully to advance the positions of citizens of color. Throughout the period Los Angeles was ranked as the nation's fifth largest city.

GOVERNMENT AND POLITICS

Municipal government in 1930s Los Angeles was directed by a mayor and a fifteen-member city council as codified in the 1925 city charter. Politics and elections had been a nonpartisan affair since the Progressive era. A coalition of reformers, labor unions, and other interest groups controlled the mayor's office during the 1920s, and in 1929 this group and the business-oriented Old Guard were defeated by an alliance headed by Protestant religious leader Robert "Fighting Bob" Shuler. Auto parts dealer John Clinton Porter was elected mayor and served one term from 1929 to 1933. In those years he managed to embarrass city residents as he snubbed foreign leaders and President Franklin D. Roosevelt, and made religious affiliation a condition of mayoral appointments. More important, he attempted to stop the city's expansion of its public water and power utilities and energized the municipal ownership advocates led by Dr. John Randolph Haynes. The latter group unsuccessfully tried to recall Porter in 1932, but succeeded in defeating him in the 1933 city election.

QUICK FACTS

LOS ANGELES, CA 1929–1941

MAYORS

John C. Porter	(1929–1933)
Frank L. Shaw	(1933–1938)
Fletcher Bowron	(1938–1953)

MAJOR INDUSTRIES AND EMPLOYERS

Petroleum refining
Aircraft production
Secondary automobile assembly
Metals and machinery manufacturing
Motion pictures and allied industries

MAJOR NEWSPAPERS

California Eagle
La Opinión
Los Angeles Times
Los Angeles Examiner
Los Angeles Daily News
Los Angeles Herald & Express

MAJOR EVENTS

1931: Repatriation of Mexicans and their American-born children begins in the city.
1932: Los Angeles hosts the tenth modern Olympic Games.
1934: Two union protesters are killed on May 15 at San Pedro Harbor during the Maritime Strike.
1938: Fletcher Bowron defeats Mayor Frank L. Shaw in the recall election on September 16.
1940: Arroyo Seco Parkway, the first Los Angeles freeway, opens.

The new mayor, Frank Leslie Shaw, was a moderate Republican and former city council member and county supervisor who styled himself as a reformer. During his first term as mayor he worked well with the city council and tried to accommodate the city's important interest groups. A staunch supporter of municipal ownership, he implemented Haynes's water and power program and backed bond measures that financed the city's power system. Shaw appeased the business elite by continuing to allow the Los Angeles Police Department's infamous Red Squad to break strikes, restrict labor organizing, and spy on left-leaning political organizations and individuals. At the same time he retained good relations with conservative labor leaders by defending unionists against restrictions proposed by business organizations. He also proved to be highly successful in acquiring federal funding for almost four hundred fifty municipal projects to boost the local economy.

Shaw's appeal to all major groups began to fade after a few years. In 1937 he faced a budding alliance of opponents, including New Deal Democrats who resented this Republican's image as an agent of their president, moderate and liberal Republicans who no longer needed his help with municipal ownership, Congress of Industrial Organizations (CIO) unions and leftists who wanted the Red Squad abolished and business power weakened, and members of the defeated religious right alarmed by rampant vice operations protected by the police. These groups joined the mayoral campaign of County Supervisor John Anson Ford, a liberal New Deal Democrat, who lost to Shaw in a close election.

Following this contest, restaurant owner Clifford Clinton and other reformers on the county grand jury initiated a vice investigation, which alarmed the city administration. The probe seemed to go nowhere until January 14, 1938, when a bomb exploded in the automobile of Harry Raymond, a private investigator employed by Clinton. The bomb blew Raymond's garage to pieces, but he miraculously survived. Three LAPD officers who were spying on Raymond were arrested, and two of them were later convicted of attempted murder. The blast and the arrests sparked a recall campaign against Mayor Shaw as a coalition ranging from archconservative religious leaders to the Communist Party formed an umbrella organization, the Federation for Civic Betterment, which won voter support and removed Shaw from office in September 1938.

The new mayor, Superior Court Judge Fletcher Bowron, was a moderate Republican jurist who would serve from 1938 to 1953, and he made the eradication of corruption his first priority. In his first year he replaced many city commissioners, particularly those on the police, public works, and civil service boards. He forced out several department heads, including the chief of police; twenty-three high-ranking police officers were shoved into retirement; and a large number of policemen were fired or transferred. He also abolished the Red Squad and spoke out in opposition to an antipicketing ordinance supported by the business establishment.

The reform momentum that brought Bowron into office began to dissipate once victory was achieved, as insurgents on the right and left quickly departed the Federation for Civic Betterment. Most of these various forces would support Mayor Bowron in his successful 1941 reelection bid, but even Bowron admitted by that time that reform "crusading" was over. Later that year, his management of the city would face a new challenge with America's entry into World War II.

INDUSTRY, COMMERCE, AND LABOR

Prior to the stock market crash in 1929, the Los Angeles economy had been regionally based on agriculture, services, and a growing industrial sector that had made it the leading Pacific Coast city in manufacturing. By that time it had also become the chief financial and entertainment center in the American West. Despite the dislocations produced during the Great Depression, the economy continued to mature in providing goods for consumption outside of the region and was supported by a strong and growing service sector composed of white-collar professionals and semiskilled workers, both self-employed and in large and small businesses. The 1930 federal census revealed that women comprised about 28 percent of the city's workforce, mostly in occupations such as teaching, dressmaking, clerical work, and nursing; in food canning and several other industries; and in domestic services, a category in which women of color were strongly represented in comparison to their overall numbers.

In 1930 the metropolitan economy was still highly agricultural (including livestock and the dairy industry), as the larger county area was the most agriculturally productive in the nation. The primary industry was petroleum refining, which had boomed with discoveries of oil in Southern California during the 1920s. The manufacturing of metals and machinery and the production of women's clothing, furniture, and rubber tires were also important. Fifteen motion picture studios employed fifteen thousand people at the time and created a variety of ancillary businesses

Oil was big business for Los Angeles in the 1930s, accounting for approximately one-fourth of the nation's supply. Oil, such as that refined at the Venice refinery above, was shipped out through the Port of Los Angeles.

Source: Popperfoto/Getty Images

to support and promote film production and distribution. These industries took advantage of inexpensive water and electrical power supplied by the city's municipal system, and plentiful oil and natural gas for fuel. Exporting the products was facilitated by the Port of Los Angeles, the second busiest harbor in the United States (in tonnage) in the 1930s. (One-fourth of the entire national oil supply came from Los Angeles County, shipped through the Port of Los Angeles.)

Like other American cities, Los Angeles was hit hard by the Great Depression. Unemployment reached 30 percent in some areas by 1933. Plants closed, wages were down 38 percent from 1927, and assessed valuation of real property declined, resulting in lower property tax revenue, which put a strain on services. The most controversial efforts by government to ameliorate the situation were a Mexican repatriation campaign and the city's "Bum Blockade" supported by conservative business and labor leaders that allowed the LAPD to act as a border patrol at the state line in early 1936 and turn back indigents attempting to enter California.

The local economy took an early turn for the better in 1935. The motion picture industry and its satellite businesses had remained strong through the downturn. Building construction of all types began to increase as Los Angeles ranked second in U.S. cities to New York in 1936. Ford, General Motors, Chrysler, and Studebaker established automobile assembly plants in the area by 1937, providing an increase in manufacturing jobs and contributing more automobiles for the increasing highway network and massive freeway system that would begin to emerge late in the decade. Additional industrial employment was supplied by Douglas, Lockheed, Hughes Aircraft, North American, Northrop, and Vultee, companies that took advantage of the region's mild weather and open space to build airplanes as war beckoned toward the end of the decade.

By 1940 the city of Los Angeles was the fifth largest producer of manufactured goods in the nation. The larger Los Angeles County was still the nation's top agricultural county as well as first in the production of airplanes and parts, metals manufacturing, shipbuilding, secondary automobile assembly, and motion picture production, and still a national leader in petroleum refining. It was second in the nation in the manufacture of tires, fourth in the production of furniture and wearing apparel, fifth in printing and publishing, and sixth in meatpacking. Fruit, vegetable, and fish canning and bakery products were also important, as was the growing service sector.

The regional economy was advanced by an entrepreneurial elite who promoted growth and business opportunity through the Chamber of Commerce and Merchants' and Manufacturers' Association. Elite boosters such as insurance executive Asa V. Call, attorney James Beebe, and *Los Angeles Times* publisher Harry Chandler encouraged the entry of large and small businesses into the area, promoted residential growth, financed industrial research, and fought any gains by organized labor by enforcing a longstanding "open-shop" policy. This effort was aided by the LAPD Red Squad, which was used by the elite to spy on labor and combat work stoppages.

Organized labor in the city had been set back early in the depression as jobs were lost. The nadir of labor occurred during the unsuccessful 1934 Maritime Strike, when two unionists died as a result of violence involving strikers, strikebreakers, the LAPD, and an employers' private security force. With a new militancy, support from New Deal legislation, and the creation of the CIO in 1935, organized labor in Los Angeles, as elsewhere in the nation, challenged its employer groups. Jurisdictional battles between the established American Federation of Labor unions and those of the more leftist CIO increased overall union membership and forced local political leaders to placate laborites. Major strikes in auto plants and other industries in Los Angeles and adjacent cities late in the decade resulted in higher wages and increased union power. With the abolition of the Red Squad by Mayor Bowron in 1938, federal investigation of anti-labor groups by the La Follette Committee in 1939, and the increase in large industrial plants offering more union jobs, the open-shop policy was clearly on the wane by 1941.

RACE, ETHNICITY, AND IMMIGRATION

During the depression era, racial and ethnic minorities faced the same prejudice and de facto and de jure restrictions as in the past. Housing for people of color was prohibited in all but prescribed areas and enforced by restrictive real estate covenants, redlining by federal housing agencies, and militant neighborhood groups. Employment was usually available only in low-paying jobs unless white workers took them in tough times, and most schools and city amenities were segregated. The leadership of these groups protested discriminatory treatment with lawsuits and peaceful campaigns, but coalition building among the groups was not successful until the 1940s. Even so, racial minorities representing about 15 percent of the city population throughout the decade had one of the highest homeownership rates of such groups in all of the largest American cities.

The African American population in Los Angeles, the largest of any city on the Pacific Coast, grew from 38,894 (3.1 percent of city population) in 1930 to 63,744 (4.2 percent) in 1940. Restrictive covenants and other devices limited their residence to the Central Avenue district southeast of downtown and two other enclaves. Most were employed in low-paying jobs such as janitors, household servants, and other positions in the service sector in 1930, and almost half had lost their jobs by 1933.

Despite segregation and economic limitations in these years, a resilient black middle class composed of professionals and business owners operated many businesses along Central Avenue, including the Golden State Mutual Life Insurance Company. Community leaders from earlier in the decade such as Betty Hill, John A. Somerville, Dr. H. Claude Hudson, and *California Eagle* publisher Charlotta Bass and younger activists such as editor Leon Washington and attorney Loren Miller roused the community to contest discrimination with boycotts and other nonviolent means. Local branches of the Urban League and NAACP, as well as religious organizations led by the First African Methodist Episcopal Church, worked to improve civil rights and economic opportunity. In 1934 Augustus Hawkins, an African American, was elected to the state assembly from the Central Avenue district in the election in which local blacks first voted Democratic in large numbers.

Mexican Americans and Mexican nationals also filled the lower levels of most jobs in Los Angeles and faced discrimination about as severely as did African Americans. Most lived east of downtown. Their population stood at 97,116 in 1930 (7.8 percent of city population) and rose to about 117,000 by 1940. The number actually dipped in the early 1930s as some returned to Mexico during the height of the depression, and thousands—including many American citizens—were forcibly repatriated by the federal, state, and county governments in order to reduce unemployment and relief expenditures.

While some Mexican nationals chose not to become American citizens, many others made efforts to assimilate and seek naturalization, especially by the end of the decade. Some were able to join labor unions led by Armando Flores and Ramona Gonzáles, who organized workers for economic gains and civil rights advancement. The National Congress of Spanish Speaking Peoples and local Mexican consuls were important in protecting their rights. Eduardo Quevedo and other middle-class civic and business leaders were active in community advancement on the east side.

Asians in Los Angeles also faced segregation and citizenship challenges, as most were prohibited by federal law from becoming American citizens and by state legislation from owning property. In 1940 most Asians lived in enclaves near downtown known as Chinatown, "Little Tokyo," and "Little Manila"; south of downtown; and at the harbor. The largest groups were the 23,321 Japanese, 4,736 Chinese, 4,498 Filipinos, and 862 American Indians, who were classified with the Asians. The 1940 total represented about 2.3 percent of the city population, the same as in 1930.

Japanese residents were primarily farmers, gardeners, and fishermen as well as small business operators and professionals. Community leaders included businessman Katsutaro Tanigoshi and younger men who formed the Japanese American Citizens League in 1929. Chinese residents, usually small business operators and laborers, were restricted to the area near the Los Angeles Plaza until it was razed late in the decade to make room for Union Station. The former residents moved to a new Chinatown and a short-lived "China City" and scattered in small numbers throughout the rest of the city. Filipinos lived and worked mostly on the east side.

Los Angeles fared relatively well in the 1930s in terms of its economic growth and the reform of its government, although the plight of citizens of color remained virtually the same. In the decade of the Second World War, much of that would change.

See also *Los Angeles, CA 1896–1929; Los Angeles, CA 1941–1952; Los Angeles, CA 1952–1989; Los Angeles, CA 1989–2011*

TOM SITTON

BIBLIOGRAPHY

Flamming, Douglas. *Bound for Freedom: Black Los Angeles in Jim Crow America*. Berkeley: University of California Press, 2005.

Hanson, Earl, and Paul Beckett. *Los Angeles: Its Peoples and Its Homes*. Los Angeles, CA: Haynes Foundation, 1944.

Kidner, Frank L. and Philip Neff. *An Economic Survey of the Los Angeles Area*. Los Angeles, CA: Haynes Foundation, 1945.

Leader, Leonard. *Los Angeles and the Great Depression*. New York, NY: Garland, 1991.

Perry, Louis B., and Richard S. Perry. *A History of the Los Angeles Labor Movement, 1911–1941*. Berkeley: University of California Press, 1963.

Rudd, Hynda, Tom Sitton, et al., eds. *The Development of Los Angeles City Government: An Institutional History, 1850–2000*. 2 vols. Los Angeles, CA: Los Angeles City Historical Society, 2007.

Sanchez, George J. *Becoming Mexican American: Ethnicity, Culture, and Identity in Chicano Los Angeles, 1900–1945*. New York, NY: Oxford University Press, 1993.

Sitton, Thomas J. "Urban Politics and Reform in New Deal Los Angeles: The Recall of Mayor Frank L. Shaw." PhD diss., University of California, Riverside, 1983.

CLEVELAND, OH 1929–1941

CLEVELAND REMAINED THE SIXTH LARGEST CITY in the United States in 1930, but its growth was slowed by the Great Depression. By 1940 it would experience a slight population loss for the first time, while its suburbs continued to grow. Its economy suffered greatly during this period, although President Roosevelt's New Deal helped to offset widespread unemployment. These conditions contributed to social unrest and labor conflict. The short-lived city manager governmental experiment ended in 1931, and the Republicans nominated their 1936 presidential candidate in Cleveland. In 1932 Howard Whipple Green began the Real Property Inventory, later imitated throughout many U.S. cities.

QUICK FACTS

CLEVELAND, OH 1929–1941

CITY MANAGERS

William Hopkins   (1929–1930)
Daniel E. Morgan   (1930–1931)

MAYORS

Raymond T. Miller   (1932–1933)
Harry L. Davis   (1934–1935)
Harold H. Burton   (1936–1940)
Edward J. Blythin   (1941)

MAJOR INDUSTRIES AND EMPLOYERS

Republic Steel
Ford
General Motors
National Acme
Zipp Manufacturing

MAJOR NEWSPAPERS

The Plain Dealer
Cleveland Press
Cleveland News

MAJOR EVENTS

1930: The Terminal Tower opens on Public Square, linking the affluent Shaker Heights suburb with downtown Cleveland.

1931: Severance Hall, the new home of the Cleveland Orchestra, and Cleveland Municipal Stadium, built on landfill on the lakefront, both open.

1931: Cleveland voters end the experiment in the city manager form of government that was initiated in the 1920s.

1936–1937: The Great Lakes Exposition and the Republican national convention both bring large numbers of visitors.

1937: Industrialist John D. Rockefeller and former mayor Newton D. Baker, both towering figures in Cleveland's history, die.

GOVERNMENT AND POLITICS

In January 1930 Cleveland's first city manager, William Hopkins, was fired by a disgruntled city council and replaced by lawyer and former Republican city councilman Daniel Morgan. Hopkins had been appointed with the agreement of Republican and Democratic Party bosses Maurice Maschke and Burt Gongwer, respectively. He alienated their allies through his ambitious plans for downtown and the lakefront. In 1931 Cleveland voters decided to end the city manager form of government adopted in 1921 and initiated in 1924. Morgan ran for mayor in 1932 but was defeated by Democrat Raymond Miller, a former county prosecutor, amid all of the problems resulting from the advent of the Great Depression. In the primary election, city councilman Peter Witt had been eliminated. This ally of former Progressive mayor Tom Johnson was previously defeated for mayor in 1915. He was a prominent critic of city manager Hopkins. His announced agnosticism was denounced by the Catholic church, contributing to his defeat.

After one term marked by corruption, Miller was succeeded by Republican Harry Davis. Davis had previously been mayor and had resigned to run successfully for governor in 1920. He was defeated in his 1924 bid for reelection. Davis was an outspoken opponent of the city manager form of government and had been involved in previous unsuccessful attempts to repeal it in 1927 and 1928.

In 1936 former city law director and Republican Harold Burton defeated Davis and Miller to become mayor. That year Cleveland hosted the Republican National Convention, which nominated Kansas governor Alf Landon to oppose Franklin Roosevelt and his New Deal. President Roosevelt appeared in Cleveland that year to visit the Great Lakes Exposition, which celebrated the centennial of Cleveland's incorporation as a city and drew more than seven million visitors to its site on the downtown shore of Lake Erie.

Less uplifting during Burton's term were the notorious and unsolved torso murders in which at least twelve victims were dismembered and killed between 1935 and 1938. Burton's public safety director, Eliot Ness (of Chicago Untouchables fame), failed to find the serial killer. Ness focused on successfully fighting police corruption and organized crime. He left in 1942 but returned to run unsuccessfully for mayor in 1947. In 1940 Burton was elected to the U.S. Senate and was succeeded by Edward Blythin. Burton was appointed to the U.S. Supreme Court in 1945.

INDUSTRY, COMMERCE, AND LABOR

In 1930 Cleveland was second only to Detroit among American cities in the percentage of its workers employed in industry. The region, including Cleveland, ranked eighth nationally in the number of industrial employees. They were mostly employed in five leading industries: transportation equipment, machinery, iron and steelmaking, metal products, and electrical machinery. Cleveland was hit hard after the stock market crash of 1929. From official unemployment of forty-one thousand in 1930, it grew to about one hundred thousand by the beginning of 1931. In February 1930 several thousand unemployed workers stormed City Hall, with recurring demonstrations in the early years of the Great Depression. Cleveland's economic mainstays of heavy industry suffered badly. Despite having Republican mayors Davis and Burton during most of Democratic President Roosevelt's first two terms and hosting the Republican National Convention in 1936, Cleveland benefitted greatly from Roosevelt's New Deal emergency relief programs to fight unemployment.

The Works Progress Administration (WPA) employed thousands of Clevelanders to build streets, sewers, schools, and other major capital improvements. Notable WPA projects included the first stretch of the Shoreway Highway, the Main Avenue Bridge, and improvements to the Cleveland Metroparks. The WPA also sponsored the Public Works of Art project and an archival compilation of early nationality, racial, and ethnic newspapers (the Annals of Cleveland project). Cleveland was a pioneer in the Public Works Administration funding of public housing projects and then additional projects after the establishment of the U.S. Housing Authority in 1937. Under the leadership of Republican Councilman Ernest J. Bohn, the first and longtime director of the Cleveland Metropolitan Housing Authority (CMHA), Cleveland replaced several slums with some of the earliest public housing projects. The Lakeview Terrace project on the site of the Angle overlooking the Cuyahoga River and Lake Erie, which had housed poor

Irish immigrants, gained architectural renown for its design and amenities, which included a community center and art works.

Before the depression virtually stopped privately financed construction, Cleveland saw the opening of several major buildings. Most noteworthy was the Union Terminal facing downtown's Public Square, which officially opened in June 1930, featuring the fifty-two-floor Terminal Tower, then the tallest building in the world outside of New York City. The complex included offices and retail over a train station. Developed by brothers Mantis and Oris Van Sweringen, the Union Terminal served as the focus of the rail connection to the newly developed exclusive suburban planned community of Shaker Heights, which was also developed by the Van Sweringens. In 1929 they had opened the Shaker Square retail center on the border between Cleveland and Shaker Heights. Unfortunately, the brothers' heavily mortgaged real estate empire went bankrupt and they died in 1935 and 1936, leaving these developments as their monuments. In 1931 the grand Severance Hall, home of the Cleveland Orchestra, opened in University Circle. That year also saw the opening of the massive Cleveland Municipal Stadium on landfill on the lakefront. The stadium would later become the home of the Cleveland Indians baseball team (and, after World War II, the Cleveland Browns football team as well).

In 1932, under the sponsorship of the U.S. Department of Commerce and the U.S. Chamber of Commerce, Cleveland pioneered a Real Property Inventory. It furnished data on family units, housing, utilities, retail stores, and industry. Under the direction of Howard Whipple Green, this became an annual survey. With federal WPA assistance, it was adopted in 140 other cities by 1934.

Not surprisingly, Cleveland saw considerable social unrest and labor strife during the Great Depression. For example, in July 1933 thousands attempted to prevent the eviction of a foreclosed homeowner, battling the police in a Cleveland neighborhood. In December 1936 auto workers protested conditions through a sit-down strike at the General Motors Fisher Body auto plant. The following year, striking steelworkers fought police protecting strikebreakers at Republic Steel. Nationally, the auto workers and the steelworkers would eventually gain recognition of their unions. With the coming of World War II, war-related production would restore prosperity to Cleveland's economy, eliminating the unemployment crisis due to the wartime mobilization that drastically reduced the labor supply.

RACE, ETHNICITY, AND IMMIGRATION

From 1920 to 1930, Cleveland's foreign-born population declined from 30 to 25 percent. The groups most represented among these foreign nationalities were Czechs, Poles, Italians, Germans, Hungarians, Yugoslavians, and Russians. While the city had ethnic neighborhoods, the earlier immigrant populations like the Germans and the Irish had begun to disperse in both the city and the nearby suburbs. In 1936 the Jewish Community Council was founded, representing 160 affiliated organizations. In 1939 the Cultural Gardens in Rockefeller Park, celebrating twenty-eight of the city's many nationalities, were formally dedicated. By 1940 the foreign-born population declined further to 20 percent.

The African American population of the city had doubled during the decade following the end of World War I, and in 1930 it comprised 8 percent of the population. Most were confined to the black ghetto in the Central neighborhood, where living conditions were harsh in overcrowded, substandard housing. When public housing was built during the Depression, while many poor blacks were eligible, CMHA Director Bohn made the decision to keep it strictly racially segregated. Cleveland's first African American mayor, Carl Stokes, and his brother, longtime Congressman Louis Stokes, both grew up during this decade in the Outhwaite Estates public housing project. The depression slowed the black migration from the South, and by 1940 the black portion of the city's population had only increased to 10 percent. During the depression, blacks were hurt even more severely than whites in terms of unemployment and poverty.

See also *Cleveland, OH 1877–1896; Cleveland, OH 1896–1929; Cleveland, OH 1941–1952*

DENNIS KEATING

BIBLIOGRAPHY

Miller, Carol Poh, and Robert Wheeler. *Cleveland: A Concise History, 1796–1990.* Bloomington: Indiana University Press, 1990.
Porter, Philip W. *Cleveland: Confused City on a Seesaw.* Columbus: Ohio State University Press, 1976.
Rose, William Ganson. *Cleveland: The Making of a City.* Cleveland, OH: World Publishing, 1950.
Van Tassel, David D., and John J. Grabowski, eds. *The Encyclopedia of Cleveland History.* Bloomington: Indiana University Press, 1996.

BALTIMORE, MD 1929–1941

ON THE BRINK OF THE GREAT DEPRESSION, the Baltimore Association of Commerce saw only a golden glow in the city's future. It predicted that the local population would pass one million by 1930 (a size it would never quite reach) and boasted of the city's attractiveness as a site for manufacturing. During the 1920s, Western Electric, Proctor & Gamble, Lever Brothers, American Sugar, and locally owned McCormick Spice had all opened new plants in the city, and Bethlehem Steel embarked on a $100 million expansion of its mill in Sparrows Point. Between 1920 and 1926, Baltimore rose from the seventh to the third most active of the nation's ports. Its construction industry was producing about six thousand homes a year.

Baltimore's Republican Mayor, William Broening, shared the business community's confidence. Months after the stock market crash of 1929, he preached boosterism at a conference he had called for one hundred executives representing "the cream of Baltimore industry." If there were a depression, he told the businessmen, it would be brief, and Baltimore would have little to worry about. Mayor Broening himself was a somewhat dissonant presence in the general display of enthusiasm. The city had been a Democratic stronghold, and its Republican mayor held office only because of paralyzing fissures in the city's Democratic organization.

QUICK FACTS

BALTIMORE, MD **1929–1941**

MAYORS

William F. Broening   (1927–1931)
Howard W. Jackson   (1931–1943)

MAJOR INDUSTRIES AND EMPLOYERS

Clothing
Foundry and machine shop products
Tin cans and other tinware
Bread and bakery products

MAJOR NEWSPAPERS

Afro-American
Baltimore American
Baltimore News
Evening Sun
Sun

MAJOR EVENTS

1931: Howard W. Jackson is elected mayor, and fellow Democrat William Curran emerges as his chief rival in the city's Democratic organization.

1931: The Amalgamated Clothing Workers strike pits the Baltimore Federation of Labor against Baltimore Industrial Council.

1933: The failure of Baltimore's Title Guarantee and Trust Company triggers a run on city banks.

1933: The Young People's Forum of the NAACP organizes the "Buy Where You Can Work" campaign, a boycott of retailers in black neighborhoods that do not hire African American employees.

1934: Mayor Jackson runs against incumbent Democratic Governor Albert Ritchie. Ritchie, with the support of William Curran, defeats Jackson in the primary but loses the general election to "New Deal Republican" Harry W. Nice.

1939: Howard Jackson is reelected mayor and reestablishes his control of the city's Democratic organization.

GOVERNMENT AND POLITICS

After losing the mayoral election to William Broening in 1927, William Curran had abandoned the pursuit of elective office to play politics as a factional leader within the local Democratic organization. After 1930 Curran's chief political rival was fellow Democrat and former mayor Howard W. Jackson. Curran represented ethnic and mostly Catholic Democrats; Jackson's constituents were primarily old-stock Protestants. In 1929, however, the two rivals joined forces in a doomed campaign to oppose Democrat Albert Ritchie's bid for an unprecedented fourth term as Maryland's governor. Both "bosslets" immediately faced open rebellion among the Democratic district leaders who had previously been their allies and retainers. Governor Ritchie, widely regarded as a contender for the presidency, was too popular to stop. Curran and Jackson capitulated. Ritchie himself refused to endorse any candidates for the legislature or other state offices in order to avoid complicating his presidential ambitions with factional entanglements. "Democrats fight among themselves," noted the *Baltimore Observer*, "without having any real factions. There are groups but they are loosely knit. It is next to impossible to tell where one group ends and the next one begins. . . . The Democratic situation in Baltimore is now more of a mess than it is anything else."

The "mess" allowed for abrupt realignments and sudden changes in political fortune. Howard Jackson had been turned out of the mayor's office by his own party in 1927 for drunkenness and because he had steered the city's fire insurance business to his own company. He did nothing to enhance his popularity by joining the unsuccessful drive to prevent the reelection of Governor Ritchie. But he made a startling comeback in 1931, when a coalition of district leaders promoted him for a second shot at the mayor's office. William Curran joined leaders from several districts in a frenzied hunt for some other candidate, but no plausible alternative emerged, and members of the anti-Jackson movement fell to fighting among themselves about issues unrelated to the mayoral election. Jackson faced no opposition in the Democratic primary and only token competition in the general election. William Curran's political prospects seemed dim. His only remaining strongholds were in the city's legislative delegation in Annapolis and Baltimore's Democratic Committee.

And Mayor Jackson had problems of his own. The depression's local impact made it impossible to sustain the optimistic boosterism of the Association of Commerce. By 1932 Baltimore's jobless rate topped 19 percent. But Jackson insisted that supporting the city's unemployed was not a municipal responsibility. It was the work of private charities like those that made up Baltimore's Family Welfare Association (FWA). Early in 1932, however, the FWA agencies announced that they had reached the limit of their resources and, not long afterward, closed their offices. In response, Jackson arranged an appropriation of $50,000 to support the unemployed, acknowledging that the sum would last no more than a few weeks. By the time the money was exhausted, Jackson had requested and received emergency powers from the city council for an indefinite period. He created an Emergency Relief Committee made up of city administrators and prominent business executives with staff support from the FWA. Then he borrowed $3 million to sustain the unemployed through the end of 1932. Governor Ritchie promised to urge the 1933 session of the state legislature to authorize a bond issue that would cover Baltimore's current and future relief expenditures.

Ritchie's presidential prospects overshadowed the Democratic primaries in the spring of 1932. The hope that a Marylander might reach the White House muted intraparty strife. Many incumbents were unopposed, and in several Baltimore districts candidates for the state legislature formed Ritchie-Jackson "harmony" slates. But Ritchie's presidential boom fizzled, and then he reneged on his pledge to see that Baltimore was reimbursed for its relief expenditures, suggesting instead that the city achieve greater economy within its own budget. Mayor Jackson responded by eliminating almost all of the city's relief expenditures. Ritchie backtracked, and the General Assembly grudgingly approved his request for a $12 million bond issue to offset relief expenditures in Baltimore, but not the $15 million requested.

Jackson had called the governor's bluff and then proceeded to go after his job. The mayor began by using patronage to consolidate Baltimore's fluidly factionalized Democratic organization—even if it meant giving jobs to William Curran's allies. While Baltimore's mayor prepared to make his bid for state leadership, he was also trying to accommodate national policy. The Federal Emergency Relief Administration, created in 1933, was to distribute half a billion dollars in federal funds among state and local relief agencies. Jackson's Emergency Relief Committee would not qualify for grants because it was not a fully public agency, but he refused to create a public welfare department in Baltimore because he feared that once an emergency relief agency became part of municipal government, "it will cling there as a budgetary barnacle most difficult to scrape off when normal business conditions are restored." Instead he established a Baltimore Emergency Relief Commission by shifting most of the Relief Committee's personnel to the public payroll, which did not impress federal field observers who were particularly dismayed by its discrimination against African Americans. Clashes with federal authorities in the Civil Works Administration were even sharper.

Mayor Jackson, like Governor Ritchie, was hostile to federal intervention and reluctant to acknowledge that either state or local governments should bear significant responsibility for unemployment relief. Ideological and policy differences had little to do with Jackson's decision to challenge Ritchie's bid for a fifth term as governor in 1934, or with Curran's endorsement of Ritchie. In fact, most Democratic political leaders in Maryland were hostile to the New Deal, and it was only Ritchie's defeat by Republican Harry W. Nice, who supported Roosevelt's plan, that finally gave Maryland a New Deal governor.

Jackson and Curran were left to fight it out with one another for control of the city. In the 1935 mayoral election, Curran's candidate was a little-known businessman whom Jackson easily defeated. Curran's man won as president of the city council, but Jackson's allies took eleven of the eighteen council seats. Curran still controlled Baltimore's Democratic Committee and the city's legislative delegations in both the Maryland Senate and the House of Delegates, but he could expect little help from the Republican governor in Annapolis. Jackson was now the sole source of patronage for Baltimore's Democrats.

William Curran embarked on a new gambit when he organized the Maryland for Roosevelt League in anticipation of the 1936 election, calling attention to the strained relationships between Mayor Jackson and the New Deal administration. The mayor responded by launching his own campaign to reelect the president. Baltimore boasted two Roosevelt campaign headquarters.

Curran's attempt to capitalize on FDR's popularity brought him no immediate gains. In the Democratic primaries, his congressional candidate suffered defeat at the hands of a Jackson ally. The city's Democratic Committee deserted Curran and collaborated with Jackson in a purge of ward executives. But Jackson had exhausted his political resources. He had already distributed what there was of city patronage, and there were more claimants than he could satisfy. There were also the purged ward executives to contend with. They drifted toward Curran, who still controlled the city's legislative delegation. Jackson's second bid for the governorship, if successful, would yield enough jobs to solve his problems. But Herbert R. O'Conor, a proven vote-getter as Baltimore state's attorney and Maryland's attorney general, emerged as a Democratic alternative to Jackson. When Curran announced that O'Conor could defeat Jackson in all six legislative districts of Baltimore, it was the signal that moved the state's anti-Jackson politicians to converge on the attorney general.

The consequences of the 1938 gubernatorial election revealed, once again, the disjointed character of politics in Baltimore. O'Conor, with Curran's backing, won both the primary and the general election. At the same time, Curran lost control of both the Baltimore Democratic Committee and the city's delegation in the state legislature. But Jackson's supposed allies in the legislature wanted to cooperate with the popular new governor and found it expedient to accommodate Curran, his leading political sponsor in Baltimore. Though they had been elected with Jackson's endorsement, a majority of the city's representatives chose a Curran ally to chair the city delegation. Another Curran partisan became speaker of the House of Delegates. Baltimore's Democratic Committee, whose members had once defected to Jackson, redefected to nominate a slate of Curran men to serve on the city's Board of Election Supervisors.

In a party organization where factional loyalties changed so readily, no alignment was likely to last. Howard Jackson was back in charge in time for the mayoral election of 1939. Jack Pollack, powerful and independent boss of West Baltimore's Fourth District, shifted his organization from Curran to Jackson; other district leaders did the same. Jackson outpolled Curran's mayoral candidate in twenty-six of the city's twenty-eight wards, and his candidates for the city council won all but three of its eighteen seats. The balance would shift again in 1940, when Franklin Roosevelt ran for a third term with the strong support of Governor O'Conor and the belated acquiescence of Mayor Jackson. It was only the Pearl Harbor attack and the American war effort that finally drove Baltimore's Democratic factions into a united front.

INDUSTRY, COMMERCE, AND LABOR

Signs of economic decline were evident in Baltimore even before the stock market crash in 1929, notwithstanding the enthusiastic optimism of the Association of Commerce. Baltimore's standing in the manufacture of clothing, the city's largest industry, dropped during the 1920s from third to fifth place among American cities, and production shifted from factories to sweat shops. Wheat exports, the original source of local prosperity, dropped by almost a third during 1921 alone and by the end of the decade would fall to levels not seen since 1910. The impact of the depression itself added only gradually to the city's economic distress. But a sharp break came with the closing of the city's Title Guarantee and Trust Company in 1933, which triggered a run on Baltimore's banks. Governor Ritchie called a state bank holiday, which merged with the national bank closing subsequently declared by President Roosevelt. Half a dozen institutions failed to reopen when the bank holiday ended. Most were back in business by the end of 1933, and one was reorganized by the Reconstruction Finance Corporation.

The city's unemployed presented a more persistent problem. The People's Unemployment League (PUL) was a distinctive creation of local socialists—a labor union for the jobless. It eventually created twenty-five neighborhood-based locals, and unlike more traditional unions in Baltimore, it was resolutely interracial. It organized under the slogan "Black and White, Unite and Fight." The PUL repeatedly picketed the offices of the Baltimore Emergency Relief Commission to protest inadequate levels of support and purges of the relief rolls. It recruited new members at Works Progress Administration (WPA) work sites, where the organization also protested low WPA wages.

Employed workers launched protests of their own. New Deal legislation encouraged them to organize—another sign of the increased federal role in local affairs. But workers were ready to act without federal encouragement. In 1932, five thousand women responded to the Amalgamated Clothing Workers' (ACW) call to go on strike. Although it affected over two hundred contract shops and factories, the strike was aimed in particular at the J. Schoeneman firm, known for low wages and poor working conditions. Police clashed with picketers outside Schoeneman's, and hundreds of women were jailed. Mayor Jackson appointed a committee headed by Johns

Hopkins University professor Sidney Hollander to investigate conditions at Schoeneman's plant and shops. The firm refused to cooperate in the study, and Hollander's report aroused sympathy for the strikers and helped to convince other garment manufacturers to recognize the ACW as the bargaining agent for their workers. The union soon represented about 70 percent of the city's garment workers.

The ACW posed a challenge, not only to employers but to the Baltimore Federation of Labor (BFL), local arm of the American Federation of Labor. The BFL did little to take advantage of New Deal legislation designed to remove obstacles to union organization. It did grant charters to workers who organized on their own and then requested affiliation with the BFL, but it systematically avoided black workers and made scarcely any attempts to organize nonunion workers until it was challenged by more radical unionists. The ACW was associated with the Baltimore Industrial Council (BIC), the local branch of the Congress of Industrial Organizations, and with the support of the Baltimore Urban League, it sponsored organizing drives among African American rag graders and the black employees of cotton garment sweatshops.

The emergent rivalry between the BFL and the BIC came to the surface in a series of strikes by Baltimore's cabdrivers. The first, in 1935, initially supported by the BFL, erupted into violence when the cab companies hired ruffians to intimidate strikers. The police moved in to protect company property from the strikers, and the BFL president immediately settled with the owners. The taxi drivers returned to work, but with unresolved grievances. The next strike, in 1936, was backed by both the BFL and the BIC. This time the cabbies attacked the first cars that attempted to leave the garages. Once again the police intervened to contain an outbreak of violence lasting more than an hour. Governor Nice negotiated a truce, which the owners used to organize a company union. Less than a month later, a renegade BFL organizer called the workers out again, and the violence that followed brought the police out too. The BFL president and a municipal judge announced a settlement. The strike organizer was sentenced to three months in jail for inciting violence. The BIC provided an attorney to defend him and denounced the BFL for abandoning the drivers.

The two labor organizations parted company even more sharply during a prolonged seamen's strike beginning in 1936. The BIC supported the strike; the BFL refused to have anything to do with it. Local Socialists and Communists joined the BIC in supporting the seamen, and their involvement was duly noted in BFL attacks on its rival organization. The seamen, represented by the National Maritime Union, eventually won wage increases and union recognition early in 1937, and the BIC gained respect and membership among Baltimore's dockworkers.

In time the BIC grew more moderate. By the end of the 1930s, it had generally stopped employing socialists from the PUL to serve as organizers and relied instead on longtime labor activists—"professional" organizers. Its collective bargaining agreements with local firms created a framework for labor relations that reduced the likelihood of strikes or violence. The BFL regained some of the ground that it had lost on the waterfront by emphasizing the radicalism of the BIC and succeeded in organizing Baltimore's autoworkers by appealing to their Americanism and identifying with Franklin Roosevelt. Still, Baltimore seemed backward to some unionists. An organizer for the International Ladies' Garment Workers complained that in Baltimore "people crawl. Nothing moves, and the earth is still flat."

RACE, ETHNICITY, AND IMMIGRATION

Baltimore's population grew by less than 7 percent between 1930 and 1940, from slightly over eight hundred thousand to almost eight hundred sixty thousand. The percentage of Baltimoreans born abroad decreased slightly during the decade, but the city's black population increased by 16.7 percent, compared to only 4.7 percent for whites, and a new activism was stirring among Baltimore's African Americans.

The Baltimore branch of the NAACP was founded in 1912, in response to a local ordinance mandating residential segregation. By the 1930s the branch was languishing, with scarcely one hundred members. But there were signs of life. In 1931 Juanita Jackson, a nineteen-year-old graduate of the University of Pennsylvania, organized the City-Wide Young People's Forum, a meeting place for the rising generation of African Americans. Its Friday night speakers and panel discussions could attract as many as two thousand participants. Two Baltimore-born graduates of Lincoln University near Philadelphia, Thurgood Marshall and Clarence Mitchell Jr., joined the forum soon after graduation. Mitchell soon became the forum's vice president, its premier orator and debater, and later Juanita Jackson's husband.

Mitchell and Marshall helped Jackson launch the forum's most ambitious offensive against racial discrimination. In 1933 the Young People's Forum organized a boycott against retailers in black neighborhoods who refused to hire African American employees. A few small businesses soon agreed to hire black clerks. But the biggest target of the "Buy Where You Can Work" campaign were the A&P supermarkets of black Baltimore, which hired no black workers. Juanita Jackson and the Young People's Forum coordinated the boycott with the support of at least forty black churches. Five hundred forum participants and many of their parents picketed every A&P outlet that was located in an African American neighborhood. In the end, the chain hired thirty-two black clerks and promised jobs for two black managers.

Success was a prelude to disunity, though. By this time the coalition supporting the boycott had expanded so far beyond the Young People's Forum that a broader organizational framework— a Citizens' Committee—was created to steer the protest. Its next targets would be smaller retail outlets on one block in West Baltimore, the epicenter of the African American shopping district. The merchants organized the Northwest Businessmen's Association in an attempt to present a united front to the boycotters. But divisions began to appear among the boycotters themselves. Not all black churches approved of the boycott, and within the boycott there were accusations of disloyalty and backsliding. Clarence Mitchell, now a columnist at the *Afro-American*, argued that such charges were distractions from the real problems of black Baltimore, which were rooted in a racist social and political system. Thurgood Marshall chaired a meeting designed to restore harmony among the black ministers whose support was essential to the boycott. The result, as the *Afro-American* reported, was a "free-for-all fight" that culminated in the explosion of stink bombs designed to disrupt the meeting. More problems emerged when the Northwest Business-men's Association filed suit challenging the picketing of their stores. The courts sided with the merchants, arguing that since the pickets were not employees of the stores, their protest was not protected by the Norris-LaGuardia Act.

Though the boycott fell short of its objectives, it had succeeded in reinvigorating Baltimore's branch of the NAACP. With the support of the *Afro-American*'s Carl Murphy, it would grow into the organization's second largest branch by the early 1940s. It backed Thurgood Marshall's first lawsuits against segregation and discrimination, beginning with the University of Maryland Law School and continuing with a series of suits to equalize pay for black and white public schoolteachers in all of Maryland's counties. *Afro-American* journalist Clarence Mitchell became the NAACP's publicity director in Baltimore. His task was not just to give visibility to the revived branch, but to hold together the coalition of groups that backed it. The branch, as historian David Terry points out, was not a freestanding organization. The city's African American leaders and activists were linked to a variety of associations and institutions; the "core leadership displayed a penchant for multiple affiliations, with the common denominator being the NAACP." All of the branch's ventures were "multi-organizational undertakings," and constant compromise and negotiation held the coalitions together. Mitchell the negotiator and Marshall the litigator would carry their work beyond Baltimore, where their efforts would culminate in *Brown v. Board of Education* and the Civil Rights Act of 1964.

See also *Baltimore, MD 1776–1790; Baltimore, MD 1790–1828; Baltimore, MD 1828–1854; Baltimore, MD 1854–1877; Baltimore, MD 1877–1896; Baltimore, MD 1896–1929; Baltimore, MD 1941–1952; Baltimore, MD 1952–1989*

MATTHEW CRENSON

BIBLIOGRAPHY

Argersinger, Jo Ann E. *Toward a New Deal in Baltimore: People and Government in the Great Depression.* Chapel Hill: University of North Carolina Press, 1988.

Brown, Dorothy M. "Maryland Between the Wars." In *Maryland: A History, 1632–1974,* edited by Richard Walsh and William Lloyd Fox, 672–772. Baltimore: Maryland Historical Society, 1974.

Rothman, Edwin. "Factional Machine Politics: William Curran and Baltimore City Democratic Organization, 1929–1946." PhD diss., Johns Hopkins University, 1949.

Skotnes, Andor. "The Black Freedom Movement and Workers' Movement in Baltimore, 1930–1939." PhD diss., Rutgers University, 1991.

Terry, David Taft. "'Tramping for Justice': The Dismantling of Jim Crow in Baltimore, 1942–1954." PhD diss., Howard University, 2002.

ST. LOUIS, MO 1929–1941

THE 1930S FOUND ST. LOUIS CONFRONTING THE GREAT DEPRESSION'S LOCAL IMPACT. During his two terms, Republican mayor Victor J. Miller improved the city's infrastructure by facilitating the passage of bond issues and garnering support for construction projects. He also secured private monies for relief, but the economic misery brought about by the depression set the stage for new political leadership, with Democrats taking over important city offices and eventually the mayor's office. With an employment rate higher than the national average during the early

QUICK FACTS

ST. LOUIS, MO **1929–1941**

MAYORS

Victor J. Miller	(1925–1933)
Bernard F. Dickmann	(1933–1941)
William Dee Becker	(1941–1943)

MAJOR INDUSTRIES AND EMPLOYERS

Food products
Chemicals and drugs
Iron and steel
Clothing
Boots and shoes

MAJOR NEWSPAPERS

St. Louis Globe-Democrat
St. Louis Post-Dispatch
St. Louis Star Times

MAJOR EVENTS

1932: Democrats are elected to key local political offices, setting the ground for the election of Bernard F. Dickmann, the city's first Democratic mayor in over twenty-five years.

1935: Voters approve a $7.5 million bond issue supporting the construction of the Jefferson National Expansion Memorial to commemorate St. Louis's contribution to westward expansion.

1936: Homer G. Phillips Hospital opens, becoming nationally recognized as a leading training center for black doctors and nurses.

1937: Emerson Electric workers stage one of the longest sit-down strikes in the country and successfully gain union recognition through the Congress of Industrial Organizations.

1940: The board of aldermen passes a smoke control ordinance banning the use of Illinois coal and creating a clean air model for other cities to follow.

1930s, St. Louis was hard hit. Mayor Bernard F. Dickmann responded with a New Deal program that trimmed the budget and secured additional relief funds, though these actions were not enough to meet local needs. He also acquired federal subsidies for public works projects such as the Jefferson National Expansion Memorial and the Homer G. Phillips Hospital and oversaw the passage of the smoke control ordinance, a clean air program adopted by other cities. St. Louis ranked seventh in manufacturing, with leading industries that included shoe, clothing, electrical, auto plants, tobacco, food products, meatpacking, chemicals, drugs, iron, and steel. Labor unrest characterized this period as food, auto, electrical, and garment workers across gender, racial, and ethnic lines waged strikes and joined unions, swelling the ranks of the Congress of Industrial Organizations (CIO) and the American Federation of Labor (AFL). The increase in union membership occurred during an era of population decline for the Gateway City. In the 1930s St. Louis was the seventh largest city in the United States, dropping from its peak at fourth place in the opening decade of the twentieth century. By 1940 the city would fall to the eighth slot. With its relatively small population of foreign-born residents, St. Louis was deeply divided along racial and ethnic lines as various groups lived in relatively distinct residential areas. There, Germans, Italians, Russians, Irish, Poles, Hungarians, Chinese, and African Americans built communities that shaped local politics and neighborhood development and life.

GOVERNMENT AND POLITICS

After an unsuccessful bid for the governorship of Missouri, Republican Victor J. Miller ran a successful mayoral campaign in 1925 and was reelected in 1929. During his second term Miller oversaw installment of the city street light network, an $8 million bond issue project approved in 1923, although corruption charges tainted the project as two municipal officials were indicted for improper use of city funds. In June 1930 Miller oversaw construction of the Civil Court Building at Twelfth and Market Streets and later, as the depression set in, established the relief Command Campaign, which raised $1.1 million from individuals and corporations.

Public and private monies donated between 1930 and 1932, namely $1.48 million from the city and $2 million from the Salvation Army, the Provident Association, and the St. Vincent DePaul Society, did not come close to adequately addressing the city's unemployment problem. Through the early years of the depression, St. Louis's unemployment rate was higher than the national rate. In 1930 the city's unemployed constituted 9.8 percent of the workforce, of which 8.4 percent were white and 13.2 percent were black. By 1931 the local unemployed were 24 percent of the workforce, and the growing economic disparity between white and black workers widened, with the black unemployment rate being twice that of whites. By the spring of 1933 the overall St. Louis unemployment rate reached 30 percent, six points higher than the national average. Fiscal crises abounded, leaving the city with a budget deficit during these early years. Still, St. Louis voters passed a $4.6 million bond issue for relief in November 1932, before federal intervention improved matters.

Franklin D. Roosevelt's New Deal message powerfully swayed St. Louis, a Republican bastion for the previous two decades. Registered voters chose the candidate who promised to revitalize the economy and improve the lives of workers by creating new job opportunities. In 1932 Democrats took most local seats, including sheriff, circuit judge, city treasurer, and coroner. The ground then was set for Democrat Bernard F. Dickmann, who ran for mayor the following year. The St. Louis Real Estate Exchange president won the 1933 mayoral race, bringing with him to City Hall fourteen Democratic aldermen who joined two others already in office. Based on a 1914 charter, St. Louis's twenty-eight wards selected their own committeewomen and committeemen based on a partisan basis, while aldermen were selected on a citywide basis. Aldermen were the lawmaking body of city government, whereas committeepersons served their party and used political patronage to deliver votes and political loyalty. St. Louis had not had a Democratic mayor in twenty-four years. With Democrats in key municipal positions, the party now controlled urban politics.

Among the new mayor's top priorities was the economic crisis. He now had control over approximately seven thousand municipal jobs and dispensed them as rewards for those who had helped him win election. During his first year Dickmann trimmed the budget by 11 percent and in February 1935 persuaded voters to pass an additional relief bond issue worth $3.6 million, to be funded by the city, the state, and local charities. Works Progress Administration (WPA), Public Works Administration, and city development funds put people to work and helped Dickmann count as a major victory a reduction in the number of relief recipients from over one hundred thousand to thirty-five thousand in one year. President Roosevelt easily won a second term and, likewise, St. Louis Democrats held onto the majority of local offices without much difficulty.

Dickmann took advantage of the call to create jobs through construction when he spearheaded plans to construct the Jefferson National Expansion Memorial. He secured $9 million of WPA funds and persuaded St. Louis voters to approve a $7.5 million bond issue in 1935. Members of the planning committee wanted the memorial to commemorate those who had led efforts to expand the borders of the United States. The park was to be built in "old St. Louis" and cover a forty-block area along the riverfront district with stone buildings, murals, gardens, and a museum. After many obstacles, the project, which included the Gateway Arch, was completed in the mid-1960s.

Furthering his commitment to new construction projects, Dickmann followed through on his campaign promise to African American voters to build a public hospital, which voters had approved in 1923, but which former Republican mayor Henry Kiel had failed to have built. African Americans only had access to the inadequate City Hospital No. 2. Incensed over the delayed construction of a new hospital, they had switched their political allegiance to the Democratic ticket. Named after an African American civil rights lawyer who fought against segregation and did not live to see its construction, the Homer G. Phillips Hospital for Colored, a public facility, opened in 1936. The hospital was a leading medical facility for African Americans in the United States, serving as a place to receive quality care and to train the next generation of black doctors and nurses.

Environmentalism distinguished the Dickmann administration, which set out to address a problem that had long plagued the city. The mayor appointed Raymond Tucker, his secretary and an engineering professor, to reduce the levels of smoke emitted when residents and companies burned soft coal. Tucker first suggested that city residents should wash coal before burning it. The board of aldermen implemented the proposal in 1937, but the measure had little effect and met vigorous opposition. Black Tuesday (November 28, 1939), however, swayed public opinion in a most dramatic fashion. A pall of black coal smoke pervaded St. Louis's daytime skies and frightened many into supporting the reform effort. In the aftermath, Tucker moved to ban use of Illinois coal and Dickmann successfully persuaded the board of aldermen to pass the plan in April 1940. The city's work in reducing air pollution gained national attention, other cities adopted Tucker's model, and in 1940 the *St. Louis Post-Dispatch* won a Pulitzer Prize for its coverage of the clean air campaign.

Dickmann sought a third term in 1941, but oppositional forces were firmly in place by this time, especially after Dickmann failed to secure a Democratic win in the 1940 governor's race. Many voters believed the mayor used corrupt tactics to prevent a Democratic defeat for over a month. When Dickmann faced his opponent in the mayor's race, Judge William Dee Becker, he won only four wards and lost by thirty-five thousand votes. Republicans largely reestablished their power as all those who ran for ward representative won. During his two terms Dickmann failed to truly alter St. Louis's ward-based political style by centralizing Democratic power, but he lessened the impact of the depression and helped define and bolster the city's civic identity.

INDUSTRY, COMMERCE, AND LABOR

Ranked seventh in manufacturing nationwide, St. Louis's economic landscape was diverse, with no single dominant industry. Leading manufacturing companies in the shoe, clothing, electrical, auto, tobacco, food products, meatpacking, chemicals, drugs, iron, and steel industries all employed a sizable number of workers. With its three thousand five hundred factories, ten thousand retail companies, and twenty-six steam railroads, St. Louis had no large industries that employed the lion's share of wageworkers. Known for "shoes and booze," St. Louis partially maintained itself after the stock market crash dramatically reduced the city's manufacturing output because the repeal of the Eighteenth Amendment in 1933 empowered large brewing companies such as Anheuser-Busch to restart production and help revive the economy. An increase in the number of women workers also helped. By 1940 women comprised 28 percent of the city's workforce, 6 percent higher than the national average. Women industrial workers, with lower rates of unemployment than men, used the meager wages they earned to take care of their families.

The number of unemployed workers in St. Louis was greater than the national average during this time. By early 1933 the unemployment rate in the city was 30 percent, with African Americans disproportionately represented. From 1929 to 1936 poor people across all races lived in Hooverville, which consisted of metal shacks lining the Mississippi River. Despite its diverse set of industries, the Gateway City was hard hit by the depression.

The pervasiveness of unemployment and meager wages for those fortunate enough to earn them created an environment ripe for protest. The Unemployed Council (UC) of the Communist Party conducted several marches to City Hall. In January 1931 activists called for the wealthy and for companies to administer aid to poor persons through taxation. After local officials announced that they would release fifteen thousand families from the city's relief rolls, UC activists waged a second demonstration in July of the same year. These actions were successful in pushing city government to take more robust action. After the protest, for example, Mayor Dickmann administered relief to one thousand unemployed workers who had been turned away. When a third march ended in casualties, Dickmann supplied additional municipal funds for relief, called for more federal aid, and restored to the relief roster those families that had been removed.

The dramatic UC confrontations unleashed a tidal wave of labor protests. Before the depression, the AFL had represented fewer than fifty thousand workers, but after the passage of section 7(A) of the National Industrial Recovery Act, which guaranteed to workers the right to collectively bargain, membership swelled to seventy-five thousand. One researcher found that the AFL chartered thirty-one locals in St. Louis after the historic legislation passed. Others followed in the footsteps of the UC demonstrators. In 1933 women nut pickers, the majority of whom were African American, joined forces with the Communist Party to successfully demand better pay and improved working conditions. Women members of the International Garment Workers Union went on strike the same year, and members and sympathizers of the American Workers Union waged a sit-down strike at City Hall when, again, fourteen thousand locals lost their places on relief rolls. During the summer of 1933 autoworkers at the Chevrolet-Fisher Body plant joined the AFL, next formed an independent union, and later became members of the

CIO. Over a thousand workers joined the new union, shut down the plant, and formed a United Auto Workers local. In 1937 Emerson Electric workers staged a fifty-three-day sit-down strike for better conditions, wages, and union recognition of its CIO local of the United Electrical Workers Union. After a series of negotiations, Emerson agreed to recognize the union.

A battle between the AFL and its philosophy of craft unionism and the CIO with its mass production organizing model resulted in a split in the St. Louis labor movement. In 1937 the Central Trades and Labor Union expunged its CIO unions after a vote of 274 to 77, with 42 abstentions. All of those expunged were CIO unions, including the Amalgamated Clothing Workers with its one thousand eight hundred members, the International Ladies Garment Workers with two thousand five hundred members, and the United Auto Workers with three thousand five hundred members. At this time the local CIO's membership topped sixteen thousand members.

RACE, ETHNICITY, AND IMMIGRATION

The fourth largest city in the United States at the turn of the century, St. Louis entered the 1930s in seventh place, with a population of 821,960. By the end of the decade and the opening of the next, the Gateway City dropped to the eighth position, having for the first time in over a century a total population that dropped, albeit slightly. The immigration restrictions of the 1920s led to a significant decline in the foreign-born population, so that in 1930 only 9.9 percent of the city's residents were foreign-born, a decline of approximately 3 percent compared to figures from the 1920 census. The depression helped further this trend as a number of immigrants chose to postpone their move or return to their country of origin. The small percentage of Chinese, for instance, dropped by 50 percent from 1929 to 1939. St. Louis's foreign-born population was small compared to major urban centers. Of the ten largest U.S. cities in 1930 and 1940, for example, St. Louis ranked ninth in the percentage of foreign-born residents.

The city was deeply divided along racial and ethnic lines even as most immigrants were segregated on the north and south sides of the city and downtown near the riverfront. Those of German ancestry, including Mayor Dickmann, comprised the largest immigrant population, followed by Italians, Russians, Irish, Poles, and Hungarians. German Americans were the most entrenched socially and economically; they generally held deep ties to the Republican Party. A divide existed between German Jews, who held prominent leadership and professional positions and were of the Reform tradition, and Russian Jews, who lived in segregated enclaves east of Grand Avenue, were less financially stable, and were committed to Orthodox teachings and practices. Irish and Poles resided in north St. Louis, while Italians lived in the southwestern section. "Dago Hill" was a thriving Italian working-class community. A well-entrenched community, the Hill had nearly 60 percent of its mostly small, shotgun homes inhabited, while only 32 percent of total city homes had occupants. Hop Alley, or Chinatown, a strip between Walnut and Market Streets downtown, was home to Chinese businesses such as laundries, grocery stores, restaurants, and community organizations. Business leader Joe Lin served as "mayor" of Chinatown because he led the On Leong Chinese Merchants and Laborers Association, an organization that met the social, legislative, political, and economic needs of its professional and working-class members.

Ethnic and racial groups played a tremendous role in bringing about the historic Democratic takeover, and ward bosses were central to the effort. Serving as justice of the peace in 1932, Anton Sestric, of Croatian descent, delivered his predominantly Slavic and Lebanese constituency by offering them jobs. Irishman Robert Hannegan, who served as 21st Ward committeeman in 1933, was the engine behind the Dickmann machine as one of the mayor's key advisors. Between the mid-1920s and early 1942, first- and second-generation Italians became increasingly involved in political issues as a means to gain better jobs and access to New Deal programs. Irish Americans were also loyal Democrats. Their Fairmont Democratic Club, founded in 1924, helped to lock in a Democratic victory. Italian American Louis Jean Gualdoni served as state Democratic committeeman from 1926 to 1941, street commissioner from 1936 to 1941, and a 24th Ward committeeman of the largest city district. With great clout Gualdoni was directly in charge of several hundred jobs, which he dispensed to his loyal base. Lou Berra, another prominent Italian American politician, served as revenue collector from 1929 to 1962 and as member of the board of aldermen from 1938 to 1954.

Jordan Chambers persuaded African Americans to abandon the party of Lincoln in record numbers. For his efforts he was elected 19th Ward committeeman in 1938, the first African American to do so. African Americans made up about 11 percent of the total city population in 1930 and over 13 percent in 1940. They mainly resided in the city's central and riverfront district but also lived in a neighborhood called the Ville, which was west of Grand Avenue on the city's north side. Less than one square block, the Ville had been bought and developed by Charles M. Elleard in 1860 and annexed by the city of St. Louis in 1876. First home to mostly Irish and German immigrants, Elleardsville, its formal designation, grew to become a center of black life by the early twentieth century. It is estimated that the Ville's black population grew from 8 to 95 percent between 1920 and 1950. An alternative to crowded Mill Creek Valley and other points further east, the north St. Louis hub of African American institution-building reached legendary status, becoming home to the first black high school constructed west of the Mississippi, prominent African Methodist Episcopal and Baptist churches, and black beauty shops and other businesses.

See also *St. Louis, MO 1854–1877; St. Louis, MO 1877–1896; St. Louis, MO 1896–1929; St. Louis, MO 1941–1952*

KEONA K. ERVIN

BIBLIOGRAPHY

Primary Source

Labor Folder, Local History File St. Louis, St. Louis County Library, Special Collections, St. Louis, Missouri.

Secondary Sources

Corbett, Katharine T. *In Her Place: A Guide to St. Louis Women's History*. St. Louis: Missouri Historical Society Press, 1999.

Feurer, Rosemary. *Radical Unionism in the Midwest, 1900–1950*. Urbana: University of Illinois Press, 2006.

————, ed. *The St. Louis Labor History Tour*. St. Louis, MO: St. Louis Bread and Roses, 1994.

Fox, Tim, ed. *Where We Live: A Guide to St. Louis Communities*. Columbia: Missouri Historical Society Press, 1995.

Primm, James Neal. *Lion of the Valley: St. Louis, Missouri, 1764–1980*. 3d ed. Columbia: University of Missouri Press, 1998.

Stein, Lana. *St. Louis Politics: The Triumph of Tradition*. Columbia: University of Missouri Press, 2002.

BOSTON, MA 1929–1941

BOSTON CELEBRATED ITS TRICENTENNIAL IN 1930, and for this "city upon a hill," which had long looked more fondly upon its historic past than upon its uncertain future, the opening of its fourth century posed severe new challenges. Not only would the difficult times of the depression decade intensify the city's already-evident economic stagnation, but they would also exacerbate the city's social divisions, mocking John Winthrop's vision of establishing a "Modell of Christian Charity." Politics as practiced in Boston proved incapable of producing a leader who could harness the city's resources or bridge its chasms.

In 1941 the *Boston Evening Transcript*, founded 111 years earlier and the oldest of the city's eight daily newspapers, published its last edition. Best known for its genealogical charts of Massachusetts' first families, the *Transcript* upheld the genteel tradition for which Boston had long been famous and which was now increasingly only a pleasant memory. The death of the *Transcript* was yet another break with Boston's past, leaving the city still more unsure about its future.

GOVERNMENT AND POLITICS

Just as he had during the prior decade and a half, James Michael Curley, a Democrat, dominated the politics of Boston for the dozen years between the stock market crash and the attack on Pearl Harbor. Three times a candidate for the legally nonpartisan post of mayor during this period, Curley also placed his name on the statewide ballot for three elections. He encountered more setbacks than successes, but he was a ubiquitous force that always had to be reckoned with, and the political obituaries written in 1941 following his fourth consecutive defeat were premature.

Curley took the oath for the third time as Boston's chief magistrate on January 6, 1930, under the widening and darkening clouds of economic depression. He addressed the growing problem of unemployment in his inaugural speech, pledging an expansive program of public construction that would supply "work and wages" to those unable to find jobs in the private sector. Since Curley had built his political career on providing such services and opportunities, this policy was nothing new, but the hard times of the early 1930s gave added urgency to his plans and highlighted the liabilities he brought to the fulfillment of these worthy objectives.

QUICK FACTS

BOSTON, MA **1929–1941**

MAYORS

Malcolm Nichols	(1926–1930)
James Michael Curley	(1930–1934)
Frederick W. Mansfield	(1934–1938)
Maurice Tobin	(1938–1942)

Boston Evening Globe
Boston Globe
Boston Herald
Boston Post
Boston Record
Boston Traveler

MAJOR INDUSTRIES AND EMPLOYERS

Wholesale and retail trade
Manufacturing
Domestic service
Clerical
Transportation and communications

MAJOR NEWSPAPERS

Boston American
Boston Evening Transcript

MAJOR EVENTS

1929: James Michael Curley is elected to his third (nonconsecutive) term as mayor.

1932: Lee, Higginson & Co., a prominent Boston investment banking house, collapses.

1934: Sumner Tunnel opens under Boston Harbor, the first road connection between North End and East Boston.

1935: Prominent religious radio figure Father Charles Coughlin is greeted warmly on a visit to Boston.

1937: Former Curley protégé Maurice J. Tobin defeats Curley in the mayoral election.

1941: Tobin once again defeats Curley, who thus suffers his fourth consecutive loss at the polls.

Boston's controversial mayor had to contend not only with the Republican-controlled state legislature, which did not trust Curley to spend public monies honestly or efficiently, but also with the Democratic governor, Joseph B. Ely, a member of an old New England Protestant family from western Massachusetts, whose election in 1930 Curley had opposed because Ely was "an enemy of the Irish." Not surprisingly, Curley received only a fraction of the resources he sought. Fortunately for the rising number of Bostonians without jobs, the city's public welfare department, a legacy of its Puritan heritage and one of the most generous in the nation, helped fill the breach.

Blocked at the state level, Curley fared little better in Washington. Although he enjoyed the distinction of being the only prominent Bay State Democrat to endorse Franklin D. Roosevelt for the presidency prior to the party's national convention, he could not overcome the stain of corruption that had become irrevocably attached to him. Roosevelt's administration denied Curley the prestigious cabinet and ambassadorial appointments he coveted and delayed sending federal funds until bureaucratic safeguards to assure their honest disbursement could be implemented.

Boston voters delivered their own rebuke to Curley (prohibited by state law from running for a consecutive term) in 1933, when they chose his defeated opponent from 1929 to succeed him. Frederick W. Mansfield, although an Irish Catholic like Curley, was his antithesis in almost every other way. "As spectacular as a four-day-old codfish and as colorful as a lump of mud" was how Curley described him, and Mansfield's fiscal conservatism won him plaudits from the very "goo-goos," good government reformers, Curley despised. When the former mayor, riding the New Deal wave, won the governorship in 1934, Mansfield received the same treatment Ely had given Curley.

Curley's single term as governor (1935–1936) was a disaster for the commonwealth, its largest city, and Curley's political fortunes. Federal funding was again held back as New Deal officials attempted to keep the money away from Curley's control; Mansfield and Curley traded charges of corruption and intimidation, and the governor suffered a series of personal misadventures that damaged his image. Seeking a broader stage, Curley ran for the U.S. Senate in 1936 but lost, in a year extremely favorable to most Democratic candidates, to that epitome of Boston's elite caste, Henry Cabot Lodge Jr.

James Curley, a Democrat, dominated Boston politics during four nonconsecutive terms as mayor during four decades of the twentieth century. Curley had earlier served in the House of Representatives and was elected governor of Massachusetts during the 1930s. Here, Curley stands with candidate Franklin Roosevelt, whom he supported, in the 1932 presidential election.   *Source: AP Photo*

In 1937 Curley attempted yet again to recapture the mayor's office. He encountered voter fatigue as well as an attractive challenger, whose candidacy demonstrated Curley's failure to groom a successor. Never interested in building a structured political organization because it might put limits on him, Curley provided his allies with no indication of where they stood in his plans for the future. One of those supporters who tired of waiting for Curley to step aside was Maurice Tobin, an Irish Catholic member of the elected school committee, who had not yet been born when Curley first won public office in 1899. Good-looking and an effective stump speaker, Tobin could count on backing from many school department employees as well as fellow workers at the telephone company, where he was a manager. Tobin attacked Curley for piling up the municipal debt in his previous administrations and benefitted from a court ruling ordering the former mayor to repay the city more than $40,000 he had allegedly siphoned from the municipal treasury.

One incident in the 1937 contest became part of the city's political folklore. On election day the *Boston Post*, a newspaper widely read in the Irish neighborhoods, printed the following statement in a front-page box above the morning daily's masthead: "VOTERS OF BOSTON: Cardinal O'Connell, in speaking to the Catholic Alumni Association, said, 'The walls are raised against honest men in civic life.' You can break down these walls by voting for an honest, clean, competent young man, MAURICE TOBIN, today. He will redeem the city and take it out of the hands of those who have been responsible for graft and corruption." Only if readers paid close attention to the punctuation would they see that the Cardinal had not in fact endorsed Tobin. Curley immediately sent an emissary to the Cardinal's residence seeking to have O'Connell repudiate the *Post*'s ploy, but His Eminence, no admirer of the former mayor, kept his silence. Whether the ruse was as decisive as legend would have it is not clear, but Tobin captured nearly 40 percent of the ballots in a four-man field, outpolling Curley by twenty-five thousand votes.

Tobin improved the city's relationships with both the federal and state governments; brought many non-Irish professionals into his administration; and imposed hiring freezes, salary reductions, and service cuts to bring the budget into balance. But his long-term solution to the city's financial ills, a city sales tax, failed to gain the Republican-controlled state legislature's approval. Austerity may have been a sound response to Boston's problems, but it was not a popular one.

No one could better exploit the electorate's unhappiness with a reduced municipal government than Curley. Thwarted in his 1938 bid to regain the governorship, he challenged Tobin in 1941. Tobin could be a candidate to succeed himself because the state legislature had repealed the law barring consecutive terms. The measure was a Republican display of support for a responsible Irish Catholic mayor and a sign that Bay State politicians thought Curley's day had finally passed. But with his pledge to restore city services and his attacks on Tobin's close ties to Republicans, Curley almost pulled off an upset. He cut the incumbent's margin of victory by 60 percent, losing by less than ten thousand votes. If this was indeed Curley's last hurrah, he had gone down fighting.

INDUSTRY, COMMERCE, AND LABOR

Boston entered the depression decade better positioned than many of the nation's other large cities to cope with the damage inflicted by the collapse of the economy. Besides having a more highly developed public welfare system that could succor the rising number of needy families, Boston also had a diversified economic base that shielded the city from the sharp declines in both industrial and agricultural production. Nevertheless, the Hub came out of the 1930s weaker than it had gone in.

Although Boston capitalists financed the development of the massive textile factories that made New England the manufacturing center of the country in the middle of the nineteenth century, the city itself was not home to large-scale industry. It had neither the open spaces nor the ready access to the cheap sources of power that were required. At the onset of the Great Depression, less than a third of Boston's labor force of three hundred fifty thousand was engaged in any form of manufacturing, and not one of the ten most important industrial categories employed as many as seven thousand workers. Small-scale clothing and shoe manufacturers, textile mills, printing companies, and food-processing firms generated the bulk of the jobs where employees operated machinery.

From its colonial beginnings, Boston had based its economy on trade, and commerce remained the lifeblood of the city three centuries later. The Boston wool market was the largest in the nation and the importation of leather was also a major enterprise; together, the wholesale and retail trades employed over one hundred thousand workers. On the other hand, the quantity of cargo passing through the Port of Boston had long been falling, with the European trade practically drying up and most of this movement of goods consisting of imports.

The key commodity of colonial trade, fishing, continued in that role. A fleet of five hundred vessels sailed from the harbor, making Boston the largest fishing port in the Western Hemisphere. "The Sacred Cod," a wooden codfish that had hung prominently in the Massachusetts House of Representatives chamber since the eighteenth century, symbolized the commonwealth's reliance on the rich fishing areas of the Atlantic.

By contrast, neither of Boston's two most prestigious investment banking houses, Kidder, Peabody and Company, and Lee, Higginson and Company, survived the harsh economic climate. Short of capital and led by plodding executives, Kidder, Peabody collapsed in 1931 and was bailed out by J. P. Morgan and Company. Lee, Higginson suffered an even more ignoble end the following year, the victim of a great swindle by the Swedish "match king," Ivar Kreuger.

If Lee, Higginson's humiliation cast a shadow over the reputation of Boston's financial community as prudent trustees of other people's money, other members of this community were expanding their operations in a relatively new field of asset management. The Massachusetts Investors Trust, established in 1924 in Boston, was the first modern mutual fund, and the 1930s saw the formation of competitors, notably Putnam. Boston became the center of the industry, and in 1943 Boston attorney Edwin Johnson II assumed command of, and turned into a powerhouse, what would become Fidelity Investments.

Mutual funds, fishing, and wholesaling and retailing aside, the 1930s witnessed a general deterioration of the Boston economy. The industrial work force declined 25 percent, and laborers in this sector earned more than a third less in 1939 than they had a decade earlier. Employment in the shoe and leather trades fell 50 percent, while the ranks of garment workers slipped by 30 percent. Thanks to the New Deal, union membership rose, but since Boston had generally been a leader in the movement to organize labor, it actually lost ground to other large urban areas in respect to wages as they saw even bigger increases in the number of unionized workers. The mobilization of the economy for defense at the start of the 1940s put Boston at a further disadvantage, as it did not have the industrial base that could capitalize on the vast flow of federal spending.

The 1940 Census reported that Boston, for the first time since the federal government began conducting the decennial counts in 1790, had lost population. Although the decline of 1.3 percent was hardly noticeable in the still highly congested city, it was yet another indication of the toll the depression decade had exacted on the metropolis.

RACE, ETHNICITY, AND IMMIGRATION

The "great knife of the Depression," to use Robert and Helen Lynd's famous phrase, left Boston not only a poorer city materially, but also a more divided community socially. Long torn by the ancient Anglo-Irish conflict brought to these shores by the massive Hibernian migration beginning in the 1840s, Boston saw cultural discord assume new forms and wider dimensions during the 1930s, as the difficult local economic circumstances and a rise in international tensions brought new players into the mix.

No dramatic demographic shifts occurred in the 1930s to challenge the continued labeling of Boston as the "Dublin of America," but the dominance of the Irish majority would be tested. By the close of the decade, Italians broke the control that the Irish had exercised over representation of the North End (an Italian neighborhood for decades) and the West End (where Italians increasingly were displacing Irish residents) on the city council, and for a few years in the middle of the decade Jews were able to double their seats on the council from one to two. Yet as the succession of mayors from Curley to Mansfield to Tobin demonstrated, in citywide contests the Irish prevailed.

No individual personified the Irish Catholic grip on Boston's politics and social outlook more than the archbishop, Cardinal William O'Connell. Without formally endorsing either Mansfield or Tobin, O'Connell still let the faithful know where his preferences lay on election day. At the state level, O'Connell successfully blocked a proposed state lottery and defeated a referendum to loosen the restrictions on birth control.

If O'Connell confined himself to issues close to the Church's doctrine, Father Charles E. Coughlin, the Detroit "radio priest," found a receptive audience in Boston for his attacks on international bankers. Governor Curley, who called Boston the "strongest Coughlin city in America," welcomed the priest to the Hub in August 1935, where he received a standing ovation at the State House.

As the thinly veiled anti-Semitism of Coughlin's earlier sermons gave way to the fully blown version as the 1930s wore on, his Boston listeners were prone to turn his vicious talk into vicious action. Ever since Jews began arriving in Boston in significant numbers starting in the 1880s, they had suffered social and economic bigotry at the hands of Brahmins and Yankees, making for common ground with the Irish. But inspired by Coughlin's words, Irish youths targeted Jews walking neighborhood streets as fair game for physical attacks.

If in the difficult times of the depression the Boston Irish rallied around a religious figure, the city's Italians latched on to a political icon—and a foreign one at that. Denied an influential role in municipal governance, and coming out on the short end in gaining relief jobs as a consequence, Boston's Italians looked abroad for solace and took comfort in the apparent success of Benito Mussolini in restoring Italy to its former grandeur. Ethnic identity, always strong among Italians, reached even higher levels in the depression as their economic woes were slow to disappear and Mussolini swaggered through continental politics. Indicative of their frustrations with conditions at home and their fear of war against their ancestral country, Italians supported Roosevelt with noticeably less enthusiasm in 1940 than they had in 1932.

By contrast, Boston's Jews united around the president, with more than 86 percent of the ballots cast in Ward 14 endorsing his bid for a third term. Although still barred from important elected positions by Protestant domination of the GOP and Irish control of the Democratic Party, Jews received unprecedented recognition from the national administration in presidential appointments. The growing anti-Semitism of the 1930s, in the city and in Europe, also led Boston's Jews to pull together as never before. They became the first Jewish community to combine its charitable fundraising into one joint appeal, and their diverse collection of synagogues established an umbrella organization to facilitate consultation.

Although Boston's African American population expanded from 2.6 percent of the city total in 1930 to 3.1 percent in 1940, the black community in the Hub was still a much smaller fraction of the whole than in other large northeastern and midwestern municipalities. As elsewhere, the depression hit blacks the hardest, making it harder for them to progress in the job market and intensifying residential segregation. Possessing no political clout, they remained, aside from an occasional protest against discrimination, practically invisible in the life of the city.

See also *Boston, MA 1776–1790; Boston, MA 1790–1828; Boston, MA 1828–1854; Boston, MA 1854–1877; Boston, MA 1877–1896; Boston, MA 1896–1929; Boston, MA 1941–1952*

MARK I. GELFAND

BIBLIOGRAPHY

Beatty, Jack. *The Rascal King: The Life and Times of James Michael Curley, 1874–1958*. Reading, MA: Addison-Wesley, 1992.

Lapomarda, Vincent A. *The Boston Mayor Who Became Truman's Secretary of Labor: Maurice J. Tobin and the Democratic Party*. New York, NY: Peter Lang, 1995.

O'Connor, Thomas H. *The Boston Irish: A Political History*. Boston, MA: Northeastern University Press, 1995.

Sarna, Jonathan, Ellen Smith, and Scott-Martin Kosofsky, eds. *The Jews of Boston*. Rev. and updated ed. New Haven, CT: Yale University Press, 2005.

Stack, John F. Jr. *International Conflict in an American City: Boston's Irish, Italians, and Jews, 1935–1944*. Westport, CT: Greenwood Press, 1979.

Trout, Charles H. *Boston, The Great Depression, and the New Deal*. New York, NY: Oxford University Press, 1977.

PITTSBURGH, PA 1929–1941

BY 1929 PITTSBURGH HAD ALREADY SURRENDERED ITS TITLE AS THE STEELMAKING CAPITAL of America. The city's iron and steel, glass, food processing, and electrical machinery industries still prospered in the 1920s; new skyscrapers, such as the Koppers and Grant Buildings, arose downtown; planners laid out a regional highway system; and three new bridges spanned the Allegheny River. Yet the earlier invention of by-product coke ovens had greatly weakened Pittsburgh's geographical advantage in steelmaking, which steadily migrated to places like Gary, Indiana, closer to the source of iron ore. Thus, it was a severely vulnerable Pittsburgh that by 1931 found itself mired deep in the Great Depression. Pittsburgh's steel, glass, and electrical machinery economy limped through the depression until orders for war materiel in 1939, and the onset of World War II in 1941, triggered a short-lived resurgence in the city's capital-intensive industrial economy.

MAYORS

Charles Howard Klein   (1926–1933)
William Nissley McNair   (1933–1936)
Cornelius Decatur Scully   (1936–1946)

MAJOR INDUSTRIES AND EMPLOYERS

Carnegie-Illinois Steel Corporation
   (aka U.S. Steel)
Westinghouse Electric and
   Manufacturing Company
Jones and Laughlin Steel Corporation
National Tube Company
Allegheny Ludlum Steel Corporation

MAJOR NEWSPAPERS

Pittsburgh Post-Gazette
Pittsburgh Press
Pittsburgh Sun-Telegraph

MAJOR EVENTS

1932: Father James R. Cox, Pittsburgh's "Mayor of Shantytown," leads a Hunger March from Pittsburgh to Washington, D.C., to aid the jobless.

1934: Pittsburgh politician David L. Lawrence becomes chairman of the Pennsylvania Democratic Party. Lawrence later orchestrated Franklin D. Roosevelt's 1936 victory in Pittsburgh and the rise of Democratic power in the city.

1936: Eccentric "Single Taxer" Mayor William N. McNair, who viscerally opposed all New Deal aid in the city, resigns, paving the way for his successor, Cornelius D. Scully, to welcome federal assistance and aid the rise of David Lawrence.

1936: On St. Patrick's Day, flood waters engulf downtown Pittsburgh. The crisis deepens the aura of despair and forces civic and business leaders to seek federal flood control and other city improvements.

Late 1930s: Brought to Pittsburgh in the wake of the 1936 flood at the behest of Howard Heinz, New York Park Commissioner and planning consultant Robert Moses drafts the celebrated Arterial [City] Plan for Pittsburgh, which greatly influences the future Pittsburgh Renaissance.

GOVERNMENT AND POLITICS

When Wall Street crashed in October 1929 Republican Charles Howard Kline was serving as Pittsburgh's mayor. Once a state legislator, Kline was tapped for the post by the city's powerful Republican luminary and President Calvin Coolidge's Secretary of the Treasury, Andrew Mellon. At that time the blessing of Pittsburgh's and Pennsylvania's powerful Republican machine led by William Larimer Mellon, William S. Vare, and Joseph Grundy was tantamount to victory. However, political infighting among state Republicans during the 1920s convulsed Pennsylvania's Grand Old Party, rendering it vulnerable to independents and even the enfeebled Democratic Party.

In 1929 Kline, now considered a maverick who favored public spending for massive public works, won reelection over the protest of boss William Larimer Mellon. Three years later a scandal involving unexplained expenditures in the city Department of Supplies resulted in charges of malfeasance in office directed against Kline. He was convicted in March 1932.

Scandal, party discord, and the incubus of economic depression, replete with long soup lines and ramshackle "Hoovervilles," climaxed politically in 1932 when Democratic presidential candidate Franklin Delano Roosevelt crashed the gates of once-impregnable Republican Pittsburgh. Behind the huge fifty-thousand-person FDR rally at Pittsburgh's Forbes Field stood David L. Lawrence and Joseph Guffey, who, eyeing GOP carrion, mobilized the city's large Italian, Polish, Hungarian, Slovak, and African American population behind FDR and the upstart Democratic Party. The African American editor of the nationally circulated *Pittsburgh Courier* urged city blacks to "turn Lincoln's picture to the wall."

Roosevelt's Pittsburgh triumph in November 1932, and the resurgence of the long dormant Pittsburgh Democratic Party, inspired Lawrence to seat a Democrat in the mayor's office. Doubtful that a Catholic like himself could win, Lawrence slated as the mayoral candidate William Nissley McNair, a Gettysburg College and Michigan Law School graduate, perennial Democratic candidate, devout follower of single-tax apostle Henry George, and old-line Pittsburgh Presbyterian. McNair had run unsuccessfully for district attorney in 1911 and for the U.S. Senate in 1928. But in 1933 he fit Lawrence's bill: a long-time Democrat, a protestant, and an anti-machine, good-government crusader with strong appeal for independents. He won handily by 103,117 votes.

During the campaign McNair never disguised his Henry George bias and like earlier progressives, attacked evil utilities and espoused the five-cent trolley fare. However, he also praised FDR and the National Industrial Recovery Act (NIRA). A vote for McNair, he exhorted, was a vote for FDR. Following Lawrence he likewise courted Pittsburgh's new Democratic constituency, Poles, blacks, and Italians, addressing the latter in surprisingly presentable Italian.

McNair's victory proved a disaster for Lawrence and his nascent Democratic political organization, which he had hoped to harness to New Deal–generated patronage. Despite McNair's pro–New Deal rhetoric, the new mayor clung to the single tax, convinced that a high tax on land, not buildings, would usher in an urban utopia. In 1933, with thousands of Pittsburghers jobless and hundreds living in a squalid shanty town or Hooverville bordering the city's rail yards, McNair stubbornly rebuffed all New Deal relief programs, including Harry Hopkins's Federal Emergency Relief Administration (FERA) and Civil Works Administration (CWA), created to provide work relief to the jobless during the bitter winter of 1933–1934. Instead, McNair set up a desk in the hallway of City Hall and personally interviewed jobless clients seeking assistance. With over ten thousand still jobless in 1935, McNair proposed housing the needy in tents located at the city's poor house. That same year McNair barred from the city Hopkins's Works Progress Administration (WPA), viewing all New Deal public works programs as nothing more than fodder for the Lawrence-Guffey machine. When Pittsburgh's chief engineer defended WPA, McNair fired him. Year after year McNair's actions defied not only Lawrence but, indeed, reason. He slashed city payrolls, including the young city planning department. In January 1936 he declared all but one of the city council seats vacant after members failed to attend a meeting he had called. Then in early October 1936 McNair fired the city treasurer, whose signature was required by law on all city checks. For McNair the act proved fatal. When the city council refused to appoint a new treasurer, city operations ceased and McNair was forced to resign on October 6, 1936.

McNair's successor, Cornelius Decatur Scully (who as president of the city council assumed the mayor's office) warmly embraced the New Deal. Like McNair, Scully too followed Henry George, but unlike McNair, his discipleship never precluded loyalty to the New Deal. In 1937, with Lawrence's support, Scully won the mayor's office on his own and eagerly cooperated with Washington in an ambitious program of public works, including the building of the Parkway East.

Scully reinvigorated Pittsburgh's planning department, which, aided by the WPA, conducted a major topographical study, a real estate survey, and an air quality investigation. WPA labor paved miles of city streets, laid water and sewer pipes, catalogued books at the Carnegie Library, and built walkways and trails at Schenley and other city parks. It developed city playgrounds, executed a master plan for city recreation, and undertook a significant countywide road, bridge, and airport project vital to Pittsburgh's future. For jobless Pittsburgh women, the WPA operated a large-scale sewing project; other projects served both artists and musicians, including the Pittsburgh WPA symphony.

In the wake of the 1936 St. Patrick's Day flood, Scully regularly traveled to Washington to win federal Public Works Administration (PWA) backing for key flood control, highway, bridge, and other major infrastructure projects that helped lay the groundwork for what became after World War II the Pittsburgh Renaissance.

INDUSTRY, COMMERCE, AND LABOR

Urban renaissance seemed unimaginable in 1931 as the city's heavily capitalized iron, steel, glass, and electrical goods industries plunged into depression. Pittsburgh, prosperous in the lush 1920s, edged down slowly from 1929 to 1930 and then steeply declined in 1931. That year the city's steel industry operated at less than 40 percent of capacity. Between 1930 and 1931 the city's glass output fell from 105,827,000 square feet to just over 83,000,000. By 1933 overall production in Pittsburgh had dropped a third from its 1929 high. Meanwhile, unemployment skyrocketed. In January 1931 more than sixty thousand Pittsburghers searched in vain for work. Two years later over two hundred thousand of Allegheny County's residents were unemployed; about 16 percent of the city's labor force was without work. That figure rose to 43 percent for African Americans and certain ethnic groups. Many families lived on potatoes; Mayor Kline helped set up the jobless at apple stands. In the classic, vividly etched novel *Out of this Furnace,* Thomas Bell revealed the experience of Pittsburgh's ethnic workforce during this period. He described the life of the demoralized jobless, especially those evicted from their homes or facing imminent eviction, who for food and mutual support often turned to Marxist groups such as the Workers Alliance or the Unemployed Council. These groups regularly demonstrated at eviction sites.

Fearful in 1930 that even meager public aid to private social agencies amounted to the dreaded dole, Pittsburgh's conservative business community mobilized to raise relief money among the private sector. As the Allegheny County Emergency Association (ACEA), these businessmen fashioned the Pittsburgh Plan whereby businesses allocated a sum to the ACEA equivalent to their total payroll for 1929. The ACEA hoped to raise $3 million but raised merely $1.3 million, a sum spent mainly for work relief wages at $4 a day. With limited resources the experiment, which Herbert Hoover's President's Organization on Unemployment Relief had fulsomely lauded, failed. By late 1931 another of the city's voluntary relief agencies, the Helping Hand, sheltered and fed between one thousand five hundred and three thousand men nightly. In January 1932 Father James Cox of St. Patrick's Church led an "army" of the unemployed from Pittsburgh to Washington seeking federal assistance. They were cheered along the way and Hoover met with Cox; but the president promised no immediate aid. These would be the same Pittsburgh jobless that welcomed FDR's New Deal and eagerly awaited the federal direct and work relief assistance of Harry Hopkins's FERA, CWA, and WPA, only to be frustrated by the obstructionism of Mayor McNair.

The Pittsburgh industrial establishment, including U.S. Steel, Westinghouse Electric, and H. J. Heinz, initially welcomed the New Deal, especially NIRA and Harold Ickes's PWA, which undertook massive road, dam, and bridge-building projects, boosting the demand for steel. Likewise, Roosevelt's termination of the prohibition experiment increased demand for steel beer cans. An early spike in automobile sales had a similar salutary impact on steel demand, encouraging Jones and Laughlin Steel to launch a $40 million plant expansion by installing new strip and sheet mills at its Pittsburgh Works. Yet despite the turnaround, by 1936 Pittsburgh steel mills still operated at under 40 percent of capacity. In fact, among Pittsburgh businessmen, the New Deal honeymoon ended between 1935 and 1936 as economic recovery slowed, the Supreme Court declared NIRA unconstitutional, and the 1936 presidential election approached.

For Pittsburgh's downtown, the glimmer of industrial recovery meant little. Depressed downtown real estate values and the anti–New Deal antics of Mayor McNair only thickened the black cloud of economic depression. The famous Point itself, the confluence of the Monongahela, Allegheny, and Ohio Rivers, languished as a mélange of abandoned rail yards, warehouse buildings, and unkempt row houses. Soot caked the banking houses on Fourth Avenue, Pittsburgh's architecturally distinguished Wall Street. Downtown real estate assessments declined by over $200 million during the 1930s, which meant a loss of $6 million per year in city taxes. New construction in the district halted with the completion of the forty-four-story Gulf Tower. Asked by a *Pittsburgh Sun-Telegraph* reporter in 1931 what might be done to improve downtown Pittsburgh, architect Frank Lloyd Wright responded, "It's cheaper to abandon it." On St. Patrick's Day in 1936, with an early spring thaw, the three rivers crested at the Point forty-six feet above flood stage, engulfing the city in a torrent of swirling, debris-filled muddy water.

But, rather than delivering a *coup de grace*, the flood energized the city. In the wake of the flood Congress passed the Copeland Omnibus Flood Control Bill, which provided federal monies for massive flood walls, flood control dams, and other navigational improvements. Likewise, the crisis catalyzed Pittsburgh's planning movement. Two months after the flood, Howard Heinz reconvened the Pittsburgh Citizens' Committee on the City Plan (an early casualty of the Great Depression), to take immediate action to revitalize the beleaguered city. Several years later he took a step further. In 1938, while in New York he persuaded the New York State park commissioner and Triborough Bridge Authority chief, Robert Moses, to visit the Steel City and offer planning recommendations, especially for improved traffic flow at, and the aesthetic appearance of, the Point. The resulting Arterial Plan for Pittsburgh, as Moses promised, essentially digested and effectively synthesized several decades of planning decision making and provided the hoped-for direction and impetus for decisive action, which would ultimately come after World War II under the aegis of Lawrence and Richard King Mellon, not Heinz, who died on February 9, 1941. Moses's Arterial Plan called for a parkway or boulevard system skirting the river edges and converging at the Point, where a park and symbolic monument would be built, providing the desired template for a postwar Renaissance.

RACE, ETHNICITY, AND IMMIGRATION

Pittsburgh's population rose almost 14 percent from 588,343 in 1920 to 669,817 in 1930. However, the war, immigration restriction laws in the late 1920s, and the Great Depression slowed foreign immigration to a trickle. Pittsburgh's population during the 1930s rose barely 1 percent to 671,659. In 1930 foreign-born households comprised 16.3 percent of the city's population, down from one-fifth in 1920. By including families headed by offspring born of foreign parentage, in 1930 51 percent of Pittsburghers were of "foreign stock." However, at the end of the depression decade, the number of foreign-born had slipped to 13 percent. Despite the Great Depression, Pittsburgh's African American population continued to rise from almost fifty-five thousand in 1930 (8.3 percent) to over sixty-two thousand in 1940 (9 percent).

Eastern and southern European immigrants created tightly knit ethnic neighborhoods in Pittsburgh, Poles in "Polish Hill" and Italians in Bloomfield and Lawrenceville. African Americans, victims as in other cities of segregation patterns, moved into Manchester, East Liberty, Hazelwood and the city's Hill District, the latter adjacent to downtown and, in the 1930s, one of the most densely settled, poorest, but also integrated ethnic/racial neighborhoods in Pittsburgh. The city's topography of hills and hollows and the system of chain migration helped give these neighborhoods a strong ethnic character; the hard times of the 1930s, which compelled ethnic groups to lean more heavily on kinship networks for survival, added to the stability. Subjected to labor union and other forms of discrimination, African American families suffered most from joblessness and poverty; thus, they moved their residences more frequently, unlike Poles and Italians.

During the 1930s the Hill District remained a busy hive of black, Russian Jewish, Greek, and Italian settlement. Segregation patterns hardened during the decade as joblessness and labor union activity bred racial and ethnic rivalries and hostility rather than brotherhood. For Pittsburgh's ethnic and racial minorities, austere economic conditions endured despite the short-lived recoveries. By 1936 over fifty thousand Pittsburgh families, many of them black or foreign-born, still collected relief checks, and housing conditions had worsened.

In 1932 the city's Buhl Foundation unveiled Chatham Village, the "modern," "affordable," garden city–type housing on Mount Washington designed by Clarence Stein and Henry Wright. Few, if any, working-class families could afford to live there, and housing conditions for Pittsburgh's growing population of the poor further deteriorated. Finally, with the passage in 1937 of the Wagner-Steagall Act and the creation of the Pittsburgh Housing Authority, three "modern," low-rise public housing projects arose atop the Hill District: the Bedford Homes, Terrace Village I, and Terrace Village II. While they were "safe and sanitary," afforded magnificent views of the

Allegheny Valley, and were racially integrated, they hardly satisfied the city's desperate need for adequate shelter as socially and environmentally besieged Pittsburgh was plunged into World War II.

See also *Pittsburgh, PA 1896–1929*

JOHN F. BAUMAN

BIBLIOGRAPHY

Bauman, John, and Edward K. Muller. *Before Renaissance: Planning in Pittsburgh, 1889–1943.* Pittsburgh, PA: University of Pittsburgh Press, 2006.

Bell, Thomas. *Out of this Furnace: A Novel of Immigrant Labor in America.* Pittsburgh, PA: University of Pittsburgh Press, 1976.

Bodnar, John, Roger Simon, and Michael Weber. *Lives of Their Own: Blacks, Italians, and Poles in Pittsburgh, 1900–1960.* Urbana: University of Illinois Press, 1982.

Lorant, Stefan. *Pittsburgh: The Story of a City.* New York, NY: Doubleday, 1964.

Lubove, Roy. *Twentieth-Century Pittsburgh, Volume 1: Government, Business, and Environmental Change.* Pittsburgh, PA: University of Pittsburgh Press, 1995.

Weber, Michael. *Don't Call Me Boss: David L. Lawrence, Pittsburgh's Renaissance Mayor.* Pittsburgh, PA: University of Pittsburgh Press, 1988.

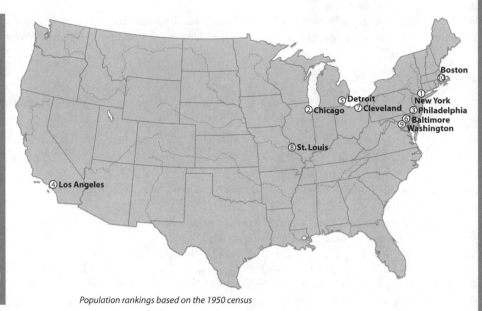

Population rankings based on the 1950 census

CHAPTER 8

CITIES DURING WORLD WAR II AND IN THE POSTWAR PERIOD, 1941–1952

Between 1941 and 1945 American society was transformed by World War II. Over ten million American troops fought throughout the Pacific, in Northern Africa, and in Europe; more than three hundred thousand were killed (compared to total casualties of roughly fourteen million), and hundreds of thousands more injured. Industrial production for the war effort involved unprecedented government spending that revived the economy, and the United States emerged from the struggle as the most powerful country in the world, and the first with nuclear weapons, matched only by the Soviet Union.

With the return of Americans from the war, and the immigration of African Americans northward from the South, the populations of American cities swelled in the 1940s. Collectively, the ten cities covered in this chapter grew by 9 percent,

484

slightly less than twice the rate they had in the 1930s, yet they were still outpaced by population growth of 14 percent nationally, resulting in a country of 151 million people in 1950, a smaller proportion of which (roughly 14 percent) lived in the ten largest cities.

The country's big cities were increasingly surrounded by larger suburban populations. The U.S. Census measured metropolitan populations differently in 1940 and 1950, making comparisons difficult, though still instructive. The total population of the central cities in the 168 "standard metropolitan areas" counted by the census in 1950 was 15 percent greater than the central city populations of the 140 "metropolitan districts" measured in 1940, yet the population in those same areas outside the central cities was 74 percent greater in 1950 than it was in 1940.

By 1950 all but three of the cities covered in this chapter (New York, Los Angeles, and Boston) had black populations proportionately greater than in the country as a whole, in which 10 percent of the total population was black. The proportionately largest black populations were in Washington (35 percent), Baltimore (24 percent), Philadelphia (18 percent), and Detroit (16 percent). In many cities white residents thwarted diversity with racial deed covenants, specifying that their homes were to be sold only to other white people. These deed restrictions were declared unconstitutional by the Supreme Court in 1948 (in *Shelley v. Kraemer*, involving a racial covenant in St. Louis), though they had already done their part, along with other factors, to create racially segregated neighborhoods in American cities. Japanese Americans were even more forcibly segregated, as they were forced to sell their property and move into concentration camps from 1942 to 1944.

Black people, white people, and others were in large part moving to cities in response to available industrial jobs, especially in Detroit and Los Angeles. Unprecedented government spending during the New Deal paled in comparison to spending for the war. The United States took on more than $250 billion in new debt and significantly raised income taxes. Much of the money was invested in ships, aircraft, and related infrastructure, especially in and around Los Angeles, due to its proximity to the Pacific war effort, which turned the city into a major industrial center and explains in part the 31 percent increase in population the city experienced during the 1940s. In Detroit (whose population increased by 14 percent in the 1940s), much of the productive capacity of the automotive industry was used to produce weapon systems for the military.

In response to labor shortages created by World War II, the number of women working outside the home during the war increased by 60 percent, and more than one-third of all teenagers between the ages of fourteen and eighteen had some sort of employment during the war. The need for labor also gave leverage to African Americans. Under pressure from A. Philip Randolph, president of the International Brotherhood of Sleeping Car Porters, who was threatening a massive march on Washington in 1941, Roosevelt established the Fair Employment Practices Commission.

Building on the base established by New Deal labor legislation, union membership soared to more than thirteen million by 1945. Yet in Congress, conservative Democrats and Republicans (who made electoral gains in 1942 and who won majorities in both chambers in 1946) successfully dismantled portions of the New Deal, eliminating the Civilian Conservation Corps and the Works Progress Administration and weakening protections in the National Labor Relations Act in 1947, by which time the war had been over for two years, Roosevelt had died in office, and Harry Truman was president.

BY THE NUMBERS: **THE MOST POPULOUS CITIES IN 1950**

	TOTAL POPULATION[1]	WHITE POPULATION[1]	BLACK POPULATION[1]	OTHER POPULATION[1]	% WHITE POPULATION[1]	% BLACK POPULATION[1]	% OTHER POPULATION[1]	FOREIGN-BORN POPULATION[1]
NEW YORK, NY	7,891,957	7,116,441	747,608	27,908	90.2	9.5	0.4	1,784,206
CHICAGO, IL	3,620,962	3,111,525	492,265	17,172	85.9	13.6	0.5	526,058
PHILADELPHIA, PA	2,071,605	1,692,637	376,041	2,927	81.7	18.2	0.1	232,587
LOS ANGELES, CA	1,970,358	1,758,773	171,209	40,376	89.3	8.7	2.0	247,054
DETROIT, MI	1,849,568	1,545,847	300,506	3,215	83.6	16.2	0.2	276,470
BALTIMORE, MD	949,708	723,655	225,099	954	76.2	23.7	0.1	51,434
CLEVELAND, OH	914,808	765,264	147,847	1,697	83.7	16.2	0.2	132,799
ST. LOUIS, MO	856,796	702,348	153,766	682	82.0	17.9	0.1	41,819
WASHINGTON, DC	802,178	517,865	280,803	3,510	64.6	35.0	0.4	39,497
BOSTON, MA	801,444	758,700	40,057	2,687	94.7	5.0	0.3	144,092

	% WHITE POPULATION FOREIGN-BORN[1]	% POPULATION 7–13 YEARS OLD ENROLLED IN SCHOOL[1]	% POPULATION 25 AND OLDER COLLEGE EDUCATED[1]	% CIVILIAN LABOR FORCE UNEMPLOYED[2]	% EMPLOYED POPULATION IN MANUFACTURING[2]	MEDIAN FAMILY INCOME[3]	LAND AREA (SQ. MI.)[4]	POPULATION DENSITY (PER SQ. MI.)[4]
NEW YORK, NY	25.1	94.5	7.1	6.9	28.0	$3,526	315.1	25,045.9
CHICAGO, IL	16.9	96.4	5.7	4.8	36.7	$3,956	207.5	17,450.4
PHILADELPHIA, PA	13.7	94.5	4.7	6.4	35.2	$3,322	127.2	16,286.2
LOS ANGELES, CA	14.0	97.3	8.6	8.5	22.9	$3,575	450.9	4,369.8
DETROIT, MI	17.9	96.7	5.0	7.3	46.0	$3,955	139.6	13,249.1
BALTIMORE, MD	7.1	95.2	5.2	5.8	29.0	$3,275	78.7	12,059.4
CLEVELAND, OH	17.4	96.2	4.1	5.5	42.4	$3,531	75.0	12,197.4
ST. LOUIS, MO	6.0	94.0	4.4	4.5	33.9	$3,205	61.0	14,045.8
WASHINGTON, DC	7.6	96.2	13.0	3.9	7.3	$3,800	61.4	13,064.8
BOSTON, MA	19.0	96.2	6.4	7.4	23.7	$3,249	47.8	16,766.6

[1] Source: Census of Population: 1950, Volume II, Characteristics of the Population. Table 34.
[2] Source: Census of Population: 1950, Volume II, Characteristics of the Population. Table 34.
[3] Source: Census of Population: 1950, Volume II, Characteristics of the Population. Table 34.
[4] Source: Campbell Gibson, *Population of the 100 Largest Cities and Other Urban Places in the United States: 1790 to 1990.* (1998) Table 18.

By 1944 the Allies had liberated France from the Nazis and were heading from both the east and west toward Germany. Surrounded, Hitler killed himself in 1945. Allied forces destroyed the Japanese navy in the Pacific, and Truman gave an ultimatum to the Japanese government to surrender. The ultimatum was not met, and the United States dropped atomic bombs on Hiroshima and Nagasaki, killing approximately one hundred eighty thousand people and compelling a Japanese surrender.

Nuclear weaponry, probably the most significant of the many technological innovations that characterized World War II, was developed through a U.S. government research program carried out in secret laboratories, the most well-known being in Los Alamos, New Mexico. The Soviet

Union successfully exploded an atomic bomb in 1949, compelling Truman in 1950 to authorize the development of a more powerful hydrogen bomb, thus initiating the nuclear arms race that would be one of the defining elements of the Cold War between the United States and Soviet Union.

After the war, much of the world quickly divided into separate spheres of influence—a product of Stalin's expansionist strategy and the American and western European policy of containment. This policy provided support through the Marshall Plan to countries such as Greece and Turkey that were at risk of being taken over by Soviet-allied Communists and established the North Atlantic Treaty Organization, the twelve-member nations of which agreed to retaliate against an attack on any of the other members.

The resultant Cold War worked in many ways at cross-purposes to the goal of an international civil society, as embodied in the creation of the United Nations in 1945. In the case of the Korean conflict, the strategy of containment became one of open military conflict, involving, on one side, pro-Western South Koreans, the United States, and the United Nations and, on the other side, North Korean Communists and China, under the new government of the People's Republic of China, led by Mao Zedong.

The unpopularity of the Korean War, which dragged on until 1953 with heavy casualties, was one of several factors that hurt Truman's standing among the American public, and he declined to run for office in 1952 (the Twenty-Second Amendment, ratified in 1951, limited presidents to two terms, though Truman would still have been eligible to run). He had won the 1948 election against Republican nominee and New York governor Thomas Dewey, despite the fracturing of Democratic support through a third party—the States' Rights Party, formed in protest against approval of a civil rights platform at the Democratic convention. The States' Rights Party won the electoral votes of Louisiana, Mississippi, Alabama, and South Carolina.

Despite Democratic electoral victories in 1948, the country was clearly becoming more conservative, inspired in part by a deep fear of communism. In control of Congress in 1947, Republicans used the House Un-American Activities Committee to investigate whether Democrats had permitted subversive Communist activities in the government. The issue was used in Republican campaigns across the country, not least by Richard Nixon and Joseph McCarthy, who was elected to the Senate in 1950 and whose name would become synonymous with postwar anti-Communist demagoguery and persecution. In 1952 Nixon was selected to run as the vice presidential candidate on the campaign of former military general Dwight Eisenhower, who handily beat Democratic nominee Adlai Stevenson, a favorite of liberal intellectuals who for the same reason was seen as weak on communism.

NEW YORK, NY 1941–1952

WHILE NEW YORK CITY HAD BEEN THE COMMERCIAL CAPITAL OF THE UNITED STATES since before the nation was born, World War II and its aftermath marked a further ascendancy as the city assumed and solidified its place as the preeminent financial center of the postwar global order. With the establishment of the United Nations in its iconic new headquarters on the east side of Manhattan, the city became a

QUICK FACTS

NEW YORK, NY 1941–1952

MAYORS

Fiorello LaGuardia   (1934–1945)
William O'Dwyer   (1946–1950)
Vincent R. Impellitteri (1950–1953)

MAJOR INDUSTRIES AND EMPLOYERS

Finance
Manufacturing—principally light
    industry
Shipping
Publishing
City, state, and federal government

MAJOR NEWSPAPERS

New York Times
New York Herald Tribune
The Sun (until 1950)
New York Post
New York World-Telegram and Sun
New Amsterdam News
Daily News
Daily Mirror
Wall Street Journal

MAJOR EVENTS

1941–1945: The city's massive manufacturing base is mobilized for wartime production, Mayor LaGuardia serves as chief of the Office of Civilian Defense, and a number of German spies are captured in New York before a sabotage plot could be executed.

1942–1945: Columbia University physicists play a central role in the Manhattan Project. Deep beneath the streets of Morningside Heights, early steps in the development of the nuclear chain reaction are made, nudging the world toward the nuclear age. All told, there were at least ten secret locations, spread throughout Manhattan, where work was done toward the development of an atomic bomb.

1943: In an early sign of the larger racial strife to come, the shooting of an African American soldier by a white police officer in Harlem explodes into overnight looting and fighting between citizens and police.

1945: Widespread labor discontent results in dockworker strikes, prompted by wartime wage freezes and labor controls, overflowing into one of the largest strikes in American history, momentarily halting commerce and war mobilization.

1952: The postwar order, characterized by both U.S. leadership and multilateral action, is symbolized by the completion of the UN's headquarters in Manhattan.

center of postwar international politics as well. As a lens through which the rest of the world was introduced to the era of American leadership, New York's ambitious self-assurance and self-conception as, in the words of a contemporary WNYC station identification, "a city where more than seven million people live in peace and enjoy the benefits of democracy," indicated a place of heightened optimism and bustling energy. While there was never a moment in which all conflict was entirely absent, this era also marked the continuation of mayor Fiorello LaGuardia's inclusive liberal coalition (and later under a resurgent local Democratic Party, which finally overcame the hegemony of the old Tammany machine to represent a broader coalition of interests and groups) centered on extensive provision of public goods, the continued development of the city's infrastructure, and economic growth.

The early 1940s were dominated by wartime mobilization efforts. Government demand heightened manufacturing activity and revived the local economy. While small industrial firms helped turn out materiel and supplies for the war effort, the top-secret Manhattan Project was funded shortly after physicists at Columbia University split the uranium atom in 1939; the project eventually led to the atomic bomb and the onset of the nuclear age. New York leaders, from Mayor LaGuardia (who served as head of the Office of Civilian Defense) to Governor Lehman (who was the first head of the nascent United Nations) to President Roosevelt himself, played pivotal roles in navigating the crisis at home and abroad. The iconic images of celebration in Times Square on VE Day and VJ Day (celebrating victory in Europe and Japan) reflected the confidence and leadership New Yorkers carried into the postwar era.

In hindsight, however, we can see the beginnings of the decline of the colossus on the Hudson even in this period. Most obviously, 1950 marked the city's highest population levels—subsequent censuses revealed a declining population. Just as the city's population was peaking, William Levitt began construction of the first of his Levittowns, the suburban tract developments that would open the suburbs to the working class. Together with urban renewal and massive highway construction projects, such private developments began to sap the strength of major cities across the nation. The 1950s saw the beginnings of middle-class white flight, and the departing residents were often replaced by less-affluent newcomers, a phenomenon that put multiple strains on the local welfare state, the city's finances, and intergroup relations generally.

The optimism of the 1950s would famously erode in the "urban crisis" of the 1960s, 1970s, and 1980s. However, few signs were apparent in the immediate postwar era that New York was anything but a beacon for cultural, economic, and political progress. This was the culmination of a century of urbanization in the United States, and New York was the epitome of that phenomenon—the most populous, most diverse, richest, densest agglomeration of persons in the nation, and perhaps in the world. Suburbanization had already begun to erode the place of the central city in the nation's demography—the peak share of total population in central cities had been achieved in the 1930s—but the visible decline of the city had not begun yet. Instead, faith in a brighter future was centered in places like New York, with its seemingly boundless energy and bustling activity.

GOVERNMENT AND POLITICS

New York was the world's largest city in the mid-twentieth century, and its politics and governance initiatives reflected all the complexity inherent in this reality. With vast fiscal authority and a system that balanced partisan electoral institutions with famously powerful autonomous bureaucrats enjoying long tenures within public authorities such as the Port Authority of New York (and New Jersey) and the Triborough Bridge Authority, the stakes of New York City politics were high and the conflicts between elites over budgets and authority would have lasting effects on the city's political and physical development.

LaGuardia had narrowly defeated the Democrat William O'Dwyer in 1941 to win a third term. LaGuardia did not run in 1945—he was in ill health and deeply involved in setting up the nascent United Nations Relief and Rehabilitation Administration—and O'Dwyer handily defeated his rivals in that contest to win the first of two terms. Though LaGuardia's interlude of reform had badly weakened the Tammany Hall corruption of earlier years, the recurrent scandals of the O'Dwyer years, in which party bosses and police officials were implicated in corrupt dealings with underworld kingpins, as well as Mayor O'Dwyer himself (though he was not officially charged with anything) were reminders of persistent corruption. Ironically, O'Dwyer had initially garnered much of his political reputation as the prosecutorial adversary of the "Murder, Inc." mob ring of the late 1930s and early 1940s. Much of this corruption was later revealed in the sensational hearings of the Kefauver Commission in 1952, in which mob boss Frank Costello's close ties to Democratic club leaders throughout much of the city were revealed. O'Dwyer resigned as the scandal was breaking, amid suspicious circumstances, to take a post as Ambassador to Mexico, and City Council President Vincent Impellitteri took the reins of government. Impellitteri did not retain the support of Democratic Party leaders, however, and failed to win the party's nomination for the special election following O'Dwyer's resignation. He therefore ran on the "Experience" Party line and defeated the Democratic nominee, Ferdinand Pecora, by over half a million votes. This third-party incumbent victory was indicative of the extent to which the Democratic Party clubs' grip over city politics had been broken; though Democrats continued to dominate the electorate and public offices, an increasing majority of elected officials were also sponsored by other parties such as the American Labor or Liberal Parties.

While electoral politics was notable for intrigue, the more durable developments in New York government were less obviously headline worthy. The first was the expansion of the local fiscal state, especially the provision of generous social benefits, such as welfare benefits, cultural and educational amenities, and pensions for city workers. City spending expanded much more rapidly than the population over the period of 1940–1955 (from $978 million to $1.393 million in constant dollars; per capita spending rose from $130 to $150 over that time, again in constant dollars). Around 40 percent of these expenditures by the city were devoted to pensions, social welfare, and education and libraries, and nearly two-thirds of revenues were drawn from local taxes. O'Dwyer presided over the city's first budget over $1 billion; Impellitteri and his successors further increased city revenues and expenditures, ushering in the era of New York's distinctive brand of liberal, inclusive, local politics. A multitude of well-organized and powerful civic groups, including the Citizens Union and the Citizens Budget Committee, brought more organized groups onto the local political playing field, with more insistent demands being made on policymakers at many levels. With the increasing mobility of capital, the attractive pull of suburban life to the middle class, and the evaporation of intergovernmental support from the national government, however, this model of civic governance led to fiscal and political crisis over the next decades.

The second important development in New York government was the continued expansion of the power of public authorities, which built the city's infrastructure over the course of the twentieth century. Significantly, Mayor O'Dwyer appointed Robert Moses to the newly created post of city construction coordinator, enhancing the powerful administrator's position for planning a comprehensive development approach for the city. According to Robert Caro in *The Power Broker*, Moses became even stronger under Impellitteri. From his position, he effectively became the face of New York City in negotiations for development funds from Washington, and the revenue flow gained through tolls from his Triborough Bridge Authority helped contribute to other transportation infrastructure projects throughout the city, including the many highways that carved up the outer boroughs by the end of this era, often heightening the spatial separation between class and racial groups and undermining what his rival visionary Jane Jacobs praises as the lifeblood of the city—street-level personal interaction.

All of Moses's projects were indicative of the prevailing high-modernist conception of the city, an aesthetic and social vision that was replicated in cities throughout the nation but fell out of favor in subsequent decades. These large projects—financed through intergovernmental aid, bond issues, and the insulated income streams Moses's public authorities enjoyed—were characterized by their grand scale and the displacement of neighborhoods and persons. Areas designated as slums were identified for clearance and replaced with highways, high-rise public housing developments, or public buildings. Moses's contributions to New York's civic geography were controversial from the start, and he was criticized for his autocratic style and for his car-centric vision of the modern metropolis. The ultimate effects of his legacy are as complex as the city itself. Lincoln Center, for instance, remains a global center of culture, while Penn Station is reviled as a poor replacement for its predecessor. The rusting remnants of Moses's World Exposition Flushing Park remain as odd curiosities, but the eleven massive swimming pools he built continue to attract millions of visitors during the sweltering summer months. Moses also helped oversee the construction of the United Nations headquarters, which was completed in 1952 and remains today a monument to the centrality of New York in the postwar geopolitical order.

INDUSTRY, COMMERCE, AND LABOR

As the commercial and industrial capital of the world, New York enjoyed commercial preeminence throughout this era. The city's enormous manufacturing base was mobilized for war production, helping to pull the city (along with the nation itself) out of the doldrums of the Great Depression, and expansion in public and private development continued apace during the era of postwar prosperity. A few significant developments sowed the seeds for the eventual erosion of some pieces of this impressive economic jigsaw puzzle.

While World War II was obviously a moment of historic disjuncture, there was much continuity in New York's role in the national and international economic order. Wall Street was the center of international finance, billions of dollars passed through the hands of the city's banks every day, and it was the world's busiest seaport as well. On top of that, around forty thousand manufacturing firms operated within the city, with nearly a million industrial workers in the force—a figure itself greater than the *total population* of all but four other American cities. Throughout the postwar boom, New York would remain a primary symbol of this prosperity and industry, and it would use the proceeds of this wealth to develop a modern vision of urban political economy.

New York's mobilization for World War II was total. It was widely believed (and later confirmed) that German forces desired to bomb the city as they had London. No aerial bombardment did take place, despite many alarms sounded in the city—though at least one industrial sabotage plot was uncovered and foiled before any damage could be done. The ongoing close ties between the state and city of New York and the Roosevelt administration were reinforced when FDR brought Mayor LaGuardia to his cabinet as the director of the Office of Civilian Defense. This added responsibility forced him to travel throughout the country, touring and inspecting defense preparations.

Nearly nine hundred thousand New Yorkers joined the armed forces to serve in the war effort, and the manufacturing sector converted to wartime production, bringing employment numbers up and creating the economic recovery that had been so long in coming. Mobilization also changed the role of different groups in the New York workforce. The wartime labor shortage attracted African Americans from the South to relatively high-paying industrial jobs in northern cities in the last big wave of the long Great Migration, and women—who had always been central to New York's manufacturing sector, albeit in "lighter" industries such as sewing and textile manufacture—were assimilated into heavier industry as well. By 1944, one hundred thirty-four thousand women (28 percent of the workforce) were employed in the city's 341 major war production plants. The integration of these "Rosie the Riveters" into the wartime workforce was an important step toward eroding segregation in employment, though it must be noted that these women earned about 40 percent less than their male colleagues. Additionally, more than eighty thousand recruits to the WAVES and SPARS corps—the female divisions of the Navy and Coast Guard, respectively, during the war—were trained at Hunter College as well. While demobilization saw some of these integrative gains rolled back as servicemembers returned, some lasting effects were felt, as in the creation of the new Women's Program and Women's Council within the New York State Commerce Department.

If wartime mobilization woke the New York economy from the depression, postwar demobilization unleashed a wave of strikes and labor conflict that had been suppressed by the exigencies of national mobilization. While wildcat strikes had occurred in some industries during the war, the cessation of hostilities made workers eager to share in the gains of peace and to see wage controls lifted from the emergency levels. In 1945, longshoremen in New York began what would become decades of labor strife, walking off the job repeatedly and against the wishes of their union bosses. The increasing assertiveness of the rank-and-file unionists broke apart the tripartite bargaining system of the wartime era and made national waves of strikes more likely, and the highly publicized labor strife contributed to the rollbacks of New Deal–era labor legislation, including the Taft-Hartley Act and Portal-to-Portal Act of the late 1940s, which limited the rights of organized labor to organize and strike, and ultimately contributed to the long-term atrophy of American unions.

Even as the New York longshoremen were working for better pay and working conditions, a parallel development occurred that would ultimately undermine New York's place in the national distribution network more than anything else: in 1948 the Interstate Commerce Commission reversed its previous rulings and allowed shippers to charge New York wholesalers the charge for loading and unloading to cross the Hudson River. This was the beginning of the end for the Port of New York, as shipping activity eventually shifted entirely to the west side of the Hudson in New Jersey—though still under the auspices of the Port Authority. The departure of blue-collar commerce was accompanied by the beginning of manufacturing and middle-class flight from the city as well, though both developments were not particularly apparent in the late 1940s and early 1950s.

RACE, ETHNICITY, AND IMMIGRATION

Two major historic waves of arrivals to the city accelerated during the war and postwar periods, continuing the basic story of New York—the arrival of millions of newcomers, different from the established and already diverse community, reshaping the city's society and politics. First, the era was the heart of the Great Migration, as millions of African Americans left the Jim Crow South and sought jobs and comparative improvement in social conditions in the industrial cities of the North. During the 1940s the African American population of the city grew from about half a million to about seven hundred fifty thousand, making up nearly 10 percent of the city's residents; this growth would continue until a leveling off in the 1980s. Most African American New Yorkers lived in upper Manhattan or Brooklyn, though there were growing communities in the other boroughs as well.

While not a paradise for newly arrived blacks by any means, New York had developed a reputation for acceptance of diversity and relative social peace, at least compared to other northern cities such as Detroit and Chicago. William Clayton Powell was a highly visible black leader who developed a relationship of mutual respect and engagement with Mayor LaGuardia; the two were national as well as local leaders on a range of urban issues. Powell went on to serve for decades on Capitol Hill, representing his base in Harlem. The most violent blemish on the city's record of racial comity in this era was the riot of 1943, in which an altercation between a black soldier and a white police officer led to a night of looting in Harlem. Even this episode lasted only one night, however, in marked contrast to similar incidents in other cities. LaGuardia's rapid response and the visible leadership and calls for calm by black leaders were credited with restoring order.

The second major wave of immigration in this era was the beginning of the Caribbean-Latino immigration, which brought to the city substantial numbers of Puerto Ricans, the first large group of Latin Americans in New York, who could travel to and from the continental United States as citizens. Though it is difficult to ascertain precise numbers of arrivals from Puerto Rico from census data, the 1950s saw the largest single wave of Puerto Rican immigration to the city, with hundreds of thousands arriving and settling with significant density on the Lower East Side, in Spanish Harlem, and in Williamsburg (Brooklyn). The influx of such large numbers of Hispanic persons complicated the ethnoracial politics of the city, presaging later events in other places and in American politics more generally after the 1965 Immigration Act reforms, which erased the existing European-centered quota system with a new preference system that led to massive immigration flows from Latin America and Asia over the pursuant decades.

As in many cities across the industrial North, patterns of ethnoracial segregation were formalized and solidified during the midcentury era, despite the end of legal restrictive covenants and similar discriminatory measures. The 1949 Housing Act included the now notorious Urban Renewal and Slum Clearance program, a provision that provided massive resources to cities and funded the large public housing projects so notoriously symbolic of the urban isolation of racial minorities and the urban poor. Separated spatially from their surrounding neighborhoods and sited to remedy what planners such as Robert Moses saw as significant urban blight, these buildings were placed around the city and began as racially segregated homes for the working class. These concentrations of persons, initially seen as the Progressive ideal, became infamous symbols of urban dysfunction later in the century.

Politically, New York's multiracial ruling coalition—with liberal whites and Democratic regulars joined with junior partners in the African American community—continued to evolve during this era, in marked contrast to the manner in which ethnoracial minorities were demobilized and marginalized in many other American cities, where racial tensions were often more explosive.

See also *New York, NY 1776–1790; New York, NY 1790–1828; New York, NY 1828–1854; New York, NY 1854–1877; New York, NY 1877–1896; New York, NY 1896–1929; New York, NY 1929–1941; New York, NY 1952–1989; New York, NY 1989–2011*

TOM OGORZALEK

BIBLIOGRAPHY

Capeci, Dominic J., Jr *The Harlem Riot of 1943*. Philadelphia, PA: Temple University Press, 1977.
Caro, Robert. *The Power Broker: Robert Moses and the Fall of New York*. New York, NY: Vintage, 1975.
Connolly, Harold X. *A Ghetto Grows in Brooklyn*. New York, NY: New York University Press, 1977.
Doig, Jameson W. *Empire on the Hudson*. New York, NY: Columbia University Press, 2002.
Jackson, Kenneth T. *The Encyclopedia of New York City*. New Haven, CT: Yale University Press, 2010.
Sayre, Wallace, and Herbert Kaufman. *Governing New York City: Politics in the Metropolis*. New York, NY: W. W. Norton, 1965.

CHICAGO, IL 1941–1952

DURING AND AFTER WORLD WAR II, the Chicago metropolitan area experienced fundamental transformations in its population and spatial organization. These changes, however, were firmly rooted in its prewar industrial and transportation base and its longstanding practices of residential racial segregation. The city's industrial foundation and role as the continent's interior crossroads combined to make it an ideal location for war-related production. Chicago's industries reorganized their operations to produce goods required for the war effort. The associated influx of war workers, many of whom were racial and ethnic minorities, swelled Chicago's population and strained its already decayed housing supply. City officials responded by loosening restrictions on apartment living and promoting public housing. Real estate developers created new private, single-family housing on Chicago's northwest and southwest sides and in the region's suburbs once the end of war production made residential construction possible again. As a result, while African Americans were concentrated into an expanded South Side "Black Belt" and a new ghetto on the West Side, white Chicagoans dispersed to the new areas of housing available within the city and its suburbs.

QUICK FACTS

CHICAGO, IL **1941–1952**

MAYORS

Edward J. Kelly   (1933–1947)
Martin H. Kennelly   (1947–1955)

MAJOR INDUSTRIES AND EMPLOYERS

Machinery
Primary metal industries
Food and kindred products
Fabricated metal products

MAJOR NEWSPAPERS

Chicago Tribune
Chicago Herald-American
Chicago American
Chicago Daily News
Chicago Daily Law Bulletin
Chicago Daily Drovers Journal

Daily Calumet
Chicago Journal of Commerce
Daily Times
Chicago Sun
Chicago Sun-Times
Chicago Defender

MAJOR EVENTS

1941–1945: Chicago residents participate in block watches and scrap drives, city government changes local regulations to make housing war workers easier, and businesses transform their operations to a war footing, all in support of the Allied effort in World War II.

1942: The world's first self-sustaining nuclear chain reaction occurs on the University of Chicago campus on December 2.

1940–1970: The period known as the Second Great Migration results in the relocation of numerous African Americans from the South to points northward, particularly Chicago.

1947: Manufacturing employment in Chicago peaks.

Late 1940s: The Second Chicago School of architecture begins to develop.

GOVERNMENT AND POLITICS

During the Great Depression Mayor Anton Cermak, who served from 1931 to 1933, had founded Chicago's infamous Democratic machine as a "house for all peoples," forging a multi-ethnic political coalition that returned members of the party to the office throughout the rest of the twentieth century. Cermak's successor was Edward J. Kelly (1933–1947), the first of three Roman Catholic, Irish American mayors who epitomized the power of the machine in Chicago politics. Kelly worked in close cooperation with Patrick A. Nash, Cook County's Democratic Party chairman, to increase the role of the mayor in the nominally "weak mayor" system. In this model, however, elected officials, even the mayor, were still subject to the discipline of the party's will. A vast patronage network for city employment, as well as tolerance for organized vice like gambling, ensured both the hold of the Kelly-Nash machine and its reputation for corruption. Kelly also tried to bring the city's burgeoning black population within the political fold by encouraging the construction of public housing and desegregation of the public schools. This rapprochement with African Americans revealed a racial liberalism that prompted the very machine that elevated Kelly to decide in 1947 that he should be replaced as mayor by the more malleable Martin H. Kennelly (1947–1955).

Despite running a "wide-open city," the Kelly administration was not indifferent to the problems that confronted Chicago during the war. Mayor Kelly personally ran Chicago's civilian defense efforts, standing at the pinnacle of an organization that had twenty thousand block clubs rallying residents to the cause, cultivating victory gardens, collecting scrap, and observing blackouts. Local officials also recognized the difficulty of housing hundreds of thousands of new residents in a city whose housing stock had only deteriorated since the 1920s. Because the demands of war production made the construction of new private homes largely impossible, the city council agreed to relax the building code to make it possible to cut up apartments to accommodate more family units in relative privacy. Rent controls protected Chicagoans from unmanageable rents under the press of the wartime crowd. The Chicago Housing Authority's (CHA) Cabrini, Lawndale Gardens, Bridgeport, and Brooks public housing projects opened during the war. To comply with the federal priority on supporting the war effort, public housing units were set aside for low-income war workers and veterans. Several more high-rise and low-rise CHA projects were opened in the decade after the war's end.

At the same time, the Kelly administration began to anticipate how the city would have to change once the war ended. In 1942 and 1943, the Chicago Plan Commission published a two-volume survey that detailed how all the land within the city limits was used, as well as the condition of residential properties. Despite the exigencies of the Great Depression, a few signs hinted at the postwar shift of corporations and residents to the suburbs. To facilitate suburbanites' access to the Loop—and therefore the continued financial importance of Chicago's downtown—the city promoted improved transportation links that ultimately radiated south, west, and northwest beyond city limits. In the late 1940s and early 1950s, construction began on several new expressways, which took decades to complete, and the subway system was expanded. In addition, the legislative groundwork for an ambitious program that combined land clearance, urban renewal, and additional public housing was laid with the Illinois legislature in the late 1940s. Most of these redevelopment programs were initiated in the mid-1950s and early 1960s under the administration of Mayor Richard J. Daley (1955–1976).

INDUSTRY, COMMERCE, AND LABOR

With the German invasion of Poland in 1939, Americans understood that the crisis implicated the United States. In Chicago, the two leading newspapers hotly debated the propriety of U.S. involvement in the European war, with Robert McCormick's *Chicago Tribune* arguing against American intervention and William Franklin Knox's *Chicago Daily News* weighing in for it. When the Japanese attacked Pearl Harbor on December 7, 1941, Chicago residents, like other Americans, lined up to support the war effort. The city's historic role as the interior hub of the nation's rail and water transportation networks and as the national center of manufacturing and distribution meant that Chicago was well positioned to capture much of the production associated with the war. Although the U.S. government initially sought goods from companies on the continent's coasts, intensive lobbying by Mayor Kelly and hundreds of corporate officials brought federal contracts to the city in 1942. By the end of 1944, only Detroit produced more war materiel than Chicago.

Many Chicago companies that survived the Great Depression had cut back production and employment. Despite the capital costs associated with retooling to transform their productive capacity from civilian consumption to military needs, the city's companies embraced the opportunity to support the war, employ workers, and return to profitability. Across the range of the region's productive capacity, Chicago firms made what the federal government needed, from food to vehicles to weapons. The iron and steel plants concentrated in the city's far South Side and southern suburbs turned out metals required to make other products. Kraft Foods supplied tinned rations to the military. Wrigley Company continued to make chewing gum, but contracted its entire supply for soldiers. Pharmaceutical manufacturers, such as Abbott Laboratories and the G. D. Searle Company, devoted their research efforts to swiftly making drugs to prevent disease and infection among members of the military. Arnold, Schwinn and Company, practiced in making metal tubes for its bicycles, turned its skills to military purposes. The Pullman Company diverted some of its manufacturing away from railroad cars and produced sub chasers, while the Pressed Steel Car Company built tanks. The McCormick Reaper Works made torpedoes instead of farm equipment. Several different companies built parts for or assembled entire airplanes. The Douglas Corporation constructed the giant C-54 Skymaster at its plant in Park Ridge. After the war ended, that site became O'Hare International Airport and was annexed into the city, ensuring Chicago's continued eminence as one of the nation's major transportation hubs in the jet age.

Of course, all of these industrial developments required workers who previously had received little consideration from employers. Although the unemployment created by the Great Depression left a pool of Chicagoans eager to go back to work, the demand for war workers was so great that hundreds of thousands of migrants headed for the city, dramatically and permanently rearranging its demographics. Women, many of whom were also urban migrants, similarly took up manufacturing positions previously closed to them.

The war also highlighted Chicago's importance in the world of advanced physics. At the University of Chicago, a team of physicists led by Enrico Fermi generated the world's first self-sustaining nuclear chain reaction. This development, which occurred under a squash court on the campus's Stagg Field, confirmed the theory that would enable the production of the atomic bombs that were dropped on Hiroshima and Nagasaki, ending the war in the Pacific in 1945. The University's physicists were also central to the creation of Argonne National Laboratory, the first federal nuclear laboratory, in suburban Lemont in 1946.

Labor relations in Chicago were largely peaceful during the war. Unions, especially those affiliated with the Congress of Industrial Organizations, used the war as a building period. After the war was over, the shape of the Chicago region continued a shift away from the central city that had begun in the 1920s but stalled during the Great Depression. Shedding many of their wartime workers and reducing opportunities for local employment, corporations moved their operations into the surrounding metropolitan area. Reflecting these tensions, in the early postwar years Chicago was part of a nationwide wave of strikes, as workers sought improved wages, conditions, and benefits. Iron- and steelworkers struck repeatedly, walking out of Inland Steel in 1947 and 1952. Packinghouse workers struck in 1946 and 1948. Workers enjoyed mixed successes in protecting their interests.

The end of the war also saw the revival of high-rise construction in and around the city's center, the beginning of half a century of downtown redevelopment. The leading edge of new building came in the form of residential construction designed in the Modernist style, using steel and glass to emphasize a building's underlying structure. The major figure in this movement was Ludwig Mies van der Rohe, but he influenced so many architects that the period is understood as having constituted the Second Chicago School of architecture. New commercial skyscrapers, also in the Modernist style and designed by firms such as Skidmore, Owings and Merrill, emerged in the later part of the 1950s.

RACE, ETHNICITY, AND IMMIGRATION

This period saw enormous transformations in the racial and ethnic composition and spatial organization of Chicago's population. The war was the impetus for many of the changes in *who* lived in Chicago, while a combination of racism and white suburbanization help account for *where* Chicagoans lived during and after this decade. For a variety of war-related reasons, many Americans migrated to Chicago in the 1940s, most in search of the newly available jobs. Among the hundreds of thousands of migrants were some sixty-five thousand black Southerners who responded to the job opportunities created by the end of the depression, the departure of young white men for the military, and the lack of European immigration by moving to Chicago. Employers recruited a smaller population of about fifteen thousand Mexican Americans to the city. Approximately twenty thousand Japanese Americans, forcibly dispossessed of their West Coast homes, chose to relocate to Chicago rather than stay in American internment camps. Hundreds of thousands of soldiers stayed in Chicago temporarily as they passed through Chicago on their way to military destinations.

Young, single, white women crowded into the North Side of the city, sharing apartments, living in rooming houses, and sleeping in basement "rooms" created by curtains. African Americans were confined almost exclusively to the traditional South Side "Bronzeville" area, which had already been crowded and dilapidated during the depression. The rapidly increasing numbers of African Americans put pressure on whites who lived in the areas adjacent to Bronzeville and would not tolerate integrated blocks. Migrants who did not fit into the neat black/white racial dichotomy lived in between the two largest racial groups. Aided by religious groups such as the Brethren and the Quakers, Japanese Americans who moved to Chicago during the war located apartments in those neighborhoods where African Americans were starting to move in and whites were moving out. As those neighborhoods later became all-black, the Nisei moved out along with the last whites. Mexicans, whose population in Chicago had fluctuated throughout the twentieth century depending on the federal government's attitude to a population easily deported, absorbed the World War II *braceros* into existing communities. The fact that Chicago lacked the kinds of racial upheavals that

This photo of 37th Street in Chicago's South Side illustrates the conditions in the postwar period that prompted the construction of new and affordable public housing in this area of the city.

Source: Mildred Mead/Chicago History Museum/Getty Images

occurred in Harlem and Detroit during World War II did not mean that all was well racially in the city. Mayor Kelly's 1943 establishment of the Mayor's Committee on Race Relations testified to the ongoing tension between whites and blacks. Whites adamantly, sometimes violently, refused to live with black neighbors throughout the century. Although the postwar period saw many housing developments opened in new locations, none broke the pattern of segregation.

The influx of workers during the war and the formation of new families during the postwar years caused an enormous shortage in housing. After the end of hostilities freed up materials and labor needed for construction, developers seized on the opportunity to build new homes for space-hungry Chicagoans. The northwest and southwest portions of Chicago, which had been annexed in the nineteenth century but remained largely undeveloped, filled in with new construction between the late 1940s and the 1960s. Suburban developers also attracted new residents, part of the national trend of white migration out of central cities. Most of these properties were single-family homes. The expansion in the amount of housing available for whites gave them a place to move to in order to avoid the city's growing black population, which increased from an official census total of 277,731 in 1940 to 492,265 in 1950.

By 1960 Chicago's 812,637 African Americans constituted almost 23 percent of the city's total population. Bronzeville could not contain that many people, despite the use of "kitchen-ettes," which were used to convert larger apartments into smaller, private facilities. Blacks were also displaced from established neighborhoods by postwar slum clearance and redevelopment projects. Although much of the new public housing built in the postwar period was justified as temporary replacement housing, the supply was insufficient to the need. African Americans sought relief from crowding at the edges of the neighborhoods where blacks already lived, first expanding southward from the familiar South Side community. In addition, a small black enclave west of downtown provided the jumping-off point for the second large African American community, on the city's West Side, as blacks expanded the area of settlement open to them over the next two decades. Although whites ultimately moved away from the growing black population, they often resisted first. They routinely threatened the first black families who move into all-white neighborhoods and sometimes rioted, making the immediate postwar period what historian Arnold R. Hirsch has called "an era of hidden violence." To contain the growing black population and appease whites, under Mayor Kennelly the city began to promote urban renewal and the construction of massive public housing complexes, a policy that came to fruition under Mayor Richard J. Daley.

By 1952, the built-up part of the region had expanded dramatically, pushed by the economic jolt of World War II. This development signaled the metropolitan trajectory of the next half-century. But the segregated foundations of Chicago remained essentially unchecked.

See also *Chicago, IL 1854–1877; Chicago, IL 1877–1896; Chicago, IL 1896–1929; Chicago, IL 1929–1941; Chicago, IL 1952–1989; Chicago, IL 1989–2011*

AMANDA I. SELIGMAN

BIBLIOGRAPHY

Biles, Roger. *Big City Boss in Depression and War: Mayor Edward J. Kelly of Chicago*. DeKalb: Northern Illinois University Press, 1984.

Bowly, Devereux, Jr. *The Poorhouse: Subsidized Housing in Chicago, 1895–1976*. Carbondale: Southern Illinois University Press, 1978.

Brooks, Charlotte. "In the Twilight Zone between Black and White: Japanese American Resettlement and Community in Chicago, 1942–1945." *Journal of American History* 86, no. 4 (2000): 1655–1687.

Condit, Carl W. *Chicago, 1930–1970; Building, Planning, and Urban Technology*. Chicago, IL: University of Chicago Press, 1974.

Duis, Perry, and Scott LaFrance. *We've Got a Job to Do: Chicagoans and World War II*. Chicago, IL: Chicago Historical Society, 1992.

Hirsch, Arnold R. *Making the Second Ghetto: Race and Housing in Chicago, 1940–1960*. 2d ed. Chicago, IL: University of Chicago Press, 1998.

McEnaney, Laura. "Nightmares on Elm Street: Demobilizing in Chicago." *Journal of American History* 92 (March 2006): 1265–1291.

PHILADELPHIA, PA 1941–1952

THE YEARS FROM 1941 TO 1952 BROUGHT GREAT DEMOGRAPHIC, ECONOMIC, AND POLITICAL CHANGES to Philadelphia. The city's population grew by some one hundred forty thousand people during this time (to just over two million), with almost all of the growth attributable to the arrival of African Americans. Those who came in the early 1940s found a revitalizing economy as war contracts jump-started industries that had faltered during the Great Depression. Unfortunately for many working Philadelphians, good economic times faded when the war came to an end. Through most of the 1940s the city remained under the control of the corrupt Republican political machine, but by the end of the decade Democratic reformers led by Joseph Sill Clark Jr. (1952–1956) and Richardson Dilworth (1956–1962) had begun to win offices and change the city's political leadership.

GOVERNMENT AND POLITICS

The Republican political machine that controlled Philadelphia's government in the first four decades of the twentieth century continued its dominance through most of the 1940s. Bernard Samuel (1941–1952) served as mayor throughout the decade. Known more as a party functionary than a political leader, Samuel used the backing of the Vare political machine to win a seat on the city council. He rose to become that body's president and from there became mayor when Robert Lamberton (1940–1941) died in office. In mayoral races, Samuel defeated William C. Bullitt, a native Philadelphian known more for his work in the foreign service, in 1944 and the reformer Richardson Dilworth in 1948. In total, Samuel served eleven years as mayor, the longest continual span in the city's history. Despite Samuel's longevity, his tenure had few highlights and is best remembered for its inertia and corruption.

Whatever Samuel's limitations, he did shepherd Philadelphia through the difficult years of World War II. During the war one hundred eighty thousand residents joined the armed forces and some five thousand died. Despite this loss of life, overall the war was beneficial to the city, providing in many ways the last hurrah for the once-robust regional industrial economy. Textiles, metal manufacturing, and other industries boomed during the war, and the population grew by nearly fifty thousand people as workers flocked to the city looking for defense jobs. Many Philadelphians hoped the war signaled a new beginning for their city. But with the lethargic Samuel administration in charge, Philadelphia emerged from World War II looking, in the words of the *Saturday Evening Post*, "shabby," with thousands of decrepit homes, dirty streets, and raw sewage emptying into many streams and rivers. It would take bold leaders to chart a new future for Philadelphia.

After the war those leaders emerged among the city's business and social elites. For nearly a century men and women of that class had withdrawn from Philadelphia's civic life, content to reside in their Main Line suburbs and let the Vare machine run the city. After World War II, they developed the bipartisan Greater Philadelphia Movement and asserted more control over the city. Their efforts became known as the Philadelphia Renaissance, a movement that

QUICK FACTS

PHILADELPHIA, PA 1941–1952

MAYORS

Robert Lamberton	(1940–1941)
Bernard Samuel	(1941–1952)
Joseph Sill Clark Jr.	(1952–1956)

MAJOR INDUSTRIES AND EMPLOYERS

Durable goods manufacturing
   (metals, furniture, machinery)
Clerical/secretarial work
Nondurable goods manufacturing
   (textiles, apparel, food)
Service work (watchmen, waitresses,
   elevator operators)
Sales (wholesale and retail)

MAJOR NEWSPAPERS

Philadelphia Bulletin

Philadelphia Inquirer
Philadelphia Record (until 1947)

MAJOR EVENTS

1944: A "hate strike" at Philadelphia Transportation Company highlights racial tensions building in the city.

1945: The end of World War II brings mass layoffs and growing concerns about the city's economic future in the postwar period.

1948: The Greater Philadelphia Movement, a bipartisan movement intent on revitalizing the city, forms.

1949: Joseph Clark and Richardson Dilworth are elected city controller and city treasurer, respectively. Their victories help sweep out the corrupt Republican political machine that had dominated Philadelphia's politics for decades.

1951: Voters ratify a new city charter, making Philadelphia's government more streamlined, transparent, and accountable.

modernized the city government, improved sanitation, built new schools, and expanded the airport. The Renaissance focused on Center City and over the next decade changed the face of that area by remaking the Independence Hall neighborhood, tearing down the Pennsylvania Railroad tracks west of City Hall, and redeveloping Society Hill. These changes in some ways improved the city, but Philadelphia's Renaissance—like the large-scale urban renewal projects that swept through most of America's large cities after World War II—destroyed working-class neighborhoods and paid little attention to the problem of jobs leaving the city.

At the same time as reformers remade the physical face of Philadelphia, Clark and Dilworth ran for office in an attempt to change the city's political leadership. Dilworth, an ethical and liberal son of a wealthy Pittsburgh family, ran for mayor in 1947, claiming he would "sweep the rascals out" of office. He lost the election, but his charges of corruption were so specific and so damning that the city council had to set up a committee to investigate his accusations. Within a year, that committee discovered some $40 million missing in municipal funds, and four city employees committed suicide over the scandal.

The corruption outraged Philadelphians enough that they sought change at the ballot box. Dilworth ran for city treasurer and Clark for controller in 1949, and they defeated the political machine candidates by over one hundred thousand votes. These jobs were only the first step for the pair as Clark went on to win the race for mayor in 1951 and U.S. Senator in 1956, and Dilworth became district attorney in 1951 and mayor in 1955. Once in office, Clark and Dilworth worked to consolidate a coalition of black, Jewish, and liberal white Philadelphians. That coalition has helped keep a Democrat in the mayor's office every term since 1951, but its electoral power stands in marked contrast to the suburban counties where the Republicans have dominated.

As Clark and Dilworth gained political power, the Greater Philadelphia Movement pushed through a new city charter in 1951. The "Home Rule" charter created a "strong mayor" form of government that greatly reduced the power of the city council, essentially limiting that body to legislative activities. The mayor received the right to appoint and remove the city's administrative officers, including the managing director, director of finance, and city solicitor. The charter created clearer lines of authority, making it easier for voters to know who to hold responsible for unethical or illegal actions. And it strengthened the civil service system to eliminate cronyism in the distribution of city jobs. Overall, the charter made Philadelphia's government more streamlined, transparent, and accountable to its citizens.

INDUSTRY, COMMERCE, AND LABOR

Government spending for World War II revived an economy devastated by the Great Depression. Unemployment had peaked at 40 percent in 1933, with another 20 percent of Philadelphians working only part-time. For black neighborhoods the situation was even graver: the jobless rate there reached over 50 percent. As late as 1940, 20 percent of Philadelphians were still unemployed. But over the course of 1941 the federal government invested $130 million in Philadelphia industries, reinvigorating the city's manufacturing base. By the end of the war Pennsylvania had received $11.7 billion in defense contracts (the sixth largest total in the nation), with Philadelphia holding the lion's share of that amount.

Across the city one out of every four workers found employment in the three thousand five hundred plants that produced war goods. Philadelphia's largest employers regained their footing. Baldwin Locomotive retooled to produce tanks, the Navy Yard and Cramp's shipyard made warships, Philco manufactured radar equipment, textile mills produced uniforms and blankets, and Frankford Arsenal rolled out countless weapons. Philadelphia, in the words of one commentator, produced everything "from battleships to braid."

The demand for workers was so great that employers turned to women and African Americans to staff open positions. By the end of the war, some three hundred thousand women were employed outside the home. Most began in service jobs, but by 1944 they made up 40 percent of the manufacturing workforce. The great majority lost these higher-paying industrial jobs after the war, but the percentage of women in the workforce continued to rise in the late 1940s and 1950s. African Americans similarly found employment in area industries, the exigencies of war overcoming employers' historic unwillingness to hire them. The number of black workers in manufacturing rose from fourteen thousand in 1940 to fifty-four thousand in 1944, with Midvale Steel and, just outside the city, Sun Shipyard being key employers. The employment of black workers periodically led to racial conflicts, the worst of which took place at the Philadelphia Transportation Company (PTC) in 1944. The company promoted eight African Americans to the position of driver, which led to a mass walkout of its white workforce. At a time when gas rationing forced most people to take mass transit to work, the "hate strike" at the PTC shut down Philadelphia. To end the strike and restart war production, President Franklin Roosevelt ultimately sent five thousand heavily armed troops into the city. African Americans kept their driving jobs, but the strike did not bode well for the city's future race relations.

The end of the war brought the end of government contracts, and prospects for Philadelphia companies and their employees quickly dimmed. In the months immediately after the war, Baldwin and Midvale laid off half their employees, Sun Ship contracted from thirty-four thousand to four thousand workers, and Cramp closed entirely. A few plants, such as Budd Manufacturing and the Navy Yard, prospered through the Korean War, and Philco remained a major manufacturer of electronics, but overall the economic outlook was gloomy.

More than the evaporation of government contracts was at work, as it became obvious that World War II had only temporarily arrested Philadelphia's prewar industrial slide. In the immediate postwar decade, many textile manufacturers shifted their operations to the South; King of Prussia drew SKF, General Electric (GE), and other industries to the suburbs; and Yale and Towne, Budd, and B. F. Goodrich left the city as well. Philadelphia's industrial areas, employers argued, were too cramped and too reliant on nineteenth-century transportation (railroads and water). As the companies moved, opportunity disappeared. Fifty thousand of the city's three hundred fifty thousand industrial positions vanished in the 1950s (two hundred thousand more would go by 1985), with the textile industry especially decimated by the loss of jobs. As industrial work left the city, residents of suburban Bucks and Montgomery Counties saw their wages rise by 46 percent and 26 percent, respectively, while Philadelphians' wages remained stagnant. These trends, which accelerated later in the 1950s, had their origins in the immediate postwar period, and they particularly hurt African Americans, who were increasingly segregated into inner-city neighborhoods just as work disappeared.

Labor leaders were troubled by the end of government funds, the dispersal of jobs, and the long-term decline of the city's industries, but also by wages and contractual issues at stronger plants. To deal with these concerns, they joined a nationwide strike wave in 1945 and 1946 that hit industries ranging from steel and oil to electronics and meatpacking. In Philadelphia, workers walked out at Baldwin, GE, and Westinghouse, with the GE strike being the largest. There, over the course of some eight weeks in early 1946, thousands of workers and police clashed on several occasions. The situation grew so chaotic that Mayor Samuel brokered a peace agreement between GE and its employees, one that ultimately led to the workers receiving a raise of $1.48 a day, three-quarters of what they demanded.

GE's employees were jubilant at first, but the strike signaled the end, rather than the beginning, of postwar labor activism in the city. In the last years of the 1940s, Philadelphia employers joined a nationwide anti-union offensive that, drawing on the Cold War and McCarthyism, tarred labor radicalism as Communistic and un-American. Instead of unions marching on City Hall as they had in the 1930s, 1949 witnessed an eleventh-hour American Legion parade. While

Philadelphia's business elites reasserted their control by the end of the 1940s, the dispersal of the city's jobs continued.

RACE, ETHNICITY, AND IMMIGRATION

Philadelphia's total population grew from approximately 1.93 million in 1940 to 2.07 million in 1950, the latter figure being the high point in the city's history. The greatest growth came in the black population, which jumped from some two hundred fifty thousand to three hundred seventy-six thousand people. African Americans moved from representing 13 percent of the total city population in 1940 to 18 percent in 1950, and they eclipsed the number of immigrants from foreign countries for the first time. The city in 1950 still had a sizable number of residents born in Italy (forty-nine thousand), Ireland (twenty-five thousand), Poland (twenty thousand), and Germany (twenty thousand). Residents born in the Soviet Union (mostly Eastern European Jews) were the largest group, with a total of nearly fifty-four thousand, while Philadelphians of Asian and Latin American descent numbered fewer than five thousand. Although the foreign-born population had dropped to its lowest level since 1880, one-third of all Philadelphians in 1950 were still immigrants or the children of immigrants.

World War II provided black Philadelphians with their best employment prospects in decades, if not in the history of the city. African Americans gained employment at the Pennsylvania Railroad, Sun Ship, Midvale Steel, city hospitals, and elsewhere. At many of these companies, especially Sun Ship, they got skilled jobs for the first time, which meant their pay often doubled from the prewar years. But the good times did not last. The problem came at war's end when many companies drastically reduced their workforces. African Americans faced the typical problem of being "last hired, first fired," with Sun Ship, for example, laying off 80 percent of its black workforce in 1945–1946. Most black workers found no market for their skills after the war and returned to lower-paid manual and service work. A few found good jobs with the city government or in construction, but most were underemployed or unemployed.

The hardening of residential segregation made black Philadelphians' lives even more difficult. The late 1940s and early 1950s saw rising racial tensions as the black population grew. Some longstanding ethnic neighborhoods (Irish Kensington, for example) had frequent racial clashes as African Americans sought housing. Elsewhere, the racial composition of neighborhoods changed quickly, as people with sufficient money to move chose to relocate to new suburbs in Bucks, Montgomery, and Delaware Counties rather than have black neighbors. African Americans could not move to the suburbs because they lacked the income to buy a home and because of overt discriminatory housing policies. From 1940 to 1950, South Philadelphia lost 27 percent of its Italian population, West Philadelphia lost 24 percent of its Irish population, and North Philadelphia lost 19 percent of its Jewish population. The latter two areas became the largest black neighborhoods in the city. The federal and city governments furthered the concentration of black Philadelphians with policies that placed public housing in inner-city neighborhoods. Any attempt to put public housing in white areas met stiff opposition. In the late 1940s Philadelphia still had large European ethnic enclaves (for example, Jews in Strawberry Mansion, Italians in South Philadelphia, Irish in West Philadelphia), but the familiar pattern of whites in the suburbs and blacks in the city was becoming increasingly obvious.

African Americans attempted to cope with their employment and residential problems through legal remedies. They pressured politicians, most successfully in the Democratic Party, to attend to their interests, which resulted in fair housing and fair employment laws. Yet such laws unfortunately proved to be inadequate tools to solve the problems confronting black Philadelphia.

Philadelphia changed greatly from 1941 to 1952, and by the end of that decade the origins of what scholars have called the "urban crisis" were apparent. The government was in more responsible hands, but it tended more to the interests of Center City businessmen than to those of ordinary people. Industry, which had revived during World War II, had begun a decline that would rob working people of decent jobs and diminish the city's tax base. And Philadelphia's population was splitting along the racial divide as the suburbanization of jobs and housing changed the face of the city.

See also *Philadelphia, PA 1776–1790; Philadelphia, PA 1790–1828; Philadelphia, PA 1828–1854; Philadelphia, PA 1854–1877; Philadelphia, PA 1877–1896; Philadelphia, PA 1896–1929; Philadelphia, PA 1929–1941; Philadelphia, PA 1952–1989; Philadelphia, PA 1989–2011*

JAMES WOLFINGER

BIBLIOGRAPHY

Bauman, John. *Public Housing, Race, and Renewal: Urban Planning in Philadelphia, 1920–1974.* Philadelphia, PA: Temple University Press, 1987.

Licht, Walter. *Getting Work: Philadelphia, 1840–1950.* Cambridge, MA: Harvard University Press, 1992.

Miller, Fredric, Morris Vogel, and Allen Davis. *Philadelphia Stories: A Photographic History, 1920–1960.* Philadelphia, PA: Temple University Press, 1988.

Reichley, James. *The Art of Government.* New York, NY: Fund for the Republic, 1959.

Scranton, Philip, and Walter Licht. *Work Sights: Industrial Philadelphia, 1890–1950.* Philadelphia, PA: Temple University Press, 1986.

Simon, Roger. *Philadelphia: A Brief History.* University Park: Pennsylvania Historical Association, 2003.

Weigley, Russell, ed. *Philadelphia: A 300-Year History.* New York, NY: W.W. Norton Co. 1982.

Wolfinger, James. *Philadelphia Divided: Race and Politics in the City of Brotherly Love.* Chapel Hill: University of North Carolina Press, 2007.

LOS ANGELES, CA 1941–1952

THE PERIOD FROM 1941 TO 1952 WITNESSED THE FINAL TRANSFORMATION of Los Angeles from a rising regional hub to a leading American metropolis. The city's politics and government were modernized, although strained by Cold War ideologies. The booming regional economy fueled by federal spending made it one of the nation's top manufacturing centers. During the 1940s events and changes in racial and ethnic relations spurred the decline of segregation and discrimination that would continue in later decades. By 1952 Los Angeles had surpassed Detroit as the nation's fourth most populous city, and it was the largest city in terms of square mileage.

QUICK FACTS

LOS ANGELES, CA 1941–1952

MAYOR

Fletcher Bowron   (1938–1953)

MAJOR INDUSTRIES AND EMPLOYERS

Aircraft production
Petroleum refining
Motion pictures
Secondary automobile assembly
Metals and machinery manufacturing

MAJOR NEWSPAPERS

California Eagle
La Opinión

Los Angeles Times
Los Angeles Examiner
Los Angeles Daily News
Los Angeles Herald & Express

MAJOR EVENTS

1942: Franklin Roosevelt's Executive Order 9066 initiates the internment of Japanese Americans in California.

1943: "Zoot Suit Riots" primarily involving Mexican American youths and servicemen rage for a week in June.

1943: The first major smog alert occurs in Los Angeles in July.

1949: The "Vicecapades" scandal involving the Los Angeles Police Department ends the police chief's career and almost topples the Bowron administration.

1951: The city council votes to rescind a $100 million public housing contract with the federal government.

By 1952 Los Angeles had emerged as a major U.S. city in population, size, industrial production, and cultural influence. It was becoming the prototypical postwar American urban center with its varied manufacturing and large service sector, sprawling suburbs, rising middle class, and popular-culture attributes, all fueled by massive federal spending and media coverage.

GOVERNMENT AND POLITICS

By the municipal election in the spring of 1941, Mayor Fletcher Bowron (1938–1953), a Republican in a nonpartisan position, had expanded his governing coalition. Business elites who had opposed his candidacy in the 1938 recall of Frank Shaw reached an accommodation with him and joined many of his conservative, liberal, and leftist supporters during the war years.

After the attack on Pearl Harbor in December 1941, Bowron directed most of his attention toward civil defense in protecting Los Angeles from enemy attack and threats to limiting wartime production, and in keeping order in the city. The business establishment worked with him to increase industrial output in military necessities, as did most labor unions, which held to a no-strike pledge during the war (with the exception of workers in the Department of Water and Power). Bowron's weekly "fireside chat" radio program kept citizens informed of municipal efforts to support the war as Angelenos pitched in by rationing and other means. Despite his efforts to improve race relations, strains in his relationship with minority groups became evident as he led calls for the internment of West Coast Japanese Americans and protected the Los Angeles Police Department (LAPD) in its discriminatory treatment of African and Mexican Americans.

Still, Bowron remained a popular leader. In the 1945 city election he faced former reform ally Clifford Clinton and a few others in the mayoral contest. With the support of the business elite and organized labor, and even the unwanted endorsement of the local Communist Party, Bowron was easily reelected in the municipal primary.

The end of the war brought changes in Los Angeles as labor unions tried to make up for wartime sacrifices by initiating work stoppages. Bowron moved rightward as he sided most often with his business allies, and leftists deserted him when the wartime popular front eroded. His conflict with the city council became more intense as he found it harder to compromise with the city's legislative body. He also faced competition from influential department heads such as City Engineer Lloyd Aldrich and Police Chief William Parker (appointed in 1950), both of whom organized their own political following among special interest groups and the mayor's political opponents. Race problems continued, with the LAPD's mistreatment of minorities revealed in court trials and the beatings and deaths of arrestees. While Bowron would spearhead several important initiatives in these years, such as the 1946 Master Plan for zoning (heralded by professional planners as a national model), the expansion of the airport, and efforts to modernize budget procedures, his governance faced increasing opposition. He defeated Aldrich in the 1949 city election just before a major LAPD vice scandal was exposed, resulting in the removal of the police chief. Bowron then survived a recall election the following year, resulting from the police scandal.

The city's postwar housing crisis would become Bowron's downfall. Before and during the war he had supported government-subsidized housing, and with the influx of servicemen and their families exacerbating an already overcrowded city, he helped to negotiate a $110 million federal grant to build ten thousand public housing units in 1949. The city's entrepreneurial elite organized a campaign against this initiative by making it a target in the nation's growing anti-Communist crusade and pushed Bowron to the left in his defense of the city's contract with the federal government. The Campaign Against Socialist Housing (CASH) convinced enough city council members to reverse their initial approval and vote to rescind the contract in December 1951. Bowron continued his fight to uphold the contract through the 1953 municipal election, when he was defeated by CASH-backed Republican Congressman Norris Poulson.

INDUSTRY, COMMERCE, AND LABOR

The onset of World War II had a profound effect on the Los Angeles regional economy as it accelerated manufacturing output already in progress. Although Los Angeles County was still the top-producing agricultural county in the early 1940s, Los Angeles was a major West Coast defense center during the war, with the infusion of federal funds to establish military installations and contracts to manufacture armaments. The local aircraft industry vastly expanded production as it supplied planes for the Allies. The California Shipbuilding Corporation, Bethlehem Shipbuilding Corporation, Consolidated Steel Corporation, and other shipbuilders at the Port of

Los Angeles fabricated war ships and support vessels, employing about ninety thousand workers in 1944. The local motion picture industry contributed to the war effort by producing training and propaganda films as well as its usual entertainment fare, which the U.S. government tried to influence as promoting an idealized view of American society.

The massive increase in manufacturing employment at the same time that many young workers were joining the armed forces created new job opportunities in the plants for women and people of color. The Great Migration of African Americans arriving in Los Angeles to find work and the entrance of many women into the industrial workforce for the first time helped make Los Angeles one of largest industrial centers in the United States, with the attendant environmental pollution to prove it. The thick smoke and fumes—smog—mostly from defense factories that triggered an alert in 1943 was but a preview of things to come with the addition of motor vehicle emissions.

After the war the regional economy contracted and quickly rebounded. The population increased with the arrival of veterans and their families and others seeking opportunity, and the construction industry expanded as housing materials became available. Manufacturing plants switched from military to consumer durable goods aimed at distant markets. The region's service sector increased exponentially to serve the larger population and new businesses.

Defense industries witnessed their ups and downs after the war as they initially converted to peacetime production and then retooled during the buildup to the Korean War. Aircraft construction took off again in the late 1940s and became the top employer in the region. With additional federal funding Los Angeles became a center for military-oriented research as well as manufacturing for the expanding arms race.

By 1951 the Los Angeles metropolitan area ranked third in industrial production in the United States. The most important locally included aircraft and related parts, petroleum refining and products, motion pictures, secondary automobile assembly, metals and machinery manufacturing, women's apparel, furniture, printing, agriculture and food processing, chemicals and paints, and electronics. Many of these commodities were shipped through the Port of Los Angeles, which would soon surpass all West Coast ports in the value of import-export cargoes as well as in net waterborne tonnage.

In the early 1940s organized labor in Los Angeles increased the gains made in the late 1930s with the help of the New Deal and Congress of Industrial Organizations' (CIO) support for the Bowron administration. The increase in jobs at large defense plants created opportunities for more members, and corporation executives from outside Los Angeles did not always share the anti-union views of the city's entrepreneurial elite. During the war most unions cooperated with national and local governments to support the war effort and broke down the "open-shop" policy enforced by the business community over the previous half century.

Industrial peace ceased with the end of the war as Los Angeles laborers resumed work stoppages to raise wages and improve working conditions. CIO unions were particularly militant, as they continued to combat industrialists and compete with the more conservative American Federation of Labor. During the "red scare" of the later 1940s, many Communist leaders in the labor movement were forced out and Los Angeles unions became less aggressive, but would still be a force in local politics.

The city's entrepreneurial elite lost ground in its open-shop program of limiting the gains of labor, but this well-organized interest group was still influential in directing economic expansion and influencing politics. Insurance executive Asa Call, attorneys James Beebe and Frank Doherty, furniture retailer Neil Petree, and other leaders of the Chamber of Commerce and Merchants and Manufacturers Association continued to oppose unions, support research and planning to enhance the economy, and offer opinions on most political issues. Although the majority in this group initially opposed Mayor Bowron, an accommodation was reached early on and Bowron became much closer to their way of thinking as labor became more active after the war.

RACE, ETHNICITY, AND IMMIGRATION

The Japanese attack on Pearl Harbor in December 1941 brought calls by state and local groups and politicians for the evacuation of all persons of Japanese ancestry from the West Coast, and President Roosevelt responded by ordering such residents to internment camps in March 1942. Little Tokyo and other Japanese American enclaves were soon deserted as an estimated sixty thousand Angelenos were confined in several camps in the West. Local Chinese citizens whose homeland had been invaded by Japan fared much better in the community and in the nation, as a sympathetic United States eased the ban on Chinese immigration in 1943.

During this time the former homes and businesses in Little Tokyo were occupied by African Americans who came to Los Angeles looking for defense jobs. Roosevelt's Executive Order 8802 in 1942 prohibited discrimination in defense industries, but did not help African Americans with living arrangements. A housing shortage and restrictive real estate covenants limited their residence to just a few areas in the city, and soon Little Tokyo became known as Bronzeville. The influx of blacks from mostly rural areas of the South clashed with the city's black middle class and the LAPD, whose dwindling ranks (as its members joined the armed forces) were filled by less-qualified and oftentimes more prejudiced officers. Established black leaders continued to defend their constituents through the local NAACP and National Negro Congress chapters with political and economic methods such as the "Double V" campaign (victory over discrimination at home and victory overseas).

Mexican and Mexican American residents faced the wrath of the LAPD and its allies in the crackdown on Latino juveniles. In 1942 the death of a young man after a party near Sleepy Lagoon, a locality just east of the city limits, erupted into a campaign sensationalized in newspaper headlines labeling all Mexican youths as violent juvenile delinquents. The LAPD and other agencies took over six hundred Mexican youths into custody, and in the following trial seventeen were convicted of various felonies, although all were eventually found not guilty after an appeal. In the following year Mexican youths wearing stylish "zoot suits" became involved in altercations with U.S. Navy personnel stationed in their neighborhood, and riots broke out for a week in June 1943, during which the LAPD allowed servicemen and others to beat anyone wearing that costume at will. This violence brought protests from the government of Mexico and the U.S. State Department and cast the city in a highly negative and racist light.

Race continued to be a major issue after 1945. African Americans in Los Angeles lost some of their housing and business structures when Japanese Americans returned to reclaim Little

Tokyo, and they lost many wartime jobs to returning white veterans. In addition, they faced a hostile LAPD, as evidenced by many documented instances of police brutality. Despite these setbacks, blacks tried to join other minority groups in political coalitions. Black leaders such as *California Eagle* editor Charlotte Bass, Dr. Claude Hudson, Rev. Clayton Russell, and Urban League director Floyd Covington continued to crusade for equal rights and economic opportunity. Attorney Loren Miller championed the demise of real estate covenants barring blacks and others from owning homes in white districts. His legal campaign resulted in precedents used by the NAACP legal team, which included Miller convincing the U.S. Supreme Court to render the covenants unenforceable in *Shelley v. Kraemer* in 1948. Segregation did decrease, but resistance from white residents persisted in the form of bombings and other violence. Such opposition, along with continued discrimination in employment and a lack of black municipal officeholders, proved that African Americans still had a long fight ahead for acceptance by many of their neighbors.

A large number of Mexican Americans served in the armed forces during the war, and upon their return they became more militant in the civil rights movement. Aided by the Congress of Spanish-Speaking Peoples and the Community Service Organization and led by union leaders Bert Corona and Tony Rios (and other community activists such as Edward Roybal, Eduardo Quevedo, Josefina Fierro de Bright, and Manuel Ruiz Jr.), they achieved major gains compared to previous decades. Roybal became the first Latino in the twentieth century to win a seat on the Los Angeles City Council when in 1949 he was elected in his second attempt, and he served until moving on to the U.S. Congress in 1963.

Japanese Americans began returning from internment camps just before the war ended, and they experienced a tense relationship with blacks in Little Tokyo/Bronzeville. Within a short time Japanese Americans were seen as the "model minority" and slowly dispersed throughout the county and eventually into the mainstream middle class. Their community leaders, including reporter Togo Tanaka, Japanese American Citizens League activists Frank Tsuchiya and Eiji Tanabe, and leftists Shugi Fujii and Karl Yoneda, were prominent organizers for their civil rights during and after the war. Many Chinese and Filipino residents also began moving out of their old enclaves to other areas of the city and county and gradually became more accepted by Anglos.

The 1950 U.S. Census revealed that Los Angeles was divided racially and ethnically about the same as it had been in 1940. The total population had expanded almost 25 percent during the previous decade, from 1.5 million in 1940 to almost 2 million in 1950. While the black population had almost doubled, from 4.2 percent to 8.5 percent since 1940, the ratio of other groups remained constant. Those of Mexican descent numbered 136,901 (almost 7 percent, as in 1940), and Asians represented a total of just over 2 percent (25,502 Japanese, 8,057 Chinese, 5,851 other Asians and races, and 956 American Indians included in this category), virtually the same as in 1940. The 83 percent white population contained a substantial number of ethnic Europeans previously clustered in the northeast portion of the city.

See also *Los Angeles, CA 1896–1929; Los Angeles, CA 1929–1941; Los Angeles, CA 1952–1989; Los Angeles, CA 1989–2011*

TOM SITTON

BIBLIOGRAPHY

Baisden, Richard Norman. "Labor Unions in Los Angeles Politics." PhD diss., University of Chicago, 1958.

Escobar, Edward J. *Race, Police, and the Making of a Political Identity: Mexican Americans and the Los Angeles Police Department, 1900–1945.* Berkeley: University of California Press, 1999.

Horne, Gerald. *Class Struggle in Hollywood, 1930–1950: Moguls, Mobsters, Stars, Reds, and Trade Unionists.* Austin: University of Texas Press, 2001.

Kurashige, Scott. *The Shifting Grounds of Race: Black and Japanese Americans in the Making of Multiethnic Los Angeles.* Princeton, NJ: Princeton University Press, 2008.

Leonard, Kevin Allen. *The Battle for Los Angeles: Racial Ideology and World War II.* Albuquerque: University of New Mexico Press, 2006.

Parson, Don. *Making a Better World: Public Housing, the Red Scare, and the Direction of Modern Los Angeles.* Minneapolis: University of Minnesota Press, 2005.

Sides, Josh. *L.A. City Limits: African American Los Angeles from the Great Depression to the Present.* Berkeley: University of California Press, 2003.

Sitton, Tom. *Los Angeles Transformed: Fletcher Bowron's Urban Reform Revival, 1938–1953.* Albuquerque: University of New Mexico Press, 2005.

DETROIT, MI 1941–1952

DETROIT WAS A STUDY IN CONTRADICTIONS between 1941 and 1952. It was the epicenter of American wartime production, leading to its nickname as the "Arsenal of Democracy." The expansion of production created a new boom, causing the migration of hundreds of thousands of job seekers to the city. Managing this growth was complicated, as the increasing population placed strains on the city's housing infrastructure and led to significant racial tensions as large numbers of African Americans came into frequently violent clashes with white residents, culminating in the 1943 Belle Isle riots. The postwar era was marked by the outward migration of both manufacturing and white residents and by significant labor protests as unions sought greater benefits from the profitable automobile industry.

GOVERNMENT AND POLITICS

Local politics in Detroit during the 1940s was strongly influenced by the industrial growth required by the wartime economy. Whereas the city's manufacturing base was already established by 1941, the demands for expanded production created new problems of growth management. The influx of job seekers and the demands on Detroit's infrastructure (particularly housing and transportation) posed significant challenges for local and national politicians. Growing racial tensions would complicate governance in the city, as ethnic whites felt threatened by plans to accommodate newly arriving African American residents. As World War II ended, white suburbanization and accelerating deindustrialization created new political challenges.

QUICK FACTS

DETROIT, MI 1941–1952

MAYORS

Edward Jeffries	(1940–1947)
Eugene Van Antwerp	(1947–1949)
Albert Cobo	(1949–1957)

MAJOR INDUSTRIES AND EMPLOYERS

Motor vehicle manufacturing

Durable goods manufacturing (steel, railway equipment, chemicals)

Sales (retail and wholesale)

Service work (professional and personal services)

Transportation and utilities

MAJOR NEWSPAPERS

Detroit Free Press
Detroit News
Detroit Times
Michigan Chronicle
Polish Daily News

MAJOR EVENTS

1941–1945: The city is dubbed the "Arsenal of Democracy" as its manufacturing base is mobilized for wartime production. Massive in-migration, including an influx of African Americans seeking manufacturing jobs, places great strain on the city's housing infrastructure.

1941–1942: Signs of racial tension emerge as street fights occur between African Americans and Polish youths. There are separate protests as the federally funded Sojourner Truth housing project, for African American workers, is built in a white neighborhood.

1943: In early June, twenty-five thousand Packard plant workers stop work in response to the promotion of three African American workers.

1943: The Belle Isle riots begin on June 20, with clashes between whites and blacks. Federal troops are required to quell the riots, in which thirty-four people die (including twenty-five African Americans). Detroit police are criticized for their uneven treatment of the rioters.

1945–1946: Organized labor calls strikes as unions vie with capitalists to shape the postwar economy. Over three million workers in the auto, steel, and mining industries strike between November 1945 and June 1946.

1950: Detroit's population peaks at 1,849,568. The city ranks as the fifth largest in the United States, but its population soon declines due to deindustrialization and white migration to the suburbs.

Detroit's local politics was balanced by two broad voting constituencies. The African American population tended to vote as part of a tenuous coalition with white liberals and the city's powerful organized labor wing, led by the United Auto Workers (UAW) and the Congress of Industrial Organizations (CIO). Despite being a predominantly Democratic city, this coalition was capable of splintering and was counterbalanced by a conservative electorate that prevailed at the ballot in most local elections between 1941 and 1952. Aside from the brief mayoralty of Democrat Eugene Van Antwerp (1947–1949), Detroit was governed by two Republicans—the personable reformer Edward Jeffries (1940–1947), who defeated staunch pro-labor Democrat candidate Richard T. Frankensteen in the 1945 election, and former businessman Albert Cobo (1949–1957), a staunch advocate for the rights of white homeowners associations and for the interests of business.

By 1941 Detroit was only beginning to emerge from the problems of the Great Depression. Mayor Jeffries had spent the first year of his administration reforming local government and quickly had to shift to manage the new problem of rapid urban growth created by the onset of World War II. Over one hundred ninety thousand migrants seeking jobs moved to the city between 1940 and 1943, overwhelming the city's available housing supply and affecting other areas of the city, including education, recreation, and transportation infrastructure. Jeffries used these pressures, and the cover provided by wartime conditions, to restructure Detroit's finances and to reconstruct the city's built environment by applying for funding from several federal agencies.

By 1944 Jeffries turned his attention to planning for peacetime Detroit. He sought to modernize the city by redeveloping the central core and constructing a network of express highways. His desire to forge closer bonds between government and the local automobile industry contributed to the 1946 Detroit Plan disregarding alternate transportation modes, including public transportation—Jeffries' administration developed a model that exacerbated and accelerated Detroit's dependence on private automobile transportation. His proposed highway system was linked to planned slum clearance in areas that greatly affected traditional African American ghetto neighborhoods and would force these residents to seek housing in traditionally white areas of the city.

Housing problems and policy in Detroit featured prominently in local politics through the years 1941–1952. Because of the wartime expansion of manufacturing employment, the city's population grew by over two hundred twenty thousand residents during the 1940s, including one hundred fifty thousand new African American residents. Such explosive population growth required the federal government to develop several projects for wartime worker housing. Aware of the racial tensions generated by the new migrants, the Detroit Housing Commission (DHC) stated that housing projects for war workers would not "change the racial characteristics of any neighborhood in Detroit." However, the Sojourner Truth public housing project contradicted this pledge, creating considerable tension in 1941. The project was designated for African American war workers, yet its location near a Polish neighborhood caused significant agitation for local residents. A campaign by local activists led to Sojourner Truth being designated for settlement by white workers, causing the NAACP and Urban League to protest the racially discriminatory housing policies that they were also campaigning against in other cities. The DHC again designated Sojourner Truth for African American workers, prompting a cross burning by the Ku Klux Klan, which escalated to a riot with armed whites preventing African Americans from moving in. The fighting caused the housing project to remain unoccupied for three weeks, creating a public relations nightmare for Detroit and the United States, eventually resolved by over two thousand troops protecting the arrival of the first tenants.

The problems of race and public housing did not end with World War II. In the 1949 mayoral election between former UAW activist George Edwards and Republican Albert Cobo, Cobo staunchly supported the right of white homeowners associations to use restrictive housing covenants to prevent non-Caucasian families from purchasing property in their neighborhoods. Cobo was explicitly committed to opposing public housing and the "Negro invasion" of Detroit's white neighborhoods, and he won the election by playing to the fears of ethnic white neighborhoods. Once in office, Cobo pursued a policy that opposed public housing projects, vetoing eight of twelve proposed developments, and quickly attacked Detroit's existing public housing programs.

INDUSTRY, COMMERCE, AND LABOR

Detroit's rapid growth from 1941 on was a direct consequence of opportunities created by its role as a significant hub for industrial production. As the United States entered World War II, Detroit's manufacturing resources were marshaled to produce the planes, tanks, and munitions required for the war effort. The city was a centerpiece of wartime production plans, as the region's industrial infrastructure could be rapidly transitioned to military purposes, providing new employment and training opportunities to the men and women who worked in the massive manufacturing plants, including Willow Run and River Rouge. The postwar period was marked by significant labor strife as workers sought greater rewards from the profitable automobile industry, and the consequent plant location decisions of the large auto firms began to reshape Detroit's economic geography as manufacturing activities shifted beyond the city's borders.

Organized labor was a powerful component of Detroit's economy during this period, with union organizing during the 1930s turning the city into a leading union town by May 21, 1941, when Ford Motor Company, the last significant holdout, finally allowed its workers the right to organize. The entry of the United States into World War II was met with pledges by the leaders of the UAW and CIO to fully support the country's war effort by voluntarily taking a no-strike pledge. Labor mobilization was rapid and enhanced union strength during the war—two hundred sixty thousand Detroit women worked in manufacturing occupations during the war, supported by UAW policies intended to provide gender equality in the workplace.

The World War II compromise between industry and labor did not last long after the cessation of hostilities. The end of the war meant manufacturing firms needed to reduce production capacity at their plants, and the return of servicemen to Detroit led to the displacement of the workers who had migrated to fill the wartime labor needs. Adding to the unrest was the fact that wartime wage growth had not kept pace with the cost of living. The reluctance of management to reward workers with higher wages created significant labor unrest in Detroit and other cities. By November 1945 the labor actions against working conditions in local plants escalated, with two hundred twenty-five UAW members voting on November 21 to strike at General Motors (GM). These strikes were quickly supported by workers in other unions nationwide.

The Detroit strikes shut down ninety-six plants as local union leaders, led by UAW organizer Walter Reuther, demanded wage increases of 30 percent linked to auto firm agreements to not raise the price of new cars. GM management was opposed to this deal on the principle that the American firms should retain the ability to set conditions as they saw fit. The situation remained at an impasse for 113 days, marking the longest strike to affect the automobile industry. The compromise deal eventually struck included wage raises without the clause limiting price increases on new cars.

By 1950 motor vehicle manufacturing in metropolitan Detroit accounted for two hundred eighty-five thousand direct jobs, out of total metropolitan employment of 1.1 million jobs. The importance of automobile manufacturing to Detroit was even more important once associated sectors (including transportation, finance, and professional services) were included. Ford, GM, and Chrysler provided the opportunity for employment in well-paying jobs, and they had the strength to shape the city's built environment and economic fortunes by the location decisions they made. During World War II and in the years immediately after, Detroit provided more jobs than the outlying suburbs, yet the significance of the central city was gradually decreasing. Ford, GM, and Chrysler built twenty new factories between 1947 and 1955, employing over seventy thousand workers as postwar demand for automobiles rose. None of the factories built during the postwar period were located within the City of Detroit, as the companies preferred to build in outlying suburbs such as Warren, Ypsilanti, Livonia, and Trenton. The relocation of jobs to these suburban areas occurred for at least three reasons. First, the land was inexpensive and could accommodate the large single-story buildings needed for modern production; second, spreading employment across a region could enhance the firms' ability to reduce union control, potentially preventing labor action on the scale witnessed in 1946; and third, the new freeway system meant less reliance on the old transportation geographies, giving firms more freedom in choosing where they located their production facilities.

The consequences of manufacturing decentralization would prove highly significant to Detroit's future development. White residents, already concerned about the movement of African Americans into their neighborhoods, shifted outside the city limits and toward the new industrial plants. The flight of auto manufacturing facilities and residents created cascade effects, as auto-related industries followed the exodus from Detroit. This process, which began in the postwar period, left behind a changed urban landscape of empty factories, vacant land, reduced tax revenue, and higher unemployment within the city.

RACE, ETHNICITY, AND IMMIGRATION

The period from 1941 to 1952 was characterized by a great degree of racial and ethnic tension, as better-established communities struggled to accept the arrival of new migrant communities. In 1940 Detroit comprised mainly ethnic white, Catholic residents. Between 1940 and 1950, the city's racial composition shifted with the arrival of over one hundred fifty thousand African Americans pushed from the Jim Crow South by discrimination and high poverty rates and pulled to Detroit by the promise of high-paying jobs in the manufacturing sector. The neighborhoods of Paradise Valley and West Side were the epicenters of Detroit's African American population in 1940, a pattern created by the presence of a great amount of social capital such as churches, businesses, and entertainment venues, yet exacerbated by discriminatory housing policies that restricted the location choices of African American families. By 1952 the African American population accounted for over 16 percent of Detroit's population and had shifted beyond the traditional neighborhoods as a consequence of sustained legal pressure against restrictive housing policies.

Racial tensions escalated as Detroit's African American population grew. The intersection of wartime stresses, ethnic communities coming into contact for the first time, and perceptions from both blacks and whites of unfair and racially based hiring practices at local firms created a volatile environment. In early 1941 clashes occurred between African Americans and Polish youths who were accused of agitating African American neighborhoods. Such episodes, combined with the labor unrest and strike in 1942 at the Packard plant over the planned promotion of three African American workers, and the protests over the planned Sojourner Truth housing project led *Life* magazine to declare in 1942 that "Detroit is Dynamite—it can either blow up Hitler or blow up the U.S." This prediction was borne out in June 1943 with the wide-scale Belle Isle riots. Clashes between whites and blacks on Belle Isle spilled over into the downtown and Paradise Valley areas. Looting of white-owned businesses by African Americans in Paradise Valley was answered by a mob of over ten thousand whites that rampaged through Paradise Valley. The Detroit police were predominantly sympathetic to the white rioters and were later accused of heavy-handed treatment against African American protesters; seventeen African Americans were shot by police, and of the thirty-four people killed during the riots, twenty-five were African American. The riots were eventually quelled by federal troops, yet the discontent between racial groups in Detroit continued to simmer.

The suspicion of new African American residents by white communities was apparent in the restrictive housing covenants developed by neighborhood associations. In the postwar period, nearly all of Detroit's neighborhoods beyond the inner city were covered by some type of racially based covenants that white residents developed to prevent non-white families from buying property. Neighborhood covenants were supported by political figures such as Mayor Cobo and by court decisions in Detroit and Michigan, yet the U.S. Supreme Court ruled in *Shelley v. Kraemer* (1948) that it was a violation of the Fourteenth Amendment for courts to enforce restrictive covenants in deeds. At the same time that restrictive covenants were removed, white residents were beginning to move to the suburbs, leaving Detroit for neighboring communities such as Grosse Pointe and Bloomfield Hills. Suburban flight from the city was not only due to Detroit's growing African American population—jobs were also decentralizing as industrial production shifted away from the city. As was the case with other American cities in the postwar period, the combination of white suburbanization and the decentralization of employment meant that by 1952 Detroit was more predominantly African American with less access to employment.

Despite Detroit's racial problems, the city was also the site of a burgeoning music scene, fostered in the African American enclaves of Paradise Valley, Black Bottom, and West Side. Throughout the 1940s, Detroit's already strong jazz community continued to grow and develop the new style of music known as bebop. This musical innovation was enabled by the supply of talented musicians and a growing selection of nightclubs, along with the demand of postwar Detroit residents for new entertainment options. The downtown area (bounded by Grand Boulevard) saw thirteen new jazz clubs open during the 1940s, while the gradual diffusion of African American residents beyond Paradise Valley was matched by the development of new jazz clubs across Detroit's North End. Clubs such as the Paradise Theatre, Club Juana, and the Flame Show Bar were popular venues for live jazz music and attracted a diverse range of customers from the city's white and African American communities. While the NAACP continued to campaign against racial discrimination policies that affected entertainment and dining venues, including these clubs, the growth and popularity of Detroit bebop provided sites for peaceful racial integration and interaction.

See also *Detroit, MI 1896–1929; Detroit, MI 1929–1941; Detroit, MI 1952–1989*

MICHAEL R. GLASS

BIBLIOGRAPHY

Bjorn, Lars, and Jim Gallert. *Before Motown: A History of Jazz in Detroit, 1920–1960*. Ann Arbor: University of Michigan Press, 2000.

Capeci, Domenic J., Jr., ed. *Detroit and the "Good War": The World War II Letters of Mayor Edward Jeffries and Friends*. Lexington: University Press of Kentucky, 1996.

Kenyon, Amy Maria. *Dreaming Suburbia: Detroit and the Production of Postwar Space and Culture*. Detroit, MI: Wayne State University Press, 2004.

Sugrue, Thomas J. *The Origins of the Urban Crisis: Race and Inequality in Postwar Detroit*. Princeton, NJ: Princeton University Press, 1996.

Vexler, Robert I. *Detroit: A Chronological and Documentary History*. Dobbs Ferry, NY: Oceana, 1977.

Widick, B. J. *Detroit: City of Race and Class Violence*. Revised edition. Detroit, MI: Wayne State University Press, 1989.

BALTIMORE, MD 1941–1952

THE ARRIVAL OF DEFENSE WORKERS BEFORE AND DURING WORLD WAR II significantly increased Baltimore's population and expanded the responsibilities of municipal government. Local shipbuilding and aircraft industries flourished. The leaders of rival Democratic factions declared a truce for the duration of the war, but the suspension of combat among leaders preceded a collapse of discipline among their followers. The unraveling of the local Democratic Party contributed to the victory of a Republican mayor, Theodore R. McKeldin, in 1943. McKeldin's administration was necessarily nonpartisan, but Baltimore's lone Republican officeholder succeeded in providing the city with a new airport, revising the municipal charter, and creating a new redevelopment authority. Wartime housing shortages triggered a revival of submerged racial issues. Postwar controversies about segregation in the city parks marked the administration of McKeldin's Democratic successor, Thomas D'Alesandro, who created a human relations commission in an effort to preserve racial peace.

GOVERNMENT AND POLITICS

Baltimore's municipal government emerged from the Great Depression with an enlarged workforce and expanded responsibilities. Mayor Howard Jackson had grudgingly assented to the creation of a city housing authority and a welfare department. The city had eleven thousand employees in forty-five departments, and under Jackson, departments with overlapping responsibilities were consolidated. He centralized support services such as payroll, purchasing, and vehicle maintenance and created a single office to handle citizen complaints. His administration introduced a retirement plan for city workers and a civil service commission to oversee employment practices. But the depression had been hard on stable setups and definite programs, and even the mayor's insistence on administrative efficiency did not preclude graft.

QUICK FACTS

BALTIMORE, MD 1941–1952

MAYORS

Howard W. Jackson   (1931–1943)
Theodore R. McKeldin   (1943–1947)
Thomas J. D'Alesandro Jr. (1947–1959)

MAJOR INDUSTRIES AND EMPLOYERS

Fabricated metal products
Transportation equipment
Primary metal industries
Chemicals and allied products
Men's and boys' suits and coats

MAJOR NEWSPAPERS

Baltimore Afro-American
Baltimore American
Baltimore News-Post
Baltimore Sun

MAJOR EVENTS

1945: Maryland approves the creation of the Baltimore Redevelopment Commission.
1947: Baltimore creates the nation's first housing court.
1950: Voters approve funds for a major league baseball stadium.
1951: Mayor D'Alesandro creates the Human Relations Commission. The city parks department integrates city golf courses and allows for interracial sports competitions.
1953: Municipal employees go on strike for the first time in the city's history.

World War II brought more growth in municipal responsibilities. Even before Pearl Harbor, the city's public services had to accommodate thousands of new workers in local defense plants and shipyards, and public schools had to provide for their children. The war also suspended some political rivalries. Jackson and his chief Democratic rival, party boss William Curran, cited the war as an occasion for a truce. Curran endorsed Jackson's reelection as mayor, and the two leaders agreed on a common slate of candidates for the state legislature. Jackson was even open to cooperation with Governor O'Conor, the man who had most recently dashed his gubernatorial ambitions. A "harmony conference" met in July 1942, at which Curran, Jackson, and O'Conor were able to agree on a partial slate of candidates for the General Assembly from Baltimore.

Baltimore's top political leaders could not establish order among their fractious followers, though. The Democratic primary brought forth not only "harmony" candidates for the legislature, but an array of recalcitrant Jackson candidates and Curran candidates, along with some who supported both Jackson and Curran but not O'Conor, and still others who ran under the banners of district leaders like Jack Pollack. In one district, there were seventeen candidates for three seats in the House of Delegates. The election yielded a motley collection of Democratic legislators and only a narrow victory for Governor O'Conor over Republican Theodore R. McKeldin—the smallest plurality for any Democratic gubernatorial candidate in more than twenty years. Jack Pollack crowed that the results had laid bare the "dead leadership" of William Curran.

Curran reiterated his support for Jackson's reelection in 1943, and Jackson endorsed two of Curran's allies for the offices of comptroller and city council president. Neither Curran nor Jackson endorsed any candidates for the city council, perhaps because they recognized just how little influence they exercised in district-level politics. Jackson made a strong showing in the Democratic primary, and Curran's candidates for comptroller and city council president were also successful. But in the general election, Jackson lost his bid for a fifth term as mayor to Theodore McKeldin by more than twenty thousand votes, while every other Democratic candidate was victorious.

Mayor McKeldin commanded no machine. A lone Republican in an otherwise Democratic regime, his influence depended almost entirely on his personal skills. The unanimously Democratic city council went its own way. William Curran and the defeated Jackson had agreed that the council's patronage should be divided evenly between their two camps. Instead, the supposed partisans of Jackson deserted their fallen leader and joined three council members controlled by Fourth District boss Jack Pollack to deny the Curran faction any share of the spoils.

At first, McKeldin dispensed mayoral patronage among council members without much regard to faction, a strategy designed to maintain goodwill with the council as a whole, but one that infuriated the mayor's fellow Republicans, who gained almost nothing tangible from his victory. The mayor offered them only a plea to rise above partisanship.

One of McKeldin's most vexing problems emerged from the intersection of party politics and race. Months before his election, the War Manpower Commission had directed the Federal Public Housing Administration (FPHA) to build as many as two thousand temporary housing units in Baltimore for African American workers in defense plants and shipyards. The FPHA selected a site for the project in industrial East Baltimore, convenient to many of the city's mills and factories, but the proposal was met with fervent opposition. The chairman of the Baltimore housing authority then suggested a different site, but stressed that it was only a recommendation, as the final decisions were to be decided by the FPHA.

Candidate McKeldin had criticized Mayor Jackson for failing to "take any part in the discussion of the Negro housing project." Mayor McKeldin appointed an Interracial Commission on Negro Housing to consider the matter and to resolve the impasse between local and federal officials. He took care to emphasize, however, that he had "no authority to determine where these houses shall be built." It was a point that he returned to repeatedly in the discussions that followed his creation of the commission. McKeldin had won the mayor's office with strong support from black voters. For him and for other Baltimore politicians, the game was to express concern for the housing needs of African Americans, but to avoid suggesting a specific location for black housing that might annoy whites.

The city solicitor, a mayoral appointee, issued a politically convenient legal opinion holding that only the city council could select public housing sites. McKeldin promptly called a special session of the all-Democratic council, giving them fifteen days to designate locations for African American housing. The council, just as promptly, enacted a legally absurd but politically expedient ordinance prohibiting the federal government from "constructing any war housing in Baltimore without the approval of the Mayor, City Council, and Board of Estimates."

A politically astute Democratic congressman from Baltimore, Thomas D'Alesandro Jr., finally engineered the outcome that minimized local political fallout. He arranged a conference between Baltimore city officials and the head of the FPHA. The meeting settled on a plan that distributed housing for black defense workers among four small sites close to defense plants. The local Urban League complained that three of the sites were too remote, but it was precisely their remoteness that made this settlement acceptable to white residents and allowed local politicians to put the issue behind them.

The Republican mayor had proven capable of the political footwork needed to dance his way around a potentially dangerous decision. Democrats, however, persisted in their attempts to maneuver him into politically precarious positions or prevent him from building a record of accomplishments. Democratic state legislators torpedoed his proposal for a cross-town expressway. With the help of the city's Democratic delegation in Annapolis, Baltimore's police commissioner bypassed the mayor and submitted proposed police pay increases directly to the state legislature. (Civil War–era legislation had made the city's police department a state agency.) But McKeldin would have to fund these increases from the city budget along with the pay for other city employees whose compensation was pegged to the police pay scales. The Democratic city council refused to back the mayor in a tax dispute with the Baltimore Transit Company because they wanted to deny the McKeldin administration an opportunity to pose as "the champions of the people against the great vested interests."

In the face of Democratic obstructionism and criticism, McKeldin nevertheless managed to ready the city for postwar renewal. He gave Baltimore an up-to-date airport, a school construction program and a civic center, a new reservoir to secure its water supply, and a tunnel to carry water to the city. He appointed a commission to revise the city charter. It produced the first major overhaul of the document since 1898. McKeldin got authorization from the state legislature to create the Baltimore Redevelopment Commission, whose assignment was to shrink the city's slums. McKeldin also introduced another innovation in city government: He appointed the first African American—George W. F. McMechen, a local attorney—to Baltimore's Board of School Commissioners.

But factional divisions in the mayor's own party weakened his defense against Democratic challenges. The intraparty feud grew more intense when McKeldin was advanced as a candidate for the Republican gubernatorial nomination in 1946. Fellow Republicans challenged the honesty of the finance reports that he had filed in his mayoral campaign. McKeldin lost the governorship by a wide margin. He even lost his own city—an outcome that may have figured in his decision not to run for reelection as mayor in 1947.

The Democrats may not have been so sharply divided as the Republicans, but they had problems of their own. The city council alliance between Curran and Pollack fell apart in a petty patronage dispute over the appointment of election judges. In 1946, when the two bosses aligned themselves with different Democratic gubernatorial candidates, the city's district leaders chose to join Pollack in his support of William Preston Lane, who won the Democratic primary, defeating Curran's candidate, J. Millard Tawes. Curran had been able to carry only one of the city's six districts for Tawes. A majority of his candidates for the General Assembly survived the Democratic primary, but once the legislature convened they could be expected to succumb to the patronage at Governor Lane's disposal.

Curran's defeats in the state elections of 1946 may help to explain his shaky leadership as he approached the municipal elections of 1947. In February he called a meeting of the ward executives, party committee members, and elected officials who made up the Curran organization to settle on a mayoral candidate. The eighty-three politicians in attendance failed to give majority support to any candidate. Pollack offered a full-throated endorsement of Congressman D'Alesandro, who won the Democratic primary with 48 percent of the vote, a near majority over his eight opponents, and then the general election by more than twenty-four thousand votes.

The mayor's election had been achieved by a coalition of "bosslets," and they were not ready to surrender their independence to the mayor or any other boss. Pollack, whose support had been critical to D'Alesandro's nomination, emerged as the principal beneficiary of mayoral patronage. The other bosslets resisted his elevation and squabbled among themselves about the allocation of city jobs. Almost everyone claimed to be shortchanged. The vacancy created by the death of a council member created a new surge of contention. Rejecting the candidate favored by the mayor (and allegedly by Pollack), the council chose a replacement not identified with either one, then mobilized the new voting alignment resulting from the appointment to oust the council's clerk, a Pollack adherent.

The repeated formation and collapse of council coalitions limited progress on Mayor D'Alesandro's priority policy initiatives: Construction of a cross-town expressway, construction of a baseball stadium (and, by implication, the acquisition of a major league team to use it), and consolidation of the various agencies concerned with Baltimore's harbor into a single port authority.

The mayor's vision of a cross-town expressway was a revival and revision of Mayor McKeldin's previous highway proposal. As originally, the freeway would have crossed the city diagonally from northeast to southwest. One by one, city council representatives from districts in the path of the road eliminated the segments that would have cut through their territories. In the end, only a little more than a mile of highway would remain—enough to link up with a new highway built by the federal government from Washington to a military base just southwest of the city. The new link would give Baltimoreans easy access to the new airport begun under Mayor McKeldin.

At first, D'Alesandro's stadium project seemed more promising than his highway proposal. The voters had approved a $2.5 million stadium bond issue in the same election that had made D'Alesandro mayor. The money was to finance the replacement of an existing city stadium built in the early 1920s and used primarily by college and high school football teams and, later, by the Baltimore Colts and minor league Orioles. Engineers and architects, however, estimated that it would cost twice as much as the amount approved by voters. Of twenty-two possible sites for the new arena, the 33rd Street location was chosen by a team of engineers, and the state courts finally disposed of the neighbors' objections; persuading the voters to authorize an additional $2.5 million bond issue proved more difficult. Having approved a stadium loan in 1947, voters were unwilling to approve another in 1948, especially since the size and design of the new arena were still uncertain. By 1950, after city leaders began to talk about getting a major league baseball team, the electorate was ready to approve the money for a bigger stadium. In the meantime, D'Alesandro had already been building as much stadium as he could afford with the money in hand.

As a port city, Baltimore was already in the big leagues, but it was threatened by competition with East and Gulf Coast cities and soon to face the St. Lawrence Seaway. Unlike its rivals

Baltimore had no port authority, no agency with the power to issue bonds or levy taxes for harbor improvements, acquire property through eminent domain, or take ownership of harbor facilities. In 1920 Baltimore had created a port development commission. It issued bonds to finance loans to some of the railroads that converged on the harbor for the construction of new piers, expansion of warehouse space, and development of rail access to shipping. The commission, however, shared its authority over the port with five other agencies and had undertaken only two major projects from the time of its formation to the end of World War II.

Baltimore was distinctive not only for the fragmented governance of its port, but also for the extent to which its harbor facilities were owned and operated by private interests—especially railroads. Not surprisingly, trucking companies operated at a disadvantage in Baltimore, and the divergent interests of the older and newer modes of transport made it difficult for politicians to arrive at plans for the development of the city's harbor that commanded wide support. D'Alesandro appointed a committee to come up with a coherent program of port improvements, partly because "the division among the shipping people in Baltimore" made it "difficult to determine what is necessary here." The committee, noting that the railroad companies were opposed to the building of any trucking facilities that could compete with their own facilities, proposed to sponsor an independent study to estimate how much truck traffic the port handled and how much more it might attract with a program of improvements.

Baltimore had been a railroad pioneer, and its early backing of the steam locomotive enabled it to leap ahead of its competition. But the city's commitment to railroads had now become a drag on its economic progress. Baltimore specialized in the bulk cargoes that railroads carried, like coal or potash or gypsum; it was short on facilities for handling the kinds of shipments that trucks carried—everything from textiles to machinery to shoes. At the railroad-owned piers, wharfage fees discriminated against cargoes carried by truck and, it was argued, diverted business to New York, where fees and facilities were more favorable to the trucking industry.

A New York engineering firm conducted a comprehensive study of port operations and facilities. Its recommendations included the creation of a centralized port authority with the power to take property by eminent domain and to issue its own bonds to pay for harbor improvements. Nine port-related organizations and agencies got an opportunity to pick the report apart before the mayor's port committee could issue its conclusions. D'Alesandro at first refused to comment on the consultants' study. But the president of the Western Maryland Railroad was ready to state his views even before receiving the report: "Baltimore has become a great port primarily because the railroads have kept a steady, lower freight rate for goods handled through Baltimore. Let the trucks with their hodge-podge rates, which can never be relied upon, take control and see what a great port that will be."

The Harbor Advisory Board, one of the agencies to be phased out under the study's recommendations, delivered a negative verdict on the study. Not long afterward, D'Alesandro expressed reservations about the condemnation powers assigned to the proposed commission, and the influential Association of Commerce rejected almost all of the study's conclusions, arguing in favor of a slightly modified version of the existing port development commission, one that was likely to increase private ownership of the port. Projects financed by commission loans would revert to private ownership once the borrowers paid off the debt.

Members of the new Port of Baltimore Commission were soon complaining that they lacked the powers to upgrade the port and were too dependent on city government to carry out their spending and development plans. By 1953 commission members were discussing the authorization of yet another study to "determine the feasibility of a single body operating all harbor activities and using money from the rental of piers and other facilities for port promotion and improvement work." Two years later a new city business organization, the Greater Baltimore Committee, persuaded the state legislature to create an independent Maryland Port Authority with its own earmarked stream of funds from state corporate tax revenues. The port no longer belonged to the city.

Baltimore's public improvements rose up against a background of private squalor. Much of the city's housing stock was old, deteriorating, and overcrowded. The city's redevelopment commission could only whittle away at the slums, and public housing could accommodate only a small fraction of their residents. A new civic organization, the Citizens' Planning and Housing Association, formed in 1941 to promote a new approach to the problem. It persuaded the city council to specify minimum standards for housing: Basic plumbing, ratio of windows to floor space, square footage per occupant, and so on. Fire, health, police, and public works officials were to carry out a strict enforcement program demanding that landlords bring their properties up to code. This "Baltimore Plan" drew national attention, and in 1947 a city housing court, the first in the country, began to hear cases generated by the plan. Two-and-a-half years later, it had cleared ninety thousand complaints. In 1949 D'Alesandro created a special Office of Housing and Law Enforcement in the city's health department with sole responsibility for the Baltimore Plan.

In 1951 the Housing Office targeted a twenty-seven-block section of East Baltimore for strict enforcement. But this time the landlords complained of harassment. Instead of making needed repairs, they expelled hundreds of tenants and sold their buildings. Rents soared. A subsequent study of the Baltimore Plan estimated that the human costs of the code enforcement campaign exceeded the benefits.

During D'Alesandro's 1951 reelection campaign the city council was in a state of paralysis. The resignation of one member created a tie between the council's two factions, and they were unable to agree on a replacement. The mayor stood aloof from the council's squabbles, not even bothering to take a position in the four-way contest for the Democratic nomination as council president. Virtually all of the Democratic combatants in the contest for council presidency supported D'Alesandro for reelection, and the remnants of Curran's organization advanced no candidate to challenge him. The mayor coasted to easy victory in the Democratic primary, as did his candidate for city comptroller.

Another surprise followed. C. Markland Kelly, the incumbent city council president, filed with the board of elections as an independent candidate for mayor. Kelly had often been at odds with D'Alesandro, and now he launched a full-scale attack. Corruption was pervasive in the D'Alesandro administration, Kelly said, and his position as chair of the city's board of estimates gave him a ringside view of the unsavory processes by which municipal contracts were awarded. The voters apparently disagreed. D'Alesandro defeated his Republican opponent by a margin of two to one, and Kelly finished a distant third. The mayor led a complete Democratic sweep of the municipal election, and the party's success seemed to heal its most persistent internal divisions.

INDUSTRY, COMMERCE, AND LABOR

Wartime industry brought money as well as migrants to Baltimore. The federal government's Reconstruction Finance Corporation supplied $70 million for the construction of defense plants in Maryland and funneled raw materials and working capital to factories in and around the city. The output of the city's factories was notable for its diversity. One firm turned out miles of chain link fence for the Army and Navy; another, three hundred fifty thousand tons of asphalt. A bottling company switched from stamping out bottle caps to nose caps for armor-piercing ammunition. A local chemical company shifted entirely to production of synthetic rubber. But steel, airplanes, and ships were the area's biggest defense industries. The Glenn L. Martin Company built the largest aircraft assembly plant in the world on the city's outskirts. Baltimore's Fairfield Shipyard launched five hundred Liberty ships and Victory ships. The assembly process began at one end of a 1,540-foot-long building, and a completed ship emerged at the other end. In April 1942, the process took about 110 days; by August the average had been reduced to 52 days.

Wages flowed into more Baltimore households than ever before. Though the city had many people and much money, there was little to spend it on, and some worried what would happen when the war ended and the wages stopped flowing. The anxiety took concrete form in October 1945, when forty-five thousand defense workers were laid off and thirty-five thousand veterans came home. The *Evening Sun* predicted that one hundred sixty thousand Marylanders might be unemployed by spring.

But peace did not bring depression. As in other cities, the forced savings of wartime, new technologies developed in defense industries, and the baby boom provided a basis for postwar economic growth. At the local Westinghouse plant, for example, wartime work on radar, automatic pilots, and X-ray inspection of armor plate led to industrial uses of X-rays, a postwar Aerospace Division, and a Molecular Electronics Division that manufactured integrated circuits. Bethlehem Steel converted Liberty ships into scrap to feed its mill, which pushed out the steel for new freighters and, eventually, supertankers and container ships at the company's shipyard.

But cars and the construction of suburban single-family homes drove economic growth in the Baltimore region and propelled the city's population outward. Governor McKeldin orchestrated a massive highway construction plan that made it possible for Baltimoreans to drive from suburban houses to jobs downtown or in the suburbs themselves. The city's population continued to grow into the 1950s, but the numbers concealed an urban infirmity. The city's share of the metropolitan area's population had been declining sharply since 1940.

Perhaps the city's residents overlooked Baltimore's downturn because so many of them had joined unions. Barred from striking so long as the country was at war, organized labor went to war when the country made peace. A wave of walkouts in 1946 contributed to a rise in local wages. Members of the United Auto Workers local got supplemental unemployment benefits and cost-of-living adjustments that made them more financially secure than most Americans. Throughout the 1950s the wages of Baltimore workers exceeded inflation by 7 percent.

But postwar labor activism flowed into some previously untouched institutions. For the first time in the history of the city, municipal employees went on strike. On New Year's Day in

1953, three thousand three hundred city laborers, represented by Teamsters' Local 825, walked out when the mayor rejected their demand for a 10 percent wage increase. The strikers included garbage collectors, school janitors and furnacemen, maintenance workers for the city's sewer and water systems and its streets. Some schools had to close because there was no one to tend the furnaces; frozen or broken water mains went unrepaired; garbage piled up in the streets unless citizens carried the waste by car to a city dump. The strike lasted for over two weeks. D'Alesandro made small concessions on overtime and sick pay and appointed a committee, headed by the city solicitor, to recommend improvements in the city's employer-employee relationships. But there would be more strikes.

RACE, ETHNICITY, AND IMMIGRATION

For the city's African Americans, the race issue was a matter of life and death. In 1942 a Baltimore police officer shot a uniformed black soldier in the back and killed him. The homicide grew out of a scuffle on Pennsylvania Avenue, the chief artery of entertainment and commerce in black Baltimore. The officer was not disciplined even though the soldier was the second black man he had killed in two years.

This killing and the exoneration of the officer responsible for it triggered a mass protest in the city's black community. Led by Carl Murphy, publisher of the *Baltimore Afro-American*, two thousand African Americans joined in a caravan of cars and buses to confront Governor Herbert O'Conor in Annapolis and to demand action—not just an end to police brutality, but the hiring of more black officers (there were only three) and the appointment of black police magistrates. The governor promised only the appointment of an interracial commission to investigate the problems facing black Baltimoreans.

The eighteen-member commission worked on its report for almost a year. It recommended the hiring of black police officers and appointment of blacks to government bodies like school boards. It did not, however, challenge the regime of segregation. It urged greater financial support for teacher training at black colleges. The commission paid particular attention to housing for African Americans, perhaps because it was the black problem most likely to disturb whites. Black neighborhoods were already overcrowded, and wartime migration to Baltimore aggravated the problem. Overcrowding in black neighborhoods threatened to push blacks into white neighborhoods. As the commission pointed out, housing was "at the root of many of the stresses that arise between the white and colored races." It called for additional black housing, with the proviso that it be "contiguous to existing Negro neighborhoods."

The commission had little to say on the issue of black employment. Its members were split on the question of initiating a fair employment practices investigation of Baltimore industry. An investigation would have shown that barriers to black employment persisted even in the face of wartime manpower shortages. The *Afro-American* celebrated the employment of thirteen thousand six hundred blacks in Baltimore-area defense plants "as job barriers fall." The defense plant jobs represented a gain for black workers, although by the end of 1942 they accounted for less than 7 percent of the city's war workers, but more than 20 percent of Baltimore's labor force. In many cases, employment did not lead to desegregation. The Glenn L. Martin plant and the

Koppers Company confined black workers to separate facilities. Attempts to create integrated workplaces at Western Electric and Maryland Drydock triggered strikes by white workers.

The migrations set in motion by World War II changed Baltimore's ethnic composition. The percentage of the city's population born abroad was slowly shrinking. In spite of the arrival of war refugees, the city's foreign-born population, never very large, actually declined by more than one-fifth. Baltimore's new immigrants were whites from Appalachia and the South. Defense industries in and around the city resisted the hiring of African Americans until late in the war, and the racial restrictions on employment opportunities shaped the stream of migration that flowed into Baltimore. About 89 percent of the one hundred fifty thousand to two hundred thousand new arrivals were white, and their coming reduced the demand for black workers. Employers refused to hire African Americans or restricted them to the least desirable jobs. When pressed, writes historian Kenneth Durr, they explained that they were deferring to the wishes of their white workers. They were mostly right. The massive influx of southern whites, says Durr, reinforced racist sentiments among whites who were native Baltimoreans.

See also *Baltimore, MD 1776–1790; Baltimore, MD 1790–1828; Baltimore, MD 1828–1854; Baltimore, MD 1854–1877; Baltimore, MD 1877–1896; Baltimore, MD 1896–1929; Baltimore, MD 1929–1941; Baltimore, MD 1952–1989*

MATTHEW CRENSON

BIBLIOGRAPHY

Brugger, Robert J. *Maryland: A Middle Temperament, 1634–1980*. Baltimore, MD: Johns Hopkins University Press, 1988.

Callcott, George H. *Maryland and America, 1940–1980*. Baltimore, MD: Johns Hopkins University Press, 1985.

Durr, Kenneth D. *Behind the Backlash: White Working-Class Politics in Baltimore, 1940–1980*. Chapel Hill: University of North Carolina Press, 2003.

Rothman, Edwin. "Factional Machine Politics: William Curran and the Baltimore City Democratic Organization, 1929–1946." PhD diss., Johns Hopkins University, 1949.

Terry, David Taft. "'Tramping for Justice': The Dismantling of Jim Crow in Baltimore." PhD diss., Howard University, 2002.

CLEVELAND, OH 1941–1952

DURING AND AFTER WORLD WAR II, CLEVELAND MODELED THE TRENDS that were present throughout urban America, especially in the manufacturing cities of the industrial North and Midwest. During the war years, population and prosperity soared. High levels of industrial employment tempered the dislocations of the Great Depression. Central business districts reached the zenith of their regional economic and political significance. Spatial diffusion across a suburban landscape, fueled by rising rates of homeownership and automobility, transformed coherent cities into metropolitan political

QUICK FACTS

CLEVELAND, OH **1941–1952**

MAYORS

Frank J. Lausche   (1941–1944)
Thomas A. Burke   (1945–1953)

MAJOR INDUSTRIES AND EMPLOYERS

Thompson Aircraft Products Company
Republic Steel
Jones & Laughlin Steel
Chase Brass & Copper
General Electric
Fisher Body
Ford Motor Company
Shipping

MAJOR NEWSPAPERS

The Plain Dealer
Cleveland Press
Cleveland News

MAJOR EVENTS

1941–1945: Wartime causes a significant boost to Cleveland's manufacturing sector, with manufacturing employment increasing from one hundred ninety-one thousand in 1940 to three hundred forty thousand by the war's end.
1943: The local housing vacancy rate falls to less than 1 percent.
1946: The Cleveland Browns football team begins playing in the American Football Conference.
1949: Clevelanders elect Jean Murrell Capers to the city council, the first African American woman to hold the position.
1952: On November 3 an oil slick on the Cuyahoga River catches fire, causing significant damage.

---

economies. By most measurements, the largest American cities such as Cleveland peaked during this period.

For thirty years beginning in 1944, the Cleveland Electric Illuminating Company promoted its growth ambitions by advertising Cleveland as the "Best Location in the Nation." Urban boosterism came easily to Clevelanders in the 1940s, animated by the bragging rights that accompany success in professional sports. In 1946 Cleveland's new football team began playing in the newly created American Football Conference. Named the Cleveland Browns (after Paul Brown, the team's first coach), the team was immediately successful. And in 1948 Clevelanders' pride swelled when their Indians baseball club won its second World Series. Urban rivalries decided on athletic playing fields were a welcome respite from the global war that had just ended.

GOVERNMENT AND POLITICS

Ohio's political affinity for Republicans made Cleveland's progressive politics stand out in contrast. Ohio voters sent generations of conservative Buckeyes to Washington, where they occupied the White House and held influential seats in both houses of the U.S. Congress. However, during the mid-twentieth century, manufacturing employment dominated the Cleveland-area economy, with the result that organized labor influenced local, state, and federal elections. The interests of labor transcended those of groups divided by factors such as race, religion, or ethnic background, making Cleveland and Cuyahoga County a reliable bastion of Democratic strength. During the 1940s and 1950s, Clevelanders voted for Democrats and, at the local level, elected them. Cleveland's mayor from 1941 to 1944 was Frank J. Lausche, who later served as Ohio's governor and as a U.S. senator. Lausche's successor as mayor was Thomas A. Burke, who served from 1945 until 1953 and was also briefly a U.S. senator. His successor, Anthony J. Celebrezze, won five consecutive mayoral elections. All were moderate Democrats who later held higher state and national offices. Celebrezze served in the cabinets of President John F. Kennedy and Lyndon B. Johnson as secretary of the Department of Health, Education, and Welfare.

Politically, postwar Cleveland responded to the interests and engagement of its growing black citizenry. Black Clevelanders had served on the Cleveland city council beginning in 1927, having run as Republican Party candidates. The New Deal gradually drew Cleveland's black voters into the Democratic Party, an alliance that strengthened after 1948, with President Harry Truman's explicit support for civil rights. Postwar councils adopted municipal ordinances that assured blacks' equal treatment in public accommodations, and in 1949 Clevelanders elected the first black woman to the city council, Jean Murrell Capers. However, persistent segregation in housing and in public schools increasingly damaged race relations in Cleveland, setting the stage for the chaotic 1960s.

Public transportation in Cleveland consisted of an extensive bus network and a local passenger rail system that shared some right-of-way with the heavy freight and long-distance passenger railroads whose tracks paralleled the Lake Erie shore. The local light rail network was the Cleveland Rapid Transit, or simply "the Rapid." It was the successor to a set of light passenger rail operations that had been consolidated in 1942 by the City of Cleveland under the aegis of the Cleveland Transit System. During the postwar administration of Mayor Burke, Cleveland obtained $30 million in federal loans to modernize and expand the Rapid into its modern routes. Ultimately, it had its eastern terminus at Windermere Station, in East Cleveland, while the western segment ended at Cleveland Hopkins Airport. Both segments met at Union Station beneath the downtown Terminal Tower. There, passengers could connect to long-distance rail service or board a bus for local destinations. A successful light rail passenger service dating from the 1920s called the Shaker Rapid also joined the Rapid system and operated from Union Station. It served a number of suburban stations in the affluent suburb of Shaker Heights and points east.

Since the 1930s traffic congestion had plagued Cleveland-area motorists. The city responded with plans for a limited-access highway spanning the Cuyahoga River, connecting the east and west side waterfront commercial districts. Construction on the initial segment of the so-called Shoreway began with financial help from the federal Works Progress Administration. By the end of World War II, plans were ready to expand the Shoreway and connect it to other freeways. However, problems with financing and land acquisition delayed connecting projects such as the Innerbelt freeway until the early 1950s. By then, commuters and through-travelers needed more relief, and Cleveland joined other major U.S. cities in lobbying for federal highway construction downtown. Cleveland's network of limited-access urban expressways eventually became part of the federal Interstate Highway System authorized by Congress and signed into law by President Dwight Eisenhower in 1956.

Cleveland's rich aviation history fostered local support for airport development. Beginning in 1929 Cleveland hosted the annual National Air Races at its new municipal airport nine miles southwest of downtown. In 1947, to supplement the main airport, the city opened a waterfront general aviation airfield on dredged land just east of downtown. In 1951 the municipal airport was named in honor of former city manager William R. Hopkins, who had been an early aviation visionary and had pushed the city council to acquire the land for the airport. The downtown waterfront airport was later named for Mayor Burke, whose post–World War II administration financed and developed the new facility.

INDUSTRY, COMMERCE, AND LABOR

During the 1940s, Cleveland reached the zenith of its population and economic productivity. The 1950 census recorded Cleveland's population at nine hundred fourteen thousand, making it the seventh largest U.S. city. (With every subsequent census, Cleveland's population and its national rank-order fell.) As with many other places in America, war transformed Cleveland economically and demographically, and propelled the city and region into a postwar economic boom. However, by 1952 Cleveland's long postindustrial decline was underway, though it was not yet manifest. The city's business and political leaders sought to capitalize on the area's wartime growth, which they anticipated would continue through the postwar decades. Planners readied designs for expanded infrastructure to serve a larger population. Meanwhile, during and after World War II, changes to the city's racial and ethnic geography accelerated, owing to in-migration from other regions of the United States, including the South. Simultaneously, growing numbers of mainly white residents moved out of Cleveland to newer homes in suburban communities.

The shoreline of Lake Erie was the region's major geographic feature. Cleveland, founded where the Cuyahoga River meets the lake, became important to the Great Lakes' commerce in iron ore and coal, borne by the distinctive fleet of ore-carrying vessels called "ore boats." Many of these vessels were built in Cleveland by firms such as American Shipbuilding. Shipping made Greater Cleveland's twentieth-century growth as a center of manufacturing possible, which also benefitted the trades and small businesses that existed in the orbit of the larger firms. Major railroads such as the Pennsylvania and the New York Central ran along the Lake Erie shore through Cleveland, and the major east-west state and federal highways in the northern Midwest, including U.S. 20, ran directly through Cleveland, carrying passenger vehicles and the growing volume of freight trucks that, in the postwar era, began to eclipse rail shipping.

The important nexus for freight transshipment that existed around the mouth of the Cuyahoga River grew and spread to Cleveland's eastern and western suburbs. During the 1940s and 1950s, a social and political cleavage persisted between the neighborhoods on Cleveland's east and west sides. Limited street and highway connections between the two sections impeded relations between their populations. Residents of the east or west side tended to work, shop, and attend schools on "their" side of town. The boundary was the river, spanned by a series of high-level rail and highway bridges. However, by mid-century the Cuyahoga River in downtown

Cleveland was an odiferous sewer of industrial waste surrounded by ore and coal stacks, refineries, steel mills, and related commercial activities. In 1952 an oil slick caught fire on the river, causing over a million dollars in property damage. A pollution crisis obviously impended, and within two decades Cleveland's Cuyahoga River became an ironic symbol of America's emerging environmental awareness by again catching fire, this time focusing international publicity on the city's history of polluting Lake Erie.

Manufacturing in the Cleveland area centered around large corporations such as Republic Steel, Jones & Laughlin Steel, Chase Brass & Copper (a subsidiary of Kennecott Copper), General Electric, and Fisher Body (a division of General Motors). All expanded and prospered during World War II, but by the beginning of the 1950s their employment and output had reverted to prewar levels. However, in the late 1940s the Ford Motor Company increased its manufacturing capacity in Cleveland by opening a new engine plant in Brookpark, where the company introduced automated production techniques allowing it to reduce the number of assembly-line jobs at older plants. Other important firms with local roots included Thompson Aircraft Products Company (which later became Tapco, and ultimately TRW), Lubrizol, White Motor Company (a major truck builder that eventually merged with Freightliner), Bailey Meter (owned by the boiler manufacturer Babcock and Wilcox), Parker Hannifin, and the Sherwin-Williams Paint Company. During the postwar years, Cleveland manufacturing enterprises that sought to modernize or expand often did so by building new facilities in the suburbs, as Bailey Meter did in 1954 with its Wickliffe plant. Land was cheaper there than in the established central manufacturing districts. Workers who were already suburbanites welcomed the shortened commute, while those who had been deferring a move had further reason to act.

The preponderance of large manufacturing employers in Cleveland strengthened the role of organized labor. From the 1930s until 1958, Cleveland's labor unions aligned themselves with the Cleveland Federation of Labor (affiliated with the American Federation of Labor) or the Cleveland Industrial Union Council (affiliated with the Congress of Industrial Organizations). Labor law reforms that came out of the Great Depression and the New Deal served increasingly during the 1940s and 1950s to benefit Cleveland's working-class citizens. Wages and benefits won through union action helped promote the rise of a broad middle class of citizens who enjoyed steady, secure employment with health and retirement plans and who could afford what their parents' generation had regarded as luxuries, such as multiple automobiles, vacations, homeownership, and the prospect of sending their children to college.

In banking, the venerable Cleveland Trust Company was the only major local institution to survive the early Great Depression and the 1933 nationwide bank holiday. By the 1950s Cleveland Trust dominated commercial financial services throughout Cuyahoga County and was rapidly expanding into suburban commercial locations. During the same postwar period, federal initiatives such as the Federal Housing Administration, the Veterans Administration, and the Federal National Mortgage Association served as powerful stimulants to homeownership. Cleveland's savings and loan institutions originated most residential mortgage loans. Broadview Savings and Loan became Cleveland's (and Ohio's) largest, facilitating and profiting from the long postwar boom in land development, homebuilding, and real estate.

Cleveland's central business district lay just east of the river and south of the lake shore, surrounding Public Square and radiating further eastward along Euclid and Superior Avenues. On the southwest corner of Public Square itself stood the imposing Terminal Tower complex, including a 701-foot-tall skyscraper built in 1927 atop the Cleveland Union Terminal station. Clevelanders claimed the Terminal Tower as the nation's tallest building outside of New York City, a distinction that it held until 1964. During the 1940s and 1950s, the tower's size and architectural grandeur reinforced downtown Cleveland's carefully cultivated image as the political and economic hub of northeast Ohio, though the process of commercial and residential diffusion had already begun.

In terms of economy and demographics, no event influenced Cleveland more than World War II. The demands of war production fueled local manufacturing contracts and caused rapid growth in industrial employment. Within three years the Thompson Aircraft Products Company grew into Cleveland's largest employer, with some twenty-one thousand workers on three shifts. Citywide, manufacturing employment increased from one hundred ninety-one thousand in 1940 to three hundred forty thousand by the war's end. The demand for labor drew newcomers to the Cleveland area, and the increased population overtaxed local housing resources. Home and apartment construction had stagnated throughout the 1930s, owing to the effects of the depression. During the war years, rationing made construction materials scarce, while skilled workers from the building trades shifted to factory work in one of Cleveland's many defense plants or entered the military. By 1943 the local housing vacancy rate had fallen to less than 1 percent. (In a normal market, a residential vacancy rate of 5 percent equates to virtually full utilization.) Cleveland's planners braced for a boom in homebuilding as soon as wartime restrictions ended.

While the war was underway, the age, density, and obsolescence of Cleveland's existing housing stock drove such new homebuilding as there was out into suburban communities such as Euclid, Wickliffe, and Mentor to the east and Parma, Bay Village, and Avon Lake to the west. Thanks to New Deal financial innovations such as mortgages guaranteed by the Federal Housing Administration, and later by the Veterans Administration, area homebuilders quickly sold new houses to buyers who obtained affordable mortgages with down payments of 5 percent or less. Growing automobile use allowed workers to live farther from their places of employment and to become independent of streetcars and other mass transit. Cleveland's streetcar system ended operations in 1954. The suburbs experienced a surge of shopping center development, in which the traditional downtown department stores such as Higbee's, Halle's, and the May Company participated by building new stores far from downtown, but close to where their customers lived. The new shopping centers emphasized their acres of free parking, something notably absent from the city's central business district. Cleveland's decentralization also gained from the increasing use of motor trucks for shipping freight, which allowed businesses to locate farther away from rail lines.

RACE, ETHNICITY, AND IMMIGRATION

In the first half of the twentieth century, immigration from central and eastern Europe helped fuel Cleveland's population growth. During the twilight of the Austro-Hungarian Empire, Slavic immigrants to the United States found work in Cleveland's booming industrial enterprises.

Following World War II, the city's critical mass of Serbs and Slovenians helped attract larger numbers of their countrymen to the greater Cleveland area. This generation of Eastern European immigrants included many who were fleeing the Soviet Union's postwar occupation of the Baltic states (such as Latvia, Lithuania, and Estonia) or Poland, Czechoslovakia, and the neighboring countries. Throughout the city, coherent ethnic neighborhoods supported churches, stores, and taverns catering to Germans, Italians, Croatians, Slovenians, Hungarians, and Poles as well as synagogues established by Jews from throughout Europe. Immigrant communities celebrated their cultural identity through associations that preserved traditional dances and music, such as variations on the polka. On Cleveland's near east and west sides, the steeples of neighborhood churches and parishes punctuated the skyline, built and supported by congregants from the surrounding neighborhoods. Those residents held fast to culture and traditions brought directly from their European homelands or inherited from their immigrant ancestors. Cleveland's Jewish community generally settled in the city's east-side neighborhoods, despite hostility from non-Jews who attempted to impose restrictive covenants.

As Cleveland's racial demographics shifted, strong, coherent ethnic neighborhoods became the setting for whites' resistance to black in-migration. In 1940 Cuyahoga County's black population stood at 84,504. By 1950 it had grown to 147,850, propelled during World War II by the demand for labor, which accelerated the migration of southern blacks to the urban industrial North. No other racial or ethnic group in Cleveland gained population on anything like such a scale, and the trend continued through the 1950s. By 1960 Cleveland's black population exceeded 250,000. During the war years, African American housing was concentrated among older, near east-side neighborhoods, along the Central Avenue corridor running east out to near East 40th Street. From there, Cleveland's black population expanded further east to the Hough Avenue and Glenville neighborhoods, from which whites were simultaneously relocating to suburbs further east. Racial boundaries in housing sharpened. Neighborhoods that experienced in-migration by new black residents realized the heightened racial tensions that accompanied similar changes then occurring in America's industrial cities of the Northeast and Midwest. As elsewhere, real estate agents deployed profitable tactics such as "blockbusting," which accelerated white flight from neighborhoods undergoing change. During the postwar period, cities such as Cleveland moved toward greater racial segregation, resulting in the spatial isolation of black citizens who would eventually constitute the majority within Cleveland's city limits.

See also *Cleveland, OH 1877–1896; Cleveland, OH 1896–1929; Cleveland, OH 1929–1941*

ALAN BLISS

BIBLIOGRAPHY

Fogelson, Robert M. *Downtown: Its Rise and Fall, 1880–1950*. New Haven, CT: Yale University Press, 2001.

Krumholz, Norman, W. Dennis Keating, and David C. Perry, eds. *Cleveland: A Metropolitan Reader*. Kent, OH: Kent State University Press, 1995.

Kusmer, Kenneth L. *A Ghetto Takes Shape: Black Cleveland, 1870–1930*. Urbana: University of Illinois Press, 1976.

Phillips, Kimberley L. *AlabamaNorth: African-American Migrants, Community, and Working-Class Activism in Cleveland, 1915–1945*. Urbana: University of Illinois Press, 1999.

Van Tassel, David, and John Grabowski, eds. *The Encyclopedia of Cleveland History*. 2d ed. Bloomington: Indiana University Press, 1996.

ST. LOUIS, MO 1941–1952

DURING THE FIRST HALF OF THE TWENTIETH CENTURY, ST. LOUIS DEVELOPED A DIVERSE ECONOMIC BASE supported by a growing population and a strong working class. Despite this success, by the 1930s city officials were concerned about stagnating property values in the heart of downtown and the movement of industries out of the urban core, trends exacerbated by the Great Depression. America's entry into World War II pulled St. Louis out of the depression, but much of the city's economic rebound was driven by wartime industries that would prove unsustainable in the long run, such as ordnance production. The city experienced population loss, economic decline, and worsening urban blight in the postwar years. Indeed, by 1960 the city's population fell to 750,026, a 12.5 percent decline. City officials tried to preempt and respond to these trends, using whatever political and economic tools they had at hand.

GOVERNMENT AND POLITICS

Deindustrialization and job and population loss were the biggest challenges facing city officials in 1941. There were three main policy strategies city officials used in their attempt to revitalize the city, regardless of party affiliation: urban renewal, reindustrialization, and promotion of tourism. To implement urban renewal and reindustrialization policies, entire swaths of blighted housing and vacant businesses needed to be cleared. Partisan control of the mayor's office generally made little difference in terms of the strategies used to address these problems; Republican and Democratic mayors used land clearance policies to promote revitalization, advocated for increased tax and bond revenue, and attempted to annex rapidly expanding suburban areas to offset the decline of the city's tax base. Only Democratic mayor Joseph M. Darst distinguished himself by aggressively pursuing a policy of providing safe and affordable housing to city residents using federal funds and court-approved tax-exempt status for public housing.

The first major land clearance project was completed in 1940. It was intended to become a park and memorial site to honor those who had made territorial expansion in the United States possible, and elected officials hoped this would spur a tourism industry in downtown St. Louis. Despite a great deal of local effort to identify the land, secure funds, pass local bond issues, and solicit memorial designs—the catenary arch design, by Eero Saairnen, was selected for the memorial in 1948—the land sat vacant for years, used primarily as a parking lot. The iconic arch was not completed until 1965 due to land disputes and funding problems.

QUICK FACTS

ST. LOUIS, MO **1941–1952**

MAYORS

Bernard Francis Dickmann   (1933–1941)
William Dee Becker   (1941–1943)
Aloys P. Kaufmann   (1943–1949)
Joseph M. Darst   (1949–1953)

MAJOR INDUSTRIES AND EMPLOYERS

Manufacturing
Wholesale and retail trade
Personal services
Transportation, communication, and
    public utilities
Finance, insurance, and real estate

MAJOR NEWSPAPERS

St. Louis Post-Dispatch
St. Louis Globe-Democrat
St. Louis Daily Record
St. Louis Star Times

MAJOR EVENTS

1941: The charter revision changes the process of electing city alderman to allow for election by ward, in addition to at-large elections, increasing the number of alderman to twenty-eight and guaranteeing representation of different neighborhoods and demographic interests in the city.

1944: The Post-War Public Improvement Program, combined with a 1935 $7.5 million bond issue, funds the acquisition and clearance of land for the Jefferson National Expansion Memorial and other blight clearance and urban renewal projects, the expansion of city facilities and services, and jobs for discharged servicemen following World War II.

1948: The Missouri legislature passes the Earning Tax Ordinance, which allows for the collection of local income tax and helps St. Louis compensate for its declining property tax base as residents move into suburban areas.

One of the primary problems with promoting blight clearance and tourism as strategies of revitalization was that urban renewal often tore down blighted, but occupied, housing. This required families—often those experiencing economic hardship—to find new, safe, affordable housing. This proved to be a challenge because, as a 1947 City Planning Commission Report said, St. Louis was not a "livable" city, with thirty-three thousand homes relying on shared toilet facilities and eighty-eight thousand families living in housing constructed before 1900. Slum clearance throughout the 1940s and the development of tourist attractions did not address this problem.

State officials tried to address the lack of safe and affordable housing in urban areas by passing the Missouri 353 statute in 1943. This legislation was designed to encourage new housing development by allowing cities (primarily St. Louis and Kansas City) to grant tax abatement for twenty-five years on properties used to develop quality housing. St. Louis also helped developers by allowing them to "borrow" the city's eminent domain rights to acquire areas declared as blighted. This made land acquisition easier for developers, but it impaired the city's ability to raise tax revenue, which ultimately hurt city schools and other services. Despite this, Mayor Darst aggressively pursued the development of safe and affordable rental housing in the city to accommodate the growing need, and under his administration the development of five low-rent apartment complexes was initiated.

To address the city's declining tax base, city officials passed a local income tax in 1946. Locally imposed income taxes were not common outside of Pennsylvania and Ohio, but the fiscal situation of St. Louis required such measures by local authorities. The Missouri Supreme Court declared the ordinance unconstitutional, but passage of state legislation in 1948 allowed the tax ordinance to become law. A second attempt to get rid of the income tax ordinance was launched in 1953, but the state legislature made the law permanent that same year. Despite this, the declining population of St. Louis limited even this source of revenue.

Another strategy that St. Louis officials attempted in order to maintain tax revenues was to expand the city limits to incorporate the growing suburban areas to which city residents were moving. Mayors Dickmann (D; 1933–1941), William Dee Becker (R; 1941–1943), and Aloys P. Kaufmann (R; 1943-1949) all attempted to consolidate city and county government. These efforts were unsuccessful, however, because the Missouri state constitution explicitly separated St. Louis County from the City of St. Louis under the same provision that allowed the city to establish its own charter. Thus, repeated attempts to enlarge the city through annexation were rejected as unconstitutional. Moreover, the more problems the city of St. Louis encountered, the less supportive county voters were of a constitutional amendment to allow city-county consolidation.

All of these attempts, successes, and eventual failures produced a city in crisis. By the early 1950s transportation and transit ways were in disrepair, traffic congestion was terrible, and half the city was considered blighted. Despite the efforts of many city officials and planners, as well as urban reformers and advocates, St. Louis continued a downward spiral.

INDUSTRY, COMMERCE, AND LABOR

In the early twentieth century, St. Louis had a diverse economic base, with lumber yards and mills, graineries, breweries (including Anheuser-Busch), clothing and shoe factories, and heavy industry, including steel. While northern St. Louis retained a strong economic base throughout the early twentieth century, as early as the 1910s and 1920s the center city began experiencing deindustrialization, as heavy industry relocated to East St. Louis on the Illinois side of the river, in large part because of tariff, or "bridge arbitrary," battles over shipping goods and raw materials across the Mississippi River. The migration of industry to Illinois weakened the city's economic base and diminished employment opportunities, a phenomena that persisted throughout the Great Depression.

World War II ended the depression in St. Louis, but much of the industrial growth spurred by the war took place in the county, concentrating economic benefits in suburban areas rather than the urban core. Indeed, the greater St. Louis region emerged from the war in good shape: There was a substantial manufacturing base in areas surrounding the city, and the region had become the second largest rail and trucking hub in the country, serving as a gateway to the

South and Southwest. The division between St. Louis County and the City of St. Louis strained city resources: people looking for work flooded the city, increasing the population and need for services, including housing. This spurred movement out of the city by those who could afford it. Unable to draw on the economic resources of the surrounding county, the city experienced declining economic and living conditions, despite modest economic growth as a result of the war.

The economic vitality of the City of St. Louis declined following the war, compounding worsening economic conditions for its government and residents. Between 1950 and 2000 the city's share of regional employment declined from 50 percent to just over 10 percent, with loss of manufacturing jobs leading the decline. During this time, manufacturers were not only moving outside city limits, increasing the tax base and job opportunities in surrounding areas, they were also leaving the region entirely and relocating to the Sun Belt. Even wholesaling and retailing activity, the second largest employment sectors in the city, declined: In the 1940s St. Louis's retail base accounted for 80 percent of regional sales, but just over 65 percent by 1954. Importantly, this did not amount to job loss in low-skill, skilled, and trade labor only. Managerial positions were also migrating to the county, as suburban cities and towns used proximity to new suburban housing and better services to attract Fortune 500 firms and white-collar jobs.

Neither local nor federal policies helped to alleviate these trends in the city. Suburbs and towns surrounding the city were able to use local land use and zoning laws to attract housing development (often including racial covenants) and industrial (re)location. Missouri tax law allowed "point of origin" cities to keep their share of locally generated sales tax, which allowed less cash-strapped regional cities and towns to compete with each other for business by lowering tax rates. The City of St. Louis had less flexibility in this regard because of its unstable financial situation—it needed tax revenue and could not lower its tax rates enough to compete. Moreover, in the 1950s federal depreciation rules allowing businesses to write off investments in buildings incentivized new construction rather than rehabilitation, promoted growth in areas surrounding the city rather than investment in the existing industrial center within the city.

While suburban policies worked against city officials in St. Louis trying to stimulate their economic base, the decisions of policymakers in the city did not help either. In response to deindustrialization, local officials focused on developing tourism, cultural institutions, and research and development as the industries to lead St. Louis out of its troubles. The problem with this strategy was that these types of industries did not rely on large-scale employment of both working-class and managerial labor, which meant that they did not support a broad tax base or develop the vibrant communities that large-scale industry once supported. City officials also focused almost entirely on reindustrialization policy, rather than comprehensive community development strategies. This meant that the city engaged in massive slum clearance to make way for new industrial development, but did not promote housing, transit, and community development beyond large-scale construction of public housing. This strategy overlooked the fact that incentivizing reindustrialization requires more than providing land for new business; it also requires housing, transportation options, and services for workers—amenities that suburbs could offer.

Taken together, these trends and policies produced an urban core that by the late 1950s was struggling to survive. Indeed, by 1953 no new office buildings had been built in St. Louis in two decades and little reindustrialization had occurred, though the city tried to spur reinvestment by opening Busch Stadium and completing the St. Louis Arch in 1965. While there was some industrial activity remaining in the city the 1970s, the City of St. Louis never fully recovered from the deindustrialization that began prior to World War II and that was accelerated in the postwar era.

RACE, ETHNICITY, AND IMMIGRATION

In addition to struggling with the depression and early deindustrialization of the inner city, the 1940 census showed that the population of the City of St. Louis declined for the first time in 120 years to 816,048, down from 821,960 in 1930. Much of the population loss was a result of increased population growth in the areas surrounding the city. The majority of the population of St. Louis was white (86 percent) and 13 percent was African American. Seven percent of the total population was foreign-born. Germans were the largest segment of the foreign-born and immigrant population, but by 1940 they were well established in the fabric of city life: They owned department stores and clothing factories, and they held prominent positions in the city and state as doctors, lawyers, and politicians.

Other foreign-born ethnic groups included Russians, Irish, Italians, Hungarians, Austrians, and Poles. One of the largest ethnic enclaves in the city was Little Italy, or "Italian Hill," which was located in the heart of downtown. Prior to World War II, there was a great deal of anti-immigrant, anti-Catholic, and anti-Jewish sentiment in the city, but the service of Italian servicemen during World War II and the efforts of foreign-born war workers during the war softened the cultural divide between the native- and foreign-born in the city. Indeed, anxious to assimilate and build upon this goodwill, Italian neighborhoods broke apart in the postwar era as Italian families moved out. Italian Hill became blighted, rundown, and dominated by dilapidated rental units in the 1950s. The area has since been revitalized and remains largely an Italian neighborhood, thanks to the efforts of local activists looking to preserve the heritage of the area.

The population of the city increased to 856,796 by 1950 as a result of the influx of workers looking for employment during the war, but this would prove to be the last decade in which the city's population would grow. Significantly, the African American community grew to 18 percent of the city's population by 1950, while the white population fell to 82 percent.

This demographic shift is particularly important because racial segregation in the city compounded the problems city officials were having with urban decay. African Americans had traditionally lived on the fringe of downtown, which by 1937 was one of the most dilapidated parts of the city and was plagued by a number of problems and posed serious health risks to residents. A report in 1937 showed that this part of town, along with the Beaumont, Mill Creek, and Soulard neighborhoods, housed one-third of the city's population but accounted for three-fourths of the city's illegitimate children, one-half of the city's infant deaths, and two-thirds of the city's tuberculosis cases.

In response, the city developed its first federally funded, low-income housing projects, which were completed in 1942. Despite this effort, the 1947 City Planning Commission report found that half of the city's residential areas were blighted or overrun with obsolete housing. The Land Clearance for Redevelopment Authority worked throughout the 1950s to clear blighted areas and use the reclaimed land for reindustrialization and revitalization efforts, while city officials and planners continued to develop low-income housing, including the Pruitt and Igoe Apartments, comprising thirty-three eleven-story apartment buildings housing almost three thousand families. This was one of the nation's largest low-income housing projects and was quickly plagued with problems due to lack of recreational space, nearby retail or health services, public transit, and job opportunities. These efforts became the target of criticism: The NAACP called the work of the Land Clearance for Redevelopment Authority "Negro removal," as many in the black community felt specifically targeted for relocation into increasingly segregated, isolated, and high-poverty areas.

Besides such notorious projects as Pruitt-Igoe, St. Louis was also home to the dispute that led the U.S. Supreme Court, in *Shelley v. Kraemer* (1948), to declare the enforcement of racially restrictive covenants in deeds to be a violation of the equal protection clause of the Constitution. The Shelleys were a black family, originally from Mississippi, who purchased a house on Labadie Avenue in St Louis. The deed to the house included a covenant barring its sale to African Americans and other nonwhites, but the owner sold it to the Shelleys regardless. Louis Kraemer, a white man who owned another house on Labadie Avenue, then sued to have the restrictive covenant on the Shelleys' home enforced. The Missouri Supreme Court ruled in 1946 that the covenant should be enforced, a decision that was reversed by the U.S. Supreme Court two years later.

Despite the minor population spike in 1950 and the subsequent precipitous population decline in the city, the population of the county grew substantially between 1940 and 1950 and beyond. Between 1940 and 1950 the population in St. Louis County grew by almost 50 percent, from 274,230 to 406,349. This population shift from city to county was a constant reminder of the challenges the city faced as a result of the political division between city and county, and the inability of the city to annex other portions of the county as a result of Missouri's state constitution. Moreover, the city's continued investment in low-income and public housing made it difficult to attract middle-class homeowners and market-rate renters to a city that was already struggling to meet its service needs, while the increased concentration of low-income families in the city increased demand on city services. This further diminished the tax base of the city and the resources city officials had to incentivize industrial and residential relocation to the City of St. Louis. Coupled with failed reindustrialization efforts, by the 1950s the city was struggling to reinvent itself even before the next wave of deindustrialization hit cities in the 1970s.

See also *St. Louis, MO 1854–1877; St. Louis, MO 1877–1896; St. Louis, MO 1896–1929; St. Louis, MO 1929–1941*

AMY WIDESTROM

BIBLIOGRAPHY

Gibson, Campbell. *Population of the 100 Largest Cities and Other Urban Places in the United States: 1790–1990.* Washington, DC: U.S. Bureau of the Census, Washington, 1998. http://www.census. gov/population/www/documentation/twps0027/twps0027.html

Gordon, Colin. *Mapping Decline: St. Louis and the Fate of the American City.* Philadelphia: University of Pennsylvania Press, 2008.

Heathcott, Joseph, and Máire Agnes Murphy. "Corridors of Flight, Zones of Renewal: Industry, Planning, and Policy in the Making of Metropolitan St. Louis, 1940–1980." *Journal of Urban History* 31 (2005): 151–189.

James, Herman G. *Local Government in the United States.* New York, NY: D. Appleton, 1921.

Perkins, Albert T. "The Municipal Bridge and Terminal Commission of St. Louis." *Journal of Political Economy* 15, no. 7 (July 1907): 412–420.

Primm, James Neal. *Lion of the Valley: St. Louis, Missouri, 1764–1980.* St. Louis: Missouri Historical Society Press, 1998.

"To Avoid Bridge Tolls." *New York Times,* August 11, 1887.

Watts, Anne, Kirwin Roach, Tom Pearson, Barbara Knotts, and Laura Liebertz. *St. Louis Mayors Quick-Facts.* St. Louis, MO: St. Louis Public Library, 2001. http://exhibits.slpl.org/mayors/default.asp

Williams, Scott K. *St. Louis City/County Census Demographics 1772–2000.* http://www.usgennet.org/usa/mo/county/stlouis/census.htm

WASHINGTON, DC 1941–1952

WORLD WAR II AND THE POSTWAR ERA BROUGHT LASTING CHANGE TO WASHINGTON. War mobilization rapidly increased the size of the federal government and the city, propelling Washington toward a peak population of 802,178 in 1950. This growth challenged the numerous federal entities responsible for Washington's governance and infrastructure to provide a framework for subsequent development. Because the federal government was the city's single biggest employer, the location of future federal offices figured prominently in this planning. Residents also worked to shape their city. Although a campaign to obtain self-governance failed during this period, the sustained efforts of African American residents and numerous civic organizations to desegregate the city brought positive results. Desegregation also spurred migration of white residents to the suburbs during the 1950s.

GOVERNMENT AND POLITICS

A plethora of federal officials and bodies governed Washington. Residents lacked both representation in Congress and self-government or "home rule." Federal hegemony and disenfranchisement frequently resulted in the subordination of local needs and aspirations to federal ones. Many federal entities also sought to use Washington as a national model of urban redevelopment, highway construction, and coordination of urban and suburban planning, further subjecting the city and its residents to the pull and sway of federal power.

Article 1, Section 8 of the Constitution grants Congress legislative power over the national capital. Since 1878 a three-member, presidentially appointed board of commissioners had helped Congress govern the District. In 1949 Congress also granted the president the authority to reorganize departments of the District's government, but the legislative branch still retained preponderate power, particularly through the House and Senate's Committees on the District

QUICK FACTS

WASHINGTON, DC **1941–1952**

PRESIDENT BOARD OF COMMISSIONERS

Melvin C. Hazen	(1941)
John Russell Young	(1941–1952)
F. Joseph Donohue	(1952)

MAJOR INDUSTRIES AND EMPLOYERS

Federal government
Retail trade
Self-employed
Domestic service
Professional services and organizations
Military service

MAJOR NEWSPAPERS

Washington Daily News
Washington Evening Star
Washington Post
Washington Times-Herald

MAJOR EVENTS

1941: U.S. entry into World War II brings rapid population growth and construction of new federal government buildings, most notably the Pentagon.

1943: A biracial citizens group organizes pickets against Capital Transit for refusing to hire black streetcar operators, but the federal Fair Employment Practices Committee fails to force the company to end its discriminatory hiring practices.

1948: A bill to provide self-rule for the District of Columbia fails to pass the U.S. House of Representatives.

1950: The National Capital Park and Planning Commission publishes its comprehensive plan for the future growth of Washington and its environs, focusing on federal work centers, highways, and infrastructure.

1952: Ongoing campaigns, including peaceful sit-ins, result in the desegregation of numerous establishments in the city's central business district.

---

of Columbia. These committees essentially served as a bicameral city council, setting budgets, authorizing positions, and passing laws.

The Board of Commissioners executed laws, administered city departments such as public works, and drafted budgets, but remained subordinate to Congress. By law, one commissioner had to be an officer in the Army Corps of Engineers, a sign of the federal government's interest in the maintenance of the District's infrastructure. During World War II the commissioners struggled to ease growth problems and to support national defense mobilization. In 1940 the District's population was 663,091; by 1942 the city had added 137,000 new residents.

In April 1941 the Board of Commissioners created the District Council of Defense, which recruited volunteers to help new residents, including servicemen, find housing, but the commissioners failed to provide the council with substantial guidance or authority. The District government had more success in organizing social events for servicemen. In 1944 the Women's Battalion No. 1 sponsored almost five hundred dances, bringing together 57,851 white female volunteers with 73,012 white servicemen. Consistent with the city's racial segregation, a separate "battalion" held dances for African American women and servicemen. The Board of Commissioners also oversaw a civil defense program. Volunteer air raid wardens received helmets and whistles and trained to survey their neighborhoods during the blackouts ordered after Pearl Harbor.

After the war, calls for home rule increased. In 1948 the House considered a bill allowing District residents to elect a city council and a nonvoting delegate to the House. The House District Committee favorably reported out the bill, but Rep. Oren Harris (D-Ark.) led a successful attempt to have it tabled. Harris was one of many southern conservatives opposed to home rule. Rep. John McMillan (D-S.C.), who chaired the House District Committee from 1945 to 1947, 1949 to 1953, and 1955 to 1973 (Republican majorities in the 80th and 83rd Congresses account for the breaks), stymied subsequent home rule bills and, supported by several other southern committee members, tightly controlled local governance, making decisions on issues both large and small. Segregationists, McMillan and his allies opposed granting self-rule to the city's grow-ing black population, fearing that enfranchisement of African Americans would spell the end of segregation in Washington and encourage the civil rights movement in the South.

Other federal bodies with authority over the governance of Washington during this period included the Commission of Fine Arts (CFA), the National Capital Park and Planning Com-mission (NCPPC), and the Army Corps of Engineers. During and after the war, these agencies planned and executed numerous projects that greatly altered the landscape of Washington and the surrounding area, demonstrating the federal government's control over architecture, monu-ments, urban and regional planning, and infrastructure.

The CFA, founded in 1910, had a statutory authority to approve plans for monuments, parks, public buildings, and private developments bordering major public spaces such as the National Mall and Rock Creek Park. Its powers included enforcement of Washington's strict height limit. The CFA reviewed plans for the National Gallery of Art, West Building (com-pleted in 1941), and the Jefferson Memorial (completed in 1943). The latter project illustrates the abundance of oversight of federal architecture in Washington. The CFA rejected the memo-rial's original design by John Russell Pope, but the Thomas Jefferson Memorial Commission, created for this project, circumvented the CFA by securing President Roosevelt's approval of a revision of Pope's design.

The NCPPC, created in 1926 by Congress, had the authority to provide comprehensive, coordinated planning for metropolitan Washington. Suburban growth during and after the war underscored the pressing need for such planning. Although the District added almost one hun-dred forty thousand residents between 1940 and 1950, the metropolitan area added almost five hundred thousand. In its 1950 comprehensive plan for metropolitan Washington (defined as the District of Columbia; the city of Alexandria, Virginia; Arlington and Fairfax Counties, Virginia; and Prince George's and Montgomery Counties, Maryland), the NCPPC outlined a unified urban and suburban approach to solve the problems brought by wartime growth and to guide orderly future development. For example, it strongly recommended that the federal government disperse future employment centers well outside of the city center. Carefully chosen suburban sites, connected to a regional network of highways, would relieve traffic congestion and reduce the vulnerability of the capital to an atomic attack, a growing concern during the Cold War. As the NCPPC observed, its plan could not be realized without the strong support of other federal entities. Although most agencies and Congress opposed dispersal, construction of a circumferential highway (the Capital Beltway) similar to the one proposed by the NCPPC began in the mid-1950s.

The Army Corps of Engineers oversaw or helped with several significant projects in and near the District during the 1940s and early 1950s. Not all of these structures, facilities, or roadways directly or solely served the military services, revealing the Corps' substantial responsibility for the city and region's infrastructure and development. Washington National Airport, constructed under presidential authority and completed in June 1941, required the Corps to dredge the Potomac River and put in five hundred acres of landfill at the site. The airport was soon handling the city's commercial air traffic. The Corps helped build the Pentagon, in Arlington, Virginia, and the Suitland Parkway, in Maryland. It constructed Bolling Army Airfield and several temporary wartime bridges over the Potomac River to link the city to the military's vital facilities bordering the District. The Corps' purview also extended to Washington's aqueduct. In the early 1940s Congress asked the Corps to plan the expansion and modernization of the city and region's water supply. Work on the Corps' recommendations began in 1947. Demonstrating Washington's prominence as a model to other cities, in 1951 the Engineer Commissioner ordered the fluoridation of the city's water, a step most U.S. cities had not yet taken.

INDUSTRY, COMMERCE, AND LABOR

The dominant industry in Washington was the federal government. Federal efforts to combat the Great Depression and national defense efforts had greatly increased the federal workforce in Washington: In 1940 federal jobs accounted for 43.8 percent of all jobs in the city (139,770 of 319,317). Entry into World War II resulted in record numbers of civil servants and military personnel. By 1943 there were 284,665 federal workers in Washington, and the need for office space was so acute that military and civilian agencies erected rows of "tempos" (temporary office buildings) on federal park grounds, most prominently the National Mall. Women benefitted noticeably from the increased hiring. In 1939 women comprised 40 percent of the federal workforce in Washington (49,312 jobs); at the height of the war, in 1944, that figure increased to 58.3 percent (157,710 jobs). After the war, the nation's position as a world leader, the Cold War, and continuing domestic programs sustained a substantial workforce. Between 1945 and 1951, the number of federal workers averaged approximately 225,000, a number that rose again during the last years of the Korean War. According to the NCPPC, the amount of federal employment in the Washington region in 1948 (one-third of all jobs) was equal to the amount of manufacturing workers in other cities.

Washington's other industries remained small in comparison to the federal government. On the eve of World War II, just 7.4 percent and 16.3 percent of workers were employed in manufacturing and commerce, respectively. In some cases, the federal government created manufacturing jobs. By 1944 the Washington Navy Yard, which produced naval ordnance, employed twenty-six

During wartime, the need for federal workers in Washington ballooned to over 280,000 employees by 1943. Women became a common sight in the workforce, accounting for over 58% of federal employees in Washington by 1944. The Office of Price Administration is shown above in 1942.

Source: Myron Davis/Time Life Pictures/Getty Images

thousand people. The American Federation of Labor, which represented the construction trades, was Washington's largest union. Most of its locals refused to accept black members (the Hotel Service Industry local was a notable exception), but the smaller Congress of Industrial Organizations was integrated from its founding in 1937. Tourism and conventions contributed much to Washington's economy. In 1950 the District hosted a record number of national and regional conventions (312), which attracted more than one hundred seventy-five thousand attendees. Approximately four million visitors came to Washington as well; together, conventions and tourism contributed an estimated $150 million to the economy that year.

Due to its importance in the economy, local business leaders cultivated good relations with the federal government. The Washington Board of Trade, the functional equivalent of a chamber of commerce, supported the commission form of government; in the late 1940s its leaders viewed representation of the District in Congress as a viable alternative to home rule. However, there were drawbacks to doing business in the nation's capital, where federal property was untaxed. The central business district or downtown occupied less than 2 percent of the District's taxable land, but its businesses paid 23 percent of the city's real estate taxes in the late 1940s.

RACE, ETHNICITY, AND IMMIGRATION

Race, much more than ethnicity, figured prominently in Washington's government, politics, and economy. The District's nonwhite population was almost exclusively African American. In 1950 64.5 percent of the city's residents were white, and 35 percent were black. Among the white population, the city's sizable German American community had assimilated by 1941, while other ethnic groups—Italian Americans, Chinese Americans, and Greek Americans—proudly demonstrated their loyalty during the war, advancing their assimilation. For example, Greek American and District resident George Vournas led a national war-bond campaign. The city's Jewish population increased to approximately forty thousand by the mid-1950s. Anchored by the Jewish Community Center on 16th Street and the Jewish Community Council, established in 1938, Washington's Jews engaged in matters of importance to both their community and Washington as a whole. This activism included support for racial desegregation, the most pressing public issue of the day.

Racial segregation and discrimination in schools, public facilities, employment, and housing was prevalent in Washington during the 1940s and early 1950s. These years brought energetic and successful efforts by black Washingtonians and supporters to expel Jim Crow from both the city and the capital and to serve as a model of desegregation for the nation. The federal government proved to be an unpredictable ally of racial justice. Although Supreme Court rulings and executive branch actions aided desegregation at key points, the federal government tended to be reactive and only partially committed to enforcement. Furthermore, support for segregation remained strong in Congress, especially on the House District Committee.

Black and white pupils attended separate public schools in Washington. After World War II, white flight to suburban areas resulted in low enrollments at white schools, while black schools suffered from overcrowding. In 1947 per capita spending was $160 for white students and $120 for black students. Rejection of the requests of black parents to transfer their children to sparsely attended white schools directed attention to the growing inequities of the school system but resulted in little change. Black parents consequently sued the school system; this case, *Bolling v. Sharpe* (1954), was one of the five school suits reviewed by the Supreme Court leading to the landmark *Brown v. Board of Education* (1954) decision banning racial segregation of schools.

Restaurants, department stores, and most theaters practiced segregation, though technically such practices were illegal under antidiscrimination laws dating to the early 1870s. During the war, the Howard University Law School and the local chapter of the NAACP organized a peaceful protest against a restaurant that denied service to blacks. As a result the establishment changed its policy. After the war concern over America's image abroad—discrimination against foreign diplomats of color in Washington incurred international opprobrium—in part prompted President Truman's Committee on Civil Rights to call for a swift end to segregation in the capital, but it took organized citizens' action to bring change. In 1950 a biracial citizens group, which included the Jewish Community Council, helped bring a case against a downtown restaurant for racial discrimination. Contradictory rulings in municipal and appellate courts advanced the case to the Supreme Court, which unanimously upheld the antidiscrimination laws. During the interim, peaceful protests by African Americans led many department stores, shops, and restaurants to desegregate.

During the 1940s the federal government mandated desegregation within its own ranks and on its property in the District. Secretary of the Interior Harold Ickes banned racial discrimination in Rock Creek Park's picnic areas, on West Potomac Park's tennis courts, and on federal golf courses. In July 1948 Truman issued an order outlawing discrimination within the federal government and instructed executive agencies to appoint compliance officers. However, the Board of Commissioners ignored the order as it pertained to the District's departments.

Housing and residential patterns in Washington were highly segregated. Racial covenants helped keep more than half of the city's residential blocks all white during the 1940s. A May 1948 decision by the Supreme Court declaring racial covenants on housing deeds to be unconstitutional (*Shelley v. Kraemer*) brought some change, as the number of all-white blocks in the city decreased during the next two years. During the 1950s increasing numbers of white residents moved to the suburbs or elsewhere, resulting in a 33.3 percent drop in the city's white population. Meanwhile the black population increased. Due to these racial residential patterns, a prominent redevelopment project begun during this period disproportionately affected black residents. Efforts to eradicate Washington's substandard alley housing had failed during the 1940s, but in the early 1950s the National Capital Planning Commission (the new name of the NCPPC) and the District's Redevelopment Land Agency, along with several other federal agencies, started planning the demolition and redevelopment of a large swath of Southwest Washington where 76 percent of the residents were African American.

The issues that dominated life, politics, and work in Washington during these years—federal hegemony and the lack of home rule, the challenges of aligning urban and suburban development, and race—would continue to profoundly affect the city throughout the postwar period.

See also *Washington, DC 1790–1828; Washington, DC 1828–1854*

DAVID F. KRUGLER

BIBLIOGRAPHY

Cary, Francine Curro, ed. *Urban Odyssey: A Multicultural History of Washington, D.C.* Washington, DC: Smithsonian Institution Press, 1996.

Elfenbein, Jessica I. *Civics, Commerce, and Community: The History of the Greater Washington Board of Trade, 1889–1989.* Washington, DC: Center for Washington Area Studies of The George Washington University, 1989.

Green, Constance McLaughlin. *The Secret City: A History of Race Relations in the Nation's Capital.* Princeton, NJ: Princeton University Press, 1967.

———. *Washington: A History of the Capital, 1800–1950.* Princeton, NJ: Princeton University Press, 1962.

———. *Washington: Capital City, 1879–1950.* Princeton, NJ: Princeton University Press, 1962.

Gutheim, Frederick, and Antoinette J. Lee. *Worthy of the Nation: Washington, D.C., from L'Enfant to the National Capital Planning Commission.* 2d ed. Baltimore, MD: Johns Hopkins University Press, 2006.

Krugler, David F. *This Is Only a Test: How Washington, D.C., Prepared for Nuclear War.* New York, NY: Palgrave Macmillan, 2006.

National Capital Park and Planning Commission. *Washington Present and Future: A General Summary of the Comprehensive Plan for the National Capital and Its Environs.* Monograph No. 1. Washington, DC: National Capital Park and Planning Commission, 1950.

Scott, Pamela. *Capital Engineers: The U.S. Army Corps of Engineers in the Development of Washington, D.C., 1790–2004.* Alexandria, VA: U.S. Army Corps of Engineers, 2005.

BOSTON, MA 1941–1952

DURING THE 1940S BOSTON REGAINED THE POPULATION it had lost in the depression decade and added tens of thousands more to reach an all-time high of 801,000, sufficient to retain its place among the nation's ten largest metropolises. Yet if the struggle against fascism abroad and the difficult transition to peace at home produced conditions that drew and kept people within the city's political limits, the special circumstances of the 1940s could not halt, much less reverse, Boston's long-term economic decline.

The 1950 census marked Boston's final appearance on the list of the nation's ten largest cities. Boston's string finally ran out because of geopolitical and economic constraints. At forty-eight square miles in 1950 (the last annexation had occurred in 1912), Boston was 15 percent of the land area of New York, 38 percent that of Philadelphia's, and 62 percent that of Baltimore. Hemmed in by neighboring communities that wanted as little as possible to do with Boston politically, the city had scant open space in a period when developing large tracts of land for housing and factories became the norm.

If Boston was falling behind its old rivals, as well as newer ones, it was because its past had finally caught up with it. It could not compete effectively in the industrial economy of the twentieth century, and the deep social and cultural antagonisms that divided the city, and found expression in the political arena, prevented an effective response to the city's declining fortunes. Boston would fall even further in the third quarter of the century before it could regain its balance and prepare itself for the postindustrial challenges of the twenty-first century.

GOVERNMENT AND POLITICS

The 1940s supplied the setting for both James Michael Curley's political resurrection and his political obituary. With his defeat in the 1941 mayor's race pushing his consecutive losing streak to four, Curley's career in public life appeared to be over, but this "last of the buccaneers" had never played by the rules and he refused to accept the results as the end of the line. The following year, at age 66, he ran for the U.S. House of Representatives, the legislative body he had left nearly three decades earlier to begin his first term as Boston's mayor. Although he was not a resident of the district, Curley vanquished the incumbent, the grandson of Harvard President Charles W. Eliot, in the Democratic primary and coasted easily to victory in the general election.

QUICK FACTS

BOSTON, MA 1941–1952

MAYORS

Maurice J. Tobin	(1941–1945)
John E. Kerrigan	(1945–1946)
James Michael Curley	(1946–1950)
John B. Hynes	(1947)
(Acting Mayor)	
John B. Hynes	(1950–1960)

MAJOR INDUSTRIES AND EMPLOYERS

Clerical
Manufacturing
Domestic service
Craftsmen
Wholesale and retail trade

MAJOR NEWSPAPERS

Boston American
Boston Evening Globe
Boston Globe
Boston Herald
Boston Post
Boston Record
Boston Traveler

MAJOR EVENTS

1941: Maurice J. Tobin defeats James Michael Curley to gain second term as mayor.

1944: William Cardinal O'Connell dies after serving thirty-seven years as Archbishop of Boston; Richard J. Cushing is named his successor.

1945: James Michael Curley wins fourth (nonconsecutive) term as mayor.

1947: Curley spends five months in a federal prison after conviction on mail fraud charges; city clerk John B. Hynes is named by the legislature to serve as acting mayor.

1949: Hynes defeats Curley to win mayoralty; voters adopt changes to city charter, providing for citywide election of council members and runoff elections for mayor in a case where no candidate received a majority of the popular vote.

It was an open secret that Curley saw the House (to which he won reelection in 1944 despite his federal indictment for mail fraud involving influence peddling) merely as a way station for a return to City Hall in 1945.

Curley's conqueror in 1941 (and 1937), Maurice Tobin would not be around for a third match-up. Focusing as he had in his first term on keeping municipal spending under control, Tobin was generally successful in maintaining the city on an even keel in the years following the attack on Pearl Harbor. In 1944 he ran successfully for the governorship of the commonwealth, becoming only the second (Curley had been the first), and also the last, Boston mayor in the twentieth century to make the leap from City Hall to the State House.

Tobin's departure from the mayor's office a year before the expiration of his term created a political problem for the new Democratic governor and the Republican-controlled state legislature. The city charter called for a special election to fill the vacancy, but Tobin and the GOP leadership feared that a short campaign would give Curley an insurmountable advantage over likely opponents. Accordingly, the charter was amended to give the city council president the temporary authority he needed to keep the municipal bureaucracy operating and to delay the election until its regularly scheduled date in November 1945.

This finagling with the political calendar could not stop the Curley bandwagon. Curley had always fared best in uncertain economic times and in periods of social tension, and the months after V-J Day certainly fit that description. A crowded field of candidates also aided the former mayor; five other names appeared on the ballot, and this divided opposition enabled Curley, whose mail fraud trial was set to begin weeks after Election Day, to score the greatest triumph of his career. Carrying nineteen of Boston's twenty-two wards, Curley defeated his closest challenger, one hundred twelve thousand to sixty thousand, the largest margin of victory in any mayoral election.

The four years of Curley's fourth term would be dominated by what took place less than a month after his inauguration. In January 1946 a federal jury in Washington, D.C., convicted the Boston mayor on ten of the fourteen counts in the indictment, exposing him to a forty-seven-year prison sentence and a $19,000 fine. Curley managed to avoid jail for nearly eighteen months, but in June 1947 the judge rejected his final emotional appeal ("You are imposing a death sentence upon me") and committed the seventy-two-year-old to one year in a federal penitentiary.

With Curley refusing to resign (it was typical of Curley's attitude toward public service that he had not relinquished his House seat upon his election as mayor, but continued to collect his congressional salary until his term expired a year later, even though he never appeared on Capitol Hill during that time), and the city charter making no provision either for automatic removal of a mayor convicted of a federal crime or for the transfer of power when a mayor became incapacitated, it fell to the Republican governor and state legislature to fill the vacuum. Although there were calls from good-government groups for a law declaring the mayoralty vacant and the creation of a gubernatorially appointed commission to run the city until a special election could be held later in the year, Republican leaders were concerned this would create a popular backlash in Curley's favor. Instead, they opted to allow Curley to keep both his title and his salary, while bestowing his powers on the city clerk. Upon his release from prison, Curley would have his authority as mayor restored.

Ironically, the city clerk, John B. Hynes, who had been named acting mayor precisely because he was seen as a nonpartisan bureaucrat, became Curley's nemesis in the political arena. When President Truman commuted Curley's sentence in November 1947, Hynes resumed his old post, but in the five months that he held the reins of power he had demonstrated excellent management skills, a keen regard for fiscal prudence, and staunch resistance to corruption. Although he had never run for elected office before, Hynes became the favored candidate of Democrats and Republicans determined to deny Curley a fifth term.

Curley sought reelection in 1949 more out of habit (and the need for income) than anything else. He could point to little in accomplishment over the previous four years, and he offered no vision for the next four. Even so, Hynes was no match for Curley's colorful platform oratory; his speeches promised nothing more than a "clean, honest, and efficient administration." He did, however, have a well-financed and well-oiled organization that carried his message into the neighborhoods. Two other candidates also contested the election, but it was essentially a Curley-Hynes battle, and the challenger emerged victorious. Demonstrating that some of the old magic was still there, Curley gained even more votes (one hundred twenty-six thousand) than he had in 1945, but Hynes did even better (with one hundred thirty-eight thousand votes).

Hynes and Curley went at it again just two years later. Boston's voters had approved changes to the city charter in 1949 that altered representation on the council from twenty-two ward-based district representatives to nine at-large members, and provided for a two-stage process in the choice of a mayor in order to limit the ballot to two candidates in the general election. In the first test of this new arrangement, Hynes gained a clear majority in the primary and defeated Curley by a 2-to-1 margin in the general election.

INDUSTRY, COMMERCE, AND LABOR

As the final decade of the half-century-long Curley political saga played itself out in the 1940s, Boston's economy continued to deteriorate. The decay was neither as evident nor as dramatic as Curley's triumphant return to City Hall or the spectacle of the mayor as a defendant in a criminal trial, and the unusual circumstances of the period—total war and an uneasy peace—obscured it even more. But Boston remained in the grips of a lengthy downward economic spiral that by the close of the 1950s would bring the municipality to the brink of bankruptcy. Only with the end of the Curley era could Boston start facing up to its underlying problems, although making real progress in ameliorating them would take a quarter-century or more.

The core of Boston's difficulty was geographical. The city was the hub of a region that was still living off its past glory of being the pacesetter for the industrial revolution of the nineteenth century. New England's cotton mills and shoe factories had demonstrated the immense potential of applying new technology and energy sources to manufacturing familiar products, but by the early 1900s the focus of the industrial economy had shifted to turning out goods that were novel and required materials either not found in New England or too costly to ship there. Even the fabled textile industry had begun to migrate out of the region, in search of cheaper labor and less stringent state regulation. By the mid-1950s Boston had lost 19 percent of the manufacturing jobs it had had in 1919 and the metropolitan region had lost 27 percent.

The stagnation of the New England industrial economy carried over to the commercial sector. Boston's economic fortunes had always been tied to its port; a vibrant foreign and coastwise trade established the settlement's importance in the colonial era and continued to define the city in the first half of the twentieth century. With fewer goods to export, however, it became more difficult to attract shipping to carry goods to Boston's wharves. Lack of attention to maintaining and modernizing cargo facilities both reflected and intensified this decline.

World War II provided support to Boston's weakening industrial and commercial base, but the assistance proved only transitory. At their peak levels of activity, the Boston Naval Shipyard and the privately owned Fore River Shipyard (just over the city line in Quincy) had fifty thousand and seventeen thousand workers on their payrolls, respectively, making them by far the biggest employers in the region. Countless other companies won government military contracts, and the docks were busy sending the goods they manufactured, as well as soldiers, overseas. The end of the war would not see a return to depression-level economic activity, but the slow rise in spending on the Cold War and the pickup in the domestic sector could not sustain the flush times of the early 1940s into the latter part of the decade. Unlike other parts of the country, New England did not produce consumer products that were in great demand after the wartime shortages; the first and only automobile assembly plant in the six-state area did not start turning out cars until 1947—characteristically, it was built in a town about twenty miles from Boston. Overall, the region's and Boston's downward secular trend picked up where it had left off in 1941.

But not all of Boston's economic ills could be traced to the impersonal functioning of the marketplace; political and ethnic rivalries also played key roles, with Curley, as usual, at the center. During his fifty years in public life, Curley had succeeded in polarizing the city to such an extent that the local private funds needed to keep Boston an attractive and vibrant place to live and work were increasingly being invested elsewhere. The Great Depression and World War II had shut down commercial construction, and while the John Hancock Life Insurance Company opened a new headquarters in 1947, that would be the last major office built in Boston for the next two decades.

Boston had suffered economic blows in the past and come back, thanks largely to entrepreneurs willing to take chances. At the middle of the twentieth century, the city's most important assets, besides the cash sitting in its banks and in the large trust accounts held by the heirs of those earlier businessmen, were its institutions of higher learning and its world-class hospitals. Exploiting these resources became the goal of a new generation of Boston financiers, the venture capitalists, who first made their appearance in 1946 with the formation of the American Research and Development Corporation, headed by Georges Doriot, a professor of manufacturing at the Harvard Business School. Along with the burgeoning mutual fund industry, the venture capitalists would lead Boston and New England into a more prosperous last third of the twentieth century.

RACE, ETHNICITY, AND IMMIGRATION

"Nowhere else in the United States," journalist John Gunther observed in his classic *Inside the U.S.A.*, "does a single community dominate a metropolis in quite the manner that the Irish Catholics dominate Boston." Although Gunther qualified this sweeping statement by noting how Yankees controlled the economic life of the city, his comment was directly tied to his further point that "popularly Boston is supposed to be the most anti-Semitic town in the United States." Just as the school integration/busing crisis of the 1970s would expose working-class Irish Catholic racism, so too did the social strains generated by World War II reveal both working-class Irish Catholic religious intolerance and the failure of politicians—Irish and Yankees alike—to condemn it.

Anti-Semitism had surfaced in the late 1930s largely in response to Detroit-based Father Charles E. Coughlin's radio diatribes against international bankers and President Roosevelt's increasingly hostile stance toward Nazi Germany. The attack on Pearl Harbor temporarily silenced Coughlin, but within a matter of months he and his Christian Front organization were again blaming Jews for plunging the nation into war. Although the Roman Catholic Church hierarchy in America distanced itself from Coughlin, Boston's William Cardinal O'Connell allowed, as a matter of courtesy, a New York priest allied with Coughlin to participate in a St. Patrick's Day/

Evacuation Day event in the heavily Irish Catholic South Boston neighborhood in March 1942. Neither Mayor Tobin nor Governor Leverett Saltonstall, a Republican Yankee, chose to make any comment on the Cardinal's action or the crowd's enthusiastic response to the priest's attacks on the national administration.

The elected leaders' desire to remain silent was tested again in the fall of 1943 when *PM*, a leftist New York newspaper, ran an article under the headline "Christian Front Hoodlums Terrorize Boston Jews" and sent a reporter to question Saltonstall about the attacks by Irish youths on Jews as they walked on city streets. (It was characteristic of the Boston newspapers before the 1960s that they did not print pieces that cast the Irish community in a bad light.) At a press conference the normally unflappable governor denounced the "stinky article," told the *PM* correspondent to "get the hell out" of his office, and instructed his bodyguard to escort him from the State House. Over at City Hall, Tobin attacked the newspaper for maligning Boston, claiming that the violence was "strictly a juvenile situation" with no connection to religious bigotry.

The Boston police commissioner (a gubernatorial appointee chosen by Curley seven years earlier) backed up Tobin's characterization, but almost immediately the police department, overwhelmingly Irish in composition, itself came under fire. Four Jewish youths had been jumped on by a crowd estimated at between sixty and three hundred people; when the police arrived on the scene, they took only the Jewish boys into custody and charged them with being involved in an "affray." Despite claims by the accused that they were beaten by arresting officers at the station house, and the failure of the police to get any witness statements, an Irish American judge tried two of the defendants as adults and fined them.

The outcry in the Jewish community, as well as among other Bostonians and in some national publications, led state officials to take action. The attorney general ordered that the appeals of the convictions not be contested, and Saltonstall decided not to reappoint the police commissioner when his term expired in November 1943. Not much changed, however. The new police chief, an Irish American, maintained the line that anti-Semitism was not at the root of the violence, the city council rejected a proposal to have the public schools teach the importance of toleration, and the attacks continued. Only with the end of World War II did the problem begin to abate.

After thirty-seven years as the Archbishop of Boston, Cardinal O'Connell died in April 1944. His successor, Richard J. Cushing, was a far less imperious figure than O'Connell and much more willing to work cooperatively across denominational lines. Cushing's reaching out to other faiths put him at odds with Church practice at the time and may explain why he had to wait fourteen years before being elevated to cardinal (O'Connell had received his promotion just four years after becoming archbishop). But with a brother-in-law who was Jewish, Cushing had no patience for the anti-Semitism O'Connell had countenanced among the faithful.

As Boston's Irish sought to mend fences with the city's Jews, Boston's racial mix continued its subtle change. The 1940 census had counted fewer than twenty-four thousand African Americans, 3.1 percent of the population; a decade later the number was more than forty-two thousand, about 5 percent of the total. This still left Boston far behind most other big northeastern and midwestern cities in the racial minority's share of the population, but the Irish Catholic city Gunther had described in 1947 was on its way out. It would not directly affect politics—an unbroken string of Irish Catholic men held the mayoralty until 1993, when an Italian Catholic male (who still occupied it in 2010) filled the vacancy opened by the incumbent's resignation to become U.S. ambassador to the Vatican—but the 2000 Census reported that a majority of the city's population was nonwhite.

See also *Boston, MA 1776–1790; Boston, MA 1790–1828; Boston, MA 1828–1854; Boston, MA 1854–1877; Boston, MA 1877–1896; Boston, MA 1896–1929; Boston, MA 1929–1941*

MARK I. GELFAND

BIBLIOGRAPHY

Beatty, Jack. *The Rascal King: The Life and Times of James Michael Curley, 1874–1958*. Reading, MA: Addison-Wesley, 1992.

Glaeser, Edward L. *Reinventing Boston: 1640–2003*. Cambridge, MA: Harvard Institute of Economic Research, 2003.

O'Connor, Thomas H. *Building a New Boston: Politics and Urban Renewal, 1950–1970*. Boston, MA: Northeastern University Press, 1993.

Sarna, Jonathan, Ellen Smith, and Scott-Martin Kosofsky, eds. *The Jews of Boston*. Rev. and updated ed. New Haven, CT: Yale University Press, 2005.

Population rankings based on the 1980 census

CITIES IN THE COLD WAR ERA, 1952–1989

The period 1952 to 1989 begins with the Cold War and ends with the fall of the Soviet Union, during which time the United States became a suburban nation; a president, his brother, and the country's most influential civil rights leader were all assassinated; thousands of riots erupted in cities across the country; and the government committed itself to civil rights and desegregation, went to war in Vietnam, and waged a "war on poverty" at home.

This chapter also covers the rise of cities in the Sunbelt (stretching from Texas to Southern California) and the decline of cities in what became known as the Rustbelt, stretching from the Northeast urban corridor to Chicago and St. Louis. In 1950 the ten largest cities in the country contained roughly 14 percent of the total U.S. population and included only one southwestern city, Los Angeles. By 1990 the ten largest cities contained 9 percent of the country's population and included six southwestern cities (Los Angeles, Houston, San Diego, Dallas, Phoenix, and San

Antonio). Moreover, all of the big Northeastern cities had fewer people in them in 1990 than they had contained in 1950, yet each was also part of a metropolitan region that had gained in population during the same period. Indeed, by 1970 the census counted the majority of people who were living in metropolitan areas as living outside the central cities.

It was in large part the federal government that made massive suburbanization possible. First, the Federal Housing Administration and Veterans Administration provided insurance for home mortgage defaults to banks, which preferred to finance the houses immediately out-side cities that were being built at unprecedented rates—for families having babies at unprec-edented rates—using new mass construction techniques first developed by Levitt and Sons in their Levittown community, located within commuting distance of New York City, and copied across the country. Second, in 1956 Congress passed, and President Eisenhower signed into law, the Federal Highway Act, providing new taxes (especially on gas) dedicated to financ-ing the country's largest-ever public works project, a grid of more than forty thousand miles of high-speed, limited-access roads across the continent, which reduced the importance of cities as transportation hubs and made it easier to commute longer distances to suburban homes outside the central cities.

The television was the new hearth of the new suburban home. In 75 percent of all Ameri-can homes by 1955, TVs came preinstalled in some of the original Levittown houses, and they transformed American political campaigns. Television also exposed Americans to the indignities suffered by black Americans demonstrating against the Jim Crow system of racial apartheid in the southern states, and thus elevated the civil rights movement to a national issue. White south-ern officials declared their open opposition to the Supreme Court's ruling in *Brown v. Board of Education* (1954) that racial segregation in schools was unconstitutional, compelling the court to declare a year later that desegregation should be implemented with "all deliberate speed." The Eisenhower administration sent federal troops to enforce desegregation in Arkansas, and Con-gress passed the first-ever Civil Rights Act in 1957, followed up by more a more significant Civil Rights Act in 1964, outlawing various forms of both racial and gender discrimination.

Black southerners retaliated against white "massive resistance" to desegregation through boycotts of segregated services and nonviolent protest marches and sit-ins. The most visible leader of the civil rights movement in the South was Martin Luther King Jr., who founded the Southern Christian Leadership Conference in 1957.

The successes of the civil rights movement came at a time when massive numbers of black people were leaving the South and moving to northern cities, just as massive numbers of white people were moving to the outlying suburbs, with job opportunities following them. As a result, the percent of the African American population in the cities covered in this chapter increased from an average of 12 percent in 1950 to 30 percent in 1990 (compared to 16 percent Hispanic and 41 percent white in 1990). Blacks in northern cities faced more subtle, but no less perni-cious, forms of discrimination than in the South, such as redlining by real estate agents and job discrimination, against which the southern civil rights tactics were less successful (as was King's campaign for racial equality in Chicago in 1966).

The growing racial tensions in big cities were matched by the growing tensions of the Cold War. After the Kennedy administration's unsuccessful attempt in 1961 to overthrow Fidel

BY THE NUMBERS: THE MOST POPULOUS CITIES IN 1980

	TOTAL POPULATION[1]	WHITE POPULATION[1]	BLACK POPULATION[1]	OTHER RACE POPULATION[1]	POPULATION OF SPANISH ORIGIN[2]	% WHITE POPULATION[1]	% BLACK POPULATION[1]	% OTHER RACE POPULATION[1]	% OF SPANISH ORIGIN[2]	FOREIGN-BORN POPULATION[3]
NEW YORK, NY	7,071,639	4,294,075	1,784,337	993,227	1,406,024	60.7	25.2	14.0	19.9	1,670,199
CHICAGO, IL	3,005,072	1,490,216	1,197,000	317,856	422,063	49.6	39.8	10.6	14.0	435,232
LOS ANGELES, CA	2,966,850	1,816,761	505,210	644,879	816,076	61.2	17.0	21.7	27.5	804,818
PHILADELPHIA, PA	1,688,210	983,084	638,878	66,248	63,570	58.2	37.8	3.9	3.8	107,951
HOUSTON, TX	1,595,138	978,353	440,346	176,439	281,331	61.3	27.6	11.1	17.6	155,577
DETROIT, MI	1,203,339	413,730	758,939	30,670	28,970	34.4	63.1	2.5	2.4	68,303
DALLAS, TX	904,078	555,270	265,594	83,214	111,083	61.4	29.4	9.2	12.3	54,912
SAN DIEGO, CA	875,538	666,863	77,700	130,975	130,613	76.2	8.9	15.0	14.9	130,906
PHOENIX, AZ	789,704	665,898	37,804	86,002	116,736	84.3	4.8	10.9	14.8	44,662
BALTIMORE, MD	786,775	345,113	431,151	10,511	7,638	43.9	54.8	1.3	1.0	24,667

	% POPULATION FOREIGN-BORN[3]	% POPULATION 7–13 YEARS OLD ENROLLED IN SCHOOL[4]	% POPULATION 25 AND OLDER COLLEGE EDUCATED[4]	% WOMEN IN THE LABOR FORCE[5]	% CIVILIAN LABOR FORCE UNEMPLOYED[5]	% EMPLOYED POPULATION IN MANUFACTURING[6]	MEDIAN FAMILY INCOME[7]	LAND AREA (SQ. MI.)[8]	POPULATION DENSITY (PER SQ. MI.)[8]
NEW YORK, NY	23.6	98.3	17.3	47.1	7.7	17.4	$16,818	301.5	23,454.9
CHICAGO, IL	14.5	98.1	13.8	50.9	9.8	26.6	$18,776	228.1	13,174.4
LOS ANGELES, CA	27.1	97.9	19.8	54.2	6.8	23.0	$19,467	464.7	6,384.4
PHILADELPHIA, PA	6.4	99.7	11.4	44.4	11.4	20.9	$16,388	136.0	12,413.3
HOUSTON, TX	9.8	97.6	23.1	59.2	3.6	16.9	$21,881	556.4	2,866.9
DETROIT, MI	5.7	98.6	8.3	45.8	18.5	28.6	$17,033	135.6	8,874.2
DALLAS, TX	6.1	97.6	22.0	59.6	3.4	18.7	$19,703	333.0	2,714.9
SAN DIEGO, CA	15.0	98.7	24.0	52.8	7.0	16.2	$20,133	320.0	2,736.1
PHOENIX, AZ	5.7	98.7	14.9	54.4	5.6	18.0	$20,635	324.0	2,437.4
BALTIMORE, MD	3.1	98.1	11.3	48.2	10.8	18.8	$15,721	80.3	9,797.9

[1]Source: 1980 Census of Population: Volume 1, Characteristics of the Population, Chapter B, General Population Characteristics. Table 15.
[2]Source: 1980 Census of Population: Volume 1, Characteristics of the Population, Chapter B, General Population Characteristics. Table 16.
[3]Source: 1980 Census of Population: Volume 1, Characteristics of the Population, Chapter C, General Social and Economic Characteristics. Table 116.
[4]Source: 1980 Census of Population: Volume 1, Characteristics of the Population, Chapter C, General Social and Economic Characteristics. Table 119.
[5]Source: 1980 Census of Population: Volume 1, Characteristics of the Population, Chapter C, General Social and Economic Characteristics. Table 120.
[6]Source: 1980 Census of Population: Volume 1, Characteristics of the Population, Chapter C, General Social and Economic Characteristics. Table 122.
[7]Source: 1980 Census of Population: Volume 1, Characteristics of the Population, Chapter C, General Social and Economic Characteristics. Table 124.
[8]Source: Campbell Gibson, *Population of the 100 Largest Cities and Other Urban Places in the United States: 1790 to 1990*. (1998) Table 21.

Castro's new government in Cuba, Castro in 1962 allowed the Soviets into Cuba to construct missile bases. Discovering the missile bases, the United States blockaded Cuba, thus bringing the United States and the Soviet Union nearly to the point of a potentially nuclear conflict, until the Soviet Union agreed to not build its bases in Cuba if the United States agreed never to invade Cuba. At the same time, the United States was getting increasingly embroiled in attempts to support an unstable pro-Western government in South Vietnam against allies of the North Vietnamese leader, Ho Chi Minh.

Kennedy was assassinated in November 1963, and Lyndon Johnson thus became president. That summer, black neighborhoods in Rochester, Philadelphia, and New York erupted into what would turn out to be the first of many waves of violence and looting in cities across the country, leading to the establishment in 1967 of the National Advisory Commission on Civil Disorders, which came to the conclusion in its 1968 report that the causes of the race riots were poor housing conditions, police brutality, and economic isolation of inner-city black ghettos.

By the time of the riots, Lyndon Johnson, who had handily won election in 1964 against the conservative Barry Goldwater, had expanded upon the "war on poverty" that had been germinating in the last year of the Kennedy administration. Among the many policies that composed Johnson's Great Society were the establishment of the Department of Housing and Urban Development, increased funding for low-income housing, educational and employment programs, and the creation of Medicare and Medicaid, providing aid to the elderly and poor for medical care. Also significant was the Immigration Act of 1965, which lifted the limits on immigrants from Asia and Africa, thus changing the nature of immigration.

The Great Society vastly increased government spending, as did Johnson's expansion of the U.S. role in Vietnam. Responding to what now appear to be dubious reports of North Vietnamese attacks on American military ships in the Gulf of Tonkin, Congress gave the president wide authority to protect American interests in South Vietnam. By 1968 there were more than half a million American troops in Vietnam and a vibrant antiwar movement in the United States.

The unpopularity of the war, and mounting American casualties, led Johnson to decline to run for reelection in 1968. John Kennedy's brother, Robert Kennedy, was a frontrunner for the Democratic nomination but was assassinated in June of that year, two months after Martin Luther King Jr. had been assassinated, which led to a new round of riots in black neighborhoods in dozens of American cities. The 1968 presidential election was also marked by the rise of a third party in the South. Previously Democratic whites who broke from their party on account of its support for civil rights and desegregation nominated as their candidate former Alabama governor George Wallace, who captured the electoral votes of Arkansas, Louisiana, Alabama, Mississippi, and Georgia, thus helping Richard Nixon win the presidency with a plurality of the popular vote.

In 1972 George Wallace was shot and paralyzed, and Nixon won reelection against liberal Democratic candidate George McGovern, capturing the electoral votes of every state but Massachusetts. During his first four years, Nixon drastically lowered troop levels in Vietnam, and right before the 1972 election, the country appeared on the verge of peace. Yet the accords collapsed and the war continued until 1975, when the North captured the southern capital and united the country.

Before the end of the Vietnam War, Nixon had resigned as a result of his connection to the 1972 break-in at Democratic National Committee headquarters at the Watergate Hotel, and Gerald Ford became president. The nation was in the midst of a deep recession, in large part a result of rising energy prices that were the result of an energy embargo by Arab oil-producing countries in response to U.S. support for Israel during its 1973 war with Egypt and Syria, which once again brought the United States and Soviet Union close to nuclear war.

For these and other reasons (including his unpopular pardon of Nixon for any crimes related to Watergate), Ford was defeated by Jimmy Carter in the 1976 presidential election.

Record-high inflation (a function of government monetary policy and high energy prices, including a second Arab oil embargo in 1979) and the seizure of fifty-three American diplomatic and military personnel as hostages in Iran (the result of the overthrow of a pro-Western government in that country), who were not released for more than a year, combined with an unpopular leadership style provided Carter with record-low popularity ratings by 1980, and he lost the election that year decisively to conservative Ronald Reagan.

The Reagan administration was defined by massive tax cuts, especially to higher-income groups, cuts to discretionary domestic government spending, increased military spending, and a more aggressive global military presence. The tax cuts resulted in record-high government budget deficits, and the new global militarism resulted in an increase in terrorism against American targets abroad, such as the bombing of a U.S. military installation in Beirut in 1983. A remarkable economic resurgence in the country after a recession in 1982, combined with his telegenic personality and the consolidation of conservative forces nationally, resulted in Reagan decisively beating Walter Mondale in 1984.

At the beginning of Reagan's second term, Mikhail Gorbachev became the leader of the Soviet Union. Gorbachev instituted a series of political and economic reforms that, by the time Reagan's vice president, George H. W. Bush, had won election in 1988 against Michael Dukakis, had set into motion the fall of the Soviet Union, including the dramatic shift away from communism of every Eastern Bloc country in 1989, signaling the end of a bipolar world order defined by the United States and Soviet Union.

NEW YORK, NY 1952–1989

IF THE IMMEDIATE POSTWAR ERA MARKED THE CULMINATION OF NEW YORK'S LONG ASCENDANCE to global preeminence among cities, the decades immediately following marked a collapse in which an ambitious vision of local liberalism was supplanted by waves of racial conflict, fiscal crisis, and endemic crime. From the 1950s to the 1980s, New York saw the most eventful and contentious series of political upheavals of any U.S. city; these local crises were exacerbated by the same broad structural changes that were undermining the economic bases of social health in large cities across the nation. Throughout this era, the provision of basic services became more irregular, a wide range of governance crises emerged, and New Yorkers faced grave levels of personal insecurity. The city was something of a failed state. This era marks the nadir of urbanism in America, and New York was iconic in this sense, just as it was for the vision of civic optimism of the immediately preceding years.

The dominant trend of New York politics in this era was a progression from optimistic consensus to ideological and racial polarization, and from ambitious local liberalism to a real struggle to provide basic goods such as public safety; it was in many ways a slide from order to chaos. With the final death throes of the Tammany machine, there was no longer a dominant force in local politics. At the same time, the civil rights movement shone a light on the deeply unequal

QUICK FACTS

NEW YORK, NY 1952–1989

MAYORS

Vincent R. Impellitteri	(1950–1953)
Robert Wagner Jr.	(1954–1965)
John Lindsay	(1966–1973)
Abraham Beame	(1974–1977)
Edward Koch	(1978–1989)

MAJOR INDUSTRIES AND EMPLOYERS

City, state, and federal government

Finance

Real estate

Manufacturing

MAJOR NEWSPAPERS

New York Times

New York Herald Tribune (until 1966)

New York Post

New York Daily News

New York Amsterdam News

Wall Street Journal

Village Voice (beginning in 1955)

MAJOR EVENTS

1964 and 1967: Riots indicate the shaky foundations of the uneasy and unequal white-black consensus forged decades earlier.

1968: School integration and community control controversy mark the start of white ethnic pushback against the racial liberalism of 1960s and the beginning of local political realignment.

1968: Demonstrations at Columbia University mark a visible manifestation of New Left antiwar and radical black nationalist protests in the heart of the elite institution.

1973: Construction of the World Trade Center is completed, making the twin towers briefly the tallest buildings in the world.

1975: A city fiscal crisis results in massive service cuts and marks the end of high levels of local spending.

1977: A major electrical blackout results in widespread looting and marks the beginning of a long period of high crime.

---

nature of American racial politics. Impatience with complacent elites on this issue and about the Vietnam War contributed to the development of a form of politics and social conduct in which polite deference to authority was no longer seen as desirable or admirable—in the countercultural view, radical transformation required rebellious acts. New York was a principal home of this New Left, and the list of milestone political events that took place in the city is impressive: the Stonewall riots in 1969 marked the beginning of the gay rights movement, beatniks from Columbia became the hippies of the 1960s, and massive antiwar protests brought youth counterculture into antagonism with conservative forces of authority and tradition on Columbia's Morningside Heights campus and on the avenues downtown.

Compounding the governance problems associated with such cultural upheaval, this era marks the range of the postindustrial urban crisis as the basis of the American economy was transformed and population patterns became more dispersed. New York's centrality to national politics was obvious in the early twentieth century and into the postwar era, and New York's mayors and governors were routinely considered by both parties as possible presidential contenders. By the end of this period, the city was no longer the behemoth it had been, and its local dysfunction meant its mayors were more like colorful characters dealing with chronic crisis than real presidential material. Americans voted with their feet, and left the big cities, even New York. New York State, the most populous in the nation since 1810, ceded that title to California at some point in the 1960s. Even the Giants and Dodgers headed west.

Political and social fragmentation, coupled with public fiscal crisis, contributed to social decay in the late 1970s. General lawlessness was the basic impression of the city as seen from the outside. The 1977 blackout prompted widespread looting, and much of the Bronx was literally burning. Cultural representations of social disorder, from *Taxi Driver* to *Death Wish*, were not far removed from reality. Rates of violent crime in the city nearly quadrupled between 1965 and 1990, and the murder rate throughout the 1980s was nearly five times what it was in 1965 (today, it has returned roughly to early 1960s levels). In short, with inequality, unemployment, and crime at very high levels, the city was comparable to developing nations on many measures. The rebound of the city in the past two decades is an important sign of progress, but such successes were remote and far from certain over the course of the 1970s and 1980s.

Even amid the blackouts, fiscal crisis, racial division, rampant crime, and overall social decline, glimmers of hope were present. New York remained the nation's cultural capital, and the construction of the World Trade Center in 1973 was one bright spot in this era. The national sectoral shift to finance, where Wall Street has always been a dominant force, had begun in earnest by the end of the 1980s, and the fraught possibilities for gentrification-driven reinvestment in major cities were beginning to show signs of life on the ground. Still, the long decades of urban crisis hollowed out the heart of the city and tempered the optimism of previous eras in New York City's governance and society.

GOVERNMENT AND POLITICS

The 1950s occupy a romantic place in America's collective memory, and this is no less true in New York than it is elsewhere. The future seemed bright for the city, and during the administration of Robert F. Wagner (1954–1965; son of the famous senator from New York that led the liberal northern wing of the Democratic Party during the New Deal), progressive steps to consolidate liberal governance were made. In retrospect, however, the structural bases of urban prosperity were already eroding, and this had a major impact on the politics of the city as well.

New York's political development in this era was tumultuous and unpredictable. Wagner, though a product of the venerable Tammany machine, later split with it and became more self-consciously reform-minded. His convincing election to a third term in 1961 against a machine candidate marked the final demise of the organization's dominance of local Democratic politics. As a reformer, Wagner made strides to depoliticize city bureaucracies and promoted racial integration of previously all-white city organizations. He also granted collective bargaining rights to city employees and continued the urban renewal efforts common across American cities, largely using funds garnered from federal and state coffers to try to breathe new life into city infrastructure and redevelop blighted neighborhoods.

The death of the machine was also the end of stability in New York politics, however. When Wagner did not run for reelection in 1965, there was a space for the young, charismatic liberal Republican congressman John Lindsay. After winning a plurality victory in a three-way race against future mayor Abraham Beame and a young William F. Buckley, Lindsay faced high expectations for continuing the momentum of reform politics in the city. He continued to expand welfare benefits and assiduously courted support in poorer neighborhoods and among minority groups, and he gained national attention for his very personal approach to dealing with racial tensions throughout the 1960s. By all accounts a dedicated liberal on most social issues of the day, the Republican, patrician-seeming Lindsay was without a strong natural political base and became almost immediately besieged on all sides by pressure and conflict, some of which had begun to percolate before his election. Municipal strikes, race riots, major controversies over school district governance, and antiwar and New Left social protests such as the student takeover of Columbia University are what his tenure in office is most remembered for. Each could have been worse without Lindsay's moderating influence, but his institutional and political weakness in the face of rapidly mounting social forces left him with only the power to persuade, and he was often unable to maintain order amid the tumult of the age.

Abraham Beame's single term saw the largest governance crisis in the city's modern history, the fiscal crisis of 1975, when the diminished tax base brought on by migration to the suburbs collided with liberal spending policies, resulting in major budget shortfalls. The Ford administration famously refused to grant the city a bailout, but complete default was avoided when the teachers union agreed to purchase $150 million in municipal bonds at the last moment, allowing city finances to be restructured without collapse. However, the crisis prompted massive cuts to services and welfare provisions that had been expanded during the liberal consensus of the postwar prosperity, even as the structural underpinnings of central city preeminence weakened.

The cuts were unpopular among residents and affected quality of life. The 1977 Democratic mayoral primary reflected the political instability brought about by the transformations of the past twenty years. Beame, the incumbent, faced several high-profile rivals: the liberal Secretary of (New York) State Mario Cuomo, who would go on to win the governorship; the very liberal Congresswoman Bella Abzug; Congressman Herman Badillo, the first Latino candidate for mayor in any major city; and Congressman Ed Koch, who assembled a coalition consisting mainly of conservative ethnic whites. The primary reflected the fractured state of the city and its politics—a different candidate won each of the five boroughs in the primary, but it was Koch (the only major candidate *not* to place first in any borough) who won a plurality in the primary, and then defeated Cuomo in a Democratic runoff and again in the general election when Cuomo ran on the Liberal Party line.

Recent increases in crime following police layoffs brought on by the fiscal crisis, and the general civil disorder of the infamous citywide blackout that struck during the campaign, may have contributed to Koch's eventual success. He won reelection twice in the 1980s, and his political base has continued to serve as a relatively coherent, locally conservative coalition to the present, providing support for the subsequent candidacies of Rudolph Giuliani and Michael Bloomberg.

INDUSTRY, COMMERCE, AND LABOR

Much of the civic dysfunction that New Yorkers experienced in this era can be attributed to unfortunate timing between population flows and the massive structural changes taking place in the American economy. New York, even with its diverse economic base, was still a leading industrial center, and the shift of manufacturing jobs to the suburbs, to other regions, and overseas cut deeply at this fundamental sector of the local economy. Hundreds of thousands of manufacturing jobs disappeared from the city, at the very moment that hundreds of thousands of African Americans and immigrants arrived from the South and abroad. The concurrent trend of middle-class migration to the suburbs compounded this mistimed arrival by undermining the tax base of the city, making the high levels of public spending characteristic of the local postwar consensus unsustainable in the long run and eventually leading to the fiscal crisis and service cuts of the 1970s. Over the second half of this era, however, New York recovered its footing, and its comparative advantage in the finance, insurance, and real estate (FIRE) sectors that would become increasingly important engines of American economic growth meant that New York would regain preeminence in the era of "global cities" in the future.

The mechanisms by which the urban economic crisis developed were numerous, and a few events in New York during this era can illuminate matters. One ironic result stemmed from Mayor Wagner's decision to grant collective bargaining rights to municipal workers, thus extending the privileges of union organization to local public employees in much the same way that the Wagner Act of 1935 (named for his father, senator from New York) had afforded this right to private-sector workers decades before. These new unions became quite powerful, however, and in the 1960s Mayor Lindsay faced numerous strikes, and threats of strikes, as the unions made demands for higher wages. The most famous of these was the sanitation workers strike of 1968, during which the city's garbage went uncollected for nearly ten days, piling high on the sidewalks and vibrantly illustrating the problems of city government under conditions of labor conflict.

Demands by municipal workers were compounded by continued campaigns to extend welfare benefits to the city's poor, who were growing in number as disinvestment progressed. This combination of higher spending and dwindling revenues would prove impossible to sustain. The effects of the shift in national economic activity from manufacturing to finance, however, were mixed. About half of the manufacturing jobs in the New York metropolitan area disappeared between 1970 and 1990, but employment in finance doubled over the same period. While there are still fewer individuals in finance than there were in manufacturing, these were (and still are) typically higher-paying jobs, meaning that once finance was established as a major source of economic activity in the United States, New York would regain its centrality in the national economy. However, among the implications of this shift was a vast increase in inequality. New arrivals to the city and workers with low levels of education were forced into low-wage service-sector jobs, while the highly educated found high-paying FIRE employment. The nascent global city developing in the 1980s was a far more unequal city than the New York of the 1940s and 1950s.

The fiscal crisis of the 1970s also had an impact on the shape of public spending in the coming decades. While public sector employment recovered somewhat, operating costs had to be slashed to maintain fiscal solvency, and the city lost control of its finances for a period of years.

The most powerful public sector agencies (that is, those with the capacity to provide public goods and invest in infrastructure) became, even more than before, the "nonpolitical" public authorities that were insulated from popular control. For instance, the Port Authority of New York and New Jersey completed the World Trade Center project in the 1970s. The threat of default disciplined New York government and contributed to the consolidation of an urban development agenda much removed from popular control and very friendly to investment and property interests.

RACE, ETHNICITY, AND IMMIGRATION

Over the course of 1952–1989, the racial composition of New York's population was transformed. In 1950 about 90 percent of New Yorkers were white; by 1990 this figure had fallen to the slimmest of majorities. This was a function of two important phenomena. First, the Great Migration continued apace, and the city's African American population surpassed a million at some point in the 1950s. There were probably more black Americans in New York than in any southern state. Second, 1965 immigration reform ended the quota system that had been in place (and that was specifically designed to maintain the ethnoracial composition of the country), opening the country's borders to newcomers from new places, especially Latin America and Asia. Though New York had long had established Puerto Rican and Chinese communities, new immigrants arrived on a new scale and constituted the next chapter in the rapid demographic change that has always characterized the city. Thus at the very moment that the city faced the structural challenges of industrial decline, it also had many new arrivals—many of them poor and in search of opportunity in their new home—from many places, whose diversity set the stage for a grand experiment in the possibilities of inclusive politics. As it turned out, the ugliness of racial conflict was often more in evidence.

Upon arrival, the new New Yorkers often found life far from perfect. The most visible discontent was among African Americans. Though the American popular imagination focuses on events in the Jim Crow South in recalling the advance of the civil rights movement, the importance of race relations in New York cannot be overstated. While the enforcement of white supremacy was less overt and violent in the North than it was in the South, residential and employment discrimination persisted despite laws forbidding them, and African Americans (along with the equally rapidly growing group of newcomers from Puerto Rico) once again found themselves on the bottom of the social, economic, and political hierarchies. As time went by, the uneven progress of local race relations was marked by the development of a radical strain in black politics and recurrent episodes of explosive violence. Over the long era of urban decline, however, little *material* progress was made—nonwhite poverty rates remained very high and disparities in opportunities and outcomes persisted. The era would end on a somewhat hopeful note for minorities, however, as David Dinkins succeeded Mayor Koch to take up residence in Gracie Mansion in 1989.

Though New York did take steps to integrate its municipal bureaucracies even before this era, reformers could not keep pace with increasingly impatient demands for equality. Harlem, long the center of black culture in the North, also served as the home of burgeoning black radical leaders such as Malcolm X. Liberal New York made efforts to incorporate the growing communities of racial minorities, with Lindsay's efforts being especially conspicuous for their liberal inclusion. But despite this liberal style of politics, New York did not escape the "long, hot summers" of the 1960s. New York's recurring riots in 1964, 1967, 1968, and 1977 were smaller than those of other cities like Watts, Detroit, and Newark, but they nonetheless reflected these groups' increasing frustration with the slow pace of reform and progress.

As in other communities, school integration became an issue around which racial conflict crystallized. When unacceptable conditions in the schools in many poor neighborhoods ran into middle-class white citizens' resistance to integration, there developed a spinoff controversy over decentralization and its advanced cousin, "community control." A privately funded experiment in devolving control over school administration and curriculum to local school boards, community control pitted local activists, often radical separatists, against the teachers union, when the local board fired many teachers for allegedly trying to undermine the success of the experiment. In an era when new understandings of cultural diversity and multiculturalism were being advanced by the New Left, this dispute over education had major implications for the understanding of race and identity politics in a city increasingly divided over these issues.

White flight, riots, and racially divisive issues such as school control greatly undermined the possibilities for a cross-racial coalition in local politics. Beginning in 1977 the coalition of outer-borough ethnic whites mostly opposed a more diverse (and relatively liberal, though both sides were fairly liberal by national standards) liberal coalition electorally based in the black and Latino communities of upper Manhattan and the less-affluent areas of the outer boroughs. This basic cleavage in local politics has persisted to the contemporary era. Only once, in 1989, did the minority alliance gain city hall, when Dinkins was elected, though he would serve only one term.

See also *New York, NY 1776–1790; New York, NY 1790–1828; New York, NY 1828–1854; New York, NY 1854–1877; New York, NY 1877–1896; New York, NY 1896–1929; New York, NY 1929–1941; New York, NY 1941–1952; New York, NY 1989–2011*

THOMAS K. OGORZALEK

BIBLIOGRAPHY

Browning, Rufus P., Dale Rogers Marshall, and David H. Tabb. *Racial Politics in American Cities*. 3d ed. New York, NY: Longman, 2003.

Cannato, Vincent J. *The Ungovernable City: John Lindsay and His Struggle to Save New York*. New York, NY: Basic Books, 2001.

Caro, Robert A. *The Power Broker: Robert Moses and the Fall of New York*. New York, NY: Knopf, 1974.

Katznelson, Ira. *City Trenches: Urban Politics and the Patterning of Class in the United States*. Chicago, IL: University of Chicago Press, 1982.

Mollenkopf, John H. *The Contested City*. Princeton, NJ: Princeton University Press, 1983.

———. *A Phoenix in the Ashes : The Rise and Fall of the Koch Coalition in New York City Politics*. Princeton, NJ: Princeton University Press, 1994.

Ravitch, Diane. *The Great School Wars, New York City, 1805–1973: A History of the Public Schools as Battlefield of Social Change*. New York, NY: Basic Books, 1974.

Sleeper, Jim. *Closest of Strangers: Liberalism and the Politics of Race in New York*. New York, NY: W. W. Norton Company, 1990.

CHICAGO, IL 1952–1989

THE PERIOD FROM 1952 TO 1989 WAS A TIME OF POLITICAL, ECONOMIC, AND SOCIAL UPHEAVAL in Chicago. Mayor Richard J. Daley, the last of the big-city machine bosses, presided over a massive downtown rebuilding program that began during the 1950s and continued during subsequent decades. Daley reached out to new voters, including African American residents, as the machine's political base of white ethnic voters gave way to a more diverse population during the decades following World War II. However, the momentum of the civil rights movement during the 1960s would make it increasingly difficult to reconcile the demands of these two constituencies. More often than not, victories won by blacks were more symbolic than substantive. With the election of a progressive African American mayor in 1983, Chicago politics entered a new era in which the voices of the city's minority population would become increasingly difficult to ignore.

GOVERNMENT AND POLITICS

Unlike other cities in the post–World War II era, Chicago was governed by a highly resilient Democratic Party machine that showed few signs of weakening until the 1970s. The early 1950s was a period of transition for Chicago's political machine. The city's mayor in 1952 was Martin H. Kennelly, a weak leader who allowed power to gravitate toward the city council. This situation was reversed in 1955 when Democrat Richard J. Daley was elected mayor. Daley was a politically powerful figure who quickly brought the city council under his wing. He did so mainly through his control over patronage—city government jobs that could be used to reward and punish the city's fifty aldermen. Council members who faithfully supported the mayor's governing agenda were rewarded with patronage positions they could distribute among their constituents to build loyalty, while noncompliant aldermen saw the patronage positions at their disposal cut. At the height of his powers, Daley personally controlled some thirty thousand patronage jobs.

Daley presided over a vast downtown development boom that included construction of the Sears Tower, the John Hancock Building, and many other downtown buildings. The mayor used his unchallenged political dominance to ensure that such projects did not become entangled in the city's vast bureaucracy that controlled building decisions. For example, construction of the Sears Tower on two city blocks required the sale of a one-block segment of Quincy Street to Sears, Roebuck and Company. Under a less powerful mayor, this requirement alone could have delayed the project for months or even killed it altogether. With Daley in charge, however, the matter was largely settled through an hour-long meeting between Daley and Sears chairman Gordon Metcalf. Under Daley, Chicago earned its reputation as "the city that works."

Daley's preoccupation with downtown development enhanced Chicago's prestige around the globe, but it provided relatively few benefits for Chicago's low-income and minority residents. African Americans in particular made up a rapidly growing percentage of the city's

QUICK FACTS

CHICAGO, IL **1952–1989**

MAYORS

Martin H. Kennelly	(1947–1955)
Richard J. Daley	(1955–1976)
Michael A. Bilandic	(1976–1979)
Jane M. Byrne	(1979–1983)
Harold L. Washington	(1983–1987)
Eugene Sawyer	(1987–1989)
Richard M. Daley	(1989–2011)

MAJOR INDUSTRIES AND EMPLOYERS

Printing and publishing
Food and related products
Machinery
Primary and fabricated metals
Textiles and apparel

MAJOR NEWSPAPERS

Chicago Tribune
Chicago Daily News
Chicago Sun-Times
Chicago Defender

MAJOR EVENTS

1955: Richard J. Daley, the last of the big-city machine bosses, is elected mayor of Chicago.

1966: Martin Luther King Jr. comes to Chicago to organize protests against segregation and poor housing conditions for blacks.

1968: Rioting breaks out on the city's West Side following Martin Luther King Jr.'s assassination in April. Several months later, the Democratic Party holds its national convention in Chicago. Thousands of antiwar protestors battle with police.

1970: Ground is broken for the Sears Tower, the world's tallest building and a key symbol of Chicago's downtown revitalization.

1983: Harold Washington becomes Chicago's first African American mayor.

---

voting population. This development was potentially troublesome for Daley, since he could not continue to win elections without significant black support. Unlike machine bosses in other cities, however, Daley had the foresight to expand the beneficiaries of machine politics beyond the machine's traditional base in the city's white ethnic wards. With Daley's support, patronage positions and other material incentives were used to incorporate blacks into the machine. As a result, black Chicagoans became some of Daley's strongest supporters despite his inattention to civil rights and other policies important to African Americans at the time.

By the early 1970s, however, several developments converged to threaten the future of the machine and weaken Daley's power. First, most political hiring and firing was ruled unconstitutional in a 1972 court decision, undermining the patronage system. Second, the federal government reduced funding for cities, a key material resource Daley and other machine leaders had relied upon to reward supporters. Third, blacks, energized by the civil rights movement of the 1960s, were increasingly critical of Daley and no longer a reliable voting bloc. Finally, Daley's endorsement of heavy-handed police tactics against protestors at the 1968 Democratic National Convention in Chicago drew widespread criticism and undermined his standing in the Democratic Party nationally. When Daley died suddenly of a heart attack in 1976, the future of the machine was uncertain. In 1979 Jane Byrne defeated interim mayor Michael Bilandic, a machine loyalist elected by city council to serve the remainder of Daley's term. Byrne ran as an independent reform candidate against the machine-backed Bilandic, winning a narrow victory in part through strong support from the city's predominantly African American wards. For the first time in a half-century, the machine's candidate for mayor had been beaten.

With Byrne's election, power was divided between a self-proclaimed reform mayor and a machine-dominated city council. The new mayor found she could do little without council support. Instead of pushing a reform agenda, Byrne ultimately backpedaled on campaign promises and allowed machine leaders in the city council to dominate Chicago's governing agenda. As before, resources were concentrated on downtown development, while low-income and minority neighborhoods suffered from neglect. African American voters were particularly disappointed by Byrne's alliance with the machine. When Harold Washington, a popular black

When added together Richard J. Daley (right) and his son, Richard M. Daley, have held the mayor's seat of Chicago for more than forty years. Richard J. served as mayor from 1955–1976 and commanded a powerful political machine. During his terms in office Chicago's downtown underwent a period of significant redevelopment.   *Source: James Quinn/MCT/Landov*

congressman from Chicago's South Side, announced his candidacy for mayor in 1982, blacks quickly rallied around him. Washington was a Democrat with no ties to the machine. His solid reform credentials and progressive policy agenda earned him support not only among blacks but also among Hispanics and liberal whites. In spring of 1983 Harold Washington became Chicago's first African American mayor.

Like Byrne, Washington was forced to reach an accommodation with a city council dominated by machine politicians he had criticized during his election campaign. Unlike Byrne, however, Washington maintained his independence from the machine as mayor. His economic development plan called for "balanced growth" between downtown and the city's low-income and working-class neighborhoods. To help facilitate this, neighborhood leaders were placed in top positions in the new administration. Although obstructionist council members successfully blocked certain policies and programs, Washington still managed to redirect the benefits of government policy in favor of less-privileged city residents to a far greater extent than his predecessors. Washington's tenure proved to be short-lived, however. In fall of 1987, the mayor fell victim to a fatal heart attack. Efforts to reassemble Washington's multiracial coalition failed, and Richard M. Daley, son of the former machine boss, was elected mayor in 1989.

INDUSTRY, COMMERCE, AND LABOR

Chicago's economy, like that of other large cities in the Northeast and Midwest was dominated by manufacturing during the years following World War II. In 1952 one of every three city workers was employed in manufacturing. While factory jobs frequently involved difficult and even dangerous working conditions, such jobs typically had the advantage of providing living-wage employment without substantial formal education requirements. Many blacks and other minorities who moved to Chicago during the post–World War II period found steady, well-paying work in manufacturing despite having limited formal schooling.

This situation would soon change, however. Manufacturing in Chicago originally developed in areas of the city with the best access to rail and port facilities for the shipping and receiving of goods. Land was costly in the best locations, so industrial buildings were often constructed several stories high in order to use the land as intensively as possible. By the 1950s, however, the construction of new highways and growth of truck transportation opened up new locations for industrial development. By this time, large industries were increasingly making use of assembly-line production. Such industries preferred one-story buildings on large parcels of land over the multistory factory buildings that dominated Chicago's existing industrial areas. Large areas of vacant land for new factory buildings were difficult to find within city limits. As a result, industries began an exodus to the suburbs and beyond that would greatly diminish the contribution of manufacturing to the city's economy during the remainder of the twentieth century.

The 1970s and 1980s were the peak years of industrial decline in Chicago. Between 1972 and 1983, Chicago lost more than one hundred thirty thousand manufacturing jobs. By 1982 the combination of deindustrialization and a pronounced national economic recession drove the city's unemployment rate to 17 percent, a postwar high. African Americans and other minorities were particularly hard hit by deindustrialization. Due to racial discrimination and lack of seniority in the workplace, minority workers were frequently the first to be laid off during economic downturns. Industrial decline played a key role in the long-term joblessness that surfaced in many of Chicago's predominantly minority neighborhoods by the 1970s.

The decline of Chicago's manufacturing base was accompanied by a dramatic building boom in the downtown area, initiated during the 1950s under the Richard J. Daley administration and continued under subsequent administrations. The construction of new office towers and other development downtown created new job opportunities that helped offset the loss of manufacturing employment. Analysts began to speak of a "manufacturing-services shift" in which downtown service-sector jobs would become the major source of employment for cities like Chicago in the postindustrial era. The problem with the new service economy, however, was that positions requiring less in the way of training and formal education—such as janitorial services, clerks, and retail workers—were generally low paying. Many displaced manufacturing workers would find it difficult to match their former industrial wages with new positions in the service sector.

During the 1980s some analysts and community leaders began to take a closer look at deindustrialization in Chicago. Studies showed that, in some cases, at least, industrial companies had a strong interest in remaining in the city but were being forced to leave by unsupportive policies. For example, land adjacent to industrial districts was sometimes rezoned for residential development, producing conflicts between industries and new residents upset with the noise and odors of industrial development. The Harold Washington administration's commitment to balanced growth emphasized balance between downtown development and manufacturing. During the 1980s Washington administration officials studied ways of preserving Chicago's manufacturing base and initiated a number of retention programs targeting key industrial sectors and areas of the city determined to be most suitable for industrial development. Certain of these programs proved to be effective in preserving a role for manufacturing in Chicago's economy.

RACE, ETHNICITY, AND IMMIGRATION

Chicago has long been one of America's most segregated cities. Prior to World War II, its black population was relatively small, representing about 8 percent of the city's total population in 1940. Black residents were concentrated in a long, narrow corridor on the South Side and several smaller areas west of downtown. Living conditions were for the most part extremely poor. Many homes had been constructed to temporarily house residents following the Great Chicago Fire of 1871 and were no longer suitable for occupation. Following World War II the city's black population swelled as southern blacks migrated north to seek employment in Chicago industries. By the early 1950s the number of black residents had increased to four hundred ninety-two thousand, representing 14 percent of Chicago's total population. The boundaries of Chicago's black residential areas expanded, but not enough to accommodate the influx of new residents. Overcrowding became a pressing concern.

The post–World War II period represented an opportunity to reduce segregation in Chicago. Using funds provided by the federal Housing Act of 1949 for slum clearance and construction of public housing, city officials embarked on an ambitious urban renewal program to rebuild areas of the city designated by planning officials as blighted. Included in the program were the city's mostly black neighborhoods on the South and West Sides. The Chicago Housing Authority developed a plan to build new public housing developments for low-income residents in white areas of the city, a strategy that could have helped integrate white neighborhoods. However, the city council gained control over the location of new public housing developments and rejected the housing authority's plan. Instead, new housing developments were concentrated in mostly black areas, reinforcing existing patterns of segregation. To make matters worse, the construction of public housing in Chicago emphasized high-rise buildings such as the notorious 4,312-unit Robert Taylor Homes on the South Side. Although this strategy was consistent with the views of prominent urban planners at the time, it proved to be a colossal failure.

Public housing and urban renewal did not end the housing shortage for blacks in Chicago, since more housing units were demolished than were constructed under the program. During the 1960s expansion of the boundaries of black areas of the city did not keep pace with the continued influx of new black residents, and black leaders called for open housing policies that would prevent discrimination against black renters and homebuyers seeking to locate in white neighborhoods. In 1966 Martin Luther King Jr. led a series of marches into white areas of the city and the suburbs protesting housing discrimination. Negotiations with Mayor Richard J. Daley culminated in the signing of an open housing agreement that summer, but weak enforcement provisions limited its effectiveness. With blacks representing a growing share of the city's voting population, Daley was eager to avoid a confrontation with King. At the same time, Daley did not wish to antagonize the white ethnic voters who formed the core of his political base. It was a difficult balance to strike. When King was assassinated two years later in April 1968, the mostly black West Side erupted in violence. Daley drew widespread criticism and further antagonized the city's black population by ordering police to shoot suspected looters and arsonists on sight. By the time of Daley's death in 1976, blacks were no longer a reliable source of votes for the machine.

By the 1960s the increase in Chicago's black population was accompanied by rapid growth of the city's Latino population. In 1960 Latinos represented only 3 percent of city residents. By 1983 the number had increased to 17 percent. Settlement patterns for Latinos differed from those of blacks, with Latino residents dispersed among different areas of the city to a far greater extent than African Americans. By 1980 many of the city's fifty wards contained significant numbers of Latino residents. As a result, despite the low-income status of many Latinos, they did not experience the concentrated poverty that many blacks did. As their numbers increased, Latino voters became increasingly important in local elections. Harold Washington won mayoral elections in 1983 and 1987 due in part to support among Latino voters. Latinos also helped Richard M. Daley win his first mayoral contest in 1989.

See also *Chicago, IL 1854–1877; Chicago, IL 1877–1896; Chicago, IL 1896–1929; Chicago, IL 1929–1941; Chicago, IL 1941–1952; Chicago, IL 1989–2011*

JOEL RAST

BIBLIOGRAPHY

Biles, Roger. *Richard J. Daley: Politics, Race, and the Governing of Chicago*. DeKalb: Northern Illinois University Press, 1995.

Hirsch, Arnold R. *Making the Second Ghetto: Race and Housing in Chicago, 1940–1960*. Chicago, IL: University of Chicago Press, 1998.

Meyerson, Martin, and Edward C. Banfield. *Politics, Planning, and the Public Interest: The Case of Public Housing in Chicago*. New York, NY: Free Press of Glencoe, 1955.

Rast, Joel. *Remaking Chicago: The Political Origins of Urban Industrial Change*. DeKalb: Northern Illinois University Press, 1999.

Seligman, Amanda I. *Block by Block: Neighborhoods and Public Policy on Chicago's West Side*. Chicago, IL: University of Chicago Press, 2005.

Squires, Gregory D., Larry Bennett, Kathleen McCourt, and Philip Nyden: *Chicago: Race, Class, and the Response to Urban Decline*. Philadelphia, PA: Temple University Press, 1987.

LOS ANGELES, CA 1952–1989

IN AN AGE WHEN THE POPULATION OF THE CITY OF LOS ANGELES ALMOST DOUBLED, from roughly two million to four million between 1952 and 1989, there was extraordinary optimism as well as deep disillusionment among the city's residents. Major cultural and political events during the 1950s and 1960s brought national and international publicity, such as the 1957 arrival of the Brooklyn Dodgers, who won the World Series the following year, and the Democratic National Convention in 1960. The Music Center for the Performing Arts, which opened in 1964, provided an important venue for classical music, opera, and theater on the West Coast. A freeway system, which city officials had already begun discussing in the 1920s, rapidly expanded in the 1950s and 1960s. Many Angelenos looked upon such events with pride. At the same time, the city's residents expressed serious concerns over race relations, urban blight, and the environment. These conflicting perceptions resulted in a population divided over living conditions and how to approach the political, economic, and social challenges that Los Angeles faced.

Air quality decreased markedly during the postwar era, a result mainly of industrial and automobile pollution. The Sylmar Earthquake of 1971 demonstrated once again that seismic shifts remained a perennial threat to the region. Finally, the passage of Proposition 13 in 1978, led by Los Angeles political activist Howard Jarvis, represented a different kind of seismic shift in the form of a tax revolt and hence substantial loss of tax income to the city; the statewide initiative, which became an amendment to the California state constitution, limited the tax rate on real estate to no more than 1 percent of the property's value. Proposition 13 resulted in an immediate decline in spending on public schools, city services, and investment in infrastructure.

Despite these harsh realities, a sense of optimism pervaded much discourse on the city as Angelenos entered the 1980s. A popular mayor with an increasingly "global city" outlook suggested that a bright future lay ahead, which the celebration of the Los Angeles Bicentennial in 1981 seemed to confirm. The highlight of the decade, the 1984 Los Angeles Olympics, indeed showed not only how Angelenos wanted to view themselves, but that they could work together to achieve common goals. Residents and visitors saw a city that functioned efficiently and where smog was kept to a minimum, in part because residents cooperated to keep the freeways relatively free of congestion near events. Although the city invested relatively little in terms of infrastructure, the Olympics generated over $2 billion in estimated economic impact and ended with the unheard-of profit of $232.5 million, part of which is still invested in support of youth sports in Southern California. Yet with expanding gang-related crime in the central and southeastern sections of the city, and an escalating drug epidemic that fueled much of that crime, by the end of the decade few could ignore the serious and abiding urban problems for which there were few ready solutions.

QUICK FACTS

LOS ANGELES, CA **1952–1989**

MAYORS

Fletcher Bowron	(1938–1953)
Norris Poulson	(1953–1961)
Sam Yorty	(1961–1973)
Tom Bradley	(1973–1993)

MAJOR INDUSTRIES AND EMPLOYERS

Automobile industry
Aircraft and aerospace industries
Entertainment industry
Garment industry
City and county government

DAILY NEWSPAPERS

Los Angeles Times

Los Angeles Herald-Examiner (until 1989)
Los Angeles Sentinel
La Opinión

MAJOR EVENTS

1957: The Brooklyn Dodgers move to Los Angeles as one of the city's first major league sports teams.
1964: The Music Center for the Performing Arts opens, representing a new era in the performance and support of arts and culture in Los Angeles.
1965: The Watts Riot is the largest urban uprising in the city's history up to that time.
1971: The Sylmar Earthquake hits Southern California, killing sixty-five people and causing $500 million in damage.
1984: Los Angeles hosts the Olympic Summer Games for the second time in the city's history.

GOVERNMENT AND POLITICS

Los Angeles was never an easy city to govern. Its physical layout gives an indication of the challenges that legislators faced. After decades of annexation of neighboring cities, largely over water rights, Los Angeles grew to comprise urban, industrial, and rural sections covering a patchwork area of almost 470 square miles, with a thin corridor to the port at San Pedro to the south and the addition of the massive San Fernando Valley to the north. Progressive reforms in the early twentieth century created a decentralized system of government that theoretically distributed control of the city among different and often competing coalitions. Since the charter of 1925, the mayor, fifteen council members (each representing one district), and citizen commissions appointed by the mayor shared control in managing the city. They all contended with a board of five supervisors who governed Los Angeles County as a whole, with each supervisor elected by residents of one of five districts; a county board had been in place since 1852. The view at the time was that this system of shared governance was the only way to overcome the pervasive graft and corruption that characterized civic politics in many other American cities during the late-nineteenth and early-twentieth centuries. Led by progressive reformer John Randolph Haynes in the first two decades of the twentieth century, Angelenos spearheaded such statewide legislative landmarks as the referendum, the recall, and the initiative with the purpose of furthering the public interest. In the eyes of many reformers, then, Los Angeles would represent a fabled "city on a hill."

That goal was exceedingly optimistic. When Judge Fletcher Bowron became mayor in 1938, the city was mired in massive corruption in both local government and the Los Angeles Police Department (LAPD). While Bowron's administration successfully curbed much of the corruption, by the early 1950s his long tenure in power was coming to an end. After he lobbied for a large housing complex for low-income residents in response to the huge increase in the postwar population, his moderate Republican opponent, Norris Poulson, successfully portrayed Bowron as a backward socialist whose time was over.

Poulson enjoyed the solid backing of the *Los Angeles Times* and much of Los Angeles's business community, and as the next mayor he oversaw a dynamic economic expansion in industry, transportation, and trade. He established a program to rebuild downtown Los Angeles, which had been in decline since the 1930s, and with owner Walter O'Malley encouraged the move of the Brooklyn Dodgers to Los Angeles as part of that initiative. Poulson also worked toward racial integration in the police and fire departments and fought Detroit to build cleaner cars—essential for a city government that believed automobiles and buses represented the future of urban transportation. The subsequent demise of public rail transport by the end of the 1950s (the Red Car and Yellow Car lines), and the expansion of a freeway system based on federal funding, formed part of the dramatic change in the city's transportation networks.

In some ways, Los Angeles preceded the nation's shift to more liberal policies in the 1960s. Poulson lost his reelection bid in 1957 to Democratic challenger Sam Yorty, in part by losing the black vote over the issue of police brutality. Yorty was a renegade Democrat who campaigned for Richard Nixon over John F. Kennedy in the presidential election of 1960 and built his powerbase on a multiracial coalition with little support from the Democratic Party. Yorty's administration, which moved further to the right during his tenure in office, signaled suburban distrust with politics as usual, anger over tax increases, and the city's distinct transition to the Westside, or the western section of the city, in terms of corporate and political power; in the postwar era, many affluent Angelenos moved to the Westside, where the entertainment industry was also predominantly located.

Yorty's successor, Tom Bradley, was the longest-serving mayor thus far in Los Angeles history. Building on the idea from previous administrations of multiracial coalitions, the African American politician and former police officer joined liberal whites, many of them Jews, with the African American vote in 1973. During his first decade in office, Bradley tirelessly promoted Los Angeles as the "gateway to the world" in vaunting world trade and rebuilding downtown. He encouraged foreign investment, and by 1979 over a quarter of the major properties downtown were foreign-owned. Some estimates claim that as much as 75 percent of downtown properties were foreign-owned by 1985. Chief owners came from Canada, Japan, and Europe; Japanese real-estate investment in Los Angeles in 1988, for example, topped $3 billion. At the peak of his power, Bradley presided over a highly profitable XXIII Olympiad under the able direction of Orange County businessman Peter Ueberroth.

The city's prospects, however, appeared to wane by the late 1980s. Ambitious to become the state's first African American governor, Bradley seemed to lose his golden touch on local matters. As manufacturing and commerce in the city departed to the outer sections of Greater Los Angeles and beyond, the tax base dwindled, and those trapped in inner-city ghettoes saw little way out. The federal government reduced social welfare spending in the 1980s, and the cumulative effect of Proposition 13 continued to limit revenues, further weakening investment in public schools and infrastructure. An inability to control the rise in Latino and black gangs, which took in huge profits in part from the expanding crack cocaine trade, helped to undermine Bradley's image as a race unifier as the city's electorate became increasingly divided. Ongoing concerns over inflation, crime, smog, and even the threatened secession of the San Fernando Valley all posed significant challenges in Los Angeles city politics.

INDUSTRY, COMMERCE, AND LABOR

The economies of the city and county of Los Angeles have long been intertwined, and it is difficult if not impossible to distill one completely from the other. Several significant points about industry, commerce, and labor in the city, however, can be determined. Both manufacturing and entertainment have played central roles in the Los Angeles economy since the first half of the twentieth century. Joining the traditional industries of automobile, steel, and tire, major industries and employers in Los Angeles during this period were aircraft, aerospace, and textiles. During their peak in the 1960s and 1970s, the aircraft and aerospace industries (dominated by Douglas, Northrop, Lockheed, and Hughes Aircraft) provided over 40 percent of all manufacturing jobs in the Greater Los Angeles region, employing half a million people. While some industrial plants were within the city's boundaries, such as in North Hollywood, many of the aerospace jobs were increasingly in cities just outside of the City of Los Angeles (Canoga Park, Lancaster, Torrance, and Glendale). The sheer presence of the aircraft and aerospace industries, however, continued to lend credence to Los Angeles's self-proclaimed image as the city of the future until the end of the 1980s.

The postwar era saw an enormous upheaval in the film industry following Hollywood's Golden Age (1927–1948). Almost all of the "Big Eight" studios were based in Los Angeles or had operations in or near the city: MGM, Warner Bros., Universal, Paramount, United Artists, Twentieth Century-Fox, Columbia, and RKO. With the loss of an antitrust suit in 1948, however, coupled with declining audience attendance, these studios began divesting their theater chains in the 1950s while at the same time competing with television for audience share. As a result, most studios either were bought up by large corporations or financiers or went bankrupt: fabled studio RKO ended production in 1957, MCA purchased Universal in 1962, Gulf+Western bought Paramount in 1966, and other studios experienced similar financial and managerial turmoil. The release of major blockbusters in the 1970s, however, saw a rebound in the industry's profits and film audiences. By the 1980s the film industry was on far better financial footing and once again a major employer and tax base for the city.

Another impact on the Los Angeles economy came from federal and state grants. Under Mayors Poulson and Yorty, such grants were viewed suspiciously; under Bradley, such grants were welcomed with the goal of spurring downtown redevelopment. State and federal grants grew from $99.1 million in fiscal year 1972 to $412.7 million six years later. In 1978 alone, federal grants amounted to $275 million. Of that amount it is estimated that 66 percent went to low- and moderate-income groups. With the formation of the Community Redevelopment Agency (CRA), tax rates were frozen in areas declared "blighted," followed by the purchase of property by the CRA and the search for federal and state grants for development. The money CRA amassed was significant; in 1988 Bradley declared he would use $2 billion of CRA funds for public housing—the kind of program over which Mayor Bowron had lost his position more than three decades previously.

As the traditional manufacturing base in automobiles and steel declined in the 1980s, the garment industry exploded along with downtown redevelopment. From a handful of manufacturers in 1953, over one thousand five hundred apparel manufacturers had formed by the early 1990s (mainly Jewish-, European-, Chinese-, and Korean-owned), employing up to forty-three thousand workers (although exact numbers in the industry are difficult to determine due to the widespread use of undocumented labor). The garment industry soon occupied an area of downtown comprising eighty-eight square blocks (between Seventh Street and the Santa Monica Freeway to the north and south, and Broadway and San Pedro Streets to the east and west), making Los Angeles second only to New York City in terms of garment production. With the feminization of labor, the industry relied heavily on immigrant women from Asia and Mexico, often working in low-paid sweatshop jobs that in 1990 paid an average of $7,200 per year (when the annual minimum wage was $8,840 per year). By 1991 combined sales annually (much of it for women's wear) were $6.2 billion (or an average of $34.1 million per firm), and total annual profits of the garment industry in Los Angeles were $100 million.

Far from the city's core, one of the critical engines for the Los Angeles economy was the Port of Los Angeles. Founded in 1907 at San Pedro, the port enabled Los Angeles to become the fishing, shipbuilding, and cannery center of Southern California. Joined in 1911 by Long Beach Harbor, which forms part of the same bay, over twenty million tons of shipping passed through the city's main port by 1950. Starkist opened the largest tuna cannery in the world at Terminal Island (adjacent to San Pedro) in 1952, although the cannery closed in 1985 due to high labor costs. Automobiles were also a major part of the port business. The beginning of the Japanese auto industry in America began in 1956, when the first Toyotas arrived. While they were soon shipped back due to poor quality, the introduction in the early 1960s of the Corolla made automobile history, and the Port of Los Angeles subsequently benefited from the rapidly growing demand for Japanese cars.

The construction of the port's first container terminal in 1960, and the expansion of trade with Japan, Taiwan, Korea, and finally China, greatly increased operations. To improve shipping and distribution of consumer products, with minimal reliance on the clogged freeway system, the creation of the Alameda Corridor in the 1980s provided rail lines faster transport of crates from the port to inland distribution networks. By 1989 the combined Port of Los Angeles at San Pedro and Long Beach topped New York and New Jersey, with 66.3 million metric tons in fiscal year 1988–1989 at San Pedro and 68.9 million metric tons of cargo at nearby Long Beach, which represented an increase of 8.3 percent over the previous year.

RACE, ETHNICITY, AND IMMIGRATION

As the population of Los Angeles increased between 1952 and 1989, it correspondingly became ethnically diverse. In 1950 the city population was 1,970,358 out of a county population of 4,151,687. Almost 90 percent of the city population was white, whereas the nonwhite population was listed at 211,585, of which 171,209 were African Americans. A marked shift in demographics was already clear by 1960, however, when 83.2 percent of the city population was white, 14 percent African American, 11 percent Latino, and 3 percent Asian. Whites were thus 2,061,808 in a total population of 2,479,015, whereas African Americans comprised 334,916, Latinos 260,389, and Asians 74,592. In almost all districts of the city except the southeastern section, whites were still in the majority in 1960, in part due to "redlining" or housing restrictions based on race. African Americans were largely confined to the Central Avenue district, West Adams district, and Furlong district in southeastern Los Angeles. Latinos lived mainly in the Eastside neighborhoods of Boyle Heights and Lincoln Heights, although during the 1960s they began moving into the downtown area as whites migrated outward to the suburbs.

Arising in part from these racial divisions were several race riots in the early 1960s, which culminated in the Watts Riot of August 11–16, 1965. The riot reflected deep tensions and anger among many members of the city's black community over issues of police brutality, housing, education, and healthcare. Following the riot, Governor Pat Brown appointed a commission to investigate the reasons for the uprising, which resulted in the McCone Report, named after the head of the group, former CIA director John A. McCone. Among the results from the study were the creation of the Martin Luther King Jr. Hospital, employment programs, and a police commission to oversee relations between the LAPD and the city's residents.

By 1970 demographic trends from the previous decade picked up strength. As whites continued to migrate out of the city, they fell to 77.2 percent of the city population (2,173,600 out of 2,816,061), and that percentage continued to fall; by 1980 it was 61.2 percent (1,816,761 out of 2,966,850). Blacks achieved their peak in terms of percentage of population by 1970, with 503,606, or 17.9 percent. Similarly, Latinos saw their numbers increase from 519,842 in 1970 to 816,076 a decade later, a percentage change from 18 percent of the city population to almost 28 percent. By 1990 that number had increased to 1,391,411, or almost triple what the Latino population had been twenty years earlier.

Demographic changes also occurred within the Asian community. Predominantly Japanese in 1950, it shifted to mainly Korean, Chinese, and Southeast Asian immigrants during the 1960s and 1970s. The 1965 Immigration Act, which ended the discriminatory quota system and favored the family-preference system, contributed to the great increase in Asian and Latin American immigration. Although not growing as fast as the Latino population, Asians comprised 6.6 percent of the city population in 1980 (195,997) and 9.2 percent in 1990 (320,668). While maintaining their base in Chinatown and Koreatown in Los Angeles, Asians began migrating to the suburbs during the 1970s, especially in the eastern and central San Gabriel Valley, and that migration continued to grow in the 1980s.

See also *Los Angeles, CA 1896–1929; Los Angeles, CA 1929–1941; Los Angeles, CA 1941–1952; Los Angeles, CA 1989–2011*

KENNETH H. MARCUS

BIBLIOGRAPHY

Allen, James P., and Eugene Turner, *Changing Faces, Changing Places: Mapping Southern Californians*. Northridge, CA: Center for Geographical Studies, 2002.

Bonacich, Edna, and Richard P. Appelbaum. *Behind the Label: Inequality in the Apparel Industry*. Berkeley: University of California Press, 2000.

Bureau of Labor Statistics. http://data.bls.gov/cgi-bin/srgate

Davis, Mike. *City of Quartz: Excavating the Future in Los Angeles*. New York, NY: Vintage, 1992.

Fulton, William. *The Reluctant Metropolis: The Politics of Urban Growth in Los Angeles*. Baltimore, MD: Johns Hopkins University Press, 2001.

Los Angeles Almanac. http://www.laalmanac.com/LA/index.htm

Pitt, Leonard, and Dale Pitt. *Los Angeles A to Z: An Encyclopedia of the City and County*. Berkeley: University of California Press, 1997.

Sonenshein, Raphael. *Politics in Black and White: Race and Power in Los Angeles*. Princeton, NJ: Princeton University Press, 1993.

PHILADELPHIA, PA 1952–1989

IN THE YEARS 1952–1989 PHILADELPHIA UNDERWENT A MASSIVE REDUCTION IN POPULA-TION and a process of deindustrialization that left the city fiscally shaky and beset by poverty, racial animosity, and a shrinking middle class. By the end of the era, however, new economic vitality could be seen in the education and medical sectors, including research, and pharmaceuticals. Politically, the city's long-ruling Republican Party machine was defeated and replaced by a Democratic Party machine swept into office amid calls for reform, inclusivity, and enhanced powers for city government.

GOVERNMENT AND POLITICS

When the Pennsylvania legislature passed the First Class City Home Rule Act in 1949, it enabled the drafting and adoption of a charter for the city of Philadelphia. A bipartisan effort emerged, aided by the Greater Philadelphia Movement, a reform-minded business organization. The Philadelphia Home Rule City Charter Commission wrote the charter, and it was overwhelmingly approved by a referendum of Philadelphia voters in the spring of 1951. The charter became active on January 7, 1952, opening a new era in Philadelphia municipal governance. The

QUICK FACTS

PHILADELPHIA, PA **1952–1989**

MAYORS

Joseph S. Clark Jr.	(1952–1956)
Richardson Dilworth	(1956–1962)
James Hugh Joseph Tate	(1962–1972)
Frank L. Rizzo	(1972–1980)
William J. Green III	(1980–1984)
W. Wilson Goode	(1984–1992)

MAJOR INDUSTRIES AND EMPLOYERS

Local, state, and federal
    government

Universities and colleges (education,
    medical research, hospitals)

Chemicals, petroleum, and
    pharmaceuticals

Transportation

Financial services and insurance

MAJOR NEWSPAPERS

Philadelphia Inquirer
Philadelphia Daily News
Philadelphia Evening Bulletin

MAJOR EVENTS

1952: Joseph Clark, the first Democrat elected mayor of Philadelphia since the Civil War era, takes office.

1964: The Columbia Avenue riot, a three-day riot in North Philadelphia at the height of the civil rights era, occurs.

1968: Girard College is desegregated—a major victory for civil rights advocates, including Cecil B. Moore.

1976: The nation's bicentennial is celebrated with a major patriotic celebration held in the city. It had been planned to accompany a world's fair that ultimately never materialized due to racial strife and political dysfunction.

1984: M. Wilson Goode takes office as the first African American mayor of Philadelphia.

Home Rule Charter created a strong-mayor municipal government, with a mayor limited to two four-year terms, and established the office of the managing director, an official appointed by and answering directly to the mayor, who would oversee the increasingly complex administrative functions of the municipal government. The city council consisted of seventeen members, ten representing districts and seven elected at-large. A provision of the charter called for two of the city council's members to come from the minority party. Reform of the civil service took place immediately, doing away with a strict patronage system of city jobs awarded for political loyalty. The Civil Service Commission now served the role of putting forward names of job candidates on a merit system.

While the new home rule charter was taking shape in Philadelphia, scandals and corruption under the administration of Republican Bernard Samuel provided an opportunity for reform Democrats to challenge the longstanding supremacy of the city's Republican Party machine. Two Democratic reformers stepped forward: Joseph S. Clark and Richardson Dilworth. Dilworth, an attorney and World War II veteran, had unsuccessfully challenged Samuel in 1947, but in doing so had garnered more votes than any Democrat in a mayoral election. Clark, also a decorated World War II veteran, was elected to the city controller position in 1949. Clark and Dilworth joined forces with local members of the Americans for Democratic Action and brought together reformers for public housing, civil rights, labor, and civil service reform. Clark was elected mayor in 1951, and Dilworth was elected district attorney, both taking office in 1952.

Municipal governance in Philadelphia changed rapidly after the election of Clark, with a turn toward technocratic, professional leadership over strict party loyalty. Particularly active were the city's redevelopment authority and planning commission, under the direction of Edmund N. Bacon. Bacon returned from World War II and went to work helping to plan the 1947 Better Philadelphia Exhibition, a popular display of urban planning ideas showing what the city might look like after sustained urban renewal. Bacon ascended to the planning commission's directorship in 1949, and remained in the post until 1970. In this role, Bacon became one of the most prominent urban planners in the United States. He became associated with the type of urban renewal sweeping American cities at the time, focusing on the clearance of "slum" neighborhoods that had seen little economic investment since the Great Depression; the construction of highrise public housing, new highways, and public transportation; and the redevelopment of center city business districts. Bacon's most famous project was Society Hill, a demographically mixed working-class neighborhood in one of the city's most historically significant areas. Using eminent domain powers, the redevelopment authority and planning commission redeveloped Society Hill, clearing out hundreds of homes and creating new parks and walkways in a "greenway" system imagined by Bacon. At the highest point in the neighborhood, the Society Hill Towers, three new apartment buildings designed by modernist I. M. Pei were constructed and were marketed to upper-income Philadelphians who might decide to stay in the city and enjoy its amenities rather than decamp for the suburbs. Bacon's efforts in Society Hill landed him on the cover of *Time* magazine in 1964, the epitome of professionalism in urban renewal. Over time, however, urban renewal was more and more faulted for its excesses in the exercise of eminent domain powers, particularly when those targeted for removal were often poor and/or minority residents. By the time he left the planning commission in 1970, Bacon's ideas had become extremely controversial, and top-down planning efforts in American cities were more and more frequently met with robust community protest.

Joseph Clark left the mayor's office to successfully run for the U.S. Senate in 1956, allowing Dilworth the chance to run for mayor, which he easily won—holding office until 1962, when he resigned to run for governor. Dilworth's successor, James Tate, defeated reformer and Dilworth-Clark ally Walter Phillips. Tate came up through the city council and is widely considered to have marked a return to "machine politics" in Philadelphia, this time under Democratic control. Under Tate the city saw economic decline and civil unrest on a massive scale. At the end of Tate's two terms, the city elected its first Italian American mayor, the highly controversial and iconoclastic former police chief Frank Rizzo. Rizzo's hard-nosed policing tactics, particularly in the midst of racial strife, won him great favor in the white ethnic working-class neighborhoods of South Philadelphia and the city's river wards. Rizzo's endorsement of Richard Nixon for reelection in 1972 signaled a turn against the liberal establishment politics of the Clark-Dilworth-Tate years. Rizzo raised the city's wage tax and tried unsuccessfully to push through a charter reform that would have allowed him to run for a third term as mayor; the effort was blocked by voters

W. Wilson Goode, a Democrat and Philadelphia's first African American mayor, took office in 1984. In 1989 Goode (far right) appointed Deputy Police Commissioner Robert F. Armstrong (left) as Special Assistant to the Mayor for Drug Control.

Source: AP Photo/Bill Cramer

2-1. Following Rizzo, William Green was elected and faced an enormously challenging legacy of a shrinking tax base and public debt leftover from the Rizzo administration. Green's most significant move as mayor was perhaps in naming W. Wilson Goode to be the city's first African American managing director. Goode had been a longstanding advocate of the poor and minorities in the city and had challenged Rizzo's administration directly on the issue of minority representation in the fire and police departments. Following Green, Goode was elected in 1983 and became Philadelphia's first African American mayor—a triumph of the civil rights movement and an achievement that would have been unthinkable even in the liberal Clark-Dilworth years.

INDUSTRY, COMMERCE, AND LABOR

Deindustrialization was the predominant economic trend in postwar Philadelphia and remained so throughout the period. The city's population grew by over 7 percent in the 1940s, driven by the manufacturing needs of World War II and another great wave of African American northward migration. During World War II every industry in the city—from shipbuilding to electronics to medical device manufacturing—was operating at full steam. Philadelphia was truly, as it has been described, the "arsenal of democracy," receiving one in six federal dollars spent toward the war effort. For example, the Philadelphia Quartermaster Depot had been in operation since the nineteenth century and during the 1930s cranked out over six hundred thousand uniforms for the Civilian Conservation Corps and other New Deal programs. During World War II all uniforms (over eight million) either were made at or passed through this operation in South Philadelphia, and it grew accordingly, employing many thousands of seamstresses and tailors as well as support personnel. In 1965 the depot was downsized, and in 1993 all textile-making operations at the location ceased. This serves as a microcosm for the bigger economic picture of Philadelphia through and after the postwar years, as manufacturing swelled the city's population and led to rapid expansions of infrastructure, then declining government contracts and the movement of manufacturing to less costly locations drained the industrial lifeblood of the city. In 1950 the city's population stood at 2.07 million; by 1990 it was 1.59 million.

By the mid-1950s it was becoming clear to political leadership that a process was underway that was shrinking the demand for industrial labor. Additionally, workplace discrimination added to the difficulty of maintaining solid employment among the city's African American population. The creation of the Philadelphia Industrial Development Corporation (PIDC) as a collaboration between the city of Philadelphia and the Greater Philadelphia Chamber of Commerce in 1958 signified the recognized need for attractive industrial land, revitalized industrial facilities, and tactics to lure new industries to the region. Working with Lyndon Johnson–era programs like Model Cities, PIDC found some success in stemming the tide of job losses. However, Philadelphia—much like its industrial peers such as Detroit and St. Louis—found it very hard to use public policy effectively to convince employers not to move operations south and west, or overseas. With high rents, old infrastructure, and relatively high labor costs, manufacturers in Philadelphia were looking to move by the 1960s and 1970s. Filling the employment void left behind, the region saw the "eds and meds" sector gaining traction. By the end of the era under review, the city's anchor institutions such as the University of Pennsylvania, Jefferson Hospital and Medical College, Drexel University, and Temple University were employing tens of thousands of Philadelphians. Added to this trend, the explosive growth of the pharmaceutical industry—led by Merck, GlaxoSmithKline, and other firms—demonstrated that the region could reinvent itself as a "knowledge-based" economy. It should be noted that though Philadelphia's place as an industrial giant had been badly diminished by 1989, and the city's population showed this effect, the regional economy and population had both grown dramatically. Federal highway and home lending policies after World War II, as well as relocation of employers across the city line in favor of cheaper land and lower taxes, fed this process.

RACE, ETHNICITY, AND IMMIGRATION

Philadelphia entered the postwar era with one of the nation's largest African American communities. As such, as the civil rights movement began to take shape across the country, Philadelphia's role was substantial. After the home rule charter was passed, the city established a Commission on Human Relations. Calls for fair housing and workplace equality were frequently voiced in the African American community, with desegregation of schools another major issue, especially after *Brown v. Board of Education* (1954). At the same time that many of the reform-minded political leaders of the 1950s and 1960s were showing a willingness to address racial disparities, the city's urban renewal policies were exacerbating racial strife. With families moved from "slums" into new housing projects, often near or in traditionally white neighborhoods, racial tensions heated up in the 1960s. In the late summer of 1964, a riot broke out in North Philadelphia near Temple University. Though no one was killed, several thousand were injured and businesses and homes were destroyed, as rioting lasted for three days after a dispute between an African American woman and two policeman (one black, one white) boiled over. Police Commissioner Frank Rizzo's tough police tactics were credited by many whites (and resented by African Americans) in the city for diffusing the riots, as were the peacekeeping efforts of local NAACP director Cecil B. Moore. Civil rights demonstrations marked the era, in one example resulting in the desegregation of Girard College—a school founded by financier Stephen Girard in the nineteenth century for the education of, as Girard put it in his will, "poor, white, male, orphans." Protests and civil disobedience led by Cecil B. Moore resulted in the school's desegregation in 1968.

Throughout the 1960s the city prepared a bid—initially under the direction of Edmund Bacon—for a world's fair to be held alongside the 1976 bicentennial celebration. As planning went forward the federal oversight commission demanded that the city's world's fair Bicentennial Corporation show greater racial inclusivity in its planning. As a result a young fair housing advocate named Catherine Sue Leslie was hired to spearhead the Agenda for Action, a program to make a world's fair in Philadelphia representative of the city's diverse population. Leslie's plan for the fair ultimately settled on a neighborhood-by-neighborhood fair, where the city's multiple racial and ethnic communities could demonstrate their cultures to visitors—a vision that ran directly against the Bicentennial Corporation's desires for a "megastructure" to be built near the 30th Street Station rail complex. In a racially polarized vote, the megastructure won out and the African American community ceased to cooperate with the world's fair plan. Also involved in the planning was African American leader Charles Bowser, who had been named a deputy mayor by James Tate in 1967. By 1972 the Rizzo administration was unable to find a community in Philadelphia willing to allow a world's fair site to be built, and the idea was dropped. The bicentennial itself was largely patriotic and nostalgic, but representative of no innovative ideas and sparsely attended. This incident was just one of many in the era that demonstrated the racial divide of the city and the growing political power of African Americans. Catherine Sue Leslie's mentor, W. Wilson Goode, would go on to be the first African American mayor of the city.

In the mid-1960s the flow of immigrants into Philadelphia picked up pace, as it did across the country, leading to a continued diversification of the city and the region. Though the great majority of these immigrants were Europeans, the immigrant community increasingly included Africans, Asians, Mexicans, Puerto Ricans, and other Latin Americans.

See also *Philadelphia, PA 1776–1790; Philadelphia, PA 1790–1828; Philadelphia, PA 1828–1854; Philadelphia, PA 1854–1877; Philadelphia, PA 1877–1896; Philadelphia, PA 1896–1929; Philadelphia, PA 1929–1941; Philadelphia, PA 1941–1952; Philadelphia, PA 1989–2011*

SCOTT GABRIEL KNOWLES

BIBLIOGRAPHY

Countryman, Matthew J. *Up South: Civil Rights and Black Power in Philadelphia.* Philadelphia: University of Pennsylvania Press, 2005.

Knowles, Scott Gabriel, ed. *Imagining Philadelphia: Edmund Bacon and the Future of the City.* Philadelphia: University of Pennsylvania Press, 2009.

McKee, Guian. *The Problem of Jobs: Liberalism, Race, and Deindustrialization in Philadelphia.* Chicago, IL: University of Chicago Press, 2008.

Weigley, Russell F., ed. *Philadelphia: A 300-Year History.* New York, NY: W. W. Norton Company, 1982.

HOUSTON, TX 1952–1989

HOUSTON LIES AT THE HEADWATER OF BUFFALO BAYOU, a small, shallow watercourse forty miles from Galveston Bay and the Gulf of Mexico. Until well into the twentieth century, the barrier-island city of Galveston was the principal seaport in Texas. After a 1900 hurricane devastated Galveston, Houstonians began lobbying Congress to dredge and widen Buffalo Bayou sufficiently to allow ocean-going vessels to travel inland to load and unload. Galveston and Houston competed with one another for shipping traffic until after World War II, when continuous channel improvements allowed Houston's seaport to handle larger ships. Galveston's location advantage, just inside the entrance of Galveston Bay, was no longer competitive.

Between the censuses of 1950 and 1990, Houston's population nearly tripled, making it one of the fastest-growing American cities. Oil and gas propelled Houston's growth, which was influenced by an ambitious business elite determined to perpetuate the regional boom. In a pattern common to other growing Sunbelt places, Houston's business and political leadership simultaneously exploited federal projects and programs while avoiding regulations at every level of government. However, as in other Sunbelt cities of the postwar era, powerful elites bent on growth adapted to the democratizing effects of the civil rights movement. In Houston political change was further complicated by a Latino population that gained rapidly in numbers and influence, due in large part to Houston's proximity to Mexico, less than three hundred miles to the south.

GOVERNMENT AND POLITICS

In Houston's city government, the mayor is the administrator and chief executive officer, working with a city council. The mayor serves two-year terms, and until 1991 consecutive terms were unlimited. The office of city controller, effectively a treasurer, is also an elected position. Municipal elections are nonpartisan, as throughout Texas.

Houston's mayor in 1952, and from 1956 to 1957, was Oscar Holcombe, a millionaire building contractor and veteran of city politics who had already served ten previous nonconsecutive

QUICK FACTS

HOUSTON, TX 1952–1989

MAYORS

Oscar Holcombe	(1947–1952)
Roy Hofheinz	(1953–1955)
Oscar Holcombe	(1956–1957)
Lewis Cutrer	(1958–1963)
Louie Welch	(1964–1973)
Fred Hofheinz	(1974–1977)
Jim McConn	(1978–1981)
Kathryn Whitmire	(1982–1991)

MAJOR INDUSTRIES AND EMPLOYERS

Federal government
Oil, gas, and energy industries
Medical industry

MAJOR NEWSPAPERS

Houston Post
Houston Chronicle

MAJOR EVENTS

1961: The Manned Spacecraft Center opens in Houston (renamed the Lyndon B. Johnson Space Center in 1973).

1966: By mandate of the U.S. Supreme Court, Houston is divided from one Congressional district into three.

1969: Houston Intercontinental Airport opens (renamed George Bush Intercontinental Airport in 1997).

1979: The U.S. Justice Department suspends local elections to evaluate compliance with the Voting Rights Act.

1981: Kathryn Whitmire is elected the first female mayor of Houston.

terms as mayor beginning in 1921. In 1958 Holcombe lost his last bid for reelection over the desegregation of public swimming pools, which the mayor warned would lead to violence. From 1953 to 1955 lawyer and developer Roy Hofheinz served two terms as mayor, during which he battled the city council for political power. After leaving office, Hofheinz helped lead the financing and construction of the Houston Astrodome and the attraction of the city's first professional sports franchises.

In 1958 Oscar Holcombe was succeeded by former city attorney Lewis Cutrer, who focused on infrastructure development in the service of economic growth. Cutrer's administration helped guide the establishment of a new, larger airport north of the city to accommodate heavy passenger jets (this would eventually be called George Bush Intercontinental Airport). Cutrer also helped resolve Houston's long-term water supply problem, negotiating an intergovernmental agreement with the state's Trinity River Authority.

Cutrer's successor was Louie Welch, a real estate broker and former city councilman who served as mayor from 1964 to 1973. During Welch's tenure, voter registration among blacks rose sharply, and minority activism became meaningful in Houston politics. White politicians had long been indifferent to the concerns of African Americans and Mexican Americans, owing to overt strategies such as the white primary and the poll taxes as well as at-large elections of council members and annexation, both of which diluted minority votes. But by 1967 blacks constituted 17 percent of registered voters and had organized under the rubric of the Harris County

Council of Organizations. Candidates for local office acknowledged the power of the coalition, and in 1969 Welch was challenged by Houston's first black mayoral candidate, Curtis Graves. Although Graves lost, his polling strength among African American and Mexican American voters impressed Welch and other white politicians.

In the 1973 election Welch was defeated by Fred Hofheinz, an attorney and son of Roy Hofheinz. The younger Hofheinz promised a police review board, which black voters had sought, and won with significant support from Houston's African American and Mexican American voters, who have been increasingly critical in every mayoral election since. Throughout the 1970s Houston's energy-related businesses benefitted from increased oil prices following the 1973 Arab oil embargo, and the economies of Houston and Texas expanded.

In 1978 homebuilder and former councilman James McConn became mayor, again with important support from minority voters. McConn served for two terms, after which he was succeeded in 1982 by Houston's first female mayor, Kathryn Whitmire. Whitmire was an accountant and former two-term city controller, another office that she was the first woman to win. Whitmire won an unprecedented five consecutive elections as mayor, a run that inspired a charter amendment limiting Houston's mayors to three consecutive two-year terms.

During Whitmire's mayoral tenure, the hazards of Houston's dependence on the petroleum and gas industries became evident. A collapse in oil prices disrupted the regional economy, leading to a spike in business and personal bankruptcies, unemployment, foreclosures, and bank failures. Population growth stumbled, and real estate values fell sharply. Houstonians strove to diversify their economy, emphasizing aerospace manufacturing and medicine. The Texas Medical Center, already an important nexus for health care and education, became one of the most important such centers in the world. By the end of the 1980s, Houston's boom had regained momentum, fueled by more sustainable enterprises.

In other political developments, population growth and congressional reapportionment mandated by the Supreme Court in 1966 forced the Texas legislature to divide Houston into three Congressional districts; it had previously been represented by only one. Voters in the new 7th District, which included affluent neighborhoods in western Houston, immediately became among the first in Texas to send a Republican to Congress (George H. W. Bush) and the 7th District has elected only Republicans since, reflecting the strength of Texas's conservatism in the late twentieth century.

Houston's post–World War II growth was by 1950 already impressive, and it continued to accelerate. Between 1950 and 1960, Houston's all-time fastest decade of growth, the population soared from approximately five hundred ninety-six thousand to more than nine hundred thirty-eight thousand, an increase of 57.4 percent. The following decades posted uneven though mostly robust gains. The 1980s were complicated by Houston's role in the oil price drop of the mid-1980s. In addition, population change in postwar Houston must be considered in the context of its sprawling metropolitan geography during this period. As Joel Garreau has said, few places model America's so-called edge-city phenomenon better than Houston, with clusters of intense commercial development around the perimeter Interstate 610 loop at the points of intersection with other limited-access freeways. Houston lies at the nexus of Interstates 45 and 59, running north and south, and the nation's southernmost interstate on the east-west transcontinental axis,

Interstate 10. Houston's physical boundaries also expanded significantly during this period, from 160 square miles in 1950 to 433.9 in 1970, and growing again by 1990 to 539.9 square miles.

Houston's population density, approximately three thousand per square mile in the 1990 census, places it among the less densely populated major American cities. Houston's density was relatively stable for the second half of the twentieth century, due to regular annexations that increased the land area of the city. Some annexed areas, such as that surrounding George Bush Intercontinental Airport, lay at the end of narrow ribbons of incorporated territory, reflecting Houston's strenuous efforts to expand into its economic hinterland. Under Texas law, cities have extraterritorial jurisdiction that extends beyond the borders of their general purpose jurisdiction. Houston's reaches up to five miles, where other municipalities or their jurisdictions do not impinge. The City of Houston's robust expansion through annexation preserved its political power, as relatively few suburban enclaves were able to incorporate as municipalities in their own right. Houston thus experienced relatively less diffusion of power than comparably growing American cities in the postwar period.

Houston is the largest American city without comprehensive land-use zoning, although the city's code of ordinances provides for bulk development standards such as lot dimensions. The result is that land uses tend to be governed by deed restrictions and neighborhood covenants. This means that sanctions establishing residential land uses succeed where property owners can afford the legal costs of adopting and enforcing private restrictions and covenants. Elsewhere, residential and commercial land uses may appear close upon one another, and visible home occupations in residential subdivisions are commonplace. Zoning opponents argue that Houston's model of *laissez-faire* land use yields a larger stock of affordable housing. In general, Houston's pattern of horizontal sprawl and suburban expansion closely resembles that of other Sunbelt places.

INDUSTRY, COMMERCE, AND LABOR

Perhaps more so than any southern city, Houston owes its part in America's postwar Sunbelt phenomenon to the federal government. Early in the twentieth century, Congress began appropriating funds to dredge Houston's shipping channel, and it has continued to do so ever since. The sandy, shallow bottom of the bays and tributaries serving the Port of Houston require regular, costly maintenance dredging. Such projects are the exclusive preserve of the U.S. Army Corps of Engineers. Absent this sustained federal support, Houston would not exist as a seaport. Federal investments in the city's transportation infrastructure have continued apace.

Houston's postwar prosperity gained from its wartime role in oil production and transshipment. As the principal seaport in the western Gulf of Mexico, Houston shipped petroleum products to American industrial centers and to the U.S. military and its allies in virtually every theater of war. Texas oil supplied the Allied military on land, at sea, and in the air. The U.S. government's wartime purchases of oil exceeded anything experienced before and created a surge of wealth in Houston, and in Texas generally.

Oil and natural gas dominated the Texas economy throughout the postwar era, and Houston's largest employers usually included such firms as Brown and Root (later KBR), Halliburton, and other energy services firms as well as petroleum companies themselves, oil refineries, and chemical companies that rely on petroleum products in the manufacturing process. Houston firms have increasingly supplied other oil-producing regions with the sophisticated technology and skilled personnel to maximize petroleum recovery from well fields, both on land and offshore.

In 1961 the National Aeronautics and Space Administration (NASA) established its new Manned Spacecraft Center at Clear Lake, Texas, a southeastern suburb of Houston. Houston won the NASA facility in part because of its temperate climate and other attributes, but also due to the influence of the Texas congressional delegation, then near the peak of its power. Former U.S. senator and senate majority leader Lyndon Johnson had just become vice president of the United States. The speaker of the U.S. House of Representatives was the legendary Samuel Rayburn, and veteran congressman Albert Thomas represented the Clear Lake area. Johnson was an especially passionate advocate for the space program, which in 1973 led to the renaming of Houston's Manned Spacecraft Center complex as the Johnson Space Center, following the former president's death in January of that year. Houston's most famous connection with U.S. space programs is the Mission Control Center at the Johnson facility, referred to by NASA's manned space flight communicators simply as "Houston."

NASA's presence rapidly became critical to the region's political economy. On November 21, 1963, President John F. Kennedy visited Houston and spoke at a testimonial dinner for Democratic representative Albert Thomas. In what turned out to be his last formal public speech, President Kennedy wryly noted the large payrolls generated by federal aerospace expenditures in Houston. NASA's initial presence had consisted of 751 transferring employees and 689 new hires. Hiring continued apace, so that by the time of Kennedy's speech, NASA employed more than 2,000 people in Houston. Construction of new facilities multiplied the economic impact of the space center throughout the southeastern part of the state. Celebrating the impact of federal investments in the region was the explicit purpose for the president's trip to Texas that November.

RACE, ETHNICITY, AND IMMIGRATION

In 1958 voters elected a black member to the governing board of the Harris County School District, the first African American since Reconstruction to win election in or around Houston. During the postwar decades, Houston's experience of racial change mirrored that of many Sunbelt cities, in which minorities gained increasing rights owing to judicial breakthroughs such as the U.S. Supreme Court's 1944 *Smith v. Allwright* decision, ending white primary elections—originally a Texas case. Other important civil rights advances followed, including the Supreme Court's 1954 *Brown v. Board of Education* decision outlawing segregated public schools (at which time the Houston Independent School District was probably the largest segregated school district in the country) and the 1962 finding in *Baker v. Carr*, which opened the way for urban voters to sue for equality in legislative apportionment and helped to revolutionize urban politics. In Houston *Baker v. Carr* empowered African Americans as well as Mexican Americans, who by the 1960s had become more numerous than their political influence reflected. The 1965 Voting Rights Act converged on electoral politics along with massive reapportionment.

Even after those reforms began to act on local elections, Houston's white political leaders resisted minority empowerment by maintaining at-large council districts, in which candidates were obliged to campaign before voters throughout the city. In addition, Houston diluted minorities' voting influence by annexing predominantly white areas into the city, which it did during the 1970s in six places. By 1979 only one African American and no Mexican Americans had won election to the city council. As a result, the U.S. Department of Justice suspended that year's election to evaluate Houston's compliance with the Voting Rights Act. Subsequently, the city election laws were revised to divide the fourteen council districts into two categories. Five of the fourteen remained at-large seats, while the remainder became single-district elections. In the election that followed, Houston voters sent three African Americans and one Mexican American to the city council, and minority representation has grown steadily to reflect Houston's increasingly diverse population.

See also *Houston, TX 1989–2011*

ALAN BLISS

BIBLIOGRAPHY

Bayor, Ronald H. "Race, Ethnicity, and Political Change in the Urban Sunbelt South." In *Shades of the Sunbelt: Essays on Ethnicity, Race, and the Urban South,* edited by Randall M. Miller and George E. Pozzetta. Boca Raton: Florida Atlantic University Press, 1989.

Bueger, Walter L., and Joseph A Pratt. *But Also Good Business: Texas Commerce Banks and the Financing of Houston and Texas, 1886–1986.* College Station: Texas A&M University Press, 1986.

Garreau, Joel. *Edge City: Life on the New Frontier.* New York, NY: Doubleday, 1991.

Kaplan, Barry J. "Houston: The Golden Buckle of the Sunbelt." In *Sunbelt Cities: Politics and Growth Since World War II,* edited by Richard M. Bernard and Bradley R. Rice. Austin: University of Texas Press, 1983.

Keller, William H. *Make Haste Slowly: Moderates, Conservatives, and School Desegregation in Houston.* College Station: Texas A&M University Press, 1999.

Leon, Ruben Hernandez. *Metropolitan Migrants: The Migration of Urban Mexicans to the United States.* Berkeley: University of California Press, 2008.

Tharp, Robert N. *Trinity River Authority.* http://www.tshaonline.org/handbook/online/articles/mwt02

Valdez, Zulema. *The New Entrepreneurs: How Race, Class, and Gender Shape American Enterprise.* Stanford, CA: Stanford University Press, 2011.

DETROIT, MI 1952–1989

DETROIT CHANGED A GREAT DEAL BETWEEN the 1950s and the late 1980s. At the beginning of this period, it was the "arsenal of democracy," one of the most important industrial cities in the country. By the end of this period, Detroit was the poster child for the Rustbelt. Over half its population and the vast majority of its industrial stakeholders had fled to the suburbs or outside of the state. Further, by 1989 Detroit was the largest predominantly African American city in North America.

QUICK FACTS

DETROIT, MI **1952–1989**

MAYORS

Albert Cobo	(1950–1957)
Louis Miriani	(1957–1962)
Jerome Cavanagh	(1963–1969)
Roman Gribbs	(1970–1974)
Coleman Young	(1974–1992)

MAJOR INDUSTRIES AND EMPLOYERS

General Motors
Ford Motor Company
Chrysler Motor Company
American Motor Company
Federal government

MAJOR NEWSPAPERS

Detroit News
Detroit Free Press
Detroit Times (until 1960)
Michigan Chronicle

MAJOR EVENTS

1960: With the 1960 census, Detroit's population drops for the first time in 140 years, to 1.67 million, although many believe the exodus began after the 1967 rebellion.

1963: Jerome Cavanagh is, at the time of his election, the youngest mayor in Detroit's history and is more responsible for integrating blacks into government than any prior mayor.

1967: A Detroit police raid becomes the catalyst for an urban rebellion that marks a watershed moment in Detroit and urban history, being the second worst urban rebellion in American history up to that point.

1974: Coleman Young is one of the first big-city African American mayors, and after his election significantly increases the number of minority- and female-owned businesses with city contracts, and the number of black officers in the Detroit police department.

1984: The General Motors Poletown Assembly plant opens after significant controversy—its construction entailed the destruction of a once-vibrant multiracial Detroit community. It is the first new auto plant built in Detroit in almost seventy years.

GOVERNMENT AND POLITICS

Detroit grew substantially from the beginning of the twentieth century to the immediate post–World War II period and was considered by many to be one of the most important industrial centers in the western world. By 1950 the city's population was 1,849,568, and it was home to one of the largest African American populations in the country. The increase in the city's population can be attributed to federal decisions and to the growing importance of the automotive industry locally, nationally, and internationally. By 1957 the city's fortunes began to change as the population started to shrink, falling to 1930 levels by 1960.

Just as its rise can be traced partially to political decisions, so can its decline. Federal defense spending helped to subsidize auto plant development in the Detroit suburbs. The Federal Highway Act of 1956 created the federal highway system, 90 percent of the construction costs for which were covered by the federal government, with the rest coming from state and local government. The decision to spend federal dollars on suburban plant construction and on highway construction was touted as a matter of national security—legislators argued that it gave citizens the ability to flee cities in case of foreign attacks. The decision gave industry an opportunity to increase profits through federal subsidies but also led to Detroit population and job loss.

Albert Cobo, a Republican, was elected mayor in 1950 at the peak of Detroit's power. By making allegiances with the white homeowners associations, he was reelected handily but then died in office in 1957. His replacement, common council member Louis Miriani, had to cope with a new, falling Detroit; according to historian Robert Conot, the combination of industry exodus and highway construction alone reduced the city's coffers by $43 million. Although entrepreneurial leaders led other cities facing somewhat similar circumstances, Miriani was different. In fact, his mayoral regime was known for its hostile relationships with the state legislature, a resulting loss in state aid, and a budget deficit that itself was held over from his predecessor. Furthermore, during Miriani's five-year rule, Detroit faced a recession unlike any it had dealt with since the Great Depression.

Given the dire straits Detroit faced in the late 1950s, pundits, politicians, and everyday citizens viewed the city's turnaround with wonder. The ability of an array of Detroit civic institutions to integrate blacks into the corridors of political, economic, and social power made it unique. Black Detroiters were more rooted, made more money (even given their relatively high unemployment rates), and were much more likely to own their homes than blacks in other cities, including New York.

But as the gains of the civil rights movement invigorated blacks throughout the country, it became clear they were not enough. In 1966 white youth killed a black war veteran, blacks accused the police of killing a black prostitute, and clashes between blacks and police officers continued to the point where some thought a riot was a foregone conclusion.

It happened a year later, sparked by a police raid of a Twelfth Street blind pig (an illegal bar). A rumor spread that the cops had harassed a woman, and someone from the gathering crowd threw something at the police. The resulting rebellion was the worst the country had ever seen. Forty-one people were killed, 347 injured, and 3,800 arrested in the five-day rebellion. Furthermore, over four thousand businesses were either ransacked or burned to the ground. Some argue that white flight and business disinvestment increased as a result of the rebellion, but census data do not appear to bear this out. However, for many in and outside of Detroit this was its flashpoint event. Jerome Cavanagh, elected to replace Miriani by a coalition of white liberals, labor, and African Americans, thought by many to be presidential material before the rebellion, decided not to run for office in 1969.

Roman Gribbs, Wayne County Sheriff, stepped into the gap. The choice of white conservatives, Gribbs ran on a campaign promising to return order to Detroit, a strategy that was tinged with racism. African American Richard Austin also announced his candidacy, later receiving the support of four union leaders and a number of liberal unionists. Understanding how the election would potentially shape the city, a group of sixty prominent liberals sponsored an ad in effect asking whites to vote based on their understanding of the issues rather than on race. In a very close election, Gribbs won out.

Detroit's unemployment rate had skyrocketed by the time Gribbs took office. Almost 33 percent of Detroiters aged sixteen and over were either unemployed, out of the labor force, or simply not working. Richard Nixon's New Federalism policies scaled back the amount of direct federal aid cities received. Given the stark levels of unemployment and poverty in Detroit, the relative lack of urban aid placed a significant damper on the city's ability to provide services. It was during this time that Detroit garnered the reputation of being the "murder capital of the world."

In response Gribbs developed a plan of attack that almost forty years later still shapes Detroit sentiment. With the assistance of police commissioner John Nichols, Gribbs created a program called STRESS (Stop The Robberies, Enjoy Safe Streets). STRESS officers would dress undercover as potential victims, theoretically placing themselves in position to both arrest criminals and prevent future crime; the thought was that if criminals believed that their potential victim could be a police officer, they should be less likely to commit crime. While arrests and police shootings increased under STRESS, crime did not decrease. The Michigan Civil Rights Commission, the NAACP, United Auto Workers (UAW) Local 600, and a number of other civil rights groups organized against STRESS, urging Mayor Gribbs to make reforms. He never did. Deciding not to run for reelection, Gribbs put his weight behind John Nichols, Detroit Police Commissioner and STRESS architect. White liberals, uncomfortable with Gribbs's and Nichols's conservative stances, supported city councilman Mel Ravitz, hoping to return to Cavanagh's style of governance.

Recognizing how well Richard Austin ran against Gribbs in 1969, blacks knew they had an even stronger chance of electing a black mayor. Black leaders settled on Coleman Young, Tuskegee Airman, state legislator, and leftist political activist. Running against STRESS with the support of black moderates, liberals, and radicals, Young came in second behind Nichols in the nonpartisan primary. In the general election, Young won handily with 54 percent of the vote.

After Young was elected he was tasked with two very different political mandates. Under his watch Detroit became a majority black city. However, the vast majority of city agencies, as well as both the police and fire department, were staffed and run by whites, and few city contracts went to minority- or female-run firms. Young integrated city agencies by mandating contract quotas for female- and minority-owned firms and by integrating the police department. After dismantling STRESS, by 1980 half of the city's police commissioners were African American. Furthermore, by 1987 women constituted 20 percent of the force.

Young took an aggressive approach toward downtown development. The Detroit Lions moved from Detroit to Pontiac in 1977. That same year, Young purchased Tiger Stadium to keep the Detroit Tigers from leaving and built Joe Louis Arena to keep the Detroit Red Wings downtown. Similarly, a year earlier he broke ground on the Renaissance Center, a massive downtown office, hotel, and shopping complex located on Detroit's riverfront. In 1979 General Motors (GM) devoted $40 billion to a plant modernization program, and executives informed city leadership that to be considered for it, they had to give GM a six-hundred-acre plot located near a highway. In response Young razed the community of Poletown, relocating thousands of homeowners, hundreds of businesses, and over a dozen schools and churches. GM bought the land at a significant discount, paying only $8 million for it, while the city of Detroit paid over $200 million.

Young's economic development strategy came at a severe cost to neighborhood development and to the growing number of working-class and poor African Americans who constituted a significant percentage of Detroit's population. While the mayor strived mightily to meet the needs of corporate stakeholders, he did not put the same degree of effort into meeting the needs of low-income residents. Housing starts for low-income residents never met demand, but by the late 1980s the city spent significant resources on constructing homes for middle- and upper-income residents. Young remained a staunch Democrat throughout his career, but his governing strategy represented an urban form of trickle-down economics.

COMMERCE, INDUSTRY, AND LABOR

Detroit's status as the automotive capital of the world drew hundreds of thousands of men and women to the city. Plant workers could make enough money to own their own homes and provide for their children's education. Yet the dynamics of race and class shaped Detroit's ability to respond to widespread changes in the economy.

Detroit was the center of the automotive world from the beginning of the twentieth century until right after World War II. The automotive industry was one of the first to take advantage of technological advances in transportation and the political growth of the military industrial complex. The Federal Highway Act played a significant role in the city, but by 1956 the automotive industry had already begun to respond to the growing national and international demand for automobiles by building newer more modern plants outside of cities and by relying more on automation than on human labor. The Ford River Rouge plant in suburban Detroit was at one time the largest integrated factory in the world. As a result of automation and plant modernization in general, it saw its labor force reduced from eighty-five thousand in 1945 to only thirty thousand in 1960. The automotive industry was particularly sensitive to shifts in demand. The combination of increased plant automation and the economic recession wrecked havoc on Detroit employment, and between 1947 and 1963 Detroit lost one hundred thirty-four thousand jobs.

Plant automation reduced labor costs, enabling plants to produce more cars with fewer people. Detroit unionists fought the growing move toward automation and were able to get a number of Detroit suburbs (including Dearborn, where Ford headquarters was located) to pass legislation against decentralization, though it was largely symbolic. The UAW was one of the largest and most powerful unions in the country. Local 600, housed at the River Rouge plant, was one of the most progressive locals in the country and one of the largest as well. But even it was unable to prevent Ford from decentralizing.

The effect on Detroit was profound. By 1961 the inner core of the city had a commercial vacancy rate of 22 percent, compared to the suburban vacancy rate of only 4 percent. The economic gains made by workers through the postwar era were substantial. However, these gains fell as workers were either replaced by machines or let go because of a combination of speeding up production and awarding more overtime. Disparate employment patterns increased white incomes faster than black ones. More important, during this period homeownership became a significant source of economic and social wealth for white middle- and working-class residents.

Just as the gains were unequally distributed, the losses were as well. In 1960 Detroit's overall unemployment rate stood at 7.6 percent, but the black unemployment rate was 18.2 percent. Economic anxiety exacerbated racial differences, and this in turn made home ownership mean even more. White homeowners, whose hold on their homes was already tenuous, were fiercely protective of their neighborhoods, wanting to keep them "safe" from black encroachment.

Mayor Young attempted to rebuild Detroit's downtown, believing that attracting businesses would attract jobs. However, the few jobs that the businesses did bring could not compare to the types of jobs offered by the automotive industry—those that paid well and offered good benefits while requiring little in the way of formal education. Although Detroit remained the largest city in the region, by the end of the 1980s it lost its status as the automotive capital of the world.

RACE, ETHNICITY, AND IMMIGRATION

Given its status as the "arsenal of democracy," Detroit had always been home to a variety of racial and ethnic groups, including sizable Polish, Irish, and Italian populations. Elites played a significant role in stoking and ameliorating the resulting interracial tensions. One of the consequences of the recession of the 1950s was increased concern about crime, especially the petty crimes committed largely by unemployed blacks in and outside of black neighborhoods. Mayor Miriani used this to shore up support among whites by aggressively deploying police against black citizens. According to Conot he ordered a police crackdown, leading police to manhandle black youth in public and to frisk middle-class blacks on the street without cause, among other things. Although the 1960 Civil Rights Commission hearings uncovered significant evidence of racial harassment, nothing came of the report. Miriani was by no means equipped to deal with Detroit's changing circumstances in a way that would benefit the city's various constituencies equally. Despite the fact that he had the support of every prominent Detroit institution, Miriani was defeated by forty thousand votes in 1961 by the thirty-three-year-old Jerome Cavanagh.

Cavanagh's mayoral acts indicated how different he was from his predecessor. He appointed an African American to manage city finances and a Michigan Supreme Court Justice with a record of fighting for black rights to serve as police commissioner. And just as he was elected, the federal government began to pour money into city development projects. Through Cavanagh's efforts the city garnered over $3.6 million in federal funds. And rather than stand with white homeowners as his predecessor had, Cavanagh stood with civil rights activists.

The number of black citizens attracted to the economic opportunity offered by the automotive industry grew, to the point where they became a statistical majority by the 1970s. Their population size and their connection to the automotive industry made them unique among black urbanites. Their numbers gave them the resources to create a variety of organizations, churches, and social groups designed to cater to their political, economic, and social needs. Detroit's chapter of the NAACP was at the forefront of the national open housing movement and also organized against police harassment, forcing the city's police department to integrate its squad cars. Similarly, the Detroit chapter of the Urban League, though ideologically more conservative than the NAACP, sought to integrate the workforce by giving African Americans job skills. And the Trade Union Leadership Council was the most important black union organization in the country. Although their population was not as large as in Chicago or Harlem, African Americans' connection to union politics gave them a level of social capital that did not exist in other places.

But these organizations were primarily black middle- and upper-class organizations that sought to promote a class-inflected racial identity and politics. For instance, the black middle and upper classes were the primary beneficiaries of the open housing movement, as they were the ones most likely to have the resources to purchase homes. Similarly, when the recession hit, the Detroit Urban League dropped its various working-class job-training programs, preferring instead to focus on white-collar job opportunities.

With the onset of the 1960s, the civil rights movement moved north. Detroit became an important battleground, as referenced by Martin Luther King Jr.'s presence at a June 1963 Detroit march. Furthermore, as the political and economic climate changed, the types of organizations, and their tactics, changed. And as the civil rights movement spread across the country, a number of radical black organizations sprang up. Reverend Albert Cleage founded the black nationalist Shrine of the Black Madonna, a Pan-African Orthodox church that wed biblical and revolutionary principles. Auto plants served as the locations for a number of radical worker organizations, most important of which was the Dodge Revolutionary Union Movement. These organizations were essential in finally electing Coleman Young mayor.

Although Detroit's politics and history during this period increasingly became one that juxtaposed black interests against white ones, during this same period other ethnic groups came to the fore in two ways. First, although the number of Asian Americans in Detroit and in the metropolitan area in general was small, the rise of foreign automotive competition in the 1970s and 1980s increased resentment toward Asian Americans. In 1982 Chinese American Vincent Chin was beaten to death in Highland Park (one of two Detroit suburban enclaves) by a Chrysler plant superintendent and his stepson, who believed Chin was Japanese American and explicitly blamed him for the increase in Detroit area unemployment (due to auto plant layoffs). The Chin murder helped to spark the modern pan–Asian American movement.

The second way other ethnic groups came to the fore was through the increase in two populations: Arab Americans and Mexican Americans. Present in small numbers since the beginning of the twentieth century, Arab immigrants began to come to Detroit in large numbers in 1970, and by 1990 approximately one hundred thousand metropolitan Detroiters were Arab American; there were, among others, sizable Chaldean, Syrian, and Lebanese populations. Indeed, Detroit came to have one of the largest populations of Middle Eastern immigrants in the country. Mexican immigrants began arriving in large numbers during the postwar era, settling in Detroit's southwest section ("Mexicantown"). As had been the case with African Americans, this process was both aided and abetted by the federal government, as U.S. government policies helped to recruit Mexican workers to Detroit, and federal highway policies displaced thousands of Mexican American Detroiters.

See also *Detroit, MI 1896–1929; Detroit, MI 1929–1941; Detroit, MI 1941–1952*

LESTER SPENCE

BIBLIOGRAPHY

Abraham, Nabeel, and Andrew Shryock. *Arab Detroit: From Margin to Mainstream*. Detroit, MI: Wayne State University Press, 2000.

Conot, Robert E. *American Odyssey*. New York, NY: Morrow, 1974.

Georgakas, Dan, and Marvin Surkin. *Detroit: I Do Mind Dying. A Study in Urban Revolution*. Updated ed. Cambridge, MA: South End Press, 1998.

Gordillo, Luz María. *Mexican Women and the Other Side of Immigration: Engendering Transnational Ties*. 1st ed. Austin: University of Texas Press, 2010.

Shaw, Todd Cameron. *Now Is the Time! Detroit Black Politics and Grassroots Activism*. Durham, NC: Duke University Press, 2009.

Sugrue, Thomas J. *The Origins of the Urban Crisis: Race and Inequality in Postwar Detroit*. Princeton, NJ: Princeton University Press, 1996.

DALLAS, TX 1952–1989

DURING THE SECOND HALF OF THE TWENTIETH CENTURY, DALLAS EXPERIENCED EXPLOSIVE POPULATION AND ECONOMIC GROWTH, witnessed significant political and social change, and competed with its booming suburbs despite massive annexation efforts. During this era the city transformed itself from a prosperous regional center to a truly national and international city that boasted one of the strongest economies in the nation. Under Mayor Robert L. Thornton (1953–1961), the city experienced stable leadership and a strongly pro-business government. Although Dallas avoided much of the turmoil and unrest associated with the 1960s, by the 1980s the city appeared increasingly fragmented and witnessed tense relationships between blacks and whites. The city's success in attracting large numbers of migrants from the north as well as immigrants changed the political dynamics and led to the downfall of the Citizens Charter Association (CCA), the longtime "good government" organization that had dominated Dallas politics since the 1930s. By the 1980s Dallas had experienced significant political, demographic, and economic transformation.

GOVERNMENT AND POLITICS

Under the leadership of sometimes combative mayor J. B. (Tiste) Adoue, the city altered the way it selected its mayor and continued its aggressive annexation campaign meant to capture the growing suburban population. Between 1946 and 1953, Dallas made sixty-five annexations, the most in the state. Because of such efforts, the area of Dallas grew from 117 square miles in 1950 to slightly over 277 square miles by 1960. As councilman, Adoue led a campaign for the direct election of the city's mayor since the city council, and not the voters, had selected the mayor up to that point. That successful effort allowed him to become the city's first popularly

QUICK FACTS

DALLAS, TX **1952–1989**

MAYORS

Jean Baptiste Adoue	(1951–1953)
Robert L. Thornton	(1953–1961)
Earle Cabell	(1961–1964)
J. Erik Jonsson	(1964–1971)
Wes Wise	(1971–1976)
Adline Harrison	(1976)
Robert Folsom	(1977–1981)
Jack Evans	(1981–1983)
Starke Taylor	(1983–1987)
Annette Straus	(1987–1991)

MAJOR INDUSTRIES AND EMPLOYERS

Texas Instruments
LTV Corporation (aerospace)
Dallas Independent School District
City of Dallas
E-Systems

MAJOR NEWSPAPERS

Dallas Morning News
Dallas Times Herald

MAJOR EVENTS

1961: Racial integration of public and private facilities begins.
1963: President John F. Kennedy is assassinated in Dallas.
1971: Judge Jason William Taylor hands down an order to desegregate the Dallas Independent School District by busing students.
1974: Dallas-Fort Worth International Airport opens.
1975: A court ruling by federal Judge Elton Mahon declares Dallas's at-large system of voting unconstitutional, accelerating the demise of the Citizens Charter Association.

elected mayor under the council-manager system of government that had been established in 1930. Adoue's tenure as mayor proved controversial, however, as he constantly fought with the city manager and council.

His decision in 1953 not to seek reelection allowed the CCA to nominate bank president and civic leader Robert L. Thornton for mayor, a position that he held until 1961. He had helped found the Dallas Citizens Council in 1937, an organization of the city's leading bankers, industrialists, and newspaper publishers who had access to their companies' money and could fund major projects. The new body, limited in size, seemed to provide better efficiency and coordination than other business-led groups and quickly emerged as the most powerful civic organization in the city's history. As mayor, Thornton clearly represented the views of that body. During his time in office the economy expanded greatly to include not only oil but aviation and electronics as well.

In response to the city's growth, Thornton called for a new comprehensive master plan, but unlike the city's two earlier ones this was to be developed by a group of laymen rather than by a hired professional master planner. Although it was supposed to cover sixteen phases of city development, the committee only issued three substantial reports: one on thoroughfares, one on parks, and one on the central business district. The focus on downtown was not accidental. Despite an impressive building boom of office buildings (twenty-four multistory buildings erected between 1945 and 1957), civic leaders worried about the decline of retail sales as traffic congestion made downtown less accessible. Movie houses and other entertainment venues started to suffer as suburban alternatives began to appear. Although some leaders wanted to use the federal government's urban renewal program to help eliminate blight and slums encircling the central business district, the lack of state enabling legislation until 1957 thwarted the earlier momentum, and by the late 1950s an escalating fear of federal intervention doomed that program.

Bruce Alger, elected in 1954 as Dallas's first Republican congressman, became a major player in the city's growing distrust of federal government programs. He aggressively opposed public housing, the federal school lunch program, and the federally developed urban renewal program, and he rallied supporters by suggesting that the national government was moving toward socialism. Concerns about creeping socialism also seemed to splinter civic leadership, which helped Earle Cabell, former CCA member, defeat the CCA nominee for mayor in 1961. The fear of an expanding federal government and hysteria over communism came to a head in Dallas during the early 1960s as right-wing extremists mobbed vice presidential candidate Lyndon B. Johnson and his wife Lady Bird. In another incident, on October 26, 1963, right-wing demonstrators disrupted a speech by U.N. Ambassador Adlai Stevenson. Even worse, the ambassador was hit and spit at when leaving the auditorium where he delivered his talk. The following month brought the tragic assassination of John F. Kennedy in Dallas, not by a right-wing extremist, but by Lee Harvey Oswald, a Marxist.

The assassination came as a severe shock to the image-conscious city, and the national condemnation of Dallas helped rally the city together and reinvigorate the CCA. In response to the bad press, citizens defeated Congressman Bruce Alger, the most visible sign of extreme right-wing fanaticism, and elected Mayor Earle Cabell to replace him. J. Erik Jonsson, president of Texas Instruments, and the new mayor, rallied citizens by creating Goals for Dallas, a citywide planning program that called for citizen participation. He also promoted the development of what would become the Dallas-Fort Worth International Airport and initiated the construction of a new city hall designed by renowned architect I. M. Pei.

Although in many ways he was very successful, Mayor Jonsson proved to be the last CCA mayor elected in the city's history. In 1971, Wes Wise, running as an antiestablishment candidate, defeated a new CCA candidate for mayor. Meanwhile, the city's African American community challenged the citywide election of council members, and on January 17, 1975, the federal courts ruled in their favor. In response, the city implemented a system in which eight city council members would be elected from specific districts while two at-large council members and the mayor would represent the entire city. That made the CCA's task of dominating local elections much more difficult and helped explain its rapid decline as a political organization.

For the first time since the 1920s, local politics became more open to a variety of groups, including advocates for the poor, for neighborhood associations, and for the city's minorities. Although the city council appeared somewhat more diverse than before, conservative, business-minded, and pro-growth mayors continued to lead Dallas. As a result, officials still neglected social programs for the city's neediest and focused primarily on economic development. Relations between minorities and the police rapidly deteriorated in the 1980s thanks largely to an increase in the use of deadly force by Dallas police. The number of police shootings rose from three in 1982 to twenty-nine in 1986, and most of those dead were minorities. In response, the city council increased the power of the Police Civilian Review Board, which set off a strong reaction from Dallas police who sought to weaken the board. Only after Ross Perot intervened was a compromise agreed upon that kept the city from even greater racial polarization. Annette Straus, Dallas's first woman mayor, formed a blue ribbon committee to recommend ways to ease racial tensions, and its 1989 report characterized Dallas as "a community divided along racial, economic and educational lines." Although the larger community could rally behind the successful Dallas Cowboys, who won their first Super Bowl in 1972, there appeared few other unifying factors as fragmentation replaced consensus in the political sphere.

INDUSTRY, COMMERCE, AND LABOR

As the second half of the twentieth century started, Dallas maintained its role as the center of wholesale and retail in the Southwest. For instance, the city's fashion industry was wholesaling $60 million in women's and children's clothing in the early 1950s. By the 1960s the Dallas Market Center became the largest wholesale trade center in the world. The city also continued its role as the center of banking and insurance in the Southwest. Indeed, by 1952 Dallas not only retained its title of the insurance capital of the Southwest but had become the fourth largest insurance center in the nation. Oil also remained a driving force in the city's economy in the 1950s, with more than five hundred oil companies doing business in Dallas. But by 1978, the year the popular TV show *Dallas* first appeared, the city's economy had expanded to include much more than giant oil companies, the focus of the show.

World War II and the Cold War altered the city's economy. For instance, the abandoned North American Aviation factory, where planes had been built during World War II, became the home of the airplane manufacturer Chance Vought, which moved there from Connecticut in 1949. Defense spending had a significant impact on the city and region, as Ling-Temco-Vought (LTV) and Texas Instruments received significant defense contracts along with other regional manufacturers such as General Dynamics and Bell Helicopter. In 1983 alone those four companies received $3.8 billion in defense contracts.

Texas Instruments (TI) witnessed explosive growth thanks to its entry into the semiconductor business in 1952 and its development in 1954 of two types of silicon transistors. In 1958 one of its engineers, Jack Kilby, invented the integrated circuit, which revolutionized the electronics and computer industries. During the 1950s TI expanded into other areas, including metallurgical products, missile guidance systems, and specialized computers. Soon other companies joined TI in manufacturing semiconductors, telecommunications, and defense electronics, making Dallas the third largest technology center in the nation. By 1983 over 535 high-tech firms had made the Dallas metropolitan region their home, providing eighty-seven thousand jobs. Five years later the number of high-tech firms in metropolitan Dallas reached 602.

The completion of the Dallas-Fort Worth International Airport in 1974 had a tremendous economic impact on Dallas and the surrounding metropolitan area, now called the Metroplex.

For the next ten years the region attracted new or relocating businesses at a rate of 250 per year and became one of the so-called Sunbelt success stories. The Dallas-Fort Worth Metroplex ranked third (behind New York and Chicago) as the headquarters for Fortune 500 corporations. The new airport also brought with it more flights between Dallas and a variety of international cities, increasing both tourism and business. On the downside, the airport, located nineteen miles from Dallas, encouraged spatial sprawl and accelerated a development already adversely affecting the city: the surge of people, industry, and commerce beyond the city limits into booming suburban communities such as Irving, Arlington, and Richardson.

The tremendous economic growth associated with the airport and rising oil prices in the 1970s and early 1980s that encouraged a building boom in downtown came to an end in the late 1980s as savings and loan institutions made bad loans to finance speculators' land acquisition of undeveloped land and risky construction projects. In addition, plummeting oil prices and risky loans by the city's largest local banks threatened their solvency and forced them to merge with out-of-state banks. Not only did this humiliate a city long known as the banking center of the Southwest, but it robbed Dallas of valuable leadership since many of its most important civic leaders had been bank presidents and who were now being replaced by out-of-state executives who had less interest in Dallas and focused more on their institutions' success.

RACE, ETHNICITY, AND IMMIGRATION

The city's economic development helps explain its rapid population growth after World War II, from 434,462 in 1950 to 1,006,877 in 1990. In addition to growth, the city experienced increasing diversity, at first from African Americans and Latinos but by the end of the period from a more diverse collection of people from around the world. However, the larger story is not simply the growing diversity of Dallas but the changing relationships between the establishment and the city's two largest minority groups. In 1950 African Americans made up 13.2 percent of the city's population, and by 1990 that had jumped to 29.5 percent. The number of Latinos increased even more spectacularly during this time, from around 35,000 in 1961 to 210,240 in 1990, about 12 percent of the total population.

In 1952 Dallas was a legally segregated city with dual school systems, segregated housing, and segregation in the public and private sectors. Unlike many cities that faced confrontational tactics and then violence as a result of discrimination, blacks in Dallas worked with white leadership in an effort that paved the way for peaceful integration of public and private facilities. On occasion, blacks in Dallas demonstrated a willingness to challenge the status quo through direct-action tactics such as the picketing of the segregated State Fair in 1955 or the sit-in at a drugstore in 1960. Those efforts, and the threat of additional demonstrations, encouraged city leaders to take the demands of African Americans more seriously than they might have otherwise done. In response to demands for integration, the Dallas Citizens Council formed a biracial committee with fourteen members to address the issue of integration. It not only orchestrated the peaceful integration of Dallas public schools in 1961 but also desegregated more than forty eateries. A 1963 visit by Martin Luther King Jr. resulted in the city desegregating its parks and swimming pools. Although there was a black power movement in Dallas by 1968, the city avoided the violent confrontations that many cities faced during the 1960s. Despite some advances in opening up more political and social opportunities for blacks and Latinos in the 1970s, including council seats for two African Americans and one Latino after 1973, the growing minority community demanded more opportunities and better representation in the city. A new generation of black leaders emerged who were more confrontational than their predecessors. A series of police shootings of blacks further promoted racial tensions and led the city's first elected female mayor, Annette Straus, to appoint in 1988 a widely diversified committee to recommend ways to encourage racial harmony within the city. One of its most important aspects was its call for increased representation for minorities. This led the mayor to create a Charter Review Commission, which recommended increasing the eight district seats to ten and electing four other council members from larger quadrants of the city. Most of the minority community found this insufficient and rallied against the plan that the council passed and voters approved on August 12, 1989. Instead of improving race relations, the vote set off a new round of protests and would be overturned the following year by a federal judge.

Progress in school integration proved exceedingly slow also. Although Dallas had initiated integration of its schools in 1961, a federal court ruled in 1970 that the city still had a dual school system. When court-ordered busing started in 1971, 57 percent of the students in the Dallas Independent School District (DISD) were white. By 1976 the number of whites in DISD schools had fallen to 38 percent. By the mid-1980s that number had dwindled to 20 percent.

By this time, Latinos had also emerged as major players in Dallas politics and faced the same types of problems that blacks had: underrepresentation, police brutality, and limited economic opportunities. Starting in 1973, with the police shooting of Santos Rodriguez, a twelve-year-old boy suspected of trying to break into a service station and looting a soft-drink machine, Latinos became more vocal in their demands. The apparent lenient treatment of the police officer who shot the boy resulted in the city's only race riot in which Latinos, now more than 8 percent of the population, and blacks participated in a demonstration that turned destructive as protesters and policemen clashed and downtown stores were vandalized. Latinos often worked with African Americans in challenging discrimination and calling for more diversity in city government. At this time only twelve Mexican Americans were members of the Dallas police force, and the fire department had not one Latino firefighter.

A growing Asian community appeared by the end of the 1980s, and census data suggested the city was on the verge of even greater diversity in the next decade. By 1989 it was clear that a growing ethnic and black population had profoundly changed the Dallas of the 1950s and had been one of several factors that had encouraged massive suburbanization and altered the very social and political fabric of the city.

See also *Dallas, TX 1989–2011*

ROBERT B. FAIRBANKS

BIBLIOGRAPHY

Fairbanks, Robert B. *For the City as a Whole: Planning, Politics, and the Public Interest, 1900–1965*. Columbus: Ohio State University Press, 1998.

Graff, Harvey J. *The Dallas Myth: The Making and Unmaking of an American City*. Minneapolis: University of Minnesota Press, 2008.

Hanson, Royce. *Civic Culture and Urban Change: Governing Dallas*. Detroit, MI: Wayne State University Press, 2003.

Morgan, Ruth P. *Governance by Decree: The Impact of the Voting Rights Act in Dallas*. Lawrence: University Press of Kansas, 2004.

Payne, Darwin. *Big D: Triumphs and Troubles of an American Supercity in the 20th Century*. Dallas, TX: Three Forks Press, 1994.

Phillips, Michael. *White Metropolis: Race, Ethnicity, and Religion in Dallas, 1841–2001*. Austin: University of Texas, 2006.

SAN DIEGO, CA 1952–1989

AS SAN DIEGO ENTERED THE 1950s, IT WOULD SOON LOSE ITS LONGSTANDING NICKNAME AS A "SLEEPY" TOWN attracting tourists to relax in the sunny southwestern corner of the country. The popularity of the automobile—combined with a population explosion created by World War II military personnel—contributed to the area's geographical expansion and a changing pattern of retail shopping. The city's downtown, suffering from neglect and outdated public transportation, gave way to the modern suburban shopping mall. It was a familiar story; the increase in automobiles meant better highways but less money for public transit, which therefore became less efficient.

Nevertheless, a single autonomous government in charge of large city departments widened the city's tax base and, with annexation of outlying areas, kept San Diego under the control of a powerful city manager, a cooperative mayor, and a pliable city council. During the period from 1952 to 1989, San Diego made remarkable progress, founded a major university, elected a U.S. senator, suffered some major business scandals, built the first Atlas missile, lost the Republican National Convention, saved Balboa Park buildings, and won the America's Cup. Formerly followed mainly by yachtsmen, the race for the cup gave San Diego national coverage. Whatever was happening, San Diego was definitely not asleep.

GOVERNMENT AND POLITICS

Although a city manager form of government had been in place in San Diego since the adoption of a new charter in 1931, several attempts were made to amend it during the following decades, but the charter, with modifications, was still in effect in 2010. Under the original 1931 charter, there were seven members of the city council—six council members and a mayor, who was also a member of the council. The six council members were nominated in six separate districts, but elected citywide, as was the mayor. In 1963 council districts increased from six to eight, and in 1974 the mayor and council became full-time employees. By 1988 council members were nominated and elected by district, with the mayor and city attorney elected citywide. The Charter

QUICK FACTS

SAN DIEGO, CA 1952–1989

MAYORS

John D. Butler	(1951–1955)
Charles C. Dail	(1955–1963)
Francis E. Curran	(1963–1971)
Pete Wilson	(1971–1982)
Roger Hedgecock	(1982–1983)
William Cleator	(acting; 1983–1985)
Maureen O'Connor	(1985–1992)

MAJOR INDUSTRIES AND EMPLOYERS

Federal and state government
University of California, San Diego
City and County of San Diego
Hospitals and health care
Tourism

MAJOR NEWSPAPERS

San Diego Union
San Diego Evening Tribune
San Diego Daily Transcript
Los Angeles Times
San Diego Union-Tribune

MAJOR EVENTS

1957: The first intercontinental ballistic missile (Atlas), built by the Convair Division of General Dynamics in San Diego, is test-fired, leading to an escalation in the strategic arms race with the Soviet Union.

1964: The University of California, San Diego, opens its doors.

1964: Sea World Marine Life Park, one of the major sea life centers in the nation, opens on recently developed Mission Bay.

1971: The Committee of 100 saves the 1915 historic Casa del Prado in Balboa Park and paves the way for future buildings to be saved and restored.

1976: The San Diego City Council adopts the Gaslamp Quarter Urban Design and Development Manual to set guidelines for historically sensitive development.

Review Commission of 1989 increased council districts to ten, giving the mayor veto power and the council a two-thirds override. San Diego State College graduate John D. Butler, the first native-born San Diegan to become mayor, took office in 1951.

Major political issues resulted from California's post–World War II love affair with the automobile, which limited funds for public transit. Signs of a new era were in place when San Diego entrepreneur George A. Scott announced in 1954 that Walker Scott Corporation, owners of a major department store in downtown San Diego, had purchased sixty-two acres of land just outside the city limits to offer ample free parking. With the same view, the city council decided in 1957, against heavy opposition, to lease rezoned Mission Valley agricultural land to the May Company of Los Angeles. Plans for a recreational area gave way to other department stores as well as a host of small shops, automobile dealerships, and hotels. Other shopping centers spelled a major change for suburban residents. Fears that downtown merchants would lose their customers proved to be true.

Mayor Charles C. Dail, a Democrat elected in 1955, helped convince the Board of Regents of the University of California that a southern campus would be appropriate. With additional support from private donors, ground was broken for the University of California, San Diego (UCSD) in 1961. The new campus, highly specialized for research, joined the Scripps Institution of Oceanography. Dail, who had polio, also convinced Jonas Salk to build his Institute for Biological Studies in 1963 on twenty-seven acres of city lands in La Jolla.

Not everyone, however, thought Dail had done a good job. He was indicted but not convicted twice by the Grand Jury and survived a recall—all related to a proposal to move the airport to Brown Field near the border, where he owned some property. He also opposed completion of a civic center fronting on the harbor because other public buildings already occupied noncontiguous downtown areas. Because Dail pushed for construction of a new civic center and community concourse, it was named for him upon completion in 1965.

Development of Mission Bay became another controversial project of the late 1950s. An argument developed over its best use, either for tourists to stay in large hotels or for residents to enjoy water sports and a beach outing with free parking. Environmental concerns dictated that seventy-seven acres of sanctuary be set aside for wildlife, although scientists warned that the natural area would still be seriously altered. The future possibilities for San Diego, however, were so great that plans went ahead for dredging the bay, creating almost two thousand acres of navigable water, more than two thousand acres of parkland, and nearly thirty-two miles of shoreline. By the time Francis E. Curran was elected mayor in 1963, plans were being made for opening Sea World in 1964, one of the country's best-known marine life parks.

Curran, a forceful figure with a reputation for getting things done, served as mayor from 1963 to 1971. He obtained approval for the new civic center and community theater as well as a state-of-the-art sports stadium in Mission Valley for professional and amateur teams. Curran's term in office saw completion of a metropolitan sewer system and the building of a spectacular bridge to the city of Coronado and the North Island Naval Air Station. Replacing the ferry, the bridge made easy access available while traffic congestion increased through residential areas across the bay.

Unfortunately, Curran became embroiled in a bribery scandal, with allegations that he allowed the Yellow Cab Company to raise its rates in exchange for campaign contributions from the company president. He and seven council members were indicted, and even though Curran was cleared by a jury, he was long remembered for his apparent indiscretion.

Republican Attorney Pete Wilson became mayor of San Diego following a five-year term as a California state assemblyman. Wilson had begun his law practice in San Diego, and lured into politics by Richard Nixon's top aide Herb Klein, publisher of the *San Diego Union*, won his assembly seat at the age of 33. He was elected mayor of San Diego in 1971.

San Diego politics was dominated by Wilson until 1982. Among his priorities was transformation of the historic Gaslamp Quarter from a decaying eyesore to a friendly business and restaurant district. In 1972, when the Republican National Convention pulled out of San Diego for Miami, Wilson called San Diego an "unconventional city" and coined its new slogan as "America's Finest City." Wilson created a municipal environmental protection agency and encouraged light rail transit to lessen freeway congestion. He emerged as a strong mayor in control of the council and city board appointments. Unfortunately, his tax cuts, his decision to take the city out of social security, and certain budget policies paved the way for future fiscal crises.

Wilson failed in a bid for governor in 1980 but received the Republican nomination for the U.S. Senate in 1982. Although elected for two terms, Wilson resigned in 1988 to again run for California governor, winning the top job in 1990. San Diego solved its leadership crisis by electing progressive Republican Roger Hedgecock in 1982. Hedgecock had been city attorney of Del Mar in 1974 and San Diego County Supervisor in 1976. Hard-working and creative, he vowed to stop uncontrolled development and curb overcrowding and pollution. Hedgecock was forced to resign in 1985 after allegedly failing to report campaign contributions from former Del Mar mayor Nancy Hoover and J. David Dominelli, who bilked investors of more than $82 million. Hedgecock became a popular conservative radio talk show host whose conviction was later overturned.

After Hedgecock's resignation in 1985, a former city council member and port commissioner, Democrat Maureen O'Connor, succeeded in becoming the first woman elected mayor in the city. A native San Diegan, O'Connor was one of thirteen children and an avid athlete. Graduating from San Diego State University in 1970, she married Robert Peterson, founder of the Jack in the Box fast food chain. A liberal thinker, she fought for term limits and campaign finance reform. She worked to increase San Diego's fair share of federal and state funds, but lost much of the power Pete Wilson had gained over the city council. In 1988 voters approved that council members be elected by their districts—a move with far-reaching implications for future partisan politics. O'Connor served as mayor until 1992.

A policy of growth during the post–World War II years had widened the city's tax base and led to annexation of surrounding areas. San Diego grew from 99 square miles in 1950 to some 320 square miles in 1990. The idea that bigger is better prevailed into the 1980s, but then citizens began voicing concern over their lack of control of local issues. Many wanted government to remain close to the people; but to others, county or even regional planning seemed a better answer to contemporary issues. Open space, water distribution, public schools, freeway expansion, air pollution—all of these problems needed solutions aimed at overall benefits. Planning was the answer, but by whom?

INDUSTRY, COMMERCE, AND LABOR

The population of San Diego more than tripled from 1950 (333,865) to 1990 (1,110,549), creating a need for new industry and increased commerce. With a war in Korea, San Diego's military payroll reached $280 million by 1960, making the city headquarters for the second largest military establishment in the nation. The Eleventh Naval District stretched from southern California to New Mexico and included installations in San Diego Bay and the U.S. Naval Hospital in Balboa Park. San Diego's lack of natural resources limited industrial development and forced the city to rely upon imported water and outside sources of power as developed by San Diego Gas and Electric Company.

Despite population growth, San Diego's tuna industry, a major source of income since the 1920s, declined. By 1958 the Japanese had taken over 46 percent of the American market and the

Soviet Union brought additional competition. San Diego's traditionally Italian and Portuguese tuna fishermen were losing out. Tuna canneries decreased from six to one: C. Arnholt Smith's Westgate-California Corporation.

During this time the city center became merely a commercial and financial district—busy in the daytime but nearly deserted at night. The lack of people downtown led to a decline in theaters and retail stores. Under the leadership of Mayors Wilson and O'Connor, the Center City Development Corporation (CCDC), and the Chamber of Commerce, San Diego revitalized its historic Gaslamp Quarter, a thirty-eight-acre project covering sixteen blocks in the heart of downtown. A 1976 Planned District Ordinance promoted the preservation of landmarks of historic, architectural, and cultural value, and Gaslamp District owners were further aided in 1977 by the State Historic Building Code, which supported restoration rather than new construction. By 1987 the city had spent $6 million on widened brick sidewalks, period street lamps, benches, landscaping, and other improvements.

The CCDC also planned and completed two residential projects—Marina and Columbia—and the Horton Plaza shopping mall. A proposed downtown convention center, taken to the voters in 1981, met serious opposition from those who questioned its cost and the city's competence to run it. The measure lost. Four years later the San Diego Port District funded the center at a cost of $165 million.

James Mills, president of San Diego's Metropolitan Transit Development Board, was responsible for legislation creating Old Town State Historic Park while in the state assembly. As a senator, Mills strongly supported measures that benefited San Diego. His bill providing for state gasoline tax revenues to finance light-rail transit systems has had far-reaching effects in the city. The first leg of San Diego's light rail, which opened in 1981, operated 15.9 miles from the Santa Fe Depot to the Tijuana border. The second leg, the East Line, which commenced operations in 1986, involved the conversion of a freight branch line from downtown to Lemon Grove, La Mesa, and El Cajon. A third segment, added in June 1990, extended southward parallel to San Diego Bay, passing Seaport Village and the Convention Center before rejoining the main line. Additional trolley lines were planned for later decades.

San Diego newcomer Kazuo Inamori founded San Diego–based Kyocera Telecommunications Research Corporation and established the nonprofit Inamori Foundation in 1984. The San Diego Supercomputer Center (SDSC), founded in 1985 as a research unit of UCSD, pioneered a national cyber-infrastructure, providing the foundation for the next generation of science and engineering advances. With a staff of scientists, software developers, and support personnel, SDSC soon became an international leader in data management, biosciences, geosciences, grid computing, and visualization. Biotech companies were also established in La Jolla and Sorrento Valley.

Dr. Irwin Mark Jacobs, a former faculty member at UCSD, founded two successful San Diego–based telecommunications companies that developed innovative technological applications revolutionizing digital communications technology. In 1969 he cofounded LINKABIT, which grew to more than one thousand four hundred employees in 1985. Jacobs then moved on to cofound QUALCOMM, which rapidly expanded worldwide and developed many technical innovations.

The most colorful business and behind-the-scenes political leader of the period was "Mr. San Diego," C. Arnholt Smith, a multimillionaire California Republican banker who brought the major league Padres baseball team to San Diego, but who was later convicted of embezzling $8.9 million from his investors and business properties.

RACE, ETHNICITY, AND IMMIGRATION

Even though California had originally been a part of Spain and Mexico, people of Latin descent were often treated unfairly. From the beginning of statehood, the majority community had welcomed Mexican laborers, but when the Great Depression hit in the 1930s, many of these same laborers were deported. However, during the 1960s the Chicano Federation, active in local affairs affecting Spanish-speaking groups, encouraged the participation of persons of Mexican descent in San Diego's politics. State Assemblyman Pete Chacon promoted bilingual education and expanded job opportunities. After a long struggle by residents of Barrio Logan, which had been cut in half by Interstate 5, and others in the Chicano community, the area underneath the Coronado Bridge became a park featuring murals about Mexican history. As San Diego's Spanish-speaking population increased yearly, neighboring Tijuana grew to 709,340 by 1980 and in 1990 topped the one million mark.

Maquiladoras, tax-exempt export manufacturing and assembly plants based in Mexico, employed recent migrants. By the end of the 1980s, there were 638 *maquiladoras* with over sixty-seven thousand workers just across the border. Many Tijuana residents shopped in San Diego and were important in stabilizing the economy of both the city and county. Nevertheless, border issues, illegal immigration, and drug smugglers made crossing the border on a regular basis time consuming. The U.S. Immigration Reform and Control Act of 1986, in addition to tightening restrictions on employers hiring undocumented workers, granted amnesty to certain immigrants who had been continuously living in San Diego prior to 1982. Because of the family reunification policy, it allowed for many more to be given documents than expected. As a result, the issue created more animosity toward Mexican laborers than had been previously evident. By 1989 Latino residents accounted for about 20 percent of San Diego's population.

San Diego's African American community made considerable gains between 1952 and 1989 through the activities of business, educational, and religious leaders. The Reverend George Walker Smith, who served four terms on the San Diego Board of Education from 1963 through 1979, upgraded educational facilities in predominantly minority areas. Leon L. Williams became San Diego's first African American councilman in 1969. Reelected in 1971, 1975, and 1979, and elected to the County Board of Supervisors in 1982, Williams was active in the Economic Opportunity Commission, the Neighborhood House Association, and numerous youth groups. Other successful members of the African American community included judges Joe Littlejohn and Napoleon Jones; city councilmen William Jones, Wes Pratt, and George Stevens; and several professional athletes.

In 1979 Judge Louis Welsh approved a voluntary plan for integration of the San Diego school system without mandatory busing in *Carlin v. San Diego Board of Education*. San Diego in 1980 had the eighth largest school district in the nation, with a student population of one hundred ten thousand. Progress during the 1980s was made in programs of voluntary ethnic transfers, magnet schools, and part-time learning center exchanges.

Few Native Americans (less than 1 percent of the population) reside within the City of San Diego. The original Kumeyaay live within the county on five reservations to the east. Because of new income from casinos established after 1988, the Indians made considerable gains in health and education.

See also *San Diego, CA 1989–2011*

IRIS ENGSTRAND

BIBLIOGRAPHY

Davis, Mike, Kelly Mayhew, and Jim Miller. *Under the Perfect Sun: The San Diego Tourists Never See.* New York, NY: New Press, 2003.
Engstrand, Iris H. W. *San Diego: California's Cornerstone.* San Diego, CA: Sunbelt, 2005.
Naverson, Andrea. *San Diego Coming of Age: A Modern History.* Carlsbad, CA: Heritage Media, 2003.
Pourade, Richard. *City of the Dream.* Vol. 7 of *History of San Diego.* San Diego, CA: Copley Books, 1977.
Pryde, Philip, ed. *San Diego: An Introduction to the Region.* San Diego, CA: Sunbelt, 2004.
Showley, Roger. *Perfecting Paradise.* Carlsbad, CA: Heritage Media Corp., 1999.
Starr, Kevin. *Golden Dreams: California in an Age of Abundance 1950–1963.* New York, NY: Oxford University Press, 2009.

PHOENIX, AZ 1952–1989

PHOENIX CHANGED DRAMATICALLY IN THE FORTY OR SO YEARS AFTER WORLD WAR II, serving as an archetype of the emerging Sunbelt city. From a modest population of roughly one hundred thousand, it grew to nearly a million people—the fastest pace in the country—becoming the ninth largest city in the United States during this time. Its economic transformation from a prewar agricultural base in central Arizona's Salt River Valley was equally striking. The growth of tourism and the addition of military facilities were superseded by major developments in aerospace and electronics manufacturing. The massive influx of new residents, including those in new retirement communities, also provided opportunities for construction, real estate, and retail sales. A highly efficient city administration provided services to the expanding city, while cultural institutions and organizations began to flourish.

But beneath the glitter of growth and the boasts of city leaders were significant costs. Minority populations, initially left out of this system, struggled to be included. The city's prodigious spatial expansion, from 17 to 404 square miles, made it a poster child of sprawl, with mass-produced and cookie-cutter housing, traffic congestion, air pollution, and loss of the surrounding desert. And like many cities, it suffered serious deterioration in its central business district and older neighborhoods.

QUICK FACTS

PHOENIX, AZ **1952–1989**

MAYORS

Nicholas Udall	(1948–1952)
Hohen Foster	(1952–1954)
Frank G. Murphy	(1954–1956)
Jack Williams	(1956–1960)
Samuel Mardian	(1960–1964)
Milton Graham	(1964–1970)
John Driggs	(1970–1974)
Timothy Barrow	(1974–1976)
Margaret Hance	(1976–1984)
Terry Goddard	(1984–1990)

MAJOR INDUSTRIES AND EMPLOYERS

Motorola
City and state government
Allied-Signal Aerospace
Samaritan Health Service

MAJOR NEWSPAPERS

Arizona Republic
Phoenix Gazette
East Valley Tribune

MAJOR EVENTS

1950s and 1960s: Motorola spearheads the rise of the electronics industry in the Phoenix area.

1969: Chicanos por la Causa, a community development agency, is founded to provide Mexican Americans with important social and economic assistance and a political voice.

1975: Commission government ends; city government is no longer controlled by a self-selected sociopolitical group.

1982: Phoenix opts to choose its city council from districts, providing effective political representation to all areas of the city.

1988: Phoenix passes a major bond issue to fund cultural institutions, greatly stimulating cultural and downtown development.

GOVERNMENT AND POLITICS

Phoenix began the postwar era needing to make changes. Its commission form of government could not handle the city's administrative needs, and it had fostered a factionalized political system run by small business owners seeking personal and political advantage. A reform movement produced a new city charter in 1948 that established a council manager system, with a policy-oriented council and a strong manager, and implemented nonpartisan at-large elections.

Supporters of this new system established the Charter Government Committee (CGC), which drafted a slate of candidates (no volunteers were accepted) and financed and helped campaign for the slate. After all of its council and mayor candidates were elected with large majorities, the committee disbanded, but it did not disappear forever. According to plan, six months before the 1951 election, the last CGC chair chose a small organizing group, it picked a full CGC, and the process began again. Over the next twenty-five years, the CGC continued this pattern, and it won every contest for council and mayor except two until 1975.

Like many "good government" groups in other cities, the CGC focused on efficient government and economic development. Its tickets included mostly middle- and upper-middle-class businessmen and professionals, but they were relatively balanced in party affiliation and were diverse in religion, ethnicity, and gender. Experienced in civic organizations, limited by desire and committee decision to one or perhaps two terms, and not politically ambitious, these men and women functioned cohesively to push for city growth, expanded services, administrative efficiency, and fiscal prudence. With this record the city was able, starting in the late 1950s, to annex very large areas of adjacent suburban neighborhoods.

The CGC's centrist policies were attacked during the 1960s from both right and left. Conservatives organized opposing slates in all but one election during the decade, complaining about taxes, a housing code, and efforts to renovate downtown. Liberals mounted a serious challenge in 1963, but after the CGC candidates won a runoff election, they accommodated the liberals by including minority candidates on their next slate, passing antidiscrimination ordinances, and implementing various Great Society programs. The city's applications for the All-America City award in 1965 and 1966 (which it had won in 1950 and 1958) described its fundamental shift in priorities to include better housing, a housing code, minority employment, and other ways to fight poverty.

Partly influenced by national trends, city politics erupted in 1969. The CGC rejected Mayor Milton Graham's request for an unprecedented fourth nomination, abandoned the incumbent council members and their liberal policy goals, and chose a slate of white male Republicans who campaigned on a law-and-order theme. Facing a Graham ticket and a slate of conservatives, all but one of the CGC candidates were elected. In 1971 the CGC selected a more diverse slate, with liberal, minority, and women council members, but support for the kind of control typified by the CGC had begun to wane.

During the 1960s Phoenix expanded services to the vast areas it was annexing through efficient administration and by acquiring new revenues from state sales, gas, and income taxes. After 1970, with expenses still rising, the city pushed harder for federal funds. It took full advantage of the Nixon administration's programs of revenue sharing and block grants, which allowed the city significant spending flexibility, using these funds for such varied purposes as spending on police, cutting "sin" taxes, and acquiring land for the Phoenix Mountain Preserve. In a decade when many cities struggled mightily with financial problems, Phoenix merely added slightly to its property tax and added fees for sewer usage and garbage pickup.

The political system first changed in 1975, when council member Margaret Hance (1976–1984) challenged the CGC's novice candidate for mayor and won convincingly, while independent candidates won four of the six council seats. The CGC's demise came largely because the city's eightfold increase in population had created diversity in leadership, population, and interests that had not existed in 1950. A second stage in the political transition occurred in 1982, when voters adopted a district system for council elections, and in 1983, when one of the leaders of that drive, Terry Goddard (1984–1990), was elected mayor.

By the 1970s the city's celebrated suburban expansion was prompting serious questions about the economic and environmental consequences of sprawl, developing an effective strategy for downtown, and creating an effective transportation system. Goddard transformed the discussion and shifted the direction of city development from suburbs to the center city. Although he accepted some additional annexation, he pushed for stronger zoning, better planning, and more infill projects. He sought to recruit businesses to the city, including professional sports franchises, while also creating a major historic preservation program and a public art program. He pushed a countywide highway program (which voters passed) and a mass transit system (which voters rejected). Most important, he substantially advanced the redevelopment of downtown, winning public support for major spending on public facilities and starting the return of businesses and residences to the area.

INDUSTRY, COMMERCE, AND LABOR

Until World War II agriculture was the primary basis of the Phoenix economy. The city was also the commercial and financial center of the region, and tourism was a growing industry. World War II was an economic watershed for Phoenix. The construction of six air bases created postwar possibilities for aviation and military spending, while the three aviation-related factories brought in high-paying manufacturing jobs. Most important, acquiring the bases and factories was invaluable training in how to construct development proposals and use political influence.

Drawing on those wartime lessons and the model of California cities, especially San Diego, key Phoenix leaders envisioned a different postwar economy. Working through a broad-based chamber of commerce, a group of leaders including Walter Bimson (the city's leading banker), Eugene Pulliam (owner of the city's two newspapers), and lawyer Frank Snell planned an economy that would add aerospace and electronics manufacturing to the existing economic sectors and would boost tourism and military bases. While many Sunbelt cities had similar visions, Phoenix was enormously successful in implementing its plan.

The first step was persuading Goodyear Aircraft and Reynolds Metals to reopen the wartime aviation manufacturing plants. Then during the 1950s the city leadership began actively recruiting new businesses, using teams of Chamber of Commerce employees and business leaders and working with city government. The major firms they attracted included Sperry Phoenix, the computer division of General Electric, U.S. Semiconductor, and the Kaiser Corporation's aircraft and electronics division. During the 1960s major computer companies, including Digital, Honeywell, GTE, and Litton, set up plants. Together these businesses doubled the manufacturing sector in the Salt River Valley to comprise 20 percent of all employment, and, especially significant, these new employees were well paid, and many were well educated.

By far the most important of these firms was Motorola. In 1949 Daniel Noble established the company's first Phoenix unit, a research lab. The company quickly built a military research and production facility and in 1957 moved its military electronics division from Chicago to Phoenix. It next constructed a factory for consumer electronics and established a semiconductor products division. By the late 1960s it had five major facilities, it was the state's largest employer, and its more than twenty thousand employees constituted one-quarter of the Salt River Valley's manufacturing workforce. But Motorola's impact went beyond employment and buildings. Noble believed that the company's success depended on higher education for its employees. Working with other business leaders, especially those in other high-tech firms, he pushed Arizona State College in neighboring Tempe to create an engineering college and, in 1958, to become Arizona State University. Its rapid development of graduate programs in engineering and business trained hundreds of students and stimulated additional economic developments.

Establishing a positive climate for business was a high priority in the immediate postwar period. In addition, a voter initiative in 1946 established Arizona as a right-to-work state, banning the requirement of union membership for employment. In 1949 the city reduced taxes on manufacturing inventory and equipment; in 1956 the state repealed the sales tax on goods made and sold to the federal government. But the natural and labor climates had more effect than these measures. Dry air and a supply of skilled laborers, the ease of recruiting workers to the sunny area, and the lower rates of absenteeism and illness were the prime attractions for businesses. The labor movement was less strong in Phoenix than in eastern cities, but this resulted less from laws than because of the types of employment and employees in the area. Some unions did have power, especially those in the building trades.

Most economic sectors kept pace with economic expansion, including retail and wholesale sales, government employment, and financial services. The city's rapid growth boosted the importance of construction, but the industry's normal volatility was accentuated in Phoenix, which saw a long downturn from 1963 to 1968 and a sharp decline from 1974 to 1976. The 1980s saw even more boom and bust: a decline in 1980–1982 and a huge boom in the mid-1980s, followed by an even greater constriction in this sector. Tourism continued to grow exponentially during this era, attracting visitors from a wide range of income levels and for stays of several days to several months. By 1967 tourist-related revenues totaled $250 million; they reached $1.6 billion by 1979 and $2.9 billion by 1988. Finally, the high-tech sector narrowed after the mid-1970s and focused on manufacturing semiconductors.

RACE, ETHNICITY, AND IMMIGRATION

Despite the city's very rapid growth from immigration and annexation, the ethnic and racial composition of its population was virtually unchanged during the 1950s, 1960s, 1970s, and 1980s. The two largest minority groups were Mexican Americans, comprising 15 percent of the city population, and African Americans, at 5 percent, with small proportions of Native Americans (1 percent) and Asians (Chinese, Japanese, and Filipinos made up .5 percent). More than three-quarters of the population was white, or Anglo American, and nearly all of them were native-born. A small share of the new population moved from other parts of Arizona, but most came from other states: one in five came from the Midwest, nearly as many came from the Pacific Northwest or the Southwest, while the greatest number came from California.

At the beginning of the postwar era, Phoenix had de facto and de jure systems of segregation in public and private housing, education, public accommodations, and employment for African Americans and Mexican Americans. But the 1950s saw considerable progress on key civil rights issues. Lawsuits ended school segregation for both groups in 1953 and 1954, and the city banned discrimination at its airport restaurant in 1952, desegregated theaters and public housing in 1954 and 1955, and then forbade discrimination in public employment.

Despite this progress, continued residential segregation, discrimination in employment, and restricted access to public accommodations, particularly restaurants, prompted the NAACP, the Congress of Racial Equality, and the Urban League to organize picketing, boycotts, and sit-ins. Armed with information discussed at a 1962 hearing in Phoenix by the U.S. Civil Rights Commission and a report by the NAACP on employment discrimination, Reverend George Brooks and Lincoln Ragsdale successfully pressured major private employers to begin hiring minorities. The city passed a public accommodations ordinance (1964) and banned housing discrimination (1968), and city leaders worked for a state civil rights law (1965) banning discrimination in employment, voting, and public accommodations. But economic progress remained slow and incomplete. Frustration exploded in riots on July 25 and 26, 1967, near one of the largely African American public housing projects, but this ended relatively quickly, due in part to the persuasive intervention of Reverend Brooks.

Mexican Americans had a similar but not identical experience. They too suffered discrimination and poverty, responded by creating organizations and engaging in protest activities, and resided in many of the same South Phoenix neighborhoods. During the 1960s they were equally interested in programs dealing with poverty, unemployment, neighborhood improvement, and education. But partly because their population was larger and more racially diverse, and partly because of white Americans' racial attitudes, more were able to live outside of South Phoenix, to achieve greater economic success, and to obtain political influence, as evidenced by inclusion on CGC slates starting in 1953. As a result, and because they competed for limited public resources, African Americans and Mexican Americans had a somewhat uneasy relationship.

During the first decades of the postwar era, the League of United Latin American Citizens advanced the interests of Mexican Americans, as did political figures holding city office or serving in the state legislature, such as Manuel Pena (1966–1996). A new and more assertive group, Chicanos por la Causa (CPLC), began in 1970. Starting with the boycott of a high school over educational mistreatment of Mexican American students, CPLC encouraged and trained a new group of political leaders, such as Alfredo Gutierrez, who served as a state senator from 1972 to 1986. By 1980 it was one of the premier Chicano community development corporations in the nation, supplying housing, health care, education, job training, and help for small businesses and operating a credit union. Although hurt by reduced federal funding in the 1980s, the organization made necessary cuts and found other revenue sources enabling it to continue.

Both African Americans and Mexican Americans made important gains during the 1960s and 1970s. The percentage of African American high school graduates doubled, as did the median income in this community, but each of these measures equaled only two-thirds that of white Phoenicians. The distribution of occupations among African Americans improved, with a number of individuals holding white-collar jobs, but they remained more vulnerable to economic downturns and were more liable to be unemployed. They were still residentially concentrated in South Phoenix, but a third now lived in other areas of the city. Mexican Americans found greater economic success: Their family income was closer to that of Anglos, and fewer of them were on public assistance or unemployed. However, although their proportion of high school graduates rose, at 45 percent it lagged well behind all other groups. The 1980s saw little overall change in education and a decline in Mexican American income levels. Thus, while Phoenix provided improvement in a range of opportunities, growth alone would not overturn basic patterns of inequality.

See also *Phoenix, AZ 1989–2011*

PHILIP R. VANDERMEER

BIBLIOGRAPHY

Collins, William S. *The Emerging Metropolis: Phoenix, 1944–1973*. Phoenix: Arizona State Parks Board, 2005.

Gober, Patricia. *Metropolitan Phoenix: Place Making and Community Building in the Desert*. Philadelphia: University of Pennsylvania Press, 2006.

Johnson, G. Wesley, ed. *Phoenix in the Twentieth Century: Essays in Community History*. Norman: University of Oklahoma Press, 1993.

Luckingham, Bradford. *Minorities in Phoenix: A Profile of Mexican American, Chinese American, and African American Communities, 1860–1992*. Tucson: University of Arizona Press, 1994.

———. *Phoenix: The History of a Southwestern Metropolis*. Tucson: University of Arizona Press, 1989.

VanderMeer, Philip R. *Desert Visions and the Making of Phoenix, 1860 to 2009*. Albuquerque: University of New Mexico Press, 2010.

Whitaker, Matthew C. *Race Work: The Rise of Civil Rights in the Urban West*. Lincoln: University of Nebraska Press, 2005.

BALTIMORE, MD 1952–1989

BALTIMORE'S DECLINE BEGAN ALMOST IMPERCEPTIBLY during this period, then gained momentum. During the 1950s, Maryland's population grew by almost a third, but Baltimore lost just over 1 percent of its inhabitants. Those who remained in the city were less prosperous than the ones who left. In 1950 Baltimore claimed 40 percent of the Marylanders who stood in the top quartile of the state's income distribution; by 1977 only 13 percent of these high earners still lived in the city.

Baltimore's slide had political as well as economic implications. In 1940 Baltimoreans accounted for 48 percent of the votes cast in state elections; by 1980 the city could deliver only 17 percent of the state's voters to the polls.

GOVERNMENT AND POLITICS

In 1953 Mayor Thomas D'Alesandro Jr. delivered a rosy assessment of his six years as Baltimore's chief executive. But he could not ignore the city's decay. It was essential to the work of the redevelopment authority, whose job was to erase the evidence of decline by demolition. Some of the displaced residents found new homes in projects run by the housing authority, but the mayor was especially proud of the Baltimore Plan, an effort at slum prevention by strict enforcement of fire, health, and housing codes. The Baltimore Plan began as an initiative of the Citizens' Planning and Housing Association (CPHA), whose leaders sold the idea to D'Alesandro, and launched programs to improve housing for the poor and rescue neighborhoods from decay.

Party politicians had no role in the Baltimore Plan and seemed increasingly marginal to the city's existence. Even within city government itself, the big decisions were being made outside

QUICK FACTS

BALTIMORE, MD **1952–1989**

MAYORS

Thomas L. J. D'Alesandro Jr.	(1947–1959)
J. Harold Grady	(1959–1962)
Philip H. Goodman	(1962–1963)
Theodore R. McKeldin	(1963–1967)
Thomas L. J. D'Alesandro III	(1967–1971)
William Donald Schaefer	(1971–1986)
Clarence H. Burns	(1986–1987)
Kurt L. Schmoke	(1987–1999)

MAJOR INDUSTRIES AND EMPLOYERS

Food and kindred products
Apparel and other textile products
Transportation equipment
Primary metal industries
Fabricated metal products
Chemicals and allied products

MAJOR NEWSPAPERS

Baltimore Sun
Baltimore Evening Sun
Baltimore News-American

MAJOR EVENTS

1959: Charles Center, a major downtown commercial and residential development project, is announced.

1964: Mayor McKeldin proposes a comprehensive civil rights ordinance.

1966: The Congress of Racial Equality names Baltimore a "target city."

1974: There are widespread strikes by city employees.

1978: Voters approve the Harborplace waterfront development, which would open in 1980.

1986: Clarence H. Burns becomes the city's first African American mayor. A year later Kurt Schmoke becomes Baltimore's first *elected* African American mayor.

the reach of the political bosses. The city's response to the Supreme Court's 1954 *Brown v. Board of Education* decision was framed by Baltimore's board of school commissioners. It voted unanimously and without public discussion to desegregate the city's schools, even though the court had not yet decided on a plan to implement its ruling. The board's president informed D'Alesandro of the decision only after the board had voted, and politicians on the city council played no part in the decision.

The downtown businesses that formed the Greater Baltimore Committee (GBC) constituted another realm outside the baronies of the party bosses. The GBC persuaded the Maryland General Assembly to approve the creation of a Civic Center Authority, removed from city control, with the power to issue bonds to finance a downtown arena for sports events, concerts, and conventions. The GBC also issued a somber report in 1955 addressing the larger problem of urban deterioration. The spread of decayed neighborhoods with poor residents would increase the cost of city services while property assessments and tax revenues diminished.

At the GBC's recommendation, the city paid a committee of outside experts to devise a strategy for the city's revival. It called for a sweeping $900 million urban renewal program.

D'Alesandro immediately announced that he would carry out the committee's recommendation to create an urban renewal superagency. He also designated the city's first urban renewal area, Harlem Park, where the new Baltimore Urban Renewal and Housing Agency would begin its work.

Baltimore's reenergized urban renewal effort moved into new territory. The Housing Act of 1954 also made commercial districts, not just decayed residential areas, eligible for federal subsidies. D'Alesandro designated the central business district as a renewal area. But the GBC, not the city government, would hire the planning staff to design the renewal program and would oversee its implementation. The first step in the program was the Charles Center Project, which would include eight office buildings, an apartment complex, a hotel, a theater, a parking garage, and shops. Federal, state, and local funds would cover only about 20 percent of the $180 million cost.

While civic organizations and civic leaders became more prominent as urban policymakers, the old party organizations continued to falter. Their mostly white constituents decamped for the suburbs one jump ahead of a growing African American population. In West Baltimore's Fourth District, for example, where Jack Pollack had exercised nearly absolute control for almost a generation, black candidates defeated Pollack men in 1954 for a seat in the state senate and another in the House of Delegates.

In 1959 the state's attorney for Baltimore, J. Harold Grady, handily defeated the three-term D'Alesandro in the primary for mayor and then defeated former mayor and governor Theodore McKeldin in the general election. As mayor, Grady never lived up to his electoral landslide and seemed uninterested in his job. In 1962 he was named to the Baltimore Superior Court and resigned as mayor. Under the city charter, council president and Kovens lieutenant Philip Goodman succeeded him in office.

McKeldin succeeded Goodman, and equal opportunity became one of his chief preoccupations. The mayor first had to negotiate with African American ministers to ward off mass demonstrations at job sites of city-financed construction projects, and he quickly reached a settlement with the ministers. The chair of the Ministerial Alliance praised the mayor for his part in reaching agreement on apprenticeship opportunities for young African Americans as well as immediate construction jobs for black workers.

In August 1964 the mayor announced that he would submit to the city council a comprehensive civil rights ordinance that would outlaw discrimination in employment, housing, public accommodations, public and private (but not parochial) schools, and health and welfare services. In order to achieve passage, the bill's proponents sacrificed the housing provision and agreed to an exemption for bars and taverns.

Less than two weeks after the city council approved the bill, McKeldin had another top priority: the War on Poverty. By year's end, the city had set up a local antipoverty agency with a budget of $4.3 million; all but $300,000 came from the federal government, under the authority of the Economic Opportunity Act. The city agency's first director resigned after less than six months, citing unspecified "differences of opinion" with the community action commission that oversaw the local poverty program. He was succeeded by Parren J. Mitchell, a member of the West Baltimore clan that provided leadership for the local branch of the NAACP.

Mitchell was repeatedly called before the city council to face objections concerning his agency's departures from the antipoverty plan originally approved by the council. His principal interrogator was usually William Donald Schaefer, the council's representative on the community action commission. While the council reined in the city's war on poverty, Mayor McKeldin attempted to persuade council members to approve the open housing provision excised from his civil rights legislation. The council voted 13-8 to defeat open housing legislation, and the local chapter of the Congress of Racial Equality (CORE) sponsored a silent demonstration outside City Hall to protest the council's third rejection of fair housing.

In April 1966 Floyd McKissick, the national director of CORE, announced that the organization had selected Baltimore as its "target city" for the upcoming summer. Asked whether the city had the country's worst record on civil rights, he said, "If it's not the worst, it is very close to it. They're probably the only city where the council has voted down a housing law three times." If open housing had been defeated three times, of course, it must also have been introduced three times—a sign, perhaps, that Baltimore might be a soft target for civil rights protest.

CORE's summer in Baltimore followed two summers of urban race riots elsewhere, first in Harlem, then in Watts. Interim Police Commissioner George Gelston, who was also adjutant general of the state National Guard, had helped to restore order in the Eastern Shore town of Cambridge after race riots in 1963 and 1964. Gelston met with both local and national leaders of CORE to review their plans for "intense civil rights activity in Baltimore." CORE, he said, was a "responsible organization," and he was confident that they would work closely with the police to forestall incidents that might lead to violence. Gelston embodied Baltimore's response to CORE's summer campaign. The establishment embraced the revolution and absorbed it into the status quo.

In early June, McKeldin called a meeting of one hundred civic leaders to announce an official attack on racial bias. Six committees, each with two chairs, one black and one white, would address a problem of racial discrimination: Housing, education, police-community relations, employment, public accommodations, and health and welfare. The chairman of the Urban League and the president of the local NAACP branch both served on the mayor's committees. The city's liberals, both black and white, had been preemptively co-opted by McKeldin. CORE would find it difficult to use Baltimore's black leadership as a local political base.

McKeldin also attempted to circumvent the council's rejection of his fair housing proposals by negotiating directly with proprietors of large apartment buildings to achieve open housing case by case. CORE had been picketing one prominent building downtown and agreed to withdraw its pickets while McKeldin successfully negotiated open occupancy agreements with nine of the largest apartment buildings in Baltimore. At the same time, he negotiated an agreement to serve African Americans with twenty-two bar and tavern owners on Baltimore's notorious "Block."

Having disposed of CORE, Baltimore's white leadership next had to contend with the federal government and an emboldened antipoverty program. The U.S. Office of Economic Opportunity (OEO) pressured the city to broaden the membership of the community action commission and to grant it more independence from the mayor and city council. A convention of delegates from Baltimore's low-income, inner-city neighborhoods at the close of 1966 sounded the new, assertive voice of the antipoverty program's local constituency. Members of the city council countered the program's drive for independence by restricting a proposed "self-help" housing program that would employ about ninety residents to make household repairs in poor neighborhoods and clean trash from the streets. The council insisted that the program's laborers be hired from a list maintained by the Department of Public Works. Council members doled out places on the list as patronage. In response to the council's action, about two hundred supporters of the local antipoverty program demonstrated in front of City Hall. The council backed down at its meeting later that evening when it learned that the OEO would withdraw all funds for the self-help program if the city insisted on the hiring restrictions that the council had imposed.

McKeldin, citing deep divisions among Baltimoreans on such issues as taxes and civil rights, announced that he would not run for reelection. In the Democratic primary, Thomas D'Alesandro III was opposed by former city council member Peter Angelos. The Angelos ticket also included an African American for city council president, state senator Clarence Mitchell III. His counterpart on the D'Alesandro ticket was city councilman William Donald Schaefer.

As in previous municipal elections, bossism and reform emerged as the principal focus of the campaign, beneath which lay the more seismic issue of race. D'Alesandro walked into a meeting of an all-white Democratic club just as a speaker declared, "We've got the guts to stand up for you—the white people." "What we want and need," said D'Alesandro, "is a guarantee all men can live in peace and dignity. I hope you can agree." Later in the campaign, he rejected the endorsement of the National States Rights Party "with distaste and disgust" for "its philosophy of bigotry." Republican Mayor McKeldin defended D'Alesandro against Republican attacks on his commitment to racial equality. But the voters split sharply along racial lines. Schaefer won the primary for city council president, but lost every black precinct to his African American opponent. Though his victory over Angelos was overwhelming, D'Alesandro nevertheless trailed Angelos in the city's black neighborhoods.

The general election produced a complete sweep for Democratic candidates. African Americans increased their representation on the city council from two seats to four. In his inaugural address, the new mayor promised to "root out every cause or vestige of discrimination." One of his first official acts was the appointment of Baltimore's first black city solicitor, George Russell.

The *Afro-American* saw D'Alesandro stepping up to the mayor's office at "a time when civil unrest is extremely high in this city." Baltimoreans seemed torn between self-congratulation for having avoided a race riot and apprehension that it might break out at any time. D'Alesandro did what he could to avert the explosion. One can only guess whether Baltimore might have been able to avoid a race riot had Martin Luther King Jr. not been assassinated in Memphis. In Baltimore, after two days of shock and mourning, came four days of looting and arson. Schaefer tried to distinguish Baltimore's riot from the ones that broke out simultaneously in approximately one hundred other cities. "We had looting," he said, "but not with the vengeance they had elsewhere."

In the aftermath of the riot, the things that D'Alesandro had done seemed irrelevant. The mayor was jeered by local businessmen at a meeting where he had hoped to offer assistance in repairing riot damage. A new organization, Responsible Citizens for Law and Order, attracted a crowd of one thousand two hundred to a meeting where speakers criticized D'Alesandro for his handling of the riot.

The D'Alesandro administration was soon under attack again. The East-West highway had been under consideration for decades, and the debate had progressed to route selection. One leg of the proposed highway would cut through white ethnic and working-class neighborhoods that traditionally yielded heavy majorities for Democrats like D'Alesandro, but not for civil rights legislation. At meetings about the expressway, hundreds of Baltimoreans shouted down their own elected representatives. One red-faced councilman thundered, "Let's get something straight. Not you or the Pope or nobody else is going to stop the road from going through these neighborhoods. It's passed. It's done." The audience's booing and shouting could be heard two blocks away. And it was hardly done. A coalition of community groups in white, working-class southeast Baltimore would eventually kill the expressway project.

The *Sun* had once called D'Alesandro the "super-charged mayor," who was "undaunted by the magnitude of the city's problems and convinced that Baltimore is of a size to be manageable." The riot was only the most obvious sign of the city's unmanageability. In its aftermath, the city's antipoverty agency unraveled when its three top administrators resigned. The city council rejected the mayor's nomination of a former CORE activist to lead the agency, an act that D'Alesandro regarded as a personal affront. Almost half of the community action commission resigned. D'Alesandro also had to address garbage, transit, and symphony orchestra strikes.

In April 1971 D'Alesandro announced that he would not run for reelection, saying that the reasons for his decision were personal. City council president Schaefer announced his candidacy for mayor just two days after D'Alesandro bowed out. Schaefer would enter the race as a political hybrid who combined the backing of a party organization with the support of newer civic organizations. In addition to the GBC, he had support in the Citizens' Planning and Housing Association, where he was a member of long standing and the recipient of the association's first Annual City Statesmanship Award.

Schaefer faced half a dozen announced candidates for the Democratic primary. One by one, other white candidates for mayor dropped out, leaving Schaefer with only one white competitor, a vestigial representative of Pollack's former empire who was given no chance of success. Two major black candidates ran against Schaefer—and one another. George L. Russell, city solicitor and a former judge, was the first to announce his candidacy. State senator Clarence Mitchell filed a few weeks later. Many black political leaders decried the anticipated division of the African American vote between the two candidates and expressed apprehension about its long-term implications for black political unity in Baltimore. African American political leaders hoped to settle on a consensus candidate whose obvious strength would induce both Russell and Mitchell to withdraw, but none stepped forward, and neither Mitchell nor Russell could be persuaded to drop out.

The primary election results were not quite as predicted. The combined votes of the two black candidates fell thirty thousand short of Schaefer's total. The vote did not split cleanly along racial lines. Although Schaefer won the support of almost all whites, about 15 percent of black voters also cast their ballots for him. In the general election, Schaefer defeated his Republican opponent with about 87 percent of the vote. Because D'Alesandro had been absent from the city, Schaefer became acting mayor even before the election and began to issue mayoral pronouncements while the campaign was still under way. He announced that he would create four new posts: a development coordinator and liaison officers for education, drug problems, and national relations. He also urged the voters to support a $3 million industrial development bond that was on the ballot. After the voters approved both his bond issue and his candidacy, Schaefer asked the GBC to help him develop an "economic master plan" for the city. It was to include industrial development, a comprehensive scheme for improving the retail district, and a new stadium.

Shortly after moving into the mayor's office, Schaefer announced another initiative: the Outer City Conservation Program. It would provide loan and grant funds for neighborhoods left out of the antipoverty and Model Cities programs. But in order to take part in the program, neighborhoods would have to organize. Schaefer's idea was to prevent sound and stable neighborhoods from deteriorating, but it would also mobilize a political constituency that could enhance both his stature in the city and his leverage with city bureaucracies. And unlike the programs for poor neighborhoods, this one came with relatively little federal oversight.

Schaefer's mayoral strategy combined a systematic drive to centralize power in his own office with a decentralization of municipal services to neighborhood mayor's stations and service centers. The four liaison officers announced before he was elected were part of this effort. Another component was a cabinet structure through which the mayor could oversee the performance of the city's departments.

One agency, the city's school system, was less amenable to mayoral control than others. Under the city charter, Schaefer and the council exercised limited control over the school budget, and the school board appointed the superintendent. Not long before Schaefer became mayor, the board appointed Roland Patterson, the city's first African American superintendent and a racial militant from Seattle. During Patterson's tenure, the U.S. Department of Health, Education, and Welfare (HEW) declared that the city's efforts to achieve school integration were "legally insufficient." Patterson insisted, and HEW agreed, that a legally sufficient solution need not include busing. But in the white, working-class neighborhoods of southeast Baltimore, anger and anxiety boiled up in protest against "forced busing"—even though no one had proposed it

Many of Baltimore's black residents regarded the white protests against busing as an eruption of code words for racism. Against the background of heightened racial tension, city council president Walter Orlinsky demanded an audit to determine whether Superintendent Patterson had shifted funds intended for supplies and materials to pay school system salaries. Patterson responded that the audit was a racist ploy intended to undermine any desegregation plan that he might propose to HEW. Schaefer only made things worse. George Russell, one of his black opponents in the Democratic primary, submitted a frosty letter informing Schaefer that he would resign as city solicitor on June 30, 1974. Without informing Russell, the mayor appointed a successor to take over on June 4. The discourtesy added to the racial antagonisms of the moment and offended the sensibilities of the city's black leaders, some of whom issued a statement warning that Baltimore's black residents would not be pushed around.

With racial tensions at the boiling point, Schaefer turned to face an outburst of militant unionism among city employees. The sanitation workers were the first to walk out, in July, leaving piles of garbage to ferment in the summer heat. Soon they were joined by groundskeepers at the city schools, many guards at the city jail, and the sewer workers. The police began a "job action," issuing nuisance tickets. The mayor's limousine got one. When Schaefer failed to respond to their pay demands, many officers stopped showing up for work, and an outbreak of looting ensued. While fifty policemen picketed the Western District police station, looters were carrying off the contents of liquor stores just two blocks away.

Schaefer chose this moment in 1974 to announce a new promotional campaign to present Baltimore as "Charm City," a tourist destination. Racial tensions and public employee strikes did not deter him from announcing his plan to build a $24 million convention center. The downtown stadium, a more controversial project, would have to await a referendum. Unlike the stadium, the convention center would not pay for itself with ticket revenues. But Schaefer argued that it would yield significant revenue for downtown hotels, restaurants, and shops. Another new initiative, promoted by housing commissioner Robert Embry, would create an alternative to demolition for vacant and dilapidated houses. The city would sell them for a dollar apiece to prospective homesteaders, who would be eligible for low-interest loans to cover the costs of rehabilitation. For Schaefer, the homesteading program was one of several hopeful ventures designed to draw middle-class households back to Baltimore.

In 1975 Patterson's contract as school superintendent was up for renewal, and Schaefer faced reelection. During his first term, Schaefer had appointed several new members to the school board, which now had an African American majority. Supporters of Patterson held prayer vigils outside school headquarters while the board discussed Patterson's future inside. Parren Mitchell, formerly director of the local antipoverty program, but now a congressman, declared himself a candidate for mayor, and some observers suggested that his candidacy might also be related to the renewal of Patterson's contract.

Mitchell's venture assumed that the city's African American leaders and voters would unify behind him, but his base was in West Baltimore, and one of the deepest fissures in black Baltimore separated African Americans on the east and west sides of the city. State delegate John Douglass and city council member Clarence "Du" Burns, both East Baltimore leaders, hoped that Mitchell's challenge might push the mayor in their direction. Schaefer took the hint. Burns became his floor manager in the council. Schaefer's shrewd political alliance with black politicians from proletarian East Baltimore helped to reinforce the division that separated them from the college-educated political dynasts of the West. When council president Orlinsky was convicted of bribery in 1982, Burns's successful bid to take his place would have the mayor's forceful backing.

Schaefer also weakened black support for Patterson. The mayor's appointment of a majority-black school board made Patterson's retention seem less essential to African Americans. The Board fired Patterson in June 1975. Mitchell withdrew as a mayoral candidate not long afterward, and Schaefer and his ticket prevailed. Turnout, according to one election official, was at its lowest in 15 years. "It's not that people don't care," said Schaefer. "The people of Baltimore are satisfied. There are no problems, no issues. Everything is okay."

Though Baltimore was hardly problem-free, Schaefer's satisfaction with the state of affairs was understandable. City schools had carried out federally mandated desegregation guidelines with little friction. Much of the credit for restoring calm went to John L. Crew, Patterson's successor. Crew was an African American and, while not a native Baltimorean, had lived in the city for twenty years, working his way up from school psychologist to superintendent. He was more attuned to Baltimore's racial sensibilities than Patterson, the outsider from Seattle. When Crew made his public debut at Memorial Stadium, before thousands of teachers, principals, and staff members, the school board president introduced him as "one of the family."

Schaefer practiced a kind of grassroots authoritarianism. By his second term, he was working with ninety-two neighborhood advisory committees. The community groups soon discovered that when he responded to their demands, he usually had demands of his own. If they wanted a playground, they would have to raise money for swings and a slide. Protest demonstrations, grandstanding, and posturing met stone-cold indifference. By the time he left the mayor's office in 1986, he had expanded his base to about 350 community groups. Some of them received city grants; some of their leaders held city jobs. He had converted the neighborhood associations into a citywide political organization that embraced both white and black communities.

Within City Hall, Schaefer could be positively dictatorial. After a city councilwoman challenged him on his subway project and tax policy, her husband lost his job as deputy executive director of the GBC. When the city council cut $10 million from his budget, he announced that constituent requests addressed to council members would henceforth be routed through the mayor's office. It was up to the mayor to monitor the cost of requests made by council members on behalf of their constituents. The agencies responsible for delivering on those constituent requests withered under his wrath if they failed to deliver promptly.

The passion that Schaefer invested in public sanitation and pothole repair rose to grander projects downtown designed to uplift both the city's spirit and its economy. Harborplace was the symbolic integration of these goals, an expression of city pride and commercialism. The idea of harborside development had been in the air since McKeldin mentioned it in his 1963 inauguration address. As Schaefer's second term approached its end, the old warehouses and rotting piers had been cleared away, leaving a desolate emptiness on the city's doorstep. He demanded that something be done. The Charles Center/Inner Harbor Management Corporation landscaped the waterfront. The corporation was one of several quasi-public bodies created outside the boundaries of official government to carry forward the city's development initiatives. Its beautification efforts created a waterfront park so attractive that it became a popular gathering place for Baltimoreans.

The mayor had already gotten approval and full or partial financing for a convention center several blocks west of the Inner Harbor, a science center to the south, and an aquarium on the east, and the city had become a shareholder in a new Hyatt Regency to be built near the convention center. The lynchpin that transformed these isolated projects into an integrated development was the strip of parkland marking the place where Baltimore met the water along the north and west margins of the Inner Harbor. For that land, Schaefer backed a scheme conceived by developer James Rouse to create a $22 million "festival mall" on 3.2 acres that would house shops and restaurants. Citizens for the Preservation of the Inner Harbor embarked on a petition drive for a ballot question to prevent any commercial development on the basin's perimeter. Schaefer countered with a ballot question of his own that would preserve 26 acres of open space while permitting the construction of the mall. The Citizens for Preservation needed ten thousand signatures to get their proposition on the 1978 election ballot. Schaefer needed only the support of ten city council members to get his measure before the voters.

The battle of the ballot questions drew far more attention and emotion than the contests for governor or state legislature. But it also confused the voters. In order to express their preferences effectively, they had to vote for one of the propositions and against the other. The Citizens for Preservation charged that the mayor had deliberately attempted to mystify the electorate and stepped up their efforts to defeat Schaefer's proposition. According to the *Baltimore Sun*, they portrayed their crusade as a David-and-Goliath struggle. But the preservationists' claim to speak for the city's grassroots was vigorously contested. Schaefer's long cultivation of community and civic organizations paid off. The Citizens' Planning and Housing Association sided with Schaefer and Rouse, as did a diverse array of neighborhood associations. About one hundred thousand citizens cast their votes on the Harborplace ballot questions, and the mayor's question won by about seventeen thousand votes.

After the victory of Harborplace, Schaefer's 1979 reelection seemed anticlimactic. His opponents in the Democratic primary were political nonentities. But the criticisms were more prominent than the candidates. The Charm City offensive seemed to overlook those citizens who were short on charm. While the city courted middle-class households for its homesteading program, twenty-four thousand Baltimoreans were on the waiting list for public housing, and Schaefer had no plans to build additional housing projects. In its effort to attract tourists and taxpayers, the city had spent one-third of its federal urban renewal and community development aid on Harborplace and a new housing development for middle-income residents. Federal authorities would later rule that some of these expenditures were illegal. Under Schaefer, the public schools' share of the budget remained constant, but only because of increased state aid. Local expenditures on the schools actually declined during his administration.

In 1980 the focus of criticism shifted from what Schaefer had done to how he had done it. A series of newspaper articles disclosed that his administration had created a so-called shadow government of quasi-public, or completely private, corporations able to evade charter requirements that city expenditures be reviewed by the planning commission or the city council, or approved by the voters through referenda. At the center of the shadow government were the city's finance director and treasurer (the "Trustees"), who controlled a $100 million fund derived from federal grants, bond issues, or loan repayments. The money was used to make further loans to private developers or direct capital expenditures through a network of twenty-five quasi-public corporations. The Trustees stood at the center of a private government created to circumvent the time-consuming procedures under which the official government labored.

Instead of provoking outrage, the public exposure of the shadow government initially prompted talk about revising the city charter so as to accommodate the Trustees' operations. City council president Walter Orlinsky, one of Schaefer's most consistent political antagonists, attempted to get the state legislature to dismantle the "corporate" branch of city government, but hardly anyone supported his effort. More than a year and a half after the shadow government had come to light, the most drastic countermeasure proposed by the city council was an annual audit of its shadowy finances. The plan went nowhere, and the funds controlled by the Trustees continued to grow.

An article in *The New Republic* criticized Schaefer for neglecting the city's low-income and African American residents, but conceded that his "positive thinking" had engendered "a genuine atmosphere of achievement and hope." Harborplace may have been less important as a business proposition than as a symbol of Baltimore's renaissance. Schaefer himself had become the city's "father figure," according to one city council member. A *Sun* poll in 1982 found that almost two-thirds of Baltimoreans believed that their city had improved during the previous five years, though African Americans were less likely than whites to see progress. When asked what they disliked about Baltimore, respondents mentioned crime and concerns for safety.

In 1983 a credible black candidate challenged Schaefer's bid for a fourth term: Circuit Court Judge William H. Murphy, a graduate of MIT. His great-grandfather had founded the *Baltimore Afro-American* in 1892, and the paper was still in the family. Murphy attacked Schaefer for giving too much attention to building projects and too little to the people of his city, especially its low-income black people. Julian Bond, Jesse Jackson, and Atlanta's first black mayor, Maynard Jackson, all visited Baltimore to promote Murphy's candidacy. But Schaefer got the endorsement of a powerful organization of black clergy, the Interdenominational Ministerial Alliance, and bested Murphy by more than one hundred thousand votes in the Democratic primary. Against an African American candidate, Schaefer won a majority of the African American vote. Du Burns, running on Schaefer's ticket, became Baltimore's first black city council president.

In his final term as mayor, Schaefer suffered his most grievous defeat: The Colts left Baltimore for Indianapolis. In 1970, the year before Schaefer won his first mayoral election, the Colts had won the Super Bowl. Schaefer had engaged in extended negotiations with the team's owner, Robert Irsay, while Irsay shopped around the country seeking a more profitable field for his team. Facing defeat, Schaefer persuaded the General Assembly to pass legislation that would authorize him to seize the Colts by eminent domain. In the dark of night, Irsay packed up his team's equipment, and its franchise, and carried them beyond the reach of Maryland's laws to Indianapolis.

The mayor would spend the rest of his term trying to secure the money and the site for a new stadium that would attract a new team. Meanwhile, he quietly prepared to run for governor in 1986, without an official declaration of his candidacy. Polls showed that he was the most popular public official in Maryland. In mid-June 1985 he confirmed that he would run for governor in conversations with other public officials, but stopped short of an official announcement. A month earlier State's Attorney Schmoke held a spectacularly successful fundraiser for his mayoral candidacy that attracted almost seven thousand guests and raised $200,000. Schmoke was a black graduate of Yale and Harvard Law School who had attended Oxford as a Rhodes Scholar. At his public high school in Baltimore, he had been a star quarterback and president of the student body.

Schaefer's victory in the gubernatorial election elevated Burns from city council president to mayor and positioned him to run for the office in 1987. Robert Embry, former housing commissioner, resigned as president of the school board to consider entering the race himself. If Schmoke and Burns split the black vote, Embry might have been able to win on the strength of the white vote. But Embry eventually took himself out of consideration. Early polls showed him running third, even among white voters.

Baltimore, which had never elected a black mayor, now headed for a Democratic primary in which both of the candidates were black. Yet they could hardly have been more different from one another. Burns had attended high school in East Baltimore and spent twenty-two years handing out towels in the locker room of a West Baltimore high school. In 1947 he had formed his own political club and rounded up votes for Thomas D'Alesandro Jr. The job as a locker room attendant was his reward. It took him twenty-seven years to move up from precinct, to ward, to district leadership, until 1971 when he was elected to the city council. To become Baltimore's first elected black mayor, he would have to defeat a Rhodes Scholar and Harvard-trained lawyer. Early polls put him more than 30 percentage points behind Schmoke. His campaign had far less money than Schmoke's, and it suffered from internal tensions. But as the September primary approached, a new poll showed that he had gained 21 percentage points on Schmoke, and though Schmoke would win, it was a narrow victory.

INDUSTRY, COMMERCE, AND LABOR

In 1950, when Baltimore reached its peak population of almost one million, it was a decidedly blue-collar town. Over 34 percent of its labor force was employed in manufacturing, and the city's factories generated much of the business that kept the rest of its economy afloat. Bethlehem Steel was one of the larger employers; in fact, it was the biggest steel mill in the world, but like many other Baltimore companies, it was not locally owned. At the end of the 1950s, Bethlehem had thirty-five thousand workers, some of whom used steel produced by the mill to build freighters and tankers at the Sparrow's Point shipyard. The Point had started out as Bethlehem's company town outside the bounds of Baltimore, but as the mill's workforce grew steelworkers began to populate southeast Baltimore, unless they were black. African American steelworkers lived in West Baltimore, segregated at home as they were at the plant.

The pay was good. After the steelworkers union became the bargaining agent for the Bethlehem employees in 1941, they got health benefits, paid vacations, and sick leave. Their circumstances approached those of the middle class, and they could afford the hope that their children might attend college. But in 1971 a surge of steel imports reduced demand for domestic product, and Bethlehem laid off three thousand workers. Foreign competition was fueled not just by cheap labor abroad, but by management inertia at home. Bethlehem's executives, for example, delayed adoption of the basic oxygen furnaces developed in Austria because the equipment was still undergoing refinements, and the open hearths already in operation were relatively new. Management overlooked the fact that the oxygen furnaces could produce 200 tons of steel every forty-five minutes, while the open hearths needed eight hours to make 425 tons.

By the late 1980s Bethlehem's workforce had been reduced to eight thousand, its decline paralleling the downward path of other Baltimore industries. The city's industrial workforce dropped by 75 percent between 1950 and 1995. But industry was not alone in losing ground. Baltimore's retail businesses also suffered. In 1954 80 percent of the region's retail trade was concentrated within the city limits. By 1992 all but 18 percent occurred in the suburbs. The consequences of deindustrialization had been compounded by suburbanization, and both were reflected in the racial composition and poverty of the city's population. Twenty percent of its residents lived below the poverty line, and Baltimore accounted for a majority of all the poor people in Maryland.

Schaefer's Charm City offensive was an attempt to remake Baltimore's economy. In the decade beginning in 1976, the redevelopment campaign spearheaded by the shadow government packaged opportunities for developers that generated $800 million in private investment, about half of it in downtown projects. Downtown property assessments quadrupled. Harborplace was even more successful; during the 1980s it drew $1.2 billion in investment, and public funds accounted for only 10 percent of the total. But at the end of the 1980s, the combined effects of changes in the federal tax code and a national recession interrupted the boom. It would revive in the mid-1990s when the downtown stadium envisioned by Mayor Schaefer was realized by Governor Schaefer, paired with another stadium intended for Baltimore's new football team. A $150 million expansion of the convention center and two publicly subsidized hotels for conventioneers rounded out the city's economic stimulus package.

Schaefer's strategy was to make up for Baltimore's loss of industry by converting the blue-collar town into a tourist destination. Improbable as it seemed, the transformation was rather successful. The city became the sixteenth most popular tourist destination in the United States, and visitors left $1 billion in Baltimore annually.

But tourism was a poor substitute for manufacturing. The service employees who staffed the harborside tourist attractions earned only 60 percent as much as other Baltimoreans. And Harborplace itself was not a complete success. Several projects failed, and a 1992 study of the city's development loans since the 1970s found that $60 million had never been paid back. Other projects were profitable, but not for the city. The new stadiums generated $4 million in annual expenditures for the city's businesses, but at a cost of $28 million to city government.

The greatest failing of Baltimore's "renaissance" was that it seemed to have little impact beyond Harborplace and the central business district. Middle-class residents—black and white—continued to leave Baltimore for the suburbs. The city's poverty rate continued to rise. Abandoned housing and vacant lots were tangible testimony to the abandonment of Baltimore.

RACE, ETHNICITY, AND IMMIGRATION

Baltimore's economic decline reduced its attractiveness to immigrants from abroad. By 2000 only 4.6 percent of the city's population was foreign-born. Of the nation's one hundred largest cities, the immigrant share of Baltimore's population ranked eighty-third. Most had come to the city from Europe or Asia. Its small Latino population was relatively dispersed, unlike its African American residents, who were more segregated than in most other cities.

Though immigration dwindled, black in-migrants continued to settle in Baltimore. Between 1940 and 1960, the city gained about one hundred thousand black residents. A few were from the West Indies, but the vast majority came from the southern United States.

They arrived at an inconvenient time. During the 1940s Baltimore, like other American cities, faced a wartime housing shortage. In the 1950s urban renewal reduced the stock of housing available to low-income families, and from 1951 to 1971, seventy-five thousand Baltimoreans were moved to make way for renewal projects. Between 80 and 90 percent of those uprooted were black.

Many of those displaced would wind up in public housing. When the first projects had opened in the 1940s, they were officially segregated. Still, they represented a step up for many of Baltimore's black households. African American families flooded the housing authority with applications, partly because housing was in short supply and partly because public housing was superior to the housing that they could afford on the private market. To live in public housing, however, applicants had to meet a variety of standards. In addition to income limits, applicants were screened to exclude "undesirable" tenants. Single mothers were generally turned down. Only a handful of those accepted were welfare recipients.

But when urban renewal displaced low-income people from their homes, it made no distinction between worthy and "undesirable" poor people. Public housing officials were under pressure to relax their selection criteria in order to accommodate families made homeless by public policy. These households would later be joined by some of the Baltimoreans living in the path of the city's ill-fated East-West expressway.

Welfare recipients and single-parent households became more numerous in the city's public housing projects. To provide apartments for these and other applicants on the public housing waiting list, the city built its first high-rise housing projects beginning in the mid-1950s. Housing officials had sought to reduce land acquisition costs by acquiring vacant property on the city's fringe, a strategy that might have enabled them to avoid the use of high-rise buildings. But outer-city residents and their city council representatives imposed severe restrictions on that option. Housing officials therefore embarked on the laborious and expensive task of assembling land parcels for the new high-rise projects in poor neighborhoods, often in proximity to preexisting public housing.

A further complication arose from new federal requirements for the racial desegregation of public housing. In Baltimore, the local housing authorities approached the race issue with the same conflict-averse caution as the school authorities. They deliberately avoided a press campaign to promote desegregation. They selected "wholesome" black families for transfer to white projects, taking care to exclude those "whose behavior might be subject to criticism." African Americans engaged in professional training under the GI Bill were also excluded because poor whites might regard them as "snobbish." As an additional precaution against outbreaks of racial conflict, the housing authorities allowed white tenants to move from integrated projects to ones that were still all white.

But "wholesome" two-parent families and black veterans getting educated on the GI Bills were more likely than other black households to achieve income levels that priced them out of the projects. The high-rises filled up with households made homeless by urban renewal and highway construction along with others who would not have qualified for apartments under the old selection standards. They became towers of concentrated poverty, decay, and crime.

Similar concentrations were emerging in inner-city Baltimore as black families with stable incomes moved into housing abandoned by whites leaving the city for the suburbs. Soon relatively prosperous African American families would head for the suburbs themselves, achieving segregation by class as well as race. The high-rises would go on to be demolished in the early 1990s.

See also *Baltimore, MD 1776–1790; Baltimore, MD 1790–1828; Baltimore, MD 1828–1854; Baltimore, MD 1854–1877; Baltimore, MD 1877–1896; Baltimore, MD 1896–1929; Baltimore, MD 1929–1941; Baltimore, MD 1941–1952*

MATTHEW CRENSON

BIBLIOGRAPHY

Bachrach, Peter, and Morton Baratz. *Power and Poverty: Theory and Practice.* New York, NY: Oxford University Press, 1970.

Callcott, George H. *Maryland and America, 1940–1980.* Baltimore, MD: Johns Hopkins University Press, 1985.

Durr, Kenneth D. *Behind the Backlash: White Working-Class Politics in Baltimore, 1940–1980.* Chapel Hill: University of North Carolina Press, 2003.

Durr, W. Theodore. "The Conscience of a City: A History of the Citizens' Planning and Housing Association." PhD diss., Johns Hopkins University, 1972.

Levine, Marc V. "'A Third World City in the First World': Social Exclusion, Racial Inequality and Sustainable Development in Baltimore." In *The Social Sustainability of Cities: Diversity and the Management of Change,* edited by Mario Polese and Richard N. Stren, 123–156. Toronto: University of Toronto Press, 2000.

Reutter, Mark. *Making Steel: Sparrows Point and the Rise and Ruin of American Industrial Might.* Urbana: University of Illinois Press, 2004.

Smith, C. Fraser. *William Donald Schaefer: A Political Biography.* Baltimore, MD: Johns Hopkins University Press, 1999.

Williams, Rhonda Y. *The Politics of Urban Renewal: Black Women's Struggles Against Urban Inequality.* New York, NY: Oxford University Press, 2004.

CHAPTER 10

Population rankings based on
the 2010 Census Bureau estimate

CITIES IN THE NEOLIBERAL ERA, 1989–2011

The period from 1989 to 2011 begins with the fall of the Soviet Union and the end of the bipolar world order that defined the Cold War. A new "war on terror" took its place, marked in 2001 by the joint attacks on the World Trade Center and the Pentagon, leading to American-led invasions of Afghanistan and Iraq under the authority of a president elected in a controversial contest in which he received less of the popular vote than his main opponent. The 1990s saw one of the world's greatest economic expansions, while the first decade of the twenty-first century was marked by the Great Recession and the election of the first African American president.

There were 24 percent more people living in the United States in 2010 (nearly 309 million in total) than there had been in 1990. The majority of population growth occurred in the southern and western states, whose cities thus also grew proportionately faster than those in the Northeast and Midwest. By 2010 only three midwestern or northeastern cities (New York, Chicago, and Philadelphia) remained among the ten largest in the country, with the rest located in Texas, Arizona, and California. All of these cities increased in population during the 1990s and 2000s (and all but Chicago and Philadelphia reached historic peak populations by 2010), but the Sunbelt cities grew the fastest, especially San Antonio (whose population increased by 44 percent between 1990 and 2008), Houston (38 percent), and Phoenix (59 percent).

With some exceptions, the Sunbelt cities are demographically distinct from the northeastern and midwestern cities. New York, Chicago, and Philadelphia all have proportionately larger black populations than the rest of the country, with the highest being in Philadelphia (43 percent black) and the lowest in New York (27 percent). Similar to New York, Houston and Dallas were both approximately one-quarter black in 2000, compared to 11 percent in Los Angeles, and less than 10 percent in Phoenix, San Diego, San Antonio, and San Jose. At the same time, however, the percentage of the population that is black in New York and Chicago has been declining since at least 1990 (as it has in other eastern cities, such as Washington, D.C.), while the Latino population in each of the country's ten largest cities has been expanding. By 2000 at least a quarter of the populations of the ten largest cities was Latino, with the exception of Philadelphia, which was 9 percent Latino.

The increasing Latino presence in big American cities is a reflection of a larger resurgence in immigration to the United States since the 1980s, with the majority of new arrivals coming from Latin America, South Asia, and Southeast Asia. Between 1981 and 1985 slightly less than three million immigrants arrived in the United States, compared to nearly five million between 1986 and 1990. During the 1990s more than eleven million immigrants arrived, and nearly eight million came between 2001 and 2005. By 2009 there were more foreign-born residents in the United States (thirty-nine million) than there had ever been in the country's history. The new immigrants have compensated for an increasingly older native-born workforce (the result of steadily decreasing birth rates since the 1960s), which has put increasing pressure on government programs for the elderly, such as Social Security and Medicare.

Increased immigration has raised new political issues, mostly focusing on the possible legalization of undocumented workers, and caused increased security along the U.S.-Mexico border. Unlike the efforts to reduce the free flow of people between the United States and Mexico, the period covered in this chapter is notably marked by an increase in the free flow of money and products across U.S. borders, a result of the North American Free Trade Agreement (NAFTA) passed by the Clinton administration in 1994, over the objections of many traditional Democratic constituencies, including labor.

Bill Clinton was elected president as a centrist Democrat in 1992, defeating the incumbent Republican George H. W. Bush in a three-way race that included the independent Texas billionaire Ross Perot, who captured 19 percent of the popular vote, thus allowing Clinton to win with a 43 percent plurality. Bush had achieved popularity for his administration's successful execution in 1990 and 1991 of the first Gulf War—an American-led, UN-sponsored international effort in response to Iraq's invasion of Kuwait, which involved relatively few casualties and was resolved quickly. Yet Bush was also forced to renege on a campaign promise when he approved a federal budget in 1990 that included significant tax increases, which

BY THE NUMBERS: THE MOST POPULOUS CITIES IN 2010

	TOTAL POPULATION[1]	WHITE ALONE NON-HISPANIC POPULATION[1]	BLACK OR AFRICAN AMERICAN ALONE NON-HISPANIC POPULATION[1]	ASIAN ALONE NON-HISPANIC POPULATION[1]	OTHER RACE NON-HISPANIC POPULATION[1]	HISPANIC POPULATION[1]	% WHITE ALONE NON-HISPANIC[1]	% BLACK OR AFRICAN AMERICAN ALONE NON-HISPANIC[1]	% ASIAN ALONE NON-HISPANIC[1]
NEW YORK, NY	8,175,133	2,722,904	1,861,295	1,028,119	226,739	2,336,076	33.3	22.8	12.6
LOS ANGELES, CA	3,792,621	1,086,908	347,380	420,212	99,299	1,838,822	28.7	9.2	11.1
CHICAGO, IL	2,695,598	854,717	872,286	144,903	44,830	778,862	31.7	32.4	5.4
HOUSTON, TX	2,099,451	537,901	485,956	124,859	31,067	919,668	25.6	23.1	5.9
PHILADELPHIA, PA	1,526,006	562,585	644,287	95,521	36,002	187,611	36.9	42.2	6.3
PHOENIX, AZ	1,445,632	672,573	86,788	43,894	52,500	589,877	46.5	6.0	3.0
SAN ANTONIO, TX	1,327,407	353,106	83,365	30,596	21,388	838,952	26.6	6.3	2.3
SAN DIEGO, CA	1,307,402	589,702	82,497	204,347	54,836	376,020	45.1	6.3	15.6
DALLAS, TX	1,197,816	345,205	294,159	33,609	17,534	507,309	28.8	24.6	2.8
SAN JOSE, CA	945,942	271,382	27,508	300,022	33,394	313,636	28.7	2.9	31.7

	% OTHER RACE NON-HISPANIC[1]	% HISPANIC[1]	% POPULATION FOREIGN-BORN[2]	% POPULATION 25 AND OLDER COLLEGE-EDUCATED[3]	% WOMEN IN THE LABOR FORCE[4]	% CIVILIAN LABOR FORCE UNEMPLOYED[4]	% EMPLOYED POPULATION IN MANUFACTURING[5]	MEDIAN FAMILY INCOME[6]	LAND AREA (SQ. MI.)[7]	POPULATION DENSITY (PER SQ. MI.)[7]
NEW YORK, NY	2.8	28.6	35.7	34.0	58.0	10.2	4.1	$56,054	302.6	27,016.3
LOS ANGELES, CA	2.6	48.5	39.7	30.3	60.2	11.6	10.2	$52,966	468.7	8,091.8
CHICAGO, IL	1.7	28.9	20.6	33.1	62.2	13.1	9.3	$52,101	227.6	11,843.6
HOUSTON, TX	1.5	43.8	28.5	27.9	60.0	8.3	9.2	$47,329	599.6	3,501.4
PHILADELPHIA, PA	2.4	12.3	11.6	23.2	56.8	13.8	7.3	$45,769	134.1	11,379.6
PHOENIX, AZ	3.6	40.8	21.7	24.7	60.0	11.3	8.1	$53,906	516.7	2,797.8
SAN ANTONIO, TX	1.6	63.2	13.2	23.1	58.4	8.0	5.3	$51,002	460.9	2,880.0
SAN DIEGO, CA	4.2	28.8	24.9	41.3	60.3	8.6	9.6	$73,648	325.2	4,020.3
DALLAS, TX	1.5	42.4	24.8	28.3	59.5	9.3	7.6	$42,699	340.5	3,517.8
SAN JOSE, CA	3.5	33.2	38.1	35.6	61.8	11.1	19.7	$84,274	176.5	5,359.4

Source: American FactFinder (http://www.census.gov).
[1]*Source:* American FactFinder: Census 2010 Redistricting Data SF (PL 94-171). Table P2.
[2]*Source:* 2009 American Community Survey 1-Year Estimates. Table B05006.
[3]*Source:* 2009 American Community Survey 1-Year Estimates. Table B15002.
[4]*Source:* 2009 American Community Survey 1-Year Estimates. Table B23001.
[5]*Source:* 2009 American Community Survey 1-Year Estimates. Table B24030.
[6]*Source:* 2009 American Community Survey 1-Year Estimates. Table B19113.
[7]*Source:* American FactFinder: Census 2010 Redistricting Data SF (PL 94-171). Table G001.

played poorly in a country that was in recession in 1992, in part a result of higher oil prices resulting from the Gulf War.

Clinton entered office in 1993 with Democratic majorities in the House and Senate. He succeeded in getting Congress to pass an initial budget, which reversed some Reagan and Bush policies, and free-trade legislation such as NAFTA, but he failed to pass the centerpiece of his agenda, health care reform. His policy choices narrowed in 1994 when Republicans won majorities in both the House and Senate, leading to a standoff between the president and Congress that stalled passage of a federal budget and thus shut down large parts of the federal government for several days in late 1995 and early 1996.

Despite his problems with Congress, and personal issues that ultimately led to his impeachment by the House in 1998, Clinton's presidency benefited from a booming economy during the 1990s. This economic prosperity was partly the result of business restructuring in response to the recessions of the 1970s and 1980s as well as the massive increase in new technologies and the industries responsible for their development and production—the Internet boom, which was followed in 2000 by the dot-com crash resulting from overspeculation in high-tech companies.

The benefits of the 1990s boom were captured to a greater extent than in previous economic upswings, by upper-income groups, at the same time that low unemployment created greater demand for low-wage workers. To bring more poor people into the labor force, the Republican Congress and the Clinton administration collaborated to create a massive reform to the cash assistance welfare program that had been created during the New Deal. The new program included work requirements and a lifetime limit of five years for receiving federal cash assistance.

Clinton was reelected handily in 1996, and his vice president, Al Gore, ran on the Democratic ticket in 2000, against George W. Bush, the son of the former president. Gore won the popular vote by roughly 0.5 percent, but the election ultimately hinged on Florida, where the vote was close enough to require a recount, which became a legal battle that was ultimately decided by the U.S. Supreme Court in favor of Bush, in a highly controversial 5-4 decision.

The beginning of the second Bush presidency was marked by the terrorist attacks against the Pentagon and World Trade Center. The United States quickly invaded Afghanistan, and the anti-American Taliban government collapsed. The suspected mastermind behind the attacks, Osama bin Laden (whom the Taliban had likely been supporting), was not captured for another decade, when he was killed by American special forces in Pakistan. Bush declared the anti-American regimes in North Korea, Iran, and Iraq an "Axis of Evil" and began to slowly build up support for an invasion of Iraq, which began in 2003.

Unlike the first Gulf War, the Second Gulf War had only limited international support and was fought for the better part of a decade, resulting in far greater casualties than the earlier war. While combat forces were withdrawn in 2010, tens of thousands of American troops remain.

Bush's presidency was marred by an inadequate response to flooding in New Orleans after Hurricane Katrina in 2005, which decimated the city and turned many of its residents into refugees; by revelations of Iraqi prisoners tortured by American troops; and by the economic collapse that began in 2008, which would become one of the biggest challenges facing the next president, Barack Obama.

NEW YORK, NY 1989–2011

NEW YORK CITY BECAME A SYMBOL OF URBAN RENAISSANCE in the 1990s. Crime was down, population was up, and the economy was thriving on finance and real estate. Mayor Rudolph W. Giuliani (1994–2001) won praise for his focus on quality-of-life concerns and ushered in two decades of Republican leadership in the heavily Democratic city.

The terrorist attacks of September 11, 2001 (9/11) triggered dire predictions for skyscraper New York, but the city proved remarkably resilient. Under Mayor Michael R. Bloomberg (2002–) crime plunged to new lows, Wall Street soared to new heights, and there was an easing of the racial tensions that welled up from aggressive policing and a singularly diverse population. In 2008, however, the nation's financial crisis struck New York and underscored the risks of an economy dependent on Wall Street.

GOVERNMENT AND POLITICS

In 1989 significant changes occurred in New York City politics. The U.S. Supreme Court declared the city's Board of Estimate unconstitutional because borough presidents with equal power represented populations that ranged from 379,000 in Staten Island to 2.3 million in Brooklyn. Charter revisions abolished the Board of Estimate and shifted its powers to an expanded, fifty-one-member city council. Emasculated borough presidencies continued to attract mayoral aspirants but no longer served as a meaningful check in a strong-mayor system.

Also in 1989 voters made history when they elected the city's only African American mayor, David N. Dinkins (1990–1993). Despite the city's liberal reputation and nonwhite majority, Dinkins's election was exceptional. As numerical equals, blacks and Latinos were rivals for power, and both groups were fractured by internecine struggles between foreign- and native-born. Meanwhile, whites maintained an electoral plurality. The mild-mannered Dinkins appealed to liberal whites, who were alarmed by escalating racial tensions and political corruption under Mayor Edward I. Koch (1978–1989), and mobilized exceptionally high black voter turnout to defeat Koch in the Democratic primary and edge out Republican Rudy Giuliani in the general election.

In office Dinkins was a weak leader who could do little for his black and Latino supporters. Facing a severe recession, billion-dollar deficits, and diminished federal aid, he trimmed spending and raised taxes. He acceded to business pressure and continued Koch's practice of subsidizing Manhattan development. His lackluster responses to a race riot in Crown Heights and a black boycott of Korean grocers antagonized white supporters. Despite hiring additional police officers and making a dent in crime, he appeared no match for crack-fueled crime rates.

Dinkins lost his 1993 reelection rematch with Giuliani, a former prosecutor who promised to get tough on crime. As mayor, Giuliani sweetened corporate subsidies and tightened social control. New policing strategies included a crackdown on minor offenses, a computerized tracking system, and extensive stop-and-frisk encounters. Welfare recipients faced stringent eligibility

QUICK FACTS

NEW YORK, NY 1989–2011

MAYORS

Edward I. Koch	(1978–1989)
David N. Dinkins	(1990–1993)
Rudolph W. Giuliani	(1994–2001)
Michael R. Bloomberg	(2002–)

MAJOR INDUSTRIES AND EMPLOYERS

The City of New York
New York-Presbyterian Healthcare System
Citigroup
J. P. Morgan Chase
Verizon Communications

MAJOR NEWSPAPERS

Daily News
El Diario La Prensa
Hoy
Newsday
New York Post
New York Times
Staten Island Advance
Wall Street Journal

MAJOR EVENTS

March 22, 1989: U.S. Supreme Court declares the New York City Board of Estimate unconstitutional.

August 19–22, 1991: A three-day riot pitting blacks against Jews occurs in Crown Heights, Brooklyn.

September 11, 2001: Terrorists attack the World Trade Center.

2002: State lawmakers grant Mayor Michael R. Bloomberg control over city schools.

2008: Mayor Bloomberg and the city council amend the city's term limits law to allow three terms for the mayor.

---

and workfare requirements. Homeless people were ticketed and arrested for "camping" in parks and obstructing sidewalks. Crime plummeted to its lowest level in forty years; welfare rolls hit a thirty-five-year low.

Although New Yorkers reelected Giuliani in 1997 by a double-digit margin over a liberal white opponent, Manhattan borough president Ruth Messinger, they soured on his hard-edged style. Instances of police brutality toward blacks, including an unarmed African immigrant killed by forty-one police bullets and a Haitian immigrant tortured by police in a precinct house restroom, magnified the mayor's alienation from the black community, while an ugly public saga of infidelity and divorce exposed Giuliani's callous mistreatment of family. Giuliani staggered toward the end of his two-term limit.

With a 5-1 advantage in voter registration, Democrats appeared poised to reclaim City Hall in 2001—until terrorists struck on the day of the primary, September 11, fundamentally altered the race. The shift in focus, from economic opportunity for poor and working-class residents to economic recovery for a wounded city, undercut Bronx borough president Fernando Ferrer's message and momentum. Although Ferrer still garnered a plurality in the rescheduled primary, he lost the nomination to public advocate Mark Green, a white liberal, in a racially

The September 11, 2001, terrorist attacks on the World Trade Center destroyed the iconic buildings and killed more than 2,600 people. Reconstruction is underway for new buildings and a memorial on the site.

Source: PH2 Jim Watson, USN/Department of Defense

charged runoff that played on Ferrer's Puerto Rican background and overtures to Reverend Al Sharpton, a polarizing black leader.

Giuliani's exceptional leadership after 9/11 earned him hero status as "America's mayor," and his late-game endorsement helped snatch a victory for Bloomberg, a billionaire businessman who switched parties to run as a Republican rather than join a fight with established Democrats. Bloomberg also benefited from racial voting patterns, winning among whites in Queens, Brooklyn, and Staten Island who abandoned Green, while Green struggled to motivate Latinos and blacks angered by his alleged race-baiting against Ferrer.

Mayor Bloomberg mingled super-sized economic development with an activist social agenda that included smoking bans in restaurants, bars, parks, and other public spaces; a ban on the use of trans fats in restaurants; and hundreds of miles of new bike lanes. He made educational improvement the cornerstone of his mayoralty and, after winning control over the city's public schools in 2002, pushed through wide-ranging reforms against strong opposition from parents and a powerful teachers union. To address recurring fiscal crises, Bloomberg favored tax increases—even alienating outer-borough supporters with an 18.5 percent property tax hike—over deep spending cuts. Although he took a tougher stand on corporate subsidies, he vigorously promoted vast new postindustrial development for the West Side of Manhattan, the Atlantic Yards in Brooklyn, Willets Point in Queens, and elsewhere.

In 2005 voters rewarded Bloomberg for the city's rebound with a historic 20-point victory over Ferrer. When the financial crisis struck in 2008, Bloomberg argued that he was uniquely qualified to be steward and muscled the city council into amending the city's term limits law—enacted and reaffirmed by popular votes in 1993 and 1996—to allow him a third term. Bloomberg's willingness to spend another $80-million-plus out of pocket snuffed the competition (dependent on public financing with spending caps) and positioned him to overpower a lone Democratic challenger, comptroller William C. Thompson Jr., the city's highest-ranking African American. In the end, Bloomberg's five-point margin of victory over a lackluster opponent—at a cost of more than $100 million, or nearly $200 per vote—was a sobering indication of public resentment over his term limits coup.

Although Bloomberg stood among the powerful mayors that had defined New York since the 1970s, he was repeatedly humbled by state lawmakers who blocked his efforts to tax commuters, construct a West Side stadium (dooming his bid for the Olympics), and impose a toll on Manhattan motorists. Tellingly, the mayor was shunned in the state-led rebuilding of Ground Zero.

INDUSTRY, COMMERCE, AND LABOR

At the turn of the twenty-first century, more than 25 percent of New York City's workforce was employed in one million jobs in finance, insurance and real estate, and professional and business services, while just over one in twenty workers labored in fewer than two hundred thousand manufacturing jobs. This marked an inversion of the economy in 1950, when one million manufacturing jobs occupied more than a quarter of the city's workers.

The decline of manufacturing and growth in service-sector employment was intertwined in New York. As manufacturing relocated around the globe, new demand arose for specialized services in finance, law, accounting, management consulting, insurance, and advertising to facilitate the operation of global enterprises. From its nadir in the 1970s, New York restructured its economy around the production and provision of these advanced services and became a command center in the global economy.

Global prominence enhanced New York's value as a terrorist target. A 1993 truck bomb attack on New York's World Trade Center killed six and injured more than 1,000. Eight years later terrorists used commercial jetliners for the devastating 9/11 attack on the World Trade Center's Twin Towers that killed more than 2,750 people, destroyed thirteen million square feet of office space, and deepened an economic downturn. President George W. Bush committed $21 billion for rebuilding, and Congress acted quickly to provide compensation for those injured and killed in the attacks, though thousands of rescue, recovery, and cleanup workers endured years of bitter conflict over treatment for illnesses caused by exposure to the toxic stew at Ground Zero.

In the post-9/11 world, New Yorkers lived with the fear that another attack was imminent. Yet as indicated by the growing number of affluent families with children in Manhattan, this fear was tempered by continued optimism regarding the city's future.

Indeed, 9/11 did not alter the city's economic position. A deeper structural problem, however, was the city's vulnerability to the boom-and-bust cycles of Wall Street. Stock market–induced recessions resulted in hundreds of thousands of lost jobs and multi-billion-dollar municipal deficits in 1989–1993, 2001–2003, and 2008 on, although New York was cushioned against this latest crisis by billions of dollars in federal bailout money injected into the ailing financial markets.

Finance also sparked economic growth in the boom years. From 2003 to 2006 Wall Street was responsible for 40 percent of the city's job growth and over 50 percent of its income gain. In 2006 Wall Street employed 5 percent of the city's workers but paid 23 percent of all wages—more than double the industry's impact in 1986. New York was home to six of the world's ten largest financial firms and nearly half of all equity trading worldwide.

Finance fueled a real estate boom as the city was refashioned around places of work, rest, and play for highly paid managers and professionals. Between 2000 and 2007 the city added over fifty major office buildings to its crowded skyline. More than one hundred seventy-five thousand new housing units were built, many of them luxury condominiums seeding gentrification around the Manhattan core, from Harlem to the Lower East Side and across the East River into the industrial waterfront and brownstone neighborhoods of Brooklyn and Queens. Home prices ballooned as much as 500 percent in these neighborhoods and almost 125 percent citywide between 1996 and 2006.

Upscale commercial districts, featuring trendy restaurants and boutique clothing shops, accompanied luxury residential development in old industrial neighborhoods like SoHo, Tribeca, and Williamsburg. The publicly subsidized redevelopment of Times Square reinvigorated the Broadway theater industry, provided high-rise headquarters for global media corporations, and produced a dazzling entertainment district that ranked among the nation's top tourist destinations. A Disney theater on once-notorious 42nd Street epitomized New York's family- and business-friendly image.

While economic restructuring sparked demand for highly educated, highly skilled managers and professionals, it also created a proliferation of low-skilled service jobs. Bankers and lawyers depended on security guards and custodians at work, nannies and housekeepers at home. This generated more polarized incomes. From the early 1980s to the first decade of the twenty-first century, the top fifth of New York City families saw their share of the city's income grow while others lost ground. Wall Street employees enjoyed record wages in 2006, but despite marginal improvement nearly one in five New Yorkers still lived in poverty. Meanwhile, the city's middle class continued to contract.

The remaining middle class was rooted in half a million government jobs (including some three hundred thousand for New York City, the city's largest employer) and another half-million jobs in health care and social services. These sectors supported a level of unionization in 2000 (30 percent) that matched the nation's rate in 1950. Leading the pack were Health and Hospitals Workers Local 1199, under Dennis Rivera; the United Federation of Teachers, led by Randi Weingarten; and the largest municipal public employee union, District Council 37 (AFSCME), whose executive director, Stanley Hill, was ousted for corruption.

Despite their numbers the unions were fighting defensive battles. In 1991 workers at the *Daily News* prevailed after a five-month strike that enjoyed broad public support, but the paper reemerged with a slimmed-down workforce and payroll. In 2005 the city's militant Transport Workers Union mounted an illegal 2.5-day strike, halting buses and subways during the

Christmas rush, when confronted with a rollback of benefits. The outcome was mixed: workers won on pensions but gave ground on wages and health care, and union president Roger Toussaint was ultimately pressured into renouncing any future strike.

Organized labor had been crucial to the election of a new Democratic mayor in 1989, but by the mid-1990s major unions were endorsing Republicans. Their accommodation reflected the realities of the era, in which economic restructuring and federal government retrenchment strengthened the hand of employers and undercut labor.

RACE, ETHNICITY, AND IMMIGRATION

New York City entered the new millennium unparalleled in its diversity. More than a million new immigrants arrived in New York during the 1990s, reversing decades of population decline and contributing to a record 2.9 million foreign-born residents among an all-time-high of 8 million inhabitants. This foreign-born share of the population, more than one in three, was unsurpassed since European immigrants had transformed the city a century earlier.

The 2000 census showed the city's population to be 35 percent non-Hispanic white, 26.6 percent black, 9.8 percent Asian, and 27 percent Hispanic (any race). But these categories blurred the diversity produced by immigrants from across the globe—roughly one-third from Latin America, one-quarter from Asia, and one-fifth each from the non-Hispanic Caribbean and Europe. The three largest sources of immigration during the 1990s were the Dominican Republic, China, and Jamaica; the countries of the former Soviet Union combined would rank fourth.

Whereas New York's blacks and Latinos once hailed mainly from the South and Puerto Rico, respectively, by 2000 this was no longer true. One-third of the city's black population was foreign-born, including almost one hundred thousand Africans along with Jamaicans, Haitians, and Guyanese. Puerto Ricans were barely more than a third of all Latinos, and their numbers declined during the 1990s as others increased, most notably Dominicans, Ecuadorians, and Mexicans.

Immigration contributed to the city's racialized class structure, in which whites earned the highest incomes, followed by Asians, then blacks, and finally Latinos, while poverty rates increased inversely. This reflected wide variation in immigrants' human capital. In general, Asians and European immigrants arrived with more education and skills than those from Latin America and the Caribbean. Over 60 percent of Filipinos and Russians were college graduates, compared to less than 15 percent of Dominicans and Mexicans; this translated into incomes that were among the highest and lowest in the city, respectively. Still, other factors such as English proficiency and occupational niches also affected socioeconomic achievement. Anglophone Jamaicans without college degrees found middle-class jobs in burgeoning health care; highly educated Koreans with limited English struggled as neighborhood greengrocers.

For all its diversity New York was no melting pot. Race was a key organizing principle in the settlement of immigrants, as evidenced by mushrooming clusters of blacks in Central Brooklyn, Latinos in Upper Manhattan and the South Bronx, and Asians in Queens. Guyanese of African descent joined Jamaicans and Haitians in Central Brooklyn, but Guyanese of Asian

Indian background settled in southwest Queens with Trinidadians and Tobagonians of similar roots. Latin Americans from Ecuador and Colombia resided in Queens, near Asians and whites, while Puerto Ricans and Dominicans settled closer to blacks in Upper Manhattan and the South Bronx. Europe was the largest source of immigrants in Staten Island, the only majority-white borough in the city.

Demographic change fueled racial tensions in the late 1980s and 1990s. The volatility was captured in Spike Lee's 1989 film *Do the Right Thing*, which explored uneasy relationships in Bedford-Stuyvesant, Brooklyn, among black residents, Italian pizzeria workers, a Korean green-grocer, and white police officers and gentrifiers. A year later blacks in Flatbush, Brooklyn, mounted a prolonged, racially charged boycott of two Korean-owned groceries following allegations that employees had assaulted a black customer. In 1991 tensions between blacks and Jews in Crown Heights, Brooklyn, exploded in three days of rioting and the stabbing death of a Jewish man after a black child was killed by a car in a Hasidic motorcade.

Many blacks resented the aggressive police tactics championed by Mayor Giuliani during the 1990s. The city's most prominent black leader, Reverend Al Sharpton, channeled black anger into public protests over police brutality and racist violence. In 1999 Sharpton rallied protesters after police shot dead an unarmed African immigrant, Amadou Diallo; a decade earlier he had led marchers through a hostile crowd in Bensonhurst, Brooklyn, a white stronghold, after a mob of white youths set upon four black teens in the neighborhood, killing one.

Racial tensions eased notably after Giuliani left office, even though aggressive policing continued. Mayor Bloomberg earned praise for reaching out to black leaders, including Sharpton. The 9/11 tragedy also overwhelmed prior racial divisions, and Mayor Giuliani preempted new conflicts by condemning violence against the city's Muslims.

See also *New York, NY 1776–1790; New York, NY 1790–1828; New York, NY 1828–1854; New York, NY 1854–1877; New York, NY 1877–1896; New York, NY 1896–1929; New York, NY 1929–1941; New York, NY 1941–1952; New York, NY 1952–1989*

ALEXANDER J. REICHL

BIBLIOGRAPHY

Brash, Julian. *Bloomberg's New York: Class and Governance in the Luxury City*. Athens: University of Georgia Press, 2011.

Fainstein, Susan. *The City Builders: Property Development in New York and London, 1980–2000*. 2d ed. Lawrence: University Press of Kansas, 2001.

Foner, Nancy. *From Ellis Island to JFK: New York's Two Great Waves of Immigration*. New Haven, CT: Yale University Press, and New York, NY: Russell Sage Foundation, 2000.

Kasinitz, Philip, John H. Mollenkopf, and Mary C. Waters, eds. *Becoming New Yorkers: Ethnographies of the New Second Generation*. New York, NY: Russell Sage Foundation, 2006.

Mollenkopf, John H. "New York: Still the Great Anomaly." In *Racial Politics in American Cities*, 3d ed., edited by Rufus P. Browning, Dale Rogers Marshall, and David H. Tabb, 115–139. New York, NY: Longman, 2003.

Sanjek, Roger. *The Future of Us All: Race and Neighborhood Politics in New York City*. Ithaca, NY: Cornell University Press, 1998.

Sassen, Saskia. *The Global City: New York, London, Tokyo*. 2d ed. Princeton, NJ: Princeton University Press, 2001.

Sites, William. *Remaking New York: Primitive Globalization and the Politics of Urban Community*. Minneapolis: University of Minnesota Press, 2003.

LOS ANGELES, CA 1989–2011

THE LATE TWENTIETH AND EARLY TWENTY-FIRST CENTURIES WITNESSED DRAMATIC CHANGES in the economy, politics, and demographics of Los Angeles. At 469.3 square miles, Los Angeles remains one of the largest cities in the country, and it is the second largest in terms of population. In 2000 there were 3,694,820 residents, an increase from 3,485,398 in 1990, and by 2009 the city's population had grown to 3,831,868.

While the city remained one of the key "gateways to the Pacific," with a growing Latino and Asian population, serious problems persisted. The loss of the aerospace and aircraft industries deeply affected the local economy, while the film industry struggled to keep production in Los Angeles. The late 1980s and early 1990s saw a dramatic growth in the crime rate, especially in central Los Angeles, and congestion on the city's freeways and streets continued to pose a major challenge for commuters. A decentralized political structure and the relatively weak position of mayor compared to other cities—the result of progressive reforms passed in the 1910s and 1920s—made it difficult for city government to solve these and other problems.

GOVERNMENT AND POLITICS

The end of Tom Bradley's tenure as mayor—the longest in Los Angeles history—was not a happy one. After an extraordinary series of successes, including the intensified renovation of downtown, the promotion of Los Angeles for international trade, and the hosting of the XXIII Olympiad in 1984, the late 1980s brought racial tensions; crime; declining performance in the city's public schools; unemployment; an aging infrastructure of streets, bridges, and buildings; and the continued impact of lost property tax revenue from Proposition 13 (passed in 1978). Bradley seemed hapless in trying to solve these and other mounting problems, and the Los Angeles riot of April 1992, ignited after the acquittal of police officers in the beating of a speeding motorist, Rodney King, proved to be the last straw for his administration. Before retiring in 1993 he hired the city's first African American police chief, Willie Williams, in the ensuing effort to rebuild trust between city residents and the Los Angeles Police Department (LAPD). With his gubernatorial ambitions thwarted, Bradley was succeeded by moderate Republican Richard J. Riordan, a lawyer with substantial investments in real estate.

Although relatively unknown among voters prior to taking office, Riordan oversaw a modest renewal in the civic spirit of the city, with strong efforts to improve city services, public education, and infrastructure. Following Bradley's efforts, one of Riordan's most important tasks was

QUICK FACTS   LOS ANGELES, CA **1989–2011**

MAYORS

Tom Bradley	(1973–1993)
Richard J. Riordan	(1993–2001)
James Hahn	(2001–2005)
Antonio Villaraigosa	(2005–)

MAJOR INDUSTRIES AND EMPLOYERS

Tourism
Entertainment industry
Garment industry
Higher education
City and county government

MAJOR NEWSPAPERS

Los Angeles Times

Los Angeles Sentinel
La Opinión

MAJOR EVENTS

1990: The opening of the first Metro rail line signifies a return to commuter rail transportation, which was largely abandoned by the 1950s.

1992: The Los Angeles riot is the largest urban uprising in the city's history.

1994: The city hosts most of the games of the FIFA World Cup, setting attendance records and indicating the rising popularity of soccer.

1996: The first *Los Angeles Times* Festival of Books takes place, which eventually becomes one of the largest book fairs in the nation.

2003: The opening of the Walt Disney Concert Hall, designed by Frank Gehry, symbolizes the renovation of downtown Los Angeles.

to improve relations between the LAPD and the city while simultaneously bringing down the spiraling crime rate. With the slogan of "Tough Enough to Turn L.A. Around," he worked closely with Chief of Police Williams and also named his successor, Bernard Parks, a thirty-two-year veteran of the LAPD. In the interest of improving the city's sagging reputation in public K–12 education, Riordan in 2000 hired a forceful superintendent of the Los Angeles Unified School District, Roy Romer, who had been a three-term governor of Colorado. Further, Riordan continued Bradley's strategy of promoting downtown redevelopment, the renewal of light rail for public transportation, and the expansion of the Port of Los Angeles. Several major cultural events also occurred during his tenure in office, including the city's hosting of the FIFA Soccer World Cup in 1994 and the creation of the annual *Los Angeles Times'* Festival of Books, which has become one of the largest book festivals in the country. By the end of his second term, Riordan still enjoyed the support of much of the city's populace.

Riordan's successor was Democrat James Hahn, the son of a much-loved Los Angeles County supervisor. Hahn had less of Riordan's flair for publicity but prided himself on being an effective administrator. Although only serving one term—the first Los Angeles mayor since the 1930s to do so—he continued the focus on improving relations with the LAPD by hiring William Bratton in 2002 as chief of police, who had been a highly effective police commissioner in

New York City. Building on the successful implementation of community policing that Willie Williams had emphasized, Bratton applied the "broken windows theory" that he had applied in New York, which states that with a deterioration of infrastructure comes an increase in crime. With the full support of the mayor, Bratton argued for improvements in city infrastructure while using a computer tracking program, together with an expanded police force, to curb crime. Aided by a "three strikes" law that California voters passed in 1994, there was a steady decline in the crime rate and general improvement in community relations with the LAPD.

The election of mayor Antonio Villaraigosa in 2005 was a momentous event: The first Latino mayor of the city since 1872. As a liberal Democrat, Villaraigosa brought much hope to many Angelenos with his vibrant persona and political connections from his days as speaker of the California State Assembly. Yet he was soon waylaid by a harsh economy, struggles with the teachers union, and ethical issues. Concerns over Villaraigosa's hiring policies mounted; his staff of 205 employees was far larger than Hahn's and almost double what Riordan's had been. Although reelected in 2009, his real achievements after five years in office were relatively meager, despite an intensive campaign to renew the city's aging infrastructure; the extension of public rail service across Greater Los Angeles; and the hiring of a popular new chief of police, Charlie Beck, in November 2009. Ongoing concerns over unemployment, poor schools, insufficiency of water reservoirs, and even the threatened secession of the San Fernando Valley all continued to pose significant challenges in Los Angeles city politics in the early twenty-first century.

INDUSTRY, COMMERCE, AND LABOR

While Los Angeles remained a major manufacturing center in the West, this period witnessed the decline of the aerospace and aircraft industries, which had been critical to the city's post–World War II economy. Dominated by companies such as Douglas, Northrop, Lockheed, and Hughes Aircraft, these industries had provided over 40 percent of all manufacturing jobs in the Greater Los Angeles region, employing half a million people. With the end of the Cold War, jobs were lost mainly in the areas of aircraft and parts, missiles, and search and navigation products. Shipbuilding, also an important part of the local economy, declined as well. Nonetheless, manufacturing in Los Angeles in 2009 still continued in the fields of apparel (68,300 jobs), computer and electronic products (60,000 jobs), transportation products (54,600 jobs), fabricated metal products (49,900 jobs), food products (44,800 jobs), and furniture (27,400 jobs).

Beset by two recessions, ominous economic trends arose between 2001 and 2008. The two sectors of the city's economy that registered the highest job losses were manufacturing and information, the latter of which includes the entertainment industry. Manufacturing lost 47,500 jobs, whereas information lost 17,800 jobs, and both sectors tend to offer middle- to upper-middle-class salaries. Although figures for the City of Los Angeles alone are difficult to extract, the entertainment industry of film, television, and music in Los Angeles County as a whole generated $113 billion in revenue and provided 304,400 jobs in 2009. After tourism, the entertainment industry continued to be the second largest business sector for both the city and the county. One of the most serious challenges for the film industry was to keep production companies filming in

Los Angeles, due to the increasing attraction of other cities in the United States and abroad for film location and production, mainly to avoid paying high union fees.

Despite these economic challenges, the Port of Los Angeles remains an important engine of the city's economy. The completion of the Alameda Corridor in the 1980s, a twenty-mile express route from the port to the city's railroad hub, greatly expanded container traffic, and a federal grant of $16 million in 2010 enabled the port to develop its rail services further. The combined Port of Los Angeles at San Pedro and Long Beach topped New York and New Jersey in terms of tonnage in 1989: 66.3 million metric tons were recorded in fiscal year 1988–1989 at San Pedro and 68.9 million metric tons at nearby Long Beach. Container traffic by 2002 reached 6,105,864 TEUs (twenty-foot equivalent units, the standard measurement for containers) at San Pedro and 4,524,038 at Long Beach, up from 1989 figures of 2,056,980 and 1,575,117, respectively. Container traffic continued to rise in 2010, with a total of 7,219,250 TEUs compared to 6,186,004 the previous year, representing an increase of 16.7 percent. The peak in container traffic occurred before the latest recession, however, with 8,469,853 TEUs in 2006.

Despite a dynamic economy on several fronts, and the presence of a large financial services sector downtown, poverty remained endemic in Los Angeles. According to the 2000 U.S. Census, almost a quarter of city residents worked at jobs that did not pay a living wage. Further straining city resources was a large skid row that developed south of downtown, consisting of over forty city blocks that had been all but abandoned by the rest of the city's residents. It resulted mainly from the loss of government support for the mentally ill during the 1980s, as well as the attraction of the metropolitan region for homeless transients and drug and alcohol addicts. Skid row has become an official district within the city; named the Central City East by the Community Redevelopment Agency in the 1980s and now with its own website, its population comprised 17,740 in 2000—one of the largest homeless districts in the United States—with Latinos numbering 51.4 percent, whites 25.5 percent, and blacks 16.7 percent.

RACE, ETHNICITY, AND IMMIGRATION

Demographic trends from the previous two decades continued their steady progression during this period, with a decline in white and black populations and an increase in Latino and Asian populations. Although whites still represented the majority of the city's inhabitants in 1990, with almost 53 percent out of a total population of 3,485,398, their numbers were clearly waning. For the first time since the nineteenth century, by 2000 less than half of the city's residents (46.9 percent) were white: 1,734,036 out of a total population of 3,694,820. Recent estimates from the 2010 census suggest a slightly different picture, with just under half of the city's residents (49.8 percent) being white: 1,908,225 out of a total population of 3,831,868. In marked decline was the city's African American population, which in 2000 comprised 13.9 percent (415,195 residents), a clear drop from its peak of 17.9 percent in 1970; this trend was even more in evidence by 2009, with African Americans comprising only 9.7 percent of the population (371,325 residents).

By contrast, the Latino population grew dramatically, in part the result of substantial immigration from Mexico, El Salvador, and Guatemala. Latinos made up just over 39 percent or 1,391,411 city residents in 1990, a tripling of their numbers since 1970. By 2000 the number

Antonio Villaraigosa (right), first elected mayor of Los Angeles in 2005 and reelected in 2009, tours the Edward R. Roybal Metro Gold Line Eastside Extension in October 2009. Light rail projects such as this have attempted to ease the city's notorious traffic problems. Mayor Villaraigosa has been a strong proponent of public transportation including an extension of the Purple Line trains to Santa Monica—also known as the "subway to the sea."

Source: AP Photo/David Longstreath

of Latinos roughly equaled the number of whites, with 46.5 percent or 1,719,073. The Latino population increased further a decade later, with 48 percent or 1,841,119 residents in 2009. The election of Villaraigosa in 2005; the hiring of the first Latino music director of the Los Angeles Philharmonic, Venezuelan conductor Gustavo Dudamel, in 2009; and the increasing audiences for Spanish-language radio, television, and newspapers all attest to the power of the Latino presence in the city.

Although relatively fewer in number, Asians were also a growing community, comprising 9.2 percent of the city's population in 1990 (320,668) compared to 6.6 percent in 1980 (195,997). By 2000 the Asian population (mainly Chinese, Filipino, Korean, and Japanese) had increased to 369,254, or almost 10 percent of the city's population. That number climbed further by 2009, when Asians represented 10.6 percent or 405,425 of the city's residents. Continuing a trend since the 1970s, Asians also migrated out of the city to the suburbs, mainly in the eastern and central San Gabriel Valley (Monterey Park, Temple City, Rosemead, San Gabriel, Arcadia, San

Marino). Further, 2.7 percent of the city's residents (105,035) identified with two or more racial groups in 2009, pointing toward the growing trend of a mixed-race population that did not necessarily adhere to any one particular ethnicity.

Although racial tensions have been present since the city's founding in 1781, those tensions exploded in one of the most violent events in the city's history, the Los Angeles riot of 1992. The conflict proved to be the culmination of many problems facing the city's population, among them unemployment, immigration, police brutality, and the escalation of street gangs. It began in April 1992 after the acquittal of four police officers accused of beating a speeding African American motorist, Rodney King. Like the Watts riot of 1965, it endured for almost a week (April 29 to May 5), National Guard troops were called in to quell the disturbance, and the financial cost was enormous, estimated at between $785 million to $1 billion. The uprising was unlike the Watts riot, however, on at least three counts: It quickly spread to neighboring communities (chiefly Koreatown, Hollywood, West Los Angeles, and Long Beach), the majority of those arrested were Latino (51 percent) rather than African American (36 percent), and whites and Asians also took part in the looting. Above all, the riot revealed deep racial antagonisms that subsequent community groups have sought to overcome; the Korean community, in particular, was targeted by black and Latino participants due to the relatively large number of shops under Korean management in south Los Angeles.

Despite the upheaval, racial trends have continued up through the first decade of the twenty-first century, with Latinos and Asians steadily outnumbering whites and blacks in the city. Employment reflected racial dynamics, with apparel manufacturing, county government, light industry, and food and hospitality services providing the majority of the employment opportunities for nonwhites, while whites continued to dominate the entertainment industries of film and television as well as the financial services and banking sectors.

See also *Los Angeles, CA 1896–1929; Los Angeles, CA 1929–1941; Los Angeles, CA 1941–1952; Los Angeles, CA 1952–1989*

KENNETH H. MARCUS

BIBLIOGRAPHY

Allen, James P., and Eugene Turner. *Changing Faces, Changing Places: Mapping Southern Californians.* Northridge, CA: Center for Geographical Studies, 2002.

City-Data, Los Angeles: Economy. http://www.city-data.com/us-cities/The-West/Los-Angeles-Economy.html

Los Angeles Almanac. http://www.laalmanac.com/LA/index.htm

Los Angeles Downtown Industrial District. http://www.centralcityeast.org

Pitt, Leonard, and Dale Pitt. *Los Angeles A to Z: An Encyclopedia of the City and County.* Berkeley: University of California Press, 1997.

Port of Los Angeles, TEU Statistics (Container Counts). http://www.portoflosangeles.org/maritime/stats.asp

Southern California Association of Governments. http://www.scag.ca.gov

U.S. Census Bureau, Los Angeles (City), California. http://quickfacts.census.gov/qfd/states/06/0644000.html

CHICAGO, IL 1989–2011

IN THE LAST DECADES OF THE TWENTIETH CENTURY, Chicago faced most of the same problems that most older American industrial cities struggled with, including a politically and racially divided population, deindustrialization, a declining tax base, pollution, a poorly performing public school system, a collapsing public housing system, a deteriorating downtown, and a burgeoning fiscal crisis. Chicago, however, has been able to call upon its diverse political and business leadership as well as its multifaceted economy to avoid some of the mistakes other cities have made. As in many large American cities, government remains the largest employer in Chicago. The city's top five employers are all in the public sector. In the first decade of the twenty-first century, Chicago has hardly solved all of its troubles, but it has made progress and firmly joined the list of truly global cities.

GOVERNMENT AND POLITICS

On April 24, 1989, Richard M. Daley was elected the fifty-fourth mayor of Chicago, continuing the domination of the city's politics by the Democratic Party, which has controlled the mayoralty and city council since 1931. The special election was held to fill out the remaining years of Harold Washington's (1983–1987) term, the city's first African American mayor, after his untimely death. The city council chose Eugene Sawyer as acting mayor on December 2, 1987, and a special election was set for 1989 to elect someone to finish out Washington's term. For some, Daley's victory over Sawyer, another African American, was seen as a restoration of the Daley family to power in City Hall.

After Richard J. Daley's passing on December 29, 1976, it seemed as if the city had fallen into political chaos. Five mayors followed the elder Daley. The younger Daley inherited a city that had gone through various difficult economic, racial, and political times. The political infighting of the Washington years led pundits to refer to Chicago as "Beirut on the Lake," a reference to that war-torn city in the Middle East. Chicago's famous downtown or Loop, looked tired and was in many parts desolate. The city had already lost much of its industrial base in the previous twenty years. Middle-class families continued to leave for the suburbs, and the Chicago Public Schools were rated among the worst in the country. Certainly, the city's legendary political clout seemed to be ebbing away as its population declined.

Like his father, the younger Daley benefited from incredible political luck. Some of the programs initiated by his predecessors began to bear fruit. Slowly, the Loop came back to life. More important, so did the national economy and especially the economy of the Midwest. Also before the end of Daley's first term, the Democrats stood on the verge of retaking the White House for the first time in twelve years, as well as Congress. All of this portended well for big-city Democrats who could look to the nation's capital to help with redevelopment plans and social programs. Early in his administration Daley made several bold moves, including taking over both the Chicago Public Schools and the Chicago Housing Authority in the 1990s.

QUICK FACTS

CHICAGO, IL 1989–2011

MAYORS

Eugene Sawyer   (1987–1989)
Richard M. Daley   (1989–2011)
Rahm Emmanuel   (2011–)

MAJOR INDUSTRIES AND EMPLOYERS

U.S. government
Chicago Public Schools
City of Chicago
State of Illinois
Cook County

MAJOR NEWSPAPERS

Chicago Tribune
Chicago Sun-Times

MAJOR EVENTS

1989: Richard M. Daley, son of former mayor Richard J. Daley, is elected mayor and goes on to serve until 2011.
1995: Chicago begins to knock down public housing high-rises.
2004: Millennium Park opens on the shore of Lake Michigan.
2009: Chicago loses its 2016 Summer Olympic bid to Rio de Janeiro.
2010: In *McDonald v. City of Chicago,* the U.S. Supreme Court rules unconstitutional Chicago's ban on handguns.
2011: Former congressman and presidential chief of staff Rahm Emmanuel is elected mayor with over 55 percent of the vote.

Chicago faced difficult challenges as Daley moved to consolidate his power. The city council saw the biggest turnover in decades in 1991 when twenty-one new aldermen took seats. Many of these had won with Daley's support. Daley also was able to appoint replacements for aldermen who resigned or died in office. Consequently, the mayor enjoyed the support of the overwhelming majority of the council.

Daley created a new political machine that relied on both old and new methods of organization. While the Shakman Decree (1972) seemed to tie Daley's hand as to patronage, his administration proved adroit at maneuvering around the prohibition, which forbade political hiring and firing except in a certain number of pertinent policy positions. Several of Daley's appointees were indicted or forced to resign because of various scandals involving patronage, including the Hired Truck Scandal, which broke in 2004. The scandal involved the hiring of trucking firms owned by politically connected companies to do the city's business. Two years later Daley's patronage chief, Robert Sorich, along with three other members of the administration, were found guilty of continuing the practice of political hiring and sentenced to jail.

Despite these setbacks the Daley administration proved both powerful and durable. Daley built a power base that reached beyond Chicago's borders. With Democrats in control across Illinois in 2009, Daley's influence grew. Not the least of the sources of influence was that fact that Daley came out early in support of the presidential ambitions of Illinois Senator Barack Obama. In addition, political advisors once close to Daley held high positions in the Obama

The 24.5 acre Millennium Park, located near the shores of Lake Michigan, opened in 2004. The site includes public art, green space, and a concert venue designed by Frank Gehry.

Source: Carol Highsmith/Library of Congress

administration, including William Daley, the mayor's brother, who has become President Obama's chief of staff.

In addition to charges of corruption, the Daley administration faced various setbacks in 2009, including widespread voter anger over the mayor's municipal privatization policy, especially in the sale of the city's parking meters to Chicago Parking Meters LLC. Rates immediately went up and were raised again on January 1, 2010. In addition, the city lost its bid to host the 2016 Summer Olympics after Daley and his supporters made a well-publicized and expensive bid for the games. This and other issues, such as the viability of public transportation, marred the last few years of Daley's administration. On September 7, 2010, he announced that he would not run for another term as mayor of Chicago. This shocked the media and the city's residents, and immediately started a scramble for the office that everyone had felt Daley would continue to occupy for years to come. On February 22, 2011, Rahm Emmanuel won the mayoralty by putting together a citywide coalition not unlike his predecessor's. The new mayor took office on May 16, 2011, a day that ushered in a new era in Chicago history, one without a Daley at the helm.

INDUSTRY, COMMERCE, AND LABOR

Both before and since 1989 Chicago witnessed a tremendous amount of deindustrialization. Between 1979 and 2000 real manufacturing wages fell 17 percent, compared to 10 percent nationally. After 1985 the region settled into a slow but steady decline, with an average manufacturing job loss of 1.6 percent; between 2000 and 2003, however, one hundred three thousand industrial jobs disappeared from the Chicago area, or about 18 percent of total industrial employment. The 2008–2010 recession only increased the problem. Not surprisingly, these shifts in job opportunities hurt minority communities the most. Growing economic insecurity came to be a reality in Chicago and across the Midwest.

The loss of great manufacturing concerns across the city, such as Western Electric, which once employed over forty-five thousand people in its Hawthorne Plant (Cicero) alone, crippled many neighborhoods and suburbs. As plants closed, the huge industrial expanses of Chicago's once flourishing industrial base left a vast amount of polluted "brown" fields that proved to be difficult to clean up.

Gentrification meant further problems for Chicago's industrial base in the 1980s and later. Urban pioneers put pressure on industry across the city. The city attempted to protect industrial districts with a zoning law designed to ensure the continued presence of manufacturing, but this has met with limited success. The Clybourn District has largely turned retail and residential in character. The Haymarket District seems to be going through the same process. The Stockyard Industrial District, on the other hand, has been largely successful in providing a home for industry.

Nevertheless, despite its decline as a manufacturing center, the Chicago area has gained new investment and remains a major transportation and communication center. Chicago's renaissance since the early 1990s has largely been predicated on its emergence as a truly global city while maintaining its considerable position as a leader in transportation and, despite losses, its title as a manufacturing center. Since the early 1990s the value of exports from the Chicago region has steadily increased and has had a positive effect on both employment and local economic development. During the period 1993–1999, Chicago stood in sixth place in the nation in export sales (1999 alone saw over $21 billion). Despite manufacturing losses Chicago has added more jobs than Boston and Los Angeles combined since 1993.

Many corporations have found Chicago attractive. The Daley administration's attempt to rejuvenate the Loop, and its use of Tax Increment Financing Districts (TIFs) proved appealing to corporations looking to relocate their headquarters. In March 2001 the Boeing Corporation moved its headquarters to Chicago, and in 2009 United Airlines agreed to move its headquarters to the Willis Tower (formerly the Sears Tower). While critics have pointed out that the incentives given to these corporations do not create a tremendous number of actual jobs, they do not take into account their overall impact on the city's reputation and attractiveness in the world market.

Chicago's central geographic location and its continued dominance of the nation's transportation center have helped it maintain its economic position despite setbacks. In 2006 the city ranked as the nation's tenth largest international freight gateway, the only one not situated along an international border or waterway. Over 3,200 miles of national highways, 2,000 miles of active Class I railway lines, 142 intermodal facilities, 163 cargo ports, and four major airports converge on the Chicago area. Chicago ranks third among all American airports in value of international airfreight and fifth in volume. It leads the nation in intermodal terminal capacity and is rated as the third largest intermodal container port in the world. Chicago's hold on the nation's freight lines has proven crucial in a deindustrializing economy.

Despite Chicago's role as a transportation nexus, the area is not without its problems, especially with an infrastructure that dates back to the nineteenth century. Railroads converging on the city create giant traffic jams, and these delays create substantial cost overruns. The only answer seems to be the outward expansion of the rail system to break the freight logjam. In 2002 the Burlington Northern Santa Fe Railroad (BNSF) opened an intermodal facility in Will County that covers some 600 acres. ProLogis acquired 184 acres in Wilmington for a new distribution park to serve the BNSF facility. The Union Pacific Railroad opened its Global III Intermodal Facility in 2003, an even larger facility in Ogle County eighty miles west of Chicago.

RACE, ETHNICITY, AND IMMIGRATION

While immigration continues to shape the city's demography, race remains an important demographic, social, economic, and political factor. Over the past twenty years, Chicago's racial profile has changed considerably. The great migration of African Americans from the South has come to an end. Since 1975 black Chicagoans have been part of a remigration to the South and Southwest. Nevertheless, African Americans remain a large and powerful group in the city and the metropolitan area, making up 36.8 percent of the city's population in 2000. Non-Latino whites made up 31.3 percent of the city's population in 2000. Since the 2000 census Chicago has lost two hundred thousand residents, most of whom were African American. Many people have flocked to outlying areas such as Will, Kane, and McHenry Counties, which have experienced double-digit growth for the second decade in a row. Others have left the region entirely, settling in the Sunbelt.

Chicago's African American middle class has grown, and many black middle-class neighborhoods and suburbs dot the metropolitan area. Class has become an important issue in the black community, as many African American middle-class families have purchased homes in traditional ghetto neighborhoods, unleashing gentrification and driving poor black families from areas such as North Kenwood-Oakland on the city's South Side. Gentrification across the city has presented class issues, without regard to race or ethnicity, among the city's working-class and poor neighborhoods.

Despite gains seen by African Americans, Chicago remains one of the most segregated cities in the United States. One of the greatest failures in Chicago's long and checkered racial past has been that of public housing. Once seen as permanent fixtures of the city' physical and social landscape, large public housing projects with a residential population more than 90 percent African American have disappeared across the city as a result of changes in federal law and local initiatives led by the Daley administration. After 1995, when Congress eliminated the requirement that new developments provide a one-to-one replacement for demolished public housing units, the wrecking balls were set to go. Occupants feared the destruction of their homes and their placement in other neighborhoods. Many of these Chicago Housing Authority (CHA) tenants protested the program, but lost. By 1999 CHA received nearly $160 million in six HOPE VI grants, and the program moved from renovation toward destruction as CHA demolished over twelve thousand units.

Despite the destruction of public housing high-rises, the traditional South Side and West Side ghettoes remain in place. While some neighborhoods and suburbs have become more racially integrated, the overall picture still places the Chicago area as one of the most segregated in the nation. White flight to both the suburbs and exurbs continues as jobs and schools in the city proper and in many close-in suburbs continue to present problems for middle-class families of all races. The old black-white segregation patterns have become more complex with the addition of large numbers of Latino immigrants and their offspring. Black-brown racial confrontations take place more frequently as clashes between these two large inner-city groups have increased. Many times these confrontations include battles over gang turf, especially in those areas where racially divided neighborhoods come in contact.

Chicago has always been an immigrant city. While the number of European immigrants has declined, Latin Americans and Asians have replaced them. Since 1965 Chicago has witnessed a large influx of Latin Americans, particularly Mexicans. Also, significant numbers of immigrants from the Caribbean and Africa have made their way to the city. Among Europeans, Polish immigrants remain the leading group, maintaining a traditional tie between Chicago and Poland. In 2000, 133,797 Polish immigrants lived in metropolitan Chicago, joining an estimated 900,000 Polish Americans. In addition, a large numbers of "vacationers" from Poland entered the country, often disappearing into the Polish American underground economy for various periods of time. From 1986 to 1996 Poles provided the largest total number of legal immigrants to Chicago proper. During the 1990s two out of every five Polish immigrants to the United States settled in the Chicago area. Only Mexican immigrants outnumbered them in the metropolitan region. They also provided the second largest number of illegal immigrants to Chicago, ranking just behind Mexicans.

Like the Poles, Mexicans have a long history in Chicago, dating back to as early as 1884. Most of their population growth, however, took place after the 1965 immigration reforms. Between 1986 and 1996 Mexico sent some 54,000 immigrants to the Chicago area. In 2004 Mexicans accounted for 1,271,710 residents of Greater Chicago, with more Mexicans living in the suburbs (725,561) than in the city (546,149). In Chicago the Pilsen and Little Village (South Lawndale) neighborhoods acted as the port of entry for many Mexican immigrants. Other large Mexican neighborhoods include South Chicago, East Side, Back of the Yards, Gage Park, and Chicago Lawn. Cicero, Berwyn, and Melrose Park, all western suburbs, have seen a tremendous growth in their Latino population. More than 40 percent of all immigrants in the Chicago area came from Mexico, ranking them far ahead of other immigrant groups. The Mexican labor force in the area is greater than the combined total of the next ten largest immigrant groups. Unfortunately, they are clustered in the lowest-paying occupations.

Chicago continued to attract immigrants from other parts of Eastern Europe and Latin America. Many of these, such as Russians, Lithuanians, El Salvadorans, Guatemalans, and Colombians, fled their homelands for political as well as economic reasons.

Over the past thirty years, the Asian population of the metropolitan area has also grown rapidly. Since 1970 Chinese, Japanese, and Filipino immigrants have been joined by large numbers of Asian Indians, Koreans, and Vietnamese. Pakistanis have also grown in number since the 1990s. In 2000 Indians made up the largest Asian group in the Chicago area, with 121,753 foreign-born. Filipinos ranked second (96,632), Chinese third (75,305), and Koreans fourth (48,467). The Japanese (23,267) and Vietnamese (17,326) populations, while growing, remained far behind. Many of these Asian immigrants have opted for Chicago's suburbs. Suburban DuPage County may be the fastest-growing Asian Indian community in the United States. In the future the Chicago area will remain an important destination for immigrants.

See also *Chicago, IL 1854–1877; Chicago, IL 1877–1896; Chicago, IL 1896–1929; Chicago, IL 1929–1941; Chicago, IL 1941–1952; Chicago, IL 1952–1989*

DOMINIC A. PACYGA

BIBLIOGRAPHY

Green, Paul M., and Melvin G. Holli. *Restoration 1989: Chicago Elects a New Daley.* Chicago, IL: Lyceum Books, 1991.

Greene, Richard P., Mark J. Bouman, and Dennis Grammenos, eds. *Chicago's Geographies: Metropolis of the 21st Century.* Washington, DC: Association of American Geographers, 2006.

Koval, James B., Larry Bennett, Michael I. J. Bennett, Fasil Demisie, Roberta Garner, and Kijong, Kim, eds. *The New Chicago: A Social and Cultural Analysis.* Philadelphia, PA: Temple University Press, 2006.

Pacyga, Dominic A. *Chicago: A Biography.* Chicago, IL: University of Chicago Press, 2009.

Pattillo, Mary. *Black on the Block: The Politics of Race and Class in Chicago.* Chicago, IL: University of Chicago Press, 2007.

HOUSTON, TX 1989–2011

DURING THE LAST DECADE OF THE TWENTIETH CENTURY and first decade of the twenty-first, Houston's remarkable growth resumed and accelerated. Its population gained through immigration and became increasingly diverse. The local economy also diversified, as business and political leaders became wary of their boom-and-bust experiences of the previous decades. The large trends that influence *fin de siècle* Houston revolve around its internationalization, in business and in people. The tensions that accompany these trends come as the city strives for global relevance while protecting its human and commercial borders. Houston's political economy has modeled the developing opportunities and complexities associated with America's Latino diaspora.

QUICK FACTS

HOUSTON, TX **1989–2011**

MAYORS

Kathryn Whitmire	(1982–1991)
Bob Lanier	(1992–1997)
Lee P. Brown	(1998–2004)
Bill White	(2004–2010)
Annise Parker	(2010–)

MAJOR INDUSTRIES AND EMPLOYERS

Federal government
Food service industry
Oil, gas, and energy industries
Health care and medical education

MAJOR NEWSPAPERS

Houston Chronicle
African-American News and Issues

MAJOR EVENTS

1991: Following Mayor Kathryn Whitmire's departure from office after five terms, all elected positions for the City of Houston are given term limits.

1997: Lee P. Brown is elected the first African American mayor of Houston.

2001: Tropical Storm Allison hits Houston, causing massive damage and twenty-two deaths due to flooding.

2001: Enron, one of the largest Houston-based corporations, goes bankrupt due to revelations of corruption.

2004: Houston's new mode of public transportation, the METRO light rail, opens its first track to the public.

2005: Thousands of Hurricane Katrina refugees relocate to Houston, many permanently.

2010: Annise Parker is elected the second female and first gay mayor of Houston. She is the first openly gay person elected mayor of a major U.S. city.

GOVERNMENT AND POLITICS

Houston's first female mayor, Kathryn Whitmire, served from 1982 until 1991 and oversaw the city's passage through a near depression during the oil glut of the mid-1980s. As mayor, Whitmire appointed Houston's first African American chief of police, Lee Brown, who also later became mayor. In Houston, municipal elections are nonpartisan, as they are throughout Texas.

Whitmire lost her bid for a sixth term to developer Bob Lanier, who campaigned against a downtown transit project favored by Whitmire. Lanier drew support from conservative suburban voters. After serving three terms, Lanier was succeeded by former police chief Lee Brown, who thus became Houston's first black mayor. Brown had also previously served in the administration of President Bill Clinton, as head of the federal Office of National Drug Control Policy.

In 2001, Brown's third and final election (due to a three-term limit), his challenger was Cuban American city councilman Orlando Sanchez, who sought to become Houston's first Latino mayor. The campaign initially focused on downtown transportation infrastructure but became infused with racial contrasts. Brown and Sanchez both brought national figures to Houston to campaign for them, former president Bill Clinton for Brown and then-president

George W. Bush for Sanchez. Latino and white support went to Sanchez, while Brown drew critical support from black and Asian voters. Turnout among the latter was heavier than in Latino precincts, and Brown won the election with 51 percent of the vote.

Brown's successor as mayor was Bill White, a moderate white lawyer with deep connections to the state's Democratic Party. Like Brown, White had served in the Clinton administration, as a deputy energy secretary. White's challenger in the 2003 election was Orlando Sanchez, who lost to White by a greater margin (62.5 percent to 37.5 percent) than in the contentious 2001 election. In the 2005 election, White defeated four challengers to win with an unprecedented 91 percent of the vote. White drew praise and support for his handling of the evacuee crisis following that summer's Hurricane Katrina disaster. In 2007 there was again no need for a runoff, as White defeated two challengers to win with 86.5 percent of the ballots cast. After completing his final term as Houston's popular mayor, White unsuccessfully challenged incumbent Texas governor Rick Perry, a conservative Republican.

In a state that is often noted for its conservative politicians, Houston's complex racial and ethnic demography can foster coalitions that make its elections seem anomalous. In 2010 Houstonians elected city comptroller Annise Parker to succeed White as mayor. She is the second woman and the first openly gay person to hold the office. Parker is also the first openly gay person elected to lead a major U.S. city. She campaigned on fiscal responsibility and won, with the support of conservative Democrats along with minorities, against a conservative African American opponent, former city attorney Gene Locke.

The City of Houston employs twenty-three thousand workers in some five hundred buildings. The seat of government is an eleven-story limestone edifice built in 1939 with the help of a federal Works Progress Administration grant. The building followed the spare, modernist style then common in government architecture and was the first public structure in Houston to be fully air conditioned. In 1990 it was listed on the National Register of Historic Places. Following a 1992 renovation, it has become the aesthetic as well as functional anchor of a downtown municipal complex and public park just east of Interstate 45.

Although Houston's human and economic geography were shaped by automobiles during most of the twentieth century, recent multimodal transportation projects illustrate local frustration with seemingly endless highway traffic congestion. For example, downtown Houston's public spaces are connected by a series of air-conditioned tunnels and skywalks, allowing pedestrians to move about while avoiding the torrid summer climate as well as city traffic. In 2004 the city's METRO light rail line began service over a 7.5-mile north-south route, which the city plans to expand as funds become available. A train arrives at each station every twelve minutes, but automobiles and highways continue to dominate Houston's transportation geography. The metropolitan area's highway network is built around interstates and their connecting feeders. Interstate 610 constitutes an inner-loop highway entirely within the City of Houston. Beltway 8, the Sam Houston Tollway, is a combination of state toll roads and free highways circling Houston in the extended Harris County area. Regional surface transportation is the responsibility of a local intergovernmental agency, Houston Transtar, formed in 1996, with jurisdiction covering four counties.

During the four postwar decades, a robust annexation campaign more than tripled Houston's land area. By 2010 the city's area, at nearly six hundred square miles, exceeded that of any of the ten largest U.S. cities, although Houston's population density remained relatively stable, at approximately three thousand people per square mile. Under Texas law, cities have unusual latitude to annex surrounding territory. In addition, urban centers such as Houston enjoy extraterritorial jurisdiction extending up to five miles beyond their corporate boundaries. Annexed land parcels around Houston sometimes lie at the end of a narrow highway corridor, thus making the city's area technically contiguous, if diffuse. "Edge cities," so named by journalist Joel Garreau, are characteristic of Houston's pattern of territorial growth and diffusion, in which express highway interchanges become peripheral hubs that foster high land values and dense, concentrated centers of commercial and residential growth.

Houston anchors the nation's sixth largest metropolitan statistical area. Known as Houston-Sugar Land-Baytown, its 2010 population was 5.9 million. Houston's commercial and civic institutions thus draw from an imposing demographic and economic base, helping to explain the city's ability to support, for example, three major trauma center hospitals within blocks of each other in the downtown core.

The city's low, flat topography and proximity to the Gulf of Mexico make it vulnerable to dangerous flooding and destructive winds. In June 2001 the city suffered severe damage when the slow-moving Tropical Storm Allison flooded the city, resulting in twenty-two deaths. During and after the 2005 Hurricane Katrina disaster, some 1.5 million residents evacuated southern Louisiana, Mississippi, and Alabama, many from New Orleans. It was the largest and most sudden evacuation in U.S. history. The majority of evacuees took refuge in metropolitan centers in the surrounding states of Texas, Tennessee, Georgia, Florida, and Arkansas as well as in the northern interior counties of their home states. Houston was one of the most accessible evacuation destinations for the Katrina evacuees. Approximately one hundred twenty-five thousand found temporary shelter in the Houston Astrodome and other large public facilities as well as in local shelters and homes. Many found it impossible to resume their previous lives in Louisiana and remained to become permanent residents. The demand for social services, combined with a surge in the local labor force, created tensions in the host communities. A 2008 study by the U.S. Bureau of Labor Statistics found that Katrina evacuees who remained in cities where they had taken shelter, such as Houston, experienced higher unemployment than those not affected by the storm. When compared with Katrina evacuees who returned to their city of origin, nonreturning evacuees also fared worse. Although local authorities feared increased crime as a result of the influx of evacuees, subsequent statistics reflected little if any such increase in Houston. Initial concerns about the possible negative impacts of the so-called Katrina diaspora have gradually receded.

INDUSTRY, COMMERCE, AND LABOR

Energy from fossil fuels drove Houston's economy into the new century. The 2010 list of Fortune 500 companies based in Houston includes Conoco Phillips Petroleum, Marathon Oil, Anadarko Petroleum, and Frontier Oil, to name a few. Related energy services firms on the list include Plains All American Pipeline and Halliburton. Houston's fastest-growing firms were those serving the offshore oil drilling industry, such as Atwood Oceanics, National Oilwell Varco, Gulfmark Offshore, and Diamond Offshore Drilling. At the end of the twentieth century, one of Houston's most famous businesses was Enron Corporation, a publicly traded energy and financial services conglomerate. Enron grew out of the 1985 merger of Houston Natural Gas with another pipeline company based in Omaha, Nebraska. In 2000, at its peak, Enron had become an online trading agent for energy-related commodities and services. The company reported annual revenue of $100 billion and was the seventh largest company on the Fortune 500 list. However, a Securities and Exchange Commission investigation revealed that company executives had deceived stockholders and analysts about Enron's huge corporate debt, and the company collapsed abruptly, creating chaos in the energy industry and financial markets, and ruining Enron's national auditing firm, Arthur Andersen. The scandal and economic consequences affected thousands of Houstonians who had allied themselves both as employees and investors with Enron despite its inscrutable business model.

Houston's aerospace economy evolved from wartime aircraft manufacturing and grew steadily after the 1961 establishment in the city of NASA's Johnson Space Center. In 2010 the space center employed some fifteen thousand civil servants and associated contractors, constituting the majority of local aerospace employment. Most workers were educated beyond high school, and many held postgraduate degrees. However, with the cessation of the space shuttle program's manned flight operations, and the cancellation of the proposed next-generation Constellation project, prospects for the Johnson Center's mission control center are uncertain. NASA anticipated the initial loss of some two thousand five hundred positions there.

Houston's twenty-first-century political economy draws most of its new strength from medical education and associated health care initiatives. For example, Houston is home to the internationally noted M. D. Anderson Cancer Center, affiliated with the University of Texas and Baylor University. The Anderson Cancer Center is perhaps the flagship among forty-nine other medical institutions located near each other in Houston under the aegis of the Texas Medical Center. Three medical schools and six nursing schools are also part of the Medical Center complex, which occupies thirty-three million square feet in 162 buildings across one thousand acres near downtown. The affiliated institutions serve a broad range of human health needs and include the Memorial Hermann Hospital, the Ben Taub General Hospital, the John Sealy Hospital (all Level One trauma centers), the Shriners Hospitals for Children, St. Luke's Episcopal Hospital, and the Texas Heart Institute. All are nonprofit. More than ninety-three thousand people are directly employed throughout the Texas Medical Center, and it helps support an additional one hundred twenty-one thousand jobs indirectly. The Anderson Cancer Center draws physicians, patients, and medical students from around the world to participate in innovative cancer treatment research and programs. Together, the affiliated institutions of the Texas Medical Center attract some one hundred sixty thousand visitors daily to the largest such medical center in the world, with far-reaching economic impacts.

Houston's health care industry has emerged as a major local source of economic activity, but its presence is not new. The Anderson Cancer Center has existed since 1941, and it moved to its present downtown location in 1954. In 1971 the National Cancer Act designated M. D. Anderson as a Comprehensive Cancer Center, one of three in the United States. (In 2009 forty-one such comprehensive cancer centers existed.) Anderson's growth since then has mirrored as well as enhanced that of Houston. It has become one of the principal recipient institutions in the United States of research funding from the National Cancer Institute. Its Houston facility consists of a six-hundred-bed treatment facility with additional expansion underway, and it has spawned off-campus treatment centers in other states, operating under the M. D. Anderson name. A 2009 study reported that the Anderson Cancer Center's total operational spending reached $7.3 billion, most concentrated in the Houston metropolitan area, which accounted for approximately 2 percent of the local economy.

RACE, ETHNICITY, AND IMMIGRATION

By 2000 Houston's Latino population of 730,865 (out of a total city population of 1,953,631) ranked fourth among U.S. cities (trailing New York, Los Angeles, and Chicago). Houston's 2010 census count of 2.1 million made it the nation's fourth most populous city. Of that number, 919,668 (43 percent) reported Hispanic or Latino ethnicity, elevating Houston's Hispanic population to the third largest in the United States, following New York and Los Angeles. African American respondents totaled approximately 513, 000, or 24.4 percent of the population. Houston is also home to a significant and growing Asian population, especially people of Indian and Pakistani origin. These racial and ethnic groups sometimes coalesce around political campaigns and sometimes divide along their perceived boundaries of identity and interests. Clearly, though, at the end of the twentieth century and the beginning of the twenty-first, Houston's demographic story is an increasingly Latino one.

See also *Houston, TX 1952–1989*

ALAN BLISS

BIBLIOGRAPHY

Davis, Mike. *Magical Urbanism: Latinos Reinvent the U.S. City.* London: Verso, 2000.

Hernandez-Leon, Ruben. *Metropolitan Migrants: The Migration of Urban Mexicans to the United States.* Berkeley: University of California Press, 2008.

Klineberg, Stephen L. *The Houston Area Survey, 1982–2005: Public Perceptions in Remarkable Times—Tracking Change Through 24 Years of Houston's Surveys.* Houston, TX: Rice University, 2005.

Miniola, Tatcho. *Black-Brown Relations and Stereotypes.* Austin: University of Texas Press, 2002.

PHILADELPHIA, PA 1989–2011

AT THE TURN OF THE TWENTY-FIRST CENTURY, Philadelphia struggled to remain financially solvent and to reshape itself as a vital postindustrial urban center. By the turn of the twenty-first century, the local economy was dominated by service industries, including universities, health care, government, education, banking, and insurance. Mayor Edward G. Rendell (1992–2000) concentrated on downtown development, in particular boosting tourism. His successor, John F. Street (2000–2008), focused

QUICK FACTS

PHILADELPHIA, PA 1989–2011

MAYORS

W. Wilson Goode	(1984–1992)
Edward G. Rendell	(1992–2000)
John F. Street	(2000–2008)
Michael Nutter	(2008–)

MAJOR INDUSTRIES AND EMPLOYERS

Federal government
City government
School district
Hospitals and universities
Finance, banking, business services

MAJOR NEWSPAPERS

Philadelphia Inquirer
Philadelphia Daily News

MAJOR EVENTS

1990–2003: The formation of the Center City [Business Improvement] District in 1990, creation of an Avenue of the Arts on Broad Street, and opening of the Kimmel Center (2001) and the Constitution Center (2003) sparks a revitalization of the Center City.

1991: Mayor Ed Rendell's contract with city unions is a turning point in controlling the city's chronic budget deficits.

2001: Mayor John Street's Neighborhood Transformation Initiative commits the city to improving deteriorated neighborhoods and to improving housing conditions.

2002: The state takes over the school district, provides more funding for public schools, and opens the door to alternative school programs.

2007: The recession leads to a drop in employment, property values, and tax revenues, forcing Mayor Michael Nutter to make sweeping budget cuts in 2009 and 2010.

more on neighborhood improvement. Street's successor, Michael Nutter (2008–), struggled with the devastating erosion of the city's revenue resulting from the recession. During these years the city experienced gentrification in select neighborhoods. After 2000 the population stabilized, grew slightly, and became more ethnically diverse even though the number of new immigrants remained lower than in other major cities. In addition, as the city continued to lose businesses and population to the suburbs, more of its residents struggled with poverty.

GOVERNMENT AND POLITICS

Population decline, erosion of the city's economic base, and generous contracts for municipal employees and teachers culminated in 1988 with Mayor W. Wilson Goode's (1984–1992) revelation of a city budget deficit of nearly $100 million. While seeking a tax increase of nearly $60 million, the mayor blamed the shortfall primarily on increased social spending and a reduction in federal and state aid. For the remainder of Goode's second term, the city's finances deteriorated while the mayor remained deadlocked with the city council over how to best balance the municipal budget. By 1991 Philadelphia was on the verge of default.

Consequently, the 1991 mayoral election loomed as particularly contentious. Former district attorney Ed Rendell captured the Democratic nomination while the Republicans chose combative former mayor Frank Rizzo (1972–1980). Rizzo died that summer, however, and Rendell defeated the little-known Republican replacement in a landslide.

The new mayor confronted a $250 million budget deficit. After contentious negotiations, Rendell gained substantial concessions from the unions, which agreed to limit wage increases and streamline work rules. He continued Goode's program of privatizing certain municipal functions and ultimately won national praise as "America's Mayor" for saving Philadelphia's finances.

Rendell then turned his attention to economic growth, determined to counter the loss of industrial jobs by reshaping Philadelphia's economy toward culture and tourism. By embracing such ideas as an Avenue of the Arts along South Broad Street, Rendell worked to transform Center City into an entertainment magnet. Meanwhile, the drain of industrial employment continued, including the federal government's 1995 closure of the Philadelphia Naval Shipyard. Some Philadelphians complained that Rendell neglected neighborhood issues, including unemployment and crime, in favor of Center City development. Yet Rendell's initiatives benefited greatly from the nationwide economic boom of the 1990s, and he earned high approval ratings for restoring the city's self-esteem. In 1995 he won reelection in another landslide against another weak opponent.

In pursuing economic growth and fiscal discipline, Rendell forged a close partnership with city council president John Street, an African American who had been raised in poverty and worked as a street vendor while completing law school. Rendell energetically supported Street's campaign for mayor in 1999. After winning the Democratic nomination, Street faced white Republican businessman Sam Katz, who presented himself as an authority on municipal finance. Street won with a 1 percent margin despite the Democratic Party's substantial edge in registration. Although both campaigns avoided racially themed rhetoric, Philadelphia's perennial racial fault line was evident, with Street capturing more than 70 percent of the black vote while Katz took approximately the same share of the white vote.

Street lacked Rendell's communication skills, but he was an engaged mayor who achieved some important results. He began an ambitious Neighborhood Transformation Initiative to reverse blight in the city's neighborhoods and continued Rendell's promotion of tourism, Center City development, and the arts. During Street's tenure the city successfully hosted the 2000 Republican National Convention. Street also negotiated agreements that led to new sports facilities for the Eagles of the National Football League and the Phillies of Major League Baseball.

Running for reelection in 2003, Street again faced Sam Katz. The election took an unexpected turn when an FBI listening device was discovered in Street's office. The Republican U.S. Attorney asserted the device was part of a corruption investigation into Street's administration. If the probe was a political tactic to discredit Street, it backfired, adding a racial tinge to the contest. Street was reelected with a greater margin than four years before. The federal probe continued, however, and a number of Street's associates were convicted of peddling city contracts in exchange for political support. The corruption allegations gained Street the dubious, and probably unfair, distinction of being labeled one of the nation's worst mayors by *Time* magazine.

During his second term, Street introduced new initiatives, including a Safe Streets program assigning additional police to high-crime neighborhoods. In 2004 he proposed a citywide Wi-Fi network to promote widespread computer use and give Philadelphia a technology-friendly reputation, but implementation was repeatedly delayed and eventually cancelled. Street's second term also benefited from the national housing boom that substantially boosted property values. A jump in property transfer tax receipts added to the city's revenues. Although a surge in homicides during 2006 tarnished the city's image, over the next three years the number of murders fell by 25 percent. For the decade as a whole, major crime dropped by the same percentage.

Michael Nutter, an African American and vocal opponent of Street on the city council, won an overwhelming mayoral victory against a little-known Republican challenger in 2007, based largely on his image as a clean, business-like administrator. The worsening national economy eroded the city's revenue in all categories, and within months Nutter faced a fiscal crisis that he labeled of "incredible proportions." Projections showed a five-year $1 billion budget gap. The state authorized the city to collect an additional 1 percent sales tax, but the added revenues did not meet expectations. City services suffered deep cuts across the board.

INDUSTRY, COMMERCE, AND LABOR

As the new century dawned, Philadelphians found themselves engaged in a postindustrial economy. Health care and education drove economic growth and accounted for the largest proportion of the city's work force. The largest employers were the federal, state, and local government and the school district, followed by the University of Pennsylvania, Temple, Drexel, and Thomas Jefferson Universities and their hospital networks. The largest private employers were Wachovia Bank (now Wells Fargo), PNC Financial Services, US Airways, Blue Cross, Amtrak, Verizon, and Comcast Communications. The regional economy was more diverse and stronger than the city's, particularly in the pharmaceutical, biotechnology, and information technology industries. In 2008, only forty-six thousand Philadelphians worked in manufacturing jobs, many of which were in the suburbs. In the recession, only health care and education witnessed job growth.

A variety of local, state, and federal programs sought to attract new employment to the city with tax abatements and subsidies, but their aggregate effect was modest. Jobs in the city continued to decline. During the first decade of the new century, Philadelphia's unemployment rate remained as much as 40 percent higher than that of the region. The recession that began in late 2007 devastated the city's workforce, though ironically somewhat reducing the gap between the rate of joblessness in the city and that in its hard-hit broader metropolitan area. In May 2010 the unemployment rate in the Philadelphia region stood at 9.1 percent, while for city residents it had reached 11.8 percent. The region did not experience the explosive housing bubble of some parts of the country, so prices did not fall as much as elsewhere. Nor were foreclosures as serious, although there were still a large number of foreclosures in the city, weakening many already vulnerable neighborhoods. The sharpest decline in property values was found in the poorest areas and a few, but not all, wealthy neighborhoods.

The key economic development was the revival of Center City (Spring Garden to South Streets between the Schuylkill and Delaware Rivers) and the gentrification of surrounding neighborhoods. The catalysts for downtown revival came with the completion of a rail tunnel linking several commuter lines (1984); a 945-foot office tower, 1 Liberty Place by developer Willard Rouse (1986); and a new convention center (1993). By the early 1990s a cluster of new office towers between 17th and 21st Streets from Market to Race Streets reshaped the city's skyline. However, except for the dramatic Cira Center at 30th Street (2005) and Comcast Tower, at 975 feet the city's tallest building (2007), new office construction in the city slowed after 1993, while it continued to grow in the suburbs. Although top-quality downtown office space rented for less than comparable suburban space, Philadelphia's share of regional office space dropped to 27 percent by 2005, and it ranked only tenth among the largest cities in percentage of regional office space in the central business district. However, in 2009 the vacancy rate for Center City prime space was lower than similar space in a number of comparable markets.

Government at all levels invested heavily to keep Center City competitive as a tourist destination and an attractive residential district. In 1991 the city chartered a business improvement district for Center City that aggressively lobbied for additional support and provided supplemental services to keep the district clean and safe. The federal government upgraded the historic district around Independence Hall with a new Independence Visitors Center (2002), Liberty Bell pavilion (2003), and Constitution Center (2003). Over 2.7 million tourists visited the site in 2009. The Avenue of the Arts project transformed South Broad Street into a vibrant cultural destination with a revitalized streetscape and new theaters. The centerpiece of the plan, the spectacular Kimmel Center, opened in 2001 to national acclaim. At decade's end construction began on a new museum on the Benjamin Franklin Parkway for the world-renowned Barnes Foundation art collection.

The city's professional sports teams provided an occasional but much-needed boost to civic pride. The Eagles played in the 2005 Super Bowl; the Flyers appeared in the 1997 and 2010 Stanley Cup finals; and the Phillies won the 2008 World Series, also playing in the 1993 and 2009 contests.

As mayor and then as governor, Ed Rendell pushed for legalized casinos to augment revenue. In 2006 Pennsylvania authorized slot-machine casinos in locations statewide, with two designated for Philadelphia. However, intense community opposition to proposed sites along the Delaware waterfront delayed implementation. In 2010 SugarHouse casino opened in the Fishtown section of Northern Liberties, but the fate of the other casino remained uncertain.

While tourism and office employment expanded, retailing continued to erode. By 2003 the city's share of regional retail sales had dropped to 16 percent. Meanwhile, downtown department stores, once major civic institutions, passed from local ownership. In 1997 John Wanamaker's became a branch of Lord & Taylor and later Macy's. In 2006 Strawbridge and Clothier closed entirely.

By the late 1980s Philadelphia had a number of gentrified neighborhoods around the edges of Center City. The city continued to encourage gentrification even when longtime residents opposed the disruption of social networks and the increased property taxes that it brought. In

1997 the city adopted a ten-year tax abatement to convert nonresidential to residential property, which it later extended to new residential construction, thus sparking additional gentrification as residents and developers sought older properties to upgrade. The Old City neighborhood completed a transition already underway, and the process took hold in Spring Garden and in Powelton Village in University City, both areas with handsome Victorian homes. Even more dramatic was development in Northern Liberties, the city's oldest manufacturing district. A local "loft district" took form in warehouses and factory buildings between Vine and Spring Garden Streets around North Broad Street. Six miles from downtown, factories became residences and shops and restaurants flourished in Manayunk. A proliferation of sidewalk restaurants added an ambiance of vitality and a sense of safety that further attracted tourists, visitors, and new residents. By 2006 Philadelphia had the nation's third largest downtown residential population, almost ninety thousand people.

RACE, ETHNICITY, AND IMMIGRATION

Although Philadelphia's population declined slightly in the 1990s, it became more ethnically and racially diverse. In 1990 more than 50 percent of Philadelphians were non-Hispanic whites, approximately 40 percent were African Americans, 5 percent were Hispanics, and less than 3 percent were Asians. By 2010, 37 percent of the population was non-Hispanic white; the non-Hispanic black or African American population had risen to 42 percent, the Hispanic population had doubled to 12 percent (two-thirds of Puerto Rican ancestry), and the Asian population jumped to more than 6 percent.

While increased immigration underlay much of the new diversity, the city failed to attract new immigrants at the same rate as other large cities, which partially accounted for its population decline in the 1990s. In 2008 one hundred fifty-one thousand Philadelphians (10.5 percent of the population) were foreign-born. Of those, 39 percent came from Asia and 27 percent from Latin America. One-third of the total arrived after 2000. The new immigrants clustered in a number of neighborhoods. People from the former Soviet Union, Eastern Europe, and India concentrated in the far Northeast. Cambodians, Koreans, West Indians, and Latin Americans moved into a narrow corridor between the black neighborhoods of North Philadelphia and white areas closer to the Delaware River. Vietnamese and Cambodians in large numbers lived in South Philadelphia neighborhoods straddling Broad Street. A Mexican community rapidly emerged in the Italian Market area. In the far Southwest, in Elmwood, could be found Vietnamese, Africans, and Cambodians. Indicative of the diversity of the public schools, the code of student conduct was published in eight foreign languages.

The recent arrivals rejuvenated several neighborhoods but also engendered some resentment and occasional violence from established residents. Sporadic street fights broke out between African Americans and Asians in West Philadelphia, between Latinos and whites in Kensington, and between Polish immigrants and native-born whites (including Polish Americans) in Port Richmond. Furthermore, although the chronic black-versus-white racial hostility of earlier decades subsided somewhat in the Rendell and Street years, Philadelphia remained deeply segregated.

Philadelphia is a poor city: A quarter of the population, and one-third of all children, manage on incomes below the poverty level. The median cash household income in 2008 was $37,000. Deindustrialization and the changing city job market, combined with educational deficits and job discrimination, hit the black and Latino populations especially hard, contributing to their high unemployment rates. While gentrifiers revived Center City, Philadelphia led the nation in abandoned buildings per capita. A lack of jobs, high crime rates, drug abuse, and poor schools characterized large sections of the city. Rates of violent crime increased into the early years of the new century, enabled in part by a persistent climate of distrust between African Americans and city police.

At the grassroots level, community development corporations and volunteer agencies worked, against enormous odds, to create jobs and improve neighborhoods. As mayor, Rendell did not ignore decaying neighborhoods, but clearly his focus was Center City. The city established additional business improvement districts but provided few resources to support them, although the city's Office of Housing and Community Development did build new affordable housing units and assisted first-time homebuyers. After the federal government briefly took over and reorganized the mismanaged Philadelphia Housing Authority (PHA), that agency demolished its oldest housing projects and replaced them with lower-density homes. The federal government briefly took control of the PHA again in 2011, after revelations of mismanagement surfaced in the local press.

Mayor Street made neighborhood revival the centerpiece of his administration. In 2001 he launched the Neighborhood Transformation Initiative (NTI), funded with almost $300 million in long-term bonds. Street expected to leverage the money to acquire parcels for both private capital and nonprofits to invest in new housing. Over the next seven years, the NTI removed thousands of abandoned cars and demolished over five thousand six hundred abandoned buildings. Empty lots were cleaned up, and many became community gardens and recreational space. Yet NTI demolished far fewer units than planned, in part because of neighborhood opposition and high demolition costs. It also built fewer housing units than hoped, relying heavily on private capital for new construction. In 2009 NTI funding ended. And under Nutter's austerity budget, money to clean up empty lots was slashed, further eroding the quality of life in many fragile neighborhoods.

The chronically underfunded public schools failed to adequately serve the population, and their poor reputation was one of the principal reasons families moved out of Philadelphia. The conspicuously segregated student population was 85 percent black, Latino, and Asian and poorer than the population as a whole: Half the students qualified for free school lunches. In 2002 the State of Pennsylvania largely took control of the schools and a five-member School Reform Commission replaced the elected Board of Education. Outside organizations, including the for-profit Edison Schools, as well as Temple University, the University of Pennsylvania, and even Microsoft, were brought in to operate some schools. Although the state takeover improved school management, funding levels remained far below that of suburban schools, while class sizes were larger. Student scores on standardized tests did improve substantially throughout the decade. By 2009 half of public school students were rated proficient or advanced in reading and almost half in math. Yet Philadelphia still spent over $2,000 less per student than the average of all the surrounding communities.

See also *Philadelphia, PA 1776–1790; Philadelphia, PA 1790–1828; Philadelphia, PA 1828–1854; Philadelphia, PA 1854–1877; Philadelphia, PA 1877–1896; Philadelphia, PA 1896–1929; Philadelphia, PA 1929–1941; Philadelphia, PA 1941–1952; Philadelphia, PA 1952–1989*

ROGER D. SIMON AND BRIAN ALNUTT

BIBLIOGRAPHY

Adams, Carolyn, T. "The Philadelphia Experience." *Annals of the American Academy of Political and Social Science* 551 (May 1997): 222–234.

Bissinger, H. G. "Buzz." *A Prayer for the City.* New York, NY: Random House, 1997.

Countryman, Matthew. *Up South: Civil Rights and Black Power in Philadelphia.* Philadelphia: University of Pennsylvania Press, 2006.

Dilworth, Richardson, ed. *Social Capital in the City: Community and Civic Life in Philadelphia.* Philadelphia, PA: Temple University Press, 2006.

Kromer, John. *Neighborhood Recovery: Reinvestment Policy in the New Hometown.* New Brunswick, NJ: Rutgers University Press, 2000.

Simon, Roger D., and Brian Alnutt. "Philadelphia, 1982–2007: Toward the Postindustrial City." *Pennsylvania Magazine of History and Biography* 131, no. 4 (2007), 395–443.

PHOENIX, AZ 1989–2011

THE PURSUIT AND CONSEQUENCES OF GROWTH shaped the history of Phoenix during this era. One of the nation's largest cities in 1989, Phoenix grew even larger over the next two decades, totaling more than 1.45 million people in 2010 and ranking sixth in the nation. Like many Sunbelt cities it increased through extensive annexation, expanding from 404 to 519 square miles, an area larger than that of any major U.S. city except Houston. Yet its metropolitan area grew even more rapidly. Some of its satellite suburbs—Scottsdale, Chandler, Gilbert, and Peoria—were among the nation's fastest-growing cities, and a number of them developed separate identities and economic and political interests.

Partly because of this growth, a number of the issues confronting Phoenix, such as transportation, the environment, and growth control, required metropolitan solutions. Certain economic problems were also becoming metropolitan, most notably the boom/bust housing and construction sector after 2000, but among the twenty-five municipalities in Central Arizona's Salt River Valley, Phoenix was the dominant player in searching for an economic driver to replace the declining high-tech electronics sector. Growth also changed the demographic composition of the area, which had important political and cultural implications. Finally, after a long period of decline and malaise, the Phoenix downtown experienced significant improvement.

QUICK FACTS

PHOENIX, AZ **1989–2011**

MAYORS

Terry Goddard	(1984–1990)
Paul Johnson	(1990–1994)
John B. Nelson	(1994)
Thelda Williams	(1994)
Skip Rimsza	(1994–2004)
Phil Gordon	(2004–)

MAJOR INDUSTRIES AND EMPLOYERS

City of Phoenix
State of Arizona
Honeywell International
Maricopa County government
American Express

MAJOR NEWSPAPERS

Arizona Republic
Phoenix Gazette
East Valley Tribune

MAJOR EVENTS

1992: The Martin Luther King Jr. holiday is adopted by popular vote.
1997–2007: The city witnesses the collapse of Motorola.
1998: The Arizona Diamondbacks baseball team opens a new stadium.
2002: Translational Genomics Research Institute comes to Phoenix.
2009: Phoenix is named All-America City for fifth time.

GOVERNMENT AND POLITICS

Governance and politics in Phoenix reflected consensus building more than conflict, partly because of the city's politically skillful mayors and a council of few members with large districts. Some council elections were uncontested, most were won easily by incumbents, and incumbents generally served for a number of terms. Even the selection of mayors seemed almost predetermined, influenced by the ability of a favored candidate to raise a significant campaign fund and often reflected in a consensus among council members about mayoral hopefuls among their number.

Mayor Terry Goddard (1984–1990) was a visionary leader, instituting new programs and seeking to change the direction of city development. His greatest success was beginning the redevelopment of the city's downtown, culminating in the passage of a major bond program in 1988. Goddard's successor, Paul Johnson (1990–1994), focused on the administration of existing programs more than on new initiatives, although his approach was partly dictated by an economic downturn that forced him to make budget cuts. He did, however, continue downtown development and press for acquiring mountain parkland and a recycling program. Skip Rimsza (1994–2004), Johnson's successor and friend, began with limited goals and approached the position as if he were a business executive. He continued the existing policies of downtown and infill development, as well as adding to the city's parks and police force. After 1998, however, Rimsza became more ambitious, pushing successfully for the adoption of a light rail system, an expanded convention center, and a biomedical campus. The final mayor of this era, Phil Gordon (2004–), entered office known for focusing on neighborhood-level concerns more than a broader vision for the city, but he actively advanced the development of light rail, the convention center, and the biomedical campus. Most significantly, Gordon worked to create a sizable, city-supported downtown campus for Arizona State University.

During the 1980s the city initiated a major shift in its planning philosophy. It adopted an "urban village" model, which divided the city into (initially) nine sections, each of which was supposed to contain the full range of services, features, and amenities. While the larger aspects of this model were not attained, it did encourage more decentralized, citizen-responsive planning. It also led to city policies that encouraged neighborhood development. The most significant of these involved creating special planning districts, and some older neighborhoods were also established as historic districts. More generally, however, there was support for the development of neighborhood associations of various types, and by 2010 their numbers were well over a thousand.

Additional annexation did generate debate in the city council. Opponents argued that annexing more land would oblige current residents to subsidize new developments. Proponents contended that growth was inevitable, that annexation would impose the city's stricter building codes on new developments, and that the additional businesses provided crucial sales tax revenues. The debate about annexation and sprawl spilled over into state politics from 1997 to 2000. A proposal for strict control was defeated in 2000, but the threat of this measure has prompted the governor and the state legislature to adopt measures requiring greater municipal planning and control of development.

Downtown redevelopment was the dominant issue during these decades. Although downtown had remained the center of government and finance, it had seen virtually no building activity since the early 1950s, and its dilapidated state prompted Mayor Johnson to call it a "rat hole." But change began in the late 1980s, starting with a residential complex, a sports arena, and two commercial centers. The 1990s saw the construction of various government buildings, two museums, several theaters, and a baseball stadium. But even the addition of major office buildings had not created the necessary critical mass to make the downtown bustling during the day and vibrant at night. Post-2000 developments gave city leaders some hope. First, a variety of housing developments were completed, bringing residents into the downtown area. Second, attracting a major biomedical institute and a research consortium along with a branch of the University of Arizona Medical School created a nucleus of professionals. Third, establishing a campus of Arizona State University, which was planned to attract fifteen thousand students, promised to provide the numbers of people that would support a range of services and attract still more people to the area.

INDUSTRY, COMMERCE, AND LABOR

The Phoenix area economy continued to expand rapidly during this era, attracting and supporting a burgeoning population. Tourism saw a rise, as revenues jumped from $2.9 billion in 1989 to $11 billion in 2005. This spawned the continued development of resorts as well as related amenities like golf courses, which numbered over two hundred. While many visitors stayed in more modest locations instead of the expensive resorts, others, especially after 2002, bought second homes as part-year residences.

Aviation benefited from more tourists, but it also played a larger role in the economy. From 1985 to 2005 passenger traffic tripled at Sky Harbor Airport, which built a new terminal and additional facilities to accommodate the traffic. America West Airlines (founded in 1983) benefited from this growth, and after a merger in 2005 it operated as US Airways, the nation's fifth largest airline. Aviation opportunities flourished in the Salt River Valley, with a feeder airport in Mesa and six general aviation airports. Airports also developed significant economic roles as business centers. Sky Harbor became the second most important economic area in the Valley, providing direct or indirect employment to more than one hundred thirty-five thousand people, while the Scottsdale Airport was the third largest employment center.

Other booming parts of the economy included traditional areas of strengths, such as finance and retail, which grew because of the area's population increase. New employers included USAA insurance company and credit card operations centers for various national banks, which had more than ten thousand local employees by 1999.

But the economy also provided grounds for concern. The most significant of these was the decline of per capita income. Until 1988 Phoenix had ranked above the national median; thereafter it fell below that level. One reason for this change was the economy's increasing dependence on the service sector, including tourism and retail businesses. Related to the income decline was the rising level of poverty, as Phoenix ranked seventh worst among the nation's largest twenty-five metropolitan areas in 2000. While the city remained generally more affordable than other large cities, low wages combined with the increased cost of housing meant that Phoenix ranked only twelfth in affordable housing.

The economy was also afflicted with structural problems. Following the loss of large locally owned department stores and construction firms in the 1960s and 1970s, the years after 1985 saw the takeover by outside owners of the area's banks and grocery stores. The loss of local economic leadership was compounded by the Valley's failure to provide much venture capital to finance new local businesses.

The most disturbing failure was the dramatic decline in manufacturing, especially in high tech. After Phoenix built up strength in this area during the 1950s, it maintained roughly 20 percent of the workforce in manufacturing into the 1980s, but by 2005 that declined to only 6 percent. Aerospace firms generally maintained their positions, but most electronics firms did not. By the 1980s the Valley's electronics sector consisted largely of semiconductor manufacturing. Intel expanded its operations through the 1990s, and in 2005 it decided to make a substantial investment in new facilities. But in 2007, facing competition and a weakening market, it began laying off employees, while several other major firms decided to simply abandon their activities in the Valley. The most dramatic failure during these years was Motorola. In the early 1990s, the Valley's headline electronics employer, with a workforce of over twenty thousand, laid off two-thirds of its employees, spun off two subsidiaries, and ended with only one thousand employees by 2005.

In the late 1980s the construction industry suffered a severe contraction caused by over-building earlier in the decade. Arizona banks had participated in this speculative behavior, but savings and loan institutions had wallowed in it, and the real estate collapse effectively elimi-nated these financial institutions. Construction activity resumed by 1992 and then boomed in the late 1990s. The profits and competition for markets led to another wave of buyouts, as major national construction companies purchased most of the remaining Arizona builders.

Investors perceived real estate as a profitable opportunity after 2000. Housing construction then boomed tremendously, and housing sales jumped, as speculators bought and resold new homes while others bought, refurbished, and sold older homes. This substantially increased con-struction-related employment pushed a huge increase in prices, with related demands for easier financing. The result was a variety of unsafe mortgage financing schemes. By 2007 Phoenix, like the rest of the country, began witnessing waves of foreclosures and another looming financial disaster, and starting in 2008 the Valley was near the top of the housing disaster charts.

By the early 1990s economic groups and various analysts saw that Phoenix needed a new stimulus for economic growth. Like in a number of cities and states, they decided on bio-medicine as the solution. A concerted effort begun in 1999 by state, city, and industry leaders succeeded in attracting the Translational Genomics Research Institute and the International Genomics Consortium to Phoenix in 2002. The following year Arizona State University began collaborative programs with Mayo Clinic in medical research and development, as well as in clinical work. In 2004 the University of Arizona, with cooperation from the other two state universities, began planning a branch campus of its Medical School, which it opened in 2007. That joined with the other biomedical institutions, as well as the National Institute of Diabetes and Digestive and Kidney Disorders labs, as part of a Phoenix Biomedical Campus. While the initial enthusiasm was muted by the economic difficulties mounting after 2007, the basic commitment remained in terms of shifting the economy to one based on information and that offered high-paying jobs.

RACE, ETHNICITY, AND IMMIGRATION

Phoenix continued its rapid growth after 1989, increasing by 47 percent to a population of 1,445,632 in 2010, yet this rate was slower than in previous decades. It also trailed the growth rates for nearly all suburbs, which had become the areas with the fastest and most sizable expan-sion. Their increase and the substantial size of some suburbs—five of them had more than two hundred thousand people—reduced Phoenix's population from half to slightly over 40 percent of the metropolitan population.

Growth brought not only more people but also people from a greater range of places, as refu-gees from Afghanistan, North Africa, and Bosnia joined immigrants from Russia, Vietnam, and Micronesia, among others. The greatest population change was the increase of Latinos, primar-ily from Mexico. Totaling 17 percent of the city's population in 1990, that group doubled to 34 percent in 2000 and rose to 41 percent in 2010. This increase affected many aspects of Phoenix. Although this population spread to neighborhoods throughout the city, significant concentra-tion continued. By 2000 Hispanics comprised over half the population in the area extending two miles north of downtown, and a U.S. Census Bureau study ranked Phoenix as one of the five most segregated metropolitan areas for Latinos.

The core of this area also comprised the city's most impoverished neighborhoods, with over half the residents living below the poverty level. Although city services improved over time, they were largely inadequate for this population, and voluntary organizations offered key assistance. This started with Friendly House, a social service organization founded in 1920, and was aided by the subsequent formation of social service groups like Centro de Amistad and Valle del Sol. A fourth organization, Chicanas Por la Causa, was a community development corporation that not only offered social services but also provided assistance in housing, business and commercial development, neighborhood revitalization, and a range of educational programs.

The growth of this population had economic consequences. By 2000 Hispanic businesses controlled over twenty-five neighborhood shopping centers and innumerable small strip malls. Marketing firms specifically targeting Hispanic consumers increased from only a few in 1990 to thirty by 2005. This involved using Spanish, which became an increasingly audible presence in the Valley—on the streets, on ten radio stations and two television stations by 2000—and employers sought workers fluent in both English and Spanish.

Language also became a divisive political issue. In 1988 Arizona voters declared English the state's official language. Although overturned by court decisions, its passage reflected growing worries about Latino assimilation; the issue reappeared in 2000, when state voters banned bilingual education. Increasing public fear and anger over illegal immigration led to a state law in 2007 that stiffened penalties for hiring illegal immigrants, while the county sheriff instituted "sweeps" allegedly to catch them. Tension heightened in 2010 with state legislation requiring police to seek and arrest those in the country illegally. Concerns about civil liberties and economic impacts led to protests and boycotts. A U.S. district judge halted enforcement of the law, but the State of Arizona appealed to the U.S. Supreme Court. In 2011 the state legislature considered but then defeated five additional measures to punish illegal immigrants. With illegal immigrants constituting a quarter of the Latino population and immigration primarily a federal issue, the only certainty was that no solution would be found quickly.

Other minorities did not experience the same population boom. African Americans remained at roughly 5 percent, while Native Americans increased slightly to 2 percent. The latter group became more visible because suburban sprawl abutted nearby reservations. After the federal government allowed gambling on reservations in the 1990s, Indians built casinos that provided a much-needed economic stimulus. The condition of African Americans changed little from previous decades. Greater numbers appeared in middle-class occupations and neighborhoods, while the levels of poverty and unemployment fell slightly below national norms, but the basic problems of inadequate housing, education, and employment continued. The city did experience a major struggle over a civil rights issue that involved the state and caught national attention. After the state legislature dawdled on enacting a Martin Luther King Jr. holiday, Governor Bruce Babbit declared the holiday by executive order in 1986. His successor, Evan Mecham, disagreeing with the substance and method of the order, rescinded it. African Americans and civil rights supporters mobilized, marched, and organized boycotts. For the next five years the state struggled through a confusion of laws and conflicting referenda. Cities established a paid

King holiday, starting with Phoenix, and by 1991 including Glendale, Tempe, and Scottsdale. Despite polls showing clear majorities favoring such a law, particularly in Phoenix, not until 1992 were Arizona voters able to vote on a single state law creating a King holiday. They passed the measure overwhelmingly, the only state to create the holiday by popular vote.

See also *Phoenix, AZ, 1952–1989*

PHILIP R. VANDERMEER

BIBLIOGRAPHY

Gammage, Grady, Jr. *Phoenix in Perspective: Reflections on Developing the Desert*. Tempe: Herberger Center for Design Excellence, Arizona State University, 1999.

Gober, Patricia. *Metropolitan Phoenix: Place Making and Community Building in the Desert*. Philadelphia: University of Pennsylvania Press, 2006.

Johnson, G. Wesley, ed. *Phoenix in the Twentieth Century: Essays in Community History*. Norman: University of Oklahoma Press, 1993.

Luckingham, Bradford. *Minorities in Phoenix: A Profile of Mexican American, Chinese American, and African American Communities, 1860–1992*. Tucson: University of Arizona Press, 1994.

———. *Phoenix: The History of a Southwestern Metropolis*. Tucson: University of Arizona Press, 1989.

VanderMeer, Philip R. *Desert Visions and the Making of Phoenix, 1860 to 2009*. Albuquerque: University of New Mexico Press, 2010.

Whitaker, Matthew C. *Race Work: The Rise of Civil Rights in the Urban West*. Lincoln: University of Nebraska Press, 2005.

SAN ANTONIO, TX 1989–2011

SAN ANTONIO EXPERIENCED CONSIDERABLE GROWTH during the late twentieth and early twenty-first centuries. In 1980 its population stood at 785,940; by 2008 it was an estimated 1.35 million, making it the seventh largest city in the United States. That rapid increase was linked to a booming economy consistent with other Sunbelt cities: hospitality and tourism, along with health care and financial services produced the most new work; the federal government (military and civilian defense workers) provided the next largest share. The political response to this robust economy has been to invest millions of public dollars in the construction of tourist amenities in the downtown core (the River Walk and convention facilities especially); and in building expressways that loop around and radiate out from the city, facilitating urban sprawl. To ensure that San Antonio did not lose suburban tax dollars, every mayor since World War II has used Texas's liberal annexation laws to expand its political boundaries. In 1940 the city covered 36 square miles; in 2008 it had swelled to 412. This pattern of low-density development also produced several intersecting environmental consequences. As a direct result of heavy automobile commuting, the city in the late 1990s began to exceed the federal Environmental Protection Agency's national ambient air quality standards; the related expansion of new subdivisions on the city's north and west sides compromised the

QUICK FACTS

SAN ANTONIO, TX **1989–2011**

MAYORS

Henry G. Cisneros	(1981–1989)
Lila Cockrell	(1989–1991)
Nelson W. Wolff	(1991–1995)
William E. Thornton	(1995–1997)
Howard W. Peak	(1997–2001)
Edward D. Garza	(2001–2005)
Phil Hardberger	(2005–2009)
Julián Castro	(2009–)

MAJOR INDUSTRIES AND EMPLOYERS

Government
Trade, transportation, and utilities
Education and health services
Professional and business services
Leisure and hospitality

MAJOR NEWSPAPERS

San Antonio Express-News
San Antonio Light (until 1997)

MAJOR EVENTS

1991: Passage of strict term limits for the city council and mayor complicated the city council's capacity to govern.

1995: The closure of Kelly Air Force Base signals a major transition in the city's economic dependence on military spending.

1997: With the completion of flood-control tunnels on San Pedro Creek and the San Antonio River, the city's downtown is effectively protected against devastating flash floods.

2003: The opening of Toyota's $1.3 billion truck manufacturing plant helps diversify San Antonio's economy.

2009: The River Walk extension project, slated to be complete in 2013, will expand San Antonio's pedestrian experience north and south of the central core.

recharge zone of the Edwards Aquifer, San Antonio's single most important source of potable water. Together, these issues, and the debates that have erupted in response to them, have profoundly shaped the community's political life, economic development, and environmental health.

GOVERNMENT AND POLITICS

Located in south-central Texas, a state whose political culture tends to distrust politicians and politics, San Antonio enacted one of the strictest term limit laws in the nation in 1991. After a series of high-profile scandals in the 1980s, voters passed laws limiting the mayor and city council to two two-year terms, with a lifetime ban on returning to these offices. This regulation, of which the conservative Homeowner-Taxpayer Association was a key advocate, came coupled with regular demands for decreases in property taxes (which were already among the lowest in the state), a reduction in city services, opposition to spending tax dollars on air conditioning in classrooms in the San Antonio Independent School District, and fluoridating public water. Although these pressures complicated the political maneuverability of the mayor and city council, and troubled the city's bond ratings throughout the 1990s, the most difficult aspect of local politics was the restrictive term limits themselves. Since 1989 there have been eight mayors and more than fifty city council representatives. Local politics had become a game of musical chairs: in the first year in office, council members learned their job; in year two they ran for a second term; if they were reelected, then in year three they governed; in year four they either ran for mayor or looked for another line of work.

This revolving door had another curious outcome: stability lay with city staff, whose power thus increased with a weakened city council, already diminished by design in the reigning council-manager system of government. Stark disparities in salary were reflective of differences in clout; council representatives are paid $20 per day per session; the mayor earns an annual salary of $4,000; in 2008 the city manager's base pay was $275,000. Realistically, only those who could afford to work without an income, or those who held a second, full-time job, could hold office. That awkward situation further decreased the elected representatives' capacity to govern effectively. Yet voters rebuffed several attempts to loosen the strict term limits law, and thus recalibrate the tenor and balance of local politics. In fall 2008, however, they accepted a modest revision granting council members and the mayor the possibility of two four-year terms.

These complicated challenges to governance did not paralyze the city's political representatives from pursuing significant development projects. Indeed, because of these constraints, individual mayors recognized that a major portion of their work was serving as the city's public face, and with varying degrees of success they launched a number of key initiatives. Mayor Henry Cisneros invested local, state, and federal dollars in tourist, sports, and convention center infrastructure, particularly focusing on the city's great pedestrian space, the River Walk. His successors followed suit, using tax abatements to subsidize new hotels and recreational attractions. And every mayor from Cisneros to Howard Peak had oversight responsibilities for two major flood-control tunnels bored beneath the city to protect the River Walk. They also pushed forward a number of signature projects: Nelson Wolff completed construction of the football arena, the Alamodome; Bill Thornton started work on Port San Antonio, located on the site of the closed Kelly Air Force Base; Ed Garza, an urban planner, developed City South, a New Urbanism live-work community; and Phil Hardberger rehabilitated the Spanish "heart of the city," Main Plaza, purchased Voelcker Park, and underwrote significant extensions of the River Walk, north and south of the central core. Elected in 2009, Julián Castro was quickly dubbed the "utility mayor" because of the immediate steps he took to reduce the city's investment in the South Texas Nuclear Plant and negotiate with the San Antonio Water System over establishing a more reliable water supply. Planning for more mass transit to enhance regional air quality was also a critical component of his early agenda.

These achievements were counterbalanced by difficulties each mayor faced in resolving pressing environmental issues. Peak, for instance, negotiated a new urban development code intended to control runaway suburbanization and increase density, but developers and contractors weakened its regulations before final passage; they also girdled a tree preservation ordinance that would have greened up the city. Water has long been the community's most tenacious and complex issue. Since the 1950s, council after council has tried to procure more water through reservoir construction projects, cross-watershed pipelines, and desalinization projects. Most met with defeat. In 1991 and 1994 voters rejected the city's decision to construct Applewhite

Reservoir, sited along the Medina River south of town, which maintained the city's dependence on the Edwards Aquifer.

Citizens were riled, too, whenever major construction was slated over the Edwards Aquifer's recharge features and contributing zone. This included big-box malls, residential projects, and a massive golf course community and resort called PGA Village. Coalitions of environmentalists, suburban residents, inner-city activists, and others periodically rallied to pressure city council to rescind such development agreements, with some success. After years of fighting over how to protect this essential resource, in 2000 the city council proposed and the voters approved Proposition 3, a one-eighth-cent sales tax increase to purchase undeveloped lands over the aquifer; five years later, Proposition 1 added more funds to this crucial initiative, as did a similar proposition in 2010. To build on these achievements, Mayor Hardberger, as he left office in 2009, offered the community a forward-looking plan called Mission Verde. Time will tell what impact the economic downturn that began in 2007 will have on his successors' ability and willingness to adopt its "green" aspirations to embrace clean technologies, alternative energy sources, high-performance buildings, and multimodal transportation.

INDUSTRY, COMMERCE, AND LABOR

San Antonio never fully experienced the industrial revolution, as did cities such as New York, Detroit, and Chicago. Like many southwestern cities, its former focus on agriculture and ranching was first supplemented and then supplanted by federal spending and an emerging service economy. Dubbed "Military City USA," it was home to five major facilities—Fort Sam Houston, and Kelly, Lackland, Brooks, and Randolph Air Force Bases—as well as a spate of ancillary installations. During World War II and the Cold War, billions of Defense Department dollars poured into the city, creating thousands of well-paying jobs, one consequence of which was the establishment of a vibrant and growing Mexican American middle class. This intense economic stimulus began to decrease after the Vietnam War, and in the late 1980s, with the formation of the Defense Base Closure and Realignment Commission (BRAC), the city began to lose once-munificent military contracts. In 1995 BRAC closed Kelly Air Force Base, a major maintenance center. Brooks, which specialized in aerospace medicine and research, became Brooks-City Base after its closing in 2005. Although the remaining military bases, as of 2009, employed upwards of twenty-seven thousand civilians, federal spending has declined substantially, so much so that it no longer makes up the single largest component of the city's economy.

Taking its place in recent decades has been the hospitality and health care industries. Tourism has been a leading economic factor since the late nineteenth century, as first the Alamo, site of the famed 1836 battle of the Texas Revolution, and later the River Walk drew countless visitors to the city. In 2008 an estimated twenty million people traveled to San Antonio for business or leisure, generating an $11 billion impact; the tourism industry employed more than one hundred thousand people who received approximately $2 billion in wages. Somewhat more significant is the younger health care and biomedical sector, which, in 2007, employed one hundred sixteen thousand, paid wages of $4.8 billion, and had a reported $16.3 billion impact. Each industry suffered during the 2007 economic downturn; as budgets shrank, jobs were cut. But these losses did not undermine the leading roles that these economic actors play in the local economy.

Uncertain is whether the same will be said of the $1.3 billion Toyota Motors Manufacturing plant that opened in City South, a planned community located on the city's south side. The factory's construction began in 2003 amid considerable fanfare, and it was slated to produce Tundra trucks, the largest in the company's fleet. But the market for these vehicles, even in pickup-mad Texas, sharply declined with the economy soon after the first vehicles rolled off the gleaming assembly line in 2006. Expected to hire over three thousand workers, instead the company began to furlough its employees; it even shuttered production for a time, before consolidating all its U.S. Tundra production in San Antonio. In 2009 it added its Tacoma truck to the local operations. Whether this new work will enable the factory to live up to earlier predictions that it would usher in a new industrial era in the city is questionable. With two thousand two hundred employees, Toyota placed third on the 2011 list of the leading manufacturers in the city, behind Harland Clarke (check printing) and Cardell Cabinetry (custom woodworking).

Because it has long sold itself to prospective employers as a "cheap-wage" town, with strong anti-union sentiments, San Antonio got what it (apparently) wanted: Lots of entry-level employment. Until the late 1990s tourism had been the key source for this kind of work. Subsequently, the city has become a national hub for back-office operations for a number of financial service giants such as Citicorp, Wachovia, American Funds, and Washington Mutual; their large call centers found their parallels in QVC Network's order center and Caremark Prescription Center's mail-order facility. While these entities offer higher-than-minimum-wage salaries and benefits, the local service economy does not present the kind of job security or opportunity for upward mobility that the military bases once provided.

RACE, ETHNICITY, AND IMMIGRATION

San Antonio is one of the nation's first majority-minority cities, and it is the largest with a Latino majority. That seems unsurprising, given that the Spanish founded the community in the late seventeenth century, it flew the Mexican flag from 1821 until the Texas Revolution of 1836, and it did not enter the Union until 1845. But for the first half of the twentieth century, non-Hispanic whites were the majority. Following World War II, however, the Latino population began to surge, and by the 2000 census it accounted for more than 58 percent of the citizenry; whites totaled 32 percent and African Americans 7 percent.

Through much of San Antonio's modern history, this racial and ethnic composition was segregated in specific neighborhoods. Latinos dominated the west side, whites populated the north side, the east side was the site of the city's small black population, and the south was a mix of poor whites and Latinos. This pattern broke down in the last decades of the twentieth century; as the number of Mexican Americans grew, they sought housing throughout the city, and by 2000 they constituted the majority on the south and east sides. With greater prosperity, many also moved into once-white enclaves on the north side. This demographic shift altered the city's electoral dynamics, boosting the successful mayoral campaigns of Ed Garza (2001) and Julián Castro (2009). Like Henry Cisneros before them, they reached out to all sectors of the community, but by winning huge majorities among Latino voters they captured City Hall.

For all these successes at the polls, the income of more than 22 percent of San Antonio's Latino population falls below the federal poverty line; in 2007 that percentage equaled approximately one hundred sixty-five thousand residents, a large proportion of whom were children. Although this is a considerable improvement from the grinding poverty that many Mexican Americans endured for much of the twentieth century, these data from the early twenty-first century remain alarming because young and poor Latinos face an additional hurdle: The schools many attend receive some of the worst ratings in Texas. This is a partial result of residual discrimination: San Antonio contains sixteen independent school districts that, when they were established, only reinforced prevailing forms of racial and ethnic segregation. Inequitable school funding has not helped matters. Local property taxes underwrote school budgets until the mid-1990s, so that richer and whiter districts on the city's north side spent exponentially more money per child than their poorer counterparts on the west, east, and south sides. In 1993, after a series of lawsuits demonstrating this system's discriminatory impact, the Texas state legislature finally adopted a court-mandated equitable school funding mechanism (promptly dubbed the "Robin Hood Plan" by its opponents). In time this new formula may bolster the educational possibilities for those in the city's Latino-majority schools. But as of 2010 the San Antonio, Edgewood, Southside, and South San Antonio Independent School Districts record the city's highest dropout rates and the lowest graduation rates. The social ramifications of this are disturbing: Nearly 50 percent of those who did not graduate from high school live below the poverty line, an indication of systemic failure. These troubling outcomes have led every modern mayor to demand school reform, but because they have no authority over the independent school districts they have been unable to influence education policy.

Political figures, civic leaders, grassroots activists, and ordinary citizens are well aware that providing a high-quality education for all children is key to San Antonio's ability to create greater economic opportunities and a more just society. Vital too will be resolving the community's interlocking environmental problems—notably clean air and plentiful clean water—that, if left unaddressed, will threaten its ability to live sustainably in the rugged south Texas landscape. Yet no American city fully controls its destiny. Global politics, climate, and economics, like political forces emanating from the national and state level, help set the context of its actions. How well San Antonio adapts to these external pressures, how thoroughly it meets the needs of its people and the environments they inhabit, will determine its future quality of life.

CHAR MILLER

BIBLIOGRAPHY

Fisher, Lewis. *Saving San Antonio: The Precarious Preservation of a Heritage.* Lubbock: Texas Tech University Press, 1996.

Hernández-Ehrisman, Laura. *Inventing the Fiesta City: Heritage and Carnival in San Antonio.* Albuquerque: University of New Mexico Press, 2008.

Johnson, David R., John Booth, and David Harris, eds. *The Politics of Power: Community, Progress, and Power*. Lincoln: University of Nebraska Press, 1983.

Miller, Char. *Deep in the Heart of San Antonio: Land and Life in San Antonio*. San Antonio, TX: Trinity University Press, 2004.

———, ed. *On the Border: An Environmental History of San Antonio*. San Antonio, TX: Trinity University Press, 2005.

Rosales, Rodolfo. *The Illusion of Inclusion: The Untold Political Story of San Antonio*. Austin: University of Texas Press, 2000.

Sanders, Heywood G. "Communities Organized for Public Service and Neighborhood Revitalization in San Antonio." *Public Policy and Community: Activism and Governance in Texas*, edited by Robert Wilson, 36–68. Austin: University of Texas Press, 1997.

Wolff, Nelson. *Mayor: An Insider's View of San Antonio's Politics, 1981–1995*. San Antonio, TX: San Antonio Express News, 1997.

SAN DIEGO, CA 1989–2011

SAN DIEGO, A CITY THAT RANKED SIXTH IN POPULATION IN THE UNITED STATES, had slipped to number eight by 2009. As the twenty-first century began, city politics suffered as pension fund irregularities were uncovered, the city lost its bond rating, and, in 2005, Mayor Dick Murphy was forced to resign. Dubbed "Enron by the Sea" by *USA Today* in October 2004, San Diego had finally gained national recognition, but not as city leaders had hoped. When Mayor Jerry Sanders took office, the worldwide recession of 2008–2010 slowed recovery. Nevertheless, San Diego in 2011, still blessed with a highly desirable climate and location, looked to a brighter future.

As the decade of the 1990s dawned, San Diego had emerged as a city with a new skyline—more cosmopolitan and more complex—with planners facing challenges that involved water, energy, pollution, traffic congestion, border issues, and the onset of a slight recession. Having revitalized the downtown area with theaters and high-rise condominiums, city leaders recognized the need for planning and proposed an expanded convention center, a new ballpark, and a well-developed harbor front.

By March 1992, a five-year drought had come to an end, but future water problems still loomed. San Diego, a city that relies on deliveries from the Colorado River and the State Water Project to some 97 percent of its population, has placed a heavy emphasis on conservation, reclamation, storage, and desalination. Despite an economic downturn in 1993, the telecommunications and biotech industries surged ahead. Housing trends showed increasing activity in the county, and downtown businesses, along with new residences, were once again in the city's center.

Unemployment resulting from the 2008–2010 recession has been felt across all segments of the population, but San Diegans and Mayor Jerry Sanders are ever optimistic about the city's recovery.

QUICK FACTS

SAN DIEGO, CA 1989–2011

MAYORS

Susan Golding   (1992–2000)
Richard M. Murphy   (2000–2005)
Jerry Sanders   (2005–)

MAJOR INDUSTRIES AND EMPLOYERS

Federal, including military, and state government
University of California, San Diego
City and County of San Diego
Hospitals and health care
Qualcomm

MAJOR NEWSPAPERS

San Diego Daily Transcript
San Diego Union-Tribune
San Diego Business Journal
Diario San Diego

MAJOR EVENTS

1990s: Major biotechnology and biomedical companies are founded in San Diego, boosting the economy during the decade of the 1990s.
1992: San Diego hosts the internationally televised America's Cup race, giving the city greater visibility.
1996: The Republican National Convention is held in San Diego.
September 11, 2001: San Diego, headquarters for the Eleventh Naval District, is put on alert following the terrorist attacks in New York and Washington, D.C.
2003: Wildfires in east San Diego burn 2,232 homes and kill fifteen people.
2004: The San Diego Padres, World Series contenders in 1998, move downtown to new state-of-the-art stadium, Petco Park.
2007: Wildfires burn 1,500 homes and cause $1 billion in damages.
2010: Storms bring major flooding to San Diego in December, causing severe damage but signaling a temporary end to drought conditions.

GOVERNMENT AND POLITICS

Republican Susan Golding served two terms as San Diego's mayor from 1992 to 2000. Previously chairing San Diego County's Board of Supervisors, she had also served in state government and as a San Diego city council member. Under her mayoral leadership the percentage of violent crime overall decreased for the first time in a decade, and Golding launched the Safe School Initiative. She led the city council to cut the license tax for small businesses, cut water and sewer capacity fees, and put in place a one-stop city, county, and state permitting center. Golding encouraged international commerce, established the San Diego World Trade Center, and opened the San Diego Business Development Office-Asia in Hong Kong.

Mayor Golding and city promoters lobbied successfully to host a national political convention. In 1996 San Diego's reputation as fiscally conservative and socially moderate appealed to Republicans scheduling their national convention. Since San Diego's harborfront convention center held fewer than twenty thousand, alternative viewing sites were planned for the thirty to forty thousand delegates and guests expected, and the August 1996 convention proved to be a success. The event brought an estimated $100 million in tourism income to San Diego.

Critics of Golding's administration, however, complained that the city's minority districts were polluted, lacked necessary police protection, and suffered from unemployment. Taxpayers opposed the $78 million stadium expansion package, which, in 1995, broke down into a $60 million bond guarantee by the city and an $18 million amendment, money later picked up by telecom giant Qualcomm for naming rights at the stadium. The money allowed San Diego to host Super Bowls in 1998 and 2003. Despite some criticism, Golding was reelected by 78 percent of the voters, setting a record for mayoral elections in California.

Former Superior Court Judge Richard M. (Dick) Murphy became the thirty-third mayor of San Diego in December 2000. Many considered him a fresh face in the world of San Diego politics. He had been appointed a Municipal Court judge by Governor George Deukmejian in 1985 and, in 1989, moved to the Superior Court.

Murphy, a San Diego city council member from 1981 to 1985, chaired the Mission Trails Regional Park Task Force and Metropolitan Transit Development Board, leading the effort to build the East Line of the San Diego Trolley that relieved traffic congestion to San Diego State University and East County. As mayor, Murphy set forth a bold agenda for city improvements and the appointment of an ethics commission. His administration, however, became tainted by the federal prosecutors' indictment of three council members for allegedly taking bribes of tens of thousands of dollars to relax the city's "no-touch" regulations regarding strippers. The council members, pleading innocence, continued to serve on the city council. Only one was ultimately convicted.

Despite its reputation as "America's Finest City," San Diego had its share of poor governance through the years. Mayor Murphy's first term began well with open space acquisitions, creation of the San Diego River conservancy, completion of new branch libraries, easing of border traffic, and a profitable Super Bowl held in 2003. Then, however, when federal investigators found a $1.7 billion gap in the city workers' pension fund, the city manager and city auditor quit in disgrace. This financial debacle, which began when the city opted out of social security in 1982, ended Murphy's second term as *Time* magazine in April 2005 listed him as one of the three worst big-city mayors in the country. Although the economic recession accounted for a serious portion of the deficit—some say as much as 70 percent—many felt that better supervision, protection, and funding should have been in place. Murphy resigned on July 15, 2005.

Voters in November 2005 elected Jerry Sanders, former police chief, as the first mayor to head a new strong-mayor type of government. Popular in fundraising circles and effective in supporting victims of the widespread Cedar fire in 2003, Sanders received 54 percent of the vote over Donna Frye, city council member who led the opposition against Murphy. In 2007 Sanders, a San Diego State University alum, reversed his stance against same-sex marriage when he announced that his daughter was gay. Reelected in 2008, Sanders essentially rescued the city's reputation and believed that San Diego's financial woes were nearly over.

Mayor Sanders's accomplishments have ranged from water conservation and environmental concerns to promoting city opportunities for small business contractors. After the city's financial crises of the previous several years, his proposal for a new City Hall was met with skepticism, but other plans, especially a new downtown library in combination with a new charter school, were approved in 2010. A planned extension of the trolley line to the north has been a landmark event in relieving freeway gridlock.

INDUSTRY, COMMERCE, AND LABOR

The decade of the 1990s brought a new wave of biotechnology development into San Diego. In 1978 University of California, San Diego (UCSD) assistant professor Ivor Royston and his research assistant Howard Birndorf had founded Hybritech to explore the use of monoclonal antibodies. Its sale in 1986 to Eli Lilly encouraged other academic scientists to form companies, and scores of biotechs were created by scientists from UCSD, the Salk Institute, the Scripps Research Institute, and other local institutes. By 2003 San Diego could count some five hundred biomedical companies employing about twenty-four thousand people. In 2000 those companies reported a collective $1.75 billion in revenue and had nearly two hundred products in development. By 1992 UCSD's San Diego Supercomputer Center had become an international leader in data management, biosciences, geosciences, grid computing, and visualization. In a different area of computer technology, UCSD graduate Michael Robertson developed music software and founded MP3.com.

Qualcomm, founded by Irwin M. Jacobs and Andrew Viterbi in 1985, introduced in 1995 Code Division Multiple Access (CDMA), a digital wireless technology that quickly became one of the world's fastest-growing wireless technologies. In 1999 the International Telecommunications Union selected CDMA as the industry standard for new "third-generation" (3G) wireless systems. Qualcomm employs nearly ten thousand local residents.

Cable television or Community Antenna Television (CATV) in San Diego reached a new high during the 1990s. By 1991 over seven hundred thousand, or about 70 percent of the population, subscribed to cable, providing upwards of thirty simultaneous broadcasts. At the end of the decade, coaxial cables enabled bidirectional carriage of signals, allowing two cable companies—Cox Communications and Time Warner—to provide Internet access.

San Diego sports can be considered big business. The Major League San Diego Padres, seldom a national contender, command a popular fan base, and 1998 marked the most significant event in Padres history: Passage of a ballot issue approving construction of a new downtown ballpark with an opening date of 2004. The construction of Petco Park, at a total cost of $453.4 million, and the changing nature of a newly named downtown "East Village" area, was not without problems. The San Diego Padres and then-owner John Moores, in conjunction with the Centre City Development Corporation and the Historical Site Preservation board, did their best to save historic buildings and relocate sensitive businesses. New owner Jeff Moorad, former CEO of the Arizona Diamondbacks, purchased the team in February 2009 for a reported $500 million.

San Diego's climate and proximity to the Pacific have made it a major tourist destination and haven for sports enthusiasts. The city hosted the 1992 America's Cup sailing race.   *Source: Carol Highsmith/Library of Congress*

San Diego's National Football League franchise spent nearly a decade on a rough downhill ride from the "Cinderella Chargers" playing in the 1995 Super Bowl to a team with sporadic success. The Chargers' complaints over an "inadequate Qualcomm stadium" have not convinced the general public of the need to move since some $78 million was spent to enclose and improve the stadium for the 1998 Super Bowl.

Tourism, San Diego's third largest moneymaker, also relies on visitors to historic sites. Old Town San Diego State Historic Park is third largest in California in terms of attendance—some seven million per year. For sporting participants, golfing, water sports, and all team sports attract tourists as well as local residents. Yacht racing also ranges from local and national competition to Olympic winners and the America's Cup. Surfing is a favorite sport year round on San Diego's popular beaches.

Lindbergh Field, San Diego's International Airport built on dredged fill from San Diego Bay on the outskirts of downtown in 1928, is one of the smallest but also busiest single-runway commercial service airports in the country. It covers a mere 526 acres and serves nearly twenty million passengers per year, but has often been deemed inadequate. It has been remodeled to expand the terminals and give better access, but plans for relocation have been discussed and researched continuously since the early 1950s, when it became obvious that its potential for growth was limited by geography. In 1999 the Joint Airport Advisory Committee concluded that if no changes were made to air transportation services, growth in the region would be limited.

In 2002 the San Diego Port District gradually began to give responsibility for Lindbergh Field to a new nine-member San Diego County Regional Airport Authority, which took over complete control in July 2005. It became the lead land-use planning agency for the county's sixteen airports (one international, four military, and eleven general aviation) as well as for nearby property. Each time new international airport sites are selected, none are acceptable. Military sites are not a viable option in view of national defense needs. Critics near any proposed site range from environmentalists, land-use planners, and residents. Since Lindbergh Field is remaining in place, the airport authority has been criticized as a problem rather than a solution. Consequently, Mayor Sanders has been looking at high-speed rail service.

The switch from the Port District to the Regional Authority also affected land-use plans for the Naval Training Center redevelopment project, which borders the airport. Primary concerns included protecting the public from excessive noise and aircraft emergencies or crashes. Liberty Station, a successful planned community developed on Naval Training Center grounds, opened in 2008.

Despite the closing of numerous military bases in the United States under the George W. Bush administration, San Diego retained the majority of its facilities so that by 2010 it became home to one of the largest naval fleets and the largest concentration of naval facilities in the world. It houses the supercarriers USS *Nimitz* and USS *Ronald Reagan*, the Bob Wilson Naval Hospital, and the Space and Naval Warfare Systems Center, among other naval and marine bases.

The world-famous San Diego Zoo, a major part of the Balboa Park complex, continues to attract crowds from all parts of the globe. With such popular exhibits as the Chinese giant pandas, who came to the zoo in 1996, and its unparalleled vegetation and design, the zoo's two hundred acres provide an important tourist destination. Nevertheless, attempts to expand the zoo have met with public and private disapproval.

The still-unsolved parking problem continues to plague park planners and those visiting the Balboa Park complex of museums during peak times. Ideas proposed over the years include a multilevel parking structure, shuttles to the park from other areas, or a trolley line from downtown. Introduced in 2003, a free tram service from the lot across Park Boulevard handles the problem sufficiently on most days. Other problems affecting Balboa Park are building repairs, removing automobiles from the main Plaza de Panama, cutbacks in school funding for students visiting the park, and lack of public and private support resulting from the 2008–2010 economic downturn.

RACE, ETHNICITY, AND IMMIGRATION

Native Americans, who occupy nine reservations in the county and also live throughout the city, have received a boost in their economy. Indian gaming, although not within the city, attracts a number of San Diego residents to its casinos. The Valley Branch contains the Pala, Pauma, Rincon, and Valley View Casinos and the La Jolla slot arcade. The Southern Branch includes Barona, Viejas, Sycuan, and Golden Acorn with the Paradise casino in Imperial County. The reservations have expanded into the hotel business, golf resorts, and RV parks. They have purchased

Singing Hills Golf Course in East County as well as the U.S. Grant Hotel in downtown San Diego. Their management of these enterprises has brought them sufficient income for increased health care, housing, education, and retirement pensions. The Barona Band has completed a Cultural Center and Museum with a collection of over two thousand ancient items dating as far back as ten thousand years.

According to the 2000 U.S. Census, the City of San Diego had 1,223,400 residents, making it the second largest city in California and the seventh largest in the United States. According to the 2010 U.S. Census, the population was listed at 1,307,407 and San Diego, still second in California, had slipped to eighth place in the nation.

From 2000 to 2010 the diverse racial makeup of the city changed from 60.18 percent non-Hispanic white to 45 percent; from 25.4 percent Hispanic or Latino/a of any race to 29 percent; from 7.7 percent African American to 6.5 percent; from 0.6 percent Native American to 0.3 percent; and from 13.7 percent Asian and 0.5 percent Pacific Islander to 15.6 percent Asian alone and 0.4 Pacific Islander. In 2000 12.4 percent were from other races and 4.4 percent from two or more races; in 2010 only 0.25 percent were classified as "some other race" and 3.25 percent as "two or more." In 2010 it was estimated that Latinos were the largest group in all ages under 18. In 2010 the percentage of Hispanic or Latino/a residents was just under twice the national average (16 percent) and of Asians, four times the national average (4.8 percent).

Racial tensions affecting the Hispanic or Latino/a population in San Diego increased with the passage of California Proposition 187 in 1994, prohibiting undocumented migrants from using health care, public education, and social services. Although the law was declared largely unconstitutional in 1999, many hard feelings were left. Tensions again became prevalent with the building of the federal border fence under the Bush administration and passage by Arizona of a bill aimed at identifying, prosecuting, and deporting illegal immigrants despite having families born in the United States. As numbers of immigrants increase and heavy unemployment continues, no solution seems workable. On the other hand, gains have been made by longtime resident black and Hispanic business owners.

See also *San Diego, CA 1952–1989*

IRIS ENGSTRAND

BIBLIOGRAPHY

Davis, Mike, Kelly Mayhew, and Jim Miller. *Under the Perfect Sun: The San Diego Tourists Never See.* New York, NY: New Press, 2003.

Engstrand, Iris H.W. *San Diego: California's Cornerstone.* San Diego, CA: Sunbelt, 2005.

Erie, Steven P., Vladimir Kogan, and Scott A. MacKenzie. *Paradise Plundered: Fiscal Crisis and Governance Failures in San Diego.* Palo Alto, CA: Stanford University Press, 2011.

Hendrickson, Nancy. *San Diego Then and Now.* San Diego, CA: Thunder Bay Press, 2004.

Naverson, Andrea. *San Diego Coming of Age: A Modern History.* Carlsbad, CA: Heritage Media, 2003.

Pryde, Philip, ed. *San Diego: An Introduction to the Region.* San Diego, CA: Sunbelt, 2004.

Showley, Roger. *Perfecting Paradise.* Carlsbad, CA: Heritage Media, 1999.

DALLAS, TX 1989–2011

THE PAST TWO DECADES SAW BOTH DALLAS'S CITY HALL AND SCHOOL BOARD PARA-LYZED by corruption and racial conflict, as the city underwent a dramatic demographic transformation due to a massive influx of Mexican and Mexican American immigrants. Latinos dramatically increased from 17 percent of the total population in 1990 to just shy of 40 percent by 2009, according to recent estimates. Democrats, long a distant second to Republicans in local politics, swept all countywide offices in 2006, largely as a result of greatly increased minority voting power. The greater Dallas area remained a regional center of high-tech and communications technology, as well as a retail center, though corporate headquarters continued to migrate to outlying suburbs in a continuation of trends begun in the 1970s. Overall, the population in Dallas increased from just over 1 million in 1990 to 1.3 million by 2009.

GOVERNMENT AND POLITICS

The implementation of a 14-1 city council election plan deeply shaped municipal politics in the past twenty years. Under this system, only the mayor was elected at-large, while the other council members were elected from smaller districts. Previously, Dallas followed a national trend after the 1965 federal Voting Rights Act, in which white-run city governments minimized the impact of an increased number of minority voters by relying on at-large elections. Then, in 1975, Dallas African American community activists Al Lipscomb, Marvin Crenshaw, and sixteen others filed a federal lawsuit charging that Dallas City Council elections systematically disempowered minority voters. The federal courts ordered Dallas to implement an 8-3 system in which only three council members would be elected at-large. Even with this change, no more than three African Americans and Hispanics had been elected at any one time until 1988.

In 1990 federal judge Jerry Buchmeyer ruled that the 8-3 plan was unconstitutional. In 1991 Buchmeyer ordered that city elections be held under a 14-1 plan. Dallas's City Council became more diverse, but racial divisions played a major role in white flight to the suburbs, a drain of not just people but capital.

Many overoptimistically hoped that Dallas had moved past racial divisiveness when in 1995 the city elected its first-ever African American mayor, Ron Kirk. Kirk was a Democrat who enjoyed support from conservative Republicans and was widely credited with bridging the racial divides that had plagued Dallas from the early 1980s to the mid-1990s. When the National Basketball Association's Dallas Mavericks and the National Hockey League's Dallas Stars both indicated they would move to the suburbs unless the city built a new sports arena, Kirk played a lead role in winning voter approval for construction of the $20 million American Airlines Center. Kirk also won from voters a go-ahead for the Trinity River Development project, which called for $246 million to provide flood protection and build roads, parks, and a nature preserve in economically depressed South Dallas. Critics charged that Kirk's big-ticket projects amounted to corporate welfare for the wealthiest developers.

QUICK FACTS

DALLAS, TX **1989–2011**

MAYORS

Annette Strauss	(1987–1991)
Steve Bartlett	(1991–1995)
Ron Kirk	(1995–2001)
Mary Poss	(2001)
Laura Miller	(2002–2007)
Tom Leppert	(2007–2011)
Dwaine Caraway	(2011)
Mike Rawlings	(2011–)

MAJOR INDUSTRIES AND EMPLOYERS

Health care
Transportation
Retail
High tech
Finance

MAJOR NEWSPAPERS

Dallas Morning News
Dallas Observer

MAJOR EVENTS

1967–1991: A series of lawsuits challenging Dallas's at-large voting system in the city council elections leads to a 14-1 plan in which each city council member is elected from a specific district and the mayor alone is elected at-large.

1997–2006: The Dallas school board suffers from a series of scandals, including one involving Yvonne Gonzalez, the district's superintendent, who, after serving from January to September 1997, goes to jail for misappropriation of funds.

2001: American Airlines Center opens, hosting the Dallas Mavericks basketball and the Dallas Stars hockey franchises. The center anchors Victory Park, a mixed-use development including hotels, apartments, and meeting centers.

2003: U.S. District Judge Barefoot Sanders ends thirty-two years of federal court oversight of Dallas school desegregation.

2005: In the space of six months, voters reject two referenda to expand the power of the city's mayor.

A wave of scandals between 1997 and 2000 rocked City Hall. In 1997 councilmember Paul Fielding was forced to resign before he pleaded guilty to two felony counts of bribery and extortion. The sixteen-year City Hall career of Al Lipscomb, the winner of the 14-1 lawsuit, crumbled in the face of accusations that he had used his office to enrich himself. A federal jury convicted Lipscomb in 2000 of sixty-five counts of bribery and conspiracy for accepting cash from a taxi company in return for friendly votes. His conviction was later overturned. Lipscomb died June 18, 2011.

Corruption and protests against Kirk's spending priorities fueled the candidacy of longtime political outsider Laura Miller, who had been a controversial columnist for the *Dallas Times Herald* and the *Dallas Observer*. Miller defeated the heavily favored Tom Dunning, who had the backing of the city's business establishment. She vaulted to the office of mayor during a special election to fill Kirk's unfinished term in 2002. She promised to reorient the city government's focus away from projects benefiting Dallas's business elites and toward more day-to-day concerns such as fixing potholes and improving libraries. Under Miller, who served as mayor from 2002 to 2007, Dallas saw its crime rate drop for the first time in a decade.

Miller, however, had a bad relationship with Dallas's African American community. As mayor, she locked horns with Terrell Bolton, who served as the city's first-ever African American police chief from 1999 to 2003. Many African Americans, used to dealing with a white-led police force that frequently used excessive and deadly force against suspects of color, had greeted his appointment with excitement. But Miller accused Bolton of incompetence and orchestrated his firing.

African American leaders played a key role in 2005 in twice defeating referenda that would have given Miller added power to bypass the city council while implementing anticrime and economic development policies. African Americans saw the proposal as a power grab by Miller inspired by white backlash against the growing number of African Americans and Mexican Americans heading city departments. Turnout for the referenda was exceptionally high in largely black South Dallas, with high-profile African American ministers and former Mayor Kirk leading the opposition.

Miller decided to not run for reelection in 2007. She left a mixed legacy. Her downtown revitalization program fizzled, and the Trinity River redevelopment project she supported had, by the end of her term, run badly over budget. Tom Leppert, a wealthy businessman, succeeded her as mayor, a triumph that was seen as a return to power by Dallas's traditional leadership and a signal by voters that the Dallas public had tired of the controversies of the Miller years. Unfortunately for such voters, the city became embroiled in the third major city hall scandal in a decade. In 2004 FBI agents began investigating Mayor Pro Tem Don Hill and D'Angelo Lee, a city planning commissioner, for demanding cash from vendors doing business with the city and insisting that friends get highly paid jobs with such firms. Agents also investigated Hill's wife, Sheila Farmington Hill, for laundering the illegal payments through her bogus consulting business. The Hills and Lee were convicted in 2009.

Leppert, a Republican, stepped down in 2011 and entered the U.S. Senate race to replace Kay Bailey Hutchison. Interim Mayor Dwaine Caraway, who became the city's second African American chief executive, replaced him. Controversy quickly enveloped Caraway following a January 2011 domestic disturbance incident (while he was still mayor pro tem) involving his wife, Texas State Representative Barbara Caraway. In June 2011, Mike Rawlings, at one time the chief executive officer of Pizza Hut, handily defeated former Dallas police chief David Kunkle in an election to complete Leppert's term. Rawlings, with wide support in the business community, ran on a traditional platform of encouraging downtown economic growth. He hugely outspent Kunkle, who called for a Laura Miller–type program of improving neighborhoods in lieu of expensive development projects. Kunkle was hurt not only by a disadvantage in campaign funds, but also by the opposition to his campaign by Dallas police and firefighter associations.

INDUSTRY, COMMERCE, AND LABOR

The 1990s marked a time of media consolidation. As happened in other large American cities, Dallas was left with only one daily newspaper. On December 8, 1991, Belo Corporation, the owner of the *Dallas Morning News*, bought the *Dallas Times-Herald* for $55 million and shut down the *Herald* the next day. Based in Dallas, Belo Corporation meanwhile expanded its holdings across the nation, including twenty television stations and several other newspapers.

Civic leaders sought to enliven the municipal core as a sales point to corporate leaders considering a move to the city. A brutal process of gentrification—in which neighborhoods occupied by poor whites, African Americans, Mexican Americans, and Mexican immigrants were demolished to make way for loft apartments, townhouses, and bars and restaurants targeted at a white middle-class clientele—unfolded in Dallas in the late 1980s and early 1990s. During that time, developers replaced decaying homes and empty lots in and near the city center with chain restaurants, antiques stores, private clubs, and condominiums. The city spent $20 million for improvements, such as street pavement and the upgrading of water and sewer lines.

African Americans and Mexican Americans moved in larger numbers to South and West Dallas. Meanwhile, the number of downtown residents, mainly upper-middle-class whites, climbed to thirteen thousand. They moved to new expensive apartments and condos. In the last decade of the twentieth century and first decade of the twenty-first, the Dallas-Fort Worth metropolitan area, the home base of billionaire and occasional politician H. Ross Perot and his EDS empire, acquired a reputation as the "Silicon Prairie," a low-tax center for high-tech and telecom firms like Texas Instruments, Perot Systems, and MetroPCS Communications.

To attract the well-to-do to the metropolitan core, the city invested heavily in the arts. Crews completed construction of the $85 million Morton H. Meyerson Symphony Center in 1989. A $250 million performance hall for the Dallas Opera soon joined The "Mort," as it was locally known, in the city's emerging arts district. The Nasher Foundation, with its collection of modern art, commissioned the building of the Nasher Sculpture Garden in 2003. The Latino Cultural Center, designed by highly regarded Mexican architect Ricardo Legorreta and containing major works of art by Texas artist Celia Alvarez Muñoz and muralist Judy Baca, opened in 2003.

Dallas also enhanced its reputation as a sports mecca. In 1989 Arkansas oilman Jerry Jones bought a losing Dallas Cowboys football franchise from Dallas oilman Bum Bright. Jones's entry provoked more boos than cheers. As one of his first acts, he fired legendary head coach Tom Landry, who had led the team for its first twenty-nine years, and replaced him with a college friend, college championship coach Jimmy Johnson. The Cowboys' rabid fans quickly reconciled themselves to the new regime, however, as a series of smart drafts built a dynasty that won Super Bowls in 1993, 1994, and 1996. Mayor Miller, however, refused to commit $350 million to expand and modernize the Cotton Bowl at Dallas's Fair Park, a decision that prompted Jones to move the Irving-based team to Arlington instead of back to Dallas (the team's original home from 1960 to 1971). In 1993 the city successfully lured away the Minnesota North Stars of the National Hockey League. They were rechristened the Dallas Stars and won the Stanley Cup in 1999.

One of Mayor Kirk's biggest political defeats, however, came shortly after he left office in 2001. The following year Dallas was rejected as the host city for the 2012 Summer Olympics, a cause for which Kirk heavily campaigned. A more deeply felt blow had come just six months earlier when Dallas lost an effort to become the new corporate headquarters for Seattle-based

Boeing Corporation. Boeing opted to move to Chicago. This decision was widely taken as a repudiation of Dallas as a second-rate, dull prairie town compared to the vibrant, cosmopolitan midwestern metropolis.

By 2011 a national recession accompanied by high unemployment created a fiscal crisis for City Hall and the Dallas school board. In September 2010 the city raised the property tax rate to nearly the maximum allowed under Texas law in order to close a deficit that had reached $200 million earlier that year. By June 2011, the city faced an estimated $52 million budget deficit for the coming fiscal year. City Manager Mary Suhm said that hundreds of city workers would be laid off. Library closings were also considered. In May 2011 tax revenue woes had forced the Dallas school board to cut the district budget by $90 million and lay off two hundred employees.

RACE, ETHNICITY, AND IMMIGRATION

By the 1990s the city had divided into three major and often mutually hostile racial camps. Whites represented just below 50 percent of the city's population, African Americans 28 percent, and Latinos 21 percent. Demographers predicted that Latinos would overtake African Americans as the second largest group in the city sometime in the first three decades of the twenty-first century. In the past twenty years, conflict between Latinos and African Americans often overshadowed the divisions between whites and the other two major racial groups.

This conflict intensified over the policies of the Dallas school board that now oversaw a minority-majority district. By 1996 members of the small New Black Panther Party, formed in Dallas in 1990 by radio personality Aaron Michaels, began attending school board meetings and campaigning hard to increase African American representation on the board. In May of that year, when the party threatened to attend a board meeting bearing firearms, the school district cancelled a meeting, winning the group national media attention.

Relations between African Americans and Mexican Americans bottomed out with Yvonne Gonzalez's appointment as Dallas Independent School District superintendent in 1997. Gonzalez, later imprisoned for spending district money to buy furniture for her private use and accused of sexually harassing an African American employee, manipulated the board's racial politics. She had been selected through an iron alliance between whites and Mexican Americans formed to prevent the hiring of an African American superintendent, and she had admitted publicly that she would divert attention and resources from African American students to Latino children. During Gonzalez's brief tenure, one school board member, Dan Peavy, had to resign after the release to the media of a taped conversation in which he referred to African Americans with racial slurs.

The Gonzalez interregnum launched a period of great instability in Dallas school politics, often punctuated with intense racial tension. Four permanent and three interim superintendents went through the school district leadership's revolving door from 1995 to 2005. In 2006 school district officials were investigated for using school district credit cards for private purchases, the type of charge that led to Gonzalez's ouster. In September 2008 the Dallas school district announced that it had overspent the previous year's budget by $64 million and scrambled to balance the budget with a minimum of teacher layoffs.

In a 2007 survey by *the Dallas Morning News,* 70 percent of residents rated the city's race relations as only "fair" or "poor." Just 3 percent told interviewers that the city's racial climate was "excellent." Marcy Barnes, a resident of Dallas's Oak Cliff neighborhood, expressed the frustration of many Dallasites concerning racial politics in recent years. "It seems everyone is out for themselves instead of out for the whole," she told the newspaper.

By the end of the first decade of the twenty-first century, another dimension had been added to the city's contentious race relations. Between three hundred fifty thousand and five hundred thousand people participated in a pro-immigrant rally in downtown Dallas on April 13, 2006, the largest outdoor demonstration in the city's history. The demonstration represented the increasing political power of the Latino community. Regardless, in November 2006 the city council of the Dallas suburb of Farmers Branch passed Texas's most severe anti-immigrant ordinance. Ordinance 2903 made English the official language of the city and prohibited landlords from renting to undocumented workers, with daily $500 fines imposed on property owners until they complied. A federal court overruled the Farmers Branch ordinance, and the Farmers Branch City Council passed a rewritten statue in 2008, but Judge Jane J. Boyle invalidated this law in March 2010.

See also *Dallas, TX 1952–1989*

MICHAEL PHILLIPS

BIBLIOGRAPHY

Graff, Harvey J. *The Dallas Myth: The Making and Unmaking of an American City.* Minneapolis: University of Minnesota Press, 2008.

Hanson, Royce. *Civic Culture and Urban Change: Governing Dallas.* Detroit, MI: Wayne State University Press, 2003.

Morgan, Ruth P. *Governance by Decree: The Impact of the Voting Rights Act in Dallas.* Lawrence: University Press of Kansas, 2004.

Payne, Darwin. *Big D: Triumphs and Troubles of an American Supercity in the 20th Century.* Dallas, TX: Three Forks Press, 2000.

Phillips, Michael. *White Metropolis: Race, Ethnicity and Religion in Dallas, 1841–2001.* Austin: University of Texas Press, 2006.

SAN JOSE, CA 1989–2011

WITH A POPULATION OF 945,942 IN 2010, San Jose is the newest city to have become one of the ten largest in the country. It is one of the oldest cities in California, having been founded by Spanish colonists in 1777. It was the first incorporated city in the state, and it briefly served as the first state capital upon California's introduction into the Union in 1850.

QUICK FACTS

SAN JOSE, CA 1989–2011

MAYORS

Tom McEnery   (1983–1991)
Susan Hammer   (1991–1998)
Ron Gonzales   (1999–2006)
Chuck Reed   (2007–)

MAJOR INDUSTRIES AND EMPLOYERS

Local government
Technology firms
Health care

MAJOR NEWSPAPER

San Jose Mercury News

MAJOR EVENTS

1989: The San Jose McEnery Convention Center opens, inaugurating a new era of downtown development.

1994: Cisco Systems moves from Menlo Park to San Jose and quickly becomes the city's largest private employer.

1998: The Greenline urban growth boundary, a joint city-county program, is approved, which limits suburban-style sprawl in the city and preserves rural and other open spaces.

2000: The dot-com crash leads to high unemployment in San Jose, with the rate quintupling between the years 2000 and 2003.

2008: Home price values drop by nearly a quarter in San Jose during a nationwide real estate crash.

Nestled in a sheltered valley between the Santa Cruz Mountains to the west and the Diablo Range to the east, with several small Pacific tributaries running through it, San Jose offered abundant water and fertile soil for agriculture. Farmers flocked to the growing town and surrounding areas of Santa Clara County, located southeast of San Francisco. By the end of World War II, San Jose had evolved from an agricultural center to a canning and food-processing center. At the same time, however, the growth of Stanford University's Industrial Park in Palo Alto, and the location there of several incipient high-tech giants such as Hewlett Packard and IBM, would ultimately be more important to the economic development of San Jose, which in the 1980s claimed the title of "Capital of Silicon Valley" and is today the home of such well-known high-tech companies as Cisco Systems, eBay, Novellus, and Hitachi. The dominance of the high-tech industry in San Jose has created a city that is at once very wealthy and progressive, with a policy focus on transit-oriented, downtown development, and reducing sprawl through a growth boundary. But the city also has significant problems incorporating lower-income groups, especially those who speak English as a second language.

GOVERNMENT AND POLITICS

Like many cities of the Southwest, San Jose holds nonpartisan elections, and it has a council-manager government, though one in which the mayor is also a significant player. The city council consists of ten members elected from separate districts. The mayor is officially an eleventh member of council (though elected at-large) who, like the other members, has a single vote and is limited to serving two successive four-year terms. San Jose mayors have no veto power, though they do get to appoint the city manager (the city's chief administrative officer) with the approval of the council. Unlike the mayor and council members, the city manager may serve indefinitely.

Though clearly a weak-mayor system in which the city manager can thus be a powerful force, the San Jose mayoralty has actually become a more powerful position over the past several decades, especially since the adoption of, and subsequent changes to, the 1965 charter. Before 1965 all council members were elected at-large, and the mayor was selected from among the council members without a popular election. Indeed, in the period after World War II, a notably strong city manager, Anthony "Dutch" Hamann, who served from 1950 to 1969, was generally credited with setting the groundwork for the city's expansion, due to his policy of aggressively annexing outlying land, thus expanding the size of San Jose from 17 square miles in 1950 to 136 square miles by 1970. The city today covers 174 square miles. Nearly one thousand acres of Hamann-acquired land have recently been added to the city's "green belt" park system, rather than remain open for development.

Though Hamann's expansionist policies were critical to San Jose's growth, he is also often criticized for encouraging suburban-style sprawl, to the detriment of the downtown. The 1965 city charter put the mayor in a better position to control policymaking, and the first two mayors to serve after Hamann's retirement, Norman Mineta (later a member of the U.S. House of Representatives and a two-time cabinet secretary) and Janet Gray Hayes, sought to reverse the Hamann-era growth trajectory. Mineta, in conjunction with Santa Clara officials, established a land-use plan designed to curtail outlying growth (especially in the hills around the city and in the Coyote and South Almaden Valleys), and Hayes focused on a large downtown revitalization initiative.

Despite the importance of both Mineta and Hayes, the San Jose politician given the most credit for transforming the city besides Hamann is Tom McEnery, who served as mayor from 1983 to 1991, presiding over the city's initial transformation into a high-tech hub (and coining the "Capital of Silicon Valley" moniker). McEnery built a coalition that joined together pro-growth business interests with neighborhood and minority activists, labor, and Democrats. He focused on transit-oriented development; limiting sprawl; and downtown-oriented public works projects (many of which were helped along by then-Representative Mineta) such as the San Jose light rail (established in 1988), a downtown indoor sports stadium (approved in 1988 and opened in 1993, it is now known as the HP Pavilion), the San Jose Convention Center (opened in 1989), and in 1990 a major expansion of the San Jose municipal airport. McEnery also expanded the power of the mayor's office, including increasing the number of full-time, salaried staff. He used a financial scandal in 1984, when the city lost $60 million on bad investments, to increase the authority of the mayor over the city manager, including greater budgetary powers and the establishment of an executive office of public information.

The 1990 mayoral election showed the influence of McEnery, as all three candidates had close ties to the former mayor, and all three supported McEnery-style downtown development. The race was the most competitive in the postwar history of the city, with the two final runoff candidates (none of the initial candidates received a majority of the vote, and San Jose has majority electoral rules) each spending close to $1 million on their campaigns. Susan Hammer, a former council member, won by a slim margin of approximately one thousand votes. As mayor, Hammer was a consensus builder, even as she pursued downtown development policies and attempted to slow the pace of sprawl. She won reelection in 1994 with more than 60 percent of the popular vote. Her mayoralty was defined in part by her efforts at community development (especially her success in reducing gang-related violence) and economic development (perhaps most notably the role she played in luring to the city such companies as Sony, Adobe, and Cisco Systems). But she also worked to prevent sprawl, most notably through her 1998 approval of a growth boundary around the city—the Greenline Initiative—which fortified Mineta's earlier land-use plan by severely restricting development in outlying parts of the city in order to preserve rural and undeveloped land. The Greenline Initiative had initially been passed by the city council in 1996, though its final approval and implementation was stalled by a lawsuit initiated by affected landowners.

Two of Hammer's initiatives, the Neighborhood Development Center, which offered city resources to neighborhood activists or would-be activists, and Project Diversity, which sought to fill more city commissions and boards with minorities, represented a break with much of the previous politics of City Hall. But it also represented a recognition of the growing Latino presence in the city, reflected as well in the 1998 election of Ron Gonzales, a former Hewlett-Packard executive and the city's first Latino mayor since California became a state.

One of Gonzales's chief initiatives was to mitigate congestion through an extension of the Bay Area Rapid Transit (BART) system to San Jose, for which the mayor was able to announce the support of Governor Gray Davis and U.S. Senator Diane Feinstein in his second state-of-the-city address, early in 2000. Yet the BART extension plan moved slowly throughout Gonzales's two terms in office. In 2000 it cleared a major hurdle, as a Santa Clara County referendum on a thirty-year, half-cent sales tax to fund the extension was approved by more than the required two-thirds of voters. Yet the bursting of the dot-com bubble in early 2000 reduced the expected revenue from the new sales tax, which in any case did not go into effect until 2006. In 2008 Santa Clara voters once again overwhelmingly approved a new one-eighth-cent sales tax increase for the extension, intended to cover the increased operating costs to BART.

Gonzales's tenure will likely always be associated with a string of scandals that nearly unseated him in 2002, the most damaging of which involved a behind-the-scenes contract negotiation with Norcal Waste Systems, San Jose's garbage hauling company. Seeking to either reward or curry further favor with the local Teamsters who had supported his campaign, Gonzales secretly agreed to boost Norcal's contract by over $10 million in exchange for increased employee wages. He declined calls for his resignation. Corruption charges after he left office were dropped since arguments for any direct, personal benefits to Gonzales by the arrangement were found lacking. One casualty of the garbage scandal was Cindy Chavez, Gonzales's vice mayor and intended successor, who lost by a wide margin to councilman and distinguished Gonzales critic Chuck Reed.

Reed entered office with a set of thirty-four "Reed Reforms" relating to ethics and transparency, almost all of which were instituted within two years. Dealing with significant budget shortfalls—similar to cities and states around the country—Reed has proposed efficiency measures, cutbacks in development funds, and city fee hikes. And the BART extension continues to move slowly forward, with the most recent negotiations focusing on whether the new train line will run through San Jose underground, through a tunnel, or above ground on a sixty-foot-high aerial track.

INDUSTRY, COMMERCE, AND LABOR

San Jose is a wealthy city, as indicated by its residents' exceptionally high salaries and the high values of their homes. The median household income in the city in 1999 was approximately $70,000, nearly 50 percent more than the state median income of $47,493. The city's homeownership rate of 62 percent in 2000 was also higher than the statewide rate of 57 percent, and the median value of those homes in San Jose ($394,000) was 86 percent higher than the median value of owner-occupied homes statewide. Moreover, since the crash of the housing market in 2008, San Jose homes have retained their value better than those in many other California cities.

Much of San Jose's wealth is bound up in the high-tech sector, as the list of the city's largest employers amply indicates—a product of the firms that developed around Stanford University, and in the Stanford Industrial Park, after World War II. In 1998 California had more high-tech jobs than any other state and twice as many such jobs as the state with the second greatest amount, Texas. The high-tech jobs are disproportionately concentrated in Santa Clara County, where more than a quarter of all nonfarm workers are employed in high tech. Most other large employers in San Jose are also linked to either the high-tech industry or real estate, including San Jose State University (which advertises itself as "powering Silicon Valley"), CB Richard Ellis, Colliers International, and several consulting companies and law firms.

The dominance of the high-tech sector in San Jose makes the city susceptible to downturns in that industry, such as the dot-com crash during the first few years of the twenty-first century, when the number of jobs in the city dropped by 17 percent, the city unemployment rate went from a low of less than 3 percent in 2000 to over 10 percent in 2003, and the office vacancy rate increased by tenfold, to 30 percent.

Interestingly, the dot-com crash had little effect on housing prices, which actually increased significantly during that same time period. To some extent, the imperturbability of the city's housing market might be explained by the limitations on development created by the growth boundary and other restrictions on new construction that limit the overall supply of housing, thus keeping prices high. Yet at the same time, even during the increase in unemployment during the dot-com crash, those who kept their jobs maintained their relatively high incomes and thus their ability to pay for expensive homes.

More recently, the housing crash of the recession of 2008–2010 initially had a dramatic impact on San Jose, where median home prices had dropped by nearly a quarter by the end of 2008, accompanied by an increase in unemployment that reached a high of over 13 percent by January 2010. Yet housing prices in Sacramento, San Diego, and Riverside declined even more steeply, and housing in San Jose has more recently shown evidence of healthy increases in price, even as unemployment remains high—officially, more than 12 percent throughout all of 2010.

Exceptionally high housing costs make San Jose a relatively inhospitable place for people with lower incomes, and, as noted above, lower-income groups in the city are disproportionately composed of recent immigrants who are not citizens and who do not speak English fluently. The dark side of the Capital of Silicon Valley, then, is an underclass separated not only by income but by language, and the noncitizens in this community also have fewer rights.

RACE, ETHNICITY, AND IMMIGRATION

Since 1990 San Jose has been a majority-minority city—that is, a city in which racial and ethnic minorities compose a majority of the overall population, though non-Latino whites are still the largest group by a plurality. The ethnic and racial composition of the city in 2000 was approximately 48 percent non-Latino white, 30 percent Latino (over 80 percent of whom are of Mexican descent), 27 percent Asian (composed of people primarily of Vietnamese, Asian Indian, Chinese, or Filipino origin), and 4 percent black (these percentages sum to more than 100 due to rounding and 5 percent of the population reporting two or more races). While the Latino population in the city has more than doubled since 1980, it represents a slightly smaller percentage of San Jose's population than statewide. In fact, Asian Americans are the only group overrepresented in San Jose, relative to their proportional representation statewide.

From 1990 to 2000 San Jose's total population increased roughly 14 percent while the foreign-born population increased 59 percent, with foreign-born residents representing 37 percent of the city population (compared to 26 percent of the total state population). Five groups accounted for 76 percent of San Jose's foreign-born population in 2000: Mexicans (99,496 residents), Vietnamese (67,375), Filipinos (35,872), Chinese (29,732), and Indians (17,881).

Extraordinary growth in the past twenty years has made San Jose's Vietnamese population the largest of any American city. Between 1980 and 1990 the Vietnamese population jumped from approximately eight thousand to forty thousand and then doubled to roughly eighty thousand by 2000. Vietnamese now account for nearly 9 percent of San Jose's total population.

The 2007 city council race for the seat that Reed left empty when he became mayor highlighted the increasingly politically active, and influential, Vietnamese community. In this eight-way race, two Vietnamese-born candidates ran but eventually lost out to Kansen Chu, a Taiwanese-born school board member and community leader. Presently, only one member of the ten-seat council, Madison Nguyen, is of Vietnamese descent. Nguyen found herself embroiled in a controversy in late 2007 over the naming of a Vietnamese retail area in East San Jose, which led an opposition group to successfully petition for a recall election in 2009, which Nguyen won, thus retaining her council seat to this day. More recently, Mayor Reed has nominated Nguyen to the position of vice mayor, suggesting that she may be his successor in 2014. The debate over naming a Vietnamese neighborhood in San Jose reveals underlying divisions in the Vietnamese community, in which accusations of radical anti-Communism or Communist sympathizing are often thrown about.

While the Vietnamese population in San Jose is large enough to have a neighborhood named for it, the African American community is small enough that it has not established as visible a presence in the city. The main black organization in San Jose, the African American Community

CITIES IN THE NEOLIBERAL ERA, 1989–2011

Service Agency, has, in conjunction with the Antioch Housing and Economic Development Corporation and the City of San Jose, embarked in an effort to create a Silicon Valley African American Cultural Center, which will be located in San Jose but has not yet come to fruition.

Language is a significant factor in understanding ethnicity, ethnic relations, and economic opportunity in San Jose. As of 2000, 51 percent of the city's population five years of age or older spoke a language other than English (compared to 18 percent for the United States overall). Among children nationally whose primary language is not English, approximately 8 percent report having difficulty speaking English, whereas in San Jose the figure is 27 percent. Sixteen percent of San Jose children aged five to seventeen live in households counted by the U.S. Census as "linguistically isolated," meaning that no one aged 14 or older speaks English "very well." Not unsurprisingly, linguistic barriers have been identified as a major contributing factor to people living in poverty. In San Jose the children of immigrants are roughly twice as likely as other children to live in poverty, yet immigrants who have gained citizenship are only slightly more likely than native-born residents to live in poverty. Twice the number of foreign-born, non-citizen San Jose residents live in poverty, as compared to foreign-born San Jose residents who have become American citizens.

RICHARDSON DILWORTH AND STEVEN LEITNER

BIBLIOGRAPHY

Arbuckle, Clyde. *Clyde Arbuckle's History of San Jose: The Culmination of a Lifetime of Research*. San Jose, CA: Smith McKay, 1985.

Bridges, A. *Morning Glories: Municipal Reform in the Southwest*. Princeton, NJ: Princeton University Press, 1997.

Christensen, Terry. "San Jose Becomes the Capital of Silicon Valley." In *San Jose: A City for All Seasons*, edited by Judith Henderson. Encitas, CA: Heritage Press, 1997.

Matthews, Glenna. "'The Los Angeles of the North': San Jose's Transition from Fruit Capital to High-Tech Metropolis." *Journal of Urban History* 25, no. 4 (1999), 459.

Mullin, Megan, Gillian Peele, and Bruce E. Cain. "City Ceasars? Institutional Structure and Mayor Success in Three California Cities." *Urban Affairs Review* 40, no. 1 (2004), 19–43.

Trounstine, Jessica. *Political Monopolies in American Cities: The Rise and Fall of Bosses and Reformers*. Chicago, IL: University of Chicago Press, 2008.

Trounstine, Philip J., and Terry Christensen. *Movers and Shakers: the Study of Community Power*. New York, NY: St. Martin's Press, 1982.

CHRONOLOGY

| NATIONAL EVENTS | URBAN EVENTS |

1770

July 4 – The Continental Congress adopts the Declaration of Independence, asserting the colonies' freedom from Great Britain.

1776

New England militiamen place Boston under siege and eventually force the British to evacuate.

The Providence General Assembly votes to legally separate from Great Britain.

June – The British launch a failed attack on Charles Town.

June 12 – Salem's town meeting passes resolution calling for independence from Great Britain.

August – November: Lord William Howe inflicts great losses on American forces and secures control of Manhattan. The city remains the British military headquarters for the next seven years.

September 21 – 22: Fire destroys five hundred buildings and a third of New York City's housing.

December – The British occupy Newport.

1776–1810: Boston's population swells from six thousand to well over thirty thousand.

– November the Articles of Confederation are ratified, uniting the thirteen colonies while still maintaining each state's sovereignty.

1777

1777–1779: Smallpox epidemics sweep Gloucester in three waves, each more severe than before.

September 26 – Philadelphia is invaded by British Troops and endures a ten-month siege.

1778

Privateering reaches its zenith with as many as eighteen Gloucester vessels active.

1779

British forces successfully occupy Charleston.

CHRONOLOGY

NATIONAL EVENTS		URBAN EVENTS

1780

March 1 – Pennsylvania begins the process of dismantling slavery through the Gradual Abolition Act.

Voters in Marblehead, ratify a new state constitution, which is the oldest state constitution still in use today.

1781

The Bank of North America, the first commercial bank in the United States, is chartered in Philadelphia.

1782

The British are forced to evacuate from Charleston.

1783

September 3 – The Treaty of Paris is signed, ending the American Revolution.

Gloucester vessels sail to the Grand Banks, where the Treaty of Paris has guaranteed fishing rights to Americans. Overseas trade also builds, reaching a high point in 1790 when trade begins between Gloucester and Surinam.

June – Four hundred men from the Continental Army carry out an antigovernment protest known as the Pennsylvania Mutiny, or Philadelphia Mutiny. Evacuation Day marks America's reoccupation of New York.

1784

Providence passes a law that guarantees the gradual emancipation of slaves.

1786

December 26 – Shays's Rebellion erupts in Massachusetts, where thousands of farmers riot against unfair debt and property laws.

1787

May – The Constitutional Convention convenes in Philadelphia.

A Marblehead town meeting resolves to support the Massachusetts government in its suppression of Shays's Rebellion.

July 13 – The Northwest Ordinance is passed, establishing settlement laws for the area between the Appalachian Mountains, the Great Lakes, and the Mississippi River, and defining how these territories could eventually apply for statehood.

Marblehead elects Elbridge Gerry as one of four Massachusetts delegates to attend the Constitutional Convention in Philadelphia.

The Salem vessel, *Grand Turk*, returns from China.

CHRONOLOGY

NATIONAL EVENTS		URBAN EVENTS
The Constitution is ratified.	**1788**	The Doctor's Riot in April leads to five deaths in New York City. Mobs fearful of grave robbery and autopsies of the dead attack Manhattan doctors and destroy their medical instruments.
		Marblehead delegates to the Massachusetts Constitutional Convention unanimously vote to ratify the new Constitution.
September 24 – the Judiciary Act of 1789 is passed, establishing a system of federal courts.	**1789**	A Marblehead town meeting resolved to send over six hundred pounds of fish to John Adams to celebrate his election as the first Vice President of the United States and for his support of American access to Atlantic fishing waters in the Treaty of Paris.
		March – April: The federal government is organized in New York City as Congress meets in Federal Hall. George Washington becomes president on April 30, but sixteen months later the capital leaves Manhattan forever.
The first Census is taken, determining the population of the United States.	**1790**	South Carolina's state capital moves to Columbia, signaling the end of low-country control over state politics.
July 16 – Congress passes the Residence Act, mandating the removal of the federal government to a permanent seat on the banks of the Potomac River following a ten-year stint in Philadelphia.		The College of Charleston opens.
The emergence of the Federalists and the Republicans signals the beginning of a two-party system in the United States.	**1791**	The Federal District on the Potomac is demarcated to include Georgetown, Maryland, and Alexandria, Virginia. Washington City, future seat of the federal government, is founded between Rock Creek and the eastern branch of the Potomac.
February 25 – The first Bank of the United States is chartered by Congress.		
December 15 – The Bill of Rights is ratified.		
	1792	May 17 – The *New York Evening Post*, founded by Alexander Hamilton, begins publication with William Coleman as editor.

CHRONOLOGY

NATIONAL EVENTS		URBAN EVENTS
	1793	Captain Jonathan Carnes of Salem discovers the pepper of Sumatra, thus beginning a lucrative new trade.
		A yellow fever epidemic rages in the late summer and early fall in Philadelphia, which during nearly half the city flees.
		November 17 – Albany slaves Bet, Dean, and Pomp conspired and burned a stable that damaged two blocks. They confessed they were lured by whites and were publicly hanged.
August 3 – The Treaty of Greenville is signed, signifying an end to Indian resistance to settlement in the Northwest Territory.	**1795**	The Philadelphia and Lancaster Turnpike opens as the first such road in the United States.
October 27 – A settlement with Spain, known as the Pinckney Treaty, establishes the nation's southwest border.		
	1797	The New York State legislature convenes permanently at Albany, though it is not officially declared the state capital until 1971.
	1799	December 21 – The Charleston Water Works is established as the city's first public utility.
		Work begins on the Schuylkill Water Works in the spring to bring water to Philadelphia.
		The Salem East India Marine Society established, the forerunner of today's celebrated Peabody-Essex Museum.
	1800	August – A planned rebellion involving as many as one thousand slaves and led by the slave Gabriel is uncovered and crushed by Richmond and Virginia authorities.

CHRONOLOGY

NATIONAL EVENTS		URBAN EVENTS

1800

The secret retrocession of Louisiana by Spain to France through the Treaty of San Ildefonso signed in October. The Cabildo remains the main municipal government of New Orleans until the fall of 1803.

November – Congress convensed in Washington for the first time.

1802

The Public Guard is established to protect state buildings and aid slave control in Richmond.

Nathaniel Bowditch, of Salem, publishes *The New American Practical Navigator*.

The Sharp Street Methodist Church, the first independent black congregation, is founded in Baltimore.

1803

Thomas Jefferson orchestrates the Louisiana Purchase. The size of the United States doubles with the acquisition of land west of the Mississippi River.

The United States purchases Louisiana territory from France, resulting in both New Orleans and St. Louis (still a very small town) joining the young American republic.

1804

April 22 – Alexander Hamilton denounces Aaron Burr at a dinner party held by John Tayler at 50 State Street, in Albany. Hamilton's remarks become public and lead to the Weehawken, New Jersey, duel where he is killed.

1805

The City of New Orleans is incorporated.

1806

The Cumberland Road Act is passed. Under this act, roads are built from Maryland to the Ohio River, making settlement in the west easier.

The first church built by free blacks in America, the African Meeting House, opens on Joy Street, in Boston.

1807

Aaron Burr, former vice president of the United States, stands trial for treason beginning in March in a federal court in Richmond.

CHRONOLOGY

NATIONAL EVENTS		URBAN EVENTS

1807 — April 21 – Politicians cane and punch each other on State Street in Albany. A riot ensues, and one hundred onlookers watch three Republicans attack Federalist Solomon Van Rensselaer. Five politicians sue each other for assault and battery.

August 17 – Robert Fulton's *North River Steamboat* (*The Clermont*) travels the Hudson River to Albany. Regular passenger service to the capital begins in September and initiates a transportation revolution.

1807–1815: Jefferson's embargo of 1807 and the War of 1812 profoundly cripples both Boston and the state's eastern maritime-based economy, including Salem.

1808 — The U.S. ban the importation of slaves, adversely affecting the economy of Charleston.

1810 — Richmond's boundaries expanded to cover a total area of 2.4 square miles.

Salem Athenaeum, a learned society, is established.

1811 — The Commissioner's Plan creates development grid for New York City.

A fire at the Richmond Theatre kills seventy-two people, including Virginia governor George W. Smith.

August 10 – New York's City Hall, designed by John McComb and Joseph Mangin, opens.

The War of 1812 erupts between the British and the United States. It lasts for two years until the Treaty of Ghent is signed in December 1814.

1812 — Louisiana is admitted to the United States by an Act of Congress, to take effect April 30. New Orleans becomes the first capital of the new state.

1813 — Francis Cabot Lowell and a handful of investors known as the Boston Associates open a cotton textile mill in Waltham, Massachusetts, that serves as the model for future New England industrialization.

CHRONOLOGY

NATIONAL EVENTS		URBAN EVENTS

1814

August 24 – Washington, D.C., is occupied by the British during the War of 1812. The British burn several government buildings, including the White House.

September – Defense against the British invasion in Baltimore at Fort McHenry and the Battle of North Point turn back the invasion.

1815

The Battle of New Orleans occurs in Chalmette, marked by a dazzling victory against the British. Word of the signing of the Treaty of Ghent, which ended the War of 1812 on December 24, 1814, had not yet reached New Orleans.

1817

Richard Allen's Mother Bethel Church in Philadelphia becomes the first African Methodist Episcopal Church in the United States.

1818

The Convention of 1818 is held, establishing the border between the United States and Canada.

1819

The Panic of 1819 marks the first economic crisis and recession in the United States.

February – The Adams-Onis Treaty is signed, transferring control of the eastern part of Florida from Spanish to the United States.

1820

The Missouri Compromise is reached. Missouri is admitted to the union as a slave state, and slavery is made illegal in the northern part of the Louisiana Territory.

1822

The Boston Associates establish Lowell as a factory town.

Boston abandons its town charter and is incorporated into a city.

Denmark Vesey, a free black man, is convicted of plotting a slave insurrection and is hanged in Charleston on July 2.

CHRONOLOGY

NATIONAL EVENTS		URBAN EVENTS

1823

1823–1828: Boston's "Great Mayor," Josiah Quincy, is elected to six consecutive terms, during which he builds Quincy Market, professionalizes the fire and police departments, erects the House of Industry to house displaced debtors, and reforms the sanitation department.

1824

With no presidential candidate winning the electoral majority, the selection of the president is put before the House of Representatives. John Quincy Adams defeats Andrew Jackson and William H. Crawford.

The Medical College of South Carolina is founded in Charleston, the first medical school in the South.

September 28 – General Lafayette arrives in Philadelphia for a grand procession followed by a reception at Independence Hall.

1825

October 26 – The Wedding of the Waters ceremony is held to celebrate the completion and opening of the Erie Canal. The canal extends 363 miles from Albany to Buffalo.

November 4 – The *Seneca Chief* arrives in Manhattan, having completed the first trip though the Erie Canal from Buffalo, thereby linking Lake Erie and the Atlantic Ocean.

1825–1845: Construction of the Miami and Erie Canal and Whitewater Canal in stages connects Cincinnati's water routes through the Ohio River to the Great Lakes and to fertile Indiana, vastly expanding its hinterland and fostering agricultural development.

1826

Philadelphia's Council wins the right to elect any Philadelphia citizen, not just a member of Council, to serve as Mayor.

1827

The Baltimore and Ohio Railroad is chartered as the first railroad in the United States.

1828

Andrew Jackson defeats John Quincy Adams in the presidential election carrying 178 electoral votes to Adams's 83.

Construction begins in Georgetown on the Chesapeake & Ohio Canal, which when completed stretches west to Cumberland, Maryland.

CHRONOLOGY

NATIONAL EVENTS

URBAN EVENTS

1828 — Construction of the Arcade, between Westminster and Weybosset Streets in Providence, is completed. This Greek Revival structure is the first indoor shopping mall in Rhode Island.

The *Lady Carrington*, is the first boat to travel from Providence to Worcester, Massachusetts, via the Blackstone Canal. This canal was first proposed by prominent Providence businessman, John Brown in 1796, but it took until the nineteenth century to gain funding and broad support.

1829 — Race riots and the enforcement of strict Black Codes drive nearly half of Cincinnati's black population to leave the city.

Under the Indian Removal Act, all Native Americans located east of the Mississippi River are required to move to the western part of the country.

1830 — The first passenger steam locomotive in America, the *Best Friend*, begins regular service between Charleston and Hamburg, South Carolina.

August 22 – Southampton County, Va, slave Nat Turner and a group of armed slaves kill Turner's master and his family beginning a rebellion that would kill some 60 people. Turner was executed on November 11 for his involvement.

1831 — The Hudson and Mohawk Railroad launches the *DeWitt Clinton* in Albany marking the introduction of the first passenger rail train engine in New York.

1832 — The Rhode Island General Assembly grants Providence city status, thus making it the first city in Rhode Island.

A cholera epidemic hits Albany, infecting 766 people and killing more than 320.

An epidemic of cholera is brought to Charleston, carried on the *Amelia* from New York.

A cholera epidemic kills approximately five thousand of New Orleans's forty thousand residents.

Andrew Jackson visits New Orleans to celebrate the Battle of New Orleans. A statue is dedicated to him.

NATIONAL EVENTS		URBAN EVENTS
	1832	The New England Anti-Slavery Society and the Boston Female Anti-Slavery Society are founded.
	1834	The Bank of Charleston, the largest financial institution in antebellum South Carolina, opens.
		Jacksonian Democrat Cornelius Van Wyck Lawrence defeats Gulian Verplanck by 174 votes in New York City's first direct mayoral election.
		Philadelphia mayor John Swift leads anti-abolitionist protestors in dumping abolitionist literature in the Delaware River.
	1835	Railroads from Boston open to Providence and Worcester, and soon to the north and northwest.
		The first railroad serving Rhode Island reaches Providence, traveling south from Boston. This helps to solidify the role of Providence as a hub of transportation in southern New England.
		December 16–17: A great fire devastates the East Side of Manhattan, destroying a quarter of the business district (seven hundred buildings) and incinerating the last remnants of Dutch New Amsterdam.
March 2 – Following a revolution in Mexican-held territory, the Republic of Texas is formed. The United States annexed Texas in 1845.	**1836**	New Orleans is divided into three municipalities separating Creoles, Americans, and free people of color or immigrants.
Overspeculation combined with inflation ultimately leads to the Panic of 1837, followed by a large-scale nationwide depression.	**1837**	
	1838	A yellow fever epidemic devastates Charleston.

CHRONOLOGY

NATIONAL EVENTS		URBAN EVENTS

1838 — The Massachusetts legislature establishes a police force for Boston.

1839 — Anti-rent wars commence when tenant farmers organize to riot against Albany's Van Rensselaer heirs, who tried to collect payments on overdue leaseholds. The county sheriff and the militia fail to quell protests. The conflict continues periodically until 1845, when a state law dissolved all manor rights.

John Swift wins a plurality of votes in Philadelphia's first direct mayoral election, but lack of majority sends election to the city councils—where mayors had previously been chosen—and he emerges victorious.

1840 — The drawbridge at Albany's State Street falls into the Hudson River. Many are injured, and twenty people drown.

Thousands of immigrants flee to the United States, settling in cities such as Boston and New York, in an attempt to escape the Great Potato Famine. — **1842** — October 14 – The Croton System begins operation. Designed by Charles King, it provides New York City with clean drinking water from Westchester County, makes indoor plumbing possible, and eliminates most epidemic threats.

1844 — The New York state legislature authorizes the establishment of a police force for New York City.

Samuel F. B. Morse sends the first telegraph message from Baltimore.

The United States adds to its landmass by annexing Texas.

1845–1849: Failure of the potato crop in Ireland leads to mass migration to the United States. — **1845** — Philadelphia radical George Lippard publishes *The Quaker City, or the Monks of Monk Hall*, a thinly veiled attack on the city's upper class and the best-selling American novel until *Uncle Tom's Cabin*.

The Wilmot Proviso states that all lands gained from the Mexican-American War will not have slavery. This measure is introduced in August by Rep. David Wilmot, passed by the House of Representatives, but defeated by the Senate. — **1846** — Vice president George Mifflin Dallas, a former mayor of Philadelphia, is burned in effigy in the city for casting the deciding vote in the U.S. Senate to lower the tariff duties manufacturers and mechanics believe are crucial to the prosperity of local industry.

CHRONOLOGY

NATIONAL EVENTS		URBAN EVENTS
1846–1848: The Mexican-American War is fought in the Southwest. In the Treaty of Guadalupe-Hidalgo, which ends the war, the United States gains the lands of California and New Mexico.	**1846**	Alexandria successfully petitions for retrocession to Virginia of portions of the District of Columbia south of the Potomac, leaving only 69 of the 100 square miles authorized in the Constitution for the federal district.
		August 10 – Congress passes an act founding the Smithsonian Institution in Washington, based on a bequest by a wealthy British inventor, James Smithson. Architect James Renwick's Norman Revival Smithsonian Castle is constructed between 1849 and 1855.
The movement for women's rights gains national attention with the Seneca Falls Convention.	**1848**	Water is brought to Boston from Lake Cochituate near Framingham, about twenty miles to the west.
January Gold is discovered at Sutter's Mill, California.		April – After the thwarting of a mass escape by seventy-six local slaves aboard the schooner *Pearl*, pro-slavery mobs along Pennsylvania Avenue in Washington threaten to lynch the crew and then attack the offices of the abolitionist weekly *National Era*.
	1849	The Louisiana state capital removed from New Orleans to Baton Rouge.
		Albany's State Normal School is established to educate teachers. It is the founding institution of the State University New York system.
		A cholera epidemic in Philadelphia claims 386 lives.
		May 10 – In Astor Place, New York City, a riot spurred by the rival appearances of competing Shakespearean actors, one British and one American, results in twenty-two deaths.

CHRONOLOGY

NATIONAL EVENTS		URBAN EVENTS
The Compromise of 1850 is drafted as a concession to the issue of slavery. Among its provisions it allows for California to enter the Union as a free state; abolishes the slave trade in Washington D.C., and creates a strong Fugitive Slave law.	**1850**	A special census report sponsored by the city of Boston reveals that 47 percent of the population consists of foreign-born people and their children.
	1851	A Christmas Eve fire burns two-thirds of the Library of Congress in Washington, in partial response to which the Army Corps of Engineers begins construction in 1853 of the innovative Washington Aqueduct.
	1852	The Commonwealth of Massachusetts appoints a three-man commission to plan and fill the Back Bay former tidal marsh in Boston.
		In New Orleans, three municipalities are consolidated into one city, and the city of Lafayette is annexed.
		Work begins on the New Orleans, Opelousas and Great Western Railroad and the New Orleans, Jackson and Great Northern Railroad.
The United States acquires land from Mexico with the Gadsden Purchase. Expansion of the American Southwest is now complete.	1853	The Baltimore & Ohio Railroad reaches the Ohio River.
		A yellow fever outbreak kills eighteen thousand people in New Orleans.
		Charter revision in Buffalo establishes an elected mayor, and a president of the Common Council, and expanded the size of the city to forty square miles.
		July 14 – America's first World's Fair begins in New York City as the Crystal Palace, topped by a 123-foot dome, opens at Fortieth Street and Sixth Avenue.
The Kansas-Nebraska Act is passed. It repeals the Compromise of 1820, stating	1854	The Pennsylvania legislature approves of the consolidation of Philadelphia city and county,

CHRONOLOGY

NATIONAL EVENTS		URBAN EVENTS
that territories should decide for themselves whether or not to allow slavery.	**1854**	thus expanding the size of the city from approximately 2 to 130 square miles.
		Baltimore elects a Know-Nothing (American Party) government.
		A cholera epidemic hits Buffalo.
		1854–1855: San Francisco faces a general depression, resulting in a major financial collapse and the closure of several banks.
	1855	Three days of rioting hit Cincinnati following Know-Nothing attacks on immigrants, ending the party's ascendancy in the city.
	1856	The Second Committee of Vigilance seizes San Francisco and hangs four criminals.
		The California state legislature passes Consolidation Act creating a new county and providing San Francisco with a co-terminous city and county government.
A short economic depression causes many of the factory and railway workers living in the East and Midwest to lose their jobs.	**1857**	In Philadelphia, a gathering of the unemployed in Independence Square to demand employment on public work projects marks the largest public meeting ever held in the city to date.
March 6 – In *Dred Scott v. Sandford* the U.S. Supreme Court asserts that slaves are not citizens protected by the Constitution.		
	1858	The state of Maryland takes control of Baltimore's police force.
		A Know-Nothing Riot in New Orleans results in the temporary takeover of the city by a vigilante committee.
Silver is discovered in Comstock Lode, Nevada.	**1859**	
December 20 – South Carolina secedes from the Union.	**1860**	The first-ever Japanese mission to the West visits Philadelphia and tours the Federal Mint.

CHRONOLOGY

NATIONAL EVENTS		URBAN EVENTS
April 12 – Confederate forces fire on federal Fort Sumter successfully capturing it after a thirty-four-hour battle.	**1861**	A mob attack on Union troops passing through Baltimore marks the first bloodshed of the Civil War.
May 20 – The federal government provides incentives for people to move west with the Homestead Act, a piece of legislation that grants citizens over the age of twenty-one 160 acres of land in the West if they agreed to occupy the area for five years.	**1862**	New Orleans is captured by the Union Army.
July 1 – With passage of the Pacific Railroad Act, westward expansion is opened up by the commissioning of a railroad to be built from Omaha, Nebraska, to Sacramento, California.		
January 1 – President Abraham Lincoln issues the Emancipation Proclamation, freeing slaves in the South.	**1863**	
	1864	The Great Sanitary Fair is held in Logan Square in Philadelphia to raise money for aspects of the war effort.
April 9 – General Robert E. Lee surrenders to General Ulysses S. Grant at Appomattox.	**1865**	Responding to a campaign led by Chicago entrepreneur John Jones, the Illinois legislature repeals the series of laws that bar black people in the state from owning property, serving on juries, testifying against whites, and serving in the state militia.
April 14 – President Abraham Lincoln is assassinated by John Wilkes Booth.		
December 6 – The Thirteenth Amendment is ratified, officially abolishing slavery in the United States.		February – Classes are held for the first time at the Massachusetts Institute of Technology. The campus is originally in downtown Boston, but would move to Cambridge in 1916.
April 9 – Former slaves are made citizens and given basic legal rights with the Civil Rights Act of 1866.	**1866**	Control of the Buffalo police department is removed from the city and given to a state-level commission.
		July – Republican efforts to have a constitutional convention in New Orleans erupt into a riot. More than nine hundred people are killed.

CHRONOLOGY

NATIONAL EVENTS		URBAN EVENTS
Under the Reconstruction Acts, Congress begins to oversee Reconstruction and elections in the South.	**1867**	The Fairmount Park Commission is created in Philadelphia. The state legislature gives the Commission responsibility over the city's extensive park land and open spaces.
		The grand Roebling suspension bridge connecting Cincinnati to its southern hinterland is completed.
July 9 – The Fourteenth Amendment is ratified, giving all people born in the United States citizenship, and prohibiting states from infringing on the rights of U.S. citizens.	**1868**	October – A major earthquake hits San Francisco.
May 10 – The Transcontinental Railroad is completed.	**1869**	Chicago's Union Stock Yards open.
		1869–1873: With authority from the Ohio legislature, Cincinnati launches a municipal railroad, the Cincinnati Southern Railway, to Chattanooga, Tennessee to try to shore up its economic decline.
The last four remaining states of the former Confederacy comply with Congress's rules for reentry. The Union is officially restored.	**1870**	
February 3 – The Fifteenth Amendment is ratified, guaranteeing voting rights to all U.S. citizens regardless of their race.		
	1871	Control of Buffalo's police department by the city is reinstated.
		April – Federal troops withdraw from New Orleans.
		Octavius Catto, a prominent African American activist, is shot on election day, in Philadelphia. The Democrat accused of his murder is acquitted by an all-white jury in 1877.
		October – The Great Chicago Fire devastates the city. Over 2,100 acres of the city are burned,

CHRONOLOGY

NATIONAL EVENTS		URBAN EVENTS
	1871	17,420 buildings are destroyed, and at least 300 people are killed.
		October 27 – New York City's William "Boss" Tweed is arrested for corruption and fraud.
The first edition of federal circuit judge John F. Dillon's *Treatise on the Law of Municipal Corporations* is published.	**1872**	November 9–10: A massive fire causes extensive damage to downtown Boston.
Overspeculation in railroads on behalf of New York banks contributes to a widespread financial panic.	**1873**	
The Civil Rights Act of 1875 bans racial discrimination and segregation.	**1875**	The Bank of California in San Francisco, the premier bank in the West, closes its doors for two months.
	1876	Federal investigators uncover the Whiskey Ring fraud that diverted millions of dollars of federal tax revenues, initially to support St. Louis's leading Republican newspaper, but later to profit the ring leaders.
		Philadelphia celebrates its centennial.
The Great Railroad Strike of 1877 lasts for one month; spreads to a number of cities, including Chicago, Baltimore; and is the largest strike in the history of the United States.	**1877**	The New Orleans White League bands with former Confederates to stage a coup taking over the city, only to be put down by the Louisiana militia.
The Compromise of 1877 calls for the withdrawal of all troops from the South, and thus the end of Reconstruction.		Workingmen's Party of California emerges in San Francisco, an explicitly anti-Chinese party that dominates city politics for four years.
		Railroad strikers shut down St. Louis for nearly a week before they are arrested by police and community leaders.
The Timber and Stone Act calls for land in the West that is not useable for farming to be sold.	**1878**	The Veiled Prophet, an anonymous civic organization that hosts a city parade, is started by business leaders in St. Louis.
		Subscription telephone service is introduced to St. Louis.

CHRONOLOGY

NATIONAL EVENTS		URBAN EVENTS

1879

At least sixty thousand citizens welcome former President Ulysses S. Grant to Philadelphia in a parade through the city.

Thousands of former slaves arrive in St. Louis during the Exodus of 1879 as they flee the post–Reconstruction South for homes in Kansas.

1880

The first electric lights are installed in St. Louis.

1881

The American Federation of Labor is founded, seeking better wages and working conditions for its members.

President James Garfield is assassinated by a disgruntled man who had been denied an appointment in the federal government.

1882

The Chinese Exclusion Act serves as the first law to exclude a specific group of people as undesirable for immigration to the United States.

Patrick Collins becomes the first Boston Irishman elected to Congress.

John D. Rockefeller forms the Standard Oil Trust, headquartered for several years in Cleveland, the most powerful monopoly in the country.

1882, 1885: Cleveland Rolling Mill strikes characterize the struggle of the emerging labor movement to improve working conditions.

1883

A professional civil service system, whereby individuals are hired on merit, is created with the Pendleton Civil Service Reform Act.

1883, 1884: Statewide civil service reform created the New York State Civil Service Commission, which allowed Buffalo's Mayor Scoville to create rules governing competitive and non-competitive examinations for candidates running for some elected offices in the city, creating a merit-based system for filling public office in the city of Buffalo.

The First issue of the *Philadelphia Tribune* is printed. Founded by Christopher Perry, it is the first lasting African American newspaper in the city.

CHRONOLOGY

NATIONAL EVENTS	URBAN EVENTS

1884

Hugh O'Brien is elected as the first Irish-born mayor of Boston.

March – The burning of the county jail and court house and the subsequent riots, which last for three nights, reflect the growing tension between business elites and the working class in Cincinnati.

1886

Significant transit strikes hit New York City.

The St. Louis Browns baseball club wins the American Association Pennant and the World Series.

May 4 – A bomb is thrown in Haymarket during a protest march in Chicago. The incident is blamed on political anarchists who are convicted in a show trial.

1887

Cincinnati's renowned Colored Schools close when segregated public schools are abolished by Ohio law.

February – A broad coalition of Cincinnati workers organizes a local branch of The United Labor Party.

1889

A majority of black workers at San Francisco's Palace Hotel are fired due to accusations of theft. More than likely, it is the result of pressure from the Cooks and Waiters' Protective and Benevolent Union. White workers replaced them.

1890

The passage of the Sherman Antitrust Act allows companies holding monopolies in a specific market to be prosecuted.

December 29 – The Battle at Wounded Knee symbolizes the end of major conflicts between Indians and American soldiers in the West.

Chinese Consolidated Benevolent Association is founded in New York City.

The downtown (Old) Arcade opened in Cleveland.

Construction of St. Louis's new City Hall begins.

CHRONOLOGY

NATIONAL EVENTS	URBAN EVENTS

1890

July – The New Croton Aqueduct begins delivering water from Westchester County to the Bronx (and on to Manhattan).

1891

The charter revision of 1891 creates a three-year term for Buffalo's mayor and a bicameral city legislature comprised of the Board of Alderman and a Board of Councilmen; divides the city into twenty-five aldermanic districts, each represented by one alderman; and established at-large elections of council members.

The Drexel Institute of Art, Science and Industry is founded by Antony J. Drexel in Philadelphia.

1892

Cleveland adopts the Federal Plan (strong mayor) form of government.

January 1 – Ellis Island opens in New York Harbor to process the thousands of immigrants coming into the United States.

Uncertainties in the stock market and banking systems cause a national panic, one of the worst financial crises in U.S. history.

1893

Philadelphia's Broad Street Station is expanded under the direction of architect Frank Furness.

Chicago hosts the World's Columbian Exposition, the greatest world's fair of the era, which served as a showcase for Chicago's meteoric rise.

October 30 – Popular Chicago mayor Carter Harrison Sr. is assassinated by Patrick Eugene Prendergast, a disgruntled job-seeker.

1894

The New York State Senate establishes a committee to investigate corruption in the New York City Police Department. The Lexow Committee, as it came to be known, reveals widespread corruption, leading to a new wave of reform, including the election of William Strong as mayor.

Labor unrest hits the "model" planned industrial community of Pullman, built by the railroad car manufacturer south of Chicago.

CHRONOLOGY

NATIONAL EVENTS		URBAN EVENTS
	1894	San Francisco holds the California Midwinter International Exposition in Golden Gate Park.
		St. Louis's Union Station opens, at the time the largest railroad station in the United States.
		November – New York voters approve a referendum on the consolidation of Manhattan and surrounding municipalities into a "Greater New York."
	1895	Josiah Quincy elected to Boston's first two-year mayoral term.
In *Plessy v. Ferguson*, the U.S. Supreme Court rules that segregation is acceptable as long as each race's facilities are equal.	**1896**	The first electric current is sent from Niagara Falls to Buffalo in August.
		The People's and Electric Traction companies and Peter A. B. Widener's Philadelphia Traction Companies merge, forming the Union Traction Company, possessing a virtual monopoly on the Philadelphia's public transport.
		The Baltimore and Ohio Railroad goes into receivership.
		Cleveland holds its Centennial celebration.
		Banker James Phelan is elected mayor of San Francisco, marking the rise of businessmen reformers on the city's political scene.
		June 16–18: The Republican National Convention is held in St. Louis. William McKinley wins the presidential nomination.
		November 9 – Illustrating the movement into the automotive age, the last horse-drawn streetcar shutters operation in Detroit.
The U.S. goes to war with Spain. In victory the U.S. expands territorial holdings.	**1898**	The Maryland legislature approves a new city charter for Baltimore, enhancing the powers of the mayor.

CHRONOLOGY

NATIONAL EVENTS		URBAN EVENTS

1898 — Greater New York City is established by act of the state legislature, bringing the five boroughs together with a central city government.

1900

The Socialist Party is formed in part to combat the pitiable conditions caused by urbanization and industrialization.

New York passes the New York State Tenement House Bill, outlining building requirements to improve living conditions and sanitation. Other states soon adopt similar laws.

September 5 – President William McKinley is assassinated in Buffalo. Vice President Theodore Roosevelt assumes office.

Newspaper exposés (commonly known as muckraking) on political corruption and the deplorable conditions of city life become popular. Muckraking becomes an important tool in shedding light on social problems and bringing about reform.

1901 — The formation of the United States Steel Corporation under the financial auspices of J. P. Morgan included the purchase of Carnegie Steel and several other smaller plants in the Pittsburgh area.

1903 — Boston's Good Government Association is formed.

A committee led by the City Beautiful architect Daniel Burnham recommends the grouping of public buildings around a new downtown mall in Cleveland.

December 30 – The fire at Chicago's Iroquois Theatre caused the largest loss of life in any fire in a building in the 20th century.

1904 — The third modern Olympic Games were held in St. Louis during the Louisiana Purchase Exposition, attracting millions of visitors.

Muckraker Lincoln Steffens concludes that Philaia is "the most corrupt and contented" city in the United States in his popular book *The*

CHRONOLOGY

NATIONAL EVENTS		URBAN EVENTS
	1904	*Shame of the Cities,* which includes chapters as well on St. Louis, Minneapolis, Pittsburgh, Chicago, and New York.
		February 7–8: Fire destroys most of Baltimore's commercial district.
		October 27 – The New York subway opens.
In *Lochner v. New York*, the U.S. Supreme Court overturns a New York law limiting a worker's day to ten hours. The Court states that employers have the right to set the conditions of employment, including long working hours.	**1905**	A bond is passed for the creation of a Los Angeles Aqueduct after the *Los Angeles Times* warns of an impending drought.
	1907	March 4 – The Market Street subway-elevated opens as Philadelphia's first rapid transit line.
		William O'Connell is named Archbishop of Boston.
		The Pennsylvania state legislature approves the annexation of Allegheny City by Pittsburgh despite the fact that the residents of Allegheny City voted overwhelmingly against the annexation. In *Hunter v. Pittsburgh* the U.S. Supreme Court upholds the act of the Pennsylvania legislature.
In *Muller v. Oregon,* the U.S. Supreme Court highlights the harmful effects of long workdays on women's health. The Court decides to uphold Oregon's law limiting the workday to ten hours.	**1908**	
	1909	Boston's new city charter is adopted.
	1910	The Baltimore City Council approves an ordinance mandating the racial segregation of residential areas.
		The Los Angeles Harbor at San Pedro and Wilmington is completed.
		October 1 – The *Los Angeles Times* building is partially destroyed by a bomb. The event, and the subsequent trial, served as the climax of *Times* publisher Harrison Gray Otis' anti-union campaign.

CHRONOLOGY

NATIONAL EVENTS		URBAN EVENTS
	1911	The Pennsylvania legislature passes bills that reduce Pittsburgh's two city councils to one.
		March 25 – The Triangle Shirtwaist fire kills 146 workers in New York City, sparking calls for industrial safety regulation.
		May 15 – The U.S. Supreme Court orders the breakup of John D. Rockefeller's Standard Oil Trust, a company with significant ties to Cleveland.
		December 30 – President William Taft dedicates Philadelphia's new John Wanamaker department store, the largest department store in the world at that time.
With a plurality, Progressive Democrat Woodrow Wilson beats both Theodore Roosevelt and William Howard Taft in the Presidential election.	**1912**	The Baltimore branch of the NAACP is founded.
The Sixteenth Amendment is ratified, enabling Congress to collect income taxes.	**1913**	
	1914	New York City is hit by financial crisis.
		James Michael Curley is elected mayor of Boston.
	1915	St. Louis adopts a residential segregation ordinance.
	1916	1916–1920s: Chicago is a major destination city of the Great Migration, a major influx of African American migrants from the South.
1917–1918: The United States fights in World War I.	**1917**	
1918–1919: A global influenza pandemic kills tens of millions of people worldwide.	**1918**	

CHRONOLOGY

NATIONAL EVENTS	URBAN EVENTS

1919

January 16 – The Eighteenth Amendment is ratified, putting Prohibition into effect. Key supporters of the Prohibition movement include industrial employers and those who oppose the growing number of immigrants who drink.

The first all-black hospital opens in Detroit.

The Boston Police Strike fails, dealing a blow to labor power locally and nationally.

The worst race riot in Illinois history points to strife resulting from segregation and rapid demographic change in Chicago.

A national steel strike is met in Pittsburgh by the steel companies with brutal repressive tactics. The striking workers are defeated, and the industry returns to harsh pre–World War I working conditions.

1920

August 18 – The Nineteenth Amendment is ratified, giving women the right to vote.

1924

Congress approves the Immigration Quota Act, setting restrictions on the number of immigrants admitted to the United States, setting limits based on "national origin" to begin in 1927, and establishing a cap of one hundred fifty thousand people a year.

Cleveland adopts the city manager form of government by charter amendment.

Los Angeles voters approve the Major Traffic Street Plan, which would modernize the city's infrastructure.

1926

Charles Lindbergh, with funding from St. Louis businessmen, flies the first transatlantic flight from New York to Paris.

1927

The Holland Tunnel opens in New York City.

1928

The Ambassador Bridge, connecting Detroit and Canada, opens as the longest suspension bridge in the world.

1928–1932: A Democratic coalition begins to coalesce in Philadelphia under the leadership of Jack Kelly, Albert Greenfield, and J. David Stern.

1929

October 29 – The Stock market crashes, precipitating the Great Depression.

Construction on the Empire State Building begins in New York City.

CHRONOLOGY

NATIONAL EVENTS	URBAN EVENTS

1929

Voters of Pittsburgh and Allegheny County narrowly defeat a new charter that would have maintained a federated structure of municipalities while consolidating many functions into a metropolitan government.

James Michael Curley is elected to third (non-consecutive) term as Boston's mayor.

February 14 – The St. Valentine's Day Massacre, a grisly Prohibition-era mob murder, comes to symbolize the violence of the 1920s in "gangland" Chicago.

June 17 – The Smoot-Hawley Tariff is signed into law to help protect American goods against foreign imports, but instead it worsens the economy by causing a disintegration of international trade.

1930

The Bank of Philadelphia and Trust Company fails, bringing the Depression home to thousands of Philadelphians.

Detroit's Communist Party organizes a protest against unemployment that draws fifty thousand people downtown.

Cleveland's Terminal Tower skyscraper opens.

1930, 1931: The Chrysler and Empire State Buildings open in New York City.

1931

The Amalgamated Clothing Workers strike pits the Baltimore Federation of Labor against the Baltimore Industrial Council.

Severance Hall and Cleveland Municipal Stadium open.

Cleveland voters end the experiment in the city manager form of government.

Chicago's most famous Progressive reformer, Jane Addams, wins the Nobel Peace Prize.

Repatriation of Mexicans and their American-born children begins in Los Angeles.

CHRONOLOGY

NATIONAL EVENTS		URBAN EVENTS

1932

January 22 – The Reconstruction Finance Corporation is created to aid financial institutions in distress.

November 8 – Franklin D. Roosevelt is elected President, amid soaring unemployment.

St. Louis Democrats elected to key local political offices, setting the ground for the election of Bernard F. Dickmann, the city's first Democratic mayor in more than twenty-five years.

Father James R. Cox, Pittsburgh's "Mayor of Shantytown," leads a Hunger March from Pittsburgh to Washington, D.C., to aid the jobless.

Mayor Jackson of Baltimore creates the Emergency Relief Commission, a quasi-governmental agency for assisting the unemployed.

Boston's prominent Lee, Higginson & Co. investment banking house collapses.

July 30 – August 14: Los Angeles hosts the tenth modern Olympic Games.

September 1 – New York City mayor Jimmy Walker resigns in a corruption scandal, and business-led reformers found the Citizens' Budget Commission, which remains a respected and influential good-government watchdog organization.

1933

President Roosevelt presses for New Deal legislation, creating services such as the Civilian Conservation Corps, and the Tennessee Valley Authority, and passing the National Housing Act to help stimulate the economy and provide jobs and services to help those in poverty due to the recession.

December 5 – Prohibition is repealed by the Twenty-First Amendment, making the sale of alcohol legal once again.

Failure of Baltimore's Title Guarantee and Trust Company triggers a run on city banks.

The Young People's Forum of the NAACP organizes a "Shop Where You Can Work" campaign which entails a boycott of retailers in black neighborhoods of Baltimore who do not hire African American employees.

February 15 – Chicago's mayor Anton Cermak is shot in Miami in an assassination attempt on President Franklin D. Roosevelt.

CHRONOLOGY

NATIONAL EVENTS		URBAN EVENTS
	1933	1933–1934: The "Century of Progress" Exposition in downtown Chicago's Grant Park.
A large-scale drought known as the Dust Bowl hits the Great Plains, causing extensive agricultural losses.	**1934**	Sumner Tunnel opens under Boston Harbor, the first road connection between the North End and East Boston.
		First Houses, the nation's first public housing project, opens in New York City. The venture is founded by the Transport Workers Union.
		May 15: Two union protesters are killed at San Pedro Harbor during the Maritime Strike in Los Angeles.
The U.S. Supreme Court, in two separate rulings, declares that the federal government cannot use eminent domain for the purposes of "slum clearance" and public housing, because it usurps the powers of the states. These rulings lead states to establish semi-independent local housing authorities in cities to serve as the recipients of federal funds for public housing.	**1935**	United Autoworkers (UAW) is founded, increasing the wages and quality of life for tens of thousands of Detroit automotive workers.
		President Franklin D. Roosevelt designates a national park in a portion of St. Louis along the Mississippi River, and the City of St. Louis issues $7.5 million bonds to finance construction of the Jefferson National Expansion Memorial, where the city's iconic arch would later be built (construction was completed in 1965).
August 15 – The Social Security Act is signed into law, giving pensions to those over the age of sixty-five, and establishing federal and state unemployment programs.		
	1936	President Franklin D. Roosevelt, at the height of his popularity, carries Philadelphia with some 62 percent of the vote.
		St. Louis's Homer G. Phillips Hospital opens, becoming nationally recognized as a leading training center for black doctors and nurses.
		March 17 – Flood waters engulf downtown Pittsburgh.
		July 11 – The Triborough Bridge opens in New York City, creating a new transportation connection between Manhattan, the Bronx, and Queens.

CHRONOLOGY

NATIONAL EVENTS		URBAN EVENTS
	1936	1936–1937: A Seamen's strike wins recognition for the National Maritime Union and gives the Baltimore Industrial Council favored position among dockworkers.
		1936–1937: The Great Lakes Exposition and Republican National Convention are held in Cleveland.
President Franklin D. Roosevelt proposes his court-packing plan in an effort to introduce additional justices more favorable to his New Deal plan. His plan fails.	**1937**	Former James Michael Curley protégé Maurice J. Tobin defeats Curley in Boston's mayoral election.
		Emerson Electric workers in St. Louis stage one of the longest sit-down strikes in U.S. history and successfully gain union recognition through the Congress of Industrial Organizations.
		May 26 – Members of Ford Motor Company's internal security department in Detroit attack United Auto Workers organizers pushing for better wages and shorter hours in "The Battle of the Overpass."
		May 30 – Memorial Day massacre at Chicago's Republic Steel, ten people are killed and dozens wounded as striking workers clash with police.
June 25 – The Fair Labor Standards Act is signed into law, creating a national minimum wage and establishing a host of labor regulations.	**1938**	September 16 – Fletcher Bowron defeats Los Angeles Mayor Frank L. Shaw in a recall election.
	1939	Howard Jackson reelected mayor of Baltimore and reestablishes his control of city's Democratic organization.
		April 30 – The New York World's Fair opens in Queens.
President Franklin D. Roosevelt is elected to an unprecedented third term.	**1940**	The Arroyo Seco Parkway opens as the first Los Angeles freeway.
		Federal defense spending leads to Philadelphia firms receiving approximately $1 billion in contracts, which finally begins to ameliorate unemployment and pull the city out of the Depression.

CHRONOLOGY

NATIONAL EVENTS	URBAN EVENTS

1940

The Interborough Rapid Transit and Brooklyn-Manhattan Transit companies consolidate with the Independent City Owned Rapid Transit Railroad to form a unified New York City subway system.

Forty city blocks in St. Louis are cleared for the Jefferson National Expansion Memorial, which is to include the now-famous arch.

1940–1970: The Second Great Migration of African Americans from the South occurs, with many resettling in Chicago.

1941

March 11 – The United States supplies the Allied forces with armaments after the Lend Lease Act is approved.

The Ford Motor Company headquartered outside Detroit, recognizes the United Auto Workers.

U.S. entry into World War II brings rapid population growth and construction of new federal government buildings in Washington, D.C., most notably the Pentagon (completed in 1943).

June 25 – The Fair Employment Practices Commission is established to investigate instances of racial discrimination in the workplace.

Maurice J. Tobin defeats James Michael Curley to gain a second term as mayor of Boston.

President Franklin D. Roosevelt issues Executive Order 8802 prohibiting discrimination in war-related industries.

A charter revision in St. Louis changes the process of electing city alderman to allow for election by ward, in addition to at-large elections, increasing the number of alderman to 28 and guarantee representation of different neighborhoods and demographic interests in the city.

December 7 – Pearl Harbor is attacked by Japanese forces; U.S. formally declares war.

1941–1942: Signs of racial tension emerge in Detroit as street fights occur between African Americans and Polish youths. There are separate protests as the federally funded Sojourner Truth defense housing project for African American workers is built in a white neighborhood.

1941–1945: Detroit is dubbed the "Arsenal of Democracy," as its manufacturing base is mobilized for wartime production. Massive

NATIONAL EVENTS

URBAN EVENTS

1941

in-migration, including an influx of African Americans seeking manufacturing jobs, places great strain on the city's housing infrastructure.

1941– 945: New York City's massive manufacturing base is mobilized for wartime production, Mayor LaGuardia goes on to serve as chief of the Office of Civilian Defense, and a number of German spies are captured in New York before a sabotage plot could be executed.

1941–1945: Wartime causes a significant boost to Cleveland's manufacturing sector, with manufacturing employment increasing from one hundred ninety-one thousand in 1940 to three hundred forty thousand by the war's end.

President Franklin D. Roosevelt's Executive Order 9066 initiates the internment of Japanese Americans in California.

1942

November 28 – The Cocoanut Grove nightclub fire kills 492 people in Boston.

December 2 – The world's first self-sustaining nuclear chain reaction is produced, at the University of Chicago campus.

1942–1945: Columbia University physicists play a central role in the Manhattan Project. Deep beneath the streets of Morningside Heights, early steps in the development of the nuclear chain reaction were made, nudging the world toward the nuclear age.

1943

Cleveland's local housing vacancy rate falls to less than 1 percent.

A biracial citizens group organizes pickets against Washington, D.C.'s Capital Transit for refusing to hire black streetcar operators.

Attacks upon Jewish youths by Irish gangs cast anti-Semitic cloud over Boston's national image.

The subway system opens in Chicago.

CHRONOLOGY

NATIONAL EVENTS		URBAN EVENTS
	1943	1943: The shooting of an African American soldier by a white police officer in New York City's Harlem explodes into overnight looting and fighting between citizens and police.
		The First major smog alert in Los Angeles appears.
		June – Zoot Suit Riots rage for a week in Los Angeles.
June 22 – The G.I. Bill is approved, giving veterans a variety of benefits, including those pertaining to employment and education.	**1944**	William Cardinal O'Connell dies after serving thirty-seven years as Archbishop of Boston.
August 1944: Allied forces liberate Paris from the Nazis.		A hate strike at Philadelphia Transportation Company highlights racial tensions building in the city.
		Maurice Tobin is elected Governor of Massachusetts, the last Boston mayor to gain higher elective office.
April 12 – President D. Franklin Roosevelt dies in office. Vice President Harry Truman assumes the presidency.	**1945**	James Michael Curley wins a fourth (non-consecutive) term as Boston's mayor.
The United States drops atomic bombs on the Japanese cities of Hiroshima and Nagasaki. Japan soon surrenders, and the Allies declare victory.		1945–1946: Organized labor calls strikes as unions vie with capitalists to shape Detroit's postwar economy. Over three million workers in the auto, steel, and mining industries strike between November 1945 and June 1946.
October 24 – The United Nations is created.		
March 12 – President Harry Truman issues the Truman Doctrine, stating that the United States will be the ally of any people or nation being suppressed or denied basic freedoms.	**1947**	Baltimore creates the nation's first housing court.
		Boston Mayor James Michael Curley spends five months in a federal prison after conviction on mail fraud charges.
June 23 – The Taft-Hartley Act is enacted, restricting the power of labor unions, and giving judges the power to end select union strikes.		Chicago reaches its highest point of manufacturing employment.
1947–1949: The National Security Act calls for the creation of the Central Intelligence Agency and unifies the military under the Secretary of Defense.		

CHRONOLOGY

NATIONAL EVENTS		URBAN EVENTS
	1948	A bill to provide self-rule for Washington, D.C., fails to pass the U.S. House of Representatives.
		The Greater Philadelphia Movement, a bipartisan movement intent on revitalizing the city, forms.
		The Missouri legislature passed the Earning Tax Ordinance, which allows for the collection of local income tax and helped St. Louis compensate for its declining property tax base as residents move into surrounding suburban areas.
		The initial construction of Ludwig Mies van der Rohe's Lake Shore Apartments signals the beginning of the Second Chicago School of Architecture.
April 4 – The North Atlantic Treaty Organization is created. It includes twelve member states that pledge to defend each other if ever attacked.	**1949**	Clevelanders elect Jean Murrell Capers to the city council, the first African American woman to hold the position.
July 15 – The Housing Act of 1949 vastly increases the authority of the federal government to provide funding for "slum clearance," funding the construction of low-income housing, and for guaranteeing the mortgages of homebuyers.		John Hynes defeats Michael Curley to win Boston's mayoralty. Voters also adopt changes to the city charter, providing for selection of councilors on a citywide basis and a runoff election for mayor.
1949–1952: President Harry Truman signs a series of legislative acts known as the Fair Deal. They prove beneficial to many workers by increasing the minimum wage, building more affordable housing, and expanding the Social Security Program.		The "Vicecapades" scandal involving the Los Angeles Police Department almost topples the Bowron administration.
		Joseph Clark and Richardson Dilworth are elected Philadelphia's city controller and city treasurer, respectively. Their victories help sweep out the corrupt Republican political machine that had dominated Philadelphia's politics for decades.
		Detroit's population peaks at 1,849,568. The city ranks as the fifth largest in the country, but its population soon declines due to deindustrialization and white migration to the suburbs.

CHRONOLOGY

NATIONAL EVENTS   **URBAN EVENTS**

The United States sends troops to join the **1950** The National Capital Park and Planning
Republic of Korea's war effort. Commission publishes its comprehensive plan
for the future growth of Washington, D.C., and
its environs, focusing on federal work centers,
highways, and infrastructure.

Baltimore voters approve funds for major league
baseball stadium.

1951 John Hynes handily defeats James Michael
Curley for the Boston mayoralty, effectively
ending Curley's political career.

The Los Angeles City Council of Los Angeles
votes to rescind $100 million public housing
contract with the federal government.

Philadelphia voters ratify a new city charter,
making the city's government more streamlined,
transparent, and accountable.

Baltimore Mayor J. D'Alesandro Jr. creates the
Human Relations Commission, and the parks
department integrates city golf courses and
allows for interracial sports competition.

Congress overrides a presidential veto to pass **1952** Ongoing campaigns, including peaceful sit-
the McCarran-Walter Immigration and ins, result in the desegregation of numerous
Nationality Act. establishments in the Washington, D.C.,'s central
business district.

The postwar order, characterized by both U.S.
leadership and multilateral action, is symbolized
by the completion of the United Nations
headquarters in Manhattan.

November 3 – An oil slick on the Cuyahoga River
in Cleveland catches fire, causing significant
damage.

1953 Baltimore's municipal employees go on strike for
the first time in city's history.

NATIONAL EVENTS

URBAN EVENTS

1954

May 17 – In *Brown v. Board of Education of Topeka*, the U.S. Supreme Court rules that segregation in schools is unconstitutional.

August 2 – The Housing Act of 1954 shifts the direction of federal urban development policy, away from public, low-income housing, and toward commercial development.

1955 — Richard J. Daley is elected mayor of Chicago and serves for over twenty years.

1956 — The Highway Act is passed, providing funding for the federal interstate system. This helps lead to the suburbanization of the United States.

1957 — Civil rights leader Martin Luther King Jr. founds the Southern Christian Leadership Conference.

The Brooklyn Dodgers move to Los Angeles as one of the city's first professional sports teams.

The First Intercontinental Ballistic Missile (Atlas) is built and test-fired by the Convair Division of General Dynamics in San Diego.

1960

Massachusetts Senator John F. Kennedy is elected president.

1961 — Racial integration of public and private facilities begins in Dallas.

1962 — President John F. Kennedy and his administration diffuse the Cuban Missile Crisis.

1963 — President John F. Kennedy is assassinated by Lee Harvey Oswald; Vice President Lyndon Johnson becomes president.

The Manned Spacecraft Center opens in Houston. In 1973 it is renamed the Lyndon B. Johnson Space Center.

1964 — July 2 – The Civil Rights Act of 1964 is passed, calling for an end to racial and sex discrimination in employment as well as an end to racial discrimination in education and public space.

The Music Center for the Performing Arts opens in Los Angeles, representing a new era in the performance and support of arts and culture in the city.

CHRONOLOGY

NATIONAL EVENTS	URBAN EVENTS

1964

July 9 – Congress approves the Urban Mass Transportation Act of 1964, to allocating funds to urban transportation systems.

The University of California, San Diego, opens.

Sea World Marine Life Park opens on San Diego's recently developed Mission Bay.

Baltimore Mayor Theodore McKeldin proposes a comprehensive civil rights ordinance.

1964, 1967: Riots in New York City indicate the shaky foundations of the uneasy and unequal white-black consensus forged decades earlier.

August 28 – 30: The three-day Columbia Avenue Riot occurs in North Philadelphia at the height of the civil rights era.

1965

Medicare and Medicaid are created to provide medical care for the elderly, impoverished, and disabled.

The Housing and Urban Development Act of 1965 is passed, creating programs to support a wide variety of urban concerns and establishing the Department of Housing and Urban Development.

The Immigration and Nationality Act of 1965 (Hart-Cellar Act) is signed into law, creating immigration ceilings from the Western and non-Western hemispheres.

1965–1973: The United States engages in the Vietnam War, a controversial military conflict in which the United States supports the South Vietnamese against the Communist North Vietnamese.

The Watts Riot in Los Angeles is the largest urban uprising in the city's history up to that time.

1966

November 3 – Congress approves the Demonstration Cities and Metropolitan Development Act of 1966 to improve urban slums and blighted areas.

Martin Luther King Jr. visits Chicago to organize protests against segregation and poor housing conditions for blacks.

The Congress of Racial Equality names Baltimore as a summer "target city."

CHRONOLOGY

NATIONAL EVENTS		URBAN EVENTS

1967

August 30 – Thurgood Marshall, the first African American to serve on the U.S. Supreme Court is confirmed by the Senate 69-11.

A Detroit police raid becomes the catalyst for major urban rebellion.

1968

Martin Luther King Jr. is assassinated, leading to riots in Chicago and Baltimore, among other cities.

Philadelphia's Girard College is desegregated— a major victory for civil rights advocates.

The Report of the National Advisory Commission on Civil Disorders is published, an investigation to the causes of the inner-city riots erupting throughout the country. The report famously concluded, *"Our nation is moving toward two societies, one black, one white—separate and unequal."*

School integration and community control controversy in New York City mark the start of white ethnic pushback against the racial liberalism of the 1960s and the beginning of local political realignment.

Spring 1968: Demonstrations at Columbia University in New York mark visible manifestation of New Left antiwar and radical Black Nationalist protests in heart of the elite institution.

August – Thousands of antiwar protestors battle with police as the Democratic Party holds its national convention in Chicago.

1969

Houston Intercontinental Airport opens. In 1997 it is renamed the George Bush Intercontinental Airport.

Chicanos por la Causa, a community development agency, is founded in Phoenix to provide Mexican Americans with important social and economic assistance and a political voice.

1970

October 15 – Congress approves the Urban Mass Transportation Act of 1970 to provide $3.1 billion to local and state governments for mass transportation projects.

Ground is broken for the Sears Tower, the world's tallest building when finished in 1974 and a key symbol of Chicago's downtown revitalization.

December 29 – The Occupational Safety and Health Act is approved by Congress, requiring the government to impose health and safety standards in the workplace.

1971

The Committee of 100 saves the 1915 historic Casa del Prado in Balboa Park in 1971 and paves

CHRONOLOGY

NATIONAL EVENTS	URBAN EVENTS

1971

the way for future buildings to be saved and restored in San Diego.

February 9 – The Sylmar Earthquake hits southern California, killing sixty-five people and causing $500 million in damage.

July 16 – Judge Jason William Taylor hands down an order to desegregate the Dallas Independent School District by busing students.

1972

President Richard Nixon becomes involved in the Watergate Scandal, ultimately leading to his resignation from office in 1974.

The first of the buildings are demolished in the Pruitt-Igoe public housing complex in St. Louis. The remaining thirty-two buildings are demolished over the next four years.

1973

April 4 – Construction of the World Trade Center in New York is completed, making the twin towers briefly the tallest buildings in the world.

November 6 – Coleman Young is elected first African American mayor of Detroit. After his election, Young significantly increases the number of minority- and female-owned businesses with city contracts and integrates the Detroit Police Department.

1974

August 22 – The Housing and Community Development Act of 1974 is approved, to provide support for "viable urban communities".

November 26 – The National Mass Transportation Assistance Act of 1974 is approved, providing $11.9 billion in assistance to help urban transit systems meet their expenses.

Dallas-Fort Worth International Airport opens.

Baltimore sees widespread strikes by city employees.

1975

A court ruling by federal judge Elton Mahon declares Dallas's at-large system of voting unconstitutional accelerating the demise of the Citizens Charter Association.

New York City's fiscal crisis results in massive service cuts and marks the end of high levels of local spending.

NATIONAL EVENTS

URBAN EVENTS

1975 — Baltimore school superintendent Roland Patterson dismissed by the school board.

1976 — The nation's bicentennial is celebrated with a major patriotic celebration in Philadelphia.

The San Diego City Council adopts the Gaslamp Quarter Urban Design and Development Manual to set guidelines for historically sensitive development.

1977 — A major electrical blackout results in widespread looting and marks the beginning of a long period of high crime in New York City.

1978 — Voters approve Baltimore's Harborplace development.

Former actor (and conservative California governor) Ronald Reagan is elected president. — **1980**

September 21– The first female U.S.Supreme Court justice, Sandra Day O'Connor, is confirmed by the Senate 99-0.

1982 — Phoenix opts to choose the city council from districts, providing effective political representation to all areas of the city.

1983 — Harold Washington is elected Chicago's first African American mayor.

1984 — The Colts football team leaves Baltimore for Indianapolis.

M. Wilson Goode takes office as the first African American mayor of Philadelphia.

The GM Poletown Assembly plant opens. after significant controversy—its construction entailed the destruction of a once-vibrant multiracial community—and is the first new auto plant built in Detroit in almost seventy years.

CHRONOLOGY

NATIONAL EVENTS		URBAN EVENTS
	1984	July 28 – August 12: Los Angeles hosts the Olympic Summer Games for the second time in the city's history.
	1987	Kurt Schmoke becomes Baltimore's first elected African American mayor.
	1988	Phoenix passes a major bond issue to fund cultural institutions, greatly stimulating cultural and downtown development.
The Berlin Wall falls, marking a significant step in the end of the Cold War.	**1989**	March 22 – The U.S. Supreme Court declares the New York City Board of Estimate unconstitutional.
		April 4 – Richard M. Daley elected Chicago's mayor.
		November 7 – New York City elects its only African American mayor, David N. Dinkins.
	1990	Philadelphia forms the Center City [Business Improvement] District.
August 2 – The Persian Gulf War begins with Iraq's invasion of Kuwait.	**1991**	August – A three-day riot pitting blacks against Jews occurs in Crown Heights, Brooklyn.
December – The Soviet Union dissolves.		San Antonio passes strict term limits for city council and mayor.
		Mayor Ed Rendell's contract with city unions is a turning point in controlling Philadelphia's chronic budget deficits.
		1991–1997: San Antonio completes flood control tunnels on San Pedro Creek and San Antonio River
Democrat Bill Clinton defeats incumbent President George H. W. Bush.	**1992**	April 29 – Racial tensions erupt, resulting in the Los Angeles Riots in South Central Los Angeles, which cause extensive damage over a number of days.
		May – San Diego hosts the internationally televised America's Cup.

CHRONOLOGY

NATIONAL EVENTS		URBAN EVENTS
December 8 – The North American Free Trade Agreement is signed into law, allowing for free trade between Mexico, Canada, and the United States.	**1993**	February 26 – Terrorists detonate explosives in a World Trade Center parking garage.
	1994	Cisco Systems moves from Menlo Park to San Jose and quickly becomes the city's largest private employer.
	1995	San Antonio's Kelly Air Force Base closes.
		Chicago begins to demolish public housing high rises.
Welfare reform is passed by Congress, giving states more control over the allocation of welfare money.	**1996**	August 12–15: The Republican National Convention is held in San Diego.
	1997	1997–2007: The Collapse of Motorola Corporation has significant effects on Phoenix's economy.
December 19 – President Bill Clinton is impeached by the House of Representatives.	**1998**	The Arizona Diamondbacks baseball team opens a new stadium in Phoenix.
		San Jose's "Greenline" urban growth boundary receives final approval.
		January – Lee P. Brown is sworn in as Houston's first African American mayor.
The Dow Jones surpasses 10,000 points, signifying a rise in economic prosperity.	**1999**	
December 12 – *Bush v. Gore* ultimately decides the presidential election in favor of George W. Bush.	**2000**	The dot-com crash leads to high unemployment in San Jose, with the rate quintupling between 2000 and 2003.
September 11 – Terrorists launch the most significant attacks in U.S. history, on the World Trade Center and Pentagon.	**2001**	Philadelphia establishes its Avenue of the Arts, and the Kimmel Center for the Performing Arts opens.
October 7 – The United States begins an invasion of Afghanistan in an effort to drive the Taliban from power and dismantle al Qaeda.		American Airlines Center opens hosting the Dallas Mavericks and the Dallas Stars franchises.

CHRONOLOGY

NATIONAL EVENTS		URBAN EVENTS
October 26 – President Bush signs the USA PATRIOT Act into law.	**2001**	Pennsylvania assumes control of the Philadelphia school district.
December 18 – Congress passes the landmark No Child Left Behind Act		Philadelphia mayor John Street initiates the Neighborhood Transformation Initiative.
		June – Tropical Storm Allison causes extensive flooding and damage in Houston.
		September 11 – The terrorist attacks on the World Trade Center in New York City result in more than two thousand five hundred deaths and massive destruction.
		December 2 – The Houston-based energy firm Enron files for bankruptcy and soon thereafter lays off some four thousand out of approximately seven thousand five hundred Houston employees.
November – Congress passes legislation creating the Department of Homeland Security.	**2002**	State lawmakers grant Mayor Michael R. Bloomberg control over New York City schools.
U.S. forces invade Iraq in search of weapons of mass destruction, toppling Saddam Hussein's longstanding regime.	**2003**	U.S. District Judge Barefoot Sanders ends thirty-two years of federal court oversight of Dallas school desegregation.
		Toyota's $1.3 billion truck manufacturing plant opens in San Antonio.
		Wildfires in east San Diego, burn 2,232 homes and kill fifteen people.
	2004	Chicago's Millennium Park opens on the shores of Lake Michigan.
June 23 – In *Kelo v. New London* the U.S. Supreme Court rules that private property can be transferred from one private owner to another for "public use" if there is a promise of good economic development in the area.	**2005**	Voters reject two separate referenda to expand the power of Dallas's mayor.
		July 1 – Antonio R. Villaraigosa is sworn in as the first Latino mayor of Los Angeles since the nineteenth century.

CHRONOLOGY

NATIONAL EVENTS		URBAN EVENTS
August 29 – Hurricane Katrina strikes the city of New Orleans with devastating effects.	**2005**	September 2005: More than one hundred thousand refugees from Hurricane Katrina relocate to Houston.
December – Recession is officially declared in the United States.	**2007**	Wildfires burn one thousand five hundred homes in San Diego, with a $1 billion loss.
June 26 – The U.S. Supreme Court strikes down Washington, D.C.'s strict handgun regulations in *District of Columbia v. Heller.*	**2008**	Home price values drop by nearly a quarter in San Jose during a nationwide real estate crash.
		September 19 – Detroit mayor Kwame Kilpatrick, facing several charges of corruption, resigns.
November 4 – Barack Obama wins the presidential election and becomes the first black president.		October 23 – New York Mayor Michael R. Bloomberg and city council amend the city's term limits law to allow three terms.
	2009	The River Walk extension projects, slated to be complete in 2013, will expand San Antonio's pedestrian experience north and south of the central core.
		October 2 – Chicago loses the 2016 Summer Olympic bid.
March 23 – Landmark health care reform, a centerpiece of President Barack Obama's agenda, is signed into law.	**2010**	June 28 – In *McDonald v. City of Chicago* the U.S. Supreme Court rules unconstitutional Chicago's ban on handguns.
May 1 – President Obama announces the death of Osama bin Laden by U.S. forces in Pakistan.	**2011**	Rahm Emmanuel is elected mayor of Chicago.

INDEX